CHILD PSYCHOLOGY

CHILD PSYCHOLOGY

A Handbook of Contemporary Issues

edited by
Lawrence Balter
Catherine S. Tamis-LeMonda

USA	Publishing Office:	PSYCHOLOGY PRESS *A member of the Taylor & Francis Group* 325 Chestnut Street Philadelphia, PA 19106 Tel: (215) 625-8900 Fax: (215) 625-2940
	Distribution Center:	PSYCHOLOGY PRESS *A member of the Taylor & Francis Group* 47 Runway Road, Suite G Levittown, PA 19057-4700 Tel: (215) 269-0400 Fax: (215) 269-0363
UK		PSYCHOLOGY PRESS *A member of the Taylor & Francis Group* 27 Church Road Hove E. Sussex, BN3 2FA Tel: +44 (0)1273 207411 Fax: +44 (0)1273 205612

CHILD PSYCHOLOGY: A Handbook of Contemporary Issues

1 2   3   4   5   6 7 8   9   0

Printed by Edwards Brothers, Ann Arbor, MI, 1999.
Cover design by Joe Dieter Visual Communications.

A CIP catalog record for this book is available from the British Library.
∞ The paper in this publication meets the requirements of the ANSI Standard Z39.48-1984 (Permanence of Paper).

Library of Congress Cataloging-in-Publication Data
Child psychology : a handbook of contemporary issues / edited by
   Lawrence Balter, Catherine Tamis-LeMonda.
      p.   cm.
      Includes bibliographical references and index.
      ISBN 1084169-000-7 (case : alk. paper)
      1. Child psychology.   I. Balter, Lawrence.   II. Tamis-LaMonda,
   Catherine.
   BF721.C5155   1999
   155.4—dc21   99-26296
                                                              CIP

ISBN 1-84169-000-7 (case)

To Karen, for her endless dedication and support.
—LB

For Brittany, Christopher, and Michael, who taught
me many truths about child development.
—CTL

CONTENTS

CONTRIBUTORS

Linda P. Acredolo
University of California at Davis

Stephanie Aubry
Yale University

Jay Belsky
Pennsylvania State University

Robert H. Bradley
University of Arkansas at Little Rock

Lisa Chen
Temple University

Robert F. Corwyn
University of Arkansas at Little Rock

Judy S. DeLoache
University of Illinois at Urbana-Champaign

Jacquelynne S. Eccles
University of Michigan

Nancy Eisenberg
Arizona State University

Yvonne D. Emmons
University of California at Davis

Richard A. Fabes
Arizona State University

Carol Freedman-Doan
Eastern Michigan University

James Garbarino
Cornell Univeristy

Susan Golombok
City University, UK

Susan W. Goodwyn
University of California at Davis

Wendy S. Grolnick
Clark University

Paul L. Harris
University of Oxford

Lowry Hemphill
Harvard Graduate School of Education

Karen D. Horobin
California State University

Carollee Howes
University of California at Los Angeles

Judith A. Hudson
Rutgers University

Diane Hughes
New York University

Jennifer C. Hurley
Reed College

Aletha C. Huston
University of Texas at Austin

Robert D. Kavanaugh
Williams College

Deanna Kuhn
Columbia University

Carolyn O. Kurowski
Clark University

Michelle D. Leichtman
Harvard University

Linda L. Liu
Northwestern University

Jannette M. McMenamy
Clark University

Gilda A. Morelli
Boston College

Barbara Alexander Pan
Harvard Graduate School of Education

Paul C. Quinn
Brown University

Robert Roeser
Stanford University

Susan Rose
Albert Einstein College of Medicine

Diane N. Ruble
New York University

Ellyn G. Sheffield
Rutgers University

Laura B. Silverman
Yale Child Study Center

Catherine Snow
Harvard Graduate School of Education

Stephen J. Suomi
Laboratory of Comparative Ethology, NICHD

Catherine S. Tamis-LeMonda
New York University

Holli Tonyan
University of California at Los Angeles

Paola Uccelli
Harvard Graduate School of Education

Marion K. Underwood
University of Texas at Dallas

David H. Uttal
Northwestern University

Heidi Verhoef
Boston College

Theodore D. Wachs
Purdue University

Allan Wigfield
University of Maryland

PREFACE

The field of child psychology has experienced a number of prominent changes over the course of its relatively short history. These include increased emphases on: (1) individual variation in developmental processes, (2) the transactional and multidimensional nature of development, (3) the multiple contexts within which development unfolds, and (4) the processes and mechanisms that explain and underlie development in a particular domain. In addition, recent innovative methodologies have further stimulated new areas of inquiry and insights into children's social-emotional, cognitive, and linguistic development. This is an exciting and dynamic era in the field of child psychology, because new research findings have incited reexamination, modification, and extension of long-standing developmental theories.

Evident throughout the field of child psychology is the increased interest in the variation that exists within and across children in virtually all domains of development. During the first half of the 20th century, and well into the later half of the century, the study of child psychology had been traditionally a search for normative and systematic developments in children's thoughts and actions. The principle goal of developmental psychologists had been to describe species-typical progressions, that is, developmental sequences that were common to all children. During the last two decades the field has shifted away from the almost exclusive pursuit of universal principles. Researchers have become increasingly interested in understanding intra- and inter-individual variation across stages of reorganization, and have underscored the need for developmental theories to accommodate and account for this variation. Variation within and across children is no longer considered to be random "noise" in the system; instead, it is considered a critical key to describing, explaining, and predicting change.

Second, researchers in child psychology have increasingly recognized the transactional and multidimensional nature of development. Development is transactional insofar as children influence, and are influenced by, their experiences with persons and objects in the world around them. Development is multidimensional insofar as cognition, emotions, language, and temperament operate synergistically to moderate and mediate relations between children's experiences and development. Though many researchers focus on a specific area of development in their research, there is widespread recognition that multiple domains act in concert as part of a complex, multifaceted system. As one example, perception, cognition, affect, and socialization all affect children's language—thus, the acquisition of language is best conceptualized within this multidimensional, rapidly developing system.

Third, researchers in child psychology have increasingly emphasized the context-dependent nature of development. Families, schools, communities, and the overarching beliefs, ideologies, and practices of cultures and subcultures operate simultaneously in children's development, as do the co-relations that exist among these systems. When the uniqueness of individual children is added to the equation, the challenges that are encountered in interpreting and generalizing findings to other populations are notable. Given these challenges, overarching conclusions are rare in current child psychology. Instead, researchers are cautious in interpreting findings, and prudent in applying them to children in other ecological contexts. Consequently, developmental researchers must take into account the broader implications of new knowledge with respect to children's development as well as to their families, schools, and communities.

Finally, the field of child psychology has shifted away from an emphasis on description to one focused on theory and explanation. It does not suffice to merely identify a particular pattern or direction of change across two or more ages. Instead, developmental researchers ask *why* a particular pattern exists and what mechanisms or processes underlie the observed change. As children develop from one stage to another, identifying the start and end points of a specific development is only the first step. The nature of the observed changes, the laws or factors that govern the changes, the mechanisms underlying the changes, and the rules by which the changes occur are of primary interest.

In summary, a great deal of exciting and recent research in developmental psychology has advanced our knowledge about processes and changes in child development within various contexts. Together, these recent foci—on individual differences, transactional processes, multiple dimensions and contexts of development, and underlying mechanisms—are all reflected in the contemporary research that is presented in this handbook. This handbook contains original research by prominent investigators who address various issues in contemporary developmental research within their individual areas of expertise. Each chapter is organized to include an introduction to the topic within a cogent historical context leading up to a presentation of the researcher's current empirical work. Aside from this general organizational structure, a flexible format was adopted in order to retain the distinct voices of the authors.

The book is divided into five sections. Three of these represent a traditional, chronological approach to developmental achievements: *Infancy, Preschool,* and *Childhood.* The individual chapters in each of these sections address contemporary research on a specific domain of development, such as learning, cognition, and social and emotional development. The topics included in these sections are considered salient to particular age groups. However, the chapters are not locked into an arbitrary parallelism.

The fourth section, *Cross-Cutting Themes,* consists of chapters that are less bound to developmental achievements within a specific age group than the preceding ones. Instead, these more topically-based chapters emphasize issues that have significance across ages. In this section, highly relevant topics such as the impact of gender, poverty, violence, as well as the nature of parenting, are examined in the context of child development.

The fifth section, *New Frontiers,* consists of chapters that explore a wide variety of themes. These scientific investigations are not easily grouped under one heading, but clearly represent topics that are significant to the study of child development. This section presents research on child development with specific reference to family life-style issues, cross cultural differences in child care, early childhood amnesia, racial socialization, and nonhuman primate development.

☐ Section I: Infancy

In Chapter 1, *Emotional Self-Regulation in Infancy and Toddlerhood,* Grolnick, McMenamy, and Kurowski examine the origins of infants' self-regulatory capacities. They suggest that babies initially rely on outside sources, particularly caregivers, to aid them in their emotional self-regulation. Gradually, as part of an innate propensity, infants demonstrate the capacity "for autonomous, flexible, smooth, and adaptive regulation." In a series of studies with infants and toddlers (aged 12–32 months), the authors observed emotional regulatory strategies in separation and delay of gratification tasks. In addition, they assessed mothers' behaviors and reactions to their children in the two situations. They discuss both developmental changes and individual differences in mothers' and children's strategies in these emotionally challenging tasks.

In Chapter 2, *The What, Why, and How of Temperament: A Piece of the Action,* Theodore Wachs expresses dissatisfaction with the traditionally narrow focus on temperament as an isolated process. He proposes a model in which temperament is viewed as one part of a larger system. He argues that multiple factors of the child, such as age, gender, cognition, motivation, and biomedical status, act in concert with the individual's social context to explain the nature of, and changes to, various dimensions of temperament over time. His inclusion of biological, biosocial, and contextual influences on infant temperament locates his mood in an ecological framework.

Jay Belsky's chapter, *Infant-Parent Attachment,* traces the origins and determinants of individual differences in infant-parent attachment security. He places the formation of attachment relationships in its broader contextual framework, emphasizing the important roles of temperament, childcare, social support, marital quality, and work-family relations. His findings are largely drawn from his longitudinal research over the past two decades, referred to as the Pennsylvania Child and Family Project. He re-conceptualizes secure and insecure attachments as a function of "reproductive and life history strategies that are flexibly responsive to contextual and caregiving conditions and which evolved in the service of evolutionary goals."

Rose and Tamis-LeMonda's chapter, *Visual Information Processing in Infancy: Reflections on Underlying Mechanisms,* presents research on infants' visual information processing as assessed by habituation, novelty preference, visual expectation formation, and cross-modal transfer paradigms. They speculate about the mechanisms thought to underlie these diverse infant tests. They suggest that individual differences in infant performance on these paradigms are explained by speed of processing, memory, deployment of attention, perceptual organization and abstraction, and the development of a knowledge base. Social factors are also implicated in explaining the stability of infant cognition over time.

Paul Quinn's research on infant recognition and categorization, as presented in Chapter 5, *Development of Recognition and Categorization of Objects and Their Spatial Relations in Young Infants,* is guided by three concerns:

How do infants analyze complex patterns into visual elements to provide the building blocks for recognition of objects and spatial relations?

What visual properties and spatial relations of objects contribute to the process of categorization?

What factors control infant visual attention toward complex stimulus patterns?

In Quinn's series of visual experiments, babies are initially familiarized with complex spatial configurations and subsequently presented with variations of test stimuli. Babies' reactions to these "novel" arrangements are taken as evidence of the organization of the infant's mental representation of the familiar stimuli. Quinn demonstrates a considerable degree of coherence and order in infants' basic tendencies to group elements, objects, and spatial relations.

In Chapter 6, *The Signs and Sounds of Early Language Development,* Acredolo, Goodwyn, Horobin, and Emmons contend that the facility with which infants acquire symbolic gestures reveals much about early language development. Their focus begins during the preverbal period and continues through the onset of early combinations of words and gestures. Based on their early observations of spontaneous gestures, they launched a series of longitudinal studies in which parents trained their infants to use particular symbolic gestures. They found that sign-trained babies consistently exceeded control group infants on indices of later language and cognition. They draw attention to the ways in which their research on symbolic gesturing and early language development addresses the issues of asynchrony between comprehension and production, the vocabulary spurt, and onset of symbol combinations.

☐ Section II: Preschool Years

In Chapter 7, *Peer Relations,* Howes and Tonyan examine the role of peer groups on children's development of social interaction skills and the construction of social relationships. In their view, early peer relationships lay the groundwork for social relationships in childhood, adolescence, and adulthood. They provide a systematic review of their observational research on the complexity and quality of peer interactions, the processes of friendship formation over the course of early development, and the stability of children's social interactions with peers over the preschool years. They emphasize the importance of various functions of friendship such as experiences of support, trust, intimacy, and attachment, as well as the need to place the study of peer relations in its broader sociocultural context.

Kavanaugh and Harris examine children's ability to engage in pretense and counterfactual thinking in Chapter 8, *Pretense and Counterfactual Thought in Young Children.* They present their own research on 2-year-olds' abilities to reason and talk about pretend transformations. The authors contend that the capacity to reason about hypothetical causal sequences is grounded in children's understanding of literal or actual events. In fact, they demonstrate that 2-year-olds are capable of imagining events that they have not witnessed. They show that in addition to encoding events that have occurred, toddlers can also imagine alternate scenarios. They draw together four domains of cognition: pretense comprehension, counterfactual thinking, text comprehension, and the understanding of displaced utterances, suggesting a common underpinning to these abilities.

In Chapter 9, *Taking a Hard Look at Concreteness: Do Concrete Objects Help Young Children Learn Symbolic Relations*? Uttal, Liu, and DeLoache challenge the notions that concreteness is a complete characterization of young children's thought, and that the use of concrete instruction and materials improves children's understanding of symbols. They note that it has been long accepted that young children are more concrete than older children in their understanding of events. Moreover, it has been commonly assumed that younger children are bound to the "here and now," whereas older children are capable of more abstract symbolic thought—consequently, instruction with young children has emphasized the use of concrete materials. In a series of empirical demonstrations, they examine the conditions under which children treat models as concrete and interesting objects in themselves, as opposed to symbolic representations.

In Chapter 10, *The Role of Reminders in Young Children's Memory Development*, Hudson and Sheffield are motivated by the question of why memories from the infant and toddler years are less likely to be recalled over time than memories of events occurring after the age of three years. In a series of studies with toddlers, they examine memory reinstatement, a process whereby children are reminded of a past activity by reexperiencing a portion of the event. Through a systematic examination of a wide variety of "reminders," the authors specify the conditions under which children younger than three are able to "remember" (reenact) earlier experiences. They demonstrate that over time, preschoolers develop their ability to use partial information, and nonmatching and abstract representations, as memory cues because of their emerging understanding of the function of representations.

In Chapter 11, *Telling Two Kinds of Stories: Sources of Narrative Skill*, Uccelli, Hemphill, Pan, and Snow take the position that children develop skills in personal narratives and fantasy stories through ongoing activities and discussion with adults, for example, a joint focus of attention on a specific toy. They undertake a series of longitudinal investigations of preschoolers with their parents in relation to social interactions and narrative attainments at five years of age. They suggest that "experience in talking about the nonpresent, practice in negotiating, shifts between talk about the 'here-and-now' and talk about the nonpresent, and engagement in a broad range of communicative interchanges may be crucial preparation for the attainment of autonomous narrative production."

☐ Section III: Childhood

In Chapter 12, *Emotion Regulation in Peer Relationships During Middle Childhood*, Underwood and Hurley review research on children's peer relations and friendships during middle childhood, the correlates and determinants of peer status, and children's emotional regulation in peer interactions. The authors present findings from their empirical research on peer status and children's emotions, the development of display rules for anger in middle childhood, and relations between display rules and peer status. They draw attention to the importance of examining children's insights into their own emotions, and to individual differences in children's strategies for controlling emotions.

In Chapter 13, *Metacognitive Development*, Kuhn provides a framework for conceptualizing developments in children's metacognitive abilities from the preschool years through early adolescence. In a series of studies with children of different ages, she examines developmental changes in children's metastrategic knowing (children's "knowing" about procedural knowledge) and metacognitive knowing (children's "knowing" about declarative knowledge). In her research, children engage in a task over multiple sessions and are asked to identify the causal and noncausal factors that influence the outcome of physical events (for example, what factors determine how fast a toy boat traverses water). By examining changes to children's strategy choices and inferences over time, as well as at different developmental stages, she addresses fundamental issues regarding the nature of change in metacognitive thought. She points out that attention to children's developing metastrategic and metacognitive competencies has the potential of informing educators' efforts to enhance student thinking, and discusses the implications of her findings for educational interventions with children.

In Chapter 14, *Academic and Motivational Pathways Through Middle Childhood*, Eccles, Roeser, Wigfield, and Freedman-Doan review the literature on changes in academic self concepts and motivational orientations from middle childhood to early adolescence. In a series of longitudinal investigations, they examine relations among children's academic self-concept, school success, and emotional development. They present the psychological and situational bases for declines in children's academic motivation and school engagement over the elementary school years. Teacher and self-report instruments are shown to yield different patterns of decline and reasons for those declines differ in individual children. The authors also identify "academically resilient" children who achieve positive school adjustment despite early difficulties. They point to the importance of identifying ways in which children compensate for difficulties experienced in the academic domain.

Eisenberg and Fabes discuss the role of emotion and emotion-related regulation in children's empathy, problem behavior, and competent social behavior in Chapter 15, *Emotion, Emotion-Related Regulation, and Quality of Socioemotional Functioning*. They integrate various methodologies including parent and teacher reports, self-report, facial and physiological markers, and observation. Moreover, by employing a multimethod approach they are able to show the relative value of particular approaches to the study of socioemotional development at different ages for different outcomes for children. The model they present points to the importance of attending to both moderation and mediation in thinking about the prediction of children's social status and social behavior.

☐ Section IV: Cross-Cutting Themes

In Chapter 16, *Parenting*, Bradley and Corwyn emphasize "parenting as the most powerful and enduring external force in the lives of children." They provide a comprehensive overview of their programmatic research using the HOME at different developmental stages and in different cultural groups. Their contribution addresses four key questions concerning parenting: What is parenting? What difference does parenting make in the lives of children? How does context affect parenting? Who performs the task of parenting?

After providing a review of pertinent research on gender preferences in Chapter 17, *The Role of Gender Knowledge in Children's Gender-Typed Preferences*, Aubry, Ruble, and Silverman examine the stereotyped knowledge and preference trends in children's gender typing. Although knowledge of gender stereotypes may guide and influence children's interests and behaviors, they argue that there are several relevant factors that may also play a significant role. For example, factors such as "motivational/attidudinal processes are also likely to be important determinants of children's responsiveness to gender norms." Specifically, they call for a better understanding of the relationship between gender knowledge and preferences at different stages in early and middle childhood, using novel methodological approaches.

In Chapter 18, *Effects of Poverty on Children*, Huston reviews current research on pathways through which poverty exerts an influence on children's development. In particular, she reviews her own research on mass media and childcare as two potentially salient factors. Huston describes an intervention project in which resources are provided to working poor adults in order to examine their effects on children and families. The major components of the intervention are guaranteed minimum income, work requirement, subsidized health insurance, subsidized childcare, and job search services. Her aim is to determine the extent to which these services influence the quality of family life and, in turn, effect children's sense of well-being and social competencies.

In Chapter 19, *The Effects of Community Violence on Children*, Garbarino introduces the concept of the "urban war zone" as a way of understanding the developmental issues faced by children exposed to chronic community violence. His in-depth and poignant interviews with school-aged children and youth lend themselves to a model of risk accumulation in the area of inner-city violence. He draws parallels between refugee camps and low-income public housing projects in the United States. As a result of their exposures to violence and trauma, he asserts that children construct "social maps" and worldviews that influence their contemporary and future attitudes and interactions with the people that inhabit their worlds. He contends that community violence and its consequences "can make children prime candidates for involvement in social groups that augment or replace families. . . ." In many urban war zones, this means gangs.

☐ Section V: New Frontiers

As lifestyles change, so does research into the effects of parenting on child development. Golombok's chapter, *New Family Forms: Children Raised in Solo Mother Families, Lesbian Mother Families, and in Families Created by Assisted Reproduction*, focuses on children who are raised in various family forms. Golombok presents findings from a series of longitudinal investigations with participants who were drawn from countries in northern and southern Europe. She looks at children's psychological adjustment by comparing and contrasting different groups such as naturally conceived children versus children conceived by assisted reproduction, and children reared in lesbian households versus children raised by single heterosexual women.

The topic of childhood amnesia has had a long and provocative history in the psychological literature. Leichtman's chapter, *Cultural, Social, and Maturational Influences on Childhood Amnesia*, focuses on the role of experiential and maturational factors in accounting for childhood amnesia. She reviews relevant recent research on three aspects of memory: adult memories of early childhood, children's long-term memory, and children's suggestibility. She concludes that both the timing and character of early recollections are influenced by a myriad of factors including maturation, language, early interactions, and cultural milieu.

In Chapter 22, *The Nature of Parents' Race-Related Communications to Children: A Developmental Perspective*, Hughes and Chen maintain that for children to function effectively in a pluralistic society they will need to develop attitudes and competencies that enable them to interact with people from different ethnic backgrounds. Accordingly, they turn their attention to "racial knowledge," which they define as "children's attitudes toward various racial groups as well as their understandings of racial hierarchies, systems of social stratification, and associated processes such as prejudice and discrimination." They assert that parents are key socializing agents in the process of acquiring racial knowledge. Their research focuses on parents' racial socialization practices at different periods across development (4–12 years-of-age). They examine similarities and differences in socialization practices across racial and ethnic groups.

In Chapter 23, *Who Should Help Me Raise My Child? A Cultural Approach to Understanding Nonmaternal Child Care Decisions*, Morelli and Verhoef draw from the fields of cultural psychology and anthropology in an effort to explain the factors that inform parent's decisions about child care. They examine the child care practices and beliefs among the Efe, hunter and gatherers of the Democratic Republic of Congo (formerly, Zaire), and the Nso community of Cameroon. Through extensive qualitative interviews and observations of members of various communities, they shed light on the role of cultural beliefs and ethnotheories in parents' decisions concerning child care.

Suomi's chapter, *Behavioral Inhibition and Impulsive Aggressiveness: Insights from Studies with Rhesus Monkeys*, presents basic issues of developmental continuity and change, and of stability of individual differences in behavioral inhibition and impulsive aggressiveness. The author addresses these issues by examining the response patterns in rhesus monkeys in order to inform and advance our understanding of the same processes in humans. He highlights the manner and degree to which environment interacts with heritable factors in shaping individual developmental trajectories. He asserts that parallel principles exist regarding the basic issues of nature-nurture, continuity-discontinuity, and inter-individual stability throughout development.

In summary, each of the chapters in the five sections of this handbook presents thought-provoking questions and current perspectives and methodologies on diverse topics in child psychology. The contributors to this handbook represent an impressive group of experts who have invested a tremendous amount of thought and intellectual effort in discussing the essence of their programmatic research. As such, this handbook should appeal broadly to professionals and advanced students who seek to better understand the nature, processes, and outcomes of child development within its many ecological settings.

—Lawrence Balter, Catherine S. Tamis-LeMonda

INFANCY

1
CHAPTER

Wendy S. Grolnick
Jannette M. McMenamy
Carolyn O. Kurowski

Emotional Self-Regulation in Infancy and Toddlerhood

☐ Introduction

Emotion regulation has become an area of increasing interest in the field of child development. The topic encompasses research by theorists representing temperamental, neurophysiological, relational, motivational, and personality viewpoints on development and intersects areas of affective, cognitive, behavioral, and even motor development. One of the reasons the topic has become so popular is that it is a broad rubric which subsumes many interesting questions about emotional development and helps us to understand key developmental outcomes such as depression and peer relationships (e.g., Calkins, 1997a; Cole, Michel, & Teti, 1994). In addition, it is a topic relevant to the life span (Cicchetti, Ganiban, & Barnett, 1991): Emotion regulation can be conceptualized as ranging from the rudimentary skills seen in the newborn to the complex strategies used by adults.

In our work we have highlighted the changing role of the self in the development of emotion regulation. In particular, we have been interested in the processes by which children develop the internal mechanisms to "self-regulate" emotion; that is, to be the origin of such capacities. Relying on self-determination theory (Deci & Ryan, 1985), we conceptualize the development of emotional self-regulation as a movement from reliance on outside sources or control-related processes to a growing capacity for autonomous, flexible, smooth, and adaptive regulation. We see this movement as an active process, part of the organism's innate propensity to master and become autonomous with respect to both his or her internal and external environments. Self-determination theory provides a way for us to understand the processes through which the development of emotion regulation takes place, including its energization and the factors which facilitate or forestall it.

In this chapter, we present a theory of the development of emotional self-regulation, focusing in particular on the toddler and early preschool years. We open our discussion by reviewing recent definitions of emotion that are grounded in a functionalist approach and tying this view to more specific definitions of emotion regulation. Next, we describe our motivational theory through which we view the development of emotional self-regulation. Given the varied use of terminology in the literature, we include a section on key distinctions such as those between emotion control and emotion regulation and emotion management versus emotional integration. Following this, we provide an in-depth discussion of our framework for understanding the development of emotional self-regulation that includes a review of empirical support for our theory. Drawing on our own work and that of others (e.g., Calkins, 1994; Kopp, 1989), we also present a model of factors that contribute to emotional self-regulation, including those within the child (such as temperament and aspects of the caregiving environment). We conclude by considering some of the conceptual and methodological issues facing emotion regulation researchers as well as the implications of emotion regulation for later adaptation.

☐ Defining Emotional Self-Regulation

We begin our discussion of definitions of emotion regulation with a more general view of emotion. In contrast to views of emotion as being necessarily disruptive, recent functionalist views argue that emotions are adaptive responses that have motivating and organizing functions which help individuals in the pursuit of their goals (Campos, Campos, & Barrett, 1989). Stressing the goal-directed nature of emotion, Barrett and Campos (1987) described the functions, both intra- and interpersonal, of emotions in individuals' goal-oriented behavior. According to their theory, anger, for example, could be viewed as the result of a person trying to overcome an obstacle. It signals to the self to mobilize energy to try and overcome the obstacle as well as to others that they should submit to the individual. Joy has the function of maintaining the individual's behavior and of signaling to others to keep the interaction going (Emde, 1988). If emotions are viewed in this way, the goal of emotion regulation processes would not necessarily be to diminish or suppress emotions but, rather, to facilitate the adaptive use of emotions. Such a view is integral to recent conceptualizations of emotion regulation.

Current definitions of *emotion regulation* have focused on the adaptive benefits of being able to flexibly alter or adjust one's emotional state. Campos, Mumme, Kermoian, and Campos (1994) described emotion regulation as the process of maintaining or changing an emotional stance. Fox (1994) described emotion regulation as the ability to modulate affect in terms of socially and culturally defined norms. In his comprehensive definition, Thompson (1994) defined emotion regulation as "the extrinsic and intrinsic processes responsible for monitoring, evaluating, and modifying emotional reactions, especially their intensive and temporal features, to accomplish one's goals" (pp. 27–28). Inherent in this definition is the notion of modulation or management of emotion—the common thread across most definitions—as well as the assumption that the way one expresses and experiences emotion may affect behavior in the individual's pursuit of various ends. In our own work, we have defined emotional self-regulation as the set of processes involved in initiating, maintaining, and modulating emotional responsiveness, both positive and negative (Grolnick, Bridges, & Connell, 1996). Two aspects of this definition merit further discussion.

First, this definition includes both positive and negative emotions. In accord with recent research, we recognize, as described above, that both positive and negative emotions serve adaptive functions for the child. Given this focus on the adaptive functions of emotions, it is reasonable to consider together issues involved in the regulation of both positive and negative emotions.

Second, in defining emotion regulation, we not only include the modulation and termination of emotional responsiveness but also its initiation and maintenance. While most research on emotion regulation has focused on the dampening of negative emotions, the goals of children and adults might well be served by the enhancement and maintenance of emotional arousal, both negative and positive (Thompson, 1994). For example, initiating positive emotions may involve caretakers in play and other positive exchanges. Intensification of anger might help to mobilize action, such as enabling oneself to stand up for one's rights or state one's needs. The inclusion of the initiation and maintenance of emotional states allows for a more comprehensive account of the function of emotion regulation in goal-directed behavior.

☐ A Developmental View

Using our definition of emotion regulation, we suggest that emotion regulation is a developmental phenomenon influenced by both individual differences among children and the relational context within which the child is developing. Our developmental view is organized around the construct of autonomy and is based on self-determination theory which stresses the key roles of three psychological needs—autonomy, competence, and relatedness—for motivated action. In order to explicate this view, we begin with a discussion of self-determination theory. We then relate this view to emotional self-regulation.

Self-determination theory can be characterized as an organismic theory stressing that development is a motivated process which emanates from the organism (Deci & Ryan, 1985). According to this viewpoint, individuals are born with innate tendencies to operate on their inner and outer environments in attempts to master them. Underlying this tendency to master, organize, and overtake oneself is the energy source referred to as *intrinsic motivation*. Intrinsic motivation, then, fuels the seeking out of novelty, pursuit of challenges, and other growth-promoting experiences. In short, intrinsic motivation is the fuel behind development.

The theory further postulates three psychological needs underlying intrinsic motivation. The first need is to feel autonomous or to feel that one's actions emanate from oneself. A second is to feel competent in dealing with the environment, including both the internal and external environments. A third need is for relatedness or connectedness with important others. These needs are complementary. For example, one can fulfill needs for autonomy and relatedness by being choicefully connected to another person.

From this viewpoint, children will naturally move toward autonomy, competence, and relatedness, as long as the environment does not thwart this movement. Applying this concept to emotional development, movement toward more active, self-initiated regulation is an expression of children's natural tendencies toward growth and development more generally in the direction of autonomy, competence, and relatedness. Children fulfill needs for autonomy as they experience a greater sense of agency in the expression of emotion as well as a greater capacity to use the information contained in their emotional experiences to serve their goals. Autonomous regulation is the converse of being other-reliant in one's emotion regulation or of being overwhelmed by emotional experiences, both of which lack a sense of self as an active regulator of one's experience. Also, as children take more responsibility for regulating emotion, they obtain a sense of competence as they master impulses and emotions rather than being overtaken by them. Finally, as children move toward greater self-regulation of emotion, they are able to fulfill the goals that others have for them, such as expressing emotions in a socially acceptable manner (Kopp, 1989). In addition, they are more likely to be able to initiate and maintain positive interactions with others. Both of these tendencies bring them closer to others and increase their sense of relatedness to others. In these ways, autonomy and relatedness work together and enhance one another.

While children will naturally move toward greater autonomy, competence, and relatedness with respect to emotional processes, there are aspects of development in relation to emotion regulation that are not natural or spontaneous. For example, modulating the expression of strong negative emotions is not something that children are intrinsically motivated to do but, rather, it represents the social expectations of children's caregivers and social groups. Such regulation first must be accomplished through caregiver prompts and interventions. The taking on of initially externally regulated behaviors or strategies falls under the rubric of internalization (Ryan, Connell, & Deci, 1985). *Internalization* is the means through which regulatory processes that originally are external in origin become transformed into part of the personal repertoire of the child. Intrinsically motivated activities as well as the internalization of extrinsically afforded regulations are the two major strands of development. As such, they both are fueled by intrinsic motivation and the underlying needs for autonomy, competence, and relatedness.

Another relevant aspect of this theory is the specification of environments that facilitate or inhibit intrinsically motivated activity and the internalization of externally afforded regulations. A corollary of the theory is that environments which support the child's needs for autonomy, competence, and relatedness will facilitate the two processes of intrinsic motivation and internalization, and those undermining these needs will forestall them. In particular, we have suggested that environments characterized by support for autonomy, structure, and involvement facilitate the development of behavioral self-regulation (Grolnick & Ryan, 1989), and we have now expanded this theory to the emotional realm (Ryan, Deci, & Grolnick, 1995). We will return to this social-contextual aspect of the theory in the Caregiver Contributions section.

☐ Key Distinctions

Emotional Control Versus Regulation

In our viewpoint, as in that of others, the regulation of emotions and impulses is not just a matter of controlling or stifling these internal responses. In managing their arousal, some children will exert great effort, forcing themselves to push emotions out of awareness. The experience of such regulation is one of feeling pressured or controlled. Controlling emotions in this way requires energy and attention and diminishes the child's capacity to engage with the environment. It also does not allow one to adaptively use the information inherent in the emotional experience. The chronic stifling or controlling of emotions may play a role in problem behavior or psychopathology (Buck, 1984). Other children may regulate emotions, even relatively strong distress, by engaging in alternative activities or by talking about their disappointment. They may be able to more flexibly choose strategies to manage emotions that allow them to engage the environment in the particular situation. Such emotion management has more of the quality of autonomous emotion regulation.

A distinction between emotion control and emotion regulation also has been made by others, notably Kopp (1982) and Block and Block (1980). Kopp (1982), for example, discussed self-control and self-regulation as stages in the child's development of behavior regulation. In the stage of self-control, the child has the ability to comply with the caregiver's demands and directives in the absence of the caregiver. Though emitted by the child, the behavior is rigid, conforming to the original directive. In contrast, the stage of self-regulation involves the flexible guiding of behavior. The child's behavior at this point is actively and flexibly adjusted to meet the demands of new situations. We concur with this distinction between control and regulation; however, we do not see these as developmental stages but, rather, as a continuum of regulation which is a function both of development and individual differences among children. While for Kopp (1982) the stage of self-control is not considered to begin until the second year, our emotional self-regulatory continuum is relevant from birth. As children develop, they move toward greater autonomy. In addition, within any age, children can be characterized as being at a more or less self-regulated point on the continuum.

In related work, Block and Block (1980) described the concepts of ego resiliency and ego control. *Ego control* involves the expression or inhibition of feelings, desires, and impulses. *Ego overcontrol* involves the suppression of action and expression across contexts regardless of the appropriateness of such actions and expressions. *Ego undercontrol* involves the expression of impulses regardless of context. *Ego resiliency*, on the other hand, is the extent to which ego control is modifiable based on contextual input. It is the extent to which the individual can meet contextual demands by altering the expression or containment of impulses and behavior. Similar to the concept of ego resiliency, the goal of emotional self-regulation is not to inhibit emotion, but to flexibly modulate the expression and containment of emotional arousal and to adaptively use the information provided by one's emotional arousal.

Also related to the issue of emotional control versus emotion regulation is work on delay of gratification. Research on delay of gratification focuses on children's abilities to restrict behavior in tempting situations (Mischel, 1974). The typical paradigm involves placing a desired object near the child and asking the child to refrain from touching the object until a certain time. The dependent variable in such experiments is time to delay behavior. Though informative in terms of assessing children's inhibition of impulses, the paradigm does not allow one to determine the nature of the regulatory processes through which children are able to delay. For example, delay behavior can be accomplished through self-imposed pressure which results in the experience of tension and discomfort and the suppression of other adaptive behaviors. Alternately, individuals can delay smoothly through the use of attention deployment and diversion which allows for engagement in other adaptive behaviors. Our experimental paradigms are designed to examine behavior during mildly stressful periods so that the specific processes through which distress is regulated can be examined.

Emotion Management Versus Emotional Integration

In discussing the issue of emotion regulation, we distinguish between emotion management per se, which involves the face of expression to the outside world, and emotional integration. When autonomously regulating emotions, individuals use emotions as guides to behavior, choicefully integrating the information inherent in them. The goal of emotional integration not only is to comply with social norms or act in opposition to one's experiences, but also to use one's inner experiences in acting flexibly. Sometimes individuals may choose to act counter to the urge or emotion and, at other times, to act consistently with it. For example, having a toy taken away often elicits anger in children. A child who is capable of emotion management without integration might respond to the situation in a socially appropriate manner (e.g., by walking away from the situation). However, this child will be unable to actively resolve his or her present anger or find ways to prevent himself or herself from becoming angry in the future. In contrast, a second child who is also capable of emotion integration may respond in the same way, but also may be able to recognize his or her feelings of anger and use that information adaptively (e.g., by seeking the assistance of an adult or by not playing with the offending child again). The key point is that whether or not an emotion is integrated cannot be judged on the basis of socially appropriate behavior alone. A child's ability to recognize his or her emotions and use them adaptively is equally as important. Thus, the concept of emotional self-regulation includes two aspects: (a) emotion management, whereby emotional arousal can be modulated appropriately; and (b) emotional integration, whereby emotions are assimilated and utilized.

Other-Reliance Versus Emotions In-Relation

Autonomous self-regulation of emotion is not synonymous with regulation that is independent from others or is accomplished alone. Autonomous regulation may actively involve others. To illustrate this point, we make the distinction between strategies in-relation and those that are other-reliant. For example, in a waiting situation, self-regulating emotion may involve engaging the mother in a game, a strategy that clearly is in-relation. This is strikingly different from a child who waits for the mother to intervene and allows her to take responsibility for providing distracting activities. Such a strategy would be considered other-reliant. While, in the first situation, the child is active and self-initiating in his or her regulatory attempts, the second situation involves passivity and dependence. Therefore, in our work examining the emotion regulation strategies that parents and children use, we note who is initiating the strategy as well as who is maintaining it.

The adaptiveness of engaging others in one's regulatory attempts and, thus, its status as in-relation versus other-reliant, depends on the context. For example, when others are unavailable or temporarily unresponsive, it is not particularly adaptive to try to involve them (Grolnick, Bridges, & Connell, 1996). However, when they are available and willing to be involved, such strategies may be most helpful. We return to this issue later in the chapter in the Conceptual and Methodological Issues section.

☐ Our Framework

In our theoretical and empirical framework, we posit that the capacity for emotional self-regulation is composed of two interrelated processes: emotional responsiveness and emotional self-regulation strategies (Grolnick, Bridges, & Connell, 1996). *Emotional responsiveness* represents the degree to which an individual responds both expressively and experientially to arousing events. This process is evident in characteristics of an individual's emotional expressions, such as intensity, latency to respond, and duration. Emotional self-regulation strategies are the various behaviors that can be used to modify or alter emotional responses.

Consistent with the self-determination framework outlined above, we conceptualize the development of these processes as involving movement from more passive, stimulus-bound, and other-reliant strategies to more active, autonomous forms of regulation. In our recent work, we have identified strategies that young children use to regulate distress in mildly stressful situations. These strategies are viewed as lying along a continuum from passive, reactive, and stimulus-bound to more active, proactive, and reorienting strategies. Below, we describe three sets of strategies from which six specific strategy codes are derived. These sets of strategies are drawn from our work in delay and separation situations, along with related work by others.

Our first set of strategies involves processes which allow for shifts in attention away from arousing stimuli. Attentional processes play an important role in modulating arousal from infancy onward (Rothbart & Posner, 1985). The newborn is equipped with rudimentary mechanisms for disengaging from stimuli (Kessen & Mandler, 1961) and overstimulating interactions (Gianino & Tronick, 1988), although the more voluntary shifting of attention begins to occur between 3 and 6 months (Rothbart, Posner, & Boylan, 1990). Redirection of attention away from a distressing stimulus and toward another object, person, or event is a strategy used frequently by older infants, toddlers, and their parents (Grolnick, Kurowski, McMenamy, Rivkin, & Bridges, 1998).

While particular strategies can be seen as ranging from those that are more passive and stimulus bound to those that are more active and autonomous, it is important to note that any type of strategy can be more or less active and sustained. Redirection of attention can be conceptualized in this way. It can range from brief looks away in the newborn period (Fox, 1989) to sustained toy play in toddlers. Thus, one can conceptualize attentional deployment strategies as being more or less active. We have tried to capture this distinction in our categorization by coding two strategies: active engagement with objects and more passive exploration and object use.

The usefulness of attentional distraction, and, particularly, more active kinds of attention deployment including abilities to shift and maintain attention, has been demonstrated by several researchers. Rothbart and her colleagues (e.g., Rothbart, Ziaie, & O'Boyle, 1992) demonstrated that the ability to control attention was associated with low levels of negative emotion in infants. Mischel (1974) found that children who are most able to delay obtaining an object are those who use a variety of self-distraction techniques.

Braungart and Stifter (1991) differentiated between toy play (engaged and sustained behavior) and looking at objects and people (less sustained behavior). These authors examined the use of these strategies and their relations with distress in separation episodes. Their findings indicated that higher levels of distress were associated with less toy play.

A second set of behaviors used by children to regulate their emotions are those for comfort or reassurance. We include three types of comforting strategies: physical comforting, other-directed comforting, and symbolic self-soothing. Comfort behaviors can be self-directed, including physical self-soothing behaviors such as thumb sucking or using familiar or special objects to obtain comfort (Klackenberg, 1949; Passman & Weisberg, 1975). Stifter (1993) described the prevalence of physical self-soothing strategies in 5- through 10-month-olds and noted their effectiveness in decreasing distress levels in children of this age. Comfort behaviors also can be directed toward a caregiver, such as in attempts to attain proximity and contact (e.g., Ainsworth & Wittig, 1969).

Comforting behaviors also can be symbolic in nature. Piaget (1954) noted that the use of the symbolic function, such as in play or imitation, helps children to master a difficult situation. The child may evoke a representation of an object or situation causing distress and develop game-like activity in the service of emotion regulation. For example, a child may pretend that he or she has obtained a desired object. Such behaviors differ from engagement in alternative activities since the child remains focused on the distressing object. Yet, by using his or her representational capacities, the child transforms the situation into one that is manageable and, thus, is comforted. The child's repertoire of symbolic self-soothing strategies is expanded by the acquisition of language. Linguistic abilities can help children to state their feelings, to obtain verbal feedback about appropriate regulation, and to hear about and think about ways to manage emotions (Kopp, 1989). Self-directed speech also may facilitate the child's ability to bring action and emotion under control. Flavell (1966) used the term *private speech* to describe this self-directed speech, and noted that the function of such speech was self-guidance. Berk (1986) demonstrated that private speech helped children to inhibit off-task behavior in a task situation, and Bivens and Berk (1990) demonstrated greater use of private speech in older versus younger elementary children.

Finally, the distressed child can maintain or increase focus on the distressing stimulus and attempt to alter a temporarily unresponsive environment. For example, during a separation, the child can search for his or her mother or, while in a delay situation, he or she can focus on the desired object. We thus include focus on the desired object/search for mother as a final strategy. Supporting the less adaptive nature of this type of strategy, Bridges and Connell (1991) found that, during a brief separation, the child's search for his or her mother was positively correlated with distress. Mischel (1974) demonstrated that, when a child's attention was directed toward the goal, voluntary delay was diminished.

We have conducted several studies examining the use of these six strategies (see Figure 1.1), their relations to emotional responsiveness, and the effects of context on their use. The first study examined the emotional responses and strategy use of 37 24-month-old children. We observed the children in two paradigms: a separation paradigm and a delay paradigm, each with two variants. In one of the two delay situations, children had to wait to receive a present and, in the other, they had to wait to eat some goldfish crackers and raisins. Further, the delays were conducted under one of two conditions: under one condition, the mother was free to do anything she wanted while her child waited (parent-active); under the other, she was asked to read a magazine and remain relatively passive, though she could respond to her child (parent-passive) during the waiting period. In the separation paradigm, children participated in a modified strange situation. Our focus was on the portion of the session when the mother left the room and the child was with an experimenter (experimenter-present) and the portion when the child was alone (child-alone).

For each of the four situations (two delay and two separation), we rated the children's affect in 5-second intervals using Thompson's facial and vocal scales which range from positive to negative. Also coded in the same intervals was children's use of the six strategies: active engagement with substitute objects, passive use of objects and exploration, symbolic self-soothing, physical self-soothing, other-directed comforting, and focus on the desired object/search for mother (see Figure 1.1).

Among these 2-year olds, active engagement with substitute objects was the most frequently used strategy, followed by focus on the desired object/search for mother. These results indicate that children of this age are able to use active distraction during mildly stressful situations, though their attention is also vulnerable to pulls by the stimulus. We also examined the relations between children's use of the various strategies and their levels of distress. These results appear in Table 1.1. Use of active engagement was

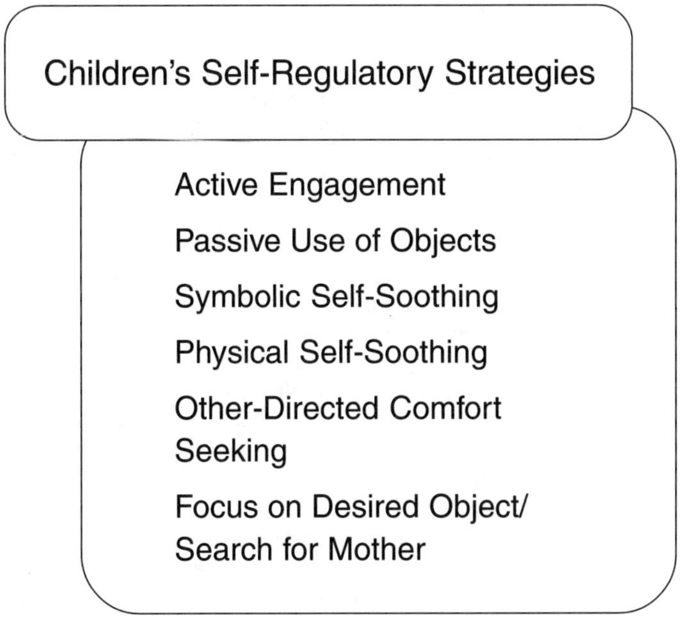

FIGURE 1.1. Self-regulatory strategies displayed by children in delay and separation situations.

highly negatively associated with children's distress while, as expected, focus on desired object/search for mother was positively related to distress in all situations. Relations between other strategies and distress levels varied by situation, but generally supported the continuum model, whereby those strategies defined as more active and reorienting were most negatively correlated with distress while those defined as more passive, other-directed, and stimulus-bound were most positively correlated with distress. In general, our findings supported the continuum of autonomy in which active, autonomous strategies are more adaptive than passive, other-reliant ones.

We also were interested in the effects of context on children's strategy use. For example, children more actively engaged in toy play when an adult was present and participatory than when an adult was not present or passive. Conversely, when an adult was unavailable, children tended to be more focused on the desired object. This finding was replicated in a longitudinal study of 12- and 14-month-olds (Bridges, Grolnick, & Connell, 1997). In both instances, children were able to use the most active and adaptive strategies when regulating in relation to their caregivers. These findings illustrate the relative dependence of children on caretakers for regulatory assistance during the first 2 years.

TABLE 1.1. Within situation correlations between strategy use and emotional expressiveness

	Separation		Delay	
	Experimenter Absent	Experimenter Present	Parent Active	Parent Passive
1. Active engagement with substitute objects	−.56***	−.84***	−.54***	−.27
2. Passive use of objects and exploration	−.49**	−.35*	−.09	−.39*
3. Symbolic self-soothing	−.10	−.19	−.02	−.22
4. Physical self-soothing	−.004	.48**	.25	.30*
5. Other-directed comforting	—	.31*	.00	.15
6. Focus on the desired object/ search for mother	.63***	.63***	.47**	.02

* $p < .05$. ** $p < .01$. *** $p < .001$.

☐ Developmental Evidence

Beyond this descriptive work on strategies, our model postulates developmental trends in the use of more active, autonomous strategies with age. Other investigators have provided data relevant to this issue and we have extended our own work with 2-year-olds to 12-, 18-, and 32-month-olds.

While not specifically categorizing their strategies along an active to passive continuum, Mangelsdorf, Shapiro, and Marzolf (1995) found that, relative to 6- and 12-month-olds, 18-month-olds were more likely to attempt to direct interactions with strangers during separations. They also found that 12-month-olds were more likely to self-soothe than 18-month-olds. Parritz (1996) found that, in "challenging situations" (e.g., presentation of a mechanical toy), 18-month-olds were more likely to attempt to control the situation with various behavioral strategies than 12-month-olds. These findings support the notion that older children are more able to utilize active strategies than their younger counterparts.

In our work (Bridges, Grolnick, & Connell, 1995), we examined children's use of our six strategies in a cross-sectional study of 150 12-, 18-, 24-, and 32-month-olds using the delay and separation paradigms described above. Results indicated that 12- and 18-month-olds were less likely to actively engage with substitute objects, either alone or with a caregiver, during these situations relative to 24- and 32-month-olds. Conversely, the older children were less likely to use other-directed strategies, such as comfort seeking, relative to the younger children. This work supports the expected developmental progression toward increasingly autonomous forms of regulation outlined above.

In another study, Grolnick, Cosgrove, and Bridges (1996) focused on the initiation of positive affect during free play in 140 toddlers. First, all expressions of positive affect by children were identified. Next, we coded whether these affective displays were child-initiated (i.e., spontaneous), prompted (i.e., following some maternal verbal or nonverbal behavior that did not involve the expression of positive affect), or mother-initiated (i.e., following a maternal affective display). Results indicated that the proportion of prompted episodes increased with age, particularly between 12 and 18 months, and then leveled off. Thus, by 18 months, children were able to respond with positive affect to neutral actions and verbalizations by their mothers at a rate comparable to older children. The proportion of child-initiated displays also increased with age, particularly between 24 and 32 months. Finally, mother-initiated episodes decreased with age. The results support our thesis that, as they become older, children take greater responsibility for regulating affective exchanges with others. We speculate that the transition between 12 and 18 months in prompted episodes may be due to children's emerging representational capacities. Such capacities, including recall memory, enable the child to evoke representations of earlier positive exchanges and enact them in the present (Kopp, 1989). However, children still require concrete prompts to exercise these capacities. By 24 months, children have developed their representational capacities to the point that they are able to initiate positive exchanges in an unsupported manner.

☐ Contributors to Emotion Regulation Capacities

We now turn to a discussion of some of the factors that contribute to children's emotional self-regulatory abilities. In our model (see Figure 1.2) we focus on individual differences (i.e., temperament) that children might bring to the task of emotion regulation. Within any age group, a range of strategies and various levels of emotional responsiveness can be observed in response to our procedures, differences which tend to be cross-situationally consistent (Grolnick, Bridges, & Connell, 1996). Such differences may be linked to children's temperaments. We also examine caregiver contributions to developmental and individual differences in children's emotional expressiveness and strategy use.

Temperament

While there are many different conceptualizations of temperament, there is relative agreement that *temperament* describes a collection of behavioral tendencies thought to have some biological basis as well as a certain degree of continuity over the life span (Goldsmith et al., 1987). These tendencies or styles of responding are thought to be distinct from specific behaviors, but are believed to influence how different individuals act and feel about similar circumstances and events.

Several recent conceptualizations of temperament focus on individuals' dispositions to express emo-

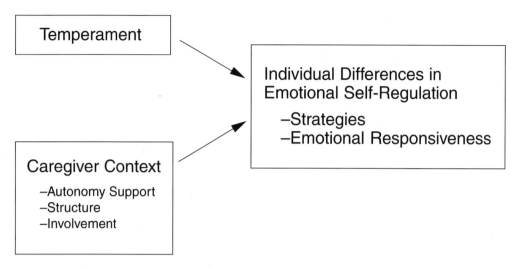

FIGURE 1.2. Factors influencing children's emotional self-regulation.

tions, including the intensity of emotional experiences, emotional reactivity, or both, constructs with obvious relevance to emotion regulation. For example, Goldsmith and Campos (1982) defined temperament as individual differences in the expression of basic emotions such as anger and sadness, fear, pleasure, and interest. In an approach that perhaps is most relevant to our work, Rothbart and her colleagues (e.g., Rothbart & Derryberry, 1981; Rothbart & Posner, 1985) defined temperament as constitutionally based individual differences in reactivity and self-regulation. According to this theory, reactivity is the quality of individuals' responses to changes in the environment. A key aspect of reactivity is susceptibility to distress (i.e., how much stimulation is needed to generate arousal). The second component of temperament, self-regulation, encompasses children's capacities for dealing with various levels of arousal. Conceptualized in this way, it is clear that temperament affects both the extent to which regulation is required as well as the ways in which children might acquire regulatory strategies.

Fox (1989) used this conceptualization of temperament to account for differences in the types of strategies that children need to regulate their emotions. He argued that children's reactivity levels shape the sort of emotion regulation strategies they need to acquire. For example, a child who is highly reactive, but possesses few regulatory skills, may become aroused too quickly and may be prevented from exercising existing strategies. He or she thus may be forced to rely on the assistance of caregivers more often than another, less reactive child. Under such circumstances, highly reactive children would have fewer opportunities to elaborate or expand their repertoire of regulatory strategies compared to less reactive children or those who possess some self-regulatory skills. Fox also claimed that temperamental factors, such as mood lability and domination by only one or a couple of emotions, can be linked to less adaptive emotion regulatory processes, such as lack of access to the full range of emotions and inability to make fluid shifts between affective states (Fox, 1997).

Eisenberg and Fabes (1992) similarly conceptualized the importance of the dimensions of reactivity and regulation in their work with preschoolers. They postulated that individuals high in emotional intensity and low in regulatory ability would be prone to emotional regulatory problems. Thus, those children whose extreme emotional responses most require regulation would be least capable of providing it. Supporting their view, they found that such children tended to have less constructive anger reactions (Fabes & Eisenberg, 1992). Again, their work supports the idea that temperament may be an important contributor to individual differences in emotion regulation processes.

Researchers also have linked temperament to individual differences in the types of strategies that children employ when experiencing stressful circumstances. Mangelsdorf et al. (1995) found that wary 12-month-olds tended to engage in more passive types of strategies, such as self-soothing and proximity seeking with their mothers, when placed in the company of strangers. Less wary children, on the other hand, tended to use more active strategies, like self-distraction, when placed in the same situation. Similarly, Parritz (1996) found that infants described as wary by their mothers engaged in more self-soothing as well as whining and proximity seeking with their mothers than less wary infants. Perhaps the emotional responses of more wary and reactive infants are too overwhelming, causing such infants to rely on others to assist them in regulating their emotions or reverting to less active and adaptive strategies when such assistance is unavailable. This research suggests that temperamental characteristics may play a role in determining where children's strategies for regulating distress may fall on the continuum of autonomy.

Recent work by Morales and Bridges (1997) further supports the notion that temperament is associated with the types of strategies children use. In their work, they used a research paradigm similar to our own and focused on the relations between mothers' perceptions of their children's temperament and children's strategy use during delay episodes. More specifically, they asked the mothers to report on aspects of their children's emotional responses in various situations. Children who were seen as experiencing more negative emotionality focused more on the desired object and engaged in more other-directed comfort seeking and low level play in the laboratory delay. Children who were seen as exhibiting less negative emotionality engaged in more active play with the parent. At the same time, children who were seen as more positive and responsive by their mothers were found to engage less in passive forms of regulation, including physical self-soothing, focusing on the desired object, and other-directed comfort seeking.

Finally, a number of researchers have identified physiological mechanisms underlying temperamental dimensions of reactivity and self-regulation. Recent advances in the study of the biological and physiological aspects of temperament indicate that these factors may contribute to individual differences in children's capacities for emotion regulation. Calkins, Fox, and Marshall (1996) found that different patterns of activation in the frontal regions of the brain were associated with differences in arousal thresholds and affective expressions. Autonomic activity, as indexed by heart rate and vagal tone, have been related to temperamental characteristics (Stifter & Fox, 1990). Specifically, infants with high vagal tone exhibit greater sociability and outgoingness, while infants with low vagal tone appear more inhibited. Research by Gunnar and her colleagues (e.g., Gunnar, 1980) on the adrenocortical system indicated that adrenocortical stress reactivity predicts temperamental characteristics such as proneness to distress. Research such as this promises to increase our understanding of the biological mechanisms through which children come to acquire regulation and through which they carry out regulatory strategies.

Caregiver Contributions

A number of researchers have conceptualized emotion regulation as developing within the context of the parent-child relationship (e.g., Gianino & Tronick, 1988). Tronick (1989) described this context as potentially responsive and coordinated, in which case the parent acts in accordance with a child's emotional needs and capacities. The context also may be characterized as more unresponsive and poorly coordinated; in which case, the parent fails to recognize the child's emotional needs or ignores the child's existing capabilities. The influence of such contexts on the development of emotion regulation can also be understood in terms of the theoretical work of both Winnicott and Greenspan. Both theorists characterized parents as early regulators of their children's levels of arousal and distress. Winnicott (1960), for instance, described the "holding environment" as one in which the infant's impulses, affects, and frustrations are satisfied by the parent before they become overwhelming. He further claimed that these experiences of having been soothed in the presence of the caretaker lead the child to be able to soothe himself or herself. In contrast, when infants are not responded to and are left with strong unsatisfied urges, the child may respond either by suppressing these urges or being overwhelmed by them, thus not making steps toward self-regulation.

Greenspan (1981) similarly discussed the growth-promoting early environment as one that balances the child's need for stimulation with his or her need to experience homeostasis or self-regulation. According to his view, the parent initially provides soothing or comforting to supplement the child's emerging capacities. As the child becomes older, the parent helps the child integrate affective polarities into organized interpersonal responses. Without such availability, whereby comfort and a sense of security in the manageability of emotions is offered, the infant cannot stabilize emerging cycles and patterns and build on his or her own capacities for comforting. These theoretical works highlight the importance of caregivers' responses to their children in children's emotion regulation development.

In our recent work, we have been interested in whether and how parents adapt the strategies they use to help their toddlers modulate mild distress. We assume that parents, at least in part, mold the strategies they use with their infants and toddlers in response to changes in children's capacities to modulate distress. During the infant and toddler periods, numerous neurophysiological and cognitive changes occur which most certainly impact children's emotion regulation capacities. Neurophysiological development allows for more modulated reactions to stress (Stansbury & Gunnar, 1994), and increased control over arousal (Fox, 1994). The cognitive advances that, at least in part, stem from these neural maturations (including increased planfulness, self-awareness, and understanding of causality) certainly contribute to developmental changes in the use of the emotion regulatory strategies described above (Kopp, 1989). Parents are able to capitalize on these changes in their attempts to regulate their children's distress. For example, very young infants primarily are able to vary arousal by shifting visual control (Tronick & Weinberg, 1990), thus allowing caregivers to use visual distraction as a soothing strategy (Thompson, 1994). Children's developing linguistic abilities during the second year (Ridgeway, Waters, & Kuczaj, 1985) provide caregivers with more opportunities to engage in language-based regulation strategies. Increases in motor capabilities and the fact that attention mechanisms become more flexible and object oriented during toddlerhood (Gunnar, Mangelsdorf, Larson, & Hertsgaard, 1989) allow caregivers to engage children in more active, sustained play with toys.

Although changes in caregiver strategies are likely to be linked to children's changing capacities, we assume that caregivers, in tailoring their strategies to their children, are doing more than simply responding to their children's existing abilities. We speculate that caregivers also are striving to create environments in which their children are challenged to engage in strategies that are just above their current abilities. This perspective, consistent with the Vygotskian notion of the zone of proximal development (Vygotsky, 1962), emphasizes that, through such challenging interactions with others, children increasingly internalize or take on the strategies they practice with those others. We have suggested that, as children become older, there will be a transition in the source of the initiation of strategies from the mothers to the children themselves. We argue that these shifts in the initiation of strategies will provide evidence that children are internalizing the strategies initially introduced to them by their parents.

In order to investigate strategies that mothers use with their children, we examined the behavior of mothers of 12-, 18-, 24-, and 32-month-old children during the delay situation in which mothers were free to be active. We developed a coding system for rating mothers' behavior that paralleled our child strategy coding system (see Figure 1.3). Categories were placed along a continuum from those that were more reorienting for the child to those that were more stimulus-focused. In particular, we coded six maternal strategies in 5-second intervals. The strategies were active game-like engagement (mother engages the child in game-like activity), redirection of attention (mother distracts child), reassurance (mother assures child that he or she will obtain the desired object), following (mother reflects, extends, or elaborates on the child's distress or preoccupation with the frustrating object), physical comforting, and focus on the desired object. When active engagement or comforting was coded, raters noted whether the mother or the child initiated the activity or whether the behavior was continued from a previous interval.

Across all ages, active engagement was the strategy most used by mothers. Mothers' use of several strategies, including active engagement, distraction, and reassurance, occurred more often when their children were more distressed. We also found age differences in mothers' use of various strategies (see Table 1.2). As expected, mother-initiated active engagement showed a linear decrease with age while child-initiated and ongoing episodes of active engagement increased. These results support the idea that mothers take less responsibility, and children take more responsibility, for children's affect regulation with children's increasing ages. We believe that this shift occurs both because of children's developing abilities and because mothers are scaffolding their children's skills. There also were changes in the use of verbal strategies, such as reassurance, redirection, and following, with increases between 12 and 18 months and decreases thereafter. This finding provides support for our claim that mothers tailor their strategies to children's changing capacities. As children become more verbal between 12 and 18 months, mothers are more able to use linguistic strategies. The explanation for the decreases in the use of such strategies after 18 months is less obvious. It could be that children are increasingly employing their own self-directed speech to self-regulate and may require less of such intervention. Future research might examine these transitions and explore whether children do, in fact, take over these verbal functions.

Finally, also of interest were differences in the strategies that mothers used with their sons and with their daughters. In particular, mothers used more active emotion regulation strategies, such as redirection of attention and reassurance, with their daughters while remaining more passive with their sons. This pattern suggests that mothers may facilitate independent emotion regulation more with their sons than with their daughters by providing their sons with more opportunities to independently regulate emo-

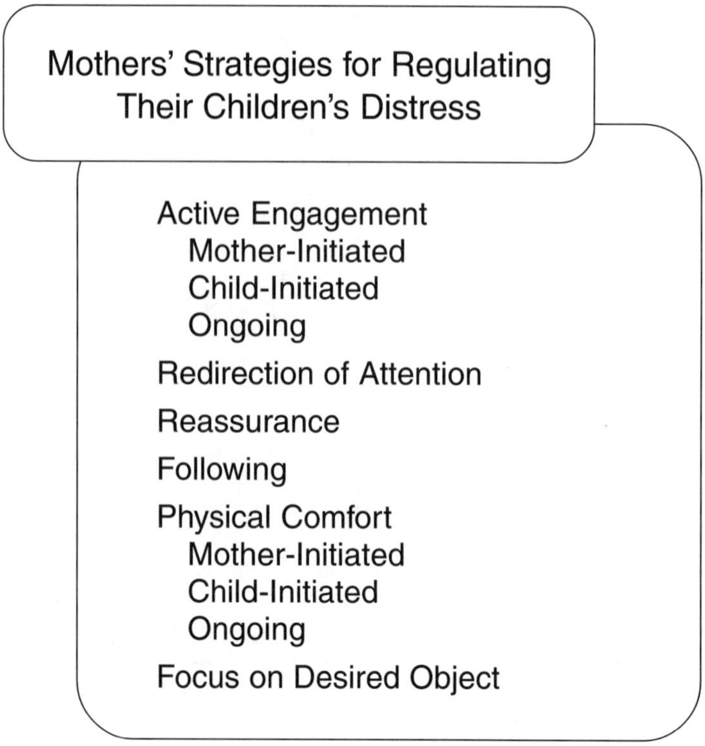

Mothers' Strategies for Regulating
Their Children's Distress

Active Engagement
Mother-Initiated
Child-Initiated
Ongoing

Redirection of Attention

Reassurance

Following

Physical Comfort
Mother-Initiated
Child-Initiated
Ongoing

Focus on Desired Object

FIGURE 1.3. Strategies mothers use to help their children regulate distress during the parent-active delay situation.

tions. This finding links up with work on older children which has suggested that boys show different patterns of problem solving and expressing emotion than girls (Zahn-Waxler et al., 1994). Whether these differences in problem solving are linked to different emotion regulation socialization strategies used by mothers remains a question for future research.

The work described above focused on developmental changes in mothers' use of various strategies. Also of interest in our work, as well as in that of others (e.g., Calkins, 1997b), is the effects of individual differences in caregiver styles and strategies on children's emotion regulation. In order to organize research in this area, we return to the self-determination model presented above. As discussed in our model, characteristics of the context provided by caretakers will determine whether children actively internalize strategies presented in their environments (Grolnick & Ryan, 1989; Ryan, Connell, & Grolnick, 1992). In particular, in order to move along the autonomy continuum, the context that the caregivers create must support the child's activity and initiation, provide the structures that can be internalized, and provide the proximal support that children need to be successful in their regulatory attempts. The environment thus must provide structure, involvement, and autonomy support. First, the context must provide adequate structures to be internalized. Included in the provision of such structures are that caregivers set up conditions which are optimal, make sure that regulatory tasks are not overwhelming, and provide strategies which are not too complex to be used and incorporated into children's repertoires. Second, parents must be involved and available for assistance. Children thus can be supported in their attempts and supplemented by adults' interventions before experiences become overwhelming. Third, caregivers must provide structures and be involved in an autonomy supportive manner (i.e., they must allow the child to take increasing responsibility for initiating and maintaining emerging strategies). If strategies are provided in a controlling manner without opportunities for self-regulation, the child's activity and internalization may be undermined.

While no studies to date have specifically examined the three dimensions of the environment in relation to children's emotional self-regulation, much work is relevant to these dimensions. With regard to parents' involvement and availability, research in the domain of social referencing has described the pow-

TABLE 1.2. Analyses of covariance illustrating effects of age (and linear trends) on maternal strategies

Strategy	Age	Linear Trend
	F	t
Active engagement		
Mother-initiated	8.30***	−4.80***
Child-initiated	4.55**	2.62**
Ongoing	7.16***	3.25**
Redirecting attention	7.02***	−.22
Reassurance	11.65***	.38
Following	4.36**	1.32
Physical comfort		
Mother-initiated	1.71	−1.08
Child-initiated	.65	−1.01
Ongoing	1.00	−.94
Focus on object	2.31	.17
Other behavior	7.96***	1.77
Passive	5.31**	−2.32*

Note. Sex and Age × Sex interactions also were included in these analyses. Distress was included as a covariate.
* p < .05. ** p < .01. *** p < .001.

erful effects of mothers' availability as a resource for children in their attempts to regulate affect (Walden & Ogan, 1988). The assumption in much of this work is that regulation involves an appraisal process in which primary emotional reactions are modulated by the meaning ascribed to the situation. Caregivers' facial and vocal expressions are important sources of meaning in ambiguous situations.

The effects of mothers' availability as referencing resources have been demonstrated in several studies. For example, Sorce and Emde (1981) presented a robot toy to children under one of two conditions: Either the mother was asked to read a newspaper or to be available for referencing. Infants whose mothers were available (not reading) showed more positive affect, more smiling, and more vocalization. In addition, they were more positive in relation to a stranger also in the room and touched the toy more. Diener, Mangelsdorf, Fosnot, and Kienstra (1997) examined children's self-regulatory behaviors (mother-related, self-soothing, engaging the stimulus) during a fear-inducing situation under conditions in which either the mother was available or unavailable. Children exhibited more self-soothing when the mother was unavailable and more engagement of the stimulus in the mother-available condition. These studies are consistent with our claim that caregiver involvement is crucial for children's attempts to regulate emotion, and suggest that systematic differences in availability might influence the types of strategies children acquire, use, or both.

Caregivers also influence their children's acquisition of emotional self-regulation through the autonomy supportiveness versus controllingness of their interactions with their children. While not proposing such a model, several studies have examined parent behaviors that can be related to an autonomy support to control continuum. Silverman and Ragusa (1990) examined children in a compliance task with their mothers (cleanup) and in an independent delay task. These authors found that mothers who were more active in the compliance task had children who performed more poorly on the delay task, even controlling for performance on the compliance tasks. Nachmias, Gunnar, Manglesdorf, Parritz, and Buss (1996) examined the strategies that mothers used to help their wary children deal with a mildly fear-inducing stimulus. Mothers who forced their children to focus on a novel event had children with higher postsession cortisol levels, indicating less effective regulation and possible interference with the children's own attempts to regulate proximity and contact with an arousing stimulus. Calkins (1997a) examined mothers' styles of interacting with their children and their children's tendencies to become distressed when frustrated as well as the behaviors children used to manage that distress. Maternal preemptive action (i.e., mothers doing activities for the child rather than allowing the child to do them for himself or herself) was related to tendencies to display distress. Conversely, toddlers whose mothers used more positive feedback and guidance when interacting with their children tended to use distraction and constructive coping. Thus, it appears that whether mothers are involved in an autonomy supportive or a controlling manner may be related to children's developing abilities to utilize effective regulatory strategies.

In our study, we were interested in whether mothers' use of certain strategies would be related to children's distress when required to regulate alone. We thus examined relations between the six strategies in the parent-active situation and children's distress in the parent-passive situation. To do so, we computed both zero-order correlations between strategies used in the parent-active delay and distress in the parent-passive delay as well as partial correlations between these two variables controlling for both children's ages and distress in the parent-active delay. Therefore, in our analyses, we focused on the relations between strategies mothers used in the parent-active situation and children's distress in the parent-passive situation beyond what would be expected by children's levels of distress in the parent-active situation. Notably, levels of distress tended to be consistent across the two situations.

Our results (see Table 1.3) showed that mothers who used more ongoing active engagement in the parent-active situation had children who were more distressed in the parent-passive situation (controlling for distress in the parent-active situation). Interstingly, this finding did not occur for mother-initiated active engagement, indicating that it is not mothers' responses per se (which tend to be reactions to child distress) but, rather, the maintenance of engagement despite decreases in distress that appears to undermine children's active self-regulation. Mothers who were more passive in the parent-active situation had children who were less distressed when required to regulate with relative independence.

These results suggest that mothers who behave in a controlling manner with regard to their children's emotion regulation, either by maintaining strategies beyond what the child needs to decrease distress or by not allowing opportunities for children to practice more self-regulating strategies, may undermine their children's capacities to develop more autonomous self-regulatory capacities. On the other hand, mothers who provide their children with opportunities to actively regulate, while being available to provide assistance when needed, encourage the internalization of emotion regulation strategies.

☐ Conceptual and Methodological Issues

Studies of emotion regulation are burgeoning. While this certainly is positive given the importance of this construct, the field has a number of challenges ahead. Tackling these conceptual and methodological

---

TABLE 1.3. Zero-order and partial correlations (controlling for children's distress in parent-active delay and age) between maternal strategies and children's distress in parent-passive delay

Strategy	Zero-Order	Partial
Active engagement		
Mother-initiated	.28**	.13
Child-initiated	−.17	.01
Ongoing	−.06	.24**
Redirecting attention	.28**	.01
Reassurance	.29***	.06
Following	.10	.12
Physical comfort		
Mother-initiated	.17*	.13
Child-initiated	.03	.05
Ongoing	.17*	.10
Focus on object	.00	−.06
Other behavior	−.32***	−.22*
Passive	−.20*	−.26**

$*p < .05.$ $**p < .01.$ $***p < .001.$

challenges will help to increase our understanding of emotion regulation processes and their potential for predicting behavioral and emotional outcomes.

First, the conceptual overlap between various domains is striking. This is particularly relevant to the concepts of temperament and emotion regulation. Are these constructs distinct entities, or are they capturing the same phenomenon? For example, Derryberry and Rothbart's (1988) definition of temperament as reactivity and emotion regulation overlaps a great deal with the strategies and emotional expressiveness components in our conceptualization: Reactivity and emotional responsiveness both represent the degree to which an individual responds to stimulation. Regulation and emotion regulation strategies both encompass those behaviors that children use to modulate arousal.

It can be argued, however, that both concepts merit retention. First, temperament tends to be regarded as a relatively static trait of an individual. Assumptions of a rather high degree of cross-situational consistency and biological underpinnings mark temperament as a primarily personological variable. Emotion regulation, on the other hand, is more often thought of as a set of behaviors or capabilities that children acquire over the course of infancy and childhood. These behaviors are expected to change with development and are not assumed to be consistent across situations, given the contextually specific nature of emotional regulatory strategies. In fact, given such specificity, temperament-strategy relations may not be direct but may depend on environmental constraints and other issues such as the level of threat of the situation (Lazarus & Folkman, 1984). Nevertheless, delineating the boundaries of these constructs remains a challenge.

Another set of challenges concerns the generality versus specificity of the adaptiveness of emotion regulation processes. As discussed above, the adaptiveness of various strategies depends on the context within which they are occurring. For example, the functionality of the use of caregivers depends on their availability and other situational constraints. If this is so, a taxonomy of adaptive strategies and developmentally appropriate emotion regulation is highly dependent on the situation. This issue is paralleled in the coping literature in which researchers stress that the same coping strategy may be adaptive or nonadaptive, depending on the situation (Lazarus & Folkman, 1984). For example, denial and avoidance-like processes may be constructive in situations in which no direct action can overcome the harm or threat. Conversely, problem-focused strategies are presumed to be more useful with potentially controllable stressors (Lazarus & Folkman, 1984). Specifying the domains in which emotional self-regulatory processes are adaptive and nonadaptive remains a task for future research.

A consideration of how regulation may vary according to the particular emotion involved is a potentially fruitful avenue for future research. Emotion regulation, including its developmental progression and the significance of its components, is likely to be dependent on the affect involved. Different affects appear to have different hormonal response patterns (Mason, 1975) and are likely to have different developmental progressions and features. The development of specific affects will be determined, at least somewhat, by cultural variability in the meaning of these emotions and expectations for the expression of these emotions. For example, in Japan, the goal in socialization attempts is to facilitate harmony and avoid conflict. Thus, Japanese parents attempt to shield their children from frustration and anger expressions (Miyake, Campos, Kagan, & Bradshaw, 1986). The developmental progression of the regulation of anger is likely to be quite different in such a culture relative to one in which anger is more readily tolerated. Again, research addressing the regulation of specific emotions, including their meaning in the cultural and situational context, is necessary to fully explore emotion regulation processes.

Finally, we delineate some challenges and future directions for our own research. First, those of us who are interested in the origins of emotion regulatory capacities will need to develop models and provide data on the interplay between factors in the child and factors in the context (including the caregiver environment) that predict emotional self-regulation. For instance, how do different temperamental characteristics and caregiver styles interact to create specific patterns of emotional responsiveness and strategy use? Do temperamental factors have more of an influence in certain domains relative to others? The answers to these and other questions will provide us with a more complete understanding of the development of emotional self-regulation.

Another future area of research concerns the origins of caregiver reactions and strategies. For example, parents' attitudes toward and comfort with the expression versus the containment of strong emotions may determine the types of strategies that they use to help their children regulate distress. The ways in which emotions were handled in parents' families of origin may be one crucial factor in determining such attitudes.

Finally, the roles of various caregivers (e.g., mothers, fathers, siblings, peers) in children's development of emotion regulation is an area for future research. Research on emotion regulation has tended to focus on the contributions of mothers to children's developing emotion regulation. Fathers and siblings therefore represent an interesting and potentially distinct source of influence on children's self-regulation. It also has been found that, as children become older, peers play an increasingly important role in their social and emotional lives (Parker & Gottman, 1989). This role may be particularly important as children begin to face the emotional experiences and concerns associated with early adolescence and to look for ways to deal with these new feelings. Attention to these issues will expand our understanding of early emotion regulation and extend research into middle childhood and adolescence.

☐ Emotion Regulation and Later Adaptation

In this final section, we explore some implications of our model of emotional self-regulation for later adaptation. Included are possible links between early emotion regulation processes and later social competence, coping, and psychopathology.

The attainment of a reasonable level of emotional self-regulation can be considered a major developmental task of toddlerhood and early childhood (Kopp, 1989). Consistent with the developmental psychopathology perspective, effective negotiation of this stage should predict competence on developmentally salient tasks in later stages. Such continuity can be explained by the need for self-regulatory capacities for other processes such as task engagement, concentration, and maintaining interchanges with others (Shields, Cicchetti, & Ryan, 1994). Thus, emotion regulation may serve as a foundation for maintaining the homeostasis that allows individuals to engage with their environments and with others. Children who do not develop these abilities therefore would be more likely to develop intra- and interpersonal problems (Calkins, 1997b; Eisenberg & Fabes, 1992).

One of the key developmental tasks of the early childhood years is the engagement with peers in cooperative, mutual play. In line with a recent focus on intersystem (Cicchetti, Ackerman, & Izard, 1995) connections, studies have examined relations between emotion regulation abilities and children's social competence. Calkins (1997a) looked at patterns of emotion regulation in preschoolers indexed physiologically through vagal tone. She also rated children's play patterns in the preschool including solitary, social/active, and reticent behavior. The results of her study indicated that children who engaged in high levels of solitary play were more regulated in their affect as indexed by greater vagal suppression (decrease in vagal tone from baseline to affect-eliciting episodes) relative to those who engaged in more social/active (including aggressive) or reticent behavior. This author concluded that physiological regulation makes possible immersement in solitary activity and the negotiation of one-on-one interactions with peers. Fabes and Eisenberg (1992) found that frequent displays of anger were related to lower levels of social competence in children, and Raver (1997) found that toddlers' emotion regulation strategies were related to social competence above and beyond measures of attentional control.

Similar connections can be found in middle childhood. Shields, Cicchetti, and Ryan (1994) examined 8- through 10-year-olds interacting with peers and assessed appropriate and inappropriate displays of positive and negative affect. They also looked at behavioral difficulties such as aggressive and withdrawn behaviors. Children were rated on social competence by observers and teachers. These authors found relations between emotion regulation indexes and ratings of social competence and cooperative play beyond those predicted by behavior problems alone. Their findings highlight the important and independent effects of emotion regulation processes in predicting social competence.

While these studies provide links between emotion regulation processes and social competence, measures taken in these studies were concurrent. Thus, it is difficult to know whether behavior problems or difficulties in interacting with others were apparent before affect regulation problems or whether they were a consequence or concomitant of them. Of need are longitudinal studies addressing whether early emotion regulation is related to later social outcomes.

There also is a need for studies delineating the processes through which relations between emotion regulation and social difficulties might occur. For example, Kobak and Cole (1994) conducted such a process-oriented study with adolescents in which they argued that links can be found between social withdrawal and the dampening down of undesired emotions. Specifically, they claimed that deactivating attachment strategies divert attention from attachment needs and cues. These strategies are used by the adolescent to dampen undesired emotions. This dampening is then linked to social withdrawal. Such process-oriented studies help us to understand *how* emotion regulation relates to social outcomes.

Possibly more direct are potential links between emotional self-regulation and coping in children and adults. *Coping* has been defined as strategies directed at managing or altering problems causing distress or emotional responses to problems (Lazarus & Folkman, 1984). Coping strategies, such as avoidance or denial, can be directly linked to attentional emotion regulation strategies described above. Altshuler and Ruble (1989) examined age-related (ages 5 through 11) changes in children's suggested coping strategies. Children were given scenarios involving a child having to wait (e.g., to receive a large candy bar) and asked to suggest strategies that the child might use. The results of their study showed that avoidance/distraction type strategies were most frequently named by children of all ages. At the same time, there was an increase with age in cognitive types of distraction (i.e., thinking about something else) and a decrease in escape strategies. The developmental component of these coping strategies provides a potential link between emotional self-regulation and this coping work, and future longitudinal studies might examine the origins of coping strategies in early emotion regulation processes. For example, are children who are able early to use attention deployment strategies more able to use cognitive strategies as they become older? What sorts of caregiver influences impact on individual differences in the use of coping strategies? Finally, we note the possibility of links between emotional self-regulation and psychopathology. Emotion dysregulation has been described as the common dimension of most categories of psychopathology (Cole, Michel, & Teti, 1994). Cole, Michel, and Teti (1994) described emotional dysregulation as emotional patterns that disrupt other processes such as attention and social relations. Similarly, Cicchetti et al. (1995) defined emotional dysregulation as existing control structures that operate in a maladaptive manner and direct emotion toward inappropriate sources. Researchers have described pathological consequences of both overcontrol (e.g., internalizing behavior, depression) and undercontrol (e.g., externalizing behavior, aggression). Furthermore, several investigators have linked problem behavior in preschoolers to difficulties in self-regulation (Cole, Zahn-Waxler, & Smith, 1994). For example, preschoolers with behavior problems have intense and prolonged distress and protest during separations (Speltz, Greenberg, & DeKlyen, 1990). Cole, Teti, and Bohnert (1997) examined 4- and 5-year-olds in emotionally challenging situations and coded facial expressions as inexpressive, modulated, or full blown. Inexpressive children reported more symptoms of anxiety and depression.

While research has begun to explore links between emotion regulation and later problems, a number of questions remain to be addressed. When does the use of less autonomous strategies become emotional dysregulation? What roles do temperament and caregiver styles play in extreme forms of dysregulation? How early are these difficulties evident? In addressing these and other questions, the study of emotion regulation promises to provide important insight into the development of problem behaviors and clinical disorders.

☐ Conclusion

In this chapter, we have presented a model of the development of emotional self-regulation in infancy and toddlerhood that is organized around the construct of autonomy. In our framework, we focus on children's emotional responsiveness as well as the strategies children use to modulate that responsiveness. We argue that movement along a continuum of autonomy toward more active, flexible strategies for regulating affect is a natural phenomenon fueled by children's innate propensities to master their environments and to take on or internalize regulatory structures provided by caregivers. We provide evidence that emotional self-regulation is a developmental phenomenon, with more autonomous strategies evident with increasing age, as well as an individual difference phenomenon, influenced by both temperamental characteristics and caregiver influences. The complex nature of emotional self-regulation is illustrated by the contextual and situational nature of adaptive strategies, specificity to particular emotions, and the key influence of cultural factors.

While a complex phenomenon, emotional self-regulation may provide important links with later coping, peer relations, and psychopathology. A challenge for the field is to specify the processes through which emotional self-regulation might impact these key developmental outcomes.

☐ References

Ainsworth, M. D. S., & Wittig, B. (1969). Attachment and exploratory behavior of one-year-olds in a strange situation. In B. Foss (Ed.), *Determinants of Infant Behavior* (Vol. 4, pp. 111–136). London: Methuen.

Altshuler, J. L., & Ruble, D. N. (1989). Developmental changes in children's awareness of strategies for coping with uncontrollable stress. *Child Development, 60*, 1337–1349.

Barrett, K., & Campos, J. J. (1987). Perspectives on emotional development: II. A functionalist approach to emotions. In J. D. Osofsky (Ed.), *Handbook of infant development* (2nd ed., pp. 555–578). New York: Wiley.

Berk, L. E. (1986). Children's private speech: An overview of theory and the status of research. In R. M. Diaz & L. E. Berk (Eds.), *Private speech: From social interaction to self-regulation.* Hillsdale, NJ: Erlbaum.

Bivens, J. A., & Berk, L. E. (1990). A longitudinal study of the development of elementary school children's private speech. *Merrill-Palmer Quarterly, 36*, 443–467.

Block, J. H., & Block, J. (1980). The role of ego-resiliency in the organization of behavior. In W. A.Collins (Ed.), *Minnesota Symposia on Child Psychology* (Vol. 13, pp. 39–101). Hillsdale, NJ: Erlbaum.

Braungart, J. M., & Stifter, C. A. (1991). Regulation of negative reactivity during the strange situation: Temperament and attachment in 12-month-old infants. *Infant Behavior and Development, 14*, 349–364.

Bridges, L. J., & Connell, J. P. (1991). Consistency and inconsistency in infant emotional and social interactive behavior across contexts and caregivers. *Infant Behavior and Development, 14*, 471–487.

Bridges, L. J., Grolnick, W. S., & Connell, J.P. (1995). *Developmental change in emotional self-regulation.* Unpublished manuscript, University of California at Riverside.

Bridges, L. J., Grolnick, W. S., & Connell, J. P. (1997). Infant emotion regulation with mothers and fathers. *Infant Behavior and Development, 20*, 47–57.

Buck, R. (1984). *The communication of emotion.* New York: Guilford.

Calkins, S. D. (1994). Origins and outcomes of individual differences in emotion regulation. In N. Fox (Ed.), The development of emotion regulation: Biological and behavioral considerations. *Monographs of the Society for Research in Child Development, 59* (2–3, Serial No. 240), 53–72.

Calkins, S. D. (1997a). *Physiological regulations and the control of emotion during toddlerhood.* Paper presented at the biennial meeting of the Society for Research in Child Development, Washington, DC.

Calkins, S. D. (1997b). *Maternal interactive style and emotional, behavioral, and physiological regulation in toddlerhood.* Paper presented at the biennial meeting of the Society for Research in Child Development, Washington, DC.

Calkins, S. D., Fox, N. A., & Marshall, T. R. (1996). Behavioral and physiological antecedents of inhibition in infancy. *Child Development, 67*, 523–540.

Campos, J. J., Campos, R., & Barrett, K. C. (1989). Emergent themes in the study of emotional development and emotion regulation. *Developmental Psychology, 25*, 394–402.

Campos, J. J., Mumme, D. L., Kermoian, R., & Campos, R. G. (1994). A functionalist perspective on the nature of emotion. In N. Fox (Ed.), The development of emotion regulation: Biological and behavioral considerations; *Monographs of the Society for Research in Child Development, 59* (2–3, Serial No. 240), 284–303.

Cicchetti, D., Ackerman, B., & Izard, C. (1995). Emotions and emotion regulation in developmental psychopathology. *Development and Psychopathology, 7*, 1–10.

Cicchetti, D., Ganiban, J., & Barnett, D. (1991). Contributions from the studies of high-risk populations to understanding the development of emotion regulation. In J. Garber & K. A. Dodge (Eds.), *The development of emotion regulation and dysregulation* (pp. 15–48). Cambridge, England: Cambridge University Press.

Cole, P. M., Michel, M. K., & Teti, C. O. (1994). The development of emotion regulation and dysregulation: A clinical perspective. In N. Fox (Ed.), The development of emotion regulation: Biological and behavioral considerations. *Monographs of the Society for Research in Child Development, 59* (2–3, Serial No. 240), 73–100.

Cole, P. M., Teti, L. O., & Bohnert, A. M. (1997). *Challenges for the study of the development of emotion regulation.* Paper presented at the biennial meeting of the Society for Research in Child Development, Washington, D.C.

Cole, P. M., Zahn-Waxler, C., & Smith, K. D. (1994). Expressive control during a disappointment: Variations related to preschoolers' behavior problems. *Developmental Psychology, 30*, 835–846.

Deci, E. L., & Ryan, R. M. (1985). *Intrinsic motivation and self-determination in human behavior.* New York: Plenum.

Derryberry, D., & Rothbart, M.K. (1988). Arousal, affect and attention as components of temperament. *Journal of Personality and Social Psychology, 55*, 958–966.

Diener, M., Mangelsdorf, S. C., Fosnot, K., & Kienstra, M. (1997). *Effects of maternal involvement on toddlers' emotion regulation strategies.* Paper presented at the biennial meeting of the Society for Research in Child Development, Washington, DC.

Eisenberg, N., & Fabes, R. A. (1992). *Emotion and its regulation in early development. New directions for child development* (Vol. 55). San Francisco: Jossey-Bass.

Emde, R. (1988). Development terminable and interminable: I. Innate and motivational factors from infancy. *International Journal of Psychoanalysis, 69*, 23–42.

Fabes, R., & Eisenberg, N. (1992). Young children's coping with interpersonal anger. *Child Development, 63*, 116–128.

Flavell, J. (1966). Le langage prive [private language]. *Bulletin de Psychologie, 19*, 698–701.

Fox, N. A. (1989). Psychophysiological correlates of emotional reactivity in the first year of life. *Developmental Psychology, 19*, 815–831.

Fox, N. A. (1994). Dynamic cerebral processes underlying emotion regulation. In N. A. Fox (Ed.), The development of emotion regulation: Biological and behavioral considerations, *Monographs of the Society for Research in Child Development, 59* (2–3, Serial No. 240), 152–166.

Fox, N. A. (1997). *The role of anterior cortical brain systems in the development of the regulation of emotions.* Paper presented at the biennial meeting of the Society for Research in Child Development, Washington, DC.

Gianino, A., & Tronick, E. Z. (1988). The mutual regulation model: The infant's self and interactive regulation and coping and defensive capacities. In. T. M. Field, P. M. McCabe, & N. Schneiderman (Eds.), *Stress and coping across development* (pp. 47–68). Hillsdale, NJ: Erlbaum.

Goldsmith, H. H., Buss, A. H., Plomin, R., Rothbart, M. K., Thomas, A., Chess, S., Hinde, R. A., & McCall, R. B. (1987). Roundtable: What Is temperament? Four approaches. *Child Development, 58*, 505–529.

Goldsmith, H. H., & Campos, J. J. (1982). Toward a theory of infant temperament. In R. N. Emde & R. J. Harman (Eds.), *The development of attachment and affiliative systems: Psychobiological aspects* (pp. 161–193). New York: Plenum.

Greenspan, S. I. (1981). *Psychopathology and adaptation in infancy and early childhood: Principles of clinical diagnosis and early intervention.* New York: International Universities Press.

Grolnick, W. S., Bridges, L. J., & Connell, J. P. (1996). Emotion regulation in two-year-olds: Strategies and emotional expression in four contexts. *Child Development, 67*, 928–941.

Grolnick, W. S., Cosgrove, T. J., & Bridges, L. J. (1996). Age-graded change in the initiation of positive affect. *Infant Behavior and Development, 19*, 153–157.

Grolnick, W. S., Kurowski, C. O., McMenamy, J. M., Rivkin, I., & Bridges, L. J. (1998). Mothers' strategies for regulating their toddlers' distress: Developmental changes and outcomes. *Infant Behavior and Development.*

Grolnick, W. S., & Ryan, R. M. (1989). Parent styles associated with children's self-regulation and competence in school. *Journal of Educational Psychology, 81*, 143–154.

Gunnar, M. R. (1980). Control, warning signals and distress in infancy. *Developmental Psychology, 16*, 281–289.

Gunnar, M. R., Mangelsdorf, S. C., Larson, M., & Hertsgaard, L. (1989). Attachment, temperament and adrenocortical activity in infancy: A study of psychoendocrine regulation. *Developmental Psychology, 25*, 355–363.

Kessen, W., & Mandler, G. (1961). Anxiety, pain and the inhibition of distress. *Psychological Review, 68*, 396–404.

Klackenberg, G. (1949). Thumbsucking: Frequency & etiology. *Pediatrics, 4*, 418–424.

Kobak, R., & Cole, H. (1994). Attachment and meta-monitoring: Implications for adolescent autonomy and psychopathology. In D. Cicchetti & S. L. Toth (Eds.), *Rochester Symposium on Developmental Psychopathology: Vol. 5. Disorders and dysfunctions of the self* (pp. 267–298). Rochester, NY: University of Rochester Press.

Kopp, C. B. (1982). Antecedents of self-regulation: A developmental perspective. *Developmental Psychology, 18*, 199–214.

Kopp, C. B. (1989). Regulation of distress and negative emotions: A developmental view. *Developmental Psychology, 25*, 343–354.

Lazarus, R. S., & Folkman, S. (1984). *Stress, appraisal, and coping.* New York: Springer-Verlag.

Mangelsdorf, S. C., Shapiro, J. R., & Marzolf, D. (1995). Developmental and temperamental differences in emotion regulation in infancy. *Child Development, 66*, 1817–1828.

Mason, J. (1975). Emotion as reflected in patterns of endocrine integration. In L. Levi (Ed.), *Emotions: Their parameters and measurement* (pp. 143–181). New York: Raven Press.

Mischel, W. (1974). Processes in delay of gratification. In L. Berkowitz (Ed.), *Progress in experimental personality research* (Vol. 3, pp. 249–292). New York: Academic Press.

Miyake, K., Campos, J., Kagan, J., & Bradshaw, D. (1986). Issues in socioemotional development in Japan. In H. Azuma, I. Hakuta, & H. Stevenson (Eds.), *Kodomo: Child development and education in Japan* (pp. 239–261). San Francisco: Freeman.

Morales, M., & Bridges, L. J. (1997). *Relations between parental attitudes concerning emotional expression, temperament, and emotion regulation.* Unpublished manuscript, University of Miami, FL.

Nachmias, M., Gunnar, M., Mangelsdorf, S., Parritz, R. H., & Buss, K. (1996). Behavioral inhibition and stress reactivity: The moderating role of attachment security. *Child Development, 67*, 508–522.

Parker, J. G., & Gottman, J. M. (1989). Social and emotional development in a relational context. In T. J. Berndt & G. W. Ladd (Eds.), *Peer relationships in child development* (pp. 95–131). New York: Wiley.

Parritz, R. H. (1996). A descriptive analysis of toddler coping in challenging circumstances. *Infant Behavior and Development, 19*, 171–180.

Passman, R. H., & Weisberg, P. (1975). Mothers and blankets as agents for promoting play and exploration by young children in a novel environment: The effects of social and non-social attachment objects. *Developmental Psychology, 11*, 170–177.

Piaget, J. (1954). *The origins of intelligence in children.* New York: International Universities Press.

Raver, C. C. (1997). *Relations between effective emotional self-regulation and low-income preschoolers' social competence.* Paper presented at the biennial meeting of the Society for Research in Child Development, Washington, DC.

Ridgeway, D., Waters, E., & Kuczaj, C. A., II. (1985). Acquisition of emotion-descriptive language: Receptive and productive vocabulary norms for ages 18 months to 6 years. *Developmental Psychology, 21,* 901–908.

Rothbart, M. K., & Derryberry, D. (1981). Development of individual differences in temperament. In M. E. Lamb & A. L. Brown (Eds.), *Advances in developmental psychology* (Vol. 1, pp. 37–86). Hillsdale, NJ: Erlbaum.

Rothbart, M. K., & Posner, M. I. (1985). Temperament and the development of self-regulation. In L. C. Hartlage & C. F. Telzrow (Eds.). *The neuropsychology of individual differences* (pp. 93–123). New York: Plenum.

Rothbart, M. K., Posner, M., & Boylan, A. (1990). Regulatory mechanisms in infant development. In J. T. Enns (Ed.), *The development of attention: Research and theory* (pp. 47–66). New York: Elsevier Science.

Rothbart, M. K., Ziaie, H., & O'Boyle, C. G. (1992). Self-regulation and emotion in infancy. In N. Eisenberg & R. A. Fabes (Eds.), *Emotion and its regulation in early development, new directions in child development* (Vol. 55). San Francisco: Jossey-Bass.

Ryan, R. M., Connell, J. P., & Deci, E. L. (1985). A motivational analysis of self-determination and self-regulation in education. In C. Ames & R. E. Ames (Eds.), *Research on motivation in education: The classroom milieu* (pp. 13–51). New York: Academic Press.

Ryan, R. M., Connell, J. P., & Grolnick, W. S. (1992). When achievement is not intrinsically motivated: A theory of self-regulation in school. In A. K. Boggiano & T. S. Pittman (Eds.), *Achievement and motivation: A social-developmental perspective* (pp. 167–188). New York: Cambridge University Press.

Ryan, R. M., Deci, E. L., & Grolnick, W. S. (1995). Autonomy, relatedness and the self: Their relation to development and psychopathology. In D. Cicchetti & D. J. Cohen (Eds.), *Developmental Psychopathology* (Vol. 1, pp. 618–655). New York: Wiley.

Shields, A., Cicchetti, D., & Ryan, R. M. (1994). The development of emotional and behavioral self-regulation and social competence among maltreated school-age children. *Development and Psychopathology, 6,* 57–75.

Silverman, I. W., & Ragusa, D. M. (1990). Child and maternal correlates of impulse control in 24-month-old children. *Genetic, Social and General Psychology Monographs, 116,* 435–473.

Sorce, J., & Emde, R. (1981). Mothers' presence is not enough: The effects of emotional availability on infant exploration and play. *Developmental Psychology, 17,* 737–745.

Speltz, M. J., Greenberg, M. T., & DeKlyen, M. (1990). Attachment in preschoolers with disruptive behavior: A comparison of clinic-referred and non problem children. *Development and Psychopathology, 2,* 31–46

Stansbury, K., & Gunnar, M. R. (1994). Adrenocortical activity and emotion regulation. In N. Fox (Ed.), The development of emotion regulation: Biological and behavioral considerations. *Monographs of the Society for Research in Child Development, 59* (2–3, Serial No. 240), 108–134.

Stifter, C. A. (1993). *Infant emotion regulation: The effectiveness of certain behaviors to modulate negative arousal.* Paper presented at the biennial meeting of the Society for Research in Child Development, New Orleans, LA.

Stifter, C. A., & Fox, N. A. (1990). Infant reactivity: Physiological correlates of newborn and 5-month temperament. *Developmental Psychology, 26,* 582–588.

Thompson, R. A. (1994). Emotional regulation: A theme in search of definition. In N. A. Fox (Ed.), The development of emotion regulation: Biological and behavioral aspects. *Monographs of the Society for Research in Child Development, 59,* (2–3, Serial No. 240), 25–52.

Tronick, E. Z. (1989). Emotions and emotional communication in infants. *American Psychologist, 44,* 112–119.

Tronick, E. Z., & Weinberg, M. K. (1990, April). *The stability of regulation behaviors.* Paper presented at the biennial meeting of the International Conference on Infant Studies, Montreal.

Vygotsky, L. S. (1962). *Thought and language.* Cambridge, MA: MIT Press.

Walden, T., & Ogan, T. (1988). Development of social referencing. *Child Development, 59,* 1230–1240.

Winnicott, D. W. (1960). The theory of the parent-infant relationship. *International Journal of Psychoanalysis, 41,* 585–595.

Zahn-Waxler, C., Cole, P., Richardson, D., Friedman, R., Michel, M., & Beloud, F. (1994). Social problem solving in disruptive preschool children: Reactions to hypothetical situations of conflict and distress. *Merrill-Palmer Quarterly, 40,* 98–119.

CHAPTER

Theodore D. Wachs

The What, Why, and How of Temperament: A Piece of the Action

☐ Introduction

A recent chapter on temperament and development by Rothbart and Bates (1998) has extensively reviewed evidence on the history of the study of temperament; measurement and definitional issues; the origins of temperament; and relations between temperament, attachment, and behavior problems. The nature and extent of the biological underpinnings of temperament have been extensively reviewed in chapters in an edited volume by Bates and Wachs (1994). Existing and potential linkages between temperament and personality have been covered in chapters in the edited volume by Halverson, Kohnstamm, and Martin (1994) and in a new review chapter by Caspi (1998), while the uses of temperament in clinical settings have been reviewed in chapters in the edited volume by Carey and McDevitt (1989).

Given this wealth of information, a very obvious question is, Does the world really need another chapter on temperament? Answering this question in the affirmative is based on an idiosyncratic view of temperament, not as a phenomena but, rather, as a field of study. Specifically, I would argue that, with some notable exceptions, our study of the nature and consequences of individual differences in temperament have focused on temperament in isolation rather than temperament as part of a linked system of multiple influences and outcomes. A fundamental thesis of this chapter is that, by focusing just on temperament per se as a single main effect predictor or outcome variable, we severely limit our ability to deal with critical issues like delineation of the domains of temperament, discordance between parent reports of their child's temperament, the modest stability of temperament traits over time, the etiology of individual differences in temperament, and the consequences of individual differences in temperament. Rather than viewing temperament in isolation, I will argue it is essential that we view temperament as one part of a system of linked multiple influences and outcomes. Other parts of this system would include:

1. other developmental domains like cognition and motivation;
2. nontemperament child characteristics like age, gender, and biomedical status;
3. changes in the structure and functioning of the central nervous system or gene action patterns;
4. different levels of the individual's context including:
    a. proximal environmental characteristics such as parental sensitivity, involvement, and responsivity as well as environmental "chaos" in the home;
    b. quality of parental marital relationship;
    c. distal environmental characteristics such as cultural values and beliefs about the desirability of various child characteristics or the availability of environmental "niches" that are open to the individual.

As will be discussed below, by viewing temperament as part of a system rather than in isolation, we are far better able to understand the nature and changes in different dimensions of temperament, how best to measure temperament, and the role temperament plays in various aspects of individual development.

The seeds for both the mainstream approach to temperament in isolation and the alternative view of temperament as part of a system were sown in the pioneering work of Thomas and Chess (Thomas & Chess, 1977; Thomas, Chess, & Birch, 1968). A major rationale underlying the New York Longitudinal Study of Thomas and Chess was to document how the prevailing view of the etiology of behavior disorders—inadequate or inappropriate parenting—was insufficient given the potential importance of biologically based individual differences in children's behavioral styles (temperament). By contrasting temperament as etiology versus parenting as etiology, Thomas and Chess laid the groundwork for later researchers who focused on temperament as an isolated influence. One result has been the increasing number of studies which have focused on two variable questions, with temperament serving as either the predictor or the outcome. Questions addressed by these types of two variable studies include whether specific temperament dimensions are heritable, whether individual differences in attachment reflect individual differences in temperament, whether differences in child temperament produce differences in parent behavior, whether parent reports of children's temperament primarily reflect parent characteristics, and how well children with certain temperaments perform in school or test situations. (For a review of evidence on these questions, see references cited in the first paragraph of this chapter or chapters in the volume by Kohnstamm, Bates, & Rothbart, 1989.) For example, there have been multiple studies using point-to-point correlations which have focused on the stability of specific dimensions of temperament or on the degree of linkage between temperament and Big Five personality dimensions. In much of this research, little consideration has been given to nontemperament influences which could act to moderate or mediate observed correlations (Wachs, 1994).

While Thomas and Chess may have sparked our focus on temperament in isolation, in their research and conceptualization, they always have been careful to emphasize that the developmental consequences of individual characteristics like temperament cannot be understood without detailed consideration of the context within which an individual with specific temperament characteristics functions—their well-known concept of "goodness of fit." By focusing on the match between temperament and context as the major contributor to individual differences in adjustment, Thomas and Chess also laid the groundwork for an alternative viewpoint; namely, that we cannot understand the impact of temperament on behavior without also understanding the nature of the context within which individuals with different temperaments function. This alternative viewpoint is best reflected in studies that have looked at the joint contributions of temperament and contextual characteristics to behavioral disorders (see Rothbart & Bates, 1998, for the most up-to-date review of these studies). An excellent example of this alternative approach to temperament as part of a system of linked multiple influences is seen in the elegant theoretical and empirical work of Kochanska (1993, 1995), in which the contributions of temperament to children's development of internalized conscience are considered in the context of parental discipline style.

There seems to be no doubt that the study of temperament in isolation was a necessary and critical step in terms of helping researchers understand the nature of temperament, the development of specific dimensions of temperament, and the contributions of temperament to development. However, I argue that the extent of our database on temperament is more than sufficient to allow us to take the next necessary step; namely, moving from the artificial world of temperament in isolation to the real world of temperament as part of a system. For purposes of the present discussion, I will use a simplified structural definition of a system; namely, a set of organized multiple elements, with each element linked to and interacting with at least some of the other elements in the set (Fogel, 1993; Miller, 1978). As I will illustrate in the following sections, viewing temperament as part of a system has two advantages. First, it allows us to deal better with certain perennial problems involving the conceptualization and measurement of temperament which have not been satisfactorily resolved by looking at temperament in isolation. Second, viewing temperament as part of a larger system allows us to develop a more comprehensive picture, both about the etiology and development of individual differences in temperament as well as about the extent and nature of temperament's contributions to individual variability in behavior and development. The advantages of viewing temperament as part of a larger system will be illustrated below through use of questions involving what, why, and how. Specifically, the following questions will be addressed: (a) What are the domains of temperament? (b) Why are levels of interparent agreement on child temperament characteristics and stability of temperament so modest? (c) What accounts for individual variability in the development of temperament? (d) How does temperament influence context? (e) How does individual variability in temperament translate into variability in individual developmental patterns?

☐ What Are the Domains of Temperament?

At present, there is neither a single agreed on definition of temperament nor agreement on what constitutes the domains of temperament (Belsky, Hsieh, & Crnic, 1996). This problem is not unique to temperament; similar problems are also found in other areas studied by psychologists, such as intelligence. Given the social nature of science (Kuhn, 1970), the existence of multiple definitions and domains has not proven to be a major hindrance to progress as long as there is general consensus among researchers as to the major definitional features of a given construct and the domains that fit under this construct (McCall, 1986). While there are multiple definitions of *temperament*, for all intents and purposes, the majority of researchers in the field would accept as a "working definition": "Biologically rooted individual differences in behavior tendencies that are present early in life and are relatively stable across various kinds of situations and over the course of time" (Bates, 1989, p. 4). There also appears to be agreement that the individual differences referred to in the working definition should bear some resemblance to later appearing personality traits (Buss, 1989; Goldsmith et al., 1987; Strelau, 1987).

While a variety of individual characteristics have been listed under the rubric of temperament, from the relatively restricted focus on emotionality by Goldsmith and Campos (1982) to the Big Nine of Thomas and Chess (1977), there does appear to be general agreement that the following list defines the major domains of temperament (Bates, 1989):

1. negative emotionality (e.g., fear, anger),
2. difficultness (e.g., high intense, easily evoked negative moods),
3. adaptability to new situations or people (e.g., inhibition),
4. activity level,
5. self-regulation (e.g., soothability),
6. reactivity (e.g., how intense a stimulus is needed to invoke a response),
7. sociability-positive emotionality (e.g., pleasure in social interactions).

Even with the existence of a working definition and a working set of dimensions, a continuing problem for researchers studying temperament has been the difficulty in defining what distinguishes the behaviors that we call temperament from similar behaviors in other domains. Certainly, if we look at the major features of the working definition of temperament (early appearing, relatively stable, biologically rooted), these criteria easily could be applied to a variety of behaviors from distinctly different domains, such as intelligence or motivation. While there has been some progress in developing criteria that allow us to differentiate temperament from personality (Strelau, 1987), once we look beyond these two traits, it becomes harder to find distinguishing criteria.

For example, a fundamental dimension of Rothbart's theory of temperament involves individual differences in self-regulation, which are based on mechanisms such as selective attention and attention span (Rothbart, 1991). Similarly, in Strelau's theory of temperament, activity level is linked to goal-directed behavior, with individual differences appearing in the difficulty and complexity of activities in which the individual engages (Strelau, 1989). Nontheoretical approaches to the dimensions of temperament often utilize constructs like attention span and goal-directed task orientation as essential elements of persistence (Caspi, 1998). Unfortunately, constructs such as selective attention and goal-directed behavior also are commonly found in research and theory from areas of psychology other than temperament. Self-regulation is viewed by many cognitive theorists as the "hallmark" of cognition and cognitive processing (Borkowski & Dukewich, 1996). Goal directed persistence and preference for challenging tasks have been claimed as fundamental aspects of mastery motivation (Barrett & Morgan, 1995).

While temperament theorists have long been aware of such conceptual confusions (McCall, 1986), for the most part, attempts to deal with cross-domain construct overlap have not been particularly fruitful. For example, Rothbart (1986) has argued that attention as cognition refers to what the person is attending to, whereas attention as temperament refers to how fast the person can shift attentional focus across content domains or how long the person can maintain attentional focus on a given domain. Unfortunately, this distinction becomes problematical, given that both attentional flexibility and attentional control (e.g., vigilance) also have been claimed as domains of information processing by cognitive theorists (Kinchla, 1992).

While questions such as to what domain a given construct "truly" belongs could be viewed as a form of semantic nit-picking, I see this problem as potentially much more fundamental. One of the major criticisms of social science theories is their lack of preciseness (Dar, 1987). I would argue that such imprecision is more likely to occur when theories that are designed to explain the nature of a particular domain (e.g., temperament) simply assimilate constructs from other domains as an essential part of the theory, without due regard for the origins of such constructs. As seen in the case of classic psychoanalysis, theories that are definitionally imprecise ultimately become overelastic: being able to explain everything while truly explaining nothing. While current theories of temperament cannot be considered as overelastic, I believe there is a danger of these theories evolving in this direction, unless they attempt to deal with perennial questions such as what criteria can be used to define the realm in which a particular individual characteristic best fits. I would further argue that we cannot adequately deal with this perennial question unless we go beyond studying temperament in isolation and look at how and how much the various domains of temperament noted above overlap with similarly named constructs from other nontemperament domains.

There are two ways to proceed in dealing with the question of potential overlap between similarly named constructs from different domains. As exemplified in our working definition, the first way is to acknowledge that we do have a construct definition problem. Among other things, this means not assuming that, because a trait fits our working definition of temperament, the trait is uniquely temperament in nature. Particularly for individual characteristics involving early personality traits, some individual traits do appear to fit better within the domain of temperament than in other domains. Traits fitting into this category would include emotionality, reactivity, difficultness, and activity. For other individual traits, such as attention or task orientation, where nontemperament domains appear to have equivalent claims, I would argue for viewing these as a separate "hybrid" class. Hybrid traits, while sharing some features with more classic temperament characteristics, also share features with characteristics from nontemperament domains. This situation is illustrated in Figure 2.1.

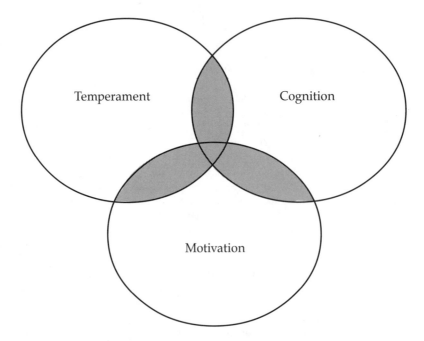

FIGURE 2.1. Example of a hybrid grouping of traits. Unshaded areas refer to trait characteristics that are unique to a specific domain. Shaded areas refer to aspects of trait characteristics that overlap multiple domains.

Viewing individual characteristics such as attention or task orientation as a hybrid class is not a semantic "sleight of hand" device. There are conceptual and analytic tools available that are designed to deal with situations where the boundaries that determine classification of a trait are unclear. Particularly for hybrid individual traits whose characteristics allow them to be assigned to any one of a number of domains, one potential approach is to apply what has been called "fuzzy logic" (Massaro, 1987). Fuzzy logic involves both a theory and a method that can be used in situations where there are multiple, nondichotomous constructs that have overlapping boundaries (e.g., the boundaries of attention because temperament may well overlap with the boundaries of attention as cognition). Fuzzy logic is designed to answer such questions as the degree to which a specific construct shares similar characteristics with a larger membership class. Using fuzzy logic, it is possible to assess the degree of resemblance of a specific characteristic to the characteristics of a larger class, with the degree of resemblance ranging from zero (no overlap) to 1.0 (total overlap). For what appear to be nonhybrid traits, like emotionality or reactivity, we would expect the degree of resemblance between characteristics of these traits and characteristics of traits drawn from cognition or motivation to be essentially zero order. For what appear to be hybrid traits, like attention or persistence, we would expect the degree of resemblance to characteristics drawn from cognition or motivation to be more than zero order, but less than perfect in magnitude.

Use of fuzzy logic approaches would make it possible not only to determine to what degree a trait fits the criteria for membership in the domain of temperament versus the degree to which it is a hybrid trait, but also to determine what characteristics of the traits are more likely to fall under the membership criteria for each class. For example, for the hybrid dimension of attention, experts in cognition and temperament could be given lists of characteristics defining attention and their task would be to rate such characteristics as more likely to reflect attention as cognition or attention as temperament. Using fuzzy logic analytic procedures similar to those applied to understanding how individuals categorize objects or make social judgments (Massaro, 1987), such ratings could be used to determine which characteristics are most salient in defining the temperament components of attention versus those that are more applicable to attention as cognition. The former class of characteristics would be those we would want to emphasize when designing temperament assessment devices that include attention as a salient dimension. Obviously, this is a very different line of research from what temperament researchers have done in the past. However, going beyond temperament to use alternative strategies, such as fuzzy logic, would seem to be a necessary line of research if we are to truly understand what temperament means and what defines those individual characteristics that uniquely or primarily fall within the domain of temperament.

☐ Why Is There Only Modest Interparent Agreement and Stability of Temperament?

As noted above, one of our major assumptions underlying the construct of temperament is that temperament is a stable individual characteristic. Stability of temperament is assumed to occur both across situations and across time. Given this central assumption, it is extremely troubling to find only moderate agreement on characteristics of a child's temperament being reported by those who best know the child; namely, the child's parents. Concerns about the relatively modest level of interparent agreement were raised over 15 years ago (Hubert, Peters-Martin, & Gandour, 1982), and more recent reviews have not reported major alleviation of this concern (Slabach, Morrow, & Wachs, 1991). Perhaps reflecting a glass half full–glass half empty phenomena, some temperament researchers seem to be content with relatively moderate levels of interparent agreement. For example, in one of the most recent studies on instrument development, across five temperament dimensions mother-father agreement correlations ranged from .29 to .54 with a mean of .41 (Goldsmith, 1996). While noting the relatively modest level of agreement Goldsmith (1996) did not appear to find this as much a cause for concern as the relatively low levels of mother-teacher agreement, found both in his own research and in earlier research. However, there is at least one obvious and potentially important cause for discordance between mother and teacher ratings; namely, the possibility of different contexts influencing children's expression of temperament at home and at school (Goldsmith, Rieser-Danner, & Briggs, 1991; also, see below for a fuller discussion of this point). Contextual differences are less likely to occur with mother-father ratings of their child's temperament, given that parent ratings occur in a similar environmental context—the home. The modest levels of interparent agreement shown for ratings of children's temperament are problematical if for no other reason than their implications for the stability of temperament. How can we propose individual stability of a child's inhibition or activity level across time when there is disagreement at the initial measurement point of how temperamentally inhibited or active actually is the child?

Congruent with what has been discussed earlier, I argue that it will be difficult to deal with issues involving modest interparent agreement by looking only at temperament in isolation from nontemperament characteristics that also could act to influence the degree of agreement shown. Attempts to deal with this issue by focusing primarily on temperament per se have not been particularly fruitful. For example, while the hypotheses that children systematically vary their temperament related behaviors for each parent or that fathers' ratings are less accurate because fathers spend less time with their children have not received strong empirical support (Slabach et al., 1991). Some studies have reported that level of agreement between parents varies as a function of the temperament dimension being considered. Specifically, higher interparent agreement has been found to occur for scales assessing negative emotionality (e.g., fear, fussy, difficultness) and activity level than for scales assessing positive emotionality, attention, or persistence (Goldsmith, 1996; Goldsmith & Campos, 1990; Mebert, 1989). These data suggest that parents may be more attuned to those aspects of their child's temperament, such as high activity or negative emotionality, that call for more active parental control (Bell & Chapman, 1986). However, even for these domains, the level of parental agreement rarely exceeds .50, suggesting that other factors are operating besides just some temperament dimensions being more salient for parents. With regard to the possibility that the structure of temperament may differ for mothers and fathers (e.g., mothers and fathers may be using different behaviors to represent the same temperament dimension for their child), the evidence is mixed. When subscales from temperament questionnaires are the basis of analysis some studies show different factor structures underlying mothers' and fathers' ratings of their child's temperament (Goldsmith & Campos, 1990). In contrast, other studies suggest little difference in the types of behaviors used by mothers and fathers to rate specific temperament characteristics of their child (Hubert, 1989). The extent to which such differences reflect methodological differences among studies in regard to what parents are rating remains unclear.

It is possible that the moderate level of interparent agreement is a narrow methodological issue that is unique to questionnaire measures of temperament, and that such concerns become irrelevant when we utilize objective laboratory-based assessments rather than parent questionnaires. However, such a conclusion is problematical on several grounds. First, it seems clear that parental report measures of their child's temperament are not purely subjective, but also assess real existing differences in those domains of individual characteristics which we call temperament (Bates, 1994). For example, if parental report measures of their infant's temperament were purely subjective, we would not expect to see the significant levels of relation between parent report measures and objective laboratory assessments of temperament that repeatedly have been documented in the literature (Rothbart & Bates, 1998; Slabach et al., 1991). Second, although interobserver agreement in laboratory assessments of temperament rarely is a problem (Matheny, 1991), assessments of stability of such laboratory assessments yield patterns of results that are remarkably similar to those found in studies of interparent agreement. Specifically, even over relatively short time periods, stability of laboratory assessments of child temperament tend to be moderate, again barely exceeding .50 (Goldsmith & Rothbart, 1991; Matheny, 1991). While statistically significant, this level of short-term stability of laboratory assessments should give us cause for concern, given the theoretical emphasis on temperament as a stable individual trait.

Overall, this data suggests that attempting to deal with the moderate level of interparent agreement by focusing only on measurement issues related to temperament, without considering the role of nontemperament factors, is a strategy that is not likely to prove fruitful. This is not to deny the possibility that some gains in parent agreement can occur from better measurement strategies such as aggregating parent report measures across occasions and contexts. Aggregation reduces the errors of measurement that are inherent in a single measured occasion or context (Rushton, Brainerd, & Pressley, 1983). However, we not only must keep in mind that aggregated data can be more costly to obtain since it requires repeated assessments, but also that parent reports themselves are a form of aggregated data based on the parents relating to their child across a variety of occasions and contexts (Carey, 1983). Thus, I would predict only limited gains in our ability to understand the source of moderate levels of interparent agreement if we use just a temperament-in-isolation strategy.

If the moderate levels of interparent agreement documented above cannot be understood solely by reference to issues involving the measurement of temperament per se, what other possibilities are there? One possibility is that nontemperament individual characteristics of both parent and child may play a role in explaining the modest level of interparent agreement. Evidence has suggested that mothers' ratings are influenced more by the age of their child while fathers' ratings tend to be influenced more by their child's gender and parity (Slabach et al., 1991). Differences in mothers' and fathers' ratings also have been associated with parental differences in factors like the level of parental anxiety or depression (Mebert, 1991).

Recent reviews of the biological foundations of temperament have offered another potential explanation for the modest levels of interparent agreement. Both Nelson (1994) and Rothbart, Derryberry, and Posner (1994) made two fundamental points about central nervous system contributions to the development and expression of temperament. First, there are multiple central nervous system areas involved in the development and expression of temperament. For example, behavioral inhibition appears to develop as a function of coordinated interaction between the hippocampus, prefrontal cortex, and portions of the motor system. Second, the different central nervous system areas which underlie the development of specific dimensions of temperament reach functional maturity at different times. For example, the hippocampal region matures earlier than does the prefrontal cortex (Nelson, 1994). What are the implications of these biological foundations for understanding levels of interparent agreement? As pointed out by Nelson (1994), while young infants have the capacity for short-term reactivity to stimulation, they may not have the capacity during the first year of life to store emotional memories associated with such reactivity. What this means is that the developing central nervous system structure of young infants may not permit consistency across different situations until the relevant central nervous system structures that allow emotional memory storage have reached functional maturity (sometime between 12 and 24 months). As a result, mothers and fathers may be seeing fairly inconsistent reactions from their young child to particular stimuli, making it difficult for them to come up with a coherent and agreed on characterization of their infant, particularly if mothers and fathers treat their infant differently (Wachs & King, 1994). This does not mean that the young infant is deliberately tailoring different reactivity patterns to their mothers and their fathers but, rather, that the nature of the early central nervous system may not permit infants to display consistent emotional reactivity patterns. This neurobiological approach to the question of moderate interparent agreement is one that could not have been developed by focusing on the measurement of temperament in isolation.

A similar issue also can be seen in regard to questions on the stability of specific dimensions of temperament over time.[1] As with interparent agreement moderate stability of individual temperament dimensions appears to be the norm, both for parent report measures (Slabach et al., 1991) and for laboratory assessments (Goldsmith & Rothbart, 1991; Riese, 1987). For example, mean stability of parent ratings of their children between 18 and 48 months on five temperament dimensions assessed by the Toddler Behavior Assessment Questionnaire was $r = .35$, with a range from $r = .06$ to $r = .54$ (Goldsmith, 1996).

For the most part, temperament researchers rarely have considered factors other than temperament that might influence stability. Some investigators have emphasized the high stability levels shown for individuals at the extremes of a given temperament dimension (e.g., Kagan, Reznick, & Snidman, 1989). Less often emphasized is the notably lower stability found for nonextreme populations or evidence that instability can be found even in extreme samples (Kerr, Lambert, Stattin, & Larson, 1994; Prior, Sanson, & Oberklaid, 1989). A second approach has been to focus on the possibility that individual temperament dimensions combine over time to form new temperament systems (Rothbart & Bates, 1998). However, evidence on this approach is relatively limited (Caspi, 1998), and at least some studies show that factor structures of children's temperament are relatively stable when assessed over time (Pedlow, Sanson, Prior, & Oberklaid, 1993).

While improvements in measurement and analytic strategies (a temperament in isolation approach) do yield higher stability coefficients (Pedlow et al., 1993), a survey of the available evidence has suggested that stability or instability of temperament cannot be fully understood without also considering the contributions of nontemperament factors. As noted above, the development of specific temperament dimensions is based on the functioning of different central nervous system areas which mature at different rates. It is not surprising that we find only moderate stability of temperament early in life, when different neural systems needed for specific complex temperament-related behaviors reach functional maturity at different age points (Wachs & King, 1994). Further, genetic influences have long been implicated in both the development and expression of individual variability in temperament (Goldsmith, 1989). While we traditionally think of gene systems as being switched on prenatally and continuing to operate unchanged throughout the life span, this traditional picture clearly is oversimplified. More recent models of gene action have illustrated how different gene systems can turn on or turn off at different points of development (Plomin, DeFries, McClearn, & Rutter, 1997). If gene systems underlying specific dimensions of temperament change across the life span, again we would not necessarily expect a high degree of stability for those dimensions of temperament that are coded by such a gene system.

Going beyond biology, contextual influences also may play a role in the degree of stability or instability shown over time for specific temperament dimensions (see below). Besides context, other nontemperament characteristics that can impact on the stability of temperament include prenatal biomedical status (Garcia-Coll, Halpern, Vohr, Seifer, & Oh, 1992; Riese, 1987) and individual differences in intelligence (Asendorpf, 1994). Taken together, these findings again highlight how perennial temperament measurement issues are not likely to be satisfactorily resolved unless we go beyond temperament in looking for solutions.

☐ Contextual Contributions to the Etiology, Development, and Consequences of Individual Differences in Temperament

Temperament traditionally has been defined and conceptualized as a phenomena with strong biological roots (Strelau, 1987). Research on both genetic (Goldsmith, 1989; Plomin & Saudino, 1994) and central nervous system influences on temperament (Calkins & Fox, 1994; Kagan et al., 1989; Strelau, 1994) have confirmed and deepened our understanding of the extent and nature of the biological foundations of temperament. However, even among temperament theorists who have a strong biological orientation, there is agreement that temperament is not just a biological phenomena (Buss & Ploman, 1984; Rothbart & Derryberry, 1981). Indeed, one of the surprising conclusions drawn from a recent major review of biological contributions to temperament was that contextual influences, such as the nature of the child's psychosocial environment, or environmental processes such as learning, cannot be ignored in the study of temperament (Bates & Wachs, 1994). What is the role that context plays in the study of temperament? I would argue that temperament-contextual linkages can be seen in five areas.

1. Context can act to change the nature of the individual's temperament, certainly on the behavioral level and possibly on the biological level.
2. The expression of temperament, in terms of issues like stability, can be influenced by the overall cultural context within which the individual develops.
3. Temperament can act to influence the nature of the individual's microcontext.

Once we understand the issues involved in areas 1–3, we are in a position to look at the developmental consequences of individual variability in temperament.

4. In understanding linkings between temperament and environment, it is essential to remember that such findings are bidirectional and not unidirectional in nature.
5. Temperament and environment may interact in a nonlinear fashion to produce developmental outcomes that could be predicted neither by temperament or environment acting in isolation nor by linear combinations of temperament and environment.

My choice of evidence to address the above issues will be based on methodological considerations. As Crockenberg (1986) has noted, in studies that concurrently measure temperament and context, it all too often becomes difficult to distinguish the direction of influence. For example, in studies based on concurrent correlations, it often is difficult to establish whether it is the child's temperament influencing their caregiver's rearing style or the caregiver's rearing style influencing the child's level of temperament. Given this potential confound, my conclusions on temperament and context will be based on: (a) longitudinal investigations in which the measurement of temperament precedes the measurement of context or vice versa; (b) studies assessing aspects of the environment that are unlikely to be influenced by the child's temperament, thus allowing inferences to be made about directionality when relations between temperament and environment are found; and (c) intervention studies that allow causal inferences to be made. Obviously, there still will be interpretive problems, even with these types of designs. Longitudinal predictive relations may be carried by the autocorrelation of either temperament or environment over time, while the absence of intervention effects may not mean that environment does not influence temperament but only that the wrong aspects of environment were chosen. However, even with these limitations, these types of studies serve to advance my argument that understanding the what and the how of temperament depends on studying more than just temperament per se.

Contextual Influences on Temperament

While not in any way negating the essential biological roots of individual differences in temperament, evidence also has shown that the level and course of temperament can be influenced by environmental characteristics. Three lines of evidence are of particular relevance.

Longitudinal Studies.   A number of longitudinal studies have shown how changes in individual temperament are not random but, rather, are associated with the nature of the child's environment. Particularly in the first year of life, evidence shows that negative emotionality may be a temperament dimension for which environmental influences are particularly relevant. For example, Belsky, Fish, and Isabella (1991) have shown that infants who shifted from low to high negative emotionality during the first year of life had fathers who both were less involved with them early in infancy and who had greater feelings of marital dissatisfaction, as compared to infants whose level of negative emotionality remained low during this time period. In contrast, infants whose level of negative emotionality declined over the first year of life had parents who had better marital relations and whose mothers displayed greater sensitivity, as compared to infants whose level of negative emotionality remained high during this time period. Similarly, Fish (1997) has reported that infants whose level of negative emotionality declined over the first year of life had mothers who received higher levels of social support, whereas infants whose levels of negative emotionality remained low had parents who were in a more harmonious marital relationship. Interestingly, relations between environment and positive emotionality in these studies were generally either nonsignificant or inconsistent. The generalizability of findings relating context to negative emotionality also is seen for infants living in non-Western, less developed countries. Using a sample of rural Egyptian toddlers studied between 18 and 30 months, we attempted to determine if we could replicate the results found for North American infants that parental nonresponse to infant distress leads to even more negative infant emotionality (Bell & Ainsworth, 1972; Crockenberg & Smith, 1982). Based on repeated naturalistic observations of both toddler behavior and parents' reactions to these behaviors, our results did show that parental nonresponsivity to toddler distress was related to higher levels of toddler distress from 24 to 29 months, even after statistically controlling for level of toddler distress from 18 to 23 months (Wachs et al., 1993).

The relevance of contextual characteristics to changes in temperament is not restricted only to negative emotionality or to the period of early infancy. Arcus and Kagen (1995) have reported that infants who were overreactive to stimuli in the first year of life exhibited less inhibited behavior during the second year of life if their mothers set firm limits, did not reinforce infant distress signals by extra attention, and made age appropriate demands of their infants. Similarly, Engfer (1986) has reported that children who switched from easy to difficult temperament between 4 and 18 months were in families with more marital problems, as compared to children who continued to display easy temperaments; children who switched from difficult to easy temperament had mothers who were higher in sensitiveness than mothers of children who continued to display difficult temperaments. Going into the adolescent period, Feldman and Weinberger (1994) have reported that boys who demonstrated increasing levels of self-regulation between 12 and 16 years of age were more likely to come from cohesive families, even after controlling for initial levels of self-regulation.

Environmental Chaos and Temperament.   In distinguishing contextual influences on child temperament from influences of child temperament on context, one approach would be to look at aspects of the environment which are potentially less sensitive to the influence of child temperament. One such aspect is the physical environment: the stage or setting on which social transactions between child and caregiver take place (Wohlwill & Heft, 1987). The various ways in which childrens' individual characteristics, such as temperament, can influence caregiver behavior patterns have been discussed repeatedly in the literature (e.g., Sameroff, 1995; Scarr & McCartney, 1983). For example, parents of highly inhibited children are more likely to attempt to increase the level of their child's interaction with the environment than are parents of less inhibited children (Bell & Chapman, 1986). The extent to which a child's temperamental characteristics can act to influence dimensions of the physical environment, such as number of wall decorations or rooms to people ratio, is less likely and less intuitively obvious. Rather, it is more likely that specified dimensions of the physical environment can act to influence child temperament characteristics. One such dimension is environmental chaos, which involves factors such as crowding (e.g., rooms to people ratio), and levels of nonhuman noise in the home. Several studies provide converging evidence of the importance of environmental chaos as an influence on child temperament. Matheny, Wilson, and Thoben (1987) have reported that higher levels of environmental noise and confusion in the homes of 18-month-old toddlers was related to behavior indicating less tractable temperaments. In my own research, direct observations of home physical environments were used to assess noise level, crowding, and home traffic pattern (number of people coming and going in the home), while parent responses to the Toddler Temperament Questionnaire were used to assess temperament characteristics of the infant (Wachs, 1988). Results indicated that higher levels of home crowding were related to 12-month-old infants being characterized as lower in approach, less adaptive, and having more intense negative moods. These results held even after statistically partialling out the potential influence of parent temperament, based on parent self-report scores on the revised Dimensions of Temperament Scale.

Intervention Studies.   Perhaps the strongest evidence for contextual environmental influences on child temperament comes from studies where specific aspects of the child's environment are manipulated to determine to what degree such manipulation can influence later temperament. While such intervention studies are relatively scarce, they do provide converging evidence on the role of environment in the development of early temperament. In terms of global interventions, MacPhee, Burchinal, and Ramey (1997) compared the temperament patterns of disadvantaged infants who were enrolled in a special day care program designed to remediate cognitive deficits. While not all dimensions of temperament were influenced by day care intervention, infants in the special day care did show significantly greater increases in measures of task orientation over a 2-year period, as compared either to control infants who did not receive intervention or to infants who were in routine family care situations. These results may, in part, reflect the hybrid nature of task orientation, as discussed earlier in this chapter. Evidence which is more relevant to temperament per se comes from research by Van den Boom (1994) using a sample of highly irritable 6-month-old infants, whose mothers were enrolled in a special 3-month program designed to increase maternal sensitivity and appropriate responsivity. As compared to infants whose mothers did not receive this special intervention, infants in the intervention group were rated by observers as being more sociable, more self soothing, and displaying lower levels of negative emotionality at 9 months of age.

Taken together, the evidence from these three lines of evidence clearly converge on the conclusion that at least some aspects of temperament are sensitive to contextual influences. This evidence does not contradict conclusions about the essential biological nature of temperament, but does underline the fact that an understanding of individual variability in the development of temperament will require focusing on both the biology and the context of the child. This may be particularly true for those aspects of temperament that are likely to prove problematic for parents, such as negative emotionality or fearfulness. Whether this reflects a greater sensitivity of these domains to contextual influences, or a greater effort by parents to change aspects of infant temperament that they regard as problematical, remains an unanswered question.

Given that environment can act to influence the characteristics and course of individual temperament, a fundamental question is the level at which environmental influences on temperament operate. Bates (1989) has proposed a conceptual scheme wherein temperament can be viewed as operating simultaneously on three levels: the behavioral, the neural, and the constitutional (e.g., genetics, hormones). While it would be easy to assume that environmental influences on temperament operate only on the behavioral level, such a conclusion is not necessarily warranted (Calkins & Fox, 1994; Wachs & King, 1994). Environmental factors have been shown to influence both central nervous system development (Greenough & Black, 1992) and the operation of temperament-related neural-hormonal systems (Gunnar, 1994). In addition, environmental influences also can act to turn on or turn off specific regulator genes that determine which structural genetic influences actually are operating (Plomin et al., 1997).

Experimental research at the infrahuman level has documented how physiological reactivity can be influenced by variations in early handling experiences (Wiener & Levine, 1978). While empirical evidence on the role of environmental influences on levels of temperament other than the behavioral are relatively sparse at the human level, DiPietro, Larson, & Porges (1987) has reported that breast-fed infants show different patterns of both behavioral and physiological reactivity than do formula-fed infants. Whether these differences are a function of nutritional influences or of psychosocial stimulation characteristics associated with breastfeeding is not clear. However, this evidence does suggest that it may be premature to conclude that environmental influences on temperament operate only at the behavioral level.

Cultural Influences on the Expression of Individual Differences in Temperament

Differences in the level and pattern of temperament have been observed across different population or cultural groups (Kohnstamm, 1989). What accounts for such differences is an open question. We cannot necessarily assume that population or group differences are due purely to cultural influences. Population groups also differ in biological characteristics, such as diet during pregnancy, which have the potential to influence infant physiology and, thereby, subsequent individual differences in temperament (Chisholm, 1981). For example, rural Egyptian populations typically have diets low in animal protein, which is a major source for vitamin B_6. Egyptian neonates, whose mothers had low vitamin B_6 status, as measured in breast milk, were far more likely to demonstrate poor self-regulation when assessed with the Brazelton scale (McCullough et al., 1990). In addition, measurement issues also may be critical. As noted by Lewis, Ramsey, and Kawakami (1993), the belief that Japanese infants are less stress reactive than American infants holds only at the behavioral level; physiologically, Japanese infants appear to be more stress reactive than American infants.

These cautions notwithstanding, it also is important to recognize that we cannot fully understand the expression of individual differences in temperament without taking into account cultural context. Kagan, Arcus, and Snidman (1993) have speculated that population differences in temperament can influence the nature of cultures within which individuals reside. Specifically, Kagan et al. (1993) have suggested that cultures are less likely to develop philosophies that contradict the temperamental characteristics of the majority of individuals within the culture. For example, in cultures where the majority of individuals are highly reactive, philosophies based on calmness and placidity (e.g., Buddhism) are less likely to be accepted as valid. While clearly speculative, this argument does raise the question of direct linkages from temperament to culture. While there is little direct evidence for the position taken by Kagan et al. (1993), some evidence does exist for the operation of a reverse process; namely, that the expression and consequences of temperament can be moderated by cultural characteristics. Perhaps the most dramatic example of this phenomena is seen in evidence indicating that fussy difficult infants are more likely to survive during drought conditions (DeVries, 1984) or in regions of less developed countries characterized by high levels of infant mortality (Scheper-Hughes, 1987). Differential survival rates appear to be based, in part, on culturally driven beliefs about the desirability of certain infant characteristics. Less dramatic, but equally valid, are studies documenting how the meaning, consequences, or stability of individual differences in temperament can be moderated by cultural characteristics.

With regard to the meaning of temperament, Thomas and Chess (1986) have noted how concepts like difficult temperament may have very different meanings in different cultural contexts. Characteristics that are viewed as difficult in one culture may not be viewed in the same way in other cultural contexts. For example, in cultures like Kenya where caregiving by multiple siblings is the norm, infants who are less soothable or who are less able to adapt to multiple caregivers are more likely to be considered as difficult than in cultures where multiple caregiving is not utilized (Super & Harkness, 1986). Similarly, the infant's ability to get on a regular schedule (regularity) is a far more meaningful temperament trait for caregivers in time-driven Western cultures (Super & Harkness, 1999) than for parents in non-Western cultures, such as India, where time demands are not central (Malhotra, 1989).

Again we see the importance of cultural context in regard to the consequences associated with different temperament traits. In the traditional goodness-of-fit model described by Thomas and Chess (1986), adjustment is a function of the degree to which the individual's characteristics match or fit the characteristics of the microcontext within which the individual lives (e.g., the home environment). We also can extend the concept of goodness of fit to culture, given evidence indicating that children whose temperamental characteristics provide a better fit to culturally based values and preferences are more likely to show better adjustment (Ballantine & Klein, 1990; Korn & Gannon, 1983). For example, the long-term negative consequences found for inhibited males in the United States are less likely to be seen in Sweden, where inhibited behavior by males is not necessarily viewed as a negative trait (Kerr, 1996).

A similar role for culture can also be seen in regard to developmental issues like the stability of temperament. Differential stability of temperament may be seen for individuals whose trait characteristics either fit or do not fit cultural beliefs about the value of such characteristics. For example, in cultures where inhibition is valued, females who were inhibited as toddlers were far more likely to be inhibited as adolescents, whereas females who were uninhibited as toddlers were far less likely to be uninhibited as adolescents (Kerr et al., 1994).

At this point, there are far more studies based on simple cross cultural comparisons of group differences in temperament than there are studies looking at specific cultural contributions to the nature, consequences, and development of temperament. However, it does seem clear from available evidence that we cannot understand the expression of individual differences in temperament in isolation from the cultural context in which the individual resides.

How Does Temperament Influence the Nature of the Individual's Context?

A fundamental assumption in the pioneering work of the New York Longitudinal Study was that children with specific temperaments elicit specific patterns of reactivity from their parents (Thomas et al., 1968). Viewed in this way, temperament can be seen as an influence on the subsequent environment of the child. The process whereby children with specific temperaments are more likely to elicit certain types of reactions from others is an example either of *reactive covariance* (Plomin, DeFries, & Loehlin, 1977) or *control system theory* (Bell & Chapman, 1986). For example, when children's behavior becomes overly intense (e.g., fussy difficult temperament, high activity level), caregivers are more likely to react by attempting to lower the level or the intensity of the child's behavior. In contrast, when children's behavior is overly passive (e.g., inhibited temperament), caregivers are more likely to react by attempting to raise the level or intensity of their child's behavioral style through techniques such as reward or prompting.

Though not deriving directly from the New York Longitudinal Study, a related concept is that of *active covariance* (Plomin et al., 1977), wherein individuals with different temperaments attempt to seek out niches in the environment that best fit the characteristics of their specific temperament. For example, evidence derived from Strelau's psychobiological model suggested that individuals with a low threshold for arousal would be less likely to prefer being in highly stimulating situations (e.g., heavy metal concerts) or occupations (e.g., air traffic controller), whereas individuals with a relatively high threshold for arousal would be more likely to prefer such contexts (Strelau, 1983). While active covariance processes do not necessarily change the nature of the individual's environment, they do change the likelihood of individuals with different temperaments encountering certain types of environmental settings.

In understanding how active and reactive covariance processes relate to the influence of temperament on context, two points are essential. First, as noted above, the meaning of different dimensions of temperament and the nature of reactivity of others to children with different types of temperament may well vary as a function of cultural context (Chess & Thomas, 1991). Second, for both active and reactive covariance, relations between temperament and context are probabilistic and not deterministic in nature. Having a specific temperament increases the probability of certain reactions from others, or the probability that one will prefer to be in certain environments, but does not guarantee either differential reactivity or differential exposure. Probabilistic and not deterministic linkages occur because a variety of nontemperament factors can serve to accentuate or attenuate the degree to which individual temperament characteristics influence the nature of the individual's subsequent environment. Potential moderators of temperament-environment linkages include, but are not limited to, nontemperamental child characteristics such as age or gender, individual parental characteristics such as preference for certain types of child behavior patterns, child and parent nutritional status, and contextual characteristics like the level of chaos or flexibility in the environment (Slabach et al., 1991; Wachs, 1992). For example, experienced mothers and mothers who believe they have the ability to deal effectively with their infant's behavior appear to be less reactive to temperamentally fussy and difficult behavior by their infants than are less experienced mothers or mothers who have doubts about their ability to cope (Cutrona & Troutman, 1986; Lounsbury & Bates, 1982).

Keeping these constraints in mind, what is the nature of evidence linking variability in individual temperament to the characteristics of the individual's environment? In regard to the question of reactive covariance, particularly during the first 2 years of life, some individual longitudinal studies have recorded evidence suggesting that variability in infant temperament influences subsequent parenting behavior. For example, Van den Boom and Hoeksma (1994) have found that over time mothers of irritable infants show less visual and physical contact, less effective stimulation, less involvement, and less responsivity to positive signals from their infants as compared to mothers of nonirritable infants. Similarly, in a controlled laboratory study, Lounsbury and Bates (1982) have reported that adult raters expressed more irritation at the cries of difficult temperament infants than they did to the cries of easy temperament infants. However, other well-designed, large sample studies have reported few significant relations between early infant temperament and later caregiver interaction patterns (Pettit & Bates, 1984; Worobey & Blajda, 1989). These complex and inconsistent patterns of findings have led reviewers to conclude that there is a gap between the level of theoretical attention given to processes like reactive covariance and the degree of empirical validation of the operation of these processes, at least for the first several years of life (Crockenberg, 1986; Slabach et al., 1991).

There are a number of reasons why links between infant temperament and subsequent caregiver behavior patterns have not been consistently demonstrated. Some researchers have questioned whether parent report measures of infant temperament are the best approach for dealing with this question (Seifer, Schiller, Sameroff, Resnick, & Riordan, 1996). There is also the possibility that existing methodological practices may limit our ability to detect existing links between infant temperament and caregiver behavior. Methodological factors may be particularly important for the many studies in this area that use single short-term observations of caregiver-infant interaction. Average within week stability of single short term observations of mother-infant interactions is $r = .35$, a value which clearly raises doubts about the representativeness of caregiver behavior patterns toward infants which are based on single short-term observations (Wachs, 1987a). Going beyond only measurement issues, there also is the issue of whether or not reactive covariance between infant and temperament and later caregiver behavior is best assessed by point to point correlations over two time periods. If we look at trajectories of caregiver behavior over time across such dimensions as soothing (Van den Boom & Hoeksma, 1994) or teaching efforts (Maccoby, Snow, & Jacklin, 1984), results suggest a pattern of declining involvement by parents toward their more fussy difficult infants. Thus, depending on the time point chosen, we could see either differences or no differences in parent reaction to fussy difficult infants.

However, measurement and methodological issues are not the whole story, given evidence suggesting that, for some caregiver dimensions like physical contact stimulation or responsivity to fussing, there is little difference in maternal behavior toward irritable versus nonirritable infants, even when maternal behaviors are looked at across time (Van den Boom & Hoeksma, 1994). One hypothesized possibility is that reactive covariance is more likely to be found for infants with extreme temperament traits, who are viewed as being more likely to have an influence over their environment than are infants with less extreme temperament traits (Clarke & Clarke, 1988). Unfortunately, evidence on this hypothesis is sorely lacking and the available evidence often is methodologically flawed. For example, Sullivan and McGrath (1995) have found that correlations between infant and caregiver behaviors shown for extreme temperament infants are not found when a full sample is studied, including both extreme and nonextreme temperament infants. Unfortunately, since the correlations were taken concurrently, it is difficult to determine if the pattern of results reflects extreme temperament infants being more likely to influence their environment or environment being more likely to influence the behavior of extreme temperament infants.

More probable as an explanatory framework is evidence documenting how reactive covariance patterns between infant temperament and subsequent caregiver behavior patterns can be moderated by a variety of nontemperamental infant and adult characteristics (Slabach et al., 1991). For example, trajectories of caregiver response patterns toward their difficult infant have been shown to be moderated by factors such as infant gender (Maccoby et al., 1984), maternal substance abuse (Schuler, Black, & Starr, 1995), and maternal attitudes about how responsive they should be toward their infant (Crockenberg & McCluskey, 1986). The overall pattern of findings supports a hypothesis that infant temperament is a necessary, but not sufficient, condition for producing variability in subsequent caregiver behavior patterns. This means that, if we are to understand the processes underlying reactive covariance between infant temperament and caregiver behavior, it is essential to go beyond temperament per se, and look at temperament as part of a larger system involving linked contributions between other aspects of the system such as nontemperamental child characteristics and caregiver preferences and attitudes.

While the concept of active covariance (niche picking) has been the focus of much theoretical speculation (e.g., Plomin, 1994; Scarr & McCartney, 1983), remarkably little research exists that actually documents how individuals with different temperaments act in ways that result in their inhabiting different types of contexts. One of the few examples we have of the process of active temperament-context covariance is seen in the work of Matheny (1986), showing how more active children, or children with less tractable temperaments, have a higher probability of putting themselves in dangerous situations that result in a greater frequency of physical injuries. Based on an underlying model of low arousability → high sensation seeking (Strelau, 1994), individual differences in sensation seeking have been linked to a variety of contextually relevant behavioral characteristics, such as substance abuse, sexual patterns, and reckless behavior, that could act to increase the individual's level of exposure to physical danger (Zuckerman, 1994). Alternatively, Gunnar (1994) has provided an elegant documentation of how, even in the same classroom, highly inhibited or uninhibited children experience different microenvironments, with inhibited children being more likely to be involved in familiar low peer contact activities while uninhibited children are more likely to be engaged in unfamiliar activities and have higher levels of peer social interactions and peer conflict.

Unfortunately, in terms of understanding the extent and impact of active temperament-context covariance we essentially are restricted to these few examples. There is a variety of reasons why our database is so limited. One obvious reason involves the effort required to document such covariance. Obviously, we need highly accurate measures of individual temperament. Perhaps even more critically, we need detailed measures of the physical and social contextual characteristics that individuals with different temperaments inhabit. Such contextual measures are time consuming to obtain and cannot be derived from global, social address context assessments. However, even if we had such detailed assessments, I predict that we would not find the strong relations between individual temperament and subsequent contexts predicted by some theories (e.g., Scarr & McCartney, 1983). In good part, this is because active covariance processes will be moderated by, or will act in concert with, a variety of nontemperamental characteristics. The operation of such nontemperament moderators is seen in some of the examples presented above. Thus, Matheny (1991) has reported that, in addition to child temperament, risk of child injury is also influenced by aspects of the child's context that are not likely to be influenced by the child's temperament, such as home chaos. Gunnar (1994) has noted that the degree to which inhibited children engage in unfamiliar classroom activities will depend on nontemperament aspects of classroom characteristics, such as organization level in the classroom and degree of teacher sensitivity and support.

The fact that links between an individual's temperament and an individual's context can be attenuated by a variety of influences other than temperament illustrates a larger issue directly related to the active covariance process itself. In general, the assumption underlying both theory (Scarr & McCartney, 1983) and research in this area (Schulenberg, Wadsworth, O'Malley, Bachman, & Johnston, 1996) is that individuals have a high degree of freedom to self-select into a variety of different contextual niches. In contrast, I would argue that there will be multiple limitations on one's ability to self-select into different types of contexts. Specifically, a variety of biological (e.g., malnutrition, chronic illness), caregiver belief (e.g., tolerance of child independence, authoritarian rearing styles), cultural (e.g., racism), and nontemperamental individual characteristics (e.g., attachment, cognitive ability) can act both to influence the individual's exposure to different environmental contexts as well as the individual's ability to self-select into different contexts (Wachs, 1996). For example, children with an extremely difficult temperament over time may be more likely to find themselves limited not only in terms of the types of peer groups available to them (Cairns, Cairns, Neckerman, Crest, & Gariety, 1988), but also in terms of educational and employment opportunities (Caspi, Elder, & Bem, 1987). Thus, even in a situation where there are ongoing active temperament-context covariance processes occurring, it will be essential to go beyond only temperament per se when attempting to understand how individuals with specific temperament characteristics have a higher probability of encountering and staying in different types of contexts.

The Nature of Temperament-Context Linkings

In previous sections, I have documented temperament influences on environment and environmental influences on temperament. However, it also is important to consider the possibility that transactional processes (Sameroff & Fiese, 1990), involving mutual bidirectional influences between temperament and environment operating over time, may be a better way of understanding relations between environment and temperament. One such example of mutual influences is seen in the work of Maccoby et al. (1984), who assessed both level of child difficultness and degree of maternal involvement during task situations at 12 and 18 months. Maccoby et al. reported that, while boys whose mothers were highly involved in teaching activities became less difficult between 12 and 18 months (environment → temperament), mothers with more difficult boys became less involved in teaching activities over the same time period (temperament → environment). A similar pattern of bidirectional reactivity was shown by Engfer (1986), who measured maternal sensitivity and child emotionality from the neonatal period through 18 months of age. Engfer's results indicated that, while maternal sensitivity in the neonatal period related to lower child difficultness at 4 months of age, child difficultness at 4 months of age related to lower maternal sensitivity at 8 months of age which, in turn, predicted lower child difficultness at 18 months of age (environment → temperament → environment). Bidirectional relations between infant sociability and maternal responsivity (Thoman, 1990), between infants' negative emotionality and maternal responsivity and sensitivity (Crockenberg & McCluskey, 1986), and between children's emotional self-regulation capacity and patterns of peer interaction also have been reported (Eisenberg & Fabes, 1992). Such bidirectional influences between temperament and context reinforce the basic hypothesis of this chapter; namely, that one cannot understand the nature or development of temperament in isolation from context. However, such findings also support the hypothesis that one cannot understand the nature or impact of context without also considering the temperamental characteristics of individuals in specific contexts.

How Do Temperament and Context Interact?

Relations between temperament and subsequent development can be either conceptualized in main effect terms (temperament → development) or in terms of multiple main effects (additive coaction: temperament + environment → development). However, main effects and additive coaction are not the only means by which temperament can influence development. There also is the possibility of interactions among different temperament dimensions, as seen in evidence showing that linkages between negative emotionality and subsequent behavior problems will vary depending on the individual's level of self-regulation (Eisenberg et al., 1996). In addition, evidence has further suggested the possibility of nonlinear interactions between temperament and context.

By temperament-context interactions, I refer to the same environments having a different influence on individuals with different temperament characteristics, or the same temperament characteristics having a different influence on individuals living in different environments. In looking for temperament-context interactions, it is essential to keep in mind the multiple methodological and statistical problems that limit our ability to detect existing interactions. Such problems include, but are not limited to, the insensitivity of traditional analytic designs to interaction effects, the likelihood that interactions will appear in only certain segments of a given population group, and the need for highly sensitive measures to detect interaction effects (McClelland & Judd, 1993; Wachs & Plomin, 1991).

Given the multiple methodological and statistical problems that limit our ability to detect interactions, it is remarkable that there is a consistent body of evidence showing context by temperament interactions. One set of findings has shown how the impact of the environment can be moderated by individual differences in temperament (Wachs, 1992). An excellent example of this type of interaction is seen in studies indicating that the impact on development of *environmental stressors,* such as crowding (Wachs, 1987b), maternal anger (Crockenberg, 1987), maternal unavailability (Lumley, Ables, Melamed, Pistone, & Johnson, 1990), or divorce (Hetherington, 1989), is significantly greater for difficult temperament children than for children with easy temperaments. For example, in a sample of 6-month-old infants, relations between an index of home background noise (number of stimulus sources on simultaneously) and the infant's verbal imitation skills and understanding of cause-effect relations were negative and significant for infants with difficult temperaments but were nonsignificant for infants having easy temperaments; the difference between the two sets of correlations was statistically significant (Wachs & Gandour, 1983). Available evidence also has indicated that higher levels of stimulation were needed to facilitate the development of low active infants but that the same levels of stimulation either were unrelated to or even inhibited the development of infants with higher activity levels (Gandour, 1989; Schaffer, 1966). For example, higher levels of parent object mediation (e.g., naming objects) were associated with higher levels of object mastery motivation in low active 12-month-old infants but tended to inhibit mastery motivation in more active 12-month-olds (Wachs, 1987b).

A mirror image set of findings has documented how the consequences of individual differences in temperament can be moderated by characteristics of the individuals' psychosocial environment (Rothbart & Bates, 1998). One example of this type of interaction is seen in a series of studies by Kochanska (1993, 1995, 1997; Kochanska, Mordhorst, & Reschly, 1997) showing how inhibited children are more likely to develop internal regulation mechanisms if their parents use gentle discipline than if they use more arousing forms of discipline. A similar set of findings has documented how relations between children's early resistance to parental control and later externalizing problems will vary as a function of the level of maternal control, with highly resistant children being less likely to show later externalizing problems when their mothers were high in control (Bates, Pettit, Dodge, & Ridge, 1997).

The pattern of findings presented in this final section shows how the contributions of temperament to development do not necessarily reflect the operation of temperament in isolation but, rather, can vary as a function of contributions from another domain; namely, characteristics of the child's environment. Obviously the converse also holds; namely, that we should not necessarily assume environmental main effects without also considering the temperamental characteristics of the individual on whom the environment impinges.

☐ Conclusions

Our understanding of both the nature of children's development and the factors influencing variability in children's development has benefited greatly from research and theorizing on the role played by individual differences in temperament. As a result of this research and theorizing, we have gained a greater understanding of the contributions that the individual makes to his or her own development as well as the dimensions of temperament, such as self regulation and reactivity, that are fundamental to understanding these individual contributions. In these endeavors, we also have benefited from advances in the measurement of temperament, whether done by parent report or by observation of children's behavior. Of necessity, much of our past and present research in this area has focused primarily on temperament per se, without giving due consideration either to contributions from nontemperamental influences, such as motivation, the structure of the central nervous system, and the child's age and gender, or to the proximal and distal context within which the individual resides. This narrow focus is not unique to studies of temperament. Early studies in behavioral genetics focused essentially on demonstrating that genetic influences were relevant for an understanding of behavioral developmental variability; it is only recently that behavior genetic researchers have focused on process questions such as how genetic and nongenetic influences combine to impact on behavioral developmental variability (Plomin, 1994). It seems clear that we have reached a similar point in regard to temperament. We have established beyond doubt the relevance of temperament, both as an independent field of study and as a major contributor to individual behavioral and developmental variability. I would argue that the time is now ripe to broaden the range of both our research and theorizing by looking at how temperament fits into a larger system of multiple influences on development and how temperament, in combination with other developmental influences, relates to individual differences in behavior and development.

An example of such a system is shown in Figure 2.2, illustrating patterns of bidirectional influences between temperament and nontemperament factors. One of the major implications to be drawn from Figure 2.2 is that, in order to understand how temperament relates to development, we need to understand how temperament is related to biological, biosocial, and contextual influences on behavioral development. Focusing on temperament as part of a larger system of multiple developmental influences will allow us to go beyond temperament, while not losing our understanding of the unique role that temperament plays in development.

☐ Note

1. A critical distinction is between stability (maintenance of rank order on a trait for a population of individuals, traditionally assessed by trait correlations over time) versus continuity (change in the level of the trait traditionally assessed by mean changes in a trait over time) (McCall, 1986). Clearly, the level of temperament traits change over time (Eaton, 1994; Worobey & Blajda, 1989). However, it is entirely possible for there to be changes in a trait over time (discontinuity), while stability (rank order of individuals) is still maintained. For the present discussion, I will be focusing on stability.

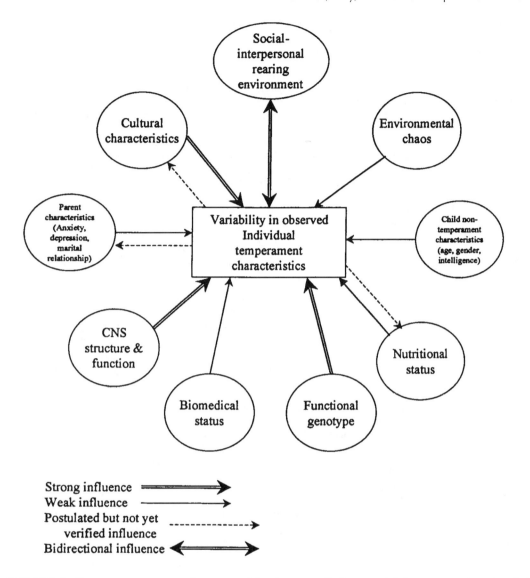

FIGURE 2.2. Temperament as part of a system of developmental influences. It is important to keep in mind that many of the nontemperament influences pictured in this figure are themselves linked. For example, the social interpersonal rearing environment covaries with genotype, nutritional status, culture, and environmental chaos; central nervous system (CNS) structure covaries with both biomedical and nutritional status which, in turn, covary with each other.

☐ References

Arcus, D., & Kagan, J. (1995, March). *Tempermental contributions to social behavior.* Symposium presentation at the Society for Research and Child Development, Indianapolis, IN.

Asendorpf, J. (1994). The malleability of behavior inhibition. *Developmental Psychology, 30,* 912–919.

Ballantine, J., & Klein, H. (1990). The relationship of temperament and adjustment in Japanese schools. *Journal of Psychology, 124,* 299–309.

Barrett, K., & Morgan, G. (1995). Continuities and discontinuities in mastery motivation during infancy and toddlerhood. In R. MacTurk & G. Morgan (Eds.), *Mastery motivation: Origins, conceptualizations and applications* (pp. 57–94). Norwood, NJ: Ablex.

Bates, J. (1989). Concepts and measures of temperament. In G. Kohnstamm, J. Bates, & M. Rothbart (Eds.), *Temperament in childhood* (pp. 3–27). New York: Wiley.

Bates, J. (1994). Parents as scientific observers of their children's development. In S. Friedman & C. Haywood (Eds.), *Developmental follow-up* (pp. 197–216). San Diego, CA: Academic Press.

Bates, J., Pettit, G., Dodge, K., & Ridge, B. (1997, April). *The interaction of temperamental resistance to control and restrictive parenting in the development of externalizing behavior.* Symposium presentation at the Society of Research and Child Development, Washington, DC.

Bates, J., & Wachs, T. D. (1994). *Temperament: Individual differences at the interface of biology and behavior.* Washington, DC: American Psychological Association.

Bell, S., & Ainsworth, M. (1972). Infant crying and maternal responsiveness. *Child Development, 43,* 1171–1190.

Bell, R., & Chapman, M. (1986). Child effects and studies using experimental or brief longitudinal approaches to socialization. *Developmental Psychology, 22,* 595–603.

Belsky, J., Fish, M., & Isabella, R. (1991). Continuity and discontinuity in infant negative and positive emotionality. *Developmental Psychology, 27,* 421–431.

Belsky, J., Hsieh, K., & Crnic, K. (1996). Infant positive and negative emotionality. *Developmental Psychology, 32,* 289–298.

Borkowski, J., & Dukewich, T. (1996). Environment covariations and intelligence. In D. Detterman (Ed.), *Current topics in human intelligence: The environment* (Vol. 5, pp. 3–16). Norwood, NJ: Ablex.

Buss, A. (1989). Temperament as personality traits. In G. Kohnstamm, J. Bates, & M. Rothbart (Eds.), *Temperament in childhood* (pp. 49–58). New York: Wiley.

Buss, H., & Plomin, R. (1984). *Temperament: Early developing personality traits.* Hillsdale, NJ: Erlbaum.

Cairns, R., Cairns, B., Neckerman, H., Gest, S., & Gariety, J. (1988). Social networks and aggressive behavior. *Developmental Psychology, 24,* 815–823.

Calkins, S., & Fox, N. (1994). Individual differences in the biological aspects of temperament. In J. Bates & T. D. Wachs, (Eds.), *Temperament: Individual differences at the interface of biology and behavior* (pp. 199–218). Washington, DC: American Psychological Association.

Carey, W. (1983). Some pitfalls in infant temperament research. *Infant Behavior and Development, 6,* 247–254.

Carey, W., & McDevitt, S. (1989). *Clinical and educational applications of temperament research.* Amsterdam: Swets & Zeitlinger.

Caspi, A. (in press). Personality development across the life course. In N. Eisenberg (Ed.), *Handbook of child psychology: Social emotional and personality development* (Vol. 3, pp. 311–388). New York: Wiley.

Caspi, A., Elder, G., & Bem, B. (1987). Moving against the world: Life course patterns of explosive children. *Developmental Psychology, 23,* 308–313.

Chess, S., & Thomas, A. (1991). Temperament and the concept of goodness of fit. In J. Strelau & A. Angleitner (Eds.), *Exploration in temperament* (pp. 15–28). New York: Plenum.

Chisholm, J. (1981). Prenatal influences on Aboriginal-White Australian differences in neonatal irritability. *Ethology and Sociobiology, 2,* 67–73.

Clarke, A., & Clarke, A. (1988). The adult outcome of early behavioral abnormalities. *International Journal of Behavioral Developement, 11,* 3–19.

Crockenberg, S. (1986). Are temperamental differences in babies associated with predictable differences in caregiving? In J. Lerner & R. Lerner (Eds.), *Temperament and interaction in infancy and childhood* (pp. 53–73). San Francisco: Jossey-Bass.

Crockenberg, S. (1987). Predictors and correlates of anger toward and punitive control of toddlers by adolescent mothers. *Child Development, 58,* 964–975.

Crockenberg, S., & McCluskey, K. (1986). Change in maternal behavior during the baby's first years of life. *Child Development, 57,* 746–753.

Crockenberg, S., & Smith, P. (1982). Antecedents of mother infant interaction and infant irritability in the first three months of life. *Infant Behavior and Development, 5,* 105–120.

Cutrona, C., & Troutman, B. (1986). Social support, infant temperament and parenting self-efficacy. *Child Development, 57,* 1507–1518.

Dar, R. (1987). Another look at Meehl, Lakatos and the scientific practice of psychology. *American Psychologist, 42,* 145–151.

DeVries, M. (1984). Temperament and infant mortality among the Masai of East Africa. *American Journal of Psychiatry, 141,* 1189–1194.

DiPietro, J., Larson, S., & Porges, S. (1987). Behavioral and heart rate pattern differences between breast fed and bottle fed neonates. *Developmental Psychology, 23,* 467–474.

Eaton, W. (1994). Methodological implications of the impending engagement of temperament and biology. In J. Bates & T. D. Wachs (Eds.), *Temperament: Individual differences at the interface of biology and behavior* (pp. 259–274). Washington, DC: American Psychological Association.

Eisenberg, N., & Fabes, R. (1992). Emotion, regulation and the development of social competence. In M. Clark (Ed.), *Review of personality and social psychology* (Vol. 14, pp. 119–150). Newbury Park, CA: Sage.

Eisenberg, N., Fabes, R., Murphy, B., Karbon, M., Smith, M., & Maszk, P. (1996). The relations of children's dispositional empathy-related responding to their emotionality, regulation and social functioning. *Developmental Psychology, 32,* 195–209.

Engfer, A. (1986). Anticendents of perceived behavior problems in infancy. In G. Kohnstamm (Ed.), *Temperament discussed* (pp. 165–180). Lisse, the Netherlands: Swets & Zeitlinger.

Feldman, S., & Weinberger, D. (1994). Self-restrainnt as a mediator of family influences on boys' delinquent behavior. *Child Development, 65,* 195–211.

Fish, M. (1997, April). *Stability and change in infant temperament.* Paper presented at the Society for Research in Child Development, Washington, DC.

Fogel, A. (1993). *Developing through relationships.* New York: Harvester Wheatshaft.

Gandour, M. (1989). Activity level as a dimension of temperament in toddlers. *Child Development, 60,* 1092–1098.

Garcia-Coll, C., Halpern, L., Vohr, B., Seifer, R., & Oh, W. (1992). Stability and correlates of change in early temperament in preterm and full term infants. *Infant Behavior and Development, 15,* 137–153.

Goldsmith, H. (1989). Behavior genetic approaches to temperament. In G. Kohnstamm, J. Bates, & M. Rothbart (Eds.), *Temperament and childhood* (pp. 111–132). New York: Wiley.

Goldsmith, H. (1996). Studying temperament via construction of the Toddler Behavior Assessment Questionnaire. *Child Development, 67,* 218–235.

Goldsmith, H., Buss, A., Plonin, R., Rothbart, M., Thomas, A., Chess, S., Hinde, R., & McCall, R. (1987). Round table: What is temperament? *Child Development, 58,* 505–529.

Goldsmith, H., & Campos, J. (1982). Toward a theory of infant temperament. In R. Emde & R. Harmon (Eds.), *The development of attachment and affilative systems* (pp. 161–193). New York: Plenum.

Goldsmith, H., & Campos, J. (1990). The structure of temperamental fear and pleasure in infants. *Child Development, 61,* 1944–1964.

Goldsmith, H., Rieser-Danner, L., & Briggs, S. (1991). Evaluating convergent and discriminant validity of temperament questionnaires for preschoolers, toddlers and infants. *Developmental Psychology, 27,* 566–579.

Goldsmith, H., & Rothbard, M. (1991). Contemporary instruments for assessing early temperament by questionnaire and in the laboratory. In J. Strelau & A. Angleitner (Eds.), *Exploration of temperament* (pp. 249–272). New York: Plenum.

Greenough, W., & Black, J. (1992). Induction of brain structure by experience. In M. Gunnar & C. Nelson (Eds.), *Developmental behavioral neuroscience* (pp. 153–232). Hillsdale, NJ: Erlbaum.

Gunnar, M. (1994). Psychoendocrine studies of temperament and stress in early childhood. In J. Bates & T. D. Wachs (Eds.), *Temperament: Individual differences at the interface of biology and behavior* (pp. 175–198). Washington, DC: American Psychological Association.

Halverson, D., Kohnstamm, G., & Martin, R. (1994). *The developing structure of temperament and personality from infancy to adulthood.* Hillsdale, NJ: Erlbaum.

Hetherington, E. (1989). Coping with family transitions. *Child Development, 60,* 1–14.

Hubert, N. (1989). Parental reactions to perceived temperament behaviors in their six and twenty-four month old children. *Infant Behavior and Development, 12,* 185–198.

Hubert, N., Wachs, T. D., Peters-Martin, P., & Gandour, M. (1982). The study of early temperament: Measurement and conceptual issues. *Child Development, 53,* 571–600.

Kagan, J., Arcus, D., & Snidman, N. (1993). The idea of temperament: Where do we go from here? In R. Plomin & G. McClearn (Eds.), *Nature nurture & psychology* (pp. 197–212). Washington, DC: American Psychological Association.

Kagan, J., Reznick, J., & Snidman, N. (1989). Issues in the study of temperament. In G. Kohnstamm, J. Bates, & N. Rothbart (Eds.), *Temperament in childhood* (pp. 133–144). New York: Wiley.

Kerr, M. (1996, June). *Temperament and culture.* Paper presented at the Netherlands Institute for Advanced Studies Conference on Temperament in Context, Wassenaer, the Netherlands.

Kerr, M., Lambert, W., Stattin, H., & Larson, I. (1994). Stability of inhibition in a Swedish longitudinal sample. *Child Development, 65,* 138–146.

Kinchla, R. (1992). Attention. *Annual Review of Psychology, 43,* 711–742.

Kochanska, G. (1993). Toward a synthesis of parental socialization and child temperament in early development of conscience. *Child Development, 64,* 325–347.

Kochanska, G. (1995). Children's temperament, mother's discipline and security of attachment. *Child Development, 66,* 597–615.

Kochanska, G. (1997). Multiple pathways to conscience for children with different temperaments. *Developmental Psychology, 33,* 228–240.

Kohnstamm, G., Mordhorst, M., & Reschly, A. (1997, April). *Child temperament and maternal discipline as contributors to emerging restraint in infancy.* Paper presented at the Society for Research in Child Development, Washington, DC.

Kohnstamm, G. (1989). Historical and international perspectives. In G. Kohnstamm, J. Bates, & M. Rothbart (Eds.), *Temperament in childhood* (pp. 557–566). New York: Wiley.

Kohnstamm, G., Bates, J., & Rothbart, M. (1989). *Temperament in childhood.* New York: Wiley.

Korn, S., & Gannon, S. (1983). Temperament, cultural variation and behavior disorders in preschool children. *Child Psychiatry and Human Behavior, 13,* 203–212.

Kuhn, T. (1970). *The structure of scientific revolutions* (2nd ed.). Chicago: University of Chicago Press.

Lewis, M., Ramsey, D., & Kawakami, K. (1993). Differences between Japanese infants and Caucasian American infants in the behavioral and cortisol response to inoculation. *Child Development, 64,* 1722–1731.

Lounsbury, M., & Bates, J. (1982). The cries of infants of differing levels of perceived temperamental difficulties. *Child Development, 53,* 677–686.

Lumley, N., Ables, L., Melamed, B., Pistone, L., & Johnson, J. (1990). Coping outcome in children undergoing stressful medical procedures. *Behavioral Assessment, 12,* 223–238.

Maccoby, E., Snow, M., & Jacklin, C. (1984). Children's disposition and mother child interactions at 12 and 18 months. *Developmental Psychology, 20,* 459–472.

MacPhee, D., Burchinal, M., & Ramey, C. (1997, April). *Individual differences in response to interventions.* Paper presented at the Society for Research in Child Development, Washington, DC.

Malhotra, S. (1989). Varying risk factors in outcomes: An Indian perspective. In W. Carey & S. McDevit (Eds.), *Clinical and educational applications of temperament research.* Amsterdam: Swets & Zeitlinger.

Massaro, D. (1987). *Speech perception by ear and eye.* Hillsdale, NJ: Erlbaum.

Matheny, A. (1986). Injuries among toddlers. *Journal of Pediatric Psychology, 11,* 163–176.

Matheny, A. (1991). Play assessment of infant temperament. In C. Schaefer, K. Gitling, & A Sandgrund (Eds.), *Play diagnosis and assessment.* New York: Wiley.

Matheny, A., Wilson, R., & Thoben, A. (1987). Home and mother: Relations with infant temperament. *Developmental Psychology, 23,* 323–331.

McCall, R. (1986). Issues of stability and continuity in temperament research. in R. Plomin & J. Dunn (Eds.), *The study of temperament* (pp. 13–26). Hillsdale: NJ: Erlbaum.

McClelland, G., & Judd, C. (1993). Statistical difficulties of detecting interactions and moderator effects. *Psychological Bulletin, 114,* 376–390.

McCullough, A., Kirksey, A., Wachs, T. D., McCabe, G., Bassily, N., Bishry, Z., Galal, D., Harrison, G., & Jerome, N. (1990). Vitamin B6 status of Egyptian mothers. *American Journal of Clinical Nutrition, 51,* 1067–1074.

Mebert, C. (1989). Stability and change in parents' perceptions of infant temperament. *Infant Behavior and Development, 12,* 237–244.

Mebert, C. (1991). Dimensions of subjectivity in parents' ratings of infant temperament. *Child Development, 62,* 352–361.

Miller, J. (1978). *Living systems.* New York: McGraw-Hill.

Nelson, C. (1994). Neural basis of infant temperament. In J. Bates & T. D. Wachs (Eds.), *Temperament: Individual differences at the interface of biology and behavior* (pp. 47–82). Washington, DC: American Psyhological Association.

Pedlow, R., Sanson, A., Prior, M., & Oberklaid, F. (1993). Stability of maternally reported temperament from infancy to 8 years. *Developmental Psychology, 29,* 998–1007.

Pettit, G., & Bates, J. (1984). Continuity of individual differences in the mother infant relationship from six to thirteen months. *Child Development, 55,* 729–739.

Plomin, R. (1994). *Genetics and experience.* Thousand Oaks, CA: Sage.

Plomin, R., DeFries, J., & Loehlin, J. (1977). Genotype environment interaction and correlation in the analysis of human development. *Psychological Bulletin, 84,* 309–322.

Plomin, R., DeFries, J., McClearn, G., & Rutter, M. (1997). *Behavioral genetics* (3rd ed.). New York: Freeman.

Plomin, R., & Saudino, K. (1994). Quantitative genetics and molecular genetics. In J. Bates & T. D. Wachs (Eds.), *Temperament: Individual differences at the interface of biology and behavior* (pp. 143–174). Washington, DC: American Psychological Association.

Prior, M., Sanson, A., & Oberklaid, F. (1989). The Australian temperament project. In G. Kohnstamm, J. Bates, & M. Rothbart (Eds.), *Temperament in childhood* (pp. 537–556). New York: Wiley.

Riese, M. (1987). Longitudinal assessment of temperament from birth to two years. *Infant Behavior and Development, 10,* 347–363.

Rothbart, M. (1986). Longitudinal observation of infant temperament. *Developmental Psychology, 22,* 356–365.

Rothbart, M. (1991). Temperament: A developmental framework. In J. Strelau & A. Angleitner (Eds.), *Exploration in temperament* (pp. 61–74). New York: Plenum.

Rothbart, M., & Bates, J. (1998). Temperament. In N. Eisenberg (Ed.), *Handbook of child psychology* (Vol. 3, pp. 105–176). New York: Wiley.

Rothbart, M., & Derryberry, D. (1981). Development of individual differences in temperament. In M. Lamb & A. Brown (Eds.), *Advances in developmental pscyhology* (Vol. 1, pp. 37–86). Hillsdale, NJ: Erlbaum.

Rothbart, M., Derryberry, D., & Posner, M. (1994). A psychobiological approach to the development of temperament. In J. Bates & T. D. Wachs (Eds.), *Temperament: Individual differences at the interface of biology and behavior* (pp. 82–116). Washington, DC: American Psychological Association.

Rushton, P., Brainerd, C., & Pressley, M. (1983). Behavioral development and construct validity. *Psychological Bulletin, 94,* 18–38.

Sameroff, A. (in press). General systems theories and developmental psychopathology. In D. Cicchetti & D. Cohen (Eds.), *Developmental psychopathology* (Vol. 1, pp. 659–695). New York: Wiley.

Sameroff, A., & Fiese, B. (1990). Transactional regulation and early intervention. In S. Meisels & J. Shonkoff (Eds.), *Handbook of early childhood intervention* (pp. 119–149), Cambridge, England: Cambridge University Press.

Scarr, S., & McCartney, K. (1983). How people make their own environments. *Child Development, 54,* 424–435.

Schaffer, H. (1966). Activity level as a constitutional determinant of infantile reaction to deprivation. *Child Development, 37,* 595–602.

Scheper-Hughes, N. (1987). Maternal estrangement and infant and death. In C. Super (Ed.), *The role of culture in developmental disorder.* San Diego, CA: Academic Press.

Schulenberg, J., Wadsworth, K., O'Malley, P., Bachman, J., & Johnston, L. (1996). Adolescent risk factors for binge drinking during the transition to young adulthood. *Developmental Psychology, 32,* 659–674.

Schuler, M., Black, M., & Starr, R. (1995). Determinants of mother infant interaction. *Journal of Clinical Child Psychology, 24,* 397–405.

Seifer, R., Schiller, M., Sameroff, A., Resnick, S., & Riordan, K. (1996). Attachment, maternal sensitivity and infant temperament during the first year of life. *Developmental Psychology, 32,* 12–35.

Slabach, E., Morrow, J., & Wachs, T. D. (1991). Questionnaire measurement of infant and child temperament. In J. Strelau & A. Angleitner (Eds.), *Exploration in temperament* (pp. 205–234). New York: Plenum.

Strelau, J. (1983). *Temperament, personality and activity.* New York: Academic Press.

Strelau, J. (1987). Concepts of temperament in personality research. *European Journal of Personality, 1,* 107–117.

Strelau, J. (1989). The regulative theory of temperament as a result of East-West influences. In G. Kohnstamm, J. Bates, & M. Rothbart (Eds.), *Temperament in childhood* (pp. 35–48). New York: Wiley.

Strelau, J. (1994). The concepts of arousal and arousability as used in temperament studies. In J. Bates & T. D. Wachs (Eds.), *Temperament: Individual differences at the interface of biology and behavior* (pp. 117–142). Washington, DC: American Psychological Association.

Sullivan, M., & McGrath, M. (1995, April). *The linkage between dimensions of maternal interaction and child temperament.* Paper presented at the Society for Research in Child Development, Indianapolis, IN.

Super, C., & Harkness, S. (1986). Temperament, development and culture. In R. Plomin & J. Dunn (Eds.), *The study of temperament* (pp. 131–150). Hillsdale, NJ: Erlbaum.

Super, C., & Harkness, S. (1999). The environment in cultural and developmental research. In S. Friedman & T. D. Wachs (Eds.), *Conceptualization and measurement of the environment across the lifespan* (pp. 279–326). Washington, DC: American Psychological Association.

Thoman, E. (1990). Sleeping and waking states of infants. *Neuroscience and Biobehavioral Reviews, 14,* 93–107.

Thomas, A., & Chess, S. (1977). *Temperament and development.* New York: Brunner-Mazel.

Thomas, A., & Chess, S. (1986). The New York Longitudinal Study: From infancy to early adult life. In R. Plomin & J. Dunn (Eds.), *The study of temperament* (pp. 39–52). Hillsdale, NJ: Erlbaum.

Thomas, A., Chess, S., & Birch, H. (1968). *Temperament and behavior disorder in children.* New York: New York University Press.

Van den Boom, D. (1994). The influence of temperament and mothering on attachment and exploration. *Child Development, 65,* 1457–1477.

Van den Boom, D., & Hoeksma, J. (1994). The effect of infant irritability on mother-infant interaction: A growth curve analysis. *Developmental Psychology, 30,* 581–590.

Wachs, T. D. (1987a). Short term stability of aggregated and nonaggregated measures of parent behavior. *Child Development, 58,* 796–797.

Wachs, T. D. (1987b). Specificity of environmental action as manifest in environmental correlates of infants' mastery motivation. *Developmental Psychology, 23,* 782–790.

Wachs, T. D. (1988). Relevance of physical environmental influences for toddler temperament. *Infant Behavior and Development, 11,* 431–445.

Wachs, T. D. (1992). *The nature of nurture.* Newbury Park, CA: Sage.

Wachs, T. D. (1994). Fit, context and the transition between temperament and personality. In C. Halverson, G. Kohnstamm, & R. Martin (Eds.), *The developing structure of personality from infancy to adulthood* (pp. 209–222). Hillsdale, NJ: Erlbaum.

Wachs, T. D. (1996). Known and potential processes underlying developmental trajectories in childhood and adolescence. *Developmental Psychology, 32,* 796–801.

Wachs, T. D., Bishry, Z., Sobhy, A., McCabe, G., Galal, O., & Shaheen, F. (1993). Relation of rearing environment to adaptive behavior of Egyptian toddlers. *Child Development, 64,* 586–604.

Wachs, T. D., & Gandour, M. (1983). Temperament, environment and six month cogntive-intellectual development. *International Journal of Behavioral Development, 6,* 135–152.

Wachs, T. D., & King, B. (1994). Behavioral research in the brave new world of neuroscience and temperament. In J. Bates & T. D. Wachs (Eds.), *Temperament: Individual differences at the interface of biology and behavior* (pp. 307–336). Washington, DC: American Psychological Association.

Wiener, S., & Levine, S. (1978). Perinatal malnutrition and early handling. *Developmental Psychobiology, 11,* 335–352.

Wohlwill, J., & Heft, H. (1987). The physical environment and the development of the child. In I. Altman & J. Stokols (Eds.), *Handbook of environmental psychology.* New York: Wiley.

Worobey, J., & Blajda, V. (1989). Temperament ratings at two weeks, two months and one year. *Developmental Psychology, 25,* 257–263.

Zuckerman, M. (1994). Impulsive unsocialized sensation seeking. In J. Bates & T. D. Wachs (Eds.), *Temperament: Individual differences at the interface of biology and behavior* (pp. 219–258). Washington, DC: American Psychological Association.

CHAPTER Jay Belsky

Infant-Parent Attachment

☐ Introduction

The topic of the infant's emotional tie to mother has been a focus of theorizing for hundreds if not thousands of years. Freud (1964), however, is probably responsible for modern scientific interest in the topic, as he asserted that the relationship between mother and baby served as a "prototype" that would shape the remainder of the developing individual's life, especially his capacity to love and to work. But, it is Bowlby (1982), the recently deceased and eminent British psychiatrist who broke from the ranks of Freudian psychoanalysts to develop the prevailing theory of attachment that guides most developmental research on the topic today. Rather than considering the full scope of research and thinking about the infant-parent attachment relationship in this chapter, I focus on results from four longitudinal studies that I have carried out over the past two decades as part of what I have come to refer to as the Pennsylvania Child and Family Project. In this chapter, I report on findings pertaining to the origins or determinants of individual differences in infant-parent attachment security. In addition to considering the classical question of how the quality of maternal care affects the development of secure and insecure infant-mother attachment relationships, I address the role of temperament, individual differences in infant-father attachments, and broader contextual influences on infant-parent attachment security including early child care, social support, marital quality, and work-family relations. Before describing this work and summarizing results, it is appropriate to review some core tenets of attachment theory that guided my research as well as that of many others.

Bowlby's Theory of Attachment and its Derivatives

Attachment theory can be viewed, in large part, as a theory of personality development, one which emphasizes the role of early experiences in shaping psychological and behavioral development. In contrast to the psychoanalytically trained psychiatrists whose ideas Bowlby came to reject, Bowlby regarded Freudians as inappropriately emphasizing the role of the individual's inner fantasies in shaping personality, at the expense of actual environmental influences. There were many possible aspects of early experience that could be considered developmentally important. Bowlby's (1944) clinical experience alerted him to the adverse effects of early separations from the mother on emotional well being, both in terms of the short-term distress it evoked and the longer-term consequences it appeared to have on children. In pondering such phenomena, Bowlby found himself dissatisfied with existing, secondary drive explanations which suggested that, because the mother satisfied the infant's primary need for nourishment, she became associated with feelings of satisfaction and, thereby, came to be regarded positively by the infant.

Drawing on a variety of theoretical perspectives, Bowlby fashioned an evolutionary theory of the child's tie to the mother: The child's intense affective tie to his or her mother, which was dramatically revealed by

Work on this chapter was supported by Grants RO1 MH45527 from the National Institute of Mental Health.

his or her behavior when away from her, was not the result of some associational learning process but, rather, the direct consequence of a biologically based desire for proximity and contact with adults that arose as a direct result of Darwinian natural selection. That is, infants and young children who protested separation, sought to maintain proximity to caregiver, and engaged in other behaviors which are now considered attachment behaviors were more likely than others not evincing them to be well cared for in ancestral human environments and were less likely to be consumed by predators or to become lost. As a result, they were more likely to survive and reproduce. In consequence, these genetically determined proclivities of infants to become attached to their caregivers became part of the human behavioral repertoire (Bowlby, 1969/1982, 1973, 1980).

One of Bowlby's first students, and certainly his most distinguished, Ainsworth, used his theoretical insights to develop a procedure for measuring individual differences in the security of the infant-mother attachment relationship that I adopted to address many of the same questions that interested Bowlby, Ainsworth, and an entire generation of attachment researchers (for review, see Belsky & Cassidy, 1994). Noting the complementary activation and inhibition of two distinct behavioral systems, one which kept the child close to the mother and thereby promoted safety and survival (i.e., the attachment system) and another which fostered exploration and thus promoted learning (i.e., the exploratory system), Ainsworth (Ainsworth, Bell, & Stayton, 1971) came to refer to an "attachment-exploration balance" and the child's inclination to use the caregiver as a "secure base from which to explore"(Ainsworth, 1963, p. 70). Most infants balance these two behavioral systems, responding with flexibility to a specific situation after assessing both the environment's characteristics and the caregiver's availability. For instance, when the attachment system is activated (perhaps by separation from the attachment figure, illness, fatigue, or by unfamiliar people and environments), infant exploration and play decline. Conversely, when the attachment system is not activated (e.g., when a healthy, well-rested infant is in a comfortable setting with an attachment figure nearby), exploration is enhanced.

Appreciating in Bowlby's theory the inherently stressful—and attachment-evoking—nature of being in an unfamiliar place, encountering unfamiliar people, and being separated from mother, Ainsworth purposefully designed all these features into a brief, 20-minute, 8-episode laboratory procedure in order to experimentally elicit infant attachment behavior (see Table 3.1). Just as important as the creative insight which led Ainsworth to invent such an experimental paradigm was the fact that she studied, in the Strange Situation, a small sample of 26 infants from middle-class homes whom she had been systematically observing throughout their first year of life in their own homes. It was Ainsworth's goal to account for variation in infant attachment behavior in the Strange Situation by carefully considering the nature and course of mother-infant interaction during the first year of life, as it was her thesis that it was the quality of care the child received at the hands of his or her caregiver during this developmental period that was principally responsible for individual differences in attachment security (Ainsworth, 1973).

In light of the fact that one of the most dramatic differences between infants in how they react to separation from mother, especially when left with an unfamiliar individual in a strange place (even if only for a short period of time), involves the extent to which they become distressed, many believed initially that a focus on crying would prove to be the "window" on individual differences in attachment security.

TABLE 3.1. Episodes of the strange situation

Episode	Persons Present	Time (min)
1	Experimenter, parent, infant	1
2	Parent, infant	3
3	Parent, infant, stranger	3
4	Infant, stranger	3[a]
5	Parent, infant	3
6	Infant	3[a]
7	Stranger, infant	3[a]
8	Parent, infant	3

[a]Length of period reduced if infant is very distressed.

As it turned out, Ainsworth's groundbreaking research revealed that it was reunion behavior with mother that was principally reflective of the quality of the infant's emotional tie to his or her mother, a discovery of no small proportion in the history of developmental psychology (Ainsworth, Blehar, Waters, & Wall, 1978).

Indeed, on the basis of variation in the attachment behavior of the 26 infants whom she studied, Ainsworth identified three distinct *patterns of attachment* that have guided research ever since (Ainsworth et al., 1978). Infants classified as securely attached (pattern B) use the mother as a secure base from which to explore, reduce their exploration, and may be distressed in her absence but greet her positively on her return, and then return to exploration. Secure infants classified into subcategories B1 and B2 are less distressed by separation than those subcategorized as B3 and B4 and greet mother following separation by vocalizing, smiling, or waving across a distance rather than by immediately seeking physical contact and emotional comfort (see Figure 3.1).

Initially, two patterns of insecurity were identified using the Strange Situation. (A third pattern, D, has since been recognized but is not discussed here because it has not played a significant role in my own research.) Infants classified as insecure-avoidant (pattern A) explore with little reference to the mother, are minimally distressed by her departure, and seem to ignore or avoid her on return. Infants classified as insecure-resistant (pattern C) fail to move away from mother and explore minimally. These infants are highly distressed by separations and often are difficult to settle on reunions.

Importantly, Ainsworth's contribution to our understanding of attachment went well beyond the development of an important method for measuring individual differences. Most significantly, it was she who first theorized in detail about why some infants would develop secure and others would develop insecure attachments to their mothers and published data addressing this issue. Using highly detailed ratings of the quality of maternal behavior based on repeated observations of her sample of 26 middle-class families, Ainsworth (1973) found that it was maternal sensitivity that accounted for why some infants behaved in a secure manner in the Strange Situation when 1 year of age while others behaved insecurely. Central to the notion of sensitivity was the mother's ability to read the infant's behavioral and, especially, emotional cues and respond in a timely and appropriate manner that served the infant's needs. Thus, mothers who reared secure infants responded in a timely manner to their infants' crying, were ready and able to physically handle the infant in a comforting manner, and were neither intrusive nor ignoring of the infant. In fact, it was Ainsworth's contention that insecure-avoidance developed in response to maternal rejection of the infant, especially when it came to the baby's desire for physical contact. Insecure-resistance, in

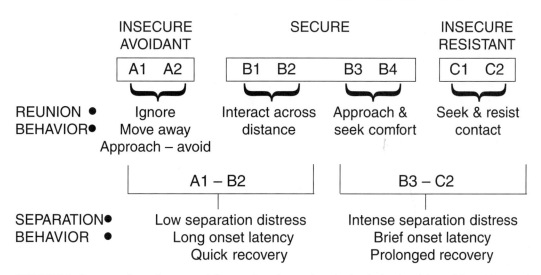

FIGURE 3.1. Patterns of attachment and distress: Reunion and separation behavior. Adapted from Ainsworth, Blehar, Waters, and Wall, 1978).

contrast, was the result of inconsistent caregiving in which the mother sometimes was available and responsive but frequently was not. Thus, the different patterns of insecurity were theorized, and found, to derive from different ways in which mothers were insensitive in their care of the infant.

Such findings which buttressed attachment theory led to a first round of investigations by Sroufe and his colleagues (1993) at the University of Minnesota examining the sequelae of individual differences in attachment. This was of central importance because what might now be regarded as Bowlby-Ainsworth attachment theory not only was a theory of the nature of the infant's tie to the mother and of the determinants of individual differences in attachment security but, as noted at the outset, of personality development. Thus, there were theoretical grounds for expecting that infants securely and insecurely attached to their mothers would develop differently. Importantly, the work by Sroufe (1983) and his colleagues further buttressed the theory by providing evidence consistent with expectations. Specifically, preschoolers with secure attachment histories proved to be more sociable toward strangers than age-mates with insecure histories (Pastor, 1981). These same children also were less emotionally dependent on their teachers, yet more willing to call on them for assistance when faced with a challenge they could not manage on their own (Sroufe, Fox, & Pancake, 1983). In addition, children with secure attachment histories evinced more empathy and positive affection toward peers (Sroufe, 1983), perhaps accounting for their greater popularity with classmates (Sroufe, Fox, & Pancake, 1983). These children also were less likely to be victimized by peers or to bully them (Troy & Sroufe, 1987). In fact, whereas insecure-avoidant attachment proved to be predictive of increased aggressiveness during the early elementary school years, insecure-resistance forecast passive-withdrawn behavior (Renkin, Egeland, Marvinney, Sroufe, & Mangelsforf, 1989). Clearly, a foundation of a secure attachment history appeared to be an asset which the child brought into the classroom (Waters, Wippman, & Sroufe, 1979), whereas an insecure history was a risk factor or liability when it came to getting along well with others.

☐ The Pennsylvania Child and Family Development Project

The Minnesota group's research validating classifications of attachment security based on behavior in the Strange Situation proved to be extremely important in shaping my investigatory endeavors. Having received only minimal training in attachment theory as a graduate student at Cornell University in the mid 1970s, but a great deal on the the the role of family, community, cultural, and historical context in shaping human development (Bronfenbrenner, 1979), I found the prospect of integrating these two distinct research traditions pregnant with opportunity. In fact, because my doctoral research had focused on parenting and infant development, with a special concern for fathering as well as mothering and husband-wife as well as parent-child relationships (Belsky, 1979a, 1979b), it proved rather easy to extend my research horizon to incorporate ideas from attachment theory into my ecologically oriented program of research on early human experience in the family. What was principally required was the inclusion of Strange Situation assessments into what developed into a series of four short-term longitudinal studies focused on the opening years of life that I have come to refer to collectively as the Pennsylvania Child and Family Development Project, which I have directed over the past two decades.

Inclusion of infant-mother and infant-father attachment assessments in these longitudinal studies enabled me to address a number of theoretically important questions that I will consider in the remainder of this chapter. These concern the determinants of individual differences in infant-parent attachment security, including infant temperament, quality of parenting, early child care, and the social context in which the parent-child dyad is embedded. At the same time that this work was going on in central Pennsylvania, my collaboration with colleagues in a 10-site study of infant day care also enabled me to address issues of child care and attachment with greater precision than was possible in my more "local" investigations. In what follows, I summarize many of the results of these inquiries. I first consider work pertaining to parenting and temperament influences on attachment security, before proceeding to consider the broader ecological context in which attachment relationships are embedded. Finally, before making some closing remarks intended to "modernize" the evolutionary basis of attachment theory, I review my research on nonmaternal child care and infant-parent attachment security. It should be noted that no attempt will be made to extensively review related research on these and other topics pertinent to the study of attachment in infancy. For such reviews, see Belsky and Cassidy (1994) and Colin (1996).

Mothering and Attachment Security

Even though Ainsworth (1973) had theorized and found that the sensitivity of maternal care during the first year of life predicted attachment security when the child was 1 year of age, her work was limited in two important respects. First, her sample of 26 was quite small in size. Second, and more importantly, her evaluations of children's attachment security were informed by what she already knew about the quality of care that the children received at home. Thus, her assessments of maternal sensitivity and attachment security were not independent and this compromised the confidence that could be placed in the results of what, in some respects, had to be regarded as a (remarkable) "pilot" study (Lamb, Thompson, Gardner, Charnov, & Estes, 1984).

Like others, I was fascinated by Ainsworth's (1973) sensitivity hypothesis and used my first longitudinal study of marital change across the transition to parenthood to examine the relation between mothering observed on three occasions during the first year of the infant's life and infant-mother attachment security assessed at 12 months. In this study, 56 Caucasian mothers and their infants from working- and middle-class Caucasian families residing in and around the semirural central Pennsylvania community of State College, where Pennsylvania State University is located, were observed at home when infants were 1, 3, and 9 months of age. During each observation period, mothers were directed to go about their everyday household routine, trying as much as possible to disregard the presence of the observer. This naturalistic observational approach is one that I have used in all the research to be described. In order to record maternal and infant behavior, we noted the presence or absence every 15 seconds of an extensive series of maternal and infant behaviors, and one particular kind of dyadic exchange in which the infant or mother emits a behavior, the other responds to it, and the first then contingently responds to the other (i.e., three-step interchange).

Because we did not employ the same rating system as did Ainsworth, we needed a way of conceptualizing and parameterizing the frequency scores of particular behaviors that we generated into indexes of sensitivity. Toward this end, we theorized that more was not inherently better and thus hypothesized that infants who established secure relationships with their mothers would have experienced neither the most frequent nor least frequent levels of reciprocal mother-infant interaction. In order to create an index of reciprocal interaction, we factor analyzed a set of 15 mother, child, and dyadic frequency scores. At each of three separate ages, the factor structure proved quite similar, with the principle factor reflecting reciprocal interaction. Loading highly on this factor were measures of maternal attention and care (e.g., undivided attention, vocalize to infant, vocally respond to infant, express positive affection, stimulate/arouse infant), infant behavior (e.g., look at mother, vocalize to mother), and dyadic exchange (i.e., three-step interaction).

We theorized that insecure-avoidance might develop in response to intrusive, overstimulating maternal care (which would force the child to turn away from mother) and that insecure-resistance might be the consequence of insufficiently responsive, unstimulating care. Thus we predicted, and found, that mothers of secure infants would score intermediate on the resulting composite index of reciprocal mother-infant interaction (see Figure 3.2). Moreover, as anticipated, we found that mothers of insecure-avoidant infants scored highest on this index, and that mothers of insecure-resistant infants scored lowest (Belsky, Rovine, & Taylor, 1984). In fact, when the reciprocal interaction composite variable was decomposed into indexes of maternal involvement and infant behavior, it was clear that it was the former rather than the latter that distinguished attachment groups.

On the basis of these results, a graduate student at the time, Russ Isabella, extended this work in our second and third longitudinal studies by focusing not solely on the raw, composited frequencies of maternal and infant behavior on which our original index of reciprocal interaction was based but, rather, on the close-in-time co-occurrence of mother and infant behaviors which was theorized to reflect synchronous and asynchronous exchanges in the dyad. The subjects of this work were 153 working- and middle-class Caucasian families rearing firstborns drawn from the same community as our first study. Once again, mother-infant dyads had been observed for 45 minutes, this time at two distinct ages—6 and 9 months— using the same time-sampling methodology described above, and infants had been seen with their mothers in the university laboratory at 12 months to measure attachment security using the Strange Situation. Isabella pursued for his dissertation the hypothesis that dyads that fostered secure attachment would be characterized by interactions that appeared synchronous, whereas those that fostered insecurity would

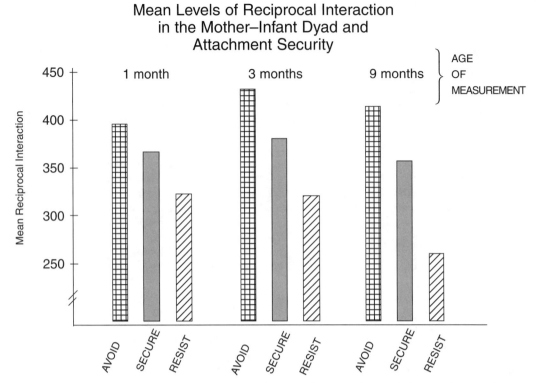

FIGURE 3.2. Reciprocal interaction at 1, 3, and 9 months as a function of 1-year infant-mother attachment classification. Adapted from Belsky, Rovine, and Taylor (1984).

look asynchronous. And, based on our earlier findings, it was predicted that insecure-avoidant dyads would be characterized by intrusive, overstimulating interactions and that insecure-avoidant dyads would be characterized by unresponsive-detached caregiving.

To generate indexes of synchrony and asynchrony, it was necessary to inspect the behaviors checked off on our behavior checklist during each and every 15-second observation period, along with those checked off in each of the two adjacent 15-second sampling periods. This enabled Isabella to determine whether the infant and mother behaviors that were recorded within three adjacent periods reflected synchronous and asynchronous interactions. Then, relying on a sophisticated point-prediction analytic technique, results again substantiated our hypotheses (Isabella & Belsky, 1991; Isabella, Belsky, & von Eye, 1989). Thus, findings from the first inquiry were replicated and extended. In fact, not only had interaction processes reflective of overstimulation been related to insecure-avoidance and those reflective of unresponsive-detachment proven predictive of insecure-resistance in three separate samples which relied on similar approaches to recording mother-infant interaction (i.e., time-sampled behaviors) but dramatically different approaches to parameterizing interaction processes, similar results were obtained in a number of other inquiries (e.g., Lewis & Feiring, 1989; Leyendecker, Lamb, Fracasso, Schjolmerich, & Larson, 1997; Malatesta, Culver, Tesman, & Shepard, 1989; Smith & Pederson, 1988). Significantly, all these findings were generally consistent with Ainsworth's (1973) original theorizing linking sensitive and appropriately responsive care with the establishment of a secure attachment to mother by infant.

The Role of Temperament

An alternative explanation of individual differences in attachment to that proposed by Ainsworth (1973) emphasizing the quality of maternal care draws attention to the infant's temperament, especially the dimension of negative emotionality or difficulty (e.g., Goldsmith & Alansky, 1987). In particular, it was argued that insecurity reflects distress in the Strange Situation, which itself is a function of temperament

(Chess & Thomas, 1982; Kagan, 1982). A fundamental problem with this interpretation, of course, was that infants classified as both secure and insecure evince great variation in distress in the Strange Situation. Consideration of Figure 3.1 makes it clear that some secure infants typically evince a great deal of distress in the Strange Situation (i.e., those classified B3 and B4), whereas others do not (i.e., B1, B2), and that some insecure infants typically express a great deal of negativity in the Strange Situation (i.e., C1, C2), whereas others do not (i.e., A1, A2).

A possible way of bringing together competing perspectives on the role of temperament in the measurement of attachment security in the Strange Situation occurred to me on considering results of findings generated by Thompson and Lamb (1984) and by Frodi and Thompson (1985). When it came to the expression and regulation of negative emotion in the Strange Situation, these investigators observed that secure infants receiving classifications of B1 and B2 looked more like insecure infants receiving classifications of A1 and A2 than like other secure infants (i.e., B3, B4); and that secure infants receiving classifications of B3 and B4 looked more like insecure infants classified C1 and C2 than like other secure infants (i.e., B1, B2). This observation raised the following question in my mind: Might temperament shape the way in which security or insecurity is manifested in the Strange Situation (A1, A2, B1, B2 vs. B3, B4, C1, C2), rather than directly determine whether or not a child is classified as secure? That is, might early temperament account for why some secure infants became highly distressed in the Strange Situation (i.e., those classified B3 or B4), whereas others did not (B1, B2), and why some insecure infants became highly distressed in the Strange Situation (C1, C2), whereas others did not (A1, A2)? To address this question, we examined data available on 184 firstborn infants participating in our second and third longitudinal studies.

As theorized, we found that measures of temperament obtained during the newborn period, using the Brazelton Neonatal Behavior Exam, and when infants were 3 months of age, using maternal reports, discriminated infants classified as A1, A2, B1, and B2 (i.e., the ones who cried little in the Strange Situation) from those classified as B3, B4, C1, and C2 (i.e., those who tended to cry more). These measures did not distinguish infants classified secure (B1, B2, B3, B4) from those classified insecure (A1, A2, C1, C2), however (Belsky & Rovine, 1987). More specifically, although secure and insecure infants did not differ on any of the temperament measures in either of the two longitudinal samples, those most likely to express negative emotion in the Strange Situation at 12 months of age scored lower as newborns on orientation (i.e., visual following, alertness, attention) and evinced less autonomic stability (i.e., regulation of state) and scored higher at 3 months of age on a cumulative difficulty index. Thus, consistent with my theorizing and the Thompson and Lamb (1984) analyses of emotion expression within the Strange Situation, early temperament appeared to affect the degree to which infants became overtly distressed in the Strange Situation but not how they regulated—with or without the assistance of their mother—their negative affect. In sum, early temperament was systematically related to how much distress infants evinced in the Strange Situation but not whether they were secure or insecure.

In these first investigations, we, like all other investigators, focused solely on temperament at a single point in time (i.e., during the newborn period or at 3 months of age). Such an approach was generally consistent with the then prevailing view of temperament as an inborn, stable, constitutional trait not particularly subject to change. Because we had obtained identical temperament reports from mothers when infants were 3 and 9 months of age, we found ourselves in the enviable position of being able to reconceptualize temperament as a characteristic of the infant that was, in theory at least, subject to change. And, when we examined change in temperament, as reported by mother, using data from our first longitudinal study, especially interesting results emerged: Infants who at 1 year of age were classified as secure became more predictable and adaptable from 3 to 6 months, whereas the exact opposite was true of infants who would develop insecure attachments to their mothers (Belsky & Isabella, 1988).

Such results raised the prospect that change in temperament may be what security of attachment, at least in some cases, is all about—a notion that Cassidy (1994) has argued recently in efforts to interpret attachment from an emotion-regulation perspective. That is, what security of attachment reflects is children's ability to regulate on their own, or to coregulate with the expected assistance of their mother, their emotions. Secure children are ones who have developed, in the context of the mother-infant relationship, the ability to manage negative affect and share positive affect. Insecure children, in contrast, are inclined to suppress negativity, lose control of it, or fail to share positive feelings. Theorizing, then, that change in the manifestation of emotion over time might reflect emotion-regulation processes and, thereby, be related to attachment security, we examined, using 148 firstborn infants participating in our second and third longitudinal studies, stability and change in two separate dimensions of temperament—positive and negative emotionality—each based on composited observational and maternal-report measures obtained when infants were 3 and 6 months of age (Belsky, Fish, & Isabella, 1991). More specifically, at each age, we relied on maternal reports of how often infants smiled and laughed, as well as cried and fussed, and frequencies of these same behaviors observed during the course of two separate observations: one when the mother was home alone with the infant and another when the mother and father were at home with the child.

To be noted is that it was consideration of the emotional expressions in the Strange Situation of insecure-avoidant and some secure infants, especially those classified B1 and B2, which led us to think about positive emotions as well as negative emotions with respect to temperament change and attachment security. Central to such thinking was the observation that one characteristic that distinguished these two groups of children (i.e., A1/A2 vs. B1/B2) was that the secure children classified as B1 or B2 in the Strange Situation openly greeted their mothers on reunion—with smiles, gestures, and vocalizations—whereas insecure-avoidant infants classified A1 or A2 seemed to suppress any proclivity to greet and express positive sentiment. Also influencing our separate focus on infant positive and negative emotionality was evidence from the literature on emotions and moods in adulthood highlighting the need to distinguish positive and negative emotionality (for review, see Belsky & Pensky, 1988).

Relying on our repeatedly measured (at 3 and 6 months) composites of infant positivity and negativity, we created four groups of infants with respect to each emotionality dimension: those scoring high on the dimension in question at both points in time, those scoring low at both points in time, those who changed from high to low, and those who changed from low to high. Figure 3.3 graphically illustrates the stability and change groups in the case of negativity. When we examined attachment security at 1 year of age as a function of these stability and change groups, several interesting findings emerged (Belsky, Fish, & Isabella, 1991). First, changes in negative emotionality were not as strongly related to later attachment as changes in positive emotionality. Consistent with the results of Malatesta et al. (1989), however, we discovered that

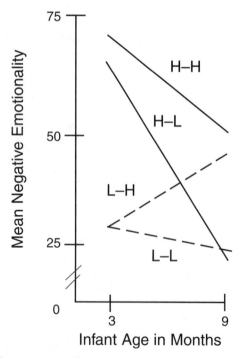

STABILITY AND CHANGE GROUPS:
Raw Negative Emotionality Mean Scores

FIGURE 3.3. Infant negativity change groups. Adapted from Belsky, Fish, and Isabella (1991).

it was infants who declined in the positivity they expressed between 3 and 9 months who were most likely to be classified as insecure in their attachment at 1 year of age. This suggested to us that change in the temperamental dimension of positivity might reflect processes of emotion regulation and, thus, that emotion regulation and attachment were very much related (see Cassidy, 1995). Moreover, these data made intuitive sense in suggesting that children who ended up insecure at the end of the first year of life were the ones whose lives, at least while with their mothers, became less pleasurable over time.

Even though change in positive emotionality by itself, but not change in negative emotionality by itself, predicted attachment security, it was not the case that stability and change in negativity were not at all related to attachment security. This is because we discovered that certain combinations of stability and change in negative and positive emotionality predicted attachment security. Specifically, insecurity was most likely to be observed (i.e., 53% of the time) when (1) infant negativity remained high over time (i.e., high-high group) or increased (i.e., low-to-high group) and when (2) infant positivity remained low over time (i.e., low-low group) or decreased (i.e., high-to-low group). In contrast, when none of these conditions obtained, insecurity was quite rare (i.e., 6%). To be noted is that, in all this work looking at change in various dimensions of temperament or in positive and negative emotionality more specifically, we purposefully did not contrast effects of change against those of temperament or emotionality at a single point in time. And, the reason for this was that we were explicitly pursuing a developmental approach which focused on how specific emotional features of temperament change, not simply where they end up at some later time point or where they begin. Indeed, in our mind, one error often made in much temperament research, whether related to attachment or not, involves the assessment of dimensions of temperament at a single point in time. Such an approach fails to acknowledge that dimensions of temperament develop, or at least change; that is, they are not fixed.

When considered in their entirety, all the findings summarized above regarding temperament and attachment dispel the notions that temperament determines attachment security in some simple, straightfoward fashion or that there is no relation whatsoever between temperament and insecurity. Rather, they clearly and collectively suggest that the relation between these two constructs is complex. The fact, moreover, that stability and change in infant positive and negative emotionality between 3 and 9 months could be predicted using measures of the parent and family functioning obtained before the child was born and of parenting obtained when infants were 3 months of age strongly suggests that it is a mistake to presume that emotional features of temperament reflect, exclusively, some inborn characteristic of the infant (Belsky, Fish, & Isabella, 1991). Because they can change, and because such change appears tied to experiences in the family, understanding of such change may tell us as much about the development of attachment security as it does about presumed constitutional features of the child.

The Broader Ecology of Attachment Security

Through this point, I have considered what might be referred to as "classical" determinants of attachment security; namely, those considered in most developmental theorizing about the origins of secure and insecure attachment (Belsky, Rosenberger, & Crnic, 1995a). But, an ecological perspective on human development, one that underscores the fact that the parent-child dyad is embedded in a family system (Belsky, 1981), which itself is embedded in a community, cultural, and even historical context (Bronfenbrenner, 1979), suggests that, if one wants to account for why some infants develop secure and others develop insecure attachments to mother, father, or even child care worker, then there is a need to look beyond the "proximate" determinants of mothering and temperament.

Toward this end, we undertook a series of inquiries using data collected as part of our longitudinal studies based on a contextual model of the determinants of parenting that I advanced more than a decade ago which highlights the role of parent, child, and social-contextual factors in shaping the parent-child relationship (Belsky, 1984; see Figure 3.4). As should be apparent from Figure 3.4, the model presumes that parenting and, thus, the parent-child relationship is multiply determined and that the contextual factors of work, social support, and marriage can affect parenting both directly and indirectly (through personality). Not explicit in the figure, however, but central to the conceptualization on which the model is based, is the notion that parenting and, thus, the parent-child relationship, is a well buffered system. This means that threats to its integrity stemming from limitations or vulnerabilities in any single source of influence (e.g., work) are likely to be compensated for by resources that derive from other sources of

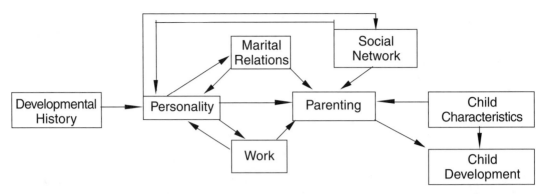

FIGURE 3.4. Determinants of parenting: A process model. Adapted from Belsky (1984).

influence (e.g., marriage). Thus, parenting and the parent-child relationship are most likely to be adversely affected when multiple vulnerabilities exist (e.g., difficult temperament plus conflicted marriage) that accumulate and undermine the effectiveness of other sources of influence in promoting parental functioning. It is just such thinking that led us to examine the cumulative impact of multiple determinants of parenting in affecting attachment security, not the impact of only one or another source of influence.

In the first work of this kind that we carried out using data collected as part of our first longitudinal investigation, linkages were examined between attachment security measured at 1 year and (a) mother's own childrearing history reported during the prenatal period, (b) mother's personality assessed using questionnaires at the same point in time, (c) change in mother-reported infant temperament between 3 and 9 months (and already discussed above), (d) change in marital quality between the last trimester of pregnancy and 9 months postpartum (based on self-reports obtained at both measurement occasions), and (e) prenatal reports by mothers of the friendliness and helpfulness of neighbors (i.e., social support). Results from univariate analyses revealed that mothers of secure infants scored higher than those of insecure infants on a personality measure of interpersonal affection, whereas mothers of avoidant infants scored lowest on a measure of ego strength; that, as indicated earlier, the (mother-reported) temperaments of secure infants became more predictable and adaptable over time, whereas the reverse was true of insecure infants; that insecure infants were living in families in which marriages were deteriorating in quality more precipitously than was so in the case of mothers of secure infants; and that the neighbors of secure infants were perceived as more friendly and helpful than those of insecure infants (Belsky & Isabella, 1988). More important than these univariate findings, however, was evidence that emerged when maternal, infant, and contextual stressors and supports were considered collectively: The more that the family ecology could be described as well resourced (i.e., positive maternal personality, positive change in infant temperament, less marital deterioration), the more likely the child was to develop a secure attachment to his or her mother.

Recently, this work has been extended using data from our fourth longitudinal study, this one of a sample consisting exclusively of 125 firstborn sons whose families were enrolled when they were 10 months of age (rather than prenatally as in the first three investigations). These subjects were recruited from the same locale as those participating in the first three longitudinal investigations, though we relied on birth announcements published in the local newspaper rather than names provided by local obstetricians to identify potential participants. Because of our interest in the multiple determinants of parent-child relations, extensive data were collected on a variety of sources of influence. At enrollment when infants were 10 months of age, mothers and fathers completed questionnaire-based personality assessments and self-reports pertaining to the social support available to them and their satisfaction with it, and whether work and family life interfered with each other or were mutually supportive. At 12 and 13 months of age, infants were seen in the laboratory to assess infant-mother and infant-father attachment, respectively. Following administration of the Strange Situation, parent and infant engaged in a short period of free play (in a separate laboratory room) and a number of procedures were implemented to evoke positive and negative emotions. For example, an experimenter tried to make the child laugh and smile using hand puppets; and the parent was directed to frustrate the child by taking a toy away from him or her while he or she was in a high chair. Videos of infant behavior following the Strange Situation were rated in terms of the extent to which the child expressed positive and negative emotion every 10 seconds; these ratings were then factor analyzed and combined with parent-report measures of temperament obtained at 10 months of age in order to create composite indexes of positive and negative emotionality.

Using these most recent data, we again have found that it is the cumulative vulnerabilities and resources of infants, parents, and families that afford the best prediction of both infant-mother and infant-father attachment security, rather than any single variable or factor (Belsky, 1996; Belsky, Rosenberger, & Crnic, 1995b). Figure 3.5 depicts results pertaining to the cumulative effect of infant, parent, and social-contextual factors in shaping infant-father attachment security (Belsky, 1996). In this research, three personality measures were composited (extraversion + neuroticism-agreeableness), as were two measures of infant temperament/emotionality (positivity-negativity), and four social-context measures ([social support satisfaction + number of people to provide support] + [work-family support-interference]). Each of these three sets of variables was then split at their respective median, with a high score on each given a value of 1 to reflect conditions considered favorable for the development of a secure infant-father relationship, and a low score given a value of 0 to reflect conditions presumed less conducive to the development of a secure relationship. These new values were then summed across sets of variables (i.e., parent, infant, social context), resulting in individual family scores ranging from a value of 0 to 3. As is apparent in the figure, the greater the family resources (i.e., cumulative resource score of 3), the more likely the infant-father relationship was classified as secure on the basis of the infant's behavior with the father in the Strange Situation (Belsky, 1996). Similar results emerged in the case of the infant-mother attachment relationship (Belsky et al., 1995b).

Nonmaternal Care

Because of the role that lengthy child-parent separations played in Bowlby's original formulations of attachment theory, concern has been raised often about the consequences of more routine, short-term separations of the kind experienced on a daily basis by children cared for by someone other than a parent when the mother is employed. The initial work addressing this issue focused almost exclusively on children being cared for in very high-quality, university-based centers and generally failed to reveal any con-

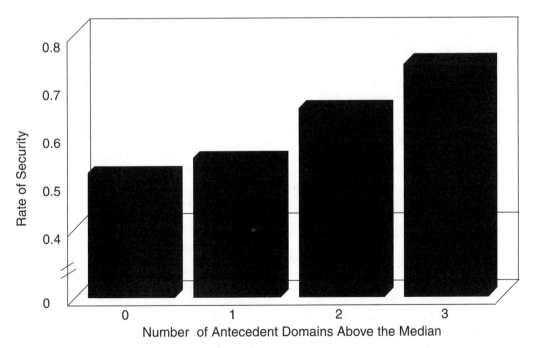

FIGURE 3.5. Probability of son-father attachment security as a function of cumulative resources (0 = low, 3 = high).

sistent association between day care and attachment insecurity (for reviews, see Belsky & Steinberg, 1978; Rutter, 1981). However, this first wave of attachment–day care research used as an index of security the extent to which the child became upset on separation from the parent, even though it never was clear conceptually whether greater or lesser distress should be considered a marker of security (or insecurity).

When we examined the issue of relations between nonmaternal care and security of infant-parent attachment in our second and third longitudinal studies, using the Ainsworth et al. (1978) reunion-based Strange Situation scoring system, two particularly interesting findings emerged. First, infants who experienced, on average, more than 20 hours per week of such care during their first year were more likely to develop insecure attachments than were children who experienced less nonmaternal care (Belsky & Rovine, 1988). In fact, when I compiled data from my own work and that from other studies of nonrisk samples that were published in the scientific literature (*n* = 491), the same pattern emerged (Belsky & Rovine, 1988). Subsequently, Clarke-Stewart (1989) and Lamb, Sternberg, and Prodromdis (1990) undertook similar analyses, drawing on both published and unpublished data. The results of these compilations of findings from research carried out in the United States across a variety of nonmaternal caregiving arrangements (e.g., day care centers, family day care homes, nanny care) all revealed a reliable association between more than 20 hours per week of such nonmaternal care in the first year of life and attachment insecurity. The magnitudes of association varied, however, with Belsky and Rovine (1988), Clarke-Stewart (1989), and Lamb et al. (1990) indicating, respectively, that the rate of infant-mother attachment insecurity was 65%, 24%, and 83% higher among infants with more than 20 hours per week of nonparental care in their first year relative to infants with less time (including none at all) in such care. More recently, though, Roggmann et al. (1995) addressed the same issue using data from five studies that they had carried out and failed to replicate these results.

The second noteworthy finding to emerge from our own work concerned infant-father attachment security. Like Chase-Lansdale and Owen (1987) before us, we found that sons with 35 or more hours per week of nonmaternal care (in the United States) were more likely to develop insecure attachments to their fathers and, thus, have two insecure attachments (one to mother and one to father) than were other boys (Belsky & Rovine, 1988). These findings seemed particularly significant as earlier work in our laboratory (Belsky, Garduque, & Hrncir, 1984) and by others (Easterbrooks & Goldberg, 1987; Howes, Rodning, Galluzzo, & Myers, 1988; Main, Kaplan, & Cassidy, 1985; Main & Weston, 1981) indicated that children with two insecure attachment relationships functioned more poorly than did children with one or more secure attachments.

A variety of observations about and explanations of these findings linking extensive nonmaternal care in the first year of life with elevated rates of insecure attachment have been offered. Consider first the fact that more than half of the children who experience early and extensive infant day care were classified as secure; such variation in response to early day care suggests that separation per se probably is not the principal cause of the elevated rates of insecurity that repeatedly have been chronicled. Consider next that the quality of child care in the United States is known to be limited; thus, elevated rates of insecurity may have as much, or more, to do with the nature of the care infants receive when cared for by someone other than their mother than by the fact that their mother is not providing the care. Especially notable in this regard is the fact that toddlers are more likely to develop secure attachments to those who care for them in child care when these caregivers are more sensitive, responsive, and available to them (Goosens & van IJzendoorn, 1990; Howes et al., 1988); and that security of attachment to the caregiver is itself related to more competent social functioning, especially in concert with secure attachment to the mother (Howes et al., 1988). These findings again would seem to implicate the quality of nonmaternal care which the child receives when it comes to understanding the developmental effects of early child care. Also to be considered is the quality of care which the child experiences at home when with his or her parents, especially since extensive time away from the parents may make it more difficult for the parents to provide the kind of care that fosters attachment security (i.e., sensitive care). Of course, the pressures that working parents experience when at home with the child also may make the provision of such care more difficult.

These varied and complex issues which remained unresolved in discussions of effects of day care led to the establishment of the National Institute of Child Health and Human Development (NICHD) Study of Early Child Care (NICHD Early Child Care Research Network, 1994), of which I am a collaborating investigator in charge of 1 of 10 sites implementing exactly the same research protocol in order to illuminate the conditions under which early child care enhances or compromises children's development. More than

1,300 children and their families were recruited into this work when infants were 1 month of age, after identifying children and families at their local hospitals shortly after birth. The sample is quite varied demographically and ethnically, but does not include any families in which the mother does not speak English fluently or in which the mother is under 18 years of age. A rather extensive research protocol has been implemented to study infant and family development, as well as child care, in this extensive project which is following the children from 1 month of age through 7 years of age (with pending prospects for further extension). Most importantly, the quality of child care received is measured in detail using observational methods that evaluate both the general child care setting, whether it be a private home or center, and the moment-to-moment experiences that the child has with caregiver(s) and other children when the child is 6, 15, 24, 36, and 54 months of age. At these same ages, multiple features of the family are measured; most important for purposes of this chapter are assessments of the sensitivity of mothering. Such assessments take the form of videotapes of mother-child interaction under free play conditions which are coded using Ainsworth-like rating scales and more naturalistic observations of maternal attentive responsiveness to the child while being interviewed. At all but 6 months of age, children are evaluated in the university laboratory using a variety of methodologies; Strange Situations were administered when children were 15 months of age.

With respect to infant-mother attachment security and the effects of early child care, the NICHD Study of Early Child Care had two specific goals. The first was to assess the validity of Strange Situation measurements in the case of children with repeated experiences of being separated from their mothers due to concerns raised about this methodology with these particular children (see below). The second goal concerned relations between early nonmaternal care and attachment security. Specifically, we sought to determine whether, or under what conditions, experience in child care increased or decreased the probability that a child would establish a secure attachment to his or her mother.

The Validity of the Strange Situation.   Ever since linkages have been chronicled between nonmaternal care and attachment insecurity, questions have been raised about whether the infant's independent and exploratory behavior in the Strange Situation is mistakenly judged to be evidence of avoidance, especially in the case of infants who experience routine nonmaternal care. Clarke-Stewart (1989), Thompson (1988), and others have argued that these children's daily separation experiences may lead them to behave more independently in the Strange Situation because they are less stressed by the separations purposefully designed into the procedure. Such a methodological artifact could then cause them to be (erroneously) classified as insecure-avoidant more frequently than children without early and extensive infant day care experience. Not only is it the case that a comprehensive review of relevant studies by Clarke-Stewart and Fein (1983) showed that infant day care experience was *not* related to less (or more) stress in the Strange Situation (as indexed by distress) but, when I carried out a small study using subjects from my second and third longitudinal investigations to directly address this proposition, I found no support whatsoever for it (Belsky & Braungart, 1991). More specifically, infants with extensive nonmaternal care experience who were classified insecure-avoidant did not evince less distress and more play than those similarly classified with limited or no nonmaternal care experience; in fact, the former actually played significantly less during reunions—exactly the opposite of what critics of the Strange Situation methodology had propositioned. Just as noteworthy as our findings are those of Berger, Levy, and Compaan (1995); these investigators found that classifications of children's attachment security based on their behavior during a standard pediatric exam (in which no separation of infant from parent occurred) are highly concordant with Strange Situation classifications for both infants with extensive child care experience in the first year (81.5% concordance) and those without such experience (76%). In other words, my own work as well as that of Berger et al. (1995) failed to find any evidence to suggest that the Strange Situation was an invalid methodology for studying one group of children in particular: namely, those with repeated separation experiences due to routine nonmaternal care.

Because these evaluations of the validity of Strange Situation classifications in the case of infants with lots of experience being separated from their mothers involved small samples, the NICHD Study of Early Child Care provided an ideal opportunity to address this issue again. Comparisons were made between children who averaged more than 30 hours per week of care from 3 through 15 months of age with others who experienced less than 10 hours per week of nonmaternal care during the same developmental period on measures of distress when separated from their mother. Not only was it the case that the two groups were not different in terms of how upset infants became when separated, but it also was true that coders' ratings of their confidence in classifying children in terms of the three primary attachment categories (i.e., avoidant, resistant, secure) did not vary as a function of nonmaternal care experience. Thus, it was concluded that there were no empirical grounds to question the internal validity of the Strange Situation in the large data set; therefore, classifications of children in this separation-based procedure could be regarded as valid even in the case of children with extensive experience with separation (NICHD Early Child Care Research Network, 1996).

Effects of Early Child Care.   Having established empirically that one could have confidence in the Strange Situation classifications of children with extensive separation experience, the NICHD Early Child Care Research Network was now in a position to powerfully address a question that had stimulated much debate and controversy. Interestingly, results of this comprehensive investigation revealed that neither the quantity of nonmaternal care, the quality of such care, the stability of care, nor the child's age of entry (within the first 15 months of life) as isolated factors accounted for variation in infant-mother attachment security. Notable, though, was that this large study discerned the same general effect of maternal sensitivity that Ainsworth's (1973) original work and my own subsequent work had had: Infants classified as securely attached in the Strange Situation at 15 months of age had experienced more sensitive care than those classified as insecure.

Even though maternal sensitivity when considered by itself did predict attachment security, (yet, features of child care when considered individually did not), it was not the case that features of early child care proved to be totally unrelated to attachment security. Consistent with Bronfenbrenner's (1979, p. 38) dictum that "in the ecology of human development the principal main effects are likely to be interactions," we found that, even though most children with early care experience were not more (or less) likely to develop insecure attachments to their mothers, this was not the case when certain ecological conditions co-occurred. More specifically, rates of insecurity were higher than would otherwise have been expected (on the basis of maternal sensitivity alone) when infants received poorer quality (i.e., insensitive) care from their mothers and low quality nonmaternal care, or more than minimal amount of nonmaternal care (i.e., > 10 hours per week), or more than one nonmaternal care arrangement in their first 15 months of life. It also was the case that boys who experienced more than 35 hours per week of nonmaternal care were somewhat more likely to develop insecure attachments to their mothers, though this also was true of girls who experienced less than 10 hours per week of nonmaternal care (including exclusive maternal care). In other words, it was under conditions of "dual-risk" that early care, for the most part, was associated with attachment insecurity. These findings not only were consistent with a controversial risk factor conclusion that I had drawn a decade earlier about the effects of infant day care as currently experienced in the United States (Belsky, 1984, 1988) but also with the results summarized above linking parent, infant, and social-contextual conditions with the probability of an infant establishing a secure or insecure attachment relationship with their mother or with their father. That is, it is knowledge of multiple features of the caregiving ecology that provides the best prediction of attachment security. And, moreover, it is when sources of risk accumulate that the probability of insecurity is greatest.

☐ Conclusion: A Modern Evolutionary Perspective on Early Attachment

Almost two decades of research on infant-parent attachment security, coupled with an emerging interest in evolutionary biology which figured so importantly in Bowlby's original formulation of attachment theory, has led me to rethink the meaning of what I have found in my work as well as what others have found in their related inquiries. Moreover, it leads me to question some of the implicit assumptions that guide the interpretation of much work on attachment. Central to this rethinking is the evidence I have summarized from my own work showing that (a) cumulative stresses and supports affect the probability that an infant will develop a secure attachment, (b) as does the sensitivity of the care provided by the child's principal caregiver, typically his or her mother, and that (c) changes in the infant's behavioral development, especially his or her emotional functioning across the first year also predict attachment security. When considered together, such findings raise the prospect of the following causal process: Contextual stresses and supports affect the sensitivity of maternal care, which affects emotional and temperamental development, which affects whether or not the child develops a secure attachment. And, as others have shown, whether or not the child develops a secure attachment affects how the child functions—especially, emotionally and interpersonally—as he or she develops.

Although it clearly is the case that the causal linkages detailed above are probabilistic rather than determininistic and, thus, that contextual effects and resulting developmental trajectories are not fixed, a question must be asked that is rarely raised by developmental psychologists: Why do developmental processes operate in the way that they do? What developmentalists usually ask are not such questions about ultimate causation, but ones about proximate causation: How does development operate? Such questions lead most developmentalists, myself included, to examine what predicts the quality of maternal care or attachment security, or what security of attachment is related to in terms of the child's future functioning. But, when we find answers to these psychological and developmental questions, as we clearly have, we rarely stop to ponder why the developmental processes we have discerned should be present in the first place. In other words, we tend to take them for granted. But, should we? And, what might we be missing by doing so? Might we be too close to the phenomena that we are studying to recognize, in some sense, what they are all about? I am beginning to believe that this indeed might be the case.

When Bowlby first discussed the evolutionary basis of attachment behavior, he stressed the survival (i.e., adaptive) value of the infant maintaining proximity to his or her caregiver. And, when attachment researchers have written about the functioning of secure and insecure children, they frequently have spoken in terms of the adaptive functioning of the former and the maladaptive functioning of the latter. By using the same terminology to discuss evolutionary-biological and psychological–mental health phenomena, it is not surprising that some have come to equate the mental health benefits of a secure attachment with evolutionary benefits. Indeed, Ainsworth (1973, p. 45) herself seemed to imply as much when she argued "that 'securely attached' babies 'developed normally, i.e., along species-characteristic lines'" (Hinde, 1982, p. 69).

Yet, as Hinde (1982; Hinde & Stevenson-Hinde, 1991) has made abundantly clear and as Ainsworth (1984) herself came to acknowledge, levels of analysis need to be distinguished when terms like "adaptation" are employed. Although it may be beneficial in the contemporary psychological or mental health sense to develop a secure attachment, it certainly is mistaken to presume that, from an evolutionary or phylogenetic perspective, a secure attachment is better or more adaptive than an insecure attachment, however much we value contextual supports and maternal sensitivity (i.e., determinants of attachment security), and that positive interpersonal relations are a presumed sequelae of security. As Hinde (1982, pp. 71–72) noted, "there is no best mothering (or attachment) style, for different styles are better in different circumstances, and natural selection would act to favor individuals with a range of potential styles from which they select appropriately. . . . Mothers and babies will be programmed (by evolution) not simply to form one sort of relationship but a range of possible relationships according to circumstances. . . . Optimal mothering (and attachment) behavior will differ according to . . . the mother's social status, caregiving contributions from other family members, the state of physical resources, and so on . . . a mother-child relationship which produces successful adults in one situation may not do so in another." In other words, while it may be the case that securely attached children develop, in contemporary Western society (or perhaps just in middle-class American society), more competently and are more likely to grow up into happy, mentally healthy adults in this ecology, it is completely inaccurate to infer from such evidence or to otherwise presume that, on the basis of natural selection theory, one attachment or mothering style is necessarily best. This is so even as we find that, under supportive and less stressful contextual conditions, and when care is more sensitive, infants and young children are more likely to develop secure attachments.

Such evolutionary thinking has led me to reconceptualize secure and insecure attachment in terms of reproductive and life history strategies that are flexibly responsive to contextual and caregiving conditions and which evolved in the service of evolutionary goals, not mental health ones pertaining to happiness or psychological well-being (Belsky, 1997; Belsky, Steinberg, & Draper, 1991; see also, Chisholm, 1996). From the perspective of evolutionary biology, the goal of all life is the replication of genes in future generations. Not only do species vary in terms of how they accomplish this task, but so do individuals within some species. Moreover, in certain species (humans included, perhaps), such variation can be determined by concurrent or developmentally antecedent experiences. Depending on the circumstances that organisms find themselves in, if they have the flexibility to adjust their behavior and development according to these life conditions, it may make sense to bear few offspring and care for them intensively (a tactic our value system tends to regard favorably) or to bear many and care for them less devotedly (an approach which contemporary norms tend to frown on and discourage).

This suggests to me that the developing attachment system evolved to provide a means through which the developing child could turn information acquired from parents about prevailing contextual conditions—via the caregiving experience—into knowledge and "awareness" of the kinds of future he or she is likely to face. More specifically, the capacity to develop different patterns of attachment in response to the quality of care received has evolved to provide a kind of "navigational" device to direct development in one direction or another depending on what would have optimized reproductive success in adulthood in the environments of evolutionary adapatation. Might it be the case, then, that security represents an evolved psychological mechanism that "informs" the child, based on the sensitive care he has experienced, that others can be trusted; that close, affectional bonds are enduring; that the world is a more, rather than less, caring place; and, as a result, that it makes reproductive sense to defer mating and reproduction, to be selective in pair bonding, and to bear fewer rather than more children but to care for them intensively? In contrast, might insecure attachment represent a similarly evolved psychological mechanism, also responsive to caregiving conditions, that conveys to the child the developing understanding that others cannot be trusted; that close, affectional bonds are unlikely to be enduring; and that it makes more sense to participate in opportunistic, self-serving relationships rather than mutually beneficial ones? In consequence, does a child who develops such a psychological orientation, in response to the caregiving he or she has received, which itself has been fostered by the less rather than more supportive conditions that his or her parents have confronted, become inclined to mate earlier and more frequently, perhaps producing more offspring who are poorly cared for, because this approach to optimizing reproductive fitness makes more sense in the world as it is understood to be than by adopting the strategy more characteristic of those who have developed secure attachments? Or, even if this is no longer the case today, might these processes have operated in the environment of evolutionary adaptation, so that what we observe today are psychological mechanisms that have evolved and are still operative even if the reproductive "payoffs" that once were associated with them no longer obtain (Buss, 1995; Cosmides & Tooby, 1987)?

While I would not want to argue definitively on behalf of these speculative propositions, I do want to suggest that the reason that our work (and that of others) linking antecedents of attachment security with attachment security generates the findings that it does may be because individual differences in attachment may be part of a complex developmental process that, in human ancestral environments, provided the means of directing development in particular ways that were reproductively strategic. To the extent that this was so, it suggests that findings linking contextual conditions and parenting processes to variation in attachment security, and variation in attachment security to variation in subsequent development, may be part of a developing system whose function was not originally understood or appreciated by Bowlby, Ainsworth, or many current students of attachment theory.

Like many others of his time, when Bowlby initially conceptualized the evolutionary basis of attachment, he wrote in terms of survival of the species. What he eventually came to understand, however, was that it is not survival alone that natural selection rewards but differential reproduction, defined in terms of the dispersion of genes in future generations. Moreover, what he also came to appreciate was that natural selection worked at the level of individuals as well as genes, not species. So, the evolutionary payoffs were to those individuals who survived to reproduce and whose genes thus came to be disproportionately represented in future generations.

In conclusion, consideration of the centrality of differential reproduction among individuals in the Darwinian process of evolution by natural selection raises the prospect that the reason individual differences in attachment may be related to rearing conditions, as my research and that of others has shown, as well as to future social and emotional development, is because patterns of attachment evolved as strategic alternatives for promoting reproductive fitness under varying circumstances in the environment of evolutionary adaptation. What this suggests is that it may be useful to move beyond a mental health orientation toward attachment to one that focuses on reproductive functioning (i.e., mating and parenting).

What is particularly intriguing about such reorientation is that it does not require the abandonment of much that has excited attachment researchers about the origins and, especially, sequelae of individual differences in attachment. This is because a reoriented focus on reproductive functioning involves many of the same processes that more mental health–oriented thinking about attachment directs attention to; namely, social and emotional development, particularly in the context of interpersonal relatedness and parenting. Thus, it is not so much that a modern evolutionary perspective on attachment suggests that attachment researchers (myself included) have been misguided in examining the antecedents and consequences of attachment that they have over the past several decades but, rather, that they may not have fully appreciated how great the significance of the early attachment system may be. Thus, by moving beyond traditional psychological and developmental questions pertaining to how development operates to ones that focus on why it operates the way it appears to do, increased insight into the developmental phenomena under investiation may be realized. This might provide new directions for research; in the case of attachment, most notably toward issues of mating and parental investment.

☐ References

Ainsworth, M. (1963). The development of infant-mother interaction among the Ganda. In B. Foss (Ed.) *Determinants of infant behavior* (Vol. 2, pp. 67–112). New York: Wiley.

Ainsworth, M. D. (1973). The development of infant-mother attachment. In B. M. Caldwell & H. N. Ricciuti (Eds.), *Review of child development research* (Vol. 3, pp. 1–94). Chicago: University of Chicago Press.

Ainsworth, M. D. (1984, April). *Adaptation and attachment*. Paper presented at the International Conference on Infant Studies, New York.

Ainsworth, M. D., Bell, S. M., & Stayton, D. J. (1971). Individual differences in strange situation behavior of one-year-olds. In H. R. Schaffer (Ed.), *The origins of human social relations* (pp. 17–52). London: Academic Press.

Ainsworth, M. D., Blehar, M. C., Waters, E., & Wall, S. (1978). *Patterns of attachment: A psychological study of the strange situation*. Hillsdale, NJ: Erlbaum.

Belsky, J. (1979a). Mother-father-infant interaction: A naturalistic observational study. *Developmental Psychology, 8*, 601–608.

Belsky, J. (1979b). The interrelation of parental and spousal behavior during infancy in traditional nuclear families. *Journal of Marriage and the Family, 41*, 62–68.

Belsky, J. (1981). Early human experience: A family perspective. *Developmental Psychology, 17*, 3–23.

Belsky, J. (1984). The determinants of parenting: A process model. *Child Development, 55*, 83–96.

Belsky, J. (1996). Parent, infant, and social-contextual antecedents of father-son attachment security. *Developmental Psychology, 32*, 905–913.

Belsky, J. (1997). Patterns of attachment mating and parenting: An evolutionary interpretation. *Human Nature, 8*, 361–381.

Belsky, J., & Braungart, J. (1991). Are insecure-avoidant infants with extensive day care experience less stressed by and more independent in the Strange Situation? *Child Development, 62*, 567–571.

Belsky, J,. & Cassidy, J. (1994). Attachment: theory and evidence. In M. Rutter & D. Hay (Eds.), *Developmental principles and clinical issues in psychology and psychiatry* (pp. 373–402). London: Blackwell.

Belsky, J., Fish, M., & Isabella, R. (1991). Continuity and discontinuity in infant negative and positive emotionalisty: Family antecedents and attachment consequences. *Developmental Psychology, 27*, 421–431.

Belsky, J., Garduque, L., & Hrncir, E. (1984). Assessing performance, competence, and executive capacity in infant play: Relations to home environment and security of attachment. *Developmental Psychology, 20*, 406–417.

Belsky, J., & Isabella, R. (1988). Maternal, infant, and social-contextual determinants of attachment security. In J. Belsky & T. Nezworski (Eds.), *Clinical implications of attachment* (pp. 41–94). Hillsdale, NJ: Erlbaum.

Belsky, J., & Pensky, E. (1988). Developmental history, personality and family relationships: Toward an emergent family system. In R. Hinde & J. Stevenson-Hinde (Eds.), *Relationships within families* (pp. 193–217). Oxford, England: Clarendon Press.

Belsky, J. Rosenberger, K., & Crnic, K. (1995a). The origins of attachment security: Classical and contextual determinants. In S. Goldberg, R. Muir, & J. Kerr (Eds.), *Attachment theory: Social, developmental and clinical perspectives* (pp. 153–184). Hillsdale, NJ: Analytic Press.

Belsky, J., Rosenberger, K., & Crnic, K. (1995b). Maternal personality, marital quality, social support and infant temperament: Their significance for infant-mother attachment in human families. In C. Pryce, R. Martin, & D. Skuse (Eds.), *Motherhood in human and nonhuman primates: Biosocial determinants* (pp. 115–124). Basel, Switzerland: Karger.

Belsky, J., & Rovine, M. J. (1987). Temperament and attachment security in the Strange Situation: An empirical rapprochement. *Child Development, 58*, 787–795.

Belsky, J., & Rovine, M. J. (1988). Nonmaternal care in the first year of life and the security of infant-parent attachment. *Child Development, 59*, 157–167.

Belsky, J., Rovine, M., & Taylor, D. G. (1984). The Pennsylvania Infant and Family Development Project: III. The origins of individual differences in infant-mother attachment: Maternal and infant contributions. *Child Development, 55*, 718–728.

Belsky, J., & Steinberg, L. (1978). The effects of day care: A critical review. *Child Development, 49*, 929–949.

Belsky, J., Steinberg, L., & Draper, P. (1991). Childhood experience, interpersonal development and reproductive strategy: An evolutionary theory of socialization. *Child Development, 62*, 647–670.

Berger, S., Levy, A., & Compaan, K. (1995, March). *Infant attachment outside the laboratory: New evidence in support of the Strange Situation.* Paper presented at the biennial meeting of the Society for Research in Child Development, Indianapolis, IN.

Bowlby, J. (1982). *Attachment and loss: Vol. 1. Attachment* (2nd ed.). New York: Basic Books. (Original work published 1969)

Bowlby, J. (1973). *Attachment and loss: Vol, 2. Separation: Anxiety and anger.* New York: Basic Books.

Bowlby, J. (1980). *Attachment and loss: Vol. 3. Loss—sadness and depression.* New York: Basic Books.

Bronfenbrenner, U. (1979). *The ecology of human development.* Cambridge, MA: Harvard University Press.

Buss, D. (1995). Evolutionary psychology: A new paradigm for the psychological sciences. *Psychological Inquiry, 6*, 1–35.

Cassidy, J. (1994). Emotion regulation: Influences of attachment relationships. In N. Fox (Ed.), The development of emotion regulation: Biological and behavioral considerations. *Monographs of the Society for Research on Child Development, 59*, (2–3, Serial No. 240), 228–249.

Chase-Lansdale, P. L., & Owen, M. T. (1987). Maternal employment in a family context: Effects on infant-mother and infant-father attachments. *Child Development, 58*, 1505–1512.

Chess, S., & Thomas, A. (1982). Infant bonding: Mystique and reality. *American Journal of Orthopsychiatry, 52*, 213–222.

Chisholm, J. (1996). The evolutionary ecology of attachment organization. *Human Nature, 7*, 1–38.

Clarke-Stewart, K. (1989). Infant day care: Maligned or malignant. *American Psychologist, 44*, 266–273.

Clarke-Stewart, K. A., & Fein, G. G. (1983). Early childhood programs. In P. H. Mussen (Series ed.) & M. M. Haith & J. J. Campos (Vol. eds.), *Handbook of child psychology: Vol. 2. Infancy and developmental psychobiology* (pp. 917–1000). New York: Wiley.

Colin, V. (1996). *Human attachment.* New York: McGraw-Hill

Cosmides, L., & Tooby, J. (1987). From evolution to behavior: Evolutionary psychology as the missing link. In J. Dupre (Ed.), *The latest and the best: Essays on evolution and optimality* (pp. 277–306). Cambridge, MA: MIT Press.

Easterbrooks, M. A., & Goldberg, W. (1987, April). *Consequences of early family attachment patterns for later social-personality development.* Paper presented at the biennial meeting of the Society for Research in Child Development, Baltimore, MD.

Frodi, A., & Thompson, R. (1985). Infants' affective response in the Strange Situation: Effects of prematurity and of quality of attachment. *Child Development, 56*, 1280–1291.

Goldsmith, H. H., & Alansky, J. A. (1987). Maternal and infant temperamental predictors of attachment: A meta-analytic review. *Journal of Consulting and Clinical Psychology, 55*, 805–816.

Goosens, F., & van Ijzendoorn, M. (1990). Quality of infants' attachment to professional caregivers. *Child Development, 61*, 832–837.

Hinde, R. A. (1982). Attachment: Some conceptual and biological issues. In C. Murray Parkes & J. Stevenson-Hinde (Eds.), *The place of attachment in human behavior* (pp. 60–70). New York: Basic Books.

Hinde, R., & Stevenson-Hinde, J. (1991). Perspectives on attachment. In C. M. Parkes, J. Stevenson-Hinde, & P. Morris (Eds.), *Attachment across the life cycle* (pp. 52–65). London: Routledge.

Howes, C., Rodning, C., Galluzzo, D. C., & Myers, L. (1988). Attachment and child care: Relationships with mother and caregiver. *Early Childhood Research Quarterly, 3*, 403–416.

Isabella, R., & Belsky, J. (1991). Interactional synchrony and the origins of infant-mother attachment: A replication study. *Child Development, 62*, 373–384.

Isabella, R. A., Belsky, J., & von Eye, A. (1989). Origins of infant-mother attachment: An examination of interactional synchrony during the infant's first year. *Developmental Psychology, 25*, 12–21.

Kagan, J. (1982). *Psychological research on the human infant: An evaluative summary.* New York: W. T. Grant Foundation.

Lamb, M., Sternberg, K., & Prodromdis, M. (1990). *Nonmaternal care and the security of infant-mother attachment: A reanalysis of the data.* Unpublished manuscript, National Institute of Child Health and Human Development, Bethesda, MD.

Lamb, M. E., Thompson, R. A., Gardner, W. P., Charnov, E. L., & Estes, D. (1984). Security of infantile attachment as assessed in the "Strange Situation": Its study and biological interpretation. *The Behavioral and Brain Sciences, 7*, 127–172.

Lewis, M., & Feiring, C. (1989). Infant, mother, and mother-infant interaction behavior and subsequent attachment. *Child Development, 60*, 831–837.

Leyendecker, B., Lamb, M., Fracasso, M., Schjolmerich, A., & Larson, C. (1997). Playful interaction and the antecedents of attachment. *Merrill-Palmer Quarterly, 43*, 24–47.

Main, M., Kaplan, N., & Cassidy, J. (1985). Security in infancy, childhood, and adulthood: A move to the level of representation. In I. Bretherton & E. Waters (Eds.), *Monographs of the Society for Research in Child Development, 50* (1–2, Serial no. 209), 66–104.

Main, M., & Weston, D. (1981). The quality of the toddler's relationship to mother and father: Related to conflict behavior and readiness to establish new relationships. *Child Development, 52,* 932–940.

Malatesta, C. Z., Culver, C., Tesman, J., & Shepard, B. (1989). The development of emotion expression during the first two years of life: Normative trends and patterns of individual difference. *Monographs of the Society for Research in Child Development* (1–2, Serial No. 219).

NICHD Early Child Care Research Network. (1994) Child care and child development: The NICHD Study of Early Child Care. In S. Friedman & H. Haywood (Eds.), *Developmental follow-up: Concepts, domains, and methods* (pp. 377–396). New York: Academic Press.

NICHD Early Child Care Research Network. (1996, April). *The effects of infant child care on infant-mother attachment security: Results of the NICHD Study of Early Child Care.* Paper presented at the bienniel meeting of the International Conference on Infant Studies, Providence, RI.

Pastor, D. L. (1981). The quality of mother-infant attachment and its relationship to toddlers' initial sociability with peers. *Developmental Psychology, 17,* 326–335.

Renkin, B., Egeland, B., Marvinney, D., Sroufe, L. A., & Manglesforf, S. (1989). Early childhood antecedents of aggression and passive withdrawal in early elementary school. *Journal of Personality, 57,* 257–282.

Rutter, M. (1981). Socioemotional consequences of day care for preschool children. *American Journal of Orthopsychiatry, 51,* 4–28.

Smith, P. B., & Pederson, D. R. (1988). Maternal sensitivity and patterns of infant-mother attachment. *Child Development, 59,* 1097–1101.

Sroufe, L. A. (1983). Infant-caregiver attachment and patterns of adaptation in preschool: The roots of maladaptation and competence. In M. Perlmutter (Ed.), *Minnesota Symposium in Child Psychology, 16,* 41–81.

Sroufe, L. A., Fox, N. E., & Pancake, V. R. (1983). Attachment and dependency in developmental perspective. *Child Development, 54,* 1615–1627.

Thompson, R. A. (1988). The effects of infant day care through the prism of attachment theory: A critical appraisal. *Early Childhood Research Quarterly, 3,* 273–282.

Thompson, R., & Lamb, M. (1984). Assessing qualitative dimensions of emotional responsiveness in infants: Separation reactions in the Strange Situation. *Infant Behavior and Development, 7,* 423–445.

Troy, M., & Sroufe, L. A. (1987). Victimization of preschoolers: Role of attachment relationship history. *Journal of American Academy of Child and Adolescent Psychiatry, 26,* 166–172.

Waters, E., Wippman, J., & Sroufe, L. A. (1979). Attachment, positive affect, and competence in the peer group: Two studies in construct validation. *Child Development, 50,* 821–829.

4

CHAPTER

Susan Rose
Catherine S. Tamis-LeMonda

Visual Information Processing in Infancy: Reflections on Underlying Mechanisms

☐ Introduction

Traditionally, the study of infant cognition has had two related foci: (a) elucidating the cognitive operations and structures that explain variation among babies in intellectual performance and (b) examining stability in intellectual functioning from infancy to later ages. The present chapter addresses these two issues by considering the mechanisms that potentially underlie measures of infant information processing and helping to explain the modest stability that has been identified between infant performance on these paradigms and later cognitive status.

In infancy, the dual efforts of describing the nature of intelligence and identifying valid predictors of later cognitive performance are fraught with difficulty, given the limitations of and rapid changes to the behavioral repertoire of the very young child. For some time, it had been suggested that qualitative reorganizations in cognitive processes during the first few years rendered it unlikely that stability of intelligence from infancy to later development would be obtained (e.g., Bayley, 1949). Reviews of the predictive validity of standardized infant tests, such as the Bayley Scales of Infant Development, have identified disappointingly low correlations (i.e., ranging from .06 to .32) between infant performance and later IQ (Fagan & Singer, 1983; Kopp & McCall, 1982). However, items on standardized infant tests largely draw from the sensorimotor repertoire of the infant. Thus, the inability of traditional infant tests to predict childhood intelligence might be viewed as a failure of convergent validity, rather than instability in early intelligence (Colombo, 1993). That is, the skills that are required for successful performance on standard infant tests differ from those that are required for successful performance on standardized intelligence measures in childhood and adulthood.

Susan Rose's research on infant cognition has been supported by grants from the National Institutes of Health (HD 13810 and HD 01799) and by Social and Behavioral Science Research Grants from the March of Dimes Birth Defects Foundation. Catherine S. Tamis-LeMonda's research was supported by an IRTA Fellowship from the National Institute of Child Health and Human Development and by grants from the National Institutes of Health (HD20559, HD20807, and HD48915). We are deeply grateful to our many colleagues and students who have contributed to this work. Susan Rose is particularly thankful to Judith Feldman, whose close collaboration through the years has been invaluable, and to Cecelia McCarton, Ina Wallace, Jeffrey Jankowski, and Lorelle Futterweit, who have given so generously of their time and effort, and to Frances Goldenberg, whose winning ways with infants and young children helped make research so much fun. Catherine S. Tamis-LeMonda is especially indebted to Marc H. Bornstein, who has continued to be an unmatched mentor and colleague through many years, and to L. Baumwell, L. Cyphers, K. Dine, R. Kalman-Kahana, J. McClure, A. Melstein-Damast, for comments and assistance. The two authors contributed equally to the preparation of this chapter. Thus, authors' names appear alphabetically.

In contrast, infant visual information processing paradigms, such as habituation, novelty preference, visual expectation formation, and cross-modal transfer are thought to reflect processes that are critical to and indicative of early learning. In all of these paradigms, assessment centers on infants' attention to incoming information and changes in the organization and allocation of attention toward that information. Consequently, these infant paradigms are regarded as promising research tools in the assessment of infant mental functioning. Independent investigators, using different stimuli, procedures, and populations, have provided converging evidence that infant visual information processing measures are successful at distinguishing at-risk (e.g., preterm) from nonrisk populations and at explaining moderate variance in IQ performance in early childhood (e.g., Benson, Cherny, Haith, & Fulker, 1993; DiLalla et al., 1990; Fagen & Ohr, 1990; Haith, Hazan, & Goodman, 1988; S. A. Rose & Feldman, 1995; S. A. Rose, Feldman, & Wallace, 1988, 1992; S. A. Rose, Feldman, Wallace, & Cohen, 1991; S. A. Rose, Feldman, Wallace, & McCarton, 1991; Sigman, Cohen, Beckwith, & Parmelee, 1986; Slater, Cooper, Rose, & Perry, 1985; Tamis-LeMonda & Bornstein, 1989, 1993). Comprehensive meta-analytic reviews of the predictive validity of information processing measures by Bornstein and Sigman (1986) and McCall and Carriger (1993) indicated that these paradigms explain between 9% and 50% variance in childhood cognitive ability.

In this chapter, we review research findings on the predictive validity of infant information processing measures and the underlying mechanisms that are thought to subserve infants' performance on these paradigms, focusing on findings from our own laboratories. We begin by describing the various paradigms that have been used to assess infant information processing. We then discuss the underlying mechanisms thought to be shared by the various measures and to serve as likely candidates for explaining long-term prediction from infancy into childhood. Following this discussion, we turn to the role of infants' caregivers in guiding their interests toward and learning about the external environment. We suggest that caregivers might influence infants' attention and motivation to explore, thereby facilitating infants' allocation of their cognitive resources to important events in their surroundings. We hypothesize that parenting interactions exert influence selectively; that is, some, but not all, of the mechanisms underlying information processing paradigms will be affected by variation in parenting styles. Finally, we discuss the unique features of the various information processing paradigms, emphasizing the varying degrees to which they tap discrete underlying mechanisms. Although each of the information processing paradigms might be subserved by a few core underlying processes they also might summon distinct cognitive operations or call on the same cognitive operations to varying degrees. Insofar as this is true, the infant information processing paradigms that we discuss might show differential prediction to diverse cognitive outcomes in childhood as well as be differentially predicted by antecedent factors.

This chapter provides an initial theoretical framework for further speculation about the meaning of information processing measures in infancy. Extensive overview of the literature on infant information processing measures, including a discussion of their predictive validity, is beyond the scope of this chapter; such reviews are readily available in the extant literature (e.g., Bornstein & Sigman, 1986; Colombo, 1993; McCall & Carriger, 1993).

☐ Background

Infant information processing paradigms, such as habituation, recognition memory (or novelty preference), and visual expectation formation are regarded as promising paradigms in the assessment of early cognitive functioning. *Habituation* is operationally defined as the infant's decline in attention to a repeated stimulus, most typically a static visual display of geometric figures or familiar objects (e.g., face). Traditionally, this response decline has been thought to reflect the formation of a mental schema by the infant (Sokolov, 1969). In the *recognition memory paradigm*, infants are initially presented with either a single visual stimulus or with two identical stimuli for a fixed period ("familiarization"), and then the familiar and a novel stimulus are presented simultaneously and differential responding is assessed ("test") (see Fagen & Singer, 1983). Provided familiarization is sufficient, infants generally spend a greater percentage of the test time looking at the novel stimulus. This "novelty" response is thought to index processes of encoding, memory, retrieval, and discrimination. Although a transitory preference for the familiar stimulus is sometimes seen early in processing, or when familiarization times are very brief, novelty responses reliably emerge with lengthier familiarization, provided the stimuli are not too complex for the infants to process (e.g., Richards, 1997; S. A. Rose, Gottfried, Melloy-Carminar, & Bridger, 1982; Wagner & Sakovits, 1986).

In *visual expectation paradigms*, infants watch a brief series of computer generated pictures that appear in a predictable sequence on the left and right sides of the monitor. In such paradigms, focus is on infants' preparatory behaviors; that is, visual behaviors that occur prior to or between events. For example, over successive stimulus presentations, the infant comes to expect a future event, as indicated by diminished reaction times to stimulus onsets and by anticipatory looks to the sites of upcoming stimuli prior to their presentation; these behaviors suggest that the infant has formed an expectation about the spatial-temporal aspects of future events and is regulating attention in preparation for these anticipated events (Haith et al., 1988).

In *cross-modal transfer paradigms*, infants are habituated or familiarized in one modality and tested for dishabituation or recognition in another modality. In many such studies, infants feel a shape during familiarization (without seeing it) and then, on test, see the previously felt shape alongside a new one. The novelty preference typically shown on the test suggests that the infants form a representation in one perceptual system (haptic) and successfully access it in another (visual). Success here also suggests that the temporally distributed information gleaned from successive palpations is integrated into a spatial gestalt, presumably an essential step for recognizing the visual instantiation of the previously felt object (e.g., Gottfried, Rose, & Bridger, 1977; Rose, Gottfried, & Bridger, 1981).

Three sets of findings have been regarded as evidence that infant information processing paradigms indeed are assessing the mental capacities of infants: (a) developmental research on age-related changes in information processing performance, (b) studies on the discriminant validity of information processing performance, and (c) studies on the predictive validity of information processing measures.

Developmental Studies

A number of developmental studies within the first year of life have identified consistent patterns of change in infants' behaviors on information processing tasks. Across age, infants show shorter durations of looking time in habituation paradigms and shorter accumulated looking times (Bornstein, Pecheux, & Lecuyer, 1988; Colombo, 1993; Colombo & Mitchell, 1990; Colombo, Mitchell, O'Brien, & Horowitz, 1987), similar novelty scores with reduced familiarization times (Fagan, 1974; S. A. Rose, 1983, 1994), a reliable shift from preferring familiar stimuli to preferring novel stimuli (Richards, 1997; S. A. Rose et al., 1982), shorter reaction times and more anticipation in expectation formation tasks (Canfield, Smith, Brezsnyak, & Snow, 1997; Canfield, Wilken, Schmerl, & Smith, 1995), and increased efficiency in transferring information across sensory modalities, as indicated by visual novelty preference scores after tactile familiarization (Bushnell, 1982; Gottfried, Rose, & Bridger, 1977; S. A. Rose, Gottfried, & Bridger, 1981).

Discriminant Validity

Infant information processing measures have been found to reliably distinguish a variety of risk groups from their age-matched low-risk counterparts. The high-risk groups include preterm infants, cocaine-exposed infants, polychlorinated biphenyis (PCB) and alcohol-exposed infants, Down's syndrome infants, and infants with health problems or nutritional deficiencies. A classic study in this area is one by Miranda and Fantz (1974) in which the visual recognition of Down's syndrome infants was compared to that of normal infants at 3, 5, and 8 months. Across a variety of stimuli (e.g., abstract patterns, faces), normal infants exhibited novelty preference several weeks earlier than Down's syndrome infants. Cohen (1981) extended such findings to habituation, showing slower habituation in Down's syndrome infants when compared to normal infants at 4, 5, and 6 months.

Others have identified deficits in performance on information processing measures in infants who have been exposed to teratogens in utero. For example, Jacobson, Fein, Jacobson, Schwartz, and Dowler (1985) demonstrated dose-dependent declines in novelty preference scores for a sample of 123 7-month-olds who had been exposed to different levels of PCB.

Research in our laboratory (i.e., by S. A. Rose and colleagues) has been instrumental in advancing the usefulness of information processing measures in identifying differences between the performance of preterm and term infants as well as between preterms who have or have not experienced respiratory distress syndrome. In these studies, preterms are generally tested at "corrected age" (i.e., age from the expected date of birth), so that performance differences are not confounded with biological maturity. In the first study (S. A. Rose, 1980), babies were brought to the laboratory when they were 6 months of age and were tested for recognition of abstract patterns and faces. Initially, when familiarization times were quite brief (5 to 20 seconds, depending on the problem), only full terms exhibited significant novelty preferences. It is noteworthy, however, that preterms' performance improved dramatically when familiarization times were increased, suggesting that they were not as quick to encode the stimuli as their full-term counterparts.

These findings were reinforced and extended in a second study in which the slower processing speed of preterms was found to persist throughout the entire first year of life (S. A. Rose, 1983). Here, 6- and 12-month-olds were tested for recognition of three-dimensional shapes after familiarization times of 10, 15, 20, and 30 seconds. At both ages, preterms required longer familiarization times than full-terms before they exhibited reliable novelty preferences (30 vs. 15 s at 6 months; 20 vs. 10 s at 12 months). Thus, while both groups encoded the stimuli faster as they became older, preterms continued to require more familiarization time than full terms.

In a more recent longitudinal study, where the sample of preterms was restricted to those of very low birth weight infants (i.e., <1,500 g at birth), preterms not only had lower novelty scores than full terms, but also took longer to accrue the required amounts of looking at the familiarization stimulus and showed less active comparison of the stimuli (S. A. Rose, Feldman, McCarton, & Wolfson, 1988). Infants with increased medical risk (as assessed by the severity and presence of respiratory distress syndrome) were shown to have especially lowered performance. Recent evidence shows that preterms' difficulties in processing speed continue well into late childhood (Rose & Feldman, 1996).

Most recently, S. A. Rose (1994) examined the discriminant validity of information processing paradigms for a group of 123 5- to 12-month-old full-term infants growing up in India, many of whom suffered nutritional deficiencies, as indicated by measurements of their weight and length. Each infant received four problems of visual recognition memory (with familiarization times of 10, 15, 20, and 30 s) and three problems of tactual-visual cross-modal transfer (with familiarization times of 30, 45, and 60 s); all problems used three-dimensional shapes as stimuli. Underweight infants performed poorly on both recognition memory and cross-modal transfer tasks relative to heavier infants and failed to show the same age-related improvements characteristic of the heavier infants. Weight and height correlated with both measures of infant cognition, $r = .25$ to $.45$, as did, to a lesser degree, head circumference. These relations persisted even after controlling for birth weight, previous illness, and parental education (see also Rose, Gottfried, & Bridger, 1978).

This research, indicating that nonoptimal conditions negatively affect infant information processing, even among full terms, accords with that of other investigators. Caron, Caron, and Glass (1983) found poor recognition memory for a group of full terms who had experienced various perinatal difficulties (such as low Apgar, abnormally long labor, small size for their gestational age), and Singer, Drotar, Fagan, Devost, and Lake (1983) found poor performance in a small group of organic failure-to-thrive infants.

Another promising measure gleaned from habituation and recognition memory paradigms is look duration; that is, the average (or peak) duration of the series of looks infants display in attending to an event or stimulus. Long looks appear to be associated with slower encoding and narrowly distributed attention (Colombo, Mitchell, Coldren, & Freesman, 1991; Colombo, Mitchell, & Horowitz, 1988; Jankowski & Rose, 1997). Longer looks are also found more frequently in high-risk groups, such as low birth weight preterms (S. A. Rose, Feldman, McCarton, et al., 1988), preterms with bronchopulmonary dysplasia (Carlson & Werkman, 1996), and full-term infants prenatally exposed to alcohol (Jacobson, Jacobson, Sokol, Martier, & Ager, 1993).

Predictive Validity

The usefulness of infant information processing measures in assessing infants' cognitive capabilities is clearly demonstrated by the moderate to strong predictive validity from such measures to later intellectual status. Reviews of this literature can be found in Bornstein and Sigman (1986) and Fagan and Singer (1983), and in a recent meta-analysis by McCall and Carriger (1993). Overall, the median predictive correlations are comparable for both habituation and recognition memory and these tend to be around $r = .45$. More specifically, infant habituation and recovery of attention have been shown to predict 1-year productive vocabulary and scores on the Bayley Scales of Infant Development (Ruddy & Bornstein, 1982), 24-month Bayley scores (Lewis & Brooks-Gunn, 1981), 2- to 4-year language comprehension (Miller et al., 1979) and 5-year verbal IQ (D. H. Rose, Slater, & Perry, 1986); habituation to a checkerboard within the first minute of presentation predicted 5-, 8-, 12-, and 18-year IQ (Sigman, Cohen, & Beckwith, 1997; Sigman, Cohen, Beckwith, Asarnow, & Parmelee, 1991; Sigman et al., 1986). Measures of infant reaction time and/or anticipation from the visual expectation paradigm predict 3-year IQ (DiLalla et al., 1990) and 4-year IQ (Dougherty & Haith, 1997). Measures of visual recognition memory have been found to predict scores on the Peabody Picture Vocabulary test (PPVT) and/or other vocabulary scores between 4 and 7 years of age (Fagan, 1984; Fagan & McGrath, 1981), 3-year IQ (DiLalla et al., 1990; Fagan & Vasen, 1997; Thompson, Fagan, & Fulker, 1991), and 3-year language (Thompson et al., 1991).

In our own research on habituation, we have demonstrated relations between various measures in habituation at 5 months and infants' representational and exploratory competencies at 13 months (Tamis-LeMonda & Bornstein, 1989, 1993). Specifically, in one study, infants were brought into the laboratory at 5 months of age and measures of baseline looking time in habituation, slope, and decrement were obtained. Infants were seen again in their homes at 13 months of age, a point in development when representational abilities in language and play are emerging. During this visit, children were videotaped during 15 minutes of free play with their mothers and measures of toddlers' symbolic play sophistication and maternal encouragement of attention were assessed. In addition, measures of children's language comprehension were obtained through maternal report. Infants showing faster habituation at 5 months demonstrated more sophisticated play, greater language comprehension, and greater representational competence at 13 months. Moreover, associations between habituation and representational abilities at 13 months maintained after covarying maternal encouragement of infant attention, which also was predictive.

In a second study, habituation measures at 5 months were assessed in relation to toddlers' exploratory competence at 13 months, a latent variable that was computed from toddlers' attention span and play sophistication. Again, infants who habituated faster were those who demonstrated greater exploratory competence, as indicated by an ability to sustain focus on play materials for longer durations and engage in greater amounts of symbolic play.

In our own research on recognition memory, we have found relations between novelty scores and later cognition in a number of studies. In two initial publications, novelty preference scores obtained by preterms at 6 months were found to predict IQ at 2-, 3-, 4-, and 6- years (i.e., Bayley, Stanford-Binet Intelligence test, and the Wechsler Preschool and Primary Scale of Intelligence (WPPSI); S. A. Rose & Wallace, 1985a) and 1-year measures of visual recognition and cross-modal transfer predicted these same outcomes (S. A. Rose & Wallace, 1985b). Like many of the early studies in this area, the samples were small and the longitudinal follow-up was bootstrapped on studies initially intended only as experimental investigations of infant attention.

These initial findings of predictive validity for infant information processing were reinforced and extended in a recently completed, prospective longitudinal study of a fairly large sample of full-term and high-risk preterm infants (born weighing <1,500 g), followed from infancy to 11 years. For both groups, measures of visual recognition memory obtained at 7 months and 1 year predicted receptive and expressive language at 2½, 3, 4, and 6 years and PPVT vocabulary at 11 years (S. A. Rose & Feldman, 1995; S. A. Rose, Feldman, & Wallace, 1992; S. A. Rose, Feldman, Wallace, & Cohen, 1991); additionally, visual recognition memory from 7 months (as well as 6 and 8 months) and cross-modal performance from 1 year predicted Bayley scores at 2 years, and IQ at 3, 4, 5, 6, and 11 years (S. A. Rose & Feldman, 1995; S. A. Rose, Feldman, & Wallace, 1988, 1992; S. A. Rose, Feldman, Wallace, & McCarton, 1989, 1991). Visual recognition memory at 1 year also predicted IQ, but the relation did not extend beyond 5 years, and was never as strong as that obtained with 7-month scores; object permanence at 1 year predicted IQ through 6 years, but not beyond. Importantly, the relations between early information processing measures and later cognitive performance that we identified were maintained after controlling for socioeconomic status, maternal education, 7-month or 1-year Bayley scores, and medical risk. Moreover, the infant-childhood relations involving 7-month visual recognition memory and 1-year cross-modal transfer were largely linear and not inflated by the inclusion of children with significant neurological handicap, very low IQ, or both (<70). Findings reported at the 3-year follow-up point to the potential clinical utility of such measures for detecting mental retardation: A cutoff of 54% novelty preference at 7 months correctly identified 8 of 11 children who had 3-year IQ scores below 70 and 42 of 45 children with IQ scores above 70 (Rose, Feldman, & Wallace, 1988; see also, Fagan & Vasen, 1997).

☐ Common Underlying Mechanisms

The above studies suggest that there exist moderate to strong relations between infants' performance on information processing paradigms and measures of current and later mental functioning. What underly-

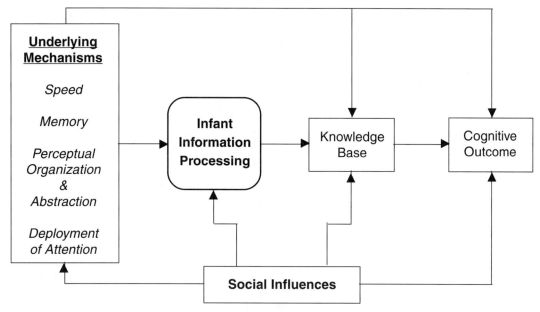

FIGURE 4.1. Mechanisms underlying infant information processing.

ing mechanisms might account for variation among infants on information processing paradigms and for the predictive validity of these measures for subsequent intellectual functioning? In Figure 4.1 we present a framework for considering some select mechanisms that potentially explain long-term prediction from early infant information processing paradigms to measures of childhood cognition. The proposed underlying mechanisms are discussed below.

Speed of Basic Processes

As a starting point, it is suggested that variation among infants on information processing measures is, in part, explained by the speed with which the infant executes basic processes involved in operations necessary for a given task. The speed of executing basic, or lower-order, processes is likened to the notion of performance components, as discussed in Sternberg's triarch theory of intelligence (1985). The construct of speed permeates the adult literature on intelligence and, to some extent, widespread conceptions of what it means to be bright: In Western Societies intelligent people are often referred to as being "quick." Certain researchers have proposed that speed of processing is a cognitive primitive; that is, a basic aspect of human cognitive architecture that limits how much can be handled by an individual at any one time (Kail & Salthouse, 1994). Empirically, age differences in speed of processing tend to be widespread (Hale, 1990; Kail, 1986, 1988), and deficits in processing speed are implicated in the relatively low childhood IQ found in high-risk preterms (S. A. Rose & Feldman, 1996). Two questions that are raised by these theoretical positions are: (a) whether mechanisms thought to explain changes in cognitive functioning across development also explain differences among individuals within a given age (particularly in infancy), and (b) whether these same mechanisms account for stability in intellectual functioning across age (e.g., from infancy to later childhood).

The construct of speed has been considered an explanatory mechanism for variation obtained among infants on information processing measures (e.g., Colombo, 1993), although its definition and scope have varied across literatures. The present conceptualization of speed is distinct from the more global term that often is used to refer to "how long" it takes an infant to process a stimulus. Instead, *speed* is defined in accord with a neurocognitive model, such as the speed in which sensory information is transferred to various regions of the brain, the speed of comparing an external stimulus to an internal representation, or the speed in which motor responses are coordinated and executed. A likely candidate for differences in speed as such might be the formation of myelin; for example, it is shown that, as myelination of the association area of the brain increases, nerve transmission is facilitated and the speed with which children process information increases (Bjorklund & Harnishfeger, 1990; Case, Kurland, & Goldberg, 1982).

In the adult literature, reaction time often has served as a proxy for speed of lower-order processing (e.g., Vernon, 1987). Reaction time measures in adults have been found to explain between 9% and 25% of the variance in standardized tests of intelligence, with even higher estimates observed in select studies. When multiple indexes of reaction time are considered together (e.g., decision speed, long-term memory accessing time, and short-term memory scanning rate), multiple Rs range between .50 and .60 (see Jensen, 1982; Vernon, 1985, 1987, for reviews).

Reaction time also has been suggested as an index of raw processing speed in infancy. There exists some evidence that reaction time in infancy, as often assessed in visual expectation formation paradigms (i.e., response latencies to graphic onsets that are obtained to the nearest millisecond), covaries concurrently with other measures of information processing, most notably novelty preference. Such a relation would suggest that the construct of speed in part explains babies' observed preferences for novel stimuli. For example, Jacobson et al. (1992) found that 6½-month-old infants' reaction times, as assessed through a visual expectation formation paradigm, predicted novelty preference and mean fixation durations as assessed with the Fagan and Singer (1983) novelty preference paradigm. Specifically, infants with faster reaction times showed higher novelty preference scores and shorter visual fixations than infants with longer reaction times.

In our research, we examined relations between infants' reaction times to graphic onsets (thought to indicate speed of processing) and infants' novelty preference measures on a modified visual-expectation paradigm (Tamis-LeMonda & McClure, 1994). Specifically, we presented 5-month-old infants with eight graphic stimuli randomly presented to the left and right visual fields of a graphics display monitor. Following these baseline trials, babies received 60 trials of a left-left-right or right-right-left alternating sequence of moving graphic stimuli. Each stimulus contained a constant visual feature (i.e., a **C** or a **G**) randomly located at various positions across stimuli. Stimuli were presented for 700 milliseconds and interstimulus intervals also were 700 milliseconds. Following the 60 trials, infants received a series of six 10-second test trials in which a novel pair of identical moving stimuli was simultaneously presented to the left and right of visual center. One member of the pair contained the "familiar" feature (e.g., **C**) and one contained the "novel" feature (e.g., **G**). Results indicated that infants showing faster baseline reaction times to graphic onsets as well as faster reaction times during the 60 anticipation trials of the experiment showed higher novelty preference scores in the test phase, suggesting that the faster infants were those that had effectively learned the constant visual feature.

Two studies from our 11-year longitudinal study provide additional evidence that infant information processing relates to the speed of executing basic processes (S. A. Rose & Feldman, 1995). We assessed aspects of information processing in infancy and a number of cognitive abilities at 11 years of age. In this investigation, speed at 11 years was assessed first with the Specific Cognitive Abilities Test (CAT; DeFries & Plomin, 1985), a paper-and-pencil battery of tasks assessing verbal ability, spatial ability, memory, and perceptual speed. Perceptual speed, which is assessed here by matching-to-sample and letter cancellations tasks, was a ubiquitous correlate of the infancy measures, and the long-term relations between infant information processing and later perceptual speed were maintained after covarying later IQ (S. A. Rose & Feldman, 1995). Moreover, in a canonical analysis of the 11-year outcomes, the single variate that emerged could best be interpreted as representing speed.

Speed also was measured using the CAT (Detterman, 1988, 1990), a computerized battery in which speed was directly assessed by decision time, a measure of reaction time unconfounded by motoric speed. This diverse battery, derived from classical experimental paradigms, assesses learning, probe recall, short-term memory search, match-to-sample, tachistoscopic threshold (inspection time), simple and choice reaction time, and the like. Two of the infant measures, 7-month visual recognition memory and 1-year cross-modal transfer, correlated with a factor analytically derived composite from this battery representing "encoding speed/working memory" (S. A. Rose & Feldman, 1997). These two studies support the notion that individual differences in early information processing are, in part, explained by early differences in the speed with which infants execute basic processes. Moreover, they indicate that individual differences in speed show some stability from infancy into childhood.

Together, these studies provide support for the idea that infants' learning in information processing paradigms, as assessed by attention to novel relative to familiar stimuli, is in part explained by the speed with which infants execute basic processes, as assessed through reaction time measures as well as stability in measures of speed over time. This notion is further supported by research documenting significant cross-age relations between reaction time in the visual expectation paradigm from 3½ months to 4 years

(Dougherty & Haith, 1997) and other findings documenting relations between infant visual reaction time in this paradigm and 3- and 4-year IQ (DiLalla et al., 1990; Dougherty & Haith, 1997) and mid-parent IQ (a proxy for projected IQ scores at later ages; Benson et al., 1993).

However, although speed more often than not has been both empirically and conceptually supported as a central mechanism that might underlie long-term relations in infant information processing studies, a simplistic model of "speed" should be approached with caution. It is possible that there exist individuals who are otherwise fast on indexes of speed, but might not show high levels of cognitive performance on other tasks. Three findings in our laboratories suggest that this sometimes is the case.

First, S. A. Rose and Feldman (1995), in their longitudinal study, discuss a paradoxical finding in which long exposure times at 7 months (thought to be indicative of slower processing) related to faster, not slower, perceptual speed at 11 years. Posthoc examination of this finding identified a subgroup of children who, despite showing quick perceptual speed at 11 years, had IQs of less than 85.

Second, Orlian and Rose (1997) found a speed-accuracy trade-off for 6½-month-olds who learned to discriminate a familiar face from a varied series of novel faces. Infants who learned the discrimination quickly failed to recognize subsequent subtle changes in the familiar face; by contrast, infants who learned the initial discrimination more slowly had no difficulty recognizing these subtle changes. For the fast learners, then, thoroughness and attention to detail seemed to have been sacrificed for speed.

Finally, Tamis-LeMonda (in preparation) also has identified a group of infants showing paradoxical relations between duration measures during habituation tasks at 5 months, and concurrent performance on expectation formation tasks. Specifically, she documented a group of infants who exhibited short habituation durations and low visual expectation scores, as indicated by fewer anticipatory looks to picture onsets during an expectation formation task. These infants did not show any novelty preference on independent assessments. She concluded that, for this group of infants, seemingly fast habituation might be indicative of inattentiveness rather than efficiency in cognitive speed.

Memory

Another mechanism that potentially underlies performance on infant information processing is that of short-term memory, an ability that has a ubiquitous role in most aspects of mental performance. Memory is putatively involved in the test phase of visual recognition tasks since a preference for novel stimuli requires that infants remember what they previously had observed. Direct support for the involvement of memory comes from findings that novelty problems in the first year of life correlate with spatial memory in the second year (Colombo, Mitchell, Dodd, Coldren, & Horowitz, 1989) and with measures of immediate and delayed memory in the third year of life (Thompson et al., 1991), and from findings that infants' retention of an instrumental response over periods of up to 2 weeks predicted 2-year Bayley scores and 3-year IQ (Fagen & Ohr, 1990).

Further support for a memory interpretation is found in three recent studies from our own laboratory, in which infant visual recognition memory was found to relate to a wide variety of measures of later memory. The first study (S. A. Rose & Feldman, 1995) showed that 7-month visual recognition memory predicted 11-year memory on versions of the tasks of picture recognition and name-face association used earlier by Thompson and her colleagues. The second study (S. A. Rose & Feldman, 1997) showed that the same infant measure related to 11-year memory for spatial location and serial position, and to memory search, all of which were measured with the computer-administered CAT (Detterman, 1988, 1990). The third study (Rose, Feldman, Futterweit, & Jankowski, 1997) provided evidence that some of the cross-age continuity was specific to recognition memory per se. In that study, not only did recognition memory from infancy correlate with recognition memory at 11 years, but this continuity remained significant after controlling for the 11-year measures of memory from the first two studies. In other words, some of the variance in the infancy measure was related uniquely to later recognition. Clearly, then, individual differences in infant information processing are, in part, explained by differences in the ability to retain information over time, and some aspects of memory may be quite specific.

Deployment of Attention

It also is suggested that variation among infants on information processing measures is explained by infants' efficiency in the deployment of attention resources to a given task (such as orienting attention, engaging attention, inhibiting attention, disengaging attention, and shifting attention to newly encountered information), processes that have been differentiated and localized in distinct regions of the brain (see Ruff & Rothbart, 1996). It essentially is established in cognitive psychology that mental resources must be allocated to various operations involved in processing, retaining, and retrieving information (Case, 1985). The adult intelligence literature often has distinguished raw processing speed, as discussed above, from executive control functions, such as attention deployment. For example, Hunt (1987) distinguished the "functional machinery that a person applies to a task" from "the cognitive program that controls the machinery." He proposed that, in some cases, efficiency in one area can be traded for inefficiency in another. In infancy, mental resources are thought to be particularly limited; accordingly, variation among infants in the efficient allocation of attention is thought to potentially explain variation in information processing abilities concurrently and to explain prediction from infant performance to cognitive abilities in childhood.

Over age, children have been shown to improve in their ability to sustain attention (e.g., Ruff & Lawson, 1990), to inhibit attention to distractors (Schiff & Knopf, 1985), and to switch attention between tasks (Pearson & Lane, 1990, 1991). Changes to these attention abilities have been theoretically and empirically linked to variation among children in task performance (e.g., Schiff & Knopf, 1985). Additionally, there exists some evidence that variation among young children in control of attention is stable in the preschool years. As an example, Ruff, Lawson, Parrinello, and Weissberg (1990) assessed variation among measures of activity, attention, and inattention in preterm and full-term children at 1, 2, and 3½ years. They found measures of attention and inattention at 1 and 2 years to be useful in predicting later attentiveness in both structured and unstructured situations.

Traditionally, the role of attention deployment in explaining variation among infants in information processing has been discussed less frequently than the construct of speed, although the past decade has seen a recent shift of emphasis to the contributing role of attention processes. For example, Sigman (1988) noted that, during information processing paradigms, the infant must be motivated enough to attend to a stimulus, as well as being capable of regulating attention initiation, maintenance, and termination; she suggests that variation in any of these processes is likely to influence infant attention as well as subsequent learning. Similarly, Lecuyer (1988) speculated that individual differences in habituation speed primarily are due to control factors of attention, with fast habituaters having greater control of processing, shorter periods of blank staring, and greater attention span than slower habituaters.

Ruff (1986) distinguished between active, effortful attention (focused attention), and more casual attention (see also Ruff & Rothbart, 1996). "Focused attention," observed during toy play, consists of looking accompanied by concentrated manual inspection (fingering and object turning) and intent facial expression. This form of attention shows considerable stability during the first 2 years of life (Ruff & Dubiner, 1979), and higher levels of focused attention at 2 years (but not earlier) are associated with higher IQ at 3 1/2 years (Ruff et al., 1990). Richards (1997) has used the natural variations in heart rate that occur during a single look to isolate different phases of attention. He proposed that maximal processing occurs during the 2–20-second phase characterized by maximal deceleration and dubbed this a period of "sustained attention." Stimuli presented during a cardiac deceleration are processed faster and more completely than stimuli presented in other phases of the cardiac cycle. Although it is not yet known whether there are stable individual differences in the presence or amount of sustained attention, and/or whether such differences would be linked to later cognition, this is a promising line of inquiry.

McCall (McCall, 1994; McCall & Mash, 1995) has suggested that the infant's ability to inhibit attention to low salient or familiar stimuli is a crucial factor underlying differential performance on tasks that assess novelty preference. In turn, inhibition of attention is central to explaining predictive relations between reaction time measures in infancy and later IQ (Benson et al., 1993; DiLalla et al., 1990, as noted above). He noted that infants who are quick to orient to a new stimulus in an expectation formation paradigm presumably are able to rapidly turn attention away from whatever else they were oriented to. Hypotheses about the role of attention inhibition in explaining variation among infants in their information processing performance articulates closely with Case's (1985) discussion of changes in processing efficiency over age. He suggested that developmental increases in processing efficiency are the result of increased efficiency in inhibitory processes over childhood, resulting in less irrelevant information entering working memory as children focus on a target task.

Empirically, little research has examined directly the role of attention regulation in early information processing, although indirect evidence speaks to its critical role. In one study discussed above (Tamis-LeMonda & Bornstein, 1993), we identified relations between infants' habituation at 5 months and their exploratory competence (based on the shared variance underlying infants' attention span and play) in the second year. Tamis-LeMonda (1995) suggested that children with greater exploratory competence are moving beyond examination of objects, instead generating ways in which they might act on or use these objects to represent past experience. As such, these children are able to: (a) inhibit lower-level object manipulation, (b) retrieve and instantiate representations of past experiences, (c) maintain attention through the termination of symbolic play episodes, and (d) inhibit attention to objects and toys that are not integral to the reenacted theme.

As noted previously, Tamis-LeMonda and McClure (1994) found that infants with greater anticipatory looking (i.e., orienting to the correct visual field prior to a stimulus presentation) during the expectation formation phase of their study attended more to the graphic containing the novel feature during test trials. A possible interpretation of this finding is that infants showing greater anticipatory looking were more able to efficiently deploy their attention which, in turn, facilitated their processing of the graphic feature. Infants who are better able to execute attention shifts between left and right visual fields are better able to learn the constant graphic feature that is a part of these rapid exposures. This idea accords with the suggestion of various researchers that the ability of infants to exhibit anticipatory looking in expectation formation paradigms indicates increased control over attentional deployment (e.g., Johnson, Posner, & Rothbart, 1991).

Perceptual Organization and Abstraction

Infants who demonstrate faster habituation, greater novelty preference scores, greater visual anticipation in expectation formation tasks, and the ability to transfer information across sensory modalities might be those who internally organize and/or represent information in more symbolic formats. Infants' propensity to extract commonalities from the perceptual flux is clearly indicated by work on categorization which shows that, from the early months of life, infants spontaneously categorize events and recognize new stimuli as instantiations of an old category (e.g., Quinn, Eimas, & Rosenkrantz, 1993). Moreover, there are clear developmental changes, with older infants invoking higher-order perceptual rules to form such categories, focusing more on internal structure and less on specific features or overall global configuration (e.g., Younger, 1993). Although information on individual differences on the presence and proclivity for categorization are lacking, Fagan (1984) suggested that infants who demonstrate high novelty preference might be those who are able to abstract commonalities in their visual world.

Another line of work suggesting that abstraction may be a common thread in some of the infant-childhood links comes from the very nature of the cross-modal task that we have used in our laboratory (see, e.g., S. A. Rose, 1986; S. A. Rose, Gottfried, & Bridger, 1983). Here, the infant is asked to store a description of an object based on tactual information and to match it to visual information about the same object. Such intermodal association seems to require some abstraction and mapping of common information that is (a) not reducible to modality-specific abilities (S. A. Rose & Orlian, 1991) and (b) shows cross-age continuity from infancy to later childhood (S. A. Rose, Feldman, Futterweit, & Jankowski, 1998). These studies raise the possibility that infants may invoke different strategies for gathering and organizing information. Individual differences in strategy use (traditionally thought to be the provenance of older children and adults) may have its origins in infancy and provide a link between infant abilities and later intelligence.

Development of a Knowledge Base

Faster execution of lower-order processes, coupled with more efficient attention deployment, are together hypothesized to eventuate in the formation of a more complete and elaborate representation of the encountered stimulus by infants, perhaps due to the freeing up of storage space (e.g., working memory capacity) for information retention and other operations (Bjorklund & Harnishfeger, 1990). Infants who repeatedly develop more elaborate mental representations of the events they encounter, over time more generally will acquire a richer and broader knowledge base. A richer knowledge base means that newly encountered information will be comprehended and assimilated with greater ease, providing a feedback cycle in which the knowledge base is further expanded. These ideas accord with those of Sternberg and Suben (1986) who stated that components of knowledge provide mechanisms for a steadily developing network that permits more sophisticated forms of later acquisition and greater ease in the execution of performance. In the cognitive literature, age differences in knowledge base have been considered central to explaining differences in the performance of younger versus older individuals on cognitive tasks (e.g., Carey, 1985) as well as performance differences between novices and experts (Chase & Simon, 1973; Chi, 1978; Schneider, Gruber, Gold, & Opwis, 1993).

How might these ideas be applied to extant empirical findings on associations between information processing measures and subsequent cognitive functioning? Consider, as an example, documented relations between measures of infant habituation and subsequent language abilities (e.g., Bornstein, 1985). Infants who perform basic operations quicker and who deploy attention efficiently in a habituation paradigm also might be quicker at developing a rich understanding of the actors, actions, attributes, and objects of the world; the relations that maintain among them; and the symbols that refer to these entities—competencies that are specifically critical to subsequent linguistic achievements and more broadly to representational or cognitive competencies. Earlier linguistic abilities, such as rapid expansion of lexicon and extraction of meanings about the world, might provide the foundation for the rapid acquisition of later abilities, such as the coordination of individual words into phrases with multiple semantic roles. Thus, in the proposed model, the development of a rich knowledge base is thought to potentially mediate relations between infant information processing and intellectual performance; in such a model, indirect relations between information processing measures and later cognition are considered.

Several investigators have documented relations between habituation and the early emergence of representational abilities, such as language and play, which may mediate long term relations between information processing and later cognitive performance. For example, as noted above, Tamis-LeMonda and Bornstein (1989) identified relations between infant's habituation at 5 months and their emerging language and play abilities at the start of the second year (i.e., at 13 months). These same children were seen again at 21 months so that measures of advanced symbolic play and productive language might be assessed in relation to their 13-month representational abilities. Not surprisingly, we found that infants who scored higher on language and play measures (as predicted by habituation) at 13 months also scored higher on measures of productive language (i.e., mean length of utterance [MLU]; vocabulary size, and semantic diversity) and symbolic play at 21 months (Tamis-LeMonda, 1995; Tamis-LeMonda & Bornstein, 1994).

A more exact test of the existence of indirect relations between information processing measures and later mental functioning, through an intermediate enriched knowledge base, also is provided by the research of S. A. Rose, Feldman, Wallace, and Cohen (1991). Using data from the first 5 years of our longitudinal study, we assessed relations between novelty preference scores at 7 months, mediating measures of language comprehension and production at 2½, 3, and 4 years, and IQ performance at 3, 4, and 5 years (using the Stanford-Binet and Wechsler Preschool and Primary Scales of Intelligence). We found that, when we removed the variance shared by novelty preference scores and language scores (particularly, comprehension), relations between novelty preference and later IQ scores were substantially attenuated. Specifically, infant novelty preference scores accounted for anywhere between 25% and 40% of the variance in later IQ, but uniquely explained between only 4% and 26% after considering the intervening variables of language performance. (Importantly, however, indirect paths to later outcomes were not completely responsible for novelty-IQ linkages, as indicated by the significant and substantial partial rs that remained after language was covaried.)

Together, the findings from these studies accord with the notion that information processing relates to the building of a richer knowledge base early on which, in turn, facilitates the process of later learning, findings which underscore the importance of considering both direct and indirect paths of prediction in infancy research. Specifically, theorists attempting to understand the mechanisms that underlie stability of cognitive functioning from infancy into later development ought to consider whether early to later relations remain after covarying mediating factors. That is, mechanisms such as speed and attention deployment might directly predict intellectual outcomes and/or indirectly predict intellectual outcomes through their relations to a rapidly developing knowledge base (as one of many potential mediators).

☐ Social Influences on Infant Information Processing Abilities

Numerous investigators have identified relations between naturalistic observations of infants and their social partners and children's current and later communicative, exploratory, and intellectual functioning, as assessed through observed child behavior (e.g., the sophistication of play and language) and direct testing (e.g., performance on standardized IQ tests). Vygotsky (1978) has noted the important role more experienced partners, often mothers, have in assisting their infants' exploration of and learning about the immediate environment. Mothers attend to infants' vocal and behavioral cues, demonstrate what to do with available objects and toys, and foster developmentally appropriate advances in their infants. It is through this close social guidance, coupled with their maturational advance, that infants increasingly become able to integrate gaze, vocalization, action, and affect (Adamson & Bakeman, 1985; Landry, 1995; Ratner & Stettner, 1991). Empirically, infants as young as 2 months have been shown to adjust their eye gaze in response to a change in the focus of attention of an adult (Scaife & Bruner, 1975) and to show increased attentiveness toward their mother or objects in response to their mother's encouragement for them to attend to themselves or to objects of the environment (Bornstein & Tamis-LeMonda, 1990).

Might certain dimensions of parenting relate to infants' performance on information processing paradigms? If so, what dimensions might be most influential and what underlying mechanisms in the infant might they affect? Studies of both biological and adoptive infants have consistently demonstrated links between sensitivity in parenting interactions and children's cognitive, linguistic, and emotional functioning (e.g., Beckwith, 1971; Tamis-LeMonda, 1996). One important dimension of maternal sensitivity is the extent to which a mother's social and didactic overtures are contingently responsive to her infant's interests (Baumwell, Tamis-LeMonda, & Bornstein, 1997; Tamis-LeMonda, Bornstein, Baumwell, & Damast, 1996; Tamis-LeMonda, Bornstein, Kahana-Kalmar, Baumwell, & Cyphers, 1998), a dimension that has been emphasized both theoretically and empirically. For example, Dunham and Dunham (1995) suggested that a contingency detection mechanism operates in infancy and that experiences with contingent social structures increase infants' ability to detect other contingent relations in their physical and social environments. Murray and Trevarthen (1985), Seligman (1975), Tronick (1989), and Watson (1985) each have discussed different versions of this mechanism, all sharing the similar conclusion that less than optimal social stimulation (e.g., a noncontingent environment) disrupts the infant's ability to detect subsequent contingent relationships, reduces their motivation to participate in subsequent contingency tasks, or both.

There exists some evidence, albeit limited and often indirect, that infants' interactions with contingently responsive partners may affect their performance on information processing paradigms by supporting their motivation and ability to effectively explore features of the environment. Landry (1995) discussed various studies in which she and her colleagues assessed relations between maternal attention-directing behaviors, the sensitivity of those interactions and toy exploration in 6-month-old premature infants. They found that sensitivity in the timing of mothers' attention-directing behaviors enhanced the toy exploration of their high-risk infants. Mothers who allowed infants to maintain their attention focus rather than shift to a different toy facilitated joint attention by placing fewer demands on these infants' limited attention abilities. The authors noted that this strategy might serve to support infants' developing autonomy and exploratory mastery; thereby, compensating to some degree for the otherwise negative effects of biological risk.

In a series of experimental studies, Dunham and Dunham (1995) exposed 3-month-old infants to contingent or noncontingent social partners. Following this manipulation, infants were tested on a transfer contingency task in which their fixation on a visual stimulus activated nonsocial multimodal stimulation. Infants placed in the noncontingent social condition were slow to orient toward the target and were unable to sustain attention to the target. The authors suggested that those infants lost interest in external events in ways that paralleled Seligman's (1975) description of learned helplessness.

Two studies in our laboratory (Tamis-LeMonda & Bornstein, 1989; Bornstein & Tamis-LeMonda, 1997) have provided additional support for the notion that mothers' contingent responsiveness per se might influence infants' motivation to explore as well as their ability to detect contingencies in their environment, thereby affecting their performance on information processing paradigms. In both studies, infants at 5 months were assessed in an infant-control habituation paradigm in the laboratory. Mother-infant dyads also were visited in their homes within a 2-week period. In both studies, measures of maternal interaction were obtained and associations between parenting and measures of infants' habituation were assessed. In the first study (Tamis-LeMonda & Bornstein, 1989), *mothers' encouragement of infant attention*, defined as the extent to which mothers directed their babies to attend to objects, events, or activities in the environment was coded from a 45-minute naturalistic interaction session. Unexpectedly, this measure of maternal interaction did not relate to infant habituation, although it did explain unique variance in children's later representational competence. In the second subsequent study (Bornstein & Tamis-LeMonda, 1997), we assessed mothers' contingent responsiveness more specifically in relation to infants' habituation and performance. *Contingent responsiveness* was defined as the mother's immediate and appropriate verbal or physical responses to infant vocalizations or explorations. Unlike in the first study, mothers who were more responsive had infants who showed faster habituation and greater novelty preference. Because these results are based on concurrent relations, the direction of effects is unclear. However, these findings tentatively suggest that sensitive social experiences (particularly, the extent to which mothers are contingently responsive to infants' overtures) effects infants' performance on information processing tasks.

What mechanisms might explain this possible relation? Infants with a history of unresponsive environments might exhibit a decreased interest in external events and fail to detect contingencies in the inanimate environment, thereby leading to decreased vigilance, lowered interest in and attention toward novel stimuli, and a lack of appreciation for the way one's own behaviors might effect dimensions of the outside world (such as the onset and offset of visual stimulation). Habituation paradigms (e.g., infant control procedures) might, in part, assess infants' learning of the contingency between their behaviors and stimulus onset and offsets, as, in such paradigms, stimulus presentation is dependent on infants' looking behaviors. Expectation formation tasks, to some extent, require vigilance and the detection of contingency between one's own direction of gaze and stimulus onsets. Novelty preference tasks directly assess infants' interest in and seeking of novel experiences. All of these competencies might be reinforced by a more responsive social environment.

If indeed information processing paradigms tap infants' abilities to effectively deploy attention, and to the extent that attention can be socially educated (e.g., Zukow-Goldring, 1996), relations between parenting and certain measures of information processing also might be expected to maintain. Rothbart, Posner, and Boylan (1990), for example, pointed to the complex interplay between biology and social interaction in addressing the problem of attentional development. What is attended to, and the intensity of that attention, will depend heavily on cultural socialization.

Alternatively, mechanisms called on by information processing paradigms might be distinct from those abilities in the infant that are influenced by very early experiences. As such, information processing and social factors together would explain greater variance in childhood cognition than either measure alone, a finding that accords with the research of Tamis-LeMonda and Bornstein (1989). It also is possible that the relation we identified between maternal responsiveness and infant information processing (i.e., Bornstein & Tamis-LeMonda, 1997) reflects the fact that mothers of infants who are better at such cognitive tasks increase in their own sensitivity to such infants over time. Increased parental sensitivity, in turn, might affect children's later cognitive performance. As such, parental interactions either might buffer the otherwise compromised performance at-risk groups or exacerbate the poorer performance of such infants. In either case, longitudinal studies that seek to examine the predictive validity of information processing tasks ought to also consider the role of infants' social experiences.

☐ Differential Accessing of Distinct Cognitive Operations

A dialectic tension has permeated the literature on the structure of human intelligence for decades. Structurally, intelligence has been considered unidimensional by some (i.e., a single underlying structure is core to all mental operations; Spearman, 1927) and multidimensional by others (i.e., the plurality of mind is stressed and dissociations among component cognitive processes, structures, or both, are underscored; Gardner, 1983). For many, an important theoretical advancement in the cognitive literature occurred around the 1980s, when it was suggested that the mind might be viewed as a modular computing device. Emphasis was placed on the multidimensionality of abilities and the specific nature of the processes required by distinct tasks. Proponents of such a perspective focused on the specificity of operations children employ in various domains, the differential motivation that is applied by children to tasks of different content, the heterogeneity of ability across domains, and the uniqueness of the biological functions that are performed (e.g., Fodor, 1983; Gardner, 1983). How would such theorists explain the fact that presumably unrelated tasks which comprise intelligence tests virtually always covary and heavily load on the first principal component in factor analytic studies? They asserted that high loadings on a single factor are a fundamental character of the way intelligence is measured rather than a reflection on the nature of intelligence (e.g., Detterman, 1987). In such a view, intelligence is comprised of independent components which, when taken together, will explain most of the variance in IQ.

A parallel thrust might be gleaned from theoretical advancements in the infancy literature around the same time. As Lewis (1983) pointed out, neither psychometric tests of infant intelligence nor nonstandardized tests of sensorimotor development (e.g., ordinal scales of psychological development; Uzgiris & Hunt, 1989) provide evidence for a single "g" or intelligence factor in infancy. That is, item analysis on these tasks fails to indicate any consistent pattern across the tests that might be likened to a unitary factor of intelligence. Is it appropriate, then, to consider the various information processing measures that have been discussed, as well as the measures obtained from such paradigms, as reflecting the same underlying mechanisms to equal degrees? Or, instead, do the various paradigms call on distinct cognitive operations to differing degrees and, hence, have potential for being linked to later cognitive abilities in more specialized ways than has yet been examined?

The information processing paradigms reviewed in this chapter often have been discussed as though they fall under a single umbrella, a perspective that might be parsimonious, yet limiting. Indeed, studies in which relations among information processing paradigms have been examined indicate that the various measures covary significantly but moderately; that is, measures such as habituation and novelty preference share approximately 16% variance and, at times, even less (e.g., Bornstein & Tamis-LeMonda, 1994).

Although in this chapter we have thus far emphasized the common processes required by the different information-processing paradigms, we also suggest that different paradigms might summon those common processes to a greater or lesser degree. Moreover, the diverse information processing paradigms might also call on distinct cognitive operations, the result being that much of the variance among the paradigms remains unshared. Certainly, unshared variance might be due to noise or to low reliability of individual measures; nonetheless, it might also provide support for the idea that there exist cognitive operations that are unique to the different information processing paradigms. In this section, some initial speculations are forwarded about the distinct cognitive operations that are summoned by the various information processing paradigms.

Although the model in Figure 4.1 presented attention as a critical factor in all paradigms, specific aspects of attention might be more central to certain paradigms than to others. As an example, expectation formation and novelty preference appear to more clearly access the common operations of engaging attention to a particular location in space and simultaneously inhibiting attention to a competing location. That is, in expectation formation tasks, infants are required to distribute attention between left and right visual fields (and, more recently, among upper and lower visual fields) in rapid succession. Similarly, in novelty preference paradigms, infants are required to select between stimuli presented to left and right visual fields. Thus, the cognitive demands of these two tasks, in particular, emphasize selection and inhibition in the deployment of attention resources. In contrast, in habituation paradigms, experimenters go to great lengths to minimize distractions, for example, by placing infants in darkened environments in which there is nothing compelling to examine except the centrally located stimulus. Thus, the challenge to inhibiting attention in habituation paradigms might not be as strong as in novelty preference and expectation formation tasks.

It also is possible that other cognitive operations not yet considered in detail, such as schema formation and stimulus comparison, differentially subserve the various infant paradigms. In both habituation and novelty preference paradigms, infant responses are driven by the content of information presented at that moment in time, in the past, or both, in contrast to expectation formation in which future information and relations among stimuli are of importance. The creation of a mental schema of an encountered stimulus, continual accessing of the internalized representation of that stimulus during the process of its construction, and comparison of the external stimulus to the internalized representation might be processes that are importantly shared by habituation and novelty preference paradigms. In contrast, expectation formation might reflect such operations to a lesser extent, but instead call on operations such as planning, foresight, and the abstraction of rules regarding the temporal and spatial aspects of a stimulus and the infants' own impact on his or her environment. As such, these constructs might be conceptually similar to those accessed by tests such as the Uzgiris-Hunt Ordinal Scales of Psychological Development, which examine infants' progressions through various conceptually unified tasks of increasing difficulty; such scales access information about means-ends analysis, appreciation of causality, visual pursuit, and the construction of object relations in space. To the extent that the various infant paradigms differentially access such abilities, relations to such outcomes might be expected to differ. As yet, the specialized nature of prediction from infant processing measures has not been systematically examined.

It also is reasonable to speculate that certain infant paradigms might summon factors of motivation more so than others. The concept of mastery motivation is rooted in the work of theorists such as White (1959), who posited an inherent motivation to affect the environment which promotes the seeking out of mastery experiences and thereby facilitates competent behavior. The tendency in infants to seek out and attempt to master challenges may determine whether and how new situations are approached and may be critical to long-term competencies. Supporting this reasoning, Yarrow, Klein, Lomonaco, and Morgan (1975) reported that early motivational measures (e.g., manipulation of novel objects) predicted Stanford-Binet IQ at 3 1/2 years while the Bayley Mental Development Index (MDI) did not. Moreover, measures of goal directedness at 6 months were better predictors of later 13-month cognitive functioning than were more cognitive measures (Yarrow, Morgan, Jennings, Harmon, & Gaiter, 1982).

Might mastery motivation also be differentially related to the three infant information processing paradigms? Both expectation formation and novelty preference share the characteristic of assessing infants' active engagement toward novel and changing environments, whereas habituation reflects the process of moving toward disengagement. That is, in expectation formation paradigms, the infant might play a more active role in information seeking; anticipatory responses index the infant's propensity to orient to fields where stimuli will appear rather than processing of information that already is present. Thus, it might be expected that expectation formation would more strongly relate to aspects of motivation than would habituation. Similarly, variation among infants on novelty preference also might be explained by differential levels of motivation, as discussed above, as the infant who attends to novel stimuli might be more motivated to learn about new aspects of the environment.

If different, yet meaningful, task demands are required by each paradigm, as suggested in the examples above, information processing paradigms might each exhibit differential prediction to particular outcomes as well as be differentially predicted by other factors. Preliminary evidence for the differential antecedents and/or outcomes of these paradigms exists in the literature. For example, in one investigation (Bornstein & Tamis-LeMonda, 1994), we conducted a prospective short-term longitudinal study in which infants visited the laboratory at 2 months of age where they were assessed on a novelty preference task. They revisited the laboratory at 5 months of age and were assessed on habituation and a tactile-visual cross-modal transfer task. During a home visit, mother-child interaction was videotaped and the mother's responsiveness was coded. In addition, mothers were given the Wechsler Adult Intelligence Scale-Revised (WAIS-R). Measures of 2-month novelty preference, maternal responsiveness and maternal IQ differentially predicted infants' 5-month habituation, novelty preference, and cross-modal transfer, underscoring the uniqueness of the different information paradigms.

Similarly, work by Jacobson (1995) has shown that measures obtained from visual expectation, novelty preference, and cross-modal transfer paradigms load in differential ways on two clearly interpretable information processing factors: processing speed and memory/attention. Additionally, teratogenic influences on these distinct information processing measures and factors can be differentiated. Specifically, PCB exposure relates to poorer recognition memory, whereas alcohol exposure relates to longer visual fixations on novelty preference and cross-modal transfer paradigms as well as to slowed reaction times on the visual expectation paradigm. This suggests that prenatal alcohol exposure specifically affects the underlying mechanism of speed.

Other research in our laboratory (i.e., S. A. Rose & Feldman, 1995) has demonstrated very different patterns of long-term prediction for diverse information processing paradigms. In this study, different performance measures taken from a 7-month visual recognition task and 1-year cross-modal transfer task showed some specific relations to various cognitive markers at 11 years. These findings suggested that, although relations between infant measures and childhood outcomes suggest some commonality, as indicated by the fact that a single canonical variate was sufficient to represent the longitudinal associations, certain specialized linkages exist. For example, infants' performance on cross-modal transfer tasks related specifically to perceptual speed, delayed memory, and spatial ability. Visual recognition memory, in contrast, showed more generalized relations to 11-year outcomes. In addition, visual recognition memory and cross-modal transfer both showed continuity from infancy to 11 years, and these cross-age relations held even when the other types of memory and other types of cross-modal performance were partialed (Rose, Feldman, Futterweit, & Jankowski, 1997, 1998).

Together, these studies suggest that, in future investigations, it may be useful to consider the specific nature of different information processing paradigms when modeling potential predictors and outcomes of infant performance on such measures.

☐ Conclusions

The aim of the present chapter was to consider the mechanisms that potentially underlie infants' performance on information processing paradigms and, in turn, explain prediction from infancy to childhood mental functioning. We began by discussing age-related changes in infants' information processing, the discriminant validity of information paradigms for groups of low- and high-risk infants, and the predictive validity of information processing paradigms for infants' current and later cognitive functioning. We then considered the mechanisms that potentially underlie infants' performance on these paradigms and proposed a model to explain empirical relations between infant information processing and long-term cognitive outcomes.

It was suggested that infants who are faster at the execution of basic processes, better able to manipulate information in working memory, better able to organize or represent information in symbolic formats, or both, and better able to deploy attention efficiently will exhibit superior performance on information processing paradigms. Over time, such children will develop a rich knowledge base that will facilitate the acquisition of newly encountered information. Individual differences among infants on factors such as arousal, motivation, memory, and problem solving as well as on the social experiences they encounter (specifically, parental sensitivity) were also suggested as contributing to variation among infants in performance on information processing paradigms.

In considering the proposed model and discussion thereof, several points serve to advance current reflections about relations between early cognition and mature intellectual functioning. First, both direct and indirect paths from infant information processing and later intellectual performance ought to be examined. Although research repeatedly has considered direct associations from early to later measures, it is possible that long-term relations between infants' information processing abilities and later cognitive performance are mediated by more short-term influences. The example provided was that mechanisms such as speed and efficient attention deployment might directly relate to the building of a rich knowledge base in the second year which, in turn, facilitates the acquisition of information at later developmental stages. This point underscores the importance of focusing on the mechanisms that underlie or explain variation among infants in information processing, in addition to a more traditional emphasis on the surface manifestations of performance (e.g., how long it takes an infant to habituate).

Second, it was suggested that studies on infants' information processing abilities be expanded to include information about infants' social engagements with others. More supportive partners, such as parents, might serve to promote infants' interest in and engagement toward the environment and, likewise, teach infants how to effectively attend to and learn about the outside world. As such, parenting interactions with infants either might explain additional variance in infants' information processing performance, buffer the otherwise deleterious effect of risk on infants' performance, or exacerbate the otherwise lowered performance of infants who show poor information processing abilities.

Finally, it was suggested that, although certain core processes (e.g., attentional deployment) are shared by the paradigms of habituation, novelty preference, and expectation formation, the diverse paradigms might also call on unique cognitive operations, a position that accords with a modular perspective of intelligence as well as the neurological structure of the brain. That is, the brain does not function as a unified whole but, rather, is composed of separate modules that operate in relative independence of one another (see Bjorklund & Harnishfeger, 1990, for discussion). The fact that diverse visual attention measures covary suggests that they reflect common underlying components. Nonetheless, the moderate size of their covariation also suggests that they measure somewhat distinct processes. Consequently, performance on certain tasks might be independent of performance on other tasks; infants might progress through a certain sequence of operations more quickly than others; certain abilities might interrelate but others might not; certain measures in infancy might predict certain outcomes but not others, depending on whether the predictor and criterion measure share, in common, the underlying requisite abilities. The theoretical speculations offered here provide a next step toward reflecting on the structures and processes that explain variability among infants on information processing measures as well as associations between these measures and later mental functioning.

☐ **References**

Adamson, L., & Bakeman, R. (1985). Affect and attention: Infants observed with mothers and peers. *Child Development, 56*, 582–593.

Baumwell, L., Tamis-LeMonda, C. S., & Bornstein, M. H. (1997). Maternal styles of maternal interaction and toddler language comprehension: The importance of maternal sensitivity. *Infant Behavior and Development, 20*, 247–258.

Bayley, N. (1949). Consistency and variability in the growth of intelligence from birth to eighteen years. *Journal of Genetic Psychology, 75*, 165–196.

Beckwith, L. (1971). Relationships between attributes of mothers and their infant's I.Q. scores. *Child Development, 42*, 1083–1097.

Benson, J. B., Cherny, S. S., Haith, M. M., & Fulker, D. W. (1993). Rapid assessment of infant predictors of adult IQ: Midtwin-midparent analyses. *Developmental Psychology, 29*, 434–447.

Bjorklund, D. F., & Harnishfeger, K. (1990). The resources construct in cognitive development: Diverse sources of evidence and a theory of inefficient inhibition. *Developmental Review, 10*, 48–71.

Bornstein, M. H. (1985). How infant and mother jointly contribute to developing cognitive competence in the child. *Proceedings of the National Academy of Sciences, 82*, 7470–7473.

Bornstein, M. H., Pecheux, M.-G., & Lecuyer, R. (1988). Visual habituation in human infants: Development and rearing circumstances. *Psychological Research, 50*, 130–133.

Bornstein, M. H., & Sigman, M. D. (1986). Continuity in mental development from infancy. *Child Development, 57*, 251–274.

Bornstein, M. H., & Tamis-LeMonda, C. (1990). Activities and interactions of mothers and their firstborn infants in the first six months of life: Stability, continuity, covariation, correspondance, and prediction. *Child Development, 61*, 1206–1217.

Bornstein, M. H., & Tamis-LeMonda, C. S. (1994). Antecedents of information-processing skills in infants: Habituation, novelty responsiveness, and cross-modal transfer. *Infant Behavior and Development, 17*, 371–380.

Bornstein, M. H., & Tamis-LeMonda, C. S. (1997). Mothers' responsiveness in infancy and their toddlers' attention span, symbolic play, and language comprehension: Specific predictive relations. *Infant Behavior and Development, 20*, 283–296.

Bushnell, E. W. (1982). Visual-tactual knowledge in 8-, 9 1/2-, and 11-month-old infants. *Infant Behavior and Development, 5*, 63–75.

Canfield, R. L., Smith, E. G., Brezsnyak, M. P., & Snow, K. L. (1997). Information processing through the first year of life: A longitudinal study using the visual expectation paradigm. *Monographs of the Society for Research in Child Development, 62*(2, Serial No. 250).

Canfield, R. L., Wilken, J., Schmerl, L., & Smith, E. G. (1995). Age-related change and stability of individual differences in infant saccade reaction time. *Infant Behavior and Development, 183*, 351–358.

Carey, S. (1985). Are children fundamentally different kinds of thinkers and learners than adults? In S. F. Chapman, J. W. Segal, & R. Glaser (Eds.), *Thinking and learning skills* (Vol. 2). Hillsdale, NJ: Erlbaum.

Carlson, S. E., & Werkman, S. H. (1996). A randomized trial of visual attention in preterm infants fed docosahexaenoic acid until two months. *Lipids, 31*, 85–90.

Caron, A. J., Caron, R. F., & Glass, P. (1983). Responsiveness to relational information as a measure of cognitive functioning in nonsuspect infants. In T. Field & A. Sostek (Eds.), *Infants born at risk: Physiological, perceptual and cognitive processes* (pp. 181–210). New York: Grune & Stratton.

Case, R. (1985). *Intellectual development: Birth to adulthood*. New York: Academic Press.

Case, R., Kurland, M., & Goldberg, J. (1982). Operational efficiency and the growth of short-term memory span. *Journal of Experimental Child Psychology, 33*, 386–404.

Chase, W. G., & Simon, H. A. (1973). Perception in chess. *Cognitive Psychology, 4*, 55–81.

Chi, M. T. H. (1978). Knowledge structure and memory development. In R. Siegler (Ed.), *Children's thinking: What develops?* Hillsdale, NJ: Erlbaum.

Cohen, L. B. (1981). Examination of habituation as a measure of aberrant infant development. In S. L. Friedman & M. Sigman (Eds.), *Preterm birth and psychological development* (pp. 240–254). New York: Academic Press.

Colombo, J. (1993). *Infant cognition: Predicting later intellectual functioning*. Newbury Park, CA: Sage.

Colombo, J., & Mitchell, D. W. (1990). Individual differences in early visual attention: Fixation time and information processing. In J. Colombo & J. Fagen (Eds.), *Individual differences in infancy: Reliability, stability, prediction* (pp.193–228). Hillsdale, NJ: Erlbaum.

Colombo, J., Mitchell, D. W., Coldren, J. T., & Freesman, L. J. (1991). Individual differences in infant visual attention: Are short lookers faster processors or feature processors? *Child Development, 62*, 1247–1257.

Colombo, J., Mitchell, D. W., Dodd, J., Coldren, J. T., & Horowitz, F. D. (1989). Longitudinal correlates of infant attention in the paired-comparison paradigm. *Intelligence, 13*, 33–42.

Colombo, J., Mitchell, D. W., & Horowitz, F. D. (1988). Infant visual behavior in the paired-comparison paradigm: Test-retest and attention-performance relations. *Child Development, 58*, 1198–1210.

Colombo, J., Mitchell, D. W., O'Brien, M., & Horowitz, F. D. (1987). The stability of visual habituation during the first year of life. *Child Development, 57*, 474–488.

DeFries, J. C., & Plomin, R. (1985). *Origins of individual differences in infancy: The Colorado Adoption Project.* Orlando, FL: Academic Press.

Detterman, D. K. (1987). Theoretical notions of intellegence and mental retardation. *American Journal of Mental Deficiency, 93*, 2–11.

Detterman, D. K. (1988). *CAT: Cognitive Abilities Test.* Unpublished test, Case Western Reserve University. (Available from Douglas K. Detterman, Department of Psychology, Case Western Reserve University, Cleveland, OH 44106)

Detterman, D. K. (1990). CAT: Computerized abilities test for research and teaching. *MicroPsych Network, 4*, 51–62.

DiLalla, L., Thompson, L. A., Plomin, R., Phillips, K., Fagen, J. F., Haith, M. M., Cyphers, L. H., & Fulker, D. W. (1990). Infant predictors of preschool and adult IQ: A study of infant twins and their parents. *Developmental Psychology, 26*, 759–769.

Dougherty, T. M., & Haith, M. M. (1997). Infant expectations and reaction time as predictors of childhood speed of processing and IQ. *Developmental Psychology, 33*, 146–155.

Dunham, P. J., & Dunham, F. (1995). Optimal social structures and adaptive infant development. In C. Moore & P. J. Dunham (Eds.), *Joint attention: Its origins and role in development.* Hillsdale, NJ: Erlbaum.

Fagan, J. F. (1974). Infant's recognition memory: The effects of length of familiarization and type of discrimination task. *Child Development, 45*, 351–356.

Fagan, J. F. (1984). The relationship of novelty preference during infancy to later intelligence and later recognition memory. *Intelligence, 8*, 339–346.

Fagan, J. F., & McGrath, S. K. (1981). Infant recognition memory and later intelligence. *Intelligence, 5*, 121–130.

Fagan, J. F., & Ohr, P. S. (1990). Individual differences in infant conditioning and memory. In J. Colombo & J. F. Fagen (Eds.), *Individual differences in infancy: Reliability, stability, prediction* (pp. 155–192). Hillsdale, NJ: Erlbaum.

Fagan, J. F., & Singer, L. T. (1983). Infant recognition memory as a measure of intelligence. In L. P. Lipsitt (Ed.), *Advances in infancy research* (Vol. 2, pp. 31–78). Norwood, NJ: Ablex.

Fagan, J. F., & Vasen, J. H. (1997). Selective attention to novelty as a measure of information processing. In J. A. Burack & J. T. Enns (Eds.), *Attention, development, and psychopathology.* New York: Guilford.

Fodor, J. A. (1983). *Modularity of mind.* Cambridge, MA: Bradford Books.

Gardner, H. (1983). *Frames of mind.* New York: Basic Books.

Gottfried, A. W., Rose, S. A., & Bridger, W. H. (1977). Cross-modal transfer in human infants. *Child Development, 48*, 118–123.

Haith, M. M., Hazan, C., & Goodman, G. S. (1988). Expectation and anticipation of dynamic visual events by 3.5-month-old babies. *Child Development, 59*, 467–479.

Hale, S. (1990). A global developmental trend in cognitive processing speed. *Child Development, 61*, 653–663.

Hunt, E. (1987). A cognitive model of individual differences, with an application to attention. In S. H. Irvine & S. E. Newstead (Eds.), *Intelligence and cognition: Contemporary frames of reference.* Boston: Martinus Nijhoff.

Jacobson, S. W. (1995, March). *Evidence for speed of processing and recognition memory components of infant information processing.* Symposium paper presented at the Society for Research in Child Development, Indianapolis, IN.

Jacobson, S. W., Fein, G. G., Jacobson, J. L., Schwartz, P. M., & Dowler, J. K. (1985). The effect of intrauterine PCB exposure of visual recognition memory. *Child Development, 56*, 853–860.

Jacobson, S. W., Jacobson, J. L., O'Neill, J. M., Padgett, R. J., Frankowski, J. J., & Bihun, J. T. (1992). Visual expectation and dimensions of infant information processing. *Child Development, 63*, 711–724.

Jacobson, S. W., Jacobson, J. L., Sokol, R. J., Martier, S. S., & Ager, J. W. (1993). Prenatal alcohol exposure and infant information processing. *Child Development, 64*, 1706–1721.

Jankowski, J. J. & Rose, S. A. (1997). The distribution of visual attention in infants. *Journal of Experimental Child Psychology, 65*, 127–140.

Jensen, A. R. (1982). The chronometry of intelligence. In R. J. Sternberg (Ed.), *Advances in the psychology of human intelligence* (Vol. 1). Hillsdale, NJ:Erlbaum.

Johnson, M. H., Posner, M. I., & Rothbart, M. K. (1991). Components of visual orienting in early infancy: Contingency learning, anticipatory looking, and disengaging. *Journal of Cognitive Neuroscience, 3*, 335–344.

Kail, R. (1986). Sources of age differences in speed of processing. *Child Development, 57*, 969–987.

Kail, R. (1988). Developmental functions for speeds of cognitive processing. *Journal of Experimental Child Psychology, 45*, 339–364.

Kail, R. V., & Salthouse, T. A. (1994). Processing speed as a mental capacity. *Acta Psychologica.*

Landry, S. H. (1995). The development of joint attention in premature low birth weight infants: Effects of early medical complications and maternal attention-directing behaviors. In C. Moore & P. J. Dunham (Eds.), *Joint attention: Its origins and role in development.* Hillsdale, NJ: Erlbaum.

Lecuyer, R. (1988). Please infant can you tell me exactly what you are doing during the habituation experiment? *European Bulletin of Cognitive Psychology, 8*, 476–480.

Lewis, M. (1983). On the nature of intelligence: Science or bias? In M. Lewis (Ed.), *Origins of Intelligence* (2nd ed., pp. 1–25). New York: Plenum Press.

Lewis, M., & Brooks-Gunn, J. (1981). Visual attention at three months as a predictor of cognitive functioning at two years. *Intelligence, 5*, 131–140.

McCall, R. B. (1994). What process mediates predictions of childhood IQ from infant habituation and recognition memory? Speculations on the role of inhibition and rate of information processing. *Intelligence, 18*, 107–125.

McCall, R. B., & Carriger, M. S. (1993). A meta-analysis of infant habituation and recognition memory performance as predictors of later IQ. *Child Development, 64*, 57–79.

McCall, R. B., & Mash, C. W. (1995). Infant cognition and its relation to mature intelligence. In R. Vasta (Ed.), *Annals of child development* (Vol. 10, pp. 27–56). London: Jessica Kinsley.

Miller, D. J., Ryan, E. B., Arbeger, E., McGuire, M. D., Short, E.J., & Kenny, D.A. (1979). Relationships between assessments of habituation and cognitive performance in the early years of life. *International Journal of Behavioral Development, 2*, 159–170.

Miranda, S. B., & Fantz, R. L. (1974). Recognition memory in Down's syndrome and normal infants. *Child Development, 48*, 651–660.

Murray, L., & Trevarthen, C. (1985). Emotional regulation of interactions between 2-month olds and their mothers. In T. Field & N. Fox (Eds.), *Social perception in infants* (pp. 177–198). Norwood, NJ: Ablex.

Orlian, E. K., & Rose, S. A. (1997). Speed vs. thoroughness in infant visual information processing. *Infant Behavior and Development, 20*, 371–381.

Pearson, D. A., & Lane, D. M. (1990). Visual attention movements: A developmental study. *Child Development, 61*, 1779–1795.

Pearson, D. A., & Lane, D. M. (1991). Auditory attention switching: A developmental study. *Journal of Experimental Child Psychology, 51*, 320–334.

Quinn, P. C., Eimas P. D., & Rosenkrantz, S. L. (1993). Evidence for representations of perceptually similar natural categories by 3-month-old and 4-month-old infants. *Perception, 22*, 463–475.

Ratner, H. H., & Stettner, L. J. (1991). Thinking and feeling: Putting Humpty Dumpty together again. *Merrill Palmer Quarterly, 37*, 1–26.

Richards, J. E. (1997). Effects of attention on infants' preference for briefly exposed visual stimuli in the paired-comparison recognition-memory paradigm. *Developmental Psychology, 33*, 22–31.

Rose, D. H., Slater, A., & Perry, H. (1986). Prediction of childhood intelligence from habituation in early infancy. *Intelligence, 10*, 251–263.

Rose, S. A. (1980). Enhancing visual recognition memory in preterm infants. *Developmental Psychology, 16*, 85–92.

Rose, S. A. (1983). Differential rates of visual information processing in full term and preterm infants. *Child Development, 54*, 1189–1198.

Rose, S. A. (1986). Abstraction in infancy: Evidence from cross-modal and cross-dimension transfer. In L. P. Lipsitt & C. Rovee-Collier (Eds.), *Advances in infancy research* (Vol. 4, pp. 218–220). Norwood, NJ: Ablex.

Rose, S. A. (1994). Relation between physical growth and information processing in infants born in India. *Child Development, 65*, 889–902.

Rose, S. A., & Feldman, J. F. (1995). Prediction of IQ and specific cognitive abilities at 11 years from infancy measures. *Developmental Psychology, 31*, 685–696.

Rose, S. A., & Feldman, J. F. (1996). Memory and processing speed in preterm children at 11 years: A comparison with full-terms. *Child Development, 67*, 2005–2021.

Rose, S. A., & Feldman, J. F. (1997). Memory and speed: Their role in the relation of infant information processing to 11-year IQ. *Child Development, 68*, 630–641.

Rose, S. A., Feldman, J. F., Futterweit, L. R., & Jankowski, J. J. (1997). Continuity in visual recognition memory: Infancy to 11 Years. *Intelligence, 24*, 381–392.

Rose, S. A., Feldman, J. F., Futterweit, L. R., & Jankowski, J. J. (1998). Continuity in tactual-visual cross-modal transfer: Infancy to 11 Years. *Developmental Psychology, 34*, 435–440.

Rose, S. A., Feldman, J. F., McCarton, C. M., & Wolfson, J. (1988). Information processing in seven-month-old infants as a function of risk status. *Child Development, 59*, 589–603.

Rose, S. A., Feldman, J. F., & Wallace, I. F. (1988). Individual differences in infant's information processing: Reliability, stability, and prediction. *Child Development, 59*, 1177–1197.

Rose, S. A., Feldman, J. F., & Wallace, I. F. (1992). Infant information processing in relation to six-year cognitive outcomes. *Child Development, 63*, 1126–1141.

Rose, S. A., Feldman, J. F., Wallace, I. F., & Cohen, P. (1991). Language: A partial link between infant attention and later intelligence. *Developmental Psychology, 27*, 798–805.

Rose, S. A., Feldman, J. F., Wallace, I. F., & McCarton, C. M. (1989). Infant visual attention: Relation to birth status and developmental outcome during the first 5 years. *Developmental Psychology, 25*, 560–575.

Rose, S. A., Feldman, J. F., Wallace, I. F., & McCarton, C. (1991). Information processing at 1 year: Relation to birth status and developmental outcome during the first five years. *Developmental Psychology, 27,* 723–737.

Rose, S. A., Gottfried, A. W., & Bridger, W. H. (1978). Cross-modal transfer in infants: Relationship to prematurity and socio-economic background. *Developmental Psychology, 14,* 643–652.

Rose, S. A., Gottfried, A. W., & Bridger, W. H. (1981). Cross-modal transfer in 6-month-old infants. *Developmental Psychology, 17,* 661–669.

Rose, S. A., Gottfried, A. W., & Bridger, W. H. (1983). Infant's cross-modal transfer from solid objects to their graphic representations. *Child Development, 54,* 686–694.

Rose, S. A., Gottfried, A. W., Melloy-Carminar, P. M., & Bridger, W. H. (1982). Familiarity and novelty preferences in infant recognition memory: Implications for information processing. *Developmental Psychology, 18,* 704–713.

Rose, S. A., & Orlian, E. K. (1991). Asymmetries in cross-modal transfer. *Child Development, 62,* 706–718.

Rose, S. A., & Wallace, I. F. (1985a). Cross-modal and intra-modal transfer as predictors of mental development in full term and preterm infants. *Developmental Psychology, 21,* 949–962.

Rose, S. A., & Wallace, I. F. (1985b). Visual recognition memory: A predictor of later cognitive functioning in preterms. *Child Development, 56,* 843–852.

Rothbart, M. K., Posner, M. I., & Boylan, A. (1990). Regulatory mechanisms in infant development. In J. T. Enns (Ed.), *The development of attention: Research and theory* (pp. 47–65). the Netherlands: Elsevier Science.

Ruddy, M. G., & Bornstein, M. H. (1982). Cognitive correlates of infant attention and maternal stimulation over the first year of life. *Child Development, 53,* 183–188.

Ruff, H. A. (1986). Components of attention during infants' manipulative exploration. *Child Development, 56,* 621–630.

Ruff, H. A., & Dubiner, K. (1979). Stability of individual differences in infants' manipulation and exploration of objects. *Perceptual and Motor Skills, 64,* 1095–1101.

Ruff, H. A., & Lawson, K. R. (1990). Development of sustained, focused attention in young children during free play. *Developmental Psychology, 26,* 85–93.

Ruff, H. A., Lawson, K. R., Parrinello, R., & Weissberg, R. (1990). Long-term stability of individual differences in sustained attention in the early years. *Child Development, 61,* 60–75.

Ruff, H. A., & Rothbart, M. K. (1996). *Attention in early development: Themes and variations.* New York: Oxford University Press.

Scaife, M., & Bruner, J. (1975). The capacity for joint visual attention in the infant. *Nature, 253,* 265–266.

Schiff, A. R., & Knopf, I. J. (1985). The effect of task demands on attention allocation in children of different ages. *Child Development, 56,* 621–630.

Schneider, W., Gruber, H., Gold, A., & Opwis, K. (1993). Chess expertise and memory for chess positions in children and adults. *Journal of Experimental Child Psychology, 56,* 328–349.

Seligman, M. E. P. (1975). *Helplessness: On depression, development, and death.* San Francisco: Freeman.

Sigman, M. D. (1988). Infant attention: What processes are measured? *European Bulletin of Cognitive Psychology, 8,* 512–516.

Sigman, M. D., Cohen, S. E., & Beckwith, L. (1997). Why does infant attention predict adolescent intelligence? *Infant Behavior and Development, 20,* 133–140.

Sigman, M., Cohen, S.E., Beckwith, L., Asarnow, R., & Parmelee, A.H. (1991). Continuity in cognitive abilities from infancy to 12 years of age. *Cognitive Development, 6,* 47–57.

Sigman, M. D., Cohen, S. E., Beckwith, L., & Parmelee, A. H. (1986). Infant attention in relation to intellectual abilities in childhood. *Developmental Psychology, 22,* 788–792.

Singer, L. T., Drotar, D., Fagan, J. F., Devost, L., & Lake, R. (1983). The cognitive development of failure to thrive infants: Methodological issues and new approaches. In T. Field & A. Sostek (Eds.), *Infants born at risk: Physiological, perceptual, and cognitive processes* (pp. 222–242). New York: Grune & Stratton.

Slater, A., Cooper, R., Rose, D., & Perry, H. (1985, July). *The relationship between infant attention and learning, and linguistic and cognitive abilities at 18 months and 4 1/2 years.* Paper presented at the biennial meeting of the International Society for the Study of Behavioral Development, Tours, France.

Sokolov, E. N. (1969). The modelling properties of the nervous system. In M. Cole and I. Maltzman (Eds.), *A handbook of contemporary Soviet psychology.* New York: Basic Books.

Spearman, C. (1927). *The abilities of man.* New York: Macmillan.

Sternberg, R. J. (1985). *Beyond IQ: A triarchic theory of human intelligence.* Cambridge, England: Cambridge University Press.

Sternberg, R. J., & Suben, J. G. (1986). The socialization of intelligence. In M. Perlmutter (Ed.), *Perspectives on intellectual development. The Minnesota Symposia on Child Psychology* (Vol. 19, pp. 201–236). Hillsdale, NJ: Erlbaum.

Tamis-LeMonda, C. S. (1995, March). *Visual attention in infancy: Covariation, prediction, and underlying processes.* Symposium paper presented at the Society for Research in Child Development, Indianapolis, IN.

Tamis-LeMonda, C. S. (1996). Maternal sensitivity: Individual, contextual, and cultural factors in recent conceptualizations. In C. S. Tamis-LeMonda (Guest Ed.), Parenting sensitivity: Individual, contextual and cultural factors in recent conceptualizations. *Early Development and Parenting, 5,* 167–171.

Tamis-LeMonda, C. S., & Bornstein, M. H. (1989). Habituation and maternal encouragement of attention in infancy as predictors of toddler language, play, and representational competence. *Child Development, 60,* 738–751.

Tamis-LeMonda, C. S., & Bornstein, M. H. (1993). Infant antecedents of toddlers' exploratory competence. *Infant Behavior and Development, 16,* 423–439.

Tamis-LeMonda, C. S., & Bornstein, M. H. (1994). Specificity in mother-toddler language-play relations across the second year. *Developmental Psychology, 30,* 283–292.

Tamis-LeMonda, C. S., Bornstein, M. H., Baumwell, L., & Damast, A. M. (1996). Sensitivity in parenting interactions across the first two years: Influences on children's language and play. In C. S. Tamis-LeMonda (Guest Ed.), Parenting sensitivity: Individual, contextual and cultural factors in recent conceptualizations. *Early Development and Parenting, 5,* 173–183.

Tamis-LeMonda, C. S., Bornstein, M. H., Kahana-Kalman, R., Baumwell, L., & Cyphers, L. (1998). Predicting variation in the timing of linguistic milestones in the second year: An events-history approach. *Journal of Child Language, 25,* 675–700.

Tamis-LeMonda, C. S., & McClure, J. (1994). Relations between expectation formation and feature learning. *Infant Behavior and Development, 18,* 427–434.

Thompson, L. A., Fagan, J. F., & Fulker, D. W. (1991). Longitudinal prediction of specific cognitive abilities from infant novelty preference. *Child Development, 67,* 530–538.

Tronick, E. (1989). Emotions and emotional communication in infants. *American Psychologist, 44,* 112–119.

Uzgiris, I. C., & Hunt, J. McV. (1989). *Assessment in infancy ordinal scales of psychological development.* Chicago: University of Illinois Press.

Vernon, P. E. (1985). Individual differences in general cognitive abilities. In L. C. Hartlage & C. F. Telzrow (Eds.), *The neuropsychology of individual differences: A developmental perspective.* New York: Plenum.

Vernon, P. E. (1987). New developments in reaction time research. In P. E. Vernon (Ed.), *Speed of information processing and intelligence.* Norwood, NJ: Ablex.

Vygotsky, L. (1978). Interaction between learning and development. In L. S. Vygotsky (Ed.), *Mind in Society* (pp. 79–91). Cambridge, MA: Harvard University Press.

Wagner, S. H., & Sakovits, L. J. (1986). A process analysis of infant visual and cross-modal recognition memory: Implications for an amodal code. In L. P. Lipsitt & C. K. Rovee-Collier (Eds.), *Advances in infancy research* (Vol. 4, pp. 195–217). Norwood, NJ: Ablex.

Watson, J. (1985). Contingency perception in early social development. In T. Field & N. Fox (Eds), *Social perception in infants* (pp. 157–176). Hillsdale, NJ: Erlbaum.

White, R. W. (1959). Motivation reconsidered: The concept of competence. *Psychological Review, 66,* 297–333.

Yarrow, L. J., Klein, R., Lomonaco, S., & Morgan, G. (1975). Cognitive and motivational development in early childhood. In B. Z. Friedlander, G. M. Sterritt, & G. E. Kirk (Eds.), *Exceptional infant: Assessment and intervention* (Vol. 3, pp. 491–503). New York: Bruner/Mazel.

Yarrow, L. J., Morgan, G. A., Jennings, K. D., Harmon, R. J., & Gaiter, J. L. (1982). Infants' persistence at tasks: Relationships to cognitive functioning in early experience. *Infant Behavior and Development, 5,* 131–141.

Younger, B. A. (1993). Understanding category members as "the same sort of thing": Explicit categorization in ten-month-old infants. *Child Development, 64,* 309–332.

Zukow-Goldring, P. (1996). Sensitive caregiving fosters the comprehension of speech: When gestures speak louder than words. In C. S. Tamis-LeMonda (Guest Ed.), Parenting sensitivity: Individual, contextual and cultural factors in recent conceptualizations. *Early Development and Parenting, 5,* 195–211.

5

CHAPTER

Paul C. Quinn

Development of Recognition and Categorization of Objects and Their Spatial Relations in Young Infants

☐ Introduction

Schyns, Goldstone, and Thibaut (1998) have recently written the following about the literatures on object recognition and categorization:

> Although these fields have not traditionally been linked, both deal with the question: "What is this object?" To recognize an object as a cart is equivalent to placing the object into the category of things called "carts." In both cases, the problem is to detect the relevant features of the object in the visual array. (p. 2)

This chapter will review what we know about the development of recognition and categorization of objects during the period of *early infancy*, roughly defined here as the first 6 to 7 months of life, with emphasis placed on research conducted in the author's laboratory. In addition, because adult observers generally experience objects in specific spatial relations with each other and in coherent spatial layouts more generally, the chapter will consider the development of recognition and categorization of common spatial relations such as above versus below and left versus right.

A number of difficult and related questions will guide our discussion. First, how does the infant begin to decompose a complex configuration of pattern information into elements that can be used as building blocks (i.e., units of visual processing) for purposes of recognition of objects and spatial relations? Second, how are the surface fragments (i.e., edge segments) of a visual scene spontaneously grouped into more complex structures (i.e., shapes or spatial primitives) that serve as the basis for recognition of objects and their spatial relations? Third, what visual properties of objects and their spatial relations mediate a common categorization response? Fourth, what factors control infant visual attention during presentation of complex stimulus patterns that contain multiple visual features?

One idea that will appear and reappear throughout the chapter, and that may provide part of the answer to each of the above questions, is that the young infant's system of recognition appears to be guided by powerful spontaneous preferences for (a) visual features such as a curvature (Quinn, Brown, & Streppa, 1997); (b) discrepancy in surface texture (Quinn & Bhatt, 1998); (c) facial information, possibly configural in nature (Johnson & Morton, 1991; Quinn & Eimas, 1996a); and (d) salient stimulus markings, overall shape, or particular parts (Behl-Chadha, 1996; Eimas & Quinn, 1994). These biases, when combined with inherent tendencies to use perceptual (and relational) similarity among surface features to organize object representations, and to group objects and spatial relations to form categorical representations, may ulti-

Much of the author's research reported in this chapter was supported by Grant HD28606 from the National Institute of Child Health and Human Development.

mately account for many of the empirical phenomena associated with the initial development of representations for objects and their spatial relations.

☐ Object Recognition

For purposes of this chapter, I will discuss object recognition and categorization in two sections: the first will consider a possible early stage of visual processing in which shapes and objects are extracted from a visual scene, and the second will consider a presumed later phase in which shapes and objects are categorized; that is, recognized as members of particular groups (see Farah, 1990, and Trick & Enns, 1997, for similar frameworks; but, see Peterson, 1994).

Parsing and Unit Formation

How are the connectedness, coherence, and outlines of objects in a visual scene established? How, during development, do we come to know which edges and contours go together to form which objects? Historically, several different answers have been given to such questions. The Gestalt psychologists argued that our nervous systems are constrained, even at birth, to follow certain principles (e.g., closure, common movement, good continuation, proximity, and similarity) that specify how small pieces of a visual scene should be organized to form larger perceptual units or perceptual wholes (Helson, 1933; Koffka, 1935; Kohler, 1929; Wertheimer, 1923/1958). Other theorists have emphasized that an extended period of perceptual learning of visual and motor associations may be needed to determine the spatial arrangement of features that comprise individual forms (Hebb, 1949; Piaget, 1952). More modern theorists working in the tradition of cognitive science have suggested that some Gestalt-like biases (e.g., common movement, connected surface) combine with or, perhaps, even are derived from an innate representational structure for objects in general (i.e., an object concept) to initially perceive the coherence or unity of objects (Spelke, 1982). The amorphous, but cohesive, object "blobs" that are the outcomes of this primitive parsing process can then be tracked to determine their precise form, color, and surface texture (Kellman, 1993, 1996; Spelke, 1982). By this view, certain of the Gestalt principles, including good continuation and similarity, are learned rather than innate (Spelke, 1982).

Empirical evidence relevant to theoretical accounts of the development of object perception has focused on when and how humans become capable of grouping parts of a stimulus together to form a coherent whole. My initial inquiry into early form perception, for example, was motivated by the straightforward question of what young infants perceive when presented with the simple stimulus shown in the left half of Figure 5.1. Do they perceive just a bunch of black on white, a simple summation of dark contour? Or, do they perceive the set of dots, or the set of spaces between dots, or possibly a subset of dots (enough to perceive a side, corner, or angle of the overall configuration), or just a single dot, or perhaps only part of a single dot? Interestingly, most adults report seeing a triangle form, despite the fact that there is nothing the least bit triangular about the individual elements (the dots) that make up the overall triangle configuration. Adult perception of the emergent property of triangularity could have been based on automatic "bottom-up" application of Gestalt principles such as closure, good continuation, proximity, and similarity. But, it also could have been based on the fact that adults have "top-down" knowledge of a category of geometric forms that have the verbal label "triangles" (cf., Xu & Carey, 1996).

To examine how young infants represent the "triangle" stimulus shown in Figure 5.1, a procedure can be used that initially familiarizes the infant with the triangle pattern and then tests the infant for response to the familiar pattern and a novel pattern, for example, the square configuration shown in the right half of Figure 5.l. This procedure relies on the well-established finding that infants from birth onward prefer novel stimulation (Fantz, 1964; Slater, 1995). The specific procedure used by the author is called the *familiarization/novelty-preference procedure* and involves presenting the infant with two identical copies of the familiar stimulus, followed by paired presentation of the familiar stimulus with the novel stimulus (for additional discussions of the procedure, see Quinn, 1998; Quinn & Eimas, 1986a, 1996b). A preference for the novel stimulus that usually is measured in looking time and that cannot be attributed to an a priori (i.e., spontaneous) preference for that stimulus is taken as evidence that the infant has formed a representation of the familiar stimulus and can differentiate between it and the novel stimulus. Note, however, that, in this example, a preference for the square over the triangle configuration, while providing evi-

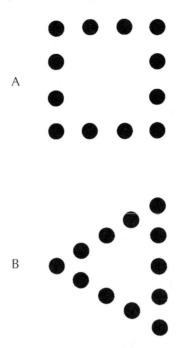

FIGURE 5.1. Patterns of elements that adults organize into "triangle" and "square" forms. The question of interest is, What do infants perceive when presented with such patterns: black on white, a set of dots, a set of spaces between dots, a subset of dots (enough to represent an angle or corner of the whole form), a single dot, part of a single dot, or the whole form?

dence of discrimination between the two patterns, would not be sufficient to claim that the patterns were experienced as coherent wholes. Discrimination between the two forms could be based on a single aspect of the overall configuration, such as the orientation difference between the left "diagonal" composing the triangle and the left "vertical" composing the square.

Adults are presumed to process the stimuli of Figure 5.1 as whole forms because of application of verbal labels like "square" and "triangle," and also because of experimental phenomena such as the *pattern superiority effect* (Williams & Weisstein, 1978). The pattern superiority effect refers to the superior identification or discrimination performance that adult subjects display for the "arrow" and "triangle" stimuli shown in panel B of Figure 5.2 compared with the right- and left-facing diagonal line segments shown in panel A (Pomerantz, Sager, & Stoever, 1977). The effect has been used as evidence to support the claim that adults represent the "arrow" and "triangle" stimuli as more than a set of independent line segments (e.g., the parts of the arrow or the sides of the triangle). If the individual line segments of the arrow and triangle were processed in isolation from each other, the prediction would be that the two forms be confused to a greater extent than the right- and left-facing diagonal line segments presented in isolation. This reasoning is based on the fact that the arrow and triangle stimuli possess two features in common (the horizontal and vertical line segments), whereas the two diagonal stimuli featurally are completely distinct. The finding that the diagonal line elements actually are confused to a greater extent than the arrow and triangle argues that subjects are extracting *emergent features*, defined as features that emerge when simple line-element features are processed in relation to each other (e.g., corners, angles, and whole configurations), and that these emergent features are processed more efficiently than simple features processed in isolation from each other (Enns & Prinzmetal, 1984; McClelland & Miller, 1979; Navon, 1977; Pomerantz & Pristach, 1989).

To determine whether stimuli like those shown in Figures 5.1 and 5.2B are perceived as emergent configurations from early in development, Quinn and Eimas (1986b) used the familiarization/novelty-preference procedure to investigate whether 3- and 4-month-old infants will display a pattern superiority effect. Consistent with the presence of the effect, Quinn and Eimas found that young infants familiarized

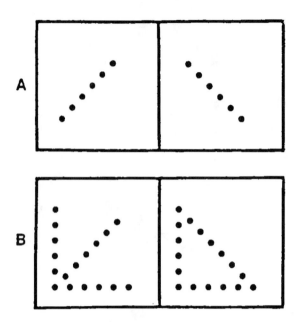

FIGURE 5.2. Line segments in isolation (A) and embedded in a right angle contextual frame (B). Even though the stimuli in (B) are more confusable in terms of individual features (i.e., the horizontal and vertical line elements common to both), both adults and young infants find them easier to distinguish relative to the stimuli in (A). This finding has been called the pattern superiority effect and has been used as evidence to support claims that form perception involves processing of emergent features (e.g., corners, angles, whole configurations). From "Pattern-Line Effect and Units of Visual Processing in Infants," by P. C. Quinn and P. D. Eimas, 1986b, *Infant Behavior and Development, 9,* p. 60. Copyright 1986 by Ablex Publishing Corporation. Reprinted with permission.

with either of the diagonal line segments did not subsequently prefer the novel diagonal. In contrast, infants familiarized with either the arrow or triangle reliably preferred the novel member of the pair. These findings provide strong evidence that the infants were not processing the arrow and triangle stimuli as a set of line segments in isolation from each other (see also Bomba, Eimas, Siqueland, & Miller, 1984; Colombo, Laurie, Martelli, & Hartig, 1984, for additional corroborating evidence). However, the findings leave open the question of precisely what aspects of the patterns the infants were representing. Were the infants using corners or angles formed by the individual line elements (or both) as a basis for their more efficient discrimination? Or might they have formed a representation of the entire "arrow-like" or "triangle-like" configuration to differentiate the two patterns? Moreover, the results do not inform us as to how the infants were able to relate the individual elements of the pattern to each other. Might the infants have used the Gestalt principles of closure, good continuation, proximity, lightness similarity, and form similarity to perceive both the coherence of the individual line elements and the whole configuration?

A second study by Quinn, Burke, and Rush (1993) hints at answers to both questions, albeit with different stimuli. The stimuli are shown in the left half of Figure 5.3. As reported by Wertheimer (1923/1958), adult subjects group together the elements of such stimuli on the basis of lightness similarity and represent the top pattern shown in panel a as a set of columns, and the bottom pattern depicted in panel b as a set of rows. Quinn, Burke, and Rush reasoned that if young infants, 3 months of age, organize the patterns shown in panels a and b of Figure 5.3 into columns and rows based an lightness similarity, then they should respond differentially to the vertical- and horizontal-grating test stimuli shown in the right half of the figure. On the assumption that there is no spontaneous preference between the vertical and horizontal stripes, infants familiarized with columns should generalize to verticals and prefer horizontals, whereas infants familiarized with rows should generalize to horizontals and prefer verticals. This is precisely the result that was obtained: a finding indicating that young infants were able to use lightness similarity to represent the row- and column-like organization of the individual light and dark squares.

FAMILIAR STIMULUS

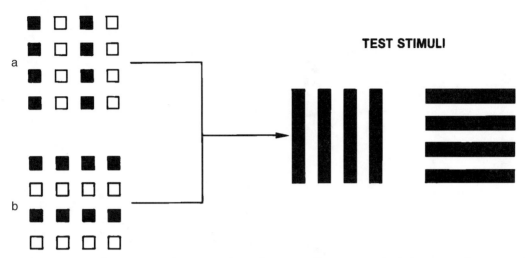

FIGURE 5.3. Familiarization and test stimuli used to test adherence to the lightness similarity Gestalt organizational principle in Quinn, Burke, and Rush (1993). The rationale is that, if infants can organize familiar stimulus (a) into columns, then the vertical column test stimulus should be perceived as familiar, and the horizontal column test stimulus should be preferred. Similarly, if infants can organize the familiar stimulus (b) into rows, then the horizontal column test stimulus should be perceived as familiar, and the vertical column test stimulus should be preferred.

One could take issue with the Gestaltist-based lightness similarity interpretation proposed by Quinn, Burke, and Rush (1993) by claiming that the apparent perceptual grouping is actually a by-product of immature peripheral filtering by the infant's visual system (Banks & Ginsburg, 1985; Banks & Salapatek, 1981). That is, one could argue that immature resolution acuity and contrast sensitivity rendered the dark squares as indistinguishable from other dark squares (and the light squares as indistinguishable from other light squares). The representation of familiar stimuli a and b resulting from such "low-pass" filtering would best be described as "two dark vertical (or horizontal) bars on a light background." Performance of the 3-month-olds could thus be explained by simple generalization from representations of this nature to the vertical (or horizontal bars) used as test stimuli, without invoking any grouping mechanism (cf., Ginsburg, 1986).

Quinn, Burke, and Rush (1993) attempted to choose between the Gestalt grouping and low-pass filtering explanations of their findings with both computer simulation and experimental evidence. First, the images of the familiar stimuli shown in Figure 5.3, and additional stimuli in which either the dark or light elements were changed from square to diamond, were fed into a low-pass spatial frequency filter that removed spatial frequencies above 4 cycles/degree, the cutoff spatial frequency for 3-month-olds as estimated by preferential looking techniques (e.g., Atkinson, Braddick, & Moar, 1977; Banks & Salapatek, 1978). Figure 5.4 shows the resulting patterns. It can be seen that the stimuli have lost some sharpness, but the individual elements comprising the patterns are clearly discernable. Figure 5.4 thus suggests that 3-month-olds have enough resolution acuity and contrast sensitivity to perceive the individual elements of the patterns, and that the initial preference results cannot be explained on the basis of peripheral immaturities in the young infant's visual system.

This suggestion was subsequently confirmed in a discrimination experiment utilizing the familiarization/novelty-preference methodology. Infants were familiarized with stimuli like those shown in the left half of Figure 5.3 and then presented with novel stimuli in which only the dark or light elements were changed from square to diamond. Figures 5.5 and 5.6 display the design of this experiment. Preference for the novel stimuli was above chance in both cases, indicating that infants were able to process shape information for both the light and dark elements. The combined findings from the simulation and discrimination experiment thus provide considerable evidence in favor of a Gestaltist interpretation of the

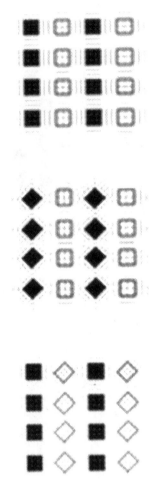

FIGURE 5.4. Patterns with spatial frequencies above 4 cycles/degree removed. While the individual elements of the patterns have lost some "sharpness," their shape (square or diamond) remains clearly discernable. From "Part-Whole Perception in Early Infancy: Evidence for Perceptual Grouping Produced by Lightness Similarity," by P. C. Quinn, S. Burke, and A. Rush, 1993, *Infant Behavior and Development, 16,* p. 26. Copyright 1993 by Ablex Publishing Corporation. Reprinted with permission.

original preference results: Infants had perceived the individual elements of the patterns and grouped these elements into alternating light and dark columns or rows on the basis of lightness similarity.

Lightness similarity may be the most robust form of grouping by similarity and, possibly, the earliest form of similarity that infants can use as a basis for perceptual grouping. Several attempts in the author's laboratory to demonstrate that young infants can use form similarity have failed to yield consistently reliable results. For example, the logic and design of Quinn, Burke, and Rush (1993) was used to investigate whether 3- and 4-month-olds could use form similarity to organize alternating rows or columns of: (a) squares and diamonds, (b) vertical and horizontal line elements, (c) Hs and Is, or (d) Xs and Os. A significant preference for vertical stripes was obtained for infants familiarized with alternating rows of squares and diamonds, and a reliable preference for horizontal stripes was revealed for infants familiarized with alternating columns of vertical and horizontal line elements. However, no significant preferences were displayed by the groups of infants participating in the other testing conditions. The most reasonable conclusion from these findings would seem to be that grouping by form similarity is more difficult than grouping by lightness similarity and may be a later developmental achievement (see Kellman, 1996; Spelke,

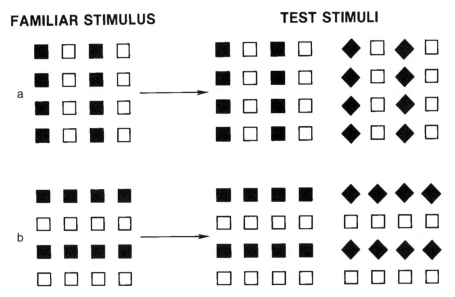

FIGURE 5.5. Familiarization and test stimuli used to assess detection of a change in the dark (filled) elements. If infants can perceive the shape of the individual dark elements in familiar stimuli (a) and (b), then the familiar test stimuli should be perceived as familiar, and the test stimuli containing the columns (a) and rows (b) of novel dark elements should be preferred. From "Part-Whole Perception in Early Infancy: Evidence for Perceptual Grouping Produced by Lightness Similarity," by P. C. Quinn, S. Burke, and A. Rush, 1993, *Infant Behavior and Development, 16,* p. 27. Copyright 1993 by Ablex Publishing Corporation. Reprinted with permission.

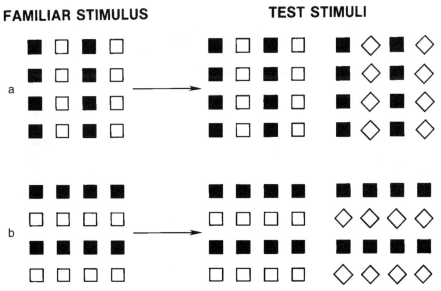

FIGURE 5.6. Familiarization and test stimuli used to assess detection of a change in the light (unfilled) elements. If infants can perceive the shape of the individual light elements in familiar stimuli (a) and (b), then the familiar test stimuli should be perceived as familiar, and the test stimuli containing the columns (a) and rows (b) of novel light elements should be preferred. From "Part-Whole Perception in Early Infancy: Evidence for Perceptual Grouping Produced by Lightness Similarity," by P. C. Quinn, S. Burke, and A. Rush, 1993, *Infant Behavior and Development, 16,* p. 28. Copyright 1993 by Ablex Publishing Corporation. Reprinted with permission.

Breinlinger, Jacobson, & Phillips, 1993, for additional theory and evidence on the difficulty that young infants may have using form similarity as a basis for perceptual organization).

When considering further the relevance of the Quinn, Burke, and Rush (1993) demonstration of Gestalt-like grouping by young infants for understanding the early development of object recognition abilities, at least two additional limitations become apparent. First, the stimuli used by Quinn, Burke and Rush (1993) are more like surface textures than they are like objects (cf., Spelke, Gutheil, & Van de Walle, 1995). Second, in many natural scenes, numerous objects appear simultaneously, and may be arranged so that their contours are partially overlapping, rather than completely visible. Such scenes must be parsed into a set of primitive contours, and these contours must be organized into coherent representations of whole shapes.

In an attempt to understand how well infants parse and organize more complex visual configurations that only begin to approximate the object processing demands of more natural scenes, Quinn et al. (1997) examined how young infants would represent the pattern shown in panel a of Figure 5.7 (adapted from one presented in Arnheim, 1974). Adults tend to parse and organize this pattern into the square and teardrop shapes shown in panel b of Figure 5.7 rather than the number 4 and open container shapes shown in panel c. Presumably adults are following Gestalt organizational principles such as good continuation and possibly closure to represent the pattern information in this manner. Explanations based on top-down readiness to perceive the pattern as objects of common experience (e.g., the square and teardrop or ice cream cone) are weakened by the fact that such readiness should be just as strong for the number 4.

To determine whether 3- and 4-month-olds would parse and organize the pattern shown in Figure 5.7a into the square and teardrop shapes perceived by adults, one group of infants was familiarized in an initial experiment with the overlapping square-teardrop configuration and then preference tested with the teardrop paired with the number 4. Another group was similarly familiarized, but then preference tested with the square paired with the number 4. There are at least three ways in which infants may represent the familiar pattern information, each of which would produce a distinct pattern of looking among the test stimuli. First, if infants parse the pattern and organize its contours into the teardrop and square shapes in accord with the Gestalt principles of good continuation or closure or both, then the teardrop and square shapes should be recognized as familiar in preference tests with the 4 shape, and the 4 shape should be preferred. Second, if infants do not parse the unitary configuration and the outcome is a representation of an unparsed whole, or if infants parse the configuration into more than one whole, but not the wholes predicted by adherence to good continuation and closure, then one would not expect a consistent preference for the 4 shape in either test. Third, infants may have spontaneous preferences for certain stimulus features (e.g., curvature, horizontal-vertical line elements that could eventuate in parsing and selective organization of the configuration into either the teardrop or square. In this case, one would expect a preference for the 4 shape in one or the other experimental group, but not both. The results were

STIMULUS   POSSIBLE ORGANIZATIONS

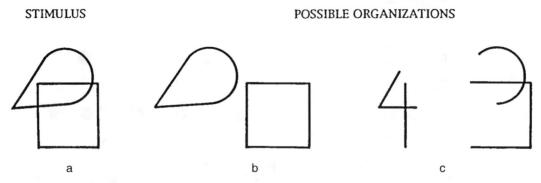

a   b   c

FIGURE 5.7. Compound pattern in (a) and two possible organizations in (b) and (c). Adherence to the Gestalt principles of good continuation or closure, or both, favor organization (b) over organization (c). From "Perceptual Organization of Complex Visual Configurations by Young Infants," by P. C. Quinn, C. R. Brown, and M. L. Streppa, 1997, *Infant Behavior and Development, 20,* p. 38. Copyright 1997 by Ablex Publishing Corporation. Reprinted with permission.

that infants in both experimental groups preferred the 4 shape, a pattern of looking that is consistent with the idea that infants had organized the familiar configuration into the square and teardrop shapes in a manner predicted by adherence to the Gestalt principles of good continuation or closure or both.

In an attempt to focus more precisely on infants' possible use of the Gestalt principle of *good continuation* to organize complex configurations of overlapping contour information into discrete, but coherent wholes, Quinn et al. (1997) familiarized 3- and 4-month-old infants in a second experiment with the pattern shown in panel a of Figure 5.8, and administered two preference tests: one pairing the circle shown in panel b with the P1 shape shown in panel c, the other pairing the square in panel b with the P2 shape shown in panel c. Adherence to the good continuation principle, in particular, would predict a representation of the pattern as the circle and square shapes, rather than the two pacman-like shapes, Pl and P2. Adherence to the closure principle would not explain why the resulting organization would favor the circle over P1 or the square over P2, since all four forms are closed. The infants responded to these conditions by preferring P1 to the circle, and P2 to the square, a pattern of outcomes that provides further evidence of Gestalt-like organization, in this case based more clearly on the good continuation of the contour information.

One rather interesting effect that was observed in the two experiments of Quinn et al. (1997) is that there was a consistent spontaneous preference for curvature observed in control groups of infants who were assessed for possible a priori preferences among the various test patterns (cf., Fantz, Fagan, & Miranda, 1975). For example, without prior familiarization experience, the teardrop was reliably preferred to the 4 shape, and the P2 shape was significantly preferred to the square. This means that the novelty preference for the 4 shape over the teardrop shape in the experimental group of the first experiment occurred despite the a priori preference for the teardrop in the control group. In addition, the novelty preference for P2 over the square in the experimental group of the second experiment occurred above and beyond that of the a priori preference for P2 in the control group. However, it is possible that the a priori preference for curvature we detected is more than just a potential confound, a noise factor to be acknowledged but then ruled out with appropriate statistical tests. The curvature preference may help answer the question, How does the infant initially begin to break down a complex whole into a set of component contours? More specifically, where on the stimulus does the infant begin the complementary processes of parsing and organization? It may be that spontaneous preferences for some stimulus features over others could play an important "Start here" role in initiating the parsing process for an unanalyzed configuration that contains a number of diverse features. A curvature preference, combined with Gestalt principles, like good continuation and closure, may have allowed infants to first develop a representation for the teardrop shape (in the first experiment) and the circle shape (in the second experiment). Once the teardrop or

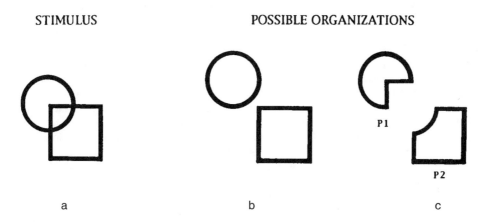

STIMULUS   POSSIBLE ORGANIZATIONS

a   b   c

FIGURE 5.8. Intersecting circle-square stimulus in (a) and two possible organizations in (b) and (c). Adherence to the Gestalt principle of good continuation favors organization (b) over organization (c). From "Perceptual Organization of Complex Visual Configurations by Young Infants," by P. C. Quinn, C. R. Brown, and M. L. Streppa, 1997, *Infant Behavior and Development, 20,* p. 41. Copyright 1997 by Ablex Publishing Corporation. Reprinted with permission.

circle were organized, infant attention then may have been free to explore other portions of the stimulus, thereby allowing for organization of the remaining contours into the square shapes in both experiments.

The proposed relation between spontaneous preferences and Gestalt principles thus implies that there may, in fact, be an order to the emergence of the representations formed for the familiar configurations of Figures 5.7 and 5.8, with the wholes containing the preferred features, the teardrop and the circle, coming to be represented slightly before wholes without the preferred features, the square in each case. In addition, there might be a difference in the robustness of the representations, with those for the teardrop and the circle being stronger than that for the square (cf., Munakata, McClelland, Johnson, & Siegler, 1997; Quinn & Johnson, 1996, 1997). If stimulus preferences for certain features facilitate parsing of complex visual configurations in the manner suggested, then it should be possible to observe the emergence of distinct representations with variation in familiarization time (cf., Colombo, Mitchell, Coldren, & Freeseman, 1991). With quite short familiarization durations, infants might not have sufficient encoding time to develop even an initial representation of the preferred features, and the prediction would be that a compound stimulus becomes represented as an unanalyzed whole. With additional familiarization, infants may have time to develop a representation of the preferred features, but perhaps not enough time to develop a complete representation for any remaining features. Finally, with an even longer familiarization period, infants should be able to form representations for preferred and nonpreferred features alike. Of interest is how infants would perform with a complex stimulus composed entirely of contours that are equally preferable. The model developed thus far would suggest that infants may have difficulty initiating the parsing of such a pattern since there is no clear start point. Additional experimentation clearly will be needed to test these predictions.

Primitive Features and Pop-Out

While Gestalt psychologists have attempted to describe the principles by which smaller elements of visual stimuli are grouped together to form perceptual wholes, a somewhat different approach to object recognition has been undertaken by some modern cognitivists. This newer approach has attempted to identify a small set of primitive features from which a much larger set of object representations can be constructed (e.g., Biederman, 1987). One specific experimental methodology to establishing "featurehood" has been to determine whether a feature "pops out" from its respective background and "calls attention to itself" (Julesz, 1984; Treisman & Gelade, 1980; Treisman, Sykes, & Gelade, 1977). For example, Julesz (1984) has demonstrated pop-out in texture segregation tasks that involve presentation of a region of one element type embedded in a larger region composed of a different element type. If a patch of +s was embedded among Ls or Ts (or vice versa), for example, the +s were detected rapidly and the speed of response was found to be independent of the number of Ls or Ts in the surround patch. In contrast, if a patch of Ls was embedded among Ts (or vice versa), detection of Ls was slow and response speed increased with increases in the number of distracting Ts in the surround patch. The critical difference between the two conditions was, according to Julesz (1984), the fact that the + contained a feature—a line crossing—not present in the Ls or Ts (but, see Bergen & Adelson, 1988), whereas the Ls and Ts were comprised of the same set of primitive features—the horizontal and vertical line elements.

Treisman (1993) also has reported evidence for pop-out using a visual search procedure in which a single unique target element is embedded amidst an array of distractors of a different element type. Thus, for example, adult subjects responded rapidly to a single oblique target positioned among a set of vertical distractors (Treisman & Gormican, 1988), and response speed again was found to be independent of increases in the number of vertical distractors. This finding led Treisman (1993) to conclude that at least some orientation differences between line elements—vertical versus oblique (and presumably vs. horizontal)—allow these elements to be registered as distinct primitive features. Additional studies by Julesz, Treisman, and others, employing either texture segregation or visual search procedures, have suggested that color, curvature, line termination points, movement, closure, contrast, and brightness, along with line-crossing and orientation information, should be included in the list of primitive features that can be combined to form object representations (Beck, 1982; Enns, 1986; Julesz, 1981; Norhdurft, 1990; Treisman, 1986a, 1986b).

Quinn and Bhatt (1998) recently have investigated whether visual pop-out of line-crossing and orientation might occur even in young infants, borrowing from the logic of a procedure first used by Rovee-Collier, Hankins, and Bhatt (1992; see also Colombo, Ryther, Frick, & Gifford, 1995). In the experiment examining possible pop-out of line-crossing information, 3- and 4-month-old infants were familiarized with homogeneous 5 by 5 arrays of Ls, Ts, or +s, like those shown in the top panel of Figure 5.9. The infants then were tested with a stimulus that contained a single novel target among 24 familiar distractors, paired with a stimulus that contained a single familiar target among 24 novel distractors. In the proposed pop-out condition (middle panel of Figure 5.9), the contrast between target and distractors was between the L (or T) and +. If a line-crossing pop-out effect occurs, then the single L (or T) should be readily detected among the +s (and vice versa). Moreover, on the assumption that the pop-out target will control attention in infants as it does in adults, if the pop-out target is familiar, infants should respond to the whole array as familiar, even though most of it is novel. Likewise, if the pop-out target is novel, infants should treat the whole array as novel, even though most of it is familiar. In contrast, in the proposed non-pop-out condition (bottom panel of Figure 5.9), the target-distractor contrast was between the L and T. In this case, a novel T is not expected to be detected among an array of familiar Ls (and vice versa), and infant looking should be directed to an array that is predominantly novel (a familiar L among an array of novel Ts). Results were in accord with expectations: Infants in the pop-out condition looked more to the array

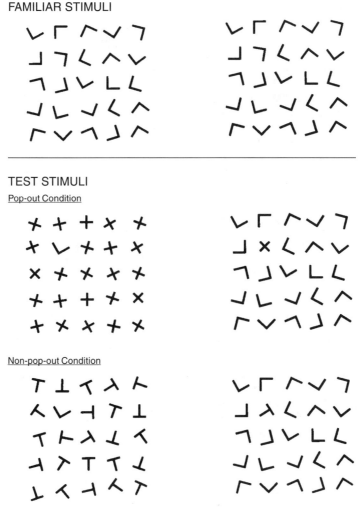

FIGURE 5.9. Examples of the familiar and test stimuli used in the line-crossing pop-out experiment of Quinn and Bhatt (1998). Infants were familiarized with homogeneous 5 × 5 arrays of Ls, Ts, or +s, and tested with an array containing a single novel character amid familiar characters paired with an array containing a single familiar character amid novel characters.

with the single novel pop-out target, whereas infants in the non-pop-out condition preferred the array with the 24 novel distractors. This pattern of looking preferences indicates that line-crossing information may serve as a primitive feature from the period of early infancy and furthermore, that mechanisms which underlie pop-out effects in adulthood may be an inherent characteristic of our system for perceiving visual pattern information.

An additional experiment by Quinn and Bhatt (1998) employed the logic of the first experiment to demonstrate that coarse orientation differences (vertical vs. oblique) may also serve as a basis for identification of primitive features from the earliest beginnings of development. Three- and 4-month-olds were, in this case, familiarized with arrays consisting of verticals (90° line elements), 135° obliques, or 45° obliques, like those shown in the top panel of Figure 5.10. They were then preference tested with a stimulus that contained a single novel orientation among 24 line elements of the familiar orientation, paired with a stimulus that contained a single familiar orientation among 24 line elements in a novel orientation. On the basis of Treisman and Gormican's (1988) work with adults, the target-distractor contrast in the presumed pop-out group was vertical versus oblique (middle panel of Figure 5.10), whereas the target-distractor contrast in the presumed non-pop-out group was oblique, 45°, versus oblique, 135° (bottom panel of Figure 5.10). The prediction of no pop-out in this latter group is based on findings obtained with both adults and infants indicating that, under some experimental conditions, oblique stimuli tend to be categorized (Quinn & Bomba, 1986; Quinn, Siqueland, & Bomba, 1985; Wolfe, Friedman-Hill, Stewart, & O'Connell, 1992). That is, obliques can be discriminated from one another, but may be treated equivalently or responded to as members of the same class of stimuli. The results were comparable to those obtained in the line-crossing experiment: Infants in the pop-out condition preferred the pattern with the single novel orientation, whereas infants in the non-pop-out condition preferred the pattern with the majority of line elements in the novel orientation. These preferences provide support for Treisman's (1988, 1993) suggestion that orientation information is coarsely coded into categories such as vertical, horizontal, and oblique, and indicate further that this manner of coding is not the product of an extensive period of perceptual learning (see also Catherwood, Green, Skoien, & Holt, 1995, for discussion of other pop-out effects in infants that appear to be categorical in nature). It is more likely a consequence of the initial architecture of the infant's system for processing visual pattern information.

Summary

The evidence reviewed in the preceding sections indicates that young infants can group together the elements of a single visual pattern, presented in isolation from other patterns, so as to form a holistic representation of that pattern. Infants also may be capable of parsing and organizing the more complex pattern information in a configuration of intersecting contours into two complete shapes. Furthermore, infants apparently are able to direct their attention to and maintain their attention on information-rich locations, points of discrepancy, in a visual array.

In achieving this degree of perceptual coherence young infants may benefit from adherence to certain Gestalt principles such as lightness similarity, good continuation, and closure, although perhaps not form similarity. In addition, infants may rely on spontaneous preferences for particular features of contour information, such as curvature, to begin parsing and organizing global conglomerations of visual pattern information that contain multiple features. Infants may also draw on tendencies to respond with allocation of attention to textural discontinuities in surface arrays. Such attentional shifts may be helpful in discovering features of contour that are associated with boundaries between objects and boundaries between distinct parts of single objects. Recognition of such features may be essential to developing individuated and wholistic representations for particular shapes in various displays of visual pattern information.

☐ Object Categorization

In addition to developing representations for coherent objects depicted in a single presentation of visual pattern information, members of the human species must, at some point during development, become capable of forming representations that are inclusive of numerous objects appearing over a more extended period of time. In compiling these representations inclusive of multiple items, individuals appar-

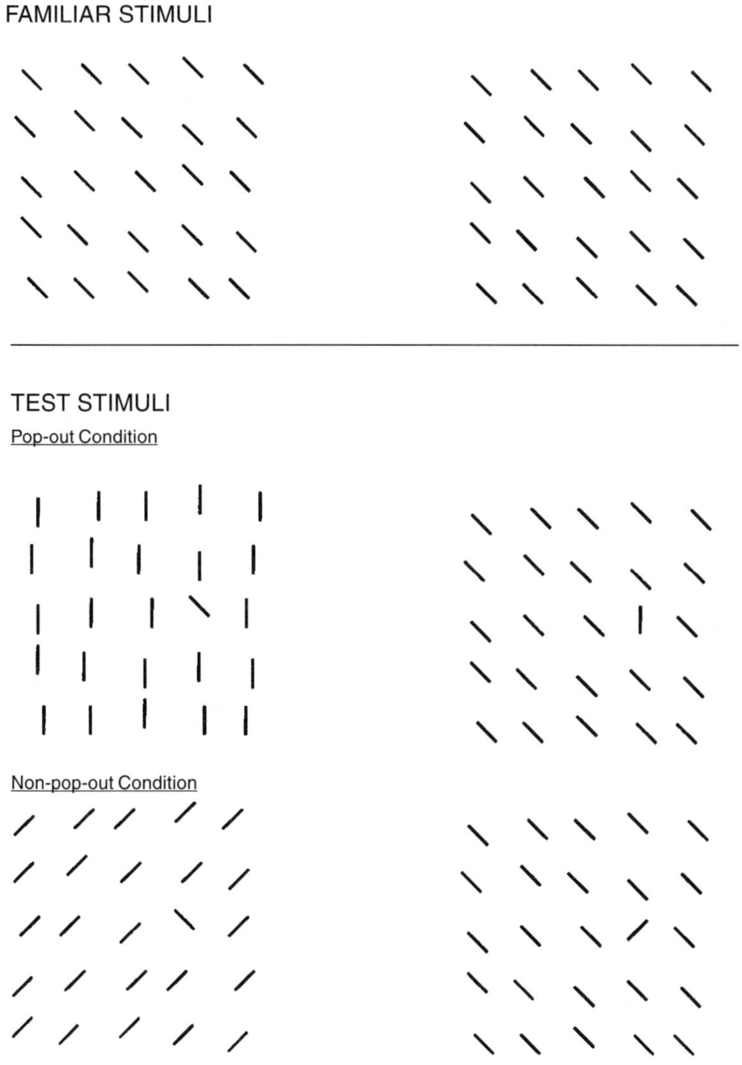

FAMILIAR STIMULI

TEST STIMULI

Pop-out Condition

Non-pop-out Condition

FIGURE 5.10. Examples of the familiar and test stimuli used in the orientation pop-out experiment of Quinn and Bhatt (1998). Infants were familiarized with homogeneous 5 × 5 arrays of vertically or obliquely oriented line elements, and tested with an array containing a single novel orientation among line elements of the familiar orientation paired with an array containing a single familiar orientation among line elements of the novel orientation.

ently are detecting some basis of equivalence among them. This basis could be perceptual, functional, conceptual, or some even more abstract combination of the attributes possessed by the items. Because representations of this nature are normally developed for categories of items (e.g., dogs, chairs), I have referred to them in past writings as *categorical representations* (Quinn, 1998; Quinn & Eimas, 1996b, 1997a). Categorical representations of many common kinds of objects may be essential to (a) organizing memory, and (b) permitting us to respond to many novel objects with familiarity, because of the recognition of equivalence among certain attributes detected from the objects and maintained in their categorical representations. Presumably, a system of mental representation that lacked categorical representations would contain a memory dominated by unrelated, individual instance information and would face the problem of having to respond anew to each novel object encountered (Smith & Medin, 1981). Indeed, the importance of categorical representations to daily cognitive functioning has led Thelen and Smith (1994) to argue that categorization is the "primitive in all behavior and mental functioning" (p. 143).

Although there has been a historical tradition among scholars of cognitive development to consider the ability to form categorical representations to be an achievement of childhood (Bruner, Olver, & Greenfield, 1966; Vygotsky, 1934/1962), more modern work has focused on the abilities of infants and toddlers to respond categorically to common object types (Cohen & Strauss, 1979; Mandler & McDonough, 1993; Mervis, 1987; Oakes, Madole, & Cohen, 1991; Quinn & Eimas, 1996b; Waxman & Markow, 1995; Xu & Carey, 1996; Younger, 1990). The chapter will now consider the evidence on categorization by these younger subjects, with emphasis on studies of categorization of simple shapes and pictorial exemplars of animals and artifacts conducted with 3- and 4-month-olds in the author's laboratory. Particular issues of current contention include exemplar versus prototype storage of category information in memory, the perceptual versus conceptual basis for early object categories, and the developmental ordering of categories formed at different levels of inclusiveness (i.e., global vs. basic).

Procedure for Assessing Categorization in Young Infants

In the familiarization/novelty-preference method of testing for categorization, infants are presented with a number of different pairs of instances from the same category during a familiarization period. The instances comprising a given pair can simply be two identical copies of the same stimulus or two nonidentical instances (see Fagan, 1978, for evidence that paired presentation of distinct exemplars during familiarization enhances recognition memory for them). Infants are then administered a paired presentation of a novel instance of the familiar category and an instance from a novel category. If infants generalize their familiarization to the novel exemplar of the familiar category, and display a preference for an exemplar from a novel category, and this pattern of looking cannot be attributed to an a priori preference or to an inability to discriminate among the familiar category exemplars, then it can be concluded that a categorical representation of the familiar category exemplars has been formed. That is, one can infer that the familiar exemplars have, in some manner, been grouped together or categorized and that the representation of this category excludes the noninstance—the novel category exemplar.

Categorization of Form

Following the efforts of Bomba and Siqueland (1983), Quinn (1987) investigated the abilities of 3- and 4-month-old infants to form categorical representations for numerous patterns of dots randomly generated from "good" Gestalt square and triangle forms. Examples of these patterns are shown in Figure 5.11. Infants were first presented with six different examples from the same form category during familiarization, and then presented with two novel patterns during a novel category preference test: one was from the familiar category, the other from a novel category. Infants responded by preferring exemplars from the novel category, a preference that control experiments demonstrated was not the result of an a priori preference for the novel over familiar category exemplars nor an inability to discriminate between the various members of the familiar category.

The pattern of findings is consistent with the idea that infants had formed a categorical representation for a series of individually distinct shapes experienced during familiarization, and had used this representation as a basis for generalizing to novel exemplars from the familiar category and for responding preferentially to novel exemplars from the novel category. Notably, the preferential responding to novel category instances was statistically even more reliable when infants were presented with exemplars from each of two form categories during familiarization (i.e., squares and triangles). Quinn argued that simultaneous experience with two categories may help the infant discover not just the features that are common among members of a category, but also those features which distinguish members of a category from members of contrast categories.

In a subsequent experiment, Quinn (1987) investigated how the infants were representing form category information in memory. Infants were familiarized as they were in the initial experiment but, in this case, during the preference test, a familiar exemplar from the familiar category was presented with the novel prototype of the familiar category (i.e., the prototype of the familiar category was not shown during familiarization). The rationale of this preference test is that, if infants are simply storing individual instances into their categorical representation, then the familiar exemplar should be perceived as familiar and the novel prototype should be preferred (cf., Posner & Keele, 1970). However, if infants are averaging

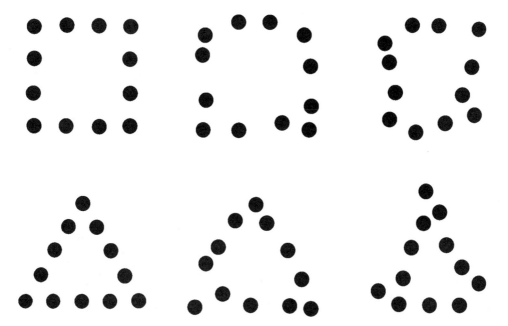

FIGURE 5.11. Square and triangle prototypes and representative distortions generated from them. From "The Categorical Representation of Visual Pattern Information by Young Infants," by P. C. Quinn, 1987, *Cognition*, *27*, p. 154. Copyright 1987 by Elsevier Science Publishers. Reprinted with permission.

the familiar category exemplars and representing them as a prototype, then the novel prototype should actually should be perceived as familiar (paradoxically), and the familiar exemplar should be preferred. The findings revealed that infants presented with 6 exemplars from a single category preferred the novel prototype, whereas infants presented with 6 exemplars from each of two categories (12 total exemplars) preferred the familiar exemplar. Thus, infants may represent a small number of exemplars from a single category as a set of exemplars, but represent a larger number of exemplars from multiple categories as prototypes one for each category (for similar findings with adults, see Homa & Chambliss, 1975). The ability to represent a series of perceptually similar exemplars as a prototype provides the young infant with an adaptive means of information processing and storage during a time of increasing experience with large numbers of exemplars from a variety of categories.

Categorization of Natural Animal Species and Human-Made Artifacts

In a series of experiments, Eimas, Behl-Chadha, and I have shown that young infants can form categorical representations for a variety of animal species and furniture artifacts (reviewed in Quinn, 1998; Quinn & Eimas, 1996b). Black and white examples of the stimuli are shown in Figure 5.12. In the experiments investigating young infants' categorical representations of various animal species, 3- and 4-month-olds familiarized with realistic, pictorial instances of 12 domestic cats, representing different breeds and depicted in a variety of stances, will generalize familiarization to novel instances of a domestic cats, but show a novel category preference for birds, dogs, horses, and tigers, although not female lions (Eimas & Quinn, 1994; Quinn & Eimas, 1996a; Quinn, Eimas, & Rosenkrantz, 1993). In addition, same-aged infants familiarized with 12 horses will generalize to novel horses, but display novel category preferences for cats, giraffes, and zebras (Eimas & Quinn, 1994). These findings indicate that young infants can form separate representations for cats and horses, each of which excludes instances of the other along with exemplars from a number of basic-level categories of related animal species.

It is important to consider the possible bases for the high degree of exclusivity in the categorical representations for animal species by young infants. Infants at 3 and 4 months are not likely to have biological

FIGURE 5.12. Black and white examples of the stimuli used in the investigations of perceptual categorization of animal species and furniture artifacts.

knowledge about animal species and, therefore, must be relying on perceptually available features that can be detected on the surfaces of the stimuli. While some of the category differentiations may be based on salient differences in parts (cats vs. birds), overall shape (cats vs. horses), and body markings (zebras vs. horses), one recent experiment has indicated that information from the head and facial region of the animals may provide the means by which infants form a categorical representation for cats that excludes dogs (Quinn & Eimas, 1996a). Three- and 4-month-olds were randomly assigned to one of three experimental conditions depicted in Figure 5.13: whole animal, face only, or body only. Infants in the whole animal group were presented with cats and tested with novel cat–novel dog pairings. The face only and body only groups were familiarized and tested with the same animals as the whole animal group, but with their bodies and faces occluded, respectively. The results were that the infants preferred the novel dog stimuli in the whole animal and face only groups, but not in the body only group. The findings suggest that information from the face and head region provides young infants with a necessary and sufficient basis to form a categorical representation for domestic cats that excludes dogs. Infants' utilization of this

Whole Animal Condition   Face Only Condition   Body Only Condition

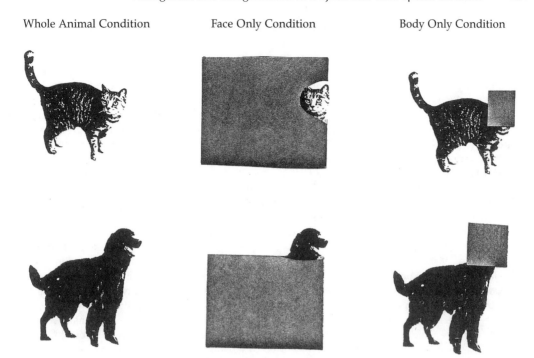

FIGURE 5.13. Black and white examples of the stimuli used in the three experimental conditions of Quinn and Eimas (1996a). In the whole animal condition, 3- and 4-month-old infants familiarized with cats preferred a dog to a novel cat. In the face only condition, infants familiarized with cat faces preferred a dog face to a novel cat face. In the body only condition, infants familiarized with cat bodies did not prefer a dog body to a novel cat body.

information may result from an inherent preference to attend to the facial configuration information in a stimulus (Johnson & Morton, 1991).

Behl-Chadha (1996) extended the findings of early basic-level differentiation among animal species to furniture. Three- and 4-month-olds familiarized with 12 pictorial instances of chairs (including arm chairs, desk chairs, kitchen chairs, rocking chairs, and stuffed chairs, depicted in a variety of colors) generalized their familiarization to novel chairs, but displayed novel category preferences for couches, beds, and tables. In addition, 3- and 4-month-olds presented with 12 couches generalized their familiarization to novel couches, but showed novel category preferences for chairs, beds, and tables. These results indicate that 3- and 4-month-olds can form individuated representations for chairs and couches, each of which excludes instances of the other as well as beds and tables. Overall, the findings provide evidence that young infants are capable of forming categorical representations for both natural kind animal species and artifactual items of furniture at a near- or child-basic-level of exclusiveness (Mervis, 1987). It is noteworthy that the infant has the ability to group stimuli into categories that correspond to many of the groupings arrived at by children and adults.

While some investigators have claimed that representations at a higher level of inclusiveness than the basic level may necessarily be conceptually based on the grounds that there is not enough within-class perceptual similarity to unite them (Mandler & McDonough, 1993), Behl-Chadha (1996; Behl-Chadha, Eimas, & Quinn, 1995) nonetheless examined how young infants would perform on perceptually based global-level categorization tasks. In one experiment, 3- and 4-month-olds were familiarized with two photographic examples from each of eight basic-level categories of mammals (e.g., deer, domestic cats, elephants, horses, rabbits, squirrels, tigers, and zebras). On a series of subsequent test trials, a novel instance from a novel mammal category was paired with (a) a novel example of a familiar mammal category, (b) a nonmammalian animal (bird or fish), and (c) an item of furniture. The infants preferred birds, fish, and furniture to instances from the novel mammal categories, but they did not prefer instances of novel mammal categories over novel members of familiar mammal categories. The findings indicate that young infants can form a global-level categorical representation for mammals that is inclusive of instances from novel mammal categories not experienced during familiarization, but that excludes at least some nonmammalian animals (birds and fish) and furniture.

In the same series of experiments, Behl-Chadha (1996) obtained evidence that 3- to 4-month-olds also can form a global-level categorical representation for furniture that includes beds, chairs, couches, cabinets, dressers, and tables, but excludes the mammals mentioned above. The evidence thus suggests that young infants can form global-level categorical representations for at least some natural (i.e., mammals) and artifactual (i.e., furniture) categories. Of theoretical importance is that the age of the subjects and the nature of the stimuli (i.e., static pictorial instances of the categories) make it improbable that the infants are relying on conceptual knowledge about the "kind of thing" something is to perform successfully in these tasks (cf., Mandler & McDonough, 1993). The studies therefore support the position that both basic and global levels of representation can have a perceptual basis.

Given the data that 3- and 4-month-olds can form categorical representations at both global and basic levels, it may be informative to speculate on the level of inclusiveness of categorical representations available to even younger infants. Might it be the case that global-level representations precede basic-level representations, as has been reported for older infants forming what were taken to be conceptually based categories (e.g., Mandler & McDonough, 1993)? Or, might it be that basic-level representations precede global-level (or superordinate) representations, as has been argued to be the case in young children (e.g., Rosch, Mervis, Gray, Johnson, & Boyes-Braem, 1976)? An additional possibility is that the basic- and global-level representations have similar temporal courses of development. In attempting to choose between these alternatives, one might reason that the information which differentiates many mammals from all furniture (e.g., presence vs. absence of faces, body hair, and tails) may turn out to be more discriminable than the information that may be used to separate mammals from one another (e.g., specific dimensional values of facial features, hair length and coloring, and tail length (cf., Quinn & Eimas, 1996b; Rakison & Butterworth, 1998). If this reasoning is correct, than a global-level categorical representation for example, for mammals, actually may emerge before basic-level representations for individual mammal species sometime during the first 3 months of life.

In correspondence with this global before basic hypothesis, a series of three layered connectionist networks (i.e., input units → hidden units → output units), supervised by a back propagation learning algorithm, were found to learn categories in a global-to-basic sequence (Quinn & Johnson, 1996, 1997). From a developmental perspective, connectionist models may be helpful for understanding the initial formation of category representations, because the models are composed of interconnected processing units that form representations as connection strengths between the units change with experience according to one or another learning algorithm (Elman, Bates, Johnson, Karmiloff-Smith, Parisi, & Plunkett, 1996). Input to the networks of Quinn and Johnson included a number of measurable dimensions taken from the surfaces of the mammal and furniture stimuli used in the studies described above (e.g., leg length, horizontal extent), and the global-to-basic prediction held true even when some of the simulations were conducted without a global-level training signal; that is, when the networks were not taught to form representations for mammals or furniture. The proposed global-to-basic order of category emergence needs to be tested by comparing the levels of category representation, global versus basic, available to infants younger than 3 to 4 months of age. Such data will be critical for our understanding of the full developmental course of category formation by infants.

A Role for Spontaneous Preferences in Early Categorization

Throughout our investigations of perceptual categorization of pictorial exemplars of various animal species and furniture artifacts, we have observed spontaneous (and, presumably, a priori) looking preferences for members of one category over members of another across a series of paired-preference trials (Behl-Chadha, 1996; Eimas & Quinn, 1994; Quinn & Eimas, 1996b). Specifically, on each of a series of eight looking periods, 3- and 4-month-olds were presented with different, randomly selected pairs of pictures from two different categories. What emerged from this procedure were reliable preferences for cats over horses, tigers over cats, chairs over tables, chairs over couches, mammals over birds, and vehicles over furniture. The basis for some of these preferences may be distinctive textural markings possessed by members of one category, but not the other, for example, the consistent dark striping and orange coloring of the tigers. However, salient stimulus markings cannot explain a number of the other preferences (e.g., cats over horses, chairs over couches). Subtle, yet consistent, differences between the categories in overall shape, particular parts, or both may be the basis for these other preferences. Whatever their eventual explanation, it would seem that these early spontaneous preferences based on preferred perceptual properties might reasonably be regarded as category preferences and, quite likely, as facilitators of early category formation. Categories marked by preferred perceptual features may be among the first to be pulled out of the continous flux of objects encountered by infants during the first few months of life.

Categorization of Humans

Any theory of knowledge acquisition about animals must account for how a categorical representation for humans arises. Given the considerable amount of evidence demonstrating the categorical differentiation of various nonhuman animal species from each other (reviewed above), it seemed reasonable to presuppose that young infants would form a categorical representation for humans that would be exclusive of nonhuman animal species. However, Carey (1985) has argued that young children may develop a naive theory of biology by organizing their knowledge of animals around people; by this view, humans may function as a prototype for the category of animals, and nonhuman animals might actually be incorporated into a broadly inclusive categorical representation of humans.

To investigate whether young infants represent humans as a category that is differentiated from other animal species, Quinn and Eimas (1997b, 1998) familiarized a group of 3- and 4-month-old infants with photographic exemplars of 12 humans, both men and women, depicted in a variety of standing, running, or walking poses, and in earth tone (i.e., nonpastel) clothing. Black and white examples are shown in Figure 5.14. Each infant was then preference tested with a novel human paired with a cat, and a different novel human paired with a horse. Somewhat surprisingly, given the exclusive representations formed by infants for nonhuman animal species, the infants did not prefer novel cats or horses to novel humans. It is possible that an a priori preference for humans could have interfered with novel category preferences for cats and horses, but a control experiment pairing humans with cats and humans with horses over a series of spontaneous preference trials indicated that this was not the case.

FIGURE 5.14. Black and white examples of the human stimuli used in the investigations of Quinn and Eimas (1996a). In the initial categorization experiment of this series, infants familiarized with 12 humans (6 men intermixed with 6 women), did not prefer a cat or horse to a novel human.

The results of our initial experiments with humans were consistent with the idea that infants either had not formed a categorical representation for humans or that they had formed a categorical representation for humans that was broadly inclusive of both cats and horses. In a follow-up series of experiments, we obtained evidence for the latter explanation. Three- and 4 -month-olds were familiarized with 12 humans or 12 horses. They then were given three novel category preference tests in which a different novel member of the familiar category was paired with a novel member of the nonfamiliar category (horses or humans, respectively), a novel fish, and a novel car. The results, when considered in conjunction with results from an experiment designed to assess a priori preferences among the categories, indicated the following: Infants familiarized with humans had formed a categorical representation for humans that included novel humans, horses, and fish, but excluded cars, whereas infants familiarized with horses formed a categorical representation for horses that included novel horses, but excluded humans, fish, and cars.

The findings from the horse familiarization condition are consistent with our previous work demonstrating a high level of perceptual differentiation among nonhuman animal categories. By contrast, the outcome of broad inclusivity obtained in the human familiarization condition indicates that humans may form a special kind of category, and possibly, a cognitive reference point for infants (cf., Rosch, 1975). A categorical representation of this nature could behave as an attractor or perceptual magnet (Kuhl, 1991; Thelen & Smith, 1994) that acts to pull in stimuli with, at least, some common attributes (e.g., facial information). The findings demonstrating an asymmetry in the exclusivity of the categorical representations for humans and horses, moreover, are suggestive that Carey's (1985) results showing that young children classify animals on the basis of their similarity to people may have an early perceptual basis.

An additional experiment provided further evidence that infants represent humans differently from nonhuman animal species. In that 3- to 4-month-olds have greater exposure to human than to nonhuman animals, even if the set of humans is limited to parents, it is an arguable consequence that infants represent the highly familiar human exemplars individually. Also plausible is the view that the less frequently encountered animals are represented by means of a summary prototype (Quinn, 1987). To investigate these possibilities, one group of 3- to 4-month-olds was familiarized with 12 humans, and another with 12 cats. Both groups were administered two preference tests. A novel cat was paired with a novel human in one (the test of categorization), and a novel member of the familiar category was paired with a familiar member of the familiar category in the other (a test of exemplar memory). The results revealed a significant interaction: Infants familiarized with cats preferred a novel human to a novel cat, but not a novel cat to a familiar one, whereas infants familiarized with humans did not prefer a novel cat over a novel human, but did prefer a novel over a familiar human. Thus, the categorical representation formed by infants for humans included novel cats and was based on exemplars, whereas the representation for cats excluded novel humans and was based on a summary representation.

It becomes interesting to speculate on what may be responsible for human infants coming to represent humans differently from nonhuman animals during the first few months of life. Our view is that frequent encounters with several familiar humans may drive infants to become human "experts" (cf., Schyns, 1991; Tanaka & Taylor, 1991). Infants thus may develop exemplar or subordinate-like representations for humans in some n-dimensional space where each dimension represents quantitative variation of an "animal" attribute (e.g., eye separation, body length). One then might ask how an exemplar-based representation for humans comes to be "magnet-like" and attractive of nonhuman animals. In the n-dimensional space noted above, the exemplar nature of the human representation could be taken as a cluster of "exemplar" points defining a "human" region, rather than a single summary "prototype" point defining "cats" or "horses." Because of the size difference between the "human" region and the "cat" or "horse" point, the representation for humans would be more accepting of a range of values along each dimension and, thus, more likely to incorporate nonhuman animals. The formation of a categorical representation for humans that incorporates nonhuman animals may be an important part of the process of infants' developing a categorical representation for animals in general. From this perspective, humans may be the "glue" that provides the coherence for a categorical representation of animals.

Summary

Several important findings are emerging from the studies examining young infants' abilities to form categorical representations for pictorial exemplars of geometric forms, animal species (including humans), and furniture. First, infants appear capable of abstracting summary level (prototype-based) information from a group of perceptually similar exemplars. Second, infants can form both basic- and global-level categorical representations for natural animal species and furniture artifacts. The emergence of some of these categorical representations may be facilitated by spontaneous preferences for perceptual properties possessed by many or all members of the categories. In addition, the formation of at least some basic-level representations for individual animal species (e.g., cats vs. dogs) may be guided by selective attention to face and head information. Third, infants appear to form a broadly inclusive, exemplar-based, categorical representation for humans that incorporates exemplars from a number of nonhuman animal species. This magnet-like representation for humans may be the mechanism by which infants compile a categorical representation for animals more generally.

☐ Categorization of Spatial Relations

The evidence reviewed above suggests that young infants are able to form categorical representations for a variety of pictorial exemplars (animal species, furniture items, people) that are representative of the kinds of objects that undoubtedly will be encountered in the world at different points during development. A question of interest is whether young infants also can form categorical representations of physical space that are defined by the positional relations of objects in the environment. That is, do young infants form categorical representations for the spatial relations that hold between objects, such as above versus below, left versus right, between, and inside versus outside? Infants experience numerous objects in various locations and in many different spatial arrangements. The ability to form categorical representations for spatial relations early in development presumably would allow infants to experience these objects in organized spatial frameworks, rather than as spatially disconnected entities located in unrelated positions. The ability to form categorical representations for spatial relations also may be a cognitive prerequisite for successful performance in tasks such as cognitive map formation (Newcombe & Liben, 1982), map comprehension (Landau, 1986), word recognition (Caramazza & Hillis, 1990), object recognition (Biederman, 1987), and reasoning about physical relations such as collision, containment, and support (Baillargeon, 1995).

Categorical Representations of Above and Below

In an initial inquiry into whether young infants could form categorical representations of spatial relations, Quinn (1994) investigated whether 3-month-olds could form categorical representations for the above and below spatial relations between a dot and a horizontal bar. The familiarization and test stimuli for this study may be observed in Figures 5.15 and 5.16. As can be seen on the left side of panels a and b in Figure 5.15, infants in the "above" group were familiarized with four exemplars, each depicting a single dot in a different position above a horizontal bar. For half of the infants in the group, each dot appeared in the above left quadrant of the stimulus (panel a); for the other half, each dot was located in the above right quadrant of the stimulus (panel b). The infants were then administered a novel category preference test that paired two novel exemplars, one in which the dot was shifted to the right (panel a) or left (panel b) of the familiar exemplars, and one in which the dot was shifted below the reference bar.

The rationale for the experimental design of the Quinn (1994) above-below study is as follows. If infants form a categorical representation of "dot above bar," then the novel above exemplar should be recognized as familiar, whereas the novel below exemplar should be perceived as novel, and, therefore, preferred. If, however, infants do not form a categorical representation of "dot above bar," and represent only information about the dot or the bar, or represent information about the dot and the bar independently of each other (cf., Cohen & Younger, 1984), then neither test exemplar should be preferred. Panels a and b of Figure 5.16 display how the same procedure and rationale was used to test whether infants also could form a categorical representation of "dot below bar."

Infants in both the "dot above bar" and "dot below bar" conditions displayed a preference for the novel spatial category, a result consistent with the idea that they had formed categorical representations for the above and below relations between the dot and the horizontal bar. A subsequent control condition supported this interpretation by demonstrating that infants could detect the changes in the location of the dot that occurred during familiarization. In addition, it should be noted that the preferences for the novel spatial category cannot be attributed to generalization based on distance information, because the dot

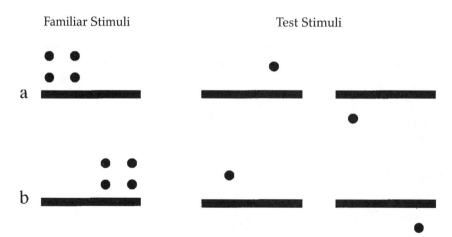

FIGURE 5.15. Panels a and b display familiarization stimuli (a composite of the four exemplars) and test stimuli used to investigate formation of the categorical representation "dot above bar." Three-month-old infants familiarized with above stimuli subsequently preferred a below test stimulus over a novel above test stimulus. From "The Categorization of Above and Below Spatial Relations by Young Infants," by P. C. Quinn, 1994, *Child Development, 65,* p. 59. Copyright 1994 by Society for Research in Child Development. Reprinted with permission.

appearing on the opposite side of the bar was moved the same distance away from the familiarization locations as the dot in the novel position on the same side of the bar.

Before reaching a definitive conclusion regarding infant performance in the above versus below categorization task, however, at least two alternative interpretations need to be considered. First, it simply could have been that infants responded preferentially to vertical (up-down) as opposed to horizontal (left-right) movement of the dot. Second, infants might have been encoding the dot locations categorically, but relative to an internal horizontal midline, rather than the externally available horizontal reference bar (cf., Huttenlocher, Newcombe, & Sandberg, 1994). That is, infants may have mentally bisected each stimulus

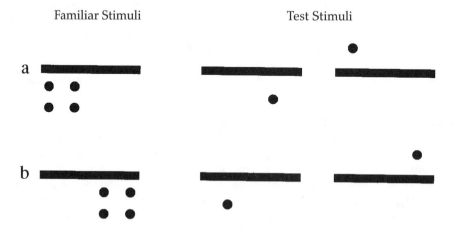

FIGURE 5.16. Panels a and b display familiarization stimuli (a composite of the four exemplars) and test stimuli used to investigate formation of the categorical representation "dot below bar." Three-month-old infants familiarized with below stimuli subsequently preferred an above test stimulus over a novel below test stimulus. From "The Categorization of Above and Below Spatial Relations by Young Infants," by P. C. Quinn, 1994, *Child Development, 65,* p. 60. Copyright 1994 by Society for Research in Child Development. Reprinted with permission.

into top and bottom halves and encoded the dot locations in relation to the line of bisection. To assess the validity of these alternative accounts, the initial categorization experiment was repeated, but, in this case, with stimuli that contained only the dot and not the horizontal reference bar. If infants performed in this control experiment as they did in the initial categorization experiment, then both the dot movement and internal bisection explanations would be supported. Alternatively, if infants divided their attention between the two test stimuli in this experiment, then the intepretation that infants had categorically represented the above and below relations in the initial experiment would be upheld. Infants in the no bar control did not prefer either test stimulus, thereby supporting the conclusion that infants had formed categorical representations of the dot's above and below relations with the horizontal reference bar.

☐ The Specific Versus Abstract Nature of Categorical Representations for Above and Below

One issue that Quinn (1994) did not address is whether young infants are able to form more abstract spatial relations for above and below that can be maintained independently of the particular objects depicting the relations. Children (at least from the age of 2½ under some circumstances; Deloache, Kolstad, & Anderson, 1991) and adults in cognitive activities such as object recognition, word recognition, and map learning experience various objects, object parts, symbols, and features in different spatial relations and are able to maintain their spatial concepts, despite the variation in the entities displaying the relations. In other words, children and adults are capable of encoding the equivalence of a spatial relation across contexts, despite changes in the particular identities or precise locations of the objects portraying the relation.

To determine whether the abilities of infants to categorize spatial relation information are functionally equivalent to those possessed by children and adults, Quinn, Cummins, Kase, Martin, and Weissman (1996) investigated whether 3- and 4-month-old infants could form categorical representations for above and below that were independent of the objects used to signal these relations. The first step was to replicate and extend the findings of Quinn (1994) to a new set of stimuli that displayed a diamond in different above and below positions relative to a horizontal bar which itself was composed of a row of square elements (shown in Figure 5.17). The Quinn (1994) results were replicated: Infants familiarized with above preferred below, and infants familiarized with below preferred above.

In a second experiment, Quinn et al. (1996) examined the effect of object variation on above-below categorization by repeating the familiarization procedure used in the first experiment but, in this instance, with four distinct shapes appearing above or below the bar. The shapes were randomly selected for each infant from among seven shapes shown to be discriminably different from each other in a control experiment: an arrow, a diamond, a dollar sign, a dot, the letter E, a plus sign, and a triangle. Infants were then preference tested as they were in the first experiment, but with the change that a novel shape in the familiar spatial relation was paired with the same shape in the novel spatial relation. The stimuli and design of this experiment may be observed in Figure 5.18. In contrast to the infants tested in the first experiment, the 3- and 4-month-olds tested in the object variation version of the above-below categorization task did not show a preference for the novel spatial category test stimulus, dividing their attention instead across both test stimuli. This result indicates that the 3- and 4-month-olds did not form more abstract categorical representations for above and below that existed independently of the particular objects signaling the relation. Apparently, the categorical representations formed by the young infants in the first experiment of Quinn et al. (1996) and Quinn (1994) specifically entailed the two objects depicting the relations: the dot or diamond, and the horizontal bar.

A third experiment conducted by Quinn et al. (1996) attempted to determine at what point during development infants will display an ability to categorically represent abstract spatial relations that are independent of the objects portraying these relations. The object variation version of the above-below categorization task thus was repeated but, this time, with a group of 6- to 7-month-olds. The older infants responded by preferring the novel spatial relation in the test phase, indicating that they were able to maintain their categorical representations for above and below, despite changes in the identity of the objects during both familiarization and test. The results from both age groups, when considered together, support the idea that categorical representations of spatial relations may initially be limited to objects depicting the relations, but that they later become more abstract so that various objects can be presented

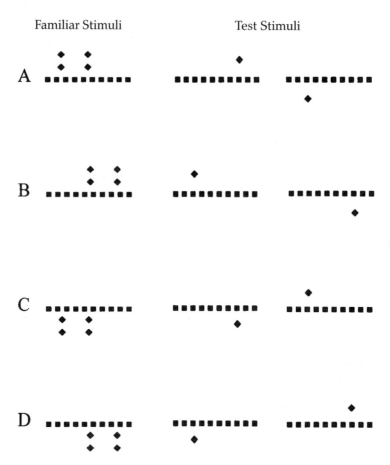

FIGURE 5.17. Panels A, B, C, and D display familiarization stimuli (a composite of the four exemplars) and test stimuli used to investigate formation of the categorical representations "diamond above bar" and "diamond below bar" in Quinn, Cummins, Kase, Martin, and Weissman (1996). Three- and 4-month-old infants familiarized with a diamond located in different locations, but consistently above and below the reference bar, subsequently preferred a test stimulus in which the diamond was located in a novel spatial relation with the bar over a test stimulus in which the diamond was located in a novel position, but in the familiar spatial relation with the bar.

in the same relation and the equivalence of the relation is maintained despite this variation. In this respect, the spatial categorization abilities of the 6- and 7-month-olds may be more like those of children and adults, although it is possible that even the abilities of the older infants might have broken down had the identity of the reference bar also changed from trial to trial. Of current interest is whether the developmental trend from specific to abstract spatial relations is driven by biological maturation, environmental experience, or both.

Several related questions were left unanswered by the Quinn et al. (1996) investigation. For example, why did object variation disrupt the spatial categorization performance of the 3- and 4-month-old infants? Also what representation(s) did infants form in the object variation version of the spatial categorization task? Furthermore, is it the case that young infants simply cannot form abstract categorical representations for above versus below under a variety of experimental conditions or that they did not form such representations under one particular set of experimental conditions? One possibility is that the trial-to-trial changes in object identity in the object variation version of the above-below categorization task recruited infant attention away from the spatial nature of the task. That is, object variation may have prompted the infant to focus attention on the objects, at the expense of processing the spatial relation between the

Familiar Stimuli   Test Stimuli

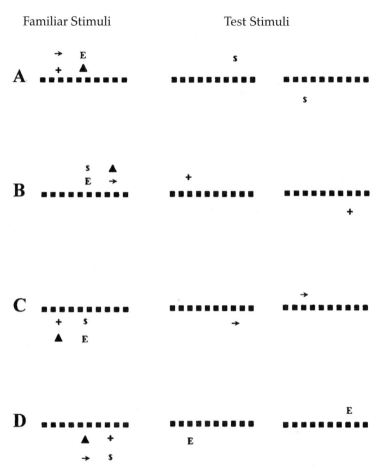

FIGURE 5.18. Panels A, B, C, and D display familiarization stimuli (a composite of the four exemplars) and test stimuli used in the object variation version of the above-below categorization task in Quinn, Cummins, Kase, Martin, and Weissman (1996). Six- and 7-month-olds, but not 3- and 4-month olds, familiarized with stimuli depicting different objects above or below the bar, subsequently preferred a test stimulus in which a novel object was depicted in a novel spatial relation over a test stimulus in which the same novel object was depicted in a novel location, but in the familiar spatial relation.

objects and the bar. This possibility is consistent with arguments that independent neural systems for processing "what" and "where" information may compete for general attentional capacity (Vecera & Farah, 1994). Reasoning from within such a framework, one way of increasing the likelihood that infants will process information about both the objects and the reference bar, and the spatial relation between them, is to provide the infants with additional familiarization experience. To this end, Quinn, Polly, Dobson, and Narter (1998) repeated the object variation version of the above-below categorization task with 3- and 4-month-olds but, in this case, increased the length of each familiarization trial by 10 seconds (from 15 to 25 s). However, despite the added encoding time, infants still failed to display a reliable preference for the novel spatial category.

There is a rather different and more "functionalist" interpretation of young infant performance in the Quinn et al. (1996) object variation version of the above-below categorization task. While it is possible that infants are not representing any information regarding the spatial relation of the objects and the reference bar, it also is possible that infants may be representing the spatial relations between specific objects and the reference bar. That is, infants could be forming individual representations for "arrow above bar," "plus sign above bar," "E above bar," and "triangle above bar," but not join these representations together into a more abstract representation of "thing above bar" or "above." By this account, spatial categorization may serve primarily as an aid to spatial memory during early development. For young infants, what may adaptively be most important is to remember the location of one particular object relative to another specific object (e.g., mobile above crib bars). It may only be later in development, and for higher order cognitive activities such as reading and map comprehension, that the ability to form more abstract categorical representations comes to be functional. According to this interpretation, the ability to form a specific categorical spatial representation for object 1 above object 2 may have developmental primacy over the ability to maintain a more abstract spatial representation for objects 1-n above objects 2-n (see Cohen & Oakes, 1993, for similar arguments in the development of infant perception of causal relations).

To test the developmental primacy of encoding specific spatial relations, Quinn et al. (1998) repeated the object variation version of the above-below categorization with a group of 3- and 4-month-olds, but now with one of the familiar shapes appearing above and below the bar during the preference test phase. The stimuli and design of this study may be viewed in Figure 5.19. Infants responded in this version of the object variation task by preferring the novel spatial relation, indicating that the younger infants are en-

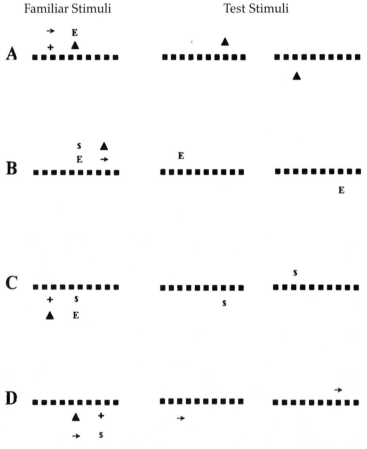

FIGURE 5.19. Panels A, B, C, and D display familiarization stimuli (a composite of the four exemplars) and test stimuli used to investigate formation of specific categorical representations for above and below in the object variation version of the spatial categorization task used by Quinn, Polly, Dobson, and Narter (1998). Three- and 4-month-old infants familiarized with stimuli depicting different objects above or below the bar, subsequently preferred a test stimulus depicting one of the familiar objects in a novel spatial relation over a test stimulus in which the same familiar object was depicted in a novel location, but in the familiar spatial relation.

coding the spatial relation between the objects and the bar during familiarization. However, based on the difference in performance on the two types of preference tests (familiar object vs. novel object), the younger infants are not generalizing their familiarization to a novel object depicted in the same spatial relation. The younger infant's categorical representation of above and below information thus is limited to the particular objects depicting the above and below relations and is not extended to novel objects depicting those same relations. This manner of encoding spatial information, while deficient or immature in its abstractness, may be adaptively sufficient for the primary problem that a spatial memory system must confront; namely, remembering the location of an object previously experienced relative to other objects previously experienced.

Summary

The evidence reviewed indicates that infants from 3 months of age have the ability to categorically represent at least some spatial relations such as above and below (see also Behl-Chadha & Eimas, 1995, for evidence that infants can form specific categorical representations for left vs. right). At 3 and 4 months of age, these spatial representations appear to be tied to the particular objects presented but, by 6 to 7 months of age, categorical representations of spatial information can be more abstract and extended to novel objects depicting a familiar spatial relation. Future work should focus on whether young infants form categorical representations for possibly more complex spatial relations such as between and inside versus outside, and whether a common specific-to-abstract developmental trend is observed for representations of all spatial relations.

☐ Conclusion

Since the writings of Piaget (1952), theorists of early perceptual-cognitive development have debated the question of "how to build a baby" (Carey, 1985; Elman et al., 1996; Karmiloff-Smith, 1992; Keil, 1989; Mandler, 1988, 1992; Quinn & Eimas, 1996b, 1997a; Rutkowska, 1993; Spelke, 1994). What mechanisms and knowledge does one build into the infant? What structure is available in the environment? The approach taken in the present chapter has been to document the representations for objects and their spatial relations that can emerge from a young infant's adherence to fundamental organizational or grouping principles in combination with certain inherent preferences or biases.

We have observed that coherent representations for individual shapes may develop through the application of Gestalt principles such as similarity, good continuation, and closure. In the more complex case of viewing stimulus patterns consisting of overlapping contours, the deployment of Gestalt principles may need to be guided by preferences for specific stimulus features such as curvature. Spontaneous preferences for particular stimulus features may dictate the location of a complex pattern where the infant will begin the complementary processes of parsing and organization. Attention to regions of discontinuity in stimulus patterns also may facilitate the detection of object boundaries.

The ability to use perceptual similarity to group individual elements of a single visual pattern may be extended to the formation of categorical representations for multiple stimulus patterns presented over time. Extraction of regularities from a set of exemplars and summarizing those regularities by means of a prototype representation may occur for stimulus classes such as geometric forms, nonhuman animal species, and furniture items. Just as the formation of coherent representations for individual patterns appears to be guided by spontaneous preferences, so also does the formation of categorical representations for groups of patterns. Differential salience of textural markings, global shape, and particular parts are likely to play a strong facilitative role in the categorical differentiation of a number of animal species and furniture items. In addition, an inherent preference to attend to and process facial information may underlie much of our ability to pick out conspecifics, categorically differentiate among certain animal species, and form even more global categorical separations marked by face presence versus absence (e.g., mammals vs. furniture). Finally, differential experience with humans versus other categories of stimulation may facilitate a kind of representational magnification for humans, with the consequence that the representation for humans becomes simultaneously exemplar based and magnet-like.

In addition to the grouping of objects into categorical representations, at least some of the spatial relations in which objects are located relative to each other are processed categorically. Initially, categorical representations for spatial relation information appear to be concrete and specific and, with development, become more clearly abstract and conceptual-like. This specific-to-abstract developmental trajectory may be measured against the spatial tasks that must be mastered over time: at first, remembering the locations of objects relative to each other, and later on, reading and map comprehension.

It would seem that a considerable degree of coherence and order emerges in the application and reapplication of basic tendencies to group elements of objects to form perceptual wholes, to group multiple objects into perceptual categories, and to group the spatial relations in which those objects appear into categories like above and below. Nevertheless, despite the perceptual and conceptual stability that can be achieved by the deployment of these basic processes, it is obvious that children and adults come to learn more about animal species (including humans), furniture items, and objects in general than can be found on their surfaces. It also is clear that children and adults can reason about large-scale spaces involving buildings, physical landmarks, and barriers in ways that infants likely are not capable. Exactly how this later acquisition of knowledge occurs and drives early representations for objects and space to higher levels of richness and abstraction remains to be explicated in detail (for differing views, see Carey, 1985; Elman et al., 1996; Mandler, 1992; Karmiloff-Smith, 1992; Keil, 1989; Quinn & Eimas, 1996b, 1997a). However, it surely is the case that an accounting of the full course of conceptual development cannot proceed without an understanding of its earliest beginnings, and it is in this respect that the present chapter makes its contribution.

☐ References

Arnheim, R. (1974). *Art and visual perception: A psychology of the creative eve*. Berkeley: University of California Press.

Atkinson, J., Braddick, O., & Moar, K. (1977). Development of contrast sensitivity over the first 3 months of life. *Vision Research, 17,* 1037–1044.

Baillargeon, R. (1995). A model of physical reasoning in infancy. In C. Rovee-Collier & L. P. Lipsitt (Eds.), *Advances in infancy research* (Vol. 9, pp. 305–371).

Banks, M. S., & Ginsburg, M. S. (1985). Infant visual preferences: A review and new theoretical treatment. In H. W. Reese (Ed.), *Advances in child development and behavior* (Vol. 19, pp. 207–246). New York: Academic Press.

Banks, M. S., & Salapatek, P. (1978). Acuity and contrast sensitivity in l-, 2-, and 3-month-old human infants. *Investigative Ophthalmology and Visual Science, 17,* 361–365.

Banks, M. S., & Salapatek, P. (1981). Infant pattern vision: A new approach based on the contrast sensitivity function. *Journal of Experimental Child Psychology, 31,* 1–45.

Beck, J. (1982), Textural segmentation. In J. Beck (Ed.), *Organization and representation* (pp. 285–317). Hillsdale, NJ: Erlbaum.

Behl-Chadha, G. (1996). Basic-level and superordinate-like categorical representations in early infancy. *Cognition, 60,* 105–141.

Behl-Chadha, G., & Eimas, P. D. (1995). Infant categorization of left-right spatial relations. *British Journal of Developmental Psychology, 13,* 69–79.

Behl-Chadha, G., Eimas, P. D., & Quinn, P. C. (1995, March). *Perceptually driven superordinate categorization by young infants*. Paper presented at the meeting of the Society for Research in Child Development, Indianapolis, IN.

Bergen, J. R., & Adelson, E. H. (1988). Early vision and texture perception. *Nature, 333,* 363–364.

Biederman, I. (1987). Recognition-by-components: A theory of human image understanding. *Psychological Review, 94,* 115–147.

Bomba, P. C., & Siqueland, E. R. (1983). The nature and structure of infant form categories. *Journal of Experimental Child Psychology, 35,* 294–328.

Bomba, P. C., Eimas, P. D., Siqueland, E. R., & Miller, J. L. (1984). Contextual effects in infant visual perception. *Perception, 13,* 369–376.

Bruner, J. S., Olver, R. R., & Greenfield, P. M. (1966). *Studies in cognitive growth*. New York: Wiley.

Caramazza, A., & Hillis, A. E. (1990). Levels of representation, coordinate frames, and unilateral neglect. *Cognitive Neuropsychology, 7,* 391–445.

Carey, S. (1985). *Conceptual change in childhood*. Cambridge, MA: MIT Press.

Catherwood, D., Green, V., Skoien, P., & Holt, C. (1995). The cat among the pigeons: Categorical "pop-out" in infant visual attention. *Australian Journal of Psychology, 47,* 1–7.

Cohen, L. B., & Oakes, L. M. (1993). How infants perceive a simple causal event. *Developmental Psychology, 29,* 421–433.

Cohen, L. B., & Strauss, M. S. (1979). Concept acquisition in the human infant. *Child Development, 50,* 419–424.

Cohen, L. B., & Younger, B. A. (1984). Infant perception of angular relations. In *Infant Behavior and Development, 7,* 37–47.

Colombo, J., Laurie, C., Martelli, T., & Hartig, B. (1984). Stimulus context and infant orientation discrimination. *Journal of Experimental Child Psychology, 37*, 576–586.

Colombo, J., Mitchell, D. W., Coldren, J. T., & Freeseman, L. J. (1991). Individual differences in infant visual attention: Are short lookers faster processors or feature processors? *Child Development, 62*, 1247–1257.

Colombo, J., Ryther, J. S., Frick, J. E., & Gifford, J. J. (1995). Visual pop-out in infants: Evidence for preattentive search in 3- and 4-month-olds. *Psychonomic Bulletin and Review, 2*, 266–268.

DeLoache, J. S., Kolstad, V., & Anderson, K. (1991). Physical similarity and young children's understanding of scale models. *Child Development, 62*, 111–126.

Eimas, P. D., & Quinn, P. C. (1994). Studies on the formation of perceptually based basic-level categories in young infants. *Child Development, 65*, 903–917.

Elman, J. L., Bates, E. A., Johnson, M. H. Karmiloff-Smith, A., Parisi, D., & Plunkett, K. (1996). *Rethinking innateness: A connectionist perspective on development.* Cambridge, MA: MIT Press.

Enns, J. (1986). Seeing textons in context. *Perception and Psychophysics, 39*, 143–147.

Enns, J. T., & Prinzmetal, W. (1984). The role of redundancy in the object-line effect. *Perception and Psychophysics, 35*, 22–32.

Fagan, J. F. (1978). Facilitation of infants' recognition memory. *Child Development, 49*, 1066–1075.

Fantz, R. L. (1964). Visual experience in infants: Decreased attention to familiar patterns relative to novel ones. *Science, 164*, 668–670.

Fantz, R. L., Fagan, J. F., III, & Miranda, S. B. (1975). Early visual selectivity as a function of pattern variables, previous experience, age from birth and conceptual and cognitive deficit. In L. B. Cohen & P. Salapatek (Eds.), *Infant perception: From sensation to cognition: Vol. 1. Basic visual processes* (pp. 249–345). New York: Academic Press.

Farah, M. J. (1990). *Visual agnosia: Disorders of object recognition and what they tell us about normal vision.* Cambridge, MA: MIT Press.

Ginsburg, A. P. (1986). Spatial filtering and visual form perception. In K. R Boff, L. Kaufman, & J. P. Thomas (Eds.), *Handbook of perception and human performance* (Vol. 2, pp. 1–41). New York: Wiley.

Hebb, D. 0. (1949). *The organization of behavior.* New York: Wiley.

Helson, H. (1933). The fundamental propositions of Gestalt psychology. *Psychological Review, 40*, 13–32.

Homa, D., & Chambliss, D. (1975). The relative contributions of common and distinctive information on the abstraction from ill-defined categories. *Journal of Experimental Psychology: Human Learning and Memory, 3*, 375–385.

Huttenlocher, J., Newcombe, N., & Sandberg, E. H. (1994). The coding of spatial location in young children. *Cognitive Psychology, 27*, 115–147.

Johnson, M. H., & Morton, J. (1991). *Biology and cognitive development.* Oxford, England: Blackwell.

Julesz, B. (1981). Textons, the elements of texture perception, and their interactions. *Nature, 290*, 91–97.

Julesz, B. (1984). Toward an axiomatic theory of preattentive vision. In G. W. Edelman, W. E. Gall, & M. W. Cowan (Eds.), *Dynamic aspects of neocortical function* (pp. 585-612). New York: Wiley.

Karmiloff-Smith, A. (1992). *Beyond modularity.* Cambridge, MA: MIT Press.

Keil, F. C. (1989). *Concepts, kinds, and cognitive development.* Cambridge, MA: MIT Press.

Kellman, P. J. (1993). Kinematic foundations of infant visual perception. In C. Granrud (Ed.), *Carnegie Mellon Symposia on Cognition: Visual perception and cognition in infancy* (pp. 121–173). Hillsdale, NJ: Erlbaum.

Kellman, P. J. (1996). The origins of object perception. In R. Gelman and T. Kit-Fong Au (Eds.), *Perceptual and cognitive development* (pp. 3–48). San Diego: Academic Press.

Koffka, K. (1935). *Principles of Gestalt psychology.* New York: Harcourt, Brace & World.

Kohler, W. (1929). *Gestalt psychology.* New York: Horace Liveright.

Kuhl, P. K. (1991). Human adults and human infants show a "perceptual magnet effect" for the prototypes of speech categories, monkeys do not. *Perception and Psychophysics, 50*, 93–107.

Landau. B. (1986). Early map use as an unlearned ability. *Cognition, 22*, 201–233.

Mandler, J. M. (1988). How to build a baby: On the development of an accessible representational system. *Cognitive Development, 3*, 113–136.

Mandler, J. M. (1992). How to build a baby: II. Conceptual primitives. *Psychological Review, 99*, 587–604.

Mandler, J. M., & McDonough, L. (1993). Concept formation in infancy. *Cognitive Development, 8*, 291–318.

McClelland, J. L., & Miller, J. (1979). Structural factors in figure perception. *Perception and Psychophysics, 26*, 221–229.

Mervis, C. B. (1987). Child-basic object categories and early development. In U. Neisser (Ed.), *Concepts and conceptual development* (pp. 201–233). Cambridge, England: Cambridge University Press.

Munakata, Y., McClelland, J. L., Johnson, M. H., & Siegler, R. S. (1997). Rethinking infant knowledge: Toward an adaptive process account of successes and failures in object permanence tasks. *Psychological Review, 104*, 686–713.

Navon, D. (1977). Forest before trees: The precedence of global features in visual perceptions. *Cognitive Psychology, 9*, 353–383.

Newcombe, N., & Liben, L. S. (1982). Barrier effects in the cognitive maps of children and adults. *Journal of Experimental Child Psychology, 34*, 46–58.

Nothdurft, H. C. (1990). Texton segregation by associated differences in global and local luminance distribution. *Proceedings of the Royal Society of London, B239,* 295–320.

Oakes, L. M., Madole, K. L., & Cohen, L. B. (1991). Infants' object examining: Habituation and categorization. *Cognitive Development, 6,* 377–392.

Peterson, M. A. (1994). Object recognition processes can and do operate before figure-ground organization. *Current Directions in Psychological Science, 3,* 105–111.

Piaget, J. (1952). *The origins of intelligence in children.* New York: Norton.

Pomerantz, J., & Pristach, E. A. (1989). Emergent features, attention, and perceptual glue in visual form perception. *Journal of Experimental Psychology: Human Perception and Performance, 15,* 635–649.

Pomerantz, J. R., Sager, L. C., & Stoever, R. J. (1977). Perception of wholes and of their component parts: Some configural superiority effects. *Journal of Experimental Psychology: Human Perception and Performance, 15,* 635–649.

Posner, M. I., & Keele, S. W. (1970). Retention of abstract ideas. *Journal of Experimental Psychology, 83,* 304–308.

Quinn, P. C. (1987). The categorical representation of visual pattern information by young infants. *Cognition, 27,* 145–179.

Quinn, P. C. (1994). The categorization of above and below spatial relations by young infants. *Child Development, 65,* 58–69.

Quinn, P. C. (1998). Object and spatial categorization in young infants: "What" and "where" in early visual perception. In A. M. Slater (Ed.), *Perceptual development: Visual, auditory, and speech perception in infancy* (pp. 131–165), East Sussex, UK: Psychology Press.

Quinn, P. C., & Bhatt, R S. (1998). Visual pop-out in young infants: Convergent evidence and an extension. *Infant Behavior and Development, 21,* 273–288.

Quinn, P. C., & Bomba, P. C. (1986). Evidence of a general category of oblique orientations in four-month-old infants. *Journal of Experimental Child Psychology, 42,* 345–354.

Quinn, P. C., Brown, C. R., & Streppa, M. L. (1997). Perceptual organization of complex visual configurations by young infants. *Infant Behavior and Development, 20,* 35–46.

Quinn, P. C., Burke, S., & Rush, A. (1993). Part-whole perception in early infancy: Evidence for perceptual grouping produced by lightness similarity. *Infant Behavior and Development, 16,* 19–42.

Quinn, P. C., Cummins, M., Kase, J., Martin, E., & Weissman, S. (1996). Development of categorical representations for above and below spatial relations in 3- to 7-month-old infants. *Developmental Psychology, 32,* 942–950.

Quinn, P. C., & Eimas, P. D. (1986a). On categorization in early infancy. *Merrill-Palmer Quarterly, 32,* 331–363.

Quinn, P. C., & Eimas, P. D. (1986b). Pattern-line effect and units of visual processing in infants. *Infant Behavior and Development, 9,* 57–70.

Quinn, P. C., & Eimas, P. D. (1996a). Perceptual cues that permit categorical differentiation of animal species by infants. *Journal of Experimental Child Psychology, 63,* 189–211.

Quinn, P. C., & Eimas, P. D. (1996b). Perceptual organization and categorization in young infants. In C. Rovee-Collier & L. P. Lipsitt (Eds.), *Advances in infancy research* (Vol. 10, pp. 1–36), Norwood, NJ: Ablex.

Quinn, P. C., & Eimas, P, D. (1997a). A reexamination of the perceptual to conceptual shift in mental representations. *Review of General Psychology, 1,* 271–287.

Quinn, P. C., & Eimas, P. D. (1997b, April). *Is the young infant's categorical representation of humans a perceptual magnet for other animal species?* Paper presented at the meeting of the Society for Research in Child Development, Washington, DC.

Quinn, P. C., & Eimas, P. D. (1998). Evidence for a global categorical representation of humans by young infants. *Journal of Experimental Child Psychology, 69,* 151–174.

Quinn, P. C., Eimas, P. D., & Rosenkrantz, S. L. (1993). Evidence for representations of perceptually similar natural categories by 3- and 4-month-old infants. *Perception, 22,* 463–475.

Quinn, P. C., & Johnson, M. H. (1996). The emergence of perceptual category representations during early development: A connectionist analysis. In G. W. Cottrell (Ed.), *Proceedings of the Eighteenth Annual Conference of the Cognitive Science Society* (pp. 638–643). Mahwah, NJ: Erlbaum.

Quinn, P. C., & Johnson, M. H. (1997). The emergence of perceptual category representations in young infants: A connectionist analysis. *Journal of Experimental Child Psychology, 66,* 236–263.

Quinn, P. C., Polly, J. L., Dobson, V., & Narter, D. B. (1998, April). *Categorical representation of specific versus abstract above and below spatial relations in 3- to-4-month-old infants.* Paper presented at the International Conference on Infant Studies, Atlanta, GA.

Quinn, P. C., Siqueland, E. R., & Bomba, P, C, (1985). Delayed recognition memory for orientation by human infants. *Journal of Experimental Child Psychology, 40,* 293–303.

Rakison, D. H., & Butterworth, G. E. (1998). Infants' use of object parts in early categorization. *Developmental Psychology, 34,* 49–62.

Rosch, E. (1975). Cognitive reference points. *Cognitive Psychology, 7,* 532–547.

Rosch, E., Mervis, C. B., Gray, W. D., Johnson, D. M., & Boyes-Braem, P. (1976). Basic objects in natural categories. *Cognitive Psychology, 7,* 573–605.

Rovee-Collier, C., Hankins, E. M., & Bhatt, R. S. (1992). Textons, visual pop-out effects and object recognition in infancy. *Journal of Experimental Psychology: General, 121,* 436–446.

Rutkowska, J. C. (1993). *The computational infant: Looking for developmental cognitive neuroscience.* New York: Harvester Wheatsheaf.

Schyns, P. G. (1991). A modular neural network model of concept acquisition. *Cognitive Science, 15,* 461–508.

Schyns. P. G., Goldstone, R. L, Thibaut, J. P. (1998). The development of features in object concepts. *Behavioral and Brain Sciences, 21,* 1–54.

Slater, A. M. (1995). Visual perception and memory at birth. In C. Rovee-Collier & L. P. Lipsitt (Eds.), *Advances in infancy research* (Vol. 9, pp. 107–162). Norwood, NJ: Ablex.

Smith, E. E., & Medin, D. L. (1981). *Categories and concepts.* Cambridge, MA: Harvard University Press.

Spelke, E. S. (1982). Perceptual knowledge of objects in infancy. In J. Mehler, M. Garrett, & E. Walker (Eds.), *Perspectives on mental representation* (pp. 409–430). Hillsdale, NJ: Erlbaum.

Spelke, E. S. (1994). Initial knowledge: Six suggestions. *Cognition, 50,* 431–445.

Spelke, E. S., Breinlinger, K., Jacobson, K., & Phillips, A. (1993). Gestalt relations and object perception: A developmental study. *Perception, 22,* 1483–1501.

Spelke, E. S., Gutheil, G., & Van de Walle, G. (1995). The development of object perception. In S. M. Kosslyn & D. N. Osherson (Eds.), *An invitation to cognitive science* (2nd ed., Vol. 2, pp. 297–330). Cambridge, MA: MIT Press.

Tanaka, J. W., & Taylor, M. (1991). Object categorization and expertise: Is the basic level in the eye of the beholder? *Cognitive Psychology, 23,* 457–482.

Thelen, E., & Smith, L. B. (1994). *A dynamic systems approach to the development of cognition and action.* Cambridge, MA: MIT Press.

Treisman, A. (1986a). Features and objects in visual processing. *Scientific American, 255,* 114B–125B.

Treisman, A. (1986b). Properties, parts and objects. In K. Boff, L. Kaufman, & J. Thomas (Eds.), *Handbook of perception and human performance* (Vol. 2, pp. 1–70). New York: Wiley,

Treisman, A. (1988). Features and objects: The fourteenth Bartlett Memorial Lecture. *The Quarterly Journal of Experimental Psychology, 40A,* 201–237.

Treisman, A. (1993). The perception of features and objects. In A. Baddeley & L. Weiskrantz (Eds.), *Attention: Selection, awareness, and control* (pp. 5–35). Oxford, England: Clarendon Press.

Treisman, A., & Gelade, G. (1980). A feature integration theory of attention. *Cognitive Psychology, 12,* 97–136.

Treisman, A., & Gormican, S. (1988). Feature analysis in early vision: Evidence from search asymmetries. *Psychological Review, 95,* 15–48.

Treisman, A., Sykes, M., & Gelade, G, (1977). Selective attention and stimulus integration. In S. Dornic (Ed.), *Attention and performance* (Vol. 6, pp. 333–361). Mahwah, NJ: Erlbaum.

Trick, L. M., & Enns, J. T. (1997). Clusters precede shapes in perceptual organization. *Psychological Science, 8,* 124–129.

Vecera, S. P., & Farah, M. J. (1994). Does visual attention select objects or locations? *Journal of Experimental Psychology: General, 123,* 146–160.

Vygotsky, L. S. (1962). *Thought and language* (E. Hanfmann & G. Vacar, Trans.). Cambridge, MA: MIT Press. (Original work published 1934)

Waxman, S. R., & Markow, D. B. (1995). Words as invitations to form categories: Evidence from 12- to 13-month-old infants. *Cognitive Psychology, 29,* 257–302.

Wertheimer, M. (1958). Principles of perceptual organization (M. Wertheimer, Trans.). In D. C, Beardslee & M. Wertheimer (Eds.), *Readings in perception* (pp. 115–135). Princeton, NJ: Van Nostrand. (Original work published 1923)

Williams, A., & Weisstein, N. (1978). Line segments are perceived better in coherent contexts than alone: An object-line effect. *Memory and Cognition, 6,* 85–90.

Wolfe, J. M., Friedman-Hill, S. R., Stewart, M. I., & O'Connell, K. M. (1992). The role of categorization in visual search for orientation. *Journal of Experimental Psychology: Human Perception and Performance, 18,* 34–49.

Xu, F., & Carey, S. (1996). Infants' metaphysics: The case of numerical identity. *Cognitive Psychology, 30,* 111–153.

Younger, B. A. (1990). Infants' detection of correlation among feature categories. *Child Development, 61,* 614–620.

6
CHAPTER

Linda P. Acredolo
Susan W. Goodwyn
Karen D. Horobin
Yvonne D. Emmons

The Signs and Sounds
of Early Language Development

☐ Introduction

When AJ was about 14-months-old, he and his mother spotted a spider. AJ caught his mother's eye, put his two index fingers together and proceeded to twist them back and forth. His mother responded "You're right, that IS a spider," whereupon AJ brought his shoe-clad foot directly down on the spider, smashing it flat. Before his surprised mother could react, AJ's face broke out in a big grin and he began vigorously moving his hand, palm down, side to side in front of him. His mother, appreciating her son's budding sense of humor, responded with a laugh: "You're right! It certainly IS allgone!"

What are we to make of these behaviors? Is this a deaf child who has been taught to communicate with sign language? Or, perhaps AJ has Down's syndrome or autism and his parents see, in sign language, a way around serious language difficulties (e.g., Abrahamson, Cavallo, & McCluer, 1985; McDade, Simpson, & Booth, 1980). The answer is "no" to all of these. Instead, what we have described is a normal, hearing infant who has been encouraged to use simple body movements as symbols in order to convey important needs and ideas to the adults around him without having to wait until he actually learns to say the words for "spider" and "allgone." Research on what we call "symbolic gesturing" over the past 15 years has revealed that infants and toddlers are capable of learning many such nonverbal symbols and, in so doing, become active participants in conversations with the important people around them. They use gestural symbols to name animals during picture book reading (e.g., fingers flapping for "butterfly"), they use gestural symbols to make requests (e.g., a knob-turning gesture for "out"), they use gestural symbols to draw attention to things they see (e.g., arms spread on either side for "airplane") , and they use gestural symbols to describe things in their environment (e.g., blowing for "hot" concrete).

But, what is the significance of symbolic gesturing for the study of language development? Is this just an interesting phenomenon that occurs among a few infants, yet remains tangential to the study of "normal" language development? In this chapter, we argue entirely to the contrary, and intend to show that the ease and flexibility infants demonstrate in acquiring symbolic gestures, and the wide range of functions for which they use them, can reveal much about language development if we know how to ask the right questions. Framing the questions, and looking at how symbolic gesturing can be used to provide new ways of seeking answers, is the organizing theme of this chapter. Our focus will be on early language learning, from the preverbal period when infants are just beginning to comprehend words until the onset of the earliest combinations of symbols.

A Historical Perspective on the Puzzle of Language Development

Understanding how infants become initiated into the spoken language of their culture is like trying to solve a complex jigsaw puzzle with many different pieces, all of which must fit together in some coherent way for us to grasp the whole picture. Historically, the pieces of this puzzle have been examined in relative isolation from each other in the search for an empirically supportable, theoretical framework. The 1950s mark the point when the study of child language was launched, a by-product of the dramatic shift from behaviorist claims that language is acquired through environmental reinforcement toward Chomsky's argument that language acquisition (particularly, grammatical regularity) must be constrained by innate structures (Chomsky, 1959, 1965). There followed several landmark studies documenting early grammatical development (e.g., Braine, 1963; Brown & Bellugi, 1964; McNeill, 1966; Miller & Ervin, 1964). In the following decade, as the shortcomings of a purely syntactic approach to language development were recognized, researchers became interested in the semantics of early child language (e.g., Bloom, 1970; Kernan, 1970; Schlesinger, 1971; Slobin, 1973).

These early studies of the different meanings conveyed by simple utterances in context (such as Bloom's now famous [1970] "mommy sock" example) soon revealed something we have come to take very much for granted: that children beginning to acquire language understand much more than they can say. This realization dovetailed nicely with a growing appreciation for the application of Piagetian constructivism to language acquisition (Piaget, 1951) and, hence, began a search for the cognitive underpinnings of language in the relationship between early words and sensorimotor achievements (particularly, object permanence), and the advent of symbolic functioning (e.g., McNeill, 1970; Slobin, 1973). In addition, and partly in reaction to Chomsky's claim that environmental input would never be sufficient in itself to ensure language acquisition, there was a dramatic surge in studies looking at the linguistic and social scaffolds available to support infant communicative efforts (e.g., Bruner, 1974; Ervin-Tripp & Mitchell-Kernan, 1977). This trend toward examining the social and environmental context in which language develops was accompanied by a growing recognition of the critical role played by the pragmatic functions of language (Austin, 1962; Searle, 1969).

As the unit of analysis shifted from the individual to the dyad engaged in the joint construction of meaning, the search was for even earlier origins of linguistic competence in the establishment of joint reference (e.g., Bates, Camaioni, & Volterra, 1975; Harding & Golinkoff, 1979) and the preverbal "proto-conversations" (Bullowa, 1979; Stern, 1977) of young infants engaged in social interactions with caregivers (e.g., Bruner, 1974). Each decade seemed to bring a new perspective, so that we now have many different pieces of the language puzzle being examined from a rich variety of theoretical specializations (e.g., syntactic, cognitive, functional, pragmatic, biological, connectionist).

How Symbolic Gestures Fit into the Language Puzzle

Clearly, the study of child language has made impressive progress over the past 40 years, but, paradoxically, it seems that the more we have learned about the multifaceted puzzle of acquiring a first language, the further we seem to be from being able to align all of its pieces. Like the proverbial blind men, each exploring different parts of an elephant's body, we have an incomplete and potentially false picture when we examine the different aspects of language development in isolation from each other. The need to view a complex development like language as the outcome of multiple interacting dynamic systems (Thelen, 1991; Thelen & Smith, 1994) has become particularly clear to us in studying how infants acquire and use symbolic gestures in comparison with vocal words. Indeed we believe that looking at language acquisition from the point of view of an infant using symbolic gestures can offer some unique insights about the self-organizing, dynamic interplay of the systems underlying the achievement of spoken language.

For example, documenting the productive and creative ways in which symbolic gestures are used in everyday settings makes it very apparent that, from the infant's perspective, many pieces of the language puzzle already must be in position before vocal words even have much of a presence in the developing communication system. That is, in order to comprehend and produce gestures symbolically, in the ways we subsequently will describe, an infant must already have, at minimum: (a) an appreciation of joint reference and the two-way sharing of information, (b) the motivation and intent to communicate, and (c) a means of representing decontextualized concepts. What does not need to be in place for symbolic gestures to be used communicatively is control over the phonological and articulatory components of speech; which, of course, is the major difference between symbolic gestures and symbolic words. This piece of the language puzzle has suffered relative neglect, to the disadvantage of the field, in descriptions and explanations of the central phenomena in early language acquisition. Hence, one of the goals of this chapter is to show how a close examination of the parallels and distinctions between the development of symbolic gestures versus words can help us understand some of the ways in which the phonological system may act as a "control parameter" (Thelen & Smith, 1994; Thelen & Ulrich, 1991) in linguistic development.

Organization of the Chapter

The chapter is organized into four main sections. We begin by providing a summary of the major studies carried out by Acredolo and Goodwyn over the past 15 years, documenting the extent and richness of the database on which ideas presented in this chapter have been developed. We go on to summarize research documenting the complexity of phonological development and the immense effort involved on the part of the infant in achieving control over the mouth, tongue, respiratory, and other articulatory apparatuses in order to vocalize words. We then discuss three central issues of early language development that have received extensive attention and outline our ideas, and evidence, for the ways in which symbolic gesturing can provide new insight into the phenomena. The topics we will be discussing are the delay between comprehension and production, the vocabulary "spurt," and the shift from single words to early combinations. Finally, we will consider future directions in theory and methodology as these pertain to symbolic gestures and their role in linguistic and cognitive development

☐ Symbolic Gesturing: What Have We Learned So Far?

> Karen saw me fill our dog's water dish and set it on the floor in its customary place. When the dog didn't immediately come for a drink, Karin went to where he was dozing on the floor, squatted in front of his face and rubbed her palms together in her "water" gesture. Although the dog ignored Karen's gesture, she had clearly tried to tell him his water was ready. (Mother of 17-month-old encouraged to develop symbolic gestures)

Defining Terms

To those outside the field of language development, the transition from babbling to words often appears fairly smooth: First, there is nonsense and then there are sounds that mean things. On closer examination, however, what seems simple and automatic has proven to be surprisingly complex. Research has revealed many interesting "way stations" along the road to even the rudimentary vocal sophistication of the 2-year-old. Motivated to connect with others around them, preverbal infants come up with a series of "successive approximations" to words, each indexing a significant leap in the child's understanding of the communicative enterprise.

The first big step is from what Bates and her colleagues call the "perlocutionary" phase to the "locutionary" phase (e.g., Bates, Benigni, Bretherton, Camaioni, & Volterra, 1977, 1979; Bates, Bretherton, & Snyder, 1988; Bates, Camaioni, & Volterra, 1975). During the former, communication occurs but without the infant understanding how or why. Marking the transition to the latter, the development of an intention to communicate creates a revolution in interactions with others. At this point, we see the development of pointing to indicate location (i.e., "deictic gestures"), sometimes with the goal of initiating joint attention ("proto-declaratives"), and sometimes to indicate a desire for an item ("proto-imperatives"). Consistent phonetic patterns, often serving as "placeholders" for the vocal symbols that will eventually follow, are another innovation late in the first year or in the first half of the second. Among these are the "communicative grunts" described by McCune (1992), exclamatory noises that seem to have roots in sounds that reflexively accompany effort. Other placeholders are more word-like and more specialized in their application. Idiosyncratic consonant vowel sequences such as "ne-ne," for example, may be used consistently when the infant is in a particular emotional state (e.g., happy, unhappy, or needful). Nonsense words like these are referred to in the literature in a variety of ways, including as "proto-words," "prewords," "call-sounds," or "quasi-words" (see Vihman, 1996, for a review).

As the infant begins to focus on the idea of specific sound patterns for specific aspects of the world, another distinction becomes relevant, that between "context bound" words (variously referred to as "prelexical," "presymbolic," or "weak words") and "context flexible" words (also called "referential," "lexical," "strong words," "symbolic words," or "vocal symbols"). The former category includes approximations to adult words which an infant can reliably produce as part of routinized interactions, presumably due to having noted a specific paired-associate relation between a sound pattern and a particular setting (e.g., "Boo!" in the game peekaboo) (Snyder, Bates, & Bretherton, 1981). It is only when the infant sponta-neously applies such a conventionalized sound pattern in a variety of appropriate settings, (i.e., to mul-tiple exemplars, absent exemplars, or both) that most researchers agree he or she has happened on the most useful communicative tool of all; the "context flexible or "truly symbolic" word.

Where Symbolic Gesturing Belongs

Symbolic gesturing differs from all of these. As briefly defined earlier, *symbolic gestures* are simple, body movements that are used by an infant in the same ways as early symbolic words tend to be used: to label objects, conditions, to answer questions, and to make requests. Eager to communicate, but hampered by the complex demands of sound production, infants fairly readily turn to nonvocal substitutes that also have predictable relations to the external world. For example, with strong encouragement from the adult world, most infants learn to wave "bye bye" or shake their heads for "yes" and "no." These conventional-ized symbolic gestures serve the child well until their vocal equivalents are conquered. We are very famil-iar with infants' use of "bye bye," "yes," and "no." What is not so well known is that infants spontaneously devise other, less conventional gestures as means to the same end—increasing the range of things they can "talk" about as they continue to struggle with the intricacies of the vocal modality.

At the time of our initial discovery of this strategy in 1982, in the spontaneous behavior of a 12-month-old girl named Kate (Acredolo & Goodwyn, 1984, 1985), the choice of the phrase "symbolic gesture" to describe what we were witnessing appeared fairly straightforward. The term "gesture" seemed an appro-priate way to index the modality being recruited, and the term "symbol" was certainly justifiable, given the flexibility with which we saw her using them. Among Kate's favorites, for example, was a gesture in which she rubbed her index fingers together to represent "spider," a movement she had learned within the context of the "Eency Weency Spider" song, but which she then spontaneously generalized at 15 months to label spiders—real, toy, or pictorial. What Kate had noticed was not only the paired-associate relation between the gesture and the word "spider" uttered in the song, but also between the word "spi-der" and its use by adults in other contexts to label little black bugs with long legs. She clearly was making a three-way connection. Another clear example of her facility with such logical connections was her spon-taneous development at 13 months of a symbolic gesture for "big." In this case, she was borrowing a hands-in-the-air gesture from a routine called, "How big's the baby? SO BIG!" in which the final word is accompanied by lifting the infants' hands in the air. Having connected the movement to the word, and the word to the condition of being large, it was easy for her to use the gesture appropriately when she encoun-tered "big" things (e.g., mommy and baby animals). Fortunately for her, the adults around her recognized her strategy and responded as they would have had she said the vocal equivalents. Had they not, of course, it is doubtful she would have persisted.

Using the criteria listed in Table 6.1 to decide what did and did not qualify as a symbolic gesture, we chronicled Kate's spontaneous development of 13 symbolic gestures between the ages of 12½ and 17½ months, many having their origins in interactive routines with adults, but some based on Kate's own experience with the referent objects (e.g., rocking torso for "swing," a hand wave from side to side for "ball"). We also began purposefully modeling gestures of our own devising, an intervention that we pur-sued much more vigorously with other infants years later.

Why Symbolic Gestures Instead of Sign?

As Kate's repertoire grew, we considered adopting the term "sign" to describe the individual gestural symbols she was routinely using. After all, her gestures seemed so clearly to function like the earliest conventionalized signs of formal sign languages (e.g., American Sign Language [ASL]). And, in fact, we have recently moved in that direction by adopting the term "baby signs" to describe symbolic gestures to the lay public (Acredolo & Goodwyn, 1996). At the time we were observing Kate, however, the term "symbolic gesture" seemed preferable for several reasons. First, we quickly realized that these gestural symbols, unlike ASL signs, were strictly transitional forms that inevitably were replaced by vocal equiva-lents before they could become truly "linguistic signs" capable of entering into complex syntactic rela-tions. (See Karmiloff-Smith, 1992, for discussion of a distinction between "linguistic signs" and "natural gestures.") Second, we were impressed with Kate's creativity in figuring out that sensorimotor schemes initially learned outside the communicative arena could be borrowed for use within it. In contrast the

---

TABLE 6.1. Criteria for assigning symbolic status to gestures

---

1. Frequency: The gesture had to be produced repeatedly in reference to conceptually similar objects or events. (Purpose: to distinguish from one-time-only pantomining of salient characteristics or actions.)
2. Form: (a) The physical movement had to be "empty handed" (i.e., not involving an object) and relatively consistent from one time to another"; (b) if a sound was involved, a nonauditory component also had to be clearly discernible. Onomatopoeic sounds occurring on their own (e.g., "rrrr" for truck, "grr" for bear) were treated as potential vocal symbols.
3. Context-flexible usage: The gesture had to be used beyond the specific situation or specific object to which it was initially attached (i.e., multiple exemplars of the concept).
4. Communicative intent: The gesture had to be serving the child as a tool for communicative interactions. Evidence included eye contact, pointing, or use during book reading. (Purpose: to distinguish between gestures used to communicate and gestures used in the context of pretend play.)
5. Noninstrumental: The gesture could not be one that the child might use to achieve a goal directly rather than by communicating with others (e.g., blowing directly on food to cool it off would not qualify, while blowing at a distance might qualify).

Note. An extensive list of criteria for assigning symbolic status to words is available in Goodwyn and Acredolo (1993).

communicative intent of ASL signs is emphasized by adult models from the very beginning. Kate's spider gesture, for example, had been modeled for her only in the very specific context of a song, no one else having ever used it to label spiders more generally. It was Kate's insight, and hers alone, that this gesture could serve more broadly. In this sense, signs of formal sign languages are much less the infant's personal creation than were Kate's gestures. Given the fact that there already were case studies in the literature of hearing infants successfully learning ASL signs modeled by their parents (e.g., Holmes & Holmes, 1980; Prinz & Prinz, 1979), it seemed important to highlight Kate's creativity by calling her behavior by a different name. Finally, in our search for an appropriate term, we were also guided by our rediscovery of Werner and Kaplan's classic 1963 book, *Symbol Formation*, in which these two theoreticians specifically posited that sensorimotor "gestures" associated with objects are natural candidates for recruitment as "symbols" by children for the purposes of communication. We were so struck by the relevance of this idea to what Kate was doing that we jokingly concluded that Kate must have read the book!

A Rose by Any Other Name

In the years since our initial use of the term "symbolic gesture," we have come across other descriptions of behavior like Kate's referred to using different, but equally appropriate, names. Volterra and Caselli, for example, just a few years earlier, had chronicled the development of such gestures in several Italian children, using the term "referential signs" to highlight their similarity to "referential words" (Caselli, 1983; Volterra, 1981; Volterra & Caselli, 1985). "Enactive names" was adopted some years ago (Escalona, 1973) to capture the idea of gestures being used symbolically to name things. Even deaf children denied access to any formal sign language symbols have been observed to develop their own idiosyncratic gestural symbols much as Kate did. Referred to as "characterizing gestures" by Goldin-Meadow and Feldman (1979), these gestural symbols arise out of a strong desire to communicate with others, the same motivation that we believe lay behind Kate's behavior.

It also occasionally has been the case that the same term, "symbolic gesture," has been used to describe quite different phenomena. O'Reilly, Painter, and Bornstein (1997), for example, use "symbolic gesturing" to describe the ability of 24-month-old children to perform pretense scenarios with substitute objects when instructed to do so (e.g., "Give the doll a drink" in the presence of a doll and a block), as well as to describe the behavior of an adult pretending to do something with an imaginary object, actions which 3- to 4-year-old children are asked to interpret. In both cases, what is of interest is the ability to mentally represent actions typically associated with specific objects, essentially to produce or comprehend "pantomime." As the researchers correctly pointed out, the fact that the ability to produce or comprehend pantomime depends on stored representations means that these behaviors should (and do) correlate with the development of vocal language. However, in neither case (producing or comprehending pantomime) is the child engaged in the language enterprise per se; that is, using a specific gesture to stand for multiple exemplars of a specific category or concept for the purpose of communicating. In other words, symbolic gesturing from our perspective is an example of language development, not just correlated with it.

Rounding Out the Picture of Spontaneous Symbolic Gesturing

The next few years were spent determining the extent to which other infants were engaging in symbolic gesturing all on their own; that is, without adults specifically encouraging the communicative use of such gestures. As the summary of these studies presented in Table 6.2 makes clear, Kate was far from unique. Other infants indeed were developing gestural symbols to label objects, describe conditions, and make specific requests. Moreover, their gestures tended to arise from the same sources as Kate's: from interactive routines and from observations of objects.

Parental reports of vocal vocabulary also were collected in these studies. As Table 6.2 indicates, the correlations between development in the two modalities tended to be positive: The more symbolic gestures (especially, object labels) a child used, the more impressive was his or her vocal vocabulary development. This relationship was tantalizing in that it seemed to fly in the face of the commonly heard warning that infants who get what they want nonverbally will be less motivated to learn to talk. It also was exciting because of the theoretical implication that development in the two modalities was interconected. Our next goal therefore, was to determine more precisely the nature of this connection. To this end, we began the most revealing experiments of all—seeing what would happen when we purposefully encouraged infants to learn symbolic gestures.

Testing the Limits: Encouraging Infants to Develop Symbolic Gestures

Kate also really was our first subject in this respect. We simply began to pair our vocal labeling of things she liked with simple movements. Rather than relying on established signs from ASL, we followed Kate's lead and simply chose gestures that seemed easy to associate with the objects, and, therefore, were easy for us to remember. For example, touching an index finger to the nose (mimicking a trunk) became our choice for "elephant" and two fingers together and apart became our choice for "scissors." The decision to forgo signs from conventionalized sign languages in favor of commonsense ones was fortuitous, not only because it made learning them easy for Kate but also because it has made the whole notion of symbolic gesturing seem easier and less intimidating for the many families who have participated in our intervention studies in the years since. By 17½ months, Kate had added 16 more symbolic gestures to the 13 she had developed on her own, for a grand total of 39, at which point word production really took off.

TABLE 6.2. Summary of studies documenting the spontaneous development of symbolic gestures

N	Age Range	Number of Gestures	Relation to Vocal Language
Acredolo & Goodwyn (1985)			
1	12–24 months	13 (plus 16 directly taught)	Vocal language developed rapidly: vocabulary at 24 months = 752 words
Acredolo & Goodwyn (1988)—Study 1			
38	17 months	148 total (M = 3.9, range 0–16)	Object gestures & vocal vocabulary at 17 months: r = .33, p < .025 (with sex, birth order, & maternal education partialled).
Acredolo & Goodwyn (1988)—Study 2			
16	11–24 months	81 total (M = 5.1, range 1–17)	Object gestures & age at 10 words: r = −.48, p < .10.
Goodwyn & Acredolo (1998)			
38	14–24 months	182 total (M = 4.8, range 0–16)	Object gestures & vocal vocabulary, r = .33, p < .025 (with sex, birth order, & maternal education partialled).

Our next effort took the form of a small-scale, longitudinal study of six infants (three males and three females) whose parents had agreed to encourage symbolic gesturing by choosing simple gestures for things their infants want to "talk" about and modeling these gestures every time they used the verbal labels. We asked each family to start by focusing on a set of eight "target" gestures, the same eight for each family, but also encouraged them to think up additional ones as they saw fit. Each child's progress in acquiring both symbolic gestures and words was chronicled on a weekly basis (via lengthy phone interviews) for at least 8 months, the intervention beginning at 11 months for five of the infants and at 8 months for one. The results were exciting. Not only did we see the infants develop impressive gestural repertoires (M = 20, range: 5 to 42), we also began to get a sense of the wide variety of ways in which the gestures were used. Parents were pleased, too, and commented on how satisfying it was to know more about what their infant was thinking. Finally, standardized language tasks indicated that the verbal development of these children was ahead of national norms. This finding, of course, was uninterpretable in the absence of a control group.

The next step, launched in 1989, was a large-scale longitudinal study involving over 130 families, all with 11-month-old infants. Each infant was assigned to one of three groups. Families assigned to the nonintervention control group simply were asked to bring their child to the laboratory for a wide variety of assessments at 11, 15, 19, 24, 30, and 36 months, with no mention on our part of any particular interest in language development. Families with infants included in the sign training group were asked to encourage symbolic gesturing the same way that the pilot families had, by pairing simple movements with verbal labels. They, too, were asked to focus on eight target symbolic gestures at the beginning, a list that included gestures for "fish," "flower," "bird," "frog," "airplane," "where is it?" "more," and "allgone." Past that, they were free to experiment with any gesture-referent pairings they believed would be of interest to their infant. Finally, families assigned to the verbal training group also experienced an intervention, but one focussed on vocalized labels rather than symbolic gestures. The purpose was to control for the effects that simply being involved in an intervention study concerning language skills might have on cognitive and language development. Parents of these children were asked to make a conscious effort to supply labels for things, starting with eight target words: kitty, doggie, ball, shoe, boat, bye bye, more, and allgone. Note that the last two words on this list, more and allgone, also were included among the target gestures for the sign training families, thereby enabling us to directly compare acquisition in the two modalities. Infants in both intervention groups were assessed at the same ages and with the same instruments as the nonintervention infants.

In addition to periodic standardized testing in the laboratory, detailed information specifically about language development was obtained during interviews every 2 weeks with parents of children in both the sign training and verbal training groups. The goal of these interviews was to chronicle the step-by-step development of both words and gestures for the sign training infants, and of words for the verbal training infants. Interviews continued until a child either had acquired 100 symbolic words or had turned age 2.

Because most of the discussions which follow involve data obtained from these interviews, it is important to appreciate the level of detail we were seeking from the parents. Each interview was carefully structured to gather the following information from both groups: (a) a list of words the infant was able to comprehend (up to 100), (b) a list of words the infant was able to produce and under what circumstances (i.e., in imitation, after being elicited with "What's that?" or spontaneously), (c) examples of the contexts in which each word was being produced, (d) any instances of multiword utterances, and (e) general observations about health and favorite activities. The parents in the sign training group also were asked questions about their child's progress with symbolic gestures—what gestures were being produced, under what circumstances, and whether combinations of gestures or gestures with words had been observed. In contrast to many studies of vocabulary development, we required both gestures and words to be used in a context flexible manner before crediting the child's vocabulary. A complete list of the criteria used to make decisions about symbolic status is available in Goodwyn and Acredolo (1993).

Summarizing the gesturing data briefly, the sign training infants acquired an average of 25.4 symbolic gestures (range: 9 to 61), most falling into one of three categories: object labels (e.g., smacking lips for "fish"), requests (e.g., finger tips tapped together to request "more"), or descriptors (e.g., blowing to represent "hot"). Comparing performances on the standardized tests, we found that the sign training infants quite consistently exceeded the other groups in their rate of verbal language development, both expressive and receptive, and in their scores on the Bayley Mental Development Inventory at 24 months. (See Goodwyn and Acredolo, 1998, for more information about these comparisons.)

As we continue to explore the rich body of data which this ambitious study has provided, we find ourselves impressed again and again with the positive nature of the effects that the symbolic gesturing had on the families in the sign training group. The gestures enabled the children to become active participants in conversational interchanges with other people, thereby reducing frustration and increasing the proportion of positive interactions. They also provided a way for the children to alert parents to specific things they had noticed, thereby increasing the chance that conversations would revolve around what they, rather than their parents, found interesting. What made all of this possible, of course, was the fact that the gestures allowed the infants a way around the difficult task of conquering the articulatory and phonological details of words. Because the world of the infant is relatively simple, a small repertoire of symbolic gestures, in combination with the vocal words the child is able to say, apparently goes a long way toward meeting the very young child's communicative needs. But, just what is it that makes learning the words themselves so difficult? This is the question we turn to next as we review the challenges posed by the articulatory and phonological demands of vocal language.

☐ Phonological Development: The Missing Link

Ask many, if not most, developmental psychologists about the slow rate of early vocal vocabulary development and their answers likely will highlight various cognitive challenges that need to be met: understanding the function of symbols, recognizing that things in the world have names and belong to categories, acquiring scripted experiences, and so forth. Ask a developmental psycholinguist the same question and the primary answer is quite likely to be more succinct, "phonological development." Both answers are right, of course. Without cognitive advances, infants would have nothing to say and, without phonological expertise, these same infants would not be able to say very much even if they wanted to. As is true of many developmental phenomena, the acquisition of language involves a constant interplay ("bootstrapping") between cognition and phonological knowledge, each one benefiting from progress in the other. It is our impression, however, that phonological development is all too often given short shrift in discussions of language acquisition in the psychological literature. This makes for an incomplete picture because, as even a cursory dip into the huge research literature on the topic shows, young children face a continuous set of challenges over the first 4 or 5 years of life as they struggle to attain the fluency that adults take for granted. Indeed, solving the mystery of how children manage to conquer the intricacies of speech production continues to keep many researchers and theoreticians busy.

The relevance of the phonological component to our discussion of symbolic gesturing should be obvious. By utilizing the gestural modality for symbol construction, infants are able to bypass their articulatory limitations and advance toward their primary goal—communicating with important people around them. In doing so, they also gain valuable phonological and conceptual information: The infant's use of a symbolic gesture for an item he or she cares enough about to label, inevitably evokes vocal responses from observant adults. These responses, in turn, provide the infant with helpful repetition of how the vocal symbol should sound while, at the same time, indicating whether or not the child's hunch about the item's identity was correct (thereby forwarding conceptual development). Even when the vocal label is finally attempted (e.g., "ba" for bottle), the symbolic gesture works to the child's advantage by helping clarify what it is the infant is trying to say. In fact, parents report such clarification as one of the many advantages to them of having an infant with a repertoire of symbolic gestures.

But, exactly why is it so hard for most 12-month-olds to say simple words like "bottle" or "ball," even though they may understand the words perfectly well? The answers are obvious once one examines the complex road to articulatory and phonological expertise. Thelen (1991, p. 239) stated, for example, that "the utterance of even a simple one-syllable word requires the coordination in time and space of over 70 muscles and 8 to 10 different body parts ranging from the diaphragm to the lips." Focusing on an even smaller unit, the individual speech sound, Smith (1988) painted a similar picture, estimating that over 100 muscles of the face, tongue, larynx, thorax, and so forth must receive neural messages for production to occur.

Learning how to control all these anatomical structures is made even more challenging by the fact that most of them undergo dramatic changes in size, shape, and relationship over the first 4 or 5 years. One becomes especially appreciative of the magnitude of the problem, given the observation that infants are born with a vocal tract that "more closely resembles that of the nonhuman primate than that of the adult human" (Kent, 1992, p. 66). Among the specific problems facing the child during the first 4 years are a vocal tract considerably shorter than an adult's, a larger tongue in proportion to the available space, inadequate control of the muscles within and outside the tongue that dictate placement, and a vocal cavity and mandible-tongue arrangement that are not suitable for the whole range of vowel sounds until 4 years of age (Kent, 1992; Kent & Miolo, 1995). Infants also must learn what specific movements yield distinctive consonant sounds (e.g., plosives, fricatives) and then master smooth movements back and forth from consonants to vowels and vice versa. Moreover, continuous growth of bone, cartilage, muscles, and teeth over the infancy and childhood years necessitates constant readjustments of even well-practiced motor schemes.

The lengthy period of babbling in the last half of the first year, of course, represents the infant's miniexperiments with these structures, each effort an example of what Piaget called "primary circular reactions." The infant produces a sound, listens to the result, and either tries to produce the same one again or modify it in some way. In this sense, the infant's efforts are no different than many other motor skills being mastered during infancy (Thelen, 1991).

As hard as infants work during the babbling period, their task becomes qualitatively more complicated at the end of the first year when cognitive and social-emotional advances motivate a shift in goals—from producing sounds merely for the sake of hearing them to producing very specific sounds in very specific sequences in order to affect the behavior of other people (i.e., words). Added to this challenge is the need to try to match this sequence as closely as possible to the sound pattern uttered (and often muttered) by others, because failure to do so results in not being understood. To this end, infants often will try to imitate words immediately after they have heard them modeled. Successful communication, however, requires spontaneous production of words, not just imitation. What is more, the words chosen must be appropriate for the situation. Meeting all these new goals presents the infant with an enormous challenge.

What enables the infant to produce a word whenever he or she deems it appropriate is the ability to commit to long-term memory the requisite sound pattern and the complex motor sequence required to produce it. To understand the scope of the infant's task, consider the difference between random finger movements on a piano and actually learning to play a complex piece and then committing it to memory. One can think of the former as analogous to babbling, the latter to spontaneous word production. Like learning to talk, learning to play even a simple melody like "Mary Had a Little Lamb" involves practicing multiple finger movements, sometimes several at once if the music mandates the use of both hands. Practice must continue until the sequence of sounds produced at least approximates the target melody and can be retrieved from long-term memory whenever desired.

This analogy also helps illustrate a critical part of the infant's task: recognizing that words consist of sequences of sounds whose combinations with other sounds are predictable. Think of this discovery as parallel to learning to play a chord on the piano. With sufficient practice, the individual finger movements necessary to produce a specific chord will become linked together, stored together, and retrievable as a unit. Discovery of such predictability in speech is what turns phonetics into phonology and prepares the infant to discover which combinations are allowed and which are not.

Although on the surface the existence of phonological constraints within a language might seem to complicate the job facing the infant, in actual fact, this internal organization is what eventually makes fluency. Out of the infants repeated efforts to produce a particular sound sequence, there eventually emerges an "articulatory score" (Browman & Goldstein, 1985) that is both encodable and retrievable as a unit (not unlike chords on the piano). Also called "production schemata" (Lindblom, 1992) or "templates" (Vihman, 1976), these articulatory packages are developed painstakingly slowly at first and are, as a consequence, very few in number as word production begins.

Infants, however, are so strongly motivated to take an active part in communicating that they find ways around the handicap posed by having a limited repertoire of articulatory scores. The strategy they use most frequently at the beginning of word production is to develop articulatory scores for entire words, even if their rendition must be far from accurate. This strategy, however, does not solve all their problems. First, the task of memorizing long sequences of sounds severely constrains the total number of words that can be retained. Second, because they are working with a limited number of well-rehearsed articulatory patterns, some words modeled by adults will be so far outside this repertoire as to be essentially impossible to even approximate. Infants deal with this problem by tending to avoid such words during the early stages of vocabulary development, favoring instead words that overlap with their existing articulatory repertoires, at least enough so that crude approximations, such as "ba" for "bottle," are possible (e.g.,

Dobrich & Scarborough, 1992; Menn & Stoel-Gammon, 1995; Schwartz & Leonard, 1982; Schwartz, Leonard, Loeb, & Swanson, 1987; Smith, 1988; Studdert-Kennedy, 1987; Tyler & Edwards, 1993). The preference for some words over others as production targets is congruent with Vihman's (1981) observation that early words tend to include the same sounds the infant produces when babbling. This bias toward target words with particular sounds is not absolute, otherwise no new sounds would ever become part of the infant's repertoire. Gradually, more and more new sound patterns are attempted and mastered, thereby increasing the number of target words that can be approximated.

All this proceeds at what appears to be a snail's pace over the first half of the second year, thereby accounting at least in part for the slowness with which the first 25 or so words are mastered. However, it all gets considerably easier as the number of available sound patterns (i.e., articulatory "chunks") increases to the point that words begin to be seen no longer as "wholes," but rather as composed of separable units. As this realization takes stronger and stronger hold, the strategy of memorizing words as wholes actually becomes more cumbersome than encoding them in terms of their component parts (i.e., phonological units): parts that can be combined and recombined with other units in a wide variety of ways to produce a wide variety of new words. Voila! We have the emergence of phonology, and along with it a combinatorial strategy that makes mastering new words, longer words, and sequences of words much easier.

Given the struggle described above, is it any wonder that many infants welcome symbolic gestures as a way around the articulatory and phonological demands of vocal words? Compared to Thelen's (1991) estimate of 70 or so movements per word (few of which are visually available for the infant to imitate), tapping one's index fingers together to ask for "more" probably seems pretty attractive. Moreover, as mentioned at the beginning of this section, infants who become adept at using symbolic gestures are in a position to garner many of the same conceptual and social-emotional benefits that the use of early vocal words inevitably generates. These infants, however, enjoy these benefits at earlier ages and need not limit their early vocabularies to objects or conditions whose names contain sounds that are easy to say. An infant who wants a parent to focus on salient features of his or her world (like flowers, pets, or even Christmas tree lights) can do so without giving a thought to the articulatory challenge that the vocal labels pose. All it takes is for parents to encourage them to do what our initial research says comes naturally: develop gestural symbols for those things that matter the most to them.

Infants are not the only ones who benefit, however. The fact that symbolic gestures enable infants to plow so easily into the naming game at such early ages has much to teach us all about how the pieces of the language puzzle come together and, particularly, how the phonological piece fits in. In the next sections, we explore three specific questions from this new point of view.

☐ A New Look at Some Old Issues

What follows is an overview of three phenomena that have received significant attention from child language researchers. Our purpose is not to provide a comprehensive review of each topic but, rather, to highlight some ways in which knowledge about symbolic gesturing can offer new evidence and insights. The issues include (a) the asynchrony between comprehension and vocal production, (b) the vocabulary spurt, and (c) the transition to early combinations.

The Comprehension-Production Asynchrony Revisited

One of the most robust findings in the language acquisition literature, and one that is known anecdotally by anyone who has had extended contact with a language-learning child, is that comprehension of language proceeds faster than vocal production. In lay terms, this means that very young children appear to understand far more than they are able to say. Researchers, of course, must be more precise.

In fact, there are at least three different ways this asynchrony has been operationalized. The most frequent strategy involves comparing the size of a child's comprehension vocabulary, typically as reported by a parent, to the size of the same child's productive vocabulary. This strategy, applied to large groups of children via the MacArthur Communicative Development Inventory (CDI), confirms the existence of a dissociation for most children, while, at the same time, documenting dramatic individual differences in its magnitude (Fenson et al., 1994). Converging data come from a second strategy, comparing "ages of onset" (i.e., the age at which each ability typically emerges). Estimates of the gap using this measure vary from 2 to 6 months, with the modal pattern being 8 to 10 months of age for the earliest comprehension of single words, compared with 12 to 14 months of age for production of the first vocal words (Fenson et al., 1994). A third strategy, the one we have used in our symbolic gesturing work, is to look at the developmental history of individual words to ascertain how long it takes before a comprehended word enters a child's productive lexicon. Although by definition narrow in its focus, this approach allows more detailed analyses of the processes that underlie development of these two capacities.

A Phenomenon in Search of an Explanation. The title of this section, taken directly from Bates, Dale, and Thal (1995, p. 113), points to an irony: The comprehension–vocal production gap is clearly a real phenomenon in language acquisition, even acknowledging marked variations in timing and rate, but it is a phenomenon which, despite extensive documentation, still lacks definitive explanation. The two activities differ in a number of subtle, but important, ways besides the obvious fact that production requires articulatory and phonological skill, and it always has been a challenge to disentangle these factors in order to assess their individual contributions. It is our belief that symbolic gesturing can shed new light on the processes underlying the comprehension-production gap by doing just that—by taking two factors, articulation and phonology, out of the mix. To the extent that the gap remains unchanged, we have evidence of other factors at work. To the extent that it disappears, we learn more precisely just how big a role the articulatory and phonological components play. Before summarizing our findings, however, we need to consider just what other factors might be involved.

There exist a number of ways in which production and comprehension can be distinguished from each other in terms of the capacities a child must have to demonstrate one or the other. First, the very fact that comprehension is a passive behavior, while production is an active behavior, has significant conceptual consequences. For example, merely registering the meaning of a word when it is heard (comprehension) does not require the child to purposefully analyze the context in enough detail to determine which words would or would not be appropriate. In contrast, during the production task, children must search through their repertoire for the best-fitting word available to them (e.g., Naigles & Gelman, 1995; Oviatt, 1980) rather than choosing randomly, or else they will not be understood. One would never expect, for example, a child who sees an airplane in the sky to say "doggie." The semantic decision making that producing words requires when communication is the goal, certainly would seem to add a burden that could delay productive vocal development past what is necessary for comprehension.

Another plausible contributor, also conceptual in nature, is the fact that production of words more so than comprehension, challenges the child to recognize the communicative partner as an intentional being with his of her own focus and goals. As Baldwin (1995) pointed out, such "intersubjective understanding" is the cornerstone of critical components of language development, including "joint attention," "social referencing," and the ability to interpret gaze, pointing, and labeling behavior as acts of reference. For example, the hypothetical child described above who labels the airplane is quite likely doing so specifically because he or she understands that the adult's attention may be elsewhere, but can be redirected via the label. In contrast, "comprehension" of a word can more easily occur without any thought on the part of the child as to the state of mind of the speaker, a situation which certainly eases the child's burden.

Having just argued that vocal production may lag behind comprehension because of the need to develop not only phonological skills, but also conceptual skills, let us now illustrate how symbolic gesturing helps disentangle these facts, thereby shedding new light on their relative contributions. The advantage of symbolic gesturing in this context is the fact that infants proficient in the use of nonvocal symbols to communicate with others are giving clear indications of having already solved the conceptual problems (e.g., intersubjective understanding, joint attention, semantic decision making). If these indeed are major stumbling blocks to vocal production, then their resolution should be followed relatively quickly by gains in the vocal modality. If nothing much changes in terms of vocal production, however, then we have evidence supporting the other candidates—the phonological and articulatory components of language—as key players.

Our strategy, representative of the third option described at the beginning of this section, was to document the development of comprehension and vocal production of two specific words, "more" and "allgone." Two groups from our intervention study provided the data, those in the sign training condition who were encouraged to develop symbolic gestures for "more" and "allgone," and those in the verbal training group

TABLE 6.3. **Mean ages (and sample size) at which children in the sign training group versus the verbal training group demonstrated comprehension and production of two target terms ("more" and "allgone")**

	Sign Training (ST) (*N* = 32)	Verbal Training (VT) (*N* = 32)
	"More"	
Comprehension	12.8 (27)	12.6 (27)
Vocal production	17.63 (32)	18.33 (30)
Gestural production	14.36 (29)	
Vocal comprehension-production gap	4.74 (27)	5.89 (29)
Vocal comprehension-gestural production gap	1.51 (24)	
	"Allgone"	
Comprehension	12.66 (22)	13.34 (32)
Vocal production	17.64 (32)	18.53 (30)
Gestural production	14.51 (31)	
Vocal comprehension-production gap	4.72 (22)	5.22 (30)
Vocal comprehension-gestural production gap	1.29 (21)	

Note. Sample sizes differ from mean to mean because (a) comprehension data were not available for all subjects, (b) not all ST subjects developed gestures for "more" and "allgone," and (c) all VT subjects developed the words "more" and "allgone."

who were encouraged to conquer the vocal versions. As briefly summarized in Table 6.3, the two groups did not differ in the age at which comprehension was achieved (as per parental report), nor did they differ in the onset of vocal production of these terms. In fact, a fairly typical delay between comprehension and vocal word production was observed (*M* = 5.31 months for "more" and *M* = 4.97 months for "allgone," averaged across both groups). But, if we look at the sign training group's average age of gestural production of these terms, then the gap between comprehension of the vocal word and production shrinks dramatically (*M* = 1.51 months for "more" and *M* = 1.29 months for "allgone").

These data can be summarized as follows: Even though infants may be able to communicate their understanding, through gestures, within a relatively short time period after comprehending a term, they are still "delayed" in vocal word production. Recalling the three differences between comprehension and production hypothesized as potential contributors to the typical asynchrony—(a) comprehension and production hypothesized versus production as an active behavior, (b) production but not comprehension demanding "intersubjective understanding," and (c) differential requirements regarding articulatory and phonological expertise—the patterns uncovered here indicate a substantial role for the last of these, the articulatory and phonological demands of spoken language. Note, however, that there still was a gap, albeit much shorter, between comprehension of the words "more" and "allgone" by the sign training children and production of the gestural symbols. This residual gap suggests that the first two factors do have roles to play, as does the gestural equivalent of the third, the motor demands of producing the specific movements involved in the gestures. The bottom line for learning words, however, is that the articulatory and phonological requirements pose a substantial challenge even once a word is comprehended.

Understanding the Vocabulary "Spurt"

One of the most fascinating and perplexing phenomena in all of language development is the *vocabulary spurt*. This term generally refers to a sudden increase at some point during the second year in the rate at which new words are acquired. This description sounds simple enough but, in reality, is very difficult to operationalize because patterns of vocabulary development are so variable from child to child. Deciding how many words must be added to what size existing vocabulary to qualify as a "spurt"—and even what kind of words these must be—is still a matter of debate. Gopnik and Meltzoff (1987), for example, defined a spurt as the addition of 10 new "names" in a 3-week period, Goldfield and Reznick (1990) as 10 new words of any kind in a 2½ week period, and Mervis and Bertrand (1995) as 10 new words, including at least 5 object words, in a 14-day period. One problem with each of these criteria as Bates et al. (1995) pointed out, is that none really captures the idea of a change in rate of acquisition. After all, 10 new words added to a vocabulary of 2 certainly would seem noteworthy, while 10 new words added to a slowly accumulated vocabulary of 70 words would not.

This criterion problem is integral to another debate: What proportion of children do and do not experience a vocabulary spurt? Goldfield & Reznick (1990), for example, collected data every 2½ weeks for 8 months (14–42 months) from mothers of 18 children and concluded that, although 13 had met their criterion (see above) for a vocabulary spurt, 5 had not. However, even though researchers disagree on whether all children experience a spurt, no one questions that there are some children for whom the change is so dramatic that concern about whether or not a spurt has occurred takes an immediate backseat to the more interesting question of what on earth is going on underneath the surface to cause such an abrupt change. Goldfield and Reznick (1990), for example, reported the addition of 60 new words to one child's vocabulary in a 2½-week period, and Dromi (1987) described a child who slowly and steadily built her vocabulary for about 25 weeks (until near the 150 word point) and then, at 16 months, suddenly added 111 new words in one 3-week period. It is hard not to agree with Bates et al. (1995) that a change of this proportion simply "cries out for an explanation" (p. 105).

Calling for an explanation is easy; finding one is not. Many reasonable suggestions have been made. Among the earliest was the hypothesis that the spurt reflects a sudden realization on the part of the child that "things have names" (Dore, 1974; McShane, 1980), or the more recent twist on this notion, that all things ought to be named (Baldwin & Markman, 1989). Others have looked to what it is that children are naming with their early words; that is, the nature of the underlying concepts. Perhaps, the spurt reflects a sudden change in the number of concepts available to be named. The common denominator among these more cognitive hypotheses is that the child's ability to see similarities and differences among the objects, events, and conditions in the world is critical. It is through such comparisons that categories are formed, contrasted with one another, and then labeled. Gopnik and Meltzoff (1987) provided data supportive of this hypothesis by documenting that the ability to efficiently sort objects into categories tended to appear in their subjects' repertoires about the same time (during the middle of the second year) as the "naming" explosion. In discussing the implications of their data, however, Gopnik and Meltzoff (1992) were careful to avoid the idea that the onset of the ability to categorize causes vocabulary to increase, opting instead for the more complex notion that the two probably interact "in intriguing ways" (p. 1102).

In fact, the idea that lexical development is multidetermined is receiving more and more serious attention, with one of the clearest and most compelling theories being contributed by Golinkoff, Mervis, and Hirsh-Pasek (1994) in the form of a "two-tier" theory of lexical development. What is most refreshing about their theory is that it includes a role for most, if not all, of the factors others have cited—lexical, cognitive, and even social. They argued that there is a set of early achievements (i.e., understanding "reference," "extendibility" of words to perceptually similar items, and the "word to whole object" principle), whose development in the child early in the second year lays the foundation for the second, more sophisticated level of achievements. These include the realization that perceptual similarity yields a "categorizable" world, that a novel name probably applies to a novel category, and that being understood by other people within one's community requires the use of the specific vocal words ("conventionality"). It is easy to see that having all these "ducks in a row" could accelerate the addition of new words, perhaps even to the point of creating a spurt for some children.

Lessons from KA.   Turning once again to the main purpose of the present chapter, symbolic gesturing, we suggest that taking a close look at infants who engage in lots of symbolic gesturing early, can provide unique data relevant to the issue of the vocabulary spurt, particularly in regard to a possible role for articulatory and phonological factors. Although not traditionally highlighted in cognitive theories of the spurt, the notion that these factors have a role to play certainly is not new with us.

Clark (1993), for example, suggested that the spurt

> has often been regarded as evidence that children have grasped the point of language as a symbolic system, that is, that there are, potentially, words for everything around them. An alternative view is that the vocabulary spurt reflects attainment of a certain level of mastery in articulatory plans for production. (p. 28)

Certainly, the previous description of phonological development, especially the discovery by the child of articulatory subunits within words, is supportive of Clark's suggestion.

In order to demonstrate that symbolic gesturing provides something new and different, let us take a closer look at both the vocal and gestural development of one child. KA was 10 months old when he entered our first, small-scale intervention study. Although his babbling had progressed in a timely fashion, he really was not much interested in vocal articulation (M. Vihman, personal communication, Nov. 14, 1988, based on reviewing the video record), and he had neither symbolic words nor gestures when his parents began to encourage the development of symbolic gestures by combining simple gestures with their vocal labels for things they thought might be important to him. Weekly interviews with his parents began at that point and, for many months, his vocal language development took very little time for them to describe. By 18½ months, KA had a grand total of only 7 context flexible words at his disposal.

All this changed very dramatically, however, during the 1-month period between 18¾ and 19¾ months when KA suddenly added 65 new symbolic words (all "context flexible") to his original 7 words and produced his first 2-word combinations. From 7 to 72 words in 4 weeks—a more dramatic and unusual example of a vocal vocabulary spurt is hard to imagine. Moreover, 55 of these 65 additional words functional as context flexible symbols from the very beginning of their appearance during this month.

With just this vocal language history to consider, and no physical handicaps to blame, it is certainly hard to see how KA could have learned enough about reference, extendibility, categories, conventionality, articulation, or any of the other advances hypothesized to be necessary for such a dramatic gain in vocabulary. It is true, of course, that comprehending words garners a child some knowledge of concepts and even sound patterns at the receptive level. However, as Elbers (1995) argued persuasively, learning to talk is an active process that requires lots of work on the part of the child: testing hypotheses about category membership, evaluating feedback, learning to value the social rewards of successfully communicating, honing the memory skills necessary to recall semantic information and articulatory patterns. Without time spent as an active partner in conversations with those around him, it is very hard to explain how KA could have achieved so much so fast.

The secret to KA's success, we believe, is the fact that he indeed had been an active partner in conversations during the months leading up to his vocal word explosion at 19 months; he just had not been using vocal words to do so. Instead, KA had developed a repertoire of 40 symbolic gestures (starting with 10 acquired between 12 and 13 months) that apparently helped him learn almost all those things he needed to know. With 40 gestures and seven words at his disposal, he had already spent lots of time verifying his hypotheses about reference and category membership ("You're right! That IS a crocodile!"), he had garnered lots of examples about how vocal words sound, he had been able to direct the attention of adults to the things he was interested in, and he certainly had learned how much fun it is to communicate with other people. He also had been combining a handful of "pivot" gestures ("more," "allgone," "where is it?") with other gestures and with his few words since he was 15 months old.

Just why the flood gates opened so suddenly, however, is a mystery we can never really solve. Perhaps, some change at the neurological level was enough to make mastery of articulation patterns easier at this point. The cortico-subcortical fibers of the pyramidal tract that are involved in motor control of speech (Eisele & Aram, 1995), for example, make gains in myelination around this time (Brody, Kinney, Klonman, & Gilles, 1987). It also is possible that KA's store of knowledge about the world was now extensive enough to make him want to express ideas not easily translated into symbolic gestures, thus motivating him to struggle with the vocal modality. Evidence to support these possibilities comes from examining just what words KA chose to add during this spurt. Sudden insights about the phonological component of vocal language, for example, is suggested by the fact that 31% of the new words (20 out of 65) began with "b," another 9% with "m," and another 9% with "h." The remaining 50% were scattered with respect to the consonant and vowels with which they began. Analysis of these early words also indicates an interest in expanding the things he could talk about:

- Of his 65 new words only 6 were direct replacements for symbolic gestures. The rest of the additions were true extensions of the things he could talk about.
- Many of his new words allowed him to make more fine-grained distinctions than had his gestures. For example, his symbolic gesture for "food" (noisy smacking of lips) was replaced not by the equivalent word "food," but by labels for eight different foods (e.g., apple, cookie, banana).

• At least 18 of his new words would have been difficult to depict in gesture, some because they were too easily conveyed by pointing to need to be depicted (e.g., nose, eye, ear, mine, hair), or were proper names (e.g., Susan, Mama, Daddy), or were too indistinct to be good candidates (e.g., people, hole, stairs, box, block).

KA's history is more extreme in its imbalance between gestures and words than that of most of the gesturing infants in our studies and, therefore, can only point us in the general direction of answers to our questions. What his history makes clear, to repeat once again the theme running throughout our discussion, is that gains in the phonological domain must be included among the potential factors accounting for vocabulary spurts when they occur. Of course, the relative contributions of the various factors (e.g., categorization knowledge, the naming insight, intersubjective understanding, the emergence of phonological units) will vary from child to child. For infants who are not developing symbolic gestures, for example, it is quite likely that the Golinkoff et al. (1994) two-tier model (with the addition of attention to phonology) is right on the mark. Even for infants developing symbolic gestures, there will be individual differences in the relative roles of these factors. Unlike KA, many infants learning symbolic gestures develop their verbal repertoires in tandem with their gestural vocabularies. The good news is that we are hearing about gestural vocabularies twice as large as KA's from parents outside our studies who have learned about the potential for symbolic gesturing to open a channel for communication between them and their children. Surely, examining such cases only can add to our understanding of how the pieces of the language puzzle come together.

Symbolic Gestures and the Onset of Two-Word Speech

> Having lived his short life entirely in California 15-month-old KA was very impressed with the snow he encountered on a trip to Chicago. Sensing his fascination, his parents came up with a gesture for snow (palms down, fingers cupped, downward motion) which KA took to immediately, using it appropriately to label pictures of snow as well as the real thing. But, it was upon their return to California that KA made his interest in snow most obvious. Exiting the airport door, KA looked around in a puzzled fashion, glanced at his mother, and by combining a favorite old gesture with his favorite new one, asked the question uppermost in his mind: "WHERE" (arms extended, palms up) is the "SNOW"?

The transition from single-word speech to two-word combinations has intrigued developmental researchers for a number of reasons, not least of which is the question of why it takes so long for children to make this advance. For the average child, the delay is 6 to 12 months between the beginning of single-word speech (about 12 months of age) and the onset of true two-word combinations (between 18 and 24 months of age). Notable exceptions to this modal pattern have been reported by Bates et al. (1995) and Fenson et al. (1994) but, despite evidence of impressive individual differences, these researchers felt comfortable in concluding that children rarely begin combining words before 16 months, and that it is unusual for combinations not to have begun by 26 months.

The central issues on which researchers have focused in regard to the development of combinational language have been (a) describing how the transition from single words to combinations takes place, and (b) explaining why it takes place at the time and in the manner that it does. Taking each of these in turn, we will briefly summarize what is known to date about the developmental path children follow from single-word speech to early word combinations. We will then consider some of the proposed explanations for the timing of this transition and discuss how the evidence from symbolic gesturing can provide an additional means by which to evaluate the various hypotheses.

Describing the Transition from Single Words to First Combinations.   As the evidence cited above makes clear, children do not move quickly from communicating single ideas using one word at a time to combining independently meaningful words in order to convey more complicated messages. The one-word period typically occupies a significant portion of the second year. It is not, however, without its own developmental milestones. Careful scrutiny of the kinds of words the child acquires and the ways in which they are used reveals numerous subtle advances assumed to be related to children's subsequent ability to combine words. One such change is growth in the lexicon during the single-word period, growth that initially proceeds relatively slowly but, then, accelerates rapidly after a few months. The result is that by the time children begin combining independent lexical entries, they typically can choose from 50 to 100 words (Bates et al., 1995). Another shift is in the abstractness or complexity of the concepts being conveyed by the individual words that are added to the lexicon, both in terms of their definitions (e.g., "blue" is more abstract than "kitty") and in terms of the variety of grammatical functions they serve within a context. The word "mama" for example, may be uttered in relation to the mother's hat, thereby indicating possession.

During the single-word period children also begin to express more complex relationships by combining a word with nonverbal, nonsymbolic indicators of intention and meaning, such as reaching and pointing gestures, or by establishing deictic reference through deliberately staring at a person or object as they say a word. A similar "practicing" of a combinatorial form prior to the actual onset of two-word speech can be seen in the repeated pairing of a single word with dummy syllables (e.g., "ma baby," "te baby"), as reported by Dore, Franklin, Miller, and Ramer (1976).

A final approximation of two-word combinations takes the form of "successive single-word utterances" composed of two words separated by a noticeable pause, yet manifesting the intonation pattern of a single utterance. The pauses between the single words gradually shorten as the child nears the point where true combinations appear. Clearly, the boundary between one- and two-word speech becomes quite blurred, given all these small, incremental achievements. Indeed, as Shore (1986) argued, the fact that so many of the elements necessary for combinatorial language already are present during the one-word phase makes the delay between these two particularly teasing. We turn now to the kinds of explanations that have been suggested for the transition to combinatorial language and, finally, to an examination of where symbolic gesturing fits into the picture.

Explaining the Transition.   Although everyone who studies language development realizes at some level that explanations will not be found solely in a single domain, there is still a strong tendency for researchers to favor one particular strand over others in proposing causal relationships. Explaining the transition to early combinations is no exception to this tendency, and candidate hypotheses fall largely into two categories; (a) those that stress advances in general or specific cognitive functioning, and (b) those that favor specifically linguistic advances.

The cognitive approach, which subsumes many different proposed correlates of the transition from one- to two-word speech, places the emphasis primarily on changes in the child's cognitive processing that increase efficiency and make possible the coordinating of two separate ideas into one organized unit. Support for this hypothesis comes from observations of other changes that occur around this time, changes taking place in domains relevant to language, including: (1) changes in symbolic play, particularly, the ability to combine multiple symbolic elements in a specific sequence (e.g., Casby & Ruder, 1983; Kelly & Dale, 1989; McCune-Nicolich, 1981; McCune-Nicolich & Bruskin, 1982; Shore, 1986; Shore, O'Connell, & Bates, 1984); (b) improvement in imitation abilities, both for sound patterns (Kelly & Dale, 1989) and action sequences (McCall, Parke, & Kavanaugh, 1977); (c) more efficient encoding and retrieval from memory of stored symbolic representations (Rescorla & Goossens, 1992); (d) advances in classification skills (Sugarman, 1983); and (e) general progess in cognitively based skills such as solving jigsaw puzzles and constructing with blocks (Case & Khanna, 1981; Greenfield, 1978). Of course, the fact that there are correlations between development in these cognitive domains and the advent of two-word speech cannot be interpreted as proof that the specific cognitive changes in question are causing utterance length to increase. In fact, Cromer (1988) suggested that the cognitive hypothesis not only is unsustainable in its strong form, but even is questionable in a weaker version based on evidence that language processes themselves influence cognitive functioning.

A second approach explains the transition to combinatorial speech in terms of specifically linguistic advances. Proponents of this position emphasize that the beginning of two-word utterances represents the child's first foray (at least among English speakers) into the grammatical representation of meaning. Hence, the onset of combinations is regarded as the beginning of a qualitative shift in language acquisition, one that represents a move away from the reliance on single words in context to convey meaning (i.e., a semantic and pragmatic emphasis) toward the conveyance of meaning through linguistic devices such as word order and, later, grammatical morphology (i.e., a syntactic emphasis). In other words, what was once done using strategy A is now done using strategy B.

The idea that the appearance of two-word combinations reflects some kind of linguistic "switch" being thrown, seems a good deal less persuasive in light of the many incremental changes in one-word use that proceed it and the myriad cognitive changes that co-occur with it. Another reason to question whether a strictly linguistic process is at work is provided by the fact that the appearance of two-word combinations is highly correlated with vocabulary size (Bates et al., 1995; Fenson et al., 1994; Marchman & Bates, 1994), a relationship which suggests that both a gradual enrichment of the semantic system and gains in the ability to process and retain speech sounds have some kind of role to play.

In addition to these two major approaches to explaining the transition, there is a much less frequently cited, yet highly relevant, literature suggesting that advances in articulatory and phonological development also contribute to the onset of combinatorial speech. An indication of the role played by phonological constraints in the onset of two-word combinations was reported nearly 20 years ago by Waterson (1978), who documented the reappearance of phonological simplification with the onset of combinatorial speech among infants who had overcome this simplification of phonological forms in their single-word utterances. Similar findings of articulatory and phonological production constraints at the two-word level have been reported in examples of children first beginning to produce two-word combinations. There are consistent error patterns in which children are less accurate in their pronunciation of each word in the combination sequence than when either of these are produced alone (e.g., Donahue, 1986; Matthei, 1989). Typically, these "on-line" errors (Menn & Stoel-Gammon, 1995) in vocal pronunciation take the form of truncations of the individual words (e.g.: "mama's key" becomes "ma ke").

Focusing on the related issue of articulatory proficiency, Clark (1993) reasoned that the later onset of two-word combinations for some children might be causally associated with a slower rate of achieving good motor control of word production:

> children who take longer to set up articulatory programs for the words they are attempting are more likely to delay trying to produce two or more words in sequence because the motor coordination required is still too complicated for them. These children prefer to try just one word at a time for up to several months until they perfect some of the necessary articulatory skills. Others whose articulatory plans get established more quickly can move on to longer sequences and so produce multi-word utterances sooner. (p. 27)

Not only are children potentially limited in their ability to articulate two-word combinations, there is also the possibility that memory for phonological sequences may play a role in slowing down the advent of combinatorial speech. For example, in a series of studies with 4- to 5-year-olds, Gathercole and Baddeley (1989, 1990) demonstrated that phonological storage in working memory is strongly associated with vocabulary growth and that deficits in this storage system are significantly correlated with specific language impairments.

In summary, the exact mix of processes underlying the transition from one- to two-word speech remains a mystery. Correlations with cognitive advances are suggestive of a role for factors such as the ability to coordinate ideas, manipulate symbols, and plan ahead. The adherence to word order constraints and the expression of specific grammatical functions, even at the two-word stage, also imply a role for purely linguistic factors. Finally, there seems good reason to suspect that advances in the motor and phonological components of word production are involved. It is for the specific purpose of shedding additional light on the last of these factors that we now turn to the data from children whose early lexicons include symbolic gestures.

Symbolic Gestures: A Shortcut to Symbol Combination.   Perhaps the behavior we found most surprising in our early studies of symbolic gesturing was the spontaneous production of two-gesture and gesture + word combinations. For example, the 17-month-old who told her mother the dog wanted to go out by combining her gesture for "dog" (panting) with her knob-tuning gesture for "out." Because we found these combinations so intriguing, we made sure to collect information about symbol combinations during our weekly or biweekly interviews with the parents in our intervention studies. The types of combinations we asked about included the following: gesture + gesture (e.g., more + book as a request to read another book), gesture + word (e.g., more + "cheez" as a request for more cheese), and word + word (e.g., "more + "juice"). We were not disappointed. At least an occasional gesture combination was produced by 24 (75%) of our gesturing infants (the sign training group), with 11 of these infants producing such combinations to a very noticeable degree ("frequent combiners"). The last infants clearly were making use of the traditional "pivot-open" strategy by combining a wide variety of nouns with "pivot" gestures for the concepts "more," "allgone," and "where is it?" We also had information about word + word combinations, both for the sign training infants and for the 37 infants in the verbal training group whose parents also were interviewed biweekly, but who knew nothing about symbolic gesturing. These data allow us to compare the age that gesture combining first appears with the age that the more traditional, two-word combinations are seen. To the extent that there is a difference, we will have garnered at least some support for the hypothesis that articulatory and phonological demands constrain the onset of two-word combinations.

In Table 6.4, we present a summary of the mean ages at which gesture + symbol combinations (GS = gesture + gesture or gesture + word) and word + word (WW) combinations were first seen. It is important to remember that, in contrast to many studies, the term *gesture* here is meant to refer exclusively to symbolic gestures, not pointing. It also is important to keep in mind the difficulties inherent in any effort to judge "onset" of combining, a problem that is especially difficult when parental reports (minus timing and intonation details) are one's only source of information. While acknowledging these issues, we feel justified in making the comparisons we do between WW combinations and GS combinations given that our judgments were based on comparable data.

For purposes of more detailed analyses of the sign training group, the 24 (of 32) infants who exhibited any GS combinations at all were subdivided into those who produced them sporadically ("occasional combiners") and those who produced them relatively frequently ("frequent combiners"). Both GS ages and WW ages were obtained for both groups. Because the infants in the verbal training group were not engaged in symbolic gesturing, only WW data were available for them.

Looking first at the results for the sign training group, it is clear that children began combining symbolic gestures with other symbols significantly earlier than they began combining words. The mean gap between the onset of GS combinations and WW combinations was 1½ months for the occasional combiners, and 3¼ months for the frequent combiners. The earlier appearance of GS combinations clearly demonstrates that infants have the cognitive ability to produce combinations in the gestural mode, even when they are not yet doing so in the vocal mode. We interpret this finding as support for the idea that infants who rely exclusively on the vocal modality to communicate are being held back from expressing combinations not only by the inevitable demands of appreciating syntactic relations, but also by the articulatory and phonological requirements inherent in vocalizing longer utterances.

If we now compare the sign training and verbal training infants in terms of the age at which WW combining began, we find a mean difference of 1.82 months favoring the sign training group, $F (1, 60) = 8.14$, $p = .0059$, suggesting that the sign training infants were gaining something through their experiences with symbolic gesturing which facilitated the onset of vocal combinations. Moreover, this advantage was not limited to the onset of speech, but was also evident at 24 months in significantly higher MLUs, (sign training: $M = 2.3$, verbal training: $M = 1.90$, $p = .017$) as reported in Goodwyn and Acredolo (1998). What might account for this advantage? Two possible candidates come to mind, possibilities which by no means are mutually exclusive: (a) The experience sign training infants had had at relatively early ages in combining gestures and gestures with words may have provided important practice in the process-

TABLE 6.4. Mean age of onset for combining symbolic words and/or symbolic gestures among infants in the sign training group and the verbal training group

	Word + Word	Gesture + Symbol*	Total Gesture Vocabulary
Sign training group (N = 32)	18.38 months[a]		
Frequent combiners (n = 11)	18.66 months[b]	15.41 months[b,f]	32.18[d,e]
Occasional combiners (n = 13)	17.65 months[c]	16.17 months[c,g]	13.85[d]
Noncombiners (n = 8)	19.00 months		14.38[e]
Verbal training group (N = 31)	20.2 months[a,f,g]		

Note. Means that share superscripts are significantly different at least at $p < .05$.
*Includes symbolic gestures paired with other symbolic gestures or with vocal words (G + G and G + W).

TABLE 6.5. Comparisons of the total number of symbols (gestures and words) produced by infants in the sign training group and the verbal training group assessed at monthly intervals from 12 to 18 months

Age (months)	Sign Training		Verbal Training		ANOVA Results	
	M	(SD)	M	(SD)	F (1, 62)	p
12	6.16	(5.56)	3.19	(3.33)	6.72	.012
13	11.69	(7.92)	6.59	(6.00)	8.4	.005
14	20.62	(11.22)	11.09	(9.72)	13.19	.0006
15	29.66	(14.84)	19.00	(17.53)	6.89	.011
16	43.53	(21.96)	29.31	(28.59)	4.98	.029
17	57.75	(28.92)	39.72	(37.31)	4.67	.035
18	70.94	(31.77)	52.75	(42.26)	3.79	.056

Note. N = 32 in both the sign training group and the verbal training group.

ing and memory skills needed for relating two symbolic representations in a single production, or (b) the availability of a larger lexicon at an earlier age (see Table 6.5) may have provided the sign training infants with a "critical mass" (Marchman & Bates, 1994) of vocabulary which then "kick-started" their combinatorial productions.

Evidence for the second possibility, as shown in Table 6.5, comes from comparisons of the total number of symbols (gestures and words) available in the infants' repertoires at monthly intervals from 12 to 18 months. At each of the seven comparison points, the infants in the sign training group had more symbols at their disposal than those in the verbal training group. This pattern—larger vocabulary and earlier combining—is consistent with reports from the MacArthur CDI that the size of the symbolic lexicon (whether words, gestures, or both) is associated with the onset of early combinations. It also is consistent with one final comparison shown in Table 6.4. When the subgroups within the sign training group, the occasional and frequent combiners, were compared in terms of the total number of symbolic gestures they had acquired, the results clearly favored the frequent combiners, M = 32.18, over the occasional combiners, M = 14.05. In other words, those infants who were most heavily engaged in combining gestures with other gestures or gestures with words, were also the infants with the largest gestural repertoires from which to choose, F (1, 30) = 27.6, p = .0001.

Taken together, the results of our comparisons of gesture combining and word combining suggest that the cognitive prerequisites for two-word speech may well be available earlier than we generally are led to believe based on the appearance of WW combinations. In the search for why the two-word stage is so long in coming, it would seem that among the more likely culprits are the articulatory and phonological requirements of vocal speech.

☐ Future Directions and Conclusions

Our goal in this chapter has been to describe the phenomenon that we call symbolic gesturing, and demonstrate its utility as a new window into language development. By enabling infants to bypass the articulatory and phonological demands of vocal symbols, symbolic gestures provide them with a way to become active participants in conversation at early ages. Because they denote specific objects and conditions in the world, just as words do, symbolic gestures can function for the child in ways that simple pointing cannot. Babies whose parents encourage them to acquire gestural symbols are in a position to label objects, make requests, describe things, and answer questions without having to wait for the equivalent words to enter their vocabularies. We believe that, as a consequence of this active participation, infants garner valuable information about the meanings of words, the scope of categories, and how language can function in interpersonal interactions. Moreover, because an infant's use of a symbolic gesture inevitably elicits a flood of vocal language from adults who see it, the infant also has an opportunity to learn more about the sound patterns (i.e., words) associated with the very items about which he or she really cares. In view of these advantages, it should come as no surprise that our sign training infants also ended up learning vocal language faster than the other two groups (Goodwyn & Acredolo, 1998).

To illustrate how symbolic gesturing can provide new perspectives on old problems, we focused on three specific issues: the comprehension-performance gap, the verbal spurt, and the onset of symbolic combinations. In each case, we provided evidence showing that infants with symbolic gestures in their productive repertoires were behaving differently than those dependent on words alone: (a) the gap between comprehension and symbol production was narrowed, (b) the vocal vocabulary spurt was atypically abrupt (i.e., case study of KA), and (c) symbol combining occurred at earlier ages. What these patterns reveal, we believe, is that cognitive advances can occur independently of articulatory and phonological progress and that anyone interested in language acquisition would be well advised to take seriously the challenges posed by these two pieces of the language puzzle.

We also believe our research contains an important message for researchers whose main focus is cognitive development. Because symbolic gestures take the demands of speech production out of the mix, they can be used to open up a channel of communication not only between infant and parent but also between infant and researcher. In the hope that the following examples will whet their appetites for more, we would like to close by illustrating for our readers some specific questions that symbolic gesturing can contribute to answering. In each case, we cite just one or two examples from our own files to make our point. Note, in particular, how young these infants are. Although anecdotal in nature and therefore open to multiple interpretations, these vignettes are tantalizing in what they hint about development. Sometimes, it seems to us, a simple story conveys an idea more clearly than pages of scholarly prose.

What Things Do Infants Perceive as Alike Enough to Be Called by the Same Name?   In order to understand more about concept development, researchers often look at over- and underextensions of labels. The infant's early words certainly are useful in this regard, but require waiting for gains in vocal vocabulary. Symbolic gestures help eliminate this constraint, enabling even very young infants to show us how they are organizing their worlds.

> MB (11¾ months)—Despite only a few weeks exposure to the "allgone" gesture her parents were modeling (palm down, back and forth movement), MB spontaneously produced the gesture when her cat ran away with the ball she had tossed to him. She was already using the gesture appropriately to indicate when she had finished her food.

How Keenly Do Infants Attend to Details of the World Around Them?   In order to build a knowledge base about the world, infants have to do the same thing we do: pay attention to what is going on around them. If our research participants are any indication, infants make it a habit to attend closely to what they see and hear around them, and take particular pride in sharing their observations with others.

> KA (13 months)—After passing by a record store window, KA enthusiastically began producing his gesture for "crocodile." When his mother returned with him to the window, KA pointed at what had caught his eye: In the corner of a record jacket was a tiny picture of a crocodile emerging from the water.

What Abstract Concepts Are Infants Mastering?   For obvious reasons, most investigators of early conceptual development focus on object concepts. The following two examples suggest that, in doing so, we are underestimating the capacity of young infants to think in more abstract terms.

> ZW (16 months)—Presumably based on his mother's tendency to put hand to chest when she was startled or afraid, ZW spontaneously developed a symbolic gesture (patting his chest) to indicate the same thing about his own emotional state and communicate his desire to be comforted. Starting at 16 months, he used this gesture in a wide variety of appropriate situations: when he saw scary (to him) pictures, on being approached by strangers, when startled by hearing large dogs bark, when a wave hit his feet, and on seeing his grandmother dressed up like a clown. The fact that he was often already in his mother's or grandmother's arms when he produced the gesture suggests that his goal was to communicate about his emotional state, not just solicit protection.

> KP (18 months)—Having used a petting gesture to label cats for several months (one hand stroking the opposite forearm), KP was suddenly confronted with her first tiny kitten. Her response was to look up at her mother and make tiny, quick gestures with the tips of her fingers along the fingertips of her other hand. When her mother asked if she was trying to tell her they were "little" cats, KP smiled.

What Can Infants Remember about Past Experiences? It is notoriously difficult to assess long-term memory for events in nonverbal infants and toddlers. One way around the problem has been to assess deferred imitation, the assumption being that the ability to repeat an action seen earlier depends on the ability to retain some kind of mental representation. The drawback to this approach is that the type of memory being assessed is "procedural" rather than semantic or episodic. The following anecdote suggests that symbolic gesturing may prove to be a useful alternative.

> KA (16 months)—Within days of learning to use a gesture to label spiders (index fingers together and twisted), KA began to routinely and insistently produce the gesture when he and his mother would settle down on his bed to read stories at bedtime. At first puzzled by his behavior, his mother subsequently remembered that KA had been badly frightened about a month earlier by a large spider on the wall above his pillow. Now in elementary school, KA continues to be phobic about spiders.

What Do They Know about the Pragmatics of Language? It is no secret that infants use their early words to label objects, make requests, and answer questions. They even learn to use social conventions like "please" and "thank you" appropriately. The following example, told to us by the director of the infant center on our campus, illustrates that, at least by 22 months, this child was much more sophisticated than that.

> CR (22 months)—During "circle time" in nursery school, CR watched as her teacher asked another child, using words and gestures, to "stop" (palm forward) "eating" (fingers to lips + smacking lips) his popsicle until after the singing was "done" (palm down, moved back and forth). When CR subsequently saw him sneak a lick anyway, she got up, came all the way across the circle, stood in front of the teacher, and pointed at the child. In what seems pretty clearly an effort to "tattle" on him, she proceeded to combine three gestures: "eat" + "no" + "alldone." These three gestures "said" it all!

As even a quick look at the questions listed above makes clear, the quest to understand how humans acquire language has come a long way since Skinner's day (Skinner, 1957). The notion that feedback from the environment is all the child needs to begin talking seems enormously simplistic, as does the idea that the environment is irrelevant, that language unfolds like the petals of a flower. Instead, we now appreciate the centrality of the "active organism" to any satisfactory explanation, and acknowledge that language cannot be viewed independently of that organism's abilities and proclivities to perceive, understand, and remember things about the world. We also understand, as our interest in pragmatics demonstrates, that the child is first and foremost a social being for whom learning to talk is not an end in itself, but rather a means to an end. These enlightened views of language development, at the same time as they increase the validity of our conclusions, do not make the challenge of studying the phenomenon any easier. What we need are ways to disentangle the strands that contribute to language development without losing sight of the tapestry they form. It is our belief that symbolic gesturing represents one way to do just that. By enabling young infants to "speak" to us without having to wait for all the necessary words, it is hard to believe we will not end up learning much more about them than we know today. All this and we also end up with less frustrated infants and happier families. How is that for a winning combination?

☐ References

Abrahamsen, A. A., Cavallo, M. M., & McCluer, J. A. (1985). Is the sign advantage a robust phenomenon? From gesture to language in two modalities. *Merrill-Palmer Quarterly, 31,* 177–209.

Acredolo, L. P., & Goodwyn, S. W. (1984). *Symbolic gesturing in language development: A case study.* Paper presented at the annual meeting of the American Psychological Association, Toronto, Ontario, Canada.

Acredolo, L. P., & Goodwyn, S. W. (1985). Symbolic gesturing in language development: A case study. *Human Development, 28,* 40–49.

Acredolo, L. P., & Goodwyn, S. W. (1988). Symbolic gesturing in normal infants. *Child Development, 59,* 450–466.

Acredolo, L. P., & Goodwyn, S. W. (1996). *Baby signs: How to talk with your baby before your baby can talk.* Chicago: NTB/Contemporary.

Austin, J. (1962). *How to do things with words.* Cambridge, MA: Harvard University Press.

Baldwin, D. A. (1995). Understanding the link between joint attention and language. In C. Moore & P. J. Dunham (Eds.), *Joint attention: Its origins and role in development.* Hillsdale, NJ: Erlbaum.

Baldwin, D. A., & Markman, E. M. (1989). Establishing word-object relations: A first step. *Child Development, 60,* 381–398.

Bates, E., Benigni, L., Bretherton, I., Camaioni, L., & Volterra, V. (1977). From gesture to the first word. In M. Lewis, N. Lewis, & L. Rosenblum (Eds.), *Interaction conversation and the development of language.* New York: Wiley.

Bates, E., Benigni, L., Bretherton, I., Camaioni, L., & Volterra, V. (1979). *The emergence of symbols: Cognition and communication in infancy.* New York: Academic Press.

Bates. E., Bretherton. I., &.Snyder, L. (1988). *From first words to grammar: Individual differences and dissociable mechanisms.* Cambridge, England: Cambridge University Press.

Bates, E., Camaioni, L., & Volterra, V. (1975). The acquisition of performatives prior to speech. *Merrill-Palmer Quarterly, 21,* 205–226.

Bates, E., Dale, P. S., & Thal, D. (1995). Individual differences and their implications for theories of language development. In P. Fletcher & B. MacWhinney (Eds.), *The handbook of child language* (pp. 96–151). Cambridge, MA: Blackwell.

Bloom, L. (1970). *Language development: Form and function in emerging grammars.* Cambridge, MA: MIT Press.

Braine, M. D. S. (1963). The ontogeny of English phrase structure: The first phase. *Language, 39,* 3–13.

Brody, B. A., Kinney, H. C., Klonman, A. S., & Gilley, F. H. (1987). Sequence of central nervous system myelination in human infancy: I. An autopsy study of myelination. *Journal of Neuropathology and Experimental Neurology, 46,* 283–309.

Browman, C. P., & Goldstein, L. (1985). Articulatory gestures as phonological units. *Phonology, 6,* 102–151.

Brown, R., & Bellugi, U. (1964). Three processes in the child's acquisition of syntax. *Harvard Educational Review, 34,* 133–151.

Bruner, J. S. (1974). From communication to language—a psychological perspective. *Cognition, 3,* 255–287.

Bullowa, M. (1979). *Before speech.* Cambridge, England: Cambridge University Press.

Casby, M. W., & Ruder, K. E. (1983). Symbolic play and early language development in normal and MR children. *Journal of Speech and Hearing Research, 26,* 404–411.

Case, R., & Khanna, F. (1981). The missing links: Stages in children's progression from sensorimotor to logical thought. In W. Fischer (Ed.), *New directions for child development* (pp. 21–32). San Francisco: Jossey-Bass.

Caselli, M. C. C. (1983). Communication to language: Deaf children's and hearing children's development compared. *Sign Language Studies, 39,* 113–143.

Chomsky, N. (1959). Review of B. F. Skinner's Verbal Behavior. *Language, 35,* 16–58.

Chomsky, N. (1965). *Aspects of the theory of syntax.* Cambridge, MA: MIT Press.

Clark, E. V. (1993). *The lexicon in acquisition.* Cambridge, England: Cambridge University Press.

Cromer, R. F. (1988). The cognition hypothesis revisited. In E. S. Kessel (Ed.), *The development of language and language researchers. Essays in honor of Roger Brown.* Hillsdale, NJ: Erlbaum.

Dobrich, W., & Scarborough, H. S. (1992). Phonological characteristics of words young children try to say. *Journal of Child Language, 19,* 597–616.

Donahue, M. (1986). Phonological constraints on the emergence of two-word utterances. *Journal of Child Language, 13,* 209–218.

Dore, J. (1974). A pragmatic description of early language development. *Journal of Psycholinguistic Research, 4,* 423–430.

Dore, J., Franklin, M. B., Miller, R. T., & Ramer, A. L. H. (1976). Transitional phenomena in early language acquisition. *Journal of Child Language, 3,* 13–28.

Dromi, E. (1987). *Early lexical development.* Cambridge, England: Cambridge University Press.

Eisele, J. A., & Aram, D. M. (1995). Lexical and grammatical development in children with early hemisphere damage: A cross-sectional view from birth to adolescence. In P. Fletcher & B. MacWhinney (Eds.), *The handbook of child language* (pp. 642–664). Cambridge, MA: Blackwell.

Ervin-Tripp, S., & Mitchell-Kernan, C. (1977). *Child discourse.* New York: Academic Press.

Escalona, S. (1973). Basic modes of social interaction: Their emergence and patterning during the first two years of life. *Merrill-Palmer Quarterly, 19,* 205–232.

Fenson, L., Dale, P. S., Reznick, J. S., Bates, E., Thal, D. J., & Pethick, S. T. (1994). Variability in early communicative development. *Monographs of the Society for Research in Child Development, 59* (5, Serial No. 242).

Gathercole, S. E., & Baddeley, A. D. (1989). Evaluation of the role of phonological STM in the development of vocabulary in children: A longitudinal study. *Journal of Memory and Language, 28,* 200–213.

Gatthercole, S. E., & Baddeley, A. D. (1990). Phonological memory deficits in language disordered children: Is there a causal connection? *Journal of Memory and Language, 29,* 336–360.

Goldfield B., & Reznick, J. S. (1990). Early lexical acquisition: Rate, content, and the vocabulary spurt. *Journal of Child Language, 17,* 171–183.

Goldin-Meadow, S., & Feldman, H. (1979). The development of language-like communication without a language model. *Science, 197,* 401–403.

Golinkoff, R. M., Mervis, C. V., & Hirsh-Pasek, K. (1994). Early object labels: The case for a developmental lexical principles framework. *Journal of Child Language, 21,* 125–155.

Goodwyn, S. W., & Acredolo, L. P. (1993). Symbolic gesture versus word: Is there a modality advantage for onset of symbol use? *Child Development, 64,* 688–701.

Goodwyn, S. W., & Acredolo, L. P. (1998). Encouraging symbolic gestures: A new perspective on the relationship between gesture and speech. In J. Iverson & S. Goldin-Meadow (Eds.), *The balance between gesture and speech in childhood* (pp. 61–76). San Francisco: Jossey-Bass.

Gopnik, A., & Meltzoff, A. (1987). The development of categorization in the second year of life and its relation to other cognitive and linguistic developments. *Child Development, 58,* 1523–1531.

Gopnik, A., & Meltzoff, A. (1992). Categorization and naming: Basic level sorting in 18-month-olds and its relation to language. *Child Development, 63,* 1091–1103.

Greenfield, P. M. (1978). Structural parallels between language and action in development. In A. Lock (Ed.), *Action, gesture and symbol* (pp. 415–445). London: Academic Press.

Harding, C. G., & Golinkoff, R. (1979). The origins of intentional vocalization in prelinguistic infants. *Child Development, 50,* 33–40.

Harris, M., Yeeles, C., Chasin, J., & Oakley, Y. (1992). Symmetries and asymmetries in early lexical comprehension and production. *Journal of Child Language, 22,* 1–18.

Holmes, K. M., & Holmes, D. W. (1980). Signed and spoken language development in a hearing child of hearing parents. *Sign Language Studies, 28,* 239–254.

Karmiloff-Smith, A. (1992). *Beyond modularity: A developmental perspective on cognitive science.* Cambridge, MA: MIT Press.

Kelly, C. A., & Dale, P. S. (1989). Cognitive skills associated with the onset of multi-word utterances. *Journal of Speech and Hearing Research, 32,* 645–656.

Kent, R. D. (1992). The biology of phonological development. In C. A. Ferguson, L. Menn, & C. Stoel-Gammon (Eds.), *Phonological development: Models, research, implications* (pp. 65–89). Timonium, MD: York Press.

Kent, R. D., & Miolo, G. (1995). Phonological development. In P. Fletcher & B. MacWhinney (Eds.), *The handbook of child language* (pp. 303–334). Cambridge, MA: Blackwell.

Kernan, K. T. (1970). Semantic relations and the child's acquisition of language. *Anthropological Linguistics, 12,* 171–187.

Lindblom, B. (1992). Phonological units as adaptive emergents of lexical development. In C. A. Ferguson, L. Menn & C. Stoel-Gammon (Eds.), *Phonological development: Models, research, implications* (pp. 131–163). Timonium. MD: York Press.

Marchman, V., & Bates, E. (1994). Continuity in lexical and morphological development: A test of the critical mass hypothesis. *Journal of Child Language, 21,* 339–366.

Matthei, E. (1989). Crossing boundaries: More evidence for phonological constraints on early multi-word utterances. *Journal of Child Language, 16,* 41–54.

McCall, R., Parke, R., & Kavanaugh, R. (1977). Imitation of live and televised models by children one to three years of age. *Monographs of the Society for Research in Child Development, 42* (No. 5, Serial No. 173).

McCune, L. (1992). First words: A dynamic systems view. In C. A. Ferguson, L. Menn, & C. Stoel-Gammon (Eds.), *Phonological development: Models, research, implications* (pp. 313–335). Timonium, MD: York Press.

McCune-Nicolich, L. (1981). Toward symbolic functioning: Structure of early pretend games and potential parallels with language. *Child Development, 52,* 785–797.

McCune-Nicolich, L., & Bruskin, C. (1982). Combinatorial competency in play and language. In D. Pepler & K. Rubin (Eds.), *The play of children: Current theory and research.* New York: Karger.

McDade, H., Simpson, M. A., & Booth, C. (1980). The use of sign language with handicapped normal-hearing infants. *Journal of Child Communication Disorders, 4,* 82–89.

McNeill, D. (1966). Developmental psycholinguistics. In F. Smith & G. A. Miller (Eds.), *The genesis of language* (pp. 15–84). Cambridge, MA: MIT Press.

McNeill, D. (1970). *The acquisition of language.* New York: Harper & Row.

McShane, J. (1980). *Learning to talk.* Cambridge, England: Cambridge University Press.

Menn, L., & Stoel-Gammon, C. (1995). Phonological development. In P. Fletcher & B. MacWhinney (Eds.), *The handbook of child language* (pp. 335–360). Cambridge, MA: Blackwell.

Mervis, C. B., & Bertrand, J. (1995). Early lexical acquisition and the vocabulary spurt: A response to Goldfield & Reznick. *Journal of Child Language, 22,* 461–468.

Miller, W., & Ervin, S. (1964). The development of grammar in child language. In U. Bellugi & R. Brown (Eds.), The acquisition of language. *Monographs of the Society for Research in Child Development. 29* (92, Serial No. 149).

Naigles, L. G., & Gelman, S. A (1995). Overextensions in comprehension and production revisited: Preferential-looking in a study of *dog, cat,* and *cow. Journal of Child Language, 22,* 19–46.

O'Reilly, A. W., Painter, K. M., & Bornstein, M. H. (1997). Relations between language and symbolic gesture development in early childhood. *Cognitive Development, 12,* 185–197.

Oviatt, S. L. (1980). The emerging ability to comprehend language: An experimental approach. *Child Development, 51,* 97–106.

Piaget, J. (1951). *Play, dreams, and imitation in childhood.* New York: Norton Press.

Prinz, P. M., & Prinz, E. A. (1979). Simultaneous acquisition of ASL and spoken English (in a hearing child of a deaf mother and hearing father). Phase I: Early lexical development. *Sign Language Studies, 25,* 283–296.

Rescorla, L., & Goossens, M. (1992). Symbolic play development in toddlers with expressive specific language impairment. *Journal of Speech and Hearing Research, 6,* 1290–1320.

Schlesinger, I. M. (1971). Production of utterances and language acquisition. In D. I. Slobin (Ed.), *The ontogenesis of grammar.* New York: Academic Press.

Schwartz, R., & Leonard, L. (1982). Do children pick and choose? An examination of phonological selection and avoidance in early lexical acquisition. *Journal of Child Language, 9,* 319–336.

Schwartz, R., Leonard, L., Loeb, D. F., & Swanson, L. (1987). Attempted sounds are sometimes not: An expanded view of phonological selection and avoidance. *Journal of Child Language, 14,* 411–418.

Searle, J. R. (1969). *Speech acts.* London: Cambridge University Press.

Shore, C. (1986). Combinatorial play: Conceptual development and early multi-word speech. *Developmental Psychology, 22,* 184–190.

Shore, C., O'Connell, B., & Bates, E. (1984). First sentences in language and symbolic play. *Developmental Psychology, 20,* 872–880.

Skinner, B. F. (1957). *Verbal behavior.* New York: Appleton-Century-Crafts.

Slobin, D. I. (1973). Cognitive prerequisites for the acquisition of grammar. In C. A. Ferguson & D. I. Slobin (Eds.), *Studies of child language development* (pp. 175–208). New York: Holt, Rinehart & Winston.

Smith, B. L. (1988). The emergent lexicon from a phonetic perspective. In M. D. Smith & J. L. Locke (Eds.), *The emergent lexicon: The child's development of a linguistic vocabulary* (pp. 75–109). New York: Academic Press.

Snyder, L., Bates, E., & Bretherton, I. (1981). Content and context in early lexical development. *Journal of Child Language, 8,* 565–582.

Stern, D. (1977). *The first relationship: Infant and mother.* London: Fontana/Open Books.

Studdert-Kennedy, M. (1987). The phoneme as a perceptuomotor structure. In A. Allport, D. Mackay, W. Prinz, & E. Scheerer (Eds.), *Language perception and production* (pp. 67–84). London: Academic Press.

Sugarman, S. (1983). Empirical versus logical issues in the transition from prelinguistic to linguistic communication. In R. M. Golinkoff (Ed.), *The transition from prelinguistic to linguistic communication* (pp. 134–144). Hillsdale, NJ: Erlbaum.

Thelen, E. (1991). Motor aspects of emergent speech: A dynamic approach. In N. A. Krasnegor, D. M. Rumbaugh, R. L. Schiefelbusch, & M. Studdert-Kennedy (Eds.), *Biological and behavioral determinants of language development.* Hillsdale, NJ: Erlbaum.

Thelen, E., & Smith, L. (1994). *A dynamic systems approach to the development of cognition and action.* Cambridge, MA: MIT Press.

Thelen, E., & Ulrich, B. D. (1991). Hidden skills. *Monographs of the Society for Research in Child Development, 56* (1, Serial No. 223).

Tyler, A. A., & Edwards, M. L. (1993). Lexical acquisition and acquisition of initial voiceless stops. *Journal of Child Language, 20,* 253–273.

Vihman, M. M. (1976). From pre-speech to speech: On early phonology. *Papers and Reports on Child Language Development, 3,* 51–94.

Vihman, M. M. (1981), Phonology and the development of the lexicon: Evidence from children's errors. *Journal of Child Language, 8,* 239–264.

Vihman, M. M. (1996). *Phonological development: The origins of language in the child.* Cambridge, MA: Blackwell.

Volterra, V. (1981). Gestures, signs, and words at two years: When does communication become language? *Sign Language Studies, 33,* 351–362.

Volterra, V., & Caselli, M. C. C. (1985). From gestures and vocalization to signs and words. In W. Stokoe & V. Volterra (Eds.), *Proceedings of the Third International Symposium on Sign Language Research* (pp. 1–9). Silver Spring, MD: Linstock Press.

Waterson, N. (1978). Growth of complexity in phonological development. In N. Waterson & C. Snow (Eds.), *The development of communication* (pp. 415–442). London: Wiley.

Werner, H., & Kaplan, B. (1963). *Symbol formation.* New York: Wiley.

PRESCHOOL YEARS

7
CHAPTER

Carollee Howes
Holli Tonyan

Peer Relations

☐ Introduction

In playgrounds, playrooms, their bedrooms, and in any number of public spaces, children play with their peers. Toddlers play peekaboo, run-and-chase, or simple pretend games like "I am pulling you in my wagon. We are going to the store." Preschoolers include elaborate scripts and costumes in their pretend games. "We are going camping, and pretend that there is a bear, and you are the baby in your pajamas." "And I climb out of the tent and try to give the bear a cookie." To the adult observer, these games seem almost magical. Where do the children get these ideas and how do they manage to communicate the meaning of their play to peers, sometimes to a peer that they have just encountered? We will explore these ideas by tracing theory and research in peer relations over a particular historical period—the 1970s through the 1990s—and by using Howes' research program as an exemplar of this historical period.

We will argue that, within groups of peers, children develop social interaction skills and construct social relationships. These social interactions and relationships become the basis of peer group social structure. Through these early developmental experiences, children internalize representations of social relationships and social network that we assume influence their individual orientations to the social world as older children, adolescents, and adults. The chapter traces three periods of research: the acquisition of structurally complex interaction, individual differences in peer interaction, and relationship construction and quality. Each period of research was influenced by sociocultural trends and by the developmental theory that was dominant at the time. Description of the three periods is marked by an initial emphasis on the acquisition of structurally complex social interaction skills, followed by a focus on individual differences in peer interaction, and concluded with the current emphasis on the importance of relationship construction and relationship quality.

☐ Learning to Interact: Early Research in the Development of Peer Relations

The ideas represented in this chapter illustrate a tension between a focus on the individual development of children and a focus on the wider social context within which individual development occurs. As developmental psychologists, we are concerned with ages and stages. We assume that development occurs in an orderly fashion. We expect that children's behavior is organized, that organizational structures which are common across children can be identified and described, and that less complex organizational forms precede more complex organizational forms. However, because we work from within a feminist political perspective and are committed to a methodological orientation based largely on naturalistic observation, we do not separate children's development from the social context of development. In this work, *social context* is defined along a continuum. It can be defined narrowly as in examining the social interaction skills of an individual as influenced by a social partner and it can be defined more broadly as the quality of the child care environment in which the child interacts with peers.

To illustrate this tension between a focus on individual development and a focus on social context, we will describe an early transformation in the study of peer relations. In this example, shifts in the social contexts of the research led to a broadening of the focus of the research. From the 1920s and 1930s until the early 1970s, the study of peer relations in the United States was dominated by early descriptive research about the ways in which individuals' social skills developed. Buhler (1931), Maudry and Nekula (1930), and the later defining and classic work of Parten (1932) provided the basis for much of the work in this area. These early researchers argued, based on naturalistic observations of peer groups, that, across age, all children progressed through a set of social participation categories from solitary play, through parallel play, to true social participation in the form of cooperative play.

In retrospect, we can see that the development captured in these theories was closely linked to the context in which the observations typically took place: nursery schools. Nursery schools were part of a social movement which was based in a particular political belief system. Within this belief system, it was assumed that the ideal child rearing environment for preschoolers consisted of a "stay-at-home mother" and, two or three mornings a week, a socialization experience with children of similar backgrounds. The ideal child rearing environment for younger children did not include peers. According to Reed (1950), "The nursery school is a place where young children learn as they play and as they share experiences with other children" (p. 3).

> Living with a group of equals is a significantly different experience for a child from that of being a member of a family group. As students in the nursery school laboratory we can add to our understanding of what relationships mean to people as we observe the children in their living group. (Reed, 1950, p. 332)

The first and most influential nursery schools were physically located in colleges and universities and served as laboratories for the study of child development and for training professional teachers. Because research in peer relations and teacher training was confounded with a particular social organization, for 50 years, early childhood teachers in training and parents seeking advice were told that 2- and 3-year-olds were solitary or parallel players, while 5-year-olds were cooperative players.

Current research and theory on peer interaction supports an alternative perspective. The forms of play identified by Parten (1932) are not an invariant sequence based on age but, instead, are categories of play which tend to be used by children of all ages as the play they engage in with peers gradually shows more signs of structure, cognitive ability, and communicative ability (Bakeman & Brownlee, 1980). When research begins with a different set of assumptions and takes place in a different context, children as young as 10 to 12 months of age can be seen engaging at least one peer in play, which is more social than expected based on early theories (Howes, 1988a).

This alternative perspective was established because of two sociocultural changes: (a) research on peer relations moved out of laboratory schools, and (b) a social movement changed our beliefs about appropriate child rearing environments. In the 1970s, the women's movement and changes in the structuring of the United States economy led to an influx of mothers of very young children into the workforce. Part-day nursery schools could not accommodate the child care needs of these women. There was a dramatic increase in full-day child care centers that served infants and toddlers, instead of just preschoolers. These social changes changed the social context for constructing peer interactions, peer relationships, and peer social networks. In the social context of child care, peer interactions and relationships developed within long periods of "everyday life events" rather than within relatively brief "socialization experiences." Children in child care centers were with their peers every day and stayed in child care from breakfast time, through nap, until the end of the day. The nursery school experience might be compared to a date, while the child care experience is more like living together.

Beyond structural changes in the social context of peer encounters, the women's movement changed the context in which the researchers were formulating their questions. They began to ask questions about the function of peers and peer relationships. Rather than simply being part of enrichment experiences, peers potentially could function to provide the child with experiences of social support, trust, and intimacy in the absence of the child's mother. Children who grew up together sharing the common resources of the child care center might engage in close rather than conflictual interaction. Cross-sex or cross-ethnic peers who became friends in a different environment than a traditional nuclear family might form different kinds of relationships. In the context of these questions, research on developmental changes in the complexity of peer interaction structure began.

☐ Complexity in the Structure of Peer Interaction

Casual observations of infants and toddlers within these settings suggested that they were not behaving according to Parten's (1932) observations: Their play was more interesting and complex than that of an onlooker or parallel player. Faced with this discrepancy, Howes conducted a qualitative study of two sets of infants from their first encounters in child care through the end of their first year together. Based on detailed narrative observations, both sets of children appeared to form friendships (Howes, 1981). This led to a new program of research designed to understand how infants and toddlers constructed their play encounters.

To answer these new questions, we needed new tools for looking at peer interaction. In 1972, Blurton-Jones published an influential collection of observational studies of peer behaviors using ethological methods, with careful attention to the description and functional meaning of behaviors. Ethology had its roots in biology and the study of animal behavior. It provided a method for close, detailed observations of behavior. Subsequently, a generation of researchers including Eckerman, Davis, and Didow (1989), Hay (1985), Howes (1988), Ross and Goldman (1976), and Vandell, Wilson, and Buchanan (1980) applied ethological methods to the task of identifying and describing changing structures underlying peer interaction.

Remember that the goal of this research was to understand the behaviors and social organizations of children with their peers within full-time child care. Ultimately, Howes wished to address questions such as whether early or late entrance into child care was more beneficial. Would a 4-year-old who had constructed his or her peer interactions and relationships within a particular group of age-mates over a 3-year period have different kinds of interactions and relationships than a 4-year-old who had spent those 3 years with a changing group of peers or without regular peer contacts? In order to meet this goal, Howes spent approximately a decade developing a system for describing and documenting the level of complexity of peer play for children within peer groups. This system is called the Peer Play Scale (Howes, 1980, 1988a; Howes & Matheson, 1992). Because each of the points of the scale represent increases in the complexity of play, we will use the scale to frame our discussion of the structure of play.

The theoretical framework that provided the basis for the Peer Play Scale was developed under the mentorship of Mueller. At the time, Mueller was arguing that very young children construct increasingly complex schemas for acting on peers, much as Piaget hypothesized that they do on objects (Mueller & Brenner, 1977). Howes (1983, 1996) reasoned that a necessary condition for children to be considered friends is that adult observers could infer from their behavior that each child understood the other to be a social actor and that social actions between partners could be coordinated and communicated. Therefore, as a starting place, research had to establish that children behaved as if they had these understandings. Similarly, Howes (1983, 1996) reasoned that later development in social play could occur only as the child increasingly understood the role of the other, incorporated symbolic play, and communicated shared meaning. These understandings are the bases for the behaviors that are captured in the Peer Play Scale. Initially, children are expected to show signs of each of these three components but, eventually, they are expected to use them fluidly and communicate negotiations with each other about their play.

Howes identified two key aspects of early play which presuppose such social understanding: mutual social awareness and coordination of action. Together, these two markers represent the necessary components for what Howes (1980) called complementary and reciprocal play. Specifically, each play partner's actions reverse the actions of the other. A child chases his or her partner, then is chased. One child peeks at his or her partner, the partner says boo, and then peeks back. Research in cognitive and communicative development (Howes, 1988a) has suggested that the representational underpinnings of these understandings are present in children as young as the toddler developmental period. Naturalistic observations (Howes, 1980, 1988a) established that toddler-age children constructing their peer interactions within full-time child care centers were indeed engaging in complementary and reciprocal play.

The next developmental step is to incorporate symbols into shared play. Children in peer group settings first begin to use symbols or to play pretend alone or with a competent adult player (Howes, 1985a, 1992), but symbolic play soon enters the realm of peer play. Pretend play with a partner requires both that the child manipulate symbolic transformations and communicate the resulting symbolic meaning to a partner. We see the simplest form of social pretend play, called *cooperative social pretend play* in Peer Play Scale terminology, among toddlers in full-time child care centers. Central to this level of structure is that children enact nonliteral role exchanges (Howes, 1985a; Howes, Unger, & Seidner, 1989). Play partners integrate their pretend actions by using a familiar pretend theme or script such as a tea party. Similarly to complementary and reciprocal play, cooperative social pretend play requires that children reverse the actions of the other but, in this form of play, the actions are nonliteral or symbolic. The actions of the children presuppose that each partner understands that each player may engage in the symbolic behaviors. The children are able to share understanding about the symbolic meaning of their play, but this is communicated through the implicit script of the play rather than explicit talk about the play. For example, when a toddler offers a cup to a partner who is holding a pitcher, the child is engaged in a very simple form of social pretend play compared to the preschool-age child who discusses the play script, sets the table, brings festively dressed toy bears to the table, and gives the bears a tea party. Nonetheless, toddler-age children are beginning to understand the role of the partner in constructing social sequences.

Despite the new skills incorporated into cooperative social pretend play, it remains a pale imitation of the well-developed fantasy play of older children which we label complex social pretend play. Toddlers have only just begun to transform symbols so their transformations are not fluid and may be only partially developed.

By preschool age, children's symbolic, linguistic, and communicative development permits meta-communication about social pretend play. Children can plan and negotiate the sequences of symbolic actions with fluidity, modify the script as it progresses, and step out of the pretend frame to correct the actions or script. These behaviors, such as those seen in a tea party for the toy bears, indicate the most structurally complex play captured in the Peer Play Scale. This play form is labeled *complex social pretend play*.

The Peer Play Scale is based on a set of measurement assumptions: the play forms develop in the predicted sequence and children develop particular play forms before or during particular age intervals predicted by theories of cognitive and communicative development (Howes, 1987, 1992). Longitudinal (Howes & Matheson, 1992) and cross-sectional studies (Howes, 1980, 1985a) which focused on validating the Peer Play Scale supported these two assumptions. (Howes, 1987, 1992). In a longitudinal study of 48 children observed at 6-month intervals, we calculated each child's highest level of the Peer Play Scale during each observation period (Howes & Matheson, 1992). More than half of the children had engaged in complementary and reciprocal peer play by 13 to 15 months and nearly all by 19 to 23 months. More than half of the children had engaged in cooperative social pretend play by 30 to 35 months, and nearly half of the children had engaged in complex social pretend by 42 to 47 months. Seventy-four percent of the children followed the predicted sequence for emergence of play forms: complementary and reciprocal play, cooperative social pretend play, and complex social pretend play. Furthermore, children who showed earlier emergence of complementary and reciprocal play also showed earlier emergence of cooperative and complex social pretend play (Howes & Matheson, 1992).

As a measure of structural complexity, the Peer Play Scale makes no distinctions among positive, aggressive, or agonistic (instrumental aggression such as toy taking) social bids. A structurally complex interaction could reflect prosocial behavior, a conflict, or any number of social styles. As we discuss below, research examining associations between the structure and content of peer interaction appeared later in the 1980s and 1990s.

Perhaps because it captures structural complexity rather than the content of peer play, the Peer Play Scale has been successfully used in cultures other than the United States. Farver has used the Peer Play Scale to describe and examine peer interaction in such diverse cultures and ethnic groups as Mexican children (Farver, 1992), Latino and African American Head Start children in Los Angeles (Farver, 1996; Farver & Frosch, 1996), Indonesian children (Farver & Howes, 1988; Farver & Wimbarti, 1995), and Korean American children (Farver, Kim, & Lee, 1995). Across studies, children's play was represented at each structural play level and play forms emerged at similar ages. When differences emerged, they were in the frequency of play forms rather than in different play forms or a different sequence of play. Farver (1996) suggested that the sociocultural context influences the style or frequencies of peer play.

Gender also appears to influence the style rather than the structure of peer play. There are well-established differences in the content of the play of boys and girls (Maccoby, 1984). However, consistent with the lack of cultural and ethnic differences in the structure of peer play, there appear to be few differences in the complexity of the structure of children's peer play (Howes, 1980, 1988a; Howes & Matheson, 1992;

Howes & Wu, 1990). Girls and boys of the same age engage in structurally similar play, although the content may differ. For example, both a game of mother, sister, and baby among girls and a game of the day the tigers ate the village among boys are very likely to be rated as complex social pretend play.

However, consistent with a Vygotskian perspective, the complexity of the structure of play is influenced by the skill level of the play partner. Toddlers play more skillfully with their peers when their partner is somewhat older and presumably more skilled at play (Howes & Farver, 1987a; Rothstein-Fisch & Howes, 1988). In contrast, the presence of the child's mother appears to reduce the complexity of peer interaction (Smith & Howes, 1994). Although the mother is a more skilled play partner than either child, peer play may be less skillful because three partner interaction is more difficult than dyadic interaction or because mother-child play content is different from child-child play content (Howes, 1992).

☐ Individual Differences in Structure of Peer Interaction and the Content of Social Interaction: Peer Acceptance, Aggression, Withdrawal, and Prosocial Behaviors

Howes' work on the development of structural complexity of peer play addressed the questions of whether and how young children constructed peer interaction. In order to move closer to the ultimate issue of whether the social experience of full-time child care influenced children's ways of relating to others, it was necessary to describe peer networks. Once again, the scope of the research widened; this time, to fit social interaction skills into the social context of friendships and other relationships.

Young children's peer interaction is organized around networks of play partners (Howes, 1983, 1988a). Within any child care group, there are children who prefer to play with each other, and children who prefer not to play with each other. Some children have no problem finding and keeping play partners, while others have difficulty entering peer groups and sustaining play. Children as young as 3 years old who have experienced full time child care in stable peer groups can describe these patterns of peer acceptance within their classroom (Howes, 1988a).

In the late 1970s, a series of longitudinal studies were published suggesting that children's peer acceptance in middle childhood was associated with positive mental health outcomes in adulthood (Parker & Asher, 1987). These studies precipitated a period of intense research into children's sociometric status (e.g., Coie & Dodge, 1983; Ladd, 1983). The term *sociometric* refers to ways of measuring peer acceptance and friendships. *Sociometric nominations* involve asking each child in a defined group to identify the children that he or she likes and the children that he or she dislikes as one means to determine peer acceptance. Children with reciprocated nominations of liking are usually considered friends. Children also can be assigned a *sociometric rating* based on the average of ratings provided by each of the children in the group. Social status groups (popular, rejected, neglected, and average) are formed using either nominations or ratings. Popular children have high liking and low disliking profiles. Rejected children have low liking and high disliking profiles. Neglected children have low liking and low disliking profiles. Average children fit none of the other profiles. Peer acceptance refers to high ratings or many positive and few negative nominations.

Studies of sociometric status found that children who were classified as popular or more socially accepted were more friendly and prosocial, and less likely than children who were not accepted to engage in aggressive behaviors with peers (Asher & Coie, 1990). Furthermore, sociometric status tended to be stable over time (Asher & Coie, 1990). These findings based on sociometric measures raised two questions about the Peer Play Scale. First, if the Peer Play Scale represents socially competent behavior with peers, would children who engage in structurally complex play also have higher peer acceptance and engage in prosocial, nonaggressive interactions with peers? Second, is competent peer play stable over developmental periods? That is, does demonstrating marker behaviors of structurally complex peer interaction during an earlier developmental period predict engaging in marker behaviors of structurally complex peer interaction during a later developmental period?

Two longitudinal studies addressed the first question. In the first, 48 children were observed with their peers in their child care centers at 6-month intervals beginning at age 13 to 24 months (Howes & Matheson, 1992; Howes, Phillipsen, & Hamilton, 1993). Within developmental periods, children who engaged in more complex play were rated by independent observer as more prosocial and sociable, and less aggressive. Children tended to be stable over time in positive, gregarious, and aggressive behaviors. Children who engaged in more complex play at earlier developmental periods were observed and rated as more prosocial and sociable, and less aggressive and withdrawn, during subsequent periods.

Another longitudinal study followed 55 children from 12 months through 9 years of age. Children were observed soon after entering group child care (Galluzzo, Matheson, Moore, & Howes, 1988) and again at 4 years of age (Howes, Matheson, & Hamilton, 1994). In addition, both preschool teachers and independent observers rated aggression and social withdrawal when the children were toddlers and, again, when they were preschoolers. When the children were 9 years of age, aggression, social withdrawal, and prosocial behaviors with peers were rated by elementary school teachers. Children who engaged in more complex play with peers as toddlers were more prosocial, engaged in more complex play, and were less withdrawn as preschoolers, and were less aggressive and withdrawn at age 9. Children who were either more aggressive or more withdrawn as preschoolers were more aggressive as 9-year-olds (Howes & Phillipsen, 1998).

To further examine stability in social skills with peers, 329 children between the ages of 12 and 53 months participated for 1, 2, or 3 years in a study of the development of social interaction with peers (Howes, 1988a). Naturalistic observations of peer play were conducted on a yearly basis. Complementary and reciprocal play in the early toddler period (13–23 months) predicted cooperative social pretend play in the late toddler period (24–35 months). Cooperative social pretend play predicted sociometric ratings in the preschool period. An extension of this longitudinal study, limited to 45 children who remained in the same school from prekindergarten through third grade, found that sociometric ratings in prekindergarten and kindergarten were associated with sociometric ratings in third grade (Howes, 1990). That is, children who more often engaged in complex social pretend play in their fourth year of life were rated as more popular with their peers 3 years later.

These studies suggest that there is considerable stability in toddlers' and preschoolers' social competence with peers as measured by the Peer Play Scale in both developmental periods and by peer acceptance in preschool. Furthermore, children who more frequently engage in structurally complex forms of play also engage in more frequent prosocial behaviors, and less frequent aggressive and withdrawal behaviors. The findings that prosocial behaviors are positively associated with peer acceptance, and that aggression and withdrawal behaviors are negatively associated with peer acceptance, lend further support to the use of the Peer Play Scale as a measure of social competence with peers.

Associations Between the Context of Peer Relationship Development and Individual Differences in Social Competence with Peers

If the social interactions that a toddler constructs with a peer partner predict social competence with peers 8 years later, it is important to differentiate between contexts of toddler peer interaction that promote rather than inhibit skillful interaction. If we can define social contexts that promote a positive orientation toward peers and discincline children toward aggressive interactions with peers we may be able to prevent maladjustment in peer relations. Therefore, Howes investigated several potentially important variations in social context: familiarity of the peer partners, the stability of the peer group, and the quality of the child care environment in which the peer interaction occurs.

The natural variation in familiarity and stability of peer partners provides an opportunity to examine variations in peer social contexts. An example of this natural variation is found in the Howes (1988a) monograph sample. In the first year of the study, children were recruited from child care classrooms with peer groups which remained intact for 1 year. In each subsequent year of the study, investigators both returned to the original peer groups and followed children who moved to different child care centers. Thus, in the second year of the study, the sample included four distinct groups of children: (a) the children who had been in the toddler room of a particular child care center the previous year and who had moved "up" to the preschool room in the same center; (b) the children who had been newly enrolled in the original child care centers to fill in preschool classroom peer groups (generally, group size increases with age); (c) the children who were in the sample in year 1, but had changed child care centers; and (d) the children who were in the same child care center classrooms as the children from year 1 who had moved to different child care centers. The results of this study suggested that toddler and preschool peer interaction is more skillful when children enroll in group settings at earlier ages, and when they remain with the same peer group for longer periods of time (Howes, 1988a). That is, it appears to be advantageous for children to enter peer groups as younger children and to maintain a familiar and stable peer network. Some children who moved between child care centers actually moved with a peer group, as opposed to moving to a child care center with an entirely new peer group. Those children who were able to move with a peer group, and who therefore did not have to reestablish relationships, were more competent in peer interaction (Howes, 1988a).

In a second set of studies, the influence of child care quality on social competence with peers was examined. In these studies, child care quality was measured by standard instruments that rate environments, activities, and teacher effectiveness. Not surprisingly, peer play is more skillful when child care quality is higher (Howes & Matheson, 1992; Howes, Phillips, & Whitebook, 1992; Howes & Stewart, 1987). These findings point to the importance of adults' use of their formal education in early childhood education to structure an environment which supports the construction of positive and skillful peer interaction.

☐ Relationships

In the last line of research to be discussed in this chapter, Howes and colleagues focused on understanding peer relationships as opposed to social interaction structure. Again, both theoretical and sociocultural influences were important in shaping this emphasis on relationships. As intense research on social acceptance with peers and its correlates grew, so did a renewed interest in relationships as a context for development. In 1976, Hinde, an ethologist, introduced the theoretical notion that relationships are more than a bidirectional effect of the influences of both partners. According to Hinde, a relationship is a new formation understood by examining not only the behaviors of both partners and their contingencies, but the pattern of relating unique to the two individuals.

Furthermore, the processes of relationship formation embedded in Bowlby's (1969/1982) attachment theory began to be understood as also applicable to relationships other than the child-mother attachment (Howes, 1996). According to this reinterpretation of attachment theory, relationships (whether attachment or playmate relationships) develop through multiple and recursive interactive experiences. Recursive interactions are well-scripted social exchanges which are repeated many times with only slight variation (Bretherton, 1985). Examples include infant caregiver interaction around bedtime or repeated toddler-age peer run-and-chase games. From these experiences, the infant or young child internalizes a set of fundamental social expectations about the behavioral dispositions of the partner (Bowlby, 1969/1982). These expectations form the basis for an internal working model of relationships. Therefore, through repeated experiences of social and social pretend play with a particular peer, a child forms an internal representation of playmate relationships. Some playmate relationships become friendship relationships. It is important to note that both the structure and content of experiences interacting with a partner are part of the child's representation of the partner. Children who engage in more complex interactions are more likely to recognize the partner as a social other and construct a relationship. Furthermore, the content of the interaction is likely to influence the quality of the resulting relationship.

Sociocultural influences also played a role in the research interest in friendships between very young children. Once infants and toddlers had daily experiences within the stable peer groups of child care, parents and child care teachers began to notice that the children had preferences among their peers (Hartup, 1983; Rubenstein & Howes, 1976; Rubin, 1980). These preferential playmate relationships appeared to parents and teachers as friendships. Teachers and parents reported that these emerging friendships helped children separate from their parents at the beginning of the child care day. The children would greet the preferred peer and join in play with him or her as part of the ritual for parents saying good-bye.

In the following sections, we will discuss the process of friendship formation in very young children and the functions of these early friendships. We will then discuss the relations between child-adult attachment relationships and peer relations.

The Process of Friendship Formation

As early as 1983, Howes (1983) began to argue that some peer playmate relationships from the toddler period become affective relationships. An *affective relationship* is one that includes feelings of affection or what would be called "love" in adult-child relationships. Toddler affective relationships have attributes of friendship common to the "best friendships" which provide older children with emotional security and closeness (Howes, 1992, 1996). These early friendship relationships appear to be formed in a way similar to adult-child attachment relationships (Howes, 1996). In the following section, we will examine the research program that supports these assumptions about early friendship formation.

In a similar manner to the research on structural complexity of peer interaction, the friendship studies began with the collection of observational data. Since toddler-age children cannot report on their friendships, we must use behaviors to distinguish friendship relationships from playmate relationships in prelinguistic children. This results in some discontinuity in research about friendships because later research relies heavily on a child's ability to talk about friendships. For example, reciprocity of friendship is an important dimension of later friendship research, but cannot be explored in early childhood. Because early friendships can be defined only based on observed behavior, the earliest identified friendships must be reciprocal, with both partners engaging in defining behaviors.

Throughout her work, Howes has used a three-part criteria for *friendship*: preference, recognition of the other as a social partner, and enjoyment (Howes, 1983, 1988a, 1996; Howes & Phillipsen, 1992). Within this definition, children must prefer the company of the friend over the company of others and must enjoy the time they spend together to be considered friends. To operationalize these constructs for observational research, the following criteria were developed: (a) proximity (being within 3 feet of each other at least 30% of the observational period), (b) at least one instance of complementary and reciprocal play to indicate recognition of the other as a social partner, and (c) shared positive affect (both children expressing positive affect while engaged in interactive social play).

This definition was first used in a year-long longitudinal study of five peer groups (Howes, 1983). The children ranged in age from 10 months to 5-years. Each peer group was composed of same-age children. Eight times over the course of the year, we observed each child's interaction with every potential partner in the group. These observations were used to identify friend pairs.

To test the assertion that toddler friendships were indeed affective relationships, we compared the three components of the behavioral definition (preference, recognition of the partner, and shared affect) to determine which component would identify the fewest friend pairs. The most stringent component was assumed to be most essential to friendship. Using shared positive affect to define friends identified the fewest friendships and, thus, was the most stringent part of the definition (Howes, 1983). This supports the premise that early friendships are affective relationships based on mutual affection.

What remained to be explored, however, were the processes of friendship formation. The 1983 study included three groups of typically developing children in full time child care and two groups of children in therapeutic settings. The processes of friendship formation were somewhat different in the typical and atypical children, providing a glimpse of how this process occurs as well as the aspects which might be essential for typical social development.

Typical Children. As found in the first longitudinal descriptive study of infants and toddlers new to peer groups, the earliest friendships appeared when the children were 10 months old (Howes, 1983). Children in this early toddler period (10 to 24 months) tended to form only one or two friendship relationships. In three different longitudinal samples, these early toddler friendship relationships tended to be very stable, lasting a year in the first study (Howes, 1983). That is, once identified, friend pairs appeared at every subsequent observation period. In two subsequent 3-year studies, discussed above, we again identified friend pairs at each observation period and found that friend pairs formed in the early toddler period reappeared for the 3 years of the longitudinal study (Howes, 1988a; Howes & Phillipsen, 1992). That is, at each observation period, we identified friendship pairs within peer groups using observers blind to previous friendships. We then computed the probabilities of a particular friendship pair reappearing in more than one observation period. Friendship pairs formed when the children were toddlers were most likely to reappear in subsequent periods.

Of particular interest, given the prevalence of same-gender friendships in preschool and older children, friendships formed in the early toddler period are as likely to be same- as cross-gender in composition (Howes & Phillipsen, 1992). Further, cross- and same-gender friendships are equally likely to be maintained over time if formed in the toddler period (Howes & Phillipsen, 1992). This is in sharp contrast to the friendships of preschool- and school-age children who tend to form and maintain same-gender friendships.

Children in the late toddler period (24 to 36 months) have more friendship relationships than younger children, perhaps because they begin to differentiate between the different functions of friendship (Howes, 1987, 1988a). Some peers become friends, while others remain playmates. To be considered a playmate, but not a friend, a pair meets the criteria for preference and the recognition of the partner portions of the friendship definition but not the affective sharing component. In the late toddler period, friendships must still be identified by behaviors as children under 3 years of age cannot reliably complete a sociometric task. Again, the affective component of behaviorally defined friendship is critical in distinguishing friends from playmates (Howes, 1983).

By preschool age, children can play with children that they do not consider to be friends. Toddler age children's social interactions are more fragile and more dependent on rituals and routines than the social interactions of preschoolers. Therefore, toddlers, more often than preschoolers, play only with their friends. We assume that this is because patterns of interaction between toddlers are highly ritualized.

Although behavior identification of friends is still a reliable measure in preschool (Howes, 1988a; Howes & Phillipsen, 1992), children also can reliably identify friends using sociometric ratings and nominations (Howes, 1988a). Beginning at age 3 and if they are enrolled in full-day child care and have a stable peer group, children select the same children in sociometric procedures as do observers (Howes, 1988a). This ability to communicate friendship status to another is a new skill. Perhaps this skill develops because preschoolers are now able to communicate the meaning of the construct of friendship. They use the language of friendship to control access to play ("I'll be your friend if you let me play").

While preschool age children are no longer dependent on rituals to sustain play, their play is still easily disrupted. For example, a pair of children may spend 10 minutes establishing the roles and scripts for a pretend play episode: "You be the lion and I'll be the little boy who finds you in the forest and then . . . " "No, I want to be a baby . . . " "OK, how about you be a baby lion and I'll be the little boy who finds you in the forest and . . . " "OK, and then when you take me home, you feed me with a bottle . . . " If a third child attempts to join, the play negotiations may have to start all over again and may not be successful. If the child attempting to enter the group is a friend, the other children appear more willing to undergo the negotiation process (Howes, 1988a). Children who are rejected by peers (using sociometric measures) but who have reciprocated friendships are more likely to be able to enter play groups because of having friends within the group (Howes, 1988a). Continuing the lion example, a child who is a friend might enter the play by saying, "Remember the time, I was the baby lion and then I got to be a great big lion and I roared but I didn't really hurt you. I'm going to be the daddy lion."

Just as there is stability in children's social interaction skills with peers (children who engage in complex play with peers in early developmental periods are the same children who are competent with peers in middle childhood), there is stability in children's friendship quality over developmental periods. In a longitudinal study that began when children were infants and continued until they were age 9, children whose teachers had identified them as having good friendships at age 4, reported that their friendships were close and supportive at age 9 (Howes, Hamilton, & Phillipsen, 1998).

Atypical Children.   Using observations rather than sociometric nominations to identify friends makes it possible to study friendship development in children who lack the social, cognitive, or linguistic skills to reliably complete sociometric interviews. Howes (1983, 1984, 1985b) used behavioral identification of friends to study relationships among peers in two groups enrolled in outpatient programs for emotionally disturbed children directed by the child psychiatry unit of a mental hospital. These children were diagnosed as severely emotionally disturbed with a predominance of nonorganic disorders. One group of children included toddlers, the other preschoolers. The children were observed eight times over the course of a year. Although the children in these groups formed fewer friendships than typical children, they did form friendships. That is, they demonstrated preference, recognition of the partner, and shared positive affect. However, unlike those of typical children, friendships among these atypical children were not sustained over time.

A second study examined friendship formation among abused toddlers who attended a daily child care program (Howes, 1984, 1988c; Howes & Eldredge, 1985; Howes & Espinosa, 1985). Again, these toddlers were found to form friendships as defined by preference, recognition of the partner, and shared positive affect. It is important to note that all of these children were enrolled in intervention programs which supported children's attempts to be prosocial and cooperative with peers. When abused children who were not enrolled in such programs were observed with their peers, a much different picture emerged. These children did not engage in shared positive affect, a necessary condition for friendship (Howes & Espinosa, 1985). These findings suggested that, in a context that supports positive relationships, very young children who have endured major disruptive life events can construct friendship relationships. Understanding which social contexts and which aspects of a particular social context can facilitate and enhance the development of trust and positive relationships among children who come from difficult life circumstances is an important area of future research.

The Functions of Friendships

In her initial program of research described above, Howes identified developmental progressions in the construction of social interaction and friendship relationships with peers. The next step was to build on this work and return to some of the questions that originally shaped the research: Could peers provide the child with experiences of social support, trust, and intimacy? Do children who grew up together sharing the common resources of the child care center have a different kind of social interaction than acquaintances? Do cross-sex peers and cross-ethnic peers who became friends in the context of child care form nontraditional relationships? Each of these questions describes a potential function of friendship: experiences of social support, trust, and intimacy; a context for mastering social interaction; and a context for engaging with children who are unlike the self. The first of these functions has received the most research attention; research on the third function is just emerging.

Friendships Provide Experiences of Social Support, Trust, and Intimacy.   We expect children who are good friends as older children or adolescents to derive feelings of social support, trust, and intimacy from these relationships (Howes, 1996). It is difficult to directly apply these constructs to the friendships of very young children. There are, however, several pieces of evidence that support the idea that children who form friendships as preverbal children in child care do experience social support, trust, and intimacy within these relationships. The children who were used for the early case studies of friendship (Howes, 1981) are now young adults. Informal conversations with these children suggest that their toddler friend partner, although no longer a "best friend" remains a person of importance in their lives. And, as discussed above, toddler friend pairs tend to remain stable friends. This suggests that toddler friendships function to provide affective support, rather than functioning merely as a context for play, when the child's life history allows for continuity of those friendships.

If toddler-age friend pairs are serving as sources of social support, we would expect them to respond to the distress of their friend. In one study of toddler-age children, we identified friends according to the behaviors identified above. We then used event coding to describe distress incidences in the classroom. The identity of the crier, the context of the distress, and the identity and behaviors of adults and peers who responded to the child were recorded. We found that children were most likely to respond to another child's crying if that child was a friend (Howes & Farver, 1987a).

Finally, we suggest that, once children become experts at social pretend play, friends use the context of play to explore issues of trust and intimacy (Howes, 1992). In an exploratory study of these issues, we compared ratings of self-disclosure in the play of 4-year-old children who were asked to engage in pretend play with a particular partner (Howes, 1992). One group of children had been in a longitudinal study, had been identified as friends as toddlers, and had kept these friendships. A second group of children were paired with short-term friends, developed within the prior 6 months. In the third group, children were paired with a child who was not an identified friend. Self-disclosure ratings were higher in the long-term friend group than in either the short-term or the nonfriend groups.

Child Care Friendships as a Context for Mastering Social Interaction.   In this chapter, in Howes' research program, and in general, the construction of social interaction has been treated as semi-independent of the construction of friendships (Howes, 1988a). The data does suggest that more socially skilled children tend to have friends and children who have friends tend to be more socially skilled. In particular, children who engage in more complex play have less difficulty than less skilled children in entering play groups (Howes, 1988a). One reason that these socially skilled children can easily enter play groups is because they are likely to be friends with children within the play group.

Friendships appear to be a particularly important context for the construction of complex peer interactions during early developmental periods. In a year-long longitudinal study, infants and toddlers made the greatest increases in complexity of social play when they were engaged with stable friends, as opposed to acquaintances or playmates (Howes, 1983). Social pretend play, which involves the communication of symbolic meaning, also appears first within friendship dyads and then within playmate dyads (Howes, 1985a, 1992). Likewise, preschoolers who had been friends for 3 years were better able to use communicative behaviors to extend and clarify pretend play than preschoolers who had been friends for 6 months or less (Howes, Droege, & Matheson, 1994). Children who are friends do not have to simultaneously devise the game structure and integrate or communicate pretend meanings. Instead, they integrate new pretend meanings into well-developed and routine-like games.

The mastery of social skills within friendships is not limited to typical children. Friendships appear to facilitate conflict resolution and conflict avoidance in children enrolled in an intervention program for emotionally disturbed children (Howes, 1985b). Toddler-age friends were more likely than acquaintances to avoid conflict. Similarly, preschool friends were less likely than acquaintances to misinterpret prosocial bids and to avoid conflict.

Friendships as a Context to Engage with Children Who Are Unlike the Self.   To the extent that children of different genders and ethnic backgrounds have different social styles, friendships appear to give children access to these diverse social styles. As discussed above, toddler-age children do not select their friends on the basis of gender (Howes, 1988b; Howes & Phillipsen, 1992). Instead, toddlers form and maintain cross-gender friendships into preschool. Likewise, in a study of young children in an ethnically diverse school, we found that children were able to form and maintain cross-ethnic friendships (Howes & Wu, 1990).

Child-Adult Attachment Relationships and Peer Relations

Until the mid-1980s, research on peer interactions and relationships was based in the ethological tradition and viewed the peer social system and development of social competence with peers as separate from the adult-child social system. Children were perceived to construct their social interactions and relationships as if adults did not exist within the social context of these developments. Even as this research was being conducted and published, there was, of course, a literature that suggested that children's social development was enhanced by positive encounters with adults (Hay, 1985; Maccoby, 1984). However, this literature, by and large, was ignored.

Inspired by the more traditional literature on the influence of adults on children's peer relations, Howes and colleagues' most recent 3-year longitudinal study of the development of peer relations included a focus on a large number of adult behaviors that could be expected to enhance peer interaction (Howes & Clements, 1994). These behaviors included teaching toddlers turn-taking games and structuring their peer interactions to support these games, intervening to redirect agonistic encounters, and so forth. Therefore, as well as coding the structure and content of children's interactions with peers, we also noted any simultaneously occurring adult behaviors. The findings of this study suggested that adults working with groups of children rarely engaged in such behaviors and whether or not they did so had no association with the development of toddlers' and preschoolers' social competence with their peers.

We then turned to another traditional literature, that of child-mother attachment. Secure child-mother attachments are linked to more positive peer interactions in childhood (e.g., Elicker, England, & Sroufe, 1992; Jacobson & Wille, 1986; LaFreniere & Sroufe, 1985; Sroufe, 1983; Turner, 1991). Children who have secure mother-child attachment relationships are more competent as older children in their social interactions with peers, more sought after by others as partners, and are more likely to construct friendships with others than children with insecure attachment relationship histories. Theoretically, these associations exist because children use their internal model of their mother-child relationship when they encounter peers. Thus, if a child's expectations, based on his or her relationship with his or her mother, are that they are loved and lovable, then the child will approach peers with a positive orientation and expect that the peer encounter will be positive. However, most children in the United States in the 1990s have attachment relationships with other caregiving adults beyond their mothers (Howes, 1999). Consequently, children are more likely to be constructing peer relationships in the presence of that alternative caregiver than they are with their mother. The alternative caregivers most likely to be present during the construction of peer relationships are child care providers. The term *child care provider* in this context refers to any adult other than the parent who is caring for the child and at least one other child. The setting can be a child care center, a family child care home, or the child's home as long as a peer is present.

This reasoning about alternative caregivers led Howes and her colleagues to a series of studies on the associations between attachment relationships to child care providers and social competence with peers. These studies confirm the findings noted above: Adult caregiving behaviors intended to shape peer interaction do not influence children's social competence with peers. Instead, adult caregiving behaviors directly influence children's attachment relationships which, in turn, influence peer relations. More specifically, more securely attached children have caregivers who are rated as more sensitive and responsive to the children in their care (Howes, 1997; Howes, Hamilton, & Matheson, 1994; Howes, Matheson, & Hamilton, 1994; Howes, Phillips, & Whitebook, 1992). In turn, children who are more securely attached to their child care providers are more socially competent with their peers (Howes, 1997; Howes, Hamilton, & Matheson, 1994; Howes, Matheson, & Hamilton, 1994; Howes, Phillips, & Whitebook, 1992). When children's attachment relationships with their child care provider are contrasted with their attachment relationships with their mothers, the child care attachment relationship is more powerful in predicting social competence with peers (Howes, Matheson, & Hamilton, 1994). We suspect that this is because they are part of the wider social context for the child's development of peer relations. The children can use the child care provider as a secure base as they explore the world of peers.

Unfortunately, child care providers are not a stable presence in children's lives. In contrast, mothers usually remain constant. Timing and changes in alternative attachment relationships as well as the quality of the relationship appear to influence children's competence with peers. In our longitudinal studies, we found that the first relationship with a child care provider may be the most influential relationship with an alternative caregiver. The quality of the attachment relationship a child constructed with the first child care provider best predicted social adjustment at age 9 in our longest longitudinal study (Howes, Hamilton, & Phillipsen, 1998).

Changing child care providers also appears to have implications for children's social competence with peers. In a 3-year longitudinal study, children who had the most changes in primary child care providers were most aggressive with peers (Howes & Hamilton, 1993). In this study, some of the caregiver changes had a positive effect in the short term: The child was able to construct a more secure relationship with the new provider than with the old and, simultaneously, became more skilled with peers. However, it appears that the cumulative effect of instability in child care caregivers is detrimental to the development of positive social competence with peers.

Broadening the study of peer relations to include a more careful examination of child-caregiver relationships has led to a particularly fruitful series of research studies. The evidence that children construct affective relationships with their peers from infancy onward highlights the importance of these early peer relationships. Likewise, the relationships that children form with the adults who supervise their encounters with peers influence social competence. It is noteworthy that both of these types of relationships, with peers as friends and with child care providers, are relationships outside of the family. While these results should in no way downplay the importance of family influences on child development, carefully examining alternative relationships underscores the value of social networks both inside and outside of the family.

☐ Future Directions

Historically, the study of peer relations has been influenced by both theoretical frameworks and the sociocultural influences of the historical period of the research. We suspect that these joint forces will continue to influence the study of the processes by which children construct and maintain their relationships with peers. One emerging sociocultural influence that appears to be influencing research on peer relations is based on changing urban demographics. In most urban areas of the United States, there is a large influx of families from societies that generally are considered more collectivist in their values than traditional families in the United States. Within collectivist societies, there is a greater emphasis placed on the individual within the group than on the individual self. These collectivist values are not dissimilar to the values of the visionaries that opened child care centers to infants and toddlers in the early 1970s. Those involved in the intersection of the women's movement and child care in the 1970s also dreamed of a society that valued the collective and helped children to be prosocial, altruistic members of a group. These values are somewhat different than the premise expressed in traditional early childhood education that the development of the individual child is paramount. As more children and families from subcultures based on collectivist ideas enter child care settings, there may be renewed tension between constructing groups of children that support and help one another while simultaneously helping each child within the group to reach their individual potential. This sociocultural trend may influence the next set of studies of peer relations.

Attachment theory, once expanded beyond the study of early parent-child relationships, also is likely to be a powerful influence on the study of peer relationships. This work has suggested that attachments with alternative caregivers are influential to peer relations. Furthermore, descriptive studies have established that relationships between young children are stable affective bonds. In order to account for this stability, we suspect that researchers will need to move beyond description to the level of representation. The question of what internal representations are derived from early peer affective relationships and how these representations shape children's working models of relationships is far from answered. In this context, it is important that the earliest friendships appear to be based on some "chemistry" that leads toddlers to prefer each other rather than on matches between children of similar gender and ethnicity. If children have opportunities to form important relationships with persons unlike themselves at such young ages, will they be more open to respectful relationships with others unlike themselves as older children and adults?

☐ References

Asher, S. R., & Coie, J. (1990). *Peer rejection in childhood.* Cambridge, England: Cambridge University Press.

Bakeman, R., & Brownlee, J. R. (1980). The strategic use of parallel play: A sequential analysis. *Child Development, 51,* 873–878.

Blurton-Jones, N. (Ed.) (1972). *Ethological studies of child behavior.* Cambridge, England: Cambridge University Press.

Bowlby, J. (1969/1982). *Attachment and loss: Vol. 1. Attachment.* New York: Basic Books.

Bretherton, I. (1985). Attachment theory: Retrospect and prospect. In I. Bretherton & E. Walters (Eds.), Growing point of attachment theory and research. *Monograph of the Society for Research in Child Development, 50* (1–2, Serial No. 209), 3–35.

Buhler, C. (1931). The social behavior of the child. In C. Murchison (Ed.), *A handbook of child psychology.* New York: Russell & Russell.

Coie, J. D., & Dodge, K. A. (1983). Continuities and changes in children's social status: A five year longitudinal study. *Merrill Palmer Quarterly, 29,* 261–282.

Eckerman, C. O., Davis, C. C., & Didow, S. M. (1989). Toddlers' emerging ways of achieving social coordination with a peer. *Child Development, 60,* 440–453.

Elicker, J., England, M., & Sroufe, L. A. (1992). Predicting peer competence and peer relationships in childhood from early parent-child relationships. In R. D. Parke & G. W. Ladd (Eds.), *Family-peer relationships: Modes of linkage* (pp. 77–106). Hillsdale, NJ: Erlbaum.

Farver, J. A. (1992). An analysis of young American and Mexican children's play dialogues. In C. Howes (Ed.), *The collaborative construction of pretend* (pp. 55–66). Albany, NY: SUNY Press.

Farver, J. A. (1996). Aggressive behavior in preschool social networks—Do birds of a feather flock together? *Early Childhood Research Quarterly, 11,* 333–350.

Farver, J., & Frosch, D. L. (1996). Los Angeles stories—Aggression in preschoolers' spontaneous narratives after the riots of 1992. *Child Development, 67,* 19–32.

Farver, J. A., & Howes, C. (1988). Cross-cultural differences in social interaction: A comparison of American and Indonesian children. *Journal of Cross-Cultural Psychology, 19,* 203–215.

Farver, J. A., Kim, Y. K., & Lee, Y. (1995). Cultural differences in Korean- and Anglo-American social interaction and play behaviors. *Child Development, 66,* 1088–1099.

Farver, J. A., & Wimbarti, S. (1995). Indonesian children's play with their mothers and older siblings. *Child Development, 66,* 1493–1503.

Galluzzo, D. C., Matheson, C. C., Moore, J. A., & Howes, C. (1988). Social orientation to adults and peers in infant child care. [Special issue: Infant day care: II. Empirical studies.] *Early Childhood Research Quarterly, 3,* 417–426.

Hartup, W. W. (1983). Peer relations. In P. H. Mussen (Series Ed.) & E. M. Hetherington (Vol. Ed.), *Handbook of child psychology: Vol 4. Socialization, personality, and social development* (4th ed., pp. 103–196). New York: Wiley.

Hay, D. (1985). Learning to form relationships in infancy: Parallel attainments with parents and peers. *Developmental Review. 5,* 122–161.

Hinde, R. (1976). On describing relationships. *Journal of Child Psychology and Psychiatry, 17*, 1–19.

Howes, C. (1980). Peer play scale as an index of complexity of peer interaction. *Developmental Psychology, 16*, 371–372.

Howes, C. (1981). *Danny and Robyn, Becca and Amy: Making friends at child care.* Unpublished manuscript.

Howes, C. (1983). Patterns of friendship. *Child Development, 54*, 1041–1053.

Howes, C. (1984). Social interactions and patterns of friendship in normal and emotionally disturbed children. In T. Field (Ed.), *Friendships between normal and handicapped children.* Norwood, NJ: Ablex.

Howes, C. (1985a). Sharing fantasy: Social pretend play in toddlers. *Child Development, 56*, 1253–1258.

Howes, C. (1985b). The patterning of agonistic behaviors among friends and acquaintances in programs for emotionally disturbed children. *Journal of Applied Developmental Psychology, 6*, 303–311.

Howes, C. (1988a). Peer interaction of young children. *Monographs of the Society for Research in Child Development, 53*(217, No. I).

Howes, C. (1988b). Same- and cross-sex friends: Implications for interaction and social skills. *Early Childhood Research Quarterly, 3*, 21–37.

Howes, C. (1988c). Abused and neglected children with their peers. In G. T. Hotaling, D. Finkelhor, J. T. Kirkpatrick, & M. A. Straus (Eds.), *Family abuse and its consequences: New directions in research* (pp. 99-108). Newbury Park, CA: Sage.

Howes, C. (1990). Social status and friendship from kindergarten to third grade. *Journal of Applied Developmental Psychology, 11*, 321–330.

Howes, C. (1992). *The collaborative construction of pretend: Social pretend play funtions.* New York: SUNY Press.

Howes, C. (1996). The earliest friendships. In W. M. Bukowski, A. F. Newcomb, & W. W. Hartup (Eds.), *The company they keep: Friendship in childhood and adolescence. Cambridge Studies in Social and Emotional Development* (pp. 66–86). New York: Cambridge University Press.

Howes, C. (1997). Teacher sensitivity, children's attachment and play with peers. *Early Education and Development, 8*, 41–49.

Howes, C., & Clements, D. (1994). Adult socilization of children's play in child care. In H. Goelman (Ed.), *Play and child care* (pp. 20–36). Albany, NY: SUNY Press.

Howes, C., Droege, K., & Matheson, C. C. (1994). Play and communicative processes within long- and short-term friendship dyads. [Special issue: Children's friendships.] *Journal of Social and Personal Relationships, 11*, 401–410.

Howes, C., & Eldredge, R. (1985). Responses of abused, neglected, and non-maltreated children to the behaviors of their peers. *Journal of Applied Developmental Psychology, 6*, 261–270.

Howes, C., & Espinosa, M. P. (1985). The consequences of child abuse for the formation of relationships with peers. *Child Abuse and Neglect, 9*, 397–404.

Howes, C., & Farver, J. A. (1987a). Social pretend play in 2-year-olds: Effects of age of partner. *Early Childhood Research Quarterly, 2*, 305–314.

Howes, C., & Farver, J. A. (1987b). Toddlers' responses to the distress of their peers. *Journal of Applied Developmental Psychology, 8*, 441–452.

Howes, C., & Hamilton, C. E. (1993). The changing experience of child care: Changes in teachers and in teacher-child relationships and children's social competence with peers. *Early Childhood Research Quarterly, 8*, 15–32.

Howes, C., Hamilton, C. E., & Matheson, C. C. (1994). Children's relationships with peers: Differential associations with aspects of the teacher-child relationship. *Child Development, 65*, 253–263.

Howes, C., Hamilton, C. E., & Phillipsen, L. (1998). Stability and continuity of child-caregiver and child-peer relationships. *Child Development, 69*, 418–426.

Howes, C., & Matheson, C. C. (1992). Sequences in the development of competent play with peers: Social and social pretend play. *Developmental Psychology, 28*, 961–974.

Howes, C., Matheson, C., & Hamilton, C. E. (1994). Maternal, teacher and child care history correlates of children's relationships with peers. *Child Development, 65*, 264–273.

Howes, C., Phillips, D. A., & Whitebook, M. (1992). Thresholds of quality in child care centers and children's social and emotional development. *Child Development, 63*, 449–460.

Howes, C., & Phillipsen, L. (1992). Gender and friendship: Relationships within peer groups of young children. *Social Development, 1*, 230–242.

Howes, C., & Phillipsen, L. (1998). Continuity in children's relations with peers. *Social Development, 1*, 340–349.

Howes, C., Phillipsen, L., & Hamilton, C. (1993). Constructing social communication with peers: Domains and sequences. In J. Nadel (Ed.), *Early communication* (pp. 215–232). London: Routledge.

Howes, C., & Stewart, P. (1987). Child's play with adults, toys, and peers: An examination of family and child-care influences. *Developmental Psychology, 23*, 423–430.

Howes, C., Unger, O., & Seidner, L. B. (1989). Social pretend play in toddlers: Parallels with social play and with solitary pretend. *Child Development, 60*, 77–84.

Howes, C., & Wu, F. (1990). Peer interactions and friendships in an ethnically diverse school setting. [Special issue: Minority children]. *Child Development, 61*, 537–541.

Jacobson, J. L., & Wille, D. E. (1986). The influences of attachment behavior on developmental changes in peer interaction from the toddler to preschool period. *Child Development, 57,* 338–347.

Ladd, G. W. (1983). Social networks of popular, average, and rejected children in school settings. *Merrill Palmer Quarterly, 29,* 283–308.

LaFreniere, P. J., & Sroufe, L. A. (1985). Profiles of peer competence in the preschool: Interrelations among measures, influence of social ecology and peer competence. *Developmental Psychology, 21,* 56–69.

Maccoby, E. E. (1984). Socialization and developmental change. *Child Development, 55,* 317–328.

Maudry, M., & Nekula, M. (1930). Social relations between children of the same age during the first two years of life. *Journal of Genetic Psychology, 54,* 193–215.

Mueller, E. & Brenner, J. (1977). The origins of social skills and interactions among playgroup toddlers. *Child Development, 48,* 854–861.

Parker, J., & Asher, S. R. (1987). Peer acceptance and later personal adjustment: Are low-accepted children at risk? *Psychological Bulletin, 102,* 357–389.

Parten, M. B. (1932). Social participation among preschool children. *Journal of Abnormal and Social Psychology, 27,* 243–269.

Reed, K. H. (1950). *The nursery school: A human relationships laboratory.* Philadelphia: W. B. Saunders.

Ross, H., & Goldman, B. (1976). Establishing new social relations in infancy. In T. Alloway, L. Kramer, & P. Pliner (Eds.), *Advances in communication and affect* (pp. 202–251). New York: Plenum.

Rothstein-Fisch, C., & Howes, C. (1988). Toddler peer interaction in mixed-age groups. *Journal of Applied Developmental Psychology, 9,* 211–218.

Rubenstein, J., & Howes, C. (1976). The effects of peers on toddler's interactions with mother and toys. *Child Development, 47,* 597–605.

Rubin, Z. (1980). *Friendships.* Cambridge, MA: Harvard University Press.

Smith, E., & Howes, C. (1994). The effect of parents' presence on children's social interactions in preschool. *Early Childhood Research Quarterly, 9,* 45–59.

Sroufe, L. A. (1983). Infant-caregiving attachment and patterns of maladaption in preschool: The roots of maladaption and competence. In M. Permutter (Ed.), *Minnesota Symposium on Child Psychology* (Vol. 16, pp. 41–81). Hillsdale, NJ: Erlbaum.

Turner, P. J. (1991). Relations between attachment, gender, and behavior with peers in preschool. *Child Development, 62,* 1475–1488.

Vandell, D., Wilson, K., & Buchanan, N. (1980). Peer interaction in the first year of life. *Child Development, 51,* 481–488.

8

CHAPTER

Robert D. Kavanaugh
Paul L. Harris

Pretense and Counterfactual Thought in Young Children

☐ Introduction

A number of researchers have noted a striking change in the social-cognitive development of children beginning at approximately age 2 years. Piaget's (1951) emphasis on the shift away from "pure" sensorimotor functioning to the symbolic accomplishments of stage 6 provides one example. For Piaget, the culmination of the object concept and the emergence of deferred imitation and symbolic (pretense) play signaled an important change in cognitive function. However, Piaget was not alone in noting developmental changes around age 2 years, particularly the emergence of thinking and reasoning about objects and events that are not immediately present. Language development researchers have long noted a shift away from here and now talk beginning roughly at the same time (Sachs, 1983), while more recent research on autobiographical memory shows that, by the beginning of the third year, both children and parents are primed to talk about the past (Engel, 1986; Fivush & Hammond, 1990). A host of other investigators has noted that pretense also begins to blossom toward the end of the second year (cf., Bretherton, 1984; Fein, 1981; McCune-Nicolich & Fenson, 1984), including joint or shared pretend play that involves understanding and responding to the nonliteral actions of another person (Dunn & Dale, 1984; Haight & Miller, 1993).

The thesis proposed here is that, beginning around age 2 years, children become capable of thinking and reasoning about two different types of unreal or hypothetical situations. First, they are able to produce pretend actions (McCune, 1995), and to make sense of similar actions on the part of others (Harris & Kavanaugh, 1993). In particular, we argue that 2-year-olds understand the causal consequences of make-believe actions. For example, during pretend play, the actions of the pretender often effect an imaginary change in props used in the make-believe scenario. Thus, pretend tea "spilled" onto an objectively dry table makes the surface all "wet." Second, there is evidence that preschool children's causal thinking not only involves an awareness of the temporal and spatial contiguity between an antecedent and consequent event (Leslie & Keeble, 1987; Oakes & Cohen, 1990), but also includes the power to reason counterfactually about outcomes that did not occur but might have occurred. Thus, preschoolers who learn of a mishap endured by a protagonist understand that a different course of action would have prevented the mishap (Harris, German, & Mills, 1996). We argue that the earliest manifestations of this type of counterfactual thought may be present among 2-year-olds, and review some preliminary data to support our contention (Kavanaugh & Harris, 1997).

The authors gratefully acknowledge the support of North Atlantic Treaty Organization Collaborative Research Grant CRG.931462.

In short, broadly conceived, our research on pretense and counterfactual thought suggests that, roughly by age 2 years, children can understand causal sequences that do not actually materialize. We contend that the capacity to reason about hypothetical causal sequences is an emerging skill grounded in 2-year-olds' understanding of literal or actual events. However, before turning to these theoretical issues, we review the evidence we have gathered on children's capacity to engage in pretense and counterfactual thinking.

☐ Pretense

In his seminal work, *Play, Dreams, and Imitation in Childhood,* Piaget (1951) established the importance of studying pretense by carefully documenting the early emergence of symbolic thought, and by providing a well-respected theoretical account of pretending that emphasized the young child's ability to differentiate between signifier (e.g., a piece of cloth) and signified (e.g., a pillow). This influential work inspired a number of studies of children's pretend actions (cf., Fein, 1981), and also proposed a sharp contrast between what Piaget saw as the iconic signifiers of pretense which bear a perceptual similarity to the signified, and the more developmentally advanced signs of language which bear a truly arbitrary relationship to the signified.

Piaget's (1951) account of pretense emphasized the importance of isolated pretend play and its relationship to other expressions of the semiotic function (Golomb & Cornelius, 1977; Nicolich, 1977). More recently, researchers have turned their attention to the social context of pretense by focusing on joint or shared pretend play. This body of work shows that children engage in shared pretend play with primary caregivers, siblings, and peers beginning as early as the second year (Haight & Miller, 1993; Howes, Unger, & Seidner, 1989; McCune, 1995). A pretend tea party between adult and child provides a ready example of this type of play. An adult may pick up a teapot, tilt it over a cup, pretend to "pour" tea, and then hand the empty cup to the child. Thus, during the course of shared pretend play, young children observe everyday actions, such as tipping a teapot over a cup, but these actions do not produce their expected physical outcome. To make sense of the play partner's intentions, children must suspend their usual expectations of the physical world and accept the partner's stipulation of a make-believe scenario. Stipulation can take the form either of an action (e.g., pretending to "pour" tea) or a statement about a make-believe event ("Would you like some tea?"). In either case, the child is asked to interpret the partner's behavior as an invitation to continue the pretend theme. In the above example, the make-believe theme could be continued by holding out a cup so that the imaginary tea can be poured, or by answering the partner's rhetorical question in a manner that implies an understanding of the pretense theme ("Want tea"). Failure to grasp the make-believe nature of the partner's stipulation violates the expectation of a response that will extend the pretend play.

A number of investigators have sought to determine the parameters that influence shared pretend play. One consistent finding is that young children engage in more sustained and elaborate pretense when playing with a familiar caregiver than when playing alone or with a partner who is uninvolved in the child's play (Fiese, 1990; O'Connell & Bretherton, 1984; Slade, 1987). Other researchers have reported that an adult's modeling of specific pretend actions enhances the young child's ability to generate related pretend actions (Bretherton, O'Connell, Shore, & Bates, 1984; Fenson, 1984; Wolf, Rygh, & Altshuler, 1984). One interpretation of these findings is that children are able to understand and elaborate on their play partner's initiative. However, we know very little about what children actually understand when they watch a partner engage in pretense. Although children might understand pretend "pouring," realizing that it implies a pretend transfer of liquid to the cup that they subsequently drink from, is it also possible that children who see one pretend gesture (such as pouring) produce other apparently related gestures (such as "drinking") simply because of the props that are placed at their disposal or because pouring and drinking are related to the same tea party script.

We have assessed children's understanding of pretense more directly by using a design in which an experimenter initiates a pretend sequence that the child is then required to complete. We have varied the way in which the experimenter initiates the sequence, the response required of the child, and the complexity of the pretend scenario. In the main, our studies have focused on children whose mean age was either just below or just above 2 years. We chose these two groups because we anticipated that 2 years would be a watershed in children's understanding of pretense. However, on occasion, we have included somewhat older children to address the question of children's ability to provide a verbal description of make-believe sequences.

Stipulating Pretense

One of the hallmarks of true dyadic play is the ability to respond contingently and appropriately to the play partner's overtures. As noted above, this means responding in a fashion that at least continues, and ideally embellishes, the stipulated pretend theme. We reasoned that if children understand a play partner's pretend overture they should be able to produce a make-believe response tailored to the stipulated theme. Furthermore, because shared pretend play often involves multiple make-believe themes invoked for brief periods of time, we felt that children should be able to produce appropriate nonliteral responses to different pretend scenarios using a single set of toys or props. The ability to respond in this way should be a crucial component of truly collaborative pretend play.

To examine these issues, we carried out two studies in which an experimenter enacted pretend scenarios embedded within two familiar routines: a bedtime and a breakfast script (Harris & Kavanaugh, 1993, Experiments 3 & 4). The two scripts contained three distinct episodes in which the experimenter initiated a particular pretend sequence which the child was asked to complete. Each episode involved a key prop used to stipulate a particular make-believe identity. For example, during the breakfast script, after simulating pouring tea from an empty teapot into an empty cup containing a popsickle stick, the experimenter handed the cup to the child saying, "Show me how you stir Teddy's tea with the spoon." A key feature of this study was testing children's ability to use a single prop (e.g., popsickle stick) to invoke two different pretend themes. Thus, on one trial of the bedtime script, children watched as the experimenter simulated squeezing toothpaste from a closed tube onto the popsickle stick saying, "Show me how you brush Teddy's teeth with the toothbrush." Two other key props were used in the same manner (i.e., children were required to recognize that the prop could assume a different make-believe identity depending on the experimenter's stipulation).

Our particular focus was children's ability to produce "dual" responses. These were defined as pretend actions, such as bringing the popsickle stick to Teddy's mouth and making brushing movements, appropriate to the stipulated identity of the key prop. Thus, children were credited with a dual response if they used the popsickle stick to "stir" Teddy's tea in the breakfast scenario and to "brush" his teeth in the bedtime scenario. As Figure 8.1 shows, in both studies, we found that children above 2 years (mean age =

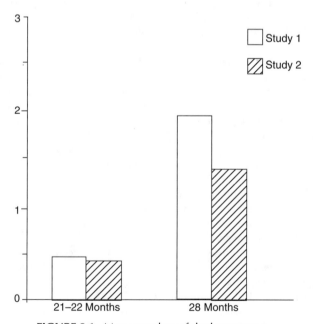

FIGURE 8.1. Mean number of dual responses.

28 months) produced a relatively large number of dual responses, whereas children below 2 years (mean age = 21–22 months) produced relatively few such responses. The design of the two studies was identical except that, in the second, the experimenter refrained from using key words, such as "stirred" and "brushed," that might have cued children to make a particular response. Instead, the experimenter substituted a more general phrase such as "Show me what Teddy does."

Our results suggested that 2-year-olds performed quite well. Even in the absence of verbal cues, they produced dual responses roughly 50% of the time. Furthermore, an error analysis showed little interference across scripts, such as treating the popsickle stick in accordance with its prior pretend identity (e.g., spoon) rather than its current identity (e.g., toothbrush). Approximately 90% of children's errors consisted of using the props in a literal manner (e.g., manipulating the popsickle stick) rather than making an inappropriate pretend action. Overall, the results suggested that 2-year-olds understand that the stipulated make-believe identities of props are not fixed, but vary according to the imaginary theme invoked by the pretender.

In sum, this first set of studies demonstrated that, by early in the third year, children have grasped one of the fundamental characteristics of shared pretend play. They understand that the make-believe identity of an object is not a property of the object itself but depends on the pretender's stipulation. Consequently, the pretend identity of a given object is tied only to a particular make-believe scenario. One can change or modify an object's nonliteral identity if the object becomes part of a different imaginary scenario.

Pretend Transformations

Shared pretend play often involves more complicated scenarios in which the pretender's actions change or transform the make-believe status of a key prop. Consider again the opening example of a pretend tea party between mother and child but, this time, the following scenario unfolds. As the mother reaches for the child's cup, she knocks over the teapot and declares that the table is "all wet." She then asks the child to use her napkin to "wipe up the tea." To understand the mother's behavior, the child must make several inferences. The first is that the table has changed from "dry" to "wet" as a result of the imaginary mishap. In turn, this inference should permit the child to understand why it is appropriate to "wipe up" the tea. From our perspective, pretend transformations offered a critical test of children's understanding of others' nonliteral actions. Whereas in our first set of studies pretend actions were embedded within everyday scenarios (e.g., breakfast and bedtime routines) whose familiarity may have aided children's comprehension, in our transformation studies children observed unexpected violations of everyday events that, while comprehensible, should not have been predictable.

Responding to Pretend Transformations.   The basic design of the transformations studies involved an experimenter-manipulated hand puppet, known to the children as Naughty Teddy, who obligingly carried out a series of make-believe misdemeanors. For example, on one trial of a representative study (Harris & Kavanaugh, 1993, Experiment 5), children watched as Naughty Teddy picked up an empty teapot and pretended to pour tea over the head of one of two identical toy pigs. The experimenter then asked the child to "dry the pig who is all wet." With position effects controlled, children who understood such a request should have inferred that the pig directly beneath the teapot was the one that was "wet" and in need of "drying." As in the first set of studies, children below (mean age = 20 months) and above 2 years (mean age = 28 months) participated. Once again we found that age 2 years was an important developmental milestone. As Figure 8.2 shows, 2-year-olds performed well on this task, but those under 2 years were considerably less successful. Statistical analyses confirmed this impression by revealing that the older, but not the younger, children exceeded chance expectations. One point of interest was a strong indication of individual differences among the children below 2 years. Approximately one third of these children made no response to the experimenter's request, perhaps indicating that they did not understand what was required of them. However, those under 2 years who did respond often were correct.

In a related study, Walker-Andrews and Harris (1993) manipulated the complexity of the make-believe transformations that children observed. They asked a group of 2-, 3-, and 4-year-olds to observe either a single or a double transformation. Single transformations were similar to those described above; double transformations involved a reversal or negation of the original pretend action. For example, on a single transformation trial, the experimenter produced a single transformation by "pouring" pretend cereal into one of two identical (empty) bowls. Children were then invited to give the cereal to a doll. They were

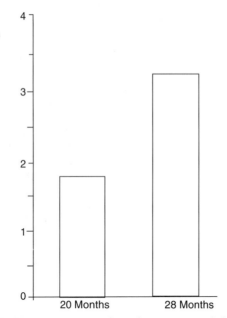

FIGURE 8.2. Mean number of correct remedial responses.

credited with understanding the request if they pretended to "feed" the doll from the bowl containing the make-believe cereal. On a double transformation trial, the experimenter first "poured" pretend cereal into each of the two bowls and then carried out a second transformation by simulating eating cereal from one of the bowls. Once again, children were required to choose the bowl containing "cereal" but, in this case, they had to recognize that the initial pretend action (filling the bowl with cereal) had been negated by the second action (pretending to eat the cereal). Figure 8.3 shows that children in all three age groups,

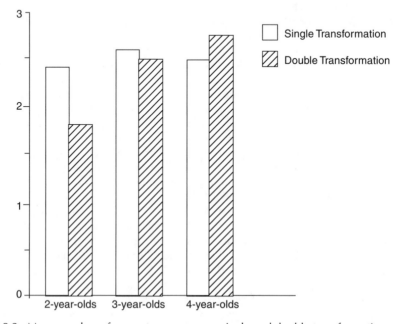

FIGURE 8.3. Mean number of correct responses on single and double transformations.

2-year-olds included, performed well on the single transformations, a finding consistent with the results of our previous experiments. Although double transformations were reliably more difficult for 2-year-olds than for the 3- and 4-year-olds, performance on double transformations was generally strong with the majority of responses correct for children in each of the three age groups. This overall pattern is noteworthy because, in this experiment as in the transformations experiments described above, it might be argued that children did not have to understand the experimenter's nonliteral intentions to respond correctly but could adopt the simple heuristic of acting on the last object the experimenter pointed to, touched, or approached. However, such a strategy would have led to systematic error on the double transformation trials where the last prop the experimenter touched was the one that children needed to ignore.

The transformation experiments demonstrated that, by early in the third year, children could imagine the consequences of make-believe actions. They understood that, if a pretend substance "spilled" onto a surface or was "poured" over an unsuspecting animal, the stipulated scenario had changed: The surface was now "wet" or the animal "messy." Moreover, they realized that further make-believe transformations were possible, such as remedial actions that "dry" the surface or "clean" the animal. Impressively, 2-year-olds did not require any perceptible markers of these transformations: Nothing actually spilled onto a surface or poured from a container. Rather, children relied on their imagination and their causal knowledge to determine the consequences of the experimenter's actions.

Talking About Pretend Transformations.   Several different investigators have reported that, beginning around age 2 years, children's language is no longer confined to the here and now. For example, research on autobiographical memory has shown that young children both understand and talk about past events (Engel, 1986; Fivush & Hammond, 1990; Nelson, 1989). However, as Fenson (1984) noted, less is known about children's ability to talk about make-believe events. Our experiments on children's understanding of make-believe transformations provided some tantalizing evidence that children were capable of using language nonliterally. For example, in the course of responding to the experimenter's requests, we noted that some children occasionally used words such as "wet" or "messy" to comment on the state of a surface or a toy animal. Although we could not rule out the possibility that children simply were repeating phrases used by the experimenter, we were intrigued enough to pursue more systematic studies.

To determine whether children could describe make-believe transformations, we first had them watch while Naughty Teddy carried out a single make-believe transformation, such as pretending to squeeze toothpaste from a closed toothpaste tube over the ears of a toy rabbit (Harris & Kavanaugh, 1993, Experiment 6). We then asked questions that required children to describe what happened (e.g., "What did Naughty Teddy put on the rabbit's ears?"). In related follow-up work (Harris, Kavanaugh, & Meredith, 1994, Experiments 1 & 2), we conducted two studies that required children to describe the consequences of *two* successive transformations. For example, with the aid of a hand puppet that resembled a duck, the experimenter might pretend to pour milk from a milk carton or to sprinkle talcum powder from a talcum powder container into a small tray. The experimenter then made Duck pretend to pour the contents of the tray over the head of a toy animal. To work out the make-believe outcome, children first had to imagine the consequence of "pouring" a particular substance into the tray, followed by the consequence of "spilling" that substance over the animal. A group of younger (mean age = 28–31 months) and older (mean age = 34–36 months) 2-year-olds participated in these studies. As Figure 8.4 shows, both younger and older children frequently named the make-believe substance that was squirted or poured over the target animal in each of the three studies described above. Impressively, this was true even when children observed the more complex scenario in which a substance was first transferred to a neutral container and then tipped over the head of the animal. Furthermore, in studies 1 and 3 of this series, we posed an open-ended question that inquired about the consequences of the make-believe actions (e.g., "Naughty Teddy made the monkey all . . . ?") Children in both age groups produced a variety of appropriate terms. For example, the rabbit with pretend toothpaste all over its ear was described as "mucky," "messy," or even "toothpastey." The victim of the milk episode was described as "wet," "covered in milk," or "milky." As one would expect and, as confirmed in Figure 8.5, this question proved more difficult than simply naming the pretend substance. Nonetheless, on the whole, the children in these experiments performed reasonably well. The majority of younger 2-year-olds produced appropriate descriptions on at least one trial out of four, and the majority of older 2-year-olds were majority successful on at least two trials out of four. Importantly, errors

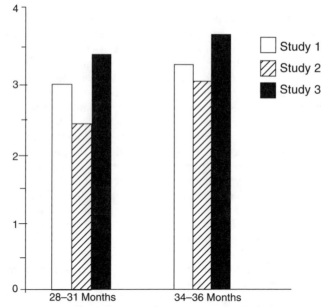

FIGURE 8.4. Mean number of correct descriptions of make-believe substances.

rarely involved inappropriate descriptions; rather, children simply remained silent. Finally, we should note that, in two experiments in this set of studies, we asked children to imagine the consequences of pretend actions directed toward a key prop that served as a substitute object. For example, on a typical trial, the experimenter might say to the child, "The horse wants to eat chocolate. Let's give him some chocolate" as she placed a small brown brick in front of the horse. The experimenter's familiar accomplice, Naughty Teddy or Duck, then performed its usual mischievous deed. In this case, Naughty Teddy "squeezed" toothpaste all over the pretend bar of chocolate (Harris & Kavanaugh, 1993, Experiment 7). In

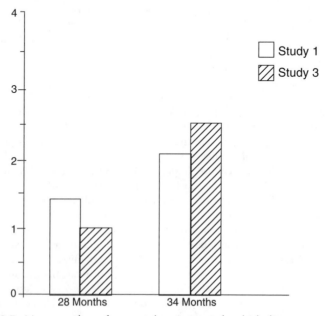

FIGURE 8.5. Mean number of correct descriptions of make-believe outcomes.

a related study (Harris et al., 1994, Experiment 3), Duck picked up a toy animal and placed it on top of the key prop (brown brick) which had been given a similar pretend identity (chocolate). As before, the experimenter then posed a series of graded questions to determine if children could describe the make-believe transformations. One question asked explicitly about the identity of the substitute object which children had successfully identified by its literal name in a pretest. Note that the design of these experiments involved an additional step in children's understanding and description of pretense. Children could describe the substitute object by reference to its familiar name (brick) or by referring to its make-believe identity (chocolate). As Figure 8.6 shows, in both studies, younger and older 2-year-olds frequently referred to the substitute object by its pretend identity. Errors consisted primarily of no response to the experimenter's question rather than a reference to the object's literal identity.

Taken together, the studies reported in this section demonstrate that, when prompting, cuing, and script knowledge are controlled, 2-year-olds can describe accurately the make-believe actions of others. Once a make-believe scenario has been established, 2-year-olds are able to use language in nonliteral fashion to refer to events unfolding within the scenario. They respond contingently and appropriately to requests that assume an understanding of pretense, and they can suppress their usual terms of reference for objects imbued temporarily with a make-believe identity.

Representing Pretend Stipulations

Young children's competence in responding to pretense overtures raises questions about how they are able to interpret others' make-believe actions. In earlier work, we have suggested that children may use a partner's action as a scaffold that guides their construction of a coherent pretend scenario (Harris, 1994; Harris & Kavanaugh, 1993). Thus, if they see a play partner pick up an empty milk carton and tip it over a toy pig, they use their causal understanding of real events to imagine the missing elements of the situation: milk flowing out and drenching the pig (Harris, 1994). Such an interpretation explains two key findings: (a) the ability to perform remedial actions such as "drying" the objectively dry pig, and (b) the ability to use language in nonliteral fashion to offer a description of the imaginary action.

If this interpretation is correct, we reasoned that young children should be able to watch an imaginary transformation and then choose among several different representations of the pretend action they had observed. For example, after watching an experimenter use a gloved hand puppet to carry out some make-believe deed, such as pretending to pour milk over a cat, children were asked to select a picture that

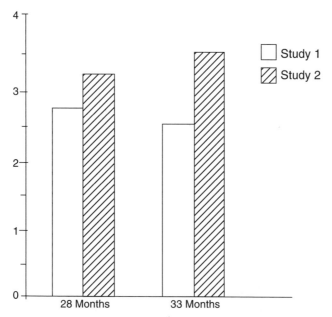

FIGURE 8.6. Mean number of correct descriptions of the make-believe identity of a prop.

"shows how the cat looks now" (Kavanaugh & Harris, 1994). In a similar study, we examined the effect of the mode of representation by comparing children's response to choice arrays involving either pictures or toy models depicting the imaginary transformation (Harris, Kavanaugh, & Dowson, 1997).

Note that this method has the advantage of overcoming a possible objection to our earlier studies, where it could be argued that the task we chose led us to underestimate the competence of children under 2 years. It is possible that the older 1-year-olds we tested understood the make-believe transformations they observed but either could not make an appropriate remedial response or could not describe what occurred. However, to be correct on the picture task outlined above, children needed only to make a simple choice response following the enacted transformation. This change in method meant that even very young children should be able to comply with the task demands.

The essential feature of the first study (Kavanaugh & Harris, 1994) was to present children with a pictorial representation of an enacted make-believe transformation. Children participated first in a warm-up session in which they were shown pictures of familiar objects in trios (e.g., a flower, a mouse, and a frog) and asked to point to each item in succession. Next, the experimenter invited the children "to play a game of pretend" and then introduced a series of make-believe transformations involving different toy animals similar to the procedure used in our earlier studies. For example, in one protocol, the experimenter placed a cat in front of the child and pretended to pour milk from an empty milk carton over the cat's body (Kavanaugh & Harris, 1994, Experiment 2). However, rather than requiring the child to remedy or to describe the situation, three pictures of the cat were positioned in front of the child who was asked, "How does the cat look now? Does he look like this picture, or like this picture, or like this picture?" The three pictures, whose location varied systematically, depicted the cat (a) in an unaltered state, (b) in a make-believe transformed state (milk all over its body), and (c) in an irrelevant transformed state (green stripes on its back). The irrelevant transformation was included as a control to ensure that children did not select the picture of the correct pretend transformation (cat covered in milk) simply because it was novel or interesting. Once again we compared the performance of a group of older 1-year-olds (mean age = 21 months) with a group of younger 2-year-olds (mean age = 27 months). As Figure 8.7 shows, the 2-year-olds performed very well on this task. They selected the correct picture on approximately 80% of trials, a performance that far exceeded chance expectations. However, 1-year-olds, who selected the correct picture on only about 40% of trials, performed no better than chance. An error analysis elaborated the

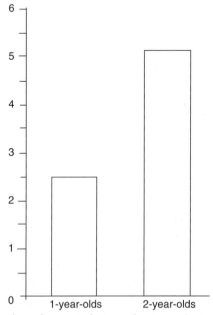

FIGURE 8.7. Mean number of correct choices of pictures depicting pretend transformations.

difference between the two groups. When 2-year-olds made an error, they usually selected the animal in its unaltered state and rarely chose the irrelevant transformation. One-year-olds were less consistent. On one or more trials, 40% of the children in this group made no response and, on the remaining trials, they chose either the picture of the animal in its unaltered state or the irrelevant transformation.

Although these results again suggest that pretense comprehension undergoes significant change in the early part of the third year, roughly between ages of 2 to 2½ years, there are several reasons for caution. One is that children who failed the task, particularly those under age 2 years, may have done so because they did not appreciate fully the experimenter's invitation to engage in pretense. Recall that test trials began with a simple statement that the child and the experimenter were going to play a game of pretend. Arguably, older 1-year-olds may not have understood this invitation or may have failed to keep it in mind throughout the test trials. If so, they may have perceived the experimenter's actions as literal rather than pretend and, thus, would not have been prompted to select a picture that depicted an imaginary transformation. A second possibility is that the younger children could imagine make-believe transformations but had difficulty recognizing that these events were shown in pictures. DeLoache and her colleagues (DeLoache & Burns, 1994; Pierroutsakos & DeLoache, 1996) have shown that children under 2 years have difficulty understanding that a picture is not only an entity in itself but also serves as a representation of what is depicted. This latter possibility would suggest that younger children would perform better if presented with a choice array of actual objects. Third, it is possible that children under 2 years have difficulty understanding the relationship between the enacted transformation and its representation. To succeed on this task, children must "map" from the actions performed on the toy animal to the representation of the animal. Thus, the difficulty that 1-year-olds experience may lie in understanding the representing relationship itself. If this interpretation is correct, then young children will find it difficult to identify any representation of a make-believe event, either pictures or actual toys. Furthermore, children under 2 years should have difficulty understanding a literal (e.g., milk actually poured over the cat's body) as well as a pretend transformation.

We explored these issues in a subsequent study that involved two distinct experiments (Harris et al., 1997). In Experiment 1, a younger (mean = 21 months), intermediate (mean = 28 months), and older (mean = 37 months) group of children first participated in an elaborate warm-up session in which they were encouraged to enact two pretend episodes each consisting of two different pretend actions. For example, the experimenter might place a toy animal before the child with a teapot and cup on one side of the animal and an empty cereal box, bowl, and spoon on the other side. Children were encouraged to "play a game of pretend" and then asked to give the monkey some tea and some cereal. Following the warm-up session, children participated in test trials similar to those described above (Kavanaugh & Harris, 1994) except that, on half the trials, the choice array consisted of three colored pictures and, on the other half, it consisted of three specially constructed toy animals. Both choice arrays presented children with the three choices noted earlier (unaltered target, correct transformation, and irrelevant transformation), but a further control was added by pairing target animals and pretend actions in such a way that the irrelevant transformation on one trial became the correct transformation on a subsequent trial involving the same animal, and vice versa. Thus, a red mark on an animal's leg was irrelevant when pretend milk was poured over the animal, but became the correct transformation when pretend ketchup was squirted on the animal's leg. On this latter trial, milk on the animal's body became the irrelevant choice. The majority of children in each age group successfully performed 75% or more of the warm-up actions, providing some assurance that they entered the test trials engaged in the pretend nature of the task. However, as Figure 8.8 shows, children below 2 years performed no better than chance on the test questions, a result that held true for both the picture and toy animal choice arrays. By contrast, children in the two older groups performed above chance on both types of choice array. An error analysis showed that the youngest children often failed to make a response and were unable to differentiate reliably between the correct and the irrelevant transformation. Children in the two older groups rarely failed to make a response and reliably distinguished the correct from the incorrect transformations.

These findings seem to eliminate two of the concerns noted above about children under 2 years: (a) that they do not participate fully in the experimenter's game of pretense, and (b) that they have a special difficulty with pictorial representations of imaginary transformations. Children under 2 years produced as many pretend warm-up actions as children in the intermediate group yet, on test trials, they identified far fewer correct transformations. The youngest children also experienced equal difficulty with picture

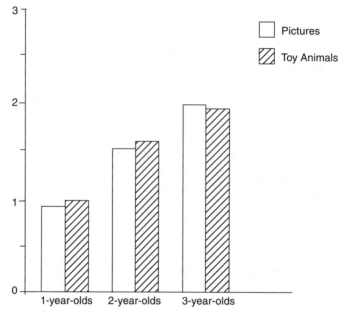

FIGURE 8.8. Mean number of correct choices of pictures and toy animals depicting pretend transformations.

and toy animal choice arrays. However, the results leave open the third possibility noted above; namely, that children under 2 years may fail because they have difficulty mapping from the enacted event to its representation. We reasoned that, if this is the source of their difficulty, then both literal (animal covered with actual substance) and pretend transformations should be equally difficult to understand.

We pursued this question in an experiment that assessed whether 2-year-olds find it easier to understand symbolic representations of actual (visible) as opposed to imaginary events (Harris et al., 1997, Experiment 2). Children were divided into a group of older 1-year-olds (mean age = 22 months) and

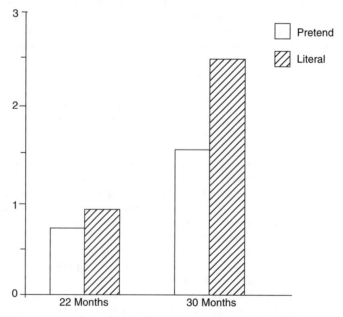

FIGURE 8.9. Mean number of correct responses on pretend and literal episodes.

younger 2-year-olds (mean age = 30 months). The procedure was similar to the previous experiment, except that half the episodes involved literal transformations (e.g., squeezing actual toothpaste from a tube) and half involved make-believe transformations (e.g., pretending to squeeze toothpaste from a tube) onto a toy animal. The choice array consisted of pictures because we observed no difference between toy models and pictures in the previous experiment. A pretend warm up, equivalent to the one used in Experiment 1, preceded the make-believe episodes and a literal warm up (e.g., encouraging children to pour and feed real cereal) preceded the literal test trials. The results, shown in Figure 8.9, revealed that the 1-year-olds performed poorly on both the literal and pretend episodes, failing to exceed chance expectations on either type of episode. Two-year-olds did better on literal than pretend episodes, but exceeded chance expectations on both types of episode. As in the previous experiment, 1-year-olds often failed to make a response and differentiated poorly between the correct and irrelevant transformation on both the literal and pretend trials. By contrast, 2-year-olds rarely failed to respond and frequently chose the correct over the irrelevant transformation on both types of episode.

The results of these experiments suggest that 2-year-olds have the capacity to understand the symbolic relationship involved in mapping from an enacted event to its pictorial representation. Moreover, they appear to be able to do this for both real and imagined situations. The superior performance of 2-year-olds on the literal trials suggests the possibility of a developmental sequence in which children first understand that pictures can refer to actual situations and then extend that insight to imaginary situations. Although this remains only an intriguing hypothesis at present, what seems certain is that 2-year-olds understand that iconic symbols, either pictures or actual objects, can be used to represent unreal situations. This finding suggests that, by the beginning of the third year, children are primed to understand one of the major functions of iconic symbols often found in children's storybooks—the depiction of imaginary objects and events.

The performance of children under 2 years is more difficult to assess, but the cumulative findings suggest that they do not understand the symbolic relationship involved in mapping from the enacted event to its representation. This appears to be a problem that is neither confined to the difficulty involved in representing imaginary events nor due to a failure to recognize the similarity between an object and its representation. On literal episodes, a transformed animal (e.g., toy animal with real tea on its body) remained visible as children chose a representation of the action. Yet, older 1-year-olds still had difficulty choosing the correct picture. This suggests that difficulties in mapping did not arise because children failed to notice the perceptual similarity between the event and its representation. Rather, it would appear that children have difficulty with the mapping relationship itself. Such a difficulty may be similar to the problem noted by DeLoache and her colleagues in their provocative series of experiments in which children are asked to treat pictures and models as representations of another situation (DeLoache, 1991; DeLoache & Burns, 1994). A recurrent finding from this work is that young children do not understand the relationship between a model and what it represents until roughly age 3 years, although they are accurate at a younger age (roughly 28 months) when pictures are used to represent the situation. Although there are notable differences between DeLoache's task and the one we have used, a convergent finding is that children's understanding of iconic symbols begins to crystallize during the third year.

Agentive Expressions of Pretense

Pretend play appears to assist children with one of the fundamental discoveries of early childhood—the knowledge that people have capacities that are different from those of inanimate objects. One of the core features of this knowledge is an understanding of agency, a concept that incorporates the notions of animacy and intentionality. As early as the first year, infants are sensitive to certain stimulus properties, such as self-propelled movement, that help to differentiate agents from inanimate objects (Gergely, Nádasdy, Csibra, & Bíró, 1995). During the latter part of the second year, the notion of agency continues to develop and receives concrete expression in children's play, particularly pretend play with inanimate replica toys such as dolls and toy animals. Young children infuse these objectively inanimate objects with the power to carry out animate actions such as walking, feeding, and bathing (Wolf et al., 1984). Several investigators have reported that children ascribe a variety of different actions or states to replica toys pretending, for example, that a doll placed on a bed is "sleeping" or that a mother doll can "feed" a baby doll (Bretherton et al., 1984; Fenson, 1984; Wolf, 1982). Typically, children first ascribe passive agency (e.g., doll "sleeps" on bed), followed by active or independent agency in which dolls and other replica toys carry out their own make-believe actions (e.g., mother doll "feeds" baby doll) (Wolf et al., 1984).

We have pursued the question of when, and under what circumstances, children understand pretense expressions of independent agency. In our early experiments, we noted that children often characterize the actions of agents, such as Naughty Teddy or Duck, in terms of their goal or outcome. Thus, children used the term "pour," rather than its literal complement, "tilt" or "lift," to describe what transpired when Naughty Teddy placed an empty teapot over the head of a toy animal (Harris & Kavanaugh, 1993, Experiment 5). Recently, we examined more directly children's understanding of the pretend actions of independent agents (Kavanaugh, Eizenman, & Harris, 1997). The design of this study incorporated a mother and baby doll who were involved in pretend scenarios in which the mother doll offered assistance (e.g., feeding, bathing) to the baby doll. For example, one of the pretend scenarios involved a hungry baby doll accompanied by props (spoon, empty bowl) that could be used to "feed" the doll. On some trials, children were required to complete the experimenter's pretend initiative by making the mother doll enact some or all of the following actions: pick up a spoon, dip it into an empty bowl, and then bring the spoon to the baby's mouth. On other trials, children observed the experimenter perform some or all of these actions and were then asked to describe what happened or, in the case of a partially completed scenario, to indicate "what the Mommy doll will do next."

As Figure 8.10 shows, older 2-year-olds were reliably better than younger 2-year-olds in understanding pretense expressions of independent agency. Several error analyses also were conducted to gain a better sense of younger children's difficulty with the task. The most revealing was that, on trials requiring children to enact a conclusion to a make-believe scenario, the most common mistake was for children to perform the pretend action themselves rather than using the doll to enact it. These self-errors appeared far more often than either of the other two possibilities: no response or simple manipulation of the props. The preponderance of self-errors likely reflects the difficulty of understanding others' nonliteral actions when faced with complex pretend scenarios. When make-believe play involves independent agency, children must appreciate the once-removed quality of the pretender's actions. It appears that children do not fully comprehend this form of pretense until relatively late in the third year.

Overview of Pretense Studies

Our research suggests that young children's accomplishments in understanding pretense are considerable. We have found that the majority of 2-year-olds can make sense of an experimenter's make-believe

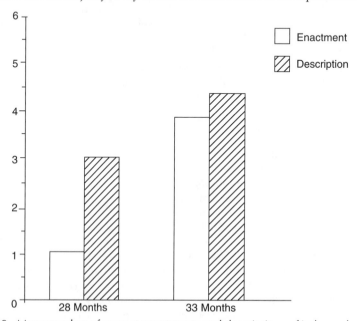

FIGURE 8.10. Mean number of correct enactments and descriptions of independent agency.

transformation of objects and events during pretend scenarios. They are able to generate appropriate responses that allow the scenarios to continue, including the ability to use language nonliterally to describe the imaginary events that have unfolded. We also have found that 2-year-olds can select an appropriate iconic representation of the pretend transformation and that, by the latter part of the third year, they comprehend pretense expressions of independent agency.

As noted elsewhere (Harris, 1994; Harris & Kavanaugh, 1993), we believe that young children's competence in understanding pretend scenarios is the result of a twofold process. First, when interacting with a play partner, 2-year-olds recognize make-believe actions as a variant on familiar activities that are common place in their physical world. For example, young children routinely see liquid poured from containers into cups or notice that it sometimes spills onto dry surfaces. What is different in pretense is that actions such as lifting, pouring, and spilling are not accompanied by their usual physical outcomes. Second, children process what transpires in a constructive slot-filling fashion. The partner's actions become a scaffold that permits children to use their imagination to restore the missing components of the scenario. Thus, when 2-year-olds observe a play partner pick up an empty teapot and tip it over the head of a toy animal they are able to visualize the outcome of imaginary actions. Such a process generates the prediction, confirmed in two studies, that 2-year-olds should be able to observe a pretend scenario and then select an iconic representation that depicts the outcome of the make-believe transformation.

When children imagine the missing components of the experimenter's actions constructively, they are not misperceiving the situation or suffering from a perceptual illusion. Rather, they are supplementing the reality of what has transpired (teapot tipped over toy animal) with assumptions about what could happen (tea flows out and wets animal). There is no reason to believe that subsequent encounters with real teapots will lead children to misconstrue reality because such assumptions are stored only in relationship to the ongoing pretend episode. As soon as a new episode begins, the assumptions from the previous episode are discontinued (cf., Harris & Kavanaugh, 1993). Note that this model can account for the fact that 2-year-olds recognize that an object with one physical identity can have a different make-believe identity (Harris & Kavanaugh, 1993, Experiments 3 & 4) in different, successive episodes. Thus, a popsicle stick can serve as a spoon in a pretend breakfast scenario and then as a toothbrush in a pretend bedtime scenario.

In sum, at roughly 2 years, children begin to use their imagination to envision the outcome of make-believe episodes generated by a play partner. This ability to understand and reason about actions that do not actually materialize would appear similar to the skills involved in thinking counterfactually about outcomes that did not occur but might have occurred. Below we discuss our findings on the development of counterfactual thought during the toddler and preschool years. We then conclude with a perspective on pretense and counterfactual thought.

☐ Counterfactual Thought

As Hume (1739/1978) noted in his well-known treatise on human nature, inferences about one event causing another often depend on people's awareness of the temporal or spatial contiguity between the two events. For example, if we observe the regular association of event A leading to event B we may well conclude that a causal relationship (A causes B) exists between the two events. Although Hume's analysis is helpful, and can be shown to apply to inferences drawn by young children (Bullock, Gelman, & Baillargeon, 1982), causal reasoning also is characterized by the contrasts people draw between what occurred and what might have occurred (i.e., a consideration of how a consequent event might have been different if the antecedent conditions were changed). Examples of this type of reasoning abound in film and literature, exemplified in emotional discussions of how a loss of love or territory might have turned out differently if only a prior set of circumstances could have been changed. Such expressions of regret exemplify the type of contrary-to-fact thinking that occurs when a clear factual outcome can be linked to an alterable antecedent event. Thus, counterfactual thought typically takes the form of a conditional proposition about an alternative view of the past that negates an established fact (Roese, 1997).

Research on causal reasoning by infants and young children has tended to focus on their sensitivity to spatial-temporal contiguities between antecedent and consequent events (Bullock et al., 1982; Leslie & Keeble, 1987). Nonetheless, some investigators have noted young children's ability to comment on things that have not actually happened but might have occurred were circumstances different. For example, although they do not produce fully formed conditional propositions, children as young as 2 and 3 years use terms such as "almost" and "nearly" to describe events (often mishaps) that come close to occurring (Au, 1992; Bowerman, 1986; Harris, Neave, & Phillips, 1996). Thus, Bowerman (1986) observed a 2-year-old exclaim "almost fall" as she grabbed a pitcher about to tumble into a sandbox.

Recently, we have investigated whether young children can understand and reason about counterfactual situations (Kavanaugh & Harris, 1997). To accomplish this, we showed children a "factual event" that involved a brief episode with a toy animal, followed by a "let's pretend" question about an alternative contrary-to-fact outcome. In one experiment, we first pretested a group of younger (mean age = 28 months) and older (mean age = 34 months) 2-year-olds on their understanding of the key words in the counterfactual questions. Following the pretest, the experimenter used three toy animals in brief scenarios that involved a change in the animal's physical state. For example, the experimenter placed an elephant in a bowl of water and then asked a forced-choice factual question about what transpired (e.g., "What happened to the elephant? Is the elephant wet or dry?"). After the child responded to this factual question, the experimenter used different props to pose two questions that began with the phrase "let's pretend" and concluded by asking the child to imagine a counterfactual situation that would produce either an altered (e.g., elephant is dry) or similar (e.g., elephant is wet) physical state. For example, in the presence of a bowl of popcorn, the experimenter said, "Let's pretend that I put the elephant in this bowl of popcorn. Would the elephant be wet or dry?" A similar question was posed with a bowl of milk serving as the accompanying prop. We found that both younger and older 2-year-olds performed near ceiling on the factual questions. Furthermore, the two groups performed very well on both altered and similar state counterfactual questions. Adjusting for knowledge of the pretest questions improved the performance of most children but, even without this measure (using raw scores only), the performance of both the older and younger groups exceeded chance expectations.

Recently, Harris, German, and Mills (1996) conducted a series of experiments that constituted a more direct exploration of children's ability to deploy counterfactual reasoning. In the first experiment, they asked 3 to 5-year-olds to observe a sequence in which event A (e.g., doll with dirty feet walks on clean floor) causes event B (clean floor becomes dirty). Children were then asked to imagine the counterfactual condition ("What if the doll first takes off her shoes?") and predict the outcome ("Floor dirty or not dirty?"). The majority of children responded correctly. In a second experiment, a group of older 3-year-olds (mean age = 43 months) first observed event A and then were asked to differentiate between two antecedent events, one that would and one that would not have caused event B. Thus, having observed the incorrigible Naughty Teddy hand puppet deface a clean floor by painting it with a paintbrush, children were asked to determine what would have happened if Teddy had (a) not painted the floor with his brush and (b) painted the floor with his fingers. Children successfully articulated the difference between these two antecedent events. A third experiment constituted the most stringent test of causal reasoning about counterfactual propositions. A group of 3- and 4-year-olds listened to stories involving a protagonist whose actions (e.g., drawing with a black pen) led to a minor mishap (getting inky fingers). In the experimental version of the story, the protagonist rejects an option (drawing with a pencil) that would have prevented the mishap, while in the control version, the protagonist chooses an option (drawing with a blue pen) that would have led to the same outcome. Children were asked to explain the cause of each mishap and to say how it might have been avoided. For example, children heard about Sally who wanted to draw a picture and was offered a choice between a black pen and a pencil (experimental story) and a black pen and a blue pen (control story). In both versions, Sally opts for the black pen and then gets ink all over her fingers. In their explanations, both 3- and 4-year-olds mentioned the failure to adopt a different course of action and, particularly in experimental stories, focused on the rejected alternative as the cause of the mishap (e.g., "She should have used a pencil").

In short, it appears that preschool children have a firm grasp of counterfactual propositions. They understand that a particular set of events could have turned out differently had antecedent circumstances or actions been different. In addition, we have provided some preliminary evidence that, if 2-year-olds observe a simple event that produces a particular physical state, they are able to imagine circumstances that would produce either an opposing or a similar state. Thus, it appears that the roots of counterfactual reasoning may emerge prior to the preschool years.

☐ A Perspective on Pretense and Counterfactual Thinking

Our results show that 2-year-olds are adroit at imagining events that they have not actually witnessed. In the context of pretense, they do this when they make sense of the gestures and props that their play partner deploys by working out what make-believe event or transformation their partner has enacted. They also do it when, having observed an actual event, they step back and conceive of ways in which that event might have turned out differently. Thus, in each case, toddlers do not simply encode what has actually taken place, they also can imagine some other episode. These observations lead us to conclude that 2- and 3-year-olds can readily set up in their mind's eye what we might call a working model in which they imagine the unfolding of imagined events. In this concluding section, we want to explore other plausible functions for such a working model. We have stressed its role in pretense and in counterfactual thinking but, in some ways, these are rare and somewhat exotic modes of thought. Do children put their working model to more prosaic or widespread use?

Before answering this question, it will be useful to backtrack briefly to an earlier discussion of our findings on pretense comprehension (Harris & Kavanaugh, 1993). In that discussion, we noted several intriguing analogies between the cognitive processes that underlie text comprehension among adults, and the processes that children deploy in understanding pretense. In particular, we noted that the two modes of comprehension involve causal inferences that connect successive parts of an episode and yield an interconnected, memorable representation.

We now argue that what we presented as an intriguing parallelism between text and pretense comprehension is better interpreted as a deep equivalence between the two cognitive modes. More specifically, we propose the following hypothesis: The mental model posited by researchers to explain the way that adults process textual material is essentially equivalent to the working model that we have proposed as an explanation for children's facility in thinking about imagined episodes, whether in the context of pretense or in the context of counterfactual thinking. We also propose that the same working model underlies a skill that we alluded to in our introduction: Young children's emerging ability to understand displaced utterances concerning past or possible events. After all, there are obvious continuities between text comprehension and the understanding of displaced utterances. Although the former involves written language and the latter involves spoken language, in each case, the events that are being described do not take place just before or concurrent with the utterance. Thus, the child needs to construct a mental representation of the event in question without any scaffolding from perceptual input.

In sum, we wish to draw together four apparently different domains: pretense comprehension, counterfactual thinking, text comprehension, and the understanding of displaced utterances. Below, we attempt to show that the working model that underpins each of these four domains of cognition is one and the same. In each of the four domains, subjects elaborate on the input that they actually receive by interpolating or postulating various causal connections. Such causal elaborations routinely are guided by the default assumption that the events under consideration obey the ordinary causal laws of the real world.

The Working Model and Causal Inferences

Evidence for this default mode of causal elaboration is clear cut in our studies of pretense comprehension. When children watched a play partner pretend to pour liquid from a container, they readily assumed, even though there was no visible feedback to guide them, that the liquid would not squirt up into the air, evaporate, or freeze—it would fall onto the surface immediately below the container and make it wet just as it would in the real world. Two-year-olds provided evidence that they were making this default assumption in various ways: They produced pretend remedial gestures that were appropriate to the imagined outcome (e.g., "drying" the relevant surface); when asked to say what had happened, they described the surface as "wet"; and, when asked to point to a picture illustrating what had happened, they indicated appropriately a picture depicting a wet surface. In all of these cases, of course, the children actually were confronted by a dry surface since only pretend liquid had been poured onto it. Nevertheless, their responses were systematically guided by default causal elaborations.

In our studies of counterfactual thinking, children deployed the same causal understanding of liquids and surfaces. Asked to explain, for example, why a story protagonist had ended up with wet socks, the children posited a counterfactual situation. They pointed out that she had ended up with wet socks because she had not worn boots. By implication, in the counterfactual world that they posited, liquids would still wet a surface if they came into contact with it but it would be the outer surface (the boots) rather than the socks that would get wet. In another story, the protagonist ended up with inky fingers. Again, children posited a counterfactual scenario in which the causal fabric of the ordinary world still operated but the specific outcome was different. They suggested, for example, that the protagonist might have worn gloves to avoid getting inky fingers (Harris et al., 1996, Experiment 3).

Research on text comprehension likewise has highlighted the fact that, although a story or narrative description typically consists of a set of causally connected episodes, the text does not contain an explicit statement of every link in the causal chain. Studies of text memory and on-line reading times indicate that readers interpolate unstated causal links (van den Broek, 1990). Singer and his colleagues (1992) provided a neat illustration of this process of interpolation. They gave participants sentence pairs in which a causal link between the two sentences was implied but not explicitly stated (e.g., "Mary poured the water on the bonfire. The fire went out." Alternatively, subjects read control sentence pairs in which no such causal link was implied (e.g., "Mary placed the water by the bonfire. The fire went out." Immediately following either type of sentence pair, participants were asked to answer causal knowledge questions such as "Does water extinguish fire?" As expected, participants given sentence pairs that had implied just such a causal connection answered these questions faster, suggesting that they had mentally constructed that causal link on reading the sentence pair and benefited from that reinstatement of the relevant causal knowledge when reading the test questions (Singer, Halldorson, Lear, & Andrusiak, 1992).

Such causal interpolations typically depend on the default assumption that the world described in the text obeys the causal principles of the everyday world. Indeed, that default assumption appears to be sufficiently automatic and potent in text comprehension that it can lead participants to override their more considered or reflective judgments about causal possibilities. For example, in reading a text about God, participants in Barrett and Keil's (1996) study made the default assumption that, like mere mortals, He cannot be omniscient or omnipresent. As a result, they misremembered what was actually stated in the text, falsely "recognizing," for example, a sentence asserting that God first finished one task before turning to another, even though the text left it open as to whether God had carried out the two tasks simultaneously or successively. This distortion was not because subjects lacked the relevant metaphysical knowledge. In a separate questionnaire study, they were much more likely to judge that God could be omnipresent and engage concurrently in many tasks.

Research on the development of displaced utterances has focused mainly on children's increasing ability to produce such utterances (Morford & Goldin-Meadow, 1997). Research on comprehension of displaced utterances by very young children is sparse. Nevertheless, existing research lends considerable support to the claim that children elaborate on what is actually said explicitly to them, by building a working model based on their understanding of everyday causal regularities. Consider the following pioneering observational research by Huttenlocher (1974). Craig, age 19½ months, was seated in the kitchen with his mother and a visitor, Jane, who was about to depart. His mother asked him to "get Jane's coat." He was given no information about the location of the coat. Nevertheless, he left the kitchen and went directly to a bench at the entry to the house where Jane had left her coat on arrival. By implication, his understanding of object permanence guided his understanding that her coat remained where he had seen her leave it on arrival. Admittedly, such a default assumption may not have come into play on line, at the exact moment that Craig processed the sentence. Nonetheless, it must have been used by Craig at some point in mapping from the adult's request to a plan of action. Thus, Craig did not simply focus on the identity of the coat, and then search the house until he located it. Rather, he made a beeline for its location.

Further evidence for the deployment of causal knowledge in dealing with requests emerges if we look closely at the behavior of Alia, whose language comprehension was tested extensively between the ages of 18 and 24 months (Savage-Rumbaugh et al., 1993). Alia was given a variety of different requests, and her accuracy in responding to each request is reported in some detail. Alia's responses to requests demanding some prior enabling action or transformation were particularly revealing. Thus, when asked to "open the milk," Alia sought to comply by getting a container of milk and trying to get the cap off. After failing to do so, she got a fork and tried to pry off the cap (p. 140, observation 359A). Use of the fork was not mentioned explicitly: It was Alia's own idea. On another occasion, she was told to "put the milk in the water," the milk being in a closed plastic container. Alia first tried to open the milk container and, having failed, made a pouring gesture over the water but nothing came out. She was then told to "put the whole thing in the water." Instead of putting the unopened container in the water, she continued to try to pour milk from the container after attempting to open it (p. 164, observation 456A). A similar revealing miscommunication occurred when Alia was told to "put the peaches in the tomatoes." Rather than putting the nearby can of peaches in with the tomatoes, Alia repeatedly tried to open the can, asked for help to open it, and eventually tried to pour the peaches out of the unopened can. These examples, prosaic as they are, illustrate how the child's compliance with a request prompts elaborative causal thinking. The enabling actions are not explicitly mentioned in the request—they are interpolated by the child, guided by knowledge of how they will permit attainment of the presumed outcome. Occasionally, as with the milk and the peaches, the child's causal elaborations block a simpler solution (e.g., relocating the container, plus its contents), rather than trying to gain access to the contents.

In summary, this brief review makes it clear that elaborative causal thinking, based on the default assumption that the imagined world enjoys the same causal regularities as the actual world, can be found in apparently disparate domains. For the most part, research in these domains has been conducted independently. In particular, there has been very little interchange between research on text comprehension by adults and research on the comprehension of pretense, counterfactuals and displaced utterances in very young children. If our hypothesis is correct, such an interchange is overdue.

☐ References

Au, T. K. (1992). Counterfactual reasoning. In G. R. Semin & K. Fiedler (Eds.), *Language interaction and social cognition* (pp. 194–213). London: Sage.

Barrett, J. L., & Keil, F. C. (1996). Conceptualizing a nonnatural entity: Anthropomorphism in God concepts. *Cognitive Psychology, 31*, 219–247.

Bowerman, M. (1986). First steps in acquiring conditionals. In E. C. Traugott, A. ter Meulen, J. S. Reilly, & C. A. Ferguson (Eds), *On conditionals* (pp. 285–307). Cambridge, England: Cambridge University Press.

Bretherton, I. (Ed.). (1984). *Symbolic play: The development of social understanding.* New York: Academic Press.

Bretherton, I., O'Connell, B., Shore, C., & Bates, E. (1984). The effect of contextual variation in symbolic play: Development from 20 to 28 months. In I. Bretherton (Ed.), *Symbolic play: The development of social understanding* (pp. 271–298). New York: Academic Press.

Bullock, M., Gelman, R., & Baillargeon, R. (1982). The development of causal reasoning. In W. J. Friedman (Ed.), *The developmental psychology of time* (pp. 209–254). New York: Academic Press.

DeLoache, J. S. (1991). Symbolic functioning in very young children: Understanding of pictures and models. *Child Development, 62*, 111–126.

DeLoache, J. S., & Burns, N. M. (1994). Early understanding of the representational function of pictures. *Cognition, 52*, 83–110.

Dunn, J., & Dale, N. (1984). I a daddy: 2-year-olds' collaboration in joint pretend play with sibling and with mother. In I. Bretherton (Ed.), *Symbolic play: The development of social understanding* (pp. 131–158). New York: Academic Press.

Engel, S. (1986). *Learning to reminisce: A developmental study of how young children talk about the past.* Unpublished doctoral dissertation, City University of New York.

Fein, G. G. (1981). Pretend play: An integrative review. *Child Development, 52*, 1095–1118.

Fenson, L. (1984). Developmental trends for action and speech in pretend play. In I. Bretherton (Ed.), *Symbolic play: The development of social understanding* (pp. 249–270). New York: Academic Press.

Fiese, B. H. (1990). Playful relationships: A contextual analysis of mother-child interaction and symbolic play. *Child Development, 61*, 1648–1656.

Fivush, R., & Hammond, N. R. (1990). Autobiographical memory across the preschool years: Toward reconceptualizing childhood amnesia. In R. Fivush & J. Hudson (Eds.), *Knowing and remembering in young children* (pp. 223–248). New York: Cambridge University Press.

Gergely, G., Nádasdy, Z., Csibra, G., & Bíró, S. (1995). Taking the intentional stance at 12 months of age. *Cognition, 56,* 165–193.

Golomb, C., & Cornelius, C. B. (1977). Symbolic play and its cognitive significance. *Developmental Psychology, 13*, 246–252.

Haight, W. L., & Miller, P. J. (1993). *Pretending at home: Early development in a sociocultural context.* Albany, NY: SUNY Press.

Harris, P. L. (1994). Understanding pretence. In C. Lewis & M. Mitchell (Eds.), *Children's early understanding of mind: Origins and development.* Hillsdale, NJ: Erlbaum.

Harris, P. L., German, T., & Mills, P. (1996). Children's use of counterfactual thinking in causal reasoning. *Cognition, 61,* 233–259.

Harris, P. L., & Kavanaugh, R. D. (1993). Young children's understanding of pretense. *Monographs of the Society for Research in Child Development, 58* (1, Serial No. 231).

Harris, P. L., Kavanaugh, R. D., & Dowson, L. (1997). The depiction of imaginary transformations: Early comprehension of a symbolic function. *Cognitive Development, 12,* 1–19.

Harris, P. L., Kavanaugh, R. D., & Meredith, M. C. (1994). Young children's comprehension of pretend episodes: The integration of successive actions. *Child Development, 65,* 16–30.

Harris, P. L., Neave, E., & Phillips, N. J. (1997). *Talking about outcomes that almost happen.* Unpublished paper, University of Oxford, England.

Howes, C., Unger, O., & Seidner, l. B. (1989). Social pretend play in toddlers: Parallels with social play and with solitary pretend. *Child Development, 60,* 77–84.

Hume, D. (1978). *A treatise of human nature.* Oxford, England: Oxford University Press. (Original work published 1739)

Huttenlocher, J. (1974). The origins of language comprehension. In R. Solso (Ed.), *Theories in cognitive psychology: The Loyola Symposium* (pp. 331–368). Potomac, MD: Erlbaum.

Kavanaugh, R. D., Eizenman, D. R., & Harris, P. L. (1997). Young children's understanding of pretense expressions of independent agency. *Developmental Psychology, 33,* 774-770.

Kavanaugh, R. D., & Harris, P. L. (1994). Imagining the outcome of pretend transformations: Assessing the competence of normal children and children with autism. *Developmental Psychology, 30,* 847–854.

Kavanaugh, R. D., & Harris, P. L. (1997). *Counterfactual thinking in two-year-olds.* Unpublished manuscript, Williams College, Williamstown, MA.

Leslie, A. M., & Keeble, S. (1987). Do six-month-olds perceive causality? *Cognition, 25,* 265–288.

McCune, L. (1995). A normative study of representational play at the transition to language. *Developmental Psychology, 31,* 198–206.

McCune-Nicolich, L., & Fenson, L. (1984). Methodological issues in studying early pretend play. In T. D. Yawkey & A. D. Pellegrini (Eds.), *Child's play: Developmental and applied* (pp. 81–104). Hillsdale, NJ: Erlbaum.

Morford, J. P., & Goldin-Meadow, S. (1997). From here and now to there and then: The development of displaced reference in Homesign and English. *Child Development, 68,* 420–435.

Nelson, K. (1989). Monologue as re-presentation of events. In K. Nelson (Ed.), *Narratives from the crib.* Cambridge, MA: Harvard University Press.

Nicolich, L. (1977). Beyond sensorimotor intelligence: Assessment of symbolic maturity through analysis of pretend play. *Merrill-Palmer Quarterly, 23,* 89–99.

Oakes, L. M., & Cohen, L. B. (1990). Infant perception of a causal event. *Cognitive Development, 5,* 193–207.

O'Connell, B., & Bretherton, I. (1984). Toddler's play, alone and with mother: The role of maternal guidance. In I. Bretherton (Ed.), *Symbolic play: The development of social understanding* (pp. 337–368). New York: Academic Press.

Piaget, J. (1951). *Play, dreams, and imitation in childhood.* London: Heinemann.

Pierroutsakos, S. L., & DeLoache, J. S. (1996, April). *Understanding the object of a picture.* Paper presented at the biennial meeting of the International Conference for Infant Studies, Providence, R I.

Roese, N. J. (1997). Counterfactual thinking. *Psychological Bulletin, 121,* 133–148.

Sachs, J. (1983). Talking about the there and then: The emergence of displaced reference in parent-child discourse. In K. E. Nelson (Ed.), *Children's language* (Vol. 4, pp. 1–28). New York: Gardner Press.

Savage-Rumbaugh, E. S., Murphy, J., Sevcik, R. A., Brakke, K. E., Williams, S. L., & Rumbaugh, D. M. (1993). Language comprehension in ape and child. *Monographs of the Society for Research in Child Development, 58* (3–4, Serial No. 233).

Singer, M., Halldorson, M., Lear, J. C., & Andrusiak, P. (1992). Validation of causal bridging inferences in discourse understanding. *Journal of Memory and Language, 31,* 507–524.

Slade, A. (1987). A longitudinal study of maternal involvement and symbolic play during the toddler period. *Child Development, 58,* 367–375.

van den Broek, P. (1990). Causal inferences and the comprehension of narrative texts. In A. C. Graesser & G. H. Bower (Eds.), *The psychology of learning and motivation: Inferences and text comprehension* (Vol. 25, pp. 175–194). San Diego, CA: Academic Press.

Walker-Andrews, A., & Harris, P. L. (1993). Young children's comprehension of pretend causal sequences. *Developmental Psychology, 29,* 915–921.

Wolf, D. (1982). Understanding others: A longitudinal case study of the concept of independent agency. In G. Forman (Ed.), *Action and thought: From sensorimotor schemes to symbol use* (pp. 297–328). New York: Academic Press.

Wolf, D. P., Rygh, J., & Altshuler, J. (1984). Agency and experience: Actions and states in play narratives. In I. Bretherton (Ed.), *Symbolic play: The development of social understanding* (pp. 195–217). New York: Academic Press.

9
CHAPTER

David H. Uttal
Linda L. Liu
Judy S. DeLoache

Taking a Hard Look at Concreteness: Do Concrete Objects Help Young Children Learn Symbolic Relations?

☐ Introduction

The ability to understand and manipulate symbols is one of the most important milestones of human development. Symbols allow us to contemplate ideas and concepts after they cease to be directly perceived. Symbol systems such as language provide the means for conveying this information to others, allowing learning to occur independent of direct perception or experience. Symbols such as numbers also serve a notational role, obviating the need to manipulate physical quantities, making it possible to perform operations on abstract representations of the quantities.

Given the importance of symbols, it is not surprising that considerable research has been devoted to improving children's understanding of symbols. Much of the research on symbolic development shares a common assumption with other research on children's thinking—the idea that the thinking of young children is very concrete. Developmental psychologists typically have characterized younger children as thinking in the "here and now" and older children as being capable of reasoning beyond their direct experience (Bruner, 1966; Piaget, 1951; Vygotsky, 1934/1962; Werner & Kaplan, 1963). Young children are seen to rely heavily on tangible, real-world information while older children possess general concepts that integrate the essence of these concrete experiences. In sum, the idea that concrete thinking precedes abstract thought lies at the heart of many prominent theories of development.

The assumption that young children's thinking focuses on concrete properties has led to further assumptions about children's understanding of symbols. Specifically, from the belief that children attain understanding at a concrete level first, it has been inferred that the most appropriate means for teaching them about symbols is to make the symbols palpable and perceptually salient (Ball, 1992; Montessori, 1917). Using concrete objects for instruction is supposed to train children to think about objects apart from their physical reality and to lay the foundation for the ability to use and understand abstract symbols. Bruner (1966) described this training process as learning to "empty the concept of specific sensory properties [in order to] grasp its abstract properties" (p. 65).

In this chapter, we argue for a different perspective on the role of concreteness in children's thinking. Reducing development to a concrete-to-abstract shift may both oversimplify the nature of children's early thinking and overestimate the extent to which objects are appropriate for the instruction of young children. We question the view that concrete materials necessarily improve children's understanding of symbols and abstract concepts. Furthermore, we suggest that concreteness is a two-edged sword: It can help young children to detect symbolic relations but also can make it more difficult for them to comprehend the abstract concepts represented by the symbolic objects. In support of this claim, we review research on children's understanding of symbolic relations in several domains. We begin, however, with a brief discussion of the traditional theoretical basis for assuming that concreteness is of paramount importance in the development of young children's understanding of symbolic relations. We also review the work of some theorists who have challenged this assumption.

☐ Symbols and General Cognitive Development

The idea that children understand symbols best through concrete objects is derived, in part, from the work of many classic developmental theorists. The acquisition of symbolic competence is seen to proceed through a concrete-to-abstract shift: the progression from thinking that is rooted in concrete reality to thinking that is unconstrained by context. Sigel (1993) described this developmental progression as the child's attempt to "separate him- or herself mentally from the ongoing here and now, and project him- or herself to some other temporal plane (past or future or the nonpalpable present), in turn transforming the received communication into some symbol or sign system" (p. 142). The end result of this progression is that the concepts of older children are no longer direct, iconic representations of their original encounter with specific instances of an object; they are reconceptualizations or abstractions based on the original stimulus. Consequently, development often has been characterized as children's struggle to transcend their shallow and shortsighted view of the world (Bruner, 1966; Piaget, 1951; Werner & Kaplan, 1963).

The idea that young children's thinking is based on concrete concepts runs through almost all classic theories of cognitive development more generally and symbolic development more specifically. For example, Inhelder and Piaget (1955/1958) considered the ability to use abstract, hypothetical information, without reference to more concrete information, to be a hallmark of the qualitative shift to formal-operational reasoning. The ability to perform logical deductive reasoning from false propositions (i.e., independent of reality) is one test of the type of abstract thought characteristic of Piaget's stage of formal operations. Given a set of statements such as "If mice are bigger than dogs and dogs are bigger than elephants," young children typically have trouble making the correct deduction "then mice are bigger than elephants." Since none of these relations exist in reality, young children are left without a concrete basis from which to reason and solve the problem (Moshman & Franks, 1986).

Indeed, it is children's attempt to rely on familiar, real relations among entities that makes counterfactual reasoning especially difficult for them. Thinking of a real mouse and a real dog, they have trouble mentally reversing the usual size relations among them. Consistent with this, Dias and Harris (1988, 1990) have shown that young children perform better when counterfactual reasoning tasks are presented in a make-believe rather than a literal mode. For example, they presented children with pairs of premises that clearly violated the children's real-world knowledge such as "All cats bark" and "Rex is a cat." Dias and Harris found that children were more likely to correctly answer "yes" to the question, "Does Rex bark?" when they were first told to pretend they were on another planet or when the experimenter presented the premises using "make-believe intonation." Thus, in some situations, the concreteness of children's real-world knowledge presents an obstacle to their ability to perform abstract reasoning.

Other theorists have discussed the concrete-to-abstract shift under various guises. In studies of early categorization, Bruner, Goodnow, and Austin (1956) described conceptual development as a perceptual-to-conceptual shift; children first think of objects only in terms of the properties directly available to their senses but can later begin to consider their abstract properties. Children may, for example, initially categorize birds and bats together because they share the perceptually salient feature of being flying creatures. As children become aware of the abstract basis of the categories, however, they not only realize that birds and bats belong in separate categories but that flightless penguins belong in the bird category. Thus, according to this view, children learn to rely less on concrete physical attributes for categorization and more on the underlying structure of the categories.

Similarly, Vygotsky (1934/1962) extended the idea of concreteness through two lines of study. First, Vygotsky introduced the notion of situational thinking, proposing that children demonstrate a thematic-to-taxonomic shift in how they classify objects. Thematic categories (e.g., bee, hive, honey) capture the fleeting but salient relations between objects in a common setting rather than the deeper structure that defines the systematic relations among objects of like kind. Thus, the developmentally primitive categories are, in essence, highly concrete because they are rooted in a specific situation that is salient to the child. Progression to taxonomic categorization (e.g., bee, fly, grasshopper) requires that the child reject the perceptually salient features of the objects in favor of their deeper similarities.

In a second line of study, Vygotsky proposed that children learn to consider the deeper similarities between objects through make-believe play. He noted that, when children play make-believe, they often substitute concrete objects for objects in the real world (e.g., a stick for a horse). He theorized that these concrete objects essentially serve as symbols because the game of make-believe strips them of their typical identity. Consequently, children become capable of seeing the physical object as being separable from its abstract meaning or identity.

The concrete-to-abstract idea also has been applied to the development and understanding of symbols. Werner and Kaplan (1963) conceptualized development as a holistic-to-analytic shift in which young children first attend to "physicochemical stimuli" from the environment which are later converted into "stimulus-signs or signals" by the developing child (p. 9). For example, young children presented with the number "3" might attend to the concrete properties of the stimulus (e.g., its curvature and symmetry). On the other hand, older children more likely would be capable of analyzing or focusing on the deeper, abstract symbolic meaning of the number.

☐ Implications of the Concrete-to-Abstract Shift

Theorists proposing a concrete-to-abstract shift have not necessarily advocated an inflexible, dichotomous view of early versus later development. Unfortunately, the oversimplified assumption often has been made that younger children benefit from, and indeed require, concrete instruction. Ball (1992) characterized this assumption as "Concrete is inherently good; abstract is inherently not appropriate—at least at the beginning for young learners" (p. 16). Concreteness thus has come to be regarded as a panacea for improving young children's learning of abstract symbols and concepts; educators often have assumed that abstract or symbolic information can best be communicated by making it concrete.

Researchers recently have become wary of taking the educational value of concreteness for granted. The notion of an inflexible concrete-to-abstract shift increasingly has been challenged as evidence accumulates showing that younger children do not rely on or benefit from concreteness as much as previously thought (Simons & Keil, 1995; Uttal, Scudder, & DeLoache, 1997). Concrete-to-abstract theories typically presume not only that concrete thought precedes abstract thought, but that it precludes it.

Simons and Keil (1995) went so far as to suggest that children's development of biological thought may, in fact, proceed in an abstract-to-concrete shift. They argued that children may first learn to make causal explanations for events at an abstract level because they lack specific physical knowledge about the events. For example, a child explaining the function of a camera might describe its ability to capture "brief temporal slices of reflected light patterns," but might not provide a mechanistic account detailing how light enters the lens and how the various parts of the camera interact (p. 131). In other words, children's earliest causal explanations may be general and abstract rather than concrete because they lack the domain-specific knowledge required to describe the specific components of the camera. Simons and Keil (1995) summarized their viewpoint stating that, "Although ignorance of the physical components of a system may preclude a concrete explanation for the system's behavior, it is quite possible to generate a principled, abstract explanation without any knowledge of the physical components" (p. 131). Thus, they emphasized that, although young children's explanations are abstract, they are not ignorant.

Similar arguments for young children's ability to think in abstract terms were presented by Gelman and Wellman (1991). They suggested that children understand that certain objects have an internal "essence" that is distinct from the outward appearance of the objects. Like Simons and Keil (1995), they claimed that this understanding can exist in the absence of detailed scientific understanding of the essence. Gelman and Wellman tested children's understanding of this "inside-outside" distinction using a categorization task: Children were presented with triads of objects from which they could either choose the pair sharing the same outside (e.g., an orange and an orange balloon) or the pair sharing the same inside (e.g., an orange and a lemon). Counter to the idea that object concreteness exerts the primary influence on children's object categorization, they found that children as young as 3 years of age could correctly report both that oranges and lemons "look alike" and that oranges and orange balloons "share the same insides." Thus, young children's understanding of objects is not inevitably bound to external appearances. Rather, Gelman and Wellman argued that children's understanding of the inside-outside distinction demonstrates that nonobvious and abstract object properties also are available to children. Their findings highlighted the need for questioning the unqualified characterization of young children's thinking as being concrete.

The difficulty that children have in translating concrete representations of objects into abstract knowledge is summarized by Ball's (1992) pithy observation that "understanding does not travel through the fingertips and up the arm" (p. 47). In other words, having a concrete object does not guarantee understanding of the abstract concept. In accordance with this view, Sigel (1993) noted that attaining abstract representations requires that children be active agents in creating them. Sigel proposed that children achieve abstract representations of objects gradually through distancing acts, which "separate the child cognitively from the immediate behavioral environment" (p. 142). These distancing acts allow children to understand that symbols stand for referents by requiring that children form mental representations that are abstract rather than palpable. In other words, the translation of abstract knowledge from concrete representations is not inevitable.

In support of this view, we will present research on children's use and, in some cases, failure to understand symbols. Specifically, we will explore symbolic development through a set of tasks designed to tap children's understanding of symbol-referent relations. The difficulties children have in completing these tasks shed light on the question of whether concrete objects do, in fact, facilitate children's learning of symbolic relations.

☐ Children's Use of Scale Models

Much of our work has focused on children's understanding of a specific symbol system—scale models. This kind of symbol and the task that children are asked to perform using it have several advantages in terms of working with very young children, and the results have implications that extend to children's understanding of other kinds of symbols. The results of several studies clearly indicate that the relation between the concreteness of an intended symbol and its effect on children's comprehension of the symbolic relation is far more complex, and interesting, than previously has been assumed.

The basic task that we have used is quite simple: Children are asked to use a model to find a toy that is hidden in the room that the model represents. In most versions of the task, the model looks very much like the room; the walls are the same colors, and the model and room are furnished with highly similar (although appropriately scaled) pieces of furniture in the same spatial arrangements. For example, there is a miniature couch in the model and a full-size couch in the room; both are covered with the same fabric and in corresponding locations in the two spaces.

The tasks began with an extensive orientation that was designed to help the children grasp the relation between the model and the room. First, the experimenter showed the children the two toys that would be hidden. One toy, a miniature dog, was labeled "Little Snoopy"; the second toy, a full-size stuffed dog, was labeled "Big Snoopy." The experimenter then pointed out the correspondences between the model and the room. The experimenter said, "This is Big Snoopy's big room; Big Snoopy has lots of things in his room." The experimenter then named each of the furniture items. Next, the experimenter pointed to the model and said, "This is Little Snoopy's little room. He has all the same things in his room that Big Snoopy has." The experimenter then labeled each of the furniture items again and pointed out the correspondence between each item in the model and the corresponding item in the room. To do this, the experimenter carried each item from the model into the room. The miniature furniture item was held next to its counterpart in the room, and the experimenter said, for example, "Look—this is Big Snoopy's big couch, and this is Little Snoopy's little couch. They're just the same."

Next, the experimenter attempted to communicate that there was a relation between actions in the model and actions in the room. For example, the experimenter told the child that, "Big and Little Snoopy like to do the same things. When Big Snoopy sits on his chair, Little Snoopy likes to sit on his chair, too." The experimenter also illustrated the correspondence by placing the toys in the appropriate positions.

The final part of the orientation involved an imitation trial in which one toy was placed in a location in either the model or the room, and the child was asked to place the corresponding toy in the correct location in the other space. For example, the experimenter placed Little Snoopy on the table in the model and said, "Little Snoopy is sitting on his table. Can you put Big Snoopy in the same place in his room?"

The test trials followed immediately after the orientation. On each of the test trials, the experimenter first hid the toy in one of the hiding locations in the model. The experimenter called the child's attention to the act of hiding, but not to the specific hiding location, by saying, "Look, Little Snoopy is going to hide here." The child was told that an assistant was going to hide Big Snoopy in the same place in the big room.

The experimenter and child then entered the room, and the child was asked to find Big Snoopy. On each trial, the experimenter attempted to remind the child of the relation between the model and the room by saying, "Remember, Little Snoopy is hiding in the same place as Big Snoopy." If the child could not find the toy, he or she was encouraged to continue searching at other locations, and the experimenter reminded the child again that the toy was in the "same place" as the other toy. Increasingly explicit hints were provided until the toy was found, but a search was counted as correct only if the child found the toy in the first location that he or she searched.

After the child found the toy on each trial, he or she was taken back to the model and was asked to find the miniature toy. This search provided a memory check that was critical to interpreting any difficulties that children may have had in finding the toy in the room. If the children were able to locate the miniature toy in the model, then difficulties that they encountered finding the toy in the room could not be attributed to simply forgetting where the toy was in the model. Instead, poor performance would reflect a failure to appreciate that the location of the miniature toy in the model (the symbol) could be used to find the larger toy in the room (the referent).

Several aspects of this task are important regarding the role of concreteness in children's insight into symbol-referent relations. First, and most importantly, the model is a concrete object (or set of objects). The symbols involved in the task are concrete. The model itself, and the furniture in the model, are tangible, manipulable replicas of larger real objects. Thus, each item is both a real object and a symbolic representation of something other than itself.

Second, successful performance requires that the child comprehend and use a symbolic relation—the relation between the model and the room. To solve the task, the child must understand that the location of the toy in the model specifies the location in the room. The concreteness of the model is useful to children only if it helps them understand the stands-for relation between the model and room.

Third, children are required to solve a seemingly familiar task (searching for a toy) in a novel way. Typically, when young children search for hidden objects, they do so on the basis of previous direct experience; like adults, they often search where they have last seen an object (DeLoache & Brown, 1983). But, to solve our task, children have to put aside this well-honed strategy and rely instead on information provided by a symbol. The model task thus allows us to examine children's first use of a novel symbol system.

Results of Research on Children's Understanding of Models

Research on children's understanding of models has revealed that, despite the apparent simplicity of the model, very young children have surprising difficulty using it. These results are summarized in Figure 9.1. Children younger than 3 years of age usually perform very poorly (only about 20% correct retrievals). The difficulty that children encounter cannot be attributed to forgetting the location of the toy that they observed being hidden. Almost all children succeed on the memory-based search in which they return to the model to retrieve the miniature toy. Thus, 2½-year-olds can remember the location of the toy in the model, but they tend not to use this knowledge to find the toy in the room. Figure 9.1 also reveals that most 3-year-old children typically succeed in the standard model task (averaging over 80% correct searches).

The success of the 3-year-olds whose performance is shown in Figure 9.1 is not, however, the end of the developmental story. The difficulty that 3-year-olds have experienced in some tasks provides much of the basis for our claim that the concreteness of the model is a dual-edged sword in terms of children's performance. What, at first, seemed to be trivial manipulations often have had disastrous consequences for children's performance. The causes of the dramatic drops in children's performance illustrate the importance of understanding that the model represents the room. Concreteness can help young children to see that the model and room are similar, but there is more to appreciating the symbolic nature of the model than perceiving this similarity. We believe that the concrete nature of the model plays a role both in children's success and in the fragility of their performance. In this section, we discuss the results of a

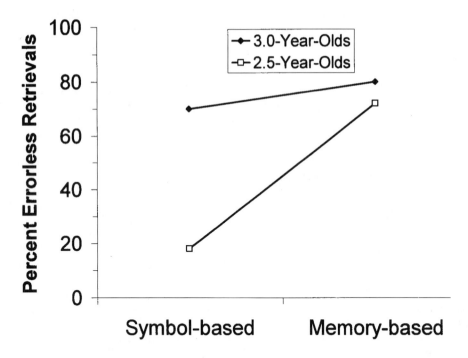

FIGURE 9.1. Children's performance in the original model study. Adapted from "Rapid Change in the Symbolic Functioning of Very Young Children," by J. S. DeLoache, 1987, *Science, 238*. For the symbol-based retrieval, children saw the miniature toy hidden in the model and then searched for the corresponding larger toy in the room. For the memory-based retrieval, children returned to the model and searched for the miniature toy. Note that only the symbol-based retrieval requires that children use the relation between the model and the room to find the toy.

series of experiments that illustrate both why concreteness can help young children in some ways and why it also can hurt them.

Several different lines of research have illustrated the fragility of children's performance. For example, DeLoache, Kolstad, and Anderson (1991) demonstrated that young children's performance depends very much on the physical similarity between the model and the room. When the furniture in the model and room were not identical, 3-year-olds performed at chance levels. Similarly, if the furniture in the model and in the room did not occupy the same relative spatial positions, performance deteriorated substantially (DeLoache, 1995).

Subsequent studies have highlighted that the concreteness of the model both helps and hurts young children. On the one hand, as the results of the studies of the effects of perceptual similarity suggest, concreteness does seem to help young children to see that there is a relation between the model and what it is intended to represent. On the other hand, subsequent research has shown that there is more to using the model than simply seeing that the model and the room look alike. The children must understand that the model is a representation of the room, and the concreteness of the model may actually make this understanding more difficult to gain than if the model were less concrete.

Children's performance also depends very much on instructions. Recall that, in the standard model task, the experimenter explicitly points out correspondences between the model and the room. If less elaborate instructions are given, 3-year-old and even 3½-year-old children's performance is again near chance (DeLoache, 1989; DeLoache, DeMendoza, & Anderson, in press). For example, telling the children that Little and Big Snoopy's rooms are alike and that the toys are hidden in the corresponding places in the two rooms is not adequate; the experimenter also must explicitly describe and demonstrate the correspondence between the objects within them for the children to be successful. Thus, the concreteness of the model per se is no guarantee that it will be used as a symbol; young children need to be told and shown how the two are related.

With age, children become increasingly less dependent on information from the experimenter about the nature of the task (DeLoache et al., in press). Four-year-olds can succeed in the task with the reduced instructions described above, although they still need explicit information about the general model-room relation. Older children are more able to detect the relation on their own. A group of 5- to 7-year-old children was shown the model and room and the two toys. They then observed a hiding event in the model and were asked to find the larger toy in the room (with no explanation of the relations between the spaces or the hiding events). Most of these older children inferred the "rules of the game" from this very minimal information and successfully retrieved the toy.

Additional research has shown that, even when children do initially grasp the relation between the model and room, they can easily lose sight of the relevance of this relation for finding the toy. In a series of studies, Uttal, Schreiber, and DeLoache (1995) showed that having to wait before using the information in the model to find the toy in the room caused 3-year-olds' performance to deteriorate dramatically. As in the standard task, the children witnessed the hiding of the toy in the model and then were asked to find the toy in the room. The only difference was that we inserted delays between when children saw the toy being hidden in the model and when they searched in the room. The delays were of three different lengths: 20 seconds, 2 minutes, and 5 minutes. Across the six search trials, all children experienced each of the delays twice. Different groups of children received the delays in one of three different orders. The groups were labeled in terms of the delay that they experienced first: the short-delay-first group had a 20-second delay first, the medium-delay-first group had a 2-minute delay first, and the long-delay-first group had a 5-minute delay first. After the initial trial, the children in each group received trials at the other delays, with delay length counterbalanced over trials.

As shown in Figure 9.2, there was a dramatic effect of the initial delay the children experienced. The long-delay-first group performed poorly, not just on the initial 5-minute delay trial, but on all subsequent trials. In contrast, the performance of the short-delay group was quite good on most of the trials. It is important to stress that the difficulty that the long-delay-first group encountered was not due simply to forgetting the location of the toy in the model during the initial delay. If this were the case, then we would expect the children to perform well on the shorter delay trials that followed the initial long delay. But,

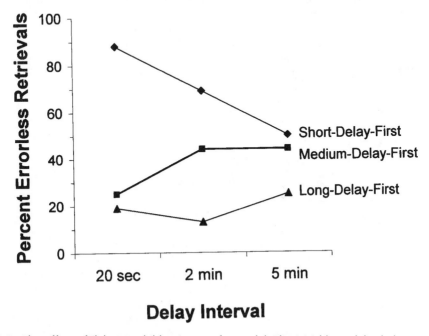

FIGURE 9.2. The effect of delay on children's use of a model. The initial long delay led to much worse performance, even on the subsequent shorter delays.

most of the children in the long-delay group performed poorly on all subsequent trials, even those trials with the short (20-s) delay that normally would give them little, if any, problem. In addition, performance on the memory-based retrievals, in which children returned to the model to find the miniature toy, were quite good, even on the long-delay trials.

Uttal et al. (1995) concluded that, during the initial long delay, the children in the long-delay-first group lost sight of the relation between the model and the room. Consequently, when they entered the room to search for the toy, they were not able to use the location of the toy in the model as a guide for searching in the room. Instead, the children conceived of the search for the toy in the model as unrelated to what they had seen in the model. In other words, the initial long delay caused the children to forget about the relevance of the model for finding the toy. Once the knowledge that the model could help was lost, the children continued to perform poorly, even on the subsequent, shorter delay trials. The children apparently construed the task as two separate and unrelated searches: One search was for the larger toy in the room, and the other was for the smaller toy in the model. The 5-minute delay caused the children to lose their insight into the relation between these two searches.

Support for our interpretation of the effects of the initial long delay on children's performance comes from a series of follow-up studies in which we were able to ameliorate partially the devastating effects of the initial 5-minute delay on 3-year-olds' performance. In these studies, all children experienced an initial 5-minute delay. However, after the delay, we inserted a reminder of the relevance of the model. For example, in one follow-up study, children were asked after the 5-minute delay to return to the model and find the miniature toy before they entered the room to find the larger toy. This simple manipulation led to a dramatic improvement in performance; the children now performed much better on all of the trials, including the initial 5-minute delay trial. A subsequent follow-up study indicated that simply pointing to the model and verbally reminding children that the model could help them find the toy also helped to inoculate children against the deleterious effects of the 5-minute delay.

The results of the follow-up studies provide additional support for the claim that, during the initial long delay, the children lost sight of the relation between the model and the room. Consequently, they had no basis of using the location of the toy in the model as a guide for search in the room. In contrast, in the follow-up studies, the reminders helped to reactivate the children's understanding of the relevance of the model and, consequently, many of the children were much less affected by the initial long delay.

In sum, the results of our research on children's use of models lead to one central conclusion: Children's success depends on their appreciation that the model is a symbolic representation of the space that it represents. When this understanding is taken away (e.g., by inserting a 5-min delay), the children have no basis for using the model. Even though the model is a highly concrete representation of the room, the concreteness alone is not enough to ensure success. Concreteness can help children to appreciate the similarity between the intended symbol and the intended referent, but perceiving this similarity alone is not the end of the story. Children must still detect the "stands-for" relation between one object and another. Concreteness alone will not ensure that children comprehend this relation.

☐ Explaining Children's Performance: The Dual Representation Hypothesis

Why is young children's comprehension of the relation between the model and the room so fragile? Taken together, the results of our studies suggest that, ironically, the concreteness of the model is part of the problem. Our results indicate that concrete objects that are interesting and attractive as objects may actually be more difficult for young children to use as symbolic representations than materials that are less interesting as objects in their own right. This interpretation highlights the dual nature of the influence of concreteness on children's performance. While concreteness may help children to perceive similarities between symbols and their referents, it also may make it more difficult for them to think about a symbolic relation between the two.

A scale model such as the one used in our task has a dual nature; it is both a symbol and an object (or set of objects) with a very high degree of physical salience. The very features that make it highly interesting and attractive to young children as a concrete object to play with obscure its role as a symbol of something other than itself. To use a model as a symbol, children must achieve *dual representation* (DeLoache, 1989, 1995; Uttal et al., 1997): They must represent the model itself as an object and at the same time, as a symbol for what it represents. In the model task, the child must form a meaningful mental representation of the model as a miniature room in which toys can be hidden and found, and the child has to interact physically with it. At the same time, the child must represent the model as a term in an abstract, "stands for" relation, and he or she must use that relation as a basis for drawing inferences.

According to the dual representation hypothesis (DeLoache, 1989, 1995), the more salient a symbol is as a concrete object, the more difficult it is to appreciate its role as a symbol for something other than itself. Thus, the more young children are attracted to a model as an interesting object, the more difficult it will be for them to detect its relation to the room it stands for.

The dual representation hypothesis leads to several interesting predictions. For example, it suggests that factors that decrease children's attention to the model as an interesting object should increase their use of the model as a symbol. In one study, 2½-year-old children's access to the model was decreased by placing it behind a window (DeLoache, 1998). The children could still see the location of the toy in the model, but they could have no direct contact with the model. This manipulation led to better performance. Conversely, our interpretation suggests that factors that increase children's attention to the model as an object should lead to a decrease in their use of the model. This prediction also was confirmed. Allowing 3-year-old children to play with the model for 5 to 10 minutes before they were asked to use it as a symbol led to a decrease in performance when children were asked to use the model to find the toy in the room (DeLoache, 1998).

Another finding that supports the dual representation hypothesis concerns children's use of photographs, rather than the model, to find the toy. Two-and-one-half-year-olds, who typically perform very poorly in the standard model task, perform much better when a photograph is substituted for the model (DeLoache, 1991; DeLoache & Burns, 1994). In some ways, a photograph could be considered less concrete than a model. Most obviously, the model is a three-dimensional representation, whereas the photograph is only two-dimensional. Nevertheless, the 2½-year-olds performed much better with a photograph than their age-mates did with the model. In sum, the results indicate that a more concrete object, a model, may be more difficult to use than a less concrete object, a photograph.

Recently, DeLoache, Miller, and Rosengren (1997) have provided especially strong support for the dual representation hypothesis. In this research, 2½-year-old children were led to believe that a shrinking machine could shrink (and, subsequently, enlarge) a room. The idea was that if children believe that a scale model actually is a room that has been shrunk by a machine, then there is no symbolic relation between the two spaces; to the child, the model simply is the room. Hence, dual representation is not required, so they should have no trouble reasoning between the two spaces.

Each child was first given a demonstration in which a "shrinking machine" (an oscilloscope accompanied by random computer-generated sounds described as the "sounds the machine makes while it's working") apparently caused a troll doll to turn into a miniature version of itself. The machine then supposedly "enlarged" the troll back to its original size. Next, the machine seemed to cause the "troll's room" (a tent-like room used in many previous model studies) to turn into a scale model identical to it except for size. It then enlarged the room.

The child then watched as the experimenter hid the larger troll somewhere in the portable room. After waiting while the machine "shrunk" the room, the child was asked to find the hidden toy. (The miniature troll was, of course, hidden in the same place in the model as the larger troll was in the room.) Thus, just as in the standard model task, the child had to use his or her knowledge of where the toy was hidden in one space to figure out where to search in the other. Unlike the standard task, there was no stands-for relation between the two spaces. As predicted on the basis of the dual representation hypothesis, performance was significantly better in this nonsymbolic task than in the standard model task.

Applying the Dual Representation Hypothesis to Educational Symbols

Our perspective on the dual nature of symbolic representations can be applied directly to other kinds of symbols, including those commonly used in American classrooms. The idea that concrete representations best foster young children's learning is very popular in early childhood education.

One domain to which our perspective is directly applicable is early mathematics education. Full competence in mathematics requires mastering complex concepts such as addition and subtraction and, at the same time, mastering the symbols that are used to represent these concepts. Teachers and researchers have noted, for many years, that neither is an easy task for young children. On the one hand, mathematical concepts may be difficult for young children to comprehend if they cannot understand the symbols that are used to represent these concepts. On the other hand, symbols are difficult to teach to children who lack an understanding of the concepts the symbols represent. Not surprisingly, considerable effort has been devoted to making their initial forays into mathematics more interesting and more meaningful for young children (Hiebert & Carpenter, 1992; Stevenson & Stigler, 1992).

Many of the attempts at improvement have involved what are commonly called manipulatives. These are concrete, tangible objects such as rods and blocks that are used to represent mathematical concepts or symbols. Children are encouraged to work out mathematics problems with the tangible manipulatives, by combining units or groups of manipulatives to represent parts of the problems. The theoretical justification for the use of manipulatives is similar to, and is derived from, the more general belief in the inherent importance of concreteness in early cognition. The hope has been that, by using a concrete object, children can draw on implicit or informal mathematical concepts that might otherwise remain inaccessible. For example, by dividing a pie or candy for friends, children might gain insight, at least implicitly, to the concepts of divisions and particular fractions. The teacher could then have children recreate this process in the classroom through the use of manipulatives. In essence, the argument has been that manipulatives give teachers and children a way around the seeming opaqueness of mathematical symbols.

Manipulatives have been touted as solutions for children of a wide range of ages and ability levels; they have been offered as appropriate for all ability levels, ranging from the disabled to the gifted (Kennedy & Tipps, 1994; Tooke, Hyatt, Leigh, Synder, & Borda, 1992). Manipulatives have been incorporated into the curriculum of the National Council of Teachers of Mathematics, whose official position is as follows:

> Children come to understand numbers meanings gradually. To encourage these understandings, teachers can offer classroom experiences in which students first manipulate physical objects and then use their own language to explain their thinking. This active involvement in, and expressions of, physical manipulations encourages children to reflect on their actions and to construct their own number meanings. In all situations, work with number symbols should be meaningfully linked to concrete materials. (1989, p. 38)

Unfortunately, research on the effectiveness of manipulatives has not confirmed the anticipated benefits. Several studies have shown, at best, inconsistent or weak advantages for manipulatives in comparison to more traditional techniques for teaching children mathematics (Ball, 1992; Resnick & Omanson, 1987; Wearne & Hiebert, 1988). Longitudinal and intensive studies of the use of manipulatives in classrooms have shown that children often fail to establish connections between manipulatives and the information that the manipulatives are intended to communicate (Sowell, 1989).

We believe that part of the reason that manipulatives have been less successful than hoped concerns problems very similar to those that younger children encounter when using a scale model. There are at least two general similarities between what is required to succeed in our model task and to what is required to effectively use a manipulative. The first is that the relation between a manipulative and what it is intended to represent may not be transparent to young children. In other words, the concreteness of a manipulative (or of our model) does not guarantee that children will understand that it is intended to represent something other than itself. Our model is extremely concrete, and parents are amazed when it proves difficult for intelligent, interested children. We believe that similar issues may arise when older children are asked to use manipulatives; to the teacher, the relation between the manipulative and a more abstract concept may be simple and direct but this relation may be, and may remain, obscure to young children, particularly if the relation is not pointed out explicitly.

The second similarity between children's difficulties with our model and with manipulatives is that dual representation is relevant to both. As was true of our model, manipulatives have a dual nature; they are intended to be used as representations of something else, but they also are objects in their own right. In the next section, we review some difficulties that children encounter when using manipulatives, difficulties that parallel younger children's problems with our scale model and that are consistent with the dual representation perspective.

Children Often Fail to Grasp the Relation Between Manipulatives and What the Manipulatives Are Intended to Represent

From a teacher's point of view, the goal of using a manipulative is to provide support for learning more general mathematics concepts. However, this is no guarantee that children will see the manipulative in this way. Previous work on the use of manipulatives has documented numerous examples of mismatches between teachers' expectations and students' understandings. Even when young children do learn to perform mathematical operations using manipulatives, their knowledge of the two ways of solving the problems may remain encapsulated; that is, children often fail to see the relation between solving mathematics problems via manipulatives and solving the same or similar problems via abstract symbols (see Uttal et al., 1997, for a review).

Evidence that children often fail to draw connections between manipulatives and more traditional forms of mathematical symbols comes from Resnick and Omanson's (1987) intensive studies of children's use of manipulatives and their understanding of mathematical concepts. Resnick and Omanson systematically evaluated third-grade children's ability to solve problems both with and without manipulatives. Much of the work involved Dienes blocks, which are a systematic set of manipulatives that are designed to help children acquire understanding of base 10 concepts. Most of the children understood and appeared to enjoy working with the blocks.

Unfortunately, however, the children's ease with and knowledge of the blocks was not related to their understanding of similar kinds of problems expressed in more formal mathematical terms. The children did not relate approaches they had used to solve problems with manipulatives to the solution of similar problems involving written symbols. For example, children who were successful in using Dienes blocks to solve subtraction problems involving two or three digits had trouble solving simpler written problems. Indeed, the child who performed best with the Dienes blocks performed worse on the standard problems. Clearly, success with a manipulative did not guarantee success with written symbols; in fact, success with one form of mathematics expression was unrelated to success with the other.

Other researchers have provided additional evidence of the nonequivalence of concrete and more abstract forms of mathematical expressions. For example, Hughes (1986) investigated young elementary school children's ability to use simple blocks or bricks to solve addition and subtraction problems. What is most interesting about this study for the current discussion is that the children were explicitly asked to draw connections between solutions involving concrete objects and those involving more abstract, written problems. The children were asked to use the bricks to represent the underlying concepts that were expressed in the written problems. For example, the children were asked to use bricks to solve written problems, such as 1 + 7 = ?.

Overall, the children performed poorly. Regardless of whether they could solve the written problems, they had difficulty representing the problems with the bricks. Moreover, the children's errors demonstrated that they failed to appreciate that the bricks and written symbols were two alternate forms of mathematical expression. Many children took the instructions literally, using the bricks to physically "spell out" the written problems (Figure 9.3). For example, they might make a line of bricks to represent the "1" and two intersecting lines to represent the "+" and so on. These results again highlight that children may treat solutions involving manipulatives and those involving written mathematical symbols as cognitively distinct entities.

The research on children's understanding of manipulatives also highlights the conditions under which manipulatives are likely to be effective. Specifically, the results of several studies suggest that manipulatives are most effective when they are used to augment, rather than to substitute for, instructions involving written symbols. In these cases, teachers have drawn specific connections between children's use of a manipulative and the related expression of the underlying concept in written form. For example, consider Wearne and Hiebert's (1988) program. It focuses on fractions, but the results are relevant to other mathematical concepts. At all stages of the program, the teacher draws specific links between manipulatives and written symbolic expressions. The manipulative is used as a bridge to the written expressions rather than as a substitute or precursor for written symbols. As a result, the manipulative scaffolds the learning of the written symbols by gradually leading children away from the concrete properties of the manipulative to the more foreign properties of the written symbols. Thus, the focus of this and similar successful programs is on the relation between manipulatives and other forms of mathematics expression.

Letters as a Symbol System.   The questions raised in this chapter regarding children's acquisition of symbols also are relevant to the early development of reading. In learning to read, children must master the relation between an abstract symbol system and its referents. The assumption of a concrete-to-abstract shift leads to the further assumption that young children would benefit if the abstract system of letters were transformed into a concrete form they could more readily understand.

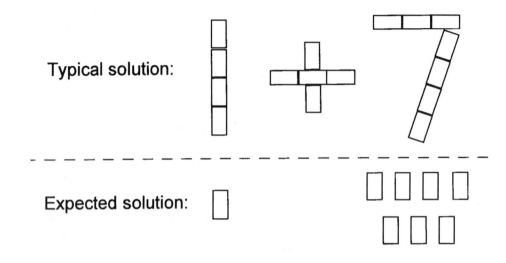

FIGURE 9.3. An example of how children might use small bricks to represent the problem 1 + 7 = 8. From *Children and Numbers: Difficulties in Learning Mathematics,* by M. Hughes, 1986, pp. 99–103. Copyright 1986 by Basil Blackwell. Adapted with permission. The children often copied written problems with the bricks rather than using the bricks as an alternate representational system.

Given that children's use of symbols does not unequivocally benefit from concreteness, however, challenges to the concrete-to-abstract shift concept may change ideas of how the development of reading is best supported. Research on notational symbol systems provides further evidence against the idea that concrete and abstract thinking develop independently. Understanding letters is difficult because letters are noniconic symbols. Unlike pictographs, there is nothing inherent in the structure of letters that reflects what they represent. In essence, understanding letters as notational symbols requires that children appreciate nonanalogous, noniconic symbolic relations (Bialystok, 1992).

Bialystok (1992) proposed that children must relinquish their hold on the specific perceptual properties of objects to understand them as symbols. Symbol acquisition emerges in three stages as children's initially fragile understanding of symbols becomes more flexible. Children may first learn a set of symbols without understanding their relation to what they represent. For example, they may be capable of verbally reproducing a sequence of symbols (e.g., counting in a series or reciting the alphabet). They may then begin to observe the relation of these objects to their referents. In this second stage, children tend to assume that the relations between symbols and referents are iconic and analogous. For example, they may believe that the word "ant" is shorter than the word "elephant" because ants are smaller than elephants. Similarly, Spanish and Italian children associate bigger words with bigger objects, in spite of the fact that this relationship is even less perfect in both of these languages (Ferreiro, 1988, as cited in Bialystok, 1992). Both Spanish and Italian languages use the suffix "ita" to demarcate diminutives of root words, so that longer words actually denote smaller objects. When children finally acquire full symbolic competence in Bialystok's third stage, they are capable of understanding that symbols may be noniconic and nonanalogous (e.g., "car" is shorter than "banana," even though cars are larger than bananas). Thus, Bialystok (1992) demonstrated that the acquisition of symbols such as letters and numbers occurs in a gradual three-step process, not as an abrupt concrete-to-abstract shift.

Once children know the correspondences between the written forms (graphemes) and auditory forms (phonemes), they have the requisite knowledge to read and write any word in the language (Adams, 1990). Learning individual grapheme-phoneme correspondences, however, is neither easy nor a guarantee that children will learn to read. In fact, Landsmann and Karmiloff-Smith (1992) found that children's understanding of letters as part of a notational symbol system does not necessarily co-occur with their understanding of how the letters are used in referential communication. They asked children age 4 through 6 to invent nonletters, nonnumbers, and nonwords. Children in all age groups imposed different constraints on what qualified as nonletters and nonnumbers, demonstrating their understanding that letters and numbers were separate domains of symbols but also that they are not in the same domain as drawings. For example, one child produced "tttt" when asked to generate a nonword (p. 297). Only the older children, however, understood that symbols serve a referential role as well as a notational role. Rather than simply using strings of repeated letters to create nonwords, 5- and 6-year-olds generated nonwords that were unpronounceable and, thus, could serve no referential function.

If, in fact, making letter learning concrete were the best way to foster reading skills, one might expect that children would quickly learn to identify symbols that are embedded in real-life situations and require communication. Landsmann and Karmiloff-Smith (1992) suggested that learning the symbolic role of letters is a task in its own right and separate from children's use of these symbols in reading or in communication. This interpretation suggests that, although the role of symbols in referential communication is more salient and more concrete to young children, it does not play a prominent role in children's early understanding of symbols as a notational system.

Given the importance of the alphabet and the problems children may have in learning it, parents often turn to other means of making letter learning more concrete. Concrete manipulatives such as alphabet blocks potentially can provide a tactile means of teaching reading in much the way that Dienes blocks allow hands-on learning of mathematics. Like mathematics manipulatives, alphabet blocks transform the abstractness of graphemes and phonemes into familiar, perceptually rich objects. Although the use of manipulatives for reading instruction has not been investigated as the use of manipulatives in math education has been, it seems likely that similar caution is appropriate. Simply putting the letters of the alphabet on colorful blocks does not guarantee that children will learn to use them for spelling rather than as building blocks.

According to the dual representation hypothesis, attempts to make alphabet blocks colorful and engaging as objects might detract from the child seeing the letters on them as symbols. The physical features or concreteness of the blocks actually may obfuscate the symbol-referent relation. Alphabet blocks, for example, typically are constructed in different colors, which facilitates children's perceptual differentiation of different letters when they are learning the alphabet early on. The elaboration of individual letters is similarly evident in the topical organization of *Sesame Street*, which typically focuses on only two letters of the alphabet per episode (i.e., "This episode brought to you by the letter 'E'") and in different skits used to interest children in learning their letters (e.g., the letter beauty pageant). Such attempts to make individual letters interesting may distract from the collective function the letters serve within the notational system as a whole. Emphasizing letters as perceptually salient objects in their own right may, in fact, make it more difficult to see each letter as being a component of a word and as serving an equivalent notational role in the alphabet.

One might predict, however, that alphabetic manipulatives may not share all of the problems associated with mathematics manipulatives. Although individual letters, like numbers, have different critical features such as curves and straight lines, letter blocks are the same size and, thus, equate the physical characteristics of different letters to some extent. It might be argued that one of the steps to understanding the notational function of letter symbols is understanding that individual letters are functionally equivalent when they constitute words. In alphabet blocks, children can create strings of letters simply by combining various blocks, without being distracted by differences in letter size. Interestingly, the mistake that children make by using Dienes blocks to spell out mathematics equations is precisely the correct way to use alphabet blocks. In this regard, alphabet blocks may be more iconic symbols for letters than manipulatives are for mathematical equations, because collections of blocks are assembled in a way that is physically analogous to how words are put together.

☐ Implications

Our review of children's understanding and use of concrete symbols has several important implications for the use of concrete objects in educational contexts. These implications emphasize that concrete objects can help young children understand symbol-referent relations, but that the ultimate goal must remain to help children comprehend more abstract relations.

1. Concreteness is not a panacea. The most important implication of our review is that concreteness alone is not sufficient to help children learn symbolic relations. Under the right circumstances, concrete

objects can help children make initial insights into symbol-referent relations. However, if the objects are not explicitly linked to less concrete representations, the knowledge about their use is likely to remain encapsulated. The best concrete object symbols may well be ones that possess elements of their own destruction, designed to become less necessary or relevant as children come to understand the more abstract representation.

2. Concreteness is a two-edged sword. Our review of research suggests that concreteness may both help and hinder young children's appreciation of the relations between symbols and their intended referents. On the one hand, concreteness, in some ways, can facilitate children's use of symbols. For one thing, concrete objects are generally attention getting and more interesting to young children. For another, some symbol-referent relations are more obvious with concrete objects as symbols. For example, children often can solve mathematics problems with manipulatives before they can solve similar problems with more abstract mathematics symbols.

On the other hand, the characteristics that make concrete objects interesting to young children may simultaneously make them difficult for young children to move beyond them. If an object is too interesting as a thing in itself, then children may have more difficulty using it as a symbol for something else. This suggests that the best concrete objects may be those that are interesting enough as objects to engage young children's attention, but not so attractive as to make it difficult to focus on the relation between the object and its intended referent. Thus, manipulatives that are selected specifically because they are interesting and attractive to young children actually may be counterproductive.

Observations of manipulative use in other countries have supported the idea that a good manipulative is not necessarily an inherently interesting object. For example, in Japan, children use the same set of manipulatives throughout the early elementary school years. Stevenson and Stigler (1992), who have conducted several cross-national comparisons of mathematics achievement in Asia and the United States, have observed the following:

> Japanese teachers . . . use the items in the math set repeatedly throughout the elementary school years. . . . American teachers seek variety. They may use Popsicle sticks in one lesson, and marbles, Cheerios, M&M's, checkers, poker chips, or plastic animals in another. The American view is that objects should be varied in order to maintain children's interest. The Asian view is that using a variety of representational materials may confuse children, and thereby make it more difficult for them to use the objects of the representation and solution of mathematics problems. Multiplication is easier to understand when the same tiles are used as were used when the children learned to add. (pp. 186–187)

3. Concrete objects are not a substitute for instruction. Our review clearly indicates that instructions are a critical part of learning about symbol-referent relations, regardless of whether the symbols are concrete or abstract. As the research on children's use of mathematics manipulatives has demonstrated, concrete objects assist children's understanding of more abstract symbols only when explicit links are made between the two forms of symbolic expressions. Children cannot be expected to make the connections on their own. Concrete objects should be thought of as a potentially helpful aid to instruction, but only in combination with instruction in their use.

☐ Conclusions

Mastering symbol systems is one of the most important and challenging tasks of childhood. It is not surprising that teachers and parents have attempted to make the task easier by providing children with sets of concrete objects that seem, at least ostensibly, to make the task of learning symbol systems easier. Despite the criticisms that we have raised in this chapter, we do not believe that the original assumptions regarding the value of concreteness for learning symbol-referent relations are inherently wrong. Concrete objects can help young children, at least initially, to gain insight into the basic relation between a symbol and its referent. Concrete objects can provide a scaffold on which an understanding of more abstract relations can be built.

The problems with concrete objects that we have discussed arise only when the concrete object is used as a substitute, rather than a scaffold, for an understanding of more abstract symbols. Objects that are particularly attractive as objects may be particularly harmful in this regard, by focusing children's attention on the objects themselves rather than on what the symbols were intended to represent. The impulse to make objects interesting and engaging to young children actually may detract from the ultimate goal of helping children understand how abstract symbols relate to concepts. In sum, it is important to consider both the advantages and disadvantages of using concrete objects to help children learn symbolic relations. Concrete objects are useful to the extent that they assist in, rather than substitute for, the learning of abstract concepts.

☐ References

Adams, M. J. (1990). *Beginning to read: Thinking and learning about print.* Cambridge, MA: MIT Press.

Ball, D. L. (1992). Magical hopes: Manipulatives and the reform of math education. *American Educator, 16,* 14–18.

Bialystok, E. (1992). Symbolic representation of letters and numbers. *Cognitive Development, 7,* 301–316.

Bruner, J. S. (1966). *Toward a theory of instruction.* Cambridge, MA: Belknap Press.

Bruner, J. S., Goodnow, J. J., & Austin, G. A. (1956). *A study of thinking.* New York: Wiley.

DeLoache, J. S. (1987). Rapid change in the symbolic functioning of very young children. *Science, 238,* 1556–1557.

DeLoache, J. S. (1989). Young children's understanding of the correspondence between a scale model and a larger space. *Cognitive Development, 4,* 121–139.

DeLoache, J. S. (1991). Symbolic functioning in very young children: Understanding of pictures and models. *Child Development, 62,* 736–752.

DeLoache, J. S. (1995). Early symbol understanding and use. In D. Medin (Ed.), *The psychology of learning and motivation* (Vol. 33, pp. 65–114) . New York: Academic Press.

DeLoache, J. S. (in press). Dual representation and young children's use of scale models. *Child Development.*

DeLoache, J. S., & Brown, A. L. (1983). Very young children's memory for the location of objects in a large scale environment. *Child Development, 24,* 888–897.

DeLoache, J. S., & Burns, N. M. (1994). Early understanding of the representational function of pictures. *Cognition, 52,* 83–110.

DeLoache, J. S., DeMendoza, O. A. P., & Anderson, K. M. (in press). Multiple factors in early symbol use: The effect of instructions, similarity, and age in understanding a symbol-referent relation. *Cognitive Development.*

DeLoache, J. S., Kolstad, V., & Anderson, K. (1991). Physical similarity and young children's understanding of scale models. *Child Development, 62,* 111–126.

DeLoache, J. S., Miller, K. F., & Rosengren, K. S. (1997). The credible shrinking room: Very young children's performance with symbolic and nonsymbolic relations. *Psychological Science, 8,* 308–313.

Dias, M. G., & Harris, P. L. (1988). The effect of make-believe play on deductive reasoning. *British Journal of Developmental Psychology, 6,* 207–221.

Dias, M. G., & Harris, P. L. (1990). The influence of the imagination on reasoning by young children. *British Journal of Developmental Psychology, 8,* 305–318.

Gelman, S. A., & Wellman, H. M. (1991). Insides and essences: Early understandings of the non-obvious. *Cognition, 38,* 213–244.

Hiebert, J., & Carpenter, T. P. (1992). Learning and teaching with understanding. In D. A. Grouws (Ed.) , *Handbook of research on mathematics teaching and learning,* (pp. 65–97) . New York: Macmillan.

Hughes, M. (1986). *Children and number: Difficulties in learning mathematics.* Oxford, England: Basil Blackwell.

Inhelder, B., & Piaget, J. (1958). *The growth of logical thinking from childhood to adolescence: An essay on the construction of formal operational structures.* New York: Basic Books. (Original work published 1955)

Kennedy, L. M., & Tipps, S. (1994). *Guiding children's learning of mathematics* (7th ed.). Belmont, CA: Wadsworth.

Landsmann, L. T., & Karmiloff-Smith, A. (1992). Children's understanding of notations as domains of knowledge versus referential-communicative tools. *Cognitive Development, 7,* 287–300.

Montessori, M. (1917). *The advanced Montessori method.* New York: Frederick A. Stokes.

Moshman, D., & Franks, B. A. (1986). Development of the concept of inferential validity. *Child Development, 57,* 153–165.

National Council of Teachers of Mathematics. (1989). *Curriculum and evaluation standards for school mathematics.* Reston, VA: Author.

Piaget, J. (1951). *Play, dreams, and imitation in childhood.* New York: Norton.

Resnick, L. B., & Omanson, S. F. (1987). Learning to understand arithmetic. In R. Glaser (Ed.), *Advances in instructional psychology* (Vol. 3, pp. 41–96). Hillsdale, NJ: Erlbaum.

Sigel, I. E. (1993). The centrality of a distancing model for the development of representational competence. In R. R. Cocking & K. A. Renninger (Eds.), *The development and meaning of psychological distance* (pp. 141–158). Hillsdale, NJ: Erlbaum.

Simons, D. J., & Keil, F. C. (1995). An abstract to concrete shift in the development of biological thought: The *insides* story. *Cognition, 56,* 129–163.

Sowell, E. J. (1989). Effects of manipulative materials in mathematics instruction. *Journal for Research in Mathematics Education, 20,* 498–505.

Stevenson, H. W., & Stigler, J. W. (1992). *The learning gap: Why our schools are failing and what we can learn from Japanese and Chinese education.* New York: Summit Books.

Tooke, D. J., Hyatt, B., Leigh, M., Synder, B., & Borda, T. (1992). Why aren't manipulatives used in every middle school mathematics classroom? *Middle School Journal, 24,* 61–62.

Uttal, D. H., Schreiber, J. C., & DeLoache, J. S. (1995). Waiting to use a symbol: The effects of delay on children's use of models. *Child Development, 66,* 1875–1891.

Uttal, D. H., Scudder, K. V., & DeLoache, J. S. (1997). Manipulatives as symbols: A new perspective on the use of concrete objects to teach mathematics. *Journal of Applied Developmental Psychology, 18,* 37–54.

Vygotsky, L. (1962). *Thought and language* (E. Hanfmann & F. Vacar, Trans.). Cambridge, MA: MIT Press. (Original work published 1934)

Wearne, D., & Hiebert, J. (1988). A cognitive approach to meaningful mathematics instruction: Testing a local theory using decimal numbers. *Journal for Research in Mathematics Education, 19,* 371–384.

Werner, H., & Kaplan, B. (1963). *Symbol formation: An organismic approach to language and the expression of thought.* New York: Wiley.

CHAPTER 10

Judith A. Hudson
Ellyn G. Sheffield

The Role of Reminders in Young Children's Memory Development

☐ Introduction

Over the past two decades, a burgeoning literature has documented the impressive memory capabilities of young children. Research has shown that preschool children can retain event memories for several years (e.g., Fivush & Hamond, 1991; Hudson & Fivush, 1991), children as young as 30 to 36 months can verbally recall unique experiences that took place when they were 14 to 18 months old (Hudson, 1993) and even 13-month-olds show behavioral evidence of recalling an event from 4 months in the past (Meltzoff, 1995).

These impressive abilities indicate that important developments in children's memory abilities take place during the years 1 to 3. One such development is the transition to verbal recall that allows children to enter into verbal conversations about their memories and verbally reflect upon the past. Participation in memory conversations has been shown to affect the development of children's event recall and narrative development during the preschool years (McCabe & Peterson, 1991; Reese, Haden, & Fivush, 1993). Another important development is young children's expanded flexibility in using different types of reminders to reinstate event memories. From 14 to 36 months of age, children may be reminded of past events via an increasingly broad range of external representations such as live models, videos, photographs, and verbal conversations. This is important for the development of long-term memory because increased opportunities for reminding can increase the degree to which early event memories are reinstated in memory. Reinstatement has been shown to inoculate against forgetting and provides a mechanism sustaining memories over longer intervals (Campbell & Jaynes, 1966; Howe, Courage, & Bryant-Brown, 1993; Rovee-Collier & Shyi, 1992). Research on memory reinstatement in young children also explores how children's event memories are represented and stored in memory. Our research program examines the role of reinstatement in sustaining young children's memories over time and also probes the processes of memory storage and retrieval during the toddler years.

☐ Research on Young Children's Event Recall

Evidence from converging lines of research indicates that, from infancy, children are capable of retaining information from novel experiences. Because very young children lack the verbal skills to demonstrate their recall of the past, four paradigms using behavioral measures have been used extensively to examine infants' and toddlers' memory: (a) response-contingency tasks, (b) deferred imitation tasks, (c) elicited imitation tasks, and (d) relearning experiments. A brief summary of each paradigm follows.

In response-contingency tasks, infants learn to respond to a stimulus to produce a target behavior during one or more training sessions. If the same or a highly similar stimulus is presented within a specific time interval, infants recognize the stimulus and reproduce the target behavior. After being trained with an operant procedure in a response-contingency task, even 2-month-old infants can remember a novel stimulus for 2 to 3 days (Davis & Rovee-Collier, 1983). However, if 2-month-olds are reexposed to the stimulus on Day 4, it is viewed as a new event and they do not respond to it. Using the same paradigm at different ages, it has been shown that infants can remember training experiences for increasingly longer periods of time (Boller, Rovee-Collier, Borovsky, O'Connor, & Shyi, 1990; Howe & Courage, 1993). By 6 months of age, infants remember training for up to 20 days (Boller et al., 1990) and, by 9 months, infants can recall training experiences for up to 56 days (Rovee-Collier, 1995).

Research with older infants and toddlers has capitalized on their interest in and ability to imitate modeled actions. In deferred imitation experiments, a unique action or sequence of actions is modeled by an experimenter. Children are restricted from producing the action(s) during this initial training period. Some time later, children are encouraged to produce the target action(s). Originally, deferred imitation over periods of 1-2 days had been found in infants at 9 months (Meltzoff, 1988b), 11 months (McDonough & Mandler, 1994), and 14 months (Meltzoff, 1988a). More recently. Mandler and McDonough (1995) have found evidence of deferred imitation by 11-month-olds over a 3-month interval and Meltzoff (1995) has found evidence of deferred imitation by 14- to 16-month-olds over a 4-month interval.

In elicited imitation research, children are given the opportunity to imitate two- and three-step action sequences immediately after observing an experimenter's demonstration. Some time later, children return to the training context and are encouraged to reproduce the learned action sequences. This procedure differs from deferred imitation in that children are encouraged to reproduce the modeled activities immediately after observation to ensure that children have attended to the model and are capable of producing the target actions. However, the single opportunity for reproduction after modeling is not equivalent to the prolonged training period required for infants to learn a contingent response in response-contingency paradigms. Using elicited imitation paradigms, it has been shown that children from 11 to 16 months of age at time of encoding can recall action sequences for intervals ranging from 1 week to 8 months (Bauer & Hertsgaard, 1993; Bauer, Hertsgaard, & Dow, 1994; Bauer & Mandler, 1990; Bauer & Shore, 1987; Mandler & McDonough, 1995).

Using primarily relearning measures, another line of research has produced evidence suggesting that memory for early experience can persist for many years and may become accessible to verbal recall (Myers, Clifton, & Clarkson, 1987). Children who had participated in an experiment involving reaching for luminous objects or sounds in a darkened chamber at 6½ months of age showed evidence of recall at 2½ years of age. As compared to control subjects, they were more comfortable in the testing situation, they were more likely to repeat the reaching actions that they had performed in the past, and one child verbally labeled a salient object from the original testing situation. In another study, 10-month-olds who learned to operate a toy were tested for recall 4, 18, and 50 months later (Myers, Perris, & Speaker, 1994). As compared to naive, age-matched subjects, children who had participated in the training at 10 months attended more to the toy, played with it for longer periods of time, and relearned the target actions more quickly.

Although these various lines of research show that children are capable of long-term memory in the second year of life, it is not clear whether such memories can be sustained over very long intervals, even after multiple experiences. For example, McDonough and Mandler (1994) found that 11-month-olds were able to recall action sequences over a 1-week interval, but when tested 1 year later, children recalled only a single action sequence, feeding a teddy bear with a schematic bottle, which was a highly familiar routine that could have repeated numerous times during the 1-year interval. Boyer, Barran, and Farrar (1994) failed to find evidence of long-term recall in testing 3-year-olds' recall of an event they had enacted 12 to 22 months in the past. Twenty-month-olds learned how to enact a nine-step sequence of making Play Dough over 1 or 3 training experiences. One week later, children in the three-visit condition performed more actions than children in the one-visit condition. However, when subjects returned for testing 12 to 22 months later, there was no effect of repeated training and there was no indication of long-term recall of the event.

Thus, results of behavior enactment research are mixed and, even when evidence of long-term memory is found, it is not known how long memories from before the age of 3 are retained. Studies of adults' recollections of childhood consistently have found that adults report few, if any specific memories from the first 3 years of life, a phenomenon referred to as *infantile amnesia* (White & Pillemer, 1979). The lower frequency of memories for early childhood as compared to memories of middle childhood, adolescence, and adulthood are too great to be attributed to simple memory decay.

Several theories have been proposed to account for infantile amnesia. Originally, Freud (1966) proposed that memories from before the age of 3 are repressed. More recently, memory theories have focused on important cognitive and social developments during the preschool years that may render earlier memories inaccessible (for a review, see Howe & Courage, 1993; Pillemer & White, 1989). Howe and Courage (1993) contended that infantile amnesia ends when children develop a cognitive sense of self that allows them to store early event memories as autobiographical memories. Alternatively, Fivush (1991), Hudson (1990), and Nelson (1990, 1993) have proposed that sharing event memories in conversations with adults allows young children to understand the social significance of autobiographical memories and provides a context for adults to assist children in constructing personal memory narratives.

In this chapter, we examine the effects of another type of cognitive development; the development of memory reinstatement in young children. *Reinstatement*, as originally defined by Campbell and Jaynes (1966) is a process whereby an organism is reminded of a past activity by reexperiencing a portion of it, through a very brief exposure to a specific part of the original event, a small amount of practice with the task, or returning to the context in which the event took place. During reinstatement, original event information is activated and refreshed, and the retrievability of the memory is thereby strengthened (Howe et al., 1993; Rovee-Collier & Shyi, 1992). New information from the reinstating context also may be conjoined with old information, both strengthening and modifying information in long-term storage (Howe, 1991; Howe & Brainerd, 1989). Our research suggests that, with increasing age, children are able to be reminded of event memories by an increasingly broad range of experiences, allowing for more opportunities for reinstatement to occur. Developments in children's ability to use reminders to reinstate memories may help to explain why memories from the infant and toddler years are less likely to be retained over very long periods of time than memories of events occurring after the age of 3 years.

☐ Effects of Reminders on Children's Long-Term Recall

Several experimental paradigms have examined effects of reminders on children's long-term recall. As in elicited imitation, in reenactment paradigms, children originally are shown how to produce a series of actions with objects and, at a later time, are encouraged to physically reproduce all or a subset of the original actions prior to final recall testing. Reenactment in nonverbal memory research is similar to repeated recall trials used in studies of verbal recall. If reenactment is complete, it also can provide additional practice. The benefits of multiple experiences and practice are not unique to young children: Positive effects of retraining have been obtained in research with older children, adults, and animals (Postman & Knecht, 1983; Underwood, Kaplak, & Malmi, 1976). However, research on effects of reenactment on toddlers' event memory is fairly recent.

Fivush and Hamond (1989) found that 24- and 28-month-old children who reenacted several five-step action sequences 2 weeks after their initial training recalled more actions after 3 months than children who were not given the chance to reenact the actions. Bauer (1995) and Boyer et al. (1994) found that reenacting action sequences one to three times improved recall performance of 15- and 20-month-olds over intervals of 1 week and 1 month. (However, as discussed above, Boyer et al. failed to find long-lasting effects when children were retested at 3 years.)

Reinstatement paradigms are distinguished from reenactment procedures in that children are not given the opportunity to reproduce an event in its entirety. Rather, they are passively exposed to partial information about a past event. Howe et al., (1993) investigated reinstatement of preschool children's memories using a hiding task. Two- and 3-year-old children were shown the hiding places of 16 toys located in a playroom. One week later, half of the children returned to the room and were shown the toys, but not the locations. In recall testing 3 weeks later, children who had participated in the reinstatement session recalled more locations than children who received no reinstatement.

Research by Rovee-Collier has found that passive exposure to a moving mobile can reinstate infants' memory for a learned response (Rovee-Collier & Shyi, 1992; Rovee-Collier, Sullivan, Enright, Lucas, & Fagan, 1980). Using a conjugate reinforcement paradigm, infants learn to produce movement in a crib mobile by kicking (a ribbon tied to the infant's ankle is connected to the mobile to produce the movement). After a time delay, memory for the learned response contingency is assessed by reintroducing the mobile without the ribbon attached and measuring infants' kicking response. When tested for memory 14 days after training, 3-month-old infants do not demonstrate retention of training; they no longer kick above baseline levels when presented with the mobile. However, their memories can be reinstated by a brief, noncontingent visual exposure either to a training cue or to the context in which training occurred (Rovee-Collier, Griesler, & Earley, 1985; Rovee-Collier et al., 1980). For example, if 3-month-olds view a moving mobile 13 days after training (the movement is produced by an experimenter and is unrelated to infants' movements), they demonstrate retention when tested at 14 days and they continue to recognize the mobile for up to 28 days (Rovee-Collier et al., 1980).

Further research has shown that the kind of information provided during the reminder session is critical to successful retrieval. Greco, Hayne, and Rovee-Collier (1990) demonstrated that reminders are effective only if they contain matching functional information. In this study, infants were trained to kick to produce movement in several different mobiles. Exposure to another, different mobile was effective in reinstating recall of initial training but exposure to a nonmoving mobile did not produce reinstatement.

Moreover, effects of reinstatement vary depending on when the reminder is administered. Reminders are most effective for infants when presented after a significant delay, just prior to the onset of forgetting (Rovee-Collier, 1995).

Rovee-Collier referred to the administration of reminders after the time that functional forgetting occurs as reactivation. However, reactivation and reinstatement are very similar in that both procedures involve presenting children with a reminder of a past event sometime during the interval between the initial experience and long-term recall testing. Howe et al. (1993) argued that reactivation and reinstatement are variants of the same process and are similar in all respects, except for the time at which they occur. Both procedures allow children to retrieve memories that seemingly are inaccessible but, nevertheless, still in storage.

Despite the extensive research on reinstatement effects in infant memory, less research has focused on the role of reminders in children's recall during the years 1 to 3. As discussed earlier, however, this may be an important period in the development of long-term recall because of the transition from nonverbal to verbal recall. Our research examines the role reminders in 1- and 2-year-olds' long-term memory to better understand the variables affecting long-term retention in early childhood and to investigate changes in very young children's ability to utilize reminder information.

We have investigated effects of four types of reminders on toddlers' long-term recall. As discussed above, reenactment occurs when a child physically reexperiences all the components of the original event. In a modeling experiment, children do not perform actions themselves, but watch someone else perform actions. With a video simulation reminder, children watch a video tape of an event instead of a live model. With photograph reminders, children view photographs of past events with or without accompanying verbal narration.

Each type of reminder provides information about events in a different format. Both reenactment and modeling involve live events; either children reenact an event themselves or watch someone else. In contrast, videos, photographs, and verbal reminders use representations in the form of images and words to give children information about past events. By examining effects of these different types of reminders, we are able to examine children's ability to use different types of representations to cue their memories. DeLoache and her colleagues (DeLoache, 1990; DeLoache & Burns, 1994; DeLoache, Pierroutsakos, & Troseth, 1996) have found that children under 3 years of age often fail to appreciate how external representations such as scale models, photographs, and videos can be used to represent specific real-world contexts. They proposed that young children lack representational insight; that is, the understanding of how external representations function as symbols of real-world referents. Studies of children's use of external representations as reminders provide another paradigm to examine children's understanding of the symbolic functions of different representational media.

In addition, we can manipulate the amount of information provided in different types of reminders to examine how much information is needed in order for a reminder to be effective. For example, during reenactment, children may reenact all or only part of an event. Similarly, a video tape may show children all of the actions they experienced in the past or only some of the actions. However, because of the nature of the representational format, some types of reminders necessarily provide less information than other. In live events and videos, action information can be kinetically presented, whereas the action information must be inferred from the images provided by photographs. Reminders therefore can vary in terms of the medium of representation as well as the amount of information provided about a past event and each of these variables may affect their effectiveness in reinstating young children's memories.

Reenactment

We began this line of research by studying effects of reenactment on 18-month-olds' long-term memory (Hudson & Sheffield, 1998). Because reenactment involves physically reproducing all of the actions learned in the past, this can be considered the most comprehensive and most concrete type of reminder. If this is an ineffective reminder, it is unlikely that less complete abstract types of reminders would be effective.

Our reenactment procedure was conducted in the following manner: During the training session, children visited our laboratory playroom and were shown how to perform eight novel, two-step activities using an elicited imitation procedure. An experimenter demonstrated an activity, the child performed the activity, then the experimenter demonstrated a second activity, and so on. The activities were designed to be interesting for 18-month-olds, but not to be things that they could discover on their own without training (such as finding a hidden box of fish food so that they can feed the goldfish or pressing a stuffed bear's paw to make it talk). Objects used in the activities were placed in various locations around a laboratory playroom and some activities involved finding hidden props (e.g., the fish food) to perform the target actions.

Some time after training, children returned to the laboratory for a reenactment session. During this session, children were first allowed 10 minutes of free play in the playroom to see if they would spontaneously produce the target actions. Then, the experimenter provided verbal prompts for any of the activities the child had not performed, such as "What could we do with this toy?" If children failed to produce the target actions after prompting, the experimenter demonstrated the action for the child and encouraged the child to imitate so that all children reenacted all of the activities during the reenactment session. Finally, children returned to the laboratory for a recall test session when they were encouraged to reproduce the target actions in the same way as in the reenactment session.

Effects of Timing of Reenactment.   In our first experiment we examined the effects of varying the timing of the reenactment session. In studying effects of memory reminders with infants, Rovee-Collier (1995) has shown that reminders are more effective when presented after a significant time delay. In this study, we examined whether effects of reenactment also vary depending on when reenactment occurs.

We examined the performance of children in three reenactment conditions (see Table 10.1). An immediate reenactment group reenacted the activities on the same day as their training. They were shown how to perform the activities, then left the playroom for 15 minutes, and returned for the reenactment session. They returned to the laboratory 8 weeks later for a recall test session. Children in the 2-week reenactment condition returned 2 weeks after training for reenactment and were also tested for recall 8 weeks later, 10 weeks after training. Children in the 8-week reenactment condition returned 8 weeks after training for reenactment and were tested for recall 8 weeks later, 16 weeks after training. Thus, the interval between training and reenactment varied across conditions, but the interval between reenactment and testing was the same for all groups.

We compared children's performance in the reenactment conditions to three control groups. The one-visit control group was not provided with training, but participated in a recall session just like the other groups. This group controlled for the potential for children to simply figure out what to do with the toys when given verbal prompts. Children in two no-reminder conditions were trained to perform the activities and were tested for recall 8 weeks later, but did not participate in a reenactment session. Children in the 18-month no-reminder condition were 18 months old at the time of training, so they were the same age as the immediate and 2-week reenactment groups at time of testing (20 months old). Children in the 20-month no-reminder condition were 20 months old at the time of training so that, at time of testing, they were matched in age to children in the 18-week reenactment condition who were 22 months old at time of testing.

Figure 10.1 shows the proportion of actions recalled by children in the test session broken down into spontaneous and prompted recall. Spontaneous recall refers to target actions performed during free play.

TABLE 10.1. Schedule of conditions, reenactment experiments

Condition	Training	Reenactment	Test	Long-Term Test
		Experiments 1 and 2: Effects of Timing		
Reenactment conditions				
Immediate	Day 1	Day 1	8 weeks	8 months
2-week	Day 1	2 weeks	10 weeks	8 months
8-week	Day 1	8 weeks	16 weeks	10 months
Control conditions				
1 visit	—	—	8 weeks	
No reminder (18 months)	Day 1	—	8 weeks	
No reminder (20 months)	8 weeks	—	16 weeks	
1 visit (26 months)	—	—	—	8 months
	Experiment 3:	**Subset**	**Reenactment**	
Subset A	Day 1	2 weeks	8 weeks	
Subset B	Day 1	2 weeks	8 weeks	

Prompted recall refers to target actions performed after verbal prompts were provided. In spontaneous recall, children in the 8-week reenactment group (0-8-16) recalled more activities than all other groups, including children in the immediate (0-0-8) and 2-week (0-2-10) reenactment conditions who, nevertheless, recalled more than children in the control conditions. For total number of activities performed, children who reenacted the activities 2 or 8 weeks after training recalled more activities than children who reenacted the activities immediately after training. However, children in the immediate reenactment condition recalled more actions than the control groups.

This experiment showed that reeenactment can extend 18-month-olds' recall: All reenactment groups recalled more activities than the control groups. But, more importantly, it also showed that timing of

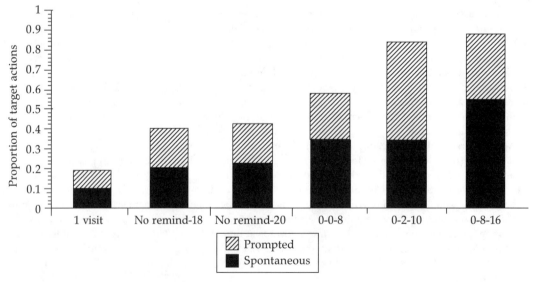

FIGURE 10.1. Recall performance by condition and type of prompt in reenactment Experiment 1. "Deja Vu All Over Again: Effects of Re-enactment on One-Year-Olds' Event Memory," by J. A. Hudson and E. G. Sheffield, 1998, *Child Development, 69,* p. 61.

reenactment strongly influences children's recall. Reenactment was more effective after a significant time delay. As found in infant research, reminders may be more effective when presented after an experience has been stored in long-term memory. Memory retrieval at this point may involve more reconstruction than when memory traces are new and more coherent.

Very Long-Term Effects of Timing of Reenactment.

After completing this experiment, we wondered if timing effects would still be evident in very long-term recall. We contacted subjects from the reenactment conditions and asked them to return to the laboratory 6 months after their last visit. We were interested in whether children who were now approximately 26 months of age could recall activities that they performed 6 to 10 months in the past and whether effects of timing of reenactment would still be evident. We compared the performance of the returning subjects to the performance of naive 26-month-olds to test whether the returning subjects actually were remembering their prior experiences and were not simply better able to infer how to use the props.

Figure 10.2 shows the total number of activities recalled combining spontaneous and prompted recall. As is evident from this figure, timing effects were even stronger in long-term recall. Children who had reenacted the activities after 8 weeks (0-8-16 group) recalled more activities than children in the other 2 reenactment groups. Children in the 2-week reenactment condition (0-2-10) recalled more than children in the immediate condition (0-0-8). In fact, children's performance in the immediate reenactment condition was not significantly better than that of children in the one visit control group. All children in the reenactment conditions had performed the activities three times in the past. However, the timing of their second visit strongly affected how much they could recall over a 6-month delay.

These results suggest that early memories may be retained for very long periods of time if children are given the opportunity to reenact events and if reenactment occurs at an opportune time. If reenactment occurs too soon after the original experience, children may remember it for a limited amount of time, but over the long term. But, if reenactment occurs after a longer delay, children's recall does not decline even over a 6-month delay. These timing effects support a large body of research indicating that distributed training is more effective for learning than is massed training (Bahrick, 1979; Bahrick, Bahrick, Bahrick, & Bahrick, 1993; Schmidt & Bjork, 1992; Underwood et al., 1976).

Effects of Partial Reenactment.

Although these experiments showed that reenactment effectively extends 1-year-olds' long-term memory, in everyday life, children may also reenact only parts of events. We conducted another experiment to investigate whether reenacting a subset of the activities also enhances children's recall. In this experiment, two groups of 18-month-olds reenacted four of the original eight activities (either subset A or subset B) 2 weeks after training and were tested for memory of all

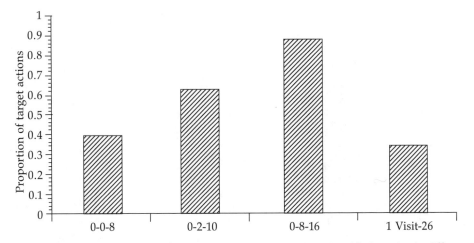

FIGURE 10.2. Recall performance in long-term retention test. "Deja Vu All Over Again: Effects of Reenactment on One-Year-Olds' Event Memory," by J. A. Hudson and E. G. Sheffield, 1998, *Child Development, 69*, p. 61.

activities 8 weeks later (see Table 10.1). We were interested in whether performing half of the activities could remind children of the other activities that were not reenacted. We did not vary the timing of reenactment in this experiment and the 2-week point was selected as a convenient point of comparison.

As shown in Figure 10.3, there were no significant differences in level of recall between the full and subset reenactment conditions. Reenacting half of the activities successfully reminded children of the activities that had not been repeated so that they recalled both reenacted and nonreenacted activities equally well. These findings indicate that event memories can be recovered by exposure to a portion of the original event, and that 18-month-olds encode and store memories in an associative network. The separate activities may have been associated in memory by the common temporal and spatial context of the event. Reexperiencing some of the activities activated memory of the remaining activities so that recall of all of the activities was high when tested 8 weeks later. Finally, these results provide evidence of memory reinstatement in 18-month-olds: Exposure to part of an original experience improved recall of the entire event.

These results led us to consider what other kinds of reminders could be effective in reinstating toddlers' event memories. Our next study examined effects of modeling as a reminder for toddlers' long-term recall.

Reinstatement with Modeling

In this experiment (Sheffield & Hudson, 1994), we tested whether toddlers could be reminded of a past event by viewing an experimenter perform some of the activities they had learned previously. As in the reenactment research, we were interested in whether children could be reminded of a past event by exposure to a subset of activities from the original event. Unlike the reenactment studies, the reminder in this study involved passive viewing of a model, not physical enactment.

Two studies using subset reinstatement with infants and preschool children had produced mixed results. Timmons' (1994) found evidence for spreading activation from subset information in reinstatement of 6-month-olds' memories. Infants were trained on two separate contingencies, kicking to make a mobile spin and arm pulling to activate a music box. Viewing either response (the moving mobile or tinkling music box) during a reactivation session reminded infants of the other contingency so that their level of performance for both actions was significantly higher during recall testing than during their original baseline assessment. In contrast, Howe et al. (1993) found only limited evidence for subset reinstatement in a study of preschoolers' memory for object locations. Three-year-olds were shown 16 items hidden in different locations. Three weeks later, children observed 8 of the items again and then 1 week later, children were tested on their recall of the locations for all 16 items. Although children who received reinstatement recalled more locations than children who had not received reinstatement, the reinstate-

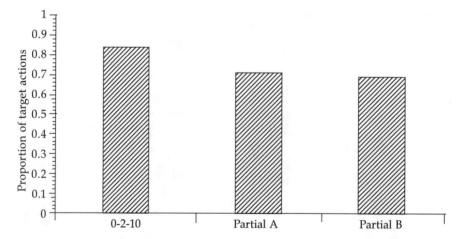

FIGURE 10.3. Recall performance in partial and full (0-2-10) reenactment conditions. "Deja Vu All Over Again: Effects of Re-enactment on One-Year-Olds' Event Memory," by J. A. Hudson and E. G. Sheffield, 1998, *Child Development, 69*, p. 63.

ment subjects did not recall reinstated locations better than nonreinstated locations. However, memory for observed hiding locations may be different than memory for performed activities.

This experiment examined effects of viewing an experimenter model half of the activities as a reminder for 14- and 18-month-olds. We selected children at different ages to see whether there were developmental differences in children's ability to use subset reminders. Three conditions were used in this experiment (see Table 10.2). Children in the train/remind and train only (no reminder) conditions were trained to perform six novel activities similar to those used in the reenactment studies. Eight weeks after training, 14-month-olds in the train/remind condition participated in a reminder session while 10 weeks after training, 18-month-olds in the train/remind condition participated in a reminder session. Different intervals were selected because pilot research had shown that the retention interval varied for children at different ages. In the reminder session, children viewed an experimenter model three of the six activities they had learned previously, but children did not perform the activities themselves. Both ages were tested for recall 24 hours later. Children in the train only conditions did not participate in a reminder session and were tested for recall 8 or 10 weeks after training. Children in the reminder only condition never were trained to perform the activities, but viewed an experimenter perform three of the activities and then were tested on their ability to perform all of the activities 24 hours later. This condition provided a test of children's ability to perform the actions simply by imitating the experimenter. Because results from deferred imitation research suggested that 14- and 18-month-olds would be able to remember actions seen the day before and reproduce them in a test session (Meltzoff, 1988a), we expected recall of modeled actions to be high for both the reinstatement and reminder only conditions. However, if reinstatement occurred, recall should also be high for the nonreminded actions for children in the reinstatement condition, but not for children in the no-reminder condition.

Results are shown in Figure 10.4. As expected, recall of modeled activities was high for both the train/reminder and reminder only conditions, indicating that children were capable of deferred imitation. However, recall of unmodeled activities was higher in the train/remind condition for both ages than in either the train only or the reminder only conditions. These results indicate that a subset reminder effectively reinstated both 14- and 18-month-olds' memory for all of the activities. Again, this finding supports the interpretation that children's representations of the activities were stored holistically, linked together by the common spatial context or by temporal proximity. This experiment also provided another demonstration that partial reminders are effective, even when children are not active participants. Finally, there were no developmental differences in reinstatement effects for 14- and 18-month-olds. Both older and younger children were reminded by the subset modeling procedure.

Representational Reminders: Videos and Photographs

Our next set of experiments focused on children's ability to use information presented in various media as reminders of past events (Hudson & Sheffield, 1996; Ryder, Sheffield, Hudson, 1995; Sheffield, 1997). In real-world situations, children regularly may come in contact with reminders that simulate or represent their experiences in different media such as watching videos or viewing photographs in a family album. Little is known about whether these potential reminding situations actually reinstate children's memories.

Research on children's use of representational information has produced mixed results. Research by DeLoache and Burns (1994) indicated that young children may not understand how photographs repre-

TABLE 10.2. Schedule of conditions, modeling experiment

Condition	Training	Reminder	Test
14-month-olds			
Train/remind	Day 1	Week 8	Week 8
Train only	Day 1	—	Week 8
Reminder only	—	Week 8	Week 8
18-month-olds			
Train/remind	Day 1	Week 10	Week 10
Train only	Day 1	Week 10	Week 10
Reminder only	Day 1	Week 10	Week 10

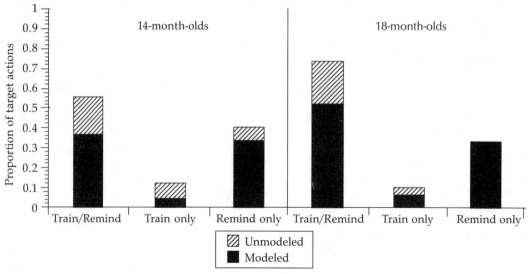

FIGURE 10.4. Recall of modeled and unmodeled actions by age and condition. "Reactivation of Toddler's Event Memories," by E. G. Sheffield and J. A. Hudson, 1994, *Memory, 2,* p. 459.

sent objects or experiences until approximately 30 months. In their research, 24-, 27-, and 30-month-olds were asked to find a hidden toy in a room after viewing a photograph indicating the toy's location. Thirty-month-olds were able to use photographs to help them find the hidden toy, but 24- and 27-month-olds were unable to understand the relationship between the room and the photograph. DeLoache and Burns proposed that children have difficulty using the information depicted in the photographs to find the hidden objects in the room because they do not understand the "representational specificity" of photographs; that is, that the photographs were representations of a specific room and not generic room representations. They argued that infants' and toddlers' initial experience with photographs typically consisted of viewing generic photographs of objects in picture books. This early experience leads them to interpret photographs as representing generic objects, but not specific realities.

This line of research also has shown that very young children have difficulty understanding videos as representations. A recent investigation found that 27-month-olds, but not 24-month-olds, were able to use location information represented in a video to retrieve a hidden toy (Troseth & DeLoache, 1996). Again, DeLoache et al. (1996) proposed that children's difficulty in this task can be attributed to their prior experience with the medium. They argued that, by the age of 2 years, children have extensive experience with videos as forms of entertainment and their expectations for how the medium is used interferes with their ability to understand that a video representation can represent a current reality. To support this view, one experiment showed that when 24-month-olds believed they were watching a live event through a window, when in fact they were looking at a large video screen, their retrieval performance improved (DeLoache et al., 1996).

This lack of understanding about the relationship between a representation and its referent suggests that children also may have difficulty using photographs or even videos as reminders of past events. However, it is possible that children's ability to use representational information may vary in terms of the specific task at hand. Although DeLoache and Burns (1994) found that children less than 30 months old were unable to use information specified in a photograph to find a hidden toy, a recent study by Harris, Kavenaugh, and Dowson (1997) found that 2-year-olds were able to use photograph information to depict imaginary transformations in pretend play. In this study, children observed an experimenter pretend to perform a transformation on a toy object such as sprinkling white talcum powder on a teddy bear's back. When shown photographs of a teddy bear with a white back, a teddy bear with a blue head, or an unchanged teddy bear, 2-year-olds (26 to 30 months) performed well, indicating that they were able to imagine a pretend transformation and select a photograph representation of its outcome. However, children under 24 months performed at chance levels. Thus, children from 24 to 30 months of age may be able to appreciate the symbolic relationship between their internal representations and external, photograph representations in tasks which do not require the mapping of spatial relationships.

Research on children's use of video information has supported this view. Meltzoff (1988b) demonstrated that 14-month-old children were able to imitate action sequences 24 hours after viewing simple, one-step actions modeled on television by an experimenter. Children's ability to perform actions on three-dimensional objects after viewing a two-dimensional television representation suggests that video representations also could be used as reminders. However, it also is plausible that imitating actions depicted in a video may involve different cognitive processes than understanding the relationship between a video and a particular past experience. If young children have difficulty in understanding videos as representations of past events, these representations would not be effective reminders.

Video Reminders.   In the first experiment using a representational reminder, we were interested in whether toddlers could be reminded of a past event by watching a video simulation of their original experience (Ryder et al., 1995). Although video simulations provide as much information as viewing a live model, they are presented in a representational format and are not live events. Viewing a video simulation would be effective in reinstating children's event memory only if children were able to relate their internal memory representation of the event to the external, video representation of the event.

Eighteen-month-olds were trained to perform eight novel, two-step activities and returned to the laboratory for a reminder session 2 weeks later, as in the original reenactment experiment. During the reminder session, the laboratory playroom was stripped of all the props associated with the original event and children in the video reminder condition viewed a videotape depicting a preschool child performing the original activities with an experimenter similar to their initial training sessions. Eight weeks later (10 weeks after training), children returned to the laboratory for testing. We compared their performance to that of children in a reenactment condition who were trained to perform the activities, returned to the laboratory and reenacted the activities after 2 weeks, and then were tested for recall 8 weeks later, 10 weeks after training (see Table 10.3). A third group of children in the no-reminder condition were tested for recall 10 weeks after training, but did not receive any reminder.

TABLE 10.3.   Schedule of conditions, video and photograph reminder experiments

Condition	Training	Reminder	Test
Experiment 1: Effects of Video Reminders			
Reenactment	Day 1	2 weeks, reenactment	10 weeks
Video reminder (0-2-10)	Day 1	2 weeks, video simulation	10 weeks
No reminder	Day 1	—	10 weeks
Nonsimulation video	Day 1	2 weeks, unrelated video	10 weeks
Reminder only	—	Video simulation	8 weeks
Experiment 2: Immediate Recall after Reinstatement			
Immediate recall (0-10-10)	Day 1	10 weeks, video simulation	10 weeks
Reminder only	—	Video simulation	10 weeks
Experiment 3: Delayed Recall after Reinstatement			
Delayed recall (0-10-12)	Day 1	10 weeks, video simulation	12 weeks
Experiment 4: Video Versus Photograph Reminders			
Video reminder	Day 1	10 weeks, video simulation	10 weeks
Photo reminder	Day 1	10 weeks, photos + narrative	10 weeks
Video reminder only	—	10 weeks, video simulation	10 weeks
Photo reminder only	—	10 weeks, photos + narrative	10 weeks
Experiment 5: Object Only Video Reminder			
Objects + actions	Day 1	10 weeks, full video simulation	10 weeks
Objects only	Day 1	10 weeks, objects only video	10 weeks
No reminder	Day 1	10 weeks, unrelated video	10 weeks
Reminder only	—	10 weeks, full video simulation	10 weeks

We were concerned that returning to the laboratory context could have a reinstating effect independent of the information children derived from viewing the video simulation. A study of reinstatement in 3-month-olds (Boller et al., 1990) found that infants could be reminded of past training simply by returning to the training context. To control for context effects, another group of children in the nonsimulation video condition were trained to perform the activities and also returned to the laboratory 2 weeks later. However, these children viewed an unrelated video of a segment from *Sesame Street*. They also returned for testing 8 weeks later, 10 weeks after training.

We also were concerned that children might be able to imitate the activities shown in the video without necessarily recalling their training experience. To control for this possibility, a fifth group in the reminder only condition never were trained to perform the activities, but viewed the video simulation of the activities and were tested for recall 8 weeks later.

If viewing the videotape was an effective reminder, then children in the video reminder condition would recall more activities than all of the control groups. If viewing the videotape was as effective as reenactment, there would be no difference in recall performance between the reenactment and video reminder groups. As shown in Figure 10.5, this was not the case. Children who watched the video recalled fewer activities than children who reenacted the activities and no more than the children who did not receive any type of reminder, the children who viewed the video simulation without prior training, or the children who viewed an unrelated video.

Effects of Timing of Video Reminders.   Were children unable to use the video as a reminder or were the effects of the video reminder no longer apparent after the 10-week delay? In a second experiment (Ryder et al., 1995), we tested whether 18-month-olds' memories could be reinstated if they were tested immediately after viewing the video (see Table 10.3). Children in an immediate recall condition (0-10-10) returned to the laboratory 10 weeks after training and viewed the video simulation. They then left the playroom and were occupied in other parts of the building while the props were replaced in the playroom. After this 15-minute break, children returned to the playroom for testing. We compared their performance to age-matched subjects who were not trained, but who simply viewed the video and were allowed to play with the props 15 minutes later. This reminder only condition controlled for the possibility that children might be able to imitate the activities after viewing the videotape without prior training (see Table 10.3).

Figure 10.6 shows the number of actions recalled in the immediate recall condition (0-10-10), compared to recall of children in the 2-week video reminder condition (0-2-10) from the previous experiment, as well as that of children who watched the video without prior training (reminder only) and were tested for recall 15 minutes later and children who received no reminder. Children in the 0-10-10 condition enacted more activities than children in the 0-2-10 condition and more actions than the control groups. These results indicate that 18-month-olds were able to use the information contained in a video representation

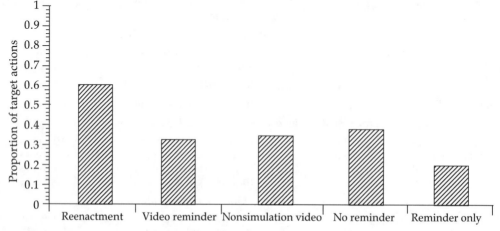

FIGURE 10.5. Recall performance in video reminder Experiment 1 comparing reenactment to video reminders (see Table 10.3) (from Ryder, Sheffield, & Hudson, 1995).

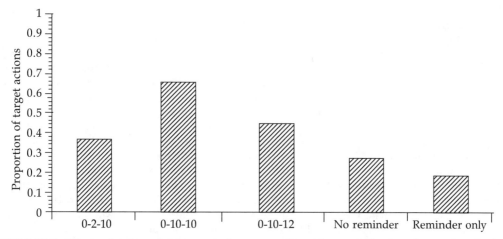

FIGURE 10.6. Effects of timing of video reminders on recall in video reminder Experiments 2 and 3 (see Table 10.3 for full description of timing of reminder presentation and recall tests).

to reinstate their memories of the original training. However, it appeared that the effects of a video reminder were not as long-lasting as reenactment, as evidenced by performance in the 2-week reminder condition (0-2-10).

It is interesting to note that children's performance in the reminder only condition was relatively low, indicating that children were not able to reproduce the activities after seeing the video if they had not been given prior training. The poor performance of children in this condition established that exposure to the reminder was insufficient to produce new learning, which is a critical component of the reinstatement paradigm (Campbell & Jaynes, 1966; Spear & Parsons, 1976). Yet, these findings are inconsistent with Meltzoff's (1988b) research showing that 14-month-olds were able to imitate actions demonstrated by a televised model. However, the actions used in Meltzoff's study were very simple ones that were repeated several times by the televised model. In contrast, the activities used in our research were more complex, two-step activities that often involved moving props from different locations in the playroom, and the activities were presented only once in the video simulation. It is likely that children did not have any difficulty processing action information in the video format but, rather, they did not receive enough exposure to the more complex actions for learning to occur.

Effects of Video Reinstatement Over Time.   The previous experiment showed that toddlers' event memories could be reinstated by viewing a video simulation of the event and administering a recall test immediately afterward. But, how long-lasting would these reinstatement effects be? In a third experiment, 18-month-olds in a delayed recall condition viewed a video simulation in a reminder session 10 weeks after training but the recall test was administered 2 weeks later, 12 weeks after training (Hudson & Sheffield, 1995). (See Table 10-3.) Their performance was compared to that of subjects in the previous experiment who were tested for recall on the same day as the reminder session. As shown in Figure 10.6, children in this condition (0-10-12) recalled significantly fewer actions than children in the immediate recall condition (0-10-10) and no more actions than children in the control conditions. These findings indicate that information presented in a video was effective in reinstating 18-month-olds' event memories, but the reinstated memories did not last for very long.

Photographs Versus Video Reminders.   In our video simulation, all the relevant props were present and the entire action sequence, including the accompanying narration, was depicted just as in children's original training. In viewing a photograph, props are shown, but motion information is unavailable. With an accompanying narration, actions can be described with words but there is still no visual depiction of the action. To test how these differences in the two media affect reinstatement, we compared children's recall after viewing a video reminder to recall after viewing photographs of the activities along with a verbal narration 10 weeks after training.

We hypothesized that a photograph reminder would not be effective for 18-month-old children. As discussed above, research by DeLoache and Burns (1994) indicated that, under 30 months of age, children are unable to use photographs as symbolic representations of a large-scale space in a search task. Harris et al. (1997) also found that children under 2 years of age were unable to use photographs to depict imaginary transformations in pretend play. These findings suggest that 18-month-olds would not be able to understand how photographs represent past events. In addition, although many 18-month-olds have developed rudimentary language skills, they do not yet use language to participate in conversations about past events and, therefore, do not verbally evoke memories of the past.

Children in the reminder conditions in this experiment either viewed a video simulation of the activities they had learned 10 weeks prior (video reminder condition) or viewed two photographs of each activity as an experimenter narrated the action, for example, "Do you remember when you came to Rutgers and you made a crown just like that (pointing)? You took the jewels and you stuck them on the crown and then you put the crown on your head" (photo reminder condition; Hudson & Sheffield, 1996). To rule out potential context effects, all reminder sessions took place in children's homes. One day later, children returned to the laboratory for their test session. Age-matched control subjects who were not trained to perform the activities also were shown either the video or the photographs in their homes 1 day before being tested for production of target actions in the laboratory (reminder only conditions; see Table 10.3.)

As shown in Figure 10.7, children at both ages in the video reminder conditions recalled more actions than children in the video reminder only conditions and more actions than children in the no reminder conditions, indicating that the video reminder was effective in reinstating memories for both age groups. However, only 24-month-old children in the photograph reminder condition recalled more actions than children in the photograph reminder only condition; there was no significant difference in performance of 18-month-olds in these conditions. This finding suggests that photographs may be effective reminders for 24-month-olds, but not for 18-month-olds. This result is consistent with the hypothesis that children below the age of 24 months do not understand the representational nature of photographs to the degree necessary to use photographs as reminders of past events. However, this finding is inconclusive because 24-month-olds in the no reminder condition recalled many of the activities after 16 weeks without receiving a reminder; their performance was not significantly different from that of 24-month-olds in the photograph reminder condition. A more recent investigation in our laboratory (Agayoff, Hudson, & Barot, 1998) indicated that 24- and 30-month-olds are able to use photographs as reminders.

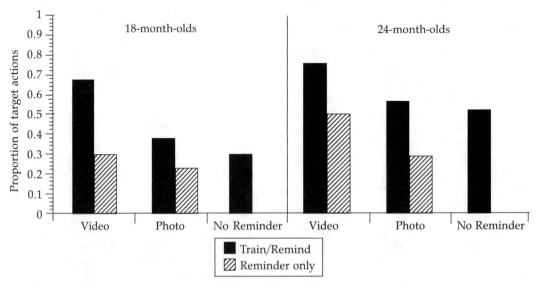

FIGURE 10.7. Effects of video and photograph reminders on 18- and 24-month-olds' recall, video reminder Experiment 4. Black bars indicate groups participating in initial training and hatched bars indicate reminder only groups (Hudson & Sheffield, 1996).

Effects of Partial Video Information.   The previous study indicated that videos were more effective than photographs in reminding children of past events, suggesting that children are able to understand the representational nature of videos before they can appreciate photographs as representations of the past. However, it also is possible that photographs provide less event information than do videos. Although in the previous experiment, an experimenter provided a verbal narrative of the actions, the video simulation provided a more complete and more detailed representation of the event. Additionally, children in the photograph and narrative condition had to attend to two different sources of information to receive event information whereas, in the video reminder condition, all information came from the same source. Our next experiment provided children with only partial information in a video representation to shed light on this issue.

In this experiment (Sheffield, 1997, Experiment 1), 18-month-olds participated in a reminder session in which they viewed a video containing only object information about the activities they had learned 10 weeks prior. Results from the previous experiment indicated that toddlers could be reminded of a past event by viewing a complete video simulation. In this experiment, however, the video did not include action information. Research with infants has indicated that they require functional information (e.g., a moving mobile) in order for reinstatement to occur (Greco et al., 1990). In contrast, research by Howe, Courage, and Bryant-Brown (1993) found that 2½-year-olds' memory for location information reinstated simply by viewing objects without actions. Would 18-month-olds' performance be more similar to infants' or to 2½-year-olds'?

The objects only video used in this experiment showed an experimenter picking up each of the props associated with each of the activities and commenting on the props, without demonstrating or describing the actions children had learned to perform in the training session, for example, "Look, here's Mickey Mouse. He has a shirt on. And shoes, too. He's my friend." Performance of children viewing the objects only reminder was compared to that of children who viewed a complete objects + actions video of the actions performed on the objects. In the object + actions video, an experimenter picked up each of the props and demonstrated each action while narrating, for example, "Look, here's Mickey Mouse. All you need to do is turn him around and pull his string. He talks!" Recall was tested 1 day after the reminder which took place in the laboratory. Children in the no-reminder condition were trained to perform the activities, returned to the laboratory 10 weeks later and viewed an unrelated video, and were tested for recall 10 weeks later. Children in the reminder only condition visited the laboratory and played with the props, but were not shown the target actions. Ten weeks later, they returned to laboratory to view the complete objects + actions video and they were tested for recall 1 day later (see Table 10.3).

As shown in Figure 10.8, toddlers in the objects only reminder condition produced significantly more target actions than children in all control conditions. This finding indicates that toddlers' event memories were effectively reinstated by viewing a video that included only object information. In contrast to very

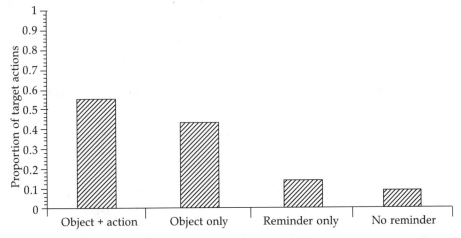

FIGURE 10.8. Recall performance of children in full video reminder (object + action), objects only video reminder, reminder only, and no reminder conditions, video Experiment 5 (Sheffield, 1997, Experiment 1).

young infants, reminders provided to 18-month-olds do not necessarily need to include functional information in order for reinstatement to occur. Thus, the lack of reinstatement effects in 18-month-olds found in the previous experiment using photograph reminders cannot be explained by the fact that photographs do not include action information. Rather, the results from this experiment suggest that 18-month-olds understand the relationship between a video and a past event, even when the video does not include action information, but they do not appreciate the symbolic relationship between photographs and memories of past events.

Results also indicated that children in the objects + actions condition produced more actions than children in the objects only condition. Although object information alone is sufficient for reinstatement to occur, recall still is better when both object and action information is provided in the reminder.

Finally, children who returned to the laboratory context and viewed an unrelated video produced no more target actions than children who did not return to the laboratory for reinstatement. Although context may be an important component in reinstating memories for young infants (Rovee-Collier et al., 1985), context appears to play a less salient role for 1-year-olds (Barnat, Klein, & Meltzoff, 1996).

Effects of New Information on Reinstatement

In all of the previous experiments, children were provided with reminders that accurately represented all or part of their original experience. In a recent experiment (Sheffield, 1997, Experiment 2), however, we examined the effects of providing children with reminders that contained discrepant information. We were interested in whether reminders that contained some new information could successfully reinstate toddlers' event memories and whether the new information provided in the reminder would overwrite toddlers' event memories.

Effects of misleading information on long-term recall have been investigated extensively in infants, children, and adults. One of the earliest paradigms designed to explore the effects of conflicting postevent information demonstrated that adults recalled past event information incorrectly after exposure to new inconsistent postevent information (Loftus, 1975; Loftus, Miller, & Burns, 1978). Loftus (1975) concluded that the original memory traces were overwritten by newly presented misinformation and that the original memory representation was no longer available for retrieval.

Other researchers have suggested that the misinformation effect may be due to new memories blocking access to the original memory, without necessarily overwriting the original representation (Berkerian & Bowers, 1983; Lindsay, 1990). Still other theorists have argued that the features (traces) of all memories decay over time and that presentation of postevent misinformation provides additional interference, effectively weakening the integrity of the trace features so that they can no longer be used to reconstruct the original memory representation (Brainerd, Reyna, Howe, & Kingma, 1990; Howe & Brainerd, 1989).

Effects of misinformation on children's long-term memory has been the topic of more than 100 research reports from 1979 to 1993 (Ceci & Bruck, 1993). Although not all studies have found that children are susceptible to postevent misinformation (e.g., Goodman & Clarke-Stewart, 1991; Rudy & Goodman, 1991; Saywitz, Goodman, Nicholas, & Moan, 1991), when effects are found, they are greater for younger children than for older children and adults (e.g., Baker-Ward, Gordon, Ornstein, Larus, & Clubb, 1993; Goodman, Aman, & Hirschman, 1987; King & Yuille, 1987; Ornstein, Larus, & Clubb, 1991). Several theorists have proposed that younger children are more susceptible to misinformation presented in suggestive questioning because they form weaker memory traces than older children (Brainerd et al., 1990; Ornstein et al., 1991). Weaker traces may be more vulnerable to the incorporation of postevent information in the form of suggestive questions (Ceci & Bruck, 1993). Another line of research by Foley (Foley & Johnson, 1985; Foley, Johnson, & Raye, 1983; Foley, Santini, & Sopaskis, 1993) indicated that young children have difficulty separating misinformation provided by suggestive questions from their original memories of events. Finally, younger children may be more vulnerable to social influences to conform to interviewers' suggestions (Ornstein et al., 1991).

Although nonverbal assessments of recall in infants do not include the kinds of social pressures found in interview studies, research using the mobile conjugate reinforcement paradigm has found evidence of misinformation effects in infant recall. Postevent misinformation introduced to infants immediately after training impaired their retention for the details of the original event and they incorporated the new information as if it were part of the original experience (Rovee-Collier, Borza, Adler, & Boller, 1993). In this study, infants were trained twice on one mobile and were briefly shown a new mobile at the end of the second training session. Twenty-four hours later, infants recognized the new mobile as if it were the original training mobile. In contrast, infants tested for recall of the original mobile did not remember it, despite the fact that they had spent two training sessions learning to respond to it. Interestingly, if the time lag between the end of training for the original mobile and presentation of the new mobile was extended to 24 hours, infants recognized both mobiles during testing (Rovee-Collier, Adler, & Borza, 1994). Rovee-Collier (1995) hypothesized that, when the memory was fresh and both representations were coactive in primary memory, new information could replace old information. However, when the representation had been stored in long-term memory, it was more resistant to the overwriting effects of new information. At this point, postevent information could be incorporated, but would not replace old information.

Can a reminder containing some original and some new information reinstate toddlers' memory? Results from our experiments using subset reenactment, subset modeling, and partial (object only) information indicated that toddlers' memories could be reinstated by exposure to partial event information. However, research showing that infants' and preschool children's memories could be overwritten by exposure to postevent information suggested that reminders containing new information might overwrite toddlers' original event memories or, at least, compete with recall of the original event. If overwriting or trace competition occurred, reinstatement effects would be very weak or nonexistent.

Toddlers in this study viewed video reminders of a past event that contained (a) all old information, (b) old object information but new action information, (c) new object information with old action information, or (d) all new information. Four groups of 18-month-olds were trained to perform novel activities during an initial training session, returned for a reminder session 10 weeks later, and were tested for recall 1 day later (see Table 10.4). The videos containing all old information were the same objects + actions videos used in the complete video condition in the previous study and showed an experimenter performing the same actions children had learned to perform on the same objects they had used. The new objects videos showed the experimenter performing the same actions using different objects, for example, pulling a string on a stuffed Alvin the Chipmunk toy instead of Mickey Mouse. In the new actions videos, the experimenter performed different actions on the same objects that children had used during training, for example, removing Mickey Mouse's shoes instead of pulling a string to make him talk. In the new objects + actions videos, the experimenter performed new actions on new objects, for example, taking the shoes off the stuffed Alvin toy. This condition controlled for the potential reinstatement effect of viewing a video involving actions on objects. Because the previous study had shown that children who viewed a video of an experimenter performing actions on objects 24 hours prior to testing, without prior training, performed no more actions than children who had been trained to perform the actions but had not been reminded, reminder only control conditions were not included in this experiment.

Results from this experiment are shown in Figure 10.9. Although there was some decrease, the difference in recall of children who viewed the new object video and that of children who viewed the video containing all old information (object + action) was not significant and children in the new object condition recalled more actions than children who viewed the video containing all new information. In contrast, the performance of children who saw the new action video was not significantly different from that of children who saw the video containing all new information. Thus, viewing a video containing new action information appeared to be equivalent to viewing entirely different actions, and reinstatement did not occur. In contrast, viewing a video with new objects, but keeping the actions constant, appeared to be equivalent to watching a video of the original experience, and reinstatement did occur.

Were children's memories in the new action condition overwritten by exposure to new information during the reminder session? To test for this possibility, an analysis was performed on the number of old

TABLE 10.4. Schedule of conditions, new information experiment

Condition	Training	Reminder Video	Test
Objects + actions	Day 1	Week 10, old objects + actions	Week 10
New objects	Day 1	Week 10, new objects + old actions	Week 10
New actions	Day 1	Week 10, old objects + new actions	Week 10
New objects + new actions	Day 1	Week 10, new objects + new actions	Week 10

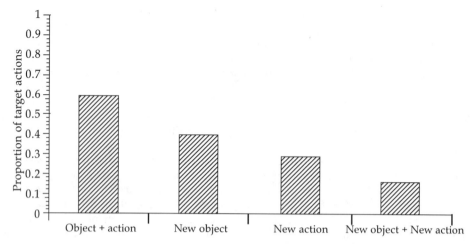

FIGURE 10.9. Effects of new information presented in video reminders (Sheffield, 1997, Experiment 2).

and new actions children performed in the test session. Children performed no more new actions (27%) than old actions (30%) and performance was low for both types of actions. This suggests that showing videos that included new actions neither reminded toddlers of their original experience nor overwrote the original memory.

Results from this experiment indicate that toddlers can be reminded of a past event by viewing a video that contains some consistent and some inconsistent information. However, all event information is not equal. Toddlers' memory for the original event was reinstated as long as the action information they viewed was consistent with their experience, but not if new actions were performed on the same objects. This finding is particularly interesting in light of the findings from the previous study indicating that reinstatement occurred even with the deletion of action information. We conclude that young children do not require that action information is specified in a reminder in order for reinstatement to occur; they can be reminded of past actions by viewing associated objects. However, viewing new action information interferes with children's recall of past actions. In this case, object information does not remind children of past actions because the new action information presented at the same time interferes with the retrieval of old action information.

☐ Implications, Unanswered Questions, and Future Directions

This line of research shows that toddlers' event memories can be reinstated by a variety of different kinds of reminders. By the age of 18 months, children can be reminded of a past experience by reenacting a subset of the activities they experienced or viewing someone else perform a subset of the activities, either in person or on a video. Reinstatement also can occur when information about objects is provided, but action information is excluded in a video. Finally, reinstatement can occur when children view the same actions performed on different objects. However, reinstatement does not occur when actions information is changed, indicating that some kinds of changes in information interfere with reinstatement, whereas others do not.

The ability to be reminded by exposure to different kinds of event information represents an important departure from the way in which reinstatement operates in infancy. If infants are trained on one exemplar, their memories will not be reinstated by partial reminders that do not contain functional information (Greco et al., 1990). In contrast, toddlers do not require action information in order for reinstatement to occur, but their recall is better when both object and action information is provided.

What developments contribute to children's increasing ability to use different kinds of retrieval cues in memory reinstatement? Children's developing ability to use both partial and nonmatching information to reinstate recall suggests that children's initial encoding of event information changes in the second year. One such change is that children may be encoding and storing more complete information about the individual components of events. An increase in encoding specificity would allow children to use various kinds of subset and partial event information to retrieve memories consisting of multiple components. In addition, toddlers may be able to appreciate that activities are composed of various components (e.g., action and object information), and that some components may be interchangeable under certain circumstances. Thus, toddlers may attend to and encode several aspects of an event simultaneously. This kind of encoding would permit their memory to be reinstated by partial information, or information that was slightly different from their original experience as long as critical event information was preserved.

Another important development is the ability to use increasingly more abstract representations as memory cues. Whereas 14- to 18-month-olds can be reminded of past events by physical reenactment, viewing enactment by a live model, or viewing a video enactment, their recall is not reinstated by exposure to photograph reminders. In contrast, photographs may be effective reminders for older children. Consistent with research by DeLoache (1989), these findings suggest that children's emerging understanding of the symbolic function of representations allows for more abstract representations to be used as memory cues. One implication of this emerging understanding is that, with age, children can be exposed to a wider array of reminder opportunities in real-world contexts.

However, our research also indicates that videos are effective in reminding children of past events at an earlier age than they are able to use video information to find hidden objects (Troseth & DeLoache, 1996). These findings indicate that children may understand the symbolic functions of various media in memory tasks before they are able to do so in object retrieval tasks. The nature of the task at hand may be a more important variable affecting children's ability to use symbolic representations than their prior experiences with the medium. Despite the fact that toddlers' experience with videos consists largely of viewing videos for entertainment, 18-month-olds had no difficulty in relating the video reminders presented in our laboratory to their own prior experiences.

Thus, several developments contribute to long-term memory improvement during the toddler years. First, children are able to retain event memories over longer periods of time (Howe & Courage, 1993; Rovee-Collier, 1995). Second, their initial encoding of components of events may be more specific so that they can be reminded of past events by exposure to various event components. Third, they may become better able to appreciate the symbolic relationships between representations and referents, allowing them to use reminders in more abstract representational formats to reinstate event memories. The ability to retain event memories for longer intervals, the decrease in the amount of information needed for reinstatement to occur, and the increase in the range of representational media that can provide reminder information all can contribute to long-term memory in young children by increasing the likelihood that children will encounter effective reminders in real-world contexts. Increased reminding opportunities results in more reinstatement which, in turn, can produce more enduring event memories.

Our research efforts also raise several unanswered questions about how reminders operate during the toddler years. One important issue concerns the long-term effects of various types of reminders. Physical reenactment and viewing a video simulation both were effective reminders for reinstating 18-month-olds' recall. However, the effects of the video reminder were no longer apparent 2 weeks later, while effects of reenactment were evident 6 months later. Additional research is needed on the long-term effects of various kinds of reminders, as well as on the effects of multiple reinstatements, to understand how reinstatement can contribute to very long-term event memory.

We also were surprised that we failed to find any evidence that returning to the context provided a form of reinstatement. Perhaps our laboratory playroom was not salient enough to reinstate toddlers' memories or toddlers may not have encoded the environment as an integrated component of the original experience. More research on the effects of context on toddlers' recall is necessary to address this issue.

Another surprising result is that we did not find overwriting effects after exposure to new postevent information as had been found in misinformation experiments with older children and adults. Further research is needed to investigate the conditions under which overwriting effects could occur in toddlers' recall. Reminders that include proportionally more of the original event information, while also including a small amount of new information, may be more effective in reminding children of past events than the videos used in Sheffield's (1997) study and also may provide a reminding context in which old and new information is conjoined in long-term memory after reinstatement.

Finally, research has examined children's ability to use different representational reminders in reinstatement (Agayoff et al., 1998). Preliminary findings have indicated that children are able to use scale models as reminders at 24 months, but are not able to use photographs as reminders until 30 months. These findings contrast with results of studies of children's use of photographs and scale models in search ranks (DeLoache & Burns, 1994). Perhaps this discrepancy occurs because using a representation as a reminder does not require understanding of the representational relationship between the representation and its referent. If this is the case, a three-dimensional scale model of the laboratory playroom and props may be a more effective reminder for young children, simply because it provides more information than a two-dimensional photograph. Alternatively, the development of representational competence may vary with the particular cognitive task at hand. Further investigation of children's use of symbolic representations in memory reinstatement will contribute to our understanding of the development of children's representational understanding.

□ References

Agayoff, J., Hudson, J. A., & Barot, H. (1998, April). *Young children's use of photographs and scale models as reminders.* Paper presented at the International Conference on Infant Studies, Atlanta, GA.

Bahrick, H. P. (1979). Maintenance of knowledge: Questions about memory we forgot to ask. *Journal of Experimental Psychology: General, 108,* 296–308.

Bahrick, H. P., Bahrick, L. E., Bahrick, A. S., & Bahrick, P. E. (1993). Maintenance of foreign language vocabulary and the spacing effect. *Psychological Science, 4,* 316–321.

Baker-Ward, L., Gordon, B. N., Ornstein, P. A., Larus, D. M., & Clubb, P. A. (1993). Young children's long-term retention of a pediatric examination. *Child Development, 64,* 1519–1533.

Barnat, S. B., Klein, P., & Meltzoff, A. N. (1996). Deferred imitation across changes in context and object: Memory and generalization in 14-month-old infants. *Infant Behavior and Development, 19,* 241–251.

Bauer, P. J. (1995). Recalling past events: From infancy to early childhood. *Annals of Child Development, 11,* 25–71.

Bauer, P. J., & Hertsgaard, L. A. (1993). Increasing steps in recall of events: Factors facilitating immediate and long-term memory in 13.5- and 16.5-month-old children. *Child Development, 64,* 1204–1223.

Bauer, P. J., Hertsgaard, L. A., & Dow, A. (1994). After 8 months have passed: Long-term recall of events by 1- to 2-year-old children. *Memory, 2,* 353–382.

Bauer, P. J., & Mandler, J. M. (1990). Remembering what happened next: Very young children's recall of event sequences. In R. Fivush & J. A. Hudson (Eds.), *Knowing and remembering in young children* (pp. 9–29). New York: Cambridge University Press.

Bauer, P. J., & Shore, C. M. (1987). Making a memorable event: Effects of familiarity and organization on young children's recall of action sequences. *Cognitive Development, 2,* 237–338.

Berkerian, D. A., & Bowers, J. M. (1983). Eyewitness testimony: Were we misled? *Journal of Experimental Psychology: Learning, Memory & Cognition, 9,* 139–145.

Boller, K., Rovee-Collier, C., Bovorsky, D., O'Conner, J., & Shyi, G. (1990). Developmental changes in the time-dependent nature of memory retrieval. *Developmental Psychology, 26,* 770–779.

Boyer, M., Barran, K. L., & Farrar, M. J. (1994). Three-year-olds remember a novel event from 20 months: Evidence for long-term memory in children? *Memory, 2,* 417–446.

Brainerd, C. J., Reyna, V. F., Howe, M. L., & Kingma, J. (1990). The development of forgetting and reminiscence. *Monographs of the Society for Research in Child Development, 55* (Serial No. 222).

Campbell, B. A., & Jaynes, J. (1966), Reinstatement. *Psychological Review, 73,* 478–480,

Ceci, S. J., & Bruck, R. (1993). Suggestibility of the child witness: A historical review and synthesis. *Psychological Bulletin, 113,* 403–439.

Davis, J., & Rovee-Collier, C. (1983). Alleviated forgetting of a learned contingency in 8-week-old infants. *Developmental Psychology, 19,* 353–365.

DeLoache, J. S. (1989). The development of representation in young children. In W. H. Reise (Ed.), *Advances in child development and behavior* (Vol. 22, pp. 1–39). New York: Academic Press.

DeLoache, J. S. (1990). Young children's understanding of scale models. In R. Fivush and J. A. Hudson (Eds.), *Knowing and remembering in young children* (pp. 94–126). New York: Cambridge University Press.

DeLoache, J. S., & Burns, N. M. (1994). Early understanding of the representational function of pictures. *Cognition, 52,* 83–110.

DeLoache, J. S., Pierroutsakos, S. L., & Troseth, G. L. (1996). The three R's of pictorial competence. *Annals of Child Development, 12,* 1–48.

Fivush, R. (1991). The social construction of personal narratives. *Merrill-Palmer Quarterly, 37,* 59–81.

Fivush, R., & Hamond, N. R. (1989). Time and again: Effects of repetition and retention interval on 2 year olds' event recall. *Journal of Experimental Child Psychology, 47,* 259–273.

Fivush, R., & Hamond, N. (1990). Autobiographical memory across the preschool years: Towards reconceptualizing childhood amnesia. In R. Fivush & J. A. Hudson (Eds.), *Knowing and remembering in young children* (pp. 223–248). New York: Cambridge University Press.

Foley, M. A., & Johnson, M. K. (1985). Confusions between memories for performed and imagined actions. *Child Development, 56,* 1145–1155.

Foley, M. A., Johnson, M. K., & Raye, C. L. (1983). Age-related confusion between memories for thoughts and memories for speech. *Child Development, 54,* 51–60.

Foley, M. A., Santini, C., & Sopaskis, M. (1993). Discriminating between memories: Evidence for children's spontaneous elaborations. *Journal of Experimental Child Psychology.*

Freud, S. (1966). New introductory lectures on psychoanalysis. In J. Strachey (Ed. & Trans.), *The standard edition of the complete psychological works of Sigmund Freud* (Vol. 15–16). London: Hogarth Press. (Original work published in 1933)

Goodman, G. S., Aman, C., & Hirschman, J. E. (1987). Child sexual and physical abuse: Children's testimony. In S. J. Ceci, M. P. Toglia, & D. R. Ross (Eds.), *Children's eyewitness memory* (pp. 1–23). New York: Springer-Verlag.

Goodman, G. S., & Clarke-Stewart, A. (1991). Suggestibility in children's testimony: Implications for child sexual abuse investigations. In J. L. Doris (Ed.), *The suggestibility of children's recollections: Implications for eyewitness testimony* (pp. 92–105). Washington, D.C.: American Psychological Association.

Greco, C., Hayne, H., & Rovee-Collier, C. (1990). The role of function, reminding, and variability in categorization by 3-month-old infants. *Journal of Experimental Psychology: Learning, Memory and Cognition, 16,* 617–633.

Harris, P. L., Kavenaugh, R. D., & Dowson, L. (1997). The depiction of imaginary transformations: Early comprehension of a symbolic function. *Cognitive Development, 12,* 1–19.

Howe, M. L. (1991). Misleading children's story recall: Forgetting and reminiscence of the facts. *Developmental Psychology, 27,* 746–462.

Howe, M. L., & Brainerd, C. J. (1989). Development of children's long-term retention. *Developmental Review, 9,* 301–340.

Howe, M. L., & Courage, M. L. (1993). On resolving the enigma of infantile amnesia. *Psychological Bulletin, 113,* 305–326.

Howe, M. L., Courage, M. L., & Bryant-Brown, L. (1993). Reinstating preschoolers' memories. *Developmental Psychology, 29,* 854–869.

Hudson, J. A. (1990). Constructive processes in children's event memory. *Developmental Psychology, 26,* 180–187.

Hudson, J. A. (1993). Reminiscing with mothers and others: Autobiographical memory in young two-year-olds. *Journal of Narrative and Life History, 3,* 1–32.

Hudson, J. A., & Fivush, R. (1991). As time goes by: Sixth graders remember a kindergarten experience. *Applied Cognitive Psychology, 5,* 347–360.

Hudson, J. A., & Sheffield, E. G. (1995). Extending young children's memory for events: Effects of reminders on 16- to 24-month-olds' long-term memory. In P. Bauer (Chair), *Stories of how we begin to remember: Developments in event memory and representation.* Symposium conducted at the meeting of the American Psychological Society, New York.

Hudson, J. A., & Sheffield, E. G. (1996, April). You must remember this: Effects of video and photograph reminders on 1- and 2-year olds' long-term memory. In H. Hayne (Chair), *Perspective on infant memory.* Symposium conducted at the International Conference on Infant Studies, Providence, RI.

Hudson, J. A., & Sheffield, E. G. (1998). Deja vu all over again: Effects of re-enactment on one-year-olds' event memory. *Child Development, 69,* 51–67.

King, M., & Yuille, J. (1987). Suggestibility and the child witness. In S. J. Ceci, M. Toglia, & D. Ross (Eds.), *Children's eyewitness memory* (pp. 24–35). New York: Springer-Verlag.

Lindsay, D. S. (1990). Misleading suggestions can impair eyewitnesses' ability to remember event details. *Journal of Experimental Psychology: Learning, Memory , and Cognition, 16,* 1007–1083.

Loftus, E. F. (1975). Leading questions and the eyewitness report. *Cognitive Psychology, 7,* 560–572.

Loftus, E. F., Miller, D. G., Burns, H. J. (1978). Semantic integration of verbal information into a visual memory, *Journal of Experimental Psychology: Human Learning and Memory, 4,* 19–31.

Mandler, J. M., & McDonough, L. (1995). Long-term recall of event sequences in infancy. *Journal of Experimental Child Psychology, 59,* 457–474.

McCabe, A., & Peterson, C. (1991). Getting the story: A longitudinal study of parental styles in eliciting narratives and developing narrative skill. In A. McCabe & C. Peterson (Eds.), *Developing narrative structure* (pp. 217–253). Hillsdale, NJ: Erlbaum.

McDonough, L., & Mandler, J. M. (1994). Very long-term recall in infants: Infantile amnesia reconsidered. *Memory, 2,* 339–352.

Meltzoff, A. N. (1988a). Infant imitation after a 1-week delay: Long-term memory for novel acts and multiple stimuli. *Developmental Psychology, 24,* 470–476.

Meltzoff, A. N. (1988a). Infant imitation and memory: Nine-month-olds in immediate and deferred tests. *Child Development, 59,* 217–225.

Meltzoff, A. N. (1995). What infant memory tells us about infantile amnesia: Long-term recall and deferred imitation. *Journal of Experimental Child Psychology, 59,* 497–515.

Myers, N. A., Clifton, R. K., & Clarkson, M. G. (1987). When they were very young: Almost-threes remember two years ago. *Infant Behavior and Development, 10,* 123–132.

Myers, N. A., Perris, E. E., & Speaker, C. J. (1994). Fifty months of memory: A longitudinal study in early childhood. *Memory, 2,* 383–416.

Nelson, K. (1990). Remembering, forgetting, and childhood amnesia. In R. Fivush & J. A. Hudson (Eds.), *Knowing and remembering in young children* (pp. 301–316). New York: Cambridge University Press.

Nelson, K. (1993). The psychological and social origins of autobiographic memory. *Psychological Science, 4,* 1–8.

Ornstein, P. A., Larus, D. M., & Clubb, P. A. (1991). Understanding children's testimony: Implications of research on the development of memory. *Annals of Child Development* (Vol. 8, pp. 145–176). London: Jessica Kingsley.

Pillemer, D., & White, S. (1989). Childhood events recalled by children and adults. In H. W. Reese (Ed.), *Advances in child development and behavior* (Vol. 22, pp. 297–340). New York: Academic Press.

Postman, L., & Knecht, K. (1983). Encoding variability and retention. *Journal of Verbal Learning and Verbal Behavior, 22,* 132–152.

Reese, E., Haden, C. A., & Fivush, R. (1993). Mother-child conversations about the past: Relationships of style and memory over time. *Cognitive Development, 8,* 403–430.

Rovee-Collier, C. (1995). Time windows in cognitive development. *Developmental Psychology, 31,* 147–169.

Rovee-Collier, C., Adler, S. A., & Borza, M. A. (1994). Substituting new details for old? Effects of delaying postevent memory on infant memory. *Memory and Cognition, 22,* 646–656.

Rovee-Collier, C., Borza, M. A., Adler, S. A., & Boller, K. (1993). Infants' eyewitness testimony: Effects of postevent information on a prior memory representation. *Memory and Cognition, 21,* 267–279.

Rovee-Collier, C., Griesler, P. C., & Earley, L. A. (1985). Contextual determinants of retrieval in three-month-old infants. *Learning and Motivation, 16,* 139–157.

Rovee-Collier, C. K., & Shyi, G. (1992). A functional and cognitive analysis of infant long-term retention. In H. L. Howe, C. J. Brainerd, & V. F. Reyna (Eds.), *Development of long-term retention* (pp. 3–55). New York: Springer-Verlag.

Rovee-Collier, C. K., Sullivan, M. W., Enright, J., Lucas, D., & Fagan, J. W. (1980). Reactivation of infant memory. *Science, 208,* 1159–1161.

Rudy, L., & Goodman, G. S. (1991). Effects of participation on children's reports: Implications for children's testimony. *Developmental Psychology, 27,* 527–538.

Ryder, M., Sheffield, E. G., & Hudson, J. A. (1995, March). *Effects of a video reminder on 18-month-olds' long-term event memory.* Paper presented at the meeting of the Society for Research in Child Development, Indianapolis, IN.

Saywitz, K., Goodman, G., Nicholas, G., & Moan, S. (1991). Children's memory for genital exam: Implications for child sexual abuse. *Journal of Consulting and Clinical Psychology, 59,* 682–691.

Schmidt, R. A., & Bjork, R. A. (1992). New conceptualizations of practice: Common principles in three paradigms suggest new concepts for training. *Psychological Science, 3,* 207–217.

Sheffield, E. G. (1997). *But I thought it was Mickey Mouse: Effects of postevent information on 18-month-olds' long-term memory for events.* Unpublished doctoral dissertation, Rutgers University, New Brunswick, NJ.

Sheffield, E. G., & Hudson, J. A. (1994). Reactivation of toddlers' event memories. *Memory, 2,* 447–465.

Spear, N. E., & Parsons, P. J. (1976). Analysis of a reactivation treatment: Ontogenetic determinants of alleviated forgetting. In D. L. Medin, W. A. Roberts, & R. T. Davis (Eds.), *Processes of animal memory* (pp. 135–165). Hillsdale, NJ: Erlbaum.

Timmons, C. R. (1994). Associative links between discrete memories in infancy. *Infant Behavior and Development, 17,* 427–439.

Troseth, G., & DeLoache, J. (1996, April). *The medium can obscure the message: Understanding the relation between video and reality.* Poster session presented at the International Conference on Infant Studies, Providence, RI.

Underwood, B. J., Kaplak, S. M., & Malmi, R. A. (1976). The spacing effect: Additions to the theoretical and empirical puzzles. *Memory and Cognition, 4,* 391–400.

White, S. H., & Pillemer, D. B. (1979). Childhood amnesia and the development of a socially accessible memory system. In J. F. Kihlstrom & F. J. Evans (Eds.), *Functional disorders of memory* (pp. 29–74). Hillsdale, NJ: Erlbaum.

Paola Uccelli
Lowry Hemphill
Barbara Alexander Pan
Catherine Snow

Telling Two Kinds of Stories: Sources of Narrative Skill

☐ Introduction

In this chapter, we explore how it is that children develop skill with two narrative genres, personal narratives and fantasy stories, and why it is that some children excel at one or the other, some at both, and some at neither. We will argue that individual differences in narrative skills emerge at least in part from children's early capacities to engage in discussions of a joint focus of attention (typically, a toy, picture, or ongoing activity) with adults. Discussions of a joint focus lead naturally into elaborations that introduce nonpresent elements; connections to the past, plans for the future, memories of related objects or events. While these discussions are not yet narrative, they provide the opportunity to deal with some of the complexities of narrative. Another activity during early mother-child conversation is fantasy play, a context for learning about plot, character, and other narrative elements. Children's opportunities for participation in discussions of joint focus and fantasy are quite variable, and this variability may explain individual differences in later skills. In the sections that follow, we first define and illustrate children's capacities with two prominent narrative genres at age 5. We then present data about children's participation at 20 and 30 months in talk about the nonpresent and about fantasy. Finally, we turn to exploring relationships between children's early experiences with social interaction and later narrative attainments.

Narratives are ubiquitous forms of oral discourse which represent shared cultural understandings of how experiences should be analyzed for purposes of communication (Berman & Slobin, 1994), how they should be represented in memory (Nelson, 1986), how the presentation of experiences should be structured and supplemented with interpretations (Labov & Waletsky, 1967), and how representations can be exploited as a mechanism for understanding the world (Bruner, 1986). Given their ubiquity in casual face to face conversation as well as in more institutional forms of discourse (lessons, medical histories, interviews), it is not surprising that children typically can tell stories by about age 5. These stories include ones based on their own lives, ones that are retellings of fictional stories, and ones that are made-up fantasy stories. The range of skill with which children as young as age 5 engage in these various narrative activities is enormous.

☐ Distinguishing Two Types of Narrative

During the preschool years, children typically have many opportunities to participate in diverse forms of narrative discourse. Two such common forms are *personal narratives*, in which children report their personal experiences in contexts like parent-child conversation and dinner table talk (Aukrust & Snow, 1998; Blum-Kulka, 1997; McCabe & Peterson, 1991; Ochs, Taylor, Rudolph, & Smith, 1992), and fictional or *fantasy stories*, produced within everyday pretend play, initially with the support of mothers or other older family members, but with increasing autonomy as children get older (Haight & Miller, 1993; Sachs, Goldman, & Chaille, 1984). Competent renditions of these two forms of narrative generally share some important features: a focus on a protagonist or protagonists and a set of related actions that these actors carry out, the reporting of supportive detail such as setting or character attributes, the use of a range of strategies for linking events together and tying actions to consequences, and the inclusion of the narrator's evaluative perspective on the reported events.

Despite these structural similarities, stories of personal experience and fantasy narratives may show different developmental courses within individual children and may draw on a somewhat separate set of pragmatic and linguistic competencies. To illustrate both the similarities in these narrative types and their different development within individuals, consider the following narratives produced by two 5-year-old girls:

Margaret: *Me and my sister went out for a snack.*

Interviewer: *Uh-huh.*

Margaret: *And Lizzie went over to the pond. And she saw a big snake. And she screamed.*

Interviewer: *Oh.*

Margaret: *And my mom didn't like it. So I went over and said, "What is it? Look, a big snake!" And then, we stayed for a little while. And then, well, we watched him go out of there.*

Interviewer: *Wow.*

Margaret: *Uh, we ate some snack. And then, we went home. And um, we missed swimming lesson.*

Margaret begins her narrative with a statement of the goal that initiated the events of the story ("Me and my sister went out for a snack") and goes on to report an elaborated series of temporally linked happenings: going to the pond, seeing the snake, screaming, reacting, investigating, and so forth. Her narrative centers on a linguistically marked climax or high point ("Look, a big snake!") and builds down from this high point with a final sequence of events which includes a practical consequence ("we missed swimming lesson"). Margaret's story makes use of a highly conventionalized narrative structure while situating its logic in the everyday world of snacks, sisters, moms, and swimming lessons. She uses orienting information to introduce the coparticipants, locate the story at a specific place, and situate the events in relation to each other with specific time markers ("then, for a little while"). These uses of orientation lend realism to the reported events and support Margaret's ability to tell the story to an audience unfamiliar with her experience. Finally, although Margaret's story is restrained in its depiction of a frightening experience, she uses a variety of types of evaluation ("screamed," "didn't like it") and the reported exclamation ("Look, a big snake!") to construct a stance in relation to the narrated events.

Margaret's personal narrative is much clearer and more fully developed than a story told by another 5-year-old, Sarah.

Sarah: *Well, I swim pretty good and I like to do banzai!*

Interviewer: *Yeah? What is that? I don't know anything about it.*

Sarah: *Well, first you have to run and then you dive in. And I was just practicing diving. And I also went off the lifeline in the deep end.*

Interviewer: *Wow.*

Sarah: *And I couldn't touch. But, I swam over to my mom.*

Sarah's story, like many personal narratives told at any age, begins in the context of general conversation; in this case, Sarah's explanation of how to do her favorite dive, the banzai. She marks her move from explanation into narration with a shift in tense ("I was just practicing diving"), but does not signal the initiation of the narrative with any other sort of framing. She reports a brief and unelaborated series of events (practicing, going off the lifeline, not touching, swimming to her mom), using simple *and* links to narrate the problematic situation and to set off the resolution. Her story is not situated in a particular place, and the central coparticipant, her mom, enters the story only at the end. Sarah's story includes minimal evaluation; only the interviewer's interjected "wow" and Sarah's factual negative ("I couldn't touch") elaborate on the stance she takes on the narrated events. However, while Sarah is not a particularly successful narrator of personal experience at age 5, she is much more skilled at fantasy narration:

Sarah: *And the dragon said to all the other animals, "I don't like you. I'm gonna eat you all up." But, they all hurried to get out of the way. But, the dragon said, "I don't care cause I can eat you all up with my huge, I can burn you all up with my huge big breath of fire"* (Makes blowing sounds). *He took a big breath and burned them all up.* (Points to dragon's mouth.) *That's fire.* (Noise from other room.) *That's just my sister.*

Interviewer: *Mm-hm. And then what happened?*

Sarah: *The trees fell over. But then, something said, "Turn!". That was the fire drill because there was a fire getting closer and closer and closer. And so they all had to get out of the way of the fire. Even the dragon. Then, they saw a fire. Cause it was burning up all the city. All everything. But, that wasn't the dragon's breath. It was a match. So they all had to get out of the way. But then, they tickled each other. I tickle my sister sometimes. She tickles me the most. I like to tickle her 'cause it makes her laugh.*

Interviewer: *What's happening in the story?*

Sarah: *The dragon had to go home. So he just went home to his cave. But then, they all got back in place. Where they should be. In the jungle, of course. So that's the end.*

With the help of an adult partner who provides a skeletal plot (a fierce dragon threatens a group of jungle animals), models narrative technique, and provides toy props to enact the fantasy, Sarah builds up a fantasy narrative. The focus of her storytelling is the elaboration of the compelling elements of the fantasy: the dragon's exaggerated threats, the menacing fire, and a satisfying resolution ("they all got back in place. Where they should be. In the jungle, of course"). In the fantasy narrative, Sarah is not burdened by the need to recapitulate a detailed real chronology of events; in fact, she can challenge typical story sequence with her side move into tickling. When reporting events would slow down the action or tax her skills of verbal improvisation, Sarah is able to enact events by manipulating the toys. Freed of most of the requirements of realism, and with the basic characters and plot collaboratively constructed with the adult partner, she can focus her verbal art on evaluation, producing expressions like the dragon's "huge big breath of fire" and the fire getting "closer and closer and closer."

Margaret, the skilled narrator of everyday happenings at age 5, is at a loss, however, when confronted with the demands of fantasy narrative:

Interviewer: *Boom-boom boom-boom. It was the dragon. Closer and closer he came. Splash!* (Places dragon in pond.) *And he sat right in the middle of the pond. Then, what happened?*

Margaret: *He blowed fire.*

Interviewer: *Yeah?* (Long pause.) *Make more story happen.*

Margaret: *Um.* (Long pause.) *I don't know.* (Touches animals.)

Interviewer: *Here, make the elephant and dragon talk with each other.* (Hands elephant and dragon to Margaret.)

Margaret: *I don't know what to say.*

Interviewer: *You can say anything.*

Margaret: *There's nothing to say.*

Interviewer: *What happened?*

Margaret: *The dragon blowed fire on him. The elephant.*

Interviewer: *Oh, then, what happened?*

Margaret: *The elephant told the other animals to hide.*

Interviewer: *Oh. And then, what happened?*

Margaret: *They hided down.* (Puts animals in between cushions on the couch.)

Interviewer: *Oh? Even the elephant hid?*

Margaret: *Uh-huh.* (Picks up dragon and turns it around.)

Interviewer: *What's happening?*

Margaret: *I don't know.* (Drops dragon.)

Interviewer: *What's happening?*

Margaret: *The dragon didn't find the other animals. The end.*

In this fantasy narrative, 5-year-old Margaret resists making up events, perhaps because she feels she lacks authority for reporting things which she has not witnessed or experienced. With repeated prompts from her adult partner, she produces a logical, but limited, chronology of events: the dragon blows fire, the animals hide, the dragon is unsuccessful in finding them. This sketchy narrative meets minimal expectations of a story, but lacks all the elements of elaboration that make Sarah's narrative a compelling fantasy. Margaret's skills at introducing characters and situating events in real places are irrelevant to the demands of fantasy narration and her focus on logical ordering misses the elements that make fantasy satisfying.

Thus, two very common types of oral narrative appear to impose different demands on young narrators. Both personal experience stories and fantasy stories require the ability to set off the narrative from the surrounding talk, to report and link happenings, and to evaluate their meaning to the story participants or to the narrator, but each genre imposes different emphases on these narrative tasks. Factual narratives require that the child select a set of happenings from the flow of past experiences that cohere and together form a satisfying story. Successful factual narratives also require that the child take account of what information is shared and unshared with the listener, and use appropriate introducing, referring, and elaborating strategies for unshared information. Successful fantasy narratives, on the other hand, require skill at plot improvisation and the ability to create tension and interest through vivid action, reported speech, and sound effects. Joint attention to a play figure or object can substitute for the more elaborate referential strategies that are characteristic of other forms of narration. These contrasting characteristics of relatively mature, 5-year-old factual and fantasy narratives reflect both the different courses of development of these two genres in the preschool years and the possibly separate contributions of different types of early communicative experience to their success.

What kinds of communicative experiences in the first 3 years of life might one expect to be relevant to the narrative skills that children are developing at age 5? In the next section, we describe the social interactionist framework within which we investigated possible connections between children's conversational and narrative skills.

Theoretical Framework

Our ideas are based on a conception of language acquisition as a process in which communication is always central (Ninio & Snow, 1996). Children clearly need to learn a great deal about the formal linguistic system and about conventional modes of expression in order to speak grammatically and correctly; such learning is impressive. Nonetheless, to think of language acquisition as consisting entirely, or even primarily, of learning about the formal, conventionalized aspects of the language system omits the aspect of language development most crucial to understanding transitions from earlier to more sophisticated stages— the child's motive to communicate, and capacity to respond to an ever widening array of communicative challenges.

The earliest uses of conventional language can be analyzed as attempts to participate in social interaction; the words children produce at this stage typically are not true lexical items but, rather, somewhat marginal linguistic forms that constitute turns in games (e.g., peekaboo) or formated responses to adult utterances ("What does the doggie say?") (Ninio, 1993). Parents recruit these semilinguistic forms for use in joint attention episodes (occasions when parents and children achieve shared attention to a real object, a toy, or a pictured object) and treat them as answers to questions about the joint focus of attention (Adult: "What's that?" Child: "Woof-woof."). Subsequently, of course, children start to learn real, conventional words in these exchanges, and eventually they are able to initiate such exchanges themselves by naming objects to establish a joint focus of attention, or by asking "What's that?"

These early naming exchanges constitute the beginning of what, within the analytic system of communicative intents proposed by Ninio and Wheeler (1984/1986), can be classified as discussions. Although these earliest discussions are limited to the here and now, they soon are expanded to incorporate information about the object of joint attention that goes beyond what is visible. For example, often when children are still in the one-word stage, mothers name animals pictured in books and then model or request information about what sounds the animals make, where they typically live, or what their babies are called. Even later, joint attentional episodes trigger discussion of jointly remembered past events; this emergence of talk about objects, attributes, or events not observable in the here and now ("nonpresent talk") constitutes the first occurrence of narrative-like structures in the talk of young children.

While children typically can participate in discussions of information somewhat displaced from the here and now with parental help between the ages of 12 and 24 months, their ability to become full conversational partners in such exchanges depends on their developing new capacities in the domain of communication. Beyond talking simply to participate socially, they discover that talk also provides the opportunity to exchange information—to request and obtain new information verbally. Though we think of this as the basic function of language, it is, in fact, one which children are able to display only after some months of using language socially. Discussion based on information exchange is, we argue, a prerequisite to the emergence of protonarrative discourse.

A further, enormous achievement in young children's communicative systems is represented by their emergent ability to take the listener's perspective. Young children provide information, but they do so in ways that are poorly adapted to the needs of the listener. With growing cognitive and social sophistication, children become more adept at predicting what information listeners need, at responding to listeners' cues, and at anticipating and taking the listener's perspective. This capacity to take the listener's perspective becomes crucial to providing satisfactory narratives, which mark explicitly for the listener how one is expected to respond to the information being provided.

Paralleling the development of skills required for exchanging information about the real world of the here and now, as well as about objects and events removed in time and space, are children's growing abilities to engage in conversation about fantasy worlds. While children can make moves into the symbolic, nonrepresentational, or fantasy domain by about the time of the first word (e.g., pushing a toy car along the table while saying "brm-brm"), organized fantasy play segments typically do not emerge until after the second birthday. It seems likely that opportunities to participate in fantasy talk interactions, in contexts where the development of the fantasy is supported by an adult, will lead to greater skill in the autonomous production of fantasy talk.

Other work also has viewed children's narratives as emerging from social (Bruner, 1986) or conversational (Eisenberg, 1985) experiences. McCabe and Peterson (1991), for example, have documented how parental questions shape children's storytelling styles, and work demonstrating cultural differences in narrative organization and structure (Heath, 1983; McCabe, 1996; Michaels, 1981) makes clear the powerful effects different interactional patterns and narrative models have on children's narratives. To these compelling points, we would add our own view that independent narrative skill depends on previous social and cognitive achievements, in particular, achievements in the child's ability to engage in true (i.e., information exchanging) conversation about topics in the here and now, in the real but nonpresent world, and in fantasy worlds. In the study reported here, we investigated whether participation in discussions of the nonpresent and participation in fantasy talk at ages 20 and 32 months is related to children's skill at producing more autonomous narratives at age 5. Specifically, we hypothesized that early experience talking about the nonpresent would allow children to practice skills necessary to later produce personal narratives, and that a 2-year-old's experience engaging in fantasy talk with an adult would build skills necessary for telling autonomous fantasy narratives at age 5.

☐ The Study

The children and their parents described in this chapter are families from the New England sample (Pan, Imbens-Bailey, Winner, & Snow, 1996; Snow, Pan, Imbens-Bailey, & Herman, 1996) for whom longitudinal data were available at child ages 20 months, 32 months, and 5 years. There were 32 children (18 girls, 14 boys) for whom data were available at all three time points. Eighteen were firstborn children. Families were English speaking, primarily middle-class families, with Hollingshead's Four Factor Index of Social Status (Hollingshead, 1975) scores ranging from 33 to 66 (mean = 55.34, SD = 10.29). Mean maternal age was 30.9 years.

At the 20- and 32-month observations, parent-child dyads were videotaped interacting in a laboratory playroom using age-appropriate toys and materials provided by the investigators. At age 5, children were asked to perform a number of tasks, including telling a personal narrative and telling a fantasy narrative using small toys and props. Resulting language samples at each observation were transcribed using the Child Language Data Exchange System (MacWhinney, 1991; MacWhinney & Snow, 1985, 1990). Children's receptive and expressive vocabularies were measured at age 20 months using an early form of the MacArthur Communicative Development Inventories (CDI), a maternal checklist (Dale, Bates, Reznick, & Morisset, 1989). Children's morphosyntactic skills at 32 months were measured using mean length of utterance (MLU; Brown, 1973) and the Index of Productive Syntax (IPSyn), a measure of emergent morphosyntax

(Scarborough, 1990). Summary statistics on these lexical and morphosyntactic measures for the present sample are presented in Table 11.1.

Nonpresent and Fantasy Talk at Ages 20 and 32 Months

In keeping with our view that traditional measures of child language (e.g., MLU) are an incomplete reflection of children's developing communicative skills, we also examined children's expression of communicative intent. Parent–child talk at child ages 20 and 32 months was segmented into communicative acts, and each act was coded using the Inventory of Communicative Acts–Abridged (INCA-A), a shortened and modified version of the system developed by Ninio and Wheeler (1984/1986) for coding the dyadic interaction of mothers and young children (see Ninio, Snow, Pan, & Rollins, 1994; Snow et al., 1996, for fuller discussions of the coding scheme). In this system, communicative intent is identified and coded at two different levels. The first is the level of interpersonally implicitly agreed-on social interchange constructed across one or more rounds of talk. In the present study, social interchange categories of interest include discussions of nonpresent people and objects; discussions of nonobservable thoughts, feelings, likes and dislikes; discussions of recent events and accomplishments; and discussions of attributes or events related to an object in the here and now ("related-to-present talk"). The second level at which communicative acts were coded is the specific speech act (e.g., whether the utterance serves the purpose of requesting, thanking, or questioning). The combination of these two levels (i.e., the number of social interchange-speech act types produced) provides one measure of children's pragmatic sophistication. We refer to this measure as pragmatic flexibility (Snow et al., 1996). Summary statistics for these pragmatic measures are also provided in Table 11.1.

The following examples illustrate the types of nonpresent talk observed in parent–child dyads at 20 and 32 months: Margaret and her mother talk about nonpresent people and objects; Elizabeth and her mother talk about an individual's nonobservable thoughts and feelings (in this case, Elizabeth's fondness for ice cream); and Sarah and her mother talk about events or accomplishments that have just occurred, but are not ongoing, and thus are no longer observable.

Margaret (32 months)

Margaret: *Where's that lady?* (Investigator has left room.)

Mother: *I don't know where she went.*

Elizabeth (20 months)

Mother: *Mmm, is that good?* (Points to picture of ice cream.) *You like that?*

TABLE 11.1. Summary statistics for the sample (*n* = 32)

	Mean (*SD*)	Range
Measures of morphosyntax (32 months)		
MLU	2.68 (.72)	1.5–4.9
IPSyn	53.29 (11.33)	36–78
Measure of vocabulary (20 months)		
CDI-Production	221.12 (164.21)	5–602
Measures of pragmatics		
Nonpresent talk (20 months)	.06 (.05)	0–.19
Fantasy talk (32 months)	.15 (.10)	.01–.34
Pragmatic flexibility (20 months)	13.84 (4.21)	4–23
Measures of narrative skill (5 years)		
PN	7.52 (4.38)	0–18.5
FAN	12.25 (6.42)	0–25
Fantasy: Genre specificity	2.94 (1.81)	0–8
Fantasy: Character voice	2.19 (1.45)	0–6

Note. MLU = mean length of utterance; IPSyn = Index of Productive Syntax; CDI = MacArthur Communicative Development Inventory; PN = personal narrative; FAN = fantasy narrative.

Elizabeth: *Mmm.* (Nods.)

Mother: *Mmm, that's ice cream, huh?*

Elizabeth: *I do like.* (Points to picture of ice cream.)

Sarah (32 months)

Sarah: *I can carry it.* (Lifts box and carries it over to table.)

Sarah: *I carried it.*

Mother: *You did. You put it right up.*

Sarah: *Yeah.*

Children's engagement in nonpresent talk is often triggered by joint attentional episodes in which the conversation moves beyond the object of joint attention to comment on nonobservable attributes of the object, or to compare the observable object to a nonobservable one, as in the following exchange:

Elizabeth (20 months)

Mother: *What's that?* (Points to picture in book.)

Elizabeth: *Yeah.* (Points to same picture.)

Mother: *Do we have one of those?* (Elizabeth nods.)

Mother: *A gate, huh?* (Mother and Elizabeth both nod.)

Mother: *We've got one of those for Sheba and you, huh?*

Elizabeth: *Yeah.*

As these examples illustrate, talk about the nonpresent between adults and very young children tends to be adult-initiated and rather brief. Children generally assume a minimal conversational role, and often rely heavily on nonverbal means to bolster their participation, as Elizabeth did in "talking" about the gate. Even very young children, however, are able to take a more active role when the topic is animal sounds:

Sarah (20 months)

Mother: *Oh, pigs!* (Referring to picture in book.) *What do the pigs say?*

Sarah: *Eek-eek.*

Mother: *Well, close.*

Mother: *He says "oink-oink. Oink-oink."*

Sarah: *Oink.*

Despite their rather routinized character, these interchanges tend to be interspersed with talk about the here and now in ways that require the child to repeatedly shift frames of reference, as in this conversation in which 20-month-old Sarah and her mother discuss a flattened rubber duck:

(Sarah blows on rubber duck, then shows her mother.)

Mother: *That's right, that's what we do with a beach ball, isn't it? We blow it up.*

(Sarah fiddles with duck.)

Mother: *Oh, it came out by itself now.* (Mother squeezes the duck.) *Peep-peep-peep-peep-peep. Sounds a little bit like a chick, doesn't it? Peep-peep-peep-peep-peep.*

Such shifts from the here and now to nonpresent frames of reference may preview shifts in genre (e.g., between personal narration and fantasy narration) as well as shifts in narrative role that are demonstrated by 4- and 5-year-olds. In the earlier excerpt from Sarah's jungle story, for example, she shifts from direct narration ("The trees fell over") to reported speech ("But then, something said, 'Turn!'") to a side explanation ("That was the fire drill because . . .").

   In addition to talk about real but nonpresent objects and talk about nonobservable attributes of referents, beginning at about age 2, children engage in talk about the fantasy world. While a child's active imagination can fashion fantasy talk around almost any object, some objects, materials, and contexts seem to be particularly inspirational in this regard. For that reason, it is difficult to estimate the frequency with which children engage in fantasy talk, either in private, with peers, or with adults. What is clear is that there are considerable individual differences in the conversational initiative and elaboration undertaken by children in these exchanges. Margaret, who we saw struggling to produce a fantasy narrative autonomously at age 5, also produced rather sparse fantasy talk at 32 months, even with considerable scaffolding by her mother:

Mother: *Who's this* [toy person]?

Margaret: *Annie.*

Mother: *That's Annie?*

Margaret: *That should be . . .*

Mother: *Who's that?* (Points to toy.)

Margaret: *Um . . . Annie.*

Mother: *That's Annie.*

Margaret: *That's a mother.*

Mother: *Mm-hm!*

Margaret: *This is Mommy!* (Places a toy next to the other toys on the floor.)

Mother: *Oh.*

Mother: *What a nice family.*

Mother: *Now, what are they going to do?*

Margaret: [unintelligible] *Play music?*

Thirty-two-month old Sarah, on the other hand, already takes an active role in assigning roles and actions to characters in a similar fantasy context:

Sarah: *There's Papa.* (Picks up doll)

Mother: *Yep, there's a papa.*

Sarah: [unintelligible] *He can get in* [the car]. (Puts doll in car.) *He can drive.*

Mother: *Is he going to drive?*

Mother: *Where's he going to go?*

Sarah: *Go in hospital.*

Mother: *The hospital? Why's he going to the hospital?*

Sarah: *He's hurt.*

Mother: *He's hurt? Why is he hurt?*

Sarah: *He needs cast.*

Mother: *He needs a cast like papa does?* (Sarah nods slightly.)

Sarah: [unintelligible] *Papa has got cast.*

The considerable skill at autonomous fantasy narration demonstrated by Sarah at age 5 may, in part, reflect her early participation in this type of adult-scaffolded fantasy world discussion. This episode begins with Sarah identifying the main character (Papa) and proposing an appropriate action for him. With her mother's help, these basic ingredients are elaborated with information about goals and explanations (going to the hospital for a cast because he's hurt). Finally, Sarah's mother ties the negotiation of fantasy world back to Sarah's real experience, validating real-world experience as appropriate material for construction of fantasy narratives.

Conversations about the nonpresent and about fantasy worlds at ages 20 and 32 months are relatively rare events in parent-child discourse, and are not engaged in by all dyads. Although 94% of dyads in this sample engaged in some nonpresent talk at 20 months, most of this talk was what we have referred to as related to present; that is, talk about nonobservable attributes of observable objects, or talk about nonpresent events tied to a present object or event. Related-to-present talk accounts for 5% of all talk at this age, while discussions of nonpresent people, objects, and events not tied to the here and now were quite rare (each accounting for less than 1% of all talk). At 32 months, nonpresent talk, though not more frequent overall, had begun to free itself from ties to the immediate context, with related-to-present talk accounting for only 2% of all talk, and discussions of objects and event not tied to an observable referent accounting for 1% to 2%. Provided with toys to stimulate fantasy dialogue and discussion (i.e., puppets and a playhouse), nearly all the 32-month-old children and their mothers engaged in brief episodes of fantasy talk. However, such talk accounted for an average of less than 2% of all talk at this age, and children rarely produced initiatory moves in these conversations. Over the subsequent 2½ years, children made considerable strides in their ability to discuss nonpresent objects, events, and people, as well as their skills in initiating and participating in fantasy dialogue and discussion, as we shall see below when we examine children's production of two types of narrative genres: personal narratives and fantasy narratives.

Personal Narratives at Age 5

At age 5, children in the New England sample were videotaped participating in a range of discourse tasks (Hemphill, Feldman, Camp, & Griffin, 1994), including telling a personal narrative to an experimenter about a recent experience and constructing a fantasy play narrative with the experimenter using small toy props.

In the personal narratives they recounted, children turned real experiences into narrative accounts of events. Five-year-olds in this sample related an average of five events in their narratives (range: 0–13), though coherent and successful narratives were sometimes produced with as few as three. Personal narratives, however, involve not only the structuring of events that advance the plot, but also require the child to provide relevant background information about space, time, and actors, and to express his or her stance toward the narrated events through the use of evaluative devices. In this study, narratives were coded for the presence or absence of three features: structure, orientation, and evaluation. Table 11.2 displays the sets of structural, orienting, and evaluative features found in these narratives and the proportion of children who included them in the narration of their personal experiences.

TABLE 11.2. Types of personal narrative elements and proportion of children producing each at age 5

Narrative Element	Example	Proportion of Children Producing Element at Age 5
Structure		
Opening	"It all started when . . . "	.09
High point	"And Sarah Clark's mother got squirted with the firehose, but she had the equipment on and *she didn't even get wet!*"	.22
Closing	"And that's it."	.19
Orientation		
Introduction of characters	"She let *Julie who is my friend* and me go."	.25
Location of action in a physical setting	"We went down *to the Cape.*"	.31
Location of action in a specific time	"*That night* I put it under my pillow."	.25
Evaluation		
Intensifiers and delimiters	"We watched fireworks *really* late."	.53
Adjectives	"It was a *pretty* costume."	.47
Defeats of expectations	"*I didn't go* to the real top of the mountain,"	.38
Causality	"It wasn't fun *because* there were too many mosquitos."	.31
Intentions and purposes	"My mother and father were *trying* to get me to bed."	.31
Compulsions	"We *had to* sing a song."	.25
Reported speech	"I said, 'yes.'"	.19
Internal states	"I *believed* her."	.19
Physical states	"It felt cold."	.16
Repetition for effect	"She did it *again and again and again.*"	.13
Hypothetical situations	"There was no gate so *she could have fallen* right down the stairs."	.13
Comparisons	"I'm *smarter than* my mother and my father."	.09

In the following paragraphs, we describe the broad range of variation present in this group of children by classifying their performances into better, average, and poor productions of personal experiences.

The better narrators at 5 years of age produced conventional narratives that followed a sequential structure and were organized around a high point or climax. These narratives clearly convey the narrator's perspective through the use of sophisticated evaluative devices. Margaret's narrative, presented above, is one example of an excellent performance. Another example is this narrative told by Elizabeth at 5 years:

Elizabeth: *Once upon a time I was in a shoe store and I had my pony with me. And I put him down. And then, my mummy said, "Do you want to buy some shoes?" And I said, "Yes." And then, I left him there for an hour. And then, I came back to get him and he was gone.*

Interviewer: *Oh no.*

Elizabeth: *We had to search all over the store, we couldn't find him.*

Interviewer: *Oh no.*

Elizabeth: *A little girl must have took him home.*

Interviewer: *Ohhh. So what happened?*

Elizabeth: *My nanna bought me a new one.*

Interviewer: *Oh, that's good.*

Elizabeth: *He had twinkle eyes.*

Elizabeth produces a highly conventional narrative: She introduces her anecdote with the appropriate background information and, only after the setting is clear for the listener, does she start narrating the sequence of events that lead to the high point (the disappearance of the pony). At this point, she conveys the frustration elicited by the lost toy through a concentration of evaluative elements ("We had to search all over the store, we couldn't find him") and, finally, closes the narrative with a resolution to the conflict described.

Narratives such as these by Margaret and Elizabeth combine both orientation, principally with reference to physical setting ("I was in a shoe store") and sophisticated evaluation, which includes reported speech, hypothetical situations ("A little girl must have took him home"), internal states ("Do you want to buy some shoes?"), and repetition for effect. Other evaluative elements more commonly used at this age, such as adjectives, defeats of expectations ("we couldn't find him"), intensifiers and delimiters ("*all over* the store"), compulsions ("We *had to* search") and intentions ("to get him") also were frequent in these narratives. These narrators had mastered a conventional pattern for telling personal anecdotes that was structured around a high point, often included conventional openers ("Once upon a time") and closings, and that skillfully integrated both orientation information and different types of evaluation.

The average performances at age 5 can be characterized as displaying one of the following two patterns:

1. a nonconventional narrative that reports a list of events with little or no evaluation; or
2. a nonconventional narrative that conveys the events as experienced by the narrator and, thus, is highly evaluated.

Interestingly, and in line with previous research on gender differences in storytelling (Peterson & McCabe, 1983), there was a tendency for boys to fall in the first category and for girls to produce narratives of the second type. The following two examples illustrate these patterns:

John (5 years)

Interviewer: *Your mom told me that something very special just happened to your sister, what happened?*

John: *She had a graduation.*

Interviewer: *Did you go?*

John: *It was at this house.*

Interviewer: *Was it fun?*

John: *Yeah.*

Interviewer: *Tell me about it.*

John: *Well, all my cousins were there, and moms and dads were there, and I had lots of fun. And I went down and played some pool ball.*

Interviewer: *Yeah?*

John: *Yep. I went up and played up in the school yard.*

Interviewer: *You did?*

John: *Yep. And we had cake and lots of junk.*

Corinna (5 years)

Interviewer: *You went a long way away to visit your grandparents.*

Corinna: *Yeah. And I went swimming. And they didn't put the dock out yet, so I didn't go too far, because I didn't know like where it was over my head and stuff like that.*

Interviewer: *Mm-hm.*

Corinna: *And so I didn't go too far. But I just swam back. And I did it slowly when I got up to here.* (Corinna points to midsection.)

Interviewer: *Uh-huh.*

Corinna: *Because I didn't want to go over my head by mistake. Because the dock wasn't there.*

Neither of these narratives makes use of conventional narrative structure (e.g., the reporting of orientative information about setting and participants preceding an event that initiates a discrete sequence of actions) nor are they organized around a high point or climax, as Elizabeth's was. Nevertheless, some evaluative elements, especially intensifiers and delimiters (John: "I had *lots of* fun" and Corinna: "I *just* swam back") and compulsions (e.g., "had to") frequently were found in these performances. Despite these common features, there were differences in what narrators foregrounded in their texts. Narrators of reportorial accounts focused on conveying a list of events and occasionally, as John's narrative shows, added some orientation ("It was at this house." "All my cousins were there"). Narrators of evaluated narratives, like Corinna, instead offered a concentration of evaluative devices, such as causality ("Because the dock wasn't there"), defeats of expectations ("I didn't go too far"), internal states ("I didn't know") and intentions or purposes ("I didn't want to go over my head"), with the primary focus on conveying not only the events but also the narrator's interpretation of the experience.

Poor narrators at age 5 conveyed unclear narratives with little evaluation and either a nonsequential structure or an obscure progression of events (as in Sarah's example). Even though these children remained on topic and within the boundaries of one anecdote, their narratives often were mixed with off-narrative talk. These least skilled narrators did not introduce actors nor offer general information to situate the action. The only evaluative elements, if any, present in their narratives were adjectives, physical states, intensifiers, and delimiters. Andrew at age 5 illustrates this case:

Interviewer: *Can you tell me about your chameleon?*

Andrew: *I got it for my birthday. And Greeney and Heidi died.*

Interviewer: *Yeah.*

Andrew: *So I got Spring and Cupcake left.*

Interviewer: *So you got more than one chameleon?*

Andrew: *Yeah. See when I had Heidi, um, I had Spring. When Heidi died, I still had Spring. When Greeney died, I still had Heidi. And the life span is about 10 days.*

Interviewer: *Their life span is 10 days?*

Andrew: *I remember that my chameleons have been living for a long time.* (Shouting into microphone.)

Fantasy Narratives at Age 5

The fantasy narrative task required children to enter the terrain of pretense and symbolic talk. With the support of toys and a provided beginning for the plot, children had to construct a coherent story using talk in combination with enactment and sound effects. Because an adult partner also participated in this fantasy task, children could narrate relatively autonomously, or they could rely on their more competent partner to introduce and reintroduce play characters and to prompt for important structural and evaluative information.

The better fantasy storytellers among our 5-year-olds used conventional narrative structure to frame and organize their fantasy performances. Structural elements present in the most successful fantasy narratives included orienting information about an imaginary setting, a buildup of events toward a narrative climax or high point, a resolution of the themes developed in the story (e.g., conflict between the animal participants), and a conventionalized closing (e.g., "Everyone lived happily ever after"). The best storytellers elaborated on the conflict theme introduced by their adult partner, weaving in subplots around themes like a search for a magic mushroom. They made abundant use of a variety of types of evaluation, including, in particular, the reporting of character intentions ("then he . . . tried to attack him") and internal states ("the mother saw the dragon and was terrified").

The most skilled fantasy storytellers built up a fully realized story world (Wolf & Polanyi, 1990), achieving genre specificity through the explicit introduction of referents ("the lion saw the dragon sitting right *in the middle of the pond*"), rather than the use of deictic expressions ("sitting right *there*"), through the use of character delineation ("there was a bird that sang a sweet song"), and often through a focus on a particular story protagonist, around whose plans, actions, and reactions the story events were developed. They also represented character voice, displaying the perspectives of story characters through reported speech ("and then when the little lion heard that, she said, 'Here I am, mother'"), as well as through direct speech ("They went in a fight. 'Arrrh!'"). These narrators used an anchor tense, typically the past tense, to hold together the diverse types of talk in the narrative, and employed strategies such as tense shifts and full nominal reintroduction of story characters to mark return to narration after stretches of nonnarrative talk. For example in Sarah's fantasy narrative, after she says, "So they all had to get out of the way. But then, they tickled each other," she digresses from the narrative to remark, "I tickle my sister sometimes. She tickles me the most. I like to tickle her 'cause it makes her laugh." Then, she reintroduces the story character with the dragon to mark return to the narrative, "The dragon had to go home. So he just went home to his cave." Table 11.3 summarizes these features of successful fantasy narratives and the proportion of the children who produced each feature at age 5.

Less successful fantasy narrators at age 5 relied on their adult partner to provide the basic elements of story structure: information about the story setting, participants, and plot (Adult: "Annie, what do all the animals do?" Child: "The lion can roar"). They also relied on the adult partner to introduce story characters with full noun phrases, making ambiguous reference to the characters themselves with pronouns ("maybe he could push him"). The least successful fantasy storytellers relied on physical enactment, rather than narrative reporting, to represent events, used an undifferentiated present tense for both narrative and nonnarrative talk ("Pretend, pretend they're saying something. Now all the lions, now all the animals say bad things to them. You see?"), and often used inconsistent tense shifts. Rather than using reported speech, less successful narrators often held up an animal to indicate that a story character was talking and, instead of using verbal strategies of story character reidentification, simply turned back to the toy figures after engaging in side conversation with the adult partner. Narrative high points and plot resolutions generally were absent from these children's narratives. Most notably, the less successful narrators provided minimal evaluation of the story, reporting few character intentions or internal states.

☐ Predictive Relationships Between Early Parent-Child Talk and Later Narrative Skill

We have seen the wide range that characterizes children's likelihood of engaging in talk about the nonpresent and fantasy talk during the first 3 years of life. A similarly wide range of accomplishment is observable in children's capacities to produce narratives, whether personal or fantasy, at age 5. To summarize the variation displayed by children in each narrative task, two composite variables were formed: a personal narrative composite score (PN) representing the sum of scores for structure, orientation, and evaluation; and a fantasy narrative composite score (FAN), the sum of scores for structure, evaluation, genre specificity, and character voice. Table 11.1 shows the means and ranges for our group of children on the PN and FAN composite scores. In the assessments of relationships with early conversational participation, these composite scores are used as outcome measures.

We undertook this study to investigate whether participation in discussions of the nonpresent and of fantasy at the earlier ages was related to children's skill in producing autonomous narratives, both personal and fantasy, later. In particular, we hypothesized that experience talking about the nonpresent constitutes opportunities to practice the language skills needed for personal narrative, and that experience engaging in fantasy talk with an adult builds skills needed to produce fantasy narratives. Alterna-

TABLE 11.3. Types of fantasy narrative elements and proportion of children producing each at age 5

Narrative Element	Example	Proportion of Children Producing Element at Age 5
Structure		
Setting	"There was a jungle and, in the jungle, they have dark trees and rocks."	.13
High point	"And he went, 'grr grr,' and he knocked over all the trees cause he got so mad, and he knocked over this, and he knocked over everything!"	.41
Resolution	"Then he kills the dragon and she kills the elephant and they live happily ever after."	.22
Closing	"The end."	.47
Genre Specificity		
Character delineation	"The father always gets mad at the little boy."	.44
Protagonist	"Then, he's [the dragon] gonna eat the elephant. Now, he's gonna eat him. Now, he's gonna throw him again. Now, him. Now, he's gonna throw the whole jungle and throw the tree."	.09
No deixis	"*The elephant* called *the lioness* on *the telephone*."	.25
Character Voice		
Direct speech	"Get off me!"	.72
Reported speech	"And the duck said, 'Stop it!'"	.13
Evaluation		
Intensifiers and delimiters	"The elephant *almost* stepped on the baby."	.41
Defeats of expectations	"The little one tried, but *he couldn't do such a big jump*."	.38
Intentions and purposes	"The dragon roared and *tried to get him*."	.41
Internal states	"The bird got *mad* at the lion."	.38
Repetition for effect	"It began to fire *more and more*."	.13
Complex temporal markers	"*Sometime, a lot later*, the elephant died."	.31

tively, of course, participation in both of these forms of early talk might support the development of narrative competence in either genre, as might early experience with more diverse forms of conversational engagement represented in our pragmatic flexibility measure.

While we are testing a set of precursors that would reflect social support for later narrative skills, another possibility is that various indexes of the child's own language competence at earlier and later ages are all highly intercorrelated, each reflecting general underlying language competence. To test this alternative explanation, we first considered the simple correlations among the variables of interest. Table 11.4 shows the results of this correlational analysis. Because somewhat different narrative tendencies were identified for boys and girls, gender also is included.

Results showed that neither morphosyntactic skill (as measured by MLU and IPSyn) nor vocabulary skill (as measured by the CDI) at 20 and 32 months was associated with narrative performance at 5 years. Thus, these measures of general language ability do not appear to help explain variability in children's later narrative development. Most of the pragmatic measures, however, were positively correlated with PN, FAN or both and, thus, invited us to further explore their predictive power. Because gender was associated with FAN, we also decided to explore its effect more closely.

Personal Narrative

To examine our more specific hypothesis that experience with past event talk would predict later skill at telling narratives of personal experience, and our more general hypotheses, that early experience with

TABLE 11.4. Correlations between narrative outcome measures and potential predictor measures

	PN	FAN	Fantasy (Genre Specificity)	Fantasy (Character Voice)
MLU				
(32 months)	−.01	.04	.05	−.06
IPSyn				
(32 months)	.05	.13	.24	.02
CDI-Production				
(20 months)	.05	.17	.28	.21
Nonpresent talk				
(20 months)	.48**	.36*	.28	.24
Fantasy talk				
(32 months)	.03	.14	.41*	.31~
Pragmatic flexibility				
(20 months)	.30~	.38*	.41*	.40*
Gender	.22	.45*	.43*	.03

Note. PN = personal narrative; FAN = fantasy narrative; MLU = mean lenght of utterance; IPSyn = Index of Productive Syntax; CDI = MacArthur Communicative Development Inventory
*$p < .05$, **$p < .01$, ~$p < .10$.

fantasy talk and pragmatic flexibility also would predict later skill in personal narrative, a series of regression models was constructed that also included gender as a predictor. The models displayed in Table 11.5 indicate that the more children engage in nonpresent talk early in life, the better narrators of personal experience they tend to be at age 5. Indeed, 23% of the variance in personal narrative is explained by nonpresent talk alone and, even when we controlled for all the other predictors, nonpresent talk still contributed predictive power. As we can see from Model M6, pragmatic flexibility and gender, as well as nonpresent talk, each explain some of the variance in personal narrative performance. It is interesting, and somewhat puzzling, that the effect of pragmatic flexibility at higher levels varies by gender. Figure 11.1 shows personal narrative scores plotted against nonpresent talk for boys and girls with high and low pragmatic flexibility scores. As the figure shows, girls with high pragmatic flexibility tended to be the best personal narrators, while boys with similarly high pragmatic flexibility scores performed at the lower extreme.

TABLE 11.5. Regression models explaining variance in personal narrative (PN) at 5 years of age ($n = 32$)

	Nonpresent Talk		Fantasy Talk		Pragmatic Flexibility		Gender		Pragmatic Flexibility x Gender			
Model	β_1	$SE(\beta_1)$	β_1	$SE(\beta_1)$	β_1	$SE(\beta_1)$	β_1	$SE(\beta_1)$	β_1	$SE(\beta_1)$	df_e	R^2 (adj)
M1	46.63**	15.36									1,30	.23 (.21)
M2			1.47	8.40							1,30	.00 (−.03)
M3	48.40**	15.71	5.23	7.52							2,29	.25 (.20)
M4	43.65*	17.60	3.24	8.25	.12	.20					3,28	.25 (.18)
M5	39.75*	18.06	2.12	8.33	.16	.20	1.43	1.46			4,27	.28 (.18)
M6	37.27*	16.97	1.20	7.82	−1.08~	.59	−8.99~	4.98	.75*	.34	5,26	.39 (.28)

*$p < .05$, **$p < .01$, ~$p < .10$

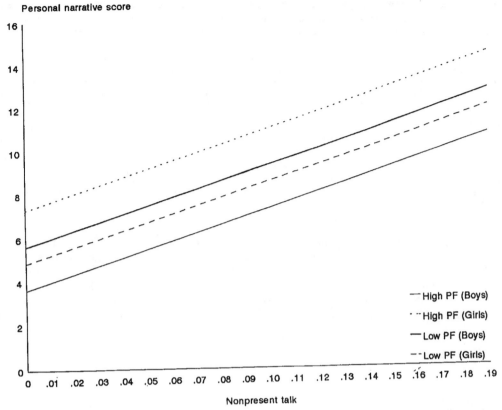

FIGURE 11.1. Predicted personal narrative score as a function of amount of nonpresent talk for boys and girls at high (75th percentile) and low (25th percentile) levels of pragmatic flexibility (PF).

Fantasy Narrative

A similar series of regression models was constructed to predict skill in fantasy narrative at 5, assessing both our more specific hypothesis, that early experience with fantasy talk would best support later competence in fantasy narration, and our more general hypotheses, that early experience with nonpresent talk and early pragmatic flexibility also would support fantasy talk at age 5. These models are displayed in Table 11.6. For fantasy narrative, even though nonpresent talk explains a portion of the variation ($R^2 =$ 13%), pragmatic flexibility and gender seem to play a more important role. Indeed, 41% of the variance in fantasy narrative is explained when these two variables are added to the regression model (see Model M5). Model M5 is illustrated in Figure 11.2, where fantasy scores are plotted against nonpresent talk for girls and boys at high and low levels of pragmatic flexibility. This figure demonstrates that the more nonpresent talk children produced at 20 months, the better fantasy narrators they tended to be at 5. In addition, the figure shows that girls tended to be better narrators of fantasy than boys, regardless of pragmatic flexibility. However, children with higher pragmatic flexibility produced better fantasy narratives than children of their same gender with lower pragmatic flexibility.

The analyses up to this point, then, have confirmed our hypothesis that degree of participation in discussions of the nonpresent around age 2 affects the performance of more autonomous narratives at age 5. In addition, pragmatic flexibility and gender have been identified as contributing additional predictive power for both personal and fantasy narrative. We were surprised, though, at the lack of relationship between fantasy talk and the fantasy narrative composite score. Therefore, we decided to look more closely at two components of the FAN score that are distinctly characteristic of fantasy narrative: genre specificity, a category that comprises the maintenance of a protagonist, character delineation, anchor tense, and lack of reliance on deixis; and character voice, which includes direct and reported speech, strategies that

TABLE 11.6. Regression models explaining variance in fantasy narrative (FAN) at 5 years of age ($n = 32$)

Model	Nonpresent Talk β_1	$SE(\beta_1)$	Fantasy Talk β_1	$SE(\beta_1)$	Pragmatic Flexibility β_1	$SE(\beta_1)$	Gender β_1	$SE(\beta_1)$	Pragmatic Flexibility x Gender β_1	$SE(\beta_1)$	df_e	R^2 (adj)
M1	50.56*	24.04									1,30	.13 (.10)
M2			9.19	12.22							1,30	.02 (−.01)
M3	55.12*	24.22	13.47	11.60							2,29	.17 (.11)
M4	40.43	26.57	7.30	12.45	.38	.30					3,28	.21(.13)
M5	24.67	24.09	2.79	11.12	.53~	.27	5.77**	1.95			4,27	.41 (.32)
M6	24.57	24.61	2.76	11.34	.48	.87	5.39	7.23	.03	.50	5,26	.41 (.29)

*$p < .05$, **$p < .01$, ~$p < .10$.

can function both for advancing the plot or for coloring the events of the story (see Table 11.3 for examples of features of each of these and Table 11.1 for means, ranges, and standard deviations for these fantasy components).

Two sets of regression models, analogous to those previously built for the composite scores, were constructed for these components of fantasy narrative. As Table 11.7 indicates, the strongest predictors for genre specificity were early fantasy talk and gender. That is, the more fantasy talk children produced early

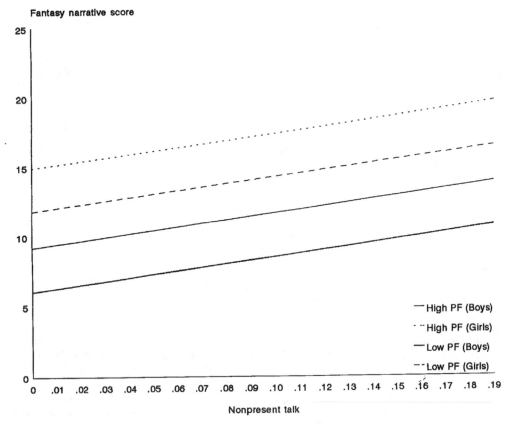

FIGURE 11.2. Predicted fantasy narrative score as a function of amount of nonpresent talk for boys and girls at high (75th percentile) and low (25th percentile) levels of pragmatic flexibility (PF).

TABLE 11.7. Regression models explaining variance in fantasy narrative genre specificity and character voice at 5 years of age (n = 32)

	Nonpresent Talk		Fantasy Talk		Pragmatic Flexibility		Gender		Pragmatic Flexibility x Gender			
	β_1	$SE(\beta_1)$	β_1	$SE(\beta_1)$	β_1	$SE(\beta_1)$	β_1	$SE(\beta_1)$	β_1	$SE(\beta_1)$	df_e	R^2 (adj)
Genre Specificity Models												
M1	11.14	6.98									1,30	.08 (.05)
M2			7.92*	3.12							1,30	.17 (.15)
M3	14.20*	6.29	9.02**	3.01							2,29	.30 (.25)
M4	11.90~	5.85	8.53**	2.78	.08	.07					3,28	.32 (.25)
M5	7.06	6.37	6.56*	2.94	.12	.07	1.47**	.52			4,27	.48 (.40)
M6	6.86	6.48	6.48*	2.99	.02	.23	.63	1.90	.06	.13	5,26	.48 (.38)
Character Voice Models												
M1	7.63	5.63									1,30	.06 (.03)
M2			4.69~	2.64							1,30	.10 (.06)
M3	9.47~	5.41	5.43*	2.59							2,29	.18 (.13)
M4	6.18	5.93	4.05	2.78	.08	.07					3,28	.23 (.14)
M5	6.12	6.20	4.03	2.86	.09	.07	.02	.50			4,27	.22 (.11)
M6	5.82	6.27	3.92	2.89	-.06	.22	-1.24	1.84	.09	.13	5,26	.24 (.10)

*p < .05, **p < .01, ~p < .10.

in life, the better they tended to perform in this particular dimension of fantasy narrative at age 5; in addition, girls once again tended to outperform boys at age 5. For character voice (see Table 11.7), nonpresent talk and fantasy talk combined accounted for 18% of the variance. For this dimension of fantasy narrative, there were not significant differences between boys and girls.

In summary, these findings indicate that participation in early discussions about the nonpresent positively influence overall performance in personal and fantasy narration at age 5. We also can conclude that early participation in fantasy talk interactions stimulates development in specific areas of fantasy narrative: the achievement of genre specificity and the representation of character voice. These relationships are further affected by children's gender and their participation in a wide variety of social interchanges and speech acts, but are not dependent on children's early morphosyntactic skills or vocabulary.

☐ Discussion

As Peterson and McCabe (1992, 1994) and Fivush and Haden have argued (Fivush, 1994, Haden, Haine, & Fivush, 1997), young children acquire understandings of culturally important elements of narrative structure through participation in joint conversation about past events with parents. The present study suggests that this interactional picture should be broadened to include other kinds of talk about the nonpresent (e.g., talk about nonobservable feelings and thoughts), as well as talk about the related to present. In a broad sense, parents who habitually engage in more nonpresent and related to present talk with their young children provide more opportunities for children to learn to represent past events; to report intentions, feelings, and reactions; and to tie experiences in one context to those in another. All of these, we believe, are skills that are critical to later autonomous narrative production. As children become more capable of extended nonpresent talk, parents' topic extensions begin to include more specific prompts for information about narrative participants, setting, consequences, and resolutions, elements of narrative structure that our most successful children were able to produce independently at age 5. Thus, the relationships demonstrated between nonpresent talk at 20 and 32 months and 5-year-olds' production of narrative structure and evaluation, both in personal narrative and in fantasy play, reflect these sorts of interactional histories.

Pragmatic flexibility assesses another feature of extended parent-child talk, the ability to engage in a variety of communicative activities and to shift between here and now and nonpresent frames of reference. This aspect of interactional experience is only moderately associated with children's later ability to produce personal narrative, but shows stronger associations with the ability to participate successfully in fantasy play. Unlike personal narrative, fantasy play is a context that requires frequent shifts between talk with the adult partner in the immediate context of joint pretense ("Oops, the lion's tail fell off!"), relatively autonomous narration of story happenings ("Out jumped the lion cub's mommy"), and shifts into the voice of story characters ("And, the dragon said to all the other animals, I don't like you. I'm gonna eat you all up"). The ability to manage these shifts in narrative role may be facilitated by early practice in shifting frames of reference in conversation with parents.

Early morphosyntactic attainment as indexed by MLU and by IPSyn at 32 months shows little association with any of these areas of extended discourse competence at age 5, though there is a hint of involvement in children's construction of a fantasy world. This may preview a larger role for morphosyntax as children begin to use more sophisticated anaphoric strategies for marking shifts in focus between central and peripheral story characters, and as they more consistently use anchor tense to bind together events in the story world.

The picture that emerges then, as we consider continuity between early and later pragmatic skills, is not simply one of homotypic continuity with early experience in relating past events or engaging in fantasy narration with an adult partner predicting later personal narrative and fantasy narrative skills. Rather, it also is one of heterotypic continuity, in which experience in talking about the nonpresent, practice in negotiating shifts between talk about the here and now and talk about the nonpresent, and engagement in a broad range of communicative interchanges may be crucial preparation for later autonomous narrative production.

☐ References

Aukrust, V. G., & Snow, C. E. (1998). Narratives and explanations in Norwegian and American mealtime conversations. *Language in Society, 27*(2), 221–246.

Berman, R. A., & Slobin, D. I. (1994). *Relating events in narrative: A crosslinguistic developmental study*. Hillsdale, NJ: Erlbaum.

Blum-Kulka, S. (1997). *Dinner talk: Cultural patterns of sociability and socialization in family discourse*. Mahwah, NJ: Erlbaum.

Brown, R. (1973). *A first language: The early stages*. Cambridge, MA: Harvard University Press.

Bruner, J. (1986). *Actual minds, possible worlds*. Cambridge, MA: Harvard University Press.

Dale, P., Bates, E., Reznick, J., & Morisset, C. (1989). The validity of a parent report instrument of child language at twenty months. *Journal of Child Language, 16*, 239–249.

Eisenberg, A. (1985). Learning to describe past experiences in conversation. *Discourse Processes, 8*, 177–204.

Haight, W., & Miller, P. (1993). *Pretending at home*. Albany: SUNY Press.

Heath, S. B. (1983). *Ways with words: Language, life and work in communities and classrooms*. Cambridge, England: Cambridge University Press.

Hemphill, L., Feldman, H., Camp, L., & Griffin, T. (1994). Developmental changes in narrative and non-narrative discourse in children with and without brain injury. *Journal of Communication Disorders, 27*, 107–133.

Hollingshead, A. (1975). The four-factor index of social status. Unpublished manuscript. Yale University, Department of Sociology, New Haven, CT.

Labov, W., & Waletsky, J. (1967). Narrative analysis: Oral versions of personal experience. In J. Helm (Ed.), *Essays on the verbal and visual arts* (pp. 12–44). Seattle: University of Washington Press.

MacWhinney, B. (1991). *The CHILDES Project: Computational tools for analyzing talk*. Hillsdale, NJ: Erlbaum.

MacWhinney, B., & Snow, C. E. (1985). The Child Language Data Exchange System. *Journal of Child Language, 12*, 271–295.

MacWhinney, B., & Snow, C. E. (1990). The Child Language Data Exchange System: An update. *Journal of Child Language, 17*, 457–472.

McCabe, A. (1996). *Chameleon readers: Teaching children how to appreciate all kinds of good stories*. New York: McGraw-Hill.

McCabe, A., & Peterson, C. (1991). *Developing narrative structure*. Hillsdale, NJ: Erlbaum.

Michaels, S. (1981). Sharing time: Children's narrative styles and differential access to literacy. *Language and Society, 10*, 423–442.

Nelson, K. (1986). *Event knowledge: Structure and function in development*. Hillsdale, NJ: Erlbaum.

Ninio, A. (1993). On the fringes of the system: Children's acquisition of syntactically isolated forms at the onset of speech. *First Language, 13*, 291–314.

Ninio, A., & Snow, C. E. (1996). The development of pragmatics: Learning to use language appropriately. In T. Bhatia & W. Ritchie (Eds.), *Handbook of language acquisition*. New York: Academic Press.

Ninio, A., Snow, C. E., Pan, B. A., & Rollins, P. (1994). Classifying communicative acts in children's interactions. *Journal of Communications Disorders, 27*, 157–188.

Ninio, A., & Wheeler, P. (1984). A manual for classifying verbal communicative acts in mother-infant interaction. *Working Papers in Developmental Psychology, No. 1.* Jerusalem: The Martin and Vivian Levin Center, Hebrew University. Reprinted as *Transcript Analysis, 1986, 3*, 1–82.

Ochs, E., Taylor, C. , Rudolph, D., & Smith, R. (1992). Storytelling as a theory-building activity. *Discourse Processes, 15*, 37–72.

Pan, B. A., Imbens-Bailey, A., Winner, K., & Snow, C. E. (1996). Communicative intents expressed by parents in interaction with young children. *Merrill-Palmer Quarterly, 42*, 72–90.

Peterson, C., & McCabe, A. (1983). *Developmental psycholinguistics: Three ways of looking at a child's narrative*. New York: Plenum.

Peterson, C., & McCabe, A. (1992). Parental styles of narrative elicitation: Effect on children's narrative structure and content. *First Language, 12*, 299–321.

Peterson, C., & McCabe, A. (1994). A social interactionist account of developing decontextualized narrative skill. *Developmental Psychology, 30*, 937–948.

Sachs, J., Goldman, J., & Chaille, C. (1984). Planning in pretend play: Using language to coordinate narrative development. In A. D. Pellegrini & T. D. Yawkey (Eds.), *Advances in discourse processes: Vol. 13. The development of oral and written lauguage in social contexts* (pp. 119–128). Norwood, NJ: Ablex.

Scarborough, H. (1990). Index of productive syntax. *Applied Psycholinguistics, 11*, 1–22.

Snow, C. E., Pan, B. A., Imbens-Bailey, A., & Herman, J. (1996). Learning how to say what one means: A longitudinal study of children's speech act use. *Social Development, 5*, 56–84.

Wolf, D., & Polanyi, L. (1990, October). *Walking into story: A five year old stumbles on the nature of semantic worlds.* Paper presented at the Conference on Language Development, Boston, MA.

CHILDHOOD

Marion K. Underwood
Jennifer C. Hurley

Emotion Regulation in Peer Relationships During Middle Childhood

☐ Introduction

Learning to regulate strong emotions in the context of peer relationships is a remarkable developmental achievement. In many ways, emotion regulation is a contradiction in terms. Emotions can be urgent and overwhelming, whereas regulation implies management and control. Children's capacity to control strong feelings in relationships with other children is particularly fascinating because these relationships are horizontal in that they require negotiation among individuals who are approximately similar in age and status (Hartup, 1989), authority figures are not present to provide structure, and children in close relationships frequently construct their own frameworks for social interaction (Laursen, Hartup, & Koplas, 1996).

This chapter will discuss previous research on emotion regulation in peer relationships in the age range of *middle childhood*, which most developmental psychologists define as age 6 to 12 (Cole & Cole, 1996). Although there has been a recent burst in research on the development of emotions, very little of this work has explored emotion regulation in older children. Perhaps researchers have concentrated more on emotion regulation in infants because early developmental advances are so dramatic. In the first 3 years of life, research has documented remarkable developments in children's emotional states, experiences, and expressions (see Lewis, 1993, for a review). Many recent volumes of current research on emotion regulation contain rich information about development during infancy and the preschool years, but only a brief mention of emotion regulation in older children (for example, Fox, 1994; Garber & Dodge, 1991; Lewis & Haviland, 1993).

However, several theories and a small, but growing, body of research have suggested that children's capacity to regulate emotions with peers may continue to develop during the middle childhood years. Comprehensive theories of development have suggested that children might be particularly well prepared to learn to regulate emotions during middle childhood. Freud (1905) characterized middle childhood as the latency stage, during which children are relatively unperturbed by sexual impulses. Piaget (1983) described these children as in the cognitive developmental stage of concrete operations, as being able to solve real world problems using logical mental procedures. Erikson (1980) portrayed middle childhood as the conflict between industry and inferiority, a time when children work to gain competence in multiple domains.

In one of the few attempts to theorize more specifically about emotion regulation in older children, Gottman and Mettetal (1986) proposed a developmental account based on careful observation of interac-

This work was partially supported by Grants MH52110 and MH55992 from the National Institute of Mental Health.

tions between peers. They suggested that young children manage emotions in social interaction by maintaining a climate of agreement and discontinuing play if disagreements arise, children in middle childhood regulate emotion by constructing elaborate rules for social interaction with same-sex peer groups to contain affective expression and avoid embarrassment, and adolescents regulate emotions by using their new skills in abstract reasoning to subject emotions to logical scrutiny in conversations with friends. The characterization of children in middle childhood as using rules to manage emotion expression fits with a large body of research demonstrating that these children value conformity, rules, and regulations (see Hartup, 1970). Gottman and Mettetal argued that the developmental function of this preoccupation with rules is to contain emotional intensity, "the external structure is the vehicle for not being so controlled by the emotions" (p. 202).

Other research and theory has suggested not only that these children are using explicit rules in their play to manage affect, but they also are starting to appreciate and obey the largely unspoken rules for expressing and controlling emotions. Saarni and von Salisch (1993) proposed that children become masters of emotional dissemblance, as they try to cope with conflicting cultural messages about emotions in social interactions: Be honest, but be careful about expressing negative feelings if you want to keep friends.

Although existing research largely supports this theoretical picture of elementary-school-age children becoming increasingly cool, calm, and collected as they deploy cultural rules for expressing emotions, much remains to be known about why some children become so competent in emotion regulation and why some struggle to manage affect and develop serious problems such as conduct disorder and depression (see Garber & Dodge, 1991, for a discussion of emotion dysregulation and psychopathology). On the specific question of how children in the age range of middle childhood learn to regulate emotions with peers, existing evidence is scant. To set the context for our current empirical work, the first part of the chapter will draw on previous work from the peer relations and emotional development literatures. Comprehensive reviews of these large bodies of work are beyond the scope of this chapter; therefore, this discussion will focus on the research that comes closest to examining the relation between peer relations and emotion regulation and refer readers elsewhere for overviews. First, the chapter will discuss previous research on children's peer relations during middle childhood: children's friendships and the correlates and determinants of peer status. Next, the chapter will present research on emotional development: what types of affect children seem to experience with peers, children's use of emotional display rules, and the few existing studies of emotion regulation in peer interaction. The majority of the chapter will present some of our current theoretical and empirical work on the following topics: the relation between peer status and children's choices for expressing and controlling emotions, the development of display rules for anger in middle childhood, the relation between peer status and reporting of display rules, observational research on anger expression, and important future directions for research on emotion regulation.

☐ Previous Research on Children's Peer Relationships

Developmental psychologists have focused on three aspects of children's peer relationships: friendships, social networks, and levels of social acceptance within the larger peer group. Friendship and peer social status seem to contribute to psychological adjustment in distinct ways (Parker & Asher, 1993). Because each of these relationship contexts demands different skills in emotion regulation, each will be considered separately here.

Friendships and Emotion Regulation

For children to maintain close friendships, they have to be able to have fun getting excited together, know when to calm down, and know how to resolve disputes when they arise (Gottman & Mettetal, 1986). Little research has focused explicitly on emotion regulation processes between friends, but the literatures on children's expectations of friends and on conflict resolution are closely related.

Overall, research on friendships has suggested that children expect to experience positive affect with peers, and to receive emotional support from friends when needed. In the middle childhood years, children reported that same-sex friends provide them with more companionship and intimacy than parents, siblings, or teachers (Lempers & Clark-Lempers, 1992). Zarbatany, Hartmann, and Rankin (1990) collected diary measures of children's activities and expectations of peer behaviors, and found that children expected that peers would provide a sense of sociability and belonging, concern for achievements and self-enhancement, and opportunities for learning. When interacting with close friends, children expected inclusion and acceptance in noncompetitive activities, and support for self-evaluation in competitive contexts (Zarbatany, Ghesquierre, & Mohr, 1992). When asked to describe upsetting events, preadolescents often mentioned social situations, but reported feeling better after talking with friends (Denton & Zarbatany, 1996). Interestingly, in this age range, friends seem to help each other cope with distress by distraction; Denton and Zarbatany found that preadolescents reported feeling better after receiving distracting social support from friends.

Although friends clearly expect and enjoy much positive interaction together, friends' interests inevitably collide and conflicts arise. A rich body of previous research has explored conflicts between friends and peers (see Laursen et al., 1996, for a thoughtful review). Aboud (1989) noted that disagreements between friends may have both positive and negative functions; disputes can prompt children to make advances in their thinking, but disputes also can disrupt relationships and generate negative affect. In a study of children's responses to discrepancies between their ratings of emotion judgments and the judgments of a friend, Aboud (1989) found that children tend to change their appraisals more when these were discrepant with the appraisals of a close friend than a "lukewarm" friend.

Several previous investigations have demonstrated that conflicts between friends are different than conflicts between children who are less closely affiliated. Hartup, French, Laursen, Johnston, and Ogawa (1993) observed third- and fourth-grade friends and nonfriends playing a board game designed to generate conflict, in a "closed field situation" (meaning that the children had little choice about what or with whom to play). Friends engaged in more conflicts than nonfriends (even when the total amount of interaction was statistically taken into account), and their disagreements lasted longer and tended to be less mild and polite than those between nonfriends. Other research has suggested that, with close friends, children respond more strongly to conflicts but also take care to protect the future of the relationship. In responding to hypothetical vignettes about anger with close friends and classmates, pre- and young adolescent children reported that, with friends, they would feel a stronger sense of violation as a result of provocation, experience more complex emotions (e.g., anger and sadness), be more likely to take partial responsibility for the dispute, and engage in more direct strategies to try to restore the relationship (Whitesell & Harter, 1996). Overall, research on conflict has suggested that close friends resolve disagreements in ways that preserve the stability of the relationship, whereas nonfriends might resort to more hostile strategies in order to prevail in a particular dispute (Laursen et al., 1996).

Social Networks and Emotion Regulation

In addition to studying dyads of friends, researchers also have explored the structure and functions of children's larger social networks. With the possible exception of research showing that young adolescents who are aggressive tend to form networks with other aggressive youth (Cairns, Cairns, Neckerman, Gest, & Gariepy, 1988), little research has explored processes of emotion regulation among children's social networks. However, research and theory has suggested that children might form networks based on similar styles of emotion management, and also socialize each other in how to manage strong feelings. For example, Kindermann (1993) studied the relation between children's naturally occurring social networks and their motivation in school, and found that children formed networks with others of similar academic motivation, but also that network members became more similar over time in their motivation for doing well in school. Given the centrality of emotion regulation in forming and maintaining relationships, it seems natural that similar processes might operate for strategies for emotion regulation. Children with similar emotion regulation styles might be attracted to form social groups and, in turn, the norms of the social network might shape individuals' styles of emotion management.

Peer Social Status and Emotion Regulation

In addition to having close friends and belonging to a group, children also value acceptance by larger peer groups such as their school classmates, neighborhood playmates, or members of their athletic teams. *Sociometric status* refers to the degree of a child's social acceptance by a group, as determined by nominations from other group members. Moreno (1934) pioneered the study of sociometry by visiting school classrooms and asking children to vote for those they would most like to sit beside. Moreno advocated sociometric testing as a way of understanding how individuals could preserve their autonomy and sponta- neity, but also participate in social groups. Moreno entitled his book *Who Shall Survive? A New Approach to the Problem of Human Interrelations.* Moreno's title hints at precisely the reason that contemporary psy- chologists have rediscovered sociometric testing; that is, that low acceptance by peers predicts later ad- justment (Kohlberg, LaCrosse, & Ricks, 1972; Kupersmidt & Coie, 1990; Parker & Asher, 1987).

In its modern form, sociometric testing is also being conducted in school classrooms, but now research- ers are presenting children with rosters of all members of their grade at school and asking them to vote for peers for a variety of types of items. Children identify those peers whom they most like (positive socio- metric nominations) and those whom they least like (negative nominations). In addition, researchers also may ask children to nominate peers for a variety of items to access specific behaviors, such as aggression ("Starts fights") and prosocial behavior ("Good leader" or "Is cooperative").

Researchers have determined children's peer status by tabulating numbers of positive and negative nominations and assigning children to status groups based on one of several classification systems. In the most commonly used of these systems (Coie, Dodge, & Coppotelli, 1982), children are designated as having five types of peer status: average, popular, rejected, neglected, and controversial. Children in the average group have average numbers of like most and like least votes. Children in the popular group receive high numbers of positive nominations, and low numbers of negative nominations. Children clas- sified as controversial receive above average numbers of both positive and negative nominations. Chil- dren in the rejected group have an above average number of like least nominations and very few nomina- tions for like most. Neglected children receive very few of either positive or negative nominations. One strength of this classification system is that it discriminates between children who are actively disliked and children who are not well known because they are shy or do not interact much socially. Also, this system works well to identify children with extreme degrees of social acceptance or rejection. Using the Coie et al. (1982) system, by far the largest group of children is either not classified or classified as having average status (approximately 52%). Other peer status groups consist of much smaller proportions of children: popular (around 12%), rejected (about 13%), neglected (approximately 13%), and controversial (about 7%).

An extensive body of research has documented the behavioral correlates of these sociometric status groups. In a comprehensive meta-analysis of research on behaviors associated with these five social status groups, Newcomb, Bukowski, and Pattee (1993) documented that popular status is associated with socia- bility and low levels of aggression and withdrawal, and rejection is related to high levels of aggression and isolation and fewer positive interactions overall. Certainly, these results confirm that the kind of extreme lack of emotional control which might be evident in aggressive behavior contributes to peer rejection (Coie & Kupersmidt, 1983). However, much remains to be known about the relation between children's sociometric status and other more normative types of emotion regulation. Many of the behavioral corre- lates described in the Newcomb et al. meta-analysis relate to emotions (such as aggression and depression and loneliness) but, because these broad categories of behavior are multiply determined, it is difficult to disentangle the role of emotion regulation. In their discussion, Newcomb et al. recommended that re- searchers broaden the types of question they ask about peer status, "especially the role of emotionality in children's peer relations" (p. 124).

Hubbard and Coie (1994) reviewed existing research on the relation between emotional responding and social competence, and suggested that positive peer status may be a reasonable criterion for social competence, at least in the peer domain. Although little empirical evidence exists, they argued that it is reasonable to expect that positive peer status would be associated with being able to recognize one's own emotions and the emotional displays of others, the ability to regulate emotional expressions, and the capacity to respond sympathetically to the emotional displays of others. To move forward in our under- standing of the relation between peer relations and emotional competence, they suggested that research- ers more thoroughly investigate differences between sociometric status groups on emotion variables.

☐ Previous Research on the Development of Emotion Regulation in Middle Childhood

Whereas peer relations researchers have focused mostly on behavioral correlates and low peer acceptance as a risk factor, emotions researchers have concentrated more specifically on the basic, normal development of emotional experience and expression. In the past 20 years, psychologists have developed much more sophisticated conceptual models of emotion and what the components of regulation might be, particularly for infants (see Walden & Smith, in press, for a review). For emotion regulation in the age range of middle childhood, our theoretical frameworks and empirical evidence are less well developed.

Saarni (1990) offered a rich description of emotional competence which includes many skills that well may develop during middle childhood. Emotional competence includes understanding one's own emotional state, discriminating others' emotional states, using a shared vocabulary of emotion terms, understanding that inner emotional experience and outer expression are not always the same, knowing cultural display rules, being able to interpret others' emotional behaviors in light of personal information about individuals, being aware of the effects of emotional expression on others, regulating negative emotions to make them less aversive, understanding that intimate relationships require reciprocity in genuine emotional expression, and having emotional self-efficacy. "Individuals view themselves as feeling, overall, the way they want to feel" (Saarni, 1990, p. 118).

For many of these components of emotional competence, empirical research on development during middle childhood is scant. This brief discussion will focus on components that have been studied most in school-age children, with special attention to research that explores emotions with peers.

Emotions Children Experience with Peers

As noted earlier, peer relations research has indicated that children expect positive affect and support when interacting with peers and friends (Zarbatany et al., 1990; Zarbatany et al., 1992). However, other research has suggested that peer relationships also may generate negative affect in preadolescents. Larson and colleagues have conducted time sampling studies, in which fifth, sixth, seventh, eighth, and ninth graders wore pagers for a week, and recorded their activities and emotions on diary forms when beeped once randomly during every 2-hour period of waking time. Larson and Richards (1991) found that older children reported less time with family; time with peers increased with age for girls and time alone increased for boys. With age, emotions with friends became more variable. Although emotional variability across contexts did not increase with age, older children reported more negative mood states overall (Larson & Lampron-Petraitis, 1989). Examination of children's explanations for negative mood states revealed that, with age, children were more likely to cite social situations with peers as their reasons for feeling bad (Larson & Asmussen, 1991). Williams and Bybee (1994) asked children and adolescents to recall guilt-inducing events, and 31% of the episodes recalled by fifth graders concerned friends. Future research should explore more fully how children regulate negative affect about peer interactions and with friends.

Children's Understanding of Display Rules for Emotions

A growing body of research has explored children's knowledge of display rules, cultural conventions for controlling emotional behavior in social interactions. Overall, this research suggests that, during middle childhood, there are sizable advances in children's understanding of social conventions for emotion expression. Saarni (1979) examined children's choices of emotional behavior for the main character in peer conflict stories, and found that older participants (11-year-olds) used display rules more, demonstrated more complex reasoning about managing emotions, and cited maintaining norms more as justification for invoking a display rule. Gnepp and Hess (1986) asked 1st-, 3rd-, 5th-, and 10th-grade children to choose facial and verbal emotional expressions for a protagonist and to explain their reasoning. The results indicated that understanding of display rules increased from Grades 1 to 5, then leveled off. Children demonstrated more sophisticated understanding of verbal than facial display rules, and reported display rules more for prosocial than for self-protective reasons.

Other research has suggested that children's choices of whether or not to invoke display rules depend on who is observing. When deciding to express anger, sadness, or pain in the presence of another person who was not the target of the emotion, first, third, and fifth grade children reported that they would mask negative emotions more with a "medium type friend" than with parents or alone (Zeman & Garber, 1996). In another study using similar methods, there were no significant differences in children's reporting of regulation with medium friends and best friends (Zeman & Shipman, 1996). Regardless of the type of observer, children reported that they expressed sadness in order to get social support, and masked anger to avoid negative consequences.

Emotion Regulation in Peer Interactions

Only a very few studies have focused specifically on children's emotion regulation in the context of peer interaction. Casey (1993) examined 7- and 12-year-olds' emotional responses to positive and negative feedback from a peer (delivered via videotape). In this very specific laboratory context, there were no clear developmental differences in children's facial expressions of emotion, understanding of emotional experience, or accuracy of self-reports of emotional behavior. Similarly, Murphy and Eisenberg (1996) did not find developmental differences in 7- to 11-year-old children's responses to anger-provoking peer conflicts. Reported anger intensity in peer conflicts was negatively related to camp counselors' reports of participants' self-regulation and social competence.

Given that successful interaction with peers and friends requires "shrewd finesse" (Saarni, 1989, p. 204) in managing emotions, research on the relation between peer status and friendship and emotion regulation could be very fruitful. Research has suggested that, for children in these age groups, teacher reports of emotionality are positively related to peer nominations for prosocial behavior (Eisenberg et al., 1996). Hubbard and Coie (1994) proposed that an important way to move forward in our understanding of peer relations and emotion regulation would be to study the relation between peer sociometric status and children's emotional understanding and behavior.

☐ Our Current Research on Peer Social Status and Emotion Regulation

Our empirical research on emotion regulation in middle childhood is guided by several goals. We focus on interactions with peers because we think that children's capacity to regulate emotions might be most apparent in contexts about which they care deeply, when authority figures are less in control. Although we acknowledge that positive emotions also may be regulated, we more carefully examine regulation of negative emotions, such as anger, because we believe that managing these is most challenging. We try to use multiple research methods; what children think and say about their emotional behaviors is interesting and important, but does not necessarily correspond to their actual behavior when provoked. Therefore, we combine self-report and observational methods. Finally, we recognize that emotion regulation may well be specific to social context, and we try to study emotional behavior in contexts that make sense for both genders.

Peer Social Status and Children's Choices about the Expression and Control of Positive and Negative Emotions

Underwood (1997a) explored the relation between peer social status and several aspects of the pragmatics of emotion regulation with peers (Parke, 1994): children's choices to express and control positive and negative emotions, and expectations of peer reactions to different emotional responses. This study contributed to previous research in several ways. Because earlier work suggested that children's choices to express or control emotions vary with the social context (Underwood, Coie, & Herbsman, 1992), this research investigated emotion expression in one particular context, in the presence of classroom peers. Peers likely provide much immediate and continuous feedback on the interpersonal consequences of expressing and controlling emotions in particular ways (Saarni & von Salisch, 1993). Whereas much previous research has focused only on children's knowledge of when they must suppress negative emotions, this study explored children's choices to express both positive and negative emotions. In fact, much research on emotions in the social sciences has seemed to presume that affect is something that always must be controlled and managed (Lutz, 1990). However, choices about emotion management may include open expression as well as dissemblance or management (Doubleday, Kovaric, & Dorr, 1990). Ekman and Friesen (1975) proposed four possible types of emotion expression: maximization (openly expressing how you really feel), minimization (showing how you feel, but at a much reduced intensity), masking (attempting to show no emotion at all), and substitution (trying to express a different emotion than you feel). In this investigation, children listened to emotion-provoking vignettes and chose an emotional response from four options, each of which represented one of these four possible types of emotion expression.

This research explored the effects of gender, age, and peer social status on children's choices to express and control both positive and negative emotions, and expectations of peer reactions to particular types of emotional expression. For choices of emotional expressions in response to the vignettes, no gender differences were predicted. Previous research showed that girls and boys report similar understandings of the rules for emotion expression in conflict situations (Saarni, 1979). Girls were hypothesized to report more negative expectations about peers' responses to intense emotional expressions than boys, because women in our culture (and, by extension, girls) may be more strongly socialized to modulate strong emotions and may fear more punishment for open expression.

Little previous research has focused on the development of emotional understanding in the middle childhood age range. Because older children might be more adept at masking emotions, and because some previous work suggests that older children are more able to mask anger and disappointment (Gnepp & Hess, 1986; Saarni, 1979), older children were predicted to report masking emotions more than younger children.

On the basis of previous research with younger samples (Fabes & Eisenberg, 1992), children rejected by peers at school were expected to more often endorse intense expressions of negative affect. Popular children were hypothesized to select moderate but honest expressions of emotions.

Method.   Participants were 200 children in the second, fourth, and sixth grades of two large elementary schools (approximate age; 8, 10, and 12 years), in a suburban community in the northwestern United States. The sample was 85% European American and most children were from lower- to middle-income families.

In a single 30 minute testing session, children responded to two measures: the Social Experience Questionnaire (SEQ; constructed for this investigation) and a sociometric measure. Participants completed the SEQ first, so that their responses to the emotion measure would not be influenced by their nominations of peers.

The SEQ includes six vignettes depicting positive and negative emotion-arousing situations that are likely to occur in school classrooms in the presence of peers: happiness at good fortune, pride in accomplishments, sadness, anger, disappointment, and embarrassment (see Figure 12.1 for a sample vignette). For each hypothetical vignette, children were asked to imagine that they were in the situation, experiencing the designated strong emotion. For each situation, children responded to two types of questions. First, they chose one of four possible responses, arranged on a continuum from most expressive to most dissembling: expressing the emotion strongly, expressing the emotion but in a subdued fashion, masking the emotion by maintaining a neutral expression, and showing another more acceptable emotion. Next, for each of the four possible responses, children were asked to imagine enacting the particular emotional response in the presence of peers, and to rate each possible type of expression on how much it would make other children "want to be your friend."

After completing the SEQ, children responded to a brief sociometric measure, including items for "like most" and "like least." On the basis of the modified Coie et al. (1982) system outlined in Terry and Coie

---

Imagine that one day you are walking down the hall to the lunchroom with the rest of your school class. You slip on a wet spot on the floor, and fall. As you fall, you hear a loud tearing sound and you realize that your pants have split. Everyone is watching you to see what you will do.
You feel really embarrassed. What would you do?

Look really upset and say   Look down and say   Keep a calm face and   Smile and say "I did
"Oh no—don't look" and   "Uh-oh!"   say nothing.   that on purpose,
walk away backwards   just to make you
as fast as you can.   laugh."

FIGURE 12.1. Sample item from the Social Experience Questionnaire (SEQ). From "Peer Social Status and Children's Choices about the Expression and Control of Positive and Negative Emotion," by M. K. Underwood, in press-a, *Merrill-Palmer Quarterly.*

(1991), children were classified as popular, average, or rejected (controversial and neglected children were not included in these analyses because these groups were small).

Results and Discussion.   Overall, the findings suggested that children's choices to express or control emotions depended on both the type of emotion and individual difference variables such as gender, age, and peer status. As expected, all children reported that they would mask negative emotions more than positive feelings, although even for the positive emotions, children rarely endorsed strong open expression. Also as expected, there were no gender differences in children's choices of emotion expression.

Interestingly, the results provided only limited support for the hypothesis that, in general, older children would mask emotions more. Table 12.1 presents means for children's responses to the six emotional vignettes by grade level (on a four point continuum from most expressive to most dissembling). Older children did report masking happiness more than younger children, but said that they would be more openly expressive of anger and disappointment. These results suggest that emotional development during middle childhood may be more complicated than just becoming more skillful in masking. The development of emotion regulation may depend very much on the specific emotion.

Contrary to predictions, there were no significant effects for peer social status on children's choices of emotional expressions. Perhaps, this was due to the fact that self-report measures were used here. Although popular, average, and rejected children may report that they would respond similarly, their behavior in live situations actually may be very different. Interestingly, though, there were consistent peer status differences in children's expectations for peer reactions to emotional behaviors. Regardless of the type of emotional expression, rejected children thought that others would respond negatively to their behaviors. This finding confirms previous evidence that rejected children perhaps are painfully aware that others react negatively to their social behaviors (see Asher, Parkhurst, Hymel, & Williams, 1990, for a review). Rejected children's uniformly negative expectations suggest that these children may be cognizant of possible reputation bias (Hymel, Wagner, & Butler, 1990) and believe that peers will dislike them no matter what they do.

All children expected the most negative peer consequences for expressing anger, both strongly and moderately. This result fits with previous theory and research which has suggested that anger may stand alone as the most taboo or "coarse" emotion (Scheff, 1984). Children may be particularly conflicted about expressing anger for several reasons. Children perceive that displays of anger often are likely to hurt others' feelings (Saarni, 1988). Tavris (1982) convincingly argued that, although some educators and psychotherapists endorse expressing angry feelings openly but appropriately, the unfortunate reality is that, for almost all forms of anger expression, the interpersonal consequences usually are negative. Children in this study may have wisely reported negative expectations for peer reactions to angry behavior, because behaving angrily means hurting others and risking rejection.

TABLE 12.1. Mean responses to emotional vignettes by grade

	Emotion					
	Happiness	**Pride**	**Sadness**	**Embarrassment**	**Disappointment**	**Anger**
Grade						
2	1.55_a	2.03	2.47	2.49	2.66_c	3.39_e
	(.62)	(.89)	(.92)	(1.06)	(1.00)	(.79)
4	1.83_b	2.02	2.34	2.40	2.69_c	2.83_f
	(.90)	(1.05)	(1.10)	(1.14)	(1.13)	(1.08)
6	1.92_b	2.08	2.30	2.42	2.25_d	2.84_f
	(1.00)	(.98)	(1.22)	(1.18)	(1.06)	(1.09)

Note. Means represent values on a 4-point scale from expressiveness to dissembling, where 1 equals *extreme honest expressions* and 4 equals *masking by showing the opposite expression*. Standard deviations appear in parentheses below each mean. Within each column, means not sharing subscripts differ at $p < .05$. From "Peer Social Status and Children's Choices about the Expression and Control of Positive and Negative Emotion," by M. K. Underwood, in press-a, *Merrill-Palmer Quarterly*.

Children's Reporting of Display Rules for Anger

Although anger may be a particularly difficult emotion for children to learn to regulate, little previous research has specifically explored children's anger. For understandable reasons, much research has focused on one worrisome form of anger expression; aggression (Averill, 1982; Lemerise & Dodge, 1993). However, most children do not behave aggressively when angered, and much remains to be known about the development of more competent strategies for anger regulation.

Underwood et al. (1992) investigated children's understanding of display rules for anger. This research assessed children's reported use of both facial and verbal display rules in response to videotaped vignettes featuring provocation in two social contexts: with teachers and with peers. An example of provocation by a teacher was a teacher falsely accusing a child of having made a mess and scolding the child harshly. An example of provocation by a peer was a child wrecking a tower of dominoes.

We predicted that children would report masking anger much more frequently for the situations with teachers. Children in these age ranges likely understand that the consequences of expressing anger toward adult authority figures are more negative than for acting angry with a peer.

For these participants in the age range of middle childhood, we expected that older children would report masking anger much more often than younger children. Older children seem likely to be more aware of the negative consequences for openly expressing anger, and have had more time to be socialized in cultural prohibitions against angry displays.

Because the sample included approximately equal numbers of boys and girls, we were able to assess gender differences in reporting display rules for anger. A large body of previous research has documented that boys are more aggressive than girls (see Maccoby & Jacklin, 1974, for a review). Also, on the basis of ethnographic work, anthropologists have observed that women in our culture are socialized to surpress anger (Lutz, 1990). Therefore, we expected that girls would report masking anger more often than boys.

Method. Participants were 85 African American children in the third, fifth, and seventh grades (with average ages of 8.4, 10.9, and 12.8 years, respectively). Children were randomly selected from six elementary and three middle schools in a small city in the southeastern United States.

The video task for the reporting of display rules was adapted from a measure developed by Dodge (1986), and consisted of 12 anger-provoking vignettes, 6 with peers and 6 with teachers. Two versions of the tapes were developed using child actors, one with boys and one with girls. Participants watched tapes with same-gender actors, because for these age groups, most social interaction at school takes place in same-gender groups. Child actors enacted each scenario, and the vignettes ended right after the provocation occurred. Participants responded to a series of questions to assess their use of display rules: how they would feel, what sort of facial expression they would have (chosen from a set of drawings developed from Ekman and Friesen's [1975] examples of facial displays of anger), and what they would say or do. Children were coded as reporting display rules if they explicitly said they would feel angry, but would do nothing. Because a significant proportion of children reported feeling sad, display rules for sadness were also coded.

Results and Discussion. The results confirmed the hypothesis that children would report masking anger more often with teachers than with peers (mean proportions of .38 and .22, respectively). Perhaps, children fear retribution from teachers for behaving angrily, which also may be why they reported that provocation by teachers would make them sad more often than provocation by peers. When angered by a teacher, children may invoke "feeling rules" (Hochschild, 1979) and manage anger by preventing themselves from experiencing the more threatening emotion and, instead, feeling sad.

Interestingly, the predicted developmental increase in reporting of display rules for anger was evident only for boys. As shown in Table 12.2, boys' masking of anger increased with age, but girls' reported use of display rules decreased with age. In the younger age groups, in accordance with hypotheses, girls reported masking anger more than boys. However, because the developmental trajectories appeared to be moving in the opposite direction for boys and girls, for the seventh-grade group, the gender difference was striking, with boys reporting masking anger much more often. Our clinical impressions from working in the schools with the same population of children is that, for adolescent males, it is fairly important to stay cool in the face of verbal provocation—to be able to "chill." However, girls seem to engage in this verbal bantering less often and, when provoked, to be strongly assertive in response. Future research will need to assess whether these same developmental patterns are evident in other samples.

TABLE 12.2. Mean proportions of children reporting they would use display rules for anger

	Grade		
	3	5	7
Boys	$.17_{a,b}$	$.11_a$	$.49_b$
Girls	$.60_c$	$.33_{c,d}$	$.13_d$

Note. Means not sharing the same subscript differ significantly at $p < .05$. From "Display Rules for Anger and Aggression in School-Aged Children," by M. K. Underwood, J. D. Coie, and C. R. Herbsman, 1992, *Child Development, 63.*

The Relation Between Peer-Rated Aggression and Peer Status and Children's Reporting of Display Rules for Anger

Because successfully engaging in peer interactions likely requires managing strong emotions (Gottman & Mettetal, 1986), we used similar methods to those described above to assess the relation between peer-rated aggression and social status and children's reporting of display rules for anger. Because aggressive children seem to express their anger in such dramatic ways, it might be reasonable to suggest that they would have less understanding of display rules for anger. However, because much aggressive behavior seems impulsive, it also may be the case that aggressive children are fully aware of how they are supposed to behave, but cannot comply with display rules because they become extremely aroused.

We expected that socially rejected children would report less masking of anger than average or popular children. Children who are unable to manage strong negative emotions and behave aggressively become socially rejected by their peers (Coie & Kupersmidt, 1983), and angry reactive aggression seems to be the type of aggressive behavior most strongly related to becoming disliked (Dodge, Coie, Petit, & Price, 1990).

Method.   To examine the relation between peer-rated aggression and reporting of display rules for anger, Underwood et al. (1992) compared the random-normal sample of the children in the study above to a group of children who had been rated as highly aggressive by their peers (with standard scores for a peer nomination item for "Starts fights" greater than 1.0).

To investigate the relation between peer social status and display rules for anger, Underwood (1992) computed peer status for 129 third and fifth graders in the same sample from the Underwood et al. (1992) study, using the sociometric procedures outlined by Coie et al. (1982). Seventh graders were not included in the peer status analyses, because middle schools in this community were structured differently enough (with much larger grade groups, and changing of classes) that it would have been difficult to interpret status differences for these older groups.

For both studies, children responded to the same video task to assess reporting of display rules for anger. Again, children were coded as using display rules for anger when they said they would feel angry, but chose to show no angry expression (either facial or verbal).

Results and Discussion.   For facial display rules for anger, there were no differences between aggressive and non-aggressive children. As seen in Table 12.3, there was not strong evidence that aggressive children reported using display rules for anger less. A significant Grade × Aggression interaction indicated that the only difference between aggressive and nonaggressive children was in the seventh-grade group. Overall, these findings suggest that even highly aggressive children talk as if they would mask anger. Therefore, understanding of display rules does not seem to account for differences in aggressive behavior.

For display rules for facial expressions for anger, Underwood (1992) found no significant effects for peer status. For the lack of status group differences on display rules for facial expressions, several explanations are possible. Perhaps socially accepted and rejected children truly do not differ on this dimension.

TABLE 12.3. Mean proportions of children reporting display rules for anger as a function of grade and peer-rated aggressiveness

	Peer-Rated Aggressiveness	
Grade	Aggressive	Random-Normal
3	.38	.37
5	.28	.29
7	.08	.24

Note. From "Display Rules for Anger and Aggression in School-Aged Children," by M. K. Underwood, J. D. Coie, and C. R. Herbsman, 1992, *Child Development, 63.*

Alternatively, perhaps this measure was not sensitive enough to what might be subtle types of differences. Very few subjects overall reported display rules for facial expressions. Also, choosing an angry face in an interview about a hypothetical situation is much different than actually showing an angry expression toward a bullying peer or an authoritarian teacher.

For display rules to manage verbal expressions of anger, the results indicated a significant interaction of Context × Sex × Status. These means are presented in Table 12.4. Follow-up comparisons of means showed that, for the peer context, the only significant differences between means indicated that rejected girls reported display rules for anger less than average status girls. Therefore, for girls, the findings supported the hypothesis that rejected children would report display rules for anger less frequently. For girls, expressing anger overtly more often is related to social rejection, perhaps because peer norms among girls require that anger be masked more than for boys. It is important to note that, for the peer context, there were no status group differences for boys on reporting of display rules. Expressing anger openly may not violate the norms of the peer culture for males.

For the teacher context, patterns of means for status groups were different for boys and girls. Popular boys reported more display rules than average or rejected boys. Therefore, although the peer culture for boys may sanction open expression of anger toward other children, overt expression of anger toward teachers seems to be prohibited, because high status is associated with masking of anger toward teachers. Rejected girls reported display rules for anger toward teachers more frequently than average or popular girls. Therefore, for girls, frequent rather than infrequent reporting of display rules for anger was associated with low social status. This is surprising, because one would expect that, especially for girls, peer norms would forbid the overt expression of anger toward teachers; therefore, popular girls would report display rules for anger the most and rejected girls the least. Perhaps, it is possible for a school-age girl to be too submissive toward teachers, to be too reluctant to act angry in the face of a punitive teacher.

Overall, these findings suggest that the relation between reporting of display rules for anger and peer status is complex, and depends on the gender of the child and the context for expression of anger. Analy-

TABLE 12.4. Display rules for verbal or physical expressions of anger

	Peer Status		
	Popular	Average	Rejected
Peer context			
Boys	.11[a,b]	.22[a,b]	.27[a,b]
Girls	.18[a,b]	.34[a]	.03[b]
Teacher context			
Boys	.72[c]	.36[d]	.34[d]
Girls	.30[d]	.42[d]	.73[c]

Note. Within row, means with different subscripts differ significantly at *p* < .05.

ses for facial display rules did not show clear differences between status groups. For display rules for angry words or actions with peers, rejected status girls reported display rules for anger less than average status girls. The clearest differences among status groups on reporting of display rules for anger emerged for the vignettes featuring teachers. However, the pattern of these differences was opposite for boys and girls. Toward teachers, rejected girls reported masking of anger toward teachers more frequently, whereas popular boys reported display rules more often than other status groups.

Observational Research on Peer Status and Coping with Angry Provocation

One serious limitation of the research described above is that it relies heavily on children's responses to hypothetical vignettes, rather than on how children behave when actually confronted with angry provocation. To try to more directly observe how children behave when angry, Underwood and Hurley (1997) developed a laboratory method to provoke a mild degree of anger in participants in the age range of middle childhood. Beginning the study of children's anger expression in the laboratory is important for two reasons. First, it allows children's expressive behaviors to be closely observed in a carefully controlled environment. Second, laboratory observation will facilitate the development of coding systems that could then be employed in more naturalistic investigations of anger expression.

Children in this study participated in a laboratory play session during which they played a competitive computer game, for a desirable prize, with a same-gender confederate whom they thought was another participant. During a 10-minute contest period, participant children were provoked in two ways: the computer game was rigged so that the participant child lost most of the rounds and the child actor was trained to make provoking comments as he or she won rounds of the game. Data with over 300 children indicates that this experience is moderately provoking, but not harmful, because we debrief children carefully and embed this 10-minute provoking period in an hour-long play session that is predominantly positive.

The goals of this research included examining developmental and gender differences in anger expression, and also the relation between coping with peer provocation and peer social status at school and peer nominations for aggression. Because of space limitations, this summary will focus on the peer status findings. Based on preliminary research, it was hypothesized that popular peer status would be associated with responding verbally to peer provocation for boys, but to keeping quiet for girls. Popular boys were predicted to respond to teasing with humorous or distracting comments. Popular children were expected to be more skillful in responding to provocation; they were predicted to assert their own needs appropriately but not to overreact in ways that would earn them scorn from their peers or disdain from their teachers. Rejected children were expected to be less skillful in responding to provocation; they would be less likely to assert their feelings verbally and more likely to respond angrily or, perhaps, not to respond at all.

Method.   Participants were 318 children (175 boys and 143 girls) who had just completed the second, fourth, and sixth grades (average age: 8, 10, and 12 years). The ethnic composition of the sample reflected that of an urban public school system in the northwestern United States (approximately 85% European American and 15% other ethnic groups).

Sociometric data were collected and peer status was determined using the modified Coie et al. (1982) method described by Terry and Coie (1991). For the peer status data reported here, the sample included true average ($n = 49$), popular ($n = 58$), and rejected children ($n = 66$). (Unclassified children, those who did not meet criteria for any of the status groups, were eliminated from these analyses to make the average group more homogeneous, following the recommendation of Terry & Coie, 1991).

During a 1-hour laboratory play session, children were invited to play a computer game with an unfamiliar child of the same age and gender, who was a peer confederate. To increase participants' motivation to do well and care about the outcome of the game, they were told that a desirable prize would be given to the winner. After a brief practice session, the computer game was programmed to repeatedly (but not obviously) give an advantage to the actor so that the actor would win approximately 75% of the rounds of the game. The child actors were trained to make a standard set of provoking remarks as they won rounds of the game. The remarks focused on the participant's competence at the game ("You're not very good at computer games, are you?" "Why don't you try a little harder?" and "That prize has my name on it").

Play sessions were videotaped. Participants' facial and verbal responses to the provoking comments were reliably coded (kappas for faces ranged from .4 to .8, kappas for verbalizations ranged from .5 to

.85). Facial responses immediately following provoking comments were coded as angry, sad, neutral, or happy. Verbal responses were coded into 39 categories of fairly specific statements related to the game and the actor. On conceptual grounds, these 39 categories were collapsed into 12 categories of verbal responses for the analyses: no immediate verbal response, strong negative, mild negative, self-negative, defensive, game not working, change situation, distracting, game-related, laughing, joking, and positive.

Results and Discussion.   Overall, children showed remarkable skill in maintaining poise in this provoking situation. Immediately following provoking comments by the actors, participants showed neutral facial expressions and gave no verbal response just over 50% of the time. The most common types of verbalizations were talking about the specifics of the game or the score, self-negative comments, or mild negative responses. More rare were strong negative verbalizations, defensive remarks, distracting statements, laughter, and positive comments. In general, the pattern of participants' verbal reactions provides support for Gottman and Mettetal's (1986) characterization of middle childhood as a time when children value containing emotional expression in order to avoid embarrassment.

Although previous research and theory has strongly suggested that peer status groups would differ on coping with angry provocation in this situation (Newcomb et al., 1993), few differences were found. For facial expressions, there were no effects for peer status. For verbal responses, there was only one main effect for peer status, and almost no interactions of peer status with gender or grade (the one exception will be reported). However, for negative gestures in response to provocation, there was a significant effect for peer status.

Table 12.5 shows verbal responses to provocation by peer status groups. There were almost no main effects for peer status group, and no interactions for peer status and grade. There was one main effect for status, for attempting to change the situation by pleading with or bribing the actor to let the child win. Follow-up contrasts showed that rejected children tended to engage in these behaviors more often. This main effect was qualified by a significant interaction of peer status and gender, for attempting to change the situation.

Table 12.6 shows that, for trying to alter the situation by pleading or bribing, there were different patterns of status group differences for boys and girls. Rejected boys were more likely to engage in these behaviors than popular or average boys. For girls, there were no clear status group differences. Ethnographic research on boys' Little League baseball teams (Fine, 1981) has suggested that boys are reluctant to show that they value an outcome too greatly. Perhaps, rejection is associated with these behaviors for boys because it violates their gender norms.

Although there was no strong evidence that rejected children differed markedly in their verbal responses to provocation, their gestures appeared more negative. Table 12.7 presents mean sums of positive

TABLE 12.5. Verbal responses to provocation by peer status

	Peer Status			
	Popular (n = 58)	Average (n = 49)	Rejected (n = 66)	F(17, 155)
No immediate verbal response	.59	.55	.52	ns
Strong negative	.06	.07	.08	ns
Mild negative	.16	.15	.20	ns
Self-negative	.19	.15	.16	ns
Defensive	.05	.04	.04	ns
Changing the situation	.01 $_a$	.005 $_a$	.03 $_b$	4.54, p < .05
Distraction	.10	.08	.08	ns
Game talk	.21	.20	.27	ns
Laughter	.07	.06	.07	ns
Joking	.003	.01	.004	ns
Positive	.07	.09	.12	ns

Note. Values represent mean proportions of verbal responses to provocations that were of each type. Within rows, means not sharing subscripts differ at p < .05.

TABLE 12.6. Changing the situation by gender and peer status

	Peer Status		
	Popular	Average	Rejected
Boys	.004$_a$	.005$_a$	.04$_b$
Girls	.02$_c$	.005$_c$	.01$_c$

Note. Values represent mean proportions of changing situation responses. $F(1, 151) = 3.17$, $p < .05$. Within rows, means not sharing subscripts differ at $p < .05$.

and negative gestures during the 10-minute provoking session. Positive gestures included gestures that indicated success, winning, or feeling good (raising hands in victory, covering mouth with glee) and humorous body movements. Although the difference was not statistically significant, rejected children tended to make fewer of these positive gestures than popular or average children. Negative gestures were body movements that indicated loss, disbelief, or frustration; invading the actor's physical space; fake punches; bumping chairs; and banging on the keyboard. Rejected children made these gestures significantly more often than popular and average children.

The overall pattern of results that begs to be explained is the lack of main effects for peer status for verbalizations, coupled with the finding that rejected children showed more negative gestures in response to provocation. Several explanations for these findings seem possible. First, perhaps more status differences would have been evident in this study had there been larger groups of extreme status children. However, this study included 58 popular and 66 rejected children, which power analyses indicated should have been large enough to detect small to medium effects.

Second, status differences in coping with provocation may not have been evident here because these children were old enough to manage their behavior in this unusual environment. Children seemed to be trying their very best to perform well in this setting and, when effort is high, older well-liked and disliked children may look similar in their verbal regulation of emotion.

Interestingly, although rejected children seemed fully capable of controlling their verbal behavior so as to respond similarly to their average and rejected peers, they were not as successful in regulating their negative gestures. Negative physical gestures had fairly low frequencies, but were extreme behaviors that are likely to be highly salient to peers. Rejected children made twice as many overt, physical expressions of negative affect as popular children. That rejected children seemed more successful in masking verbal expressions of emotion than gestures fits well with previous theory and research. Harris (1993) cogently argued that individual differences in children's understanding of emotions are likely to be subtle; this subtlety of individual differences seems even more likely for outward expressions of emotion which likely are heavily influenced by children's efforts to present themselves positively. Gnepp and Hess (1986) found that children master verbal display rules before facial display rules, suggesting that masking nonverbal expressions of emotion might be more challenging. That rejected children differed on overt physical expressions of emotion confirms that it may be important for intervention programs on improving the social relations of rejected children to focus more on helping children master their nonverbal expressions of emotion.

TABLE 12.7. Positive and negative physical gestures by peer status

	Peer Status			
	Popular ($n = 58$)	Average ($n = 49$)	Rejected ($n = 66$)	$F(2, 155)$
Positive gestures	.77	.82	.53	*ns*
Negative gestures	1.89$_a$	2.16$_a$	3.91$_b$	5.24, $p < .01$

Note. Within rows, means not sharing subscripts differ at $p < .05$.

A third reason for the lack of peer status differences for verbal reactions may have been that the rejected children with the most extreme problems with anger regulation were not able to tolerate the play session, and may have stopped participating because they were upset and before they got really angry. Chi-square analyses indicated a significant difference between peer status groups in stopping the play session, and rejected children were far more likely to stop (12 of 66, 18%, χ^2 = 8.35, $p < .05$) than popular (3 of 58, 5%) or average (6 of 87, 7%) children. Ethical considerations forced us to make it easy for children to stop the contest if they wanted, but this provision means we may have missed the opportunity to see the most dramatic angry expressions. Rejected children appeared to stop the sessions when they felt frustrated, which may have been their way of trying to regulate strong negative affect by extricating themselves from the situation. Had they been forced to continue the play sessions, we believe that we might have seen more of the extremely angry behavior which may contribute to rejected children being intensely disliked at school.

Another possible reason for the overall lack of peer status differences may have been that this laboratory task involved coping with provocation by an unfamiliar child. If rejected children had been interacting with particular types of familiar peers, status group differences might have been much more evident. Hubbard, Coie, Dodge, Cillessen, and Schwartz (1997) found that much aggressive behavior takes place within dyads of children, in which a relationship develops over time within which one or both children fight frequently. To fully understand the emotion regulation behaviors of children disliked by peers, it may be important to observe them in dyadic interactions with another child with whom they have a history of social difficulties.

Last, although we would be reluctant to conclude from nonsignificant effects that no differences indeed exist, the lack of differences between peer status groups here supports research and theory on the importance of reputational bias. Hymel and others have proposed that rejected children may not really be "architects of their own social difficulties," but that their rejected status is determined in part by a negative reputation they develop in a particular peer group (see Hymel et al., 1990, p. 151, for a review). Hymel (1986) demonstrated that children judge peer behaviors differently, depending on whether the other child is a specific liked or disliked peer. Children gave well-liked peers the benefit of the doubt and judged them less harshly for negative behaviors, whereas they viewed negative behaviors by rejected children as caused by stable personality characteristics. Coie and Cillessen (1993) argued that, once a child is regarded as rejected by the peer group, a sort of self-fulfilling prophecy develops. Peers have negative expectations of a disliked child and communicate these by behaving more negatively toward the rejected person who, in turn, responds with aversive behavior, thereby confirming others' social expectations.

Perhaps rejected and popular children showed similar verbal responses in this investigation because rejected children were not facing such negative expectations and behaviors from familiar peers. Because participants in this research were interacting with a previously unacquainted peer in a novel setting surrounded by positive and friendly undergraduate research assistants, even rejected children might have had every reason to believe that things would go well for them. Rabiner and Coie (1989) found that, when led to believe that other children would like and accept them, rejected third grade children could behave much more competently. Although positive expectations were not intentionally induced in this research, the very presence of the unfamiliar peer and the positive setting might have led even rejected children to have positive expectations for their peer success, and to behave accordingly.

To fully understand rejected children's capacity for emotion regulation, it may be important to observe them with known children in familiar environments. However, the methodological challenges of this would be considerable. Observing naturally occurring emotion-provoking episodes would require many hours, and older children might well be skillful in hiding the most important interactions from view. Creating a conflict between two known peers in the laboratory raises serious ethical questions, because researchers would be manipulating an ongoing relationship for a child with peer problems, in an age range during which peer interactions matter enormously.

Overall, the findings from this laboratory study suggest that, in middle childhood, rejected children seem as capable of controlling their verbal reactions to provocation as their popular and average peers but, perhaps, less able to regulate their gestural responses. One method that rejected children may have used to manage their strong emotions was removing themselves from the situation. The fact that rejected children responded fairly competently suggests that they may have social skills that they can deploy in novel environments. Much of the research suggesting social skill deficits in rejected children comes from studies using peer nominations or teacher checklists, both of which may well be subject to negative halo effects. Carefully examining the role of emotion regulation in peer acceptance may require observing children's emotional reactions in a variety of situations where reputation effects may be more or less influential.

Observing More Subtle Forms of Anger Expression Among Girls

One advantage of using a computer game context to provoke anger in children is that it is intense and involving; a disadvantage is that this competitive situation and playing computer games, in general, seems more relevant to boys' interests and concerns. Galen and Underwood (1997) developed a laboratory task that seems likely to elicit the more subtle ways that girls might express anger and contempt. In this study, dyads of female friends played the board game, Pictionary, with a third unfamiliar girl who was an actor trained to be a difficult play partner. The task is less competitive and there is no prize for the winner, the outcome of the game is not rigged to reduce the focus on losing as part of the provoking experience and highlight the interpersonal provocation, and children participate with a best friend to elicit social referencing and exclusionary behavior.

We developed this laboratory task as a way to try to observe what we call social aggression, more subtle ways that we think children, and girls in particular, might express anger and contempt toward one another. Social aggression consists of disdainful facial expressions, negative evaluation gossip, exclusionary behavior, or friendship manipulation (Galen & Underwood, 1997). Social aggression is directed toward damaging another's self-esteem, social status, or both and may take direct forms such as verbal rejection, negative facial expressions or body movements, or more indirect forms such as slanderous rumors or social exclusion. We chose the term "social aggression" because it aptly describes a class of behaviors that belong together because they serve the same function in ongoing social interaction: to hurt another person by doing harm to his or her self-concept or social standing. Although many of the behaviors thought to be socially aggressive (such as relationship manipulation) cannot be observed in a single laboratory session, our goal was to directly observe some of the behaviors that may be elements of social aggression among girls: disdainful facial expressions, social exclusion, and derisive remarks.

To date, we have used this method with only a small sample of seventh-grade girls. Our research plans include using this observational method with much larger samples of boys and girls in the fourth, sixth, and eighth grades, to carefully observe gender and developmental differences in social aggression.

Results and Discussion.   In this exploratory study in which we made every attempt to standardize behaviors by the provocateur, we chose to focus on the behaviors of individual girls as the unit of analysis. Participants' responses were variable, but several behaviors were evident in all sessions: staring ($M = 26.5$, $SD = 13.92$), glancing ($M = 5.36$, $SD = 2.66$), and ignoring ($M = 4.64$, $SD = 2.19$). Other frequently observed behaviors were using a snide tone of voice ($M = 3.14$, $SD = 3.75$), sarcastic comments ($M = 2.71$, $SD = 4.12$), and making a face ($M = 2.36$, $SD = 3.21$). Positive responses to the provocations (e.g., "Alright, you go first then") were relatively rare ($M = 1.36$, $SD = 1.73$), as were more direct behaviors such as verbal abuse ($M = 0.86$, $SD = 2.06$), threats of violence ($M = 0.36$, $SD = .95$), and physical responses ($M = 0.50$, $SD = 1.32$).

Girls' responses to the questionnaire they completed after the Pictionary game indicated that they viewed the confederate as mean, rude, and unpleasant. On a scale of 1 to 5, with 1 representing *not at all*, participants reported that they did not like the confederate very much ($M = 2.29$, $SD = 1.70$, corresponding to *a little* on the scale), and that they did not think the confederate was nice ($M = 2.14$, $SD = .95$, corresponding to *a little* on the scale). Girls did think she was mean ($M = 3.21$, $SD = 1.19$, representing *pretty mean* on the scale) and reported that the confederate made them mad ($M = 3.14$, $SD = 1.70$, corresponding to *pretty mad*), and that they were not eager about the prospect of being friends with her ($M = 2.64$, $SD = 1.15$).

These findings indicate that this game task was successful in eliciting elements of social aggression. Reliable coding was possible even for subtle facial expressions. Although we recognized that not all types of socially aggressive behaviors could be observed in this setting (particularly, aspects related to manipulating friendship patterns), some of the specific behaviors observed in response to an unpleasant stranger may be similar to those involved in social exclusion among friends, such as not responding to what a person says or does (ignoring) or exhibiting disdainful facial expressions (Olweus, 1991). Girls' responses to interview questions after the game indicated that the method was successful; the confederate was not well liked by the participants. The participants found her to be mean rather than nice, and indicated that she made them moderately angry. Participants' descriptions of their overall impressions of the confederate also were predominantly negative.

To further support the ecological validity of this laboratory method and to explore children's perceptions of actual samples of social aggression, we showed a separate sample of children brief video clips from these play sessions, and asked them questions about how angry and hurt they would feel if they were the targets of these behaviors. We found that girls viewed actual samples of social aggression as indicating more anger than boys, and that older children viewed socially aggressive behavior as indicating more dislike.

An important strength of this method is that it allowed us to actually see socially aggressive behaviors among girls. With the slightly different construct of relational aggression, Crick and Grotpeter (1995) have relied mostly on peer nominations to measure behaviors such as friendship manipulation. Although they sensibly argued that direct observation would be difficult because it would require prior knowledge about relationships among children, we worry about a construct that relies on only one method of measurement and that, by definition, is something that cannot really be seen. We suggest (tentatively, because of the small number of play sessions conducted here) that elements of social aggression can be elicited and reliably coded in carefully constructed laboratory situations.

To confirm this suggestion, it seems important to employ these methods with larger samples, and to include groups of boys as well as girls, and cross-gender groups. Observational research is badly needed to confirm the suggestion from questionnaire and peer nomination data that social aggression is more common and more hurtful for girls. Answering this question requires observing boys in the same laboratory tasks used to elicit social aggression among girls. Also, by middle school, cross-gender interaction is frequent enough that it seems important to observe how both boys and girls respond to this particular type of provocation by members of the opposite gender.

☐ Future Directions

In 1979, Yarrow commented that the study of emotion by developmental psychologists had a rather "checkered history." Lewis and Michaelson (1983) proposed that developmental research on emotions had been impaired by conceptual confusion about emotions, problems in identifying and measuring emotions, and the lack of an integrative theory of social, cognitive, and emotional development. In a commentary for a special edition of a journal, Underwood (1997b) noted recent accomplishments in research on the development of emotion regulation and suggested future directions. Table 12.8 presents a list of top 10 pressing questions for the study of emotion regulation, and for understanding the relation between peer status and emotion.

To move forward in our understanding of emotion regulation in the context of peer relationships, it seems particularly important that we clarify what we mean by competence. Hubbard and Coie (1994) have suggested that one way to determine what is and is not competent emotion regulation in the peer context might be to see what behaviors are associated with popular and rejected peer status. However, as seen in the studies above, sometimes clear peer status differences do not emerge, using currently available tools. Researchers may have to think conceptually about what we believe competence in emotion regulation means for children, for different emotions, and in particular types of social settings.

The studies described above also highlight that emotion regulation likely is not one construct; it depends on the type of emotion and the social context in which it is elicited. Emotions likely occur in blends (Polivy, 1981) and research has suggested that how children choose to regulate emotions with peers depends on the specific type of emotion experienced (Underwood, 1997a).

Fully understanding emotion regulation will require careful observation across different social contexts. Laboratory studies allow emotional responses to be observed at close range in carefully controlled circumstances, but suffer from problems of external validity. There is no guarantee that laboratory situations correspond to the most important naturalistic situations in individuals' lives, and laboratory investigations fail to take into account that different children select or fall prey to different types of social encounters. To date, observation in natural settings has been difficult because emotional behaviors often can be subtle and difficult to detect from afar. Observing these behaviors at close range is intrusive and

---

TABLE 12.8. Top ten pressing questions about the development of emotion regulation

---

10. On what basis can we decide which types of emotional experiences and displays are adaptive or competent?
9. To what extent does emotion regulation depend on the specific emotion experienced?
8. Does emotion regulation require that a person has experienced at least some degree of emotional arousal? Can arousal be measured independently of emotional behavior?
7. How do temperament and socialization work together to influence the development of emotion regulation?
6. How much does emotion regulation vary across situations and contexts?
5. In studying emotion regulation, how accurate are self-report measures?
4. What types of information can and cannot be gleaned about a child's capacity for emotion regulation from questionnaires completed by parents or teachers?
3. Is it possible to use more observational or even experimental methods to study the development of emotion regulation?
2. What are the developmental trajectories for emotion regulation beyond infancy and early childhood?
1. How does the development of emotional regulation differ for girls and boys?

Note. From "Top Ten Pressing Questions about Emotion Regulation," by M. K. Underwood, in press-b, *Motivation and Emotion.*

alters the social interaction. Pepler and Craig (1995) have proposed a promising solution to these methodological challenges—remote audiovisual recording in which children wear small microphones and their interactions are recorded from afar using zoom lenses. Using this kind of technology in different social settings could greatly enhance our understanding of emotion regulation.

The research described above also confirms that individual difference variables may affect emotion regulation in social interaction with peers. The particular patterns of gender and developmental differences vary some with the methods used and samples participating but, overall, girls and older children seem to hide negative feelings more. It will be important to understand other individual differences in emotion regulation with peers, and how these relate to temperament, family, and culture.

The role of gender in emotion regulation deserves special attention for several reasons. The developmental arena in which gender differences most often have been documented is social relationships (Maccoby, 1990). During middle childhood and early adolescence, girls and boys interact at school most often in same-gender groups (Gottman, 1986). Boys' relationships are characterized more by dominance and structured activities, whereas girls interact more in smaller dyads and value intimacy more (Maccoby, 1990; Thorne & Luria, 1986). Brody (1996) has noted that gender differences in emotion regulation change over the life span. In infancy, boys express emotions more intensely than girls. By adulthood, women more openly express emotions facially and verbally (although, there is some inconsistency in gender differences in anger expression). Brody argued that much more research is needed to understand how parents and peers might influence these different developmental trajectories. More systematic study of emotion regulation in middle childhood might illuminate these issues.

Perhaps the biggest challenge for research on emotion regulation in the context of peer relationships during middle childhood is understanding the role of physiological arousal. Many children in these age groups are skilled at remaining calm and poised when provoked (Underwood & Hurley, 1997). For some individuals, maintaining calm in the face of emotional provocation may be the result of successful efforts at regulation and dissemblance. For others, remaining calm may require much less effort, because they are less prone to becoming strongly aroused by emotion on account of temperamental variables or socialization histories. So far, measuring emotional arousal in ongoing social interaction has proved difficult. Because movement seriously perturbs these kinds of data, the few researchers who have attempted physiological recording with children in these age groups have been forced to record arousal while children are sitting still watching videotapes rather than taking part in live social interaction (Guthrie et al., in press). However, recent technological advances have suggested that it soon may be possible to do some physiological recording with children as they interact with others in live situations (Hubbard, 1997). It will be important for developmental psychologists to systematically use some of these better tools for physiological recording, so that we can start to amass an empirical and theoretical base for understanding how arousal relates to regulation.

☐ Conclusion

In the laboratory study in which children were provoked to anger by losing at a computer game while being taunted by a peer confederate (Underwood & Hurley, 1997), we asked children (after the provocation but before the debriefing) a series of questions about what they felt like doing to the peer provocateur, and why they did not show their true feelings. Responses to these queries differed enormously and reflected the extreme variability in strategies for emotion regulation during middle childhood. One child said he felt like "keeping my mouth shut, and smiling back at him," which he was able to do. Another reported that he felt like "teaching him a lesson, telling him how to do things to make people like him," but did not because he "didn't feel like it." A girl said, "I felt like hitting her," but did not because "I knew it wouldn't help me win the game or anything." Another girl reported, "I felt like I wanted to smack her," but did not "because I am not here to fight." This same girl told us that she usually hits people who provoke her. A boy said he felt like "just killing myself—I hate my sister when she is being sassy and naughty, that's when I feel like killing myself," but that he did not do this because "I usually hit myself in the head or stop thinking about it or stop the game." A girl said, "I felt like saying 'I am trying as hard as I can and please don't tease me,'" but did not because "I thought I would be hurting her feelings."

Why are some children able to be very strategic about controlling their emotions in a manner consistent with their social goals, and why are others so disregulated? Emotions researchers (Frijda, 1986) and peer relations experts (Dodge, 1991) alike have agreed that emotions influence all aspects of social information processing and, therefore, emotions are regulated at many different levels. Understanding emotion regulation will be further complicated by the fact that emotional arousal not only is determined by various types of regulatory processes, but also by emotional intensity—stable individual differences in emotional arousability that may be temperamental (Eisenberg & Fabes, 1992). These complex, multidimensional models of emotion and regulation have been helpful in suggesting fruitful research questions. However, these models may have tempted us to believe that the only path to understanding emotion regulation will be more and better research on its various components. Saarni (1997) has cogently suggested that only researchers think of emotions in terms of "disconnected entities" (p. 1), and that it might be productive to examine children's emotion scripts for emotion management. Most of us develop characteristic ways of experiencing and communicating strong emotions, though these might vary some for different social contexts. Given that children's interactions with peers can generate everything from high glee to intense pain, examining children's developing scripts for managing emotions with peers might provide insight into how and why emotions can energize or overwhelm us.

☐ References

Aboud, F. E. (1989). Disagreement between friends. *International Journal of Behavioral Development, 12*, 495–508.

Asher, S. R., Parkhurst, J. T., Hymel, S., & Williams, G. A. (1990). Peer rejection and loneliness in childhood. In S. R. Asher & J. D. Coie (Eds.), *Peer rejection in childhood* (pp. 253–273). New York: Cambridge University Press.

Averill, J. R. (1982). *Anger and aggression: An essay on emotion.* New York: Springer-Verlag.

Brody, L. R. (1996). Gender, emotional expression, and parent-child boundaries. In R. D. Kavenaugh, B. Zimmerberg, & S. Fein (Eds.), *Emotion: Interdisciplinary perspectives* (pp. 139–170). Mahwah, NJ: Erlbaum.

Cairns, R. B., Cairns, B. D., Neckerman, H. J., Gest, S. D., & Gariepy, J. L. (1988). Social networks and aggressive behavior: Peer support or peer rejection? *Developmental Psychology, 24*, 815–823.

Casey, R. J. (1993). Children's emotional experience: Relations among expression, self-report, and understanding. *Developmental Psychology, 29*, 119–129.

Coie, J. D., & Cillessen, A. H. N. (1993). Peer rejection: Origins and effects on children's development. *Current Directions in Psychological Science, 2*, 89–92.

Coie, J. D., Dodge, K. A., & Coppotelli, H. A. (1982). Dimensions and types of social status. *Developmental Psychology, 18*, 557–569.

Coie, J. D., & Kupersmidt, J. B. (1983). A behavioral analysis of emerging status in boys' groups. *Child Development, 54*, 1400–1416.

Cole, M., & Cole, S. R. (1996). *The development of children*. New York: W. H. Freeman.

Crick, N. R., & Grotpeter, J. K. (1995). Relational aggression, gender, and social-psychological adjustment. *Child Development, 66*, 710–722.

Denton, K., & Zarbatany, L. (1996). Age differences in support processes in conversations between friends. *Child Development, 67*, 1360–1373.

Dodge, K. A. (1986). A social information processing model of social competence in children. In M. Perlmutter (Ed.), *Minnesota Symposium on Child Psychology* (Vol. 18, pp. 77–125), Hillsdale, NJ: Erlbaum.

Dodge, K. A. (1991). Emotion and social information processing. In J. Garber & K. A. Dodge (Eds.), *The development of emotion regulation and dysregulation* (pp. 159–181). New York: Cambridge University Press.

Dodge, K. A., Coie, J. D., Petit, G. S., & Price, J. M. (1990). Peer status and aggression in boys' groups: Developmental and contextual analyses. *Child Development, 61*, 1289–1309.

Doubleday, C., Kovaric, P., & Dorr, A. (1990, August). *Children's knowledge of display rules for emotional expression and control*. Paper presented at the meeting of the American Psychological Association, Boston, MA.

Eisenberg, N., & Fabes, R. A. (1992). Emotion, regulation, and the development of social competence. In M. S. Clark (Ed.), *Review of personality and social psychology: Emotion and social behavior* (pp. 119–150). Newbury Park, CA: Sage.

Eisenberg, N., Fabes, R. A., Karbon, M., Murphy, B. C., Wosinski, M., Polazzi, L., Carlo, G., & Juhnke, C. (1996). The relations of children's dispositional prosocial behavior to emotionality, regulation, and social functioning. *Child Development, 67*, 974–992.

Ekman, P., & Friesen, W. V. (1975). *Unmasking the face*. Englewood Cliffs, NJ: Prentice-Hall.

Erikson, E. H. (1980). Elements of a psychoanalytic theory of psychosocial development. In S. I. Greenspan & G. H. Pollock (Eds.), *The course of life: Psychoanalytic contributions towards understanding personality development: Vol. 1. Infancy and early childhood* (pp. 11–61). Adelphi, MD: NIMH Mental Health Study Center.

Fabes, R. A., & Eisenberg, N. (1992). Young children's coping with interpersonal anger. *Child Development, 63*, 116–128.

Fine, G. A. (1981). *With the boys: Little League baseball and preadolescent culture*. Chicago: University of Chicago Press.

Fox, N. A. (Ed.). (1994). The development of emotion regulation. *Monographs of the Society for Research in Child Development, 59*(2–3, Serial No. 240).

Freud, S. (1905). Three essays on the theory of sexuality. In J. Strachey (Ed.), *The complete psychological works* (Vol. 7). New York: Norton.

Frijda, N. H. (1986). *The emotions*. New York: Cambridge University Press.

Galen, B. R. & Underwood, M. K. (1997). A developmental investigation of social aggression among children. *Developmental Psychology, 33*, 589–600.

Garber, J., & Dodge, K. A. (1991). *The development of emotion regulation and dysregulation*. New York: Cambridge University Press.

Gnepp, J., & Hess, D. L. (1986). Children's understanding of verbal and facial display rules. *Developmental Psychology, 22*, 103–108.

Gottman, J. M. (1986). The world of coordinated play: Same and cross-sex friendship in young children. In J. M. Gottman & J. G. Parker (Eds.), *Conversations with friends: Speculations on affective development* (pp. 139–191). New York: Cambridge University Press.

Gottman, J. M., & Mettetal, G. (1986). Speculations about social and affective development: Friendship and acquaintanceship through adolescence. In J. M. Gottman & J. G. Parker (Eds.), *Conversations with friends: Speculations on affective development* (pp. 192–237). New York: Cambridge University Press.

Guthrie, I. K., Eisenberg, N., Fabes, R. A., Murphy, B. C., Holmgren, R., Mazsk, P., & Suh, K. (1997). The relations of empathy and emotionality to children's situational empathy-related responding. *Motivation and Emotion, 21*(1), 87–108.

Harris, P. L. (1993). Understanding emotion. In M. Lewis & J. M. Haviland (Eds.), *Handbook of emotions* (pp. 237–246). New York: Guilford.

Hartup, W. W. (1970). Peer interaction and social organization. In P. H. Mussen (Ed.), *Carmichael's manual of child psychology*. New York: Wiley.

Hartup, W. W. (1989). Social relationships and their developmental significance. *American Psychologist, 44*, 120–126.

Hartup, W. W., French, D. C., Laursen, B., Johnston, M. K., & Ogawa, J. R. (1993). Conflict and friendship patterns in middle childhood: Behavior in a closed field situation. *Child Development, 64*, 445–454.

Hochschild, A. R. (1979). Emotion work, feeling rules, and social structure. *American Journal of Sociology, 85*, 551–575.

Hubbard, J. A. (1997, April). Observing children's emotion expression in a confederate-based, competitive paradigm. In M. K. Underwood (Chair), *Creating naturalistic laboratory methods to observe peer relations and emotion expression*. Symposium conducted at the biennial meeting of the Society for Research in Child Development, Washington, DC.

Hubbard, J. A., & Coie, J. D. (1994). Emotional correlates of social competence in children's peer relationships. *Merrill-Palmer Quarterly, 40*, 1–20.

Hubbard, J. A., Coie, J. D., Dodge, K. ., Cillessen, A. H., & Schwartz, D. (under review). *The role of relationship dyads in aggressive behavior.*

Hymel, S. (1986). Interpretations of peer behavior: Affective bias in childhood and adolescence. *Child Development, 57,* 431–445.

Hymel, S., Wagner, E., & Butler, L. J. (1990). Reputational bias: View from the peer group. In S. R. Asher & J. D. Coie (Eds.), *Peer rejection in childhood* (pp. 156–186). New York: Cambridge University Press.

Kindermann, T. A. (1993). Natural peer groups as contexts for individual development: The case of children's motivation at school. *Developmental Psychology, 29,* 970–977.

Kohlberg, L., LaCrosse, J., & Ricks, D. (1972). The predictability of adult mental health from childhood behavior. In B. Wolman (Ed.), *Manual of child psychopathology* (pp. 1217–1284). New York: McGraw-Hill.

Kupersmidt, J. B., & Coie, J. D. (1990). Preadolescent peer status, aggression, and school adjustment as predictors of externalizing problems in adolescence. *Child Development, 61,* 1350–1362.

Larson, R., & Asmussen, L. (1991). Anger, worry, and hurt in early adolescence: An enlarging world of negative emotions. In M. E. Colton & S. Gore (Eds.), *Adolescent stress: Causes and consequences* (pp. 21–41). New York: Aldine de Gruyter.

Larson, R., & Lampron-Petraitis, C. (1989). Daily emotional states as reported by children and adolescents. *Child Development, 60,* 1250–1260.

Larson, R., & Richards, M. H. (1991). Daily companionship in late childhood and early adolescence: Changing developmental contexts. *Child Development, 62,* 284–300.

Laursen, B., Hartup, W. W., & Koplas, A. L. (1996). Towards an understanding of peer conflict. *Merrill-Palmer Quarterly, 42,* 76–102.

Lemerise, E. A., & Dodge, K. A. (1993). The development of anger and hostile interactions. In M. Lewis & J. M. Haviland (Eds.), *Handbook of emotions* (pp. 537–546). New York: Guilford.

Lempers, J. D., & Clark-Lempers, D. S. (1992). Young, middle, and late adolescents' comparisons of the functional importance of five significant relationships. *Journal of Youth and Adolescence, 21,* 53–96.

Lewis, M. (1993). The emergence of human emotions. In M. Lewis & J. M. Haviland (Eds.), *Handbook of emotions* (pp. 223–236). New York: Guilford.

Lewis, M., & Haviland, J. M. (1993). *Handbook of emotions.* New York: Guilford.

Lewis, M., & Michaelson, L. (1983). *Children's emotions and moods: Developmental theory and measurement.* New York: Plenum.

Lutz, C. A. (1990). Engendered emotion: Gender, power, and the rhetoric of emotional control in American discourse. In C. A. Lutz & L. Abu-Lughod (Eds.), *Language and the politics of emotion* (pp. 69–91). Cambridge, England: Cambridge University Press.

Maccoby, E. E. (1990). Gender and relationships: A developmental account. *American Psychologist, 45,* 513–520.

Maccoby, E. E., & Jacklin, C. N. (1974). *The psychology of gender differences.* Stanford, CA: Stanford University Press.

Moreno, J. L. (1934). *Who shall survive? A new approach to the problem of human interrelations.* Washington, DC: Nervous and Mental Disease Publishing Co.

Murphy, B., & Eisenberg, N. (1996). Provoked by a peer: Children's anger-related responses and their relation to social functioning. *Merrill-Palmer Quarterly, 42,* 103–124.

Newcomb, A. F., Bukowski, W. M., & Pattee, L. (1993). Children's peer relations: A meta-analytic review of popular, rejected, neglected, controversial, and average sociometric status. *Psychological Bulletin, 113,* 99–128.

Olweus, D. (1991). Bully/victim problems among schoolchildren: Basic facts and effects of a school-based intervention program. In D. J. Pepler & K. H. Rubin (Eds.), *The development and treatment of childhood aggression* (pp. 411–448). Hillsdale, NJ: Erlbaum.

Parke, R. D. (1994). Progress, paradigms, and unresolved problems: A commentary of recent advances in our understanding of children's emotions. *Merrill-Palmer Quarterly, 40,* 157–169.

Parker, J. G., & Asher, S. R. (1987). Peer relations and later personal adjustment: Are low-accepted children at greater risk? *Psychological Bulletin, 102,* 357–389.

Parker, J. G., & Asher, S. R. (1993). Friendship and friendship quality in middle childhood: Links between peer group acceptance and feelings of loneliness and social dissatisfaction. *Developmental Psychology, 29,* 611–621.

Pepler, D. J., & Craig, W. M. (1995). A peek behind the fence: Naturalistic observations of aggressive children with remote audiovisual recording. *Developmental Psychology, 31,* 548–553.

Piaget, J. (1983). Piaget's theory. In P. H. Mussen (Ed.), *Handbook of child psychology: Vol. 1, History, theory and methods* (4th ed., pp. 1–25). New York: Wiley.

Polivy, J. (1981). On the induction of emotion in the laboratory: Discrete moods or multiple affective states. *Journal of Personality and Social Psychology, 41,* 803–817.

Rabiner, D., & Coie, J. (1989). Effect of expectancy inductions on rejected children's acceptance by unfamiliar peers. *Developmental Psychology, 25,* 450–457.

Saarni, C. (1979). Children's understanding of display rules for expressive behavior. *Developmental Psychology, 15,* 424–429.

Saarni, C. (1988). Children's understanding of the interpersonal consequences of dissemblance on non-verbal emotional-expressive behavior. *Journal of Non-verbal Behavior, 12,* 275–294.

Saarni, C. (1989). Strategic control of emotional expression. In C. Saarni & P. L. Harris (Eds.), *Children's understanding of emotions* (pp. 181–208). New York: Cambridge University Press.

Saarni, C. (1990). Emotional competence. In R. Thompson (Ed.), *Nebraska Symposium: Socioemotional development* (pp. 115–161). Lincoln: University of Nebraska Press.

Saarni, C. (1997, April). Emotion management and strategies for social interaction. In A. Sroufe (Chair), *What develops in emotional development.* Symposium conducted at the biennial meeting of the Society for Research in Child Development, Washington, DC.

Saarni, C., & von Salisch, M. (1993). The socialization of emotional dissemblance. In M. Lewis & C. Saarni, (Eds.), *Lying and deception in everyday life* (pp. 106–125). New York: Guilford.

Scheff, T. J. (1984). The taboo on coarse emotions. In P. Shaver (Ed.), *Review of personality and social psychology: Emotions, relationships, and health* (Vol. 5, pp. 185–209). Beverly Hills, CA: Sage.

Tavris, C. (1982). *Anger: The misunderstood emotion.* New York: Simon & Schuster.

Terry, R., & Coie, J. D. (1991). A comparison of methods for defining sociometric status among children. *Developmental Psychology, 27,* 867–880.

Thorne, B., & Luria, Z. (1986). Sexuality and gender in children's daily worlds. *Social Problems, 33,* 176–190.

Underwood, M. K. (1992, April). Peer social status and the development of anger expression. In T. A. Kinderman (Chair), *Peer group networks as contexts for children's development.* Symposium conducted at the annual convention of the Western Psychological Association, Portland, OR.

Underwood, M. K. (1997a). Peer social status and children's choices about the expression and control of positive and negative emotions. *Merrill-Palmer Quarterly, 43,* 610–634.

Underwood, M. K. (1997b). Top ten pressing questions about emotion regulation. *Motivation and Emotion, 21,* 127–146.

Underwood, M. K., Coie, J. D., & Herbsman, C. R. (1992). Display rules for anger and aggression in school-aged children. *Child Development, 63,* 366–380.

Underwood, M. K., & Hurley, J. C. (1997, April). Children's responses to angry provocation as a function of peer status and aggression. In J. L. Zeman & M. K. Underwood (Cochairs), *Affect regulation and dysregulation: A developmental perspective.* Symposium conducted at the biennial meeting of the Society for Research in Child Development, Washington, DC.

Walden, T., & Smith, M. C. (1997). Emotion regulation. *Motivation and Emotion, 21,* 7–25.

Whitesell, N. R., & Harter, S. (1996). The interpersonal consequences of emotion: Anger with close friends and classmates. *Child Development, 67,* 1345–1359.

Williams, C., & Bybee, J. (1994). What do children feel guilty about? Developmental and gender differences. *Developmental Psychology, 30,* 617–623.

Yarrow, L. J. (1979). Emotional development. *American Psychologist, 34,* 951–957.

Zarbatany, L., Ghesquierre, K., & Mohr, K. (1992). A context perspective on early adolescents' friendship expectations. *Journal of Early Adolescence, 12,* 111–126.

Zarbatany, L., Hartmann, D. P., & Rankin, D. B. (1990). The psychological functions of preadolescent peer activities. *Child Development, 61,* 1067–1080.

Zeman, J., & Garber, J. (1996). Display rules for anger, sadness, and pain: It depends on who is watching. *Child Development, 67,* 957–973.

Zeman, J., & Shipman, K. (1996). Children's expressions of negative affect: Reasons and methods. *Developmental Psychology, 32,* 842–849.

Deanna Kuhn

Metacognitive Development

☐ Introduction

Psychology began as an enterprise that relied on introspection regarding internal mental activity for much of its insight. Yet, by the middle decades of the twentieth century, when behaviorism had its strongest hold on American psychology, the role of cognition was most often defined in negative terms—as a misleading construct best bypassed in the effort to explain, predict, and control behavior. Only a few decades later, as the century draws to a close, a cognitive revolution has secured a center stage role for the study of cognition in a broad array of both laboratory and "situated" contexts. Not as widely noted, although it ultimately may prove as consequential, is an increasingly important role occupied by the second-order construct of *metacognition*—cognition about cognition.

This development is visible both at the center of academic psychology and at its borders with other disciplines. The most interesting border activity is at the intersection of psychology (particularly, neuropsychology) and philosophy. As Nelson (1996) observed, it is notable for border activity between these disciplines to be occurring at all. Only recently has there been a shift in the traditional view among philosophers that, if findings from an empirical science such as psychology become relevant to a philosophical problem, the problem mistakenly has been regarded as a philosophical one and warrants reclassification. A flurry of recent books reflects the interest among philosophers in the puzzle of consciousness, with philosophers seeing as central to this puzzle how to connect the phenomenological experience of consciousness to events that neuroscientists have identified as occurring in the brain (Baars, 1997; Cohen & Schooler, 1996; Dennett, 1991; Flanagan, 1992; Shear, in press; Weiskrantz, 1997). Since most accounts of metacognition involve conscious awareness of mental activity, psychologists' study of metacognitive phenomena stands to inform and constrain theories of consciousness (Nelson, 1996).

At the other, applied end of the disciplinary spectrum lies a more traditional area of border activity—that between psychology and education. It also is a focus of current attention. Educators have become increasingly troubled by the gap between students' rote learning and their understanding, most often reflected in their inability to apply what they have learned in new contexts (Brown, 1997; Gardner, 1991; Perkins, 1992; Resnick & Nelson-LeGall, 1998). In addition, educators increasingly see it as important for students to "take charge of their own learning" rather than accept the passive role of being recipients of what others have to tell them. In each of these cases, students' metacognitive awareness and management of their own cognitive processes is implicated. If educators are to realize such goals, they need psychological knowledge of metacognitive processes, how they develop, and how they can be fostered.

Metacognitive phenomena and the issues surrounding them also have received increasing attention in recent years within the mainstream of psychology. People have been shown to have some access to their own cognition in the form of "feeling of knowing" judgments about their factual knowledge, and these have been the focus of empirical research on metacognition in the adult literature (Metcalfe & Shimamura, 1994; Nelson, 1996). More broadly, a much debated issue within cognitive psychology has been the validity of think aloud methods in which participants are asked to provide concurrent or retrospective verbal data on their own mental processes during problem solving (Ericsson & Simon, 1980). Similarly, in social psychology, debate has occurred regarding the accuracy of verbal reports of mental processes (Nisbett & Wilson, 1977), contrasts between direct and self-reported measures of beliefs and belief change (Bassili,1996; Greenwald & Banaji, 1995; Kuhn & Lao, 1996; Miller, McHoskey, Bane, & Dowd, 1993), and the consequences of reflecting on one's beliefs (Kuhn & Lao, in press; Tesser, Martin, & Mendolia, 1995; Wilson & Brekke, 1994; Wilson & Schooler, 1991). All of these are topics that have to do directly with people's cognitions about their own cognition.

The present chapter is devoted to an examination of past, present, and potential roles of metacognition in developmental psychology. If metacognition is as influential and potentially powerful a construct as it appears, it becomes important to understand how it develops. Among the questions to be asked in this chapter are these: How and when does the capacity for awareness, understanding, or management of one's own cognition first emerge and what are the various forms it takes? How does knowledge of one's own cognition relate to knowledge of others' cognition? What mechanisms underlie the emergence and continuing development of these meta-knowing competencies? What role do they play in the development and regulation of first-order cognitive skills? Although the empirical literature in developmental psychology is, at best, incomplete in providing answers to these questions, the rapid growth of research activity in this area has established many promising leads. Impediments to progress, I will argue, have been a lack of definitional clarity and a lack of connection between different approaches to the topic.

☐ Forms of Meta-Knowing

Within developmental psychology, the roots of current interest in metacognitive phenomena are both narrow and broad. The earliest work, as I note in more detail below, dealt almost exclusively with awareness and monitoring of memory strategies (Brown, 1975, 1978). Yet, a broader conception of metacognition as "thinking about thinking" figures importantly in a wide range of both traditional and modern theories of cognitive development (Campbell & Bickhard, 1986; Case, 1997; Demetriou & Efklides, 1994; Piaget, 1950; Sternberg, 1984, 1985; Vygotsky, 1934/1962). As a theoretical construct, it has appeared in different guises in developmental psychology—traditionally, as the hallmark of Piaget's adolescent stage of formal operations, later as the executive monitoring and management of information-processing strategies, and only more recently, as a focus of the burgeoning literature on young children's "theory of mind." This theoretical fluidity, I will claim, does not signal a construct so loosely defined as to be useless but, rather, a gradually evolving, multidimensional competence. Like cognition itself, metacognition is not a zero-one phenomenon that emerges at some single, identifiable point in development. Even very young children exhibit metacognitive competencies (Brown, 1997), yet the thinking of adults reveals serious weaknesses in metacognitive awareness and control (Kuhn, 1991; Kuhn, Garcia-Mila, Zohar, & Andersen, 1995).

This conception of a gradually developing metacognitive competence offers a unifying perspective for connecting a variety of developmental phenomena that may not seem closely linked on the surface, but all have to do with the emergence and development of second-order cognition. In particular, largely unconnected bodies of work that I wish to bring together in this chapter are, on the one hand, those addressing meta-knowing about *knowing processes* (originating with the early literature on metamemory) versus *knowing products* (particularly, the concepts and theories currently studied as "theory of mind"), and, on the other hand, investigation of the meta-knowing competencies of young children versus older individuals.

I use *meta-knowing* as a broad, umbrella term to encompass any cognition that has cognition (either one's own or others') as its object. Within the relatively new research area that has come to be known as "theory of mind," the question has arisen as to the relation between these two objects or products of meta-knowing: the self's vs. the other's cognition and, in particular, the extent to which understanding of one derives from understanding of the other. This is a question to which I will return.

Another distinction in forms of meta-knowing is one between awareness of cognition (the fact that it exists or is occurring, in either self or other) and understanding of its content (which can range from implicit and intuitive to explicit and theory-like). In addition to awareness and understanding, a third form consists of the attempt to influence (rather than only observe or understand) one's cognition through processes of monitoring, resource allocation, or other forms of management. Parallel forms in the case of others' cognition include efforts to persuade or instruct another, guided by conceptions of the other's mental processes.

In each of these cases, a hierarchical cognitive system of at least two levels is implied, with cognitions of the first level serving as the object of cognitions at the second level. Note, however, that the existence of a two-level cognitive system does not necessarily imply conscious awareness (of the first level by the second level). Classical developmental theorists such as Vygotsky (1934/1962) and Piaget (1976, 1978) included conscious awareness as a defining attribute of metacognition. In an information-processing theory such as Sternberg's (1984, 1985), in contrast, "meta" components played a major role in the absence of any attribution of conscious awareness.

Finally, the broadest distinction to be drawn in this chapter is based on one of the most widely employed dichotomies in cognitive psychology: the dichotomy between procedural knowing (knowing how) and declarative knowing (knowing that). Meta-knowing, I claim, differs depending on the kind of first-order knowing that is its object. Knowing about declarative knowing (as a product) is addressed in the section, Metacognitive Knowing. Knowing about procedural knowing (as a process) is addressed in the section, Metastrategic Knowing.

One further subdivision reflects the fact that metacognitive knowing can be either specific and situational (i.e., pertaining to a particular piece of knowledge) or general and more abstract (i.e., about knowledge and knowing in general). The latter I examine in the section, Epistemological Meta-Knowing, which, in turn, can be either personal (pertaining to one's own knowing) or impersonal (applicable to anyone's knowing). All of the categories that have been identified here are summarized in Table 13.1, with references to representative research studies, most of which are discussed further at various points in the chapter.

☐ Developmental Origins of Meta-Knowing

How does meta-knowing arise? Many of the questions and issues that have arisen in studying the development of first-order cognition (particularly, questions of mechanism) are encountered in a parallel way in examining second-order, meta-knowing. We have learned enough about cognitive development to reject, for example, the view that mental representations are direct copies internalized from the physical or social environment. Yet, as socioculturalists (Cole, 1996; Rogoff, 1997) have persuasively demonstrated, the constructivist alternative does not imply that a child constructs an understanding of self and world as a solitary enterprise in a social vacuum. Children's participation in a social culture transforms their experience in powerful ways. Still, recognizing the power of culture is not sufficient to explain the process by which the child constructs meaning through participation in it. In the words of Astington and Olson (1995), "Social understanding cannot . . . proceed via 'participation' without appeal to concepts" (p. 187). Analysis must include the meaning-making activity of the participants in this collective experience.

The capacity for mental representation of meaning develops early in life, certainly by the second year, as reflected by such traditional indicators as pretend play (Leslie, 1987) and deferred imitation (Piaget & Inhelder, 1951). Not long after, there is evidence that the content of these mental representations becomes recursive (i.e., includes mental phenomena themselves). By age 3, children are able to verbalize their awareness that the world includes not only material entities but also nonmaterial ones, such as desires, intentions, thoughts, and ideas, that are the product of human mental life (Flavell & Miller, 1997). They are able to distinguish mental entities from physical ones, for example, thinking about a dog from looking at one (Estes, Wellman, & Woolley, 1989). Given explicit enough cues, they will acknowledge that another person is engaged in thinking (Flavell, Green, & Flavell, 1995). In everyday conversation, children by age 3 make reference to their own knowledge states, using verbs such as think and know (Olson & Astington, 1986) and may even express awareness of absence of knowledge, as in "I don't know which" (Feldman, 1988, p. 134). Although appearing slightly later (Fabricius, in press), reference to others' mental states of knowledge, intention, or desire also becomes common, as in "He wants the biggest one for himself" or "She knows where it is and won't tell."

How has the child achieved this capacity to make mental experience its own object—to think about thinking? As in the achievement of first-order mental representations, both social participation and constructive meaning making are implicated. As well as multiple processes, multiple sources of knowledge are involved, as the child constructs meaning based both on his or her own inner experience and the selves that others make visible in social interaction. An early contributor to this achievement is the joint attention to objects and events that emerges among infants and their caretakers and out of which the infant comes to recognize meaning making and intention on the part of the other (Tomasello, Kruger, & Ratner, 1993; Trevarthen, 1980). As children's experience, and hence awareness, of their own mental

TABLE 13.1. Forms of meta-knowing

Metastrategic (Knowing about Procedural Knowing)		Metacognitive (Knowing about Declarative Knowing)			
		Specific/Situated		General/Epistemological	
About others' knowing	About self's knowing	About self's knowing	About others' knowing	About others' knowing	About self's knowing
Awareness Flavell, Green, & Flavell (1995)	Awareness Flavell et al. (1995)	Awareness Olson & Astington (1986) Gopnik & Graf (1988) Kuhn & Pearsall (1998)	Awareness Trevarthen (1980) Wellman (1988) Wimmer et al. (1983) Flavell et al. (1992) Dunn et al. (1991) Carpendale & Chandler (1996) Lao & Kuhn (1998) Kuhn (1989)	Mansfield & Clinchy (1997) Chandler et al. (1990) Perry (1970) Kuhn (1991) King & Kitchener (1994) Leadbeater &	Dweck (1991)
Understanding Flavell et al. (1995)	Understanding Flavell et al. (1995) Kreutzer, Leonard, & Flavell (1975)	Coord. of beliefs & new evidence Kuhn et al. (1995) Kuhn & Lao (1996) Chinn & Brewer (1993) Chan et al. (1997)			
Management Persuading Clark & Delia (1976) Kuhn et al. (1997) Leadbeater (1988) Staudinger & Baltes (1996)	Management Monitoring Brown (1975, 1978) Flavell et al. (1981) Markman (1979)				
Instructing Palincsar & Brown (1984) Brown (1997) Wood et al. (1995)	Directing Brown (1987, 1997) Bisanz et al. (1978) Cross & Paris (1988)				
	Coord. of strategy & task knowledge Kuhn et al. (1995) Kuhn & Pearsall (in press)				

Note. References to research studies are illustrative only, rather than exhaustive. They appear within each column in a rough developmental order, beginning with those involving initial acquisitions early in development and ending with those pertaining to adults.

activities increases, the desire to communicate these to others may emerge, for example, when a child tells her mother a story she has invented which then becomes a topic of conversation (Feldman, 1988). At the same time, a parent scaffolds the child's understanding by making reference to the mental states of parent, child, and others, thus making the child more aware of mental states as a topic of conversation and, hence, thought. Leslie (1987) argued for the special role of pretend play in contributing to the child's understanding of mental life, because it entails the same suspension of truth and reality requirements that characterize mental states such as belief and desire.

Those involved in the current study of theory of mind have drawn a distinction between "simulation" (Harris, 1992) and "theory" (Gopnik & Wellman, 1992; Montgomery, 1992) accounts of the mechanism responsible for children's developing theories of mind, the child generalizing from his or her own inner life in the simulation account and constructing a theory based on social data in the theory account. But, there is no reason to think that a choice must be made between the two mechanisms. Both self and others serve as sources of knowledge about both self and others. Projecting my own experience helps me to understand others, but I also come to know myself more fully, including what I think and feel, by how others react to and understand me.

I turn now to the content of thinking about thinking, once this second-order representational capacity has been achieved. What do children know or believe about their own and others' thinking? We begin with metacognitive knowledge; that is, one's beliefs about one's own and others' declarative knowledge— what self or other knows and how it is known. What does such meta-knowledge consist of and how does it evolve?

Metacognitive Knowing

By the end of their second year of life, children spend significant time engaged in pretend play, a form of mental representation which, as noted above, entails the suspension of reality. One might anticipate, then, that 3-year-olds' metacognitive understanding of mental life would include the recognition that mental representations need not correspond to reality. This turns out, however, not to be the case. Although they routinely engage in pretend play, young preschool children are unwilling to accept that anyone could hold a belief that deviates from what they themselves take to be a true state of affairs. Although Leslie's (1987) conjecture may be correct that the experience of pretend play facilitates the eventual understanding that mental representations need not mirror reality, young children apparently do not have the reflective awareness of their own or others' mental states of pretense that would lead them to make this inference. They acknowledge that what another person imagines (e.g., an elephant in the room) need not reflect reality (Woolley, 1995), but this recognition does not extend to one's own or another's beliefs. Pretense, as Leslie (1987) noted, involves a temporary mental suspension of reality without obvious cause or consequent. Beliefs, in contrast, are assertions about the way the world really is. As such, they presumably derive from experiences in the world and, in turn, lead the believer to act in the world in ways consistent with these beliefs. In other words, unlike pretense, beliefs have causes and consequents that link them to the external world.

A good deal of evidence now exists suggesting that children below the age of about 4 regard the universe of assertions that people make, and the beliefs that these assertions reflect, as descriptive of and isomorphic to an external reality. An account of an event differs from the event itself only in that one exists on a representational plane while the other is perceived directly. In other words, the world is a simple one in which things happen and we can tell about them. There are no inaccurate renderings of events.

The most familiar source of evidence for this characterization is young children's poor performance in the now classic false belief task. Three-year-olds believe that a newcomer will share their own accurate knowledge that a candy container, in fact, holds pencils (Perner, 1991; Wimmer & Perner, 1983). It is impossible that the other person could hold a belief that the child knows to be false. Less widely cited is the finding that this refusal to attribute false knowledge to another extends beyond the realm of factual knowledge to values, social conventions, and moral rules that the child takes to be valid or true claims. In a study by Flavell, Mumme, Green, and Flavell (1992), preschool children were told, for example, about a girl (Robin) who thinks that it is okay to put her feet on the dinner table and then immediately were asked, "Does Robin think that it is okay to put her feet on the dinner table?" Strikingly, a large majority of 3-year-olds responded negatively to such questions as well as to parallel questions about whether someone could hold nonnormative beliefs regarding moral rules (breaking a toy), values (eating grass), and facts (whether cats can read books). Performance improved, but remained below ceiling, among 4-year-olds.

Findings in related kinds of tasks have supported the claim that young children treat mental representations as in necessary correspondence with an external reality. Once the true state of affairs has been revealed to them, 3-year-olds deny their own earlier false beliefs (e.g., that they originally had thought the container held candy; Gopnik & Astington, 1988). Also, they deny that another child possesses knowledge that they lack regarding the contents of a box immediately after witnessing the other child being given this information verbally or visually (Wimmer, Hogrefe, & Perner, 1988). Apparently, the other's knowledge cannot deviate from the child's own. Wimmer et al. have speculated that the child transforms questions about representations such as "Do you [does he] know what's in the box?" to simpler questions about reality (i.e., "What's in the box?"). The child thus can answer the "you" form correctly, by just reading off his or her own knowledge state. In the third-person form, however, the transformed question yields an incorrect answer.

Beginning at about age 4 (and largely completed by age 5), children come to recognize assertions as the expression of someone's belief—a milestone, I would claim, in their cognitive development, that lays the way for many of the achievements examined in this chapter. Perner (1991) characterized this acquisition in formal terms as the ability to metarepresent (i.e., to mentally model the human representational function). Accordingly, the child comes to recognize that, as expressions of humans' representational capacity, assertions do not necessarily correspond to reality. We do not know why this achievement occurs at exactly this time but, evidently, the child accrues enough experience with human knowing (of both self and others) to link the products of knowing—beliefs and assertions—to the generative process that gives rise to them. Their source is a human representational system that is recognized as having intent and volition to represent what it wishes to represent. Accordingly, an assertion's closest link becomes one to this source—the subject that is doing the representing, rather than the object being represented.

If assertions do not necessarily correspond to reality, they become susceptible to evaluation vis-à-vis a reality from which they are now distinguished. Although such evaluation in its rudimentary form entails no more than a simple comparison of an assertion to reality and declaration of it as true or false, it is a critical step in the development of metacognitive knowing. It also is notable as the origin of what will become scientific thinking as well as what has long been referred to as critical thinking (one traditional definition of which is in fact the evaluation of assertions). Evaluating assertions implies, at least, some distinction between an assertion and external evidence bearing on it: Assertion and evidence must exist as distinct entities if one is to be evaluated in light of the other. The resulting potential for disconfirmation is a hallmark of science. We return later to the relation of metacognition to these traditional forms of higher-order reasoning.

Evolving more directly from the recognition of assertions as belief states susceptible to evaluation is attention to the source of an assertion—the basis for claiming it to be true. If assertions mirror reality, the source from which a particular assertion arises is of little consequence. All sources offer equally authentic knowledge. As soon as assertions become potentially false, however, their sources take on new significance. A concern with the sources of assertions takes us to the heart of metacognitive knowing: Is an individual aware that and why one knows some piece of declarative knowledge? Can the individual justify, accurately, to self or others, how and why he or she knows?

Several studies have documented the metacognitive challenge entailed in maintaining awareness of the source of one's claim—the evidence that led to making it—as knowledge distinct from the claim itself. Gopnik and Graf (1988) and O'Neill and Gopnik (1991), for example, found preschool children unable to indicate whether they had just learned the contents of a drawer from seeing them or being told about them. Similarly, Taylor and colleagues (Esbensen,Taylor, & Stoess, 1997; Taylor, Esbensen, & Bennett,1994) reported preschoolers as showing little ability to distinguish when they had acquired a particular piece of factual knowledge, whether it had just been taught to them or was something they had "always known" (as most of them claimed regarding a newly learned fact).

My own recent work in this vein is situated in a framework of coordinating theory and evidence (Kuhn, 1989), as the essence of both scientific and argumentive thinking. Children from an early age construct theories as a means of understanding their worlds (Wellman & Gelman, 1998) and gradually revise these theories in the face of new evidence. What develops, I claim, is increasing awareness and control of the coordination of theory and evidence in one's own thinking. We have examined these processes in microgenetic studies of children's and adults' gradual coordination of their existing theories with an accumulating base of new evidence that they access and interpret (Kuhn, Schauble, & Garcia-Mila, 1992; Kuhn et al., 1995). Their task is to identify factors that do and do not affect an outcome in a multivariable situation. Of primary interest is the basis individuals use to justify their knowledge claims.

In a current study (Kuhn & Pearsall, 1998), we have examined developmental origins of these skills in preschoolers' ability to differentiate theory and evidence as a basis for their knowledge claims. Do young children appreciate whether they are claiming something to be true because it makes sense as a way for things to be or on the basis of specific evidence of its correctness? In our study, preschoolers were shown a sequence of pictures in which, for example, two runners compete in a race. Certain cues suggest a theory as to why one will win (e.g., one has fancy running shoes and the other does not). The final picture in the sequence provides evidence of the outcome (e.g., one of the runners holds a trophy and exhibits a wide grin). When children subsequently are asked to indicate the outcome and to justify this knowledge, younger children show a fragile distinction between the two kinds of justification—"How do you know?" and "Why is it so?"—that is, the evidence for their claim (the outcome cue in this case) versus their explanation for it (the initial theory-generating cue). The two jointly support a single representation of a state of affairs that "makes sense," with the respective cues treated as interchangeable contributors to this knowledge state. In the race example, young children often answered the "How do you know [he won]?" question, not with evidence (e.g.., "He's holding the trophy"), but with a theory of why this state of affairs makes sense (e.g., "Because he has fast sneakers"). In another instance in which a boy is shown first climbing a tree and then down on the ground holding his knee, the "How do you know [that he fell]?" question often was answered, "Because he wasn't holding on carefully." These confusions between theory and evidence diminish sharply among 5-year-olds, who are more likely to distinguish the evidence for their claim from a theory that explains it. The question "How do you know?" becomes a meaningful one, distinct from the question of whether this knowledge claim is a plausible one. It is this development, I believe, that reflects a growing metacognitive capacity to reflect on one's own knowing and, hence, to distinguish theory and evidence, rather than demonstrations of children's ability to reason about correspondences between assertions and patterns of evidence (i.e., that a particular pattern of evidence is consistent with or supports a particular claim), which have been the focus of most studies of early scientific reasoning skill (see Kuhn et al., 1995, for review of this literature).

The several lines of evidence that have been described above point to the gradual emergence of a competence in metacognitive knowing during the preschool years. With respect to developmental mechanism, it bears emphasis once again that these achievements do not arise solely from the child's internal cognitive constructive efforts. As highlighted in work such as that by Dunn and colleagues (Dunn, Brown, Slomkowski, Tesla, & Youngblade,1991), equally important is the scaffolding provided by adults in natural settings, reflected, for example, in a parent's explanation of a sibling's false belief: "He didn't know you wanted it." The dual processes of social participation and cognitive construction that begin in infancy gradually increase in complexity and support the achievements of the preschool period.

A number of studies have shown these preschool achievements to be amenable to acceleration by various forms of scaffolding. To the extent tasks are situated in everyday contexts (Dunn et al., 1991) or familiar, purposive experimental settings, for example, hiding and deceiving in a game context (Chandler, Fritz, & Hala, 1989; Hala & Chandler, 1996), performance is enhanced. Similarly, performance in the standard false belief task is enhanced if the child is provided some representational depiction of the earlier (now falsified) knowledge state, such as a photograph (Freeman & Lacohee, 1995; Mitchell & Lacohee, 1991), if the new (correct) knowledge state is made less visually salient (Zaitchik, 1991), if the child is asked to explain rather than predict an action deriving from false belief (Robinson & Mitchell, 1995), or if the child is given direct experience regarding the changeability of belief states (Slaughter & Gopnik, 1996).

It thus would be a mistake to see a particular age level or competency as marking a singular turning point in what is better conceptualized as a gradual evolution. It similarly would be a mistake to see the evolution in metacognitive knowing as complete once the child reaches the age of 4 or 5. Four-year-olds who succeed in recognizing another's failed search for an object as a product of the other's false belief have not achieved the most sophisticated understanding of the mental processes and products involved in knowing that we might hope for. Knowing at this point is explained by the knower's having perceptual exposure to the salient information. Knowing means seeing that it is so. Even inference is not fully under-stood as a source of others' knowledge (Keenan, Ruffman, & Olson,1994; Sodian & Wimmer, 1987). Ac-cordingly, false beliefs can be only the product of a lack of exposure or exposure to misinformation. The holder of a false belief has not seen the reality that is there to be seen.

Still to develop is the understanding that different minds can arrive at genuinely different and legiti-mate understandings following exposure to exactly the same information. Studies by several researchers have shown that 4- and 5-year-olds who are fully competent in reporting false beliefs attributable to incor-rect information nonetheless do not make appropriate judgments regarding the mental representations of observers exposed to misleading or ambiguous stimuli (Carpendale & Chandler, 1996; Pillow & Henrichon, 1996; Taylor, Cartwright, & Bowden, 1991), tending instead to assume that the other will interpret the stimulus in the same way they do. Even, at age 8, they may not understand the difficulty in predicting others' responses to ambiguous stimuli (Carpendale & Chandler, 1996). Although children of this age have no difficulty in accepting that people can have different tastes and values (Flavell et al., 1992), and even emotional reactions to the same object or event (Taylor et al., 1991), they do not yet accept that different people can hold genuinely different beliefs regarding this object or event, except in the case where one party's belief is misinformed and incorrect. Children at this age evidently lack the "interpre-tive" or "constructive" theory of mind (Carpendale & Chandler, 1996) that would lead them to understand conflicting representations of the same event as legitimate products of individuals' unique meaning-mak-ing efforts—to understand that, because interpretive mental processes vary across individuals, their prod-ucts also may differ. This achievement is a stepping stone in the development of epistemological under-standing, which we turn to later in the chapter. In concluding this section, it should be emphasized that the development that has been traced, leading to the beginnings of a constructive theory of mind, re-mains at best incomplete. Throughout adulthood, all of us, on occasion, fail to assess, or misassess, the knowledge states of others, most often assuming that they match our own (Kuhn & Lao, 1998).

Metastrategic Knowing

I turn now to metastrategic knowing—knowing about mental processes, as opposed to products. As noted above, the distinction rests on the first-order distinction between procedural (knowing how) and declara-tive (knowing that) knowledge. Another way of framing this distinction is knowledge as means versus knowledge as end. Declarative knowledge we know and retain as an end in itself, ordinarily without a specific use to which it is to be put, whereas procedural knowledge enables one to carry out some activity that is the end and purpose for knowing. Knowing how to play the violin enables me to perform on the instrument, whereas knowing that violin is the instrument's name enables me only to display this knowl-edge as an end in itself. Similarly, in the case of procedural meta-knowing (what we are calling here metastrategic knowing), the knower's awareness, monitoring, and management of procedural knowledge offer the potential dividend of enhancing the performance to which they pertain; again, in contrast to metacognitive knowing which typically has no immediate or specific application beyond the declarative knowledge to which it pertains. Unlike my awareness of the fact (and even origin) of my knowing the instrument name, my awareness, monitoring, and management of my own playing techniques stand to enhance my performance on the violin.

What, then, do children come to know about their cognitive processes and what impact does this knowledge have on performance? The findings described in the preceding section lead to a prediction that young children are unlikely to have much awareness (let alone, monitoring or management) of their own (or others') cognitive processes. For them, as we saw, mental representations reflect the external world more than they do the mental activity of the representer. As such, this mental activity does not assume great significance in its own right and is unlikely to be the object of the child's attention.

Recent research by Flavell and colleagues (Flavell, 1997; Flavell et al., 1995) confirmed this prediction. Although their responses make it clear that they understand thinking as internal mental activity, pre-school children show limited awareness of its occurrence or content, in themselves or others. They may not acknowledge that a person engaged in making a decision is thinking and, despite explicit cues, are poor at judging what the person has been thinking about. When they themselves are asked to "not think about anything," in contrast to older children and adults who realize the difficulty of the task, they are likely to report having been successful. They also demonstrate limited awareness of the contents of their own thought. When asked, for example, to think about the room in their house where their toothbrush is kept and asked immediately afterward what they had been thinking about, 5-year-olds failed to mention either bathrooms or toothbrushes (Flavell et al., 1995).

Flavell's recent work grew out of the earliest empirical research in developmental psychology to examine meta-knowing—a literature focused on meta-memory, originating with Flavell himself (1979; Flavell & Wellman, 1977; Kreutzer, Leonard, & Flavell, 1975), Brown (1975, 1978, 1987), and several others. This work, conducted largely in the 1970s and 1980s, has been reviewed in a number of places (Brown, Bransford, Ferrara, & Campione, 1983; Flavell & Wellman, 1977; Schneider, 1985), and will not be described in detail here. The major findings and their historical significance easily can be summarized.

The work focuses on children's knowledge and use of strategies, such as rehearsal or categorization, to aid their performance in traditional memory tasks like recalling a list of words. The ability to behave strategically is itself relevant to the present concerns since it implies some competence in the management of one's cognitive functions. It initially was thought that preschool children were incapable of using strategies to aid their memory performance, but it since has been shown that they can do so if the task is simple (e.g., remembering where a toy was hidden) and the context supportive (DeLoache, Cassidy, & Brown, 1985). In this respect, the findings parallel those described in the preceding section with respect to false belief and other theory-of-mind tasks. Like those achievements, the development of strategies that enhance cognitive performance is gradual and context sensitive, rather than sudden.

In contrast to evidence of early metacognitive achievements described in the previous section, no marked achievements in strategic memory performance or meta-memory appear during the preschool years. Early studies reported some success in teaching memory strategies to young children (Brown, 1975, 1978). The more significant finding, however, is that such teaching rarely generalizes to new situations (Brown, 1997). Unless they are prompted to do so, children tend not to apply strategies spontaneously in contexts where they would be useful. Improvements in this respect occur during the middle childhood years but, even by the end of childhood, performance is far from optimum. Such findings have led to the conclusion that children have poor metastrategic awareness and understanding of their memory processes (Brown et al., 1983; Flavell & Wellman, 1977; Schneider, 1985).

Studies that have directly assessed children's knowledge about memory support this conclusion. Preschoolers display some elementary knowledge, for example, that increasing the number of items makes a memory test harder (Kreutzer et al., 1975), but not before middle childhood do children understand, for example, that a memory strategy such as categorization aids recall (Moynahan, 1978). Older children also are able to predict their own memory performance more accurately than preschoolers, who tend to greatly overestimate it (Flavell & Wellman, 1977).

Do children who exhibit more knowledge in meta-memory assessment perform better in a related memory task? Although early studies of correspondences between meta-memory knowledge and memory performance suggested little relation between the two (Kreutzer et al., 1975), more recent research has indicated a modest correlation (Schneider & Bjorklund, 1997). Other studies have shown, however, that children do not necessarily make appropriate use of the meta-knowledge that they have as a means of enhancing their performance. For example, although both younger and older children have been shown to discriminate between recalled and unrecalled items on a memory test, only older children take advantage of this information by focusing on unrecalled items when given the opportunity for further study (Bisanz, Vesonder, & Voss, 1978; Masur, McIntyre, & Flavell, 1973). Children's failure to generalize to a new situation a strategy that they have been taught to perform successfully may be due to a lack of metastrategic awareness of the strategy's value (Kuhn, 1982). Supporting this assumption, Fabricius and Hagen (1984) found many children recognized their improved performance following use of an organizational strategy, but failed to attribute it to use of the strategy.

Although it has served the important historical role of identifying children's metastrategic understanding as a factor deserving of attention, the meta-memory literature is limited in three ways. First, correlations between memory and meta-memory performance do not establish the direction of causality or, more broadly, tell us anything about the dynamic, most likely bidirectional influence of memory skills and meta-memorial understanding on one another as the two develop over time and across a range of contexts. More will be said about this dynamic process below. I also postpone until the next section discussion of a second limitation: the fact that the traditional meta-memory literature is based on what we now understand to be an obsolete model of strategy development.

A third limitation is that this literature is based almost entirely on the study of children's memory for experimental stimuli in laboratory settings in which there is no purpose for remembering the material beyond the demands of the experimental situation. We do not know to what extent the findings from these studies generalize to more natural settings in which memorization occurs as part of some purposeful activity. Although some efforts have been made to extend work on strategic and metastrategic memory to the more natural context of learning in school (Pressley, 1997; Zimmerman & Martinez-Pons, 1986), not a great deal is known about how such skills develop during the childhood years in school contexts or in children's lives outside of school.

Nor has there been much research on metastrategic competence outside of the well-studied memory paradigm. An exception is a smaller literature on comprehension monitoring (Flavell, Speer, Green, & August, 1981; Markman, 1977, 1979; Pressley & Ghatala, 1990). Significantly, its implications parallel those from the meta-memory research. In a now classic set of studies, Markman (1977, 1979) found that children asked to read a short passage containing blatant contradictions did not report them, even when asked explicitly whether what they have read makes sense. Evidently, they do not engage in metastrategic monitoring of their processing of information, to achieve an awareness of whether it has been successful (or, at least, show no evidence of such awareness in their verbal reports). As in the meta-memory research, modest improvements can be observed through the school years, but weakness remains evident even in older children. Only if they were alerted in advance that something in the passage might not make sense, Markman (1979) found, did the performance of sixth graders exceed that of third graders, and even then their performance was far from perfect.

These findings, then, point to a more wide-ranging metastrategic deficit in children, one not limited to memory skills. Children apply cognitive skills to meet task demands but, even if capable of doing so, do not spontaneously apply metastrategies that would enable them to evaluate their performance—a first step toward the use of metastrategic understanding as a means to regulate and improve performance. Although there does not exist a substantial enough database across diverse kinds of cognitive tasks and settings to make this judgment conclusively, little if any evidence exists to refute it. It also is a conclusion consistent, certainly, with a good deal of educational literature on children's rote learning rather than deep understanding of what they are taught (Gardner, 1991; Perkins, 1992).

This brief review of research pertaining to children's metastrategic knowledge of their own cognitive processes leaves us in a different place than the earlier review of research on children's developing metacognitive understanding of the beliefs that are the products of their own and others' knowing activities. The early and rapid progress that was noted in children's achieving an understanding of human representational activity is not matched in their achievement of awareness, understanding, or management of their own cognitive processes. Before proceeding to questions of mechanism, in the next section, I explore what connections might be made between the two bodies of findings and whether there is a more extended developmental framework in which they can be viewed. Doing so will leave us in a better position to contemplate the developmental mechanisms involved.

☐ Linking Metastrategic and Metacognitive Knowing

To pursue these objectives, I turn to a line of research I have pursued for a number of years (Kuhn, Amsel, & O'Loughlin, 1988; Kuhn & Phelps, 1982; Kuhn et al., 1992, 1995) that, I believe, highlights connections between metastrategic and metacognitive knowing as well as situates them in a life span developmental framework. The latter is accomplished by addressing a key developmental question, In what directions and toward what ends are these developing competencies headed? Also, in what ways are they supported by and in what ways do they support other developing competencies? This developmental framework is critical in establishing the broader significance of the cognitive skills that researchers study.

The work I describe here is based on a task more cognitively demanding than the memory and comprehension tasks considered in the preceding section in the sense that it requires the individual to go beyond comprehension or memorization of presented material, to operate on it and generate conclusions that follow from it. The task is suitable across a wide spectrum of the life span, making it possible to examine performance in an extended developmental framework. The task involves the kinds of inferential reasoning that people of all ages engage in commonly, even if not self-consciously or explicitly. As briefly described earlier, participants engage in the task over multiple sessions, during which they gradually coordinate their existing theories with an accumulating base of new evidence that they access and interpret. Their objective is to identify the causal and noncausal factors influencing an outcome in a multivariable context. The method allows us to follow over time both their evolving knowledge base (as their theories change in the face of new evidence) and changes in the strategies by means of which they acquire that knowledge. The task can be situated in the context of several different literatures in cognitive and developmental psychology—as a task of inductive causal inference, scientific, argumentive, or critical thinking (Kuhn, 1996) as well as learning and knowledge acquisition.

Because the method is a microgenetic one in which change over time is observed, the data address fundamental issues regarding the nature of the change process. Findings by other investigators who have used a microgenetic method to examine change converge with our own in showing that individuals approach a task with a repertory of strategies that they apply variably over time, even when the task environment remains constant (for review, see Kuhn, 1995; Siegler, 1996). Such findings lead to a revised conception of change. In contrast to the traditional conception of a single transition in which a new strategy replaces an old one, with the focus on the challenge of mastering the new strategy, the newer portrayal of change features continuing shifts in the frequencies of usage of multiple strategies, with the diminished usage and eventual relinquishment of less adequate strategies a developmental challenge at least equal to that of mastering new, more adequate ones.

This revised model of strategy change has major implications with respect to the role of metastrategic factors. Rather than the traditional focus on metastrategic understanding of a particular strategy (such as categorization in meta-memory research) as a factor influencing performance, the major metastrategic task becomes the very different one of strategy selection, from the repertory of strategies the individual has available that are applicable to the task. If the strategies an individual selects shift over repeated encounters with the task, as microgenetic research documents that they do (Kuhn, 1995; Siegler, 1996), this is the change that needs to be explained in a model of the change process. Strategy selection is a metastrategic, not a strategic, function; hence, the burden of explanation shifts to the metastrategic level. Other solutions are possible, for example, that strategy selection is accomplished by a nonmetastrategic process such as competition among strategies based on associative strength (Siegler & Jenkins, 1989), but metastrategic operations are at the least a leading contender in accounting for strategy selection.

Since our task allows participants to freely choose strategies both for investigating the database we make available and drawing inferences from their observations, it is ideal for studying strategy selection, especially since our data confirm that virtually all participants have available a variety of both investigative and inference strategies that they apply variably over time. Although I will not discuss the particular strategies in detail here (see Kuhn et al., 1995, for further description), they encompass such dimensions as (a) the extent to which individuals coordinate instances (of multivariable features and accompanying outcomes) they choose to investigate with the question they have identified as the object of the investigation, (b) whether an inference is based on a single instance of evidence or whether two or more instances are compared, and (c) whether a comparison that is made is one that allows variation in nonfocal features to be excluded as a contributor to the outcome.

At the same time as it calls on metastrategic skill in the selection and monitoring of strategies, the task requires metacognitive skill in justifying knowledge claims. Individuals are not required to make any inferences (they are free to say that they do not know or cannot yet tell), but they are asked to justify each of the inferences they do make. Although there is age-related improvement, it is here that we see in adolescents and adults metacognitive weaknesses that parallel those observed among preschoolers in the research by Kuhn and Pearsall (1998) described above. Like preschoolers, many older individuals blur the distinction between theory-based and evidence-based sources of their beliefs. Rather than seeing their theories as belief states subject to disconfirmation and representing theory and evidence as distinct entities to be reconciled with one another, they merge the two into a single representation of "the way things are," with little apparent awareness of the sources of their belief.

When supportive evidence accumulates, individuals may become more convinced of the correctness of their beliefs, but even less metacognitively aware of the source of this certainty. They are certain that they know, but not how they know. They frequently substitute theory-based justifications in response to questions about the implications of evidence, suggesting an indifference to the sources of claims. Evidence serves merely to illustrate what one knows to be true, with evidence-based and theory-based justifications functioning as interchangeable supports for a claim.

In cases in which evidence discrepant with a theory accumulates over time, rather than compare theory and evidence, individuals often ignore or distort the evidence or draw on fragments of this evidence to support the theory, disregarding the rest and using the allegedly supportive evidence to illustrate what from their perspective is true. Theories do change in response to discrepant evidence, but often with the individual manifesting little awareness of the process. Like young children in the theory-of-mind research described above, the older participants in our studies are likely to deny they ever held a belief different from the one they are now professing.

A common pattern across all ages, we found, is the use of a valid strategy to interpret theory compatible evidence with respect to one feature and an invalid strategy to interpret theory discrepant evidence with respect to another feature, even though the evidence in regard to the two features is identical. Weak metacognitive awareness of the basis for one's beliefs and metastrategic inconsistency in the application of inference strategies thus reinforce one another.

The performance of one of our young subjects, Beth, a fourth grader working on the boat problem (Kuhn et al., 1992, 1995), illustrates a number of these weaknesses. Beth was allowed to construct and test boats of her choice to determine which features did and did not make a difference in how fast the boats traveled (via a weight-and-pulley mechanism) across a tank of water. The index of speed was which colored zone the boat reached in a fixed time interval (with red the fastest and yellow the slowest). (See Table 13.2 for a summary of the problem structure.)

Although Beth's attention shifted among the different features on which the boats varied and she made inferences regarding the effects of all five features during her investigations, we focus here on sail size (large or small), which was of considerable concern to her. Beth's progress with respect to the sail size feature is worthy of close examination as it illustrates that the coordination that needs to be achieved is more than a linear process of replacing an incorrect theory with a correct one dictated by the evidence. Instead, the theory itself is fluid over time, influenced, in part, by what the subject experiences as the fluidity of the evidence which, at times, seems to indicate one thing and, at other times, another. Beth, in fact, initially exhibited two conflicting strands of theory with respect to sail size (which, in fact, was a noncausal feature having no effect on outcome). At the initial theory assessment, she claimed that the large sail should yield a faster outcome than the small sail because "the wind will catch it" and make it go faster. Several weeks later, however, just prior to beginning her investigations, she changed her theory regarding sail size, claiming first that sail size makes a difference and then immediately changing her mind, "No, no it doesn't. If you have the sail on there, it will still catch the breeze."

In predicting the outcome of the first boat she constructed, Beth's causal theory regarding sail size reappeared:

Beth: *I think it will go to black, because it has a big sail so the wind would catch it.*

In interpreting the outcome, Beth continued to focus on sail size (despite the indeterminacy of which of the five variables had contributed to the outcome):

Interviewer: *What have you found out about what makes a difference in how fast or slow the boats go?*
Beth: *The sail size.*

Of greatest interest is how she justified this inference:

TABLE 13.2. Causal structures of boat problems

Summary of Outcomes				
Blue (0)	**Yellow (1)**	**Green (2)**	**Black (3)**	**Red (4)**
	L-s, LWS	L-D,LwD, L-d, Lwd Sws	SwD Swd S-s	S-d, S-D

Note. Effects are as follows. Size of boat (S or L): Small (S) advances boat two zones. Weight (w or -): Absence of weight (-) advances boat one zone, in small boats only. Depth of water (D, d, or s): Deep (D) or medium deep (d) water advances boat one zone. Sail color (R or G): No effect—red (R) and green (G) sails yield identical outcomes. Sail size (1 or 2): No effect—small (1) and large (2) sails yield identical outcomes. "Strategies of Knowledge Aquisition," by D. Kuhn, M. Garcia-Mila, A. Zohar, and C. Anderson, 1995, *Society for Research in Child Development Monographs, 60*(4, Serial No. 245).

Interviewer: *How do you know?*

Beth: *It would be easier for the wind to catch onto it.*

Interviewer: *Does the testing you've done with the boats tell you about whether the sail size makes a difference?*

Beth: *No.*

Thus, at this point Beth seemed to distinguish theory and evidence as justifications for her claim. The next boat she constructed, which differed from the first one on all five features, however, posed a problem for her theory, because a small sail co-occurred with a faster outcome than had the previous large sail. Rather than acknowledge the covariation in a direction opposite of her theory, Beth distorted the evidence by claiming that the two outcomes were equivalent and, hence, that sail size makes no difference:

Beth: *The sail still went fast no matter what size.*

Interviewer: *So does sail size make a difference?*

Beth: *No, because no matter what size it was, it caught the wind, so it will go fast.*

At this point, moreover, she implicated the evidence as supporting her inference:

Interviewer: *Does the testing you've done with the boats tell you about whether the sail size makes a difference?*

Beth: *Yes, because with the big boat* [and sail] *it went pretty fast . . . and with the small boat and small sail it went pretty fast.*

In her notebook Beth wrote, "The boat went pretty fast with a small sail and a big sail."

The noncausal theory voiced just prior to the beginning of her investigations thus reappeared, as a means of achieving compatibility between theory and evidence. In addition, the evidence itself had to be distorted (the two outcomes were not, in fact, equivalent). Both theory and evidence were adjusted to achieve a reconciliation between the two. Furthermore, Beth appealed to both evidence and theory as sources of justification for her claim, in fact, merging them into a single explanation ("no matter what size it was, it caught the wind").

At the beginning of the next session, the causal sail size theory resurfaced in Beth's interpretation of the first instance she generated:

Beth: *I found out that it didn't go further from what I said because it had a small sail.*

Interviewer: *So the small sail makes it go slower?*

Beth: *Yes.*

Interviewer: *And sail size makes a difference then?*

Beth: *Yes.*

Interviewer: *How do you know?*

Beth: *Because this small sail went to the green flag and didn't go to the black or the red. And the last test I did with the big sail* [initial instance at session 1], *and it was on a big boat, and it went past the green flag, and it almost went to the red, but it didn't.*

The two outcomes Beth compared were, in fact, identical. Thus, she again distorted the evidence to accord with what appeared to be her dominant theory (invoking sail size as causal). She wrote in her notebook, "The small sail doesn't go fast"—an entry, note, that contradicts the immediately preceding entry from the previous session.

In the next two instances she examined, Beth varied two features that were, in fact, causal (boat size and water depth), as well as sail size. Although she had stated an intention to investigate depth, her attention was diverted by the compatibility of the outcomes with the causal sail size theory and she concluded:

Interviewer: *So what have you found out?*

Beth: *That the size of the sail won't be able to go as fast as the one with the big sail, because it's small and the wind won't be able to catch on to it as much as the one with the big sail.*

Interviewer: *Does any of the testing you've done with the boats tell you about whether sail size makes a difference?*

Beth: *Yes, when I chose the one with the big sail, it went to the black flag, and this one went to the yellow flag. It didn't go as fast as the one with the big sail because it's a small sail and the wind wasn't really able to catch on to the sail.*

Thus, despite the interviewer's probe designed to focus Beth's attention on evidence-based justification, she again merged theory-based and evidence-based justification. In addition, her theoretical preoccupation with the sail size feature led her to ignore the features that were, in fact, causal and that also covaried with outcome. By the third session, Beth had accumulated a database of eight instances in which boat size covaried perfectly with outcome, yet she continued to appeal to the inconsistently covarying sail size as responsible for the outcomes. Beth eventually did acknowledge the effect of boat size, but her justification made it clear that she lacked a theoretical mechanism for explaining this effect, which may have impeded her recognition of it:

Interviewer: *So what have you learned?*

Beth: *That the big boat doesn't go as fast as the small boat.*

Interviewer: *And how do you know?*

Beth: *'Cause with the small boat, it's smaller, and it can go a lot faster than the big boat.*

Over the course of her investigations, Beth demonstrated that she had in her repertory inference strategies that enabled her to draw valid, evidence-based conclusions regarding both causal and noncausal effects. By the fifth session, she began to recognize the need to equate instances with respect to nonfocal features so as to exclude them as contributors to variation in outcome, and she exhibited multiple instances of valid causal and noncausal inference. In justifying a causal inference regarding boat size, for example, she explained: ". . . last week when I tried a small boat, it went past the green flag, and it had the same depth and same big red sail [as the present large boat, which had a slower outcome]."

Similarly, with respect to sail color, which Beth had consistently believed to be noncausal, she confidently justified her noncausal inference:

Beth: *When I tried a small red sail, it went up to the green flag, and this one* [identical except for sail color] *went to the green flag.*

Interviewer: *So what have you found out?*

Beth: *That the color of the sail doesn't make a difference.*

With respect to sail size, in contrast, powerful inference strategies such as these were never applied. The difference in the way Beth treated sail size and boat size is particularly striking at one of the later sessions, when she was asked to justify her claim that both were causal. She justified the boat size effect by contrasting the relatively slow outcome of the large boat in front of her with the faster outcome of the immediately preceding (otherwise comparable) small boat. To justify the effect of sail size, however, she resorted to an earlier instance in which the favored large sail had been paired with a small boat size and thus had a relatively fast outcome, which Beth attributed to its large sail size. In doing so, she had to ignore the fact that the instance she had just generated (which remained displayed in front of her) had an even faster outcome, although its sail was small.

Despite her progress in the use of valid strategies, invalid strategies remained in Beth's repertory, to be used when they suited her purposes. Although I will not describe it here, Beth showed similar progress in an equivalent problem she worked on during the same period, involving race cars traveling along a race track on a microcomputer. At the completion of the study, we asked Beth what she had learned. Her answer with respect to the boat problem was: "I learned that the smaller boats go faster than the big boats." In fact she learned much more, with her progress in meta-knowing the most important outcome of her activities. In attainments that subsequent studies (Kuhn et al., 1995) have shown to generalize to new content, Beth became more aware of her own knowledge claims as assertions subject to evaluation and more skilled in selecting strategies capable of evaluating them, even though her metastrategic control of these strategies awaited further development.

☐ Connecting Meta-Knowing to Performance

If meta-knowing exercises the powerful influence over performance that has been suggested, it would be important to document this influence by obtaining independent measures of the two and demonstrating their relation. Although measures of performance are easy to devise, assessing meta-knowing is less straightforward. One relevant source in our work is the notebooks that participants were given to keep records if they wished to. These notebook entries reflect the kinds of information or knowledge claims that a subject saw as relevant to the task at hand and, hence, can be regarded as indicators of metacognitive understanding. Analysis of change in notebook entries over time (Garcia-Mila & Andersen, in preparation) suggests progress paralleling that observed on the plane of performance. Some entries reflect the lack of differentiation of theory and evidence as sources of knowledge that appeared on the performance plane in Beth's case. For example, one fifth grader wrote: "Now I am sure that the small boat goes further from the testing I have done because the smaller boat is lighter than the big boat." Most subjects progressed to entries that captured aspects of their investigative activity and served as an evidence base for their inferences, but many never progressed beyond incomplete data entries, such as antecedent feature combinations without outcomes or outcomes without the full indication of features necessary for unambiguous interpretation.

In a recent study (Kuhn & Pearsall, 1998), we undertook to assess metastrategic understanding by asking fifth-graders to communicate to a new child how to do the task, thereby externalizing their metastrategic knowledge and making it available for observation. Until this point in the chapter, metastrategic knowledge has been discussed simply as knowledge about strategies. In the work described in this section, we develop a fuller and arguably more adequate conception of metastrategic knowledge as involving two components. One is understanding of the task objectives and requirements. The other is awareness and understanding of the strategies available in one's repertoire that potentially are applicable to the task. The challenge of effective metastrategic functioning can be conceived of as one of coordination of task and strategy components, so that the optimal intersection of the two is realized in performance. In the Kuhn and Pearsall (1998) study, we assessed each of these components on two occasions, once in an interview near the beginning of the 7-week period during which the child worked on the boat, car, or other equivalent tasks (Kuhn et al., 1995) and, again, in a second interview at the end of the period. Table 13.3 summarizes the levels of metastrategic understanding that were identified.

Children at the lowest level (0) in Table 13.3 (who, by definition, score no higher than level 0 on either task or strategy components) exhibit no insight regarding the task objective and, when asked about it, simply describe the procedures involved in the task. Likewise, they exhibit no knowledge of strategies nor awareness of the need for them. The following is an excerpt from the strategy portion of one child's initial metastrategic interview (with respect to the car task):

Interviewer: *Can you explain to _____ how you decide which ones to investigate?*
Child: *There are some things here that you could pick.*
Interviewer: *How do you decide?*
Child: *Ah, you just guess. To see what items you want to see in the car.*

Children progressing beyond level 0 conceive of some purpose of their activity beyond simply executing the procedural routines involved. At level 1, this purpose is focused on obtaining a good outcome, either as a task objective or a strategy (see Table 13.3). At levels 2 and above, the focus shifts from outcome to analysis of the effects operating to produce outcomes, again both as a task objective and strategy. At level 4, this analysis begins to focus on determining the effects of features as a task objective and on strategies for achieving this objective, with levels 5 and 6 incorporating the critical features, respectively, of focusing on individual features and controlling the influence of nonfocal features. (As reflected in Table 13.3, level 3 is not defined in the strategy domain and level 6 is not defined in the task domain.)

Children typically increased in metastrategic understanding from the first assessment, when they had had little experience with the task, to the final assessment, when they had been working with the task for 7 weeks. Of 47 participants, only 3 showed any decline in metastrategic level from initial to final assessment. Seven showed no change and the remaining 37 (79%) showed an increase in level (on one or both components). Because the metastrategic assessment method is a verbal one and, therefore, subject to false negatives (i.e., the child may have a higher level of understanding than he or she communicates verbally), for purposes of examining the connection to strategic performance a child was classified as exhibiting the level of metastrategic understanding that was the highest exhibited in either the task objective or the strategy portion of the interview. Thus, in effect, a child had two chances to exhibit metastrategic understanding, in communicating either the objective of the task or the strategies used to achieve it.

Taking as an indicator of strategic performance whether the child attained significant strategic mastery of the task as indicated by a proportional display of valid inference strategies greater than 50%, children at

TABLE 13.3. Levels of metastrategic understanding

	Task Objective	Strategy
Level 0	Procedural only.	None. ("Just choose anything.")
Level 1	Attain a good outome. ("Find out which goes fastest.")	Choose instances believed to yield a good outcome. ("Choose the fastest.")
Level 2	Analysis at instance level. ("Find out how fast different boats will go.")	Try different instances and observe outcomes. ("Try different ones to see how fast they go.")
Level 3	Analysis at feature level without discriminating features. ("Find out what things are making a difference.")	—
Level 4	Analysis at feature level with reference to muliple features. ("See whether the size and weight make a difference.")	Compare instances in which muliple features are varied. ("Compare a big heavy one and small light one to see if it makes a difference.")
Level 5	Analysis at feature level with focus on single features at a time. ("Find out whether each of the features makes a difference.")	Compare instances in which a single feature is varied and other features are not mentioned. ("See if the big or small one goes faster.")
Level 6	—	Compare instances in which a single feature is varied and nonvariation of other features is indicated. ("Change just the weight and see if it makes a difference.")

Note. From "Relations Between Metastrategic Knowledge and Strategic Performance," by D. Kuhn and S. Pearsall, *Cognitive Development* (in press).

metastrategic levels 0 and 1 never achieve strategic mastery. In fact, their percentages of valid inference most often remain at zero. In contrast, children at metastrategic levels 2 and above begin to show strategic mastery. Its achievement, however, remains limited to a minority of children at levels 2 through 5, not increasing greatly even when the focus of analysis shifts from instances to the more appropriate one of features (level 2 to 3). Not until metastrategic level 6 does strategic success become the norm and, even then, it is not universal, suggesting that even a high level of understanding of both task objective and strategy does not ensure strategic success and other factors may be contributory.

These results support the thesis that metastrategic knowledge is both assessable as an entity distinct from strategic performance and related to it. There is no reason, however, to predict a tight trial-by-trial linkage of functioning in the two realms. Alternatively, a model that the data support is a necessary (but not sufficient) relation, with both of the two metastrategic components necessary (but not sufficient) for mastery in strategic performance. Other factors, including simply time to consolidate the gain in metastrategic understanding, presumably play a role in exactly when and in what form this metastrategic gain is realized in strategic performance.

The finding of changes in the strategic and metastrategic realms over the same time period, however, does not establish direction of causality, and other possibilities than a necessary (but not sufficient) "gatekeeper" relation of one to the other should be considered. Perhaps, strategic success leads to greater metastrategic awareness rather than the reverse. Or, perhaps, it is strategic failure that leads to a metastrategic search for new approaches. And, even if the direction of causality is from metastrategic to strategic, multiple possibilities exist. Failure to attain what the individual construes as the task objective is a possible impetus for strategic variation, and hence improvement, but so might newly achieved metastrategic insight serve as the impetus for strategic change.

Rather than one of these possibilities being correct to the exclusion of the others, more likely is the existence of multiple directions of influence between the strategic and metastrategic—the kind of bootstrapping feedback relation that Case (1997) and others have proposed in contemplating the relations between more general and more specific cognitive structures. In other words, advances at the general level feed down to support the more local structures while, at the same time, gains in the local structures feed up to strengthen and consolidate the general ones (what Case called a "hierarchical learning loop"). In the present case, the likelihood of such a bidirectional model is enhanced by the fact that initial competence was minimal in both strategic and metastrategic realms. Metastrategic understanding was able to emerge only in the context of strategic engagement with the task. Yet, as it developed in the course of this strategic engagement, it set limits on strategic progress (but still was not sufficient to guarantee strategic success).

Also relevant in the present case, and implicative of the role of metastrategic competence, is the fact that most children continued to use a combination of less successful strategies—those in the process of being discarded—as well as more successful ones in the process of emerging. Use of successful strategies may "feed up" to the metastrategic level, strengthening awareness of the strategy and understanding of its value. But, the use of unsuccessful strategies may also feed up, strengthening awareness of the strategy's ineffectiveness and leading to recognition of the need for better strategies. Similarly, both components of metastrategic knowledge may feed down to the strategic level. Gains in understanding of the task objective feed down to guide the application of strategies. Awareness and understanding of available strategies likewise supports their effective implementation.

In contrast, the paths of influence between the two components of metastrategic knowledge are not as apparent. Knowledge of a task objective cannot supply strategies to achieve it when they are absent, nor can availability and awareness of strategies provide a task goal. The coordination of these two components of metastrategic knowledge, then, may be a central task of the metastrategic knowledge system. In our data, strategic understanding sometimes exceeded task understanding (e.g., when children's attention turned to outcomes or to features before they verbalized these as relevant to task objectives); in other cases, however, it was lack of awareness of a strategy to implement task objectives that impeded progress.

 How widely do our findings regarding the relation between metastrategic and strategic functions apply? Inclusion of multiple kinds of task content in our design allowed us to conclude that they apply across a range of content within this task domain. Do they also apply, however, to a broad range of cognitive tasks of other kinds? Siegler (1996) has questioned the extent to which metacognitive or metastrategic factors are influential in task performance, turning instead to associative strength as a more influential factor in strategy choice and, hence, developmental change in strategic performance. It is worthwhile, therefore, to compare the kinds of cognitive tasks and strategies that he and his colleagues have studied with those we have examined here, to see if the differing content might account for the differing importance attributed to metacognitive factors. An argument can be made that it does. Siegler and colleagues have focused their studies on children's mastery of the basic arithmetic "number facts" of single-digit addition and subtraction. One might anticipate a central role for associative learning mechanisms in the mastery of number facts, since associative learning is the ultimate task goal. By middle childhood, we want and expect children to have learned these facts as associative links in their knowledge base of mathematics, such that the problem statement 7 + 8 produces the response 15 rapidly and automatically, without the need for intervening mental operations. The "back-up" strategies that Siegler and his colleagues have studied, involving procedures such as counting on fingers or the "min" strategy (counting up from the larger addend), are temporary aids that are expected to drop out once the necessary associative learning has been achieved. The desired performance end state here does not involve strategy use except in the limited sense that retrieval might be called (i.e., asking oneself, "Do I know an answer to 7 + 8?") a strategy. In this domain, then, associative strengths between the various number fact problems and corresponding responses would be expected to be the most direct and strongest predictor of performance, certainly stronger than less direct measures that have been investigated such as the individual's judgments of problem difficulty (regarded as a metastrategic indicator).

In the case of the competencies we have examined here, in contrast, the ultimate developmental goal is replacement of primitive strategies not with associative learning, but with more complex and demanding strategies, ones that continue to require exacting cognitive processing each time that they are applied. This is an important difference, for it says a great deal about the anticipated role of metastrategic factors. If more effortful and exacting strategies are to be applied in lieu of more primitive ones that continue to exist in the repertory, some explanatory governing mechanism needs to be invoked to account for such a choice. It is here that metastrategic understanding can be invoked as playing an important role. Also likely to be influential is the other component of metastrategic understanding—understanding of task objective—which, as we observed, is variable and undergoes change, again in contrast to what is the case in a domain like mastery of number facts. In sum, at least within the range of cognitive tasks that entail complex, effortful cognitive processing across all degrees of mastery, most promising is a model of bidirectional paths of influence between performance and understanding.

☐ Epistemological Meta-Knowing

Before proceeding to conclusions regarding meta-knowing in a life span framework, a final form of meta-knowing, the epistemological remains to be examined. Beyond specific understandings of their own or others' cognition in particular coontexts, how do individuals conceptualize knowing and knowledge more broadly? This is meta-knowing of an abstract, theoretical (Schraw & Moshman, 1995) sort, although it also extends to one's personal theories about the self's knowing capacities and dispositions (Dweck, 1991). Although a fair amount of research has accumulated regarding the development of epistemological theories, it has remained curiously isolated from other cognitive development research and, in particular, unconnected to research on metacognitive and metastrategic knowing reviewed earlier in this chapter, especially the theory-of-mind work to which it is most directly related. A possible explanation is that theory-of-mind research largely has been confined only to children up to the age of about 6, whereas work on the development of epistemological thinking has focused on adolescents and adults. With a few isolated exceptions (Mansfield & Clinchy, 1997; Schwanenflugel, Fabricius, & Noyes,1996), no connecting research exists covering the period from middle childhood to early adolescence.

The conceptual connection between the two bodies of work is nonetheless clear. The understanding of assertions as belief states was identified above as providing an essential foundation for further developments in epistemological understanding. With this attainment, assertions are recognized as emanating from, and therefore connected to, the human activity of knowing. Nonetheless, the initial absolutist epistemological stance, the norm in childhood and into adolescence and even adulthood (Chandler, Boyes, & Ball, 1990; King & Kitchener, 1994; Kramer & Woodruff, 1986; Kuhn, 1991; Perry, 1970), does not accord a pivotal role to the knower as a constructor of knowledge. Rather, the locus of knowledge remains in the external world, where it awaits discovery by human knowledge seekers. By age 4 or 5, a child appreciates knowing as connected to and generated by a knowing agent to a sufficient extent to understand that beliefs may deviate from a single, true reality. Yet much slower to be achieved, if indeed it is achieved at all, is a truly constructivist theory of mind that recognizes the primacy of humans as knowledge constructors capable of generating a multiplicity of valid representations of reality.

The transition from a realist pre-epistemological unawareness of belief states to the initial epistemological stance of absolutism is nonetheless a profound one. It is a transition from simply knowing that something is true to evaluating whether it might be. To carry out such evaluation, absolutists rely on the concept of a certain truth, one that is known or potentially knowable through either direct apprehension or the authority of experts. Belief states can be judged as correct or incorrect in relation to this truth.

People can spend entire lifetimes within the protective wraps of either a preabsolutist stance in which assertions are equated with reality or, more commonly, the absolutist stance in which disagreements are resolvable by appeal to direct observation or authority. In the modern world, however, it is difficult to avoid exposure to conflicting assertions that cannot readily be reconciled by appeal to observation or authority. As a result, most people progress beyond absolutism, venturing onto the slippery slope that will carry them to a multiplist epistemological stance, which becomes prevalent at adolescence. A critical event leading to the first step down the slope toward multiplism is likely to be exposure to the fact that experts disagree about important issues. If even experts cannot be counted on to provide certain answers, one resolution is to relinquish the idea of certainty itself, and this is exactly the path the multiplist takes. As the next inductive leap along this path, if experts with all of their knowledge and authority disagree with one another, why should their views be accepted as any more valid than anyone else's? A better assumption is that anyone's opinion has the same status and deserves the same treatment as anyone else's. Beliefs or opinions are the possessions of their owners, freely chosen according to the owner's tastes and wishes, and accordingly not subject to criticism. In the words of one of the adolescents in my research (Kuhn, 1991), "You can't prove an opinion to be wrong because an opinion is something somebody holds for themselves." Hence, in a conceptual sleight of hand that represents the final step down the slippery slope, because everyone has a right to their opinion, all opinions are equally right.

In contrast to the absolutist stance, which is difficult to maintain in pure form, people often remain multiplists for life. Only a minority progress to an evaluative epistemology, in which all opinions are not equal and knowing is understood as a process that entails judgment, evaluation, and argument. Evaluative epistemologists have reconciled the idea that people have a right to their views with the understanding that some views nonetheless can be more right than others. They see the weighing of alternative claims in a process of reasoned debate as the path to informed opinion, and they understand that arguments can be evaluated and compared based on their merit (Kuhn, 1991).

A weakness of research on epistemological understanding has been the lack of a clear theoretical framework for conceptualizing, and developing means of assessing, the developmental progression sketched above, despite broad agreement among different investigators regarding its nature. Details of the levels and stages described by different investigators have made it difficult to identify a core of what it is that is developing. My own conception of the core dimension underlying and driving this progression is the coordination of the subjective and objective components of knowing. The absolutist sees knowledge in largely objective terms, as located in the external world and knowable with certainty. The multiplist becomes aware of the subjective component of knowing, but to such an extent that it overpowers and obliterates any objective standard that would provide a basis for comparison or evaluation of opinions. Only the evaluativist is successful in integrating and coordinating the two, by acknowledging uncertainty without forsaking evaluation. This conception is compatible with that proposed by Hofer and Pintrich (1997) in a recent summary and review of the literature on the development of epistemological thinking. Endorsing the broad three-level (absolutist, multiplist, evaluativist) progression described here, they identify four dimensions of this progression, which pertain to the simplicity of knowledge (from simple to complex), the certainty of knowledge (from certain to uncertain), the source of knowledge (from external to internal), and the justification of knowledge (from external to internal and evaluative).

Schemes for the empirical assessment of epistemological thinking have ranged from a complex seven-level multidimensional coding system developed by King and Kitchener (1994), to the more skeletal coding scheme we have favored in our research (so as to retain clarity as to the construct being assessed). Again, however, at this point, the commonalities are more important than the differences in the coding schemes used by various researchers (see Hofer & Pintrich, 1997, for review), especially since the upper levels in the most complex, seven-level scheme by King and Kitchener appear relatively rarely as empirical realities except in highly educated samples.

In empirical research, my coworkers and I have relied on two schemes for distinguishing absolutist, multiplist, and evaluative levels of epistemological thinking. One is based on individuals' answers to questions regarding their own versus experts' judgments regarding the causes of complex social problems such as school failure, crime, and unemployment (Kuhn, 1991). We have classified as absolutists those who believe that such questions have certain answers. Those who maintain that the causes of such phenomena cannot be known with certainty we have classified either as multiplists (if they maintain that their own theories are just as likely to be right as those of experts who have studied the problem for a long time) or as evaluativists (if they see the expert's study of the problem as productive of understanding more likely to be correct than the average person's).

The second coding scheme is based on understandings of how to interpret conflicting claims (Kuhn, Weinstock, & Flaton, 1994; Leadbeater & Kuhn, 1989). In one scenario, two historians have produced conflicting accounts of an historical event. Progression in epistemological understanding can be observed from a rudimentary preabsolutist level in which the individual does not acknowledge discrepancies between the accounts (equating the account with the event itself) to the absolutist stance in which discrepancies are understood simply as omissions or incomplete renderings of a factual reality, then to a multiplist stance in which differences are unreconcilable since accounts become entirely subjective renderings, and finally to the evaluative stance in which differences are understood as ones of perspective, emphasis, and interpretation (with multiple accounts nonetheless susceptible to comparison and evaluation). For absolutists, then, only one account can be correct, whereas multiplists claim both can be right since they are equally valid subjective opinions, and evaluativists claim both can be right but that one may be superior to the other (because it is better supported or argued).

Although epistemological thinking is of interest in its own right, it assumes greater significance to the extent that it has implications for other aspects of intellectual functioning. Were such implications absent, epistemology reduces to simply another domain of knowledge, equivalent in significance to botany or geography or any other intellectual domain in which people may acquire some degree of knowledge or expertise. Although much remains to be learned in this respect, a number of recent studies have established that connections do exist between level of epistemological understanding and cognitive performance across a range of tasks and populations. In other words, epistemological understanding is not encapsulated knowledge. Schwanenflugel et al. (1996), for example, reported a relation between children's differentiation of verbs that denote mental states varying in certainty (e.g., guess, think, know), which they interpret as reflecting growing appreciation of the constructivist nature of knowing, and their performance on Markman's comprehension monitoring task. Carey and Smith (1993) and Sodian and Schrempp (1997) reported relations between children's and adolescents' levels of epistemological understanding and their performance on scientific reasoning tasks. In my work on argumentive reasoning (Kuhn, 1991), I have found associations between levels of epistemological understanding and argumentive reasoning skill among adolescents and adults. Kardash and Scholes (1996) also reported relations between epistemological understanding and reasoning about conflicting views. Such associations document the relevance of epistemological understanding to intellectual functioning, in particular, to higher-order thinking and reasoning. Unless one sees the point of intellectual debate, there is little incentive to expend the effort entailed to engage in it. Put simply by one of the multiplists in our studies, "I feel it's not worth it to argue because everyone has their opinion." In such cases, educators can undertake to teach cognitive skills, but the reasons to apply them will be missing.

☐ Meta-Knowing in Developmental Perspective: A Summary

We are now in a position to bring together the diverse array of phenomena that have been considered in this chapter. Again, I propose, as a conceptual umbrella for doing so, the development of meta-knowing, defining this development as the achievement of increasing awareness, understanding, and control of one's own cognitive functions as well as awareness and understanding of these functions as they occur in others. Young children's dawning awareness of their own and others' mental functions lies at one end of a developmental progression that eventuates in complex meta-knowing capabilities not realized before adulthood, if they are realized at all. Linking these diverse attainments within a developmental framework makes it possible to investigate ways in which earlier attainments prepare the way for later ones.

Competence in meta-knowing thus warrants attention as a critical end point and goal of childhood and adolescent cognitive development. This is even more the case since meta-knowing capacities inform cognitive performance as well as being informed by it. Indeed, meta-knowing is strongly implicated in some of the most consequential intellectual skills that ordinary individuals may attain. To be competent and motivated to "know how you know" puts one in charge of one's own knowing—of deciding what to believe and why, of determining how new information should be interpreted and reconciled with one's current beliefs, and of updating and revising those beliefs as one deems warranted. In the absence of this control, beliefs are vulnerable to the twin hazards of rigidity and fluidity. They come into contact with external evidence in only an unstable manner, often with radical accommodations of one to the other. In contrast, with such control, thinking is sensitive to new evidence but not dominated by it. To achieve this control of their own thinking arguably is the most important way in which people both individually and collectively take control of their lives.

Steps in the achievement of such control have become a topic of empirical research in recent years not only in work of the sort reviewed here, undertaken from a developmental perspective, but also in recent studies by a number of researchers working within a cognitive psychology tradition (Chinn & Brewer, 1993; Chan, Burtis, & Bereiter, 1997). The continuum identified is similar. At one end, new evidence is either ignored or assimilated to one's existing beliefs, rather than examined for its implications with respect to those beliefs. At the other, theory and evidence are firmly distinguished and evaluated in light of one another—conditions that make possible what Chan et al. (1997) referred to as genuine "knowledge building." In current work (Felton & Kuhn, in progress; Kuhn, Shaw, & Felton, 1997), we are examining within a developmental framework how these processes are manifested in dialogic argument between two people. If such argument is to be productive, its participants must take a propositional attitude toward the utterances that constitute the dialogue—these utterances must assume the status of objects of cognition, available for scrutiny, evaluation, and, ultimately, reconciliation by the participants. It is here that we encounter meta-knowing at a collective or social level (see below).

One other link that remains important to make explicit is that between the development of meta-knowing as discussed here and the cognitive skills commonly discussed under the headings of higher-order or critical thinking. The latter have been the object of continuing attention and have received wide endorsement as an overarching goal of education, at all levels from preschool to postgraduate. Typically, however, they are discussed as first-order cognitive skills, rather than as second-order meta-knowing competencies (see Perkins, 1992, as an exception). Proficiency in the execution of cognitive skills by no means is to be ignored, but educational assessments of various kinds repeatedly have shown students' most significant deficits lie not in executing such skills under direct instruction, but in applying these skills in appropriate contexts in the absence of explicit instruction to do so. As already has been argued in this chapter, metastrategic and metacognitive competencies are strongly implicated in such deficits. Attention to these competencies, including epistemological understanding, has the potential to inform educators' efforts to enhance students' thinking. Olson and Astington (1993) made an explicit case for the connection between meta-knowing competencies and traditional critical thinking skills. "Higher-order thinking," they stated:

> is nothing other than competence with the set of concepts for managing how beliefs are to be held and how statements are to be taken. It is a matter of the recognition of the attitude one takes to the content of one's own thoughts, and it is a matter of the correct assignment of illocutionary force to others' statements. (p. 19)

As I have done here, they also connect critical thinking to the developmental milestone of recognizing assertions as expressions of someone's belief: "What is required for criticism of a text, then, is the recognition that texts are not repositories of the known but the product of human intention" (Olson & Astington, 1993, p. 18).

In sum, viewed in the terms proposed in this chapter, competencies in meta-knowing assume broad significance in people's lives, both individually and collectively. This portrayal stands in sharp contrast to the more circumscribed ways in which metacognitive and metastrategic skills have been examined in much of the existing literature that has been reviewed here. It is interesting then, that, even though the field did not follow his lead, Flavell (1979), in a seminal paper highlighting metacognitive development as a promising new area of inquiry, conceptualized it in extremely broad terms, going even beyond what has been discussed here to incorporate personal life management as a domain in which meta-knowing skills are strongly implicated:

> In many real-life situations, the monitoring problem is not to determine how well you understand what a message means but to determine how much you ought to believe it or do what it says to do. I am thinking of the persuasive appeals the young receive from all quarters to smoke, drink, take drugs, commit aggressive or criminal acts, have casual sex without contraceptives, have or not have the casual babies that often result, quit school, and become unthinking followers of this year's flaky cults, sects, and movements. . . . Perhaps it is stretching the meanings of metacognition and cognitive monitoring too far to include the critical appraisal of message source, quality of appeal, and probable consequences needed to cope with these inputs sensibly, but I do not think so. It is at least conceivable that the ideas currently brewing in this area could someday be parlayed into a method teaching children (and adults) to make wise and thoughtful life decisions as well as to comprehend and learn better in formal educational settings. (Flavell, 1979, p. 910)

Flavell's vision in this respect has yet to be realized. I turn finally, then, to the question of how meta-knowing competencies can be fostered and the conceptual issues that arise in undertaking to do so.

☐ Fostering Meta-Knowing Competence

In a society whose young increasingly often are growing up in endangered circumstances, more research should perhaps be devoted to the kinds of development that may occur—to the competencies that children may be capable of attaining, given a favorable combination of circumstances, rather than only the universal cognitive achievements that occur even when circumstances are less favorable. The early meta-knowing attainments that are the focus of the theory-of-mind literature can be counted on to occur, even if at this point, we have only an imperfect understanding of the mechanisms involved. The more advanced meta-knowing competencies explored later in this chapter, in contrast, may never develop in many individuals, imparting a different significance to them. I have attempted to identify some of the most important of these more fragile, less predictable achievements, which are important in the sense of enhancing the effectiveness and hence well-being of those who possess them. A final question, then, with which I conclude the chapter, is how we might best promote their attainment.

Within the life span framework adopted here, the question assumes both a theoretical and a practical form: What are the mechanisms involved in meta-knowing development and how can our knowledge of them inform the design of educational environments that will optimize this development? Cognitive construction and social participation were highlighted earlier in this chapter as dual mechanisms that play an important role in early cognitive and metacognitive development. In the case of the more advanced forms of meta-knowing considered later in the chapter, the two mechanisms are similarly implicated. Conceiving of social participation as a mechanism in the attainment of advanced forms of thinking, however, requires some reconceptualization of what it is that is being attained.

Influenced by the sociocultural movement (Cole, 1996; Rogoff, 1997), Resnick and Nelson-LeGall (1998) made a pointed contrast between the traditional view of higher-order cognitive competencies as mental entities that reside within individuals and their own view of cognitive skills as social practices, developed through processes of social participation and appropriation. In identifying what such social practices consist of, Resnick and Nelson-LeGall enlarge on the typical portrayal of social practices to incorporate a belief component into their definition. Intelligence, they specified, for example, entails "believing that problems can be analyzed and that solutions often come from such analysis, and believing that you are capable of that analysis" (thus, encompassing both the impersonal and personal dimensions of epistemological thinking; Resnick & Nelson-LeGall, in press). They suggest that this broadly defined intelligence, encompassing intellectual skills, attitudes, and values, be conceptualized as a constellation of dispositions or habits—ways of life practiced and valued in the community and, thereby, appropriated by its younger members.

This expanded conception of what gets transmitted from more to less able members of a community is an important one from the perspective that has been developed in this chapter, since one of its major theses has been that mastery of cognitive skills encompasses more than the skills themselves, as narrowly defined and performed. Meta-knowing competencies develop in conjunction with cognitive skills and are a major determinant of whether and when these skills will be practiced. In emphasizing intellectual values and beliefs as well as performance, Resnick and Nelson-LeGall (1997) were sensitive to the transfer issue. Beyond referring to the traditional construct of socialization as an explanatory mechanism, however, they do not elucidate exactly how beliefs and values, and the dispositions that are assumed to follow from them, are transmitted across generations.

A problem with the disposition conception of good thinking (Perkins, Jay, & Tishman, 1993) that Resnick and Nelson-LeGall (1997) relied on is that it leaves much of the variance unaccounted for. What determines whether someone has a disposition to behave in a particular way? If disposition is interpreted in the sense of habit, someone might get used to thinking well in the same way they are in the habit of exercising high standards of personal hygiene. Humans, however, are not simply creatures of habit—their beliefs and values regarding what is important help to shape their behavior. In the end, people think carefully and reflectively, not out of habit since such thinking is not an effortless habit to maintain, but because they are convinced of the value of doing so. This conception takes us to understanding, then, as a major determinant of disposition (and, hence, of performance) and, with it, to cognitive construction as a mechanism that operates in conjunction with social participation as joint vehicles of development.

Clearly, the intellectual skills and attitudes we wish to inculcate must be practiced widely and visibly within the communities in which young people grow up. If they are absent in the community, it is difficult, if not impossible, to instill them in individual members—a finding that, for example, led educators attempting to apply Kohlberg's theory of moral development in schools and prisons to shift their attention from the individual's moral reasoning to the moral climate of the institution in which individuals spend their time (Power, Higgins, & Kohlberg, 1989). Equal attention, however, must be accorded to the constructive cognitive activity of individuals. To understand how intellectual values are transmitted from older to younger members of a community, we must examine the sense these individuals make of the shared social practices in which they participate and how these meanings shape their own actions. In a word, the power of social practice as a shaper of human behavior can be recognized without overlooking the knowing and meta-knowing powers that allow people to attribute meaning to what they do and, in the course of so doing, to shape their own behavior.

This conceptualization leaves the educator, however, uncertain where to begin. Earlier, a reciprocal relation was postulated between performance and understanding. What are the implications of this reciprocal relation for educational intervention? Practice is essential, we know, but practice does not make perfect in the absence of understanding. The best approach, then, may be to work from both ends at once—from a bottom-up anchoring in regular practice of what is being preached, so that skills are exercised, strengthened, and consolidated as well as from a top-down fostering of understanding and the value structures associated with it—the latter imparted both by explicit discussion and the presence of abundant models within the community who both display them and scaffold their formation and development among younger members of the community.

Over time, external forms thereby become internal ones. This conceptualization appears in several lines of current educational research. It is reflected in the research my coworkers and I have done on argumentive reasoning, in which we treat participation in dialogic argument as an external representation of the argumentive forms that we hope to see also emerge on the individual plane (Kuhn, 1991; Kuhn et al., 1997). A similar conception is evident in Brown's (1997) recent work on fostering children's development as members of a "community of learners." She described her approach as relying on

> the development of a discourse genre in which constructive discussion, questioning, querying, and criticism are the mode rather than the exception. In time, these reflective activities become internalized as self-reflective practices and foster children's growing theories of learning. (p. 406)

Brown also described the community as a "metacognitive environment" in which talk is

> largely metacognitve: "Do I understand?" "That doesn't make sense," "They [the audience] can't understand X without Y," and so forth. (p. 406)

Recent work by Staudinger and Baltes (1996) also drew on this conceptualization of externalizing or "socializing" the cognitive forms that we would like to see develop within the individual. In all of these approaches, the other person is, in some sense, assuming an external role that we would like to see become interiorized in the form of metacognitive and metastrategic awareness and control. In our work (Kuhn et al., 1997), individual arguments for or against capital punishment improved in quality among both young adolescents and young adults as a function of dyadic discussions on the topic with a series of peers. Analyses of the dialogues were revealing as to how the dyadic interaction led to changes in individual thinking, a topic too complex to go into in detail here. Of particular interest, however, were the enhancements in metacognitive awareness that occurred in the adolescent group. Metacognitive statements (about one's own beliefs) became more common in the posttest assessments of individual reasoning, following the dyadic interactions, as did the appearance of two-sided arguments. The following, for example, is the opening sentence of one adolescent's posttest justification of her opinion: "I think that capital punishment is somewhat kind of fair but at the same time I think that it is not right."

This opening sentence was followed by a number of pro and con reasons—a striking contrast to the pretest justification of capital punishment on the grounds, "because if someone does something I think if the punishment fits the crime why not" (Kuhn et al., 1997). The majority of adolescents in our study, we believe, became more aware of their own thinking as an object of knowledge, as a result of their participation. The fact that their thinking had been the object of others' attention in the dialogues most likely facilitated this attainment, although the attention accorded the other's thinking also had a role to play.

The question of how to get people to be more thoughtful and reflective is a long-standing one that continues to be asked in a range of different contexts. The contribution I hope to have made in this chapter is to situate the question in a developmental framework. A well-articulated developmental framework provides guideposts (Kuhn, 1997) that identify where particular competencies have originated and where they are headed. The developmental end point highlighted in this chapter is competence in meta-knowing and the control of one's own cognitive functions that it affords. Articulating this developmental end point, and conceptualizing earlier meta-knowing achievements as steps toward it, may make clearer how it can be achieved.

☐ References

Ash, A., Torrance, N., Lee, E., & Olson, D. (1993). The development of children's understanding of the evidence for beliefs. *Educational Psychology, 13,* 371–384.

Astington, J., & Olson, D. (1995). The cognitive revolution in children's understanding of mind. *Human Development, 38*(4–5), 179–189.

Baars, B. (1997). *In the theater of consciousness: The workspace of the mind.* New York: Oxford University Press.

Bassili, J. (1996). Meta-judgmental versus operative indexes of psychological attributes: The case of measures of attitude strength. *Journal of Personality and Social Psychology, 71,* 637–653.

Bisanz, G., Vesonder, G., & Voss, J. (1978). Knowledge of one's own responding and the relation of such knowledge to learning. *Journal of Experimental Child Psychology, 25,* 116–128.

Brown, A. (1975). The development of memory: Knowing, knowing about knowing, and knowing how to know. In H. Reese (Ed.), *Advances in child development and behavior* (Vol. 10, pp. 103–152). New York: Academic Press.

Brown, A. (1978). Knowing when, where, and how to remember: A problem of metacognition. In R. Glaser (Ed.), *Advances in instructional psychology* (Vol. 1, pp. 77–165).

Brown, A. (1987). Metacognition, executive control, self-regulation, and other more mysterious mechanisms. In F. Weinert & R. Kluwe (Eds.), *Metacognition, motivation, and understanding* (pp. 65–116). Hillsdale NJ: Erlbaum.

Brown, A. (1997). Transforming schools into communities of thinking and learning about serious matters. *American Psychologist, 52,* 399–413.

Brown, A., Bransford, J., Ferrara, R., & Campione, J. (1983). Learning, remembering, and understanding. In P. Mussen (Series Ed.) & J. Flavell & E. Markman (Vol. Eds.), *Handbook of child psychology: Vol. 3. Cognitive development* (4th ed.). New York: Wiley.

Brown, A., & Palincsar, A. (1989). Guided cooperative learning and individual knowledge acquisition. In L. Resnick (Ed.) *Knowing and learning: Essays in honor of Robert Glaser* (pp. 393–451). Hillsdale, NJ: Erlbaum.

Campbell, R., & Bickhard, M. (1986). *Knowing levels and developmental stages. Contributions to human development* (Vol. 16). Basel, Switzerland: Karger.

Carey, S., & Smith, C. (1993). On understanding the nature of scientific knowledge. *Educational Psychologist, 28,* 235–251.

Carpendale, J., & Chandler, M. (1996). On the distinction between false belief understanding and subscribing to an interpretive theory of mind. *Child Development, 67,* 1686–1706.

Case, R. (1997). The development of conceptual structures. In W. Damon (Series Ed.) & D. Kuhn & R. Siegler (Vol. Eds.), *Handbook of child psychology: Vol. 2. Cognition, language, and perception* (5th ed., pp. 745–800). New York: Wiley.

Chan, C., Burtis, J., & Bereiter, C. (1997). Knowledge-building as a mediator of conflict in conceptual change. *Cognition and Instruction, 15,* 1–40.

Chandler, M., Boyes, M., & Ball, L. (1990). Relativism and stations of epistemic doubt. *Journal of Experimental Child Psychology, 50,* 370–395.

Chandler, M., Fritz, A., & Hala, S. (1989). Small-scale deceit: Deception as a marker of two-, three-, and four-year-olds' early theories of mind. *Child Development, 60,* 1263–1277.

Chandler, M., & Hala, S. (1994). The role of personal involvement in the assessment of early false-belief skills. In C. Lewis & P. Mitchell (Eds.), *Origins of an understanding of mind* (pp. 403–426). Hove, England: Erlbaum.

Chinn, C., & Brewer, W. (1993). The role of anomalous data in knowledge acquisition: A theoretical framework and implications for science instruction. *Review of Educational Research, 63,* 1–49.

Clark, R., & Delia, J. (1976). The development of functional persuasive skills in childhood and early adolescence. *Child Development, 47,* 1008–1014.

Cohen, J., & Schooler, J. (1996). *Scientific approaches to consciousness.* Mahwah, NJ: Erlbaum.

Cole, M. (1996). *Cultural psychology: A once and future discipline.* Cambridge, MA: Harvard University Press.

Cross, D., & Paris, S. (1988). Developmental and instructional analyses of children's metacognition and reading comprehension. *Journal of Educational Psychology, 80,* 131–142.

DeLoache, J., Cassidy, D., & Brown, A. (1985). Precursors of mnemonic strategies in very young children's memory. *Child Development, 56,* 125–137.

Demetriou, A., & Efkildes, A. (1994). Structure, development, and dynamics of mind: A meta-Piagetian theory. In A. Demetriou & A. Efkildes (Eds.), *Intelligence, mind, and reasoning: Structure and development* (pp. 75–109). Amsterdam: North-Holland.

Dennett, D. (1991). *Consciousness explained.* Boston: Little, Brown.

Dunn, J., Brown, J., Slomkowski, C., Tesla, C., & Youngblade, L. (1991). Young children's understanding of other people's feelings and beliefs: Individual differences and their antecedents. *Child Development, 62,* 1352–1366.

Dweck, C. (1991). Self-theories and goals: Their role in motivation, personality and development. In R. Dienstbier (Ed.), *Nebraska Symposium on Motivation, 1990* (Vol. 36, pp. 199–235). Lincoln: University of Nebraska Press.

Ericsson, K. A., & Simon, H. (1980) Verbal reports as data. *Psychological Review, 63,* 19–80.

Esbensen, B., Taylor, M., & Stoess, C. (1997). Children's behavioral understanding of knowledge acquisition. *Cognitive Development, 12,* 53-84.

Estes, D., Wellman, H., & Woolley, J. (1989). Children's understanding of mental phenomena. In H. Reese (Ed.), *Advances in child development and behavior* (pp. 41–87). New York: Academic Press.

Fabricius, W., & Hagen, J. (1984). Use of causal attributions about recall performance to assess metamemory and predict strategic memory behavior in young children. *Developmental Psychology, 20,* 975–987.

Feldman, C. (1988). Early forms of thought about thoughts: Some simple linguistic expressions of mental state. In J. Astington, P. Harris, & D. Olson (Eds.) *Developing theories of mind.* Cambridge, England: Cambridge University Press.

Flanagan, O. (1992). *Consciousness reconsidered.* Cambridge, MA: MIT Press.

Flavell, J. (1979). Metacognition and cognitive monitoring: A new area of cognitive-developmental inquiry. *American Psychologist, 34,* 906–911.

Flavell, J. (1997). Recent convergences between metacognitive and theory-of-mind research within children. In G. Schraw (Chair), *Constructing metacognitive knowledge.* Symposium conducted at the biennial meeting of the Society for Research in Child Development, Washington, DC.

Flavell, J., Flavell, E., Green, F., & Moses, L. (1990). Young children's understanding of fact beliefs versus value beliefs. *Child Development, 61,* 915–928.

Flavell, J., Green, F., & Flavell, E. (1995). Young children's knowledge about thinking. *Society for Research in Child Development Monographs, 60*(1, Serial No. 243).

Flavell, J., & Miller, P. (1997). Social cognition. In W. Damon (Series Ed.) & D. Kuhn & R. Siegler (Vol. Eds.), *Handbook of child psychology: Vol 2. Cognition, language, and perception.* (5th ed., pp. 851–898). New York: Wiley.

Flavell, J., Mumme, D., Green, F., & Flavell, E. (1992). Young children's understanding of different types of beliefs. *Child Development, 63,* 960–977.

Flavell, J., Speer, J., Green, F., & August, D. (1981). The development of comprehension monitoring and knowledge about communication. *Society for Research in Child Development Monographs, 46*(Serial No. 192).

Flavell, J., & Wellman, H. (1977). Metamemory. In R. Kail & J. Hagen (Eds.), *Perspectives on the development of memory and cognition* (pp. 3–33). Hillsdale, NJ: Erlbaum.

Freeman, N., & Lacohee, H. (1995). Making explicit 3-year-olds implicit competence with their own false beliefs. *Cognition, 56,* 31–60.

Gardner, H. (1991). *The unschooled mind: How children think and how schools should teach.* New York: Basic Books.

Garcia-Mila, M., & Andersen, C.

Gopnik, A., & Astington, J. (1988). Children's understanding of representational change and its relation to the understanding of false belief and the appearance-reality distinction. *Child Development, 59,* 26–37.

Gopnik, A., & Graf, P. (1988). Knowing how you know: Young children's ability to identify and remember the sources of their beliefs. *Child Development, 59,* 1366–1371.

Gopnik, A., & Wellman, H. (1992). Why the child's theory of mind really is a theory. *Mind and Language, 7,* 145–171.

Greenwald, A., & Banaji, M. (1995). Implicit social cognition: Attitudes, self-esteem, and stereotypes. *Psychological Review, 102,* 4–27.

Hala, S., & Chandler, M. (1996). The role of strategic planning in accessing false-belief understanding. *Child Development, 67,* 2948–2966.

Harris, P. (1992). From simulation to folk psychology: The case for development. *Mind and Language, 7,* 120–144.

Hofer, B., & Pintrich, P. (1997). The development of epistemological theories: Beliefs about knowledge and knowing and their relation to learning. *Review of Educational Research, 67,* 88–140.

Kail, R., & Hagen, J. (Eds.). (1977). *Perspectives on the development of memory and cognition.* Hillsdale, NJ: Erlbaum.

Kardash, C., & Scholes, R. (1996). Effects of preexisting beliefs, epistemological beliefs, and need for cognition on interpretation of controversial issues. *Journal of Educational Psychology, 88,* 260–271.

Keenan, T., Ruffman, T., & Olson, D. (1994). When do children begin to understand logical inference as a source of knowledge? *Cognitive Development, 9,* 331–353.

King, P., & Kitchener, K. (1994). *Developing reflective judgment: Understanding and promoting intellectual growth and critical thinking in adolescents and adults.* San Francisco: Jossey-Bass.

Kreutzer, M., Leonard, C., & Flavell, J. (1975). An interview study of children's knowledge about memory. *Society for Research in Child Development Monographs, 40* (Serial No. 159).

Kuhn, D. (1982). On the dual executive and its significance in the development of developmental psychology. In D. Kuhn & J. Meacham (Eds.), *On the development of developmental psychology. Contributions to human development* (Vol. 8). Basel, Switzerland: Karger.

Kuhn, D. (1989). Children and adults as intuitive scientists. *Psychological Review, 96,* 674–689.

Kuhn, D. (1991). *The skills of argument.* New York: Cambridge University Press.

Kuhn, D. (1992). Thinking as argument. *Harvard Educational Review, 62,* 155–178.

Kuhn, D. (1995). Microgenetic study of change: What has it told us? *Psychological Science, 6,* 133–139.

Kuhn, D. (1996). Is good thinking scientific thinking? In D. Olson & N. Torrance (Eds.), *Modes of thought: Explorations in culture and cognition.* Cambridge, England: Cambridge University Press.

Kuhn, D. (1997). Constraints or guideposts? Developmental psychology and science education. *Review of Educational Research, 67,* 141–150.

Kuhn, D., Amsel, E., & O'Loughlin, M. (1988). *The development of scientific thinking skills.* Orlando, FL: Academic Press.

Kuhn, D., Garcia-Mila, M., Zohar, A., & Andersen, C. (1995). Strategies of knowledge acquisition. *Society for Research in Child Development Monographs, 60*(4, Serial No. 245).

Kuhn, D., & Lao, J. (1996). Effects of evidence on attitudes: Is polarization the norm? *Psychological Science, 7*, 115–120.

Kuhn, D., & Lao, J. (1998). Contemplation and conceptual change: Integrating perspectives from social and cognitive psychology. *Developmental Review, 18*, 125–154.

Kuhn, D., Shaw, V., & Felton, M. (1997). Effects of dyadic interaction on argumentive reasoning. *Cognition and Instruction, 15*, 287–315.

Kuhn, D., & Pearsall, S. (2000). Developmental origins of scientific thinking. *Journal of Cognitive Development, 1*(1).

Kuhn, D., & Pearsall, S. (1998). Relations between metastrategic knowledge and strategic performance. *Cognitive Development, 13*, 227–247.

Kuhn, D., & Phelps, E. (1982). The development of problem-solving strategies. In H. Reese (Ed.), *Advances in child development and behavior* (Vol. 17). New York: Academic Press.

Kuhn, D., Schauble, L., & Garcia-Mila, M. (1992). Cross-domain development of scientific reasoning.*Cognition and Instruction, 9*, 285–232.

Kuhn, D., Weinstock, M., & Flaton, R. (1994). Historical reasoning as theory-evidence coordination. In M. Carretero & J. Voss (Eds.), *Cognitive and instructional processes in history and the social sciences* (pp. 377–401). Hillsdale, NJ: Erlbaum.

Leadbeater, B. (1988). Relational processes in adolescent and adult dialogues: Assessing the intersubjective context of conversation. *Human Development, 31*, 313–326.

Leadbeater, B., & Kuhn, D. (1989). Interpreting discrepant narratives: Hermeneutics and adult cognition. In J. Sinnott (Ed.), *Everyday problem-solving: Theory and application.* New York: Praeger.

Leslie, A. (1987). Pretense and representation: The origins of "theory of mind." *Psychological Review, 94*, 412–426.

Mansfield, A., & Clinchy, B. (1997). *Toward the integration of objectivity and subjectivity: A longitudinal study of epistemological development between the ages of 9 and 13.* Research display presented at the biennial meeting of the Society for Research in Child Development, Washington, DC.

Markman, E., (1977). Realizing that you don't understand: A preliminary investigation. *Child Development, 48*, 986–992.

Markman, E. (1979). Realizing that you don't understand: Elementary school children's awareness of inconsistencies. *Child Development, 50*, 643–655.

Masur, E., McIntyre, C., & Flavell, J. (1973). Developmental changes in apportionment of study time among items in a multitrial free recall task. *Journal of Experimental Child Psychology, 15*, 237–246.

Metcalfe, J., & Shimamura, A. (1994). *Metacognition: Knowing about knowing.* Cambridge, MA: Bradford Books.

Miller, A.G., McHoskey, J.W., Bane, C.M., & Dowd, T.G. (1993). The attitude polarization phenomenon: Role of response measure, attitude extremity, and behavioral consequences of reported attitude change. *Journal of Personality and Social Psychology, 64*, 561–574.

Montgomery, D. (1992). Young children's theory of knowing: The development of a folk epistemology. *Developmental Review, 12*, 410–430.

Moore, C., Bryant, D., & Furrow, D. (1989). Mental terms and the development of certainty. *Child Development, 60*, 167–171.

Moynahan, E. (1978). Assessment and selection of paired associate strategies: A developmental study. *Journal of Experimental Child Psychology, 26*, 257–266.

Nelson, T. (1996). Consciousness and metacognition. *American Psychologist, 51*, 102–116.

Nisbett, R., & Wilson, T. (1977). Telling more than we can know: Verbal reports on mental processes. *Psychological Review, 84*, 231–259.

Olson, D., & Astington, J. (1986). Children's acquisition of metalinguistic and metacognitive verbs. In W. Demopoulos & A. Marras (Eds.), *Language learning and concept acquisition.* Norwood, NJ: Ablex.

Olson, D., & Astington, J. (1993). Thinking about thinking: Learning how to take statements and hold beliefs. *Educational Psychologist, 28*, 7–23.

O'Neill, D., & Gopnik, A. (1991). Young children's ability to identify the sources of their beliefs. *Developmental Psychology, 27*, 390–397.

Palincsar, A., & Brown, A. (1984). Reciprocal teach of comprehension-fostering and monitoring activities. *Cognition and Instruction, 1*, 117–175.

Perkins, D. (1992). *Smart schools: Better thinking and learning for every child.* New York: Free Press.

Perkins, D., Jay, E., & Tishman, S. (1993). Beyond abilities: A dispositional theory of thinking. In "The development of rationality and critical thinking" [Special issue]. *Merrill-Palmer Quarterly, 39*(1), 1–21.

Perner, J. (1991). *Understanding the representational mind.* Cambridge, MA: MIT Press.

Perry, W. (1970). *Forms of intellectual and ethical development in the college years.* New York: Holt, Rinehart & Winston.

Piaget, J. (1950). *The psychology of intelligence.* London: Routledge & Kegan Paul.

Piaget, J. (1976). *The grasp of consciousness.* Cambridge, MA: Harvard University Press.

Piaget, J. (1978). *Success and understanding.* Cambridge, MA: Harvard University Press.

Piaget, J., & Inhelder, B. (1951). *Play, dreams, and imitation in childhood.* New York: Norton.

Pillow, B., & Henrichon, A. (1996). There's more to the picture than meets the eye: Young children's difficulty under-standing biased interpretation. *Child Development, 67,* 803–819.

Power, C., Higgins, A., & Kohlberg, L. (1989). *Lawrence Kohlberg's approach to moral education.* New York: Columbia University Press.

Pressley, M. (1997). How students construct self-regulatory knowledge. In G. Schraw (Chair), *Constructing metacognitive knowledge.* Symposium conducted at the biennial meeting of the Society for Research in Child Development, Washington, DC.

Pressley, M., & Associates. (1990). *Cognitive strategy instruction that really imrpoves children's academic performance.* Cambridge, MA: Brookline Books.

Pressley, M., Borkowski, J., & Schneider, W. (1987). Cognitive strategies: Good strategy users coordinate metacognition and knowledge. In R. Vasta & G. Whietehurst (Eds.), *Annals of child development* (Vol. 5, pp. 89–129). Greenwich, CT: JAI Press.

Pressley, M., & Ghatala, E. (1990). Self-regulated learning: Monitoring learning from text. *Educational Psychologist, 25,* 19–34.

Resnick, L., & Nelson-LeGall, S. (1997). Socializing intelligence. In L. Smith, J. Dockrell, & P. Tomlinson (Eds.), *Piaget, Vygorsky, and beyond.* London, Routledge.

Robinson, E., & Mitchell, P. (1995). Masking of children's early understanding of the representational mind: Back-wards explanation versus prediction. *Child Development, 66,* 1022–1039.

Rogoff, B. (1998). Cognition as a collaborative process. In W. Damon (Series Ed.) & D. Kuhn & R. Siegler (Vol. Eds.), *Handbook of child psychology: Vol 2. Cognition, language, and perception* (5th ed., pp. 679–744). New York: Wiley.

Schneider, W. (1985). Developmental trends in the metamemory-memory behavior relationship: An integrative re-view. In D. Forrest-Pressley, G. MacKinnon, & T. Waller (Eds.), *Cognition, metacognition, and human performance* (Vol. 1, pp. 57–109). Orlando, FL: Academic Press.

Schneider, W., & Bjorklund, D. (1997). Memory. In W. Damon (Series Ed.) & D. Kuhn & R. Siegler (Vol. Eds.), *Hand-book of child psychology: Vol 2. Cognition, language, and perception.* (5th ed., pp. 467–522). New York: Wiley.

Schraw, G., & Moshman, D. (1995). Metacognitive theories. *Educational Psychology Review, 7,* 351–371.

Schwanenflugel, P., Fabricius, W., & Noyes, C. (1996). Developing organization of mental verbs: Evidence for the development of a constructivist theory of mind in middle childhood. *Cognitive Development, 11,* 265–294.

Shear, J. (Ed.). (in press). *Explaining consciousness.* Cambridge, MA: Bradford Books.

Siegler, R. (1996). *Emerging minds: The process of change in children's thinking.* New York: Oxford University Press.

Siegler, R., & Jenkins, E. (1989). *How children discover new strategies.* Hillsdale, NJ: Erlbaum.

Slaughter, V., & Gopnik, A. (1996). Conceptual coherence in the child's theory of mind: Training children to under-stand belief. *Child Development, 67,* 2967–2988.

Sodian, B., & Schrempp, I. (1997). *Metaconceptual knowledge and the development of scientific reasoning skills.* Paper presented at the annual meeting of the American Educational Research Association, Chicago.

Sodian, B., & Wimmer, H. (1987). Children's understanding of inference as a source of knowledge. *Child Development, 58,* 424–433.

Sodian, B., Zaitchik, D., & Carey, S. (1991). Young children's differentiation of hypothethical beliefs from evidence. *Child Development, 62,* 753–766.

Staudinger, U., & Baltes, P. (1996). Interactive minds: A facilitative setting for wisdom-related performance? *Journal of Personality and Social Psychology, 71,* 746–762.

Sternberg, R. (1984). Mechanisms of cognitive development: A componential approach. In R. Sternberg (Ed.), *Mecha-nisms of cognitive development.* New York: Freeman.

Sternberg, R. (1985). *Beyond IQ: A triarchic theory of human intelligence.* New York: Cambridge University Press.

Taylor, M., Cartwright, B., & Bowden, T. (1991). Perspective taking and theory of mind: Do children predict interpre-tive diversity as a function of differences in observers' knowledge? *Child Development, 62,* 1334–1351.

Taylor, M., Esbensen, B., & Bennett, R. (1994). Children's understanding of knowledge acquisition: The tendency for children to report they have always known what they have just learned. *Child Development, 65,* 1581–1604.

Tesser, A., Martin, L., & Mendolia, M. (1995). The impact of thought on attitude extremity and attitude-behavior consistency. In R. E. Petty & J. A. Krosnick (Eds.), *Attitude strength: Antecedents and consequences* (pp. 73–92). Hillsdale, NJ: Erlbaum.

Tomasello, M., Kruger, A., & Ratner, H. (1993). Cultural learning. *Behavioral and Brain Sciences, 16,* 495–552.

Trevarthen, C. (1980). The foundations of intersubjectivity: Development of interpersonal and cooperative understanding in infants. In D. Olson (Ed.), *The social foundations of language and thought.* New York: Norton.

Vygotsky, L. (1962). *Thought and language.* Cambridge, MA: MIT Press. (Original work published 1934)

Weiskrantz, L. (1997). *Consciousness lost and found: A neuropsychological exploration.* New York: Oxford University Press.

Wellman, H. (1988). First steps in the child's theorizing about the mind. In J. Astington, P. Harris, & D. Olson (Eds.), *Developing theories of mind* (pp. 64–92). Cambridge, England: Cambridge University Press.

Wellman, H., & Gelman, S. (1998). Knowledge acquisition in foundational domains. In W. Damon (Series Ed.) & D. Kuhn & R. Siegler (Vol. Eds.), *Handbook of child psychology: Vol 2. Cognition, language, and perception* (5th ed., pp. 523–574). New York: Wiley.

Wilson, T., & Brekke, N. (1994). Mental contamination and mental correction: Unwanted influences on judgments and evaluations. *Psychological Bulletin, 116,* 117–142.

Wilson, T., & Schooler, J. (1991). Thinking too much: Introspection can reduce the quality of preferences and decisions. *Journal of Personality and Social Psychology, 60,* 181–192.

Wimmer, H., Hogrefe, G., & Perner, J. (1988). Children's understanding of informational access as a source of knowledge. *Child Development, 59,* 386–396.

Wimmer, H., & Perner, J. (1983). Beliefs about beliefs: Representation and constraining function of wrong beliefs in young children's understanding of deception. *Cognition, 13,* 103–128.

Wood, D., Wood, H., Ainsworth, S., & O'Malley, C. (1995). On becoming a tutor: Toward an ontogenetic model. *Cognition & Instruction, 13,* 565–581.

Woolley, J. (1995). Young children's understanding of fictional versus epistemic mental representations: Imagination and belief. *Child Development, 66,* 1011–1021.

Zaitchik, D. (1991). Is only seeing really believing? Sources of the true belief in the false belief task. *Cognitive Development, 6,* 91–103.

Zimmerman, B., & Martinez-Pons, M. (1986). Development of a structured interview for assessing student use of self-regulated learning strategies. *American Educational Research Journal, 23,* 614–628.

Jacquelynne S. Eccles
Robert Roeser
Allan Wigfield
Carol Freedman-Doan

CHAPTER 14

Academic and Motivational Pathways Through Middle Childhood

☐ Introduction

We have two goals in this chapter: first, we review the literature on longitudinal changes in academic self-concepts and motivational orientation, and, second, we discuss the associations among academic self-concepts, school success, and emotional development. We do this by linking different longitudinal patterns of school adjustment to individual differences in social-emotional development. By focusing on school adjustment, we test the notion that academic competence is an important part of the overall portrait of positive adjustment and more general interpersonal competency during both middle childhood and early adolescence (e.g., Eccles & Midgley, 1989; Erikson, 1968; Roeser, Lord, & Eccles, 1994).

During middle childhood, children progressively move from home into wider social contexts that exert important influences on their cognitive, behavioral, and socioemotional development. In particular, the commencement of formal schooling initiates a series of new life experiences for children. School experiences encourage the development of intellectual and interpersonal competencies, and introduce the child to new social roles wherein status is conferred based on competence and performance (e.g., Higgins & Parsons, 1983). According to Erikson (1968), the accomplishment of a "sense of industry" in school during these years, as well as a sense of cooperation and mutuality in social interactions with peers and adults outside the home, is critical to healthy development. If children fail to develop these requisite skills and, thereby, meet the challenges of adaptation associated with entry into formal schooling, Erikson suggested that a "sense of inferiority" would develop that could exert long-lasting consequences on children's intellectual, emotional, and interpersonal well-being.

Since the time of Erikson's (1959) seminal writings on children and youth, a great deal of research attention has been given to understanding how children's self-appraisals and behavioral competencies are related to the quality of their intellectual, social, and emotional functioning across the first two decades of life. Researchers interested in the development of the self-system during childhood have corroborated the notion that feelings of competence and personal esteem are of central importance for a child's psychosocial well-being (see Eccles, 1983, 1994; Harter, 1985; Rosenberg, Schooler, & Schoenbach, 1989). For instance, children who fail to develop positive self-perceptions of competence in the academic or social domains during the elementary school years report more of the symptoms associated with both "internalized" distress, such as depression and social isolation (Asher, Hymel, & Renshaw, 1984; Cole, 1991), and "externalized" distress, such as anger and aggression (Parkhurst & Asher, 1992). Studies of psychiatric difficulties during childhood and adolescence also have documented that children's feelings of competence in various activity domains, especially academics, serve as protective factors against both concurrent and later problem behaviors (e.g., Achenbach, Howell, Quay, & Conners, 1991; Lord, Eccles, & McCarthy, 1994; Rae-Grant, Thomas, Offord, & Boyle, 1989). Finally, research on children who experience difficulties with learning early in school has shown that these children are at increased risk for behavioral, academic, and psychiatric difficulties contemporaneously and subsequently—such children also are particularly likely to be retained in grade and to later drop out of school prior to the completion of high school (e.g., Alexander, Entwisle, & Horsey, 1997; Cairns, Cairns, & Neckerman, 1989; Hinshaw, 1992; Offord & Fleming, 1995; Roderick, 1994; Rutter, 1988). It could be that some learning problems are manifestations of more serious underlying pathology. Alternatively, the frequent feelings of frustration and incompetence that accompany a child's lack of success early in his or her school career may coalesce over time into a negative pattern of adaptation toward schooling (e.g., Cairns et al., 1989).

All of these results suggest that academic success during middle childhood is critical to a successful developmental trajectory through this period and into adolescence precisely because academic success is critical to developing a healthy, positive view of one's competence and a positive motivational orientation toward learning in school. Although we know that a distressingly large percentage of children in elementary and secondary schools experience academic difficulties and are at risk for academic failure and disengagement (e.g., 25%; Dryfoos, 1990, 1994), work documenting longitudinal changes in both ability self-concepts and academic motivation over this period is just beginning to emerge. There is even less work documenting the relation of early school adjustment and competence to the development of other personal difficulties in the late childhood and adolescent years. The relative lack of cross-fertilization among the researchers interested in the different areas of a child's development has resulted in a fragmented understanding of developmental patterns of intellectual, emotional, social, and behavioral functioning (see also Millstein, Petersen, & Nightengale, 1994). Although there is some cross-sectional evidence to suggest that academic problems are related to difficulties of adjustment in other domains of functioning (e.g., emotional, interpersonal, behavioral), few longitudinal studies have simultaneously examined the interweaving developmental lines of academic and social-emotional adjustment from childhood to adolescence.

☐ Developmental Patterns Across the Middle School Years in Academic Motivation

Over the years, psychologists have proposed many different components of academic motivation. In an effort to systematize this vast literature, Eccles, Wigfield, and Schiefele (1997) suggested that one could group these various components under four basic questions: (a) Can I succeed at this task? (b) Do I want to do this task? (c) Why am I doing this task? (d) What do I have do to succeed at this task? They hypothesized that the answers to these questions would determine children's engagement with academic tasks as well as their general commitment to the educational goals of their parents and teachers. Children who develop positive, productive answers to these questions are likely to engage in their schoolwork and to thrive in their school settings. Children who develop less positive, and/or less effective, answers to these questions are likely to experience school failure and to withdraw their psychological attachments from the activities associated with school, increasing the likelihood that they will turn to less productive and more risky activity settings for their psychological nurturance. In this chapter, we focus on the first three of these questions.

In this section, we review what is known about developmental changes over the middle childhood years in children's answers to these questions. We focus this summary on those constructs most directly linked to the Eriksonian perspective outlined above (i.e., those constructs linked to one's sense of industry) and to school engagement.

☐ Can I Succeed at This Task?

Several theorists have proposed constructs linked to this question. We focus on those related to ability self-perceptions and expectations of success. These include such expectancy-related theories as Eccles' (1983) expectancy-value theory, Bandura's (1997) self-efficacy, and various control theories.

Expectancy Theories

Eccles and Colleagues' Expectancy-Value Theory. Eccles and her colleagues have elaborated and tested one expectancy-value model of achievement-related choices and engagement (e.g., Eccles,

1987; Eccles, Adler, & Meece, 1984; Eccles, 1983; Eccles & Wigfield, 1995; Meece, Wigfield, & Eccles, 1990; Wigfield & Eccles, 1992). The most recent version of this model is depicted in Figure 14.1. In this model, expectancies and values are assumed to influence performance, persistence, and task choice directly. Expectancies and values are assumed to be influenced by task-specific beliefs such as perceptions of the difficulty of different tasks, and individuals' goals and self-schema. These social cognitive variables, in turn, are influenced by individuals' perceptions of other peoples' attitudes and expectations for them, by their own interpretations of their previous achievement outcomes, and by their affective memories of, or affective expectations about, similar tasks. Individuals' task perceptions and interpretations of their past outcomes are assumed to be influenced by socializer's behaviors and beliefs, by the individuals' own histories of success and failure, and by the broader cultural milieu and unique historical events.

In this expectancy-value model, ability beliefs are conceived as broad beliefs about competence in a given domain, in contrast to one's expectancies for success on a specific upcoming task. Consequently, Eccles (1983) defined *expectancies for success* as children's beliefs about how well they would do on either immediate or future tasks and *beliefs about ability* as children's evaluations of their more general level competence in different areas. However, their empirical work has shown that children and adolescents do not distinguish between these two different levels of beliefs: The children's responses to these two types of scales always load together on the same factor (Eccles & Wigfield, 1995). Apparently, even though these constructs are theoretically distinguishable from each other, in real-world achievement situations they are highly related and empirically indistinguishable.

Self-Efficacy Theory

Bandura (1977, 1997) also has proposed a social cognitive model of motivated behavior that emphasizes the role of perceptions of efficacy and human agency in determining individuals' achievement strivings. Bandura (1977) defined *self-efficacy* as individuals' confidence in their ability to organize and execute a given course of action to solve a problem or accomplish a task. In his recent writings (e.g., Bandura, 1997), he characterizes self-efficacy as a multidimensional construct that can vary in strength, generality, and

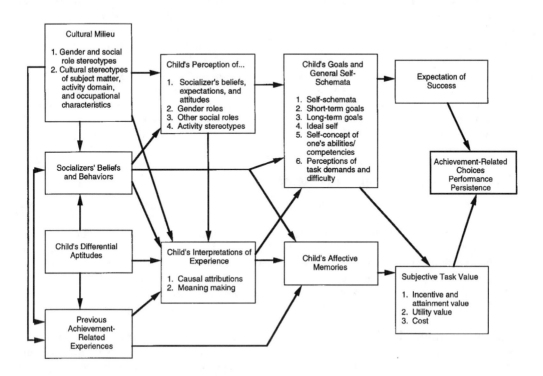

FIGURE 14.1. General model of achievement choices.

level (or difficulty). That is, some people have a strong sense of self-efficacy and others do not; some individuals' efficacy beliefs encompass many situations, whereas others have narrow efficacy beliefs; and some individuals believe they are efficacious even on the most difficult tasks, whereas others do not.

As in Eccles' (1983) expectancy-value theory, Bandura's (1997) self-efficacy theory focuses on expectancies for success. Bandura distinguished between two kinds of expectancy beliefs: (a) outcome expectations (beliefs regarding which behaviors are likely lead to specific outcomes, e.g., studying hard increases the chances of doing well on tests), and (b) efficacy expectations (beliefs about whether one can effectively perform the behaviors necessary to produce the outcome, e.g., I will be able to study hard enough to do well on the next test). Futhermore, Bandura proposed that efficacy expectations are the major determinant of goal setting, activity choice, willingness to expend effort, and persistence (see Bandura, 1997). By and large, the evidence supports this prediction. For example, high personal academic expectations (i.e., high efficacy expectations) predict subsequent performance, course enrollment and, occupational choice for all ethnic groups studied (see Gurin & Epps, 1974; Schunk, 1991; Zimmerman, Bandura, & Martinez-Pons, 1992).

Bandura (1977, 1997) proposed that individuals' efficacy expectations (also called perceived self-efficacy) are determined by four things: Previous performance (people who succeed will develop a stronger sense of personal efficacy than those who do not), vicarious learning (watching a model succeed on a task will improve one's own self-efficacy regarding the task), verbal encouragement by others, and the level of one's physiological reaction to a task or situation. Bandura primarily analyzed physiological reactions in terms of their negative consequences: when individuals are overaroused and anxious, the self-efficacy will be lower.

Bandura (1997) also outlined a theoretical analysis of the development of self-efficacy. First, he proposed that experiences controlling immediate situations and activities provide the earliest sense of personal agency. Through these experiences, infants learn that they can influence and control their environments. If adults do not provide infants' with these experiences, the infants are not likely to develop a strong a sense of personal agency. Second, because self-efficacy requires the understanding that the self produced an action and an outcome, Bandura (1997) argued that a more mature sense of self-efficacy should not emerge until children have at least a rudimentary self-concept and can recognize that they are distinct individuals, which happens sometime during the second year of life (see Harter, 1997). Through the preschool period, children are exposed to extensive performance information that should be crucial to their emerging sense of self-efficacy. However, just how useful such information is should depend on the child's ability to integrate it across time, contexts, and domains. Since these cognitive capacities emerge gradually over the preschool and early elementary school years, young children's efficacy judgments should depend more on immediate and apparent outcomes than on a systematic analysis of their performance history in similar situations (see Parsons & Ruble, 1972, 1977; Shaklee & Tucker, 1979). More work is needed to understand how children become able to integrate diverse sources of information about their performances (e.g., information about their own performance, social comparison information) to develop a stable sense of self-efficacy.

The Development of Competence-Related Expectancy Beliefs

Most of the work on the development of children's achievement-related beliefs has looked at the development of children's ability- and expectancy-related beliefs (e.g., see Eccles, 1997; Stipek & Mac Iver, 1989). Researchers have studied three kinds of age-related changes in these beliefs: change in the mean levels of children's responses to specific scales, change in the factor structure of these responses, and change in children's understanding of these concepts. We focus on the first. We also discuss various ways of assessing and describing longitudinal patterns of change at the level of the individual. However, because it is essential to understand exactly how children of different ages think about competence and ability before we can interpret the age differences in their responses to our scales, we briefly discuss this third type of change.

Changes in Children's Understanding of Competence-Related Beliefs.   Several researchers have investigated children's understanding of competence-related beliefs, focusing primarily on children's understanding of ability and intelligence. For example, Nicholls and his colleagues asked children questions about ability, intelligence, effort, and task difficulty, and how different levels of performance can occur when children exert similar effort (e.g., Nicholls, 1990; Nicholls, Cobb, Yackel, Wood, &

Wheatley, 1990). They found four relatively distinct levels of reasoning: At level 1 (ages 5 to 6), effort, ability, and performance are not clearly differentiated in terms of cause and effect. At level 2 (ages 7 to 9), effort is seen as the primary cause of performance of outcomes. At level 3 (ages 9 to 12), children begin to differentiate ability and effort as causes of outcomes, but they do not always apply this distinction. Finally, at level 4, adolescents clearly differentiate ability and effort, and understand the notion of ability as capacity; they also believe that ability can limit the effects of additional effort on performance, that ability and effort are often related to each other in a compensatory manner, and, consequently, that a successful outcome that required a great deal of effort may reflect limited ability.

Dweck and her colleagues (e.g., Dweck & Elliott, 1983; Dweck & Leggett, 1988) also have discussed how children view ability. In their view, children hold one of two views of intelligence or ability: an entity view that intelligence is a stable trait, or an incremental view that intelligence is changeable and can be increased through effort. Like Nicholls (1990), Dweck stressed how children's conceptions of ability and intelligence have important motivational consequences, particularly when children experience failure. Believing that ability is an entity increases the debilitating effects of failure. Children holding this view likely believe they have little chance of ever doing well, because their ability cannot be improved after failure. In contrast, believing that effort can improve performance should protect children from a learned helpless response to failure precisely because these children should continue to try even if they are not doing well on a given task. Although much less work has been done on the impact of an entity versus an incremental view of intelligence on children when they are doing well, some evidence has suggested that an entity view can undermine learning and motivation even when one is doing well: In particular, children with an entity view of intelligence tend to avoid challenging tasks in order to ensure their continued success (see Dweck & Leggett, 1988).

Dweck and her colleagues have done less developmental work than Nicholls and his colleagues. Consequently, we know less about the age-related changes in children's endorsement of entity versus incremental views of intelligence. Nicholls' work has suggested that younger children should be less likely to believe ability is stable or fixed: and, by and large, evidence supports this prediction (see Eccles, Wigfield, & Schiefele, 1997). Nonetheless, both Heyman, Dweck, and Cain (1993) and Burhans and Dweck (1995) found that some quite young children have doubts about their ability to do certain tasks, even if they try hard.

Change in the Mean Level of Children's Competence-Related Beliefs.   Several researchers have found that children's competence-related beliefs for different tasks decline across the elementary school years and into the middle school years (see Dweck & Elliott, 1983; Eccles et al., 1984; Eccles & Midgley, 1989; Stipek & Mac Iver, 1989). To illustrate, in Nicholls (1979), most first graders ranked themselves near the top of the class in reading ability, and there was essentially no correlation between their ability ratings and their performance level. In contrast, the 12-year-olds' ratings were more dispersed, and their correlation with school grades was .70 or higher. Similar results have emerged in cross-sectional and longitudinal studies of children's competence beliefs in a variety of academic and nonacademic domains by Eccles and her colleagues (e.g., Eccles, Wigfield, Harold, & Blumenfeld, 1993; Wigfield et al., 1998) and by Marsh (1989). These declines, particularly for math, often continue into and through secondary school (Eccles, 1983; Eccles et al., 1989; Wigfield, Eccles, Mac Iver, Reuman, & Midgley, 1991).

Some of the findings from our work are summarized in Figure 14.2, which illustrates the longitudinal changes in elementary school children's ability self-concepts for math, English, and sports. A set of predominantly White, middle-class children (N = 615) initially in kindergarten, Grade 1, and Grade 3 were given a written survey in their classrooms each year for 3 consecutive years. Together these three cohorts provide a picture of the developmental changes in ability self-concepts over the entire elementary school period. The survey included measures of their ability self-concepts in math, English, and sports. Scales were composed of several items responded to on a 7-point Likert scale anchored with verbal labels at the extreme end points and the midpoint (see Eccles, Wigfield, et al., 1993, and Wigfield et al., 1998, for full details). We have aggregated the data across cohorts to produce a single age-linked function for each domain.

Figure 14.2 illustrates a clear decline in children's ability self-concepts in reading from Grade 1 through Grade 4, followed by a slight upturn between Grades 5 and 6. Ability self-concepts in both math and sports follow a similar though less extreme picture with the biggest declines occurring between Grades 1 and 2. Follow-up data from these same children suggest that these declines continue into the early middle school years and then asymptote across the transition into high school.

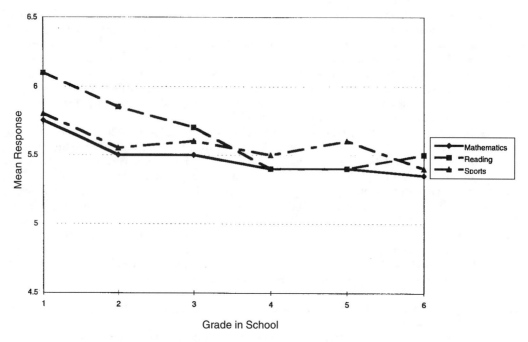

FIGURE 14.2. Developmental patterns in ability self-concepts.

Similar results have been found in the Michigan Study in Adolescent Life Transitions (MSALT; see Eccles et al., 1989, and Wigfield et al., 1991, for details of study). These students were studied at four time points over the junior high school transition (two times in the sixth grade and two times in the seventh grade). Students' confidence in their math and English abilities and self-esteem were assessed at each time point. Confidence in both academic domains showed a marked decline over this school transition and continued to decline during the first year of junior high school. Self-esteem also showed a marked drop over the school transition followed by a partial rebound during the seventh-grade school year (Wigfield et al., 1991).

Expectancies for success also decrease during the elementary school years. In most laboratory-type studies, 4- and 5-year-old children expect to do quite well on a specific task, even after repeated failure (e.g., Parsons & Ruble, 1977; Stipek, 1984). Across the elementary school years, the mean levels of children's expectancies for success both decline and become more sensitive to both success and failure experiences. Consequently, both competence beliefs and expectancies become more accurate or realistic in terms of their relation to actual performance history (see Eccles, Midgley, & Adler, 1984; Parsons & Ruble, 1972, 1977; Stipek, 1984).

In contrast to research based on self-report measures, researchers using either different kinds of questions, or observing young children's reactions to their performance on different tasks have found that not all young children are optimistic about their abilities. In a study by Heyman et al. (1993), for example, some preschool children reacted quite negatively to failure. Similarly, in Stipek, Recchia, and McClintic (1992), children as young as age 2 reacted both behaviorally and emotionally to failure experiences.

In summary, there is a drop in children's ability self-concepts and expectations for success over the elementary school years. In part this drop reflects the initially high, and often unrealistic, expectations of kindergarten and first-grade children. Stipek (1984) has argued that young children's optimistic expectancies reflect hoped-for outcomes rather than real expectations; in contrast, Parsons and Ruble (1977) suggested that, because young children's skills do, in fact, improve rapidly, high expectancies for future success may be based on experience (see also Dweck & Elliott, 1983; Eccles, Midgley, & Adler, 1984). As the rate of improvement slows, children may learn that current failures are more predictive of subsequent performance. Other changes also are likely to contribute to this decline: changes such as increased exposure to failure feedback, increased ability to integrate success and failure information across time to form expectations more closely linked with experience, increased ability to use social comparison information, and increased exposure to teachers' expectations.

Some of these changes are directly linked to the transition into elementary school. Entrance into elementary school and, then, the transition from kindergarten to first grade introduces several systematic changes in children's social worlds. First, classes are age stratified, making within-age ability social comparison much easier. Second, formal evaluations of competence by "experts" begins. Third, formal ability grouping begins, usually with reading group assignment. Fourth, peers have the opportunity to play a much more constant and salient role in children' lives. Each of these changes should impact children's motivational development. Such changes could contribute to the increase in children's response to failure feedback as they move from preschool and kindergarten into the first grade (Parsons & Ruble, 1972, 1977; Stipek, 1984). Parents' expectations for, and perceptions of, their children's academic competence also are influenced by report card marks and standardized test scores given out during the early elementary school years, particularly for mathematics (Alexander & Entwisle, 1988; Arbreton & Eccles, 1994). But, more systematic studies of the effects of transition into elementary school and transitions from kindergarten to first grade are needed.

There are significant long-term consequences of children's experiences in the first grade, particularly experiences associated with ability grouping and within-class differential teacher treatment. For example, teachers use a variety of information to assign first graders to reading groups, including temperamental characteristics like interest and persistence, race, gender, and social class (e.g., Alexander, Dauber, & Entwisle, 1993; Brophy & Good, 1974). Alexander et al. (1993) demonstrated that differences in first-grade reading group placement and teacher-student interactions have a significant effect (after controlling for initial individual differences in competence) on motivation and achievement several years later. Furthermore, these effects are mediated by both differential instruction and the exaggerating impact of ability group placement on parents' and teachers' views of the children's abilities, talents, and motivation (Pallas, Entwisle, Alexander, & Stluka, 1994).

Individual Differences in Developmental Trajectories.   All of the data reported above focused on mean level changes at the population level. Changes at this aggregate level likely reflect either shared maturational influences or shared changes in school characteristics (see Eccles, Midgley, & Adler, 1984; Eccles et al., 1997). These findings, however, mask individual differences in these developmental trajectories. Work in the arenas of underachievement, test anxiety, and learned helplessness (reviewed below) provides clear evidence of strong individual differences in these trajectories: Some children evidence a negative self-concept pattern as soon as they enter the first grade and remain low throughout their schooling years, others start high and show the type of gradual decline evident in the mean level graphs, still others start low and rebound, and others start and remain high throughout their schooling years.

We have been exploring these individual differences in our Childhood and Beyond (CAB) Study. The results summarized here are taken from Roeser, Eccles, et al. (1995). This study was designed to look at two issues: (a) individual differences in the trajectories of children's academic ability self-concept, and (b) the relation of these different trajectories to other indicators of social development and mental health. We describe the results relevant to the first goal here; the results relevant to the second goal are presented later.

To assess trajectories of academic risk and resilience, we grouped children based on their level of academic functioning at two points in time: during early elementary school and later in middle school. We then examined a constellation of related indexes of academic functioning as a means of corroborating our characterization of children and youth as "academically at risk" or "academically not at risk" during these times. To address an issue that Sroufe and Jacobvitz (1989) called the "equivalency problem" of examining coherence in risk status over time, we created indexes of academic risk status that were functionally equivalent, even though objectively different, during both middle childhood and early adolescence. Because the criteria by which children judge their academic competence are known to change with development and increasing cognitive sophistication, and because so many young children express such optimistic expectations and ability self-concepts (Eccles, Wigfield, & Schiefele, 1997; Stipek, 1984), we relied on teacher reports of children's academic competence during the early grades to assess academic risk status. We did this by asking teachers to rate each child's academic abilities (in reading and math) and chances of future academic success relative to his or her same-age peers. Other research has shown that teachers' ratings of children's competence have good concurrent and long-term predictive validity in terms of children's performance on cognitive tests and academic school achievement (e.g., Stevenson, Parker, Wilkinson, Hegion, & Fish, 1976; Wigfield et al., 1998).

When the youth were in Grades 7 and 8, we relied on their own self-reports of academic competence to assess their academic risk status. Similar to the questions asked of teachers during the early elementary school years, several of the items in the self-report academic competence scale assessed how these early adolescents felt they compared to their same-age peers in terms of their abilities in reading and math. By the early adolescent years, the use of social comparison information to determine one's abilities in a given domain is, for better or worse, a functional part of youth's self assessments (e.g., Harter, 1985; Ruble, 1983). Thus, we believe that these two assessments of children's academic competence, one based on elementary school teachers' ratings, and one based on adolescent self-reports, are more functionally "equivalent" indicators of risk than relying on self-reports at both time points. Because the younger children rate their academic abilities so high, it is quite difficult to identify a group of at-risk children in terms of their academic potential. Consequently, we felt it necessary to use the teachers' ratings for the younger children. By Grades 7 and 8, there is a very high correlation between youth and teacher ratings of academic competence. Consequently, we felt justified in using their self-reports.

To identify children at risk at time 1, we created a composite measure of teachers' perceptions of children's academic competence in reading and math as well as their expectancies for children's future academic success. The children were identified as academically at risk at time 1 if they were rated in the lowest 33% of the distribution of their teachers' ratings. Our original sample consisted of 397 first and second graders during the 1988 school year. Of these children, 137 (35%) were categorized as having poor school adjustment, and thus were designated as academically at risk. The remaining 260 children were categorized as academically not at risk. Representative numbers of girls and boys were categorized into each of these groups, $\chi^2(1,396) = 0.13$, $p = .72$.

To corroborate and triangulate our characterization of the children as either academically at risk or not at risk based on teacher ratings, we conducted a series of multivariate analyses of variance using measures from the children's teachers, mothers, and the children themselves. We also looked at group differences in measures drawn from the children's school academic records that we assumed would covary with our characterization of children's academic risk status. The results of these analyses are presented in Table 14.1. The at-risk children scored significantly worse than the other children on all of these measures.

To identify the children at risk in Grades 7 or 8, we used adolescent self-report measures of their academic competence in reading and math. Criteria similar to those used during the early elementary school years were used to characterized adolescents as academically at risk or not at risk. Youth who were in the lowest 33% of the overall sample distribution on a measure of their self-reported academic competence were designated as academically at risk. Youth in the upper 66% of the distribution were categorized as not at risk. Of the sample of 363 seventh and eighth graders who were available for follow-up during the 1994 school year, 109 (30%) were categorized as being academically at risk, and 254 as not at risk. Representative numbers of girls and boys were categorized into each of the groups, $\chi^2(1,363) = 2.68$, $p = .10$, with a trend toward boys being slightly overrepresented in the at risk group. Table 14.2 shows the results for corroborating measures of academic difficulties during early adolescence. Again the at-risk youth scored more poorly than the not-at-risk youth on all of these indicators of academic adjustment as well as an on the indicators of social adjustment.

Next we used these risk scores to identify different patterns of change in risk status across the years that span middle childhood to early adolescence. To do this, we grouped children into four "academic risk trajectory" groups. These included children who were or were not at risk at both times, children who evidenced academic risk early but not later, and children who did not evidence academic risk early but did so later. A summary of these four groups is presented in Table 14.3. As you can see, there is a great deal of stability in these trajectories (62% remained in the same risk category across time). Nonetheless, the chi-square statistic for this 2 by 2 table is significant, $\chi^2(1,289) = 17.85$, $p = .001$, indicating some instability in this matrix as well. Despite the mean level changes in academic self-concepts reported above, fewer children than the empirically generated expected frequency (given the marginals and the distribution of the sample into the two at-risk categories at both time points) fell into the decliner category and more children than the empirically generated expected frequency fell into the incliner category.

We then assessed the trajectories of change on other indicators of academic confidence, valuing, and performance to see how these four groups differed across these years. The results are illustrated in Fig-

TABLE 14.1. Teacher, parent, school record, and child self-report indexes of academic and social-emotional adjustment by academic risk status during middle childhood

Descriptive Variables	At Risk Academically (*n* = 137)	Not At Risk Academically (*n* = 260)	Significance
Teacher's ratings of child— Academic adjustment			
Academic competence[a]	3.92	5.96	$F(1, 373) = 790.48$***
Social competence	4.44	5.19	$F(1, 373) = 37.09$***
Academic effort and persistence	4.02	5.76	$F(1, 373) = 237.72$***
Adjustment to school[b]	4.90	6.12	$F(1, 289) = 75.61$***
Teacher's ratings of child— Social-emotional adjustment			
Anxiousness	3.74	3.32	$F(1, 394) = 9.99$**
Aggression/Impulsivity	3.22	2.48	$F(1, 394) = 24.92$***
Prosociability	4.95	5.61	$F(1, 394) = 28.90$***
Creativity	4.16	5.32	$F(1, 394) = 94.81$***
Mother's ratings of child			
Academic competence	5.22	6.05	$F(1, 276) = 54.92$***
Children's self-reports			
Academic competence	5.67	5.82	$F(1, 391) = 2.61$
Academic valuing	5.37	5.63	$F(1, 391) = 2.12$*
General self-esteem	2.84	3.04	$F(1, 391) = 5.35$*
School record data			
Slosson I.Q. Measure	113.60	122.01	$F(1, 305) = 20.62$***
Time 1 Academic marks[c]	9.43	10.84	$F(1, 305) = 73.17$***
Time 1 Academic effort marks[c]	9.94	11.40	$F(1, 305) = 35.86$***
Time 1 School conduct marks[c]	9.47	10.68	$F(1, 305) = 20.36$***

Note. N = 397; ns vary due listwise deletion of cases and missing data.
[a] Academic competence is the criterion variable used to designate students' academic risk status, with those students falling into the lower 33% of the distribution being categorized as being "academically at risk."
[b] Adjustment to school" was a measure taken from students' first-grade teacher regardless of their cohort in 1988, and assessed how well the first-grade teacher perceived the child's adjustment to school in general. A separate ANOVA was run for this scale due to the number of students with missing data.
[c] Academic marks consisted of teacher-rated grades of students in the core subjects of math and reading. Marks were measured on a 16-point scale, with values roughly equaling specific letter grades. For instance, 1 = F, 3 = E, 6 = D, 9 = C, 12 = B, 15 = A, and 16 = A+.
* $p \leq .05$, ** $p \leq .01$, *** $p \leq .001$.

ures 14.3 through 14.6. The four groups did not differ during their elementary school years in either their own estimates of academic competence and the value they reported attaching to doing well in school. They clearly did differ at time 4. A slightly different picture emerged for academic performance. Both the incliners and stably adjusted groups showed an increase in their academic performance between Grades 2 and 3 and Grades 3 and 4. The incliners showed an additional increase between Grades 3 and 4 and Grades 7 and 8, at which time they were performing almost as well as the stably adjusted group. Their first-grade teachers had been wrong about their potential. The four groups differed in their self-esteem at time 2. This result is discussed more below.

Apparently, although children's confidence in their academic abilities declines over time on the average, a substantial number of children identified as at risk by their teachers due to their academic limitations appear to enter adolescence with reasonably high ability self-concepts and good academic records. We discuss exactly who these children are below. But, before leaving this discussion, it is important to point out that one needs to be careful about assuming that the mean level declines in academic self-

TABLE 14.2. Youth self-reports of academic and social-emotional adjustment by academic risk status during early adolescence

Descriptive Variables	At Risk Academically (*n* = 107)	Not At Risk Academically (*n* = 247)	Significance
Youth self-reports— Academic adjustment			
Academic competence[a]	3.81	5.23	$F(1, 352) = 484.62$***
Academic valuing	3.77	4.69	$F(1, 352) = 111.95$***
Grade point average[b]	2.91	3.48	$F(1, 352) = 89.71$***
Likelihood of dropping out	1.41	1.12	$F(1, 352) = 9.18$**
Youth self-reports— Social-emotional adjustment			
Anger	3.48	2.88	$F(1, 344) = 12.02$***
Depressive-symptomatology	2.88	2.44	$F(1, 344) = 8.85$**
Life satisfaction	4.55	5.26	$F(1, 344) = 35.80$***
Self-esteem	2.87	3.15	$F(1, 344) = 17.67$***
Ego resilience	4.71	5.39	$F(1, 344) = 36.84$***

Note. N = 354; *ns* vary due listwise deletion of cases and missing data.
[a] Academic competence is the criterion variable used to designate students' academic risk status, with those students falling into the lower 33% of the distribution being categorized as being "academically at risk."
[b] Adolescents' self-reported grade point averages (GPAs) were used. In other work with adolescents, we have found self-report measures to correlate .70 with actual school record data GPAs (Roeser, Lord, & Eccles, 1994). In the measure reported here, 0 = Failing, 1 = Ds, 2 = Cs, 3 = Bs, and 4 = A.
* $p \leq .05$, ** $p \leq .01$, *** $p \leq .001$.

concepts represent the tip of a dangerous iceberg. Instead, some of this decline likely reflects the overly optimistic scores of young children and the more realistic self-concept scores of older children. Furthermore, even though first-grade teacher ratings have emerged in several studies as significant predictors of adolescent school achievement, these data clearly indicate that a nontrivial number of the children rated by their first-grade teachers as at academic risk look fine by the time they were in middle school.

Control Theories

Control theorists also have proposed motivational components with respect to the question, Can I succeed? that are related to other aspects of social development such as individual's feelings of efficacy and industry, and general mental health. More specifically, these theorists propose that individuals with a strong sense of internal locus of control will be more likely to engage in, and succeed at, academic tasks and will feel better about themselves more generally than will children with an external locus of control.

TABLE 14.3. Count of youth by academic risk status over time

	Academic Risk Status During Middle Childhood		
	Not At Risk	At Risk	Totals
Academic risk status during early adolescence			
Not at risk	122 (42%) "Stable-adjusted"	80 (28%) "Incliners"	202
At risk	29 (10%) "Decliners"	58 (20%) "Stable difficulties"	87
Totals	151	138	N = 289

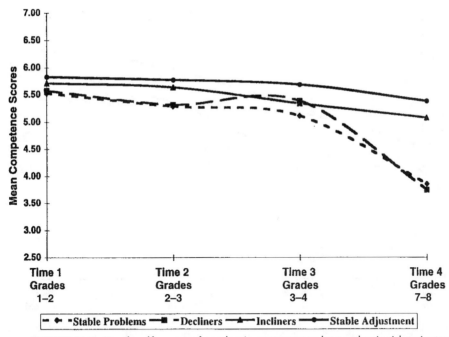

FIGURE 14.3. Youth self-report of academic competence by academic risk trajectory.

Empirical work has confirmed these predictions (see Weisz, 1984, for reviews of this evidence). In addition, contemporary control theorists have elaborated broader conceptual models of control. Connell (1985), for example, added unknown control as a third control belief category, in addition to internal (one's own effort and ability) and external control (luck and powerful others), and argued that younger children are particularly likely to use this category.

Connell and Wellborn (1991) then integrated control beliefs into a broader theoretical framework in which they proposed three basic psychological needs for competence, autonomy, and relatedness (see

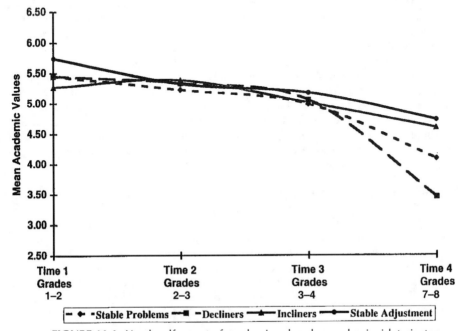

FIGURE 14.4. Youth self-report of academic values by academic risk trajectory.

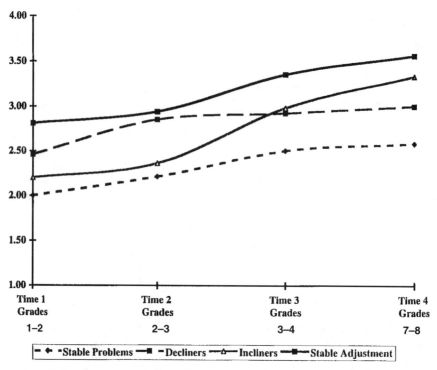

FIGURE 14.5. Academic achievement by academic risk trajectory.

also Ryan, 1992). They linked control beliefs to competence needs: Children who believe they can control their achievement outcomes should feel more competent. They hypothesized that the extent to which these three needs are fulfilled is influenced by the following contextual characteristics: the amount of structure, the degree of autonomy provided, and the level of involvement in the children's activities. Finally, they proposed that the ways in which these three psychological needs are fulfilled determine engagement in different activities. When the psychological needs are fulfilled, children will be fully engaged. When one or more of the needs is not fulfilled, children will become disaffected (see Connell, Spencer, & Aber, 1994; Skinner & Belmont, 1993, for supportive evidence). In this way, Connell and Wellborn have linked control beliefs to more general psychological functioning.

Building on Connell and colleagues' work, Skinner and her colleagues (e.g., Skinner, 1995) proposed a more elaborated model of perceived control. Focusing on understanding goal-directed activity, Skinner described three critical beliefs. *Means-ends beliefs* concern the expectation that particular causes can produce certain outcomes; these causes include Weiner's (see 1992) various causal attributions and Connell's (1985) unknown control. *Control beliefs* are the expectations individuals have that they can produce desired events. *Agency beliefs* are the expectations that one has access to the means needed to produce various outcomes.

Developmental Changes in Control Beliefs.   In her discussion of the ontogeny of control beliefs, Skinner (1995) stressed the importance of perceived contingency between individuals' actions and their successes. She also stressed the importance of success itself for developing positive control beliefs. Finally, she discussed how children's understanding of causality and explanations for outcomes likely changes over age with these beliefs, particularly the means-ends beliefs, becoming more differentiated as children get older. What is similar across all ages is the importance of fulfilling the need for competence.

In their review of studies of children who were primarily 8- to 9-years-old and older, Skinner and Connell (1986) concluded that there is an increase in perceptions of internal control as children get older. In contrast, based on a series of studies of children's understanding of skill versus chance events, Weisz

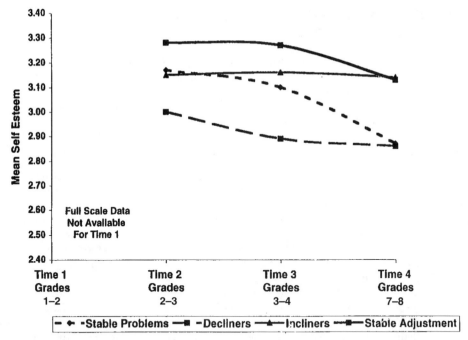

FIGURE 14.6. Youth self-report of self-esteem by academic risk trajectory.

(1984) concluded that the developmental sequence is more complex. The kindergarten children in these studies believed outcomes of chance tasks were due to effort, whereas the oldest groups (eighth graders and college students) believed that such outcomes were due to chance; fourth graders were confused about the distinction. Thus, in this work, the youngest children had internal central belief—so strong, in fact, that they believed in internal control over outcomes even when none was possible, suggesting that, with age, children came to understand better which kinds of events they can control and which they cannot. Similarly, Connell (1985) found a decrease in the endorsement of all three of his locus of control constructs (internal control, powerful others control, and unknown control) from Grades 3 through 9. Like Weisz's (1984) work, the unknown belief results suggested that older children have a clearer understanding of what controls achievement outcomes. However, the older children also rated the other two sources of control as less important, making interpretation of the findings difficult.

In summary, children's competence beliefs and expectancies for success become more negative as they get older, at least through early adolescence. The negative changes in children's achievement beliefs have been explained in two ways: (a) because children become much better at understanding, interpreting, and integrating the evaluative feedback they receive, and engage in more social comparison with their peers, many children should become more accurate or realistic in their self-assessments, leading some to become relatively negative (see Dweck & Elliott, 1983; Higgins & Parsons, 1983; Nicholls, 1984; Parsons & Ruble, 1977; Ruble, 1983; Shaklee & Tucker; Stipek & Mac Iver, 1989), and (b) because school environment changes in ways that make evaluation more salient and competition between students more likely, some children's self-assessments will decline as they get older (e.g., see Eccles & Midgley, 1989; Eccles, Midgley, & Adler, 1984; Stipek & Daniels, 1988). For example, there has been some speculation that the declines in ability self-concepts between Grades 2 and 4 reflect changes in teacher's grading practices and stress on competition among students at about third grade. However, evidence regarding this type of change is not yet widely available.

We also discussed individual differences in these patterns of change. Some children show these declines; others do not. Some start quite low and remain low; others start high and remain quite high throughout their elementary school years. Very little work has been done on identifying the characteristics of children and their social environments that distinguish these groups from each other.

☐ Theories Concerned with the Question, Do I Want to Do This Task?

Although theories dealing with competence, expectancy, and control beliefs provide powerful explanations of individuals' performance on different kinds of achievement tasks, these theories do not systematically address another important motivational question, Does the individual want to do the task? Even if people are certain they can do a task, they may not want to engage in it. The theories presented in this section focus on this aspect of motivation.

Eccles, Wigfield, and Colleagues' Work on Subjective Task Values

Eccles and her colleagues have elaborated the concept of task value. Building on earlier work on achievement values (e.g., Battle, 1966), intrinsic and extrinsic motivation (e.g., Deci, 1975), and Rokeach's (1979) view that values are shared beliefs about desired end states, Eccles et al. (1983) outlined four motivational components of task value: attainment value, intrinsic value, utility value, and cost. Like Battle (1966), they defined attainment value as the personal importance of doing well on the task. Drawing on self-schema and identity theories (e.g., Kohlberg, 1966; Markus & Nurius, 1984), as well as the work by Feather (1982, 1992) and Rokeach, they also linked attainment value to the relevance of engaging in a task for confirming or disconfirming salient aspects of one's self-schema (see Eccles, 1984, 1987). Like Harter (1997), Deci and his colleagues (Deci, 1975; Deci & Ryan, 1985; Ryan, Connell, & Deci, 1985), Csikszentmihalyi (1988), Renninger (1990), and Schiefele (1991), Eccles et al. defined intrinsic value in terms of the enjoyment the individual gets from performing the activity, or the subjective interest the individual has in the subject.

Eccles et al. defined utility value in terms of how well a task relates to current and future goals, such as career goals. A task can have positive value to a person because it facilitates important future goals, even if he or she is not interested in the task for its own sake. For instance, students often take classes that they do not particularly enjoy but that they need to take to pursue other interests, to please their parents, or to be with their friends. In one sense, then, this component captures the more "extrinsic" reasons for engaging in a task (see Deci & Ryan, 1985; Harter, 1985). But, it also relates directly to the internalized short- and long-term goals an individual may have.

Finally, Eccles and her colleagues identified "cost" as a critical component of value (Eccles et al., 1983; Eccles, 1987). Cost is conceptualized in terms of the negative aspects of engaging in the task, such as performance anxiety and fear of both failure and success as well as the amount of effort that is needed to succeed and the lost opportunities that result from making one choice rather than another.

Eccles and her colleagues have conducted extensive empirical tests of different aspects of this model. For example, they have shown that ability self-concepts and performance expectancies predict performance in mathematics and English, whereas task values predict course plans and enrollment decisions in mathematics, physics, and English and involvement in sport activities, even after controlling for prior performance levels (Eccles, 1984; Eccles, Adler, & Meece, 1984; Eccles, Barber, Updegraff, & O'Brien, 1995; Eccles et al. 1983; Eccles & Harold, 1991). They also have shown that both expectancies and values predict career choices (see Eccles, Barber, & Josefowicz, 1998).

Development of Subjective Task Values. There has been much less work on the development of subjective task values during the middle childhood years. Eccles, Wigfield, and their colleagues have examined change in the structure of children's task values as well as mean level change in children's valuing of different activities. Even young children distinguish between their competence beliefs and their task values. In Eccles et al. (1993), Eccles and Wigfield (1995), and Wigfield et al. (1998), children's competence-expectancy beliefs and subjective values within the domains of math, reading, and sports formed distinct factors at all grade levels from Grade 1 through Grade 12. Thus, even during the very early elementary grades, children appear to have distinct beliefs about what they are good at and what they value.

As with competence-related beliefs, studies generally show age-related declines in children's valuing of certain academic tasks (e.g. Eccles, 1983; Eccles & Midgley, 1989; Eccles, Wigfield, et al., 1993; Wigfield & Eccles, 1992). For instance, in longitudinal analysis of elementary school children, beliefs about the usefulness and importance of math, reading, instrumental music, and sports activities decreased over time

(Wigfield et al., 1998). In contrast, the children's interest decreased only for reading and instrumental music, not for either math or sports. The data for interest in math, reading, and sports is illustrated in Figure 14.7.

Using data from other samples, the decline in valuing of math continues through high school (Eccles, 1984). Eccles et al. (1989) and Wigfield et al. (1991) also found that children's ratings of both the importance of math and English and their liking of these school subjects decreased across the transition to middle school. In math, students' importance ratings continued to decline across seventh grade, whereas their importance ratings of English increased somewhat during seventh grade.

Researchers have not yet addressed changes in children's understandings of the components of task value identified by Eccles et al. (1983), although there likely are age-related differences in these understandings. An 8-year-old is likely to have a different sense of what it means for a task to be "useful" than an 11-year-old does. Further, it is likely that there are differences across age in which of the components of achievement values are most dominant. Wigfield and Eccles (1992) suggested that interest may be especially salient during the early elementary school grades. If so, then young children's choice of different activities may be most directly related to their interests. And, if young children's interests shift as rapidly as their attention spans, it is likely they will try many different activities for a short time each before developing a mere stable opinion regarding which activities they enjoy the most. As children become older, the perceived utility and personal importance of different tasks may become more salient, particularly as they develop more stable self-schema and long-range goals and plans. These developmental patterns have yet to be assessed empirically.

A related developmental question is, How do children's developing competence beliefs relate to their developing subjective task values? According to both the Eccles et al. model and Bandura's self-efficacy theory, ability self-concepts should influence the development of task values. In support of this prediction, Mac Iver, Stipek, and Daniels (1991) found that changes in middle school students' competence beliefs over a semester predicted change in children's interest much more strongly than vice versa. Does the same causal ordering occur in younger children? Recall that Bandura (1997) argued that interests emerge out of one's sense of self-efficacy and that children should be more interested in challenging than in easy tasks. Taking a more developmental perspective, Wigfield (1994) proposed that, initially, young children's competence and task value beliefs are likely to be relatively independent of each other. This independence would mean that children might pursue some activities in which they are interested re-

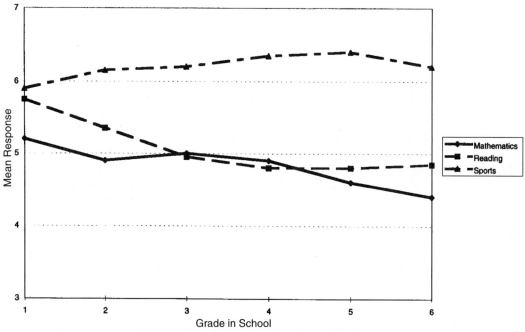

FIGURE 14.7. Development patterns for interest.

gardless of how good or bad they think they are at the activity. Over time, particularly in the achievement domain, children may begin to attach more value to activities on which they do well for several reasons: First, through the processes associated with classical conditioning, the positive affect a child experiences when doing well should become attached to activities yielding success (see Eccles, 1984). Second, lowering the value a child attaches to activities with which he or she is having difficulty can be an effective way to maintain a positive global sense of efficacy and self-esteem (Eccles, 1984; Eccles, Wigfield, Blumenfeld, 1984; Harter, 1990). Thus, at some point, the two kinds of beliefs should become positively related to one another. In partial support of this view, Wigfield et al. (1998) found that relations between children's competence beliefs and subjective values in different domains indeed are stronger in older than younger elementary-school-age children. The causal direction of this relation, however, has not yet been tested empirically.

Interest Theories

Closely related to the intrinsic interest component of subjective task value is the work on "interest" (Alexander, Kulikovich, & Jettison, 1994; Hidi, 1990; Renninger, Hidi, & Krapp, 1992; Schiefele, 1991). Researchers in this tradition differentiate between individual and situational interest. Individual interest is a relatively stable evaluative orientation toward certain domains; situational interest is an emotional state aroused by specific features of an activity or a task. Two aspects or components of individual interest are distinguishable (Schiefele, 1991): feeling-related valences and value-related valences. Feeling-related valences refer to feelings that are associated with an object or an activity itself—feelings like involvement, stimulation, or flow. Value-related valences refer to the attribution of personal significance or importance to an object. In addition, both feeling-related and value-related valences are directly related to the object or task rather than to the relation of this object or task to other objects or tasks. For example, if students associate mathematics with high personal significance because mathematics can help them get prestigious jobs, then we would not speak of interest. Although feeling-related and value-related valences are highly correlated (Schiefele, 1997), it is useful to differentiate between them because some individual interests are based primarily on feelings, while other interests are based on more personal significance (see Eccles, 1984; Wigfield & Eccles, 1992). Further research is necessary to validate this assumption.

Much of the research on individual interest has focused on its relation to the quality of learning (see reviews by Alexander et al., 1994; Renninger et al., 1992; and Schiefele, 1997). In general, there are significant, but moderate, relations between interest and text learning. More importantly, interest is more strongly related to indicators of deep-level learning (e.g., recall of main ideas, coherence of recall, responding to deeper comprehension questions, representation of meaning) than to surface-level learning (e.g., responding to simple questions, verbatim representation of text; Schiefele, 1997; Schiefele & Krapp, 1997).

Most of the research on situational interest has focused on the characteristics of academic tasks that create interest (e.g., see Hidi 1990; Teigen, 1987). Among others, the following text features arouse situational interest: personal relevance, novelty, activity level, and comprehensibility (Hidi, 1990). Empirical evidence has provided strong support for the relation between situational interest and text comprehension and recall (see reviews by Schiefele, 1997; Wade, 1992).

Developmental Changes in Interest.   Based on Piaget's (1948) theory, Travers (1978) analyzed the earliest phase of interest development. He assumed that only "universal" interests would be evident in very young children, for example, the infant's search for structure. Later, depending on the general cognitive development of the child, these universal interests should become more differentiated and individualized. According to Roe and Siegelman (1964), the earliest differentiation occurs between interest in the world of physical objects versus interest in the world of people. Todt (1990) argued that this early differentiation eventually leads to individual differences in interests in the social versus natural sciences.

The next phase of interest development— between 3 and 8 years of age—is characterized by the formation of gender-specific interests. According to Kohlberg (1966), the acquisition of gender identity leads to gender-specific behaviors, attitudes, and interests. Children strive to behave consistently with themselves and, thus, evaluate "male" and "female" activities or objects differently. Activities or objects that are consistent with the children's gender identity will be more positively evaluated than other activities or objects. As a consequence, boys and girls develop gender role stereotype interests (see Eccles, 1987; Eccles & Bryan, 1994; Ruble & Martin, 1997).

Like the work of Eccles and colleagues discussed above, several European researchers have found that interest in different subject areas declines continuously during the school years. This is especially true for the natural sciences (e.g., Baumert, 1995; Hedelin & Sjîberg, 1989; Lehrke, Hoffmann, & Gardner, 1985). For example, Hedelin and Sjîberg (1989) investigated students in Grades 1 through 9 of the Swedish comprehensive school. Similar to the findings of Eccles, Wigfield, and their colleagues in studies of American children (e.g., Eccles, Wigfield, et al., 1993; Wigfield et al., 1991), the students' ratings of their interest in mathematics and Swedish reading and writing declined over time, especially in mathematics. These researchers have identified a number of instructional variables that contribute positively or negatively to interest in school mathematics and science such as: clarity of presentation, monitoring of what happens in the classroom, supportive behavior, cognitively stimulating experiences, and achievement pressure (e.g., Baumert, 1995; Eder, 1992; Lehrke, 1992).

Intrinsic Motivation Theories

The theories described in this section deal with the distinction between intrinsic motivation and extrinsic motivation. When individuals are intrinsically motivated, they do activities for their own sake and out of interest in the activity. When extrinsically motivated, individuals do activities for instrumental or other reasons, such as receiving a reward.

Self-Determination Theory.   Over the past 25 years, many studies have documented the debilitating effects of extrinsic incentives and pressures on the motivation to perform even inherently interesting activities (e.g., see Amabile, Hill, Hennessey, Tighe, 1994; Deci, 1975; Deci & Ryan, 1985; Lepper, 1988). Interest in intrinsic motivation has grown out of two theoretical traditions: (a) traditions that assume humans are motivated to maintain an optimal theoretical level of stimulation (Hebb, 1982), and (b) traditions that posit basic needs for competence (White, 1959) and personal causation or self-determination (deCharms, 1968) underlie intrinsically motivated behavior. Deci and Ryan (1985) integrated these two traditions into their theory of self-determination. In addition, they argued that intrinsic motivation is maintained only when actors feel competent and self-determined. Evidence that intrinsic motivation is reduced by exerting external control and by giving negative competence feedback supports this hypothesis (see Deci & Ryan, 1985). Deci and Ryan (1985) argued, however, that the basic needs for competence and self-determination also play a role in more extrinsically motivated behavior. Consider, for example, a student who consciously and without any external pressure selects a specific major because it will help him or her earn a lot of money. This student is guided by his or her basic needs for competence and self-determination, but his or her choice of major is based on reasons totally extrinsic to the major itself. Finally, Deci and Ryan (1985) postulated that a basic need for interpersonal relatedness explains why people turn external goals into internal goals through internalization.

Individual Difference Theories of Intrinsic Motivation.   Until recently, intrinsic motivation researchers like Deci and Ryan (1985) and Csikszentmihalyi (1988) have dealt with conditions, components, and consequences of intrinsic motivation without making a distinction between intrinsic motivation as a state versus intrinsic motivation as a trait-like characteristic. However, interest in trait-like individual differences in intrinsic motivation has increased recently, particularly among educational and sport psychologists (see Amabile et al., 1994; Gottfried, 1990; Nicholls, 1984, 1989; Schiefele, 1997). These researchers define this enduring intrinsic motivational orientation in terms of three components: (a) preference for hard or challenging tasks, (b) learning that is driven by curiosity or interest, and (c) striving for competence and mastery. The second component is most central to the idea of intrinsic motivation. Both preference for hard tasks and striving for competence can be linked to either extrinsic or more general need achievement motivation. Nonetheless, empirical findings suggest that the three components are highly correlated. In addition, evidence suggests that high levels of trait-like intrinsic motivation facilitate positive emotional experience (Matsumoto & Sanders, 1988), self-esteem (Ryan et al., 1985), mastery-oriented coping with failure (Dweck, 1975), high academic achievement (Benware & Deci, 1984; Schiefele & Schreyer, 1994), and use of appropriate learning strategies (Schiefele & Schreyer, 1994).

Developmental Changes in Intrinsic Motivation.   Researchers in both Europe and the United States have found that intrinsic motivation in general and, for different subjects in particular, declines in elementary school years (Harter, 1981; Helmke, 1993). The transition from elementary to middle school also results in a decrease in intrinsic motivation and interest in different school subjects (see Eccles, Midgley, et al., 1993). Such changes are likely to lead to decreased school engagement. The possible origins of these declines have not been studied, but it is likely that they are similar to the causes of declines in expectations and ability-related self-confidence; namely, shifts in the nature of instruction across grade levels, cumulative experiences of failure, and increasing cognitive sophistication.

☐ Why Am I Doing This?

The last area of motivation related to issues of engagement is the new work in goal theory. This work focuses on why children think they are engaging in particular achievement-related activities and what they hope to accomplish through their engagement. Although this work has progressed independently, it has strong theoretical links to the work discussed above on the valuing of an activity and on intrinsic versus extrinsic motivation. We include it in this chapter because individual differences in goals are likely to affect both persistence and engagement, as well as the relations of performance outcomes and engagement to mental health and ability self-concepts. In addition, goal theories currently are very popular among researchers interested in both the determinants of performance and task choice (e.g., Butler, 1989a, 1989b), and the restructuring of schools to enhance motivation (e.g., Ames, 1992; Maehr & Midgley, 1991).

Goal Theories

Recently, researchers have become interested in children's achievement goals and their relation to achievement behavior (see Ames & Ames, 1989; Locke & Latham, 1990; Meece, 1991, 1994). Several different approaches have emerged. For instance, Bandura (1986) and Schunk (1990, 1991) have focused on goals' proximity, specificity, and level of challenge and have shown that specific, proximal, and somewhat challenging goals promote both self-efficacy and improved performance. Other researchers have defined and investigated broader goal orientations (e.g., Ames, 1992; Blumenfeld, 1992; Butler, 1993; Dweck & Leggett, 1988; Nicholls, 1984). For example, Nicholls and his colleagues (e.g., Nicholls, 1979; Nicholls et al., 1990) defined two major kinds of motivationally relevant goal patterns or orientations: ego-involved goals and task-involved goals. Individuals with ego-involved goals seek to maximize favorable evaluations of their competence and minimize negative evaluations of competence. Questions like, Will I look smart? and Can I outperform others? reflect ego-involved goals. In contrast, with task-involved goals, individuals focus on mastering tasks and increasing one's competence. Questions such as, How can I do this task? and What will I learn? reflect task-involved goals. Dweck and her colleagues provide a complementary analysis distinguishing between performance goals (like ego-involved goals), and learning goals (like task-involved goals) (e.g., Dweck & Elliott, 1983; and Dweck & Leggett, 1988). Similarly, Ames (1992) distinguished between the association of performance (like ego-involved) goals and mastery goals (like task-focused goals) with both performance and task choice. With ego-involved (or performance) goals, children try to outperform others, and are more likely to do tasks that they can do. Task-involved (or mastery-oriented) children choose challenging tasks and are more concerned with their own progress than with outperforming others.

Other researchers (e.g., Ford, 1992; Wentzel, 1991) have adopted a more complex perspective on goals and motivation, arguing that there are many different kinds of goals available to individuals in achievement settings. For example, Ford proposed a complex theory based on the assumption that humans are goal directed and self organized (e.g., Ford 1992; Ford & Nichols, 1987). He defined goals as desired end states people try to attain through the cognitive, affective, and biochemical regulation of their behavior. Furthermore, Ford considered goals to be only one part of motivation; in his model, motivation is the product of goals, emotions, and personal agency beliefs. Ford (1992; Ford & Nichols, 1987) outlined an extensive taxonomy of goals. Ford and Nichols distinguished most broadly between within-person goals, which concern desired within-person consequences, and person-environment goals, which concern the relationship between persons and their environment. Similar to Rokeach's (1979) human values and Eccles' attainment value (Eccles, 1983), the within-person goals include affective goals (e.g., outlined an extensive taxonomy of happiness, physical well-being), cognitive goals (e.g., exploration, intellectual creativity), and subjective organization goals (e.g., unity, transcendence). These goals include self-assertive goals such as self-determination and individuality; integrative social relationship goals such as belongingness and social responsibility; and task goals such as mastery, material gain, and safety. Finally, Ford (1992) derived a set of principles for optimizing motivation.

Development of Children's Goals.   To date, there has been surprisingly little empirical work on how children's goals develop. Nicholls (1979, 1984, 1990) suggested and documented that both task goals and ego goals are already developed by second grade (Nicholls et al., 1990). However, Nicholls (1989) also suggested that the ego goal orientation becomes more prominent for many children as they become older, in part, because of developmental changes in their conceptions of ability and, in part, because of systematic changes in school context.

Dweck and her colleagues (e.g., Dweck & Elliott, 1983; Dweck & Leggett, 1988) predicted that performance goals should become more prominent as children go through school for two reasons: (a) they develop a more entity view of intelligence as they become older, and (b) children holding an entity view of intelligence are more likely to adopt performance goals.

It also is likely that the relation of goals to performance changes with age due to the changing meaning of ability and effort. Butler's work is directly related to this hypothesis. In a series of studies looking at how competitive and noncompetitive conditions, and task- and ego-focused conditions, influence pre-elementary and elementary-school-age children's interests, motivation, and self-evaluations, she identified several developmental changes. First, competition decreases children's subsequent interest in a task only if the children also have a social-comparative sense of ability (Butler, 1989, 1990). Competition also increases older, but not younger, children's tendency to engage in social comparison (Butler, 1989a, 1989b). Second, although children of all ages engage in social comparison, younger children do it more for task mastery than for ego-related reasons; in contrast, older children do it to assess their relative abilities (Butler, 1989b). Butler concluded that "older children's concerns with evaluating relative ability may exact a considerable price in terms of their ability to use others as resources and improving task mastery" (Butler, 1989b, p. 1359). Third, whereas 5-, 7-, and 10-year-old children's self-evaluations are quite accurate under mastery conditions, under competitive conditions, 5- and 7-year-olds inflate their performance self-evaluations more than 10-year-olds (Butler, 1990). Apparently, the influence of situationally induced performance goals on children's self-evaluations depends on children's age and cognitive sophistication.

Finally, Butler and Ruzany (1993) found evidence that different patterns of socialization influence children's ability assessments and reasons for social comparison. In a study comparing kibbutz reared with city reared Israeli children, the kibbutz children adopted a normative ability concept earlier than urban children. However, only the urban children's reasons for engaging in social comparison were influenced by their concept of ability: Once they adopted a normative view they used social comparison to compare their abilities to those of other children. In contrast, the kibbutz children used social comparison primarily for mastery reasons, regardless of their conception of ability.

Developmental studies of multiple goals are truly needed. Neither Wentzel nor Ford, the major theorists in this area, have done such work. Thus, we know very little about how these kinds of multiple goals emerge during childhood and whether the relation of these different goals to performance varies across age and context.

Summary.   In this section, we have reviewed the evidence for changes in children's goals for doing schoolwork. Because interest in this area of motivation is fairly recent, much less empirical and theoretical work has been done on developmental changes; most of the work has focused instead on individual differences in goal orientation. But, the little available developmental work has revealed a pattern of change not unlike the patterns discussed above for expectancy-related beliefs and values. At the population level, there appears to be an increase in ego-focused goals and competitive motivation. Given what we know about individual differences in goal orientation, such a shift is likely to lead at least some children (particularly those doing poorly in school) to disengage from school as they get older.

In the next section, we focus more directly on work directly linking motivational constructs to healthy functioning. Much of this work has grown out of concern over particular motivational problems like test anxiety and learned helplessness. We discuss this work first. More recently, searchers have been studying the link between motivational constructs and mental functioning directly. We discuss this work second.

☐ The Development of Motivational Problems

Many children begin to experience motivational problems during the elementary school years. These problems include lack of confidence in one's abilities, anxiety, and the belief that one cannot control one's achievement outcomes. In this section, we focus on the motivational problems that have received the most research attention: test anxiety and learned helplessness.

Test Anxiety

Anxiety has long been an important topic in motivational research (see Weiner, 1992). Early research in this area was conducted by Sarason, Hill, and their colleagues using the Test Anxiety Scale for Children. In one of the first longitudinal studies, Hill and Sarason (1966) found that anxiety both increases across the elementary and middle school years and becomes more negatively related to subsequent grades and test scores. They also found that highly anxious children's achievement test scores were up to 2 years behind those of their low anxious peers, and that girls' anxiety scores were higher than boys'. These researchers also determined that test anxiety is a serious problem for many children: For example, Hill and Wigfield (1984) estimated that as many as 10 million children and adolescents in the United States experience significant evaluation anxiety.

Researchers (e.g., Dusek, 1980; Hill & Wigfield, 1984; Wigfield & Eccles, 1989) have postulated that high anxiety emerges when parents have overly high expectations and put too much pressure on their children; to date, few studies have tested this proposition. Anxiety continues to develop in school as children face more frequent evaluation, social comparison, and (for some) experiences of failure; to the extent that schools emphasize these characteristics, anxiety becomes a problem for more children as they get older (Hill & Wigfield, 1984).

The nature of anxiety also may change with age. Typically, researchers in this area distinguish between two components of anxiety: a worry component and an emotional-physical component. Wigfield and Eccles (1989) proposed that anxiety initially may be characterized more by emotionality but, as children develop cognitively, the worry aspect of anxiety should become increasingly salient. This proposal also remains to be tested, but we do know that worry is a major component of the thought processes of highly anxious fifth and sixth graders (Freedman-Doan, 1994).

Anxiety Intervention Programs.   Many programs to reduce anxiety have been developed (see Wigfield & Eccles, 1989). Earlier intervention programs emphasized the emotionality aspect of anxiety and focused on various relaxation and desensitization techniques. Although these programs did succeed in reducing anxiety, they did not always lead to improved performance, and the studies had serious methodological flaws. Anxiety intervention programs linked to the worry aspect of anxiety focus on changing the negative, self-deprecating thoughts of anxious individuals and replacing them with more positive, task-focused thoughts. These programs have been more successful both in lowering anxiety and improving performance.

An important issue that has not been adequately addressed is how programs should be tailored for children of different ages. This consideration is particularly important for elementary-school-age children (see Wigfield & Eccles, 1989). Further, because children's anxiety depends so much on the kinds of evaluations they experience in school, changes in school testing and other evaluation practices could help reduce anxiety.

Learned Helplessness

As defined by Dweck and Goetz (1978), "learned helplessness . . . exists when an individual perceives the termination of failure to be independent of his responses" (p. 157). Learned helplessness has been related to individuals' attributions for success and failure: Helpless individuals are more likely to attribute their failures to uncontrollable factors, such as lack of ability, and their successes to unstable factors (see Dweck

& Goetz, 1978). Dweck and her colleagues have documented several interesting differences between help-less and more mastery-oriented children's responses to failure: When confronted by difficulty (or failure), mastery-oriented children persist, stay focused on the task, and sometimes even use more sophisticated strategies. In contrast, helpless children's performance deteriorates, they ruminate about their difficul-ties, and often begin to attribute their failures to lack of ability. Further, helpless children adopt an entity view that their intelligence is fixed, whereas mastery-oriented children adopt an incremental view of intelligence.

Fincham and Cain (1986) provided a developmental analysis of helplessness. Citing Weisz's (1984) work, they noted the difficulties that young children have in distinguishing between contingent and noncontingent events; thus, young children may not be aware of which achievement outcomes they con-trol and which they do not. They also noted that, because young children do not understand the differ-ences between ability and effort as causes of performance, it is not likely that young children will show the differential attributional patterns linked to mastery orientation versus learned helplessness. They concluded that researchers need to look at how children's understanding of contingencies, estimations of their own competence, and attributions for their outcomes work together in determining children's evalu-ations of their achievement outcomes. This kind of theoretically integrative work on learned helplessness has not yet been undertaken.

Instead, there are a few studies of age differences in learned helpless behavior. For example, consistent with the suggestion of Fincham and Cain (1986), Rholes, Blackwell, Jordan, and Walters (1980) found that younger children did not show the same decrements in performance in response to failure as some older children do (see also Parsons & Ruble, 1972, 1977). However, Dweck and her colleagues' recent work (see Burhans & Dweck, 1995) showed that some young (5- and 6-year-old) children respond quite negatively to failure feedback, judging themselves to be bad people (see also Stipek et al., 1992). These rather troubling findings show that negative responses to failure can develop quite early. But, does this mean that some very young children already have an entity view of intelligence and are attributing their failures to lack of this entity? Burhans and Dweck did not think so. Instead, they proposed that young children's learned helplessness is based on their belief that their worth as a person is based on their performance.

But, what produces learned helplessness in children, even at these early ages? Dweck and Goetz (1978) proposed that it depends on the kinds of feedback children receive from parents and teachers about their achievement outcomes, in particular, whether children receive feedback that their failures are due to lack of ability. Recently, Hokoda and Fincham (1995) found that mothers of helpless third-grade children (in comparison to mothers of mastery-oriented children) gave fewer positive affective comments to their children, were more likely to respond to their children's lack of confidence in their ability by telling them to quit, were less responsive to their children's bids for help, and did not focus them on mastery goals. Dweck and Goetz argued further that girls may be more likely than boys to receive negative ability feed-back in elementary school classrooms (see Dweck, Davidson, Nelson, & Enna, 1978, for evidence sup-porting this view), and so are more likely to develop helplessness. Although some other researchers have not replicated Dweck et al.'s (1978) classroom findings regarding sex differences in feedback to children (e.g., Eccles et al., 1983), it is likely that children who receive feedback that their failures are due to lack of ability will be more likely to develop helplessness.

Alleviating Learned Helplessness. There are numerous studies designed to alleviate learned help-lessness by changing attributions for success and failure so that learned helpless children can learn to attribute failure to lack of effort rather than to lack of ability (see review by Forsterling, 1985). Various training techniques (including operant conditioning and providing specific attributional feedback) have been used successfully in changing children's failure and attributions from lack of ability to lack of effort, and improving their task persistence and performance (e.g., Dweck, 1975). Two problems with these approaches have been noted. First, what if the child is already trying very hard? Then the attribution retraining may be counterproductive. Second, telling children to "try harder," without providing specific strategies that are designed to improve their performance, is likely to backfire—children may put in mas-sive amounts of effort and still not succeed if they do not know how to apply that effort. Therefore, some researchers (e.g., Borkowski, Carr, Relliger, & Pressley, 1990) now advocate using strategy retraining, in combination with attribution retraining, so that the lower achieving, learned helpless, or both types of children are provided with specific ways to remedy their achievement problems. Borkowski and his colleagues, for example, have shown that a combined program of strategy instruction and attribution re-training is more effective than strategy instruction alone in increasing reading motivation and perfor-mance in underachieving students (e.g., Borkowski & Muthukrisna, 1995; Paris & Byrnes, 1989; Pressley & El-Dinary, 1963).

Self-Efficacy Training.   Self-efficacy training also has been used to alleviate learned helplessness. For example, Schunk and his colleagues have conducted several studies designed to improve elementary-school-age children's (often low-achieving children's) math, reading, and writing performance through skill training, enhancement of self-efficacy, attribution retraining, and training children how to set goals (see Schunk, 1994). Modeling often is an important aspect of the training. A number of findings have emerged from this work. First, the training increases both children's performance and their sense of self-efficacy. Second, attributing children's success to ability has a stronger impact on their self-efficacy than does either effort feedback or ability and effort feedback (e.g., Schunk, 1983). However, the effects of this kind of attributional feedback vary across different groups of children (see Schunk, 1994). Third, training children to set proximal, specific, and somewhat challenging goals enhances their self-efficacy and perfor-mance. Fourth, training that emphasizes process goals (analogous to task or learning goals) increases self-efficacy and skills in writing more than an emphasis on product (ego) goals; however, this is not true for reading (see Schunk, 1991, 1994). Finally, like the work of Borkowski and his colleagues, Schunk and his colleagues have found that combining strategy training, goal emphases, and feedback to show children how various strategies relate to their performance has a strong effect on subsequent self-efficacy and skill development.

Summary.   In summary, work on anxiety and learned helplessness shows that some children suffer from motivational problems that can debilitate their performance in achievement situations. Although most of the work in developmental and educational psychology has focused on these two problems, there likely are other important motivational problems. In particular, some children may set maladaptive achieve-ment goals, others may have difficulties regulating their achievement behaviors, and still others come to devalue achievement. More comprehensive work on these kinds of motivational problems and how they affect children's achievement is needed.

Researchers interested in the remediation of these motivational difficulties have turned increasingly to programs targeting both cognitive and motivational components. This work now needs to be extended to children of different ages to determine whether the strategy instruction and motivation enhancement techniques need to be modified for younger and older children. Further, work is needed on developing programs that integrate various approaches, particularly, those approaches associated with self-efficacy, goal setting, and self-regulation. More broadly, however, as valuable as these individually focused pro-grams are, they are likely to have little lasting benefit if home and school environments do not facilitate and support the changes. Therefore, some researchers have turned to changing school and classroom environments to facilitate motivation, rather than changing individual children.

Other theorists have focused more generally on the link between school experiences and emotional experiences. These theorists have been concerned with two issues: (a) the possible link between experi-ences in school and more general mental health, and (b) emergence of what appear to be less adaptive motivational strategies as a means to protect one's mental health. Some of this work was summarized in the introduction to this chapter. In the next section, we focus on the work by Covington (1992) and on the work by Roeser (Roeser et al., 1994; Roeser & Eccles, in press) and Eccles (Eccles, Lord, Roeser, & Barber, 1997).

Self-Worth Theory

Covington was concerned with children's need to maintain positive self-esteem across a variety of situa-tions. He was particularly concerned with how children would accomplish this goal when faced with repeated failure experiences in school. In his self-worth theory, Covington (1992) defined the motive for self-worth as the tendency to establish and maintain a positive self-image, or sense of self-worth. Because children spend so much time in classrooms and are evaluated so frequently there, Covington argued that they must protect their sense of academic competence in order to maintain their sense of self-worth. One way to accomplish this goal is by using those causal attribution patterns that enhance one's sense of academic competence and control: attributing success to both ability and effort, along with attributing failure to effort (Covington & Omelich, 1979; Eccles-Parsons, Meece, Adler, & Kaczala, 1982). Attributing failure to lack of ability is a particularly problematic attribution that students should try to avoid.

However, school evaluation, competition, and social comparison make it difficult for many children to maintain the belief that they are academically competent. Covington (1992) discussed the strategies many children develop to avoid appearing to lack ability. These include procrastination, making excuses, avoiding challenging tasks, and most importantly, not trying. Although trying is critical for success, if children try and fail, it is difficult to escape the conclusion that they lack ability. Therefore, if failure seems likely, some children will not try, precisely because trying and failing threatens their ability self-concepts. Covington called such strategies "failure avoiding strategies." Further, Covington discussed how even some high achieving students can be failure avoidant. Rather than responding to a challenging task with greater effort, these students may try to avoid the task in order to maintain both their own sense of competence and others' conclusions regarding their competence. Covington (1992) suggested that reducing the frequency and salience of competitive, social comparative, and evaluative practices, and focusing instead on effort, mastery, and improvement, would allow more children to maintain their self-worth without having to resort to the failure-avoiding strategies just described. These suggestions have been incorporated into many other motivation theorists' recommendations for changing schools to enhance motivation (e.g., Ames, 1992; Maehr & Midgley, 1991).

Academic Self-Perceptions and Mental Health

We also have begun to assess the link between academic self-perceptions and mental health with our data from the Michigan CAB Study. Earlier (see Tables 14.1 through 14.3), we summarized the patterns of change across middle childhood in children's academic risk status. We reported that a substantial number of children identified as at risk in the first grade are doing fine in terms of their academic self-concepts and their academic performance by the time they reach middle school. Now, we discuss in more detail both who these children might be and the link between academic outcomes and mental health. The first issue we will look at is the comorbidity of academic risks with mental health risks. The results reported in Tables 14.1 and 14.2 document this association. Children identified as at risk academically in both early elementary school and early adolescence also had more mental health problems than their not-at-risk peers.

But, more importantly, are variations in mental health related to the trajectories of change in risk status? Yes! These results are summarized in Figure 14.6. The incliners had significantly higher self-esteem than the decliners at time 2, even though they were performing more poorly in terms of their grades (see Figure 14.5) at that time. Furthermore, when they were adolescents (at time 4), they still had significantly higher self-esteem; in addition, they were more satisfied with their lives and reported higher levels of ego resilience and less anger than the decliner group.

We have looked at the issue of co-occurance in one other way (Roeser & Eccles, in press). Using only the middle cohort of children in the CAB Study, we clustered the children based on two indicators of academic motivation (ability self-concept and academic valuing) and one indicator of mental health (a composite of scores on depressive affect, self-esteem, and anger scales) when they were in Grade 8. Four distinct clusters of approximately equal size emerged: a well-functioning group (high on all three indicators), a poor motivation group (low on the motivation indicators but high on mental health), a poor mental health group (low on mental health but high on the motivation indicators), and a multiple risk group (low on all three indicators). The results indicate that these two sets of indicators of social adjustment sometimes co-occur in the same individual and sometimes do not. We then followed these four groups back to Grades 2 and 3 and compared their academic competence beliefs and grade point average. Several interesting patterns emerged. As one might expect, the well-functioning group scored the highest on both of these indicators. In contrast, there were no differences in academic self-competence among the other three groups at Grade 2. However, by Grade 3, the multiple risk group had the lowest self-competence scores and remained the lowest from that point on. The multiple risk group also had a lower grade point average than the other three groups in Grades 1 through 3 and 8, and they were the only group to show a decline in academic marks from Grade 4 to Grade 8. The other groups showed an increase in marks over this period.

Clearly, these four groups of children had different trajectories of change in both their academic motivation and their mental health over the middle childhood years. We present these findings because they demonstrate the importance of taking a person-centered orientation to studying developmental trajectories. These patterns of individual differences would have gone unnoticed if we had relied only on population-centered and variable-centered analyses. Our next steps will be to identify the psychological, family, school, and peer group characteristics that distinguish among these four groups of children. Recent studies by Collins and his colleagues (in press) and by Keating and his colleagues (Keating, 1997; Miller, Keating, Marshment, & MacLean, 1997) have suggested two very important influences: the child's ability to regulate his or her own behavior to the demands of the situation and the quality of family support for effective problem solving during the preschool years.

☐ Conclusion

We had two goals in this chapter: (a) to describe the developmental pathways associated with academic motivation and school engagement during middle childhood, and (b) to explore the link between academic adjustment and mental health during this same developmental period.

With regard to our second goal, the picture varies somewhat depending on whether one takes a population-centered approach, a variable-centered approach, or both, or an individual difference or person-centered approach. At the population level, there is clearly a link between psychological functioning in the domain of school and general mental health. At the individual differences level, there is a strong relation between these two domains of functioning in some children and no relation (or only a very weak relation) in other children. Additional work is needed before we can understand these individual variations.

The findings regarding our first goal also yield somewhat different conclusions depending on whether one adopts a variable-centered versus a person-centered approach. Evidence for changes at the population level points fairly consistently to declines in children's academic motivation and school attachment-engagement during the elementary school years. On average, children begin elementary school quite confident of their own abilities and quite enthusiastic about school; and, on average, both of these sets of beliefs decline over the elementary school years, particularly between Grades 2 and 4. Both psychological and situational causes for these patterns were discussed.

A different picture emerges when one conducts person-centered analyses. There are clear and consistent patterns of individual differences in these trajectories. Although it is the case that the vast majority of children do start elementary school with very high estimates of their own abilities, not all of these children evidence declines over the elementary school years, and the rate of decline varies in systematic ways across children with different psychological resources (assessed primarily in terms of self-esteem in the studies reported in this chapter).

The Roeser, Eccles, Yates, Lord, Harold, Wigfield, and Blumenfeld (1995) study identified two pathways to academic and social-emotional functioning in early adolescence: the straight path of chronic academic difficulties and the less common path of declining academic performance and feelings of competence over time. Although these pathways at least suggest the possibility of different underlying mechanisms, one common characteristic of both of these groups of children is clear: Somewhere between the later elementary years and the transition to middle school, these youth experience a serious decline in their academic motivation. It could be that children who are vulnerable in terms of academic motivation and achievement, either due to long-term problems or some other factor during childhood, are most susceptible to the stresses involved with biological-psychological-social transitions during early adolescence (e.g., Eccles & Midgley, 1989; Simmons & Blyth, 1987). Although speculative, these data certainly suggest a disruption between the late elementary and middle school years in the two groups of children who ended up academically at risk during early adolescence.

The "decliner" group certainly seemed to be a group of children who were capable, but had difficulties that went largely unnoticed in their early school years when they still appeared to be engaged in school. It could be that these children manifested their distress in an internalizing way that was not identified by their early teachers (e.g., Loeber, Green, & Lahey, 1990; Lord et al., 1994), or that the problems that they experienced later during adolescence resulted from events occurring during the later elementary school years. Whatever the case, it is clear that these children, despite their ability to do well in school, end up very disengaged from academics by the seventh or eighth grade. So much so, in fact, that they—more than any other group of children—already were entertaining the notion that they might drop out of school before graduating.

In summary, then, there appear to be two subgroups of children who are especially vulnerable to these declines: These children have lower self-esteem, less well-developed self-control and self-organizational strategies, and more problematic behavioral patterns when they enter elementary school. Emerging evidence also has suggested that they may have less supportive relationships at home and at school (Carlson et al., in press). The other group begins school looking fine and then begins to disengage as the children approach and go through adolescence. We are not sure why this downward shift occurs for these children in particular.

Roeser, Eccles, et al. (1995) also documented two pathways toward positive academic and social-emotional adjustment during early adolescence, again a straight and a deviating one. By definition, the majority of children in this study evidenced positive academic and social emotional adjustment over time. This is as one might expect. However, we also identified a group of "academically resilient" children who, despite early difficulties, went on to achieve at a fairly high level during early adolescence. What is most interesting about these children is that, despite their lower academic marks, less favorable teacher beliefs concerning their abilities, and slightly lower intelligence scores early in elementary school, they had a positive profile of academic competence, value, and self-esteem beliefs all the way from childhood to early adolescence. That is, the optimism these children felt seemed to predict their later success in school and positive adjustment. Investigating the social and personal resources and the environmental experiences that have distinguished these resilient youth represents important future research direction.

The findings presented in this chapter also raise several interesting issues concerned with how children may compensate for difficulties they experience in the academic domain. This question is important given the fact that the academic realm is a central sphere of experience and "work" for the children and adolescents, and competence and achievement in this sphere must be critically relevant to a their self-esteem (e.g., Eccles, 1983; Erikson, 1959; Harter, 1985). What happens when youth cannot claim that they feel academically competent? On the one hand, the findings of Roeser and his colleagues (Roeser & Eccles, et al., 1995; Roeser & Eccles, in press) have suggested that this is likely to lead to diminished self-esteem and social-emotional experience for many children. On the other hand, Roeser et al. (1995) also provided evidence of at least one mechanism of compensation: Youth who feel less academically competent and receive lower marks also come to devalue academics the most. Beginning with James, several theorists of the self have noted that one way to maintain self-esteem in the face of relative incompetence is to devalue that domain (Eccles, 1983; Harter, 1985; Wigfield & Eccles, 1992). This may be one explanation for what occurred with the children in the "stable difficulties" and "decliner" groups. That is, those youth who experienced more and more difficulties in school lowered their perceptions of the importance, usefulness, and interest of their core academic subjects during seventh and eighth grade. This is particularly distressing given that "not liking school" is a primary reason for dropping out of school.

Another mechanism of compensation children can use is to change their valuing of, and engagement in, achievement-related activities in other relevant life domains. Although there are several "culturally mandated" dimensions of self that are likely central to esteem, including academics (e.g. Stein, Markus, & Roeser, 1995), some children may be able to compensate for difficulties in one area by achievement in another. For instance, in her expectancy-value formulation of achievement motivation, Eccles (1983) suggested that competence and valuing of any number of achievement domains, including the performing and fine arts, sports, and the social sphere, can serve as relevant sources of esteem. Furthermore, in this model, self-perceptions of relative incompetence in one area are assumed to relate to children's feelings of competence and value in some other domain: Those children with very low academic competence beliefs may develop other strengths and competencies to compensate for their relative lack of success at school. If successful, this strategy can provide the children with another ecological niche in which to develop a sense of efficacy. Unfortunately, given that children must attend school until they are age 16, this strategy also is likely to lead them to feel quite disaffected from the setting in which they must spend a great deal of time.

☐ References

Achenbach, T. M., Howell, C. T., Quay, H. C., & Conners, C. K. (1991). National survey of problems and competencies among four to sixteen year olds. *Monographs of the Society of Research in Child Development, 56* (3).

Alexander, K. L., Dauber, S. L., & Entwisle, D. R. (1993). First-grade classroom behavior: Its short-and long-term consequences for school performance. *Child Development, 64*, 801–803.

Alexander, K. L., & Entwisle, D. R. (1988). Achievement in the first two years of school: Patterns and processes. *Monographs of the Society for Research in Child Development, 53* (2, Serial No. 218).

Alexander, P. A., Entwisle, D. R., & Horsey, C. S. (1997). From first grade forward: Early foundations of high school dropout. *Sociology of Education, 70*, 87–107.

Alexander, P. A., Kulikowich, J. M., & Jetton, T. L. (1994). The role of subject-matter knowledge and interest in the processing of linear and nonlinear texts. *Review of Educational Research, 64*, 201–252.

Amabile, T. M., Hill, K. G., Hennessey, B. A., & Tighe, E. M. (1994). The Work Preference Inventory: Assessing intrinsic and extrinsic motivational orientations. *Journal of Personality and Social Psychology, 66*, 950–967.

Ames, C. (1992). Classrooms: Goals, structures, and student motivation. *Journal of Educational Psychology, 84*, 261–271.

Ames, C, & Ames, R. (Eds.). (1989). *Research on motivation in education: Vol. 3. Goals and cognitions.* San Diego, CA: Academic Press.

Arbreton, A. J., & Eccles, J. S. (1994). *Mother's perceptions of their children during the transition from kindergarten to formal schooling: The effect of teacher evaluations on parents' expectations for their elementary school children.* Paper presented at American Educational Association Conference, New Orleans, LA.

Asher, S. R., Hymel, S., & Renshaw, P. D. (1984). Loneliness in children. *Child Development, 55*, 1456–1464.

Bandura, A. (1977). Self-efficacy: Toward a unifying theory of behavioral change. *Psychological Review, 84*, 191–215.

Bandura, A. (1986). *Social foundations of thought and action: A social cognitive theory.* Englewood Cliffs, NJ: Prentice-Hall.

Bandura, A. (1997). *Self-efficacy: The exercise of control.* New York: W. H. Freeman.

Battle, E, (1966). Motivational determinants of academic competence. *Journal of Personality and Social Psychology, 4*, 534–642.

Baumert, J. (1995, April). *Gender, science interest, teaching strategies and socially shared beliefs about gender roles in 7th graders—A multi-level analysis.* Paper presented at the annual meeting of the American Educational Research Association, San Francisco, CA.

Benware, C. A., & Deci, E. L. (1984). Quality of learning with an active versus passive motivational set. *American Educational Research Journal, 21*, 755–765.

Blumenfeld, P. C. (1992). Classroom learning and motivation: Clarifying and expanding goal theory. *Journal of Educational Psychology, 84*, 272–281.

Borkowski, J. G., Carr, M., Relliger, E., & Pressley, M. (1990). Self-regulated cognition: Interdependence of metacognition, attributions, and self-esteem. In B. Jones & L. Idol (Eds.), *Dimensions of thinking and cognitive instruction* (Vol. 1). Hillsdale, NJ: Erlbaum.

Borkowski, J. G., & Muthukrisna, N. (1995). Learning environments and skill generalization: How contexts faculty regulatory processes and efficacy beliefs. In F. Weinert & W. Schneider (Eds.), *Recent perspectives on memory development.* Hillsdale, NJ: Erlbaum.

Brophy, J. E., & Good, J. L. (1974). *Teacher-student relationships.* New York: Holt, Rinehart and Winston.

Burhans, K. K., & Dweck, C. S. (1995). Helplessness in early childhood: The role of contingent worth. *Child Development, 66*. 1719–1738.

Butler, R. (1989a). Interest in the task and interest in peers' work: A developmental study. *Child Development, 60*, 562–570.

Butler, R. (1989b). Mastery versus ability appraisal: A developmental study of children's observations of peers' work. *Child Development, 60*, 1350–1361.

Butler, R. (1990). The effects of mastery and competitive conditions on self-assessment at different ages. *Child Development, 61*, 201–210.

Butler, R. (1993). Effects of task- and ego-achievement goals on information seeking during task engagement. *Journal of Personality and Social Psychology, 65*, 18–31.

Butler, R., & Ruzany, N. (1993). Age and socialization effects on the development of social comparison motives and normative ability assessments in kibbutz and urban children. *Child Development, 64*, 532–543.

Cairns, R. B., Cairns, B. D., & Neckerman, H. J. (1989). Early school dropout: Configurations and determinants. *Child Development, 60*, 1437–1452.

Carlson, E. A., Sroufe, L. A., Collins, W. A., Jimerson, S., Weinfield, N., Henninghausen, K., Egeland, B., Hyson, D. M., Anderson, F., & Meyer, S. E. (in press). Early environmental support and elementary school adjustment as predictors of school adjustment in middle childhood. *Journal of Adolescent Research.*

Cole, D. A. (1991). Preliminary support for a competency-based model of depression in children. *Journal of Abnormal Psychology, 100*, 181–190.

Connell, J. P. (1985). A new multidimensional measure of children's perception of control. *Child Development, 56,* 1018–1041.

Connell, J. P., Spencer, M. B., & Aber, J. L. (1994). Educational risk and resilience in African American youth: Context, self, and action outcomes in school. *Child Development, 65,* 493–506.

Connell, J. P., & Wellborn, J. G. (1991). Competence, autonomy, and relatedness: A motivational analysis of self-system processes. In R. Gunnar & L. A. Sroufe (Eds.), *Minnesota Symposia on Child Psychology* (Vol. 23, pp. 43–77). Hillsdale, NJ: Erlbaum.

Covington, M. (1992). *Making the grade: A self-worth perspective on motivation and school reform.* New York: Cambridge University Press.

Covington, M. V., & Omelich, C. L. (1979). Effort: The double-edged sword in school achievement. *Journal of Educational Psychology, 71,* 169–182.

Csikszentmihalyi, M. (1988). The flow experience and its significance for human psychology. In M. Csikszentmihalyi & I. S. Csikszentmihalyi (Eds.), *Optimal experience* (pp. 15–35). Cambridge, England: Cambridge University Press.

deCharms, R. (1968). *Personal causation: The internal affective determinants of behavior.* New York: Academic Press.

Deci, E. L. (1975). *Intrinsic motivation.* New York: Plenum Press.

Deci, E. L., & Ryan, R. M. (1985). *Intrinsic motivation and self-determination in human behavior.* New York: Plenum Press.

Dryfoos, J. G. (1990). *Adolescents at risk: Prevalence and prevention.* New York: Oxford University Press.

Dryfoos, J. G. (1994). *Full service schools: A revolution in health and social services for children, youth, and families.* San Francisco: Jossey-Bass.

Dusek, J. B. (1980). The development of test anxiety in children. In I. G. Sarason (Ed.), *Test anxiety: Theory, research, and applications.* Hillsdale, NJ: Erlbaum.

Dweck, C. S. (1975). The role of expectations and attributions in the alleviation of learned helplessness. *Journal of Personality and Social Psychology, 31,* 674–685.

Dweck, C. S., Davidson, W., Nelson, S., & Enna, B. (1978). Sex differences in learned helplessness: II. The contingencies of evaluative feedback in the classroom, and III. An experimental analysis. *Developmental Psychology, 14,* 268–276.

Dweck, C. S., & Elliott, E. S. (1983). Achievement motivation. In P. H. Mussen (Ed.), *Handbook of child psychology* (Vol. 4, pp. 643–691). New York: Wiley.

Dweck, C. S., & Goetz, T. E. (1978). Attributions and learned helplessness. In J. H. Harvey, W. Ickes, & R. F. Kidd (Eds.), *New directions in attribution research* (Vol. 2). Hillsdale, NJ: Erlbaum.

Dweck, C. S., & Leggett, E. (1988). A social-cognitive approach to motivation and personality. *Psychological Review, 95,* 256–273.

Eccles, J. S. (1983). Expectancies, values and academic behaviors. In J. T. Spence (Ed.), *The development of achievement motivation* (pp. 283–331). Greenwich, CT: JAI Press.

Eccles, J. S. (1984). Sex differences in achievement patterns. In T. Sonderegger (Ed.), *Nebraska Symposium on Motivation* (Vol. 32, pp. 97–132). Lincoln: University of Nebraska Press.

Eccles, J. S. (1987). Gender roles and women's achievement-related decisions. *Psychology of Women Quarterly, 11,* 135–172.

Eccles, J. S., Adler, T. F., & Meece, J. L. (1984). Sex differences in achievement: A test of alternate theories. *Journal of Personality and Social Psychology, 46,* 26–43.

Eccles, J. S., Barber, B., & Jozefowicz, D. (in press). Linking gender to educational, occupational, and recreational choices: Applying the Eccles et al. model of achievement-related choices. In W. B. Swann, J. H. Langlois, Jr., & L. A. Gilbert (Eds.), *The many faces of gender: The multidimensional model of Janet Taylor Spence.* Washington, DC: American Psychiatric Association.

Eccles, J. S., Barber, B., Updegraff, K., & O'Brien, K. (1995). *An expectancy-value model of achievement choices: The role of ability self-concepts, perceived task utility and interest in predicting activity choice and course enrollment.* Paper presented at the AERA, San Francisco, CA.

Eccles, J. S., & Bryan, J. (1994). Adolescence: Critical crossroad in the path of gender-role development. In M. R. Stevenson (Ed.), *Gender roles through the life span: A multidisciplinary perspective.* Muncie, IN: Ball State University Press.

Eccles, J. S., & Harold, R. D. (1991). Gender differences in sport involvement: Applying the Eccles' expectancy-value model. *Journal of Applied Sport Psychology, 3,* 7–35.

Eccles, J. S., Lord, S. & Roeser, R. W., Barber, B. L., & Josefowicz-Hernandez, J. (1997). School transitions and health risks. In J. Schulenberg, J. Maggs, & K. Hurrelmann (Eds.), *Health risks and developmental transitions during adolescence.* New York: Cambridge University Press.

Eccles, J. S., & Midgley, C. (1989). Stage-environment fit: Developmentally appropriate classrooms for young adolescents. In C. Ames & R. Ames (Eds.), *Research on motivation in education: Vol. 3. Goals and cognitions* (pp. 13–44). New York: Academic Press.

Eccles, J. S., Midgeley, C., & Adler, T. (1984). Grade related changes in the school environment: Effects on achievement motivation. In J. Nicholls (Ed.), *Advances in motivation and achievement* (Vol. 3, pp. 283–331). Greenwich, CT: JAI Press.

Eccles, J. S., Midgley, C., Wigfield, A., Buchanan, C. M., Reuman, D., Flanagan, C., & Mac Iver, D. (1993). Development during adolescence: The impact of stage environment fit on adolescents' experiences in schools and families. *American Psychologist, 48*, 90–101.

Eccles, J. S., & Wigfield, A. (1995). In the mind of the actor: The structure of adolescents' achievement task values and expectancy-related beliefs. *Personality and Social Psychology Bulletin, 21*, 215–225.

Eccles, J. S., Wigfield, A., & Blumenfeld, P. C. (1984). *Psychological predictors of competence development* (Grant No. 2 R01 HD17553-01). Bethesda, MD: National Institute of Child Health and Human Development.

Eccles, J. S., Wigfield, A., Flanagan, C., Miller, C., Reuman, D., & Yee, D. (1989). Self-concepts, domain values, and self-esteem: Relations and changes at early adolescence. *Journal of Personality 57*, 283–310.

Eccles, J. S., Wigfield, A., Harold, R., & Blumenfeld, P. (1993). Age and gender differences in children's self- and task perceptions during elementary school. *Child Development, 64*, 830–847.

Eccles, J. S., Wigfield, A., & Schiefele, U. (1997). Motivation to succeed. In N. Eisenberg, (Ed.), *Handbook of child psychiatry*. New York.

Eccles-Parsons, J., Meece, J. L., Adler, T. F., & Kaczala, C. M. (1982). Sex differences in attributions and learned helplessness. *Sex Roles, 8*, 421–432.

Eder, F. (1992). Schulklima und entwicklung allgemeiner interessen. In A. Krapp & M. Prenzel (Eds.), *Interesse, lernen, leistung* (pp. 165–194). Münster, Germany: Aschendorff.

Erikson, E. H. (1959). Identity and the life cycle. *Psychological Issues, 1*, 18–164.

Erikson, E. H. (1968). *Identity, youth and crisis*. New York: W. W. Norton.

Feather, N. T. (1982). *Expectations and actions: Expectancy-value models in psychology*. Hillsdale, NJ: Erlbaum,

Feather, N. T. (1992). Values, valences, expectations, and actions. *Journal of Social Issues, 48*, 109–124.

Fincham, F. D., & Cain, K. M. (1986). Learned helplessness in humans: A developmental analysis. *Developmental Review, 6*, 301–333.

Ford, M. E. (1992). *Human motivation: Goals, emotions, and personal agency beliefs*. Newbury Park, CA: Sage.

Ford, M. E., & Nichols, C. W. (1987). A taxonomy of human goals and some possible applications. In M. E. Ford & D. H. Ford (Eds.), *Humans as self-constructing living systems: Putting the framework to work* (pp. 289–311). Hillsdale, NJ: Erlbaum.

Fosterling, F. (1985). Attributional retraining: A review. *Psychological Bulletin, 98*, 495–512.

Freedman-Doan, C. R. (1994). *Factors influencing the development of general, academic, and social anxiety in normal preadolescent children*. Unpublished doctoral dissertation. Detroit, MI: Wayne State University.

Gottfried, A. E, (1990). Academic intrinsic motivation in young elementary school children. *Journal of Educational Psychology, 82*, 525–538.

Gurin, P., & Epps, E. (1974). *Black consciousness, identity, and achievement*. New York: Wiley.

Harter, S. (1981). A new self-report scale of intrinsic versus extrinsic orientation in the classroom: Motivational and informational components. *Developmental Psychology, 17*, 300–312.

Harter, S. (1985), Competence as a dimension of self-evaluation: Toward a comprehensive model of self-worth. In R. L. Leahy (Ed.), *The development of the self*. New York: Academic Press.

Harter, S. (1990). Causes, correlates and the functional role of global self-worth: A lifespan perspective. In J. Kolligian & R. Sternberg (Eds.), *Perceptions of competence and incompetence across the life-span* (pp. 67–98). New Haven, CT: Yale University Press.

Harter, S. (1997). The development of self-representation. In W. Damon & N. Eisenberg (Eds.), *Handbook of child psychology: Vol. 3. Social, emotional and personality development* (5th ed., pp. 553–618). New York: Wiley.

Hebb, D. O. (1982). *Conceptual nervous system*. Oxford, England: Pergamon Press.

Hedelin, L, & Sjîberg, L. (1989). The development of interests in the Swedish comprehensive school. *European Journal of Psychology of Education, 4*, 17–35.

Helmke, A. (1993). Die entwicklung der lernfreude vom kindergarten bis zur 5. Klassenstufe. *Zeitschrift fär Pñdagogische Psychologie, 7*, 77–86.

Heyman, G. D., Dweck, C. S., & Cain, K. M. (1993). Young children's vulnerability to self-blame and helplessness: Relationships to beliefs about goodness. *Child Development, 63*, 401-415.

Hidi, S. (1990). Interest and its contribution as a mental resource for learning. *Review of Educational Research, 60*, 549-571.

Higgins, E. T., & Parsons, J. E. (1983). Social cognition and the social life of the child: Stages as subcultures. In E. T. Higgins, D. N. Ruble, W. W. Hartup (Eds.), *Social cognition and social development* (pp. 15–62). Cambridge, England: Cambridge University Press.

Hill, K. T., & Sarason, S. B. (1966). The relation of test anxiety and defensiveness to test and school performance over the elementary school years: A further longitudinal study. *Monographs of the Society for Research in Child Development, 31* (2, Serial No. 104).

Hill, K. T., & Wigfield, A. (1984). Test anxiety: A major educational problem and what to do about it. *Elementary School Journal, 85*, 105–126.

Hinshaw, S. P. (1992). Externalizing behavior problems and academic underachievement in childhood and adolescence: Causal relationships and underlying mechanisms. *Psychological Bulletin, 111,* 127–155.

Hokoda, A., & Fincham, F. D. (1995). Origins of children's helpless and mastery achievement patterns in the family. *Journal of Educational Psychology, 87,* 375–385.

Keating, D. P. (1997). Habits of mind for a learning society: Educating for human development. In D. R. Olson & N. Torrance (Eds.), *Handbook of education and human development: New models of learning, teaching, and schooling* (pp. 461–481). Oxford: Blackwell.

Kohlberg, L. (1966). A cognitive-development analysis of children's sex-role concepts and attitudes. In E. E. Maccoby (Ed.), The development of sex differences, (pp. 82–172). Stanford, CA: Stanford University Press.

Lehrke, M. (1992). Einige lehrervariablen und ihre beziehungen zum interesse der schuler. In A Krapp & M. Prenzel (eds.), *Interesse, lernen, leistung* (pp. 123–136). Münster, Germany: Aschendorff.

Lehrke, M., Hoffmann, L., & Gardner, P. L. (Eds.). (1985). *Interests in science and technology education.* Kiel, Germany: Institut fur die Pädagogik der Naturwissenschaften.

Lepper, M. R. (1988). Motivational considerations in the study of instruction. *Cognition and Instruction, 5,* 289–309.

Locke, E. A., & Latham, G. P. (1990). *A theory of goal setting and task performance.* Englewood Cliffs, NJ: Prentice-Hall.

Loeber, R., Green, S. M., & Lahey, B. B. (1990). Mental health professional's perceptions of the utility of children, mothers, and teachers as informants on childhood psychopathology. *Journal of Clinical Child Psychology, 19,* 136–143.

Lord, S. E., Eccles, J. S., & McCarthy, K. (1994). Surviving the junior high school transition. Family processes and self-perceptions as protective and risk factors. *Journal of Early Adolescence, 14,* 162–199.

Mac Iver, D. J., Stipek, D. J., & Daniels, D. H. (1991). Explaining within-semester changes in student effort in junior high school courses. *Journal of Educational Psychology, 83,* 201–211.

Maehr, M. L. & Midgley, C. (1991). Enhancing student motivation: A school-wide approach. *Educational Psychologist, 26,* 399–427.

Markus, H. J., & Nurius, P. S. (1984). Self-understanding and self-regulation in middle childhood. *The status of basic research on school-aged children.* Washington, DC: National Academy of Sciences.

Marsh, H. W. (1989). Age and sex effects in multiple dimensions of self-concept: Preadolescence to early adulthood. *Journal of Educational Psychology, 81,* 417–430.

Matsumoto, D., & Sanders, M. (1988). Emotional experiences during engagement intrinsically and extrinsically motivated tasks. *Motivation and Emotion, 12,* 353–369.

Meece, J. L. (1991). The classroom context and students' motivational goals. In M. Maehr & P. Pintrich (Eds.), *Advances in motivation and achievement* (Vol. 7, pp. 261–286). Greenwich, CT: JAI Press.

Meece, J. L. (1994). The role of motivation in self-regulated learning. In D. H. Schunk & B. J. Zimmerman (Eds.), *Self-regulation of learning and performance* (pp. 25–44). Hillsdale, NJ: Erlbaum.

Meece, J. L., Wigfield, A ., & Eccles, J. S. (1990). Predictors of math and its consequences for young adolescents' course enrollment. *Journal of Educational Psychology, 82,* 60–70.

Miller, F. K., Keating, D. P., Marshment, R. P., & MacLean, D. J. (1997, April), *Continuity in habits of mind: Emotion, attention, and social self-regulation from infancy to early childhood.* Poster session presented at the biennial meeting of the Society for Research in Child Development, Washington, DC.

Millstein, S. G., Petersen, A. C., & Nightingale, E. O. (1994). *Promoting the health of adolescents: New directions for the twenty-first century.* New York: Oxford University Press.

Nicholls, J. G. (1979). Development of perception of own attainment and causal attributions for success and failure in reading. *Journal of Educational Psychology, 71,* 94–99.

Nicholls, J. G. (1984). Achievement motivation: Conceptions of ability, subjective experience, task choice, and performance. *Psychological Review, 91,* 328–346.

Nicholls, J. G. (1989). *The competitive ethos and democratic education.* Cambridge, MA: Harvard University Press.

Nicholls, J. G. (1990). What is ability and why are we mindful of it? A developmental perspective. In R. Sternberg & J. Kolligan (Eds.), *Competence considered.* New Haven, CT: Yale University Press.

Nicholls, J. G., Cobb, P., Yackel, E., Wood, T., & Wheatley, G. (1990). Students' theories of mathematics and their mathematical knowledge: Multiple dimensions of assessment. In G. Kulm (Ed.), *Assessing higher order thinking in mathematics* (pp. 137–154). Washington, DC: American Association for the Advancement of Science.

Offord, D. R. & Fleming, J. E. (1995). Child and adolescent psychiatry and public health. In M. Lewis (Ed.), *Child and adolescent psychiatry: A comprehensive textbook* (2nd ed.). Baltimore: Williams & Wilkins.

Pallas, A. M., Entwisle, D. R., Alexander, K. L., & Stluka, M. F. (1994). Ability-group effects: Instructional, social, or institutional? *Sociology of Education, 67,* 27–46.

Paris, S. G., & Byrnes, J. P. (1989). The constructivist approach to self-regulation and learning in the classroom. In B. J. Zimmerman & D. H. Schunk (Eds.), *Self-regulated learning and academic achievement: Theory, research, and practice.* New York: Springer-Verlag.

Parkhurst, J. T., & Asher, S. R. (1992). Peer rejection in middle school: Subgroup differences in behavior, loneliness, and interpersonal concerns. *Developmental Psychology, 28,* 231–241.

Parsons, J., & Ruble, D. (1972). Attributional processes related to the development of achievement-related affect and expectancy. *APA Proceedings, 80*, 105–106.

Parsons, J., & Ruble, D. N. (1977). The development of achievement-related expectancies. *Child Development, 48*, 1075–1079.

Piaget, J. (1948). *Psychologie der intelligenz.* Zurich, Switzerland: Rascher.

Pressley, M., & El-Dinary, P. B. (Eds.). (1993). Strategies instruction [Special issue]. *Elementary School Journal, 94* (2).

Rae-Grant, N., Thomas, H., Offord, D. P., & Boyle, M. H. (1989). Risk, protective factors, and the prevalence of behavioral and emotional disorders in children and adolescents. *Journal of American Academy of Child and Adolescent Psychiatry, 28*, 262–268.

Renninger, K. A. (1990). Children's play interests, representation, and activity, In R. Fivush & J. Hudson (Eds.), *Knowing and remembering in young children* (pp. 127–165). Boston: Cambridge University Press.

Renninger, K. A., Hidi, S. & Krapp, A. (Eds.). (1992). *The role of interest in learning and development.* Hillsdale, NJ: Erlbaum.

Rholes, W. S., Blackwell, J., Jordan, C., & Walters, C. (1980). A developmental study of learned helplessness. *Developmental Psychology, 16*, 616–624.

Roderick, M. (1994). Grade retention and school dropout: Investigating the association. *American Educational Research Journal, 31*, 729–759.

Roe, A., & Siegelman, M. (1964). *The origin of interests.* Washington, DC: American Personnel and Guidance Association.

Roeser, R. W., & Eccles, J. S. (1997). *Academic functions and mental health in adolescence; Patterns, progressions, and routes from childhood.* Presented Sundance, Utah.

Roeser, R., Eccles, J. S., Yates, B., Lord, S. E., Harold, R., Wigfield, A., & Blumenfeld, P. (1995). *School adjustment and psychological well-being from childhood to early adolescence.* New York: American Psychological Association.

Roeser, R. W., Lord, S. E., & Eccles, J. S. (1994, February). *A portrait of academic alienation in early adolescence: Motivation, mental health and family indices.* Paper presented at the meeting of the Society for Research on Adolescence, San Diego, CA.

Roeser, R. W., Midgley, C., & Urban, T. (1995). *The middle school psychological alienation in early adolescents' self appraisals and academic engagement: The mediating role of goals and belonging.* Manuscript submitted for publication.

Rokeach, M. (1979). From individual to institutional values with special reference to the values of science. In M. Rokeach (Ed.), *Understanding human values* (pp. 47–70). New York: Free Press.

Rosenberg, M., Schooler, C., & Schoenbach, C. (1989). Self-esteem and adolescent problems: Modeling reciprocal effects. *American Sociological Review, 54*, 1004–1018.

Ruble, D. N. (1983). The development of social comparison processes and their role in achievement-related self-socialization. In E. T. Higgins, D. N. Ruble, & W. W. Hartup (Eds.), *Social cognition and social development: A sociocultural perspective* (pp. 134–157). New York: Cambridge University Press.

Ruble, D. N., & Martin, C. L. (1997). Gender development. In W. Damon & N. Eisenberg (Eds.), *Handbook of child psychology; Vol. 3. Social, emotional, and personality development* (5th ed., pp. 533–618). New York: Wiley.

Rutter, M. (1988). *Studies of psychosocial risk: The power of longitudinal data.* New York: Cambridge University Press.

Ryan, R. M. (1992). Agency and organization: Intrinsic motivation, autonomy, and the self in psychological development. In J. Jacobs (Ed.), *Nebraska Symposium on Motivation* (Vol. 40, pp. 1–56). Lincoln: University of Nebraska Press.

Ryan, R. M., Connell, J. P., & Deci, E. L. (1985). A motivational analysis of self-determination and self-regulation in education. In C. Ames & R. Ames (Eds.), *Research on motivation in education: Vol. 2. The classroom milieu* (pp. 13–15). London: Academic Press.

Schiefele, U. (1991). Interest, learning, and motivation. *Educational Psychologist, 26*, 299–323.

Schiefele, U., & Krapp, A. (1997). Topic interest and free recall of expository text. *Learning and Individual Differences.*

Schiefele, U., & Schreyer, I. (1994). Intrinsische lernmotivation under lernen. Ein uberblick zu ergebnissen de forschung. *Zeitschrist fur Padagogische Pyschologie, 8*, 1–13.

Schunk, D. H. (1983). Ability versus effort attributional feedback. Differential effects on self-efficacy and achievement. *Journal of Educational Psychology, 75*, 848–856.

Schunk, D. H. (1990). Goal setting and self-efficacy during self-regulated learning. *Educational Psychologist, 25*, 71–86.

Schunk, D. H. (1991) Self-efficacy and academic motivation. *Educational psychologist, 26*, 207–231.

Schunk, D. H. (1994). Self-regulation of self-efficacy and attributions in academic settings. In D. H. Schunk & B. J. Zimmerman (Eds.), *Self-regulation of learning and performance.* Hillsdale, NJ: Erlbaum.

Shaklee, H., & Tucker, D. (1979). Cognitive bases of development in inferences of ability. *Child Development, 50*, 904–907.

Simmons, R. G., & Blyth, D. A. (1987). *Moving into adolescence: The impact of pubertal change and school context.* Hawthorne, NY: Aldine de Gruyter.

Skinner, E. A. (1995). Perceived control, motivation and coping. Thousand Oaks, CA: Sage.

Skinner, E. A., & Belmont, M. J. (1993). Motivation in the classroom: Reciprocal effects of teacher behavior and student engagement across the school year. *Journal of Educational Psychology, 85*, 571–581.

Skinner, E. A., Chapman, M., & Baltes, P. B. (1988). Control, means-ends, and agency beliefs: A new conceptualization and its measurement during childhood. *Journal of Personality and Social Psychology, 54*, 117–133.

Skinner, E. A., & Connell, J. P. (1986). Control understanding: Suggestions for a developmental framework. In M. M. Baltes & P. B. Baltes (Eds.), *The psychology of control and aging*. Hillsdale, NJ: Erlbaum.

Sroufe, L. A., & Jacobvitz, D. (1989). Diverging pathways, developmental tranformations, multiple eiologies, and the problem of continuity in development. *Human Development, 32*, 196–203.

Stein, K. F., Markus, H. R., & Roeser, R. W. (1995). *The socio-cultural shaping of self esteem in American early adolescent girls and boys*. Manuscript submitted for publication.

Stevenson, H. W., Parker, T., Wilkinson, A., Hegion, A., & Fish, E. (1976). Predictive value of teacher's ratings of young children. *Journal of Educational Psychology, 68*, 507–517.

Stipek, D. (1984). Young children's performance expectations: Logical analysis or wishful thinking? In J. Nicholls (Ed.), *Advances in achievement motivation: Vol. 3. The development of achievement motivation* (pp. 33–56). Greenwich, CT: JAI Press.

Stipek, D. J., & Daniels, D. H. (1988). Declining perceptions of competence: A consequence of changes in the child or in the educational environment? *Journal of Educational Psychology, 80*, 352–356.

Stipek, D. J., & Mac Iver, D. (1989). Developmental change in children's assessment of intellectual competence. *Child Development, 60*, 521–538.

Stipek, D. J., Recchia, S., & McClintic, S. M. (1992). Self-evaluation in young children. *Monographs of the Society for Research in Child Development, 57* (2, Serial No. 226).

Teigen, K. H. (1987). Intrinsic interest and the novelty-familiarity interaction. *Scandinavian Journal of Psychology, 28*, 199–210.

Todt, E. (1990). Entwicklung des interesses. In H. Hetzer (Ed.), *Angewandte entwicklungspsychologie des kindes- und jugendalters*. Wiesbaden, Germany: Quelle & Meyer.

Travers, R. M. W. (1978). *Children's interests*. Unpublished manuscript, Western Michigan University, College of Education, Kalamazoo.

Wade, S. E. (1992). How interest effects learning form text. In K. A. Renninger, S. Hidi, & A. Krupp (Eds.). *The role of interest in learning and development*. Hillsdale, NJ: Erlbaum.

Weiner, B. (1992). *Human motivation: Metaphors, theories, and research*. Newbury Park, CA: Sage.

Weisz, J. P. (1984). Contingency judgments and achievement behavior: Deciding what is controllable and when to try. In J. G. Nicholls (Ed.), *The development of achievement motivation* (pp. 107–136). Greenwich, CT: JAI Press.

Wentzel, K. R. (1991). Social competence at school: Relation between social responsibility and academic achievement. *Review of Educational Research, 61*, 1–24.

Wigfield, A. (1994). Expectancy-value theory of achievement motivation: A developmental perspective. *Educational Psychology Review, 6*, 49–78.

Wigfield. A., & Eccles, J. S. (1989). Test anxiety in elementary and secondary school students. *Educational Psychologist, 24*, 159–183.

Wigfield. A., & Eccles, J. S. (1992). The development of achievement task values: A theoretical analysis. *Developmental Review, 12*, 11–41.

Wigfield, A., Eccles, J. S., Mac Iver, D., Reuman, D. A., & Midgley, C. (1991). Transitions during early adolescence: Changes in children's domain-specific self-perceptions and general self-esteem across the transition to junior high school. *Developmental Psychology, 27*, 552–565.

Wigfield, A., Eccles, J. S., Yoon, K. S., Harold, R. D., Arbreton, A. J., Freedman-Doan, C. R., & Blumenfeld, P. C. (1998). Changes in children's competence beliefs and subjective task values across the elementary school years: A three year study. *Journal of Educational Psychology*.

Zimmerman, B. J., Bandura, A., & Martinez-Pons, M. (1992). Self-motivation for academic attainment: The role of self-efficacy beliefs and personal goal setting. *American Educational Research Journal, 29*, 663–676.

15
CHAPTER

Nancy Eisenberg
Richard A. Fabes

Emotion, Emotion-Related Regulation, and Quality of Socioemotional Functioning

☐ Introduction

In recent years, interest in the role of emotion in development has grown enormously. For a long time, emotion was considered inconsequential or a nuisance variable (Campos, 1984); however, in the past decade or two, it has moved to center stage in work on social development. Thus, emotion and its regulation are foci of investigation in work on attachment, social competence, moral development, psychopathology, socialization in the home, and many other topics (see Saarni, Mumme, & Campos, 1998).

Like many other psychologists, our concern with emotion is relatively recent. It initially grew out of an interest in prosocial motivation; this interest expanded to include the role of emotion and its regulation in social competence and problem behavior more generally. Because our thinking about emotion grew out of work on empathy and its role in prosocial behavior, thinking and research on empathy-related responding and prosocial behavior are briefly summarized. Next, recent research on the relations of individual differences in emotionality and regulation to empathy-related responding is reviewed, followed by examples of research on the role of emotion and emotion-related regulation in children's problem behavior and competent social functioning.

☐ Empathy-Related Responding and Prosocial Behavior

Numerous philosophers and psychologists have suggested that empathy-related processes motivate prosocial behavior (Blum, 1980; Hoffman, 1982; Hume, 1777/1966; Staub, 1979)—that when people experience others' negative emotions, they are likely to engage in prosocial behavior. However, in 1982, Underwood and Moore published a review in which they found, contrary to most theory, no empirical relation between empathy and prosocial behavior. On careful consideration of this literature, it became clear that most of the work before 1982 had been conducted with children using self-report measures and hypothetical vignettes that were problematic and that there were conceptual problems with most of the existing research (Eisenberg & Miller, 1987).

The conceptual problems were of several sorts. One problem was that most investigators had not differentiated between different types of empathy-related responding that would be expected to involve different affective motivations. Batson (1991) first differentiated between empathy and personal distress in the late 1970s. One can further differentiate among empathy, sympathy, and personal distress. Thus, although

Work in this chapter was supported by grant DBS-9208375 from the National Science Foundation and Grant 1 R01 HH55052 from the National Institute of Mental Health to both authors and Research Scientist Award K05 M801321 from the National Institute of Mental Health to Nancy Eisenberg.

definitions differ, *empathy* can be defined as an affective response that stems from the apprehension or comprehension of another's emotional state or condition, and which is similar to what the other person is feeling or would be expected to feel. If a child views a sad person, and consequently feels sad himself or herself, that child is experiencing empathy.

In most situations, empathy with another's negative emotion is likely to evolve into one or another related emotional reactions (or into both): sympathy and personal distress. *Sympathy* is an emotional response stemming from the apprehension or comprehension of another's emotional state or condition, which is not the same as what the other person is feeling (or is expected to feel) but consists of feelings of sorrow or concern for the other. Thus, if a girl sees a sad peer and feels concern for the peer, she is experiencing sympathy. Such a sympathetic reaction often is based on empathic sadness, although sympathy also may be based on cognitive perspective taking or accessing encoded cognitive information relevant to another's situation or need (Eisenberg, Shea, Carlo, & Knight, 1991; Karniol, 1982). However, empathy also can lead to *personal distress*. Personal distress is a self-focused, aversive affective reaction to the apprehension of another's emotion (e.g., discomfort, anxiety).

The distinction between sympathy and personal distress is critical because these two empathy-related reactions are expected to result in different motivations and, consequently, different behavior. Batson (1991) hypothesized that a sympathetic emotional reaction is associated with the desire to reduce the other person's distress or need and, therefore, is likely to lead to altruistic behavior. In contrast, personal distress, because it is an aversive experience, is believed to be associated with the motivation to reduce one's own distress. Consequently, personal distress is believed to result in the desire to avoid contact with the needy or distressed other if possible. People experiencing personal distress are expected to assist others in the distressing situation only when helping is the easiest way to reduce the helper's own distress.

In studies with adults, Batson (1991; Batson et al., 1988) found some empirical evidence to support the aforementioned relations between prosocial behavior and sympathy or personal distress. However, the experimental methods and self-reports measures that he used generally were inappropriate for use with children. Thus, we conducted a series of studies designed to develop alternative methods of assessing empathy-related responding and to examine the relations of sympathy and personal distress to children's prosocial behavior.

Briefly, in this work, we used self-report, facial, and physiological markers of sympathy and personal distress. The experience of personal distress was expected to be associated with higher levels of physiological distress than sympathy, self-reports of distress, and facial distress, whereas sympathy was expected to be linked to facial concern, reports of sadness or sympathy for others, and heart rate deceleration (an index of outwardly oriented attention; Cacioppo & Sandman, 1978; Lacey, Kagan, Lacey, & Moss, 1963). In the first set of studies, we found that, in general, when children or adults were in situations likely to induce a reaction akin to personal distress (e.g., in response to a film), they exhibited higher heart rate and skin conductance than in analogous situations likely to induce sympathy. Moreover, children and adults tended to exhibit facial concerned attention rather than facial distress in sympathy-inducing contexts, and older children's and adults' self-reports also were somewhat consistent with the emotional context (although findings for report of distress are mixed; Eisenberg & Fabes, 1990; Eisenberg, Fabes, et al., 1988; Eisenberg, Fabes, Schaller, Miller, et al., 1991; Eisenberg, Schaller, et al., 1988). These findings provided some evidence that one could differentiate sympathy and personal distress with a variety of measures.

Using the aforementioned measures of sympathy and personal distress, we examined children's and adults' sympathetic or personal distress reactions to empathy-inducing films about others in distress or need. Specifically, we examined the relations between physiological, facial, and self-reported reactions to these films and actual helping or sharing with the needy or distressed individuals in the film (or others like them) when it was easy to avoid contact with the needy other (e.g., sharing of a prize or engaging in a boring task that would benefit the needy others rather than playing with toys). Consistent with theory, in general, markers of sympathy were positively related to prosocial behavior, whereas markers of personal distress were negatively related to prosocial behavior, the latter particularly for children. Thus, sympathy and personal distress seemed to reflect different motivational states (Eisenberg et al., 1989, 1990; see Eisenberg & Fabes, 1990, 1991, 1998, for reviews).

The differing relations of personal distress and sympathy to prosocial behavior are consistent with the conclusion that the subjective experiences of sympathy and personal distress are quite different. Prior to the time that sympathy and personal distress were consistently differentiated in the research, Hoffman (1982) suggested that overarousal due to empathy results in a self-focus. Consistent with this view, we (Eisenberg, Fabes, Murphy, et al., 1994) hypothesized that empathic overarousal in situations involving negative emotion results in an aversive emotional state which leads to a self-focus; that is, personal distress. Children and adults who cannot maintain their emotional reactions to others' emotions within a tolerable range (and become overaroused) would be expected to focus on their own emotional needs, a response that is likely to undermine positive social interactions in situations involving negative emotion (including one's own or that of other people). Evidence consistent with the notion that empathic over-arousal results in self-focused personal distress includes the following: (a) negative emotional arousal is associated with a focus on the self (Wood, Saltzberg, & Goldsamt, 1990); (b) people exhibit higher skin conductance, and sometimes report more distress, in situations likely to elicit person distress (in contrast to sympathy; Eisenberg, Fabes, Schaller, Carlo, & Miller, 1991; Eisenberg, Fabes, Schaller, Miller, et al., 1991); and (c) personal distress sometimes has been associated with lower heart rate variability (the degree to which heart rate goes up and down as reflected in its variance), which can be viewed as a rough index of low physiological regulation (see Fabes, Eisenberg, & Eisenbud, 1993).

Conversely, children and adults who can maintain their vicarious emotional arousal at a moderate level, which is arousing but not aversive, would be expected to experience sympathy. Consistent with this view, is the type of evidence just discussed: (a) skin conductance and heart rate are lower when people are viewing sympathy-inducing, in comparison to distressing, films (Eisenberg, Fabes, Schaller, Miller, et al., 1991; Eisenberg, Fabes, Schaller, Carlo, & Miller, 1991; Eisenberg, Schaller, et al., 1988); and (b) higher situational sympathy (as indexed by facial concern) has been correlated with high heart rate variability (which is correlated with measures of physiological regulation; see Fabes et al., 1993; also see Eisenberg, Fabes, Murphy, et al., 1996).

Conceptualizing personal distress and sympathy in this manner led to the next logical question, What factors account for individual differences in the tendencies to experience personal distress and sympathy and, on a broader level, in a host of behaviors that, at least in part, are driven by emotional reactivity? One possible set of contributing factors is environmental, including socialization; another is biological predispositions. Thus, in some research, investigators have focused on the familial or genetic contributors to emotionality and emotion-related regulation (e.g., Eisenberg et al., 1992; Parke, Cassidy, Burks, Carson, & Boyum, 1992; see Plomin & Stocker, 1989; Eisenberg, Fabes, & Losoya, 1997). Another approach is to consider person variables, which likely reflect both environmental and constitutional factors, that influence whether individuals become emotionally overaroused in social contexts involving emotion.

☐ Determinants of Emotional Arousal

We have focused on two categories of person variables that we believe influence whether children and adults become emotionally overaroused in social contexts: (a) individuals' dispositional levels of emotional responsivity, particularly the intensity, quantity of responding, or both (Rothbart & Derryberry, 1981; Thomas, Chess, & Birch, 1968); and (b) individuals' ability to regulate (modulate) their emotional reactions and cope behaviorally with the emotion and the evocative situation (Derryberry & Rothbart, 1988; Lazarus & Folkman, 1984; Rothbart, Ziaie, & O'Boyle, 1992).

Emotionality

By *emotional intensity*, we mean stable individual differences in the typical intensity with which individuals experience their emotions (i.e., affective intensity, as defined by Larsen & Diener, 1987). Both the intensity of emotional experiences and the ease with which individuals respond intensely (which likely is highly related to quantity of responding) are expected to contribute to the degree to which individuals become emotionally aroused in a given situation. Similar to others, we view emotional intensity as having a temperamental or biological-constitutional basis, and as a characteristic that is considerably consistent over time (Larsen & Diener, 1987; Rothbart & Derryberry, 1981; also see Plomin & Stocker, 1989).

In initial early work on this topic, dispositional emotional intensity was associated with the degree of positive or negative emotion experienced in specific contexts (Larsen & Diener, 1987), as well as with adults' physiological arousal to empathy-inducing stimuli (Eisenberg, Fabes, Schaller, Miller, et al., 1991).

Thus, individual differences in emotional intensity seemed to be a likely predictor of the tendency to become emotionally overaroused in emotional contexts.

Emotion Related Regulation

Conceptualization. Despite abundant interest in recent years in emotion-related regulation, there is little consensus on its conceptualization or definition. Campos and colleagues suggested that emotion regulation can take place at three general loci: at the level of sensory receptors (input regulation), at central levels where information is processed and manipulated (central regulation), and at the level of response selection (labeled output regulation; Campos, Mumme, Kermoian, & Campos, 1994). Thompson (1994) also described various domains for emotion regulation, including neurophysiological responses, attentional processes, construals of emotionally arousing events, encoding of internal emotion cues, access to coping resources, regulating the demands of familiar settings, and selecting adaptive response alternatives. Rather than include all of these processes under the rubric of emotion regulation, we find it a useful heuristic to differentiate between the regulation of internal processes or physiological states and the regulation of behavioral reactions associated with, or resulting from, internal states.

Building on the work of others, (e.g., Campos et al., 1994; Cole, Michel, Teti, 1994; Thompson, 1994), we define *emotion regulation* as the process of initiating, maintaining, modulating, or changing the occurrence, intensity, or duration of internal feeling states and emotion-related physiological processes. This type of regulation also might be labeled the regulation of internal emotion-relevant states and processes.

In contrast to emotion regulation, *emotion-related behavioral regulation* is defined as the process of initiating, maintaining, inhibiting, modulating, or changing the occurrence, form, and duration of behavioral concomitants of emotion, including observable facial and gestural responses and other behaviors that stem from, or are associated with, internal emotion-related psychological or physiological stress and goals. This type of regulation can involve the communication of emotion, often it is goal directed, and sometimes it is an attempt to change the emotion-inducing context. Attempts to manage stressful contexts, often called instrumental or problem-focused coping (Lazarus & Folkman, 1984; Sandler, Tein, & West, 1994), can be considered an aspect of emotion-related behavioral regulation, although it also may be useful to distinguish between the regulation of behaviors that involve the expression or communication of emotion and those behaviors that are attempts to alter the emotion-eliciting context. The critical distinction between what we have labeled emotion regulation and the general category of emotion-related behavioral regulation is the locus of regulation: internal psychological and physiological reactions versus overt behavior driven by or associated with aroused internal states.

These definitions are somewhat arbitrary because there is a fine line between emotion regulation and emotion-related behavioral regulation. Emotion regulation and emotion-related behavioral regulation are intricately and often inextricably associated, particularly in infancy. Not only is behavioral regulation affected by internal emotion-related processes, but the consequences of behavioral regulation often may influence the course of internal emotion-related processes and states, and may serve to modify contemporaneous and future emotion-related cognitive or physiological processes.

Another type of emotion-related regulation is *niche-picking*; that is, behaviors that act to control exposure to various aspects of the environment related to emotional experience (Carstensen, 1991). This type of regulation is similar to Aspinwall and Taylor's (1997) conception of proactive coping, or "efforts undertaken in advance of a potentially stressful event to prevent it or to modify its form before it occurs" (p. 417). Examples of niche-picking are when socially anxious individuals choose not to go to social events that elicit discomfort, whereas extroverted people seek out larger groups of peers and social gatherings. Niche-picking generally occurs prior to subsequent emotion-eliciting events, although it also may occur as a reaction to previous emotional experiences. Although niche-picking obviously is an important method of regulating emotional experience, there is little research on its use by children.

Appropriate regulation depends, in part, on the particular context. Thus, effective emotion-related regulation is viewed as flexible and relevant to one's goals (Cole et al., 1994; Eisenberg & Fabes, 1992), and individuals skilled in regulation adjust their behavior accordingly.

Prior Research and Theory on Emotion-Related Regulation. The construct of emotion regulation has been considered in several bodies of work. For example, it has been discussed in depth by

TABLE 15.1. Summary of major constructs predicting quality of socioeconomic functioning

Emotionality
1. Intensity: stable individual differences in the typical intensity with which individuals experience their emotions (one also can look at emotional intensity in specific context; Larsen & Diener, 1987).
   a. Intensity of negative emotions.
   b. Intensity of positive emotions.
   c. Intensity of general emotionality: the general tendency to feel emotions strongly, without reference specifically to valence of the emotion (positive or negative).
2. Frequency: individual differences in the frequency of experiencing emotions.
   a. Frequency of negative emotions.
   b. Frequency of positive emotions.

Emotion-related regulation
1. Emotion regulation: the process of initiating, maintaining, modulating, or changing the occurrence, intensity, or duration of internal feeling states and emotion-related physiological processes (i.e., the regulation of internal emotion-relevant states and processes).
2. Emotion-related behavioral regulation: the process of initiating, maintaining, inhibiting, modulating, or changing the occurrence, form, and duration of behavioral concomitants of emotion.
   a. Regulation of observable facial and gestural responses and other behaviors that stem from, or are associated with, internal emotion-related psychological or physiological states and goals.
   b. Attempts to alter or manage the emotion-inducing context causing the emotion, often called instrumental or problem-focused coping (Lazarus & Folkman, 1984; Sandler, Tein, & West, 1994).
3. Niche-picking or proactive coping (Aspinwall & Taylor, 1997): controlling exposure to various aspects of the environment related to emotional experience through efforts undertaken in advance of a potentially stressful event to prevent it or to modify its form before it occurs.

temperament theorists who define regulation in terms of modulating internal reactivity (Rothbart & Derryberry, 1981). In the temperament literature, emotion regulation frequently is operationalized as involving attentional processes such as the abilities to shift and focus attention as needed (Derryberry & Rothbart, 1988; Windle & Lerner, 1986). Similarly, in the literature on stress and coping, investigators have discussed attentional processes such as cognitive distraction and positive cognitive restructuring of a situation (e.g., thinking of a negative situation in a positive light) that, if successfully applied, modify the individual's internal psychological, emotional, or physiological reactions. Indeed, in their early work, Lazarus and Folkman (1984) viewed emotion-focused coping (efforts to reduce emotional distress in contexts appraised as taxing or exceeding the resources of the individual) as a major category of coping reactions.

People who can regulate their emotional reactivity in social or nonsocial contexts through allocating attention appear to respond relatively positively to stressful events. For example, the abilities to shift and refocus attention have been associated with lower levels of distress, frustration, and other negative emotions; although, until recently, most of the empirical work had been conducted with infants and adults (Bridges & Grolnick, 1995; Derryberry & Rothbart, 1988; Rothbart et al., 1992). Shifting attention from a distressing stimulus can decrease arousal. Focusing attention on positive aspects of the situation or on means by which to cope also can decrease negative emotion and increase positive emotion; further, focusing attention on nonthreatening ideas or objects can distract a person from a distressing event or cognition.

Emotion-related behavioral regulation traditionally did not play a major role in systems of temperament (Prior, 1992). However, more recently, some temperament theorists have assessed behavioral inhibition and impulsivity as part of temperament (e.g., Derryberry & Rothbart, 1988; Rothbart, Ahadi, & Hershey, 1994). Furthermore, theorists and researchers in clinical, developmental, and personality psychology frequently have discussed constructs such as inhibition of behavior, self-regulation, constraint, or ego control, all of which involve the ability to modulate the behavioral expression of impulses and feelings (Block & Block, 1980; Fox, 1989; Kochanska, 1993; Kopp, 1982; Tellegen, 1985). In addition, as noted above, behaviors aimed at regulating stressful situations have been discussed extensively by coping theorists in work on problem-focused and instrumental coping (e.g., Kliewer, 1991; Lazarus & Folkman, 1984; Sandler et al., 1994).

☐ A Multiconstruct Perspective

In our view, emotionality and emotion-relevant regulation, albeit related conceptually and empirically, are also distinct. We have proposed that they can be associated in a variety of different ways and, in combination, predict more variance in various outcomes than does either alone.

In a heuristic model (Eisenberg & Fabes, 1992), we outlined expected relations of social functioning with emotional intensity and three types of regulation. The types of regulation can be characterized as follows: (a) highly inhibited (individuals high in behavioral inhibition but low in other types of regulation such as emotion regulation and instrumental, problem-focused coping), (b) undercontrolled (individuals low in emotion regulation and emotion-related behavioral regulation, including the ability to deal instrumentally with the stressful context), and (c) optimally regulated (people high in various modes of adaptive regulation, moderately high in behavioral inhibition but not overcontrolled, and flexible in their use of regulatory behavior). People who are optimally regulated are predicted to be high in quality of social functioning (i.e., social competence) regardless of their level of emotional intensity. However, some differences were expected between optimally regulated people who are relatively high versus low in emotional intensity. For example, people high in emotional intensity and optimally regulated were predicted to be particularly high in sympathetic and prone to sympathy-based prosocial behavior. In contrast, children and adults low in intensity and optimally regulated were expected to be only moderately high in sympathy and prosocial behavior (unless they were high in cognitive perspective taking, which could engender sympathy and prosocial behavior).

Furthermore, individuals low in behavioral regulation, in the ability to cope instrumentally with the environment, and in the ability to regulate emotion through attentional and cognitive processes were expected to be prone to externalizing problem behaviors. Those people high in emotional intensity, especially intensity of negative emotion, and low in all types of regulation were expected to be particularly out of control and prone to reactive (emotionally driven) aggression and other behaviors that are based on unregulated emotion. Undercontrolled individuals low in emotional intensity also were expected to be low in social competence and high in problem behaviors, but their behavior was hypothesized to be more calculated and less emotionally driven. In contrast to externalizing types of behaviors, internalizing problem behaviors (e.g., fearfulness, social avoidance, and shyness, and behavioral inhibition to novelty and new people), as well as low social competence, were expected to be predicted by the combination of high emotional intensity with low emotional regulation (e.g., attentional control and cognitive coping mechanisms), low instrumental coping, and high levels of behavioral overcontrol (e.g., high behavior inhibition and rigidity of regulatory efforts).

The emotions associated with under- and over-control may differ somewhat (although in no absolute sense). For example, hostility appears to be associated particularly with undercontrol, whereas overcontrolled people often are anxious or fearful (e.g., Bates, Bayles, Bennett, Ridge, & Brown, 1991; Rubin, Chen, & Hymel, 1993), although some undercontrolled children evidence anxiety as well as externalizing problems (Robins, John, Caspi, Moffitt, & Stouthamer-Loeber, 1996).

In summary, we have argued that individual differences in emotionality and regulation jointly contribute to the prediction of numerous aspects of social functioning, including socially appropriate and problem behavior, popularity with peers, shyness, sympathy, and prosocial behavior. In some cases, the contributions of emotionality and regulation are expected to be additive; in other cases, we predict interactive or moderating effects (Baron & Kenny, 1986).

☐ Empirical Findings

Empathy-Related Responding

Predictions.   Because work on empathy was the genesis of our thinking about emotionality and regulation, much of our initial work on emotionality and emotion regulation concerned empathy-related responding. According to our model (Eisenberg & Fabes, 1992), and based on the notion that sympathy involves optimal regulation, we made the following predictions:

1. In general, regulation we expected to be positively and linearly related to sympathy. The exception might be if there were a substantial number of highly behaviorally inhibited people in a sample; in such a case, moderately high behavioral control or inhibition, but not extremely high behavioral control, may be related to sympathy.
2. Conversely, nonoptimal levels of regulation, particularly low levels of regulation of internal emotion-related processes (e.g., by mechanisms such as attentional control), were expected to be associated with personal distress; this is because personal distress is believed to reflect high levels of unmodulated negative emotion.
3. Emotional intensity, in general (i.e., for both positive and negative emotions) or for emotions such as sadness, was predicted to be moderately associated with sympathy (in that somewhat higher sympathy was expected for higher intensity people), although optimally regulated people were expected to be somewhat sympathetic regardless of level of emotional intensity.
4. People high in emotional intensity, especially intensity of negative emotion, were expected to be high in personal distress, particularly if they were low in the ability to regulate negative emotion.

In addition, sympathy was expected to be associated with a disposition toward experiencing positive emotions because sympathy and positive emotion may be an outcome or correlate of an optimal level of emotional regulation (Eisenberg & Fabes, 1992). Moreover, individuals who tend to experience positive emotion may be more benign toward others due to mood effects or a relation between an ongoing sense of well-being and a positive view of other people (Cialdini, Kenrick, & Baumann, 1982; Staub, 1984). In contrast, personal distress (which, by definition, involves feelings of distress, anxiety, or discomfort) was expected to be correlated with high levels of negative affectivity and low levels of positive emotion.

The Data.   In reviewing relevant data, we begin with brief summaries of initial studies with adult samples and then discuss research with children.

Dispositional Empathy-Related Responding.   In general, we have obtained empirical support for the hypothesis that individual differences in emotionality and regulation predict differences among individuals in dispositional sympathy and personal distress. In an initial study with college students (Eisenberg, Fabes, Murphy, et al., 1994), we found that self-reported dispositional personal distress (assessed with Davis', 1994, questionnaire) was related to low levels of both self-reported regulation (behavioral and attentional) and friends' reports of students' coping. Although self-reported sympathy was unrelated to regulation in zero-order correlations, it was significantly related to regulation (a composite measure of attentional and behavioral regulation) once the effects of negative emotional intensity were controlled. Consistent with the notion that empathic people are high in emotional intensity, both personal distress and sympathy were positively related with intensity of negative emotion and dispositional proneness to experience sadness. However, friends' reports of negative emotionality (both intensity and frequency) related positively with students' personal distress, but not to sympathy. The aforementioned effects generally held even when scores on social desirability were controlled.

Moreover, in regression analyses, regulation and emotionality contributed unique variance to prediction. In general, the predicted moderational (interaction) effects were not obtained in this study. Finally, frequency of positive emotion was negatively related to dispositional personal distress, whereas intensity of positive emotion was positively correlated with sympathy.

In a similar study with older adults (Eisenberg & Okun, 1996), the pattern of findings was even more consistent with expectations. Self-reported regulation, especially emotion regulation, was positively related to sympathy and negatively related to personal distress. Negative emotional intensity was positively related to both personal distress and sympathy, although the relation was older, somewhat stronger for the former. Moreover, for women only (most of the older study participants were women), there was an interaction between negative emotional intensity and regulation (a composite of emotional and behavioral regulation) when predicting personal distress. Personal distress decreased with increasing level of regulation for women at all levels of negative emotional intensity but, particularly, for women who were low or average in negative emotional intensity. Thus, the relation between regulation and sympathy was stronger for women who were not prone to intense negative emotions. Apparently, older women who were high in negative emotional intensity were somewhat more likely than other women to be overwhelmed by vicariously induced negative emotion, even if they were high in regulation. However, even these women showed a significant drop in personal distress as a function of increasing regulation; the drop simply was less dramatic than for women moderate or low in negative emotional intensity.

In a study with 82 6- to 8-year-old school children, we obtained teachers' and children's reports of sympathy (on questionnaire measures) and parents' and teachers' reports of children's emotionality and regulation (Eisenberg, Fabes, Murphy, et al., 1996). Specifically, adults reported on children's emotional intensity with regard to negative, positive, and unspecified (general) emotions; frequency of children's negative and positive emotions; children's abilities to shift and focus attention; and children's abilities to inhibit and regulate their overt behavior. In general, adults' reports of children's regulation were positively related to children's dispositional sympathy. Further, vagal tone, a marker of physiological regulation (Porges, Doussard-Roosevelt, & Maiti, 1994), was positively related to self-reported sympathy for boys (although the relation was negative for girls).

In this study with children, negative emotionality was negatively related to sympathy, but only for boys. Recall that in the research with adults, intensity and/or frequency of negative emotion was positively related to both sympathy and personal distress. It is likely the reversed pattern of findings for children is due to the types of children's negative emotions that are salient to adults. In general, researchers have found that boys exhibit more anger than do girls (Birnbaum & Croll, 1984; Fabes, Eisenberg, Nyman, & Michealieu, 1991; Maccoby & Jacklin, 1974; see Eisenberg, Martin, & Fabes, 1996). It is likely that adults' (particularly teachers') reports of children's negative emotionality predominantly reflect externalizing emotions, such as anger and frustration, as well as overt distress (see Eisenberg et al., 1993; Eisenberg, Fabes, Nyman, Berzweig, & Pinuelas, 1994); these sorts of negative emotions are likely to be particularly visible and salient to adults, and especially noticeable for boys. Parents may be likely to report internalizing negative emotions, as well as externalizing negative emotions, when reporting on children's negative emotionality; however, a dispositional tendency to experience or express internalizing negative emotions, like externalizing emotions, is expected to be related to personal distress (Eisenberg & Fabes, 1992).

Further, in the same study, there was evidence that, for boys, physiological arousal (heart rate, skin conductance) when exposed to a relatively distressing film clip was related to low dispositional sympathy. Thus, boys prone to physiological overarousal appeared to be low on dispositional sympathy. In addition, teachers', but not parents', reports of children's positive emotionality were positively related to teachers' reports of girls' sympathy and boys' self-reported sympathy.

Adults' reports of children's regulation and emotionality tended to contribute some unique as well as overlapping variance to the prediction of a composite index of children's self-reported and teacher-reported sympathy. That is, measures of regulation and emotionality sometimes predicted sympathy, even when controlling for one another. Of most interest, was the interaction between general emotional intensity and regulation when predicting teacher-reported child sympathy. *General emotional intensity* is the general tendency to feel emotions strongly, without reference specifically to valence of the emotion (positive or negative). Children low in regulation were low in sympathy regardless of their general emotional intensity; such children were likely to be overwhelmed by their vicarious emotion when it was experienced. In contrast, for children who were moderate or relatively high in their regulation, sympathy increased with the level of general emotional intensity. Thus, children who were likely to be emotionally intense were sympathetic if they were at least moderately well regulated. Such children would be expected to experience vicariously others' emotions, yet not become overaroused and overwhelmed by this emotion.

In brief, across studies, we generally (albeit not always) have found that regulation is correlated with high dispositional sympathy and low dispositional personal distress. The relation of emotionality with empathy-related responding varies depending on whether the index is adults' reports of their own emotionality or other people's reports of an individual's negative emotion (e.g., teachers' or parents' reports of children's emotionality or friends' reports of adults' negative emotionality). In general, emotionally intense adults who report they are prone to negative emotion tend to score high on both dispositional sympathy and personal distress, particularly, the latter. In contrast, friends' reports of negative emotional intensity and frequency of negative emotion were related to college students' personal distress, but not sympathy. In addition, adult-reported negative emotional intensity and frequency of negative emotion tend to be related to low dispositional sympathy in children, particularly for boys, probably because boys who exhibit high levels of negative emotionality are prone to overarousal and emotions such as anger that are unlikely to be linked to sympathy. In contrast, normal adults who report high levels of negative emotions may be those who are willing to think about and acknowledge their negative emotions; such people may be especially susceptible to vicariously induced emotion.

In addition, there is initial evidence that the joint contributions of general emotionality and regulation sometimes are useful for predicting individual differences in children's empathy-related behavior. Children who were prone to relatively intense emotions (both positive and negative) and who are well regulated were especially high in teacher-reported sympathy. Finally, it is important to note that although adults' reports of boys' negative emotionality frequently were negatively related to boys' dispositional sympathy, the tendency to be emotionally intense in general was positively related to teacher-reported dispositional sympathy for children who are moderately and highly regulated.

Situational Empathy-Related Responding.   Prior to leaving the topic of empathy-related responding, it is worth noting that relations between situational measures of empathy-related responding and measures of dispositional regulation and emotionality are considerably weaker than findings for dispositional empathy-related responding. For example, Eisenberg, Fabes, Murphy, et al. (1994) found that adults' self-reported sympathy, sadness, and distress in response to empathy-inducing films not only were positively related to measures of intensity of emotion, but also were negatively related to a self-reported measure of emotion regulation. Facial reactions to the films, including sadness, concerned attention, and distress, all were related to some of the measures of emotionality, but they were unrelated to measures of regulation. Men's heart rate acceleration during an evocative portion of the film (an index of personal distress) was correlated with frequency and intensity of dispositional negative emotion, and negatively related to emotion regulation, but primarily for men exposed to the relatively evocative film. Thus, the relations of measures of situational empathy-related responding varied with the specific measure and sex of the individual.

In a study of children age 4 to 6, more consistent relations between situational sympathy and dispositional regulation were found, at least for the measure of facial concerned attention in response to a film about peer conflict (a child being bullied; Eisenberg & Fabes, 1995). Children's facial reactions to the conflict film were videotaped and their self-reported reactions were assessed after the film. For children who viewed the conflict film first (effects were diluted for the group who viewed another film first), those high in facial concerned attention were rated by teachers as high on attentional control and low on negative dispositional emotional intensity and nonconstructive (acting out versus avoidant) coping. Facial distress and sadness reactions, as well as self-reported reactions, were infrequently related to measures of dispositional regulation and emotionality.

Moreover, in a large study of nearly 200 children in kindergarten to third grade (Guthrie et al., 1997), children who evidenced sympathy (e.g., facial sadness, mean heart rate decline, and self-reported sympathy) in response to an empathy-inducing film generally were rated higher in regulation and resiliency, although findings sometimes were obtained for only one sex and often were weak. For example, facial sadness in response to the sympathy segment of the film was positively related to teachers' ratings of attention shifting and resiliency (the latter particularly for girls), as well as teachers' and parents' ratings of general emotional intensity. Children who evidenced personal distress (e.g., facial distress) were rated relatively high in emotionality. Girls' (but not boys') reports of sympathy were positively related to teachers ratings of attentional control. Moreover, self-reports of situational sympathy for both boys and girls were negatively related to parents' ratings of negative emotionality, whereas self-reports of sadness were positively related to parents' ratings of general emotional intensity and fathers' ratings of negative emotionality (this finding particularly for boys).

Thus, although situational measures of empathy-related responding tend to be related to emotionality, and sometimes regulation, the findings are complex and relatively weak. Given that emotional responding in any particular context may or may not be a very reliable index of general empathy-related dispositions, it is not really surprising that the relations between situational measures of empathy-related responding and dispositional emotionality and regulation are weak. If numerous situational empathy-related reactions were aggregated across different events and settings, the relation of these aggregated responses to enduring personality characteristics such as emotionality and regulation probably would be stronger (Rushton, Brainerd, & Pressley, 1983).

Social Competence and Problem Behavior

Because many of the same predictions regarding the relation of individual differences in emotionality and regulation to empathy-related responding logically would be expected to apply to the broader domain of social competence and problem behavior, we also have examined the role of individual differences in emotionality and regulation in children's social competence and problem behavior.

Predictions.   As for the study of sympathy and personal distress, we have been interested in the additive and multiplicative contributions of emotionality and regulation. In general, we predicted that high emotionality (particularly, frequency and intensity of negative emotion), combined with low behavioral and emotional regulation, as well as low instrumental coping, would be associated with externalizing types of behavior problems and low social competence. In contrast, low emotional regulation (e.g., attentional control), combined with high behavioral control and high emotionality (especially negative emotionality), was expected to predict internalizing types of problems such as high levels of shyness and withdrawn behavior. For both externalizing and internalizing behavior, prediction is expected to be greater when measures of both emotionality and regulation are obtained. Further, we hypothesized that moderational effects would be found for emotionally driven internalizing or externalizing problem behaviors (e.g., that regulation would be a better predictor of externalizing problem behaviors for children prone to experience intense negative emotions).

In the past, researchers have linked negative emotionality to quality of social functioning (e.g., Barren & Earls, 1984; Teglasi & MacMahon, 1990), but intensity of emotion seldom was examined and often data on both emotionality and social functioning were provided by the same reporter. Although some investigators also have examined the relation between regulation and social functioning, such research has been limited in quantity, often a single reporter has provided all data (particularly in the studies of temperament or coping, e.g., Kyrios & Prior, 1990; Teglasi & MacMahon, 1990), the findings on regulation have pertained primarily to behavioral rather than to emotion regulation (e.g., Block & Block, 1980; Kochanska, Murray, Koenig, & Vandegeest, 1996; Pulkkinen, 1982), and the existing data on emotion regulation have been collected primarily with infants (e.g., Bridges & Grolnick, 1995; Rothbart et al., 1992). Nonetheless, the existing research has suggested that negative emotionality and low regulation are related to low levels of social competence and to high levels of problem behaviors (e.g., Caspi, Henry, McGee, Moffitt, & Silva, 1995; Rothbart et al., 1994; Stocker & Dunn, 1990).

The Data.   Due to space limitations, it is impossible to review all the work pertaining to the relation of emotionality and regulation to quality of social functioning. Thus, some selected examples of the findings are used to illustrate the general pattern of results in our work.

Social Competence and Externalizing Problem Behaviors.   In an initial study with 4- to 6-year-olds (Eisenberg et al., 1993), children's socially appropriate behavior was rated by undergraduates who observed the children's naturally occurring interactions with peers and teachers at school for extended periods of time. For example, the observers rated whether the children had good social skills, tended to get into trouble because of their actions, and acted appropriately. Moreover, peer evaluations of sociometric status (popularity) were obtained by asking children to sort pictures of their classmates into piles that indicated how much they liked to play with each peer. Teachers and mothers also rated children on their negative emotional intensity, frequency of negative emotion, attentional regulation (the abilities to shift and focus attention), and constructive (instrumental coping and seeking support) and nonconstructive (aggression and venting emotion versus avoidance) coping. Boys who were viewed as socially appropriate and who were popular with peers were high in teacher-rated attentional regulation, were reported by teachers as exhibiting high levels of constructive coping and low levels of nonconstructive coping, and were low in both intensity and frequency of negative emotion (as rated by teachers). Fewer relations were obtained for girls, although socially appropriate girls were low in nonconstructive coping and in negative emotionality intensity. Many of the correlations ranged from about .40 to .65 (and emotionality and attentional regulation, combined, accounted for about 50% of the variance in boys' and girls' socially appropriate behavior), even though information on social functioning and regulation or emotionality was obtained from different sources. In addition, children who were both low in attentional regulation and high in negative emotional intensity were particularly likely to be low in socially appropriate behavior and popularity. The findings based on mothers' reports of children's emotionality and regulation were less impressive; although, there were some interesting associations. For example, boys viewed by their mothers as being high in negative emotional intensity were rated as low in peer status and observed social competence.

Further, individual differences in regulation and emotionality predicted real-life behavior when children were angered in their social interactions at school (Eisenberg, Fabes, Nyman, et al., 1994). Real-life, naturally occurring, events involving anger and frustration were observed over the school year. Children who were relatively likely to use nonabusive verbalizations to deal with anger—a constructive strategy— were high in teacher-rated constructive coping and attentional control (both of these findings were only for boys) and low in nonconstructive coping and negative emotional intensity (for both boys and girls). In addition, such children were viewed by mothers as high in instrumental coping and coping by seeking support, and low in aggressive coping and negative emotional intensity (Eisenberg, Fabes, Nyman, et al., 1994). There were fewer findings for other modes of coping with anger; although, for example, teachers' reports of children's negative emotional intensity were related to girls' venting of emotion, children's use of physical retaliation, and low levels of avoidant behavior when angered.

We now have the results of this sample 2 and 4 years later, when children were age 6 to 8 and 8 to 10 years. At the 2-year follow-up, teachers' reports of children's socially appropriate/nonaggressive behavior and prosocial/sociable behavior were linked to contemporaneous teacher ratings of high regulation (behavioral and attentional regulation combined), either high constructive coping or low nonconstructive coping, and low negative emotionality. Thus, when the children were age 6 to 8, teachers' ratings of children's social functioning were related to their ratings of emotionality and regulation. Of more interest, teachers' reports of children's social functioning at age 6 to 8 correlated with reports of attentional regulation, constructive coping, low nonconstructive coping (for socially appropriate nonaggressive behavior only), and low emotional intensity provided by different teachers 2 years previous (at age 4 to 6). Parental reports of regulation and emotionality were infrequently related to teachers' reports of social functioning; however, such reports obtained when the children were age 6 to 8 were correlated with reports of externalizing problem behaviors in the home concurrently (at age 6 to 8). Moreover, parental reports of attentional regulation and negative emotionality taken at age 4 to 6 correlated, to some degree, with parents' reports of problem behavior at age 6 to 8, albeit primarily for boys (Eisenberg et al., 1995).

At the 4-year follow-up, when the children were age 8 to 10, a composite index of socially competent behavior was computed (see Eisenberg, Fabes, Shepard, et al., 1997). Included in this measure were teachers' reports of children's socially appropriate behavior (in the manner described above), popularity, prosocial behavior, and aggressive and disruptive behavior. Also included were ratings of how friendly versus hostile children were when they acted out with puppets what they would do in five hypothetical situations involving the potential for conflict with peers (e.g., when the child is excluded from activities or called a "baby"). This aggregate measure of social functioning generally was related to both teachers' and parents' report of high regulation and low negative emotionality (particularly, the latter), contemporaneously (at age 8 to 10) as well as when assessed 2 and 4 years earlier. Parents' and teachers' reports of children's nonconstructive coping also tended to predict quality of social functioning. Parents' reports of low regulation, high negative emotionality, and high destructive coping at age 8 to 10 as well 2 to 4 years earlier tended to predict parents' reports of problem behavior, although findings for father-reported problem behavior held primarily for boys, whereas maternal reports of emotionality and regulation also predicted girls' problem behavior. Thus, in general, regulation and low intensity and frequency of negative emotionality predicted socially competent behavior and low levels of problem behavior contemporaneously and across time, albeit primarily in the home context for parental reports of problem behavior (Eisenberg, Fabes, Shepard, et al., 1997).

As expected, we frequently found that the effects of emotionality and regulation were additive as well as overlapping when predicting social functioning within a given setting (i.e., home or school), even over time (see Eisenberg, Fabes, Shepard, et al., 1997). Of particular interest, at age 8 to 10, there was an interaction of teacher-reported general emotional intensity and regulation when predicting social competence; social competence increased with regulation at all levels of emotional intensity, but the association was strongest for children high in general emotional intensity. A similar interaction was identified at age 6 to 8 years; moreover, similar interactions were obtained when negative emotionality rather than general emotional intensity was used as a predictor. In contrast, negative emotionality did not moderate the relation between regulation and parents' reports of problem behavior. Thus, regulation generally was a predictor of social competence but, especially, for children prone to intense emotion.

The sample in the aforementioned study was relatively small (77 children), so it was difficult to obtain significant interaction effects when predicting problem behavior (due to lack of power), although some were obtained for the aggregate measure of social competence. However, we also have examined the relation of dispositional regulation and emotionality to teacher- and parent-reported problem behavior and social competence with a sample of nearly 200 children (Eisenberg, Fabes, Guthrie, et al., 1996). In this study of children in kindergarten to third grade, parents reported on a number of children's externalizing problem behaviors such as starting fights, being disobedient, breaking rules, lying, and being sneaky. The primary parent (usually, mothers) and teachers also provided information on children's attentional regulation, ego control (i.e., primarily behavioral regulation; see Block & Block, 1980), and ego resiliency (resourceful adaptation to changing circumstances and contingencies, flexible use of the available repertoire of coping strategies, the ability to rebound from stress; see Block & Block, 1980). In addition, children played a game in which their persistence and resistance to cheating were assessed; this measure was viewed as an index of behavioral regulation. Gaze aversion during a distressing film segment also was assessed as an index of attentional control (i.e., the ability to shift attention briefly when needed to lower arousal). Further, baseline facial and heart rate responding were obtained while children viewed the film. Low baseline heart rate has been associated with externalizing problem behaviors in prior work, for example, in the criminology literature (Fowles, 1993; Lahey, Hart, Pliszka, Applegate, & McBurnett, 1993).

In general, there were consistent relations between reported problem behavior and low regulation, as measured by both adults' reports and by the behavioral (persistence versus cheating) task. Moreover, reported problem behavior often was associated with low resiliency. Generally, findings were obtained when one reporter (the primary caregiving parent or teacher) provided information on emotionality and regulation and another reporter (mother, father, or the teacher) provided information on externalizing problem behavior. The primary exception was that mothers' reports of daughters' problem behaviors were unrelated to teachers' reports of regulation or resilience, or performance on the behavioral task (but were related to mothers' reports of low attentional and behavioral regulation). Additionally, children who tended to use gaze aversion while watching a distressing film segment were relatively low in problem behaviors.

Children with problem behaviors also were viewed as high in negative emotionality (frequency and intensity) and, to some degree, as high in general and positive emotional intensity by parents and teachers (although, generally, not for correlations with mothers' reports of daughters' problem behavior). Teachers' reports of children's problem behaviors were substantially predicted by parents' reports of children's emotionality and vice versa.

Of most interest was the finding that the relation between problem behaviors and regulation sometimes was moderated by children's negative emotionality. For example, teachers' reports of regulation were related to teachers' reports of low problem behavior at all levels of negative emotion; however, the relation was strongest for children high in negative emotionality. Thus, regulation was most important for predicting problem behavior of children prone to negative emotion. A moderating effect also was found when teachers' reports of regulation and emotionality were used to predict parents' reports of problem behavior (averaged across parents). In this case, the relation between regulation and parents' reports of problem behavior was significant for children moderate and high in negative emotionality, but not for children low in negative emotion (who tended to be low in problem behavior). Thus, regulation was not a predictor of problem behavior for children low in negative emotionality. Moderation effects were obtained less frequently when parents' (usually mothers') reports of emotionality and regulation were used in the analyses; however, an interaction effect was obtained for the prediction of fathers' reports of boys' problem behavior. Maternal report of regulation was unrelated to fathers' reports of problem behavior for boys low and moderate in negative emotionality (who were relatively low in problem behavior) but, for boys high in negative emotionality, problem behavior decreased with increasing regulation. Thus, in general, regulation appeared to be particularly important for children's problem behavior in children prone to frequent and intense negative emotions.

Finally, children's heart rate and facial distress during a baseline period (while seeing a calm film) were, at least marginally, negatively related to problem behavior; findings held for mother- and father-rated problem behavior for heart rate and for problem behavior as rated by all three reporters for facial distress. This finding is consistent with prior work in which children and adults with low baseline physiological arousal are prone to problem behavior. People with low baseline arousal may seek out stimulation and exciting sensations.

A recent analysis of the relations of regulation, resiliency, and emotionality to positive social functioning illustrated the importance of attending to both moderation and mediation in thinking about the prediction of social behavior. In some of the aforementioned studies, we examined moderation effects, but not mediation. In a recent study (Eisenberg, Guthrie, et at., 1967), we examined that possibility that kindergarten to third grade children's socially competent behavior was predicted by the interaction of individual differences in emotionality and regulation, and that the interactive effects of emotionality and regulation on social functioning were mediated (i.e., mediated moderation) by individual differences in ego resiliency (i.e., resourceful adaptation to changing circumstances and contingencies, flexible use of the available repertoire of coping strategies, the ability to rebound from stress). Both attentional and behavioral regulation (including parent and teacher reports as well as the puzzle box persistence task) were assessed. Regulation was expected to predict resiliency which, in turn, was expected to predict social functioning; in this case, popularity with peers and socially appropriate/prosocial behavior. However, we expected these relations to be stronger for children high in negative emotionality because regulation is more important for those children. The data were analyzed for 193 children using structural equation monitoring. Our results, including unstandardized path coefficients, are shown in Figure 15.1; the Comparative Fit Index was .962 for the model.

The effects of attentional (i.e., emotional) control on social status and socially appropriate behavior were mediated by resiliency; in addition, the path from attentional control to resiliency, albeit significant for children both high and low in negative emotionality, was higher for children prone to negative emotion. Thus, children who could regulate their attention appeared to be resilient to stress and, perhaps as a consequence, were better liked by peers and viewed as being more socially appropriate and prosocial by teachers and peers. However, level of attentional control was particularly important for predicting social functioning for children prone to negative emotion.

The relation between behavioral regulation and social functioning was not mediated by resiliency. Rather, individual differences in behavioral regulation were directly related to socially appropriate behavior (but not social status). Moreover, this direct effect held only for children high in dispositional negative emotionality. As expected, behavioral regulation was particularly important for children likely to experience negative emotions because they have to manage more frequent and intense emotions.

It is interesting to note that there also was a quadratic relation of behavioral regulation to resiliency in a regression analysis. Teacher-reported resiliency was highest at moderate levels of behavioral regulation, in comparison to low or high levels. However, this quadratic relation was only marginally significant

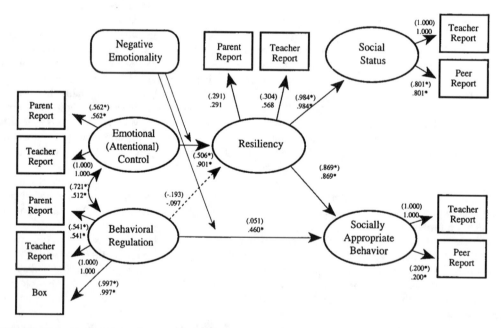

FIGURE 15.1. Model of regulation and emotionality, resiliency, and social functioning. From "The Relations of Regulation and Emotionality to Resiliency and Competent Social Functioning in Elementary School Children," by N. Eisenberg, I. K. Guthrie, R. A. Fabes, M. Reiser, B. C. Murphy, R. Holmgren, P. Maszk, and S. L. Losoya, 1997, *Child Development, 68,* p. 305. Copyright 1997 by Society for Research in Child Development. Adapted with permission.

when the effects of attentional regulation were controlled in a regression analysis; thus, the quadratic effect was not included in the model.

Shyness. As discussed above, in 1992, we hypothesized that people who are moderately high in emotional intensity, high in behavioral inhibition and behaviorally overcontrolled, and low in the use of emotional regulation and constructive coping behaviors (e.g., attention shifting, activation control, instrumental coping) are likely to be shy and prone to negative internalizing emotions such as fear and anxiety. These individuals were expected to be prone to experience relatively intense negative emotional arousal in social (as well as nonsocial) situations that they cannot effectively modulate because of their difficulty in achieving optimal regulation. High levels of unregulated emotional arousal (particularly, negative emotion) tend to be experienced as aversive and, over time, are likely to increase the probability that social interactions are viewed as aversive and uncomfortable. Although the tendencies to experience intense negative emotions and shyness appear to have a genetic basis (see Plomin & Daniels, 1986; Plomin & Stocker, 1989), negative emotionality increasingly may become associated with social interactions if the emotional person feels that he or she is not successful in social encounters (Rubin, LeMare, & Lollis, 1990).

In an initial study with adults, people who reported being shy tended to be relatively low in attention shifting, activation control, and constructive coping, and high in avoidant coping, temperamental reactivity, negative emotional intensity, and dispositional negative affect (Eisenberg, Fabes, & Murphy, 1995). Moreover, these correlations for shyness, with the exception of avoidant coping, differed significantly from similar correlations with low sociability (i.e., a nonfearful preference for not affiliating with others). Shyness also was correlated with low intensity and frequency of positive emotion. Unexpectedly, however, shyness was modestly negatively related to inhibition control (the ability to voluntarily inhibit action), perhaps because shy individuals do not feel in control of their behavior. Even though they may be inhibited in their behavior, shy people may not feel that they are skilled at voluntarily inhibiting behavior when they feel it is appropriate to do so. Clearly, the shy individuals in this study did not feel that they were in control either of their attention or the initiation of behaviors that were aversive but appropriate or necessary. Thus, these findings suggest that shy individuals were low in emotional and voluntary behavioral regulation (Eisenberg, Fabes, & Murphy, 1995). However, it is quite possible that shyness, as assessed in this study, primarily tapped social inhibition based on concern about social evaluation rather than shyness based on wariness of unfamiliar people and things. Asendorpf (1993) hypothesized that people who are temperamentally shy often are not lacking in social skills.

In one of the longitudinal studies discussed above, we obtained parental reports of children's shyness at age 6 to 8, 8 to 10, and 10 to 12. Data on teacher- and parent-reported regulation, emotionality, and coping are available at the same ages and, sometimes, at ages 4 to 6. In general, adults' reports of children's shyness were positively related to internalizing negative emotion, coping by doing nothing, and, for parent-rated shyness, avoidant coping. Shyness also was negatively related to positive emotionality, instrumental coping, and seeking support from teachers (at younger ages). Often predictions held over several years, across reporters, or both. Interestingly, teachers' reports of shyness were associated with low attentional regulation (attention shifting and focusing), whereas parents' reports of shyness were correlated with relatively high levels of regulation (behavioral inhibition/nonimpulsivity, attention focusing). This may have occurred because parental reports of shyness seemed to tap temperamental shyness (as Asendorpf, 1990, found), whereas teachers' reports of shyness likely reflected social inhibition based on social evaluative concerns (e.g., they were negatively correlated with peer popularity and unrelated to reticence with a stranger). It is also possible that involuntary inhibition (low impulsivity) may be confused with effortful control (e.g., inhibition control).

We expected children low in attention shifting (an index of emotional regulation), who also were prone to intense and frequent internalizing emotions, to be especially high on rated shyness. Such children would be likely to experience negative emotions that they could not easily regulate. This interaction effect was obtained for parental reports of children's attentional control and internalizing negative emotion (e.g., fear, sadness, and physiological reactivity) at age 4 to 6 when predicting parent- and teacher-reported shyness at age 6 to 8 and parent-reported shyness at age 8 to 10. Such interactions were not found for teachers, or at age 10 to 12, perhaps because our measure of internalizing emotion at later ages was briefer and did not contain many items related to fear or autonomic reactivity, which Clark, Watson, and Mineka (1994) argued are linked to anxiety disorders.

☐ Summary

In our work, we have tried to document the importance of individual differences in emotionality and regulation on both positive and negative aspects of social functioning. We have found that one can make more sense of the empirical data by thinking about moderational and mediational relations as well as additive effects. For example, social competence and problem behaviors often are predicted both by high regulation and low negative emotionality, although regulation is a better predictor of outcomes for children prone to negative emotion. We also have found that we can learn more by considering various types of regulation and emotional reactions and by using multiple reporters and a multimethod approach to obtaining data. Sometimes, our facial or physiological data added information that was different from that provided by self- or other-report data; for example, relations between children's prosocial behavior and empathy-related responding have been much more consistent for these nonverbal measures than for self-report measures. Children may have difficulty assessing and reporting their internal states, and their reports may be contaminated by concerns about providing socially desirable responses. In general, each type of measure has different strengths and weaknesses, and provides somewhat different kinds of information. Nonetheless, facial or physiological measures may be especially useful for younger children because their self-reports often are not very predictive of outcomes. Thus, overall, our data support the current emphasis on process (mediation) and moderating relations, as well as multimethod, multireporter data, in the study of socioemotional development.

In regard to future directions, relatively little is known about the role of positive emotionality in the development and prediction of children's social competence and problem behaviors. It is likely that children prone to positive emotionality are relatively resilient and socially competent. In addition, it would be useful to differentiate among various negative emotions when predicting outcomes for children. Anger and frustration and emotions such as anxiety and sadness probably relate to different types of problem behaviors; moreover, different types of regulation may be more effective in moderating the relations between these two types of emotions and specific outcomes. For example, behavioral regulation may be especially crucial for managing anger and frustration, whereas attention shifting may be more particularly important in moderating the relation of anxiety or sadness to social behavior and internalizing problems. Thus, in the future, more differentiation among various emotions and types of regulation is desirable in research on the role of these aspects of functioning in the quality of social functioning.

☐ References

Asendorpf, J. B. (1990). Development of inhibition during childhood: Evidence for situational specificity and a two-factor model. *Developmental Psychology, 26*, 721–730.

Asendorpf, J. B. (1993). Beyond temperament. In K. H. Rubin & J. B. Asendorpf (Eds,), *Social withdrawal, inhibition, and shyness in childhood* (pp. 265–289). Hillsdale, NJ: Erlbaum.

Aspinwall, L. G., & Taylor, S. E. (1997). A stitch in time: Self-regulation and proactive coping. *Psychological Bulletin, 121*, 417–436.

Baron, R. M., & Kenny, D. A. (1986). The moderator-mediator variable distinction in social psychological research: Conceptual, strategic, and statistical considerations. *Journal of Personality and Social Psychology, 51*, 1173–1182.

Barron, A. P., & Earls, F. (1984). The relation of temperament and social factors to behavior problems in three-year-old children. *Journal of Child Psychology and Psychiatry, 25*, 23–33.

Bates, J. E., Bayles, K., Bennett, D. S., Ridge, B., & Brown, M. M. (1991). Origins of externalizing behavior problems at eight years of age. In D. Pepler & K. Rubin (Eds.), *Development and treatment of childhood aggression* (pp. 93–120). Hillsdale, NJ: Erlbaum.

Batson, C. D. (1991). *The altruism question: Toward a social-psychological answer*. Hillsdale, NJ: Erlbaum.

Batson, C. D., Dyck, J. L., Brandt, J. R., Batson, J. G., Powell, A. L., McMaster, M. R., & Griffitt, C. (1988). Five studies testing two new egotistic alternatives to the empathy-altruism hypothesis. *Journal of Personality and Social Psychology, 55*, 52–77.

Birnbaum, D. W., & Croll, W. L. (1984). The etiology of children's stereotypes about sex differences in emotionality. *Sex Roles, 10*, 677–691.

Block, J. H., & Block, J. (1980). The role of ego-control and ego-resiliency in the organization of behavior. In W. A. Collins (Ed.), *Development of cognition, affect, and social relations. The Minnesota Symposia on Child Psychology* (Vol. 13, pp. 39–101). Hillsdale, NJ: Erlbaum.

Blum, L. A. (1980). *Friendship, altruism and morality*. London: Routledge and Kegan Paul.

Bridges, L. J., & Grolnick, W. S. (1995). The development of emotional self-regulation in infancy and early childhood. In N. Eisenberg (Ed.), *Review of personality and psychology* (pp. 185–211). Newbury Park, CA: Sage.

Cacioppo, J. T., & Sandman, C. A. (1978). Physiological differentiation of sensory and cognitive tasks as a function of warning processing demands and reported unpleasantness. *Biological Psychology, 6,* 181–192.

Campos, J. (1984). A new perspective on emotions. *Child Abuse and Neglect, 8,* 147–156.

Campos, J. J., Mumme, D. L., Kermoian, R., & Campos, R. G, (1994). A functionalist perspective on the nature of emotion. In N. A. Fox (Ed.), *The development of emotion regulation: Biological and behavioral considerations. Monographs of the Society for Research in Child Development, 59*(Serial No. 240), *59*(Nos. 2–3), 284–303.

Carstensen, L. L. (1991). Selectivity theory: Social activity in life-span context. In K. W. Schaie (Ed.), *Annual review of geriatrics and gerontology* (Vol. 11). New York: Springer.

Caspi, A., Henry, B., McGee, R. O., Moffitt, T. E.,& Silva, P. A. (1995) Temperamental origins of child and adolescent behavior problems: From age 3 to age 15. *Child Development, 66,* 55–68.

Cialdini, R. B., Kenrick, D. T., & Baumann, D. J. (1982). Effects of mood on prosocial behavior in children and adults. In N. Eisenberg (Ed.), *The development of prosocial behavior* (pp. 339–359). New York: Academic Press.

Clark, L. A., Watson, D., & Mineka, S. (1994). Temperament, personality, and the mood and anxiety disorders. *Journal of Abnormal Psychology, 103,* 103–116.

Cole, P.M., Michel, M. K., & Teti, L. O. (1994). The development of emotion regulation and dysregulation: A clinical perspective. In N. Fox (Ed.), *Monographs of the Society for Research in Child Development, 59*(No. 2–3, Serial No. 240), 73–100.

Davis, M. H. (1994). *Empathy: A social psychological approach.* Madison, WI: Brown and Benchmark.

Derryberry, D., & Rothbart, M. K. (1988). Arousal, affect, and attention as components of temperament. *Journal of Personality and Social Psychology, 55,* 958–966.

Eisenberg, N., & Fabes, R. A. (1990). Empathy: Conceptualization, assessment, and relation to prosocial behavior. *Motivation and Emotion, 14,* 131–149.

Eisenberg, N., & Fabes, R. A. (1991). Prosocial behavior and empathy: A multimethod, developmental perspective. In P. Clark (Ed.), *Review of personality and social psychology* (Vol. 12, pp. 34–61). Newbury Park, CA: Sage.

Eisenberg, N., & Fabes, R. A. (1992). Emotion, regulation, and the development of social competence. In M. S. Clark (Ed.), *Review of personality and social psychology: Vol. 14. Emotion and social behavior* (pp. 119–150). Newbury Park, CA: Sage.

Eisenherg, N., & Fabes, R. A. (1995). The relation of young children's vicarious emotional responding to social competence, regulation, and emotionality. *Cognition and Emotion, 9,* 203–229.

Eisenberg, N., & Fabes, R. A. (1998). Prosocial development. In W. Damon (Series Ed.) & N. Eisenberg (Vol. Ed.), *Handbook of Child Psychology: Vol. 3. Social, emotional, and personality development* (5th ed., pp. 701–778). New York: Wiley.

Eisenberg, N., Fabes, R. A., Bernzweig, J., Karbon, M., Poulin, R., & Hanish, L. (1993). The relations of emotionality and regulation to preschoolers' social skills and sociometric status. *Child Development, 64,* 1418–1438.

Eisenberg, N., Fabes, R. A., Bustamante, D., Mathy, R. M., Miller, P., & Lindholm, E. (1988). Differentiation of vicariously-induced emotional reactions in children. *Developmental Psychology, 24,* 237–246.

Eisenberg, N., Fabes, R. A., Carlo, G., Troyer, D., Speer, A. L., Karbon, M., & Switzer, G. (1992). The relations of maternal practices and characteristics to children's vicarious emotional responsiveness. *Child Development, 63,* 583–602.

Eisenberg, N., Fabes, R. A., Guthrie, I. K., Murphy, B. C., Maszk, P., Holmgren, R., & Suh, K. (1996). The relations of regulation and emotionality to problem behavior in elementary school children. *Development and Psychopathology, 8,* 141–162.

Eisenberg, N., Fabes, R. A., & Losoya, S. (1997). Emotional responding: Regulation, social correlates, and socialization. In P. Salovey & D. J. Sluyter (Eds.), *Emotional development and emotional intelligence: Educational implications* (pp. 129–163). New York: Basic Books.

Eisenberg, N., Fabes, R. A., Miller, P. A., Fultz, J., Mathy, R. M., Shell, R., & Reno, R. R. (1989). The relations of sympathy and personal distress to prosocial behavior: A multimethod study. *Journal of Personality and Social Psychology, 57,* 55–66.

Eisenberg, N., Fabes, R. A., Miller, P. A., Shell, C., Shea, R., & May-Plumlee. T. (1990). Preschoolers' vicarious emotional responding and their situational and dispositional prosocial behavior. *Merrill-Palmer Quarterly, 36,* 507–529.

Eisenberg, N., Fabes, R. A., & Murphy, B. (1995). The relations of shyness and low sociability to regulation and emotionality. *Journal of Personality and Social Psychology, 68,* 505–517.

Eisenberg, N., Fabes, R. A., Murphy, B., Karbon, M., Maszk, P., Smith, M., O'Boyle, C., & Suh, K. (1994). The relations of emotionality and regulation to dispositional and situational empathy-related responding. *Journal of Personality and Social Psychology, 66,* 776–797.

Eisenberg, N., Fabes, R. A., Murphy, B., Karbon, M., Smith, M., & Maszk, P. (1996). The relations of children's dispositional empathy-related responding to their emotionality, regulation, and social functioning. *Developmental Psychology, 32,* 195–209.

Eisenberg, N., Fabes, R. A., Murphy, M., Maszk, P., Smith, M., & Karbon, M. (1995). The role of emotionality and regulation in children's social functioning: A longitudinal study. *Child Development, 66,* 1239–1261.

Eisenberg, N., Fabes, R. A., Nyman, M., Bernzweig, J., & Pinuelas, A. (1994). The relations of emotionality and regulation to children's anger-related reactions. *Child Development, 65,* 109-128.

Eisenberg, N., Fabes, R. A., Schaller, M., Carlo, G., & Miller, P. A. (1991). The relations of parental characteristics and practices to children's vicarious emotional responding. *Child Development, 62,* 1393–1408.

Eisenberg, N., Fabes, R. A., Schaller, M., Miller, P. A., Carlo, G., Poulin, R., Shea, C., & Shell, R. (1991). Personality and socialization correlates of vicarious emotional responding. *Journal of Personality and Social Psychology, 61,* 459-471.

Eisenberg, N., Fabes, R. A., Shepard, S. A., Murphy, B. C., Guthrie, I. K., Jones, S., Friedman, J., Poulin, R., & Maszk, P. (1997). Contemporaneous and longitudinal prediction of children's social functioning from regulation and emotionality. *Child Development, 68,* 642–664.

Eisenberg, N., Guthrie, I. K., Fabes, R. A., Reiser, M., Murphy, B. C., Holmgren, R., Maszk, P., & Losoya, S. (1997). The relations of regulation and emotionality to resiliency and competent social functioning in elementary school children. *Child Development, 68,* 295–311.

Eisenberg, N., Martin, C. L., & Fabes, R. A. (1906). Gender development and gender differences. In D. C. Berliner & R. C. Calfee (Eds.), *The handbook of educational psychology* (pp. 358–396). New York: Macmillan.

Eisenberg, N., & Miller, P. (1987). The relation of empathy to prosocial and related behaviors. *Psychological Bulletin, 101,* 91–119.

Eisenberg, N., & Okun, M. (1996). The relations of dispositional regulation and emotionality to elders' empathy-related responding and affect while volunteering. *Journal of Personality, 64,* 157–183.

Eisenberg, N., Schaller, M., Fabes, R. A., Bustamante, D., Mathy, R., Shell, R., & Rhodes, K. (1988). The differentiation of personal distress and sympathy in children and adults. *Developmental Psychology, 24,* 766–775.

Eisenberg, N., Shea, C. L., Carlo, G., & Knight, G. (1991). Empathy-related responding and cognition: A "chicken and the egg" dilemma. In W. Kurtines & J. Gewirtz (Eds.), *Handbook of moral behavior and development: Vol. 2. Research* (pp. 63–88). Hillsdale, NJ: Erlbaum.

Fabes, R. A., Eisenberg, N., & Eisenbud, L. (1993). Behavioral and physiological correlates of children's reactions to others' distress. *Developmental Psychology, 29,* 655–663.

Fabes, R. A., Eisenberg, N., Nyman, M., & Michealieu, Q. (1991). Young children's appraisals of others' spontaneous emotional reactions. *Developmental Psychology, 27,* 858–866.

Fowles, D. C. (1993). Electrodermal activity and antisocial behavior: Empirical findings and theoretical issues. In J. C. Roy, W. Boucsein, D. Fowles, & J. Gruzelier (Eds.), *Progress in electrodermal research* (pp. 1–4). London: Plenum Press.

Fox, N. A. (1989). Psychophysiological correlates of emotional reactivity during the first year of life. *Developmental Psychology, 25,* 364–372.

Guthrie, I. K., Eisenberg, N., Fabes, R. A., Murphy, B. C., Holmgren, R., Mazsk, P., & Suh, K. (1997). The relations of regulation and emotionality to children's situational empathy-related responding. *Motivation and Emotion, 21,* 87–108.

Hoffman, M. L. (1982). Development of prosocial motivation: Empathy and guilt. In N. Eisenberg (Ed.), *The development of prosocial behavior* (pp. 281–313). New York: Academic Press.

Hume, D. (1966). *Enquiries concerning the human understanding and concerning the principles of morals* (2nd ed.). Oxford, England: Clarendon Press. (Original work published 1777)

Karniol, R. (1982). Settings, scripts, and self-schemata: A cognitive analysis of the development of prosocial behavior. In N. Eisenberg (Ed.), *The development of prosocial behavior* (pp. 251–278). New York: Academic Press.

Kliewer, W. (1991). Coping in middle childhood: Relations to competence, type A behavior, monitoring, blunting, and locus of control. *Developmental Psychology, 27,* 689–697.

Kochanska, G. (1993). Toward a synthesis of parental socialization and child temperament in early development of conscience. *Child Development, 64,* 325–347.

Kochanska, G., Murray, K., Jacques, T. Y., Koenig, A. L., & Vandegeest, K. A. (1996). Inhibitory control in young children and its role in emerging internalization. *Child Development, 67,* 490–507.

Kopp, C. B. (1982). Antecedents of self-regulation: A developmental perspective. *Development Psychology, 18,* 199–214.

Kyrios, M., & Prior, M. (1990). Temperament, stress and family factors in behavioural adjustment of 3-5-year-old children. *International Journal of Behavioral Development, 13,* 67–93.

Lacey, J. I., Kagan, J., Lacey, B. C., & Moss, H. A. (1963). The visceral level: Situational determinants and behavioral correlates of autonomic response patterns. In P. H. Knapp (Ed.), *Expression of the emotions in man* (pp. 161–196). New York: International Universities Press.

Lahey, B. B., Hart, E. L, Pliszka, S., Applegate, B., & McBurnett, K. (1993). Neurophysiological correlates of conduct disorder: A rationale and review of the research. *Journal of Clinical Child Psychology, 22,* 141–153.

Larsen, R. J., & Diener, E. (1987). Affect intensity as an individual difference characteristic: A review. *Journal of Research in Personality, 21,* 1–39.

Lazarus, R. S., & Folkman, S. (1984). *Stress, appraisal, and coping.* New York: Springer.

Maccoby, E. E., & Jacklin, C. B. (1974). *The psychology of sex differences.* Stanford, CA: Stanford University Press.

Parke, R. D., Cassidy, J., Burks, V. M., Carson, J. L., & Boyum, L. (1992). Familial contributions to peer competence among young children: The role of interactive and affective processes. In R. D. Parke & G. W. Ladd (Eds.), *Family-peer relationships: Modes of linkage* (pp. 107–134). Hillsdale, NJ: Erlbaum.

Plomin, R., & Daniels, D. (1986). Genetics and shyness. In W. H. Jones, J. M. Cheek, & Briggs, S. R. (Eds.), *Shyness: Perspectives on research and treatment* (pp. 63–80). New York: Plenum Press.

Plomin, R., & Stocker, C. (1989). Behavioral genetics and emotionality. In I. S. Reznick (Ed.), *Perspectives on behavioral inhibition* (pp. 219–240). Chicago: Chicago University Press.

Porges, S. W., Doussard-Roosevelt, J. A., & Maiti, A. K. (1994). Vagal tone and the physiological regulation of emotion. In N. Fox (Ed.), *Monographs of the Society for Research in Child Development, 59*(Serial No. 240. Nos. 2–3), 167–186.

Prior, M. (1992). Childhood temperament. *Journal of Child Psychology and Psychiatry, 33,* 249–279.

Pulkkinen, L. (1982). Self-control and continuity from childhood to late adolescence. In P. B. Baltes & O. Brim, Jr. (Eds.), *Life-span development and behavior* (Vol. 4., pp. 63–105). New York: Academic Press.

Robins, R. W., John, O. P., Caspi, A., Moffitt, T. E., & Stouthamer-Loeber, M. (1996). Resilient, overcontrolled, and undercontrolled boys: Three replicable personality types. *Journal of Personality and Social Psychology, 70,* 157–171.

Rothbart, M, K,, Ahadi, S. A., & Hershey, K. L. (1994). Temperament and social behavior in childhood. *Merrill-Palmer Quarterly, 40,* 21–39.

Rothbart, M. K., & Derryberry, D. (1981). Development of individual differences in temperament. In M. E. Lamb & A. L. Brown (Eds.), *Advances in developmental psychology* (Vol. 1, pp. 37–86). Hillsdale, NJ: Erlbaum.

Rothbart, M. K., Ziaie, H., & O'Boyle, C. G. (1992). Self-regulation and emotion in infancy. *New Directions in Child Development, 55,* 7–23.

Rubin, K. H., Chen, X., & Hymel, S. (1993). Socioemotional characteristics of withdrawn and aggressive children. *Merrill-Palmer Quarterly, 39,* 518–534.

Rubin, K. H., LeMare, L. J., & Lollis, S. (1990). Social withdrawal in children: Developmental pathways to peer rejection. In S. R. Asher & J. D. Cole (Eds.), *Peer rejection in childhood* (pp. 217–249). Cambridge, England: Cambridge University Press.

Rushton, J. P., Brainerd, C. J., & Pressley, M. (1983). Behavioral development and construct validity: The principle of aggregation. *Psychological Bulletin, 94,* 18–38.

Saarni, C., Mumme, D., & Campos, J. J. (1998). Emotional development: Action, communication, and understanding. In W. Damon (Series Ed.) & N. Eisenberg (Vol. Ed.), *Social, emotional and personality development: Vol. 3. Handbook of child psychology* (5th ed., pp. 237–309). New York: Wiley.

Sandler, I. N., Tein, J., & West, S. G. (1994). Coping, stress and the psychological symptoms of children of divorce: A cross-sectional and longitudinal study. *Child Development, 65,* 1744–1763.

Staub, E. (1979). *Positive social behavior and morality: Vol. 2: Socialization and development.* New York: Academic Press.

Staub, E. (1984). Steps toward a comprehensive theory of moral conduct: Goal orientation, social behavior, kindness and cruelty. In J. Gewirtz & W. Kurtines (Eds.), *Morality, moral development, and moral behavior: Basic issues in theory and research* (pp. 241–260). New York: Wiley.

Stocker, C., & Dunn, J. (1990). Sibling relationships in childhood: Links with friendships and peer relationships. *British Journal of Developmental Psychology, 8,* 227–244.

Teglasi, H., & MacMahon, B. H. (1990). Temperament and common problem behaviors of children. *Journal of Applied Developmental Psychology, 11,* 331–349.

Tellegen, A. (1985). Structures of mood and personality and their relevance to assessing anxiety, with an emphasis on self-report. In A. H. Tuma & J. D. Maser (Eds.), *Anxiety and anxiety disorders* (pp. 681–706). Hillsdale, NJ: Erlbaum.

Thomas, A., Chess, S., & Birch, H. G. (1968). *Temperament and behavior disorders in children.* New York: New York University Press.

Thompson, R. A. (1994). Emotional regulation: A theme in search of definition. In N. Fox (Ed.). *Monographs of the Society for Research in Child Development, 59*(Serial No. 240, Nos. 2–3), 25–52.

Underwood, B., & Moore, B. (1982). Perspective-taking and altruism. *Psychological Bulletin, 91,* 143–173.

Windle, M., & Lerner, R. M. (1986). Reassessing the dimensions of temperamental individuality across the life span: The Revised Dimensions of Temperament Survey (DOTS-R). *Journal of Adolescent Research, 1,* 213–230.

Wood, J. V., Saltzberg, J. A., & Goldsamt, L. A. (1990). Does affect induce self-focused attention? *Journal of Personality and Social Psychology, 58,* 899–908.

CROSS-CUTTING THEMES

Robert H. Bradley
Robert F. Corwyn

Parenting

☐ Introduction

Perhaps it is true that every program of research has its own gravity, a small but enduring force that contributes to its shape and momentum. Our research revolves around a single question, How does the care that children receive affect the character and quality of their lives? The actual sequence of studies involves both this persistent pursuit and happy accident. The journey began with a phone call made on a whim by a graduate student (Robert H. Bradley) during the dead space between two holidays, a phone call that led to a job with one of the leading researchers on early child care and the task of analyzing data on what was then an unknown measure of parenting, the HOME Inventory (Caldwell & Bradley, 1984). The purpose of this chapter is to present an overview of this series of interlocking investigations on children's home environments with a view toward providing a perspective on parenting as the most powerful and enduring external force in the lives of children. The hope is to invite a more defined, if more complex, portrait of parenting than would have been conceivable 25 years ago.

The chapter is organized around four questions concerning parenting: (a) What is parenting? (b) What difference does parenting make in the lives of children? (c) How does context affect parenting? (d) Who performs the tasks of parenting? Throughout we discuss issues pertaining to the measurement of *parenting* (a.k.a., the home environment) because it is through the process of measurement that answers about parenting are both realized and constrained.

☐ What Is Parenting?

It is tempting to answer this question in a glib manner: Parenting is what parents do to take care of their children, rather like the classic response to what is intelligence (i.e., it's what intelligence tests measure). The fact is, what adults do in their role as parents has changed over the centuries, a function of techno-logical, social, and economic adjustments. But, the goal of parenting has remained essentially the same, to enable children to become competent, caring adults who are able to function well within society (Maccoby, 1992). For any place and any era, attaining the goal is no mean feat. This seemingly innocuous generic prescription requires a plethora of specific parenting actions carried out over a lengthy period of time fitted to a particular child's needs and executed within the boundaries of the resources and constraints present.

The Tasks of Parenting

We recently constructed a system for organizing the tasks of parenting (Bradley & Caldwell, 1995). It derives from systems theory, and is organized around the concept that the environment (parenting) helps to regulate the course of development (Sameroff & Friese, 1991). Central to our framework is the notion that *optimal parenting* (a facilitative home environment) is best conceived of as a set of regulatory acts and conditions aimed at successful adaptation and at successful exploitation of opportunity structures for children (Saegert & Winkel, 1990). Such a conception seems in keeping with ecological developmental theories that portray human beings as phylogenetically advanced, self-constructing organisms and the environment as a regulator (actually, coregulator) of complex developmental processes (Ford & Lerner, 1992). This framework is also consonant with the idea that children are conscious agents who are active in adapting to their environments (Lewis, 1997). Starting from this basic notion, we identified five basic regulatory tasks (or functions) performed by parents: (a) sustenance, (b) stimulation, (c) support, (d) structure, and (e) surveillance.

The first three regulatory functions derive from what is known about human needs and arousal systems. Specifically, Maslow (1954) centended that human beings need environments which promote survival, provide information (including enlistment of attention), and affirm worth. Relatedly, Ford and Lerner (1992) identified three major domains of organismic functioning each with its own arousal processes: (a) biological/physical-activity arousal, (b) cognitive-attention arousal, and (c) social/emotional-emotional arousal (Ford & Lerner, 1992). For complex living systems such as human beings, the task of maintaining internal unity is quite complicated due to the large number of component subsystems involved and the elaborateness of their organization (Ford & Lerner, 1992). To deal with the child's individuality and complexity, parents must perform other functions which assure that the direct inputs designed to sustain, stimulate, and emotionally support the child are maximally fitted to the child's current needs, proclivities, and competencies; hence, structure and surveillance.

Sustenance.   "The growth, health, and functioning of the human body as a physical entity requires the ability to collect and use appropriate material/energy forms and to protect against potentially damaging ones" (Ford & Lerner, 1992, p. 103). We call *sustenance parenting* acts and conditions that are designed to promote biological integrity. Parents must provide adequate nutrients, shelter, and conditions for the maintenance of health to ensure both survival and the level of biological integrity needed for physical and psychological development (Pollitt, 1988). Parents also must protect children from pathogenic conditions such as pollutants, passive cigarette smoke, and exposure to heavy metals (Evans et al., 1991; J. L. Jacobson, Jacobson, Padgett, Brummitt, & Billings, 1992; Tong & McMichael, 1992).

Stimulation.   To ensure competence and continued effort toward life-enhancing goals, the environment must provide sensory data that engage attention and provide information (i.e., stimulation). There is an abundance of both psychological theory and empirical data to buttress the significance of stimulation for cognitive, psychomotor, and social development (Horowitz, 1987). Development in every domain of competency requires a manageable amount of meaningful information (Caldwell, 1968),

Support.   Optimal social-emotional development depends on having an environment which responds to human social and emotional needs (Bretherton & Waters, 1985). Such acts and conditions we call support. Some acts of support are given in anticipation of unexpressed needs, others following expressed needs. Emotions function to prepare human beings to take action in their own best interest (Grinker et al., 1956). Parents must assist in enlisting and modulating the motivational properties of emotions to help ensure optimal fit with environmental demands.

There also is evidence that children benefit from positive affirmation of worth (Ausubel, 1968; Roberts, 1986). That is, to be supportive, parents must be reinforcing (in a proactive sense) as well as responsive (in a reactive sense). How worth is affirmed varies substantially from culture to culture. In some societies worth is closely tied to individual accomplishments or status; in others, it is more strongly tied to collective commitments and involvement. Finally, a supportive environment is one that provides guidance or direction for adequate functioning in other environments (Pettit, Dodge, & Brown, 1988). At its base, support is motivational preparation for encountering other environments.

Structure.   Although children need sustenance, stimulation, and support for optimal growth and development, there also is evidence that the relation between these inputs and either growth or development is not constant. Receiving equal amounts of these inputs does not seem to result in equal amounts of "good" growth and development. The arrangement of inputs may be as crucial to development as amount.

In sum, optimal parenting consists not only in ensuring that sufficient amounts of stimulation, sustenance, and support reach a child, but in configuring or structuring a child's encounters with those direct inputs so that "fit" is achieved. What fits one child's needs may not be suitable at all for another child. A good example may be seen in the differential responsiveness of preterm infants and infants prenatally exposed to drugs. Such biologically vulnerable infants often are overwhelmed by levels of stimulation that are quite comfortable for normal babies (Friedman & Sigman, 1996).

Surveillance.   To be effective in the management of inputs to a system, the regulatory apparatus designed to control the system must monitor both the system and its context. This important regulatory function performed by parents (or their proxies) we call surveillance. It involves "keeping track of" the whereabouts and activities of the child and the child's surrounding circumstances. Most commonly, surveillance has been thought of as keeping track of the child and of environmental conditions to which the child is exposed so as to protect the child from harm (Darling & Steinberg, 1993; U.S. Department of Health and Human Services, 1991; Lozoff, 1989; Patterson, DeBaryshe, & Ramsey, 1989; Peterson, Ewigman, & Kivlahan, 1993). However, surveillance also includes observations of the child and the environment designed to determine how much the physical and social environment affords the child for productive and enjoyable engagements.

Does careful attention to these five parenting tasks promote positive adaptation in children? The most straightforward answer is: The research is incomplete. However, there is suggestive evidence. For example, we recently conducted a study of 243 premature, low birth weight children living in chronic poverty. The purpose was to determine whether the availability of protective factors in the home environment at age 1 and at age 3 increased the probability of resiliency. Resiliency was operationalized as being in good to excellent health, being within the normal range for growth, not being below clinically designated cutoffs for maladaptive behavior on the Child Behavior Checklist, and having an IQ of 85 or greater. Six home environment factors were considered potentially protective: (a) low household density, (b) the availability of a safe play area, (c) parental acceptance and lack of punitiveness, (d) parental responsivity, (e) the availability of learning materials, and (f) variety of experiences. The first two would be classified under the category, sustenance; the second two under the category, support; and the final two under the category, stimulation. Fifteen percent of the children with three or more protective factors present in the home at age 1 were classified as resilient. By contrast, only 2% of children with two or fewer protective factors were classified as resilient. Similarly, 20% of children with three or more protective factors present in the home at age 3 were classified as resilient, whereas only 6% of children with two or fewer protective factors were resilient (Bradley, Whiteside, et al., 1994).

The Parenting Environment

Closely related to the idea of parenting tasks is the idea of a place where parenting occurs. It seems useful to think of the environment for parenting as including all the social and physical phenomena within the child's home place (Wachs, 1992; Wapner, 1987; Wohlwill & Heft, 1977). However, it is probably counterproductive to confine the concept of the parenting environment to a particular place, even though the concepts of parenting and home are semantically linked. In a child's mind, or in a parent's mind, what constitutes "home" probably will not refer exclusively to those events, objects, and actions within the four walls of a particular residence (or within the property lines that define a place of residence). Home experiences may include any number of events seen as connected to home and family but not coterminous with the physical boundaries of a place. A walk around the block with Dad, a visit to the local library with Mom, or argument between Mom and Dad in the car on the way to McDonald's all may be strongly associated with the network of acts and events that comprise a child's home life. By the same token, the concept of the home environment as fully divorced from any place of residence probably is not useful either, because the idea of home is generally associated with identifiable places. For both parent and child, many of the ideas and attitudes connected with "home" have their roots in scenes, episodes, and "scripts" that emanate from particular concrete places where family activities occur (Abelson, 1981).

The concept of the home environment might best be defined as phenomena emanating from the family setting. The boundaries become somewhat permeable and expansive, a boundary of meaning—not just bricks or fences. Such a capacious definition is consistent with the position of social anthropologists who contend that the social boundaries of household units do not necessarily coincide with the physical boundaries of their dwellings (Altman, 1977). Such an expansive definition seems more appropriate when one considers actual living conditions for some children (e.g., families living in cars or makeshift shelters). The concept of the parenting environment as not fully confined to a specific place becomes useful because the role of parent tends to shift from that of direct provider and teacher (most of which may well take place within the family residence) to that of mentor, guide, and arranger of experiences (some of which almost certainly will occur outside the four walls of the residence) (Fagot & Kavanaugh 1993; Maccoby & Martin, 1983).

The parenting environment is best understood not only on the basis of the activities and objects it contains or generates, but also on the basis of its instrumentality for child care and child rearing (Korosec-Serafty, 1985). For individual parents there is a sense of boundary to the spaces where parenting takes place, but what actually constitutes the boundary varies across parents and time depending on an array of cultural, familial, personal, and child factors (Belsky, 1984; Bronfenbrenner, 1979). In effect, what is appropriated to the idea of the home environment is the meaning of the acts, objects, and places connected to parental caregiving. Different families may utilize different geographic settings to be part of the parenting environment (e.g., the street beside the house, the backyard, a neighborhood park). The parenting environment encompasses the locations where the activities of parental caregiving take place (Rapoport, 1985).

☐ What Difference Does Parenting Make in the Lives of Children?

Answering this question has dominated our attention for the past 25 years. To answer the question, we have relied on the HOME Inventory, perhaps the most widely used measures of the home environment in the world. HOME was created by Caldwell and her colleagues at the Syracuse Early Learning Center in the mid-1960s; and we, along with Caldwell, have continued to work with the HOME ever since. The HOME does not comprehensively cover all five of the parenting dimensions described above; nor does it fully capture the myriad aspects of home life. However, HOME is widely known and its properties are well understood. Perhaps, more importantly, the lessons we have learned from constructing the measure, doing research with it, and addressing numerous questions from others who have used it allow us a useful perspective on the meaning of parenting.

The HOME Inventory is different from some other measures of the home environment in that the data are collected from the perspective of a particular child. It is well known that children growing up in a particular family do not always have the exact same experiences. Some get more attention than others, some receive harsher punishment than others, and some are read to more than others. The current interest in within-family differences in experience and development provides ample testimony to this belief (Dunn, 1991; Plomin & Daniels, 1987). The HOME tries to capture these personal histories of experience and living conditions.

HOME is designed to assess the quality and quantity of stimulation and support available to children in the home environment (Caldwell & Bradley, 1984). There are four versions of the inventory: The Infant-Toddler version is designed for children from birth to age 3, the Early Childhood version for children age 3 to 6, the Middle Childhood version for children from age 6 to 10, and the Early Adolescent version for children age 10 to 14 (see Bradley, 1994, and Bradley, Corwyn, & Whiteside-Mansell, 1996, for reviews). Table 16.1 includes a list of the subscales from these four inventories.

The information needed to score the inventories is obtained through a combination of observation and semistructured interviews done at home when both the child and the child's primary caregiver are present. Other family members also often are present during the 45–90-minute visit as well. The visit is designed to minimize intrusiveness and to allow family members to act as naturally as possible.

HOME and Children's Development

What have we learned from our long history with the HOME? The first thing is that the HOME seems to "work" in the sense that it provides a reasonably accurate—if limited—picture of the home environment, one that is correlated with a wide range of developmental markers in a wide range of populations. In a series of studies done in the late 1970s and early 1980s, we found that scores on the Infant-Toddler and Early Childhood versions of HOME consistently showed positive correlations with cognitive and language

---

TABLE 16.1. Subscales of the HOME Inventories

Infant-Toddler HOME
1. Parental Responsivity
2. Acceptance
3. Organization of the Environment
4. Learning Materials
5. Parental Involvement
6. Variety of Experience

Early Childhood HOME
1. Learning Materials
2. Language Stimulation
3. Physical Environment
4. Parental Responsivity
5. Academic Stimulation
6. Modeling
7. Variety of Experience
8. Acceptance

Middle Childhood HOME
1. Parental Responsivity
2. Encouragement of Maturity
3. Acceptance
4. Learning Materials
5. Enrichment
6. Family Companionship
7. Parental Involvement

Early Adolescent HOME
1. Physical Environment
2. Learning Materials
3. Modeling
4. Instructional Activities
5. Regulatory Activities
6. Variety of Experiences
7. Acceptance and Responsivity

---

development from infancy through the early school years (Bradley & Caldwell, 1976a, 1976b, 1979b, 1980a, 1982, 1984b; Elardo, Bradley, & Caldwell, 1975, 1977). Importantly, we found that these relations obtained for boys as well as girls, Blacks as well as Whites, and poor as well as rich (Bradley & Caldwell, 1981; Bradley, Caldwell, et al., 1989).

Our findings have been corroborated by dozens of other researchers in the United States and throughout the world. Correlations between the Infant-Toddler HOME and measures of infant developmental status (usually the Bayley Scales) typically do not exceed .40 during the first year of life (Adams, Campbell, & Ramey, 1984; Allen, Affleck, McGrade, & McQueeney, 1984; Bakeman & Brown, 1980; Bee, Mitchell, Barnard, Eyres, & Hammond, 1984; Carlson, Labarba, Sclafani, & Bowers, 1986; Coll, Vohr, Hoffman, & Oh, 1986; Cooney, Bell, McBride, & Carter, 1989; Elardo et al., 1975; Johnson, Breckenridge, & McGowan, 1984; Lozoff, Park, Radan, & Wolf, 1995; Moore, Bushnell, & Goldberg, 1989; Pederson, Evans, Chance, Bento, & Fox, 1988; Siegel, 1982; Stevenson & Lamb, 1979; Wilson & Matheny, 1983). However, the strength of the relation increases during the second year of life, with correlations generally ranging from .20 to .50 (Bergeman & Plomin, 1988; Consullo, 1992; Palti, Otrakul, Belmaker, Tamir, & Tepper, 1984). Although the upward trend in correlations may partially reflect the fact that infant tests contain a larger proportion of language-oriented items by age 2, research by Belsky, Garduque, and Hrncir (1984) has suggested that the higher correlations are not mere artifacts of the changing content of infant tests. They obtained correlations between HOME scores and children's performance (.64 to .73), competence (.51 to .63), and executive capacity (.27 to .46), during play at 12, 15, and 18 months. Exceptions to the generally upward trend for correlations during the second year of life included poor Hispanics and poor African Americans (Adams et al., 1984; Johnson et al., 1984). Although these two exceptions may reflect a lack of measurement equivalence, they may instead reflect a more restricted range of scores on the HOME for Hispanics. They also may reflect chronic conditions of poverty that are prevalent in these minority groups (McLoyd, 1990).

Most studies have shown low-to-moderate correlations (.20 to .60) between HOME scores during the first 2 years of life and later tests of intelligence and achievement (Bee et al., 1982; Bradley & Caldwell, 1976b, 1984b; Bradley, Caldwell, & Rock, 1988; Coons, Fulker, DeFries. & Plomin, 1990; Elardo et al., 1975; Gottfried & Gottfried, 1984, 1988; Johnson, Breckenridge, McGowan, 1984; Siegel, 1982; Stevens & Bakeman, 1985; Wilson & Matheny, 1983). However, in a study of Mexican American children (Johnson et al., 1984), correlations were negligible; for lower-middle-class Costa Ricans, they were somewhat lower than correlations observed in most other groups, but still significant. The studies may indicate that different relations obtain for Latin populations, but the differences are difficult to interpret given measures of intellectual competence originally were constructed using Hispanics (Super & Harkness, 1986). The contributions of culture, social status, and recency of immigration to the observed disparate results remain unclear. The increasing magnitude of correlation from birth to age 3 probably results from a number of factors: early biological protection, the changing content of mental tests, and particular children.

HOME scores obtained when children were between 3 and 5 years old showed moderate correlations (.30 to .60) with contemporaneous measures of children's intellectual and academic performance (Billings, Jacobson, Jacobson, & Brumitt, 1989; Bradley & Caldwell, 1984b; Bradley, Caldwell, & Rock, 1988; Chua, Kong, Wong, & Yoong, 1989; Gottfried & Gottfried, 1988; Hawk, et al., 1986; McMichael et al., 1988; Sahu & Devi, 1982). The more restricted the socioeconomic status range, the more attenuated the correlations. However, no difference was found between farm and nonfarm children who otherwise had a similar diversity in socioeconomic status (S. Jacobson, Jacobson, Brunitt, & Jones, 1987).

Transactional and general systems theories of development (Ford & Lerner, 1992; Sameroff, 1983) portray development as a joint function of both what the environment affords a person by way of experiences and what the person brings to the environment by way of capabilities and behavioral tendencies. As an example, Bradley, Caldwell, Rock, Casey, and, Nelson (1987) found that, for low birth weight infants, home environment in combination with child medical status predicted 18-month Bayley scores better than either did alone. A study of language delayed, Down's syndrome, and normally developing children by Wulbert, Inglis, Kriegsmann, and Millis (1975) offered yet another view of the transactional process. A high correlation (.76) was obtained in the combined sample, attesting to the impact extreme scores can have on correlations. The results are ambiguous with respect to direction of causality. It could result from effects of the children's low capabilities on the richness of the environment that these children are afforded, as well as from effects on the children's capabilities by an environment in which stimulation and support for development are far below average.

Correlations between Early Childhood HOME scores and later academic achievement have been generally low to moderate (Bradley & Caldwell, 1979; Gottfried, Gottfried, Bathhurst, & Guerin, 1994; Hammond, Bee, Barnard, & Eyres, 1983; Jordan, 1976). In one study involving 55 Black and 30 White children, HOME scores were correlated with Science Research Associates Achievement Test scores obtained when the children were 6 to 10 years old (Bradley & Caldwell, 1978). HOME shared about 25% of variance with each achievement domain. Moderate correlations were obtained for both Black males and Black females; but significant residual correlations remained for males only when socioeconomic status and 3-year IQ were partialed out (Bradley & Caldwell, 1980a). Gottfried, Gottfried, and Bathurst (1994) found that high achieving 7- and 8-year-olds experienced more enriched home environments than classmates who had lower levels of achievement.

Our experience with the Middle Childhood and Early Adolescent versions of HOME is more limited. In one of the first studies, we obtained low-to-moderate correlations between HOME subscale scores and school performance for 11-year-olds (Bradley, Caldwell, Rock, Hamrick, & Harris, 1988). Responsivity, Learning Materials, Active Stimulation, and Physical Environment showed the strongest relations. A separate analysis of 8- to 10-year-old African American students (Bradley, Caldwell, Rock, Casey, & Nelson, 1987) revealed that Responsivity and Emotional Climate had the most consistent relations. Other researchers found that high-achieving students were living in homes characterized by more Materials for learning, more Active Stimulation, greater Family Participation in enriching activities, and a higher level of parental Responsivity (Gottfried et al., 1994).

Information on the HOME-achievement relation, though scanty, indicates that children's achievement during early and middle childhood is related to the home environment. Results from studies by Gottfried and Gottfried (1988), Gottfried et al. (1994), Bradley and Caldwell (1981), and Jordan (1976) indicated that the relation is strong for both European Americans and African Americans. Kurtz, Borkowski, and Deshmukh (1988) also found a significant relation between HOME scores and school achievement for children in Nagpur, India. However, the sex, race, and social class differences obtained in those investigations suggest a complex relation.

The total score from the Early Adolescent HOME was significantly related to the Wide Range Achievement Test-third edition (WRAT-3) in a sample of 10- to 15-year-olds (Bradley, Whiteside-Mansell, & Corwyn, 1997). So, too, were all seven subscale scores. Analyses also were performed separately for four sociocultural groups (European American, African American, Hispanic American, and Asian American). Early Adolescent HOME scores were correlated with WRAT-3 scores in all four groups, but the pattern of correlations varied according to subscales. For Asian Americans, only the Learning Materials subscale was related to achievement test performance (.58); but, for the other three groups, achievement was related to other subscales as well (particularly, Modeling). For Hispanic Americans, WRAT-3 scores were correlated with all subscales except Physical Environment. The total score, and all subscales except Regulatory Activities, were significantly related to adolescents' self-reported grades in school.

Scores on the HOME are also associated with social development. A major component of social competence is the ability of a child to enter into and sustain social relations. Bakeman and Brown (1980) followed 21 preterm and 22 full-term Black low-income children from 9 months to 3 years of age. The Responsivity scale from the Infant-Toddler HOME predicted both social participation (involvement with others) and social competence (ability to navigate the social world smoothly, gaining both material and emotional goods from others in socially acceptable ways). Other studies also indicated that the quality of the home environment in general, and Responsivity in particular, are related to adaptive social competence during early and middle childhood (Jordan, 1979; Lamb et al., 1988; Tedesco, 1981). A good example is a study of behavior problems in very low birth weight Dutch children (Weiglas-Kuperus, Koot, Baerts, Fetter, & Sauer, 1993). They found that HOME scores at ages 1 and 3½ years were correlated with clinician ratings of behavior problems. Scores on the HOME at 3½ years also were correlated with the total problems score on the Child Behavior Checklist.

Although not actually an index of social competence per se, having an internal locus of control is considered salient for good mental health and adaptive functioning (Rotter, Chance, & Phares, 1972). We reported low, but significant, correlations between the Early Childhood HOME and locus of control orientation at age 6 to 8 years (Bradley & Caldwell, 1979a).

One of the most intensive investigations of the relation between HOME and children's social and behavioral competence was a prospective longitudinal study involving 267 high-risk mothers from Minnesota (Erickson, Stroufe, & Egeland, 1985). Securely attached infants who later showed behavior problems had mothers who provided less support and encouragement during problem solving and families that scored lower on the Learning Materials and Involvement subscales from Infant-Toddler HOME. Relatedly, anxiously attached infants who later showed no behavior problems had mothers who were more supportive, and provided clearer structure and better instruction during instructional tasks. Their mothers also had better social support and better relationships. Likewise, their families scored higher on the Learning Materials and Involvement subscales. From first through third grade children were rated on peer competence and emotional health by their teachers (Stroufe, Egeland, & Kreutzer, 1990). The ratings were averaged; and this mean rating was regressed on 6-year Middle Childhood HOME, 2½-year Infant-Toddler HOME, kindergarten rank, child functioning in preschool, and infant attachment classification. All variables in the model, save attachment classification, made a significant contribution. In general, the findings tend to support Bowlby's (1958) general model of development in which both the total developmental history and current circumstances are given important roles in social competence.

We analyzed data from a multisite study of 549 low birth weight children which illustrates some of the potential complexity of the relation between home environment and adaptive social behavior during the first 3 years of life (Bradley et al., 1992). This study, involving Infant-Toddler HOME at 1 year and Early Childhood HOME at 3 years plus three measures of adaptive social behavior at 2½ to 3 years showed that: (a) correlations between 3-year Early Childhood HOME and social competence tended to be higher than correlations with 1-year Infant-Toddler HOME, though not uniformly so; (b) different HOME subscales were related to different aspects of adaptive social functioning; (c) there was little evidence that parental nurturance (e.g., Acceptance, Responsivity) during infancy was more strongly associated with 3-year adaptive social behavior than was parental nurturance around age 3, but apparently cognitive stimulation (e.g., Learning Materials, Variety) at age 3 was more important than at age 1; and (d) social behavior was predicted better by a combination of support and stimulation factors than with either alone.

We also examined the relation of both Infant-Toddler HOME and Middle Childhood HOME to classroom behavior at 10 to 11 years of age as assessed with the Classroom Behavior Inventory (CBI; Bradley, Rock, Caldwell, & Brisby, 1989). A few significant correlations emerged between Infant-Toddler HOME and the three dimensions tapped by the CBI. Many more emerged between the Middle Childhood HOME and classroom behavior. Both Active Involvement and Family Participation were moderately correlated with consideration, task orientation, and school adjustment. Responsivity also was correlated with consideration and adjustment. The researchers also used the data to examine three models of environmental action: Model I (primacy of early experience), Model II (predominance of contemporary environment), and Model III (cumulative effects in stable environments). Though all three models received some support, the strongest support was for Model II. The importance of the early environment was supported in terms of significant partial correlations between Responsivity and considerate classroom behavior, even with the intervening environment controlled. Similar results were obtained for Variety. The salience of the contemporary environment received greatest support in the case of the Family Participation and Active Involvement subscales and classroom behavior (task orientation, consideration, adjustment). The relation of Involvement to considerate behavior seems largely a function of the cumulative effects of parental involvement.

Scores on the Early Adolescent HOME were related to several measures of social competence (Bradley, Whiteside-Mansell, & Corwyn, 1997). The total score and all seven subscale scores were moderately related to three measures of self-efficacy (self-efficacy related to school, self-efficacy related to family, and self-efficacy related to peers). There were a couple of exceptions to the general pattern but most correlations were significant. The total score and scores from most subscales also were related to parents' reports of adolescent considerateness versus hostility in the home.

Findings by Bakeman and Brown (1980); Lamb et al. (1988); Erickson, Stroufe, and Egeland (1985); Mink and Nihira (1987); and Bradley, Caldwell, Rock, Barnard, Gray, et al. (1989) suggested that particular parenting practices may interact with both particular child characteristics (e.g., quality of attachment, difficult temperament, level of disability) and broader ecological factors (e.g., marital quality, support from extended family, overall family style) to affect the course of social development. Moreover, the study by Plomin, Loehlin, and DeFries (1985) showing little relation between HOME and behavior problems in adopted children but a significant, yet small (.23), relation for nonadopted children suggests that genetic factors may play a role.

We have learned one other thing in using the HOME with families: The process of gathering data about what goes on in the family changes subtly as children get older. A young mother, fresh from the experience of trying to calm a child with colic, may decry the notion that she has much control in the child's life; but parents of infants generally have far greater control over what their children do and what happens to them than do parents of 10-year-olds. Ten-year-olds are much more involved in home visits and have much more influence over what is said and done than do 2-year-olds. Adolescents are far more likely to contradict what the parent says during the interview than are 4-year-olds, and the parents of adolescents may have less certain knowledge about the adolescent's daily routine than parents of a toddler. The dynamic becomes more like that of equals as children age. Both adolescent and parent are more likely to engage in protective and deceptive behavior in the others' presence than is true of 3-year-olds and parents.

Earlier we described the basic ingredients of a good home environment (a.k.a, good parenting). There is no evidence that, at a deep level, adolescents need anything different from their environments than do infants; actually, there is no evidence that it changes at any time in the life span. However, the patterns and amounts of particular ingredients salient for well-being certainly change. The younger the child, the more life is lived in the moment. What counts is what is happening here and now. There is an immediacy and an intimacy to life's experiences. As children age, the meaning of life, its phenomenology, stretches in time and space—such is the advantage of growing memory and competence.

When constructing the four versions of HOME, we faced numerous technical concerns, but we also faced two substantive concerns: (a) What environmental dimensions or constructs are most salient to measure at each developmental period? (b) How does one most accurately capture the salient dimensions or constructs? That is, what set of processes and indicators are most informative? It has been a struggle and, though we are proud of the acceptance of the Inventories, our resolutions to these issues have been far from fully satisfactory. Our approach has been catholic. We have looked at developmental theory and we have reviewed the empirical literature on the relationship between environment and development for the major developmental periods of childhood. In addition, we have consulted with both parents and professionals regarding their beliefs concerning what is important for children at different ages.

An examination of the content of the four versions of HOME (see Table 16.1) makes concrete our judgment concerning what is salient at each of the four age periods we have assessed. Some of the dimensions or constructs measured for the various age periods are the same, some are different. For example, at each age period, we include items that measure parental responsivity, the amount and variety of materials for learning, whether harsh child management techniques are used (whether the parent is accepting of the child), whether a variety of enriching experiences are made available to the child, and so forth. However, at each developmental period, we also include items that seem particularly relevant for that age period. For example, during infancy, we assess whether parents encourage the development of particular developmental competencies (e.g., walking, talking). During early childhood, the focus shifts to an assessment of whether parents teach preacademic skills like learning colors and shapes and whether parents provide conditions that facilitate the development of the kind of social skills required to function well outside the home. During middle childhood, there is, for the first time, an assessment of the overall emotional climate in the home and an assessment of whether the family does things as a unit. During early adolescence, there is a particular concern with the kinds of rules and policies established for the adolescent and the types of monitoring practices used. Clearly, as children age, the role of parent shifts gradually from that of direct provider of experiences and conditions (caretaker) to that of guide, broker, and facilitator of experiences. Things often are done at a greater distance and over a longer period of time—monitoring the whereabouts of a baby and monitoring the life and times of an adolescent require quite different actions. Things more often are done in league with other adults and other institutions (e.g., church, school, youth organization).

How one views the issue of age differences (or similarities) in the parenting environment depends on one's level of analysis. As stated above, we measure some dimensions (e.g.. parental responsivity) at every developmental age, but the particular indicators we use to reveal those dimensions may change (responding to an infant's vocalization vs. encouraging a 10-year-old to contribute to a conversation, giving an infant a rattle vs. giving an 8-year-old a guitar, taking a 4-year-old to the park vs. arranging for an adolescent to go to a dance camp). Two things are clear. First, the particular needs that children express from moment to moment change as children age; thus, what they require from their home environments in order to do well changes accordingly. And, indeed, the home environment of a young child is quite different from the home environment of an adolescent in almost every way, including its physical arrangements (Bradley, 1995). Second, children become more competent (self-sufficient) as they grow older and they are able to fashion their environments more to meet their desires. Scarr and McCartney (1983) argued that, when children are young, their influence on the environment is mostly passive; by their actions they elicit different responses from their caregivers. That is, it is not that children are not active in trying to shape their environments, but they lack the full range of capacities needed to construct or find environments highly suited to their needs. However, as they become more competent, children seek out and construct environments that more fully meet their needs.

Parenting from the Child's Point of View

Knowing what parents do is one thing, knowing how it matters in the lives of children is quite another. In his tantalizing book, *Altering Fate*, Lewis (1997) made much of the fact that it is extraordinarily difficult to predict the course of individual lives. It is not just that the measures of parenting and the measures of children's characteristics are imperfectly reliable. It is not just that developmental theory is imprecise. It is not even just that there are a myriad biological and contextual factors that impinge on development. Lewis (1997) argued that predicting the course of individual development is difficult because accidental occurrences pervade our real lives. He also argued that predicting the course of development for individuals is difficult because we are conscious beings; thus, part of our fate is in our own hands. We make meaning of what we experience and we make choices that affect our lives.

Our own research leads us to believe that the meaning a child makes of any particular action on the part of parents is conditioned by the full tableaux of experiences within the family. Family life is complexly organized and its influence on the lives of children involves a myriad of interwoven processes. For example, there is growing evidence that actions occurring at multiple levels of the environment influence how children interpret what parents do. A specific parenting action operates at the foreground of a child's conscious awareness. That action is set against a background of other actions; and, it is this background, together with the foreground, that determines the meaning a child makes of the specific action. Figure 16.1 depicts these levels.

Most domains of parental action (or the home environment, more broadly) can be segmented into subdomains that are psychologically distinguishable by a child. For example, the domain of parental responsivity appears to be composed of several distinct subdomains (e.g., communicative responsiveness, responsivity to distress, physical responsiveness). A similar breakdown could be made of other parenting (home environmental) domains. Provision of stimulation could include language stimulation, exposing the child to an array of objects and materials, providing enriching experiences such as visits to places of commerce and culture, and so forth.

To illustrate how these multiple levels of the environment operate to determine the meaning of a parental action for a child, let us begin with a representative action (i.e., a specific action that operates in the

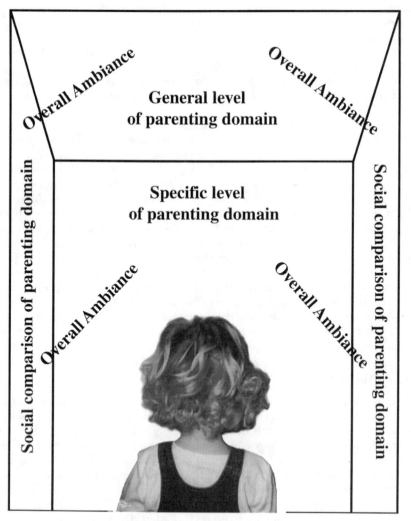

FIGURE 16.1. The multiple levels of the parenting environment experienced by children.

foreground of a child's conscious awareness). Suppose Eddie, Jr. attempts to get Dad's attention, but that Dad is only vaguely responsive to Eddie's question because Dad is busy watching television. Eddie's experiences with Dad in the area of communication may lead Eddie to conclude that Dad is not a very responsive communicator (i.e., at a specific level of communication, the child may judge Dad to be nonresponsive). But, the meaning Eddie makes of this action probably will not depend only on how responsive Dad is in this specific domain (communication), but also on how responsive in general Dad is to Eddie's needs and interests. Eddie's reaction is likely to be conditioned by Dad's general level of responsiveness (i.e., responsiveness across subdomains–responsivity to distress, responsiveness in play, and so forth). Most domains of the environment that directly involve the child (e.g., parental responsivity, object stimulation, the structuring of learning opportunities) appear to function both at a general (across subdomains) level and at a more specific (within subdomains) level in terms of their influence on behavior.

What a child makes of a particular parental action also reflects how the parent treats other household members in similar situations (in the same subdomain)—a social comparison level. That is, the child will compare his or her treatment to the treatment given others. To follow our scenario regarding Dad's low level of communicative responsiveness to Eddie, Eddie's reaction to Dad's failure to fully respond to his bid for attention will depend on the Eddie's belief about how responsive Dad is to siblings, the other parent, or whoever else lives in the house. In effect, there is an across persons level of parental action that affects how a child makes meaning of a particular parent action; that is, it generates social comparisons among family members.

A child's reaction to a particular parent action also is a function of the overall ambiance or style (e.g., the overall amount of conflict present, the degree of optimism or cohesion in the family, a general style of interaction among family members, an overall level of organization or harmony) present in the home. As a rule, these pervading conditions are more distal than behaviors aimed directly at the child by other household members present; albeit, there are exceptions such as background noise. Ambient conditions indirectly affect children and they moderate the effect of direct exchanges between children and those persons and objects in the home environment (e.g., a high level of background noise reduces the effectiveness of parental attempts to teach the child, a high degree of parental conflict may reduce the effectiveness of parental attempts to nurture the child). Darling and Steinberg (1993) proposed, for example, that parenting style is best viewed as a context that modifies the influence of specific parenting practices. Mink and Nihira (1986) identified three types of family style and, for each family type, a different set of relationships between particular parenting behaviors and children's behavioral development emerged. Cummings, Zahn-Waxler, and Radke-Yarrow (1981) observed that toddlers exposed to frequent marital conflict reacted more intensively to later episodes of parental conflict than children who experienced less frequent conflict. Research on noise indicated that persistent intensive auditory stimuli has physiological consequences and may be inimical to task performance and interpersonal exchanges (World Health Organization, 1980).

In sum, there are one foreground level of parenting action (i.e., actions within a specific subdomain) and three background levels (i.e., across subdomains, across persons, and ambiance) that function together to determine the meaning a child makes of each parenting action. As children grow older, they are increasingly able to integrate information from multiple sources (levels) within the home and to develop ideas about their meaning. Children construct a generalized set of expectancies and motivational propensities to act in accordance with the general level of responsivity, object stimulation, structured learning opportunities, and the like, that are present. Children also are aware of the specific ways that their environments are responsive or not so responsive, stimulating or not so stimulating, and so forth. They can discriminate among the various types of responsivity present, each of which may have different salience for various behavioral systems.

Cross-cultural studies of environmental dimensions are especially informative in this regard. Investigators have observed that, while broad dimensions such as stimulation or responsiveness may have similar meaning across cultures, the narrower components of these dimensions (verbal stimulation vs. physical contact stimulation, responsivity to vocalization vs. responsivity to exploration) may have different significance (Bornstein et al., 1992; Wachs et al., 1992). Recent findings from behavior genetics research on within-family versus between-family environmental effects have been notable in pointing to differential treatment of siblings within the same family and the differential developmental trajectories of those siblings (Plomin & Daniels, 1987). The magnitude of the differences in trajectories seems not to derive solely from the absolute differences in treatment, but also from the meaning siblings give to these differences.

There appears to be some independence in the operation of these four levels of parenting action such as there is independence for the different levels of biological functioning (from organ systems down to the subcellular level). The organization of action is complex: occurring within, between, and across levels. As children become older and they can comprehend more distal and general conditions, those conditions become more salient for behavioral development. Indeed, as children grow older, what they make of parental actions also increasingly reflects the features of the environment outside the home (e.g., the conditions present in the peer group, at school, or in the neigborhood, even images on TV) at even more distal levels. It is not unusual, for example, for an adolescent to judge his or her parent's actions in light of his or her perceptions regarding how friends are treated by their parents in similar situations. The adolescent may judge even a mild reprimand as being too controlling or the continuation of attentiveness as too smothering.

Research that deals with the dynamic interplay of these four levels of parenting action, for all practical purposes, is absent. Most studies concentrate on one level or another, occasionally two, but rarely all four. Our own research has been no different, but we are in the process of attempting to understand the simultaneous influence of at least three levels of parenting on children's development. Specifically as part of the National Institute of Child Health and Human Development Study of Early Child Care, we collected data on parenting style (ambiance), general parental responsivity (across subdomains), and maternal responsivity in teaching (within subdomain) and play (within subdomains) situations. We will attempt to link these three levels to measures of children's cognitive and social development.

☐ How Does Context Affect Parenting?

Having spent nearly a quarter century developing measures of the home environment and studying family environments has brought as much humility as elucidation. It is rare that, in providing training on a family measure or presenting findings from studies of family life, we are not presented with a new wrinkle on an issue we thought long since settled or a new challenge regarding the fit of what we say to some real family situation. One of the things we have learned from our experience with the HOME is that life is incredibly diverse within and across groups, be they social class or cultural (a point made by Bloom, 1964, over 30 years ago). One of the most memorable home visits made using the HOME involved a large Mexican American family in Los Angeles. During the visit, there were 14 persons present, at one time or another, from the large, tightly knit extended family group. The home was rich with language and personal exchanges between family members, and it was also rich with joy. The family offered a strong contrast to the family situation of a young Mexican American mother in San Diego, separated from the father of her only child and living with her father, who was separated from her mother. The young mother's discomfort with her living arrangement was readily apparent. So keen was this discomfort, she did not even bring her child's toys to her father's home.

In 1984, Belsky published a paper on parenting in which he argued that parenting is a joint function of the parent's own history, the context in which parenting occurs, and the characteristics of the child. Our experience with HOME provides ample evidence of the "truth" of Belsky's parenting process model. Scores on the Inventory are correlated with nearly everything (one might say confounded with nearly everything): race, family structure, neighborhood, parental personality and competence, parental history. Many of the items on the HOME Inventory index objects and parenting practices more common to better educated, wealthier families. Most investigators have found low-to-moderate correlations between HOME and social status variables (Adams et al., 1984, Bradley, Caldwell, Rock, et al., 1989; Bradley, Mundfrom, et al., 1994; Brummitt & Jacobson, 1989; Caldwell, 1967; Hollenbeck, 1978; Kurtz et al., 1988; Nihira, Tomiyasu, & Oshio, 1987; Noll, Zucker, Curtis, & Fitzgerald, 1989; Pascoe, Loda, Jeffries, & Earp, 1981; Rogozin, Landesman-Dwyer, & Streissguth, 1978; Sahu & Devi, 1982; Saxon & Witriol, 1976). However, the strength of association sometimes can be quite modest (.24), as a study of working mothers from Italy attests (Fein, Gariboldi, & Boni, 1993). Results indicated that, in cultures with a highly defined class structure such as India, the link between social status and parenting practice is likely to be tight (Kurtz et al., 1988). By comparison, in societies with more mobility across classes and nearly universal access to education (but not employment), the association may be weaker.

Studies show that scores on HOME reflect many factors in addition to parental social status (Bradley & Caldwell, 1978), including parental personality (Allen, Affleck, McQueeney, & McGrade, 1982; Bergerson,

1989; Crockenberg, 1987; Fein et al., 1993; Pederson et al., 1988; Reis, Barbera-Stein, & Bennett, 1986), parental substance abuse (Fried, O'Connell, & Watkinson, 1992; Noll et al., 1989; Ragozin et al., 1978), parental IQ (Longstreth et al., 1981; Plomin & Bergeman, 1991), family structure (Bradley et al., 1982, 1984), parental knowledge about child development and attitudes toward child rearing (Reis et al., 1986), social support (Bradley et al., 1987, 1989, 1991; Wandersman & Unger, 1983), psychosocial climate of the home (Bradley et al., 1987; Gottfried & Gottfried, 1984; Nihira, Mink, & Meyers, 1981; Wandersman & Unger, 1983), presence of traumatic events (Bradley et al., 1987), and a variety of other community and cultural factors. Ragozin, Landesman-Dwyer, & Streissguth (1980) also observed a birth order effect on Involvement and Variety.

HOME scores also vary as a function of maternal age (Coll et al., 1986, 1987; Field et al., 1980; Luster & Rhoades, 1989; Reis et al., 1986; Schilmoeller & Baranowski, 1985; von Windeguth & Urbano, 1989). Reis and Herz (1987) even found that younger teens (13 to 16 years old) had lower scores than older teens (age 16 to 19). Coll and her colleagues found that, even with total child care support and stress controlled, older mothers scored higher on HOME. But, the parenting practices of young mothers are not uniformly lower than those of older mothers. We recently conducted a study of 193 mothers ranging in age from 15 to 24 years (Whiteside-Mansell, Pope, & Bradley, 1996). Each mother was assessed with the HOME when their infants were 12 months old and again when their children were 36 months old. A cluster analysis was performed on the HOME subscale scores for both ages. Results showed that the majority of young mothers had HOME score profiles similar to those of older mothers. However, four of the five clusters had some HOME scores that were at least one standard deviation lower than those of older mothers. These profiles were related to maternal competence and family context as well as to children's development.

A little over a decade ago, we looked at the relationship of HOME and an array of demographic factors in a racially diverse sample (Bradley & Caldwell, 1984a). We found two things: (a) no one demographic factor accounted for much of the variance in HOME scores, and (b) all the demographic factors we used put together accounted for only about 50% of the variance. Recently, we repeated this study with a much larger and even more diverse sample (Bradley, Mundfrom, et al., 1994). We did it in response to a study which erroneously concluded that income accounted for most of the difference in HOME scores (that study totally confounded race, area of residence, and social class). In our analysis using data from the Infant Health and Development Program (1990) Study, we essentially reproduced the findings from the earlier study: No one factor accounted for more than about 20% of the variance and a substantial amount of variance was left unaccounted for (see Table 16.2).

In an effort to better understand how culture and socioeconomic status operate to shape the character of parenting and the parenting environment, we have undertaken several lines of investigation. One of the most comprehensive efforts was a collaborative study involving 11 investigators from six sites in North

TABLE 16.2. HOME and demographic factors

Demographic Variable	Variance Accounted for	
	12-Month HOME	36-Month HOME
Black vs. White	8%	9%
Black vs. Hispanic	1%	1%
Income	5%	4%
Maternal education	2%	6%
Gestatational age	1%	4%
Marital status	2%	3%
Maternal age	1%	1%
Parity	1%	4%
R^2	.38	.53

Note. From "The Demography of Parenting: A Re-examination of the Association Between HOME and Income," by R. H. Bradley, D. J. Mundfrom, L. Whiteside, B. M. Caldwell, P. H. Casey, R. S. Kirby, and S. Hansen. 1994, *Nursing Research, 43*.

America (Bradley, et al., 1989). In this study, correlations between HOME scores and 2-year Bayley scores were higher for European Americans than for African Americans and Hispanic Americans. However, by age 3, the correlation between child IQ and the Responsivity subscale was higher for African Americans than for European Americans, and there were no other notable differences between these two groups. The pattern of correlations for Mexican Americans was different from other groups. Reminiscent of results for poor children in rural Mexico (Cravioto & DeLicardie, 1986), correlations with social status and mental test scores were very low. Also in keeping with previous studies, HOME was found to significantly predict 3-year IQ (from .30 to .47) when it was entered into a regression equation after socioeconomic status.

More recently, we took a different approach to investigating cultural group differences in the relation between home environment and children's development. We reviewed over 70 studies conducted outside the United States which utilized HOME (Bradley, Corwyn, & Whiteside-Mansell, 1997). Although there were notable exceptions, HOME total scores were similarly correlated with family structure, family status, and child outcomes across cultures. However, ethnic group differences relating to HOME subscales were quite common; and item-level analysis was the most useful in detecting these differences. Several instances of culturally inappropriate items were found. For example, "Parent introduces interviewer to child," "Child has free access to musical instrument," and "Family member has taken the child on a trip over 50 miles from home" were considered inappropriate for Caribbean households (Dubrow, Jones, Bozoky, & Adam, 1996). Moreover, items from the Responsivity subscale were problematic in several Asian studies. Aina, Agiobu-Kemmer, Etta, Zeitlin, and Setiloane (1993) dropped the Acceptance subscale since Yoruba culture places little value on independence, and Nihira et al. (1987) found the items not reflective of the different emotional aspects of parenting in Japanese. Not surprisingly, European studies mirrored those from the United States and Canada.

According to Hui and Triandis (1985), "the continuum of universality-cultural difference of a construct closely parallels the construct's level of abstraction" (p. 134). In other words, group similarities are greatest when total scores, or subscales, are analyzed, while item-level analysis is more precise in detecting group differences. For that reason, we recently began exploring data from the National Longitudinal Survey of Youth (NLSY) to investigate item-level differences by sociocultural group and poverty status. The original NLSY sample included 6,283 women who were between the age of 14 and 21 in 1979. The sample was selected to be nationally represented; however, there was deliberate oversampling of African Americans, Hispanics, and poor European Americans. Data from this sample has been collected every 2 years. Beginning in 1986, NLSY also included a child supplement which contained short forms of the four versions of HOME.

In the first of an extended series of planned investigations using NLSY, we found that what children experience day to day and week to week in the households of Asian Americans, Hispanic Americans, European Americans and African Americans are quite different from infancy through adolescence. Overall, Hispanic American and African American home environments were somewhat less supportive and stimulating than were the home environments of European Americans and Asian Americans, even when controlling for poverty status. These differences likely reflect cultural and economic legacy as well as continued macro-level sociopolitical factors such as racism. However, poverty status almost always had a greater affect on aspects of the home environment than did ethnicity. A surprising, but perhaps the most salient finding, was that the effect of poverty status was proportional across ethnic groups for all HOME short form items.

Across all ethnic groups, nonpoor mothers were over one and one half times as likely as poor mothers to communicate effectively with the child, and approximately twice as likely to show verbal and physical affection toward the child. Across all ethnic groups, nonpoor children were approximately twice as likely in infancy, four times as likely in early childhood, six times as likely in middle childhood, and three times as likely in adolescence to have three or more children's books than their poor counterparts. Likewise, across all ethnic groups, and across all three age groups assessed, those not in poverty were more likely to have a safe home environment than those who were poor.

While there were few ethnic differences in the variety of experiences afforded the child, nonpoor children were approximately twice as likely to be taken to the museum as poor children, and one and one half times as likely to be taken to the theater as poor children. Although there were clear ethnic group differences in tutoring and teaching experiences for children, poverty status had a major affect on the likelihood that the child was read to and provided with special lessons. For each ethnic group, nonpoor mothers were twice as likely to read to their child three or more times a week than were poor mothers. Nonpoor family members also were twice as likely to help the child learn shapes, colors, numbers, and the alphabet. Also, nonpoor children were from four to five times as likely through middle childhood, and three times as likely in adolescence, to see their father daily than were poor children. Even though at all age levels, poor African American children were approximately one third as likely to see their father, nonpoor African-American children were from 1.18 to 1.38 times as likely to see their father as others. Notably, there were no ethnic group or poverty status differences in how often children saw family and friends.

Nonpoor mothers chose less harsh forms of discipline such as talking and ignoring, and were less likely to ground, spank, give a chore, send to room, or take away allowance. At all age levels, and across all ethnic groups, parents living below the poverty level were more likely to spank their children. Nonpoor mothers also were likely to expect their child to perform a number of chores around the house. Nonpoor mothers were also more likely to monitor their children's activities and whereabouts. Nonpoor children also were shown to live in more aesthetically pleasing and safer environments than poor children.

One could argue that information based on the HOME short forms collected in connection with NLSY represents a first phase of constructing a topography of the parenting environment. Certainly, it is a small first step, but the effort is perhaps more significant than is initially obvious. Determining the significance of any aspect of parenting requires an understanding of the full context of parenting. What we know about parenting and its effects from existing surveys and anthropological accounts gives nothing like the full mapping of this context. They are rather like maps of small towns, city sections, or small bits of the countryside—tiny fragments like our understanding of the U.S. territories before Lewis and Clark. At present the terrain of parenting is a frontier—we barely know the landscape. Describing its topographical features in greater detail is essential for future explorations, lest we be limited to following mostly the same bumpy trails in the foreseeable future.

☐ Who Performs the Tasks of Parenting?

Understanding what parenting means in the lives of children is more difficult as we stand on the threshold of the twenty-first century than it was at the close of World War II, just before the current era of investigations on parenting began. Economic, demographic, and technological changes of the past half century have profoundly altered the landscape of parenting. With 79% of adult Americans agreeing that it takes more than one paycheck to support a family today (Mass Mutual American Family Values Study, 1989), mothers are entering the workforce in record numbers. Only 4.5% of all married women were in the workforce in 1890 (Smith, 1979), compared to over 60% today. Other employment-related changes also have impacted children's lives. For example, more jobs now require that parents spend extended periods of time away from home, more jobs involve working hours outside the traditional 8 to 5 Monday through Friday workweek, and more jobs have variable working hours. Also, the average number of years adults work at the same job has declined, the result being that families move more often and adults more often spend time in educational experiences aimed at getting them a better job.

The second major shift in family life relates to the move away from the stable two-parent nuclear family structure as predominant. Rapid increases in divorce rates and out-of-wedlock births have contributed to a jump in the proportion of children living in single-parent families: 28% in 1998 versus only 12% in 1970 (Bureau of the Census, 1997, 1998). The rate of out-of-wedlock births to Black women is now approximately 70% (Ventura, Martin, Curtin, & Mathews, 1997). A particularly striking statistic relates to the likelihood that a child will live in a single-parent household at some point during childhood. For Whites, the figure is 70%; for Blacks, it is 94%. Not only are children more likely to live in divorced and never married households than ever before, but they are also more likely to live with stepparents than in previous decades. Approximately two thirds of adults who divorce eventually remarry (U.S. National Center for Health Statistics, 1991). About 16% of children living in married couple households are stepchildren.

How have these changes in patterns of employment and family structure affected parenting? First, men have been encouraged by necessity, and by redefinition of the male parenting role, to play a greater part in the day-to-day care of children. Although fathers have by no means lived up to the "new father" image of fifty-fifty shared parenting, the move is in that direction (Pleck, 1997). More fathers are also functioning as single parents today. In 1995, there were an estimated 3.2 million families maintained by men with no wife present in the households, a nearly threefold increase from 1970. At the same time, an increased number of divorced and never-married fathers have distanced themselves from their children (Blankenhorn, 1995); in sum, a bifurcation in the population of fathers.

Second, the fertility rate has declined from 3.5 in 1957 to 2.1 in 1995 (Ventura et al., 1995). Parents are caring for fewer children. Relatedly, the proportion of women who give birth to their first child in their thirties has increased fivefold since 1970. During the same period, the proportion of births to teenagers has skyrocketed. In 1993, 13% of all births and 29% of births out of wedlock were to teens (Ventura et al., 1995), a bifurcation in the population of mothers.

Third, grandparents play a larger caregiving role in many families, particularly in families headed by single parents (Lamanna & Riedmann, 1997). Approximately 4 million children live in their grandparent's home, a 118% increase since 1970 (Casper & Bryson, 1998). For adults who have children later in life, grandparents may also compete for parents' time. These middle-age adults now have the simultaneous responsibility for young children and elderly grandparents.

Fourth, over half of all preschoolers are now cared for by someone unrelated to the child while parents are at work. Arrangements include in-home caregivers (6%), child care homes (22%), and day care centers (24%). The older children become, the more likely they are to be cared for in more formal nonhome settings such as day care centers. During nonschool hours, elementary school children of employed mothers are most likely cared for by a parent (33%), followed by a relative (23%), care during lessons (15%), after-school day care (14%), a child care home (7%), self-care (4%), or an in-home paid provider (3%) (Hofferth, Brayfield, Diech, & Holcomb, 1991). Because parents are reluctant to admit they leave their children at home alone and because of the unreliability of some measures of child care, it is difficult to estimate how many school-age children are home alone. The 1991 Survey of Income and Program Participation (Hofferth, et al., 1991) puts the figure at 8%. The National Child Care Survey (NCCS; Miller, 1995) of 1990 puts the figure even higher (nearly 15%). As children get older, the percentage increases: SIPP estimates that over one-third of twelve-year-olds are regularly in self-care while parents are at work. As children get older, they are also more likely to spend time in multiple non-parental child care arrangements (Bureau of the Census, 1994).

Taken as a whole, what do these changes in family life signify with regard to parenting? Most fundamentally, they mean that the tasks of parenting often are distributed across an array of caregivers with varying degrees of investment in the child and varying styles of parenting. Parenting is likely to be neither consistent across caregivers and settings nor constant throughout childhood. Children are required to adapt to these variable and often unstable conditions. Relatedly, more of a parent's time is often unstable spent in preparing for and coping with distributed caregiving and its consequences. The meaning a child makes of any parenting act will depend on the child's total history and current context of care.

Parental Investment in the Lives of Children

In a recent paper, Tanfer and Mott (1997) argued that changes in family patterns, brought on by changes in social and economic conditions, "signal a weaker commitment of women to men and of men to women; a weaker commitment by the partners to their relationship, and very possibly a weaker commitment to their children " (p. 2). Trends from the past half century seem clear and compelling: smaller families, fewer and delayed marriages, increased divorce, delayed childbearing, advancing numbers of children growing up in single-parent households. Growth in materialism, stresses from work, and the rising cost of rearing children almost certainly conspire to reduce the value of children and adults' commitment to them. More and more, status (and fulfillment) is derived from outside the home, outside the role of parenting.

According to parental investment theory, "the responsibilities of caring for young, often unruly children would seem to require putting one's needs and desires on the back burner so that one can attend to the needs of one's offspring" (Bjorklund & Kipp, 1996, p. 181). The ability to inhibit one's own impulses to leave one's offspring to their own resorts, by extension, requires that one derive pleasure in caring for the child and that one identify one's own well-being with the well-being of the child (Marsiglio et al., 1997). As the trend toward disinvestment in family and child rearing has accelerated (Popenoe, 1993), our research has focused more intensively on parental involvement in the lives of children. We constructed a measure called Parents' Socioemotional Investment in Children (PIC; Bradley, Whiteside-Mansell, Brisby, & Caldwell, 1997). The PIC assesses four components of investment: acceptance of the parenting role, delight in the child, knowledge/sensitivity, and separation anxiety. A study done on 137 mothers of 15-month-old children revealed that PIC was related to the quality of caregiving, maternal depression, neuroticism, agreeableness, social support, the quality of the marital relationship, parenting stress, and perceived child difficultness.

Because of increased concerns about paternal involvement in the lives of children, we examined factors that predicted fathers' three component scores from PIC (acceptance, delight, and knowledge/sensitivity). Predictors were chosen based on Belsky's process model of parenting (Belsky, 1984), and consisted of income to needs, marital quality, mother's employment, child's compliant behavior (Adaptive Social Behavior Inventory), and child's mental competence (Bayley scores). The factors associated with investment varied as a function of the dimension of investment and time of measurement. Major contextual factors, such as family income, maternal employment status, and marital quality, showed associations with father's knowledge and sensitivity at 15 months, father's acceptance at 36 months, and father's delight at 36 months. Marital quality was associated with paternal investment in infancy and early childhood, and maternal employment was positively associated with both acceptance and delight. Interestingly, neither children's temperament or compliance was related to PIC scores, and the relation to children's competence varied with age. Overall, such findings are reminiscent of the findings of Woodworth, Belsky, and Crnic (1996).

☐ The Future of Parenting Studies

If there is anything we have learned from our long years of studying parents and children, it is how diverse life is "in the moment" for children. This "fact" has consumed us as we have struggled to develop measures that are useful representations of that broad phenomenon called parenting (a.k.a., the home environment). What, among the myriad acts, objects, conditions, and events that constitute the home environment, should be included in measures of parenting? What indicators are telling enough across the broad diversity of families in America and throughout the world that they capture what is most salient about parenting? With family life so bound up with history, culture, community, and place, it seems impossible that any one measure (given that it contains only a limited census of indicators) could sufficiently capture what is most salient about parenting for all groups and all situations. But, without "marker" measures or "indicators," how can we construct an integrated science of parenting, a theory of environment-development relationships that is anything more than parochial? This dilemma, bringing as it does conflicting seals in the service of science, has led us to recommend a dual strategy for studying parenting: It is what we call an inside and outside strategy with regard to marker measures of key parenting domains. The inside strategy means looking inside the measures themselves and, more specifically, looking at the issue of measurement invariance across groups. Using such techniques as confirmatory factor analysis, structural equation modeling, and multitrait-multimethod analysis, we are looking at whether the internal structure of measures is similar across groups and whether a measure links with similar constructs across groups (Whiteside-Mansell, Bradley, & Rakow, 1996). The outside strategy is to supplement marker measures with outside indicators that may be particularly revealing of a parenting domain in a particular group. Perhaps, the best example of the outside strategy in our own research has been our work with children with disabilities. In those studies, we added items to the Infant-Toddler, Early Childhood, and Middle Childhood versions of HOME that were designed for families having children with various types of disabilities. The thought was that these children may require additional things from their environments in order to do well. Our findings showed that the items on the HOME generally worked well in predicting how children would do on standard measures of social and cognitive functioning but, as the severity of the disability increased, the additional items became more useful in predicting the course of development (Bradley et al., 1989). When approached by researchers from other cultures, we now routinely recommend gathering information on parenting indicators of local value in addition to those found on the HOME, then analyzing data from the standard HOME and from the additional items in tandem. In addition to recommending the outside strategy with regard to the measurement of parenting, we also have begun examining the relation between parenting and children's development within cultures (e.g., our studies using the Early Adolescent HOME and our recent studies involving NLSY). There is convincing evidence for the value of within-group analyses for building a comprehensive science of human development (Coll et al., 1996).

The second major thing we have learned in our studies of families is how much the process of parenting changes from infancy through adolescence. The latter "fact" has compelled us to construct measures of the home environment unique to each developmental period, and it has forced us to struggle to identify the most meaningful and informative parenting behaviors at each age. Conducting research on parenting in the twenty-first century will present challenges only dimly foreshadowed during the past three decades. The realities of child rearing in the late 1990s present extraordinary obstacles to definitive research, with complexity and diversity in arrangements compounding the ordinary problems of linking particular parenting practices to the trajectory of development in highly evolved, phylogenetically advanced organisms living in rich, multilayered contexts. The challenge requires longitudinal designs with repeated measures of all the caregiving environments in which a child spends a meaningful amount of time (Friedman & Haywood, 1994).

The final thing we have learned from our quarter century of studying children is that the family environment is a dense, multidimensional, multilayered context. The longer we have studied parenting, the more measures of family life and the parenting process we have included as part of our studies. In recent years, we have included such measures as Moos' Family Environment Scale (Bradley, Caldwell, et al., 1987), coping style (Bradley, et al., 1989), and parental investment (Bradley et al., 1997). Our current studies include microanalytic measures of parenting, measures of parenting style, and measures of family cohesion and optimism. The future of research in parenting requires not only examining these multiple dimensions of parenting, but also examining the mediating and moderating role each plays with regard to the development of children. The importance of parenting in the lives of children is constant, but how parenting works in the lives of children is complex and ever changing.

☐ References

Abelson, R. (1981). Psychological status of the script concept. *American Psychologist, 36*, 715–729.

Adams, J. L., Campbell, F. A., & Ramey, C. T. (1984). Infants' home environments: A study of screening efficiency. *American Journal of Mental Deficiency, 89*, 133–139.

Aina, T. A., Agiobu-Kemmer, I., Etta, E. F., Zeitlin, M. F., & Setiloane, K. (1993). *Early child care, development and nutrition in Lagos State, Nigeria*. Produced by the Social Sciences Faculty, University of Lagos, and the Tufts University School of Nutrition Science and Policy for the United Nations Children's Fund (UNICEF), New York.

Allen, D. A., Affleck, G., McGrade, B. J., & McQueeney, M. (1984). Effects of single parent status of mothers on their high-risk infants. *Infant Behavior and Development, 7*, 341–139.

Allen, D. A., Affleck, G., McQueeney, M., & McGrade, B. J. (1982) Validation of the parent behavior progression in an early intervention program. *Mental Retardation, 20*, 159–163.

Allen, D. A., McGrade, B. J., Affleck, G., & McQueeney, M. (1982). The predictive validity of neonatal intensive care nurses' judgements of parent child relationship: A nine-month follow-up. *Journal of Pediatric Psychology, 7*, 125–134.

Altman, I. (1977). Privacy regulation: Culturally universal or culturally specific? *Journal of Social Issues, 33*, 66–84.

Ausubel, D. (1968). *Educational psychology: A cognitive view*. New York: Rinehart and Winston.

Bakeman, R., & Brown, J. V. (1980). Early interaction: Consequences for social and mental development at three years. *Child Development, 51*, 437–447.

Bee, H. L., Barnard, K. E., Eyres, S. J., Gray, C. A., Hammond, M. A., Spietz, A. L., Snyder, S. & Clark, B. (1982). Prediction of IQ and language skill from perinatal status, child performance, family characteristics, and mother-infant interaction. *Child Development, 53*, 1134–1156.

Bee, H. L., Mitchell, S., Barnard, K., Eyres, S. J., & Hammond, M. A. (1984). Predicting intellectual outcomes: Sex differences in response to early environmental stimulation. *Sex Roles Bulletin, 75*, 81–95.

Belsky, J. (1984). The determinants of parenting: A process model. *Child Development, 55*, 83–96.

Belsky, J., Garduque, L., & Hrncir, E. (1984). Assessing performance, competence and executive capacity in infant play: Relations to home environment and security of attachment. *Developmental Psychology, 20*, 406–417.

Bergeman, C. S. & Plomin, R. (1988). Parental mediators of the genetic relationship between home environment and infant mental development. *British Journal of Developmental Psychology, 6*, 11–19 .

Bergerson, S. (1989). *Personality characteristics of mothers whose infants are referred to early intervention programs*. Unpublished doctoral dissertation, University of Toronto, Canada.

Billings, R., Jacobson, S., Jacobson. J., & Brumitt, G. (1989, April). *Preschool HOME: Dimensions and predictive validity*. Paper presented at the meeting of the Society for Research in Child Development, Kansas City, MO.

Bjorklund, D. F., & Kipp, K. (1996) Parental investment theory and gender differences in the evolution of inhibition mechanisms. *Psychological Bulletin, 120*, 163–188.

Blankenhorn, D. (1995). Pay, papa, pay. *National Review, 47*, 34–42.

Bloom, B. (1964). Stability and chance in human characteristics. New York: Wiley.

Bornstein, M. H., Tamis-LeMonda, C. S., Tal, H., Ludemann, P. I., Toda, S., Rahn, C. W., Pecheux, M. Asuma, H., & Vardi, D. (1992). Maternal responsiveness to infants in three societies: The United States, France, and Japan. *Child Development, 63*, 808–821.

Bowlby, J. (1958). The nature of the child's tie to his mother. *International Journal of Psychoanalysis, 39*, 350–373.

Bradley, R. H. (1995). Environment and parenting. In M. Bornstein (Ed.). *Handbook of parenting* (Vol. 2, pp. 235–262). Hillsdale, NJ: Erlbaum.

Bradley, R. H. (1994). The HOME Inventory: Review and reflections. In H. W. Reese (Ed.), Advances in child development and behavior (Vol. 25, pp. 241-288). San Diego, CA: Academic Press,

Bradley, R. H., & Caldwell, B. M. (1976a). Early environment and changes in mental test performance in children from six to thirty-six months. *Developmental Psychology, 12*, 93–97.

Bradley, R. H., & Caldwell, B. M. (1976b). The relationship of infants' home environment to mental test performance at fifty-four months: A follow-up study. *Child Development, 47*, 1172–1174.

Bradley, R. H., & Caldwell, B. M. (1978). Screening the environment. *American Journal of Orthopsychiatry, 48*, 114–130.

Bradley, R. H., & Caldwell, B. M. (1981). The HOME Inventory: A validation of the preschool scale for Black children. *Child Development, 52*, 708–710.

Bradley, R. H., & Caldwell, B. M. (1982). The consistency of the home environment and its relation to child development. *International Journal of Behavioral Development, 5*, 445–465.

Bradley, R. H., & Caldwell, B. M. (1995). Caregiving and the regulation of child growth and development: Describing proximal aspects of caregiving systems. *Developmental Review, 15*, 38–85.

Bradley, R. H., Caldwell, B. M., Rock, S. L., Hamrick, H. M., & Harris, P. T. (1988). Home observation for measurement of the environment: Development of HOME inventory for use with families having children 6 to 10 years old. *Contemporary Educational Psychology, 13*, 58–71.

Bradley, R. H., Caldwell, B. M., & Rock, S. L. (1988). Home environment and school performance: A ten-year follow-up and examination of three models of environmental action. *Child Development, 59*, 852–867.

Bradley, R. H., Caldwell, B. M., Rock, S. L.. Barnard. K. E., Gray. C., Hammond, M. A., Mitchell, S., Siegel, L., Ramey, C. T., Gottfried, A. W., & Johnson, D. L. (1989). Home environment and cognitive development in the first 3 years of life: A collaborative study involving six sites and three ethnic groups in North America. *Developmental Psychology, 28*, 217–235.

Bradley, R. H., Caldwell, B. M., Rock, S. L., Casey, P. H., & Nelson, J. (1987). The early development of low-birthweight infants: Relationship to health, family status, family context, family processes, and parenting. *International Journal of Behavioral Development, 10*, 1–18.

Bradley, R. H., Corwyn, R. F., & Whiteside-Mansell, L. (1996). Life at home: Same time, different place—An examination of the HOME Inventory in different cultures. *Early Development and Parenting, 5*, 251–269.

Bradley, R. H., Mundfrom, D. J., Whiteside, L., Caldwell, B. M., Casey, P. H., Kirby, R. S., & Hansen, S. (1994). The demography of parenting: A re-examination of the association between HOME scores and income. *Nursing Research, 43*, 260–266.

Bradley, R. H., & Rock, S. L. (1985). The HOME Inventory: Its relation to school failure and development of an elementary-age version. In W. Frankenburg, R. Emde, & J. Sullivan (Eds.), *Early identification of children at risk: An international perspective* (pp. 159–174). New York: Plenum.

Bradley, R. H., Rock, S. L., Caldwell, B. M., Harris, P. T., & Hamrick, H. M. (1987). Home environment and school performance among Black elementary school children. *Journal of Negro Education, 56*, 499–509.

Bradley, R. H., Whiteside, L., Mundfrom, D. J., Blevins-Knabe, B., Casey, P. H., Caldwell, B. M., Kelleher, K. J., Pope, S., & Barrett, K. (1995). Home environment and adaptive social behavior among premature, low birthweight children. Alternative models of environmental action. *Journal of Pediatric Psychology, 20*, 347–362.

Bradley, R. H., Whiteside, L., Mundfrom, D. J., Casey, P. H., Kelleher, K. J., & Pope, S. K. (1994). Early indications of resilience and their relation to experiences in the home environments of low birthweight, premature children living in poverty. *Child Development, 65*, 346–360.

Bradley, R. H., Whiteside-Mansell, L., Brisby, J. A., & Caldwell, B. M. (1997). Parents' socioemotional investment in children. *Journal of Marriage and the Family, 59*, 77–90.

Bradley, R. H., Whiteside-Mansell, L., & Corwyn, R. (1997, August) *Early adolescent HOME Inventory: Its usefulness and validity for 4 racial/ethnic groups*. Paper presented at the annual meeting of the American Educational Research Association, Chicago, IL.

Bretherton, I., & Waters, E. (1985). Growing points of attachment theory and research. *Monographs of the Society for Research in Child Development, 50* (1–2, Serial No. 209).

Bronfenbrenner, U. (1979). *The ecology of human development*. Cambridge, MA: Harvard University Press.

Brumitt, G.A., & Jacobson, J. L. (1989, April). *The influences of home environment and socio-economic status on cognitive performance at 4 years*. Paper presented at the meeting of the Society for Research in Child Development, Kansas City, MO.

Bureau of the Census. (1994, April). National Child Care Survey. U.S. Department of Commerce Economics and Statistics Administration.

Bureau of the Census. (1997, March). Marital status and living arrangements: March 1996. Current population reports. Washington, DC: GPO.

Bureau of the Census. (1998, March). Marital status and living arrangements: March 1998 (update). Current population reports. P20-514. Washington, DC: GPO.

Caldwell, B. M. (1967). Descriptive evaluations of child development and of developmental settings. *Pediatrics, 40,* 46–54.

Caldwell, B. M. (1968). On designing supplementary environments for early child development. *BAEYC Reports, 10,* 1–11.

Caldwell, B. M.. & Bradley, R. H. (1984). Home observation for measurement of the environment. Little Rock: University of Arkansas at Little Rock.

Carlson, D. B., Labarba, R. C., Sclafani, J. D., & Bowers, C. A. (1986). Cognitive and motor development in infants of adolescent mothers: A longitudinal analysis. *International Journal of Behavioral Development, 9,* 1–13.

Casper, L. M., & Bryson, K. R. (1998). Co-resident grandparents and their grandchildren: Grandparent maintained families: March 1998. U.S. Bureau of the Census, Population Division Working Paper No. 26. Washington, DC: GPO.

Chua, K. L., Kong, D. S., Wong, S. T., & Yoong, T. (1989). Quality of the home environment of toddlers: A validation study of the HOME Inventory. *Journal of the Singapore Pediatric Society, 31,* 38–45.

Coll, C. G., Hoffman, J., & Oh, N. (1987). The social ecology and early parenting of Caucasian adolescent mothers. *Child Development, 58,* 955–963.

Coll, C. G., Vohr, O., Hoffman, J., & Oh, W. (1986). Maternal and adolescent mothers. *Developmental and Behavioral Pediatrics, 7,* 230–236.

Consullo, M. (1992, May). *Relationship of early responsiveness to one-year outcomes in preterm and full-term infants.* Paper presented at the International Conference on Infancy Studies, Miami, FL.

Cooney, G. H., Bell, A., McBride, W., & Carte, C. (1989). Neurobehavioral consequences of prenatal low level exposure to lead. *Neurotoxicology and Teratology, 11,* 95–104.

Coons, H., Fulker, D. W., DeFries, J. C., & Plomin, R. (1990). Home environment and cognitive ability of 7-year-old children in the Colorado Adoption Project: Genetic and environment etimologies. *Developmental Psychology, 26,* 459–468.

Cravioto, J., & DeLicardie, E. R. (1986). Microenvironmental factors in severe protein-calorie malnutrition. In N. Scrimshaw & M. Behar (Eds.), *Nutrition and agricultural development* (pp. 25–36). New York: Plenum.

Crockenberg, S. (1987). Predictors and correlates of anger toward and punitive control of toddlers by adolescent mothers. *Child Development, 58,* 964–975.

Cummings, E. M., Zahn-Waxler, C., & Radke-Yarrow, M. (1981). Young children's responses to expressions of anger and affection by others in the family. *Child Development, 52,* 1274–1282.

Darling, N., & Steinberg, L. (1993). Parenting style as context. An integrative model. *Psychological Bulletin, 113,* 487–496.

Dunn, J. (1991). The developmental importance of differences in siblings' experiences within the family. In K. Pillemer & K. McCartney (Eds.), *Parent-child relations throughout life* (pp. 113–124). Hillsdale, NJ: Erlbaum.

Dubrow, E., Jones, E., Bozoky, S. J., & Adam, E. (1996, August). *How well does the HOME Inventory predict Caribbean children's academic performance and behavior problems?* Poster session presented at the 14th biennial meeting of ISSBD, Quebec City, Canada.

Elardo, R., Bradley, R. H., & Caldwell, B. M. (1975). The relation of infants' home environment to mental test performance from six to thirty-six months: A longitudinal analysis. *Child Development, 45,* 71–76.

Elardo, R., Bradley, R. H., & Caldwell, B. M. (1977). A longitudinal study of the relation of infants' home environment to language development at age three. *Child Development, 48,* 595–603.

Erickson, M. F., Stroufe, L. A., & Egeland, B. (1985). The relationship between quality of attachment and behavior problems in a high risk sample. In I. Bretherton & E. Waters (Eds.), Growing points of attachment theory and research. *Monographs of the Society for Research in Child Development, 50*(1:2, Serial No. 209), 147–166.

Evans, G. W., Kliewer, W., & Martin, J. (1991). The role of the physical environment in the health and well-being of children. In H. E. Schroeder (Ed.), *New directions in health psychology assessment* (pp. 127–157). New York: Hemisphere.

Fagot, B. I., & Kavanaugh, K. (1993). Parenting during the second year: Effects of children's age, sex, and attachment classification. *Child Development, 64,* 258–271.

Fein, G. G., Gariboldi, A., & Boni, R. (1993). Antecedents of maternal separation anxiety. *Merrill-Palmer Quarterly, 39,* 481–495.

Field, T. M., Widmayer, S. M., Adler, S., & DeCubas, M. (1990). Teenage parenting in different cultures, family constellations and caregiving environments: Effects on infant development. *Infant Mental Health Journal, 11,* 158–174.

Ford, D. M., & Lerner, R. M. (1992). *Developmental systems theory.* Newbury Park, CA: Sage.

Fried, P. A., O'Connell, C. M., & Watkinson, B. (1992). 60- and 72-month follow-up of children prenatal exposed to marijuana, cigarettes, and alcohol: Cognitive and language assessment. *Developmental and Behavioral Pediatrics, 13*, 383–391.

Friedman, S. L., & Haywood, H. C. (1994). Developmental follow-up: Concepts, domains, and methods. San Diego, CA: Academic Press.

Friedman, S. L., & Sigman, M. D. (1996). Past, present, and future directions in research on the development of low-birthweight children. In L. S. Friedman & M. D. Sigman (Eds.), *The psychological development of low birthweight children* (pp. 3–22). Norwood, NJ: Ablex.

Garcia-Coll, C., Lamberty, G., Jenkins, R., McAdoor, H. P., Crnic, K., Wasik, B. H., & Garcia, H. V. (1996). An integrative model for the study of developmental competencies in minority children. *Child Development, 67*, 1891–1914.

Gottfried, A. W., & Gottfried, A. E. (1984). Home environment and cognitive development in young children of middle-socioeconomic status families. In A. W. Gottfried (Ed.), *Home environment and early cognitive development* (pp. 329–342). Orlando, FL: Academic Press.

Gottfried, A. E., & Gottfried. A. W. (1988). *Maternal employment and children's development: Longitudinal research.* New York: Plenum Press.

Gottfried, A. E., & Gottfried, A. W., Bathurst, K., & Guerin, D. W. (1994). *Gifted IQ: Early developmental aspects.* New York: Plenum Press.

Grinker, R. R., Korshin, S. J., Bosowitz, H., Hamburg, D. A., Sabshin, M., Pershy, H., Chevalier, J. A., & Borad, F. A. (1956). A theoretical and experimental approach to problems of anxiety. *AMA Archives of Neurology and Psychiatry, 76*, 420–431.

Hammond, M. A., Bee, H. L., Barnard, K. E., & Eyres, S. J. (1983). *Child health assessment: Part IV followup at second grade* (No. RO1 NU 00816). Seattle: U.S. Public Health Service.

Hawk, B. A., Schroeder, S. R., Robinson, G., Otto, D., Mushak, P., Kleinbaum, D., & Dawson, G. (1986). Relation of lead and social factors to IQ low-SES children: A partial replication. *American Journal of Mental Deficiency, 91*, 178–183.

Hofferth, S. L., Brayfield, A., Deich, S., & Holcomb, P. (1991). *National child care survey, 1990.* Washington, DC: The Urban Institute Press.

Hollenbeck, A. R. (1978). Early infant home environments: Validation of the home observation for Measurement of the Environment Inventory. *Developmental Psychology, 14*, 416–418.

Horowitz, F. D. (1987). *Exploring developmental theories: Toward a structural/behavioral model of development.* Hillsdale, NJ: Erlbaum.

Hui, C. H., & Triandis, H. C. (1985). Measurement in cross-cultural psychology. *Journal of Cross-cultural Psychology, 16*, 131–153.

Infant Health & Development Program. (1990). Enhancing outcomes of low-birth-weight, premature infants. *Journal of the American Medical Association, 263*, 3035–3042.

Jacobson, J. L., Jacobson, S. W., Padgett, R. J., Brummitt, G. A., & Billings, R. L. (1992). Effects of prenatal PCB exposure on cognitive processing efficiency and sustained attention. *Developmental Psychology, 28*, 297–306.

Jacobson, S., Jacobson, J., Brunitt, G., & Jones, P. (1987, April). *Predictability of cognitive development in farm and non-farm children.* Paper presented at the biennial meeting of the Society for Research in Child Development, Baltimore, MD.

Johnson, D. L., Breckenridge, J. N., & McGowan, R. (1984). Home environment and early cognitive development in Mexican-American children. In A. Gottfried (Ed.), *Home environment and early cognitive development* (pp. 151–196). Orlando, FL: Academic Press.

Jordan, T. E. (1976, April). *Measurement of the environment for learning and its effect on educational and cognitive attainment.* Paper presented at the meeting of the American Educational Research Association, San Francisco, CA.

Jordan, T. E. (1979). *Old man river's children.* New York: Academic Press.

Korosec-Serfaty, P. (1985). Experience and use of the dwelling. In I. Altman & C. Werner (Eds.), *Home environments* (pp. 65–86). New York: Plenum Press.

Kurtz, B. C., Borkowski, J. G., & Deshmukh, K. (1988). Metamemory and learning in Maharashtrian children: Influences from home and school. *Journal of Genetic Psychology, 149*, 363–376.

Lamanna, M. A., & Riedmann, A. (1997). *Marriages and families making choices in a diverse society (6th ed.).* New York: Wadsworth.

Lamb, M. E., Hwang, C., Bookstein, F. L., Broberg, A., Hult, G., & Frodi, M. (1988). Determinants of social competence in Swedish preschoolers. *Developmental Psychology, 24*, 58–70.

Lewis, M. (1997). *Altering fate.* New York: Guilford Press.

Longstreth, L., Davis, B., Carter, L., Flint, D., Owen, J., Rickert, M., & Taylor, E. (1981). Separation of home intellectual environment and maternal IQ as determinants of child IQ. *Developmental Psychology, 17*, 532–541.

Lozoff, B. (1989). Nutrition and behavior. *American Psychologist, 44*, 231–236.

Lozoff, B., Park, A. M., Radan, A. E., & Wolf, A. W. (1995). Using the HOME Inventory with infants in Costa Rica. *International Journal of Behavioral Development, 18*, 227–295.

Luster, T. E., & Rhoades, K. (1989). The relation of child-rearing beliefs and the home environment in a sample of adolescent mothers. *Family Relations, 38*, 317–322.

Maccoby, E. E. (1992). The role of parents in the socialization of children: An historical overview. *Developmental Psychology, 28*, 1006–1017.

Maccoby, E. E., & Martin, J. A. (1983). Socialization in the context of the family: Parent-child interaction. In P. H. Mussen (Series Ed.) & E. M. Hetherington (Vol. Ed.), *Handbook of child psychology: Vol. 4. Socialization, personality, and social development* (4th ed., pp. 1–102). New York: Wiley.

Marsiglio, W., Day, R., Braver, S., Evans, V. J., Lamb, M., & Peters, E. (1997, March). *Social fatherhood and paternal involvement: Conceptual, data, and policymaking issues.* Presented at the National Institute for Child Health & Human Development-sponsored Conference on Fathering and Male Fertility, Bethesda, MD.

Massachusetts Mutual Life Insurance Company. (1989). Mass Mutual Family Values Study. Springfield, MA: Author.

Maslow A. (1954). *Motivation and personality.* New York: Harper.

McLoyd, V. C. (1990). The impact of economic hardship on Black families and children: Psychological distress, parenting, and socioeconomic development. *Child Development, 61*, 311–346.

McMichael, A. J., Baghurst, P. A., Wigg, N. R., Vinpani, G. V., Robertson, E. F., & Robert, R. J. (1988). Port Pirie Cohort Study: Environment exposure to lead and children's abilities at the age of four years. *New England Journal of Medicine, 319*, 468–475.

Miller, B. M., (1995). How children spend out-of-school time. *Child Care Bulletin,* March/April (2), 4–5.

Mink, I. T., & Nihira, K. (1986). Family life-styles and child behaviors: A study of directions of effect. *Developmental Psychology, 22*, 610-616.

Mink, I. T., & Nihira, K. (1987). Direction of effects: Family life styles and behavior of TMR children. *American Journal of Mental Deficiency, 92*, 57–64.

Moore, M. R., Bushnell, W. R., & Goldberg, S. A. (1989). A prospective study of the results of changes in environmental lead exposure in children in Glasgow. In M. Smith (Ed.), *Lead exposure and child development. An international assessment* (pp. 371–378). London: Kluwer Academic.

Nihira, K., Mink, I. T., & Meyers, C. E. (1981). Relationship between HOME environment and school adjustment of TMR children. *American Journal of Mental Deficiency, 86*, 8–15.

Nihira, K., Tomiyasu, Y., & Oshio, C. (1987). Homes of TMR children: Comparison between American and Japanese families. *American Journal of Mental Deficiency, 91*, 486–495.

Noll, R. B., Zucker, R. A., Curtis, W. J., & Fitzgerald, H. E. (1989, April). *Young male offspring of alcoholic fathers: Early developmental and cognitive findings.* Paper presented at the meeting of the Society for Research in Child Development, Kansas City, MO.

Palti, H., Otrakul, A., Belmaker, E., Tamir, D., & Tepper, D. (1984). Children's home environments: Comparison of a group exposed to stimulation intervention program with controls. *Early Child Development and Care, 13*, 193–212.

Pascoe, J. M., Loda, F. A., Jeffries, V., & Earp, J. (1981). The association between mothers' social support and provision of stimulation to their children. *Developmental and Behavioral Pediatrics, 2*, 15–19.

Patterson, G. R., DeBaryshe, B. D., & Ramsey, E. (1989). A developmental perspective on antisocial behavior. *American Psychologist, 44*, 329–335.

Pederson, D. R., Evans, B., Chance, G. W., Bento, S., & Fox, A. M. (1988). Predictors of one-year developmental status in low birthweight infants. *Developmental and Behavioral Pediatrics, 9*, 287–292.

Peterson, L., Ewigman, B., & Kivlaham, C. (1993). Judgments regarding appropriate child supervision on prevent injury: The role of environmental risk and child age. *Child Development, 64*, 934–950.

Pettit, G. S., Dodge, K. A., & Brown, M. M. (1988). Early family experience, social problem solving patterns, and children's social competence. *Child Development, 59*, 107–120.

Pleck, J. H. (1997). Paternal involvement: Levels, sources, and consequences. In M. E. Lamb (Ed.), *The role of the father in child development* (pp. 66–103). New York: Wiley.

Plomin, R., & Bergeman, C. (1991). The nature of nurture: Genetic influence on "environmental" measures. *Behavior and Brain Sciences, 14*, 373–427.

Plomin, R., & Daniels, D. (1987). Why are children in the same family so different from one another? *Behavior and Brain Sciences, 10*, 1–16.

Plomin, R., Loehlin, J., & DeFries, J. (1985). Genetic and environmental components of "environmental" influences. *Developmental Psychology, 21*, 391–402.

Pollitt, E. (1988). A critical review of three decades of research on the effect of chronic energy malnutrition on behavioral development. In B. Schureh & M. Scrimshaw (Eds.), *Chronic energy depletion: Consequences and related issues* (pp. 77–93). Luzanne, Switzerland: Nestle Foundation.

Ragozin, A. S., Landesman-Dwyer, S., & Streissguth, A. P. (1978). The relationship between mothers' drinking habits and children's home environments. In F. Seixas (Ed.), *Currents in alcoholism: IV. Psychological, social and epidemiological studies.* New York: Grune and Stratton.

Ragozin, A. S., Landesman-Dwyer, S., & Streissguth, A. P. (1980). The relationship between mothers' drinking habits and children's home environments (Rep. No. 77–10). Seattle: University of Washington, Alcoholism and Drug Abuse Institute.

Rapoport, A. (1985). Thinking about home environments: A conceptual framework. In I. Altman & C. M. Werner (Eds.), *Home environments* (pp. 255–286). New York: Plenum Press.

Reis, J. S., Barbera-Stein, L., & Bennett, S. (1986). Ecological determinants of parenting. *Family Relations, 35*, 547–554.

Reis, J. S., & Herz, E. J. (1987). Correlates of adolescent parenting. *Adolescence, 22*, 599–609.

Roberts, W. L. (1986). Nonlinear models of development: An example from the socialization of competence. *Child Development, 57*, 1166–1178.

Rotter, J., Chance, J., & Phares, E. (1972). *Applications of social learning theory of personality.* New York: Holt, Rinehart, and Winston.

Saegert, S., & Winkel, G. H. (1990). Environmental psychology. *Annual Review of Psychology, 41*, 441–477.

Sahu, S., & Devi, B. (1982). *Role of home environment in psycholinguistic abilities and intelligence of advantaged and disadvantaged preschool children.* Unpublished master's thesis, Utkal University, Orissa, India.

Sameroff, A. J. (1983). Developmental systems: Context and evolution. In P. H. Mussen (Series Ed.), & W. Kessen (Vol. Ed.), *Vol. I. Handbook of child psychology: History, theories, and methods* (pp. 237–294). New York: Wiley.

Saxon, S., & Witriol, E. (1976). Down's Syndrome and intellectual development. *Pediatric Psychology, l*, 45–47.

Schilmoeller, G. L., & Baranowski, M. D. (1985). The effects of knowledge of child development and social-emotional maturity on adolescent attitudes toward parenting. *Adolescence, 20*, 805–822.

Siegel, L. S. (1982). Reproductive, perinatal, and environmental factors as predictors of the cognitive and language development of preterm and full term infants. *Child Development, 53*, 963–973.

Smith, R. E. (1979). *The subtle revolution.* Washington, DC: The Urban Institute.

Stevens, J. H., & Bakeman, R. (1985). A factors analytic study of the HOME scale for infants. *Developmental Psychology, 21*, 1196–1203.

Stevenson, M. B., & Lamb, M. E. (1979). Effects of infant sociability and the caretaking environment on infant cognitive performance. *Child Development, 50*, 340–344.

Stroufe, L. A., Egeland, B., & Kreutzer, T. (1990). The fate of early experience following developmental change: Longitudinal approaches to individual adaptation in childhood. *Child Development, 61*, 1363–1373.

Super, C. M., & Harkness, S. (1986). The developmental niche: A conceptualization at the interface of child and culture. *International Journal of Behavioral Development, 9*, 545–569.

Tanfer, K., & Mott, F. (1997, March). *The meaning of fatherhood for men.* Paper presented at the NICHD-sponsored Conference on Fathering and Male Fertility, Bethesda, MD.

Tedesco, L. (1981). *Early home experience, classroom social competence, and academic achievement.* Unpublished doctoral dissertation, State University of New York, Buffalo.

Tong, S. & McMichael, A. J. (1992). Maternal smoking and neuropsychological development in childhood: A review of the evidence. *Developmental Medicine and Child Neurology, 34*, 191–197.

U.S. Department of Health and Human Services. (1991). Health status of minorities and low-income groups (3rd ed.). Washington, DC: U.S. Government Printing Office.

U.S. National Center for Health Studies. (1991). Annual Summary of Births, Marriages, Divorces, and Deaths: United States, 1990. Monthly Vital Statistics Report 39 (13), August 18.

Ventura, S. J., Martin, J. A., Taffel, S. M., Matthews, T. J., & Clarke, S. C. (1995). Advance Report of Final Natality Statistics, 1993. Monthly Vital Statistics Report 44 (3, supplement), September 21. Hyattsville, MD: National Center for Health Statistics.

Ventura, S. J., Martin, J. A., Curtain, S. C., & Matthews, T. J. (1997). Report of Final Natality Statistics, 1995. Monthly Vital Statistics Report 45 (11, supplement). Hyattsville, MD: National Center for Health Statistics.

von Windeguth, B. J., & Urbano, R. C. (1989). Teenagers and the mothering experience. *Pediatric Nursing, 15*, 517–520.

Wachs, T. D. (1992). *The nature of nurture.* Newbury Park, CA: Sage.

Wachs, T. D., Sigman, M., Bishry, Z., Moussa, W., Jerome, N., Neumann, C., Bwibo, N, & McDonald, M. A. (1992). Caregiver child interaction in two cultures in relation to nutritional intake. *International Journal of Behavioral Development, 15*, 1–18.

Wandersman. L. P., & Unger, D. G. (1983, April). *Interaction of infant difficulty and social support in adolescent mothers.* Paper presented at the biennial meeting of the Society for Research in Child Development, Detroit, MI.

Wapner, S. (1987). A holistic, developmental system-oriented environmental psychology: Some beginnings. In D. Stockols & I. Altman (Eds.), *Handbook of environmental psychology* (Vol. 2, pp. 1433–1465). New York: Wiley.

Wasserman, G. A., Gruziano, J. H., Factor-Liktvak, P., Popovac, D., Morina, N., Musabegovic, A., Vrenzi, N., Capuni-Paracka, S., Lekic, V., Preteni-Redjepi, E., Hadzialjevic, S., Slavkovich, V., Kline, J., Shrout, P., & Stein, Z. (1994). Consequences of lead exposure and iron supplementation on childhood development at age 4 years. *Neurotoxicology and Teratology, 16*, 233–240.

Weiglas-Kuperus, N., Koot, H. M., Baerts, W., Fetter, W. P., & Sauer, P. J. (1993). Behavior problems of very low-birthweight children. *Developmental Medicine and Child Neurology, 35*, 406–416.

Whiteside-Mansell, L., Bradley, R. H., & Rakow, E. (1996, August). *Comparison of parental emotional involvement for mothers and fathers.* Paper presented at the biennial meeting of the International Society for the Study of Behavioral Development, Quebec City, Canada.

Whiteside-Mansell, L., Pope, S., & Bradley, R. H. (1996). Patterns of parenting behavior in young mothers. *Family Relations, 45,* 273–281.

Wilson, R. S., & Matheny, A. P. (1983). Mental development: Family environment and genetic influences. *Intelligence, 7,* 195–215.

Wohlwill, J., & Heft, H. (1977). Environments fit for the developing child. In H. McGurk (Ed.), *Ecological factors in human development* (pp. 1–22). Amsterdam: North Holland.

Woodworth, S., Belsky, J., & Crnic, K. (1996). The determinants of fathering during the child's second and third years of life: A developmental analysis. *Journal of Marriage and Family, 58,* 679–692.

World Health Organization. (1980). *Noise. Environmental health criteria 12.* Geneva, Switzerland: Author.

Wulbert, M., Inglis, S., Kriegsmann, E., & Millis, B. (1975). Language delay and associated mother/child interactions. *Developmental Psychology, 2,* 61–70.

Stephanie Aubry
Diane N. Ruble
Laura B. Silverman

CHAPTER 17

The Role of Gender Knowledge in Children's Gender-Typed Preferences

☐ Historical Overview

This chapter explores children's developing knowledge of gender stereotypes for objects, activities, and personality attributes, and the influence of this knowledge on children's own preferences. By investigating this issue, we can come to a better understanding of the role that cognitions play in children's gender related preferences and behavior. This issue has gained importance in the past twenty years as the "cognitive revolution" in psychology has led theories of gender development to become increasingly cognitive in their focus. While it is now widely accepted that children's beliefs about gender play an important role in gender development, there is still a great deal of controversy about whether these beliefs are causally related to and precede gender-typed preferences and behavior, especially early on in children's development (Huston, 1985; Martin, 1993). There is also debate about the importance of cognitive factors relative to other influences (Ruble & Martin, 1998).

The first truly cognitive model of gender development was proposed by Kohlberg in 1966. This model was revolutionary for proposing that children do not become gender typed passively by the socializing agents around them but, instead, play an active role in constructing their own gender typing. Children's understanding about gender is critical to this process, and this understanding develops as an outgrowth of cognitive development more broadly. A key feature of the theory is that, once children acquire gender constancy, the belief that their gender is an immutable trait about themselves that can never be reversed or discarded, they are motivated to seek out information about what is appropriate for their gender by carefully observing the behaviors of others. They acquire an extensive network of knowledge about the gender norms of their culture, and selectively take on those behaviors and traits that they learn are same-sex appropriate. This is suggested to take place between the age of 2 and 7. For cognitive theorists of this tradition, beliefs about gender and knowledge of gender stereotypes are antecedent and causal factors in children's gender-typed behavior and preferences.

Another set of theories which arose from the "cognitive revolution" are gender schema theories. One early schema theory was developed by Bem in 1981. She suggested that children develop an extensive associative network of knowledge about the gender norms of their culture, called *gender schemas*, which affect the way children process new information relevant to gender. Children's attention to, encoding of, and retrieval of novel, gender-related information are filtered through their preexisting gender schemas. Children's own attitudes, behaviors, and preferences become gender typed as the self-concept itself be-

Preparation of this chapter was faciliated by Research Scientist Award MH01202 and Research Award MH37215, both from the National Institute of Mental Health to Diane N. Ruble. We are grateful to Carol Martin for comments on an earlier draft.

comes assimilated into the gender schema, and children learn to evaluate their adequacy as a person in terms of the schema.

Another early model of gender-based schematic processing in children was developed by Martin and Halverson (1981). Here too, the authors suggested that gender schematic knowledge plays an important role in young children's gender-typed preferences and behavior. To illustrate how schematic processing operates in gender typing, they described an example of a girl presented with a doll. According to this model, the girl makes a series of decisions on the basis of her gender schemas which affect how she interacts with the doll. She first decides that "dolls are self-relevant." She then concludes that "dolls are for girls and I am a girl, which means that dolls are for me." She approaches the doll, plays with it, explores and learns as much as she can about it, while encoding in memory the information she has acquired. When presented with a truck instead, she decides that "trucks are for boys" and "I am a girl," and therefore, avoids playing with the truck altogether. In line with their theory, these authors predicted that children with more developed schemas would be more likely to approach toys and activities that are appropriate for their sex while avoiding those that are inappropriate, compared to children with schematic knowledge that is less well developed. Thus, in both cognitive developmental theory and the gender schema models, knowledge of one's gender and knowledge of the gender role stereotypes of one's culture lead to the acquisition of gender-typed preferences and behaviors.

Cognitive theories of gender development generally are contrasted with social learning theories, which have been extremely influential in the past 30 years. According to Mischel (1966) in an early presentation of this perspective, children acquire gender-typed preferences and behaviors as a result of learning contingencies; society rewards children for engaging in behavior appropriate for their sex and punishes them for inappropriate behavior. Children also learn gender-appropriate behaviors through observational learning; they imitate same-sex models whom they perceive as powerful in the world, such as their parents. In recent years, social learning theorists also have acknowledged the role of cognitive factors in children's gender development, renaming their theory "social cognitive theory" (Bussey & Bandura, 1992). In this new model, cognitive factors play a role in gender development in conjunction with social influences, such as parents, teachers, peers, the mass media, and cultural institutions. Together they produce gender-related standards which children use in self-regulation.

However, this model differs from cognitive developmental theory and schema theories in that knowledge about gender and gender-role stereotypes does not lead *to* gender-typed preferences and behavior. In fact, just the opposite occurs—knowledge of gender stereotypes increases as a result of children developing stronger gender-linked preferences. It is the explicit and implicit socializing influences experienced from birth that cause children to become gender typed; the learning of gender role norms occurs as an outgrowth of this process.

In summary, it is now widely accepted that cognitive factors, such as children's knowledge of gender stereotypes, play an important role in gender development. What remains of the theoretical and empirical debate is the nature and direction of the relationship between this knowledge and children's own gender-linked preferences and behavior. This issue is the focus of the remainder of the chapter.

☐ Methodological Clarifications

Before reviewing the literature on this topic, it is important to make two methodological clarifications involving the assessment of gender stereotype knowledge and preference. Signorella, Bigler, and Liben (1993) found evidence that differences in the way gender schemata are conceptualized and measured can lead to different results. Their data suggested that forced-choice measures, regardless of the specific wording of the questions, tap knowledge of existing gender stereotypes, whereas non-forced-choice measures assess either knowledge or attitudes toward stereotypes, depending on the way the questions are phrased. Questions that use wording such as "Who usually" tend to tap knowledge, while questions worded as "Who should" or "Who can" measure attitudes. Since we are interested in children's knowledge of stereotypes rather than their attitudes toward those stereotypes, we limit ourselves to discussing studies which use forced-choice measures, or are worded in a manner that assesses knowledge.

Another clarification involves the definition of preference. In the literature, researchers have used both verbal report measures as well as studies of behavior to refer to children's gender-related preferences. While these often yield similar trends, the effect of stereotype knowledge on a child's elicited choices in a controlled setting may be very different from its effect on the child's behavior in a free play situation. Thus, in this literature review, we address studies that define preference in both ways but clearly differentiate between them.

Knowledge and Preference Trends for the Preschool Years

In 1983, Aletha Huston presented an extensive review of the literature on gender development in children, investigating multiple dimensions of gender typing, including emerging knowledge of gender stereotypes and gender-typed preferences and behavior. She concluded that, as early as the age of 3, American children are aware of the gender stereotypes for most concrete activities and interests including toys, clothing, tools, household objects, games, and work. Occupational stereotypes are learned slightly later, during the end of preschool and the beginning of elementary school. She painted a similar picture of the preference literature. By the age of 3, children prefer gender-typed toys and avoid other-gender toys, even when few alternatives are made available. By kindergarten, children also develop gender-typed occupational preferences.

More recent literature has arrived at similar conclusions (see Ruble & Martin, 1998, for a review). Stereotype knowledge for concrete items emerges during the preschool years and reaches ceiling levels by age 5 or 6. This trend has been found consistently in studies that used different experimental methodologies and investigated different concrete items (Coker, 1984; Martin & Little, 1990; Perry, White, & Perry, 1984; Picariello, Greenberg, & Pillemer, 1990; Serbin, Powlishta & Gulko, 1993; Serbin & Sprafkin, 1986).

A common procedure for assessing knowledge of gender stereotypes is to have children sort pictures of stereotypical items such as toys, household objects, and adult possessions into appropriately gender-labeled boxes; the more items sorted in line with gender stereotypes, the higher the gender knowledge score. In most studies, the proper labeling of the items as feminine, masculine, or neutral is achieved a priori using adult ratings of gender stereotypes. One very frequently used method is the Sex-Role Learning Inventory (SERLI; Edelbrock & Sugawara, 1978). In this measure, children are presented with drawings of objects traditionally associated with the male gender role (e.g., car, shovel) and the female gender role (e.g., baby bottle, hairbrush, and mirror) and are asked, "Who would use this object? Boys? Girls? Or both boys and girls?" Children first respond verbally and then sort the pictures into appropriately labeled boxes. To achieve a forced-choice format, the items labeled "both" are presented again, and children are asked who would use the object more? Total knowledge is the percentage of items identified in accordance with traditional gender stereotypes. Gender stereotype knowledge also has been assessed by having children place female and male dolls into stereotypically depicted masculine or feminine scenes (Picariello et al., 1990), and by having children choose toys that a same-sex child would prefer (Perry et al., 1984).

Recent literature also has supported Huston's conclusion that children show evidence of gender typing in their own preferences and behavior as early as 3 years (Carter & Levy, 1988; Coker, 1984; Martin & Little, 1990). Interestingly, several studies measuring behavioral rather than verbal preferences have found that children show greater involvement with same- than other-gender toys in their free play behavior as young as the early toddler years (Caldera, Huston, & O'Brien, 1989; O'Brien & Huston, 1985). There is even some evidence that girls as young as 10 months show more interest in dolls than do boys of the same age (Roopnarine, 1986). Such findings raise questions about the role of stereotypic knowledge in emerging gender-related preferences because these preferences seem to be present at a younger age than relevant knowledge is typically found (Huston, 1983; Ruble & Martin, 1998).

In more highly controlled experiments, however, in which children are systematically presented with toys that vary in their gender-role appropriateness and are asked to make conscious, deliberate choices, children show only slight evidence of gender typing in the early toddler years. They show a large increase in gender typing at age 3, which is followed by moderate gains throughout the remaining preschool years (Carter & Levy, 1988; Coker, 1984; Martin & Little, 1990; Perry et al., 1984). Indeed, there is considerable evidence of parallel trends when stereotypic knowledge and preferences are measured in similar ways. For example, comparisons of 4- and 6-year-olds on the SERLI, which measures preference as well as knowledge on the same items, have found that both knowledge and preference scores increase with age and are higher for boys than for girls (Coker, 1984; Edelbrock & Sugawara, 1978; Welch-Ross & Schmidt, 1996).

However, in the SERLI, there exist instances in which preferences are not always highly gender typed, even though knowledge scores are high. This has been attributed to the fact that many of the items are household chores (e.g., ironing, sweeping), and are therefore not particularly desirable. In measures that include more play activities and toys (e.g., trucks, dolls), preferences often are highly gender typed and may reach levels as high as 80% by age 4 (e.g., Emmerich & Shepard, 1984).

In general, as reported above, gender stereotypic knowledge and verbal preferences emerge by age 3 and continue to show gains at least until age 5. Moreover, studies that have measured knowledge and preference for similar items often have found parallel developmental trends in 4- to 6-year-olds. This parallel increase in the two measures at this age would seem to make age 4 to 6 an ideal time to examine the relation between children's preference and knowledge for concrete items. Once knowledge approaches ceiling after age 5 to 6, a relation will be difficult to observe.

Knowledge and Preference Trends in the Middle Childhood Years

Because the acquisition of stereotype knowledge for concrete items generally reaches a ceiling by the time children enter kindergarten, far fewer studies have focused on the subsequent development of this knowledge during middle childhood. Nevertheless, the range and extent of children's stereotype knowledge for concrete items continues to increase during the elementary school years, as does children's recognition of the subtleties and nuances associated with these stereotypes (Ruble & Martin, 1998).

The literature on children's preferences for concrete items during middle childhood is somewhat less clear cut. Huston (1983) concluded that boys and girls follow different developmental paths after age 5 or 6, with boys becoming more gender typed, demonstrating greater interest in masculine activities, and girls becoming less gender typed, showing a declining preference for feminine items and increased interest in masculine activities. Several studies since her review have replicated this finding, including a 3-year longitudinal study conducted by Eron, Huesmann, Brice, Fischer and Mermelstein (1983). In this study, two cohorts of children (one tested in the first, second, and third grades, and one tested in the third, fourth, and fifth grades) were shown pictures of children's activities that were masculine, feminine, and neutral, and were asked to indicate which they liked the most. Over time, it was found that the girls' preference for masculine activities increased and their preference for feminine activities decreased, while boys showed high levels of preference for masculine activities and low levels of preference for feminine activities throughout all grades of the study. Studies by Katz and her colleagues using a range of different measures (Katz & Boswell, 1986; Katz & Walsh, 1991) also have found that boys' gender-typed preferences increased during middle childhood, whereas girls' preferences remained stable or declined.

Other studies have found mixed results, however. For example, in a recent longitudinal study, Trautner (1992) did not find a sex difference but, instead, found two separate trajectories for children's preferences that functioned independently of sex. Children either showed a large increase in their gender-typed preferences and behavior until the age of 7 at which point they stabilized, or they were already at a high level at the age of 5 and remained at this level. Similarly, other studies have found that preferences for both sexes were stable after kindergarten (e.g., Serbin et al., 1993) or that they declined (Welch-Ross & Schmidt, 1996). Patterns of sex differences also seem to vary depending on the kind of preference assessed, such as occupations versus toys (Etaugh & Liss, 1992), or items assessing approach toward same-gender activities versus avoidance of other-gender activities (Bussey & Perry, 1982).

In short, parallel developmental trends do not occur for children's gender-related knowledge and preferences regarding concrete items during middle childhood. After age 6, knowledge remains steady or increases only slightly, but gender-typed preferences appear to be multiply determined, often showing a decline, especially for girls. Thus, preferences during this age seem unlikely to be driven by stereotypic knowledge, although they may be related to individual differences in the flexibility of applying stereotypes (i.e., believing items are appropriate for both boys and girls), which is higher for girls and increases with age (Ruble & Martin, 1998).

Up to this point, we have focused exclusively on children's knowledge of and preference for concrete objects, activities, toys, and occupations. However, middle childhood is an important period in gender development because it also is the first time that children show knowledge of and adherence to stereotypes for personality attributes. Considerable evidence has suggested that children learn about personal-social attributes later than concepts about activities, presumably because attributes are abstractions from behavior rather than concrete, observable objects and play behaviors (Huston, 1983; Ruble & Ruble, 1982).

One of the most common methods for assessing children's knowledge of stereotypes for personal-social attributes is the Sex Stereotype Measure (SSM) designed by Williams, Bennett, and Best (1975). This tool provides children with short stories illustrating various traits traditionally associated with either the masculine role (e.g., adventurous or independent) or the feminine role (e.g., gentle). After hearing each story, children indicate who they think the story is about by pointing to the drawing of either a boy or a girl. They receive a total knowledge score based on the percentage of stories in which they made judgments that were in line with traditional stereotypes.

With the use of this measure, studies consistently have found that children show little knowledge of attribute stereotypes until 5 to 6 years, after which point their knowledge increases steadily through middle childhood (Ruble & Martin, 1998). For example, Coker (1984) studied children ages 3 to 6 and found that before the age of 5, they performed at chance levels. Their knowledge increased slightly at age 6, but still was poor. Leahy and Shirk (1984) extended this research to older children, including participants at 4, 6, and 8 years. They found that children showed increasing knowledge of stereotypes across the age range. Finally, a study by Best et al. (1977) showed a gradual linear development in knowledge of attribute stereotypes between age 5 to 11, with the knowledge of 11-year-olds still not reaching ceiling levels, suggesting that attribute knowledge continues to develop into adolescence. This general pattern of development also has been observed in children from countries other than the United States (Best et al., 1977).

One difficulty that researchers must confront when studying attribute stereotypes, is that children often demonstrate a "same-sex bias." Children attribute positive characteristics to their own sex and negative characteristics to the other sex, rather than accurately identifying gender stereotypes. This phenomenon was illustrated in a study by Albert and Porter (1983), in which children 4 to 6 years old were told stories illustrating attributes typically associated with the male and female gender roles. At important points in the stories, children were asked to decide whether a boy or girl doll should demonstrate the behavior described. It was found that, for many of the positive attributes such as leadership and nurturance, the majority of 4-year-olds associated these stereotypes with the doll of their own sex rather than accurately identifying the stereotypes. A similar pattern occurred for negative attributes such as passivity and aggression; 4-year-olds attributed these characteristics to the other sex. The author's conclusion was that "young children attempt to maintain pride in their gender role through associating with their own sex the qualities that are highly valued in their environment." Gradually after age 5 to 6, children began to lose this same-sex bias and showed evidence of gender stereotyping. Serbin et al. (1993) found that a same-sex bias for personality attributes continued to be present in children age 5 to 8 and was not replaced by more accurate stereotype knowledge until the age of 11.

What about the development of children's preferences for attribute items? It actually is not entirely correct to speak of children's "preference" for these items, but it can be asked to what degree they describe themselves according to gender typed traits. In the preschool years, children show little evidence of gender typing when attributing personality characteristics to themselves but, instead, label themselves using only positive characteristics and none of the negative traits (Cowan & Hoffman, 1986).

By the middle childhood years, however, when children are becoming aware of the gender stereotypes for attribute items, they also appear to show evidence of gender-typing themselves (Ruble & Martin, 1998), although most of the research in this area has examined positive or neutral attributes only. For example, a study by Antill, Russell, Goodnow, & Cotton (1992) found that when children age 8 to 12 were asked whether certain positive gender-typed personality attributes such as "adventurous" and "sensitive to others" were true of them, the children responded by attributing more of the gender-appropriate attributes to themselves and fewer of the gender-inappropriate items. A study by Boldizar (1991), which assessed gender typing of attribute items for children in third through seventh grades using a version of the Bem Sex Role Inventory (BSRI) adapted for children, the Children's Sex Role Inventory (CSRI), also found that, across all ages, the children were significantly gender typed. However, there also was a grade by sex interaction on the feminine scale, indicating a pattern of increased flexibility. Girls showed declining scores on the feminine items between third and sixth grades, while boys showed increasing feminine scores during the same time period. However, there was a resurgence in gender typing with the onset of adolescence in seventh grade, with girls showing increased femininity and boys showing a decline in femininity.

In summary, just as children do not show knowledge of gender-typed personality characteristics in preschool, they also do not describe themselves along gender lines. This is partly the result of same-sex bias, and also is probably related to the broader issue that children are not aware of stable personality traits in themselves or others at this young age, irrespective of gender. However, by third grade, children begin to describe themselves according to gender-typed personality traits, although this effect is not as strong as it is for concrete activities and interests. Thus, as with concrete items, there appears to be a parallel developmental increase in knowledge and preference for attribute items, but it occurs a bit later (i.e., between 5 and 12 years). It seems likely, then, that the influence of knowledge on children's tendency to describe themselves according to gender attributes probably also emerges later than for concrete items.

☐ Examining the Relation Between Knowledge and Preference

Evidence for Independence

So far, we have examined stereotype knowledge and preference trends for children from preschool through the end of middle childhood. We can now begin to explore the research which looks specifically at the relationship between these two important components of gender development. Although the development of gender-stereotyped knowledge and preference occurs during the same time period, there are conflicting views in the literature about the nature of the relationship. While some have argued that knowledge of gender stereotypes is an important influence on children's gender-typed preferences, others claim that the trends are parallel, but independent. Huston (1983) alluded to this possibility, "very early aspects of sex-typed behavior may develop independently of cognitions about gender. There is a real possibility that cognition and behavior develop along somewhat separate tracks, perhaps becoming integrated when the child reaches middle childhood or in a later period of development" (pp. 448–449).

Eisenberg, Murray, and Hite (1982) made the argument that knowledge and preference are independent in early childhood after exploring the spontaneous explanations preschoolers provide for their gender-typed choices. In one phase of the study, 3 to 4 year olds were followed during their free play session and were asked what they liked about specific toys that they were playing with at any given moment. In the second phase of the study, the same children were presented with several same- and other-gender toys, and were asked what they liked about the toy they preferred the most, and what they disliked about the toy they preferred the least. In both phases of the study, children made reference to their knowledge of gender role appropriateness less than 1% of the time, and were much more likely to provide a justification on the basis of what the toy did or its specific characteristics. From these data, the authors argued that preschool children are not making choices on the basis of their understanding of gender stereotypes but, rather, on the basis of other, more salient factors.

As the authors themselves acknowledged, however, a basic problem with this study is that it assumes children at this young age are aware of the motivations for their choices and are able to articulate them to an outside observer. This assumption does not seem realistic given that children do not develop metacognitive abilities until much later in their development. Moreover, the process by which knowledge of gender stereotypes leads to gender-typed preferences may be extremely automatic, preventing children from being conscious of these influences; this possibility is also noted in the article.

A study by Weinraub and colleagues (1984) provided additional evidence that knowledge and preference may function independently during the preschool years. In their study of 2- to 3-year-olds, they found that preference for gender-typed toys emerged as early as 26 months, but that knowledge of sex differences in toys did not develop until 5 months later, at 31 months. From this piece of data, these authors concluded that knowledge and preference may develop independently, or that it may "take some time before children's awareness of sex-role schemas begins to affect sex-typed behavior" (p. 1502).

However, certain methodological features of this experiment limit the conclusions that can be drawn from it. Most notably, the gender knowledge and preference tasks were quite different and not likely to be equivalent in their level of difficulty for preschoolers. The gender knowledge task was a classification task that involved sorting pictures of items into boxes labeled with the appropriate gender, whereas the preference measure was behavioral, involving observations of the amount of time children spent touching same-gender and other-gender toys during a structured free play session. The gender knowledge task probably was very challenging for preschoolers and required a much heavier processing load than the method used to assess preference. This fact alone could account for the earlier appearance of gender-typed preference.

Moreover, there are additional problems with the particular knowledge and preference measures chosen for this study, independent of their relation to one another. There is evidence in the cognitive developmental literature that sorting tasks are poor indicators of what preschoolers know about logical rules and their consequences (Zelazo & Reznick, 1991; Zelazo, Reznick, & Pinon, 1995). It often is the case that preschoolers are able to indicate verbally which items belong in certain categories (e.g., which things go "in the house," and which go "outside the house") and yet show a much poorer performance when asked to sort pictures of these same items into separate piles. There is an "asynchrony between knowledge and action" which is particularly marked during the preschool years, and which may be related to the immaturity of the prefrontal cortex. Thus, preschoolers actually may have known more about the gender appropriateness of toys than was evident in their performance on the gender knowledge sorting task. The preference measure also was problematic because it was a measure of children's initial interest in toys. This procedure may not have been reflective of children's actual preferences, in part, because children may be drawn to novel toys at first, which may not end up as the toys they actually prefer. The authors themselves acknowledged that the failure to find a relation between gender-related awareness and toy preference could be due to the "limited sophistication of the sex-typed toy preference measure" (p. 1502).

In a study by Perry et al. (1984), the authors made a similar argument that, because the acquisition of gender-typed preferences precedes the acquisition of gender knowledge, early gender typing cannot possibly result from children adopting as their own preferences those toys and activities they have learned is appropriate for their sex. Instead, the authors suggested, the order of causation may be the reverse: Gender-typed preferences may contribute to the acquisition of knowledge, or perhaps the two are not causally related at all. Their basis for these conclusions is that, at age 3, the boys alone showed a great increase in preference for same-gender toys, while responding only slightly better than chance on the measure of gender-stereotype knowledge. It was not until age 4 that boys' knowledge of the gender appropriateness of toys caught up with their gender-typed preference.

The advantage of this study as compared to that of Weinraub and colleagues was that the knowledge and preference measures were far more comparable. For both measures, the children were presented with similar pairs of photographed toys (either same-gender paired with neutral or neutral paired with other-gender), and were asked to indicate which toy they thought either the same-sex children shown in a photograph would prefer (for the knowledge measure), or the toy that they themselves would prefer (for the preference measure). There are a couple of limitations to their conclusions, however. First, the knowledge measure was somewhat unusual in that it did not pair same- versus other-gender items as do most measures; and, for half of the items, it required the child to infer that same-sex children would like a neutral toy more than an other-gender toy. This task may be confusing to young children.[1]

More importantly, in this study, their only method for testing the relationship between knowledge and preference was by comparing the changes over time in the knowledge and preference group means, rather than looking at individual differences. It is true that preference scores were higher than knowledge scores for boys at age 3, but this observation does not necessarily preclude the possibility that knowledge influenced choices even at this age. Their conclusions would have been much stronger had they used correlation models, regression models, or both, or other such methods better suited for testing whether scores on one variable are associated with or predict scores on a second variable. The question is whether knowledge influences preferences; it is not necessary that it be the only determinant in every case. To illustrate, a young boy's preference for a truck because his parents have given him a lot of trucks does not undermine the cognitive developmental argument. Once the boy knows that trucks are for boys, however, cognitive developmental theory would predict that he subsequently would show greater personal preferences for this toy than he had previously.

In a more recent study, Hort, Leinbach, and Fagot (1991) argued that gender is a "multidimensional construct," and that the acquisition of knowledge about gender roles in preschool and the acquisition of gender-typed preferences occur separately. The authors came to this conclusion after finding no correlation between the knowledge and preference sections of the SERLI (Edlebrock & Sugawara, 1978) in a sample of 4-year-olds. A serious problem with this measure, however, as noted above, was that many of the items, particularly the feminine ones, were unpleasant household chores such as ironing, sewing, and sweeping. Thus, girls may have been reluctant to show a preference for these activities, even once they had learned that they were same-gender appropriate. Moreover, developmental considerations discussed earlier may be important. Gender-related knowledge and preferences for concrete items both increase during age 3 to 6 years. Therefore, examining the relation at a single age (in this case, 4 years) may provide an inadequate test, particularly, if they develop at different times and rates of development. Indeed, it may be insufficient to examine only concurrent relations, in that new knowledge may influence self-regulation only after a lag in time.

Similarly, Bussey and Bandura (1992) reported that knowledge of gender stereotypes for concrete items was unrelated to gender-linked preferences in their study of preschoolers 2.4 to 4 years old. They reached this conclusion using a sorting task to assess gender knowledge, and by operationalizing gender-linked conduct as the total number of seconds children chose to play with masculine and feminine toys during a short unstructured play session. The authors claimed that they were not surprised by the lack of correlation they found between knowledge and preference in this experimental paradigm, given that "most children at an early age are fully aware of the gender-linked stereotypes but show substantial variation in gender-linked behavior" (p. 1247). They conclude that the findings taken as a whole reveal that from an early age, children adopt traditional patterns of gender-linked conduct. Neither gender constancy nor gender knowledge appear to guide this conduct" (p. 1248).

These conclusions do not seem warranted for several reasons discussed in reference to other studies. The primary reason is that gender knowledge was assessed in this experiment using a sorting task which may not have been reflective of what children actually knew about gender stereotypes, and which was far more demanding than the gender preference measure. Moreover, this method of assessing knowledge was particularly complex because it also required the "accurate" sorting of neutral items, such as xylophone, into the box for "both boys and girls." In addition, their participants were very young, representing the beginning of known developmental increases in these constructs, and, thus, it may have been too early to examine predicted relations, at least without a longitudinal analysis to allow for time lags in influence. Finally, their conclusion that knowledge must not guide gender-typed preferences and behavior simply because children who sorted more "accurately" did not show higher same-gender play (or lower other-gender play) would seem to be premature for two reasons. First, the correlation would be lowered for children who "accurately" sort, for example, the xylophone into the box for both boys and girls and then play with xylophones themselves and for boys who "inaccurately" sort robots into the box for both boys and girls and then play with it themselves. Second, as suggested above, simply because children do not always apply their gender knowledge to their own behavior and preferences does not mean that gender knowledge has no influence on preference. It is but one factor in a host of many which affect children's decisions about what they like and what behavior they choose to engage in at a given time.

Finally, Carter and Levy (1988) suggested that it is the level of children's gender schematization, rather than their gender knowledge, that should lead to greater gender-typed preferences among preschoolers. They argued that a highly schematized child, as measured by the child who rapidly picks the same-gender toy when it is paired with either a neutral- or other-gender toy, should have preferences that are more gender typed than the child who is less highly schematized. As predicted, they found that gender schematization significantly predicted gender-typed toy preference in 3- to 5-year-olds, whereas overall level of gender role knowledge as assessed by performance on a version of the SERLI did not.

This study provided an interesting twist to the literature discussed up to this point. On the one hand, the authors suggested that gender knowledge does not predict gender-typed preferences and, yet, without knowledge of which toys are masculine and which are feminine, the highly schematized children they described would be unable to choose the same-gender toy from the pair placed before them. The data suggested that individual differences in the extent to which that knowledge is salient or important influences preferences but, nevertheless, gender knowledge must certainly be playing a role in their choices. Perhaps, then, the authors' argument is that global knowledge of gender roles should not be predictive of children's preferences in a specific situation. This makes sense; as argued earlier with respect to other studies, there is no reason why children's global score on the SERLI should be associated with their toy preferences in this experiment. The absence of a correlation between measures of knowledge and preference using very different items is not necessarily informative; it is the gender knowledge of the items participants are choosing that should be predictive of the specific choices they make. Moreover, in this study, knowledge was at a ceiling level (on the average, 86% of the items were correctly recognized as stereotypically consistent or inconsistent), suggesting that this restricted range might make it difficult to find correlations with preference. Finally, it would have been useful to examine interactions with sex, because the preference measure included pairings with neutral toys which girls often prefer.

In summary, the studies discussed up to this point have all attempted to show that children's knowledge about gender stereotypes in preschool does not influence their own personal preferences and behavior, that acquiring gender stereotype knowledge and becoming gender typed are separate processes. Three general types of arguments have been used: (a) that young children do not mention gender as a basis for their choices, (b) that preferences sometimes emerge earlier in development than knowledge, and (c) that knowledge and preferences measures are uncorrelated. Although these findings certainly do raise questions about the nature of the relation between gender knowledge and personal preferences, we have suggested that, because of a variety of conceptual and methodological problems, these studies do not provide an adequate test of the hypothesis that gender knowledge influences preference.

Studies Finding a Relation Between Knowledge and Preference

Statements suggesting that preferences must, at least, be partly based on knowledge are abundant in the literature, but the evidence is often indirect. For example, on the basis of findings from a study of 2-, 4- and 6-year-olds, Blakemore, LaRue, and Olejnik (1979) concluded:

> Their behavior is certainly in line with the idea that knowledge about the sex appropriateness of toys influences preferences. Indeed, the spontaneous comments of some 6-year-olds during the preference task made it clear the concept was salient to them (e.g., "I don't like that. That's for boys. I like girls' things"). (p. 340)

The major supportive findings were that both 4- and 6-year-olds were easily able to sort toys stereotypically and also were strongly gender typed in their toy preferences, whereas 2-year-old girls neither preferred the gender-appropriate toys nor were they able to sort them "accurately." In seemingly direct contradiction to their conclusion, however, 2-year-old boys preferred same-gender toys, without showing any awareness of their gender typicality. Thus, the best case that can be made about a positive relation among these two constructs from these data is that, among children who were cognitively sophisticated enough to understand the gender dimensionality of toys, gender-typed preferences were high. Among less cognitively advanced children, the relation between cognition and gender-typed toy preference was less straightforward.

Additional indirect supportive evidence was provided in a follow-up study by these same authors. Three-year-old girls who completed the gender knowledge task first were found to be significantly more gender typed in their own preferences than were the girls who were given the preference task first. These data suggested that gender knowledge was beginning to form at this age, but it only actively influenced preference when this knowledge was made salient. These findings are interesting and suggestive; however, strong inferences about the relationship between knowledge and preference cannot be made.

Other indirect evidence that children use their stereotype knowledge in forming preferences has come from several studies showing that identifying toys experimentally as being "for boys" or "for girls" increases the likelihood of gender-typed toy preferences. For example, in a study by Montmayor (1974), children age 6 to 8 were asked to play a game that was labeled by the experimenter as either gender-appropriate, neutral, or inappropriate. After playing the game, the children assessed how much they liked it, ranging from "the worst in the world" to "the best in the world." Results showed that, when boys believed that the game was meant "for boys" or "neutral," they gave it significantly higher ratings than when they believed it was "for girls." Similarly, when girls believed that the game was "for girls" or "neutral," they rated it significantly higher than when they thought it was "for boys." These results are especially illuminating because they show that the other-sex rejection component of preferences may be more influenced by increased gender stereotype knowledge than the same-sex approach component. Learning that a game was "inappropriate" led to increased rejection (compared to when the game was labeled neutral); however, learning that the game was "appropriate" did not lead children to prefer the game more. Similar findings have been reported for actual engagement or avoidance of toys (Bradbard, Martin, Endsley, & Halverson, 1986; Martin, Eisenbud, & Rose, 1995) and when the manipulation of appropriateness is done by showing same- or other-sex models playing with the toy (e.g., Ruble, Balaban, & Cooper, 1981).

Only a few studies have found a direct association between gender-related knowledge and preferences. In a study of 3- to 6-year-olds, Coker (1984) found that the children knew the gender stereotypicality of concrete objects before showing preferences for those items, and that gender knowledge and preference scores were significantly correlated, but only for boys. Similarly, Serbin et al. (1993) examined 5- to 12-year-olds knowledge of and preference for a range of gender-typed items including activities, occupations, and traits. Knowledge was assessed using a forced-choice sorting task, and preference was measured by asking participants to rank the same items from their most favorite to their least. Results showed that the children's stereotype knowledge and preference scores were significantly correlated.

Taken together, then, the combination of indirect and direct data suggest that claims of independence between gender-related knowledge and preference may be premature. Interestingly, in the two studies that avoided some of the pitfalls of other studies, a direct relation between the two constructs was found. That is, both Coker (1984) and Serbin et al. (1993) included children at multiple ages as participants and examined correlations between knowledge and preference for the same items.

☐ Summary of Prior Findings

In summary, the relation between children's knowledge of gender stereotypes and their preferences is not clear, largely because of theoretical and methodological limitations in extant studies. Typical methodological problems in the preschool literature include using gender knowledge tasks which may not accurately assess what preschoolers know about gender stereotypes, and that are far more challenging than the measures used to assess gender preference. Equally problematic is basing inferences about the relation between gender knowledge and gender-typed preferences on developmental trends rather than on direct associations between knowledge and preference.

Even when studies do examine direct relations, however, conceptual problems affect the interpretation of both finding and not finding relations. Both the emergence and maintenance of preferences about activities and self-attribution of personality attributes are likely to be influenced by a number of factors other than gender appropriateness (such as toy attractiveness, social desirability, external support, personal skills and interests, and prior interest in and availability of the item). Knowledge of gender stereotypes may be viewed as a guideline that influences children's interests and behaviors, but this does not imply that a one-to-one correspondence between knowledge and choice should occur to the exclusion of other relevant factors. Emerging cognitive structures may change, for example, the likelihood children will play with dolls and trucks, but this does not mean that a girl will always choose the doll over the truck, even if the doll is old and ratty, and the truck is new and shiny. Motivational and attitudinal processes seem likely to be particularly important determinants of children's responsiveness to gender norms (Signorella et al., 1993). To illustrate, once children have learned that certain activities and characteristics are appropriate for their gender and others are not, their continued adherence to these norms likely will depend, in part, on how important it is to them to appear feminine and how strongly they believe that males and females should behave differently in certain arenas.

☐ Current Study

In the present study, we focus primarily on the emergence of preferences: How knowledge of gender norms influences gender-related preferences in 4- to 8-year-old children. The question is whether emerging knowledge about particular objects, activities, and characteristics influences subsequent preferences. A major issue guiding the present study concerns the developmental timing of knowledge-preference relations. There are various reasons to predict that knowledge may not affect preferences immediately. If so, measures of only concurrent relations may not detect a true relation. Two factors would seem to be especially likely to lead to a lag between the emergence of knowledge and the emergence of the associated preference: (a) when the gender-appropriate item is unattractive such as chores, or involves negative attributes such as helpless; and (b) when the new knowledge requires giving up an item that was previously viewed as fun or desirable, such as computers or being strong.

The purpose of the present study is to arrive at a better understanding of the relation between stereotype knowledge and preference, by attempting to overcome many of the common methodological and conceptual problems currently in the literature. First, we designed a preference measure that is practically identical in format and content to the knowledge measure, so that specific relations between knowledge and preference might be examined, and to reduce the possibility that the knowledge measure was more complicated than the preference measure, particularly, for the younger children.

Second, in our analysis of the data, we made use of regression models to examine direct relations between knowledge and preference, in addition to examining developmental trends in both. Moreover, our study is one of the few longitudinal studies on this topic, spanning both the preschool and early middle childhood years, allowing us to see whether knowledge predicts preference concurrently, over time, or both. It seems reasonable to suppose that the effects of new knowledge about gender appropriateness may require several months before it influences children's own preferences, especially if it means now avoiding an activity that was previously considered attractive. In addition, the procedure we developed to assess preference allows us to tease apart children's attraction to things that are gender consistent and their avoidance of things that are gender inconsistent.

Finally, we chose diverse items that involve knowledge development at different ages, incorporating a range of concrete objects, activities, occupations, and personality attributes.

☐ Method

Participants

Two hundred fifty-five children participated in this 3-year longitudinal study. Participants were divided into three cohorts based on grade placement in the first year of the study, with roughly equal numbers of girls and boys participating (see Table 17.1). Of the 255 children, 215 (84%) were present for all testing sessions during the first 2 years. In the last year of the study, an additional 13 children were absent for one or more sessions. All children were enrolled in neighborhood based preschool programs or elementary schools located within two New York Public School Districts on Long Island. The preschool sample did not differ from the elementary school samples in any significant way. Participants were from middle-class, suburban families. Two hundred fifty of the participants were White (98%), 2 were African American and 1 each were Asian, Hispanic, and Native American. Children were recruited as a part of a larger research study which examined children's cognitive and social development using a variety of measures administered during several yearly testing sessions. A letter describing the study and a consent form were sent to their homes.

Testing Sessions

Participants were interviewed during five structured testing sessions over the course of each school year. Interviews continued for three years, resulting in a total of fifteen sessions. During each interview, the cognitive and social measures were administered to participants in a fixed order. Children were interviewed at their elementary schools by one of seven female interviewers. All interviewers had previous experience working with children and completed training on the standardized test administration. In order not to disrupt the daily routine of the classroom, teachers of participants reserved specific time slots during which children could be removed from the classroom. Interviews took place in rooms designated by the host schools. All children were approached in a similar manner by interviewers, who would first introduce themselves and then explain the purpose of the study. Children were told that the research study was designed to examine "changes in kids as they grow up."

All of the data used in this study were collected during the first two interview sessions of each of the three years. A gender knowledge measure was administered during the first interview session of each year (occurring in the fall), and a gender preference measure was administered during the second interview session, a few months later.[2] Children responded to the gender knowledge measure, immediately

TABLE 17.1. Number and mean age (in months) of children in study

Grade	Boys		Girls	
	N	Mean Age	N	Mean Age
Preschool	32	50.5	39	50.3
Kindergarten	40	63.7	49	63.0
First Grade	46	74.9	49	76.3
Total N	118	—	137	—

following the administration of a picture vocabulary test and an open-ended measure of children's sense of self. Administration of the gender preference measure was preceded by a socio-metric measure (indicating which classmates children would most and least prefer to sit next to); an open-ended measure of how accessible children make themselves to peers; a subset of questions from Harter and Pike's Perceived Competence and Social Acceptance Scale; and, a measure of children's range of moods (in which participants were asked to indicate on a five point scale, how often they experienced various moods over a one week period). This order of administration of measures remained the same each year for all cohorts. At the end of each interview session, children were presented with a small prize and thanked for their help.

Measures

Gender Stereotype Knowledge.   Children's knowledge of traditional feminine and masculine gender stereotypes for both concrete items and personality attributes was assessed using a set of 19 items (see Table 17.2) chosen on the basis of previous studies which showed them to be highly stereotyped in children as young as age 4 (e.g. Williams, Bennett, & Best, 1975). The eight concrete items included gender-typed objects, activities and occupations, while the 11 attributes included items that were both positive and negative in valence and covered a range of personal-social characteristics.[3] Children were presented with cards naming the items in random order, and also were given three response cards (men, women, both). All item and response cards were simultaneously read aloud and presented by the interviewer, for children in all three cohorts. During the first phase of the administration of the measure, children were told the following instructions:

> Now, we're going to play a game where I'll ask you to match a phrase or word to whom you think it best describes; men or boys, women or girls, or both. You can tell me what you think by pointing to the card marked by the men or boys, by the women or girls, or showing both as we go through these cards. There are no right or wrong answers. I just want to know what you think.

During the second phase of the administration, the response card with the "both" option was removed, making the task forced choice. Children were now asked to look at each item card again and point to either the "men" or "women" response card.

Gender Preference.   Children's preferences were assessed using the same set of concrete and attribute items used in the gender knowledge measure. The instructions for this task were as follows:

> I've got some cards here with words on them that describe things that people do, have and feel. I'm going to read them to you, and I want you to tell me whether or not what is on the card is something that you would sometimes do or would not do, O.K? You know, whether or not it's something you like.

Children were asked to respond either "yes" or "no" for all items, even if they felt unsure of their answer. The instructions and format for this measure were the same for both concrete and attribute items, even though the nature of the task was slightly different depending on the type of item presented. For concrete items, the purpose of the measure was to assess preference (the last sentence of the instructions was included to emphasize to the children the nature of their task). However, attributes cannot be "preferred" in the same way that concrete items can. Thus, for these items, the purpose of the measure was to assess whether children identified with these gender stereotypical personality traits.

Scoring

Gender Stereotype Knowledge.   For each item of the measure, children were scored as having responded "correctly" if they labeled the item with the appropriate gender stereotype in either the first or second round of questioning (i.e., before or after the task became forced choice).

Concrete Items.   Each child received a total gender knowledge score across all concrete items, which was calculated as the proportion of these items "correctly" identified out of the total number of concrete items attempted. They also received a separate knowledge score for same-gender concrete items (those stereotypically associated with the gender of the particular child being tested). As before, this score was calculated as the proportion "correctly" identified, out of the total number of same-gender concrete items attempted. A score for other-gender concrete items (those associated with the opposite gender of the child being tested) was calculated in the same manner.

Attribute Items.   Each child received a total of four knowledge scores based on both the gender and the valence of the items. These scores included: same-gender positive-valence, same-gender negative-valence, other-gender positive-valence, and other-gender negative-valence. Once again, each score was calculated as the proportion "correctly" identified out of the total attempted in that gender-valence category.

Gender Preference.   Children were scored as showing a preference for each item if they responded "yes," indicating that it was something they liked. For all knowledge scores described above, we calculated corresponding preference scores. In each case, the score was based on the proportion of items that the child liked out of the total attempted.

☐ Results

The presentation of results is divided into two main sections. The first section includes a discussion of children's knowledge and preference for concrete items only. We begin descriptively, exploring the trends that emerged from the data and comparing our trends to those currently in the literature. We then examine whether children's knowledge of gender stereotypes for concrete items actually predicts children's preference for those same items. The second main section is structured similarly to the first but investigates children's knowledge and preference for personality attributes.

Concrete Items

Developmental Trends.   The proportion of children showing gender stereotypic knowledge and preferences for the concrete items are shown in Figures 17.1 through 17.4. There are separate graphs illustrating girls' and boys' knowledge of and preference for feminine and masculine items. Each graph also shows the cohorts separately, making it possible to compare whether children show similar levels of knowledge and preference at the same ages.

As can be seen in Figures 17.1 and 17.2, knowledge for concrete items increases steadily between preschool and third grade with children in different cohorts showing approximately the same levels of knowledge at approximately the same ages.

TABLE 17.2. Item list

Concrete Items	
Feminine	**Masculine**
Secretary	Drives a truck
Hairbrush and mirror	A shovel
Takes care of children	Boxing gloves
Reads love stories	Builds things

Attributes		
Valence	**Feminine**	**Masculine**
Positive	Polite	Active
	Good at reading	Explores strange places
	Gentle	
Negative	Sad	Angry
	Runs away from scary places	Careless
	Afraid	Gets clothes dirty[a]

[a] This item was presented to participants only during the first and second years of testing.

For the most part, the trends are consistent with those in the literature. Children in preschool show some rudimentary knowledge of gender stereotypes, responding slightly above chance on average and, by second or third grade, they reach ceiling levels. The fact that they do not reach ceiling levels as early as kindergarten is somewhat discrepant from the literature. However, this is likely due to the inclusion of occupation and activity items. When we examine the knowledge trends for individual items, we find that common concrete objects such as hairbrush and mirror or shovel are learned earlier (as the literature suggests), than are occupation and activity items such as "secretary" and "reads love stories."

The preference trends, in contrast to the knowledge trends, generally slope downward as can be seen in Figures 17.3 and 17.4. This occurs for both boys and girls, and for both feminine and masculine items, indicating that the items in our measure generally become less desirable as children get older. However, we still see clear evidence of gender typing that becomes more dramatic over time. Boys' preference for feminine items declines much more precipitously than does their preference for masculine items and also reaches much lower absolute levels. By third grade, boys are responding on average that 56% of masculine items describe them, compared to 28% of feminine items. Girls also show a steep decline in their preference for other-gender items between kindergarten and second grade (rebounding slightly in third), while their interest in same-gender items remains practically flat. By third grade, girls prefer an average of 35% of masculine items, compared to 56% of feminine items. Across all years of the study, we see that children never fall below chance in their preference for same-gender items, but fall considerably below chance in their preference for other-gender items, indicating a strong rejection of items as not "appropriate" for their sex.

Predicting Preference from Knowledge for Concrete Items.   We can now ask whether children's knowledge of the stereotypes for concrete items can predict children's preference for those items. We conducted three sets of analyses that enabled us to address this question. First, we examined whether children's preference for same-gender items in year 2 of the study was predicted by their knowledge of the gender appropriateness of those items in both years 1 and 2. This allowed us to see whether

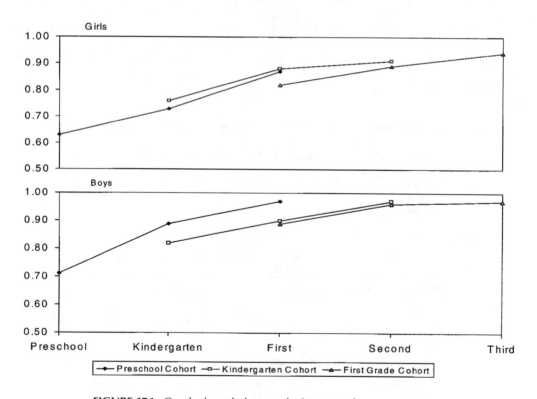

FIGURE 17.1. Gender knowledge trends: Same-gender concrete items.

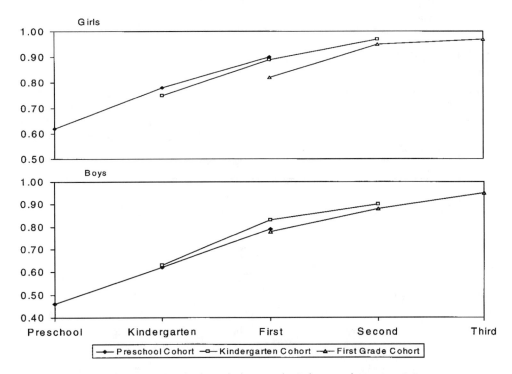

FIGURE 17.2. Gender knowledge trends: Other-gender concrete items.

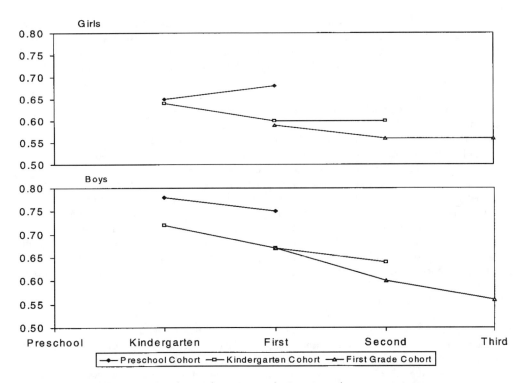

FIGURE 17.3. Gender preference trends: Same-gender concrete items.

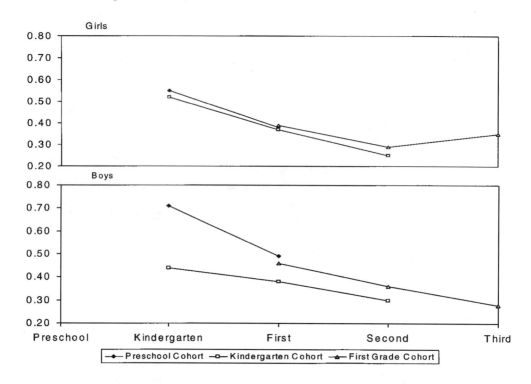

FIGURE 17.4. Gender preference trends: Other-gender concrete items.

knowledge predicts preference concurrently, or whether it takes some time for children to apply what they learn to their own preferences. We also conducted an identical analysis using data from the following year, examining whether same-gender knowledge in years 2 and 3 of the study could predict children's same-gender preference in year 3. We also investigated differences between boys and girls, and differences between cohorts.

Second, we conducted similar analyses for other-gender items, this time predicting that knowledge and preference would be negatively correlated. As children learn that certain items are appropriate for the other gender, they should manifest less interest in those items. Once again, we looked at the contribution of knowledge in both years 1 and 2, to children's preference in year 2, allowing us to see any time lag, concurrent effects, or both. As before, we also conducted an identical analysis with data from a year later in the study, and examined sex and cohort differences where needed.

The purpose of the final set of analyses was to determine whether having more knowledge about gender stereotypes for concrete items overall leads to preferences that are more gender typed. Thus, we examined whether children's total gender knowledge across all the concrete items would predict a greater preference for same-gender items relative to their preference for other-gender items (i.e., whether higher total gender knowledge is associated with greater same- minus opposite-gender preference). As with the previous analyses, we determined whether knowledge in years 1 and 2 predicts preference in year 2, and whether knowledge in years 2 and 3 predicts preference in year 3. We explored cohort and sex differences where appropriate.

The first set of analyses examines the relation between children's knowledge of gender stereotypes for same-gender items and their own preferences for these items. The following series of independent variables were entered in a regression equation in separate steps with same-gender preference in year 2 as the dependent variable: sex, cohort, gender knowledge in year 1, gender knowledge in year 2, the interaction of sex and gender knowledge in year 1, the interaction of sex and gender knowledge in year 2, the interaction of cohort and gender knowledge in year 1, and the interaction of cohort and gender knowledge in year 2.[4]

The results showed that cohort was a significant predictor of same-gender preference, $F(2, 212) = 5.56$, $p < .05$, indicating that the decline in preference for same-gender items over time, as shown in the trend data, was significant. Neither knowledge in year 1 or year 2 was a significant predictor, though there was a significant interaction between sex and gender stereotype knowledge in year 1, $F(5, 209) = 5.42$, $p < .05$. Within sex analyses indicated that girls' stereotype knowledge of same-gender items in year 1 was a significant negative predictor of their same-gender preference, $F(2, 101) = 5.07$, $p < .05$ in year 2. In direct contrast to expectations, then, girls who demonstrated greater stereotype knowledge of same-gender items in year 1, showed larger declines in their preference for those items in year 2. For boys, the relationship between knowledge and same-gender preferences was not significant, $F(2, 108) = 1.89$, $p = .17$, but was in the opposite (i.e., predicted) direction.

The same regression analysis for same-gender preference in year 3 included a new variable into the equation as the first step: children's preference for same-gender items in year 2. This independent variable was found to be a highly significant predictor, $F(1, 200) = 23.46$, $p < .001$, indicating that children's previous preference scores are a good predictor of their current scores. Cohort also was a significant predictor once again, $F(3, 198) = 7.06$, $p < .01$. There were no effects of knowledge or sex, nor any interactions.

What do these findings indicate in terms of the theories described at the beginning of this chapter? From the data presented up to this point, there is no evidence that increased knowledge of stereotypes for same-gender items leads to increased preference for those items. In fact, the findings for the girls indicate the opposite; as girls learned which items were for their sex in year 1 of the study, they showed less interest in those items the following year.

The regression analyses for other-gender preference in year 2 showed that cohort was once again a significant predictor, $F(2, 212) = 32.74$, $p < .001$. Gender stereotype knowledge in year 1 also was a highly significant negative predictor, $F(3, 211) = 15.12$, $p < .001$, indicating that knowledge of gender stereotypes for other-gender items contributed to a sizable decline in preference for those items in the following year. This finding is particularly noteworthy because it suggests that acquiring gender stereotype knowledge in 1 year can lead to changes in preference that appear the following year. The analysis for other-gender preference in year 3 showed only a significant effect for preference in year 2, $F(1, 200) = 32.27$, $p < .001$.

In summary, these findings for other-gender items indicate that children who have greater knowledge of the stereotypes are less likely to demonstrate preference for those items. In particular, having greater stereotype knowledge of other-gender items in year 1 of the study predicted less preference for those items in the following year. Other-gender preference was not predicted by stereotype knowledge in the same year, perhaps because year 1 knowledge accounted for so much of the variance in preference that the change in knowledge between year 1 and 2 did not add anything substantial. Moreover, preference in year 3 was not predicted by gender stereotype knowledge in either year 2 or 3, probably because of insufficient variation in knowledge at this age, as children hit ceiling levels.

The final set of analyses clarifies these findings even more. Regression analyses in the same basic format as those used for same and other-gender items were conducted to investigate whether children's total knowledge of gender stereotypes (i.e., across all the concrete items in the measure) predicted a greater preference for same-gender items relative to other-gender items. The results showed a significant effect for cohort, $F(2, 212) = 32.74$, $p < .001$, indicating that with increasing age, same-gender items were preferred more relative to other-gender items in year 2, as would be expected. Neither total gender knowledge in year 1, $F(3, 211) = .001$, $p = .98$, or in year 2, $F(4, 210) = 1.09$, $p = .3$ was a significant predictor of "same- minus other-gender preference" in year 2. However, there was a significant knowledge in year one by sex interaction, $F(5, 209) = 5.98$, $p < .05$, showing that for boys, total gender knowledge in year 1 predicted greater preference for same-gender items relative to other-gender items in year 2, $F(2, 108) = 4.47$, $p < .05$, whereas for girls, beta was actually *negative*, although the effect was not significant, $F(2, 101) = 3.27$, $p = .07$. The regression equation for year 3 was not significant.

In conclusion, taken together, the results reveal a relatively clear picture of the relationship between preference and knowledge for concrete items. Across all the items, and for both boys and girls, preferences decline with age. The children find the items in our measure less and less desirable, perhaps because they are becoming less developmentally appropriate, or perhaps because the children become tired of being asked about the same items year after year. More importantly, however, in addition to waning interest in the items themselves, there is also growing rejection of items that the children learn are inappropriate for their sex.

The findings from these analyses provide some support for cognitive models suggesting that gender-typed preferences are influenced by developing knowledge of stereotypes, but qualified by type of preferences and sex of participants. The results are particularly noteworthy for two reasons. First, they suggest that in some cases the influence of increasing gender knowledge on preferences may only be seen by examining the relations over time—that knowledge may not affect preferences immediately. Second, they suggest that it is the other-gender avoidance component of gender-typing that is affected by cognitions, rather than the same-gender approach component. Children who learned that certain objects and activities were inappropriate for their sex showed less interest in those things a year later. Knowing that objects and activities are appropriate for their sex, however, was not sufficient to increase preferences.

Not only were children as a whole rejecting other-gender items as their stereotype knowledge of these items increased, there were also interesting sex differences. For boys, total stereotype knowledge in the first year of the study predicted their preference for same-gender items relative to other-gender items in the following year. Even though boys rejected both same and other-gender items as they got older, the more knowledge they had of gender stereotypes, the wider the divergence between their same and other-gender preferences; boys with more knowledge of stereotypes showed greater dislike for feminine items than masculine items. For girls, greater stereotype knowledge was associated with a reduced preference for both other- *and* same-gender items. Moreover, the more girls knew about gender stereotypes, the narrower the divergence between their same and other-gender preferences. To illustrate, boys with greater knowledge of gender stereotypes were likely over time to say a truck more than a hairbrush was something for them, whereas girls with greater knowledge were less likely over time to differentiate between the two.

Attribute Items

There are certain key differences between concrete items and attributes that are important to make note of before beginning our discussion of the attribute results. For concrete items, we were able to make the relatively straightforward prediction that greater stereotype knowledge for same-gender items should lead to increased preference, while greater stereotype knowledge for other-gender items should lead to decreased preference. However, for attributes, there is an added dimension which influences the relationship between stereotype knowledge and preference—the valence of the attributes. As we discussed in the literature review, children have a tendency to attribute only positive characteristics to themselves and others of their sex, especially early in development. This "same-sex bias" can obscure children's ability to accurately identify gender stereotypes, and also can influence the degree to which their own preferences reflect their stereotype knowledge. We decided to divide the attributes into two categories that illuminate the inherent interaction between valence and gender appropriateness: attributes that present no conflict between these two dimensions (items that are either same-gender and positive or other-gender and negative), and attributes that present a clear conflict between valence and gender appropriateness (items that are either same-gender and negative or other-gender and positive). Throughout this section, we explore the ways in which "no conflict" attributes may behave differently from "conflict" attributes.

Another feature of attributes that distinguishes them from concrete items is that they cannot be "preferred" in the same way that concrete items can be. One does not "prefer" gentleness, for example, the way one can prefer building things. Instead, the relevant issue is whether children identify themselves with the gender stereotypes. Thus, in this section, we will often use identification as a more accurate term to describe children's preference for attributes; however, we will also continue to use preference when we wish to maintain consistency with the previous section on concrete items.

Developmental Trends.   We begin this section by discussing the attribute knowledge and preference trends separately and by comparing these trends to those in the literature. The data are broken down by the sex of the child, and the gender and valence of the items. As can be seen in Figures 17.5 and 17.6, the knowledge trends for the "no conflict" attributes are similar to the trends for the concrete items, although the learning curves are shifted slightly to the right. Children responded slightly above chance in preschool, and reached ceiling or close to ceiling levels in third grade. This linear increase in knowledge for attributes is relatively consistent with the literature.

The knowledge trends for the "conflict" attributes, as shown in Figures 17.7 and 17.8, are much flatter, with children showing only moderate learning. In preschool, they responded at chance levels and, by

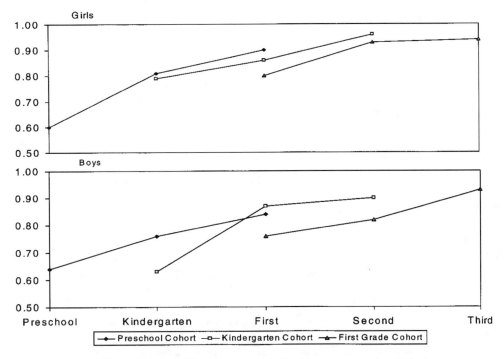

FIGURE 17.5. Gender knowledge trends: Positive same-gender attributes.

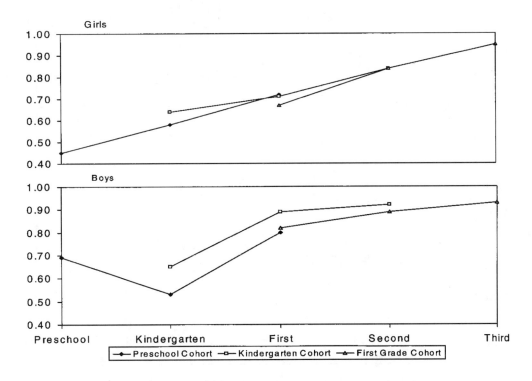

FIGURE 17.6. Gender knowledge trends: Negative other-gender attributes.

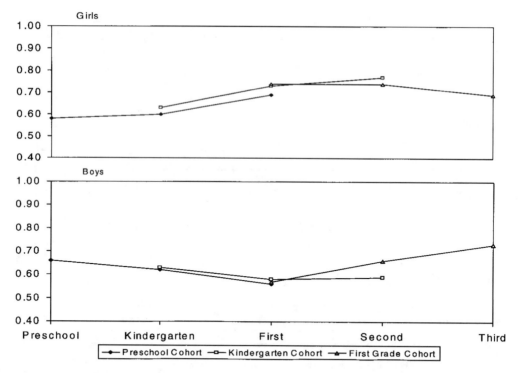

FIGURE 17.7. General knowledge trends: Negative same-gender attributes.

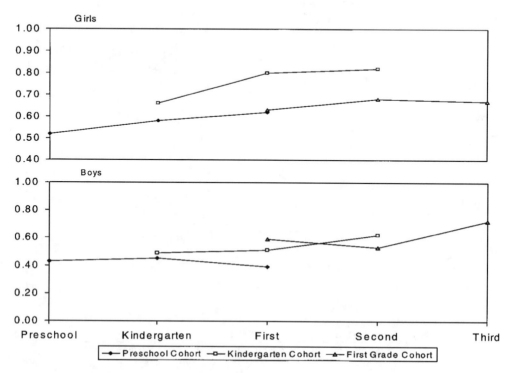

FIGURE 17.8. Gender knowlege trends: Positive other-gender attributes.

third grade, they achieved about 70% in line with traditional gender stereotypes. This finding also is consistent with studies showing that children's stereotype knowledge for attributes in preschool is influenced by a strong same-sex bias which gradually disappears during the middle childhood years, but is not replaced completely by accurate stereotype knowledge until later in development.

The preference trends for "no-conflict" attributes also are relatively consistent with what one would predict based on the trends in the literature. For same-gender positive items (see Figure 17.9), the scores of kindergartners already were substantially above chance, and increased after that point. For negative other-gender items (see Figure 17.10), the scores of kindergartners were somewhat below chance, and decreased during the remaining years. The only peculiar finding was an increase in preference among girls in the kindergarten cohort for negative other-gender items in the second year of the study.

The "conflict" preference trends are not consistent with the literature, but are interpretable nevertheless. For positive other-gender attributes, one would expect that the scores of younger children would be quite high due to same-gender bias, and would fall as the gender role appropriateness of these items becomes more salient. For boys (see Figure 17.11), the preference scores were very high in kindergarten (almost at ceiling levels), but never fell. The scores of girls in kindergarten were at only chance levels, and increased during the subsequent years. It appears that the positive valence of these items continues to have a remarkable influence on children's preferences during the middle childhood years in spite of their gender inappropriateness.

For negative same-gender attributes, one would expect younger children to show an initial dislike for these items, but show increasing interest in them as gender role appropriateness becomes more important. However, the data (see Figure 17.12) showed that children responded at chance levels on these items through all years of the study, demonstrating continued reluctance to identify themselves with negatively valenced attributes.

Predicting Preference from Knowledge for "No-Conflict" Attribute Items. The next step is to examine whether children's knowledge of gender stereotypes for personality attributes can predict their identification with them. The first two sets of analyses involve "no-conflict" items. As with the

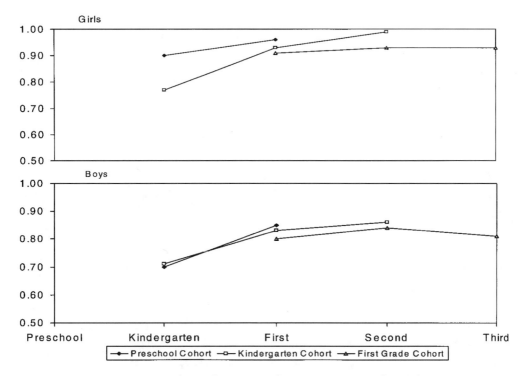

FIGURE 17.9. Gender preference trends: Positive same-gender attributes.

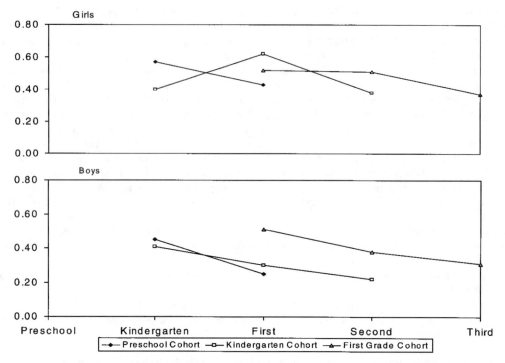

FIGURE 17.10. Gender preference trends: Negative other-gender attributes.

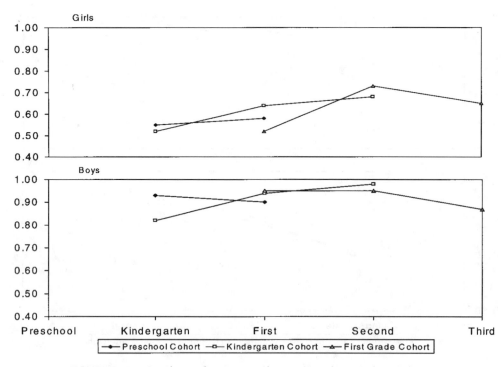

FIGURE 17.11. Gender preference trends: Positive other-gender attributes.

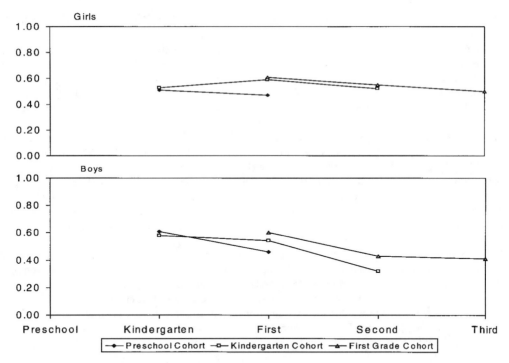

FIGURE 17.12. Gender preference trends: Negative same-gender attributes.

concrete item analyses, we examined whether knowledge in years 1 and 2 can predict preference in year 2, and whether knowledge in years 2 and 3 can predict preference in year 3. We also examined cohort and sex differences where appropriate.

The purpose of the first set of analyses was to examine whether greater stereotype knowledge of same-gender positive attributes can predict increased identification with those items. Based on the trend data, there is reason to expect to find this relation. In the first regression, preference in year 2 was regressed on the following independent variables entered in separate steps: sex, cohort, knowledge in year 1, knowledge in year 2, the interaction of knowledge in year 1 with sex, the interaction of knowledge in year 2 with sex, the interaction of knowledge in year 1 with cohort, and the interaction of knowledge in year 2 with cohort. The results showed that sex was a highly significant predictor, $F(1, 213) = 21.0$, $p < .001$. Girls were much more likely to attribute positive same-gender attributes to themselves than were the boys. None of the other factors were found to be significant predictors.

We conducted the same regression analysis using data from a year later in the study, this time including preference in year 2 as an independent variable entered in the first step. Preference in year 2 was found to be a highly significant predictor, $F(1, 200) = 12.88$, $p < .001$, showing, not surprisingly, that previous identification with same-gender positive attributes predicted current identification. Sex was found to be significant again, $F(2, 199) = 8.74$, $p < .01$. Knowledge in year 3 was also found to be a significant predictor, $F(5, 196) = 9.25$, $p < .01$, indicating that children with greater stereotype knowledge of same-gender positive attributes in the third year of the study showed greater attraction to those items. However, there was also an interaction between knowledge in year 3 and sex, $F(7, 194) = 4.0$, $p < .05$, indicating that knowledge in year 3 predicted preference for boys only, $F(4, 97) = 8.11$, $p < .01$. For girls, the effect was not significant.

A number of interesting conclusions can be drawn from this set of findings. Most importantly, they suggest that cognitions about gender stereotypes for attributes can predict children's preference for and identification with them, as was true for concrete items. Moreover, for attributes, unlike for concrete items, the same-gender approach component of gender typing was affected by gender knowledge. The fact that knowledge predicted preference for boys only also is consistent with both the results from the analyses of concrete items and with previous studies. The literature has also found that, during the middle childhood years, boys continue to be interested in masculine things while girls become less interested in feminine things.

The second set of analyses examined the other no-conflict items, negative other-gender attributes. Based on the trend data, we expected that greater stereotype knowledge should lead to a decrease in preference and identification. As was the case for positive same-gender attributes, we found that sex was the only significant predictor of preference in year 2, $F(1, 213) = 21.28$, $p < .001$. Girls were more likely to attribute negative other-gender items to themselves than were the boys. For preference in year 3, preference in year 2 was a significant predictor $F(1, 200) = 5.89$, $p < .05$, as was sex, $F(2, 199) = 4.78$, $p < .05$. In addition, a significant interaction between knowledge in year 2 and sex, $F(6, 195) = 4.05$, $p < .05$, indicated that, for boys, greater stereotype knowledge in year 2 predicted the anticipated decline in preference in year 3, $F(3, 98) = 11.11$, $p < .01$. There was no effect for the girls.

These findings provide additional support for the claim that knowledge of gender stereotypes for personality attributes can influence children's preferences. Greater stereotype knowledge not only led children to be drawn to positive same-gender attributes, but also led them to reject negative other-gender traits. However, once again, it was the boys alone who show the effect. Interestingly, for positive same-gender items, knowledge predicted an increase in preference among boys concurrently in year 3 of the study, while for negative other-gender items, there was a time lag effect, with boys' knowledge in year 2 predicting a decline in preference in year 3. Perhaps avoidance of other-gender characteristics requires more time to implement than adoption of same-gender characteristics.

In summary, the findings for the "no conflict" attributes are relatively clear cut and in line with predictions. Increased stereotype knowledge led to greater attraction to same-gender attributes and to greater avoidance of other-gender items. However, stereotype knowledge was a significant predictor of preference only among older participants and for boys alone.

Predicting Preference from Knowledge for "Conflict" Items.   The goal of the third set of analyses was to explore whether children with more stereotype knowledge of same-gender negative attributes show greater identification with those items, despite their negative valence. Regression analyses involving the same format as that for the no conflict attributes were used to explore this question. With preference in year 2 as the dependent variable, there was an interaction between knowledge in year 1 and sex, $F(5, 209) = 4.25$, $p < .05$, showing that stereotype knowledge in year 1 predicted preference in year 2 for boys $F(2, 108) = 6.85$, $p < .05$, but not for girls, $F(2, 101) = .061$, $p = .805$. This is consistent with no conflict findings that stereotype knowledge influences boys' identification with same-gender personality traits, but not girls'.

For preference in year 3, preference in year 2 was a highly significant predictor, $F(1, 200) = 16.34$, $p < .001$, and sex was also significant $F(2, 199) = 4.68$, $p < .05$, with girls showing higher levels of preference than the boys. There was also an interaction between knowledge in year 3 and sex, $F(7, 194) = 5.56$, $p < .05$, indicating that surprisingly it was the girls who were carrying the effect, $F(4, 95) = 4.74$, $p < .05$, rather than the boys, $F(4, 97) = .53$, $p = .47$.

Thus, the relationship between stereotype knowledge and preference for same-gender negative attributes shows an unusual pattern of results. In year 1 of the study, stereotype knowledge predicted preference in year 2 for boys only. Year 3 preference was predicted by stereotype knowledge in the same year, but for girls only. There is a reversal of the effects of participant sex on the relation between knowledge and preference.

What do these findings indicate in terms of our previous results, and in terms of theories of gender-role development? We now have even further support for cognitive models of gender-role development. Children with more knowledge of negative same-gender stereotypes showed greater attraction to these items, despite their negative valence. What is puzzling are the sex differences, particularly, why knowledge is a significant concurrent predictor of preference for girls in year 3, given that this has not been the case in any other analyses. However, it is important to keep in mind that the preference trends for these items remained flat throughout the years of our study, hovering around chance levels, and that the knowledge trends also never reached ceiling levels. The children never really learned or, at least, agreed with the stereotypes, nor did they embrace them. When considered within this context, the nature of the relation between knowledge and preference may differ somewhat from the earlier analyses.

The final set of analyses involve the second group of "conflict" attributes (positive other-gender items). The purpose of this set of analyses was to determine whether greater stereotype knowledge predicts a decline in preference, despite the items' positive valence. Given the trend data, this prediction seems unlikely. High or increasing levels of identification with these items was seen throughout the study, even as the children were learning that these items were gender inappropriate.

The regression analyses for preference in years 2 and 3 showed that sex was a significant predictor in both year 2, $F(1, 213) = 57.89$, $p < .001$, and year 3, $F(2, 199) = 25.92$, $p < .001$, with boys more likely to attribute these traits to themselves than the girls. Note that, for positive same-gender attributes, there also was a main effect of sex, with girls more likely to attribute these items to themselves. It seems likely that children of both sexes were identifying with the positive feminine attributes because these items (politeness, gentleness) are the types of qualities that adults often reinforce at this age. Cohort also was a significant predictor of year 2 preference, $F(2, 212) = 9.31$, $p < .01$, and year 2 preference was a significant predictor of year 3 preference, $F(1, 200) = 22.4$, $p < .001$. However, there were no main effects of knowledge and no interactions.

In summary, for the conflict attributes, the data do not suggest a straightforward relationship between knowledge and preference. This is likely due to the fact that children are being confronted with a conflict between gender appropriateness and valence.

☐ Conclusion

What do the findings indicate in terms of the relationship between knowledge and preference? For concrete items, and for attributes that do not present a conflict between gender appropriateness and valence, the findings are remarkably clear. In general, children's own preferences and identifications are affected by what they know of gender stereotypes. With respect to concrete objects and activities, children with greater other-gender stereotyped knowledge in year 1 of the study were more likely to reject those items in year 2 of the study. With respect to personality attributes, boys' attraction to same-gender traits in year 3 was predicted by greater stereotyped knowledge of those traits in the same year (i.e., a concurrent relation), and their rejection of other-gender traits in year 3 was predicted by greater stereotyped knowledge of those traits in the previous year (i.e., a lagged relation).

These data thus provide the kind of support for cognitive developmental perspectives that typically has not been observed by others and suggest reasons why relations between gender-related knowledge and preferences often have not been detected in the past. First, many of the observed relations involved lagged effects, with knowledge predicting preferences only at a later point in time. These findings suggest that the cross-sectional nature of many previous studies may have precluded their finding predicted knowledge-preference relations. It may take time for new knowledge to affect choices and behaviors, especially when it involves a conflict of some kind, such as giving up an activity or attribute that was previously part of one's repertoire, or foregoing a desirable attribute or embracing an undesirable one. It is noteworthy therefore that, in the present study, lagged effects occurred only when the preferences involved a decline in endorsement of other-gender items or when they involved self-attribution of undesirable traits. It will be interesting in future research to examine the factors that determine when concurrent versus lagged effects are found.

Second, the developmental timing of the relation varied by the type of stereotype. For concrete items, relations were observed more often for predictions from year 1 to year 2 (i.e., when children were 4 to 6 years of age). In contrast, for attribute items, relations were observed primarily for predictions to year 3 (i.e., when children were 6 to 8 years of age). The literature on the development of gender-stereotyped knowledge has suggested that these are the ages when the two types of stereotypes are being learned, with knowledge of concrete times emerging a year or two prior to knowledge of trait attributes. In other words, because attributes are being learned later, it is not surprising that the influence of this kind of knowledge on preferences occurs later. These results suggest further that the influence of gender schematic knowledge on preferences is especially discernible when such schemas are emerging. Indeed, it seems possible that the relative weak relations observed for concrete items may be due partly to the high level of knowledge already present in the younger children.

One of the most striking findings of this study was that it was primarily the preferences of the boys that were affected by stereotype knowledge. Of course, many other studies have suggested that boys are more gender typed than girls, but these often have been biased by desirability, with female-typed items involving chores and male-typed items involving fun activities. In the present study, the apparently greater responsiveness of boys to gender norms occurred even though this bias was not present. Although girls as well as boys avoided other-gender concrete items more with increasing knowledge, only boys showed the expected pattern of greater overall knowledge leading to a greater differentiation between same- and other-gender items. Unexpectedly, girls with greater knowledge showed significantly less interest in same-gender items. Similarly, three of the four sex by knowledge interactions for attributes showed that knowledge predicted preferences for boys only.

This does not mean that girls' preferences were unaffected by knowledge, however. Some of the knowledge-preference relations held for girls as well as boys and, for same-gender negative attributes, a concurrent relation in year 3 of the study was found for girls only. Thus, it does appear that girls who know, for example, that certain attributes such as sadness and fear are more associated with girls, also are more likely to see these attributes as applying to them personally. Moreover, increasing knowledge of gender stereotypes probably also is accompanied by increasing knowledge of values associated with gender. Perhaps girls not only are learning what is gender appropriate, but also are learning what is valued by society—"maleness" and all that accompanies it. Girls may be experiencing a conflict situation analogous to the conflict between gender appropriateness and valence that we discussed in reference to attributes. Perhaps, girls are being forced to choose between desiring gender appropriateness and desiring societal value. This conflict could inhibit them from developing preferences based on what they know of gender stereotypes. Furthermore, differences between feminine girls and "tomboys" may contribute to such conflicts, and it would be of considerable interest in future research to examine knowledge-preference relations separately for the two groups of girls. Of course, these ideas about the specificity of which gender norms affect girls and about the conflict they may experience in choosing between appropriateness (femininity) and prestige (masculinity) is post hoc and speculative; it remains for future research to test these interpretations directly.

More generally, these differences reinforce a point made above: that, even if stereotyped knowledge is an important influence on gender-related choices and behaviors, it is not the only influence. In a sense, then, previous research may have placed too heavy a burden on cognitive theories of gender development concerning what constitutes sufficient evidence to demonstrate the influence of cognitive factors. Yet, it also is important to be cautious about interpreting the present findings in causal terms. As suggested in previous analyses, preferences may causally influence knowledge, as well as the reverse. In the present study, this reverse direction of influence seems especially plausible for concurrent relations observed among older children or when knowledge is at a high level.

In summary, this study provides support for the idea that children are involved in their own gender typing. What they learn about gender roles in this society affects how they see themselves and the kinds of activities and toys they enjoy. Further research needs to examine how cognitive factors interact with other factors to influence children's preferences, particularly for girls. Factors such as the value of different roles, traits, and behaviors in this society may be especially important to consider, given the disparity between the status of males and females in this society.

☐ Notes

1. The overall analysis did not, however, indicate that children did worse on neutral paired with other-gender items than on neutral paired with same-gender items, but the data were not presented separately for the knowledge versus the preference scores so that they are somewhat difficult to interpret.

2. It was not possible to administer the preference measure to the preschoolers in year 1 of the study. As is described in the Method section, the preference measure was administered after several other measures—the preschoolers did not have the attention span to sit for that long a time period.

3. There originally was another positive masculine item: "good at math." Preliminary analyses with the whole sample, including adolescents, indicated that this item was not stereotyped at any age. It thus could not be included in the present analyses because of the focus on knowledge of stereotypes.

4. We were not able to control for year 1 preference in any of our analyses because the preschoolers were not present for this measure.

☐ References

Albert, A. A., & Porter, J. R. (1983). Age patterns in the development of children's gender-role stereotypes. *Sex Roles, 9,* 59–67.

Antill, J., Russell, G., Goodnow, J., & Cotton, S. (1993). Measures of children's sex typing in middle childhood. *Australian Journal of Psychology, 45,* 25–33.

Bem, S. L. (1981). Gender schema theory: A cognitive account of sex typing. *Psychological Review, 88,* 354–364.

Best, D. L., Williams, J. E., Cloud, J. M., Davis, S. W., Robertson, L. S., Edwards, J. R., Giles, H., & Fowles, J. (1977). Development of sex-trait stereotypes among young children in the United States, England, and Ireland. *Child Development, 48,* 1375–1384.

Blakemore, J. E.., LaRue, A. A., & Olejnik, A B. (1979). Sex-appropriate toy preference and the ability to conceptualize toys as sex-role related. *Developmental Psychology, 15,* 339–340.

Boldizar, J. (1991). Assessing sex typing and androgyny in children: The children's sex role inventory. *Developmental Psychology, 27,* 505–515.

Bradbard, M. R., Martin, C. L., Endsley, R. C., & Halverson, C. F. (1986). Influence of sex stereotypes on children's exploration and memory: A competence versus performance distinction. *Developmental Psychology, 22,* 481–486.

Bussey, K., & Bandura, A. (1992). Self-regulatory mechanisms governing gender development. *Child Development, 63,* 1236–1250.

Bussey, K., & Perry, D. G. (1982). Same-sex imitation: The avoidance of cross-sex models or the acceptance of same-sex models? *Sex Roles, 8,* 773–785.

Caldera, Y. M., Huston, A. C., & O'Brien, M. (1989). Social interactions and play patterns of parents and toddlers with feminine, masculine, and neutral toys. *Child Development, 60,* 70–76.

Carter, D. B., & Levy, G. D. (1988). Cognitive aspects of early sex-role development: The influence of gender schemas on preschoolers' memories and preferences for sex-typed toys and activities. *Child Development, 59,* 782–792.

Coker, D. R. (1984). The relationships among gender concepts and cognitive maturity in preschool children. *Sex Roles, 10,* 19–31.

Cowan, G., & Hoffman, C. (1986). Gender stereotyping in young children: Evidence to support a concept-learning approach. *Sex Roles, 14,* 211–224.

Edelbrock, C., & Sugawara, A. (1978). Acquisition of sex-typed preferences in preschool-aged children. *Developmental Psychology, 14,* 614–623.

Eisenberg, N., Murray, E., & Hite T. (1982). Children's reasoning regarding sex-typed toy choices. *Child Development, 53,* 81–86.

Emmerich, W., & Shepard, K. (1984). Cognitive factors in the development of sex-typed preferences. *Sex Roles, 11,* 997–1007.

Eron, L. D., Huesmann, L. R., Brice, P., Fischer, P., & Mermelstein, R. (1983). Age trends in the development of aggression, sex typing and related television habits. *Developmental Psychology, 19,* 71–77.

Etaugh, C., & Liss, M. B. (1992). Home, school, and playroom: Training grounds for adult gender roles. *Sex Roles, 26,* 129–147.

Hort, B. E., Leinbach, M. D., & Fagot, B. I. (1991). Is there coherence among the cognitive components of gender acquisition? *Sex Roles, 24,* 195–207.

Huston, A. C. (1983). Sex-typing. In E. M. Hetherington (Ed.), *Handbook of child psychology: Socialization, personality, and social development* (Vol. 4, pp. 388–467). New York: Wiley.

Huston, A. C. (1985). The development of sex typing: Themes from recent research. *Development Review, 5,* 1–17.

Katz, P., & Boswell, S. (1986). Flexibility and traditionality in children's gender roles. *Genetic, Social, and General Psychology Monographs, 112*(1), 103–147.

Katz, A., & Walsh, P. (1991). Modification of children's gender-stereotyped behavior. *Child Development, 62,* 338–351.

Kohlberg, L. A. (1966). A cognitive-developmental analysis of children's sex role concepts and attitudes. In E. E. Maccoby (Ed.), *The development of sex differences* (pp. 82–173). Stanford, CA: Stanford University Press.

Leahy, R. L., & Shirk, S. R. (1984). The development of classificatory skills and sex-trait stereotypes in children. *Sex Roles, 10,* 281–292.

Martin, C. L. (1989). Children's use of gender-related information in making social judgments. *Developmental Psychology, 25*(1), 80–88.

Martin, C. L. (1993). New directions for investigating children's gender knowledge. *Developmental Review, 13,* 184–204.

Martin, C. L., Eisenbud, L., & Rose, H. (1995). Children's gender-based reasoning about toys. *Child Development, 66,* 1453–1471.

Martin, C. L., & Halverson, C. F. (1981). A schematic processing model of sex typing stereotyping in children. *Child Development, 52,* 1119–1134.

Martin, C. L., & Little, J. K. (1990). The relation of gender understanding to children's sex-typed preferences and gender stereotypes. *Child Development, 61,* 1427–1439.

Mischel, W. (1966). A social-learning view of sex differences in behavior. In E. E. Maccoby (Ed.), *The development of sex differences* (pp. 57–81). Stanford, CA: Stanford University Press.

Montemayor, R. (1974). Children's performance in a game and their attraction to it as a function of sex-typed labels. *Child Development, 45,* 152–156.

O'Brien, M., & Huston, A. C. (1985). Activity level and sex-stereotyped toy choice in toddler boys and girls. *Journal of Genetic Psychology, 146,* 527–533.

Perry, D. G., White, A. J., & Perry, L. C. (1984). Does early sex typing result from children's attempts to match their behavior to sex role stereotypes? *Child Development, 55,* 2114–2121.

Picariello, M. L., Greenberg, D. N., & Pillemer, D. B. (1990). Children's sex related stereotyping of colors. *Child Development, 61,* 1453–1460.

Roopnarine, J. L. (1986). Mothers' and fathers' behaviors toward the toy play of their infant sons and daughters. *Sex Roles, 14,* 59–68.

Ruble, D. N., Balaban, T., & Cooper, J. (1981). Gender constancy and the effects of sex-typed televised toy commercials. *Child Development, 52,* 667–673.

Ruble, D. N., & Martin, C. L. (1998). Gender development. In N. Eisenberg (Ed.), *Handbook of child psychology: Vol. 3. Social, emotional, and personality development.* New York: Wiley.

Ruble, D. N., & Ruble, T. L. (1982). Sex-role stereotypes. In A.G. Miller (Ed.), *In the eye of the beholder: Contemporary issues in stereotyping.* New York: Holt, Rinehart, and Winston.

Serbin, L. A., Powlishta, K. K., & Gulko, J. (1993). The development of sex typing in middle childhood. *Monographs of the Society for Research in Child Development, 58*(2). (Serial No. 232).

Serbin, L. A., & Sprafkin, C. (1986). The salience of gender and the process of sex typing in three- to seven-year-old children. *Child Development, 57,* 1118–1199.

Signorella, M. L., Bigler, R. S., & Liben, L. S. (1993). Developmental differences in children's gender schemata about others: A meta-analytic review. *Developmental Review, 13,* 147–183.

Trautner, H. (1992). The development of sex-typing in children: A longitudinal analysis. *German Journal of Psychology, 16*(3), 183–199.

Weinraub, M., Clemens, L., Pritchard, S. A., Eithridge, T., Gracely, E., & Myers, B. (1984). The development of sex role stereotypes in the third year: Relationships to gender labeling, gender identity, sex-typed toy preference, and family characteristics. *Child Development, 55,* 1493–1503.

Welch-Ross, M. K., & Schmidt, E. R. (1996). Gender-schema development and children's constructive story memory: Evidence for a developmental model. *Child Development, 67,* 820–835.

Williams, J. E., Bennett, S. M., & Best, D. L. (1975). Awareness and expression of sex stereotypes in young children. *Developmental Psychology, 11,* 635–642.

Zelazo, P. D., & Reznick, J. St. (1991). Age-related asynchrony of knowledge and action. *Child Development, 62,* 719–735.

Zelazo, P. D., Reznick, J. S., & Pinon, D. E. (1995). Response control and the execution of verbal rules. *Developmental Psychology, 31*(3), 508–517.

Aletha C. Huston

Effects of Poverty on Children

☐ Introduction

The United States is facing a social problem of epidemic proportions: Approximately one fifth of our children live in poverty (Bureau of the Census, 1997). The problem is not new; with few exceptions, it has been with us for many years. In 1960, almost 27% of children under 18 years of age in the United States lived in families with incomes below the official poverty level. By the end of the 1960s, the poverty rate for children was reduced to 14%, in large measure because of the programs of the Great Society. After that, however, poverty among children increased. In 1993, it reached its highest level in 30 years—22.7% of U.S. children lived in families with incomes below the poverty threshold. In absolute numbers, that is more than 15 million children (see Figure 18.1) (Bronfenbrenner, McClelland, Wethington, Moen, & Ceci, 1996; Bureau of the Census, 1995). In 1997, 9% of children lived in extreme poverty (i.e., with family incomes less than 50% of the poverty threshold) (U.S. Bureau of the Census, 1997).

The changes in children's poverty occurred as part of a larger pattern of increasing income inequality. Since the late 1970s, the disparity between the top and bottom levels of income has been increasing (Danziger & Gottschalk, 1994). The share of income for people in the top 20%, especially those in the top 5%, increased while the share for people in the bottom 20% and for those in the middle declined (Bureau of the Census, 1997). Children are, of course, more likely to live in families at the bottom than at the top.

The United States is distinct from other industrialized nations in having both a high percentage of children living in poverty and a large disparity between incomes of the rich and poor. By comparison with children in other developed countries, the poorest U.S. children are very poor indeed, and the richest are very affluent (Rainwater & Smeeding, 1996).

☐ Background

The current wave of research on child poverty, including my own work, dates from the mid-1980s when it became apparent that the War on Poverty of the 1960s had not been permanently won. Around that time, journalists put child poverty back on the public agenda, and scholars from economics, policy analysis, and sociology began to forge some new collaborations with developmental psychologists and others studying human development (see, e.g., Huston, 1991).

In this chapter, I will consider some of the recent research investigating the influences of poverty on children, with particular attention to understanding how and why such influences occur. "Poverty" in-

Portions of this chapter were presented as part of a Presidential Address to Division 7 of the American Psychological Association in 1995 and at the Poverty Research Seminar, Joint Center for Poverty Research, Northwestern University/ University of Chicago, November 1996. Funding for various parts of the work described has been provided by the National Institute for Child Health and Human Development, the National Institute of Mental Health, the MacArthur Foundation, Children's Television Workshop, and the W. T. Grant Foundation.

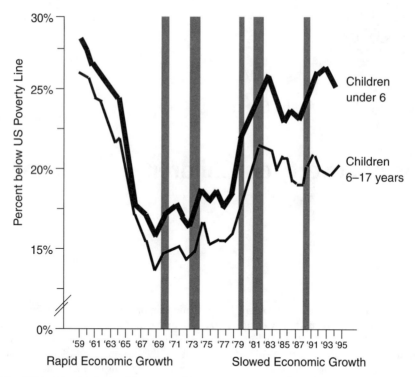

FIGURE 18.1.   Children in poverty and the state of the economy. From *The State of Americans: This Generation and Next*, by U. Bronfenbrenner, P. McClelland, E. Wethington, P. Moen, and S. J. Ceci. Copyright 1996 by the Free Press. Reprinted with permission of the author.

cludes a complex set of individual, family, community, and cultural factors that are difficult to disentangle. One issue currently under debate is whether income per se contributes to the outcomes associated with poverty, independent of the many other conditions accompanying family poverty. Although this issue is important, my work takes a different tack by trying to understand how the many conditions associated with poverty contribute to developmental outcomes. I first review some of the earlier research on poverty and income effects; then, I describe my own research investigating child care and mass media as two possible avenues by which poverty affects children's development. The chapter ends with a discussion of the New Hope Project, an experiment in providing resources to working poor adults, in which we are studying the effects on children and family life.

☐ Poverty and Child Outcomes: Some Basic Conceptual Problems

At first blush, the issues seem simple. Poverty is bad for children. There is ample evidence that poor children are at risk for problems of health (e.g., low birth weight, infant mortality, childhood death and injury, contagious diseases, and injuries), developmental delays in intellectual development, low levels of school achievement, and social-emotional and behavioral problems. By adolescence, these problems become obvious in the form of juvenile crime, early pregnancy, and dropping out of school and, in adulthood, individuals raised in poverty have lower average levels of educational attainment and income than do those from more affluent families (Chafel, 1993; Garbarino, 1992; Hill & Sandfort, 1995; Huston, 1991; Huston, McLoyd, & Garcia Coll, 1994; McLoyd, 1997, 1998).

The correlation of poverty with many problematic outcomes is not in doubt, but the reasons for that correlation are. Some conceptual muddiness results from the complexity of "poverty" as a construct. For many purposes, poverty is defined simply by cash income. If a family receives less money in a year than the federal poverty threshold, they are officially defined as "poor" for most statistical analyses. The poverty threshold originally was calculated from the estimated cost of food multiplied by three. It is adjusted for family size, but not for geographic region. Annual adjustments are made for changes in average prices. There are several problems with the threshold. A family's income is defined by pretax rather than disposable income, and there are no adjustments for such nondiscretionary expenses as the costs of child care and transportation for employed parents. On the other hand, noncash benefits (e.g., food stamps) are not counted as income. In 1995, a National Academy of Sciences expert panel (Citro & Michael, 1995) recommended changing the definition of poverty to remedy these deficiencies, but virtually all available data are based on the flawed index. The poverty threshold is an absolute dollar amount, not a percentage of the median income or a percentile. Therefore, it is theoretically possible for everyone to be above the poverty threshold.

The income-to-needs ratio (the ratio of family income to the poverty threshold) provides a continuous index reflecting how far below or above the poverty threshold a family's income falls. A family with an income at the poverty threshold has an income-to-needs ratio of 1.0; at half the poverty threshold, the ratio is 0.5, and so forth. This ratio is a better and more complete predictor of many child outcomes than a dichotomy between poor or not poor because it takes into account the depth of poverty and the variations in resources above the poverty threshold (e.g. Duncan, Brooks-Gunn, & Klebanov, 1994; Smith & Brooks-Gunn, 1994).

Still another issue is the duration of poverty. Most definitions of poverty are based on current income, but longitudinal studies of income since the 1970s have demonstrated that many people move in and out of poverty from year to year (Duncan, 1984). People whose poverty is transitory, lasting only a year or 2, are demographically similar to the rest of the population (Duncan, 1991). Although income loss can cause considerable stress (e.g., Elder, 1974), such families usually do not live in conditions of serious material hardship for long periods of time. Persistent poverty, lasting over several years, is another matter. Families in chronic poverty have fewer savings and other assets than do those in transitory poverty (Duncan, 1991). Both the depth and duration of poverty are important determinants of its effects on children's development (Huston et al., 1994; McLoyd, 1998).

Finally, poverty occurs within a complex set of social, physical, and biological conditions that are difficult to disentangle. For example, single mothers often head poor families. African Americans, Hispanic Americans, and Native Americans are more apt to be poor than are people of European or Asian ancestry. Many parents in poor families lack education and perform poorly on tests of intellectual ability. They are likely to be unemployed or to work in unstable jobs with irregular hours that pay low wages and lack benefits. Some groups of poor families live in violent or disorganized neighborhoods and in physical conditions that pose risks of environmental toxins and injury. Poor parents experience more life stress, depression, and lack of social support than do affluent parents (Duncan, 1984; Duncan & Brooks-Gunn, 1997a; Edin & Lein, 1997; McLoyd, 1998; Scarbrough, 1993).

☐ Two Research Traditions

Current research on children and poverty flows from two academic traditions: human development and economics. Scholars in the economic tradition address the issue because they are concerned with conditions that promote economic competence and well-being of adults; those in human development usually come to the topic because of their interest in conditions that promote positive developmental outcomes for children.

Economic Conditions and Welfare Policy

Economists and scholars concerned with welfare policy have been concerned primarily with how economic conditions and policies influence adults' work, income, and life choices and, secondarily, with how these aspects of parents' lives affect their children (e.g., Hauser & Sweeney, 1997; Haveman & Wolfe, 1994). Most outcomes of interest are long term (e.g., completion of high school, ultimate educational attainment, adult work effort and earnings, adolescent pregnancy). One question they often ask is, How important is family income per se, above and beyond the other factors associated with poverty? This question has a policy focus based on the assumption that it is easier to provide income to the poor than to change their family structures, education levels, and so forth. Conversely, to what extent are the correlates of poverty due to factors other than income (e.g., single mother families, low parent education)? Does income from welfare have different effects than income from parent earnings?

Human Development

For investigators in the developmental tradition, the primary goal is to understand and improve developmental outcomes for children (e.g., intellectual functioning, school achievement, social competence, and physical health). The theories that guide this work rest on the assumption that the physical and social environments of poverty are responsible for many of the developmental outcomes associated with it (see McLoyd, 1998); therefore, it makes sense to change those environments in order to improve the life chances of children.

During the War on Poverty of the 1960s, developmental psychologists enthusiastically endorsed Head Start and related preschool intervention programs that were designed to compensate for presumed gaps in the early experience of children in poor families. They assumed that one major reason for low school achievement was the absence of language, cognitive stimulation, and academic learning experiences in the homes of poor families. Some investigators tempered this "deficit" view with the hypothesis that families living in poverty provide "different" experiences that promote the development of skills and knowledge relevant for their cultural circumstances, but not for schools, which require particular types of knowledge and skills (see McLoyd, 1997, for extensive review of this topic).

The best of these early intervention studies were carried out with experimental methods, randomly assigning children to treatment or control groups. Children were followed from early childhood to adolescence and, in some cases, into adulthood. The findings are clear: Intensive and high quality early intervention leads to improved school achievement, educational attainment, and success in work (see Barnett, 1995; McLoyd, 1997). These findings, while extremely important for public policy, do not tell us much about why poor children have low achievement and attainment in the first place.

My research and that of many others in the developmental tradition have turned to these questions: How does family income, or lack of it, translate into conditions that affect children's lives? What mediates the relation of poverty to outcomes for children and adolescents? How do experiences in settings away from home—child care, school, and neighborhood—mediate or moderate the influences of poverty?

In recent years, the developmental and economic research traditions have converged to some extent, largely because of increasing interdisciplinary collaboration by the practitioners of the two. The questions addressed include: (a) How does poverty affect children's development, and by what processes? (b) What public policies can prevent or alleviate the negative effects of poverty? Although the answers to these two sets of questions are related, they are not isomorphic. Understanding the causes of a problem often provides insight about its prevention or treatment, but effective treatments that are unrelated to initial causes are also possible. For example, evidence indicates that smoking contributes to the probability of developing lung cancer, suggesting that the risk can be reduced by not smoking. But, lung cancer can also be treated with surgery—a therapy that is unrelated to its causes. Similarly, a large body of research points to television violence as one cause of aggressive behavior, suggesting that reductions in violent content might reduce aggression (Huston et al., 1992; Huston & Wright, 1997; Paik & Comstock, 1994). But, educating children about television violence can also reduce the effects of viewing it (Huesmann, Eron, Klein, Brice, & Fischer, 1983). This point is especially important in the debates about poverty because public policy can affect some aspects of people's lives (e.g., income, availability of health care, availability of quality child care) more easily than others (e.g., attitudes and values, intellectual ability, family structure).

☐ Is Income Per Se Important?

One question occupying the attention of researchers from both the economic and the developmental traditions is whether family income, poverty, or economic loss contribute to children's development, or whether the correlations of poverty with developmental outcomes are the results of "third" variables (e.g., parents' education, single parent family structure, minority group membership). That is, do poverty, economic hardship, or income loss make unique contributions, or are the correlations between family economic status and children's developmental outcomes due primarily to other factors? The most frequently used method for determining "effects" of poverty or family income is multivariate analyses of surveys and longitudinal databases, controlling statistically for a large of number of variables. The National Longitudinal Survey of Youth (NLSY), the Infant Health and Development Project (IHDP), and the Panel Study of Income Dynamics (PSID) have been analyzed in several studies investigating family income "effects."

Longitudinal Studies

In a recent edited book, Duncan and Brooks-Gunn (1997a) assembled 13 longitudinal investigations of individuals ranging from early childhood through late adulthood in which family incomes during childhood and developmental outcomes were measured. The investigators conducted parallel analyses to determine the unique contribution of family income, with controls for related demographic and family structure variables. In a final chapter (Duncan & Brooks-Gunn, 1997b), a summary of the findings indicated that family income during children's early years was related to cognitive and academic development in early and middle childhood and to adult earnings and work. Family income during adolescence was less likely to predict grades, educational attainment, or adult job characteristics. These authors then performed further analyses on the PSID data comparing the relations of family income at three points in development (age 0 to 5, 6 to 10, and 11 to 15) to the number of years of completed schooling in adulthood. Income during the child's first 5 years of life was the major predictor of completed schooling (Duncan & Brooks-Gunn, 1997b).

Prior research is consistent with this conclusion. Family income or the absence of poverty predicted performance on cognitive tests measuring vocabulary and skill in reading and math for young children (between about 3 and 8 years old) (Duncan et al, 1994; Liaw & Brooks-Gunn, 1994; Smith, Brooks-Gunn, & Klebanov, 1997). Moreover, family poverty at age 3 predicted change in children's performance between age 3 and 5 in one analysis (Duncan et al., 1994). Family poverty was only slightly related to adolescent and adult achievement—high school graduation (Haveman, Wolfe, & Spaulding, 1991) and to years of schooling completed and adult work activity (Corcoran & Adams, 1997; Duncan, 1996; Haveman & Wolfe, 1994). These relationships hold with extensive sets of controls including maternal education, maternal performance on intellectual tests, family structure, family size, and race and ethnicity.

The other outcomes examined in the summary by Duncan and Brooks-Gunn (1997b) were physical and mental health, growth, and psychosocial adjustment: Few effects of family income were found, but there were few measures of these variables by comparison to the cognitive and achievement outcomes. In other investigations, family income has been shown to be an independent predictor of social skills, aggression, internalizing, and externalizing behavior (Duncan et al, 1994; Liaw & Brooks-Gunn, 1994). Several investigations have demonstrated that children living in poverty, compared to children in nonpoor families, had higher levels of internalizing and externalizing problems (Bolger, Patterson, Thompson, & Kupersmidt, 1995; Brody et al., 1994; Duncan et al., 1994; McLeod & Shanahan, 1993; Patterson, Kupersmidt, & Vaden, 1990) and antisocial behavior (Luster & McAdoo, 1994; McLeod, Kruttschnitt, & Dornfeld, 1994), lower levels of social skills (Luster, Reischl, Gassaway, & Gomaa, 1995), lower self-esteem and popularity (Bolger et al., 1995), and higher peer-rated aggression (Guerra, Huesmann, Tolan, Van Acker, & Eron, 1995). In adolescence, poverty or economic hardship predicts delinquency (Sampson & Laub, 1994), depression and loneliness (Lempers, Clark-Lempers, & Simons, 1989), females' low psychological well-being and males' antisocial behavior (Conger & Elder, 1994).

Different conclusions were reached in a recent book by an economist, Mayer (1997a), using similar methods of analysis on many of the same datasets. She argued that the effects of income on developmental outcomes are modest at best when the many potential confounding variables are taken into account. By implication, raising the income of poor families would have negligible effects on cognitive skills, school achievement, or behavior problems. For example, according to her calculations, doubling the incomes of poor families would reduce the overall high school dropout rate in the United States from 17.3% to 16.1% and would reduce the overall teen childbearing rate from 20% to 18% (pp. 144–145). One reason, she suggested, is that government policies have ensured that many poor children receive such basic necessities as food, shelter, and health care. Because noncash government benefits (e.g., Medicaid, food stamps, child care subsidies) are not counted as "income" in most investigations, the effects of these family resources are not reflected in studies of income. In another paper (Mayer, 1997b), she demonstrated that cash income was not synonymous with material hardship (lacking food, housing, or medical care). For several reasons, then, cash income is not a very good or complete index of the material resources available to a family.

A basic methodological conundrum exists in all of these studies. Although large numbers of related family variables are controlled in regressions, there is always the possibility that other unmeasured family characteristics could have contributed to the "effects" of income or poverty. The method of choice for determining causal direction is, of course, a random assignment experiment in which income is manipulated, but experimental designs to evaluate the effects of changing income are rare. In fact, the only investigations meeting this definition, to my knowledge, are the Income Maintenance Experiments of the 1960s and 1970s and a few studies currently in progress, which I will discuss later in the chapter.

Income Maintenance Experiments

Four experiments were conducted to evaluate the impact of a guaranteed minimum income on poor families. They were in New Jersey; Gary, Indiana; Seattle/Denver; and rural areas in North Carolina and Iowa (Haveman, 1986). The populations all were poor families with one or two parents. People were randomly assigned to receive a guaranteed minimum income or to a control group. The size of the guaranteed minimum and the tax rate associated with earnings was varied. There were methodological imperfections in these studies (Haveman, 1986; Rossi & Lyall, 1978), but they are of interest as we attempt to understand how poverty and income affect families and children.

The most serious drawback for our purposes is that they were interested primarily in adult work effort and earnings, and marriage and divorce. They paid scant attention to measuring outcomes for children or parenting. Salkind and Haskins (1982) summarized available information concerning outcomes for children. I have expanded their summary, using a few other sources (Goenveld, Tuma, & Hannan, 1980; Institute for Research on Poverty, 1976; Kershaw & Fair, 1976; Mayer, 1997a; Office of Income Security, U.S. Department of Health and Human Services, 1983). In Table 18.1, the findings are summarized.

One consistent effect of the guaranteed income was increased expenditure on housing. Families in the experimental groups were more likely than controls to buy a house or spend additional money on rent. They also purchased such durable goods as major appliances. One could reasonably argue that improvements in housing might improve the physical conditions in which children were living as well as offering them better schools and better neighborhoods.

There is little evidence concerning health benefits, but what is available does not show much effect. The one notable effect was an increase in dietary intake for the rural North Carolina sample; these families were extremely poor and predominantly African American, so they may have been particularly deprived without the income guarantee (Institute for Research on Poverty, 1976).

The effects on children's school performance and attendance are somewhat mixed. For elementary-school-age children, there is some evidence of positive effects but, for high-school-age adolescents, there is little indication of a positive effect on achievement or aspirations. Nevertheless, in two studies, children in the experimental treatments were more likely to complete high school and they had higher levels of ultimate educational attainment than those in control families did. Adolescents in experimental families also were employed less than controls, perhaps because they were spending more time in educational pursuits. Other literature has indicated that extensive employment among high school students can interfere with optimal development (Steinberg & Dornbusch, 1991), so this finding may also indicate a "positive" outcome.

Measures of parent-child relations and socioemotional development are almost nonexistent, but no effects were found on the few superficial indexes that were reported.

In summary, the Income Maintenance Experiments provided some support for the conclusions from longitudinal, correlational investigations. There is a modest positive effect of family income change on academic and school-related outcomes. Given the fact that the absolute increase in income in the experimental families was relatively small, this result is particularly notable. On the other hand, no social experiment has a "pure" manipulation; the experimental effects could have been influenced by participants' awareness that they were in a time-limited experimental program and, in some studies, by a few additional counseling services provided to some subgroups.

TABLE 18.1. Summary of Income Maintenance Experiment effects on family and child outcomes

Measure	New Jersey	Gary, IN	Seattle/Devner	Rural North Carolina	Rural Iowa
Expenditures					
Housing (buy or rent)	E > C[a,b]	E > C[a]	E > C[a]	E > C[c]	E > C[c]
Migration out of city			E > C White E = C Black[a]		
Purchase durable goods	E > C[b]		E = C[a]	E > C[c]	E > C[c]
Food			E > C Single[a]		
Clothes			E > C[a]		
Medical			E > C[a]		
Health					
Health care utilization	E = C[b]				
Physical, mental health	E = C[b]				
Low birth weight		E < C in some groups, not in others[e]	E = C[a]		
Dietary intake				E > C[c,e]	E = C[c]
Fertility	Mixed E > C Black E < C White E = C P.R.[a,b,e]	E < C[a]	Mixed E = C Black E < C White E > C Chicano[a]		
School performance					
Grades in school		E < C (7–10)[e]	E = C Denver, E > C Seattle, p < .10[a,e]	E > C (2–8) E = C (9–12)[c,e]	E = C[c]
Achievement test performance		E > C (4, 6) E = C (5, 7–10)[e]		E > C (2–8) E = C (9-12)[c,e]	E = C[c]
Attendance, comportment		E>C (8-11)[e]	E=C, Denver E>C (K-12), Seattle[e]	E > C (2–8) E = C (9–12)[e]	E = C[e]
Finish high school, years of schooling	E > C[e]		E > C[e]		
Aspirations of teens				E = C[c]	E = C[c]
Employment of teens			E < C[a]	E < C[c]	E < C[c]
Delinquency				E = C[c]	E = C[c]
Family relations					
Marital dissolution			E > C Black, White, & high conflict E = C Chicano, & low conflict[d]	E = C[c]	E = C[c]
Parent-child relations (rated by mother and teen)				E = C[c]	E = C[c]

[a] Office of Economic Security (1983).
[b] Kershaw and Fair (1976).
[c] Institute for Research on Poverty (1976).
[d] Goenveld, Tuma, and Hannan (1980).
[e] Salkind and Haskins (1982).

Conclusion from Longitudinal and Experimental Studies

The overall conclusion from both longitudinal and experimental studies is that family income, especially during the early years, plays a role in children's cognitive, academic, and social development. The magnitude of the effect, relative to other family variables associated with poverty, is difficult to determine. Reported income is only a partial index of the material resources available to a family or the material hardships experienced. Moreover, the effects of income probably are not linear. The difference between incomes at 50% versus 100% of the poverty threshold is potentially more influential than the difference between incomes at 350% vs. 400% of the poverty thresholds. There probably are inflection points below which declines in income take on considerable importance.

Most of this research has not taken into account the fact that long-term persistent poverty has different consequences than transitory poverty or income loss. For example, children in persistent poverty have lower scores on cognitive and achievement tests than those in transitory poverty (Duncan et al., 1994). For many socioemotional outcomes, including aggression and antisocial behavior, however, income loss and transitory poverty are at least as strongly implicated as is persistent poverty (e.g., McLeod, et al., 1994).

☐ How Are Effects of Poverty Mediated?

The more interesting questions for me concern how family income and poverty translate into conditions that affect children's lives. It certainly is important to understand the relative contribution of family resources, family structure, and the like, but is it important to go beyond identifying particular variables to ask what experiences occur in children's worlds as a result of poverty or affluence? And, what are some of the important individual differences in the experience of poverty that lead to better or worse outcomes for children?

Two theoretical models provide hypotheses about environmental influences associated with poverty. In some respects, they overlap. In the resource model, income provides material goods and opportunities as well as a range of nonmaterial resources including parents' time, parents' ability to teach and provide guidance, parents' emotional support, quality schools, safe and supportive neighborhoods, and community resources. These are variously described as human, social, and cultural capital (Becker, 1981; Haveman & Wolfe, 1994; Johnson, 1996).

In the socialization model, broadly writ, family income influences parenting practices, values, aspirations, and modeling as well as other socialization environments (Conger, Ge, Elder, Lorenz, & Simons, 1994; McLoyd, 1990, 1998). Poverty and economic hardship are conceptualized as sources of psychological distress for adults; that distress, in turn, leads to nonsupportive or harsh, punitive parenting. This model can be extended to other socialization contexts, for example, child care settings, schools, and mass media (Huston, 1995).

A third model is based on the proposition that heritable characteristics account for the association of poverty with children's outcomes. According to this model, heritable intellectual abilities, personality dispositions, and the like are the causes of adult poverty; these same dispositions, transmitted genetically to children, are the reasons for low cognitive and academic skills, and behavior problems (Rowe & Rodgers, 1997). Although individual differences among children are partly a function of genetic endowments, they also are strongly influenced by multiple environments, particularly when those environments pose high risks (Huston, McLoyd, & Garcia Coll, 1997). The genetic hypothesis makes it even more important to use research methods that separate environmental influences from possible genetic influences; that is, to go beyond simple correlations of parent and child characteristics.

Both the resource and socialization models contain hypotheses about what processes mediate the relations of poverty to child outcomes. A basic mediational model, illustrated in Figure 18.2, describes the relations of poverty or family economic resources to some child outcomes as a function of some aspects of the child's environment. Poverty affects the proximal environment, which, in turn, influences the child.

To test any mediational model, you need to establish first that (a) family economic resources predict the child outcome, (b) family economic resources predict the environmental variable of interest, and (c) the environmental variable predicts the child outcome. If all of these are true, then you can ask whether the environmental variables "account for" the association of family economic variables with the child outcome. That is, when you take into account individual differences in the environmental variable, is the direct relation of economic resources to child outcome reduced (see Baron & Kenny, 1986)?

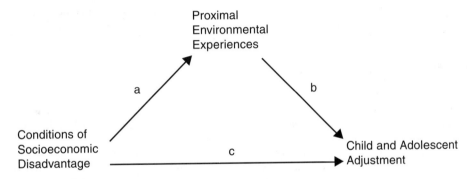

FIGURE 18.2. Ecological-mediational model of the effects of socioeconomic disadvantages on child and adolescent adjustments. Reprinted from R. D. Felner, 1995.

The preceding discussion addresses the role of poverty and family economic resources as an influence on child outcomes. The next question is, Do family economic resources predict the socialization environments in which children develop? And, to what extent do these socialization environments mediate the effects of economic resources on child outcomes? My research has been concerned with three socialization contexts: family, child care, and mass media. I will begin with what we know about the family environment.

☐ Home Environment

Family Income, Home Environment, and Parenting

Family income is related to both the social and material resources available in the home. The most frequently used index of home environment is the HOME Scale, which is based on both interview and observation of the mother and child at home. It includes ratings of maternal affection and discipline, learning opportunities, the physical quality of the home, and children's opportunities for exposure to different environments outside the home (Caldwell & Bradley, 1984). Low-income families provide early home environments that are less conducive to intellectual and social development (i.e., lower HOME scores) than do more affluent families, even when parent education, family structure, ethnic group, and a number of other child and family characteristics are statistically controlled (Brooks-Gunn, Klebanov, & Liaw, 1995; Duncan et al., 1994; Klebanov, Brooks-Gunn, & Duncan, 1994; Watson, Kirby, Kelleher, & Bradley, 1996). Perhaps more interesting is the finding that changes in income from birth to age 4 predicted changes in the HOME score (Garrett, Ng'andu, & Ferron, 1994).

Socialization theories posit parenting as a critical mediator of poverty effects on children's socioemotional development. Parents living in poverty report more financial stress, depression, and psychological distress than do more affluent parents. They worry about providing for basic needs like food and housing, racial and ethnic discrimination, dangerous neighborhoods, unemployment, lack of support systems, and lack of status in the society (McLoyd, 1990, 1998). The psychological stresses generated by poverty or income loss can affect interactions with children. Low family income is associated with: (a) harsh discipline and punitiveness (Conger & Elder, 1994; Dodge, Pettit, & Bates, 1994; Hashima & Amoto, 1994; McLeod et al., 1994; McLoyd, Jayaratne, Ceballo, & Borquez, 1994; Sampson & Laub, 1994); (b) low levels of warmth and support (Dodge et al., 1994; Hashima & Amoto, 1994; McLeod et al., 1994; McLoyd & Wilson, 1991); (c) for older children, low levels of supervision and monitoring (Sampson & Laub, 1994); (d) marital or cocaregiver conflict (Brody et al., 1994; Conger & Elder, 1994); and (e) repeated child abuse (Kruttschnitt, McLeod, & Dornfeld, 1994). Of course, not all parents respond to stress in these ways. Those with strong social networks and social support socialize their children with less harshness and more positive interactions than people who lack social support, suggesting that social networks can buffer the stresses associated with poverty (Brody et al., 1994; Hashima & Amoto, 1994; Leadbeater & Bishop, 1994; McLoyd et al., 1994).

In short, the links in Figure 18.2 of poverty to child outcomes and poverty to home environments are supported by a large body of investigation. Do home environments and parenting mediate some of the effects of poverty on children?

Home Environment as Mediator of Income Effects

Differences in home environmental conditions and parenting practices do partially mediate the relation of income to development, particularly to social and emotional development. In analyses of two samples, for example, HOME scores accounted for one third to one half of the relations of family income to IQ, vocabulary, reading, and math scores in middle childhood (Duncan et al., 1994; Smith et al., 1997). In a reanalysis of data for a sample of White, low-income adolescents studied in the 1950s, low levels of parent supervision, harsh discipline, and weak attachment to the parent partially accounted for relations of poverty to adolescent males' delinquency (Sampson & Laub, 1994). Among African American children in single mother families, adolescents' perceptions of negative relationships with their mothers predicted their anxiety and low self-esteem (McLoyd et al., 1994), and maternal nurturance mediated the effects of economic hardship on anxiety and depression (McLoyd & Wilson, 1991). In samples of midwestern farm families, parent-child conflict mediated the effects of economic hardship on behavior problems (Conger & Elder, 1994), and nurturance and inconsistent discipline mediated the effects of economic hardship on adolescents' depression and loneliness (Lempers et al., 1989).

Two additional investigations supported a mediational model, but their measures of family economic status were combinations of education and occupational status rather than income. In a longitudinal study of children from kindergarten through third grade, parents' disciplinary practices accounted for about half of the effects of socioeconomic status on children's aggression and externalizing behavior in school (Dodge et al., 1994). Among early adolescents from a poor, rural area, family climate and parental acceptance and rejection accounted for part of the effects of parent education on children's self-esteem, perceived competence, and depression, but did not mediate effects on grade point average, reading achievement, and classroom behavior problems (Felner et al., 1995).

On the other hand, two analyses of the NLSY data provided little support for the mediating effects of parents' emotional responsiveness and discipline (spanking). In one, parenting accounted for the effects of current poverty on children's internalizing and externalizing problems, but not for the effects of persistent poverty (McLeod & Shanahan, 1993). In a second analysis, there was some evidence of parenting as a mediator for White, but not for Black, families. In both groups, poverty was directly related to children's antisocial behavior (McLeod et al., 1994). The parenting measures in these analyses, however, were very superficial by comparison with most of the other investigations of mediational processes. Emotional responsiveness was the sum of three observer ratings of the mother, and discipline was based on one question to the mother about how often she had spanked the child in the past week.

In sum, a number of multivariate and longitudinal studies have supported the hypothesis that qualities of the home environment, including parental affection, discipline, and relationships with children mediate some of the effects of poverty on children's behavior. The evidence has been particularly strong for socioemotional and behavioral outcomes. Many of these investigations have included multiple measures from multiple respondents, and rigorous tests of their models. Nonetheless, because these investigations all are essentially correlational, alternative causal explanations are possible. Measured or unmeasured correlates of family income (e.g., intellectual or personality attributes of parents or children) could account for the relationships between poverty and child outcomes. The best method for establishing causal direction is, of course, the random assignment experiment but, as noted above, experiments varying family income have been rare.

☐ Early Child Care

The effects of poverty on children may be mediated not only by parents, but by the early care and educational environments in which many children spend time. American children from all income levels are likely to spend significant amounts of time in nonmaternal care during their early years. By 1990, over half of all infants under age 1 were in some form of nonmaternal care, with the majority enrolled for 30 hours or more per week. "As of 1993, 9.9 million children under age 5 were in need of care while their mothers were at work. Approximately 1.6 million of these children lived in families with monthly incomes below $1500" (Phillips, 1995, p. 1).

If we apply the mediational model in Figure 18.2 to child care, then our first question is whether family economic resources predict the qualities of the child care environments their children experience. Below, I will summarize what we know about these issues from recent research on early child care, including my own work as part of the multisite National Institute of Child Health and Human Development (NICHD) Study of Early Child Care (NICHD Early Child Care Research Network, 1994). In the NICHD study, investigators in 10 different locations around the United States are following a sample of 1,364 children recruited at birth in 1991. The children are now in first grade, and we are continuing to follow them. We have done repeated assessments of the characteristics of the families and children, and we have observed children in any nonmaternal care settings that they attended regularly, including care by grandparents and relatives, fathers, in-home caregivers, child care homes, and child care centers. Although the sample represents the entire range of family incomes, some analyses have been designed specifically to investigate the relations of poverty to children's child care experiences.

Age of Entry and Amount of Care

Family income and poverty predicted many of children's child care experiences, even when we controlled for maternal education, ethnic group, child's sex, family structure, and parents' attitudes about the costs and benefits of maternal employment for children (NICHD Early Child Care Research Network, 1997a, 1997c). Family income was a particularly important correlate of the age at which infants entered child care and the amount of time they spent in care, but the relation was complex. For the analyses of age of entry, children were grouped into five categories based on their age in months when they began 10 or more hours per week of regular child care: 0–2, 3–5, 6–11, 12–15, and not in care by 15 months.

The major reason that families use nonmaternal care for infants is to enable mothers to do paid work which, in turn, supplies family income, so it is not surprising that infants who had not experienced child care by 12 months of age came from families with lower average incomes (income-to-needs = 2.60) than those who entered child care before 3 months of age (income-to-needs = 3.26). Mothers provided the majority of the family's income (51%) in the group whose children entered early, and these families were most likely of any "age of entry" group to have been poor once, but not more than once, in the child's life. It appears that maternal employment serves to bring many of these families out of poverty. Children who entered child care between 3 and 5 months of age had families with the highest average incomes (income-to-needs = 4.01) and mothers' whose earnings supplied 45% of the family income (NICHD Early Child Care Research Network, 1997c).

Children in poor families spent less time in nonmaternal care than those in affluent families. For example, children in poor families (income-to-needs < 1.0) spent an estimated 14 hours per week less in child care than did children in affluent families (income-to-needs > 4.0 +); these estimates are adjusted for maternal education, ethnic group, family structure, and sex of child. With income held constant, children who were in care for the longest hours had mothers who worked many hours and who had relatively low levels of education, suggesting that mothers had to work relatively long hours to acquire their incomes. In the poorest families (income-to-needs < 1.0), children were less likely than other groups to receive nonmaternal care; in part, because their mothers were less likely to have paid employment (NICHD Early Child Care Research Network, 1997c).

Type of Care

The many settings in which infants received their first nonmaternal child care were classified into five groups: fathers ($N = 198$), grandparents ($N = 140$), other adults in the child's home ($N = 133$), other adults in a child care home ($N = 251$), and child care centers ($N = 106$). Children who received care by grandparents and fathers came from families with the lowest incomes (income-to-needs = 2.91 and 3.01, respectively). Families who used child care homes and centers were somewhat more affluent (income-to-needs = 3.46 and 3.78, respectively), and those using in-home care were much more affluent (income-to-needs = 5.25).

Income and Child Care Quality

The major concern of many developmentalists and policymakers, however, is the quality of the child care that children from different income groups receive (Phillips, 1995). In the first 3 years of life, most child care occurs in home settings, either with relatives or family child care providers, but there is very little information about these settings. In a widely publicized Study of Family and Relative Care, infants and toddlers cared for in home settings by relatives and nonrelatives were observed. Children from low income families received poorer quality care than those from more affluent families (Galinsky, Howes, Kontos, & Shinn, 1994).

In the NICHD study, we reported detailed observations of infants in child care at 6 and 15 months. Four indexes of quality were used. Two of these were obtained from the Observational Record of the Caregiving Environment (ORCE), a measure designed for this study to capture the quality of caregiving received by an individual child rather than by the group of children as a whole. *Positive caregiving frequency* is the frequency of eight categories of caregiving: shared positive affect, positive physical contact, responds to vocalization, asks question, talks, stimulates cognitive and social development, and facilitates infant behavior. *Positive caregiving rating* is the sum of ratings done at the end of each 30-minute observation cycle on sensitivity and responsiveness to nondistressed communication, positive regard, stimulation of cognitive development, and low detachment, absence of flat affect. In most home care settings, we also collected a version of the HOME modified for child care. Finally, in child care homes and centers, we used the Assessment Profile for Early Childhood Programs (Abbott-Shim & Sibley, 1987).

Because the types of care differed in important ways, analyses relating quality to family income were done within each of the five types of care. Family incomes were defined categorically as <1.0, 1.0–1.99, 2.0–2.99, 3.0–3.99, and 4.0+. For purposes of analysis, all income groups were compared to the "near poor" (i.e., 1.0–1.99), with controls for ethnic group, child sex, family size, and maternal education.

In all types of care except child care centers, family income was positively related to the frequency and quality of caregiver-child interactions and to measures of the physical setting and learning opportunities in many of the child care settings (NICHD Early Child Care Research Network, 1997a). Children from poor families received significantly lower quality care than children from families who were near poverty, and children from more affluent families received higher quality care than both groups.

Child care centers have been studied more extensively than home settings, and most studies have not found strong relations between family income and quality (Phillips, 1995). One reason may be that children from poor families receive slightly better care than those from lower- to middle-income families. In the National Child Care Staffing Study which investigated a large sample of centers serving infants and preschoolers, centers serving children from moderate-income families provided poorer quality care than those serving children from families with very low incomes or high incomes. It is not surprising that high income families can purchase quality center care, assuming a correlation of price with quality. Moreover, families with very low incomes or middle to high incomes have more access to government subsidies for care than those in between (Phillips, Voran, Kisker, Howes, & Whitebook, 1994). The very poorest nonworking families receive subsidized care more often than do working families with incomes of less than $25,000, and more affluent families receive greater benefit from the income tax credit for child care expenses (Hofferth, 1995).

We found a similar pattern in infant care in the NICHD study. In child care centers, children from the poorest families (income-to-needs < 1.0) received higher quality care than those whose family incomes were just above the poverty threshold (income-to-needs = 1.0–1.99). Children from relatively affluent families (income-to-needs = 3.0 or greater) were in centers that scored higher on the profile than centers serving our near-poor children. Although the sample of poor infants in child care centers was small (N = 11), most of them (7) received public subsidies (NICHD Early Child Care Research Network, 1997). These findings suggest that public policies subsidizing child care for low income families can improve the quality of care they receive.

Effects of Child Care Quality on Children

Children's early experience in nonmaternal care can make important contributions to both intellectual and socioemotional development. In the NICHD Study, we have examined the relations of child care to children's cognitive, language, and social development during the first 3 years of life. Because we have extensive measures of family and child characteristics, we can control for these to determine whether child care contributes to child outcomes independently of individual and family differences. In these analyses, the quality of care received during these early years predicted cognitive and language development at ages 15, 24, and 36 months (we have not yet analyzed data after age 3). The variance accounted for by child care ranged from 1.3% to 3.6%, after controls for maternal vocabulary score, family income, child sex, family HOME, and observed maternal cognitive stimulation were included. Children who received care that rated high on positive caregiving (particularly, when it included frequent language stimulation from caregivers), performed better on measures of general cognitive development and language skills than those who received lower quality care (NICHD Early Child Care Research Network, 1997d). One index of the magnitude of these differences is a comparison between children in the top and bottom quartiles on the observed quality scales. After adjustment for the control variables, their mean scores on the Bayley Mental Development Index at 24 months differed by 5.1 points (90.5 for the lowest quartile; 95.6 for the highest), and by 11 percentile points on Verbal Comprehension at 36 months (41.7 on the Reynell Verbal Comprehension Scale for the lowest quartile; 52.7 for the highest quartile) (NICHD Early Child Care Research Network, 1997d).

Children who had been cared for in child care centers performed better than those in other types of care, when overall quality of care was controlled, suggesting that centers provide some conditions or activities beyond adult attention and responsiveness that enhance cognitive and language development (NICHD Early Child Care Research Network, 1997d).

By contrast, we have found less consistent relations of child care experiences to mother-child interaction, attachment security, and social behavior during these early years. When children were in high amounts of care, mothers were somewhat less sensitive in interacting with them but, when children were in high-quality care, mothers were somewhat more sensitive. The variance accounted for was small—less than 1% (NICHD Early Child Care Research Network, 1997b). There were no overall relations of child care to attachment security, but for a subgroup with insensitive mothers, children were more apt to be insecurely attached if they were in high amounts, low quality, or unstable child care (NICHD Early Child Care Research Network, 1997c). There were weak effects of quality of child care on children's social behavior (NICHD Early Child Care Network, 1998). All of these analyses included controls for demographic "selection" variables, child gender, and appropriate indexes of home conditions and maternal behavior. Family, maternal, and relationship variables consistently explained considerably more variance than did the child care variables.

Other investigations following children over longer periods of time have shown relations between quality and social-emotional outcomes. For example, Howes (1988, 1990) demonstrated that quality of early care predicted children's levels of play and social competence in the child care setting and, a few years later, when they reached school age. In the Child Care Costs and Quality Study, 826 4-year-olds were observed in child care centers in four states. The quality of the adult-child interactions predicted vocabulary, math competence, children's perceptions of their own competence, and teacher ratings of positive behavior and sociability (Peisner-Feinberg & Burchinal, 1997). In another investigation, the observed quality of care at age 4 predicted children's social and academic adjustment in school at age 8 (Vandell & Corasaniti, 1990).

Experimental Studies

Much of the information on child care is correlational in nature and has the limitations on causal inference noted above. In addition, the "effects" can be estimated only for the environments that exist, not for environments that might be optimal but rare. If most existing child care is of low quality, as some have argued, then examining correlations of quality with child outcomes will not tell us how much good quality could contribute to children's development. In this domain, we do have experimental tests showing the efficacy of educational child care for children from low income families during the first few years of life (Barnett, 1995; McLoyd, 1997). For instance, children who received educational child care from infancy to school age in North Carolina performed better than controls on measures of school achievement as late as age 12 (Campbell & Ramey, 1994). Child care was more effective than interventions in the children's homes (Burchinal, Campbell, Bryant, Wasik, & Ramey, 1997). Low birth weight children were randomly assigned to an intervention that included educational child care from age 1 to 3 or to an untreated control group. The intervention had positive effects on IQ, vocabulary, and incidence of behavior problems at age 3 and 5 (Smith & Brooks-Gunn, 1994).

Does Child Care Mediate Poverty Effects?

The data indicate that children from low income families are most likely to receive low-quality child care, at least in the home care settings used by most parents. Those near the lower end of the income continuum are most likely to receive poor care in centers, and they are apt to enter care at an early age for long hours. These patterns point to working poor and near-poor families as those whose children may be most at risk for extended exposure to poor-quality center care.

A large body of correlational, longitudinal, and experimental research also identifies the quality of child care as an important contributor to children's intellectual and academic development and probably to social-emotional competence as well. The next step in testing a mediational model is to determine whether features of child care account for the relations of family poverty to children's outcomes. Testing this mediational model is one of the future directions that my own research will take.

☐ Television

Discussions of poverty usually do not include references to mass media, despite the well-known facts that virtually all American homes have television sets (usually more than one) and that people with low incomes watch more television than do affluent individuals and families (Comstock & Paik, 1991). With my colleague, friend, and husband, John Wright, I have been studying the influences of television on children for many years. We have conducted two longitudinal studies of very young children's media use. The Topeka Study followed 326 children from age 3 to 5 or 5 to 7 in a cohort sequential design. No information on income was obtained, but parents' educational levels and occupational statuses included a wide range. It is likely, however, that most had incomes above the poverty threshold (Huston, Wright, Rice, Kerkman, & St. Peters, 1990). In the second study, the Early Window Project, 235 children in families with low to moderate incomes (average income-to-needs = 1.70) were recruited and followed over a 3-year period from age 2 to 5 or 4 to 7 (Wright & Huston, 1995).

One guiding principal of our research is that television in not homogeneous; its effects depend on the content and form of the programs watched. In the Topeka Study, parents kept 1-week viewing diaries for the whole family every 6 months (a total of five diaries over 2 years). In the Early Window Study, we collected periodic 24-hour time use diaries in telephone or face-to-face interviews. In both studies, children in families with low socioeconomic status or low incomes were particularly likely to watch entertainment programs designed for older audiences and cartoons that contained violence, social stereotypes, and little of educational or social value (Truglio, Murphy, Oppenheimer, Huston, & Wright, 1996; Wright & Huston, 1995). In the Early Window Project, children in families with the lowest incomes were least likely to watch educational television for children (Huston & Wright, 1997; Wright & Huston, 1995). Hence, the link from poverty to television use is well established.

Research investigating the second link in Figure 18.2, from television to child outcomes, has been concentrated on harmful effects (e.g., televised violence and aggressive behavior) (Huston & Wright, 1997). Much less attention has been given to the lost opportunity for using television in a positive way. Our work and that of others (e.g., Singer & Singer, 1994) has demonstrated that programs designed to promote children's development can teach intellectual skills and prosocial behavior and attitudes.

In both the Topeka and Early Window Studies, children who watched educational programs at home or in child care from age 2 to 4 performed better on measures of vocabulary, prereading and math, and school readiness at age 5 than those who did not watch educational television. These effects occurred with controls for family education, home environment, and children's initial language competency (Rice, Huston, Truglio, & Wright, 1990; Wright & Huston, 1995). These longitudinal findings are supported by experimental studies of *Sesame Street* conducted in the early 1970s, showing that economically disadvantaged children learned school-related skills from viewing the program (Ball & Bogatz, 1970; Bogatz & Ball, 1971; see Huston & Wright, 1997, 1998). Although a specific test of the mediational hypothesis—that television accounts for some of the relation of poverty to children's development—has not to my knowledge been performed, this combination of longitudinal and experimental findings indicates that educational television can play a role in the intellectual development of children from low-income families. Such findings provide a solid basis for public policies promoting educational uses of television.

In fact, the corpus of research on educational television informed a major public policy initiative to increase the availability of educational and informative television for children in the past 10 years. In 1990, the Children's Educational Television Act became law. It requires broadcasters to include programming that meets the educational and informational needs of children. The law had little impact, however, until a 1996 ruling that put a specific minimal time requirement of 3 hours per week into effect. Broadcasters are required to label programs which they consider educational so that parents and others will be able to evaluate their claims. These policies are concerned with the welfare of all children, not just those in poor families, but they are likely to have particular benefits for children in low-income families.

☐ The New Hope Project

Several of these research interests have come together in an experiment that is currently underway to study the effects of the New Hope Project in Milwaukee on children and families (Bos, Huston, Granger, Duncan, Brock, & McLoyd, et al., 1999). The New Hope Project is a 3-year random-assignment demonstration experiment designed to test the effectiveness of an employment-based antipoverty program for families who are economically poor. For adults who work full time (defined as a minimum of 30 hours per week), it provides job search assistance, wage supplements that raise family income above the poverty threshold, and subsidies for health insurance and child care. Applicants were assigned to take part in the program or in a control group that did not receive its services in a rigorous random assignment experimental design. Therefore, it represents a strong test of the causal effects of improving family resources on family functioning and child development.

New Hope Inc., the nonprofit corporation operating the experiment, originally contracted with the Manpower Demonstration Research Corporation (MDRC) to evaluate its implementation and effects. While both New Hope Inc. and MDRC had an initial interest in child and family policy issues, resource constraints led their evaluation to emphasize labor market and economic outcomes for the adults. My association with the project came about as a result of my membership in the MacArthur Network on Successful Pathways Through Middle Childhood. We joined with MDRC to add an extensive assessment of family life and children's development. Of the 1,362 adults in the experimental and control groups, 745 had at least one child age 1 through 10 at the time of random assignment. These parents and up to two of their children were interviewed 24 months after random assignment when the children were age 3 to 12. Information was collected on parents' income, employment, use of child care, health care, psychological well-being, and parenting practices. Children's educational progress, aspirations, school motivation, well-being, and social behavior were assessed using information collected from parents, children, and teachers. We also are collecting ethnographic and qualitative information on subsamples of this group, and will follow them up again 60 months after random assignment.

Conceptual Model

The conceptual model guiding this research incorporates resource and socialization models of poverty effects. The major components of New Hope are a guaranteed minimum income, a work requirement, subsidized health insurance, subsidized child care, and job search services. These components were expected to increase some or all of the following: income, hours of employment, access to medical care, use of paid, formal child care, which, in turn, are expected to influence children's development. The conceptual model describing the processes by which the New Hope intervention might affect family life and children's developmental pathways is shown in Figure 18.3. Both parenting and child care are included as mediators in this model.

Effects on Parents

The most direct effects are expected to occur for parents' material resources, time allocation, and psychological well-being. Both work hours and income did increase for parents who were not employed full time when they entered the program; they were less likely than control parents to earn incomes below the poverty threshold. Parents who were already employed full time at the outset continued to work, but their

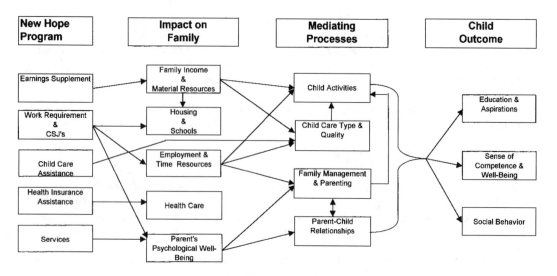

FIGURE 18.3. New Hope: Child and Family Study Conceptual Model.

total incomes did not increase. We expected that employment could have both positive and negative effects.

For the most part New Hope increased parents' sense of efficacy and reduced their stress and worries, but it increased time pressure in the lives of those who worked more in response to the program's incentive. The program also increased the social support available to participants. However, New Hope did not improve more enduring psychological dispositions—feelings of depression, mastery, or self-esteem.

Effects on children were expected to be mediated by changes in the family environment, child care and out-of-school activities, and parent-child interactions. As predicted, participants used more organized child care in centers and after-school programs, as opposed to informal care by older siblings, family, neighbors, or self-care. Children also participated in more structured activities—lessons, clubs, team sports, and recreation centers. Because New Hope improved parents' psychological well-being, we expected positive effects on parenting. These effects occurred only for parents who were employed full time when they entered the program.

The most striking findings were positive effects of the program on children, particularly the boys in the sample. Teachers, who had no knowledge about the families' participation in the New Hope study, reported that boys in New Hope families had better academic performance, stronger study skills, higher levels of social competence, and fewer behavioral problems than control group boys. Boys whose parents were in New Hope reported higher educational expectations and higher occupational aspirations and expectations, implying that the program affected their ambitions for future study and careers. Although girls were generally doing better in school and had more positive social behavior than boys, there were few differences between girls in the program and control group families (Bos et al., 1999).

Many children in New Hope families are statistically at risk for delinquency and school failure as they approach adolescence. By definition, their families are poor, most are ethnic minorities, and most are headed by single mothers. If the experiences provided through New Hope can change young boys' trajectories toward better school performance, more competent social behavior, and fewer problems of poor behavior control, the odds of school completion and socially competent adolescent development will be increased.

Access to formal child care, extended day care in schools, and structured out-of-school activities appears to be an important path by which the New Hope impacts on children occurred. If that is correct, there are clear public policy implications. Public policy can readily increase availability of child care, after-school activities, and other opportunities for supervised, structured activities for children, which may, in turn, significantly alter developmental trajectories for young boys and girls in low-income families.

☐ Conclusion

I began this chapter with questions about the processes by which family poverty influences children's development. To what extent does family income or economic condition make a unique contribution to children's development, above and beyond parent education, family structure, and many other conditions associated with poverty? What proximal conditions and experiences in the home environment and in other socialization contexts mediate the relations between family economic status and children's developmental outcomes?

The weight of the evidence has suggested that income makes a significant contribution to intellectual development, school achievement, and socioemotional development that is independent of related demographic and family structure influences. Much of the available literature, however, is fundamentally correlational; therefore, the effects attributed to income could be due to unmeasured third variables (e.g., parents' levels of motivation, personality attributes). Many of the investigations demonstrating "effects" have gone to great lengths to control for such related variables as maternal education, maternal intellectual performance, family structure, ethnic group, unemployment, and maternal age. These studies also may have underestimated the importance of material resources because cash income represents only part of the variation in material hardship and noncash resources. The Income Maintenance Studies provided modest experimental support for the hypothesis that improving incomes of people in poverty leads to improvement in resources available to children and to improvement in educational outcomes. Family income loss and poverty are associated with features of the home environment that, in turn, account for part of the relationship between poverty and child outcomes. The weakness in this body of literature is that it is difficult to exclude alternative explanations for the patterns observed.

Similarly, poverty predicts the amount and quality of nonmaternal care that children receive, and it predicts the amount and quality of the television that they watch. These features of children's experience, in turn, contribute to cognitive and social developmental outcomes, but we know little about their contribution to the overall impact of poverty on intellectual and social development. Although the amount of research on child care and television is smaller than the volume of work on family influences, the body of data available is subject to fewer methodological problems. For both topics, some solid random assignment experiments complement the correlational and longitudinal research.

Although longitudinal methods are invaluable in understanding the complexities of children's development in context, experimental designs have some unique virtues for elucidating these issues. The New Hope Project is one attempt to use such a design. It suggests that a package of benefits that make modest improvements in family material resources can have positive effects on children. A parallel experiment, the Canadian Self-Sufficiency Project (Veevers, 1996), is a test of the effects of increased income using larger income supplements than those in New Hope. Single mothers on welfare can receive wage supplements of several thousand dollars if they leave welfare to work full time. Because Canada has universal health coverage, it is not necessary to provide health benefits, but neither are extra supplements given for child care. With the decentralization of "welfare" in the United States from the federal government to the states, several states also are conducting experiments evaluating a variety of incentives and penalties that may increase or reduce incomes of single parents. Although their primary concern is the impact on adults' work, income, and receipt of welfare, some of these investigations will also obtain information about how family life and children's development is affected.

I will conclude where I started. It is important to understand the processes by which the conditions of poverty influence children for both theoretical and policy reasons. Seeking to understand these processes will provide a more sophisticated basic science of development and will inform intelligent and effective policies.

☐ References

Abbott-Shim, M., & Sibley. A. (1987). *Assessment profile for early childhood education programs.* Atlanta, GA: Quality Assist.

Ball, S., & Bogatz, G. A. (1970). *The first year of* Sesame Street: *An evaluation.* Princeton, NJ: Educational Testing Service.

Bogatz, G. A., & Ball, S. (1971). *The second year of* Sesame Street: *An evaluation.* Princeton, NJ: Educational Testing Service.

Barnett, W. S. (1995). Long-term effects of early childhood programs on cognitive and school outcomes. *The Future of Children, 5*, 25–50.

Baron, R. M., & Kenny, D. A. (1986). The moderator-mediator variable distinction in social psychological research: Conceptual, strategic and statistical considerations. *Journal of Personality and Social Psychology, 6*, 1173–1182.

Becker, G. S. (1981). *A treatise on the family.* Cambridge, MA: Harvard University Press.

Bolger, K. E., Patterson, C. J., Thompson, W. W., & Kupersmidt, J. B. (1995). Psychosocial adjustment among children experiencing persistent and intermittent family hardship. *Child Development, 66*, 1107–1129.

Bos, H., Huston, A. C., Granger, R., Duncan, G., Brock, T., & McLoyd, V. with Crosby, D., Gibson, C., Fellerath, V., Magnuson, K., Mistry, R., Poglinco, S., Romich, J., & Ventura, A. (1999). *New Hope for people with low incomes: Two-year results of a program to reduce poverty and reform welfare.* New York: Manpower Demonstration Research Corporation.

Brody, G. H., Stoneman, Z., Flor, D., McCrary, C., Hastings, L., & Conyers, O. (1994). Financial resources, parent psychological functioning, parent co-caregiving, and early adolescent competence in rural two-parent African-American families. *Child Development, 65*, 590–605.

Bronfenbrenner, U., McClelland, P., Wethington, E., Moen, P., & Ceci, S. J. (1996). *The state of Americans: This generation and next.* New York: Free Press.

Brooks-Gunn, J., Klebanov, P. K., & Liaw, F. (1995). The learning, physical, and emotional environment of the home in the context of poverty: The Infant Health and Development Program. *Children and Youth Services Review, 17*, 251–276.

Burchinal, M. R., Campbell, F. A., Bryant, D. B., Wasik, B. H., & Ramey, C. T. (1997). Early intervention and mediating processes in cognitive performance of children of low-income African-American Families. *Child Development, 68*, 935–954.

Bureau of the Census. (1995, February). *Income, poverty, and valuation of noncash benefits: 1993 Current Population Reports, Series P60-188.* Washington, DC: Author.

Bureau of the Census. (1997). *Poverty in the United States, 1977.* Current Population Reports, pp. 860–201. Washington, DC: Author.

Caldwell, B. M., & Bradley, R. H. (1984). *Home observation for measurement of the environment.* Little Rock, AR: University of Arkansas at Little Rock.

Campbell, F. A., & Ramey, C. T. (1994). Effects of early intervention on intellectual and academic achievement: A follow-up of children from low-income families. *Child Development, 65*, 684–698.

Chafel, J. A. (Ed.) (1993). *Child poverty and public policy.* Washington, DC: Urban Institute Press.

Citro, C. F., & Michael, R. T. (1995). *Measuring poverty: A new approach.* Washington, DC: National Academy Press.

Comstock, G., & Paik, H. J. (1991). *Television and the American child.* Orlando, FL: Academic Press.

Conger, R. D., & Elder, G. H., Jr. (1994). *Families in troubled times: Adapting to change in rural America.* New York: Aldine de Gruyter.

Conger, R. D., Ge, X., Elder, G. H., Jr., Lorenz, F. O., & Simons, R. L. (1994). Economic stress, coercive family process, and developmental problems of adolescents. *Child Development, 65*, 541–561.

Corcoran, M., & Adams, T. (1997). Race, sex, and the intergenerational transmission of poverty. In G. J. Duncan & J. Brooks-Gunn (Eds.), *Consequences of growing up poor* (pp. 461–517). New York: Sage.

Danziger, S., & Gottschalk, P. (Eds.) (1994). *Uneven tides: Rising inequality in America.* New York: Sage.

Dodge, K. A., Pettit, G. S. & Bates, J. E. (1994). Socialization mediators of the relation between socioeconomic status and child conduct problems. *Child Development, 65*, 649-665.

Duncan, G. J. (1984). *Years of poverty, years of plenty.* Ann Arbor: Institute for Social Research, University of Michigan.

Duncan, G. J. (1991). The economic environment of childhood. In A. C. Huston (Ed.), *Children in poverty: Child development and public policy* (pp. 23–50). New York: Cambridge University Press.

Duncan, G. J., & Brooks-Gunn, J. (Eds.). (1997a). *Consequences of growing up poor.* New York: Sage.

Duncan, G. J., & Brooks-Gunn, J. (1997b). Income effects across the life span: Integration and interpretation. In G. J. Duncan & J. Brooks-Gunn (Eds.), *Consequences of growing up poor* (pp. 596–610). New York: Sage

Duncan, G. J., Brooks-Gunn, J., & Klebanov, P. K. (1994). Economic deprivation and early-childhood development. *Child Development, 65*, 296–318.

Edin, K., & Lein, L. (1997). *Making ends meet: How single mothers survive welfare and low-wage work.* New York: Sage.

Elder, G. H., Jr. (1974). *Children of the Great Depression: Social change in life experience.* Chicago: University of Chicago Press.

Felner, R. D., Brand, S., DuBois, D. L., Adan, A. M., Mulhall, P. F., & Evans, E.G. (1995). Socioeconomic disadvantage, proximal environmental experiences, and socioeconomical and academic adjustment in early adolescence: Investigation of a mediated effects model. *Child Development, 66*, 774–792.

Galinsky, E., Howes, C., Kontos, S., & Shinn, M. (1994). *The study of children in family child care and relative care.* New York: Families and Work Institute.

Garbarino, J. (1992). The meaning of poverty in the world of children. *American Behavioral Scientist, 35*, 220–237.

Garrett, P., Ng'andu, N., & Ferron, J. (1994). Poverty experiences of young children and the quality of their home environments. *Child Development, 65,* 331–345.

Goenveld, L. P., Tuma, N. B., & Hannan, M. T. (1980). The effects of negative income tax programs on marital dissolution. *Journal of Human Resources, 15,* 654–674.

Guerra, N. G., Huesmann, L. R., Tolan, P. H., Van Acker, R., & Eron, L. D. (1995). Stressful events and individual beliefs as correlates of economic disadvantage and aggression among urban children. *Journal of Consulting and Clinical Psychology, 63,* 518–528.

Hashima, P. Y., & Amoto, P. R. (1994). Poverty, social support, and parental behavior. *Child Development, 65,* 394–403.

Hauser, R. M., & Sweeney, M. M. (1997). Does poverty in adolescence affect the life chances of high school graduates? In G. J. Duncan & J. Brooks-Gunn (Eds.), *Consequences of growing up poor* (pp. 541–595). New York: Sage.

Haveman, R. H. (1986). Review of social experimentation. *Journal of Human Resources, 21,* 586–603.

Haveman, R., & Wolfe, B. (1994). *Succeeding generations: On the effects of investments in children.* New York: Sage.

Haveman, R., Wolfe, B., & Spaulding, J. (1991). Childhood events and circumstances influencing high school completion. *Demography, 28,* 153–157.

Hill, M. S., & Sandfort, J. R. (1995). Effects of childhood poverty on productivity later in life: Implications for public policy. *Children and Youth Services Review, 17,* 91–126.

Hofferth, S. (1995). Caring for children at the poverty line. *Children and Youth Services Review, 17,* 61–90.

Howes, C. (1988). Relations between early child care and schooling. *Developmental Psychology, 24,* 53–57.

Howes, C. (1990). Can the age of entry into child care and the quality of child care predict adjustment in kindergarten? *Developmental Psychology, 26,* 292–303.

Huesmann, L. R., Eron, L. D., Klein, R., Brice, P., & Fischer, P. (1983). Mitigating the imitation of aggressive behaviors by changing children's attitudes about media violence. *Journal of Personality and Social Psychology, 44,* 899–910.

Huston, A. C. (Ed.). (1991). *Children in poverty: Child development and public policy.* New York: Cambridge University Press.

Huston, A. C. (1995, August). *Children in poverty and public policy.* Presidential address to Division 7, American Psychological Association, New York.

Huston, A. C., Donnerstein, E., Fairchild, H., Feshbach, N., Katz, P., Murray, J., Rubinstein, E., Wilcox, B., & Zuckerman, D. (1992). *Big world, small screen: The role of television in American society.* Lincoln: University of Nebraska Press.

Huston, A. C., McLoyd, V. C., & Garcia Coll, C. (Eds.) (1994). Children and poverty: Issues in comtemporary research . *Child Development, 65,* 275–283.

Huston, A. C., McLoyd, V. C., & Garcia Coll, C. (1997). Poverty and behavior: The case for multiple methods and multiple levels of analysis. *Developmental Review, 17,* 376–393.

Huston, A. C., & Wright, J. C. (1997). Mass media and children's development. In W. Damon, I. Sigel, & A. Renniger (Eds.). *Handbook of child psychology: Vol. 4. Child psychology in practice* (5th ed., pp. 999–1058). New York: Wiley.

Huston, A. C., & Wright, J. C. (1998). Contributions of television toward meeting the informational and educational needs of children. *Annals of the American Academy of Political and Social Science, 557,* 9–23.

Huston, A. C., Wright, J. C., Rice, M. L., Kerkman, D., & St. Peters, M. (1990). The development of television viewing patterns in early childhood: A longitudinal investigation. *Developmental Psychology, 26,* 409–420.

Institute for Research on Poverty. (1976). *The Rural Income Maintenance Experiment.* Madison, WI: University of Wisconsin, Institute for Research on Poverty.

Johnson, J. H., Jr. (1996). The real issues for reducing poverty in America. In M. R. Darby (Ed.), *Reducing poverty in America: Views and approaches* (pp. 337–363). Thousand Oaks, CA: Sage.

Kershaw, D., & Fair, J. (1976). *The New Jersey Income Maintenance Experiment* (Vol. 1). New York: Academic Press.

Klebanov, P. K., Brooks-Gunn, J., & Duncan, G. J. (1994). Does neighborhood and family poverty affect mothers' parenting, mental health, and social support? *Journal of Marriage and the Family, 56,* 441–455.

Kruttschnitt, C., McLeod, J. D., & Dornfeld, M. (1994). The economic environment of child abuse. *Social Problems, 41,* 299–315.

Leadbeater, B. J., & Bishop, S. J. (1994). Predictors of behavior problems in preschool children of inner-city Afro-American and Puerto Rican adolescent mothers. *Child Development, 65,* 638–648.

Lempers, J. D., Clark-Lempers, D., & Simons, R. L. (1989). Economic hardship, parenting, and distress in adolescence. *Child Development, 60,* 25–39.

Liaw, F., & Brooks-Gunn, J. (1994). Cumulative familial risks and low-birthweight children's cognitive and social development. *Journal of Clinical Child Psychology, 23,* 360–372.

Luster, T., & McAdoo, H. P. (1994). Factors related to the achievement and adjustment of young African American children. *Child Development, 65,* 1080–1094.

Luster, T., Reischl, T., Gassaway, J., & Gomaa, H. (1995, March). *Factors related to early school success among African American children from low income families.* Paper presented at the Biennial Meeting of the Society for Research in Child Development, Indianapolis. SRCD.

Mayer, S. E. (1997a). *What money can't buy: Family income and children's life chances.* Chicago: University of Chicago Press.

Mayer, S. E. (1997b). Trends in the economic well-being and life chances of America's children. In G. J. Duncan & J. Brooks-Gunn (Eds.), *Consequences of growing up poor* (pp. 49–69). New York: Sage

McLeod, J. D., Kruttschnitt, C., & Dornfeld, M. (1994). Does parenting explain the effects of structural conditions on children's antisocial behavior? A comparison of Blacks and Whites. *Social Forces, 73,* 575–604.

McLeod, J. D., & Shanahan, M. J. (1993). Poverty, parenting, and children's mental health. *American Sociological Review, 58,* 351–366.

McLoyd, V. C. (1990). The impact of economic hardship on Black families and children: Psychological distress, parenting, and socioemotional development. *Child Development, 61,* 311–346.

McLoyd, V. C. (1997). Children in poverty: Development, public policy, and practice. In W. Damon, I. E. Sigel, & K. A. Renninger (Eds.), *Handbook of child psychology: Vol. 4. Child psychology in practice* (5th ed., pp. 135–210). New York: Wiley.

McLoyd, V. C. (1998). Socioeconomic disadvantage and child development. *American Psychologist, 53,* 185–204.

McLoyd, V. C., Jayaratne, T. E., Ceballo, R., & Borquez, J. (1994). Unemployment and work interruption among African American single mothers: Effects on parenting and adolescent socioemotional functioning. *Child Development, 65,* 562–589.

McLoyd, V. C., & Wilson, L. (1991). The strain of living poor: Parenting, social support, and child mental health. In A. C. Huston (Ed.), *Children in poverty: Child development and public policy* (pp. 105–135). New York: Cambridge University Press.

NICHD Early Child Care Research Network. (1994). Child care and child development: The NICHD Study of Early Child Care. In S. Friedman & H. C. Haywood (Eds.), *Developmental follow-up: Concepts, domains, and methods* (pp. 377–396). New York: Academic Press.

NICHD Early Child Care Research Network. (1997a). Familial factors associated with the characteristics of nonmaternal care for infants. *Journal of Marriage and the Family, 59,* 389–409.

NICHD Early Child Care Research Network. (1997b, April). Mother-child interaction and cognitive outcomes associated with early child care: Results from the NICHD study. Poster session presented at the meeting of the Society for Research in Child Development, Washington, DC.

NICHD Early Child Care Research Network. (1997c). The effects of infant child care on infant-mother attachment security: Results of the NICHD Study of Early Child Care. *Child Development, 78,* 860–879.

NICHD Early Child Care Research Network. (1997d). *The relation of child care to cognitive and language development.* Manuscript submitted for publication.

NICHD Early Child Care Research Network. (1997e). Poverty and patterns of child care. In J. Brooks-Gunn & G. Duncan (Eds.), *Growing up poor* (pp. 100–131). New York: Sage.

NICHD Early Child Care Research Network. (1998). Early child care and self-control, compliance, and problem behavior at 24 and 36 months of age. *Child Development, 69,* 1149–1170.

Office of Income Security Policy, U.S. Department of Health and Human Services (1983). *Overview of the Seattle-Denver Income Maintenance Experiment. Final Report.* Washington DC: U.S. Government Printing Office.

Paik, H., & Comstock, G. (1994). The effects of television violence on antisocial behavior: A meta-analysis. *Communication Research, 21,* 516–546.

Patterson, C. J., Kupersmidt, J. B., & Vaden, N. A. (1990). Income level, gender, ethnicity, and household composition as predictors of children's school-based competence. *Child Development, 61,* 485–494.

Peisner-Feinberg, E. S., & Burchinal, M. R. (1997). Relations between preschool children, child care experiences, and concurrent development: The cost, quality, and outcomes study. *Merrill-Palmer Quarterly, 43,* 451–477.

Phillips, D. A., (1995). *Child care for low-income families: Summary of two workshops.* Washington, DC: National Academy Press.

Phillips, D. A., Voran, M., Kisker, E., Howes, C., & Whitebook, M. (1994). Child care for children in poverty: Opportunity or inequity? *Child Development, 65,* 472–492.

Rainwater, L., & Smeeding, T. M. (1996, April). *Doing poorly: The real income of American children in a comparative perspective.* Paper presented at the Workshop on Welfare and Child Development, Board on Children, Youth, and Families, National Research Council and Institute of Medicine, Washington, DC.

Rice, M. L., Huston, A. C., Truglio, R. T., & Wright, J. C. (1990). Words from *Sesame Street:* Learning vocabulary while viewing. *Developmental Psychology, 26,* 421–428.

Rossi, P. H. & Lyall, K. C. (1978). An overview evaluation of the NIT experiment. In T. D. Cook, M. L. Del Rosario, K. M. Hennigan, M. M. Mark, & W. M. K. Trochim (Eds.), *Evaluation studies review annual* (Vol. 3). Beverly Hills, CA: Sage.

Rowe, D. C., & Rodgers, J. L. (1997). Poverty and behavior: Are environmental measures nature and nurture? *Developmental Review, 17,* 358–375.

Salkind, N. J., & Haskins, R. (1982). Negative income tax: The impact on children from low-income families. *Journal of Family Issues, 3,* 165–180.

Sampson, R. J., & Laub, J. H. (1994). Urban poverty and the family context of delinquency: A new look at structure and process in a classic study. *Child Development, 65,* 523–540.

Scarbrough, W. H. (1993). Who are the poor? A demographic perspective. In J. Chafel (Ed.), *Child poverty and public policy* (pp. 55–90). Washington, DC: Urban Institute Press.

Singer, D. G., & Singer, J. L. (1994). Evaluating the classroom viewing of a television series: "Degrassi Junior High." In D. Zillmann, J. Bryant, & A. C. Huston (Eds.), *Media, children, and the family: Social scientific, psychodynamic, and clinical perspectives* (pp. 97–116). Hillsdale, NJ: Erlbaum.

Smith, J. R., & Brooks-Gunn, J. (1994, December). *Developmental effects of natural transitions in welfare receipt*. Paper presented at the Workshop on Welfare and Child Development, National Academy of Sciences, Washington, DC.

Smith, J. R., Brooks-Gunn, J., & Klebanov, P. K. (1997). Consequences of living in poverty for young children's cognitive and verbal ability and early school achievement. In G. J. Duncan & J. Brooks-Gunn (Eds.), *Consequences of growing up poor* (pp. 132–189). New York: Sage.

Steinberg, L., & Dornbusch, S. M. (1991). Negative correlates of part-time employment during adolescence: Replication and elaboration. *Developmental Psychology, 27*, 304–313.

Truglio, R. T., Murphy, K. C., Oppenheimer, S., Huston, A. C., & Wright, J. C. (1996). Predictors of children's entertainment television viewing: Why are they tuning in? *Journal of Applied Developmental Psychology, 17*, 475–494.

U.S. Department of Health and Human Services. (1996). *Trends in the well-being of America's children and youth: 1996*. Washington, DC: U.S. Government Printing Office.

Vandell, D. L., & Corasaniti, M. A. (1990). Variations in early child care: Do they predict subsequent emotional, and cognitive differences? *Early Childhood Research Quarterly, 5*, 555–572.

Veevers, R. (1996, April). *The Canadian Self Sufficiency Project*. Paper presented at the Workshop on Welfare and Child Development, Board on Children, Youth, and Families, National Research Council and Institute of Medicine, Washington, DC.

Watson, J. E., Kirby, R. S., Kelleher, K. J., & Bradley, R. H. (1996). Effects of poverty on home environment: An analysis of three-year outcome data for low birth weight premature infants. *Journal of Pediatric Psychology, 21*, 419–431.

Wright, J. C., & Huston, A. C. (1995, June). *Effects of educational TV viewing of lower income preschoolers on academic skills, school readiness, and school adjustment one to three years later*. Report to Children's Television Workshop, Center for Research on the Influences of Television on Children, University of Kansas, Lawrence.

James Garbarino

The Effects of Community Violence on Children

☐ Introduction

This chapter deals with the impact of community violence on children. In addition to reviewing "conventional" empirical data, it relies heavily on qualitative data and a narrative-phenomenological approach, including my interviews with children in war zones around the world and with youth incarcerated for murder or other forms of severe violence. It introduces the concept of "the urban war zone" as a way of accessing data and concepts drawn from the international scene to provide a framework for understanding the developmental issues faced by children exposed to chronic community violence.

A recent edited volume on the mental health issues of children in war is entitled *Minefields in Their Hearts* (Apfel & Simon, 1996). This image captures the basic truth that war presents children and youth with serious developmental challenges, challenges that, if unmet, can lead to disaster. This much is clear. Children have been involved directly in the prosecution of war in extraordinary and increasing numbers throughout the twentieth century. The United Nations Children's Fund (UNICEF) estimated that, whereas in 1900, the ratio of civilian to military casualties was about 1:9, in recent decades, this pattern has reversed and now stands at approximately 8:1 (civilians to soldiers; Garbarino, Kostelny, & Dubrow, 1991). Children constitute a significant proportion of these civilian casualties.

This shift reflects the changing nature of war. The technology of warmaking more and more has emphasized antipersonnel weapons that do not target specific individuals, and indiscriminate bombing and shelling, while the strategy of war more and more has emphasized attacks on civilian infrastructure (whether it be in the saturation bombing of "conventional war" or the struggle for the "hearts and minds" of the population characteristic of insurgency-counterinsurgency operations).

An understanding of the impact of war on children and youth is practically important in a large number of societies around the world, including countries which do not have overt war within their borders but do accept numerous refugees coming directly from foreign war zones (c.f., Garbarino, Kostelny, & Dubrow, 1991). In addition, some countries, like the United States, have chronic community violence in the "urban war zones" that affects the development of children and youth (c.f., Garbarino, Dubrow, Kostelny, & Pardo, 1992). Thus, the parallel to "minefields in their hearts," is an analysis of children in the urban war zones conducted by Kotlowitz and entitled *There Are No Children Here* (1991).

In this chapter, my goal is to focus on the processes and conditions that transform the "developmental challenge" of community violence into developmental harm in some children (and enhanced development in some others). Several themes ground this discussion in an ecological framework for understanding child and youth development. These include: (a) an accumulation of risk model for understanding how and when children suffer the most adverse consequences of exposure to community violence and exceed the limits of resilience, (b) the concept of "social maps" as the product of childhood experience, and, (c) the concept of trauma as a philosophical wound. These foundation concepts provide an intellectual context in which to understand our primary concerns: psychological and philosophical manifestations of trauma. We start, however, with a brief overview of the socioeconomics and demographics of community violence affecting children in the urban war zone.

☐ The Socioeconomics and Demographics of Violence in the Urban War Zone

Homicide rates provide only an imprecise indicator of the overall problem of violence in the lives of American children and youth, for behind each murder stand many nonlethal assaults. This ratio between assault and death varies as a function of both medical trauma technology (which prevents assaults from becoming homicides) and weapons technology (which can affect the lethality of assaults). An example from Chicago illustrates this: the city's homicide rate in 1973 and 1993 was approximately the same and, yet, the rate of serious assault increased approximately 400% during that period. Thus, the ratio of assaults to homicides increased substantially, from 100:1 in 1973 to 400:1 in 1993 (Garbarino, Dubrow, Kostelny, & Pardo, 1992).

Data from Chicago's Cook County Hospital provide another perspective on the changing nature of violence facing children in America. In 1982, the hospital responded to approximately 500 gunshot cases. In 1992, the number was approximately 1,000. However, in 1982 these cases overwhelmingly involved single bullet injuries while, in 1992, 25% involved multiple bullet injuries. Rates of permanent disability thus have increased substantially, although the homicide rate has remained about the same because of compensating improvements in medical trauma services.

Class, race, and gender exert important influences on exposure to community violence. The odds of being a homicide victim range from 1:21 for young Black males, to 1:369 for young White females, with young White males at 1:131, and young Black females at 1:104 (Bell, 1991). Being an American is itself a risk factor. The United States far exceeds all other modern industrialized nations in its homicide rate, not just for African Americans dealing with racism and deprivation, but for Whites, where the rate of 11.2 per 100,000 is far greater than the second-place country, Scotland, with 5 per 100,000 (Richters & Martinez, 1993).

Whatever the exact constellation of causes, children growing up in the United States have particularly high levels of exposure to community violence, particularly if they live in neighborhoods that simulate urban war zones. A survey of 6th through 10th graders in New Haven, Connecticut, revealed that 40% had witnessed at least one incident of violent crime within the previous 12 months (Marans & Cohen, 1993). In three high-risk neighborhoods in Chicago, 17% of the elementary-school-age children had witnessed domestic violence, 31% had seen someone shot, and 84% had seen someone "beat up" (Bell, 1991).

Some 30% of the children living in high-crime neighborhoods of major metropolitan areas like Chicago have witnessed a homicide by the time they are 15 years old, and more than 70% have witnessed a serious assault (Bell, 1991). Richters and Martinez (1993) have amplified these results. In their study, 43% of the fifth and sixth graders had witnessed a mugging in a "*moderately* violent" neighborhood in Washington, DC. Other researchers have echoed these findings (e.g. Groves, Zuckerman, Marans, & Cohen, 1993). Guns are one of the recurrent themes in the American urban war zone, and account for much of the increasing medical seriousness of adolescent conflicts. These figures are much more like the experience of children in actual war zones in other countries (Garbarino et al., 1991) than they are of what we should expect for American children living in "peace." This supports the contention that it is intellectually useful to speak of the urban war zones as a basis for understanding the long-term effects of community violence on children and youth.

Being a child becomes more and more dangerous as chronic violence becomes a fact of life for more and more Americans. Drugs, guns, and gangs conspire to create dangerous environments for children and youth in urban neighborhoods and, increasingly, elsewhere in our society. These violent external threats often are added to the risk of violence inside the family and the broader range of risk factors that afflict children in America (i.e., poverty, parental substance abuse, absent fathers, and maternal incapacity), risk factors that produce a social environment for children that is "toxic" in the sense of being poisonous and putting the child at risk for impaired development (Garbarino, 1995).

Virtually all the children living in a Chicago public housing project studied had had firsthand experiences with shooting by the time they were 5 years old (Garbarino, Dubrow, Kostelny, & Pardo, 1992). Interviews with school-age children and youth have confirmed that the "gun culture" is a potent factor in the life of children in diverse settings in the United States (Garbarino, 1995). Teen use of guns in homicides increased from 64% in 1987 to 78% in 1991. During the same period, teen arrests for crimes involving weapons increased 62% (U. S. Department of Justice, 1992). Despite the recent decline in teen arrests for violent assault, the spread of the "gun culture" into the lives of school children and youth since 1980 has been associated with a clear and present danger to their mental health, social behavior, and educational success.

Perhaps a few narrative examples in which I have been directly involved as an interviewer will help illuminate the effects of this gun culture on the experience of childhood. In Detroit, a young boy whose idolized teenage brother was killed in a gang-related attack was asked, "If you could have anything in the whole world, what would it be?" "A gun so I could blow away the person that killed my brother," he answered (Marin, 1988). In California, when a 9-year-old boy living in a neighborhood characterized by declining security was asked, "What would it take to make you feel safer here?" he replied simply, "If I had a gun of my own" (Garbarino, 1995). In a middle-class suburb of Chicago, a classroom of 8-year-olds was asked, "If you needed a gun, could you get one?" A third of the children were able to describe in detail how they would get one. In a prison in North Carolina, when three incarcerated teenagers were asked about why they had done the shooting that had landed them in prison, all three replied, "What else was I supposed to do?" (Garbarino, 1995).

To understand the urban war zone, we must understand the gun culture infusing the minds and hearts of American children and youth as well as adults, for about one half of U.S. households contain at least one gun. Of course, most children and youth who are drawn to guns, who know how to get guns, and who say that having a gun would make them feel safer will not actually end up using a gun. That parallels adult gun ownership, and even most armed police are likely to go through an entire career without actually firing their weapon in the line of duty. Whether or not a child's integration into the gun culture results in actually shooting someone depends on the particular circumstances of that child, most particularly, whether they experience an accumulation of social and psychological risk factors in the absence of compensatory opportunity factors (Garbarino, 1999).

One further example illustrates this point. It comes from a study conducted by myself and colleagues (Garbarino & Bedard, 1997) in which youth incarcerated for homicide or other crimes of severe violence were interviewed intensively over a period of months. Allan's story reveals the interplay of traumatic experience and guns in experience of the urban war zone.

Allan is a basketball star and a student of philosophy. He reads voraciously about religion, a recent favorite is *Ambivalent Zen*. At 17, he recently has completed requirements for his general equivalency diploma (GED). At 5´11´´, he worries that he will not grow the additional inches needed to make him competitive in the world of big-time basketball. And, he is serving 5 years for manslaughter (plea bargained from murder, second degree). As he talks, the words flow in intriguing circles. He is eloquent, paying close attention to his choice of words because of his constant effort to "elevate" his language. Suddenly, his language returns to the street as he talks about the scariest thing that ever happened to him.

I was 12. That was a big thing. That was a big thing for me. One time a kid was gonna shoot me because four people had spent a night at his house. He has guns there, and he was selling drugs, but they had a party, so we was too drunk and too high to go home. And we left, and he said somebody stole one of his guns, you know. So, he dealt with accusation on me and the rest of us, but nobody stole his gun. So, they had a party the next week, and I came. So, when I came to the party, he was like, "Yo." He's in my face, and he goes, "Yo. Where my gun at? Where my gun at? Where my gun at? Yo, you was there that night. You spent the night. I asked everybody else where my gun at" and I was the youngest out of them four. I was 12 years old. What was I gonna do with a gun? Even, even though I had a potential skill in me, I never thought as such. He's like, "Yo" and he pulled out a .44 caliber, a .44 Bulldog. This big. It's like the same size as a Desert Eagle. And he was like, "Yo, what's up? I better have my gun. If I hear that you got my gun, I'm gonna shoot you." And, he just point the gun down at me with this anguish in his eyes that made me break down. And, I was crying. I was, like, I couldn't believe I got threatened like that, because I never had the intentions of stealing somebody's gun. And, that shocked me. And, I was like, I was like, Yasheem, my man, the one that got shot, that was his cousin. I was like, "Yasheem, why he do that? Why he threaten me like that? Why would I take his gun when I'm cool with him, you know what I mean. I see him as my peoples." And, then, that made me disconnect from him, because it was like, if he felt that I took his gun, he would think many other things of me. So and then any other little thing that he thought that I did would trigger him for killing me. So, I stayed away from him, because he was much older than me, much older than me. I took heat when he threatened me. Because of the fact that it put me on point. And, when I mean point, this means I was aware of things. He had the capability of killing me. That turned me around—to deal with the killer instinct. Because at first I never thought that I could wrong nobody. I never thought about it, and the potential of killing anybody. I never had that heart. But, when that man put the gun on me, when he pointed that gun at me and told me that he was gonna kill me and told me that I better protect myself and do the killing before somebody else kill me. From then, I was in the way of being cannibalistic. I became a shark eating the little fishes. I've been through a lot—in my 17 years of breathing. I'm been through a lot. (pp. 7–8)

Having told the story of how it felt to be a frightened child in the urban war zone—a little fish—Allan told of how he became an armed predator—a shark, a cannibal—never leaving home without a gun or two in his backpack in the year and a half that followed this incident. His story culminated in the tale of the shooting that placed him in the youth prison system at age 13. The day after an argument and an exchange of gunfire on the street, he and a friend walked out the front door of their apartment building only to find themselves confronting three armed kids bent on finishing the earlier conflict. As he recounted the event, his language changed from that of the scholar to that of the street shark. His body hardened to the task, his face tough and wrinkled with intensity, his hands chopping the air as he laid it out step by step. He seemed to be reliving every instant. Seeing the intruders, he and his friend both pulled out their own guns—two each, one in each hand—and started shooting. Nine shots; he slammed the table nine times. All three of the enemy died.

After the final word of his story, he put his thumb in his mouth and sucked, as though completely oblivious to the fact that he was not alone, that there was someone there looking at him and listening. For 2 minutes, he who had dazzled with his words sat in this most eloquent of silences. Then, with weariness in his voice, he admitted what he had told no one else, that he goes to bed every night thinking about when he is going to die. He is afraid of dying before he has a chance to live his life and he is afraid of what happens after death. And, he cries in bed every night thinking about that.

Boys like Allan reveal the powerful accumulation of traumatic experiences in the lives of children in the urban war zone. For him, traumatic exposure occurs in the larger context of poverty, racism, father absence, and a host of other socially toxic factors (Garbarino, 1995). This accumulation of risk model is crucial both for assessing exposure to violence and for understanding its effects.

☐ Accumulation of Risk Model

Risk accumulates; opportunity ameliorates—this is one of the conclusions we draw from our observations of children coping with chronic violence in urban war zones. As negative ("pathogenic") influences increase, the child may exceed his or her breaking point. Conversely, as positive ("salutogenic") influences increase, the probability of recovery and enhanced development increases. We can term these pathogenic and salutogenic influences as risk and opportunity (Garbarino and Associates, 1992).

Although most of the children of war in the latter part of the twentieth century are found outside the first world, much of the available research dealing with risk and opportunity comes from North America and Europe. Therefore, extrapolating to the urban war zones may be scientifically feasible. The human catastrophe of the recent wars in the former Yugoslavia has been a gold mine for research since it has allowed the testing of trauma and stress models developed in the context of American community violence in a European war context, without some of the uncertain assumptions that must be made when trying to make this application across radical cultural boundaries outside of a Western framework, for example, in Cambodia (Kinzie, Sack, Angell, Manson, & Rath, 1986) and Mozambique (Boothby, 1996). Similarly, the various war experiences of Israeli and Palestinian children and youth have been a focal point for research and clinical development as a result of being one of the few settings in the late twentieth century in which highly sophisticated populations both have been exposed to war and accessible to Western-style research (Garbarino & Kostelny, 1996).

One such application of developmental research concerns models developed in the United States for understanding the impact of stressful life events on the development of competence in childhood. This research offers the hypothesis that most children are capable of coping with low levels of risk, once the accumulation moves beyond this low level, there must be a major concentration of opportunity factors to prevent the precipitation of harm. A study by Sameroff and his colleagues (Sameroff, Seifer, Barocas, Zax, & Greenspan, 1987) illustrated this point.

Sameroff explored the impact of risk accumulation on intellectual development—itself a major salutogenic factor for children facing developmental challenges. This approach is made even more relevant by the work of Perry, Pollard, Blakley, Baker, and Vigilante (1995) documenting the impact of early trauma (particularly, neglect and abuse) on brain development. Put simply, this research documents the risk that such trauma can produce deficient development of the brain's cortex (the site of higher faculties such as abstract reasoning, moral development, and impulse control). The processes involved in the link between war and brain development appear to be both direct (by stimulating a stress-related hormone, corotisal, that impedes brain growth) and indirect (by disrupting normal caregiving, with the result being neglect and abuse). For children in urban war zones, the issues are similar.

Using a pool of eight risk factors that included indicators of maternal dysfunction (e.g., mental illness, substance abuse, low educational attainment), family structure (e.g., absent father, large number of siblings) and social status (e.g., low income), Sameroff and his colleagues found that one or two major risk factors in the lives of the children studied produced little damage (i.e., IQ scores remained within, even above, the normal range). But, when risk accumulated with the addition of a third and fourth risk factor, there was a precipitation of developmental damage, and IQ scores dropped significantly below average (Sameroff et. al, 1987).

Dunst and Trivete (1992) augmented Sameroff's approach by including in the developmental equations counterpart measures of opportunity (e.g., a present and highly involved father as the "opportunity" counterpart to the risk factor of "absent father" and a flexible and highly supportive parent as the counterpart to a "rigid and punitive" parent). Such a simultaneous assessment of both risk and opportunity is essential to understand the total picture in assessing the long term effects of early developmental experience, because this more accurately captures the realities of the child's experiences (i.e., the fact that in the real world of children, this risk factors usually do not exist without some compensatory impulse in the social environment of family, school, neighborhood, and society). Indeed, one of the worst features of living in an urban war zone may be the dismantling of the compensatory, salutogenic infrastructure of the community.

This developmental model is particularly relevant to understanding the impact of community violence on children. It predicts that the children and youth most at risk for negative consequences associated with community violence are those who already live in the context of accumulated risk (e.g., the socially marginal, those with fractured families, those with mentally impaired or substance addicted caregivers). In contrast, children who approach their community violence experiences from a position of strength (i.e., with the salutogenic resources of social support, intact and functional families, and parents who model social competence) can accept better the developmental challenges posed by community violence and deal with them more positively in the long run (even if they show short-term disturbance). This model applies to actual war zones as well as to urban war zones (Garbarino & Kostelny, 1996).

There is little systematic evidence about the demography and sociology of children in actual war zones (e.g., the social class correlates of exposure to war trauma). Nonetheless, most observers note that the prewar social class system continues to operate in most war zones, most of the time. In general, the families at the bottom of the social ladder are most likely to be directly affected (Garbarino et al., 1991). In the urban war zones of the United States, social class is a critical correlate of exposure.

The experience of community violence takes place within a larger context of risk for most children. They often are poor, live in father absent families, contend with parental incapacity due to depression or substance abuse, are raised by parents with little education or employment prospects, and are exposed to domestic violence (Garbarino et al., 1991). Approximately 20% of American children live with major accumulation of risk and in situations characterized by community violence. Thus, the problem of violence clearly is a major problem with far-reaching implications for child development (Osofsky, 1995).

Students of resilience (e.g., Garmezy & Masten, 1986; Losel & Bliesener, 1990) believe that, under adverse circumstances, about 80% of children will "bounce back" from developmental challenges (particularly if they have had adequate care during the first 2 years of life). However, under conditions of extreme risk accumulation, resilience may be diminished drastically. The magnitude of risk accumulation as a pathogenic influence and the corresponding limits of resilience have been illustrated by research conducted by Tolan (1996) in Chicago. Tolan pointed out that, in some environments, virtually all youth demonstrate negative effects of highly stressful and threatening environments. In his Chicago data, for example, none of the minority adolescent males facing the combination of highly dangerous and threatening low-income neighborhoods coupled with low resource-high stress families, evidenced, resilience at age 15 when measured by neither being more than one grade level behind in school nor scoring in the "clinical range" on the Achenbach Child Behavior Checklist for a 2-year period. The concept of resilience is useful, but should not be taken as an absolute.

This finding parallels work done on the impact of chronic combat experience on adults. Studies from World War II (Wank & Marchand, 1946) indicated that, if soldiers are exposed to chronic combat conditions for 60 days, 98% of them eventually end up as psychiatric casualties. Only those classified as aggressive psychopathic personality are able to function without becoming symptomatic. Why? Grossman and Siddle (in press) concluded chillingly, that the psychopaths are so stress resistant because they do not have the same issues of arousal in the face of threat and do not face the stress of violating moral prohibitions about killing human beings by virtue of being "cold-blooded killers."

The possible implications of this finding for child development in the urban war zone are equally chilling. We might expect that the youth best able to survive functionally would be those who have the least to lose morally and psychologically. My interviews with youth incarcerated for murder and other acts of severe violence have tended to confirm this. In Gilligan's terms (1996), they already are dead and, thus, experience no fear or inhibition. They view the world as having neither emotional barriers nor moral terrain.

☐ The Social Maps of Children in Urban War Zones

Certainly one of the most important features of child development is the child's emerging capacity to form and maintain "social maps" (Garbarino, 1995; Garbarino and Associates, 1992). These representations of the world reflect the simple cognitive competence of the child (knowing the world in the scientific sense of objective, empirical fact), to be sure. But, they also indicate the child's moral and affective inclination, not just where the child has been, but how the child views pathways to the future. These "pathways" are crucial in mediating the experience of risk in later developmental outcomes (Rutter, 1989).

In considering children facing community violence, we are concerned with the conclusions about the world contained in the child's social maps. Which will it be? "Adults are powerless and unreliable" versus "Adults are to be trusted because they know what they are doing." "You can never be too careful in dealing with people" versus "People will generally treat you well and meet your needs." "The only safe place is at home" versus "school is a safe place." Interviews with children and youth conducted by the author and his colleagues confirmed the reality of these as alternative maps among children and youth exposed to community violence and war (Garbarino, 1995; Garbarino & Bedard, 1999; Garbarino et al., 1991, 1992). The forces shaping these maps are the child's social experiences in counterpoint with the child's inner life, both cognitive competence and the working of unconscious forces.

Young children must contend with dangers that derive from two sources not so relevant to adults. First, their physical immaturity increases vulnerability by placing them at risk for injury from trauma that would not hurt adults because they are larger and more powerful. But, there is a potentially compensating force at work here. This is evident in research highlighting the power of parents and teachers to buffer very young children from traumatic encounters. Consider, for example, the observation from World War II London during the height of the German bombing: "Children measure the danger that threatens them chiefly by the reactions of those around them, especially trusted parents and teachers" (Papenek, 1992).

Second, young children tend to believe in the reality of threats from what most adults would define as the "fantasy" world. This increases their vulnerability to perceiving themselves as being "in danger." These dangers include monsters under the bed, wolves in the basement, and invisible creatures that lurk in the dark corners of bedrooms. But, here too, there is a salutogenic opportunity present in this characteristic. Children are more likely than adults to believe in ghosts, angels, and other supernatural beings who can serve in supportive roles during times of crisis (Barreto & Bermann, 1992). Their social maps may contain psychologically relevant features that are not present in the maps of most adults.

Security is vitally important for a child's well-being and, thus, his or her social map. When children feel safe, they relax. When they relax, they start to explore the environment. This is clear with infants and other very young children. When a parent or other familiar person is around, a child treats the adult as a secure base from which to explore the nearby space. If frightened, perhaps by a loud sound or by the approach of a stranger the child will quickly retreat to the familiar person.

This pattern is part of the normal development of children. It is so common that it is used to assess the quality of children's attachment relations. Children who do not use their parents this way—showing anxiety when separated and relief when reunited—are thought to have a less than adequate attachment relationship (they are "insecure" or "ambivalent" or "avoidant"). Thus, for very young children, the question of security is relatively simple. As children get older, their security needs are transformed, and their social maps change accordingly. Soon they are getting on school buses and visiting friends' houses by themselves. Eventually they are on the streets at night on their own. But, security remains a constant theme for them. "Am I safe here?" "Will I be safe if I go there?" "Would I be safe then?"

Many children do not feel safe. In my interviews conducted in an urban war zone, a 6-year-old girl reported that her job was to find her 2-year-old sister whenever the shooting started and get her to safety in the bathtub of their apartment. "The bathroom is the safest place," she told me. Being responsible for the safety of another, younger, child is a rather large responsibility for a 6-year-old girl (Garbarino, 1995).

For other children, the basis for their sense of insecurity is not life in the urban war zone, but just life. A national survey conducted by *Newsweek* and the Children's Defense Fund in 1993 found that only a minority of children nationwide said they felt "very safe" once they walked out the door; most said they only felt "somewhat safe," and about 12% said they felt "unsafe." Other surveys have reported similar results. For example, a Harris (1992) poll of 6th to 12th graders revealed that 35% worried they would not live to old age because they would be shot.

Many children in the United States are experiencing a growing sense of insecurity about the world inside and outside the boundaries of their families. For one thing, they are preoccupied with kidnapping. Teachers have reported that, if they ask students what they worry about, kidnapping looms large for most. One study (Price & Desmond, 1987) reported that 43% of the elementary school children studied thought it was likely that they would be kidnapped. Having been bombarded with messages of threat via the news and more informal sources (such as worried parents and other well-meaning adults) children have drawn the logical conclusion: "If the adults are so scared, I should be too."

Television and movies present a world full of threat. In general, the more television an individual watches, the more paranoid is that individual's view of the community. Children in the United States watch a lot of television; most of it is adult television. It is not surprising that they come away from that experience with a sense that the world is a hostile and threatening place. The level of predatory behavior on television and in the movies is very high: Maniacs, killers, and thieves abound.

Whether it is real life or television imagery, it does not take much violence and terror to set a tone of threat in a child's social map. Even in the worst war zones (e.g., Sarajevo), shooting and killing is intermittent. In the worst high-crime neighborhood, it only takes shots fired a few times per month and homicides a few times a year to create a year-round climate of danger, to establish insecurity as people's dominant psychological reality. Memory of the emotions of trauma does not decay; it remains fresh (Apfel & Simon, 1996). Once the feeling of danger takes hold, it takes very little new threat to sustain it.

American children are little anthropologists as they watch and listen to what goes on around them. What are they learning from the news, their favorite television programs, the latest action movie, cartoons, current events lessons at school, and from watching and listening to their parents, aunts, uncles, and grandparents? What are they learning about the world? More and more, they are learning that the world is a very dangerous place. But, for some children, the level of their fright exceeds the actual dangers they face. For others, the fact of the matter is that they are surrounded by violence. The world *is* a dangerous place. They experience trauma.

☐ The Concept of Trauma as a Psychological Wound

Community violence and its consequences can make children prime candidates for involvement in social groups that augment or replace families, and offer a sense of affiliation and security (and, perhaps, revenge). In many urban war zones this means gangs. Based on my interviews with incarcerated youth, it is clear that the violent and illicit economy that often exists in an urban war zone offers a sense of belonging and solidarity as well as cash income for kids who have few prosocial alternatives for either. These peer alliances offer some sense of security in a hostile world. If these children do not develop a sense of confidence that adults are committed to providing a safe zone, their willingness and ability to take advantage of developmental opportunities will decrease and this will adversely affect their future.

One important process that translates war into directly pathogenic experiences for children is the social disruption of families that often accompanies it (e.g., Garbarino et al., 1991). In actual war zones, this disruption may be the explicit tactical and strategic goal of combatants. One evidence of the fact that war disrupts families is to be found in the fact that globally one of the major consequences of modern war is the creation of refugees and other displaced persons, the majority of whom are mothers and children.

How does this process affect children? Consider refugee camps as contexts for parenting and child development, and then consider their parallels in the urban war zone, particularly low-income public housing projects around the United States which often are focal points for the urban war zone. This analysis derives from my site visits to such camps in Thailand, Hong Kong, Sudan, the former Yugoslavia, and the Middle East conducted during the period 1985 to 1994.

- The "Arms race."

    Refugee camps: There is a proliferation of violence, sometimes a kind of "arms race," which exacerbates the effects of conflict. It is common for young people, particularly, males, to be heavily involved in this violence, and even to be engaged in armed attacks and reprisals. Substantial numbers of "bystander" injuries are observed.

    Public housing projects: Violence is endemic, and gun possession (particularly, by youths) also is extraordinarily high, and violent crime rates typically are many times the average for the rest of the city.
- Gangs.

    Refugee camps: Representatives of "mainstream" society have only partial control over what happens. International relief workers leave the camps at the end of the working day.

    Public housing projects: The projects are under the control of the local gangs at night. Therefore, no action during the day can succeed unless it is acceptable to the gangs that rule the community at night. Gangs may establish curfews on their own initiative and make the decision about whether or not someone who commits a crime against residents will be identified and punished.
- The Role of Mothers.

    Refugee camps: Women (particularly, mothers) are in a desperate situation. They are under enormous stress, often are the target of domestic violence, and have few economic or educational resources and prospects. Men often play a marginal role in the enduring life of families, having lost access to economically productive roles, and being absent for reasons that include participating in the fighting, fleeing to escape enemies, being injured or killed. Largely as a result, there is a major problem of maternal depression. Studies in these settings have reported 50% of the women being seriously depressed.

    Public housing projects: Survey research in public housing projects has confirmed similarly difficult conditions for mothers, including depression at rates comparable to the refugee camps (Osofsky, 1995). This, in turn, is related to problems with early attachment relationships between mothers and children. One consequence of maternal depression is neglect of children. This connection is well established in research (Osofsky, 1995). This neglect leads to elevated levels of "accidental injuries" to children as well as a more generalized lack of psychological availability.

Trauma arises when the child cannot give meaning to dangerous experiences. This orientation is contained in the American Psychiatric Association's definition of post-traumatic stress disorder (PTSD), which refers to threatening experiences outside the realm of normal experience. Trauma has two principal components: overwhelming arousal and overwhelming negative cognition. The former component is especially relevant to young children who have not developed fully functioning systems to modulate arousal (e.g., brain stem maturation that is not complete until age 8). Trauma involves an inability to effectively handle the physiological responses of stress in situations of threat.

The second component of trauma—overwhelming cognition—was captured in Herman's (1992) formulation that to experience trauma is "to come face to face with human vulnerability in the natural world and with the capacity for evil in human nature." This is the human core of the term "overwhelming negative cognition" and it illuminates the traumatic nature of living in an urban war zone for children and youth.

Experiences that are cognitively overwhelming may stimulate conditions in which the process required to "understand" these experiences itself has pathogenic side effects. That is, in coping with traumatic events, the child may be forced into patterns of behavior, thought, and feelings that are themselves "abnormal" when contrasted with those of the untraumatized healthy child. Children, particularly elementary-school-age children who are too old to profit from the parental buffering that can insulate young children, may be particularly vulnerable to the trauma caused by threat and fear. So it is that one study of nonwar trauma reported that those exposed to trauma before age 10 were three times more likely to exhibit PTSD than those exposed after age 12 (Davidson & Smith, 1990).

Children and youth exposed to acute danger may require processing over a period of months (Pynoos & Nadar, 1988). Some children in urban war zones experience the psychological symptoms of PTSD, symptoms which include sleep disturbances, daydreaming, recreating trauma in play, extreme startle responses, emotional numbing, diminished expectations for the future, and even biochemical changes in their brains that impair social and academic behavior (Osofsky, 1995). This trauma can produce significant psychological problems that interfere with learning and appropriate social behavior in school and that interfere with normal parent-child relationships. And, if the traumatic stress is intense enough, it may leave some permanent "psychic scars" (Terr, 1990). This particularly is the case for children made vulnerable because of disruptions in their primary relationships (most notably, with parents). These effects include excessive sensitivity to stimuli associated with the trauma and diminished expectations for the future (Terr, 1990). But, by and large, most children will respond positively to the return of the pretraumatic state of reality by themselves returning to normal functioning.

This is acute traumatic danger, but the more common variety in urban war zones and the specific focus of this chapter is chronic danger. Chronic traumatic danger imposes a requirement for developmental adjustment. In the terminology of developmental psychology coined by Piaget (1952), these developmental adjustments result from the inability of the child to assimilate these experiences into existing conceptual frameworks ("schemas," to use the Piagetian term). Rather, these experiences require the child to alter existing concepts to permit the new experiential information to be known, and this involves what Piaget termed *accommodation*.

What are these accommodations? They are likely to include persistent PTSD, alterations of personality, and major changes in patterns of behavior or articulation of ideological interpretations of the world that provide a framework for making sense of ongoing danger (Garbarino et al., 1992). Chronic traumatic danger rewrites the child's story, redraws the child's social map, and redirects behavior. This is particularly true when that danger comes from violent overthrow of day-to-day social reality, as is the case where communities are altered substantially, where displacement occurs, or where the child experiences the death of important member of the child's family or social network. In the case of children exposed to the chronic horrors of Pol Pot's Khmer Rouge regime in Cambodia in the 1970s, 50% of the children exhibited persistent symptoms of PTSD 8 years after exposure (Kinzie et al., 1986).

Trauma inflicts philosophical wounds by challenging the very meaningfulness of life. Van der Kolk (in press) asked incoming psychiatric patients, "Have you given up all hope of finding meaning in your life?" Among those who experienced major trauma prior to age 5, 74% answered "yes." Among those who experienced major trauma after age 20, the figure was "only" 10%. Posing this question informally to thousands of professionals, students, and other adults revealed an overall incidence of about 1% (asking people to respond anonymously, but in a public setting).

What do we make of this? It reflects the fact that trauma represents an enormous challenge to any individual's understanding of the meaning and purpose of life, the metaphysical and spiritual dimensions, and that this crisis is particularly difficult for children. Further, if the crisis of meaning and purpose cannot be acknowledged and mastered, it can result in psychological and physiological symptoms which can become debilitating to the point of requiring psychiatric care.

These data suggest that there may be a developmental context for this experience. Just as there are "critical periods" in the development of many other human attributes (e.g., vision), the initial structures of meaning are most efficiently and effectively established in early childhood. Trauma is a challenge to meaningfulness, and the enormity of this challenge is greatest for the youngest victims. They have less well-developed cognitive skills to be employed in making sense of the world, and they have not had the time to build a solid framework of meaning. Their social maps are as vulnerable to trauma at age 8 as their central nervous systems were at age 1.

What is more, we can readily acknowledge that a child's worldview is more fluid than an adult's, in the sense that their experience of reality is less constricted by social conventions regarding what is real and what is not. Thus, for example, children are generally more ready to believe that there are spirits everywhere around them (as opposed to most adults who have been trained to make clear distinctions between the culturally "acceptable" spirit world of religion and the "unacceptable" world of "fantasy"). Silverman and Worden (1992) offered documentation of this in a study of children whose parents had died. Some 57% reported speaking to the dead parent, 43% of those children felt they received an answer, and 81% believed their dead parents were watching them. In contrast, Kalish and Reynolds (1973) reported that 12% of adults reported such direct contact with the dead.

Where spirituality and religion rely on an intrinsic belief in a higher, all benevolent power, trauma can temporarily or permanently shatter this belief. It can challenge children's understanding of themselves as spiritual beings having a physical experience because it brings about a perceived threat to, or even a severance from, their spiritual connection between them and the higher power which they believe exists to protect them. Trauma creates a profound cut which separates the child from a place within where he or she believed in a higher spiritual power, whether referred to as Allah, God, Buddha, Jehovah, the Creator, or whatever language used to reflect their relationship with the larger spiritual dimension of existence. This is a profound form of "cognitive dissonance," perhaps better termed "spiritual dissonance."

That is why we often hear trauma victims—children, youth, and adults—say "If there is a God, how could He/She allow such atrocities?" (Kozaric-Kovacic, Folnegovic-Smalc, Skrinjharic, Szajnberg, & Marusic, 1995, p. 43). Of course, the spiritual dissonance engendered by confronting "the problem of evil" is itself a fundamental religious issue. Even trauma inflicted on others may trigger this kind of questioning. For example, my interviews with teenagers involved in acts of severe violence (e.g., shooting) have suggested the possible traumatic dimensions of committing assault (Garbarino, 1995). Research on combat has indicated that one of the principal sources of trauma for soldiers is the violation of the basic moral precept "Thou shalt not kill" (Grossman & Siddle, in press).

Those who have dealt with the most heinous of killers (e.g., sadistic serial killers) have outlined the nihilism that pervades their metaphysical universe (e.g., Douglas & Olshaker, 1995). Their thinking seems to be thus: How could God permit a monster like me to exist? Gilligan (1996) confirmed this insight in his exploration of profound shame as the unifying factor among men incarcerated or hospitalized for the most severe violence, these individuals who face daily the prospect of psychic annihilation. Coles (1990) put it this way: "Children try to understand not only what is happening to them but why; and in doing that, they call upon the religious life they have experienced, the spiritual values they have received, as well as other sources of potential explanation" (p. 159).

Speaking about children traumatized from having become suddenly crippled due to illness, a psychoanalyst, Lindemann (cited in Coles, 1990), made the following observation: "These are young people who suddenly have become quite a bit older; they are facing possible death, or serious limitation of their lives; It would be a mistake . . . to emphasize unduly a psychiatric point of view . . . if those children want to cry with you, and be disappointed with you, and wonder with you where their God is, then you can be there for them" (p. 173).

If adults imagine the higher power as a caring, protective, all benevolent figure—in short as the ideal parental figure—then it makes sense that children's imagery of a higher power also would include a sense of the protective, ideal parent figure. What children may add to this concept of spirituality is that, in their cases, God's persona would be magnified by the child's need for care, protection, and love.

When this need is absolutely violated, some children will seek out a negative universe on the grounds that anything is better than nothing. This is one of the origins of extreme negative behavior later in life such as exhibited by serial killers—brutal child abuse that leads to a descent into evil to provide some structure of meaning for the child (Douglas & Olshaker, 1995). It also has implications for identity in the sense that, when faced with the prospect of psychic annihilation, human beings will opt for even negative identities (Gilligan, 1996). A convicted killer once put it this way to a colleague of mine: "I'd rather be wanted for murder than not be wanted at all."

Magical thinking is an important feature of early childhood. It forms the basis for fantasy play, which itself is an important resource for children in developing and working through alternative scenarios as solutions for day-to-day issues and problems in their lives. When trauma overwhelms the child's play and constricts it in repetitive unproductive patterns, that play may be said to be "captured" (Garbarino & Manley, 1996). Captured play is often linked to traumatic experiences. In captured play, children seek unsuccessfully to find a meaningful solution to the crisis of meaning imposed by the shattered assumptions they experience in the wake of trauma. They often are literally looking for God in a world in which God has disappeared.

The origins of these shattered assumptions in the urban war zone experience of the child may be domestic (e.g., child abuse in the family) or community (e.g., living in a war zone or being a street child subject to sexual exploitation and punitive violence). Whatever the specific origins, there are common issues to be found in the challenge to meaningfulness. This rendering of trauma as a spiritual challenge has found expression in the work of many thinkers and helpers in the helping tradition who began their work in the "psychological" domain, but found their impulse to understand and to help led them inevitably to the spiritual. We see this evident in the path taken by Jung (1933), Moore (1992), and Coles (1990), among others. Frankl (1963) followed this path through the Nazi concentration camps to conclude: "It is this spiritual freedom—which cannot be taken away—that makes life meaningful and purposeful" (p. 106).

Janoff-Bulman put it this way based on her work with trauma survivors: "It may seem remarkable, yet it is not unusual for survivors, over time, to wholly reevaluate their traumatic experience by altering the positive value and meaningfulness of the event itself. The victimization certainly would not have been chosen, but it is ultimately seen by many as a powerful, even to some extent worthwhile, teacher of life's most important lessons" (Janoff-Bulman, 1992, p. 142). This is essential to the process of understanding the long-term salutogenic impact of violent trauma. When trauma engenders the search for meaning in the context of a social environment that nurtures and supports that search it can move children and youth from short-term pathogenic effects to long-term salutogenic influences.

The task of dealing with the effects of community violence as a developmental conspiracy falls to the people who teach the children of that society: their parents and other relatives, teachers, and counselors. Adults are crucial resources for children attempting to cope with the chronic danger and stress of living in a war zone. Generations of studies focusing on the experience of children living in war zones have testified to the importance of adult responses to danger as mediators of psychological responses in children exposed to war (Garbarino et al., 1991). So long as adults take charge of themselves and present children with a role model of calm, positive determination, most children can cope with a great deal of acute war-related violence. They may indeed be traumatized by their experiences, but the adults around them will be able to serve as a resource and support the child in rehabilitative efforts to cope with long-term consequences and, perhaps, even stimulate salutogenic experiences (Apfel & Simon, 1996).

However, once adults begin to deteriorate, to decompensate, to panic, children suffer in the short term (and perhaps also in the long run). This is not surprising, given the importance of the images of adults contained in the child's social maps. Traumatized children need help to recover from their experiences (Apfel & Simon, 1996). Emotionally disabled or immobilized adults are unlikely to offer the children what they need. Such adults are inclined to engage in denial, to be emotionally inaccessible, and are prone to misinterpret the child's signals. Messages of safety are particularly important in establishing adults as sources of protection and authority for children living in conditions of threat and violence. But, these adults take on this task facing enormous challenges of their own. Human service professionals and educators working in war zones are themselves traumatized by their exposure to violence (Danieli, 1996).

In the long run (i.e., in the process of accommodating to the war experience), children depend on adults as teachers. Thus, we must understand the teaching process as it relates to trauma. This leads us to the interactional model of development proposed by Vygotsky. In Vygotsky's approach (1986), child development is fundamentally social; cognitive development proceeds at its best through the process of interactive teaching. He focused on the zone of proximal development: the difference between what the child can accomplish alone versus what the child can accomplish with the guidance of the teacher. How is this relevant to the child's ability to cope with war trauma?

In the case of isolated acute trauma in a setting of peace (a single horrible incident that violates the normal reality of the child's world), the child needs help believing that "things are back to normal." This is a relatively easy teaching task—this therapy of reassurance. But, the child who lives with chronic trauma (e.g., the urban war zone) needs something more. This child needs to be taught how to redefine the world in moral and structural terms.

One major risk is an extreme loss of future orientation. This "terminal thinking" grows out of chronically traumatic situations in which youngsters come to believe that violent death is an inevitable fact of their lives, and respond accordingly; that is, with fatalistic violence, depression, and antisocial behavior

(Garbarino, 1995). Children in urban war zones need teaching that matches their developmental and experiential needs to move beyond the "default option" of terminal thinking and revenge-oriented morality. Vygotsky referred to this kind of teaching to the child's specific needs as teaching in the zone of proximal development.

Families can do much to provide the emotional context for the necessary "processing" to make positive moral sense of danger (Garbarino & Kostelny, 1996), but it takes help from outside the home. If teachers and other adult representatives of the community are unwilling or unable to demonstrate and teach higher-order moral reasoning, or are intimidated if they try to do so, then the process of moral truncation that is "natural" to situations of violent conflict will proceed unimpeded.

In Northern Ireland, for example, both Protestant and Catholic teachers in some communities learned that, if they tried to engage their students in dialogue that could promote higher-order moral reasoning, they would be silenced by extremist elements (Conroy, 1987). This is a common situation under conditions of war in which narrow concepts of loyalty and the exigencies of the immediate tactical situation may lead to the suppression of teaching dialogue. While this danger is greatest in societies that were totalitarian prior to the war situation, it may be an issue even in otherwise democratic societies. The prosocial forces in a community that are committed to moral development must remain in control of the schools, churches, and neighborhood clubs for this healing process to operate for children.

The problem of chronic gang and militia violence under conditions of war (and the related displacements of communities that it engenders) poses a threat to youngsters that parallels other situations in which there is a dramatic and overwhelming destruction of the foundations of daily life. Erikson's (1976) study of an Appalachian community devastated by flood spoke to what happens when a community loses faith with itself, when parents, teachers, and other adults are demoralized and powerless: "The major problem, for adults and children alike, is that the fears haunting them are prompted not only by the memory of past terrors but by a wholly realistic assessment of present dangers" (Erikson, 1976, p. 215)

☐ Conclusion

One focus of international initiatives (such as the United Nations Convention on the Rights of the Child) is to create "zones of peace" for children and, generally, to encourage combatants to institute and respect protected areas for children. Underlying all such efforts is an attempt to communicate a message of safety to children, to stimulate a redrawing of their social maps (Osofsky, 1995). We might go further to suggest that these zones of peace also include the freedom to engage in free play and in moral teaching in Vygotsky's zone of proximal development so that the long-term process of accommodation fosters salutogenic influences for children and youth.

International action does bring change for living in actual war zones. For example, the signing of a peace accord has meant that repatriation has come to the Khmer, and they are returning to Cambodia to take up a more genuine community life. However, without efforts to achieve reconciliation, social justice, and a major peacekeeping force in highly conflicted areas, many of the children in urban war zones will get stuck there psychologically. We might consider the following programmatic actions to translate the concept of teaching in the zone of proximal development into strategies to increase the likelihood of salutogenic influences of the children of the urban war zones.

- Programmatic efforts to alter the "legitimization of aggression" among children and youth. These efforts should include programs that start early—in the early childhood classroom and in the elementary school—to simultaneously stimulate cognitive restructuring and behavioral rehearsal of nonviolence responses to conflict, anger, frustration, injustice, and threat (e.g., Garbarino, 1993).
- Respond to trauma in early childhood. These efforts should help train and support early childhood educators to recognize and respond to traumatic experiences in the lives of young children in their care and, perhaps serve as a focal point for mental health services aimed at the parents of these children (Garbarino et al., 1992).
- Mobilize prosocial adult and youth members of the community to "take charge." The greatest threat to young children comes when positive adults are defeated by the antisocial forces of community violence. Thus, efforts to mobilize adults and prosocial youth to have a visible presence and to convey a clear message of strength and responsibility is crucial for redrawing the social maps of children living in violent communities (Garbarino, 1995).

- Recognize the critical importance of "moral" rehabilitation. Our efforts to understand the impact of war-related violence on children and youth around the world highlights several concerns: unmet medical needs, the corrosive effects of the coexperiencing of poverty and violence on personality and on academic achievement, and so forth. But, from our perspective, the most important of these is that the experience of trauma distorts the values of children. Unless we reach them with healing experiences and offer them a moral and political framework within which to process their experiences, traumatized children are likely to be drawn to groups and ideologies that legitimize and reward their rage, fear, and hateful cynicism. This is an environment in which gangs flourish and community institutions deteriorate, a socially toxic environment (Garbarino & Bedard, 1997).
- Focus on issues of trust. At the heart of this downward spiral is declining trust in adults on the part of children and youth in war zone communities. As one youth living in a small city experiencing a proliferation of gangs put it: "If I join a gang I will be 50% safe, but if I don't I will be 0% safe." He does not put his trust and faith in adults. That is what he is telling us if we are prepared to listen. There are self-serving, antisocial individuals and groups in any society prepared to mobilize and exploit the anger, fear, alienation, and hostility that many children feel growing up in a war zone. They are the competition for programs designed to build peace in place of the cycle of violence.

☐ References

Apfel, R., & Simon, B. (Eds.). (1996). *Minefields in their hearts: The mental health of children in war and communal violence*. New Haven, CT: Yale University Press.

Barreto, S., & Bermann, E. (1992, May). *Ghosts as transitional objects: The impact of cultural belief systems upon childhood mourning*. Paper presented at the meeting of the American Orthopsychiatric Association, New York.

Bell, C. (1991). Traumatic stress and children in danger. *Journal of Health Care for the Poor and Underserved, 2*, 175–188.

Boothby, N. (1996). Mobilizing communities to meet the psychosocial needs of children in war and refugee crisis. In R. Apfel & B. Simon (Eds.), *Minefields in their hearts: The mental health of children in war and communal violence* (pp. 149–164). New Haven, CT: Yale University Press.

Coles, R. (1990). *The spiritual life of children*. Boston: Houghton Mifflin.

Conroy, J. (1987). *Belfast diary*. Boston: Beacon Press.

Danieli, Y. (1996). Who takes care of the caretakers? The emotional consequences of working with children traumatized by war and communal violence. In R. Apfel & B. Simon (Eds.), *Minefields in their hearts: The mental health of children in war and communal violence* (pp. 189–205). New Haven, CT: Yale University Press.

Davidson, J., & Smith, R. (1990). Traumatic experiences in psychiatric outpatients. *Journal of Traumatic Stress Studies, 3*, 459–475.

Douglas, J., & Olshaker, M. (1995). *Mindhunter*. New York: Scribner.

Dunst, C., & Trivette, C. (1992). *Risk and opportunity factors influence parent and child functioning*. Paper presented at the Ninth Annual Smoky Mountain Winter Institute, Ashville, NC.

Frankl, V. (1963). *Man's search for meaning: An introduction to Logotherapy*. New York: Washington Square Press.

Garbarino, J. (1995). *Raising children in a socially toxic environment*. San Francisco: Jossey-Bass.

Garbarino, J. (1999). *Lost boys: Why our sons turn violent and how we can save them*. New York: Free Press.

Garbarino, J., & Associates. (1992). *Children and families in the social environment*. New York: Aldine de Gruyter.

Garbarino, J., & Bedard, C. (1997). *Making sense of "senseless youth violence: Preliminary report*. Ithaca, NY: Cornell University.

Garbarino, J., & Bedard, C. (1999). Is it self-defense? A model for forensic evaluation of juvenile violence. *Loyola Human Rights Review, 5*, 1–12.

Garbarino, J., Dubrow, N., Kostelny, K., & Pardo, C. (1992). *Children in danger: Coping with the consequences*. San Francisco: Jossey-Bass.

Garbarino, J., & Kostelny, K. (1996). The impact of political violence on the behavioral problems of Palestinian children. *Child Development, 67*, 33–45.

Garbarino, J., Kostelny, K., & Dubrow, N. (1991). *No place to be a child: Growing up in a war zone*. Lexington, MA: Lexington Books.

Garbarino, J., & Manley, J. (1996). Free and captured play: Releasing the healing power. *International Play Journal, 4*, 123–132.

Garmezy, N., & Masten. A. (1986). Stress, competence, and resilience: Common frontiers for therapist and psychotherapist. *Behavior therapy, 17*, 500–607.

Gilligan, J. (1996). *Violence*. NY: Putnam.

Grossman, D., & Siddle, R. (in press). Psychological effects of combat. In *Encyclopedia of violence, peace, and conflict*. New York.

Groves, B., Zuckerman, B., Marans, S., & Cohen. D. (1993). Silent victims: Children who witness violence. *Journal of the American Medical Association, 269,* 262–264.

Growing up fast and frightened. (1992, March 9). *Newsweek,* p. 29.

Harris, L., & Associates. (1994). *Metropolitan Life survey of the American teacher: Violence in America's schools.* (Part II). New York: Metropolitan Life Insurance.

Herman, J. (1992). *Trauma and recovery.* New York: Basic Books.

Janoff-Bulman, R. (1992). *Shattered assumptions: Towards a new psychology of trauma.* New York: Free Press.

Jung, C. (1933). *Modern man in search of a soul.* New York: Harcourt, Brace.

Kalish, & Reynolds, D. (1973). Phenomenological reality and post-death contact. *Journal for the Scientific Study of Religion, 12,* 209–221.

Kinzie, J., Sack, W., Angell, R., Manson, S., & Rath, B. (1986). The psychiatric effects of massive trauma on Cambodian children. *Journal of the American Academy of Child Psychiatry, 25,* 370–376.

Kotlowitz, A. (1991). *There are no children here.* New York: Doubleday.

Kozaric-Kovacic, D., Folnegovic-Smalc, V., Skrinjharic, J., Szajnberg, N., & Marusic, A. (1995). Rape, torture, and traumatization of Bosnian and Croatian women: Psychological sequelae. *American Journal of Orthopsychiatry, 65,* 428–433.

Losel, F., & Bliesener, T. (1990). Resilience in adolescence: A study on the generalizability of protective factors. In K. Hurrelmann & F. Losel (Eds.), *Health hazards in adolescence* (pp. 15–31). New York: de Gruyter.

Marans, S., & Cohen, D. (1993). Children and inner-city violence: Strategies for intervention. In L. Leavitt & N. Fox (Eds.), *Psychological effects of war and violence on children* (pp. 281–302). Hillsdale, NJ: Erlbaum.

Marin, C. (1988, June 21). *Grief's children.* Chicago: WMAQ.

Moore, T. (1992). *Care of the soul.* New York: Harper-Collins.

Osofsky, J. (1995). The effects of exposure to violence on young children. *American Psychologist, 50,* 782–788.

Papanek, V. (1972). *Design for the real world: Human ecology and social change.* New York: Pantheon Books.

Perry, B., Pollard, R., Blakley, T., Baker, W., & Vigilante, D. (1995). Childhood trauma, the neurobiology of adaptation, and "use-dependent" development of the brain: How "states" become traits. *Infant Mental Health Journal, 16,* 271–291.

Piaget, J. (1952). *The origins of intelligence in children.* New York: Norton.

Price, J., & Desmond, S. (1987). The missing children issue: A preliminary examination of fifth-graders' perceptions. *American Journal of Diseases of Children, 141,* 811–815.

Pynoos, R., & Nader, K. (1988). Psychological first aid and treatment approach to children exposed to community violence: Research implications. *Journal of Traumatic Stress, 1,* 445–473.

Richters, J., & Martinez, P. (1993). The NIMH community violence project: 1. Children as victims of and as witnesses to violence. *Psychiatry, 56,* 7–21.

Rutter, M. (1989). Pathways from childhood to adult life. *Journal of Child Psychology and Psychiatry, 30,* 23–51.

Sameroff, A., Seifer, R., Barocas, R., Zax, M., & Greenspan, S. (1987). Intelligence quotient scores of 4-year-old children: Socio-environmental risk factors. *Pediatrics, 79,* 343–350.

Silverman, P., & Worden, J. W. (1992). Children's reactions in the early months after the death of a parent. *American Journal of Orthopsychiatry, 62,* 93–104.

Wank, R., & Marchand, W. (1946). Combat neurosis: Development of combat exhaustion. *Archives of Neurology and Psychology, 55,* 236–247.

Terr, L. (1990). *Too scared to cry.* New York: Harper and Row.

Tolan, P. (1996, October). How resilience is the concept of resilience? *The Community Psychologist, 4,* 12–15.

U.S. Department of Justice. (1992). *Crime in the United States. 1992.* Washington, DC: Author.

van der Kolk, B. (in press). Trauma and meaningfulness. In D. Chicchetti & S. Toth (Eds.), *Rochester Symposium on Developmental Psychopathology.*

Vygotsky, L. (1986). *Thought and language.* Cambridge, MA: MIT Press.

NEW FRONTIERS

CHAPTER

Susan Golombok

New Family Forms:
Children Raised in Solo Mother Families,
Lesbian Mother Families, and in Families
Created by Assisted Reproduction

☐ Introduction

Since the birth of the first "test-tube" baby in 1978, advances in assisted reproduction have led to the creation of family types that would not otherwise have existed. With in vitro fertilization (IVF) using the father's sperm and the mother's egg, the child is genetically related to both parents. When a donated egg is used, the child is genetically related to the father but not the mother and, when donated sperm are used, the child is genetically related to the mother but not the father (donor insemination [DI] is a relatively simple procedure when used without IVF and has been widely practiced for many years). When both egg and sperm are donated, the child is genetically unrelated to both parents, a situation that is like adoption except that the parents experience the pregnancy and the child's birth. In the case of surrogacy, the child may be genetically related to neither, one, or both parents, depending on the use of donated egg or sperm or both. Thus, as Einwohner (1989) pointed out, it is now possible for a child to have five parents: an egg donor, a sperm donor, a birth mother who hosts the pregnancy, and the two social parents whom the child knows as mom and dad. In addition, an increasing number of lesbian and single heterosexual women are opting for assisted reproduction, particularly, donor insemination, to allow them to conceive a child without the involvement of a male partner. Children in these families grow up in the absence of a father from the outset, and many of those in lesbian families are raised by two mothers. In this chapter, findings will be presented from a series of studies of the psychological consequences for children of being raised in the following family types: assisted reproduction families with two heterosexual parents, families headed by a solo heterosexual mother, and lesbian mother families.

☐ Assisted Reproduction Families

Of the various concerns that have been expressed regarding the potential negative consequences of assisted reproduction for children's psychological well-being, the effects of keeping information about genetic origins secret from a child conceived by gamete donation has been the subject of great debate. As few children are told that a donated sperm or egg had been used in their conception, the large majority grow up not knowing that their father or their mother is genetically unrelated to them. Although clinicians traditionally have advised parents that there is no need to tell the child (Mahlstedt & Greenfield, 1989), it increasingly has been argued that parents should be open with their children, either on the grounds that they have a right to know, or because it is believed that secrecy will result in psychological problems for the child (Daniels & Taylor, 1993; Schaffer & Diamond, 1993).

Findings suggestive of an association between secrecy and negative outcomes for children have come from two major sources; research on adoption and the family therapy literature. It has been demonstrated that adopted children benefit from knowledge about their biological parents, and that children who are not given such information may become confused about their identity and at risk for emotional problems (Hoopes, 1990; Sants, 1964; Schechter & Bertocci, 1990; Triseliotis, 1973). In the field of assisted reproduction, parallels have been drawn with the adoptive situation and it has been suggested that lack of knowledge of, or information about, the donor may be harmful for the child (Clamar, 1989; Snowden, 1990; Snowden, Mitchell, & Snowden, 1983).

From a family therapy perspective, secrets are believed to be detrimental to family functioning because they create boundaries between those who know and those who do not, and cause anxiety when topics related to the secret are discussed (Karpel, 1980). In examining the particular case of parents keeping secrets from their children, Papp (1993) argued that children can sense when information is being with-held due to the taboo that surrounds the discussion of certain topics, and that they may become confused and anxious, or even develop symptoms of psychological disorder, as a result. Experimental studies have demonstrated that people who are deliberately trying not to disclose information often give themselves away by their tone of voice, body posture, or by saying less than they normally would in a similar situation (De Paulo, 1992). However, it remains unknown whether children conceived by gamete donation become aware that a secret relating to their parentage is being kept from them and, if so, whether this awareness has negative consequences for their psychological state.

More general concerns regarding the consequences of assisted reproduction for family functioning and child development also have been expressed, such as the potential negative impact on family relation-ships of the parents' experience of infertility investigations and treatment, often lasting over a period of several years. It has been suggested that couples who have not come to terms with their infertility may experience difficulties in relating to their children (L. H. Burns, 1990). This has been reported to be a problem for some adoptive parents (Brodzinsky, 1987; Humphrey & Humphrey, 1988). In addition, whereas some couples find that the experience of infertility has no deleterious effect on their marriage, for others the stress of infertility as well as the stressful nature of the procedures involved in infertility treatment result in marital difficulties (Cook, Parsons, Mason, Golombok, 1989). For couples whose relationship difficulties persist, problems are likely to develop for the child (Cox, Owen, Lewis, & Henderson, 1989; Howes & Markman, 1989). Furthermore, growing attention has been paid in recent years to the social context of families and to the processes through which social environments affect family relationships. It is important to remember, therefore, that negative attitudes may exist toward the reproductive technolo-gies, with procedures such as IVF and DI sometimes considered to be immoral or unnatural. As a result, families with a child conceived by assisted reproduction may experience overt prejudice not only from the wider community but also from relatives and friends.

Nevertheless, conception by gamete donation would be expected to have negative consequences for family functioning only to the extent that the lack of genetic ties interferes with the quality of parent-child relationships, either due to the effects of secrecy, or because parents feel or behave differently toward a nongenetic than a genetic child. There is a growing body of empirical evidence to show that the course of a child's social and emotional development is closely related to the quality of the child's attachment rela-tionships with parents (Bowlby, 1969, 1973; Main, Kaplan, & Cassidy, 1985). From the perspective of attachment theory, it is parental responsiveness, rather than biological relatedness, that is considered to be important for the development of secure attachment relationships (Grossmann, Grossmann, Spangler, Suess, & Unzer, 1985; Isabella, Belsky, & von Eye, 1989). Further evidence for the relatively greater impor-tance of parental responsiveness comes from the lack of difference between adopted and nonadopted infants in the proportion classified as securely attached to their mother (Singer, Brodzinsky, Ramsay, Steir, & Waters, 1985). Other aspects of parenting also have been shown to influence children's psycho-logical well-being. For example, Baumrind (1989) has demonstrated that an authoritative parenting style (i.e., a combination of warmth and discipline) has positive outcomes for children's socioemotional devel-opment. Thus, insofar as nongenetic parents do not differ from genetic parents with respect to factors such as responsiveness and control, difficulties would not necessarily be expected for the child.

In view of the conflicting opinions regarding the predicted outcomes for children conceived by assisted reproduction, and the absence of empirical data on the actual consequences for these families, we set out to examine the quality of parent-child relationships and the social and emotional development of children in families created as a result of the two most common assisted reproduction methods, IVF and DI, and to compare these families with two control groups: a group of families with a naturally conceived child and a group of adoptive families (Cook, Golombok, Bish & Murray, 1995; Golombok, Cook, Bish & Murray, 1995).

Forty-one families with a child conceived by IVF and 45 families with a child conceived by DI were obtained through infertility clinics throughout the United Kingdom. The control groups of 43 families with a naturally conceived child and 55 families with a child adopted in the first 6 months of life were recruited through the records of maternity wards and adoption agencies respectively and matched to the assisted reproduction families as closely as possible with respect to demographic characteristics such as the age of the mother, social class, and family size. The response rates ranged from 95% for IVF families to 62% for DI families. All of the children were between age 4 and 8, and there was a similar proportion of boys and girls in each group of families. Children with major congenital abnormalities, children who had experienced obstetric or perinatal complications that were thought likely to involve brain damage or risk of persisting disability, and children of a multiple birth were not included in the study.

The quality of parenting was assessed by standardized interview with the mother, using an adaptation of the technique developed by Quinton and Rutter (1988). This procedure has been validated against observational ratings of mother-child relationships in the home, demonstrating a high level of agreement between global ratings of the quality of parenting by interviewers and observers. The researchers were fully trained in the interview techniques by one of the authors of the interview procedure. The interview, which was tape-recorded, lasted for around 1½ hours and was conducted with the mother alone. Detailed accounts were obtained of the child's behavior and the parents' response to it. The mothers were asked to describe the child's daily routine focusing on waking, mealtimes, leaving for school or day care, returning home, mother's and father's play activities with the child, and bedtime. Information was obtained on the parents' handling of any problems associated with these areas, and particular attention was paid to parent-child interactions relating to issues of control and the child's fears and anxieties.

Four overall ratings of the quality of parenting were made, taking into account information obtained from the entire interview: (a) Warmth was rated on a 6-point scale ranging from 0 (*none*) to 5 (*high*). This rating of the mother's warmth toward the child was based on the mother's tone of voice and facial expression when talking about the child, spontaneous expressions of warmth, sympathy and concern about any difficulties experienced by the child, and enthusiasm and interest in the child as a person. (b) Emotional involvement was rated on a 5-point scale from 0 (*little or none*) to 4 (*extreme*). This rating, which represented anxious overinvolvement at the extreme end, took account of the extent to which the family day was organized around the child, the extent to which the needs or interests of the child were placed before those of other family members, the extent to which the mother was overconcerned, overprotective, or inhibited the child from age-appropriate independent activities, the extent to which the mother was willing to leave the child with other caretakers, and the extent to which the mother had interests or engaged in activities apart from those relating to the child. (c) Mother-child interaction and (d) father-child interaction were each rated on a 5-point scale ranging from 0 (*very low*) to 4 (*very high*). These ratings of the quality of interaction between the parent and the child were based on mothers' reports of the extent to which the parent and the child enjoyed each other's company, wanted to be with each other, spent time together, enjoyed joint play activities, and showed physical affection to one another.

In addition, mothers of children conceived by donor insemination were interviewed about their openness regarding the circumstances of the child's conception. Systematic information was obtained from these mothers with respect to whether or not they had told their child about his or her genetic origins, and whether or not they had told other members of their family or friends. Those who had not told the child were asked about their reasons for secrecy.

The short form of the Parenting Stress Index (PSI/SF; Abidin, 1990) also was administered to both parents to provide a standardized assessment of stress associated with parenting for mothers and fathers separately. This measure produces a total score of the overall level of parenting stress an individual is experiencing. Test-retest reliability for this instrument has been shown to be high over a 6-month period. Concurrent and predictive validity has been demonstrated for the full-length questionnaire, and the short form has been reported to correlate very highly with the full-length version.

The presence of behavioral and emotional problems in the child was assessed using the Rutter A and B scales which are completed by mothers and teachers respectively. Each produces an overall score of the child's psychiatric state. These questionnaires have bean shown to have good interrater and test-retest reliability, and to discriminate well between children with and without psychiatric disorder (Rutter, Cox, Tupling, Berger, & Yule, 1975; Rutter, Tizard, & Whitmore, 1970).

Each child was administered the Pictorial Scale of Perceived Competence and Social Acceptance for Young Children (Harter & Pike, 1984). This is a measure of children's perceptions of their cognitive and physical competencies, and of their perceptions of acceptance by their mother and by peers, all of which have been shown to be associated with the development of self-esteem in later childhood. A score is obtained for each of the following subscales: (a) cognitive competence, (b) physical competence, (c) maternal acceptance, and (d) peer acceptance. The higher the score, the more positive the child's feelings of competence and social acceptance. Satisfactory internal consistency has been demonstrated, and the scale has been shown to discriminate between groups of children in predicted ways (e.g., between peer acceptance and length of time at a school, and between perceived cognitive competence and academic achievement at school), indicating that it is a valid measure.

Contrary to the concerns that have been raised regarding the potential negative consequences of the new reproductive technologies for family functioning, the findings of this study indicate that the quality of parenting in families with a child conceived by assisted conception (IVF and DI) is superior to that shown by families with a naturally conceived child, even when gamete donation had been used in the child's conception. Families with a child conceived by assisted reproduction obtained significantly higher scores on measures of mother's warmth to the child, mother's emotional involvement with the child, mother-child interaction and father-child interaction. In line with these findings, mothers and fathers of naturally conceived children reported significantly higher levels of stress associated with parenting. No group differences were found for any of the measures of children's emotions, behavior, or relationships. It is important to point out that the families with a naturally conceived child were selected from the general population and did not constitute a dysfunctional group. Thus the investigation indicates that the assisted reproduction families were functioning very well, and not that the control group was experiencing difficulties.

The findings suggest that genetic ties are less important for family functioning than a strong desire for parenthood. Whether the child was genetically unrelated to one parent, in the case of DI, or genetically unrelated to both parents, in the case of adoption, the quality of parenting in families where the mother and father had gone to great lengths to become parents was superior to that shown by mothers and fathers who had achieved parenthood in the usual way. The similarity in parenting quality between DI and adoptive mothers and fathers showed that it does not seem to matter whether the child is genetically unrelated to one parent or two; an imbalance in genetic relationships between the parents and the child does not appear to disrupt the parenting process.

Nevertheless, it is striking that not one of the DI parents had told their child that he or she had been conceived using sperm from an anonymous donor. Thus, none of the a DI children was aware that their father was not their genetic parent. Most mothers (80%) reported that they definitely had decided not to tell, 16% were undecided, and 4% planned to tell their child. In contrast, half of the DI mothers had told a member of their family, and almost one third had told one or more friends, so the risk of disclosure to the child was always there. The main reasons for the parents' decision not to tell the child were (a) the concern that the child would love the father less, (b) protection of the father from the stigma associated with infertility, and (c) lack of knowledge about what, and when, to tell the child.

In spite of the recent move toward encouraging openness with children conceived by DI, it seems that parents continue to withhold information from children about their origins. Although it has been argued on the basis of research on adoption that such information is important for children's emotional well-being, it seems from mothers' reports that the areas presenting most difficulty for disclosure are precisely those in which DI differs from adoption: acknowledgment of the father's fertility problem, uncertainty about the best time and method of telling the child, and lack of information to give to the child about the genetic father.

Unlike adoption, there are no generally accepted stories of what to tell the child about DI and parents have to explain the facts of life and discuss the father's infertility in order for the child to understand. Moreover, because an anonymous donor had been used, they had little information to give the child about his or her genetic father. Due to these factors, the situation for DI parents is different than that of adoptive parents and, as a result, most DI parents seem to have concluded that nondisclosure is desirable for the protection of both the father and the child.

In the second phase of this research, we included an additional country from northern Europe (the Netherlands) and two countries from southern Europe (Italy and Spain), thus allowing an examination of the influence of culturally determined attitudes toward assisted reproduction on the functioning of families that have resulted from these techniques. Identical procedures were employed in the Netherlands, Italy, and Spain as had been used in the United Kingdom. The inclusion of these three countries brought the total number of IVF, DI, adoptive, and naturally conceived families respectively to 116, 111, 115, and 120.

The findings of the European study confirmed the findings of the original investigation (Golombok et al., 1996). Mothers of children conceived by assisted reproduction were found to express greater warmth to their child, to be more emotionally involved with their child, to interact more with their child and to report less stress associated with parenting than the comparison group of mothers who conceived their child naturally. In addition, assisted reproduction fathers were reported by mothers to interact with their child more than fathers with a naturally conceived child. Once again, whether or not donor sperm had been used in order to conceive the child seemed to make little difference to the quality of parenting in assisted reproduction families as DI parents did not differ from IVF parents for any of these variables. Further evidence that the lack of a genetic link between one or both parents and the child does not have negative consequences for parent-child relationships comes from the finding that the adoptive families were similar to the assisted reproduction families with respect to the parenting measures. Regarding the children themselves, no overall group differences were found for either psychological problems or for children's developing self-esteem. Significant group x country interactions were not identified for any of these measures, showing that the findings relating to the quality of parenting and the socioemotional development of the children were similar in each of the four countries studied.

Perhaps surprisingly, there was no evidence that attitudes toward assisted reproduction differed between northern and southern Europe. Not one of the parents with a child conceived by DI in any of the four countries studied had told their child about his or her method of conception. When mothers were asked whether they planned to tell their child in the future, most (75%) reported that they had definitely decided not to tell, 13% were undecided, and only 12% planned to tell their child. A significant difference between countries was found with respect to attitude toward telling the child. The Italian parents were most against telling, with 100% having decided never to tell, followed by the U.K. and Dutch parents of whom 80% and 76%, respectively, had decided never to tell. In Spain, the parents seemed more open to considering the idea of telling, with only 48% having definitely decided never to tell.

Although the majority of DI parents had decided against telling their child, more than half had told a friend or family member. A significant difference between countries was not identified for this variable. The mothers of DI children also were asked about which members of the family had been told. Although the majority of parents had not told the child's grandparents, more than one third of the maternal grandparents had been told, compared with less than one quarter of paternal grandparents. There was no significant difference between countries with respect to telling either maternal or paternal grandparents. In addition, there was no significant difference between countries in telling friends. Overall, 71% of the sample had not told any friends, 28% had told a very few friends, and only 1% had told many friends.

More recently, a group of 21 families with a child conceived by egg donation has been recruited in the United Kingdom, allowing a contrast to be made between families where the child is genetically related to the father but not the mother (egg donation families) and families where the child is genetically related to the mother but not the father (DI families) (Golombok, Murray, Brinsden, & Abdalla, 1999). This was not possible at the time of the initial study as the first egg donation child was not born until 1983 (Lutjen, Trounson, Leeton, Findlay, Wood, & Renou, 1984; Trounson, Leeton, Besanka, Wood, & Conti, 1983). The only difference to emerge between egg donation and DI families was that mothers and fathers of children conceived by egg donation reported lower levels of stress associated with parenting than parents of a DI child. It seems that egg donation families, like DI families, are functioning well. Only one set of parents with a child conceived by egg donation had told their child about his genetic origins.

Thus, it appears from this series of studies that children conceived by IVF, DI and egg donation have good relationships with their parents and are not at risk for psychological problems. These findings are in line with those of other investigations of both DI families (Kovacs, Mushin, Kane, & Baker, 1993) and IVF families using different samples and different methods of assessment in France (Raoul-Duval, Bertrand-Servais, & Frydman, 1993), Belgium (Colpin, Demyttenaere, & Vandemeulebroecke, 1995), the Netherlands (Van Balen, 1996), and the United Kingdom (Papaligoura, 1998; Weaver, Clifford, Gordon, Hay, &

Robinson, 1993) The studies by Colpin and Papaligoura used direct observation of mother-child interaction in addition to self-report measures.

It is important to stress, however, that not one of the DI parents and only one set of egg donation parents had told their child about his genetic origins. Although keeping the method of conception secret from a child age 4 to 8 does not appear to have a negative impact on family relationships or on the psychological development of the child, it remains to be seen whether secrecy leads to difficulties as the children grow up. It could be expected that problems are most likely to arise in adolescence, the time at which issues of identity, and difficulties in relationships with parents, become more salient. Certainly, it is the case that adopted children show a greater increase in behavioral and emotional problems at adolescence than nonadopted children (Maughan & Pickles, 1990), alongside an increased interest in their biological parents (Hoopes, 1990). In order to address this issue, a follow-up study of all of the children in Italy, the Netherlands, Spain, and the United Kingdom, as they reach age 11 to 12, is currently under way.

☐ Solo Mother Families

Research on the psychological consequences for children of growing up in a fatherless family has focused on children who had lived with their father during their early years and who had then experienced parental separation or divorce. The first studies showed father absence to have negative outcomes with respect to children's cognitive, social, and emotional development (for reviews see Biller, 1974; Herzog & Sudia, 1973). Later investigations that controlled for factors associated with, but not directly related to, father absence such as economic hardship and lower social class, found that the absence of a father in itself is not adversely related to children's social adjustment or intellectual ability (Broman, Nichols & Kennedy, 1975; Crockett, Eggebeen, & Hawkins, 1993; Ferri, 1976). However, it has been argued that economic disadvantage is a major consequence of single parenthood and as such should not be controlled for as an extraneous variable in data analysis. From their examination of four nationally representative data sets in the United States, McLanahan & Sandefur (1994) concluded that the lower income that results from lone parenthood is the single most important factor in the underachievement of young people from one-parent homes. They also found a negative effect of lone parenting, resulting from inadequate parenting and poor access to community resources, over and above that of reduced family income.

Studies that have taken account of the reason for becoming a fatherless family have shown that discordant family relationships carry psychological risks for children. In comparisons between children whose parents had divorced or separated, and those whose father had died, a higher incidence of behavioral problems (Ferri, 1976; Rutter, 1971) and greater difficulties in the transition from adolescence to adult life (McLanahan & Sandefur, 1994) have been found among children who had experienced divorce or separation. From a review of the empirical evidence in support of the various explanations of children's psychological adjustment, Amato (1993) concluded that conflict between parents is the main predictor of emotional distress among children of divorce.

Evidence for the importance of factors that predate the transition to a fatherless family comes from longitudinal studies in the United States and Great Britain in which comparisons were made between the behavior problems of children whose parents divorced or separated between the first and the second assessment, and the behavior problems of children whose families remained intact (Cherlin et al., 1991). It was found that behavior problems and family difficulties that were present before the parents' separation or divorce were strongly associated with children's difficulties after the families had broken up. Thus, it is not only what happens to children after their parents separate, but also their circumstances beforehand, that influence the impact of rearing in a fatherless family on children's social and emotional adjustment.

Almost one quarter of American families (A. Burns, 1992) and one fifth of U.K. families (Roll, 1992) are currently headed by a single mother. Although a large proportion of these families result from parental separation or divorce, a growing number of heterosexual women are becoming mothers without marrying, or living with, the father of their child (Burghes, 1993). This has resulted in an increase in the number of children being raised by "solo" mothers (i.e., mothers who have been single from the outset).

To the extent that early family experiences are important determinants of later socioemotional development, the findings of existing research on children of single heterosexual mothers who had lived with their father during their first years of life cannot be generalized to children raised without a father from infancy. Studying these families allows an examination of the effects of rearing in a female-headed family without the confound of parental separation or divorce which, in itself, is likely to lead to problems for the child (Amato & Keith, 1991; Hetherington, Cox, & Cox, 1982, 1985).

It might be expected that children raised from infancy without a father would be no more at risk for social and emotional difficulties than children raised by two heterosexual parents as they had not been exposed to parental conflict or a disruption in family relationships. Similarly, they had not experienced the emotional distress and associated reduction in parental functioning common among single mothers following divorce (Amato, 1993; Chase-Lansdale & Hetherington, 1990). However, mothers may be subject to other pressures, such as social stigma and lack of social support, that may interfere with their parenting role, and their children may be vulnerable to emotional and behavioral problems as a result.

There are very few investigations of children raised by solo mothers. From a general population study in the United Kingdom of children raised from the outset by a single heterosexual mother, Ferri (1976) tentatively concluded that these children were as well adjusted as children in father-present families. Rather more negative outcomes for children of unmarried mothers were reported by McLanahan and Sandefur (1994). However, these findings related to young adults and were largely attributed to the economic disadvantage they experienced while growing up. In addition, Weinraub and Gringlas (1995) found that, in solo mother families, more negative outcomes for children appeared to be associated with lower levels of social support and higher levels of stress. In a study of middle-class mothers who had raised their child alone from the first year of life (Golombok, Tasker, & Murray, 1997), we found the children to show greater security of attachment to the mother as assessed by the Separation Anxiety Test, a test designed to assess children's responses to a series of photographs involving separation from parents (Grossmann & Grossmann, 1991; Klagsbrun & Bowlby, 1976), but to perceive themselves as less physically and cognitively competent, than their peers from father-present families. It is important to point out that, although the children we studied had been raised in a fatherless family from infancy, they had not been exposed to economic hardship while growing up.

Single mothers, and particularly unmarried single mothers who are financially dependent on the state, have been accused in recent years of producing an "underclass" of delinquents, dropouts, and drug addicts. Whereas an association does appear to exist between single motherhood, poverty, and childhood problems (McLanahan & Sandefur, 1994), the circumstances of single-mother families can be just as diverse as those of the traditional nuclear family. It is important, therefore, not only to determine which factors associated with single parenthood place children at risk, but also to establish those aspects that do not result in psychological difficulties for the child.

There has been a great deal of controversy in recent years about whether single heterosexual women should have access to assisted reproduction to enable them to have a child without the involvement of a male partner (Englert, 1994; Shenfield, 1994). Children born to single mothers as a result of assisted reproduction have not experienced parental divorce and generally are raised without financial hardship. A small, uncontrolled investigation of 10 single women requesting DI (cited by Fidell & Marik, 1989) found that an important reason for opting for this procedure was to avoid using a man to produce a child without his knowledge of consent. DI also meant that they did not have to share the rights and responsibilities for the child with a man to whom they were not emotionally committed. Although rare, women who have never experienced a sexual relationship with either sex also have been given access to DI (Jennings, 1991). These so-called virgin births have given rise to media outcry. As yet, no study has specifically examined children of single mothers conceived by assisted reproduction procedures such as DI. What seems clear, however, is that, in making predictions about the consequences for children in such families, it is important to take social context into account. Single-mother families are not all the same, and factors such as the mother's financial situation, and social support from family and friends, are likely to have an impact on outcomes for the child.

☐ Lesbian Mother Families

Studies of children in lesbian mother families date back to the 1970s when lesbian mothers began to fight for custody of their children when they divorced. At that time, lesbian mothers were losing custody of their children on the grounds that it would not be in the child's best interests to grow up in a lesbian family. In particular, it was argued that the children would be teased and ostracized by their peers and would develop emotional and behavioral problems as a result, and also that they would show atypical gender development (i.e., that boys would be less masculine in their identity and behavior, and girls less feminine, than their counterparts from heterosexual homes).

In all that has been said and written about lesbian families, greatest attention has been paid to the consequences of being raised by a lesbian mother for children's gender development. In investigations of gender development, a distinction is generally made between gender identity, gender role, and sexual orientation. Gender identity is a person's concept of themselves as male or female, gender role includes the behaviors and attitudes which are considered to be appropriate for males and females in a particular culture, and sexual orientation refers to a person's sexual attraction toward partners of the other gender (heterosexual sexual orientation) or the same gender (lesbian or gay sexual orientation). Whether or not children of lesbian mothers will differ with respect to these different aspects of gender development from children brought up by heterosexual single mothers will depend on the extent to which it is possible for parents to influence the gender development of their children. Insofar as gender development is biologically determined, the way in which parents raise their children should make little difference. The three major psychological theories—psychoanalytic, social learning, and cognitive developmental—vary according to the psychological processes which are believed to be operative, and also in the role ascribed to parents.

Psychoanalytic theorists believe that relationships with parents early in childhood are central to the development of gender identity, gender role, and sexual orientation in adult life. According to traditional psychoanalytic theory, gender development is rooted in the phallic stage of psychosexual development which occurs at about 5 years of age (Freud, 1905/1953; 1920/1955; 1933; Socarides, 1978). It is in order to resolve the Oedipal conflict (i.e., the conflict between his sexual desire for his mother and his fear of castration by his father) that boys are believed shift their identification from the mother to the father and take on his male characteristics. The mechanisms involved in female identification are rather different and less clearly described. The resolution of the Oedipal conflict in girls is believed to be driven by penis envy, and involves transferring identification from the father back to the mother and adopting a female role.

For psychoanalytic theorists, the acquisition of nontraditional gender roles, and the development of a lesbian or gay sexual orientation, are viewed as negative outcomes resulting from the unsuccessful resolution of the Oedipal conflict. It is believed that boys who fail to identify with their father, and girls who fail to identify with their mother, at the completion of the Oedipal period are more likely to identify as gay or lesbian, respectively, when they grow up. The quality of children's relationships with their heterosexual parents is considered to be an important determinant of children's passage through the Oedipal phase. The combination of a domineering mother and a weak father for boys is thought to lead to a homosexual orientation. A lesbian orientation is believed to result from a girl's hostile and fearful relationship with her mother.

So, what can we predict from psychoanalytic theory about the consequences for gender development of being raised by a lesbian mother? Traditional psychoanalytic theorists, stressing the importance of the presence of heterosexual parents for the successful resolution of the Oedipal conflict, would expect that the lack a father figure, together with the mother's atypical female role, would influence the gender development of children brought up in lesbian families. Specifically, it has been argued that boys will not identify with the male role and therefore will be less masculine, and that girls will identify with a mother who does not conform to the traditional female role and thus will be less feminine. While studies of children raised in heterosexual families have failed to produce empirical evidence to demonstrate that the quality of parent-child relationships influences the development of children's sexual orientation, psychoanalytic theorists would predict that a gay or lesbian identity would be particularly likely for boys with a close relationship and girls with a hostile relationship with their lesbian mother, and for boys with a hostile relationship and girls with a close relationship with their gay father.

From the perspective of classic social learning theory, which has focused on the development of childhood sex-typed behavior rather than on adult sexual orientation, the two processes which are important for children's gender development are differential reinforcement, and modeling others of the same sex as themselves, particularly the same-sex parent (Bandura, 1977; Mischel, 1966, 1970). There is much empirical evidence to suggest that parents of preschool children do treat their sons and daughters differently, although the extent to which they are producing sex-typed behavior, rather than simply responding to preexisting differences between boys and girls, remains unknown (Lytton & Romney, 1991; Maccoby & Jacklin, 1974).

With respect to modeling, the idea that children acquire sex-typed behavior by directly imitating same-sex parents is now thought to be rather simplistic, and a modified version of social learning theory has been proposed (Bandura, 1986; Bussey & Bandura, 1984; Perry & Bussey, 1979). It seems that children learn which behaviors are considered to be appropriate for males and which for females by observing many men and women and boys and girls, and by noticing which behaviors are performed frequently by females and rarely by males, and vice versa. Children then use these abstractions of sexually appropriate behavior as models for their own imitative performance. Thus, children observe a wide variety of role models in their daily life and tend to imitate those whom they consider to be typical of their sex. Friends, in particular, appear to be important role models; school-age boys and girls show a strong preference for same-sex peers (Maccoby, 1988). But, it is gender stereotypes, rather than specific individuals, that seem to be most influential in the acquisition of sex-typed behavior. Gender stereotypes are pervasive in our society, and children are aware of these stereotypes from as early as 2 years old (Martin, 1991; Signorella, Bigler, & Liben, 1993; Stern & Karraker, 1989).

Thus, from a social learning theory perspective, it could be expected that different patterns of reinforcement may be operating in lesbian than in heterosexual families such that young people in lesbian families would be less likely to be discouraged from engaging in nonconventional sex-typed behavior, or from embarking on lesbian or gay relationships. Whereas contemporary social learning theorists are less likely than classical social learning theorists to emphasize the importance of the same-sex parent as a role model, it could be argued that by virtue of their nontraditional family, the sons and daughters of lesbian mothers may hold less rigid stereotypes about what constitutes acceptable male and female behavior than their peers in heterosexual families, and may be more open to nonconventional gender role behavior, or to involvement in lesbian or gay relationships themselves. It is important to remember, however, that social learning theorists believe that individuals other than parents also are important role models and reinforcers of sex-typed behavior for the child.

Like social learning theorists, cognitive developmental theorists have focused on the development of childhood gender identity and role rather than on adult sexual orientation. For cognitive developmental theorists, the role of parents is a minor one. A central tenet of this approach is that children play an active part in their own development; they seek out for themselves information about gender and socialize themselves as male or female. Parents are viewed as simply one source of gender-related information. Early studies of cognitive developmental processes focused on children's developing understanding of the concept of gender (Kohlberg, 1966; Stagnor & Ruble, 1987). Basic gender identity is established at about age 2 to 3. By this age, children know that they are male or female, and also can correctly label other people as male or female. It is not until they reach the stage of gender stability a year or 2 later, however, that they realize that gender is stable across time. Gender constancy, the understanding that gender is a characteristic which does not change, is the final stage in the development of the gender concept and is reached at about 5 or 6 years old.

More recently, gender schema theorists have examined the way in which children organize knowledge about gender (Martin, 1989, 1991; Martin & Halverson, 1981). Gender schemas refer to organized bodies of knowledge about gender, and are functionally similar to gender stereotypes. Gender schemas influence the way in which we perceive and remember information about the world around us so that we pay greater attention to, and are more likely to remember, information that is in line with our gender schemas than opposing information. From as early as age 2 to 3, soon after they begin to consistently label themselves and others as male or female, children organize information according to gender. If told that a person is male or female, children will make gender-related predictions about that person's behavior (Martin, 1989; Martin, Wood, & Little, 1990), and children as young as age 5 have been shown to have a better memory for events which fit with gender stereotypes than those which do not (Liben & Signorella, 1980; Martin & Halverson, 1983; Signorella & Liben, 1984).

Cognitive developmental theorists place even less emphasis on the role of parents in the gender development of their children. According to this theory, children integrate information about sexual identity from their wider social environment, actively constructing for themselves what it means to be male or female. It would not be predicted that children raised by lesbian mothers would differ in this process from children in heterosexual families. Cognitive developmental theorists, like social learning theorists, have focused on childhood sex-typed behavior rather than on adult sexual orientation. To the extent that cognitive processes are contributing to the adoption of a heterosexual or homosexual orientation, it would seem that young people seek out information in their social world which is in line with their emerging sexual orientation, and come to value and identify with those characteristics which are consistent with their view of themselves as heterosexual, lesbian, or gay.

The assumption that children of lesbian mothers may be more likely to experience emotional and behavioral problems than children of heterosexual parents stems from the finding that some childhood family experiences have been found to carry an increased risk of psychiatric disorder. Of particular relevance to children of lesbian mothers is the children's experience of parental divorce. A number of studies have examined the psychological adjustment of children whose parents divorce, the most noteworthy of which is the longitudinal investigation by Hetherington and her colleagues (Hetherington, 1988, 1989; Hetherington, et al., 1982, 1985). Children of divorced parents in mother custody families were compared with children of nondivorced parents at 2 months, 1 year, 2 years, and 6 years following divorce using a variety of observational, interview, and rating scale measures of the children's behavior at home and at school. It was found that, in the first year, the children from divorced families showed more behavioral problems. They were more aggressive, demanding, and lacking in self-control than their counterparts in nondivorced families. By 2 years following divorce, the girls had adapted to their new situation and had a positive relationship with their mother provided that she had not remarried. The boys, although slightly improved, still showed problems in adjustment and difficulties in their relationship with their mother. By the time of the 6-year follow-up, some of the mothers had remarried so that these children were living with their mother and a stepfather. The mothers who had not remarried continued to have good relationships with their daughters and difficult relationships with their sons. This pattern was reflected in the children's behavior. The daughters were functioning well, whereas the boys were more likely than boys in nondivorced families to be noncompliant, impulsive, and aggressive. In families where the mother had remarried, however, the situation was rather different. After the early stages of remarriage, the boys had fewer problems than boys in nonremarried families. If the stepfather was supportive, boys developed a good relationship with him. The girls, on the other hand, had more difficulties with family relations and adjustment than girls whose mothers had not remarried, and continued to reject their stepfather however hard he tried to develop a positive relationship (Vuchinich, Hetherington, Vuchinich, & Clingempeel, 1991).

When intense marital conflict continues after the divorce, it can have a more harmful effect than when it occurs in intact families (Hetherington, 1988, 1989). Wallerstein and Kelly (1980) also found that children with difficulties are those whose parents remain in conflict after the divorce, and concluded that whether or not children's problems diminish is a function of whether or not divorce improves parental relationships. The quality of children's relationships with their parents also is an important determinant of psychological adjustment. Children who have good postdivorce relationships with their parents are less likely to suffer negative effects (Hess & Camara, 1979; Hetherington, 1988).

Nevertheless, parental divorce is not directly related to rearing in a lesbian family. The expectation that being raised in a lesbian family would, in itself, increase the likelihood of psychiatric disorder in children arises from the assumption that the children would be teased about their parent's sexual orientation and ostracized by their peers. The concern is that this situation would be deeply upsetting to children, and that it would have a negative effect on their ability to form and maintain friendships. There is wide agreement in the psychological literature that satisfactory relationships with peers are important for positive social and emotional development (Dunn & McGuire, 1992; Kupersmidt, Coie, & Dodge, 1992).

It is well established that children's social and emotional development is fostered within the context of parent-child relationships (Darling & Steinberg, 1993; Maccoby, 1992). As discussed earlier in this chapter in the section, Assisted Reproduction Families, by far the most accepted and comprehensive explanation of the processes involved in the development of parent-child relationships comes from attachment theory put forward by Bowlby (Bowlby, 1969, 1973, 1980) and Ainsworth (Ainsworth, 1972, 1982; Ainsworth, Blehar, Waters, & Wall, 1978). According to this theory, interactions between the parent and the child form the basis of attachment relationships, and the type of attachment that an infant develops (i.e., secure or insecure) largely depends on the quality of interaction between the parent and the child such that parents of securely attached infants are responsive and sensitive to their infant's needs (Ainsworth, 1979). Recent research has provided empirical evidence in support of this view (Grossmann et al., 1985; Isabella & Belsky, 1991; Izard, Haynes, Chisholm, & Baak, 1991; Pederson et al., 1990; Smith & Pederson, 1988). For example, it has been demonstrated that secure attachments in infancy are fostered by synchronous interactions in which mothers are responsive to their infant's vocalizations and distress signals (Isabella et al., 1989).

Studies traditionally have focused on the development of attachment in infancy. However, in recent years, attention has turned to the examination of attachment relationships in the preschool- and school-age years. As a result, interest has grown in representational aspects of attachment. Through their early experiences with attachment figures, children are believed to form internal representations of their attachment relationships (Bowlby, 1969, 1973, 1980). Bowlby referred to these internal representations as "internal working models." According to Bowlby, the child's internal working model of an attachment figure (e.g., as available and responsive in the case of securely attached children or as unavailable and unresponsive in the case of insecurely attached children) will influence the child's expectations of, and behavior toward that person. The child's internal working models of attachment relationships are also believed to influence the child's internal representation of the self. Thus, a child who represents attachment figures as responsive and emotionally available is likely to hold an internal model of the self as lovable, whereas a child with internal models of attachment figures as unresponsive and unavailable is likely to represent the self as unworthy of being loved. The child's internal representations of attachment figures and of the self are believed to have a profound influence on the individual's relationships with others in childhood and in adult life. There is growing empirical evidence in support of Bowlby's view that individuals form internal models of their attachment relationships (e.g., Bretherton, 1985; Main et al., 1985). It also has been demonstrated that a connection exists between working models of attachment figures and the working model of the self (Cassidy, 1988).

Thus, it appears that the most important factor for a secure parent-child relationship is the quality of interaction between that parent and the child. Children in lesbian families, therefore, would be expected to have a positive relationship with their lesbian mother, provided that she is responsive to the child and sensitive to his or her needs. Whereas some researchers have claimed that attachment is characterized by a sensitive period, others have believed that attachment security can change for better or worse according to family circumstances (Thompson, Lamb, & Estes, 1982; Vaughn, Egeland, Sroufe, & Waters, 1979).

The early investigations of lesbian mother families adopted a similar design in that they compared children in lesbian mother families with children raised in families headed by a single heterosexual mother (for reviews see Falk 1989; Golombok & Tasker, 1994; Patterson, 1992). The rationale for the choice of single heterosexual mothers as a comparison group was that the two types of family were alike in that the children were being raised by women without the presence of a father, but differed in the sexual orientation of the mother. This allowed the effects of the mothers' sexual orientation on children's development to be examined without the confound of the presence of a father in the family home.

Our U.K. study centered on the two areas of child development that had been the focus of concern in child custody cases; children's gender development and their psychological well-being (Golombok, Spencer, & Rutter, 1983). Data were obtained through in-depth standardized interviews with the mothers and their children, and the mothers and the children's teachers also completed standardized questionnaires. We found that all of the boys and girls in the two family types had a secure gender identity as male or female, respectively. There was no evidence of gender identify confusion for any of the children studied (i.e., none of the children wished to be the other sex, or consistently engaged in cross-gender behavior). In terms of gender role, no differences were found between children in lesbian and heterosexual families, for either boys or girls, in the extent to which they showed behavior that was typical of their sex. Daughters of lesbian mothers were no less feminine, and the sons no less masculine, than the daughters and sons of heterosexual mothers.

With respect to the children's psychological well-being, children in lesbian families were no more likely to experience psychological disorder than children of single heterosexual mothers as assessed by a child psychiatrist who was unaware of the type of family to which the child belonged. Teacher's ratings of the children's emotional and behavioral problems at school also failed to differentiate children from the two family types, a finding which provided important validation for the mothers' reports. In addition, the children from the two family types did not differ with respect to the quality of their friendships, and children of lesbian mothers were no more likely than children of heterosexual mothers to be teased or bullied by peers. So, from this study of children with an average age of 10 to 11 years, it seems that growing up in a lesbian family has not had an adverse effect on their social, emotional, or gender development. Similar findings have been reported by other researchers who have studied samples with different geographic and demographic characteristics (Green, Mandel, Hotvedt, Gray, & Smith, 1986; Huggins, 1989; Kirkpatrick, Smith, & Roy, 1981). Regarding the parenting ability of the mothers themselves, it also has been demonstrated that lesbian mothers are just as child oriented (Kirkpatrick, 1987; Miller, Jacobsen, & Bigner, 1981; Pagelow, 1980), just as warm and responsive to their children (Golombok et al., 1983), and just as nurturant and confident (Mucklow & Phelan, 1979) as heterosexual mothers.

A limitation of these investigations was that only school-age children were studied, because it has been argued that "sleeper effects" may exist such that children raised in lesbian households may experience difficulties in emotional well-being, and in intimate relationships, when they grow up. It also has been suggested that children from lesbian homes will be more likely than those from heterosexual backgrounds to themselves adopt a lesbian or gay sexual orientation in adulthood, an outcome that is considered undesirable by courts of law.

In order to address these questions, we followed up the children first seen in 1976–1977 by Golombok et al. (1983) 14 years later when their average age was 23½ years (Golombok & Tasker, 1996; Tasker & Golombok, 1995, 1997). We were able to contact 25 young adults from lesbian families and 21 young adults from single heterosexual families, representing 62% of the original sample. The follow-up participants did not differ from the nonparticipants with respect to age, sex, or social class. Although the sample size was small, the advantage of the study was that the majority of children were recruited to the investigation before they reached adolescence, and so the results were not confounded by the knowledge of their sexual orientation in adult life. Each young adult took part in a standardized interview designed to assess four key areas of their lives: (a) family relationships, (b) peer relationships, (c) psychological adjustment, and (d) sexual orientation.

By the time of the follow-up, all but one of the original group of single heterosexual mothers had at least one new male partner who lived in the household. Similarly, all but one of the lesbian mothers had a female partner who lived in the family home. Therefore, the young adults from both types of family could report on their experience of stepfamily relationships. In terms of the quality of their current relationship with both their mother and their father, young adults from lesbian backgrounds did not differ from their counterparts from heterosexual homes. However, young adults who had been brought up in a lesbian household described their relationship with their mother's partner significantly more positively than those who had been raised by a heterosexual mother and her new male partner. This difference was found both for their recollections of their relationship with their mother's partner during adolescence, and for their current feelings toward their mother's partner. So, it seems that children from lesbian homes had been able to forge closer relationships with their mother's new female partner than had children from heterosexual households with their mother's new male partner. Detailed examination of the interview data suggested that children from lesbian households could more easily accept a stepparent in their family than children from heterosexual households because she was not necessarily seen as a direct competitor to their absent father; she was more likely to be seen as an additional parent rather than as a replacement parent.

With respect to peer relationships, data were obtained on the proportion of young adults in each group who reported having been teased or bullied during adolescence. Young adults from lesbian families were no more likely to report teasing by peers in general, than those from heterosexual single-parent homes. But with respect to teasing about their own sexuality, there was a tendency for those from lesbian families to be more likely to recall having been teased about being gay or lesbian themselves, although those from lesbian families simply may have been more sensitive to casual remarks from peers, and more likely to recollect incidents that had been quickly forgotten by their counterparts from heterosexual homes. Interestingly, those who were most negative about their experiences of growing up in a lesbian family, and who were most likely to have been teased by peers, tended to come from working-class backgrounds and to live in a social environment that was generally hostile toward homosexuality (Tasker & Golombok, 1997). It seems, therefore, that the social context of the lesbian mother family is an important predictor of the experiences of the child.

The findings relating to psychological well-being show that children raised by lesbian mothers continue to function well in adulthood and do not experience long-term detrimental effects arising from their early upbringing. No differences between young adults from lesbian and heterosexual homes were found for anxiety level or depression as assessed by standard questionnaire measures, and their scores fell within the normal range. In addition, those from lesbian families were no more likely to have sought professional help for anxiety, depression, or stress.

With respect to sexual orientation, three aspects were studied: (a) whether or not the person had experienced same-gender sexual attraction, (b) whether or not the person had experienced same-gender sexual relationships, and (c) sexual identity (i.e., whether the person identified as heterosexual, bisexual, lesbian, or gay). In terms of sexual attraction, there was no statistically significant difference between adults raised in lesbian families and their peers from single-mother heterosexual households in the proportion who reported sexual attraction to someone of the same gender. Nine children of lesbian mothers (six daughters and three sons) and four children of heterosexual mothers (two daughters and two sons) reported same-gender attraction.

Regarding actual involvement in same-gender sexual relationships, there was a significant difference between groups such that young adults raised by lesbian mothers were more likely to have had a sexual relationship with someone of the same gender than young adults raised by heterosexual mothers. None of the children from heterosexual families had experienced a lesbian or gay relationship. In contrast, six children (one son and five daughters) from lesbian families had become involved in one or more sexual relationships with a partner of the same gender.

However, in terms of sexual identity, the large majority of young adults with lesbian mothers identified as heterosexual. Only two young women from lesbian families identified as lesbian, compared with none from heterosexual families. This group difference did not reach statistical significance. So, the commonly held assumption that lesbian mothers will have lesbian daughters and gay sons was not supported by the findings of the study. The large majority of children who grew up in lesbian families (92%) identified as heterosexual in adulthood. It is, of course, possible that participants were reluctant to admit a same-gender sexual identity. However, such underreporting seems more likely among men and women from heterosexual homes, since young adults from lesbian families appeared to be more comfortable in discussing gay and lesbian issues in general.

Perhaps surprisingly, rather more is known about children born through assisted reproduction to lesbian mothers than through assisted reproduction to single heterosexual mothers. In recent years, controlled studies of lesbian couples who conceived their child through DI have begun to be reported. In our U.K. study (Golombok et al., 1997), we compared 30 lesbian mother families with 41 two-parent heterosexual families, using standardized interview and questionnaire measures of the quality of parenting and the socioemotional development of the child. Similarly, Brewaeys, Ponjaert, Van Hall, and Golombok (1997) studied 30 lesbian mother families in comparison with 68 heterosexual two-parent families in Belgium. In the United States, Flaks, Ficher, Masterpasqua, and Joseph (1995) compared 15 lesbian families with 15 heterosexual families, and Chan, Raboy, and Patterson (1998) studied 55 families headed by lesbian and 25 families headed by heterosexual parents. Unlike lesbian women who had their children while married, these mothers planned their family together after coming out as lesbian. The studies are of particular interest because they allow an investigation of the influence of the mothers' sexual orientation on children who are raised in lesbian families with no father present right from the start.

Although the children investigated in the above studies are still quite young (around age 5 to 6 on average), taking the findings together, the evidence so far suggests that they do not differ from their peers in two-parent heterosexual families in terms of gender development. It seems, therefore, that the presence of a father is not necessary for the development of sex-typed behavior for either boys or girls, and that the mother's lesbian identity, in itself, does not have a direct effect on the gender role behavior of her daughters or sons. The children were not cut off from men, however, and many had a close relationship with one or more of the mothers' male friends. In terms of socioemotional development, the children appeared be functioning well; there is no evidence of raised levels of emotional or behavioral problems among children raised in a lesbian mother family from the outset. It is possibly of relevance that, unlike the majority of children in studies of father absence, almost all of those in the present investigation lived in an intact two-parent family with a good relationship between the parents, and had not experienced family disruption as a result of parental separation or divorce. The most significant finding to emerge thus far from the studies of lesbian families with a child conceived by DI is that comothers in two-parent lesbian families are more involved with their children than are fathers in two-parent heterosexual families.

☐ Conclusions

Studying new family forms—solo mother families, planned lesbian mother families, and families created by assisted reproduction—allows us to address questions about the relative importance of family structure on one hand, and the quality of family relationships on the other, for childrens' psychological adjustment, as well as interactions between them. What the findings appear to suggest is that whether children have one parent or two, whether or not they are genetically related to their mother or their father, and whether their parents are homosexual or heterosexual may matter less for children's psychological adjustment than warm and supportive relationships with parents, and a positive family environment.

Nevertheless, research on the consequences for children of growing up in these new family forms is in its infancy and many questions remain unanswered. Of particular interest will be the outcomes for children as they progress through adolescence and into adulthood. How will they feel about their upbringing once they themselves become parents? And, what will be the influence of their family experiences on their own parenting behavior? What will be the effect of finding out that one or both parents is genetically unrelated to them? Or, that the person they thought of as an aunt or uncle is their genetic mother or father? There is a great deal of speculation about these issues. Instead of uninformed opinion, what are needed are systematic studies to establish what actually happens to children and their parents in these new family types.

☐ References

Abidin, R. (1990). *Parenting Stress Index test manual.* Charlottesville, VA. Pediatric Psychology Press.

Ainsworth, M. D. S. (1972) Attachment and dependency: A comparison. In J. L. Gewirtz (Ed.), *Attachment and dependency* (pp. 97–137). New York: Wiley.

Ainsworth, M. D. S. (1979). Attachment as related to mother-infant interaction. In J. Rosenblatt, J. Hinde, C. Beer, & M. Busnel (Eds.), *Advances in the study of behavior* (Vol. 9, pp. 1–51). Orlando, FL: Academic Press.

Ainsworth, M. D. S. (1982). Attachment: Retrospect and prospect. In C. M. Parkes & J. Stevenson-Hinde (Eds.), *The place of attachment in human behaviour.* New York: Basic Books.

Ainsworth, M. D. S., Blehar, M., Waters, E., & Wall, S. (1978). *Patterns of attachment.* Hillsdale, NJ: Erlbaum.

Amato, P. (1993). Children's adjustment to divorce: Theories, hypotheses, and empirical support. *Journal of Marriage and the Family, 55,* 23–38.

Amato, P., & Keith, B. (1991). Parental divorce and the well-being of children: A meta-analysis. *Psychosocial Bulletin, 110,* 26–46.

Bandura, A. (1977). *Social learning theory.* Englewood Cliffs, NJ: Prentice-Hall.

Bandura, A. (1986). *Social foundations of thought and action: A social cognitive theory.* Englewood Cliffs, NJ: Prentice-Hall.

Baumrind, D. (1989). Rearing competent children. In W. Damon (Ed.) *Child development today and tomorrow* (pp. 369–378). San Francisco: Jossey-Bass.

Bell, A. P., & Weinberg, M. S. (1978). *Homosexualities: A study of diversity among men and women.* New York: Simon and Schuster.

Bene, E. (1965a). On the genesis of male homosexuality: An attempt at clarifying the role of the parents. *British Journal of Psychiatry, 111,* 803–813.

Bene, E. (1965b). On the genesis of female homosexuality. *British Journal of Psychiatry, 111,* 815–821.

Bieber, I., Dain, H., Dince, P., Drellick, M., Grand, H., Gondlack, R., Kremer, R., Rifkin, A., Wilber, C., & Bieber, T. (1962). *Homosexuality: A psychoanalytic study.* New York: Basic Books.

Biller, H. B. (1974). *Parental deprivation.* Lexington, MA: Heath.

Bowlby, J. (1969). *Attachment and loss: Vol. 1. Attachment.* London: Hogarth Press.

Bowlby, J. (1973). *Attachment and loss: Vol. 2. Separation: Anxiety and anger.* London: Hogarth Press.

Bowlby, J. (1980). *Attachment and loss: Vol. 3. Loss.* London: Hogarth Press.

Bretherton, I. (1985). Attachment theory: Retrospect and prospect. In I. Bretherton & E. Waters (Eds.), Growing points in attachment theory and research. *Monographs of the Society for Research in Child Development, 50*(1–2, Serial No. 209), 3–38.

Brewaeys, A., Ponjaert, I., Van Hall, E., & Golombok, S. (1997). Donor insemination: Child development and family functioning in lesbian mother families with 4–8 year old children. *Human Reproduction, 12,* no. 6, 1349–1359).

Brodzinsky, D. M. (1987). Adjustment to adoption: A psychosocial perspective. *Clinical Psychology Review, 7,* 25–47.

Bromam, S. H., Nichols, P. L., & Kennedy, W. A. (1975). *Pre-school IQ: Parental and early development correlates.* Hillsdale, NJ: Erlbaum.

Burns, A. (1992). Mother-headed families: An international perspective and the case of Australia. *Social Policy Report, 4,* 1–24.

Burns, L. H. (1990). An exploratory study of perceptions of parenting after infertility. *Family Systems Medicine, 8,* 177–189.

Bussey, K., & Bandura, A. (1984). Influence of gender constancy and social power on sex-linked modeling. *Journal of Personality and Social Psychology, 47,* 1292–1302.

Cassidy, J. (1988), Child-mother attachment and the self in six-year-olds. *Child Development, 59*, 121–134.

Chan, R., Raboy, B., & Patterson, C. (1998). Psychological adjustment among children conceived via donor insemination by lesbian and heterosexual mothers. *Child Development, 69*, 443–457.

Chase-Lansdale, P. L., & Hetherington, E. M. (1990). The impact of divorce on life-span development: Short and long-term effects. In P. B. Baltes, D. L. Featherman, & R. M. Featherman (Eds.), *Life-span development and behavior* (Vol. 10, pp. 105–150). Hillsdale, NJ: Erlbaum

Cherlin, A., Furstenberg, F., Chase-Lansdale, P., Kiernan, K., Robins, P. Morrison, D., & Teitler, J. (1991). Longitudinal studies of effects of divorce on children in Great Britain and the United States. *Science, 252*, 1386–1389.

Clamar, A. (1989) Psychological implications of the anonymous pregnancy. In J. Offerman-Zuckerberg (Ed.), *Gender in transition: A new frontier* (pp. 111–112). New York: Plenum.

Colpin, H., Demyttenaere, K., & Vandemeulebroecke, L., (1995). New reproductive technology and the family: The parent-child relationship following in vitro fertilization. *Journal of Child Psychology and Psychiatry, 36*, 1429–1441.

Cook, R., Golombok, S., Bish, A., & Murray, C. (1995). Keeping secrets: A controlled study of parental attitudes towards telling about donor insemination. *American Journal of Orthopsychiatry, 65*, 549–559.

Cook, R., Parsons, J., Mason, B., & Golombok, S. (1989). Emotional, marital and sexual problems in patients embarking upon IVF and AID treatment for infertility. *Journal of Reproductive and Infant Psychology, 7*, 87–93.

Cox., M. J., Owen, M. T., Lewis, J. M., and Henderson, W. K. (1989). Marriage, adult adjustment and early parenting. *Child Development, 60*, 1015–1024.

Crockett, L. J., Eggebeen, D. J., & Hawkins, A. J. (1993). Father's presence and young children's behavioral and cognitive adjustment. *Journal of Family Issues, 14*, 355–377.

Daniels, K., & Taylor, K. (1993). Secrecy and openness in donor insemination. *Politics and Life Sciences, 12*, 155–170.

Darling, N., & Steinberg, L. (1993). Parenting style as context: An integrative model. *Psychological Bulletin, 118*, 487–496.

De Paulo, B. M. (1992). Nonverbal behaviour and self-presentation. *Psychological Bulletin, 111*, 203–243.

Dunn, J., & McGuire, S. (1992). Sibling and peer relationships in childhood. *Journal of Child Psychology and Psychiatry, 33*, 67–105.

Einwohner, J. (1989). Who becomes a surrogate: Personality characteristics. In J. Offerman-Zuckerberg (Ed.), *Gender in transition: A new frontier* (pp. 123–149). New York: Plenum Press.

Englert, Y. (1994) Artificial insemination of single women and lesbian women with donor semen. *Human Reproduction, 9*, 1969–1971.

Falk, P. J. (1989). Lesbian mothers: Psychosocial assumptions in family law. *American Psychologist, 44*, 941–947.

Ferri, E. (1976). *Growing up in a one parent family.* National Foundation for Educational Research, England: Slough.

Fidell, L., & Marik, J. (1989). Paternity by proxy: Artificial insemination by donor sperm. In J. Offerman-Zuckerberg (Ed.), *Gender in transition: A new frontier* (pp. 93–110). New York: Plenum Press.

Flaks, D. K., Ficher, I., Masterpasqua, F., & Joseph, G. (1995). Lesbians choosing motherhood: A comparative study of lesbian and heterosexual parents and their children. *Developmental Psychology, 31*, 105–114.

Freud, S. (1933). Psychology of women. *New introductory lectures on psychoanalysis* (pp. 3–68). London: Hogarth Press.

Freud, S. (1953). Three essays on the theory of sexuality. In J. Strachey (Ed. and Trans.), *The standard edition of the complete works of Sigmund Freud* (Vol. 7, pp. 125–243). London: Hogarth Press. (Original work published 1905)

Freud, S. (1955). Beyond the pleasure principle. In J. Strachey (Ed. and Trans.), *The standard edition of the complete works of Sigmund Freud* (Vol. 18). London: Hogarth Press. (Original work published 1920)

Golombok, S., Brewaeys, A., Cook, R., Giavazzi, M. T., Guerra, D., Mantovani, A., van Hall, E., Crosignani, P. G., & Dexeus, S. (1996). The European study of assisted reproduction families: Family functioning and child development. *Human Reproduction, 11*, (10), 101–108.

Golombok, S., Cook, R., Bish, A., & Murray, C. (1995), Families created by the new reproductive technologies: Quality of parenting and social and emotional development of the children. *Child Development, 66*, 285–298.

Golombok, S., Murray, C., Brinsden, P., & Abdalla, H. (1999). Social versus biological parenting: Family functioning and the socioemotional development of children conceived by egg or sperm donation. *Journal of Child Psychology and Psychiatry, 40*, 519–527.

Golombok, S., Spencer, A., & Rutter, M. (1983). Children in lesbian and single-parent households: Psychosexual and psychiatric appraisal. *Journal of Child Psychology and Psychiatry, 24*, 551–572.

Golombok, S., & Tasker, F. (1994). Children in lesbian and gay families: Theories and evidence. *Annual Review of Sex Research, 5*, 73–100.

Golombok, S., & Tasker, F. (1996). Do parents influence the sexual orientation of their children? Findings from a longitudinal study of lesbian families. *Developmental Psychology, 32*, 3–11.

Golombok, S., Tasker, F., & Murray, C. (1997). Children raised in fatherless families from infancy: Family relationships and the socioemotional development of children of lesbian and single heterosexual mothers. *Journal of Child Psychology and Psychiatry, 38*, 783–791.

Green, R., Mandel, J. B., Hotvedt, M. E., Gray, J., & Smith, L. (1986). Lesbian mothers and their children: A comparison with solo parent heterosexual mothers and their children. *Archives of Sexual Behaviour, 15*, 167–184.

Grossmann, K. E., & Grossmann, K. (1991). Attachment quality as an organizer of emotional and behavioural responses in a longitudinal perspective. In C. M. Parkes, J. Stevenson-Hinde, & P. Marris (Eds.), *Attachment across the lifecycle* (pp. 93–114). London: Routledge.

Gross, K. E., Grossman, K., Spangler, G., Suess, G., & Unzer, L. (1985). Maternal sensitivity in northern Germany. In I. Bretherton & E. Waters (Eds.), *Growing points of attachment theory and research. Monographs of the Society for Research in Child Development, 50* (1–2, Serial No. 209), 233–256.

Harter, S., & Pike, R. (1984). The pictorial scale of perceived competence for young children. *Child Development, 55,* 1969–1982.

Herzog, E., & Sudia, C. E. (1973). Children in fatherless families. In B. M. Campbell & H. N. Ricciuti (Eds.), Review of child development research (pp. 161–231). Chicago: University of Chicago Press.

Hess, R. D., & Camara, K. A. (1979). Post-divorce relationships as mediating factors in the consequences of divorce for children. *Journal of Social Issues, 35,* 79–96.

Hetherington, E. M. (1988). Parents, children and siblings six years after divorce. In R. Hinde & J. Stevenson-Hinde (Eds.), *Relationships within families.* Cambridge, England: Cambridge University Press.

Hetherington, E. M. (1989), Coping with family transitions: Winners, losers, and survivors. *Child Development, 60,* 1–14.

Hetherington, E. M., Cox, M., & Cox, R. (1982). Effects of divorce on parents and children. In M. E. Lamb (Ed.), *Nontraditional families: Parenting and child development.* Hillsdale, NJ: Erlbaum.

Hetherington, E. M., Cox, M., & Cox, R. (1985). Long-term effects of divorce and remarriage on the adjustment of children. *Journal of the American Academy of Psychology, 24,* 518–530.

Hoopes, J. L. (1990), Adoption and identity formation. In D. M. Brodzinsky & M. D. Schechter (Eds), *The psychology of adoption* (pp. 144–166). Oxford, England: Oxford University Press.

Howes, P., & Markman, H., (1989). Marital quality and child functioning: A longitudinal investigation. *Child Development, 60,* 1044–1051.

Huggins, S. L. (1989). A comparative study of self-esteem of adolescent children of divorced lesbian mothers and divorced heterosexual mothers. In F. Bozett (Ed.), *Homosexuality and the family* (pp. 123–135). New York: Harrington Park.

Humphrey, M., & Humphrey, H. (1988). *Families with difference: Varieties of surrogate parenthood.* London: Routledge.

Isabella, R. S., & Belsky, J. (1991). Interactional synchrony and the origins of infant-mother attachment: A replication study. *Child Development, 62,* 373–384.

Isabella, R. A., Belsky, J., & von Eye, A. (1989). Origins of infant-mother attachment: An examination of interactional synchrony during the infant's first year. *Developmental Psychology, 25,* 12–21.

Izard, C. E., Haynes, M., Chisholm, G., & Baak. K. (1991). Emotional determinants of infant-mother attachment. *Child Development, 52,* 906–917.

Jennings, S. (1991). Virgin birth syndrome. *Lancet, 337,* 559–560.

Karpel, M. (1980). Family secrets. *Family Process, 19,* 295–306.

Kirkpatrick, M. (1987). Clinical implications of lesbian mother studies. *Journal of Homosexuality, 13,* 201–211.

Kirkpatrick, M., Smith, C., & Roy, R. (1981). Lesbian mothers and their children: A comparative survey. *American Journal of Orthopsychiatry, 51,* 545–551.

Klagsbrun, M., & Bowlby, J. (1976). Responses to separation from parents: A clinical test for young children. *British Journal of Projective Psychology, 21,* 7–21.

Kohlberg, L. (1966). A cognitive-developmental analysis of children's sex-role concepts and attitudes. In E. E. Maccoby (Ed.), *The development of sex differences* (pp. 82–173). Stanford, CA: Stanford University Press.

Kovacs, G., Mushin, D., Kane, H., & Baker, H., (1993). A controlled study of the psychosocial development of children conceived following insemination with donor semen. *Human Reproduction, 8,* 788–790.

Kupersmidt, J. B., Coie, J. D., & Dodge, K. A. (1990). The role of poor peer relationships in the development of disorder. In S. R. Asher & J. D. Coie (Eds.), *Peer rejection in childhood* (pp. 276–305). Cambridge, England: Cambridge University Press.

Liben, L. S., & Signorella, M. L. (1980). Gender-related schemata and constructive memory in children. *Child Development, 51,* 111–118.

Lutjen, P., Trounson, A., Leeton, J., Findlay, J., Wood, C., & Renou, P. (1984). The establishment and maintenance of pregnancy using in vitro fertilization and embryo donation in a patient with primary ovarian failure. *Nature, 307,* 174.

Lytton, H., & Romney, D. M. (1991). Parents' differential socialization of boys and girls: A meta-analysis. *Psychological Bulletin, 109,* 267–296.

Maccoby, E. E. (1988). Gender as a social category. *Developmental Psychology, 45,* 513–520.

Maccoby, E. E. (1992). The role of parents in the socialization of children. *Developmental Psychology, 28,* 1006–1017.

Maccoby, E. E., & Jacklin, C. N. (1974). *The psychology of sex differences.* Stanford, CA: Stanford University Press.

Mahlstedt, P. E., & Greenfield, D. (1989). Assisted reproductive technology with donor gametes: The need for patient preparation. *Fertility and Sterility, 52,* 908–914.

Main, M., Kaplan, N., & Cassidy, J. (1985). Security in infancy, childhood and adulthood: A move to the level of representation. In I. Bretherton & E. Waters (Eds.). *Growing points in attachment theory and research, Monographs of the Society for Research in Child Development, 50,* (1–2, Serial No. 209), 66–104.

Martin, C. L. (1989, April). *Beyond knowledge based conceptions of schematic processing.* Paper presented at the meeting of the Society for Research in Child Development, Kansas City, MO.

Martin, C. L. (1991). The role of cognition in understanding gender effects. In H. Reese (Ed.), *Advances in child development and behavior* (Vol. 23, pp. 113–164). New York: Academic Press.

Martin, C. L., & Halverson, C. (1981). A schematic processing model of sex typing and stereotyping in children. *Child Development, 52,* 1116–1134.

Martin, C. L, Wood, C. H., & Little, J. K. (1990). The development of gender stereotype components. *Child Development, 61,* 1891–1904.

Maughan, B. L., & Pickles, A. (1990). *Adopted and illegitimate children growing up with a single parent: What hurts, what helps.* Cambridge, MA: Harvard University Press.

Miller, J. P., Jacobsen, R. B., & Bigner, J. P. (1981). The child's home environment for lesbian vs. heterosexual mothers: A neglected area of research. *Journal of Homosexuality 7,* 49–56.

Mischel, W. (1966). A social learning view of sex differences in behavior. In E. E. Maccoby (Ed.), *The development of sex differences* (pp. 56–81). Stanford, CA: Stanford University Press.

Mucklow, B. M., & Phelan, G. E. (1979). Lesbian and traditional mothers' responses to child behavior and self-concept. *Psychological Reports, 44,* 880–882.

Pagelow, M. D. (1980). Heterosexual and lesbian single mothers: A comparison of problems, coping and solutions. *Journal of Homosexuality, 5,* 198–204.

Papaligouras, Z. (1998). *The effects of in vitro fertilisation on parent-infant communication.* Unpublished Ph.D. thesis, University of Edinburgh, Edinburgh.

Papp, P. (1993). The worm in the bud: Secrets between parents and children. In E. Imber-Black (Ed.), *Secrets in families and family therapy* (pp. 66–85). New York: Norton.

Patterson, C. J. (1992). Children of lesbian and gay parents. *Child Development, 63,* 1025–1042.

Pedersen, D., Moran, S., Sitko, C., Campbell, K., Ghesquire, K., & Acton, H. (1990). Maternal sensitivity and the security of infant-mother attachment: A Q-sort study. *Child Development, 61,* 1974–1983.

Perry, D. G., & Bussey, K. (1979). The social learning theory of sex difference: Imitation is alive and well. *Journal of Personality and Social Psychology, 37,* 1699–1712.

Power, T. G., & Parke, R. D. (1982). Play as a context for early learning: Lab and home analyses. In E. Sigel & L. M. Laosa (Eds.), *The family as a learning environment.* New York: Plenum.

Quinton, D., & Rutter, M. (1988). Parenting breakdown: The making and breaking of intergenerational links. Aldershot, England: Avebury Gower.

Raoul-Duval, A., Bertrand-Servais, M., & Frydman, R. (1993). Comparative prospective study of the psychological development of children born by in vitro fertilization and their mothers. *Journal of Psychosomatic Obstetrics and Gynaecology, 14,* 117–126.

Roll, J. (1992). *Lone parent families in the European community.* London: European Family and Social Policy Unit.

Rutter, M. (1971). Parent-child separation: Psychological effects on children. *Journal of Child Psychology and Psychiatry, 12,* 233–260.

Rutter, M., Cox, A., Tupling, C., Berger, M., & Yule, W. (1975). Attainment and adjustment in two geographical areas: I. The prevalence of psychiatric disorder. *British Journal of Psychiatry, 126,* 493–509.

Rutter, M., Tizard, J., & Whitmore, K. (1970). *Education, health and behaviour.* London: Longmans.

Sants, H. J. (1964), Genealogical bewilderment in children with substitute parents. *British Journal of Medical Psychology, 37,* 133–141.

Schaffer, J., & Diamond, R. (1993). Infertility: Private pain and secret stigma. In E. Imber-Black (Ed.), *Secrets in families and family therapy,* (pp. 106–120). New York: Norton.

Schechter, M. D., & Bertocci, D. (1990). The meaning of the search. In D. M. Brodzinsky & M. D. Schechter (Eds.), *The psychology of adoption* (pp. 62–92). Oxford, England: Oxford University Press.

Shenfield, F. (1994). Particular requests in donor insemination: Comments on the medical duty of care and the welfare of the child. *Human Reproduction, 9,* 1976–1977.

Signorella, M. L., & Liben, L. S. (1984). Recall and reconstruction of gender-related pictures: Effects of attitude, task difficulty, and age. *Child Development, 55,* 393–405.

Signorella, M. L., Bigler, R. S., & Liben, L. S. (1993). Developmental differences in children's gender schemata about others: A meta-analytic review. *Developmental Review, 13,* 106–126.

Singer, L., Brodzinsky, D., Ramsay, D., Steir, M., & Waters, E. (1985). Mother-infant attachment in adoptive families. *Child Development 56,* 1543–1551.

Smith, D. B., & Pedersen, D. (1988). Maternal sensitivity and patterns of infant-mother attachment. *Child Development, 59,* 1097–1101.

Snowden, R. (1990), The family and artificial reproduction. In Bromham et al. (Eds.), *Philosophical ethics in reproductive medicine* (pp. 70–185). Manchester, England: Manchester University Press.

Snowden R,, Mitchell, G. D., & Snowden, E. M. (1983). *Artificial Reproduction: A Social Investigation*. London: Allen and Unwin.

Socarides, C. W. (1978). *Homosexuality*. New York: Aronson.

Stagnor, C., & Ruble, D. N. (1987). Development of gender role knowledge and gender constancy. In L. S. Liben & M. L. Signorella (Eds.), *Children's gender schemata: New directions for child development* (Vol. 38, pp. 5–22). San Francisco: Jossey-Bass.

Stern, M., & Karraker, K. H. (1989). Sex stereotyping of infants: A review of gender labeling studies. *Sex Roles, 20,* 501–522.

Tasker, F., & Golombok, S. (1995). Adults raised as children in lesbian families. *American Journal of Orthopsychiatry, 65,* 203–215.

Tasker, F., & Golombok, S. (1997). *Growing up in a lesbian family.* New York: Guilford Press.

Thompson, R. A., Lamb, M. E., & Estes, D. (1982). Stability of infant-mother attachment and its relationship to changing life circumstances in an unselected middle-class sample. *Child Development, 53,* 144–148.

Triseliotis, J. (1973). *In search of origins: The experiences of adopted people.* London: Routledge and Kegan Paul.

Trounson, A., Leeton, J., Besanka, M. , Wood, C., & Conti, A. (1983). Pregnancy established in an infertile patient after transfer of a donated embryo fertilized in vitro. *British Medical Journal, 286,* 835–838.

Van Balen, F. (1996). Child-rearing following in vitro fertilization. *Journal of Child Psychology and Psychiatry, 37,* 687–693.

Vaughn, B., Egeland, B., & Sroufe, L. A., & Waters, E. (1979). Individual differences in infant-mother attachment at 12 and 18 months: Stability and change in families under stress. *Child Development, 50,* 971–975.

Vuchinich, S., Hetherington, E. M., Vuchinich, R., & Clingempeel, W. G. (1991). Parent-child interaction and gender differences in adolescents' adaptation to stepfamilies. *Developmental Psychology, 27,* 618–626.

Wallerstein, J. S., & Kelly, J. B. (1980). *Surviving the breakup: How children and parents cope with divorce.* New York: Basic Books.

Weaver, S., Clifford, E., Gordon, A., Hay, D., & Robinson, J. (1993). A follow-up study of "successful" IVF/GIFT couples: Socio-emotional well-being and adjustment to parenthood. *Journal of Psychosomatic Obstetrics and Gynaecology, 14*[Special Issue], S5–S16.

Weinraub, M., & Gringlas, M. (1995). Single parenthood: In M. H. Bornstein (Ed.), *Handbook of parenting: Vol. 3. Status and social conditions of parenting* (pp. 65–87). Hove, England: Erlbaum.

CHAPTER

Michelle D. Leichtman

Cultural, Social, and Maturational Influences on Childhood Amnesia

Interviewer: *Do you have any memories from childhood?*
Participant: *No.*
Interviewer: *Do you remember any sad events or happy events that occurred when you were a child?*
Participant: *No.*
Interviewer: *Do you remember any accidents that took place when you were young? A fire, or something like that?*
Participant: *Yes. It happened. A house caught fire.*
Interviewer: *Whose house?*
Participant: *My uncle's.*
Interviewer: *How old were you then?*
Participant: *Thirty-five.*

Excerpt from an interview with a rural Indian goatherd,
translated from the regional language, Kanada.

☐ Introduction

Recent literature on memory development has been peppered by renewed interest in adults' memories of their early lives. Typically, adults have difficulty consciously recollecting experiences from childhood, particularly those that occurred before their fourth birthdays. This difficulty, termed *childhood amnesia*, varies considerably between individuals and populations. As the above excerpt illustrates, recent interviews in rural India revealed that adults there had strikingly little access to early memories—only 12% of participants could provide even one specific memory of a childhood experience (Sankaranarayanan & Leichtman, 1997).

What accounts for childhood amnesia and, further, its variations? This chapter focuses on two families of factors: experiential and maturational. Recent findings in three distinct areas of memory development have implicated both kinds of factors in adult performance on tasks calling for the recollection of childhood events. First, studies of long-term memory during infancy and early childhood have identified characteristics of the early memory system that affect later event recall. These studies have demonstrated an ontogenetic shift from implicit to explicit event memories, and illustrate how culturally transmitted narrative styles affect memory during the preschool years and beyond. Second, direct investigations of adults' memories of childhood events have revealed social environment, culture, and family structure variations that influence whether and in what form childhood events are remembered. Third, recent findings on children's suggestibility have demonstrated a pertinent relationship between source monitoring abilities and event memories. These results have suggested that frontal lobe immaturity, which appears to be related to children's source monitoring problems, also may contribute to childhood amnesia. This chapter presents a selective review of studies in each area, highlighting recent work that colleagues and I have conducted bearing on childhood amnesia. The chapter concludes with a discussion of what our findings mean to the conception of human event memory.

☐ Memory in Infancy and Early Childhood

Traditionally, researchers devoted little attention to the processes of long term memory in childhood, because of the prevailing view that infants had little capacity to make sense of their environments or to meaningfully encode events (James, 1950; Mandler, 1992). Under such circumstances, early experiences would stand little chance of later retrieval from memory in response to prompting. Thus, most work on memory development during infancy concerned only short-term processes, with retention intervals commonly limited to under several minutes (Bornstein & Sigman, 1986; McCall, 1979; Werner & Perlmutter, 1979). However, over the past two decades, researchers have developed new methodologies to study infants and toddlers. These methods have produced some of the most provocative research in developmental psychology, forcing reconsideration of the potential of memory during the first 3 years of life (e.g., Rovee-Collier & Hayne, 1987; Meltzoff, 1988, 1995).

A number of paradigms have revealed that infants and toddlers process and recall substantial information about specific events. Memories are registered earlier in life, and remain accessible to retrieval for longer periods than researchers previously thought possible (e.g., Bauer, Hertsgaard & Dow, 1994; Meltzoff, 1995; Perris, Myers, & Clifton, 1990). But, what is the nature of these early long term memories?

Discussing childhood amnesia, Pillemer and White (1989) proposed a model of long term memory in which two functionally separate memory systems emerge during the course of development. The first system is present from birth and is concerned with social and emotional information. This system operates through images, behaviors, or emotional expressions that are cued by other people, locations, or feelings. Memories of this type are not linked to specific past interactions, but afford general familiarity with emotions, people, or situations that are interpreted within narrow retrieval contexts. For example, a child may remember an uncle he or she rarely sees, but may not recall the details of his or her past encounters with him. In contrast, the second memory system forms during the preschool years, and consists of more socially accessible information. Children can retrieve specific past experiences and learned items, and can make intentional retrieval efforts. Only when this second system is in operation can the child produce memories in response to situational demands and language-based prompting, for example, remembering a specific visit with his or her uncle when asked to do so. Theoretically, children rely solely on the first memory system in the early years of life, while the two memory systems coexist throughout later childhood and adulthood.

This account of the development of event memory captures several critical differences between the memories researchers have observed in very young children and older participants. Consistent with Pillemer and White's (1989) characterization of the early memory system, studies of event memory in infancy have shown clear evidence of implicit processes. Implicit memories are those that people retrieve without the awareness that they are remembering, as is the case whenever past experience unconsciously influences present perceptions, thoughts, or actions (Schacter, 1987).

Experiments utilizing habituation paradigms to evaluate infants' long term recognition have documented evidence of implicit memory. Habituation paradigms frequently use infants' looking behavior as an indicator of their differential attention to novel and familiar stimuli. This method is based on the idea that infants show decreased visual attention to stimuli they recognize as old, while they respond with renewed attention to equivalent novel or forgotten stimuli. Studies based on habituation have revealed delayed recognition from several days to several weeks for a variety of photographs and abstract designs in 5- to 7-month-olds (Fagan, 1971, 1979; Strauss & Cohen, 1980).

Rovee-Collier and colleagues' mobile conjugate reinforcement paradigm has also revealed impressive evidence of recognition after long delays. This paradigm relies on training infants to respond to specific stimuli by kicking their feet to move a mobile. When the context in which infants learned this contingency is reinstated, their anticipatory foot kicking response indicates recognition of the original stimuli.

Results using this method indicate long term memory in 3-month-olds after an 8-day delay, and in 6-month-olds after a 21-day delay (Hartshorn & Rovee-Collier, 1997; Rovee-Collier, 1993; Rovee-Collier & Hayne, 1987).

A central problem in determining the nature of early long term memory processes is the infant's prelinguistic status. When there is no possibility that memories can be described verbally, it often is difficult to determine whether explicit memories exist. Explicit memory, which occurs when individuals knowingly recall the past, is readily apparent when adults call to mind and report the details of a past event, or when they consciously identify having encountered past material within a particular context (Schacter, 1987). These activities provide evidence of "true" memory in adulthood—the ability to sense the past and to recount it (Mandler, 1992). Such memory relies on the ability to construct a mental representation of the past, not simply to provide a conditioned response on reinstatement of a familiar situation (Leichtman & Ceci, 1993; Mandler, 1992; Mandler & McDonough, 1995). Conceptually, this is a prerequisite of the second memory system that Pillemer and White (1989) described, which allows children to dig purposefully into mental representations of past experience.

Theorists have struggled with how to capture evidence of memorial representation in the absence of language, and what constitutes compelling evidence of this in infants. While it is theoretically possible that an infant in a conjugate reinforcement experiment could have an explicit memory of the original learning experience, it would not be prudent to conclude this from his or her foot kicking response. For this reason, theorists have questioned what such studies reveal about the relationship between long-term memory in infancy and adulthood. Clearly, demonstrations of reproductive memory come closer to providing evidence of explicit memory than recognition tasks (Mandler, 1990). These paradigms require infants to act out, or reproduce some aspect of an event, which presumably relies on mental representation at some level (Mandler, 1992).

Several methods targeting reproductive processes have revealed evidence of long-term memory in children under 3 years of age. Evaluating children's anticipation of events as a function of earlier experience is one approach. For example, 5-month-olds have demonstrated the ability to use event sequences, or routines for prediction, after delays of several days to weeks (Kessen & Nelson, 1978; Smith, 1984). In addition, when researchers provided children with materials cuing them to reproduce three-step action sequences, children who were 21 months at exposure did so accurately after a 6-week delay (Bauer & Shore, 1987). Further work showed that 18-month-olds could reproduce the sequences after 8 months, although 14-month-olds could not (Bauer et al., 1994). Related work has shown increased evidence of surprise in 9- to 18-month-olds when expectations established by a past event are violated (LeCompte & Gratch, 1972).

Studies of deferred imitation, which require that participants reproduce unusual behaviors that they previously either observed or acted out, offer more rigorous demonstrations of reproductive memory. Nine-month-olds have imitated the actions they witnessed after 24 hours, and 14-month-olds have imitated modeled actions after a week (Meltzoff, 1988). In a pair of studies using a large sample of 14- and 16-month-olds, Meltzoff (1995) demonstrated significant deferred imitation of experimenter-modeled actions after both 2- and 4-month intervals. These effects were present whether or not children were allowed to practice the behavior immediately after first seeing it modeled. In other words, children imitated the behaviors even when they were not allowed to contemporaneously pair the objects involved in the modeling with specific behaviors. Thus, Meltzoff concluded that the memories children displayed with their imitation after 2 to 4 months did not involve habitual or conditioned learning. Using deferred imitation, McDonough and Mandler (1994) further provided suggestive evidence that 2-year-olds remembered and demonstrated in their behaviors a novel action that they had either observed or performed when they were 11 months old.

Using an alternative method, Perris et al. (1990) provided a striking example of early reproductive memory. Individuals who had participated in an auditory localization experiment at 6½ months, requiring them to reach for a sounding object in a dark or lit room, were brought back to the original laboratory setting and reintroduced to the procedure at either 1½ or 2½ years of age. Children in the older group showed behavioral memory of the earlier laboratory experience by reaching out and grasping the object more than controls, and by acting less startled and more persistent in the testing situation. The younger subjects did not demonstrate similar memories, although this may have been due to very high levels of reaching by control subjects in the younger group.

Also testing after a very long delay interval, Myers, Perris, and Speaker (1994) evaluated the memories of 32-month-olds. In the original study when they were 10 months old, the participants learned to operate a toy on several occasions, and were tested 4 months later. That study indicated familiarity and fast relearning of the original toy operation by the experimental subjects, when contrasted with controls. In the follow-up, children who had been involved in only one training session at 10 months were contrasted with those who had been involved in five early sessions as well as matched controls. The results indicated that any prior experience resulted in greater interest in the target toy, more touching of the toy, and more successful responses to verbal prompts toward its operation. Notably, only children with multiple past experiences were able to operate the toy without demonstration, revealing memory for a sequence of actions they had learned 18 months earlier.

In a further study of reproductive memory processes, Leichtman (1994) presented 147 experimental participants, between 4 months and 3½ years of age, with 50 minutes of interaction with a puppet, distributed over 5 consecutive days. At each session, the puppet had an edible treat hidden under one of two identical mittens. The mitten that contained the treat was removable and consistently on either the right or left hand for each child, while the other mitten was not removable. During the sessions, participants removed the mitten as many times as they desired, and it was replenished each time with a fresh treat. Participants were reexposed to the puppet 3 months, 6 months, or both, after the initial sessions, and their behaviors were evaluated against the behaviors of 64 controls, who had no prior exposure to the puppet.

A substantial portion of participants, as young as 6 months at exposure, demonstrated behavioral effects of prior experience with the puppet when tested after delays of 3 or 6 months. That is, starting at 6 months at exposure, indicators such as the behavior of looking inside the puppets' mittens, the amount of time taken to remove the mittens, and persistence in searching again and again for the treat were reliably affected by prior exposure to the puppet. The memories that these behaviors reflected in the children below 1½ years of age were almost certainly implicit—unconscious reflections of past experience that were not accessible through language. In contrast, the youngest participants to produce spontaneous linguistic references to the past experience after 3 and 6 months were 17 to 18 months of age, respectively, at the time of exposure. This early spontaneous verbal reference was quite unusual however; only 12% of children between 1½ and 2 years of age at exposure made this kind of mention after 3 months, and even fewer did so after 6 months. As would be expected, these numbers increased with age at exposure, to approximately 45% of children in the 2- to 3-year-old group at exposure, and a similar percentage who were 3 to 4 years old when they first encountered the puppet.

A few other experiments report the possibility of verbal references to long past events before the age of 3. Myers, Clifton, and Clarkson (1987) reported that 1 child in a sample of 10 participants just under 3 years old correctly named a hidden object, apparently based on a previous experience at age 11 months. Studies by Fivush, Gray, and Fromhoff (1987) and Fivush and Hamond (1990) also documented spontaneous verbal recall by 2- to 3-year-olds of specific, salient past events more than 6 months after they occurred.

Taken together, these studies indicated that, during the early years of life, long-term memories shift from being wholly implicit to being frequently explicit in nature. The onset of language allows for the clear demonstration of event memories rooted in symbolic representation. Once children acquire narrative skill, their memories, in many respects, resemble the explicit memories retained by adults. Although the contents of preschoolers' recollections may differ substantially from those of adults, by 4 years of age children encode aspects of events that may be responsive to memorial prompting after long delays (Fivush & Hammond, 1990; Pillemer, Picariello, & Pruett, 1994).

Recent studies of preschool children's narrative memories have revealed striking individual differences that appear to result from variations in the social environments in which children grow up. Most dramatically, the nature of children's early conversations with adults appears to influence their event recall in several ways. Personal memories become encoded and subsequently accessible for verbal recall through a process of "co-construction" between children and significant adults (Nelson, 1993). As children acquire linguistic fluency, they learn to talk about personal experiences through discussions about the past with adults. Engaging in such conversations allows children to absorb the dominant narrative structure with which others around them discuss events. Thus, children learn not only to discuss past events in ways that others understand, but also to build organized personal histories from a growing base of autobiographical memories (e.g., Fivush & Hudson, 1990; Nelson, 1993; Tessler & Nelson, 1994).

Current research has suggested considerable variation in maternal styles of talking with children, and investigators have identified two broad styles of parental talk about the past (Fivush & Fromhoff, 1988; Reese, Haden, & Fivush, 1993; Pillemer, 1998). While researchers have used various terms to describe the distinction between these styles (e.g., elaborative/high-elaborative vs. pragmatic/repetitive/low-elaborative), the findings have painted a consistent picture of two kinds of mothers in conversation. *High-elaborative mothers* often speak with their children about the past. They provide voluminous descriptive information about past experiences, and frequently prompt children to provide similarly embellished narratives. Even when immature language prohibits children from contributing much substantive information to conversations, these mothers persist undaunted in focusing on the details of past experience. Conversely, *low-elaborative mothers* talk relatively little about past events and provide fewer details during past-centered discussions. When these mothers ask their children about past events, they tend to pose pointed questions with single correct and incorrect answers (Fivush & Fromhoff, 1988; Reese et al., 1993).

Research has suggested a relationship between these differences in maternal style and children's narrative development. In several investigations children of high-elaborative mothers provided richer memory narratives than children of low-elaborative mothers (Haden, Haine, & Fivush, 1997; Hudson, 1990; McCabe & Peterson, 1991). Children of high-elaborative mothers tended to give longer, more detailed, and more descriptive reports about their experiences than other children, even when their mothers were not present at the interviews.

In addition, the contents of children's memorial reports appear to be potently influenced by their discussions with significant adults (Fivush, 1991; Hudson, 1990; Reese et al., 1993). In a dramatic illustration, Tessler and Nelson (1994) tape-recorded dialogues between mothers and children as they walked through a museum together. When researchers interviewed the children 1 week later, they were able to recall exclusively those museum exhibits they had talked about with their mothers. Similarly, Haden, Didow, Ornstein, and Eckerman (1997) interviewed 30- to 42-month-old children about a series of planned events that they experienced with their parents. The children displayed excellent recall of information that was discussed during the events, and poor recall of information that was not discussed.

These studies illustrate the effects of ongoing conversations during events; however, parents also affect the content of children's memories through their postevent conversations. Leichtman, Pillemer, Wang, Koreishi, and Han (1999) documented this effect in a study of 15 4- to 5-year-old children. One morning, the children experienced a surprise event in their preschool classroom. Their former teacher, Martha, whom they had not seen for 3 months, came for a visit with her new baby, Maisy. A series of scripted activities occurred during the visit: Martha placed Maisy in the center of the circle of seated children, she distributed a different baby-related item to each child (e.g., diaper pin, rattle), she received and opened several gifts, and she gave out baby biscuits as a snack. On the same day, mothers interviewed their own children individually about the event. Mothers were not present during the event and, at the outset of the interviews, researchers told them that Martha and Maisy had visited, but gave them no other details about what occurred. Researchers instructed mothers to question their children in whatever way they wished. Three weeks later, children were interviewed by a researcher who had not been present during the original event and who had no information about the content of the parent-child interviews. The researcher asked each child the same set of nine questions. She began with an open-ended question: "A few weeks ago something very special happened at school. Martha brought her baby in for a visit. I wasn't there, but I am really interested in what happened. What happened when Martha brought her baby in for a visit?" The researcher then asked eight direct questions about the event, including the following: "I heard that Mary brought a present for the baby. What was the present?" "I heard that you got to hold something. What did you get to hold?" "I heard that Martha brought other baby things for children to hold. What other things did Martha bring?" Both interviews were audiotaped and later transcribed for coding purposes.

The results of both interviews were coded on a host of variables that captured the structure and style of mother's questions and children's responses, as well as the specific content of the memories children provided. The coding of structure and style variables was adapted from previously validated schemes (Fivush & Fromhoff, 1988; Reese & Fivush, 1993). These variables included indicators of volume of speech (e.g., number of sentences spoken), number and type of questions mothers asked (e.g., memory questions such as "who" and "where" vs. yes-no questions), use of contextual statements and descriptives. Specific content variables included the number of objects, actions, time statements, and total correct details that children provided.

The results indicated that mothers' conversational style predicted the amount of information children provided during the mother-child interview. The degree to which mothers used an elaborative style of questioning their children (e.g., prompting children for details with open-ended and yes-no questions and using contextual and evaluative statements in the interviews) predicted the number of sentences children produced, the number of correct details they remembered, and the number of descriptive terms they used to explain their memories. Moreover, the mother's questioning style significantly affected children's responses during the researcher-child interview 3 weeks later. Children whose mothers gave them more elaborative-style interviews were not necessarily more talkative with the researcher than other children, but they remembered more accurate details regarding what occurred during Martha's visit. Furthermore, children's recall of the specific objects Martha distributed during the event was influenced by their conversations with their mothers. Across the sample as a whole, 83% of the items that children recalled during the researcher-child interview also had been discussed with their mothers. Thus, revisiting the details of personally experienced events in conversation with adults appears to strengthen children's memories, increasing the likelihood that talked about aspects of their experiences will remain accessible to verbal prompting at later dates.

The powerful effects of discussion on young children's memories are readily apparent in available evidence from cross-cultural studies. Recent work has suggested that parental conversational styles may vary at the cultural level, as a function of larger societal norms dictating the appropriateness of extended discussions about the personal past. For example, a key dimension along which parental conversation styles vary is the independent-interdependent distinction that Markus and Kitayama (1991, 1994) proposed. According to these theorists, Western societies typically promote an independently oriented construal of self, which emphasizes the relative importance of the unique inner attributes of the individual. Eastern cultures tend to espouse an interdependently oriented construal of self, emphasizing the relative importance of others in evaluating one's own position in society. Within the social psychological literature, these divergent perspectives show extensive effects on socialization and cognition (Fiske, Kitayama, Markus, & Nisbett, 1997). The Western perspective, which encourages individuals to "stand out," consequently deems self-expression and the sharing of self-relevant autobiographical memories desirable. In contrast, Eastern cultures may discourage excessive talk about the self and, consequently, encourage less discussion of the personal past (Markus & Kitayama, 1991; Mullen, 1994).

Mullen and Yi's (1995) analysis of naturally occurring conversation between Korean or American mothers and their 40-month-old children supported this contrast. Researchers tape-recorded 1 entire day of at-home dialogue between mothers and their children in each culture. The results indicated that the Korean dyads engaged in past event talk only about one third as often and in far less detail than the American dyads. The amount of children's contributions to each episode of past event talk was constant between cultures, although American mothers talked more than Korean mothers when discussing all aspects of past events except social norms. Mullen proposed that the divergent self-concepts associated with independent and interdependent cultures may influence socialization goals which, in turn, are reflected in conversations between parents and children.

Choi's (1992) study of Canadian and Korean mothers supported Mullen's suggestion that differential socialization is responsible for cultural variation in maternal communication styles. In an analysis of the types of questions Korean and Canadian mothers posed to children, Choi found that Korean mothers did not often seek information, but instead prompted children to confirm information already presented to them. Neither did Korean mothers encourage children to introduce their own ideas into the conversation. Korean mothers often made statements unrelated to children's previous utterances, and expected children to follow their leads. In contrast, Canadian mothers more often followed up and elaborated on children's utterances, encouraged children to contribute ideas, and took a partnership, rather than leadership role, in conversation. Notably, the conversational style of Korean mothers in Choi's sample resembled that of low-elaborative American mothers in other studies, while the conversational style of Canadian mothers resembled that of high-elaborative American mothers (e.g., Fivush & Fromhoff, 1988, Leichtman et. al., 1999).

Given the variation across cultures in parental conversational styles, questions of interest are exactly how, and at what point in development children's memorial narratives begin to reflect these variations. To address this question, Han, Leichtman, and Wang (1998) conducted a comparative study of memory in upper-middle class, urban Korean, Chinese, and American 4- and 6-year-old children. The United States is a prototypically independently oriented society, while Korea and China are two interdependently oriented societies whose cultures differ enormously in other respects, including language, politics, history, and contemporary lifestyles. Researchers interviewed 50 children from each culture in their home countries and in their native languages, asking the same series of free recall questions about recent personally experienced events (e.g., questions about what the child did at bedtime the day before, a time when the child was scolded, a recent event that was fun). In addition to this autobiographical interview, researchers showed all children an identical slide show story, and gave them a story memory test after a 24-hour delay. Researchers included the story memory test in order to explore whether predicted cross-cultural differences would be unique to autobiographical reports, or whether they would extend to general narrative skill development and answers to objective questions.

The findings pertaining to children's autobiographical narratives indicated a rich array of differences between the three cultural groups, following a general pattern reflective of the independent-interdependent distinction. The volume of children's narratives, measured in terms of both the number of words and propositions they spoke, was surprising: American and Chinese children provided voluminous reports of past events, while Korean children provided only brief reports. However, the number of words per proposition told a different story. While Americans used many words per proposition, both Korean and Chinese children used far fewer. This finding indicated that American children's units of thought were comparatively long and complex, suggesting an elaborated, descriptive style of talking about the past. Qualitatively, American children generally provided rich, fleshed out descriptions of one or two single activities (e.g., a long description of taking a bath, including a detailed description of bathtub activities, objects present, and dialogue), whereas both Korean and Chinese children provided skeletal descriptions of multiple events (e.g., "watched television, took a bath, brushed my teeth, went to bed"). The major difference between autobiographical narratives of the two Asian groups was that Chinese children talked about a greater number of activities than Korean children.

Consistent with predicted contrasts between independently and interdependently oriented societies, Americans used more descriptives (i.e., adjectives, adverbs, modifiers), more terms expressing personal preferences (e.g., "I really wanted the red bag"), more personal judgments and opinions (e.g., "The game was boring") and more personal thoughts or cognitions (e.g., "I forgot about that") in talking about their experiences compared to children from both Asian countries. Furthermore, Americans provided many more memories that qualified as "specific"; that is, memories that clearly referred to a one point in time episode as opposed to routine episodes or multiple events. Finally, when the ratio of references to other people versus the self in children's narratives was calculated, the findings revealed that American children made comparatively more self references than children in either Asian culture.

Each of the above findings is consistent with the notion that independently oriented American adults encourage children to focus on themselves, their personal feelings, reactions, and thoughts during autobiographically relevant experiences, and model a relatively elaborative style of conversing about personal life events, emphasizing the unique details and social value of discussing the past. The findings also support the suggestion of an interdependently oriented Asian perspective that encourages children to focus more on others than themselves, to conform to societal norms instead of focusing on their own preferences or immediate emotions, and to avoid excessive, potentially boastful conversation about the details of their own experiences. In terms of developmental trends, children in all cultures increased their narrative volume, memorial elaboration, and discussion of personal preferences and cognitions with age. However, by age 4, the American children provided narratives that were specific and elaborative in nature, while the Korean and Chinese children spoke about their experiences in more general and unelaborated terms. By the time the Asian children were 6 years old, their narratives were characterized by a degree of specificity similar to that of the American 4-year-olds.

Children in all three cultures recalled the objective elements of the story with equal accuracy after a day-long interval. A notable difference among cultural groups arose in questions that required children to report the emotions experienced by the story's protagonist, Bear, at various points in his adventures. Researchers posed prompted questions to probe children's recollections of the story's emotional content. For example, regarding a scene in which Bear's mother told him that it was time to leave the playground while he was playing happily with his friends, researchers asked, "How did Bear feel when he had to leave the playground?" There was no single correct answer to these questions about emotions, as each required interpretation of the circumstances in which the protagonist found himself or herself.

For all such questions, the majority of U.S. children answered that the bear felt a negative emotion such as sad, scared, or bad, while the majority of children in both Asian samples answered that the bear felt a positive emotion such as good, happy, or excited. When researchers asked children to justify their answers, American children reported that Bear was upset by his mother's request that he depart from his friends. Asian children's answers showed greater acceptance of the will of authorities; they typically reported that Bear responded positively to his mother's request because he had had the opportunity to enjoy his friends. Consistent with data indicating that Japanese children are less likely than Americans to express negative emotions such as anger (Zahn-Waxler, Friedman, Cole, & Mizuta, 1996), these data indicated that emotional reactions may vary between independently and interdependently oriented cultures. Children may be less likely to react to adult requests with contrary thoughts and emotions when they are raised in societies which place a premium on social harmony, personal discipline, and obedience. As the story memory task suggests, differences in emotional interpretation during events may subsequently contribute to differences in children's autobiographical narratives.

In sum, the building blocks of autobiographical memory are present early in infancy, when durable long-term memories of events are laid down in a form that is responsive to cuing at the implicit level. After age 2, memory emerges in a form that is increasingly explicit, consciously accessible, and responsive to linguistic prompting. During the early period of children's acquisition of narrative skills, children's narrative expression is influenced by individual differences and cultural differences that reflect the norms of discourse around them. Nonetheless, from age 4 to 6 years, the narrative system is refined (Fivush & Hudson, 1990; Nelson, 1996), and children's memories of personal events reflect a developing proficiency with language and the pragmatics of social discourse.

☐ Childhood Memories Recalled by Adults

While research only recently has begun to document the extent of young children's event memories, investigators have been aware for over a century that most adults can consciously recollect relatively few memories of early childhood (Pillemer & White, 1989; Rubin, 1982). Freud pointed out that, in turn of the century Vienna, most adults had difficulty retrieving memories from before they were 6 to 8 years old (Freud, 1920/1953). This curious fact—that adults experienced what Freud called "amnesia" for early life events—has also interested contemporary theorists (Howe & Courage, 1993; Leichtman & Ceci, 1993; Perner & Ruffman, 1995). Systematic investigations conducted in the United States have indicated that, on average, adults are unable to consciously recollect events experienced before 3½ years of age (Kihlstrom & Harackiewicz, 1982; Pillemer & White, 1989; Sheingold & Tenney, 1982). For example, an early study by Waldfogel (1948) indicated that college students had difficulty generating memories of events that occurred before age 3, while they were able to report many more memories that occurred after age 5. Similarly, Wetzler and Sweeney's (1986) analysis of Rubin's (1982) data showed greater deficits in memory for events occurring before age 3 than later in childhood.

In view of recent findings concerning cultural differences in parental conversational style and young children's narrative reports, cross-cultural data on adult autobiographical memory is particularly intriguing. Several recent studies have suggested that there are cultural variations in the date of adults' earliest memories as well as in the qualitative characteristics of autobiographical reports. A few studies that offer insight into the independent-interdependent distinction have been conducted in interdependently oriented cultures, occasionally including comparative U.S. samples. In addition to offering a perspective on how early socialization may affect long-term autobiographical memories of childhood, the studies reported below provided insight into a number of other factors in children's environments that appear to be related to the nature of adults' retrospective reports.

In a groundbreaking comparison of adult autobiographical memory across cultures, Otoya (1988) studied bilingual adults proficient in both Spanish and English. Half of the sample was monocultural, consisting of individuals who grew up in bilingual families in the United States, while the other half was bicultural, consisting of individuals who moved to the United States from Central or South America some time after their sixth birthdays. Participants reported the first three memories they could think of from before the age of 8, and then dated each memory. Otoya found that monocultural participants dated their earliest memories at 3.8 years of age on average, while bicultural participants dated their earliest memories at 5.1 years of age.

One interpretation of these results is that the abrupt shift which bicultural participants experienced in moving to the United States interfered with their ability to retrieve memories from before the move (Otoya, 1988; Pillemer & White, 1989). This interpretation fits with the proposal that any dramatic transition in a child's social environment will render preexisting memories more difficult to retrieve (Neisser, 1967; Schactel, 1947). Just as continuity in the retrieval environment should facilitate recall by providing a rich variety of contextual cues to earlier events, abrupt changes in a child's mindset may inhibit later memory by minimizing associations between the present and past.

While environmental transitions during childhood may indeed have contributed to the monocultural-bicultural difference Otoya recorded in the age of earliest memory, more recent international data has suggested another plausible explanation. This difference may have been due to subtle variations in the children's environments prior to the age at which the bicultural participants moved. Although parents of individuals in the two samples were raised in similar cultural milieus, for the participants themselves, growing up in the United States versus Central or South America may have introduced autobiographically relevant environmental differences. For example, while early parent-child conversations may have been similar for participants from the two samples, discussions with adults outside the family, in a larger society with less homogeneity and different values that those of the Latin American world, may have contributed to monocultural participants' ability to recall earlier memories.

The factors present early in life that might contribute to such effects on adult autobiography were highlighted by a number of studies conducted with Asian populations. As discussed earlier, living in a culture focused on interpersonal harmony and attention to others, in which attention to the self is discouraged and talk about the personal past is uncommon, appears to influence the nature of preschoolers' autobiographical reports. It follows that adults' reports of their own life experiences should reflect the normative differences in cultural orientation captured by the independent-interdependent distinction, and that memories of early life events—from the period during which normative narrative structures are first being absorbed—might be especially vulnerable to cultural differences.

Mullen's (1994) research appeared to support this connection. In a series of questionnaire studies, Mullen found that, on average, the earliest memories reported by a mixed group of Asians and Asian Americans were approximately 6 months later than those of White Americans. Subsequent comparison of the age of earliest memories of native Koreans and White Americans revealed an even larger difference of 16.7 months in the same direction (Mullen & Yi, 1995). These results relate provocatively to the pattern of findings reported in studies of Korean children: Korean parents' low-elaborative style of past event discussion and Korean children's abbreviated manner of discussing the past may indicate little early focus on the personal past and, consequently, few explicit, verbally accessible adult memories of specific early events.

In a study of 255 Chinese adults, Q. Wang, Leichtman, and White (1998) obtained findings that complement Mullen's (1994) Korean data. High school and college students living in Beijing were asked to write down and date their earliest memory, and then to provide three additional childhood memories. The results indicated that, on average, Chinese adults' earliest memory dated from 3 years 9 months; several months later than typical findings among U.S. populations.

In addition, this study evaluated the influence of a number of specific factors in children's environments on adult autobiographical memories. Regression models including cohort and other factors of interest as covariates were used in analyzing the results, so that the effects reported below are independent of the historical timing of participants' births. A central question was whether the memories of participants who grew up as only children ($N = 99$) would differ from those who grew up with siblings ($N = 156$). The one-child policy, in place in China since 1979, provided a unique opportunity to evaluate the role of family structure in influencing autobiographical memory among persons from otherwise equivalent backgrounds. Significant literature has suggested that the "4-2-1 syndrome" present in Chinese only child families, whereby four grandparents and two parents focus completely on one child, may create an environment that departs considerably from traditional Chinese collectivist values (Lee, 1992). Some reports have characterized Chinese only children, popularly described as "little emperors," as more self-centered, willful, and egocentric, and less disciplined, obedient, and other-oriented than children from larger families (Fan, 1994; Jiao, Ji, & Jing, 1986; Z. W. Wang et al., 1983). These differences amount to a less traditionally interdependent orientation among children from only child families. A central question was how differences in the extent to which children from each type of family were encouraged to focus on themselves would be reflected in their later autobiographical memories of childhood.

To evaluate this question, all participants completed two written questionnaires in Chinese. The first, a version of Kuhn and McPartland's (1954) Twenty Statements Test eliciting self-descriptions, asked participants to fill in blanks in repeated sentences phrased "I am _____." The second asked participants to describe and date their earliest memory and to do the same for three other childhood memories. The results confirmed expectations of differences between only child and sibling child groups on both measures. Importantly, for each analysis reported below, contrasts between only-child participants and first-borns showed the same results as those reported for only child and all sibling child participants. Thus, although firstborns were only children before the births of their first sibling (for an average of 4.37 years in this sample), this early experience did not result in their resembling only children on any relevant measures.

Each answer to the Twenty Statements Test was categorized as an expression of a private, collective, or public self-description. This scoring method has been used in past studies as an index of how self-related information is differentially organized in memory across individuals (Bochner, 1994). Private self-descriptions focus on personal traits, states, or behaviors (e.g., "I am tall, intelligent, nervous."), collective self-descriptions focus on group membership (e.g., "I am a girl, a member of the Grimaldi family, a Catholic"), and public self-descriptions focus on the way in which a person interacts with or is viewed by others (e.g., "I am a person others view as kind," "I am someone who likes to help other people") (Greenwald & Pratkanis, 1984; Triandis, 1989). Past work has indicated that participants from independent cultures typically provide overwhelmingly private self-descriptions, while participants from interdependent cultures provide more collective self-descriptions (Bochner, 1994; Trafimow, Triandis, & Goto, 1991). Such differences presumably stem from independently oriented participants giving priority to personal values and goals, and having richly furnished, highly organized, and readily accessible sets of information about the private self in memory. In contrast, interdependently oriented persons focus significantly on the values and goals of the group and, thus, have similarly rich and accessible information regarding the collective self (Markus & Kitayama, 1991; Triandis, 1989).

This same contrast was apparent in the analysis of Chinese only and sibling child participants. Only child participants reported more private self-descriptions and fewer collective self-descriptions than sibling child participants. These findings support the notion that children from the two family structures may organize self-relevant information differently, despite the fact that they are part of the same larger cultural milieu.

In terms of autobiographical memories, only child participants reported earliest memories dated from 39 months, while siblings reported earliest memories that were dated from 47.7 months, or almost 9 months later. The nature of the reported memories also differed between groups on a number of qualitative dimensions: only child participants reported fewer memories focusing on social interactions, more memories focusing on personal experiences and feelings, fewer memories focusing on family, and more memories focusing solely on themselves. In addition, only child participants reported a greater number of memories that were specific in nature (i.e., referring to one point in time events) than their sibling counterparts. Finally, only child participants' memories contained a lower ratio of other-self mentions, indicating a differentially greater focus on their own past thoughts and activities. In addition to these between group differences, across the sample as a whole, participants' scores on the self-description questionnaire were predictive of a number of the autobiographical memory measures. Private self-description scores were positively related to memory narrative volume, mentions of the self, and the specificity of autobiographical memories, while collective self-description scores were negatively related to each. This combined evidence suggests a relationship between variables in the participants' early environments that affected the extent of focus on the self, and the degree and content of the autobiographical memories that remained accessible into adulthood.

Independent of family status, participants who attended preschool reported earliest memories that were 11 months earlier than those who did not and, the earlier preschool attendance began, the earlier was the first memory reported. Similarly, the employment status of participants' mothers during their childhood years was related to participants' autobiographical memories; a striking finding, given that all participants were top scholars enrolled in highly elite Chinese schools at the time of the study. Participants whose mothers either were professionals or urban workers had memories dating from 40 and 45 months on average, respectively, while participants whose mothers were farmers during their childhoods had memories dating from the later period of 56 months. This contrast is perhaps best conceived of as a rural-urban distinction. It is possible that socialization differences, such as farmers' children's engagement in collaborative work and the urban environment's greater emphasis on competition, self-actualization, and adaptation to modernization affected the degree to which participants focused on autobiographical events during childhood and, consequently, recalled them later.

In a study that further explored memories of childhood in rural versus urban populations, Sankaranarayanan and Leichtman (1997) focused on a sample of 26 adults living in a remote village of goatherds in southern India, and 24 participants from a comparable low socioeconomic status (SES) population, living in urban Bangalore. A trained interviewer raised in the same region as the participants conducted interviews in the regional language, Kanada. The interviewer asked participants a series of scripted questions about autobiographical memory, beginning with an open-ended question asking whether they recalled any events from childhood. The interviewer asked participants to recount their childhood memories, and further prompted participants to relate any happy events and any sad events that they could recall. For each memory provided, the researcher asked participants their age at the time of the event.

Only 12% of participants in the rural sample and 30% of participants in the urban sample reported a specific event memory from childhood during the interview. Specific event memories were those that referred to a one point in time event (e.g., "the day my father fell into the well"), as opposed to routine or scripted activities (e.g., "going to school"). While all participants in the rural sample who reported a specific memory provided only one during the interview, 17% of participants in the urban sample provided two or more memories. Most participants in both samples did not know their own birth dates, and could not date their memories. However, of six urban participants who stated their age at the time of the events they recollected, age estimates ranged between 6 and 11 years.

To examine whether there were systematic differences in the qualitative aspects of the rural and urban participants' reports, 10 American raters, blind to all aspects of the study, assisted in a coding task. Raters were given a stack of 69 index cards, each with a single memory provided by a rural Indian, urban Indian, or an American control participant (one third each) in response to the same memory questions. All Indian memories that appeared on the cards were English translations, and culturally identifying information (e.g., names of Indian foods, local place references) was replaced with neutral information. (Some memories included in the rural selections were obtained from a supplementary sample of 32 rural participants who also were asked memory questions.) The memories from each group were randomly selected after eliminating all responses in which participants could not provide a memory. The number of words in each memory segment was similar, on average, for the three groups. The cards were shuffled randomly, so that memories from all three groups of participants were mixed.

Raters came to the laboratory and were told that they were to read over the cards and sort them into two approximately equal piles. They were told, "We've been interviewing people about their autobiographical memories. People differ in how vividly they remember and talk about past events. Some peoples' reports reflect very rich, vivid memories of their experiences—it seems like the events just happened yesterday and they recall every detail. Other people have fuzzier, weaker, more skeletal memories of past events, and their reports appear comparatively impoverished, lacking in vividness and richness of details." Participants were then asked to read over the cards and sort them into two approximately equal piles, placing half the cards in a box representing rich, vivid memories and the other half in a box representing relatively impoverished, skeletal reports of past events.

The cumulative results of this sorting revealed distinct patterns for memories of participants from the three populations. Sixty-three percent of those memories provided by Americans were placed in the box representing rich memories, with only 37% placed in the box representing poor memories. Similarly, 54% of memories from urban Indians were rated as rich, while 46% were rated as poor. In contrast, only 27% of rural Indian memories were rated as rich, while 73% were rated as poor. This gross rating scheme thus captured a parallel with the urban-rural difference that Q. Wang et al. (1998) found among Chinese participants: Living in an urban area appears to increase access to early event memories, and to make reports of those memories more vivid and detailed. Notably, although there was a slight difference in years of education favoring urban participants in this study, there was no significant effect of educational status on the number or qualitative characteristics of participants' memories.

By what mechanism might urbanization influence autobiographical memory? As noted in the discussion of Q. Wang et al.'s (1998) Chinese results, differences in general aspects of participants' social environments may have contributed to the later, more skeletal autobiographical reports documented among rural samples. In addition, the informal reactions of Indian participants provides insight into a broader explanation. A large percentage of rural Indian participants responded to questions about their autobiographical memories with an attitude of incredulity. Typically, participants said, "Why think about the past? The past is just as the future," or "It's a silly waste of time to think about the events of one's life; such thinking changes nothing."

When the researcher asked participants directly whether, and under what circumstances they reminisced about past events, rural participants responded almost universally that they rarely did so. In contrast, urban participants seemed more comfortable reflecting on and sharing their life memories, and did not display the same attitude of indifference toward life experiences. Even more strikingly, American participants often noted that their personal memories were an integral part of themselves, that such memories were extremely important to them, and that they commonly reflected on past experiences. These fundamentally different attitudes between groups may, in part, be a function of the need to think about the past in response to change. In rural Indian villages, lifestyles are much as they were generations ago and anticipated changes are few. In urban India or the United States, deciding on a life course and constantly adapting to the changing demands of modernized society may increase individuals' attention to the unique aspects of their personalities and situations, leading to a relatively more introspective attitude toward the personal past. This explanation remains speculative; however, it illustrates the possibility of multiple indirect channels through which particular social environments may affect the nature of autobiographical memories.

Finally, it remains to be noted that the timing and quality of childhood memories may depend, in part, on the events being recalled. Usher and Neisser's (1993) study of the memories of American college students made this point effectively. Participants remembered episodes of hospitalization or births of siblings that occurred when they were between 2 and 3 years old. However, they recalled deaths in the family or moves to new homes only if these events happened after they were 3 years of age. Participants' retrospective ratings of affect and amount of postevent rehearsal were similar across events, such that these two factors did not readily explain the differences between events. However, the amount of preparation children received prior to the events, in the form of discussion with parents and other significant adults, may have differed. While Usher and Neisser's findings indicated group-level differences between various categories of events, the characteristics of the events driving these differences remain to be explained. It is likely that, for all children, particular events share common features that are likely to affect memorial outcomes, for example, the life significance, affect inspired, salience, and associated rumination may be similar for most children facing significant life experiences such as hospitalization. However, individual differences in the context in which these events take place in children's lives also affect their memorability. The broad cultural and social contexts of children's lives affect the meanings they ascribe to various life events, and likewise the manner in which any particular event will later be remembered.

☐ The Suggestibility of Children's Memories

In addition to work on early memory and adult recollections, studies of the suggestibility of children's memory have provided surprising insight on the issue of childhood amnesia. Over the past decade, a burgeoning developmental psychology literature concerning the questions of why, and under what circumstances, children's memories are affected by suggestion has emerged (Ackil & Zaragoza, 1995; Ceci & Bruck, 1993; Leichtman & Ceci, 1995). The central phenomenon of interest is the vulnerability of children's memorial reports to distortion from influences outside the original memory trace.

A large literature currently attests to a developmental trend whereby children's suggestibility declines with age. While adults also are prone to memory distortion (Loftus, 1991; Schacter, 1995), young children's recollections show a particular vulnerability to the effects of misleading information (Ceci & Bruck, 1993, 1995; Lepore & Sesco, 1994). Typically, children's suggestibility has been documented in misinformation paradigms, in which children experience a story or event and, subsequently, receive misleading information about the details that they witnessed. For example, Ceci, Ross, and Toglia (1987) read a story about several events in the life of a protagonist to children between the age of 3 and 12. The day after the reading, a researcher interviewed the participants, asking a series of questions about the story. The researcher included subtle misinformation in his or her questions to experimental participants, while including only correct information in questions to control participants. Two days later, another researcher gave all participants two-item forced choice recognition tasks regarding the items present in the original story. The results indicated that control participants were highly accurate in recognizing the correct original items; the mean for all age groups was between 84% and 95% correct. In contrast, there was a sharp age trend in the experimental group due to younger children's incorrect selection of suggested information or "false alarms": 3- to 4-year-olds achieved a mean of 37% correct, 5- to 6-year-olds a mean of 58% correct, 7- to 9-year-olds a mean of 67% correct, and 10- to 12-year-olds a mean of 84% correct.

More naturalistic paradigms have demonstrated similar age effects. For example, Leichtman and Ceci (1995) conducted a study of 3- to 6-year-olds centering on an event staged in their preschool classrooms. The event was the unannounced visit of a man named Sam Stone. Sam Stone simply entered the children's classrooms while they were gathered in a circle, said hello, chatted, looked around the room, and left after several minutes. Researchers gave children in an experimental group a series of four misleading interviews over the course of 8 weeks. During each interview, the researchers assumed in their questioning that Sam Stone had committed clumsy acts during his visit, such as spilling and breaking things. The questions thus centered on the circumstances and details of these acts. When interviewed 10 weeks after the event, many experimental group children who participated in misleading interviews appeared convinced that Sam Stone had committed actions in line with the researchers' suggestions. In response to an open-ended question about what happened during Sam Stone's visit, 21% of 3- to 4-year-olds and 14% of 5- to 6-year-olds alleged that Sam Stone committed at least one clumsy act consistent with the suggestions. In response to direct questions regarding actions about which they had been mislead, commission error rates climbed to 53% for younger participants and 38% for older participants. In contrast, control participants of both ages, who received no misleading suggestions after Sam Stone's visit, made almost no such errors under open-ended or direct question conditions 10 weeks after the event.

The growing evidence of disproportionate vulnerability to suggestion among preschoolers has intrigued researchers, inspiring explanations on a number of different levels (e.g., Ackil & Zaragoza, 1995; Welch-Ross, Diecidue, & Miller, 1997). Certainly, under some questioning conditions, social factors play a role in children's suggestibility. Young children, for example, may consciously bow to the suggestions of adult authority figures or mentally question the accuracy of their own recollections in the face of alternative suggestions from powerful adults (Ceci & Bruck, 1993). However, while under some conditions these social factors may give rise to or enhance children's report distortion, there is compelling evidence that fundamental cognitive elements of memory also are affected by misleading information in children's environments.

In the present discussion of factors involved in childhood amnesia, one particular explanation for the suggestibility of children's memory is of central relevance. This is the hypothesis that poor source monitoring skills cause children to make the memorial errors that distort their reports. *Source monitoring* refers to the ability to identify the origin of one's own beliefs and memories. Across a number of experimental paradigms, preschoolers show particular difficulty doing so, commonly making source misattribution errors. For example, in one paradigm, participants are asked either to perform or to imagine performing a number of actions (e.g., standing up, touching their noses). After doing so, younger children are more likely than older children to make source misattributions; they remember performing actions that they only imagined, and vice versa (e.g., Foley & Johnson, 1985; Welch-Ross, 1995a). Similarly, young children have difficulty remembering the circumstances under which they acquired new information. Taylor, Esbensen, and Bennett (1994) conducted a series of studies exploring this phenomenon. They found that, after learning novel facts, 4-year-olds incorrectly stated, and acted as though they believed, that they had always known facts they had learned just minutes earlier. Thus, across tasks requiring source monitoring, young children often are unable to specify the original context in which they encountered information, although they accurately recall the information itself.

Theorists have hypothesized that source misattributions underlie the suggestibility effects induced by misleading information. In the simplest example of how this might occur, children may confuse facts or pictures they were given after an event with those that were part of the event. In suggestibility paradigms involving only verbal questions, repeated suggestive questions may induce children to create images of suggested events while they are being interviewed. During subsequent questioning (e.g., during the fifth interview after Sam Stone's visit or after multiple visualizations in Ceci, Loftus, et al.'s, 1994, card drawing paradigm), children may call to mind the images inspired during past interviews. In doing so, children may have difficulty identifying the origins of these images; that is, they may confuse these internally generated mental pictures with the actual events they experienced. Younger participants may be particularly prone to this confusion, just as they make source misattribution errors with exaggerated frequency under other circumstances.

A set of experiments focusing on 3- to 4-year-olds illustrates the potential contribution of source monitoring to suggestibility effects. In the original study, once each week for 10 weeks, children participated in an interview in which they were asked to draw from the same group of cards. Half of the cards described real events that occurred in the children's classrooms, while the other half referenced events that never happened in the children's lives (Ceci, Crotteau, Smith, & Loftus, 1994). During each one-on-one session with a researcher, the children drew one card at a time until all of the cards had been drawn. After the children drew each card, the researcher read the event described on the card aloud, and asked, "Think real hard, and tell me—did that ever happen to you?" After children answered this question with a "yes" or "no," they moved on to the next card. In the 11th and final week, a new interviewer queried children, asking a similar question for each card. In this session, however, the interviewer also asked children to elaborate. If children said that events on the cards had happened to them, the researcher asked them to tell him or her all about these events. Further, the researcher asked detailed follow-up questions after each open-ended question.

The results indicated that, by the final interview, more than one third of children reported remembering an event that never actually occurred; in most cases, events they originally denied remembering. Moreover, the children's inaccurate reports were internally consistent, full of vivid detail, and accompanied by a confident attitude. When condition-blind adult raters were asked to discriminate between the children's accurate and inaccurate memories, they were unable to do so at a level above chance.

A second study focused on the emotional nature of the imagined events, and how this might influence the children's susceptibility to incorporating the events into memory (Ceci, Loftus, Leichtman, & Bruck, 1994). Here, the manipulation was a bit more heavy handed; during the weekly sessions, researchers actively encouraged children to visualize events to which they acquiesced. The suggested events were either positive (getting a present), neutral (waiting for a bus), or negative (falling off a tricycle and cutting one leg). The results indicated that, while children were quite accurate from start to finish in reporting on the events that had actually occurred, the mean false assent rate (or rate of commission errors) rose dramatically across interviews. Three- to 4-year-olds and 5- to 6-year-olds showed similar increases in false assents across interviews, although in accordance with common development trends in suggestibility, younger children had a higher rate of baseline errors. Notably, all types of events were subject to the effects of imagining, although not equally so—negative events reflected fewer commission errors than positive. Thus, emotional content may be among the parameters that influence the difficulty of discriminating real from imagined events.

Studies of both source monitoring and suggestibility have shown substantial individual differences among children. On both types of tasks, even the performance of children in the most error-prone preschool age group varies widely; while participants on the whole make a substantial number of errors, there are individuals who consistently resist suggestions and correctly identify the origins of their past experiences. Schacter, Kagan, and Leichtman (1995) noted that children's source monitoring problems and memorial suggestibility were similar to the source amnesia and high rates of false recognition found among adults with frontal lobe damage. Given this parallel, Schacter et al. suggested that both the phenomena of suggestibility and source misattributions might be caused by immature frontal lobe development in preschoolers. Individual differences between children on both types of tasks could then be explained by differential maturity of the frontal regions.

Support for this provocative suggestion required evidence of a direct relationship between source monitoring and suggestibility performance in young children. Thus, Leichtman and Morse (1997), conducted a series of experiments to examine this relationship. In each study, the same 45 3- to 5-year-old children were given several traditional source monitoring tasks as well as multiple tasks measuring memorial suggestibility. In an illustrative study (Leichtman & Morse, 1997, Study 2), researchers gave children two measures of source monitoring, and two measures of suggestibility. The first source monitoring task was an adaptation of Gopnik and Graf's (1988) paradigm, in which a researcher showed children a set of six small drawers, each containing a different small object. Children learned what was inside each drawer by either being told, guessing from a clue provided them, or opening the drawer. Just after learning the drawers' contents, the researcher asked children to identify the object inside each of the closed drawers. Immediately afterward, he or she asked them to tell him or her how they learned what was inside each drawer—by seeing the object, being told about it, or guessing it with a clue.

The second source monitoring task was an adaptation of the do-imagine task designed by Foley and Johnson (1985). A researcher led children through a series of simple actions, and asked them either to actually perform or to imagine performing each one. After completing the entire list, the researcher asked the children to list all of the actions they remembered performing or imagining. Finally, she reminded the children of each of the actions, and asked whether they had performed or imagined each.

The first suggestibility task was a version of the misinformation paradigm often given to adults. Researchers showed children a narrated slide show story that included several target events. One day after they viewed the story, an interviewer asked children misleading questions about it. One week later, another interviewer gave children a forced-choice picture recognition task including the suggested detail and the original information. This forced-choice task required children to identify which was the original object they had seen in the story.

The second suggestibility task was similar to the visualization paradigm developed by Ceci and colleagues (Bruck, Ceci, & Hembrooke, 1997; Ceci, Crotteau, et al., 1994; Ceci, Loftus, et al., 1994). Children were questioned once per week about the same six events; three events that they actually experienced, and three events that never happened (e.g., a boy visited school with a little puppy; a teacher found $100 under a slide). Each week, children drew the events from a hat in random order. A researcher asked children whether each occurred, and then asked them to imagine the events that they said did not occur. A final interview occurred during the seventh week, when another researcher asked children to tell whether each event occurred and then to elaborate on what they remembered about the event.

The results of this series of tasks show a compelling pattern of connection between children's source monitoring skills and their ability to resist memorial suggestion. As expected, scores indicating accurate source identification on the two source monitoring tasks (i.e., the drawer and do-imagine tasks) were highly correlated with each other ($r = .62$). Scores indicating the ability to resist suggestion on the two disparate suggestibility tasks (i.e., the traditional story misinformation paradigm and visualization task) also were significantly correlated ($r = .34$). The four critical correlations—between each of the source monitoring tasks and each of the suggestibility tasks—all were highly significant ($p < .001$), ranging between -.75 and -.85. Thus, the better children were at identifying the context in which they acquired knowledge in the source monitoring tasks, the less vulnerable they were to suggestion.

Importantly, measures indexing simple recognition of story details and recall of actions performed were not significantly related to either source monitoring skills or suggestibility. It appears that the relationship between suggestibility and source monitoring was not simply the outcome of globally better memory among some children; the two measures were more specifically related. Although this relationship is not definitive evidence of frontal lobe control of both processes, it strongly supports the theoretical possibility. Other aspects of children's cognitive development that contribute to the variance in suggestibility performance also may be either directly or indirectly related to improvements in frontal lobe functioning. For example, Welch-Ross and colleagues have recently provided evidence that children's understanding of conflicting mental representations in theory of mind tasks also show strong correlations with suggestibility scores (Welch-Ross et al., 1997). Whether these are an outgrowth of improvements in source monitoring skills or independent contributors to their development remains to be seen.

The cumulative literature on children's suggestibility and source monitoring has suggested that maturational processes significantly influence whether children are prone to incorporating "false memories" into their autobiographical repertoires. This literature also has provided an alternative perspective on the timing of childhood amnesia. The strict measure of autobiographical memory in adulthood is whether memories respond to explicit, verbal cuing. For example, researchers ask participants questions such as, "Tell me about an event that you remember from childhood," "What do you remember about the birth of your younger brother?" "Remember the events of your third birthday?" These are the questions in response to which participants have a reliable dearth of memories from the first 3 to 6 years of life, and which reflect between-culture differences in terms of age boundaries.

Extrapolating from the literature on suggestibility and source monitoring, it may be that, until children reach a critical level of frontal lobe maturity, the memories they encode will not consistently respond to the kind of cues that adult autobiographical memory tasks provide. Fundamentally, children's early performance deficits reflect a failure to integrate the larger context in which an experience occurs with the core facts of that experience. Yet, the cuing of adults' early memories is a process that begins at the very place children's memories are weakest—with the context itself. Asking an adult to remember the events of his or her third birthday is, in some sense, akin to asking a child who has participated in Gopnik and Graf's (1988) drawer task to "remember that thing that you guessed one day with a clue." Many young children are unable to identify how they acquired information about a known object (e.g., by guessing), even minutes after doing so. It is unlikely, then, that being provided with the context cue (e.g., "an object you guessed") would enable these children to recall an object they had otherwise forgotten. In other words, because the associations between context and object are weak, one is unlikely to serve as an effective retrieval cue for the other over the long term. By this reasoning, the problem is not simply that adults fail to access early memories because they do not label them within useful specific contexts during childhood (e.g., "something that's happening now, while I'm 3 years old"). The problem is that the link between the context and the content of the memory is weak at encoding, and the context is the only cue researchers can provide in explicit autobiographical tasks.

This perspective explains a coincidence in the memory development literature that has received limited attention (Welch-Ross, 1995b). On average, adults' earliest autobiographical memories begin during the same period in which source monitoring skills dramatically improve, and in which children become significantly more accurate in discriminating real from suggested events. As literature on the trajectory of childhood memory has pointed out, this period—between age 3 and 5—also represents the upper cusp of an identifiable shift from implicit, behaviorally expressed memories to explicit, verbal processes. Adult autobiographical memory tasks, which probe for explicit, narrative life memories, may come up short with respect to the earliest years of life because they require memories that were encoded in a manner that supports both conscious recollection and a close, lucid, explicitly retrievable association between context and the central elements of experience.

☐ Conclusions

Current evidence regarding the factors that contribute to childhood amnesia calls for a contextualist perspective (Bronfenbrenner, 1993). As researchers discover more about each of the interrelated areas of memory development that explain adults' autobiographical memories, it becomes evident that myriad influences on cognition play a role in the timing and character of early recollections. These influences come from the internal development of children themselves as well as from the many layers of environmental systems around them.

Research on the development of memory within childhood has indicated the overwhelming importance of apparently maturational factors such as the shift from implicit to explicit event memories, and the growing ability to identify the source of acquired recollections. Only when children have achieved these developmental milestones does it appear that durable memories, ripe for conscious recollection in adulthood, can be encoded. Simultaneously, factors within children's microsystems—their most immediate, intimate early environments—shape the kinds of memories they begin to register. From the earliest point at which language is used as a tool for sharing experience, the significant adults in children's lives powerfully influence the shape of their memorial narratives. These significant others largely determine the contents of children's discussions about past events, influencing which details will be strengthened and which will soon fade. Even more important, they affect how children think generally about the meaning of personal experience, and how children allocate attention in the face of novel events that eventually will become memories.

At the broader level of children's macrosystems, or the general cultural milieus in which they live, the beliefs that define children's social experiences also dramatically influence long term memory. As a growing body of cross-cultural literature has suggested, how children think about themselves, their roles in society, and the meaning of their personal experiences emerges, in part, as a function of the cultures in which they grow up. Each of these aspects of children's belief systems, in turn, plays a role in the nature of the autobiographical memories they carry throughout their lives. As early as the preschool years, and perhaps before, whether children's memories are rich and elaborated or skeletal and utilitarian, in part, is a function of the larger values their societies endorse. Moreover, whether children view their own autobiographical memories as an integral part of who they are and who they will become is also dependent on what they learn from the society around them. Research is just beginning to unveil the varieties of autobiographical experience that result from subtle differences across individuals, families, and societies.

☐ References

Ackil, J. K., & Zaragoza, M. S. (1995). Developmental differences in eyewitness suggestibility and memory for source. *Journal of Experimental Child Psychology, 60*, 57–83.

Bauer, P. J., Hertsgaard, L. A., & Dow, G. A. (1994). After 8 months have passed: Long-term recall of events by 1- to 2-year-old children. *Memory, 2*, 353–382.

Bauer, P. J., & Shore, C. M. (1987). Making a memorable event: Effects of familiarity and organization on young children's recall of action sequences. *Cognitive Development, 2*, 327–338.

Bochner, S. (1994). Cross-cultural differences in the self concept. *Journal of Cross-Cultural Psychology, 25*, 273–283.

Bornstein, M. H., & Sigman, M. D. (1986). Continuity in mental development from infancy. *Child Development, 57*, 251–274.

Bronfenbrenner, U. (1993). The ecology of cognitive development: Research models and fugitive findings. In R. H. Wozniak & K. W. Fischer (Eds.), *Development in context: Acting and thinking in specific environments* (pp. 3–44). Hillsdale, NJ: Erlbaum.

Bruck, M., Ceci, S. J., & Hembrooke, H. (1997). Children's reports of pleasant and unpleasant events. In D. Read & S. Lindsay (Eds.), *Recollections of trauma: Scientific research and clinical practice* (pp. 199–219). New York: Plenum Press.

Ceci, S. J., & Bruck, M. (1993). The suggestibility of the child witness: A historical review and synthesis. *Psychological Bulletin, 113*, 403–439.

Ceci, S. J., & Bruck, M. (1995). *Jeopardy in the courtroom: A scientific analysis of children's testimony.* Washington, DC: American Psychological Association.

Ceci, S. J., Huffman, M. L., Smith, E., & Loftus, E. (1994). Repeatedly thinking about non-events. *Consciousness and Cognition, 3*, 388–407.

Ceci, S. J., Huffman, M. L. C., & Smith, E. (1994). Repeatedly thinking about a non-event: Source misattributions among preschoolers. *Consciousness and Cognition, 3*, 388–407.

Ceci, S. J., Loftus, E. F., Leichtman, M. D., & Bruck, M. (1994). The role of source misattributions in the creation of false beliefs among preschoolers. *International Journal of Clinical and Experimental Hypnosis, 42*, 304–320.

Ceci, S. J., Ross, D. F., & Toglia, M. P. (1987). Suggestibility of children's memory: Psycholegal implications. *Journal of Experimental Psychology: General, 116*, 38–49.

Choi, S. H. (1992). Communicative socialization processes: Korea and Canada. In S. Iwasaki, Y. Kashima, & K. Leung (Eds.), *Innovations in cross-cultural psychology* (pp. 103–122). Amsterdam: Swets & Zeitlinger.

Fagan, J. F. (1971). Infants' recognition memory for a series of visual stimuli. *Journal of Experimental Child Psychology, 14*, 453–476.

Fagan, J. F. (1979). The origins of facial pattern recognition. In M. Bornstein & W. Kessen (Eds.), *Psychological development from infancy: Image to intention.* Hillsdale, NJ: Erlbaum.

Fan, C. (1994). A comparative study of personality characteristics between only and nononly children in primary schools in Xian. *Psychological Science, 17*(2), 70–74. (in Chinese)

Fiske, A. P., Kitayama, S., Markus, H. R., & Nisbett, R. E. (1998). The cultural matrix of social psychology. In D. T. Gilbert, S. T. Fiske, & G. Lindzey (Eds.), *The handbook of social psychology* (Vol. 2, 4th ed., pp. 915–981). New York: Oxford University Press.

Fivush, R. (1991). The social construction of personal narratives. *Merrill-Palmer Quarterly, 37*, 59–81.

Fivush, R., & Fromhoff, F. A. (1988). Style and structure in mother-child conversations about the past. *Discourse Processes, 11*, 337–355.

Fivush, R., Gray, J. T., & Fromhoff, F. A. (1987). Two-year-olds talk about the past. *Cognitive Development, 2*, 393–409.

Fivush, R., & Hamond, N. R. (1990). Autobiographical memory across the preschool years: Toward reconceptualizing infantile amnesia. In R. Fivush & J. A. Hudson (Eds.), *Knowing and remembering in young children.* New York: Cambridge University Press.

Fivush, R., & Hudson, J. (1990). *Knowing and remembering in young children.* New York: Cambridge University Press.

Foley, M. A., & Johnson, M. K. (1985). Confusions between memories for performed and imagined actions. *Child Development, 56*, 1145–1155.

Freud, S. (1953). *A general introduction to psychoanalysis.* New York: Simon and Schuster.

Gopnik, A., & Graf, P. (1988). Knowing how you know: Young children's ability to identify and remember the sources of their beliefs. *Child Development, 59*, 1366–1371.

Greenwald, A. G., & Pratkanis, A. R. (1984). The self. In R. S. Wyer & T. K. Srull (Eds.), *Handbook of social cognition* (Vol. 3, pp. 129–178). Hillsdale, NJ: Erlbaum.

Haden, C. A., Didow, S. M., Ornstein, P. A., & Eckerman, C. O. (1997, April). Mother-child talk about the here and now: Linkages to subsequent remembering. In E. Reese (Chair), *Adult-child talk about the past: Theory and practice.* Symposium conducted at the biennial meeting of the Society for Research in Child Development, Washington, DC.

Haden, C. A., Haine, R. A., & Fivush, R. (1997). Developing narrative structure in parent-child reminiscing across the preschool years. *Developmental Psychology, 33,* 295–307.

Han, J. J., Leichtman, M. D., & Wang, Q. (1998). Autobiographical memory in Korean, Chinese and American children. *Developmental Psychology, 34,* 701–703.

Hartshorn, K., & Rovee-Collier, C. (1997). Infant learning and long-term memory at 6 months: A confirming analysis. *Developmental Psychobiology, 30,* 71–85.

Howe, M. L., & Courage, M. L. (1993). On resolving the enigma of infantile amnesia. *Psychological Bulletin, 113,* 305–326.

Hudson, J. (1990). The emergence of autobiographical memory in mother-child conversation. In R. Fivush & J. Hudson (Eds.), *Knowing and remembering in young children* (pp. 166–196). New York: Cambridge University Press.

James, W. (1950). *Principles in psychology.* New York: Dover.

Jiao, S., Ji, G., & Jing, Q. (1986). Comparative study of behavior qualities of only children and sibling children. *Child Development, 57,* 357–361.

Kessen, W., & Nelson, K. (1978). What the child brings to language. In B. Z. Presseisen, D. Goldstein, & M. H. Apperl (Eds.), *Topics in cognitive development* (Vol. 2). New York: Plenum Press.

Kihlstrom, J. F., & Harackiewicz, J. M. (1982). The earliest recollection: A new survey. *Journal of Personality, 50,* 134–148.

Kuhn, M. H., & McPartland, T. S. (1954). An empirical investigation of self-attitudes. *American Sociological Review, 19,* 68–76.

LeCompte, G. K., & Gratch, G. (1972). Violation of a rule as a method of diagnosing infants' level of object concept. *Child Development, 43,* 385–396.

Lee, L. C. (1992). Day care in the People's Republic of China. In M. E. Lamb & K. Sternberg (Eds.), *Child care in context: Cross cultural perspectives* (pp. 355–392). Hillsdale, NJ: Erlbaum.

Leichtman, M. D. (1994). Long term memory in infancy and early childhood. *Dissertation Abstracts International, 55,* 2024B.

Leichtman, M. D., & Ceci, S. J. (1993). The problem of infantile amnesia: Lessons from fuzzy-trace theory. In M. L. Howe & R. Pasternak (Eds.), *Emerging themes in cognitive development: Vol. 1. Foundations* (pp. 195–213). New York: Springer Verlag.

Leichtman, M. D., & Ceci, S. J. (1995). The effects of stereotypes and suggestions on preschoolers' reports. *Developmental Psychology, 31,* 568–578.

Leichtman, M. D., Pillemer, D. B., Wang, Q., Koreishi, A., & Han, J. J. (1999). *When Baby Maisy came to school: The effect of maternal interviews on preschoolers' event memories.* Manuscript submitted for publication.

Leichtman, M. D., & Morse, M. B. (1997, April). *Individual differences in preschoolers' suggestibility: Identifying the source.* Paper presented at the biennial meeting of the Society for Research in Child Development.

Lepore, S. J., & Sesco, B. (1994). Distorting children's reports and interpretation of events through suggestion. *Applied Psychology, 79,* 108–120.

Loftus, E. F. (1991). Made in memory: Distortions of recollection after misleading information. In G. Bower (Ed.), *Psychology of learning and motivation* (Vol. 27, pp. 187–215). New York: Academic Press.

Mandler, J. M. (1990). Recall of events by preverbal children. In A. Diamond (Ed.), The development and neural bases of higher cognitive functions. *Annals of the New York Academy of Sciences, 608,* 485–516.

Mandler, J. M. (1992). How to build a baby II: Conceptual primitives. *Psychological Review, 99,* 587–604.

Mandler, J. M., & McDonough, L. (1995). Long-term recall of event sequences in infancy. *Journal of Experimental Child Psychology, 59,* 457–474.

Markus, H. R., & Kitayama, S. (1991). Culture and the self: Implications for cognition, emotion, and motivation. *Psychological Review, 98,* 224–253.

Markus, H. R., & Kitayama, S. (1994). The cultural construction of self and emotion: Implications for social behavior. In S. Kitayama & H. R. Markus (Eds.), *Emotion and culture: Empirical studies of mutual influence* (pp. 89–130). Washington, DC: American Psychological Association.

McCabe, A., & Peterson, C. (1991). Getting the story: A longitudinal study of parental styles in eliciting narratives and developing narrative skill. In A. McCabe & C. Peterson (Eds.), *Developing narrative structure* (pp. 217–253). Hillsdale, NJ: Erlbaum.

McCall, R. B. (1979). The development of intellectual functioning in infancy and prediction of later IQ. In J. D. Osofsky (Ed.), *Handbook of infant development.* New York: Wiley.

McDonough, L., & Mandler, J. M. (1994). Very long-term recall in infants: Infantile amnesia reconsidered. In R. Fivush (Ed.), *Long-term retention of infant memories: Vol. 2. Memory* (4th ed., pp. 339–352). Hove, England: Erlbaum.

Meltzoff, A. N. (1988). Infant imitation after a 1-week delay: Long term memory for novel acts and multiple stimuli. *Developmental Psychology, 24,* 470–476.

Meltzoff, A. N. (1995). What infant memory tells us about infantile amnesia: Long-term recall and deferred imitation. *Journal of Experimental Child Psychology, 59,* 497–515.

Mullen, M. K. (1994). Earliest recollections of childhood: A demographic analysis. *Cognition, 52,* 55–79.

Mullen, M. K., & Yi, S. (1995). The cultural context of talk about the past: Implications for the development of autobiographical memory. *Cognitive Development, 10,* 407–419.

Myers, N. A., Clifton, R. K., & Clarkson, M. G. (1987). When they were very young: Almost-threes remember two years ago. *Infant Behavior and Development, 10,* 123–132.

Myers, N. A., Perris, E. E., & Speaker, C. J. (1994). Fifty months of memory: A longitudinal study in early childhood. *Memory, 2,* 383–415).

Neisser, U. (1967). Cultural and cognitive discontinuity. In T. E. Gladwin & W. Sturtevant (Eds.), *Anthropology and human behavior* (pp. 54–71). Washington, DC: Anthropological Society of Washington.

Nelson, K. (1993). Events, narrative, memory: What develops? In C. Nelson (Ed.), *Memory and affect in development: The Minnesota Symposia on Child Psychology* (Vol. 26, pp. 1–24). Hillsdale, NJ: Erlbaum.

Nelson, K. (1996). *Language in cognitive development: Emergence of the mediated mind.* New York: Cambridge University Press.

Otoya, M. T. (1988). A study of personal memories of bilinguals: The role of culture and language in memory encoding and recall. *Dissertation Abstracts International, 48,* 2789B.

Perner, J., & Ruffman, T. (1995). Episodic memory and autonoetic consciousness: Developmental evidence and a theory of childhood amnesia. *Journal of Experimental Child Psychology, 59,* 516–548.

Perris, E. E., Myers, N. A., & Clifton, R. K. (1990). Long-term memory for a single infancy experience. *Child Development, 61,* 1796–1807.

Pillemer, D. B. (1998). *Momentous events, vivid memories.* Cambridge, MA: Harvard University Press.

Pillemer, D. B., Picariello, M. L., & Pruett, J. C. (1994). Very long-term memories of a salient preschool event. *Applied Cognitive Psychology, 8,* 95–106.

Pillemer, D. B., & White, S. H. (1989). Childhood events recalled by children and adults. In H. W. Reese (Ed.), *Advances in child development and behavior* (Vol. 21, pp. 297–340). Orlando, FL: Academic Press.

Reese, E., & Fivush, R. (1993). Parental styles of talking about the past. *Developmental Psychology, 29,* 596–606.

Reese, E., Haden, C., & Fivush, R. (1993). Mother-child conversations about the past: Relationships of style and memory over time. *Cognitive Development, 8,* 403–430.

Rovee-Collier, C. (1993). The capacity for long-term memory in infancy. *Current Directions in Psychological Science, 2,* 130–135.

Rovee-Collier, C., & Hayne, H. (1987). Reactivation of infant memory: Implications for cognitive development. In H. W. Reese (Ed.), *Advances in child development and behavior* (Vol. 20, pp.185–238). New York: Academic Press.

Rubin, D. C. (1982). On the retention function for autobiographical memory. *Journal of Verbal Learning and Verbal Behavior, 21,* 21–38.

Sankaranarayanan, A., & Leichtman, M. (1997). *The function of autobiographical memory across cultures: A study of urban and rural Indian adults.* Unpublished manuscript.

Schactel, E. (1947). On memory and childhood amnesia. *Psychiatry, 10,* 1–26.

Schacter, D. L. (1987). Implicit memory: History and current status. *Journal of Experimental Psychology: Learning, Memory and Cognition, 13,* 501–518.

Schacter, D. L. (1995). Memory distortion: History and current status. In D. L. Schacter (Ed.), *Memory distortion* (pp. 1–43). Cambridge, MA: Harvard University Press.

Schacter, D. L., Kagan, J., & Leichtman, M. D. (1995). True and false memories in children and adults: A cognitive neuroscience perspective. *Psychology, Public Policy and Law, 1,* 411–428.

Schneider, W., & Bjorklund, D. F. (1998). Memory. In D. Kuhn & R. S. Siegler (Eds.), *Handbook of child psychology* (5th ed., pp. 467–521). New York: Wiley.

Sheingold, K., & Tenney, Y. J. (1982). Memory for a salient childhood event. In U. Neisser (Ed.), *Memory observed* (pp. 201–212). San Francisco: Freeman.

Smith, P. H. (1984). Five-month-old infant recall and utilization of temporal organization. *Journal of Experimental Child Psychology, 38,* 400–414.

Strauss, M. S., & Cohen, L. B. (1980, May). *Infant immediate and delayed memory for perceptual dimensions.* Paper presented at the International Conference on Infant Studies, New Haven, CT.

Taylor, M., Esbensen, B. M., & Bennett, R. T. (1994). Children's understanding of knowledge acquisition: The tendency for children to report they have always known what they have just learned. *Child Development, 65,* 1581–1604.

Tessler, M., & Nelson, K. (1994). Making memories: The influence of joint encoding on later recall by young children. *Consciousness and Cognition, 3,* 307–326.

Trafimow, D., Triandis, H. C., & Goto, S. G. (1991). Some tests of the distinction between the private and the collective self. *Journal of Personality and Social Psychology, 60,* 649–655.

Triandis, H. C. (1989). The self and social behavior in differing cultural contexts. *Psychological Review, 96,* 506–520.

Usher, J. A., & Neisser, U. (1993). Childhood amnesia and the beginnings of memory for four early life events. *Journal of Experimental Psychology: General, 122,* 155–165.

Wang, Z. W., Cao, D. H., Hao, Y., Cao, R. Q., Dai, W. Y., & Qu, S. Q. (1983). A preliminary study of education of only children. *Academic Journal of Shenyang Education Institute, 2,* 11–15.

Wang, Q., Leichtman, M. D., & White, S. H. (1998). Childhood memory and self-description in young Chinese adults: The impact of growing up an only child. *Cognition,* 73–103.

Welch-Ross, M. K. (1995a). Developmental changes in preschoolers' ability to distinguish memories of performed, pretended and imagined actions. *Cognitive Development, 10,* 421–441.

Welch-Ross, M. K. (1995b). An integrative model of the development of autobiographical memory. *Developmental Review, 15,* 338–365.

Welch-Ross, M. K., Diecidue, K., & Miller, S. A. (1997). Young children's understanding of conflicting mental representation predicts suggestibility. *Developmental Psychology, 33,* 43–53.

Werner, J. S., & Perlmutter, M. (1979). Development of visual memory in infants. In H. W. Reese & L. P. Lipsitt (Eds.), *Advances in child development and behavior* (Vol. 14, pp. 1–55). New York: Academic Press.

Wetzler, S. E., & Sweeney, J. A. (1986). Childhood amnesia: An empirical demonstration. In D. C. Rubin (Ed.), *Autobiographical memory* (pp. 91–201). New York: Cambridge University Press.

Zahn-Waxler, C., Friedman, R. J., Cole, P. M., & Mizuta, I. (1996). Japanese and United States preschool children's responses to conflict and distress. *Child Development, 67,* 2462–2477.

Diane Hughes
Lisa Chen

The Nature of Parents' Race-Related Communications to Children: A Developmental Perspective

☐ Introduction

This is a critically important time in our nation's history for researchers to focus on agents of socialization that shape children's racial knowledge. By *racial knowledge* we mean children's attitudes toward various racial groups as well as their understandings of racial hierarchies, systems of social stratification, and associated processes such as prejudice and discrimination.[1] By the year 2030, when today's children will reach middle adulthood, the demographic landscape of the United States will be dramatically different from what it has been in the past. Fewer than 50% of children will be non-Hispanic White, 20% of them will be African American, 28% will be Hispanic, and 10% will be Asian or Pacific Islanders (Hernandez, 1997). Ours will be the most ethnically diverse nation in the industrialized world. Thus, to function effectively, children will need to develop attitudes and competencies that will enable them to appreciate, communicate with, and interact with people from different ethnic backgrounds. Diversity holds both potentials for increased intergroup conflict, resulting from competition for resources and cultural misunderstanding, and promise for culturally rich and tolerant communities that build on difference.

Children's racial knowledge also influences the life trajectories they choose, suggesting too that researchers need to learn more about factors that influence it. Studies have found that identification with, and pride in, one's ethnic group is associated with increased competence, academic achievement, and self-esteem. Conversely, children who anticipate race-related prejudice, discrimination, and blocked opportunity may develop oppositional cultural values. Such values have been associated with poor outcomes such as academic underachievement, psychosocial maladaptation, and problem behaviors at home and at school (Biafora, Warheit, et al., 1993; Fordham & Ogbu, 1986; Oyserman & Harrison, 1998; Rumbaut, 1994; Vega, Khoury, Zimmerman, Gil, & Warheit, 1995). As researchers, policymakers, and practitioners struggle to identify factors that promote youth's resiliency, understanding the messages children receive about their race and how they interpret them may provide important clues.

Parents play a particularly important role in shaping children's racial knowledge. As key socializing agents, their values, attitudes, and behaviors transmit fundamental information to children about their own and other racial and ethnic groups. Both the mechanisms of transmission and the substantive content of race-related information vary widely across families. Some parents deliberately discuss racial issues with their children; others communicate that race is "taboo" by avoiding the topic. Some parents emphasize group differences and disadvantage; others emphasize similarities among all people. Although early studies showed that children's racial attitudes were unrelated to those of their parents (for reviews, see Aboud, 1988; Katz, 1982) recent research among families of color suggests that parents' race-related messages may have important consequences for children's identity formation and development (Marshall, 1995; Peters, 1985; Sanders Thompson, 1994; Spencer, 1983, 1985; Stevenson, 1994). Thus, children's orientations toward race are derived, in part, from parental practices and world views.

In this chapter, we focus on parental communications to children about race, a process researchers commonly refer to as "racial socialization." In doing so, we hope to stimulate interest in racial socialization, to provide a framework to evaluating what is already known about it, and to suggest steps necessary for increasing researchers' understanding of the phenomenon. We begin by discussing the concept of racial socialization, describing its most salient features and outlining the various types of messages parents may transmit to children. We also review existing empirical studies on the frequency of different types of race-related messages that parents may transmit and describe the small literature on the influences of parental socialization on children's development. Throughout this section, we illustrate our points using comments from African American parents who participated in a series of focus group interviews concerning racial socialization (Hughes & Dumont, 1993). In the second section of the chapter, we describe findings from our empirical research on racial socialization among ethnic minority parents. Our focus here is on examining the frequency and content of racial socialization, on exploring the possibility that there are shifts in parents' racial socialization practices as children get older, and on linking such shifts to accompanying shifts in children's understanding of, and experiences with, race as a social category. Finally, we consider the implications of current theoretical and empirical research on racial socialization for future research on the topic.

☐ The Concept of Racial Socialization

The concept of racial socialization originated in scholars' efforts to identify strategies that ethnic minority parents use to rear competent and effective children in a society that is largely stratified by race. The majority of research and theoretical writing on racial socialization has focused on African Americans, a group that historically has been at the bottom of the social structure in terms of access to privileges and economic resources. Consequently, current conceptualizations have emphasized parents' efforts to promote racial pride in their children and to prepare them to succeed in the face of potential racial bias. For instance, Peters' (1985) widely cited conceptualization highlighted racism as a mundane extreme environmental stressor which shapes the normative tasks of African American parents. In her view, racial socialization "includes the responsibility of raising physically and emotionally healthy children who are black in a society in which being black has negative connotations" (p. 161). Thornton, Chatters, Taylor, and Allen (1990) defined racial socialization as "specific messages and practices that are relevant to and provide information concerning the nature of race status" (p. 401). They further specified three realms of relevant information that parents may communicate: (a) information related to personal and group identity, (b) information related to intergroup and interindividual relationships, and (c) information on group position in the social hierarchy. Other conceptualizations have incorporated aspects of these definitions, focusing on the transmission of cultural practices, racial knowledge, and awareness of racism through verbal, nonverbal, deliberate, and inadvertent mechanisms (Bowman & Howard, 1985; Marshall, 1995; Sanders Thompson, 1994; Smith, Fogle, & Jacobs, in press; Stevenson, 1994, 1995).

In this chapter, we adopt a definition of *racial socialization* similar to that proposed by Thornton and colleagues (Thornton et al., 1990). Specifically, we use the term to refer generally to parental practices that communicate messages about race or ethnicity to children. This definition is both broad and limited. It is broad in the sense that it is applicable across multiple racial-ethnic groups. All parents transmit messages about race to their children, even if it is by way of silence on the topic. The definition is limited, however, in its exclusive focus on parents as the sole source of race-related messages to children. Although parents are important mediators of children's racial knowledge, children's exposure to influences outside of the family also prompts them to construct and reconstruct their notions about themselves as members of a racial or ethnic group. Smith and colleagues (Smith et al., in press) suggested that community members, community billboards, school textbooks, teachers, and the media all contain or communicate an abundance of racial messages to children about who is valued, smart, beautiful, dangerous, disruptive, rich, and so forth—and who is not. Thus, as the study of racial socialization advances, it will be critical for researchers to expand their conceptual frameworks to delineate these multiple influences.

It also is important to note that our working definition of racial socialization may exaggerate commonalties in practices across parents of various racial-ethnic groups. For instance, we know that logically similar and isomorphic behaviors may have distinct purposes and consequences among different actors and within different contexts. Thus, we would argue that similarities in broad classes of racial socialization practices (e.g., promoting pride in one's ethnic group; avoiding discussions about race), likewise, may have different meaning among different ethnic groups. Kofkin, Katz, and Downey (1995) recently found that African American and White parents' conversations about race with their children were embedded in very different underlying goals. White parents' discussions stemmed from their desire to promote views of equality among their children, whereas Black parents' discussions stemmed from their desire to prepare their children for prejudice. Similarly, there were racial group differences in parents' rationales for avoiding race-related discussions with their children. White parents were most likely to indicate that race was unimportant, whereas Black parents were most likely to believe that their children were too young to understand racial issues. Thus, although race-related information is transmitted in all families, the essence of parents' race-related messages, and their origins, may vary across racial and ethnic groups.

Having outlined the advantages and limitations of our definition, we now describe several features of racial socialization processes that may vary across individuals and, within individuals, across contexts and situations.

☐ Features of Parents' Race-Related Messages to Children

Recent efforts to delineate components of racial socialization underscore both the subtlety and complexity of the phenomenon (e.g., Smith et al., in press; Stevenson, 1994, 1995). In highlighting the multiple features of parents' race-related communications to children, and the ways in which such communications transpire, we hope to underscore the need for creative, diverse, and multiple methods in order to adequately capture and understand the phenomenon.

A Synergistic Process

The socialization process involves dynamic exchanges of information and interaction between socializers and recipients. Although scholars studying racial socialization have focused primarily on goals initiated by parents for their children, racial socialization is a bidirectional process shaped by parents and children. Parents' bring to the process attitudes, beliefs, values, and ideas about race and race-relations that form from their experiences. Parents also bring expectations regarding the competencies or coping skills their children will need to negotiate negative experiences that are based on their racial or ethnic group membership. However, children's developing racial knowledge and their experiences in extrafamilial settings also shape the content and frequency of parents' communications to them about race. Children's experiences and questions may prompt parents to share attitudes, values, and information regarding race and intergroup relations regardless of parents' intended racial socialization agendas.

Notably, qualitative studies have been better able to capture the dynamic, changing, and transactional qualities of racial socialization processes than have studies based on self-report methodologies. These qualitative studies suggest that parents are quite aware of the transactional nature of their racial socialization efforts. In a number of studies, parents' narratives feature children's queries and experiences, which prompt conversations about race. The following comment made by a focus group participant conveys this sort of awareness. The participant was a parent of an 8-year-old boy, who responded to a question about how children learn about race:

> I notice with children, children will ask questions when they're curious. And as they start to ask questions about, "Why is my skin black and this and that?" That's when you have to start, uh feeding them the information, the proper information regarding the White or other races. (Focus group participant, Hughes, 1996)

Parents in Richardson's (1981; cf., Marshall, 1995) study of mothers in Los Angeles also described the ways in which socialization about race is syntonized to children's experiences. For instance, one parent explained:

You can't just sit a child down and say, "Now listen, I'm going to tell you about what the White man is going to do to you." You can't just do that, but when you as a parent see something happen, then you sit the child down and give them as much as they need to know at that particular time. (Richardson, 1981, p. 179)

As the points of view these parents expressed suggest, children's racial knowledge and attitudes are formed and re-formed through ordinary social interaction and conversations with their parents (and others). Thus, racial socialization is primarily contained within nuanced microsocial exchanges between parents and children. Distinguishing situations in which racial socialization is child- versus parent-initiated, and elaborating the synergistic qualities of the process, will be critical if researchers are to generate and employ empirical methodologies that will adequately represent and fully capture the process.

Verbal and Nonverbal

Parents' race-related messages to their children take a variety of forms: verbal, nonverbal, explicit, and implicit. These features of racial socialization are not orthogonal: We mention them simply to underscore the complexity and subtlety of the phenomenon. The most commonly investigated messages are explicit verbalizations about race. For example, parents may teach their children racial attitudes or discuss race relations with them in a direct, conventional sense in the same manner that they would teach their children rules for conduct or moral values. Such verbal racial socialization messages may be explicit, as when parents have discussions about prejudice or cultural traditions with their children, or implicit, as when parents emphasize the importance of morality, hard work, education, and self-pride in order to prepare children for potential racial bias (Peters, 1981, 1985; Richardson, 1981; Thornton et al., 1990; cf., Peters, 1985). Importantly, then, studies that focus on verbal messages with explicit race-related content capture only one facet of a diverse array of practices in which parents engage.

Parents may also socialize race-related attitudes, values, and perspectives through a variety of nonverbal implicit mechanisms. Practices aimed at promoting children's racial and ethnic pride and their knowledge about their cultural history and heritage are often nonverbal and unarticulated (Boykin & Toms, 1985; Peters, 1985; Sanders Thompson, 1994; Spencer, 1983; Stevenson, 1995). Nonverbal and unarticulated racial socialization messages may take a variety of forms including modeling racial-ethnic behaviors (e.g., cooking traditional foods, speaking in native languages), structuring children's environments (e.g., displaying culturally based art in the home, influencing children's peer choices), or selectively reinforcing children's behaviors (Hamm, 1996; Marshall, 1995; Smith, 1996; Smith et al., in press).

In the focus group interviews that we conducted among dual-earner African American families, themes regarding unarticulated messages emerged in conversations about children's developing racial knowledge. The following remarks by parents in one of the groups is quite typical of exchanges that took place across groups. One parent explained:

Children learn about race before they ask. You don't really start talking to them about it. You instill pride in them and make them aware of their race and that they should have pride in their people and their culture. And what grows out of that is that they notice that there are White people and other people. But, you know, I don't really think you actually start saying, "You're black, you're White, this is the way it is." It's right in your face. It sort of comes naturally. (Focus group participants, Hughes, 1996)

Agreeing with this statement, another parent added:

Yeah! We do the same thing. We read to our kids constantly—black books. We have them active in preschool and active with other Black kids so they get a chance to see blacks. At Christmas, with my husband's family, we have everyone talk about what they do so there are positive black role models. I know in growing up that was really important for me and it has helped me so much when I'm faced with the racial problems. (Focus group participant, Hughes, 1996)

Deliberate and Unintended

As the above examples illustrate, parents utilize a variety of strategies to promote children's racial pride, to teach them about their culture and history, and to prepare them for potential encounters with racial prejudice and discrimination. The strategies we have described thus far are based on parents' race-related values, their goals for their children, and their views of skills and competencies children will need to be successful in the larger society. However, parents race-related messages to children may be distinguished in terms of whether they are deliberate or unintended. Deliberate messages, such as those described above, are communicated intentionally as part of a well-defined socialization agenda. In contrast, "unintended messages" are subtle, often inadvertent communications about race that may or may not be directed at children but, nevertheless, transmit information to them regarding their parents' attitudes, values, or views about race or race relations.

Most empirical studies of racial socialization focus on parents' deliberate (and explicit) race-related messages to children. This focus is inherent in researchers' reliance on self-report methods, due to the fact that such methods require that parents are aware of, and willing to report, their behaviors. In this regard, studies that have examined African American parents' reports about their current racial socialization practices (Hughes & Chen, 1997; Marshall, 1995; Peters, 1981; Thornton et al., 1990; Ward, 1996) have found that the majority of them teach their children about their racial-ethnic background, history, and heritage, and prepare them for racial bias. Studies have also found that the majority of African American adults' recall receiving messages about race from their parents (Sanders Thompson, 1994; Demo & Hughes, 1990). Child rearing among Latino and Asian parents also emphasizes the importance of preserving the cultural traditions and values of their host countries and of teaching children about prejudice and discrimination in the United States (Buriel & De Ment, 1997; Fisher, Jackson, & Villarruel, in press; Garcia Coll & Magnuson, 1997; Garcia Coll, Meyer, & Brillon, 1995; Kibria, 1997).

Although many parents have an explicit racial socialization agenda, not all of them do. Moreover, even parents who have clearly articulated beliefs about racial socialization may unwittingly transmit race-related messages to children. Thus, racial socialization processes may also occur by way of inadvertent and unintentional metacommunications that parents may be unaware of. For example, parents' reactions to situations as they present themselves, such as when a parent mumbles a snide remark in response to a racial slur, may constitute a context for transmitting values and perspectives about the meaning of race to children. These sorts of subtle and unintended messages rarely have been the focus of empirical studies, in part, because labor intensive methods such as ethnography or structured observations are required to assess them.

Again, comments by parents who participated in our focus groups illustrate these sorts of inadvertent communications to children about race. For instance, one parent described a situation in which she perceived a strangers' remarks to have racial undertones:

> My son wanted a tail, he wanted a flat top [hair style]. I never thought that at 4 years old he would say he wanted a flat top like his Uncle Spence. So, you know, I let him have it. One day I was in the store and this woman said, "Oh, are you starting kindergarten? Do they let them wear their hair like that?" I said, "Well, uh, are there any restrictions on white children in how they wear their hair?" And I said, "Excuse me" and just walked away.

Embedded in this parent's response is what Appelgate and colleagues (Appelgate, Burleson, & Delia, 1992) refered to as an interpretive logic, or, a generalized orientation that parents transmit to children and that guides children's assessment and management of situations. In this interaction, race was made salient, not by the stranger, but by the parent's interpretation of the stranger's comments. Thus, as Boykin and Toms' (1985) suggested, racial attitudes, values, and behaviors often are passed on to children by way of "cultural motifs" that are largely invisible to parents but are displayed to children in a "consistent, persistent, and enduring fashion" (p. 42). These cultural motifs typically are not accompanied by directives or imperatives from parents to learn but simply are absorbed by children and provide a basis for their "behavioral negotiations with the world."

Proactive and Reactive

Parental racial socialization messages may be proactive or reactive. That is, they may emanate from parents' preconceived values, goals, and agendas (proactive) or they may occur in reaction to discrete events in parent's or children's lives (reactive). As with anticipatory socialization mechanisms described by others (Nsamenang & Lamb, 1995), proactive racial socialization is intimately tied to parents' views of the strengths and competencies their children will need in order to function effectively in their adult social roles. Descriptions of proactive racial socialization among African American parents have emphasized that it is guided by parents' expectations that their children will inevitably encounter racism and discrimination (e.g., Essed, 1990; Peters, 1981). However, other racial socialization agendas also may be proactive. For example, parents who value diversity and pluralism may choose racially-ethnically diverse versus homogeneous settings for their children. Further, they may teach their children about experiences and perspectives of particular racial-ethnic groups or they may encourage their children to respect individuals of all racial-ethnic groups. An important feature of proactive racial socialization messages, whether subtle or overt, is that they have internally consistent structures and are intimately linked to parents' worldviews and experiences. The following remark from a focus group participant suggests the ways in which parents' proactive socialization goals are derived from their experiences and worldviews.

> When I was a little kid, I grew up in a mixed neighborhood. I used to think, "When I grow up, I can do anything." But it's not like that now and it's not going to be like that for our kids. In my job, I used to think about the whole concept of fairness, but it's no longer a concept I deal with. I see too much when mediocrity is rewarded [for Whites] and only superior performance on my part or the other Black folks' part is rewarded. There's degrees of fairness and we [Blacks] got the minimal degree. Fair is something you don't even deal with. That's the real world and you just maneuver around it. I want my own children to know that they have to be better, they have to do more. That's what my parents told me. I didn't think I would have to do this but I do. (Focus group participant, Hughes, 1996)

In contrast to racial socialization that is proactive, reactive racial socialization occurs inadvertently in response to race-related incidents that parents or children have experienced, or in response to children's general queries about racial issues. Whereas proactive racial socialization messages are likely to be internally consistent, reactive messages may or may not reflect parents' intentional racial socialization agendas. That is, parents may be uncomfortable with, or unprepared for, handling necessary discussions that children initiate concerning race. Several examples from the focus group study illustrate this sort of reactive racial socialization. In the first example, the participant, an African American father, described his discomfort with his preschool son's race-related questions:

> About three years ago, I was sitting downstairs watching television, and on Showtime they had a little bit of Denzel Washington in *Roots*. My son was sitting there next to me. I guess he was two-and-a-half, maybe three. There's a scene where they're coming in and destroying the Bantu stand. There's one vivid shot where there's a little black boy running trying to get away from the police. And, the police just leaned out and shot this little boy. And, it really kind of happened before I could think. And my son said, "Daddy, why did he shoot the little boy?" How do you explain to a two-and-a-half year old that the little boy was shot because he was black? And then my son saw them capture the guys and put the chains on them, putting them on the boat. And he kept asking "Daddy, why are they doing that to them?" And trying to explain this whole concept is so difficult. They continue to ask "Why, why, how come?" And, it's such a devilish terrible situation that you really can't explain it but you try. (Focus group participant, Hughes, 1996)

In this example, the parent's response to his child's queries appears to reflect his values and worldviews (i.e., racism still exists; racism is unfair). However, there is no evidence that this communication is part of a deliberate socialization agenda. The father simply is reacting to questions posed to him by his son. Another example from the focus groups provides an illustration of a child-initiated discussion of race in which the parent's response is clearly inconsistent with the parent's own views about race.

> Well, here's a typical question my daughter asks me. We have friends of all races and colors. Here's my daughter at age 8 "Mommy, daddy's a Muslim. What happens if I meet a White man when I get big and he asks me to marry him?" I said, "So you marry him!" She said, "It's gonna kill my daddy because he's White." I said, "You can marry a White person. . . . You have to treat each person on an individual basis." Now, it would kill me, but I would never feed the way I feel to my children. (Focus group participant, Hughes, 1996)

As these examples illustrate, reactive racial socialization is characteristically ad hoc and may or may not be a part of a deliberate socialization agenda. Moreover, parents' messages may or may not be consistent with their own views. Therein, reactive messages are less likely than are proactive messages to form a coherent entity that is consistently reproduced in interactions with children. Thus, in research on racial socialization, it may be important for researchers to differentiate between race-related messages that are proactive and those that are not. Proactive messages may be simpler to assess empirically than reactive messages, due to the fact that parents are inherently cognizant of them. Moreover, in that reactive messages may be inconsistent with other race-related attitudes and behaviors that parents present to children, it may be important to evaluate the influence of such reactive messages on children's own attitudes and behaviors.

Messages Sent Versus Messages Received

In light of the complexity and subtlety of racial socialization processes, it also is important to distinguish between messages parents intend to communicate and messages children actually receive. That is, children not only initiate racial socialization, but they can miss, misinterpret, or ignore parents' communications about race. In Marshall's (1995) study, African American parents' and their 9- to 10-year-old children's reports about family racial socialization sometimes were incongruent. For instance, 40% of children compared with 18% of parents reported that parents said nothing about race. About 3% of children compared with 12% of parents reported parental messages about racial barriers. Thirty-one percent of parents versus 22% of children reported parents' emphasis on racial pride. Only parents' and children's reports concerning communications about physical attributes and the importance of self-development were congruent. Barnes (1980) found that children of mothers who reported more frequent race-related socialization were less likely than other children to demonstrate pro-Black attitudes using forced-choice assessment techniques, suggesting that parent's efforts to instill pride in their children inadvertently led children to view Blacks negatively. Johnson (1989) also documented a lack of congruence between parents' reports about their socialization strategies and children's actual coping behavior.

Children also can disagree with parents' socialization messages, choosing instead to adhere to their own worldviews. Indeed, the low correspondence in Marshall's (1995) study may have resulted from discrepancies between children's worldviews and those of their parents. Lee and Cyn's (1991; cf., Uba, 1994) case study of conflict between a 17-year-old Korean American boy and his immigrant parents illustrates the ways in which children may choose to incorporate or ignore parents' racial socialization efforts.

> Although his parents tried to teach him to be proud to be Korean and to learn about Korean culture, Jack did not identify with Koreans as much as his parents wanted. Jack's father had threatened to disown him for being so disrespectful and attributed Jack's behaviors to being too Americanized. (Uba, 1994, p. 113)

Importantly, then, researchers' common focus on parents' explicit communications to children, has emphasized messages parents believe they send rather than those children actually receive. However, it is interesting to note that in Marshall's (1995) study, parents' reports of ethnic socialization were significantly correlated with children's ethnic identity stage, whereas children's reports were not.

☐ The Substantive Content of Racial Socialization Messages

Parents' racial socialization practices vary considerably in terms of the nature and content of the messages that are transmitted to children. In this section, we attempt to describe more fully the content of racial socialization messages that parents may communicate. We distinguish several dimensions of racial socialization including: (a) emphasizing racial and ethnic pride, traditions, and history (termed cultural socialization); (b) promoting an awareness of racial prejudice and discrimination (termed preparation for bias); (c) issuing cautions and warnings about other racial and ethnic groups, or about intergroup relations (termed promotion of mistrust); and (d) emphasizing the need to appreciate all racial and ethnic groups (termed egalitarianism) (Boykin & Toms, 1985; Thornton et al., 1990; Demo & Hughes, 1990; Sanders Thompson, 1994). We also examine empirical research that investigates the incidence of different sorts of racial socialization practices and, where available, associations between parents' racial socialization and outcomes for their children.

Although we describe dimensions of racial socialization separately, particular racial socialization messages as they occur in everyday conversation are less readily distinguishable. For instance, messages emphasizing cultural pride and history (cultural socialization) also may contain messages about historical discrimination and prejudice (preparation for bias), at least among minority populations in the United States. Similarly, parents may inadvertently embed cautions or warnings about other groups (promotion of mistrust) in their efforts to prepare children for racial bias (preparation for bias). Thus, although we describe dimensions of racial socialization separately, these dimensions are not mutually exclusive.

Cultural Socialization

> I'm a very firm believer that you have to prepare children to deal with their race. The first thing is teaching them that they're Black or, rather, African American. I had to get away from the Black thing because they did not

understand it. My daughter, who is very fair, would say "Oh, Mommy, I'm white," and I would say, "Oh, no dear, no, no," and try to explain. So, I tried as they were growing up to give them Black dolls. They'd always want the White Barbie and I'd say, "This [Black barbie] is my favorite. " I try to go into Black books, to surround them with our music, and to give them the little pieces of Black history, you know, the story of Rosa Parks. I've tried to bring their culture here (lives in a predominantly White community) because I think they need to know. They need to know where they come from before they can know where they're going. (Focus group participant, Hughes, 1996).

The term *cultural socialization* has been used commonly to refer to parental practices that teach children about cultural heritage, ancestry, and history; that maintain and promote cultural customs and traditions; and that instill cultural, racial, and ethnic pride (Boykin & Toms, 1985; Thornton et al., 1990). Cultural socialization may be evidenced in a wide range of behaviors including: talking to children, or reading books to them, about important people in the history of their ethnic or racial group; celebrating cultural holidays; exposing children to positive role models; and so forth. These sorts of practices have been central to researchers' ideas about racial socialization (Barnes, 1980; Bowman & Howard, 1985; Chen, 1998; Hughes & Chen, 1997; Knight, Bernal, Garza, Cota, & Ocampo, 1993; Ou & McAdoo, 1993; Peters, 1985; Sanders Thompson, 1994; Smith, 1996; Spencer, 1983; Stevenson, 1994; Thornton et al., 1990). That is, scholars have consistently suggested that cultural socialization promotes children's positive racial identity development and self-esteem by preparing children to interpret and cope with prejudice, discrimination, and negative group images emanating from the outside world (e.g., Barnes, 1980).

A number of studies have found that most parents of color engage in cultural socialization practices with their children. For example, in Phinney and Chavira's (1995) study of parents with adolescent children, 88% of Mexican American, 83% of African American, and 67% of Japanese American parents described behaviors associated with cultural socialization. Spencer (1983) also found that about three quarters of southern Black mothers in her sample taught their children about Black history and famous Black leaders, although only one third of them taught their children about the civil rights movement in the United States. As we will describe below, over two thirds of urban African American parents who participated in our study of racial socialization among African American parents in dual-earner married couple families reported engaging in cultural socialization practices within the previous year (e.g., reading children Black history books and storybooks, taking children to cultural events).

Notably, studies that have inductively coded parents' responses to open-ended questions about racial socialization typically find a lower incidence of cultural socialization than do those that ask about it explicitly (see Phinney & Chavira, 1995, for an exception). For instance, one third of the Black parents of 9- and 10-year-olds in Marshall's (1995) study were coded as mentioning that they instilled racial pride in their children. Thornton and colleagues (Thornton et al., 1990) found that approximately one fourth of the Black parents in their study mentioned behaviors related to racial pride or Black heritage and historical traditions. In a retrospective study of racial socialization among African American adults, Sanders Thompson (1994) reported that less than one fifth of participants had received messages related to racial pride or cultural heritage from family members when they were growing up. Similarly, 23% of African American youths age 14 to 24 in Bowman and Howard's (1985) study reported that their parents taught them about Black heritage or emphasized racial pride and Black unity.

Nevertheless, in accordance with theorists' predictions, empirical studies have suggested that cultural socialization is associated with more favorable child outcomes among minority youth, particularly in terms of children's ethnic identity and their knowledge and attitudes regarding their ethnic group. For example, Demo and Hughes (1990) found that Black adults who recalled that their parents had emphasized racial pride, cultural heritage, and racial tolerance reported greater feelings of closeness to other Blacks and more Afrocentric racial attitudes than did those who reported no racial socialization. Branch and Newcombe (1986) also found that children of parents who taught them in more of a pro-Black fashion were more likely than their counterparts to have higher racial awareness, higher racial knowledge, and greater pro-Black preferences. In Knight and colleagues' (Knight et al., 1993) study, Mexican American school-age children whose mothers taught them more about Mexican culture, and those with more Mexican objects in their homes, were more likely than their peers to use racial-ethnic self-labels correctly, to use more racial-ethnic behaviors, and to have greater same-race/ethnic preferences. Further, Mexican mothers' teachings about racial-ethnic pride were significantly correlated with children's ability to correctly sort picture stimuli by race and with their children's use of racial-ethnic behaviors. In their study of Chinese American families, Ou and McAdoo (1993) found that parents' pride in Chinese culture was related to their children's racial-ethnic preferences. Specifically, more parental cultural socialization was associated with greater preferences for same-race/ethnic peers among first- and second-grade girls. Several studies that have not differentiated multiple dimensions of racial socialization also have reported significant relationships between overall racial socialization and favorable identity outcomes among youth (Marshall, 1995; Sanders Thompson, 1994).

Cultural socialization also may be associated with positive outcomes for children in other domains, such as academic achievement. For instance, Smith (1996) found that African American parents' socialization concerning ethnic pride and racial-ethnic equality was consistently related to their children's better grades and higher test scores. Moreover, cultural socialization may have salutary influences on minority youth by way of its influence on their positive ethnic identity which, in turn, has been associated with a broad range of outcomes, such as school performance, the quality of relations with peers, and psychosocial adjustment (Phinney & Kohatsu, 1997; Porter & Washington, 1993). Thus, the consequences of cultural socialization may go beyond racial-specific child outcomes, such as ethnic identity, to reach other important aspects of children's lives.

Preparation for Bias

> My children know about race. I didn't go around saying "That person's Black that person's White." It just sort of comes up. I do not know, though, if I want to point out that there are differences and watch out for them. I don't want my kids to ever use race as a crutch. I guess that's the way I was brought up. I knew about racism but my parents used to say "You have to be better." As I got older, I understood what they meant. I just want to teach my kids the same thing too. I want them to be better because I want them to be good and they have to be better in this society to be good. (Focus group participant, Hughes, 1996)

Parents' efforts to promote their children's awareness of racial bias, and to prepare them to cope with prejudice and discrimination, also have been emphasized as a critical component of racial socialization. We use the term *preparation for bias* to refer to such practices. Several scholars have suggested that enabling children to navigate around racial barriers and to negotiate potentially hostile social interactions are normative parenting tasks within ethnic minority families (Thornton et al., 1990; Fisher et al., in press; Garcia Coll & Magnuson, 1997; Garcia Coll, Meyer, & Brillon, 1995; Kibria, 1997; Harrison, Wilson, Chan, Buriel, & Pine, 1995). Scholars also have proposed that parents' efforts in this regard protect children from threats to their self-esteem and well being posed by the race-related stressors they encounter (Spencer, 1983; Spencer & Markstrom Adams, 1990).

A number of the studies described in reference to cultural socialization also have examined the frequency of socialization about racial prejudice and discrimination (preparation for bias.) Such socialization, like cultural socialization, varies widely across samples. In some studies, the large majority of African American parents reported socialization related to racial barriers (Hughes & Chen, 1997; Phinney & Chavira, 1995). Sanders Thompson (1994) found that 48% to 58% of African American participants recalled parental messages about racial barriers. However, in Bowman and Howard's (1985) study, only 13% of youth described parental messages about racial barriers. Similarly, only 8% of respondents in the National Survey of Black Americans reported messages to their children about racial barriers (Thornton et al., 1990).

The extent to which parents discuss racial bias with their children appears to vary as a function of racial-ethnic group membership. Most notably, studies among Asian American and Latino parents have found comparatively low levels of racial socialization in this regard (Chen, 1998; Phinney & Chavira, 1995). Phinney and Chavira (1995) found that 93.8% of African American parents reported discussing racial bias and discrimination with their children, but only 73% of Mexican American parents and 44.5% of Japanese American parents reported such discussions. In Chen's (1998) study of immigrant Chinese families with children age 4 to 9 years old, about 90% of parents did not discuss racial prejudice or discrimination with their children. Kofkin and colleagues (Kofkin et al., 1995) also found that only 1% of White parents versus 19% of African American parents with 3-year-old children cited the importance of discussing race in order to prepare their children for prejudice.

Empirical studies regarding the influences of preparation for bias on youth have produced inconsistent results. A few studies have supported the view that preparation for bias serves the sorts of protective functions that scholars have proposed. In Knight and colleagues (Knight et al., 1993) study, Mexican mothers' teachings about discrimination were associated with their children's ability to correctly sort picture stimuli by race and with children's use of racial-ethnic behaviors. Similarly, in Spencer's (1983) study of African American parents of preschoolers, parents' teachings about civil rights and racial discrimination predicted children's Afrocentric racial attitudes and preferences. Bowman and Howard (1985) also found that Black youth whose parents had prepared them for racial barriers reported a greater sense of efficacy and higher grades in school. However, other studies have indicated that children are negatively affected by parental socialization regarding the existence of racial barriers (Fordham & Ogbu, 1986; Marshall, 1995; Smith, 1996). For instance, in a study of southern African American fourth-grade children, Smith (1996) found that children's perceptions of racial barriers significantly predicted lower reading and math scores on the Stanford Achievement Test. Similarly, Marshall (1995) found that African American children's reports of more parental ethnic socialization, in general, were related to lower reading grades among the 9- and 10-year-olds she studied.

In our view, inconsistencies across studies examining the influence on children of parental communications about racial barriers may be due to subtle differences in the structure or content of such communications. Practices aimed at instilling racial pride in children, and preparing them to cope with discriminatory experiences based on their race, are intended to be and often are protective. However, parents may sometimes communicate in ways that emphasize group differences, lack of common ground, and the disadvantaged status of their own group. Unless parents' messages are carefully crafted, these sorts of communications may promote children's feelings of alienation and mistrust of other groups. This possibility may underlie many parents' reluctance to emphasize racial barriers in their child rearing practices.

Socialization of Mistrust

> I teach my son and my daughter don't trust them (Whites). I don't trust them—teach them he's [the "White Man"] no good. He's not on your side. And that's the way I feel. And, you know, I say, "He might be O.K. You can hang out with them and you can play. You can dance, you can do everything. But when it comes to the bottom line, he ain't on your side." It's never too early for children to learn that. (Focus group participant, Hughes, 1996)

We use the term *promotion of mistrust* to refer to parental practices that discourage children from interacting with people of other racial-ethnic out-groups or that foster a sense of distrust across racial-ethnic boundaries. In our view, it is distinct from preparation for bias in that it does not incorporate messages regarding strategies for coping with and overcoming prejudice and discrimination (e.g., you have to be better; you have to do more). Mistrust may be communicated in parents' warnings to children about other racial-ethnic groups or in their cautions about racial barriers to success. For instance, in the comment of the focus group participant included above, there is no reference to strategies that can be used to overcome the barriers that may be imposed by race. The same pattern is evident in a second example from a focus group participant, who was describing the various contexts in which he had race-related discussions with his daughter:

> So far, I haven't experienced racism with my kids, like as far as school and stuff. But I mean, I teach her, I try to show her. That's why we watch the news together. For example, when, um, with that Hostage thing in Waco Texas? I explained to my daughter that if it had been Blacks or Hispanics they wouldn't have waited 50 some odd days to move in. If it had been a person of our color they would've moved in the same day or maybe tomorrow. So right there, I'm telling her that her skin color means a lot. (Focus group participant, Hughes, 1996)

Embedded in this description is this father's communications to his daughter about the inevitability of unequal treatment of Blacks. No corollary efforts to provide the daughter with ammunition against unfair treatment, or to socialize modes of operating that will enable her to overcome barriers, are evident.

Few empirical studies have distinguished socialization of mistrust from preparing children for racial bias, perhaps because the distinction is so subtle. However, among the studies that have differentiated the two, the incidence of explicit cautions or warnings about other ethnic groups seems to be quite low. For instance, in Thornton and colleagues' (Thornton et al., 1990) analysis of data from the National Study of Black Americans, 8.2% of parents stressed the presence of racial barriers and 6.5% of parents taught their children to recognize and accept their racial background. However, only 2.7% of parents instructed their children to maintain social distance from Whites.

As we have noted above, where preparing children for racial bias may have salutary influences on children's developmental outcomes, socialization practices that foster intergroup mistrust and alienation from mainstream values may promote maladaptive behaviors. For example, in Ogbu's (1974) research among high school students in Stockton, California, parents' overemphasis on racial barriers and discrimination seemed to undermine children's sense of efficacy and promote distrust of and anger toward mainstream institutions. Children who exhibited these attitudes were more likely to perform poorly in school. Patchen (1982) found that negative parental attitudes toward other races were associated with children's increased avoidance of cross-race peers and with their reports of negative intergroup social interactions. In a study of sixth and seventh grade Black boys, Biafora and colleagues (Biafora et al., 1993) found that racial mistrust was a significant predictor of deviant behaviors (e.g., ranging from taking small amounts of money to stealing a car) even when other factors such as socioeconomic status, peer values, family cohesion, and religiosity were statistically controlled.

Evidence that parental socialization of racial mistrust may have negative consequences for youth also comes from studies that have examined relationships between parents' attitudes (as opposed to their racial socialization practices per se) and children's experiences, or between children's feelings of mistrust and their outcomes on a range of psychosocial indicators. For example, in a study of fourth-grade children and their parents, Smith (1996) found that children whose parents reported less interracial trust reported less contact with peers of different races. In turn, children with less interracial contact had lower reading and math grades than those with more contact. Children's perceptions of racial barriers, were associated with their scores on the reading and math components of the Stanford Achievement Tests. Similarly, in a study of approximately 5,000 immigrant and nonimmigrant minority youth, Rumbaut (1994) found that adolescents who had experienced discrimination and perceived future discrimination were less likely than were their counterparts to espouse assimilative mainstream ethnic identities. They also reported higher levels of depressive symptoms. Thus, strategies that promote racial mistrust may prompt youth to withdraw from activities that are essential for access to opportunity and reward structures of the dominant society (Biafora et al., 1993). Moreover, they may motivate them to engage in rebellious activities that deviate from accepted norms.

Egalitarianism and Silence about Race

> When I discuss race with my kids, I try to be as positive as I can and let them see that everyone is the same regardless of what color they are. I tell them that we're all human. We all have blood. We breathe the same, talk the same, and everything. (Focus group participant, Hughes, 1996)

Many parents encourage their children to appreciate the values and experiences of all racial-ethnic groups or, as Spencer (1983, 1985) noted, to rear racially neutral children who notice people's individual qualities rather than their racial group membership. Theoretically, socialization that emanates from this sort of egalitarian values may manifest itself in two distinct forms: one in which parents expose their children to the history, traditions, and current experiences of many different groups, including their own, and the other in which parents avoid any mention of race during discussions with their children.

Researchers consistently have documented that many parents either focus on promoting egalitarian views or are completely silent about race. Spencer (1983) found that over half of the southern Black parents in her sample reported that they taught their children to believe that all people are equal. In Bowman and Howard's (1985) study, 38% of African American youth reported that their parents did not transmit any information to them about Blacks or Whites, and 12% reported that their parents had emphasized equality among all people. In a study of southern Black adults (Parham & Williams, 1993), 20% of respondents reported that their parents "rarely" or "never" discussed race, racial attitudes, or both, whereas 27.8% said that their parents had emphasized egalitarian views.

Few scholars have directly investigated the influences of *egalitarian socialization* or silence about race in terms of their consequences for children's development. However, scholars have emphasized that children of color socialized from an egalitarian perspective may have unrealistic expectations concerning intergroup relations. They also may be unable to comprehend and cope with experiences involving racial bias (Smith, Fogle, & Jacobs, in press; Spencer, 1983; Stevenson, 1995). In Bowman and Howard's (1985) study, Black youth who were not taught anything about race had lower self-efficacy scores than did recipients of proactive racial socialization strategies. Oyserman (1993) found that the lack of parental influence on their adolescent's racial-ethnic identity was linked to delinquent behaviors.

Scholars also have suggested that avoiding race-related discussions with children increases the likelihood that they will incorporate racial-ethnic stereotypes emerging from the larger social structure. In their investigation of family conversations about race, Kofkin and colleagues (Kofkin et al., 1995) examined correlations between parents' and children's racial attitudes for parents who reported no discussions about race, as compared to those who reported race-related discussions. Not surprisingly, parent and child attitudes were unrelated within the former group, but significantly and positively correlated in the latter. The researchers noted that, if family discussions about race did not occur, children seemed to be left to their own devices to form an understanding of the racial differences they observed. Spencer (1983) also noted that lack of direct instruction and discussion about race among parents of color means that traditional views and prevalent stereotypes remain unchallenged.

☐ A Summary

Thus far, we have described the multiple ways in which parents communicate race-related information to their children. In doing so, we have hoped to convey that racial socialization is a complex, synergistic process. Messages to children can be child- or parent-initiated, and communicated through a variety of mechanisms: verbal, nonverbal, deliberate, unintended, proactive, reactive, or a combination of these. Moreover, parents' actual messages may or may not correspond with parents' beliefs and values pertaining to race. Some parents act on intentional racial socialization agendas by engaging in a range of practices that they believe will promote particular types of knowledge, values, attitudes, and orientations in their children pertaining to race and racial issues. However, other parents may hold a set of beliefs about racial socialization that they rarely implement (e.g., the view that teaching children about race is important). There also may be instances in which parents are unaware that a particular behavior or comment is communicating race-related information and perspectives to their children. Thus, to advance researchers' knowledge about racial socialization processes, a broad array of research methods and approaches are needed that adequately capture the subtle and inadvertent aspects of the phenomenon.

We also reviewed empirical literature concerning the extent to which parents employ racial socialization practices and the consequences of such practices for children. Although this literature is small, and is marked by gaps and uncertainties, several important themes have emerged. Most notably, it has suggested that there is considerable variation in the extent to which parents transmit race-related information to their children as well as in the content of messages parents transmit. Parents' messages can be categorized according to whether they emphasize cultural heritage and pride, or the equality of all groups; transmit information about discrimination and prejudice; or caution and warn children about intra- or intergroup relations. Moreover, the consequences of racial socialization for children's development seem to depend on the nature of the messages parents transmit. Cultural socialization and preparation for bias appear to have salutary effects on children, in part, by influencing their racial identity and positive attitudes regarding their own ethnic group. However, parents' overemphasis on racial barriers may undermine children's efficacy and promote maladaptive behaviors, particularly when such an emphasis is unaccompanied by information regarding strategies for coping with racial bias. Failure to discuss race at all, especially racial bias, may also have adverse consequences for ethnic minority children.

☐ A Research Example

We now provide a brief description of select findings from a program of research on racial socialization in which we have been engaged for the past several years. The research began with a series of focus group interviews, which we have drawn on throughout the chapter, and subsequently has involved efforts to delineate: (a) the frequency and content of parents' racial socialization practices, (b) shifts in parents' racial socialization as children get older, (c) ecological and contextual correlates of racial socialization, and (d) the consequences of racial socialization for youth's well-being (Hughes, 1977, 1998; Hughes & Chen, 1997; Hughes & Dumont, 1993). Thus, an overarching goal of this research has been to unpack the concept of racial socialization and to understand its ecological antecedents and its consequences for children.

In the remainder of this chapter, we focus primarily on two issues. First, we describe findings regarding the extent to which parents engage in different types of racial socialization practices with their children. Although we have reviewed a number of studies that have examined parents' racial socialization practices, the information that these studies provide regarding the prevalence and frequency of varying racial socialization practices is limited in several ways. In some studies, multiple dimensions of racial socialization have been assessed, but they have not been retained in empirical analyses (e.g., Marshall, 1995; Thornton et al., 1990). In addition, investigators often have measured dimensions of racial socialization by inductively coding parents' responses to an open-ended question, providing limited information about the range of practices in which parents might engage. Marshall's (1995) finding that parents were more likely to indicate that they engage in specific racial socialization strategies when they were asked about them explicitly than when they were responding to open-ended questions about child rearing suggests that studies may underestimate the degree to which parents transmit race-related information to their children. Finally, most studies have provided dichotomous estimates of varying racial socialization practices (e.g., present or not), rather than assessing the frequency with which varying practices take place. In order to argue that racial socialization is an important component of child rearing in ethnic minority families with potential consequences for children's well-being, it seems important to first establish both the extent to which parents employ independent dimensions of it and the frequency with which they do so.

After examining the prevalence and frequency of racial socialization, we explore the possibility that particular racial socialization practices, most notably preparation for bias and promotion of mistrust, increase as a function of children's ages. This focus is embedded in the view that parents' interactions with their children are tailored to match their children's unfolding developmental competencies. For example, parents adjust their speech and play behaviors to their young children's current language and play skills, respectively (Bornstein & Lamb, 1992; Damast, Tamis-LeMonda, & Bornstein, 1996; Tamis-LeMonda & Bornstein, 1991). We believe that parent's race-related messages to children, in a similar manner, probably are very closely tied to parents' perceptions of children's understanding of racial issues, and perhaps also to children's race-related experiences. The study of developmental trends in parents' racial socialization practices may be especially fascinating due to information that it may provide concerning transactions between developmental processes and parents' behaviors.

The findings we describe are drawn from several studies. The sample for the first study, the Employed Parents Project (EPP), consisted of 157 African American parents of children age 4 to 14 who were lower-middle- to upper-middle-class, college-educated adults in dual-earner married couple families (see Hughes & Chen, 1997). Parents participated in 90-minute structured interviews concerning work, family, parenting, and other issues. The majority of these respondents lived in Chicago, but a subsample who participated in an initial pilot study (n = 16) lived in New York City. In the pilot study, we also conducted interviews with a randomly selected target child between the age of 4 and 14. The interview assessed children's racial awareness and constancy, among other things. We describe these pilot data simply to illustrate the possible ways in which parents' racial socialization practices may be associated with cognitive shifts in children's racial knowledge.

The sample for the second study consisted of 587 Black and Hispanic (Dominican, Puerto Rican, and Mexican) parents of children age 6 to 17. The sample consisted primarily of working class and high-school-educated adults, although there also was considerable socioeconomic diversity within the sample. Parents participated in a larger study of health and well-being among midlife adults as part of the John D. and Catherine T. Macarthur Foundation's Research Network on Mid-life Development (MIDMAC). Interviewers conducted 1- to 2-hour interviews with a quota sample of respondents drawn from randomly selected census block groups in New York City and Chicago. The interviews focused on phenomena associated with parents' race, ethnicity, and immigration experiences as well as on their health, well-being, and other social processes during midlife. All of the Black parents were born in the United States, as were approximately 50% of the Puerto Rican parents. The large majority of Mexican and Dominican parents were first-generation immigrants. Thus, the data permit us to examine racial socialization processes within a sample that is both ethnically and socioeconomically diverse.

The final study, the Early Adolescent Development Study (EADS), is an ongoing study of intergroup relations among a multiethnic (primarily White and African American) sample of over 950 elementary and middle school youth in the suburban Northeast. The targeted child sample consisted of all students who were in fourth or fifth grade in a midsized school district as of fall 1996, as well as third graders who attended selected elementary schools in the district. In the spring of 1997, 466 parents of these youth returned a survey which included a series of questions regarding their socialization practices pertaining to race and ethnicity with the participating child.

Similar measures of racial and ethnic socialization were used across these studies. The core set of items were initially generated for the EPP. For the MIDMAC and EADS studies, the items were revised to be applicable to multiple ethnic groups and to assess a broader range of racial and ethnic socialization practices. However, the core set of items focused on three of the dimensions of racial and ethnic socialization that we outlined above. These dimensions included: cultural socialization (e.g., "Have you ever encouraged your child to read books about the history or traditions of your ethnic/racial group?" "Do you ever do things with your child to remember events in [ethnic/racial group] history?"), preparation for bias (e.g., "Have you ever told your child that some people might treat him or her badly or unfairly because your child is [ethnic/racial group]?" "Have you ever talked with your child about prejudice or discrimination against [ethnic/racial group] people in this country?"), and promotion of mistrust (e.g., "Have you ever done or said things to discourage your child trusting people of a different racial/ethnic group?"). For each of the items, parents reported whether or not they had ever engaged in the behavior with their child (0 = *No*) and, if so, how often in the past year (1 = *never*; 5 = *very often*). Although items pertaining to each dimension of racial and ethnic socialization were not identical across studies, precluding comparison, the underlying constructs that emerged from principal components analyses were quite similar. In two of these studies (MIDMAC and EADS), we also included items to assess practices that reflect egalitarian values and perspectives (e.g., "Have you ever done or said things to encourage your child to appreciate people from all racial/ethnic backgrounds?"). Generally, the subscale measuring egalitarianism was highly correlated with that measuring cultural socialization, but we have retained them as distinct measures for theoretical purposes. Thus, we begin our presentation of findings with a description of the prevalence and frequency of racial and ethnic socialization across these different samples.

To What Extent Do Parents Engage in Racial-Ethnic Socialization?

As noted above, in the studies we have conducted, we have asked parents to indicate whether or not they have "ever" engaged in a series of discrete practices which we believe communicate information about race to children and, if so, the frequency with which they have engaged in such practices within the past 12 months. The advantage of this approach is that dimensions of racial socialization are assessed independently in terms both of prevalence (presence-absence) and frequency. Thus, in contrast to studies that have coded parents' responses to open ended questions regarding racial socialization practices, we have been able to ascertain whether or not parents engage in particular practices with their children and the intensity with which they do so.

In Table 22.1, we present data from each of the studies concerning both the prevalence and the frequency of particular racial or ethnic socialization messages within the past year. The estimate of prevalence was a relatively liberal one, based on the percentage of parents in each study reporting that they ever engaged in any of the behaviors or practices assessing dimensions of racial and ethnic socialization within the past year. The estimate of frequency consisted of the mean values for each dimension of racial socialization among parents who reported any such socialization within the past year.

As Table 22.1 indicates, we have consistently found that a substantial proportion of parents engage in at least some practices that communicate information about race and ethnicity to their children. For instance, in the EPP, only 3% (n = 5) of African American parents reported that they never engaged in any of the racial socialization practices we assessed within the past year. In the MIDMAC study, the large majority (94%) of parents also reported some racial socialization within the past year. Even in the EADS, which included non-Hispanic White and Jewish parents, the vast majority (over 95%) of parents in each ethnic group reported that they had engaged in at least one of the racial socialization practices we assessed within the past year.

The coefficients in Table 22.1 also suggest that, although racial socialization is evident among the large majority of parents, it occurred relatively infrequently. Moreover, it varied according both to the dimension that was measured and to the ethnic group that was responding. The mean values on dimensions of racial socialization among parents who reported any such socialization within the past year suggests that,

TABLE 22.1. Means and standard deviations of racial socialization measures for parents of children age 6 to 17 by racial-ethnic group

	Black	Dominican	Puerto Rican	Mexican	White	Jewish
EPP						
% reporting any cultural socialization in the past year (3 items; α = .84)	91.8	—	—	—	—	—
% reporting any preparation for bias in the past year (7 items; α = .91)	85.4	—	—	—	—	—
% reporting any promotion of mistrust in the past year (2 items; r = .68)	18.4	—	—	—	—	—
Mean cultural socialization among respondents reporting any in the past year	2.58	—	—	—	—	—
Mean preparation for bias among respondents reporting any in the past year	2.08	—	—	—	—	—
Mean promotion of mistrust among respondents reporting any in the past year	1.93	—	—	—	—	—
MIDMAC						
% reporting any egalitarianism (2 items; r = .65)	98.9[a]	90.8[a,b]	94.3[a,b]	88.3[b]		
% reporting any cultural socialization (2 items; r = .83)	93.2[a]	83.1[a]	81.9[a]	68.8[b]	—	—
% reporting any preparation for bias (4 items; α = .75)	93.2[a]	70.8[b]	74.1[b]	62.5[b]	—	—
% reporting any promotion of mistrust (1 item)	20.5[a]	9.2[b]	7.3[b]	8.6[b]	—	—
Mean egalitarianism among respondents reporting any in the past year	3.97[a]	3.87[a,b]	4.00[a]	3.62[b]		
Mean cultural socialization among respondents reporting any in the past year	3.52[a]	3.24[a]	3.03[a]	2.62[b]	—	—
Mean preparation for bias among respondents reporting any in the past year	2.62[c]	2.04[b]	1.87[b]	1.57[b]	—	—
Mean promotion of mistrust among respondents reporting any in the past year	2.39	3.17	3.21	3.09	—	—
EADS						
% reporting any egalitarianism in the past year (5 items; α = .73)	97.8				98.6	99.9
% reporting any cultural socialization in the past year (3 items; α = .65)	98.9	—	—	—	96.7	98.4
% reporting any preparation for bias in the past year (77 items; α =.87)	95.6[a]	—	—	—	72.0[b]	92.7[a]
% reporting any promotion of mistrust in the past year (2 items; r =.47)	20.9				13.3	12.1
Mean egalitarianism among respondents reporting any in the past year	2.79				2.67	2.46
Mean cultural socialization among respondents reporting any in the past year	3.32[a]	—	—	—	1.72[b]	2.41[c]

(Continued)

TABLE 22.1. (Continued)

	Black	Dominican	Puerto Rican	Mexican	White	Jewish
Mean preparation for bias among respondents reporting any in the past year	2.45[a]	—	—	—	.78[b]	1.13[c]
Mean promotion of mistrust among respondents reporting any in the past year	1.34				.91	.83

Note. EPP = Employed Parents Project; MIDMAC = John D. and Catherine T. McArthur Foundation's Research Network on Mid-life Development; EADS = Early Adolescent Development Study. Means with different superscripts are significantly different at *p* < .05.

within each study and within each ethnic group, cultural socialization and egalitarianism were more prevalent and more frequent than was preparation for bias which, in turn, was more prevalent and more frequent than was promotion of mistrust. For instance, in the EPP, 92% of African American parents reported cultural socialization practices within the past year and 85% of them reported some discussions about racial bias (preparation for bias) within the past year. However, only about 19% of African American parents in the EPP reported any promotion of mistrust within the past year. Moreover, parents who reported any cultural socialization engaged in it more frequently than did parents who reported preparation for bias or promotion of mistrust. A very similar pattern emerged among parents who participated in the MIDMAC study and in the EADS.

In addition to differences in racial socialization according to the dimensions measured, there were racial-ethnic group differences in the prevalence and frequency of various racial and ethnic socialization practices. In particular, the mean values for such socialization were generally higher among African American parents than among parents of other racial-ethnic backgrounds, indicating that they engaged in racial socialization practices more often. In MIDMAC, African American parents reported more frequent cultural socialization than did Puerto Rican or Dominican parents who, in turn, reported more frequent cultural socialization than did Mexican parents. African American parents also were more likely than were their Dominican, Puerto Rican, or Mexican counterparts to report any preparation for bias within the past year. The mean values among African American parents reporting preparation for bias were higher than those of their Dominican, Puerto Rican, or Mexican counterparts. African American parents also were significantly more likely than were any of the Hispanic parents to report promotion of mistrust, although ethnic group differences in the frequency of promotion of mistrust were not statistically significant at *p* < .05.

In the EADS study, African American parents were more likely than were Jewish parents to report preparation for bias, although Jewish parents also were more likely to report preparation for bias than were non-Jewish White parents. However, there were no ethnic or racial group differences in the prevalence of egalitarian practices or cultural socialization, due to the fact that the vast majority of parents reported egalitarianism and cultural socialization. Nor were there ethnic or racial group differences in promotion of mistrust, due to the fact that a small minority of parents from any ethnic group reported it. However, the frequency of both cultural socialization and preparation for bias was significantly greater among African American parents, as compared to Jewish and non-Jewish White parents. Preparation for bias also was significantly greater among Jewish parents as compared to non-Jewish White parents.

The general pattern of findings, then, suggested that very few parents completely avoided discussions with their children pertaining to race and racial issues. The most common practices in this regard were those that expose children to their own group's history, heritage, and culture (cultural socialization) and those that emphasize appreciation of ethnic and racial diversity (egalitarianism). Discussions about racial bias or poor treatment of one's own ethnic or racial group (preparation for bias) also occurred in most families at some point within the past year, but they occurred with much less frequency than did cultural socialization or practices promoting egalitarian views. Moreover, African American parents were consistently more likely than parents of other racial or ethnic backgrounds to report preparation for bias, and they reported that it occurred with greater frequency than did other parents. Promotion of mistrust was relatively rare among any group, although, again, it was typically more prevalent and more frequent among African American parents than among parents of other ethnic or racial backgrounds.

Age-Related Shifts in Racial Socialization

Parents' race-related messages to children are not static or constant throughout childhood. In the studies we have conducted to date, we have consistently found that parents of older children were more likely than were parents of younger children to engage in certain types of racial socialization practices with their children, in particular promotion of mistrust and preparation for bias (Hughes, 1998; Hughes & Chen, 1997). For instance, in the EPP, in which parents answered racial socialization questions about target children 4 to 14 years of age, the prevalence and frequency of preparation for bias and promotion of mistrust within the past year increased linearly as a function of children's ages (shown in Figures 22.1 and 22.2). In the MIDMAC study, we also found that parents of older children reported more preparation for bias and promotion of mistrust in terms of both prevalence and frequency than did parents of younger children (Shown in Figures 22.3 and 22.4).

We did not find consistent age-related trends in the frequency of these dimensions of racial socialization in the EADS, a study in which the age range of target children was only between 8 and 11 years old. As in the EPP and the MIDMAC studies, a significantly greater proportion of parents with children age 10 and 11 reported preparation for bias than did parents of children age 8 and 9 (although the large majority of parents in both groups reported such socialization). However, neither preparation for bias nor promotion of mistrust were more frequent among parents of older children, as compared to parents of younger children. The lack of significant findings in this regard may be due to the fact that children made a transition from elementary schools that were racially homogenous to one of two racially heterogeneous middle schools following fourth grade. Racial socialization was consistently highest among parents of fourth

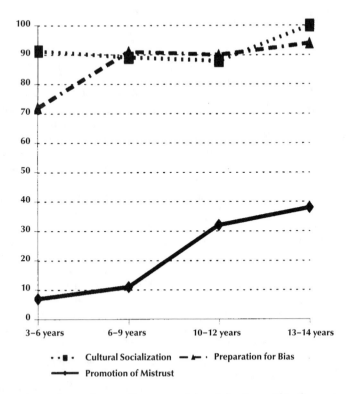

FIGURE 22.1. Percentage of parents reporting any racial socialization within the past year by target child's age category (Employed Parents Project [EPP]).

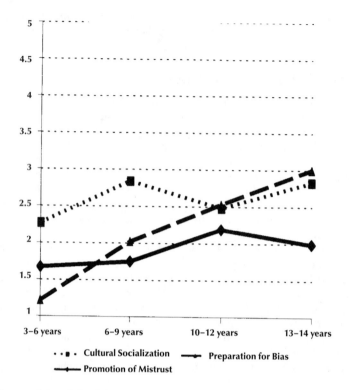

FIGURE 22.2. Mean racial socialization among parents reporting any within the past year by target child's age category (Employed Parents Project [EPP]).

graders as compared to parents of third graders or fifth graders. Thus, parents' racial socialization efforts also may be sensitive to ecological transitions.

Elsewhere, we have proposed that age-related shifts in parents race-related messages to their children may be a function of corrollary shifts in children's development. As children get older, they undergo important cognitive transitions in their understanding of race. Although children as young as 3 years old are aware that people belong to different racial groups and can classify individuals into racial-ethnic categories, they do not have an adult-like understanding of race until cognitive markers, such as racial constancy, have been achieved (around the age 7 to 10) (Aboud, 1988). Children's racial-ethnic identity and their sophisticated understanding of race as a sociostructural phenomenon emerge even later. We expect that parents of children who demonstrate only a rudimentary understanding of race as a social construct would be less likely than parents of older children to discuss issues related to racial bias with their children, or to caution or warn them about cross-race interactions.

Data from our pilot subsample of 157 African Americans permitted us to examine in a very preliminary way the possibility that age-related trends in parents' racial socialization practices corresponded to cognitive shifts in children's understanding of racial issues. The interview protocol for the pilot study included a 17-item Racial Constancy Scale, adapted from the Boy-Girl Identity Task (Aboud, 1988; Slaby & Frey, 1975), which assessed three components of racial constancy: Identification, Consistency, and Stability. The Identification subscale consisted of five items which required children to correctly identify themselves as being African American and to correctly label photographs of children and adults as being either White or African American. The Stability subscale consisted of five separate tasks that required children to demonstrate knowledge that race is stable and immutable over the life course (e.g., "When this (white/ black) (man/woman) was a baby, was he (white/black) like this child or was he (white/black) like this child?"). The Consistency subscale assessed children's understanding that race is stable and immutable despite transformation in superficial features. It was assessed by asking children questions about a set of sequential photographs in which a Caucasian girl is pictured through a series of transformations in cloth-

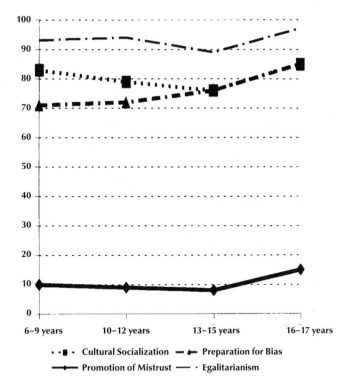

FIGURE 22.3. Percentage of parents reporting any racial socialization within the past by year target child's age category (John D. and Catherine T. McArthur Foundation's Research Network on Mid-Life Development [MIDMAC]).

ing, hairstyle, and skin color (e.g., "This girl put on clothes like these black people are wearing. Is she really a black girl or is she a white girl?"). Children with higher scores for overall constancy or for any of the three subscales answered more of the respective items correctly.

As in other studies (Aboud, 1988), children's age was strongly correlated with their overall racial constancy score ($r = .64$, $p < .01$). Almost all of the children completed the Identification task successfully: Twelve children answered all six identification questions correctly and four children answered five of the six questions correctly. However, performance on both the Stability ($r = .70$, $p < .01$) and the Consistency ($r = .61$, $p < .05$) subscales of racial constancy task varied according to children's ages. Older children were significantly more likely to demonstrate Stability and Consistency than were younger children. For the Stability subscale, which assessed children's ability to understand that one's racial group membership is constant over time, only one of three children age 3 to 5 answered all five questions correctly, six of the eight children age 6 to 9 answered all five questions correctly (all but two 6-year-old children) and all of the children age 10 and older answered all five questions correctly. For the Consistency subscale, which assessed children's understanding that one's racial group membership is consistent despite transformations in physical appearance, none of the children age 4 to 5 demonstrated Consistency (e.g., at least five of six questions answered correctly), 40% of children age 6 to 9 demonstrated Consistency, and 80% of children age 10 and older demonstrated Consistency. The average number of items correct for the full Racial Constancy Scale as a function of children's ages is shown in Figure 22.5.

Figure 22.5 also shows mean values for parents' reports about their racial socialization practices as a function of children's ages. As in the full EPP sample and MIDMAC, cultural socialization was unrelated to children's ages. Cultural socialization also was unrelated to children's overall constancy scores and (not shown) to their scores on the Stability and Consistency subscales. Thus, it seems that the motivation underlying cultural socialization may be distinctively different from that which underlies racial socialization practices that reference racial social hierarchies.

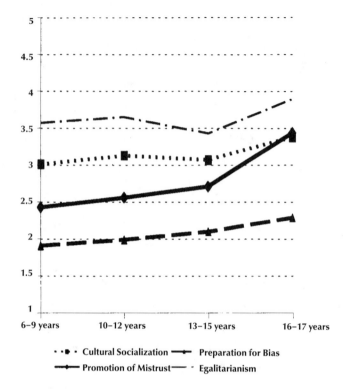

FIGURE 22.4. Mean racial socialization among parents reporting any in the past year by target child's age category (John D. and Catherine T. McArthur Foundation's Research Network on Mid-Life Development [MIDMAC]).

However, in Figure 22.5, increases in parents' preparation for bias closely mirror increases with age in children's overall racial constancy scores. Preparation for bias was positively related to children's actual racial knowledge (i.e., overall Constancy, Stability, and Consistency). Parents who were more likely to discuss with their children the possibility of future encounters with bias had children with a more sophisticated understanding of race as stable and consistent across time and transformations ($r = .63$; $p < .05$). Parents' cautions and warnings about other racial-ethnic groups had a similar parallel relation to children's overall racial constancy. However, the correlation was not statistically significant ($r = .04$; $p > .05$) due to the very low number of parents reporting any promotion of mistrust: only 3 of the 16 parents actually reported engaging in such socialization practices.

We believe that these preliminary findings regarding relationships between children's ages, children's understanding of racial issues, and parents' racial socialization practices may be both informative and useful in guiding future investigations of racial socialization processes. Specifically, as with studies of reference group orientation and racial-ethnic identity, parents' racial socialization practices need to be examined through a developmental lens that brings into focus the dynamic relationship between shifts in children's understanding of racial issues and parental messages to them regarding such issues. Parents' interactions with their children are unlikely to include repeated reference to racial issues during stages in which children evidence little understanding of the concept. Thus, researchers seeking to understanding the extent of racial-ethnic socialization among families need to be mindful of shifts in parents' racial socialization as children get older. Data from our small pilot study suggests that such shifts correspond closely to progressions in children's cognitive understanding of race.

It is important to note, however, that such progressions cannot fully account for age-related trends in parents' racial socialization practices, due to the fact that preparation for bias and promotion of mistrust continued to increase beyond the ages at which the large majority of children have achieved constancy. In future analysis of data from the EADS study, which includes multiple assessment of children and parents over a 2-year period, we will be able to examine the extent to which racial socialization practices among

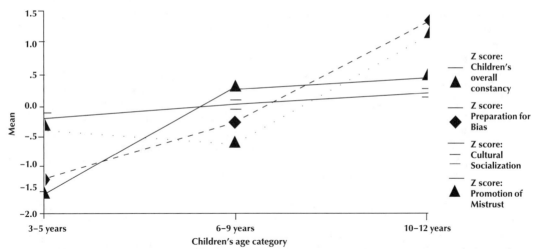

FIGURE 22.5. Children's overall racial constancy as a function of parent's reports about racial socialization by child's age category.

parents of older children change as a function of changes in children's race-related experiences in various settings.

Conclusions and Future Directions

The study of racial socialization provides insight into how parents shape their children's knowledge about racial-ethnic categories and about different groups in our increasingly pluralistic society. Parents may address racial-ethnic issues in many ways. They may provide deliberate, proactive messages concerning the maintenance of cultural traditions, they may inadvertently react to their children's experiences with prejudice, or they may attempt to promote a "color blind" approach by modeling exemplary behaviors to their children. The ways in which parents discuss race-related issues with their children—whether they choose to convey information to their children about cultural history or not; cultural traditions or ethnic pride; about racial bias, discrimination, and prejudice; and about relations with other racial-ethnic groups including mistrust or pluralism—may have important implications for children's eventual well-being and development.

Our review of the small body of literature on influences of parents' racial socialization practices on children's developmental outcomes showed that parents' messages about cultural heritage and pride consistently have salutary effects on children's racial-ethnic identity development; racial-ethnic attitudes, preferences, knowledge, and behaviors; and academic and psychosocial outcomes (Branch & Newcombe, 1986; Demo & Hughes, 1990; Knight et al., 1993; Marshall, 1995; Ou & McAdoo, 1993; Sanders Thompson, 1994; Stevenson, 1995). In contrast, parental messages that may foster mistrust of other racial-ethnic groups appear to influence children in a negative manner (Biafora et al., 1993; Ogbu, 1974; Patchen, 1982; Rumbaut, 1994; Smith, 1996). These findings suggest that parents' race-related messages to children about race and racial issues must be carefully crafted to ensure their children's healthy and successful development. Parents' socialization practices that make reference to hierarchies, barriers, and unfair treatment due to race may, on one hand, help children cope with societal realities (Bowman & Howard 1985; Knight et al., 1993; Spencer, 1983). However, on the other hand, such practices also may be related to poor child outcomes, for example, academic performance (Marshall, 1995; Smith, 1996).

Due to the differential effects that varying messages about race may have on children's development, many parents are ambivalent about engaging in race-related discussions with their children. Thus, though they may believe that it is important to inform their children about the "racial realities of the world," they may rarely do so in practice. Racial and ethnic issues may be sensitive topics for parents to approach and whether or not they choose to do so may depend on their beliefs about their children's readiness to understand and cope with such complicated topics.

We investigated the influences of children's age and racial knowledge on dimensions of parental racial socialization utilizing examples from our own empirical work. Age-related differences in children's racial knowledge may underlay the positive relationship between children's age and racial socialization messages that prepare children for racial bias. As children age from 4 to 12 years, there are marked differences in their comprehension of racial-ethnic categories as stable over time and consistent across perceptual transformations, though their ability to correctly identify racial-ethnic group members emerges early (Chen, 1998; pilot study from Hughes & Chen, 1997). We argue that parents may be sensitive to their children's greater understanding of racial-ethnic issues as they grow older and, therefore, might become more comfortable in discussing such issues with them. Indeed, we found that, as children scored higher on the Stability and Consistency subscales of racial constancy (providing evidence of gains in racial knowledge) and their parents perceived them as more knowledgeable about racial bias, parents were more likely to prepare them for future encounters with bias (pilot study from Hughes & Chen, 1997). We interpreted these findings as possible evidence that parents are more willing to discuss racial status differences and bias with their children only when they realize their children have achieved a certain level of racial knowledge development.

Among parents who rear their children from a humanistic approach, however, the types of racial socialization they are most likely to practice (i.e., cultural socialization or egalitarianism and silence) may be unrelated to children's cognitive understanding of race, their experiences, or both. Notably, few empirical investigations of pluralistic socialization and silence about race exist (e.g., Bowman & Howard, 1985; Kofkin et al., 1995; Spencer, 1983); however, specific predictors of such forms of racial socialization have yet to be investigated and warrant future attention.

To date, there also have been few studies that have attempted to investigate the similarities and differences in race-related socialization practices across racial-ethnic groups (Hughes, 1998; Phinney & Chavira, 1995). Yet, the frequency of racial socialization practices seems to be associated with racial-ethnic group membership. African American parents have reported race-related communications with their children more than parents of other racial groups (Hughes, 1998; Phinney & Chavira, 1995). Due to the unique immigration history, cultural heritage and values, and social status of each racial-ethnic group in the United States, different patterns of socialization may arise and are likely to influence children's developmental outcomes. Comparative studies of racial socialization may be useful in ascertaining how racial group categorizations, and their related implications, impact groups of different positions in American social structure. The basic nature of racial socialization and its underlying origins may be distinct across groups. As our society becomes increasingly multicultural, racial categories will become more significant for the child's developing understanding of self and others. Studying parental influences on children's racial knowledge acquisition will enable us to help children not only to have positive views of themselves and others, but also positive interactions in their social world.

☐ Note

1. In this chapter, we use the terms *race* and *ethnicity* interchangeably and very broadly to refer to social groups distinguished by physiogenomic and cultural differences. We are cognizant of scholarly debates regarding the meaning of race and its biological and social significance as well as those regarding the distinction between race and ethnicity in terms of the groups to whom the terms apply. We do not address these issues in this chapter.

☐ References

Aboud, F. (1988). *Children and prejudice*. New York: Basil Blackwell.

Appelgate, J. L., Burleson, B. R., & Delia, J. G. (1992). Reflection enhancing parenting as an antecedent to children's social cognitive and communicative development. In I. E. Sigel, A. V. McGuillicudy-DeLisi, & J. J. Goodnow (Eds.), *Parental belief systems: The psychological consequences for children* (2nd ed., pp. 3–40). Hillsdale, NJ: Erlbaum.

Barnes, E. J. (1980). The black community as a source of positive self concept for black children: A theoretical perspective. In R. Jones (Ed.), *Black Psychology*. New York: Harper and Row.

Biafora, F. A., Warheit, G. J., Zimmerman, R. S., Gil, A. G., Apospori, E., Taylor, D., & Vega, W. A. (1993). Racial mistrust and deviant behaviors among ethnically diverse Black adolescent boys. *Journal of Applied Social Psychology, 23*, 891–910.

Bornstein, M. H., & Lamb, M. E. (1992). *Development in infancy: An introduction* (3rd ed.). New York: McGraw-Hill.

Bowman, P. J., & Howard, C. (1985). Race-related socialization, motivation, and academic achievement: A study of Black youth in three-generation families. *Journal of the American Academy of Child Psychiatry, 24*, 134–141.

Boykin, A. W., & Toms, F. D. (1985). Black child socialization: A conceptual framework. In H. P. McAdoo & J. L. McAdoo (Eds.), *Black children: Social, educational, and parental environments* (pp. 33–52). Newbury Park, CA: Sage.

Branch, C. W., & Newcombe, N. (1986). Racial attitude development among young children as a function of parental attitudes: A longitudinal and cross-sectional study. *Child Development, 57,* 712–721.

Buriel, R., & DeMent , T. (1997). Immigration and sociocultural changes in Mexican, Chinese, and Vietnamese American families. In A. Booth, A. C. Crouter, & N. Landale (Eds.), *Immigration and the family: Research and policy on U.S. Immigrants* (pp. 165–200). Mahwah, NJ: Erlbaum.

Chen, L. A. (1998). *A contextual examination of parental ethnic socialization and children's ethnic attitudes and knowledge among immigrant Chinese families.* Unpublished doctoral dissertation, New York University.

Damast, A. M., Tamis-LeMonda, C. S., & Bornstein, M. H. (1996). Mother-child play: Sequential interactions and the relation between maternal beliefs and behaviors. *Child Development, 67,* 1752–1766.

DeBerry, K. M., & Weinberg, R. (1996). Family racial socialization and ecological competence: Longitudinal assessments of African American transracial adoptees. *Child Development, 67,* 2375–2399.

Demo, D., & Hughes, M. (1990). Socialization and racial identity among Black Americans. *Social Psychology Quarterly, 53,* 364–374.

Essed, P. (1990). *Everyday racism.* Alameda, CA: Hunter House.

Fisher, C. B., Jackson, F. J., & Villarruel, F. A. (in press). The study of African American and Latin-American children and youth in the United States. In R. M. Lerner (Ed.), *Handbook of Child Psychology: Vol. 1. Theoretical models of human development* (5th ed.). New York: Wiley.

Fordham, S., & Ogbu, J. U. (1986). Black students' school success: Coping with the "burden of acting White." *Urban Review, 18,* 176–206.

Garcia Coll, C. T., & Magnuson, K. (1997). The psychological experience of immigration: A developmental perspective. In A. Booth, A. C. Crouter, & N. Landale, (Eds.), *Immigration and the family: Research and policy on U.S. immigrants* (pp. 91–132). Mahwah, NJ: Erlbaum.

Garcia Coll, C. T., Meyer, E. C., & Brillion, L. (1995*).* Ethnic and minority parenting. In M. Bornstein (Ed.), *Handbook of parenting: Vol. 2. Biology and ecology of parenting* (pp. 189–209). Hillsdale, NJ: Erlbaum.

Hamm, J. V. (1996). Adolescents' cross-race peer relations as a consequence of parents' beliefs and socialization efforts (Doctoral dissertation, University of Wisconsin, Madison, 1996). *Dissertation Abstracts International, 57*(09), Z5945.

Harrison, A. O., Wilson, M. N., Pine, C. J., Chan, S. Q., & Buriel, R. (1995). Family ecologies of ethnic minority children. In N. R. Goldberger et al. (Eds.), *The culture and psychology reader* (pp. 292–320). New York: New York University Press.

Hernandez, D. J. (1997). Child development and the social demography of childhood. *Child Development, 68,* 149–169.

Hughes, D. (1998). *Contextual correlates of parents' race-related messages to children: A study of urban African American and Latino/a families.* Unpublished manuscript, New York University.

Hughes, D. (1997). *Racial socialization among urban African American and Latino families.* Paper presented at the biennial meeting of the Society for Research in Child Development, Washington, DC.

Hughes, D. (1996). Focus group transcript. Unpublished document. New York University, New York.

Hughes, D., & Chen, L. A. (1997). When and what parents tell children about race: An examination of race-related socialization among African American families. *Applied Developmental Science, 1,* 198–212.

Hughes, D., & Dumont, K. (1993). Focus groups as culturally anchored methodology. *American Journal of Community Psychology, 21,* 775–806.

Johnson, D. (1989). Identity information and racial coping strategies of Black children and their parents: A stress and coping paradigm. *Dissertation Abstract International, 48*(10-A), 2581.

Katz, P. A. (1982). Development of children's racial awareness and intergroup attitudes. In L. G. Katz, C. H. Watkins, M. J. Spencer, & P. J. Wagemaker (Eds.), *Current topics in early childhood education* (Vol. 4). Norwood, NJ: Abex.

Kibria, N. (1997). The concept of "bicultural families" and its implications for research on immigrant and ethnic families. In A. Booth, A. C. Crouter, & N. Landale, (Eds.), *Immigration and the family: Research and policy on U.S. immigrants* (pp. 205–210). Mahwah, NJ: Erlbaum.

Knight, G. P., Bernal, M. E., Garza, C. A., Cota, M. K., & Ocampo, K. A. (1993). Family socialization and the ethnic identity of Mexican-American children. *Journal of Cross-Cultural Psychology, 24,* 99–114.

Kofkin, J. A., Katz, P. A., & Downey, E. P. (1995, March). *Family discourse about race and the development of children's racial attitudes.* Paper presented at the meeting of the Society for Research on Child Development, Indianapolis, IN.

Lee, J., & Cynn, V. (1991). Issues in counseling 1.5 generation Korean Americans. In C. Lee & B. Richardson (Eds.), *Multicultural issues in counseling: New approaches to diversity* (pp. 127–140). Alexandria, VA: American Association for Counseling and Development.

Marshall, S. (1995). Ethnic socialization of African American children: Implications for parenting, identity development, and academic achievement. *Journal of Youth and Adolescence, 24,* 377–396.

Nsamenang, A. B., & Lamb, M. E. (1995). The force of beliefs: How the parental values of the Nso of northwest Cameroon shape children's progress toward adult models. *Journal of Applied Developmental Psychology, 16,* 613–627.

Ogbu, J. U. (1974). *The next generation: An ethnography of education in an urban neighborhood.* New York: Academic Press.

Ou, Y. S., & McAdoo, H. P. (1993). Socialization of Chinese American children. In H. P. McAdoo (Ed.), *Ethnicity: Strength in diversity* (pp. 245–270). Newbury Park, CA: Sage.

Oyserman, D. (1993). Adolescent identity and delinquency in interpersonal context. *Child Psychiatry and Human Development, 23*, 203–214.

Oyserman, D., & Harrison, K. (1998). Implications of cultural context: African American identity and possible selves. In J. K. Swim & C. Stangor (Eds.), *Prejudice the targets' perspective* (pp. 281–300). San Diego, CA: Academic Press.

Parham, T. A., & Williams, P. T. (1993). The relationship of demographic and background factors to racial identity attitudes. *Journal of Black Psychology, 19*, 7–24.

Patchen, M. (1982). *Black-White contact in schools.* Lafayette, IN: Purdue University Press.

Peters, M. F. (1981). Parenting in black families with young children: A historical perspective. In H. McAdoo (Ed.), *Black families.* Newbury Park, CA: Sage.

Peters, M. F. (1985). Ethnic socialization of young Black children. In H. P. McAdoo & J. L. McAdoo (Eds.), *Black children: Social, educational, and parental environments* (pp. 159–173). Newbury Park, CA: Sage.

Phinney, J. S., & Chavira, V. (1995). Parental ethnic socialization and adolescent coping with problems related to ethnicity. *Journal of Research on Adolescence, 5*, 31–54.

Phinney, J. S., & Kohatsu, E. L. (1997). Ethnic and racial identity development and mental health. In J. Schulenberg, J. L. Maggs, & K. Hurrelmann (Eds.), *Health risks and developmental transitions during adolescence* (pp. 420–443). New York: Cambridge University Press.

Porter, J., & Washington, R. (1993). Minority identity and self-esteem. *Annual Review of Sociology, 19*, 139–161.

Richardson, B. (1981). Racism and child-rearing: A study of Black mothers. (Doctoral dissertation, Claremont Graduate School, 1981). *Dissertation Abstracts International, 42*, 125A.

Rumbaut, R. (1994). The crucible within: Ethnic identity, self-esteem, and segmented assimilation among children of immigrants. *International Migration Review, 28*, 748–794.

Sanders Thompson, V. L. (1994). Socialization to race and its relationship to racial identification among African Americans. *Journal of Black Psychology, 20*, 175–188.

Slaby, R. G., & Frey, K. S. (1975). Development of gender constancy and selective attention to same sex models. *Child Development, 46*, 849–856.

Smith, E. P. (1996, March). *Racial-ethnic socialization: Family, school, and community influences.* Paper presented at the biennial meeting of the Society for Research in Adolescence, Boston, MA.

Smith, E., Fogle, V., & Jacobs, J. (in press). Assessing parental ethnic socialization: Issues and implementation. In D. Johnson (Ed.), *Racial socialization and African American children.* Berkeley, CA: Cobb and Henry.

Spencer, M. B. (1983). Children's cultural values and parental child rearing strategies. *Developmental Review, 3*, 351–370.

Spencer, M. B. (1985). Cultural cognition and social cognition as identity correlates of Black children's personal-social development. In M. B. Spencer, G. Brookins, & W. Allen (Eds.), *Beginnings: The social and affective development of black children* (pp. 215–230). Hillsdale, NJ: Erlbaum.

Spencer, M. B., & Dornbusch, S. H. (1990). Challenges in studying minority youth. In S. Feldman & G. Elliott (Eds.), *At the threshold: The developing adolescent* (pp.123–146). Cambridge, MA: Harvard University Press.

Spencer, M. B., & Markstrom-Adams, C. (1990). Identity processes among racial and ethnic minority children in America. *Child Development, 61*, 290–310.

Stevenson, H. C. (1994). Validation of the scale of racial socialization for African American adolescents: Steps towards multidimensionality. *Journal of Black Psychology, 20*, 445–468.

Stevenson, H. C. (1995). Relationships of adolescent perceptions of racial socialization to racial identity. *Journal of Black Psychology, 21*, 49–70.

Tamis-LeMonda, C. S., & Bornstein, M. H. (1991). Individual variation, correspondence, stability, and change in mother and toddler play. *Infant Behavior and Development, 14*, 143–162.

Thornton, M. C., Chatters, L. M., Taylor, R. J., & Allen, W. R. (1990). Sociodemographic and environmental correlates of racial socialization by black parents. *Child Development, 61*, 401–409.

Uba, L. (1994). *Asian Americans: Personality patterns, identity, and mental health.* New York: Guilford Press.

Vega, W. A., Khoury, E. L., Zimmerman, R. S., Gil, A. F., & Warheit, G. L. (1995). Cultural conflicts and problem behaviors of Latino adolescents in home and school environments. *Journal of Community Psychology, 23*, 167–179.

Ward, J. V. (1996). Raising resisters: The role of truth telling in the psychological development of African American girls. In B. J. R. Leadbeater & N. Way (Eds.), *Urban girls: Resisting stereotypes, creating identities* (pp. 83–99). New York: New York University Press.

23
CHAPTER

Gilda A. Morelli
Heidi Verhoef

Who Should Help Me Raise My Child?
A Cultural Approach to Understanding
Nonmaternal Child Care Decisions

☐ Introduction

This chapter is about the factors that influence women's decisions regarding who is going to care for their children on a regular basis, sometimes for extended periods of time.[1] While this issue is particularly relevant in the United States, given recent welfare reform that will result in more than 3 million women entering the labor market over the next few years, it is not a new issue for women in the United States or elsewhere.

We focus on cultural factors in this chapter because we believe they are a significant source of influence but, unlike other factors such as maternal income and educational status, they seldom have been taken into account. In order to learn more about the role of culture in the care arrangements mothers make for their children, we examine mothers' ideas about qualities of care. These ideas, referred to as ethnotheories, are part of a culture's system of beliefs, and they help to form mothers' views of child care and the role child care plays both for them and their children.

We begin the chapter by reflecting on the value of examining ethnotheories through use of writings mainly from the fields of cultural psychology and anthropology for guidance. We then present information on the need for child care and how this need has been conceptualized across time and place. This material is meant to help frame the issues raised in the next section that compares what mothers and experts look for in nonmaternal care. We make this comparison to highlight areas of divergence and overlap between the views of mothers and dominant cultural ideology. We also look more closely at child care decisions in one cultural community in West Africa, the Nso of Cameroon. Finally, we consider U.S. public policy on child care and the implication it has for the policies of other countries where women's participation in the formal and informal labor market is increasing at exceedingly high rates.

☐ Parental Ethnotheories

Parents make decisions about their children's care and upbringing based on the options available to them. Options are determined by the opportunities within parents' reach and the constraints that limit parents' access to them, both of which are mediated by cultural systems of practices and beliefs as well as by the circumstances of everyday life.

Support for this paper was provided by Grant 5-23484 from the National Institute of Mental Health to Gilda A. Morelli. The authors thank David Wilkie for his careful reading of the manuscript and technical support, and Ellen O'Donnell and Kaitlan Mulcahy for their library help.

Parents' ethnotheories about children are part of the culture's more general belief system and, as such, play a role in determining the child care options that are considered acceptable. For example, preschools in America serve more than 4.5 million children each year and are partly financed by government spending (Fuller, Holloway, & Liang, 1996). Yet, Latinos are significantly underrepresented in their use of this resource. It appears as though Latino mothers believe that the values emphasized in preschools conflict with the values emphasized at home. Thus, while preschools are physically available to Latino mothers, they are not an option for them.

Ethnotheories are perpetuated as well as revised by parents as they participate with others in culturally meaningful activities. Social exchanges can provide parents with an opportunity to develop a shared understanding of the culture—creating a commonality in beliefs among the participants that links present and past ways of knowing. Yet, even though parental ethnotheories consist of elements that make up the collective culture, they also are highly personalized. This is because parents integrate their own histories with their culture's history, and construct their own personal cultures in the process (Valsiner, 1988; Valsiner & Litvinovic, 1996). As a result, parental ethnotheories reflect both parents' personal histories and the experiences of past generations (McGillicuddy-De Lisi & Subramanian, 1996).

Personal cultures often represent innovative ways of conceptualizing the collective culture. These new perspectives may be expressed by parents in their social exchanges or through the products of their activities; if they are, they may change the personal cultures of others or even the collective culture (Valsiner & Litvinovic, 1996). In this way, parents produce as well as reproduce their cultural systems of knowledge (Corsaro & Rizzo, 1988). Valsiner and Litvinovic (1996) noted that "the role of persons as innovative carriers of the collective culture is crucial for the constant modification of the cultural form" (p. 61). However, it is not reasonable to expect that every personal revision will lead either to innovative ways of constructing cultural knowledge or to the production of new shared knowledge.

Parents' ideas about children, however, do not always relate to how they act toward them. Yet, whether we should expect a predicable relation between ideas and actions is debatable. Goodnow (1988) suggested that we should not, and offered ways to qualify the most accepted notion on parents' ideas—ideas structure action—to address this paradox. For example, inconsistencies may be a function of the relative strength of the opinion held on two or more principles that are in conflict with each other, the characteristics of the particular situation or the people studied (e.g., their income level and educational status), and the actions of interest. Considering factors such as these may lead to a better understanding of the relation between ideas and actions. However, many researchers do not expect a perfect correspondence. Besides, they believe that there is a lot of evidence supporting the position that parents' activities can be seen as an expression of their beliefs (e.g., Harkness & Super, 1996).

However, the close coupling of parents' ideas with specific actions may not be necessary for children to learn about qualities emphasized by their parents and the community. What may be important, instead, is the creation of themes in children's lives that communicate valued ways of thinking and acting. Thematicity is brought about in the way that children's activities are organized and made sense of by others across time and place (Harkness & Super, 1995). For example, research on children's sleeping arrangements has suggested that practices surrounding where children sleep and with whom, when children go to sleep, bedtime routines, and nighttime wakings and feedings as a whole communicate to children valued ways of relating to family members and others. Some have suggested that children's understanding of independence and interdependence may develop from these different experiences (Morelli, Rogoff, Oppenheim, & Goldsmith, 1992). Any particular parenting act probably would not foster this understanding, but acts that collectively promote it might. Thus, it may be more worthwhile for those interested in studying parents' ideas and actions, and children's outcomes, to focus on the relation between ideas and the cultural themes they create in children's lives rather than on the relation between ideas and specific parental acts.

Culture theory gives us insight into how parents' ideas about their children guide their actions and change over time as they interact with others whose views may be different from their own. It suggests that any efforts to provide child care services to communities must consider parents' ethnotheories, especially if parents' ideas are not consistent with dominant cultural ideology. It also suggests that ideas are dynamic, changing over time, and are modified by circumstances of everyday life. With this in mind, we look at the way child care needs have been thought about over time and place.

☐ Framing Women's and Children's Child Care Needs

Women seek out others to help with child care for many reasons, such as to improve educational and social opportunities for their children or to earn an income. For women who work, child care is intimately tied to their participation in the labor force (Meyers, Gilbert, & Duerr-Berrick, 1992) and, when possible, women will adjust their work routines to meet their child care needs. For example, Presser and Cox (1997) noted that about a third of low-educated U.S. women sampled in the 1991 Current Population Survey reported working nonstandard schedules to improve their child care arrangements. These findings are supported by the 1993 Survey of Income and Program Participation (SIPP), where about 15% of U.S. working mothers chose to work nonstandard hours to obtain better child care; this figure rose to 18% for mothers with preschool-age children (Casper, Hawkins, & O'Connell, 1994). Yet, regardless of women's employment status, child care must be seen as meeting the needs of both women and children, whatever those needs might be.

The view that children's as well as women's needs must be carefully thought about when developing nonmaternal child care opportunities is fairly recent. We know this from looking at the history of women-in-development (WID) programs in third world countries (Myers, 1992). Early concerns of development programs focused on facilitating women's involvement in income-earning positions, or in training or educational programs. During this time, children's needs were considered as an afterthought, and little attention was paid to promoting children's developmental experiences when in nonmaternal care settings. The assumption was that the additional income earned by mothers would be enough to improve the lives of their children, an assumption that has been challenged (Myers, 1992). But, because of this position, care was seen as custodial in nature, aimed primarily at protecting children from harm (see below for a discussion of when women may prefer this type of care). Child care as a service for mothers simply to sustain their employment or training, however, is no longer acceptable to many international community development workers. These individuals realize the broader implications of nonmaternal care for the child and the mother, and they advocate for programs that promote children's health, safety, and development and, at the same time, meet the needs of women (Cochran, 1995; Myers, 1992).

Child care programming in the United States shares a similar history. There is an ongoing debate within and outside of the early childhood education profession regarding the role of nonmaternal child care in the lives of women and children (Daniel, 1996). Like the differences of opinion seen among international development workers, there are some in the United States who believe that child care is meant to support mothers in their attempts to achieve self-sufficiency, while others believe that it is meant to support children's learning and development. Yet, even as this debate continues, many lawmakers in the United States realize the importance of supporting both child care goals (Smith, Fairchild, & Groginsky, 1997); however, accomplishing this will be particularly challenging with the signing of the Personal Responsibility and Work Opportunity Reconciliation Act (PRWORA; P. L. 104-193). PRWORA ended federal entitlement to child care, required individuals to work after 2 years of receiving federal subsidies, and set work participation requirements so that states must have at least half of the adults who receive Temporary Aid for Needy Families (TANF) working by the year 2002. Failure to meet this last obligation will result in states receiving less of the money allocated in their block grants. This legislation will increase the demand for child care among the nation's poor and near-poor families while, at the same time, decreasing federal resources to provide these services. Obviously, states will have to make difficult decisions regarding how to best meet their child care needs (Smith et al., 1997).

While there is a growing consensus in domestic and international arenas that child care ought to consider the needs of mothers and children alike, we are still learning about what these needs are and the factors that influence them. For example, we know that women need care that is affordable and accessible (see, for example, Kontos, Howes, Shinn, & Galinsky, 1995; Ogbimi, 1992; Phillips, 1995). Women also need child care arrangements that are flexible in the services they provide (e.g., caring for sick children) and in the hours they operate (e.g., nights and weekend hours). However, women seem able to cope with inflexible child care if their jobs or family situations are flexible. Job and family situation flexibility allow women to change their work schedules or to call on friends and family members when child care arrangements fall through or when children are sick (Oregon Child Care Research Partnership, 1997).

Mothers, early childhood education professionals, and policymakers agree that children need to be in care arrangements that promote their health and safety. However, there are differences in opinion with regard to children's other needs in these settings. Professionals and policymakers (i.e., experts who represent dominant ideology) are concerned about the quality of children's experiences, defined in terms of the structural aspects of the setting (e.g., the ratio of adults to children) and the nature of the provider's interactions with the child (e.g., sensitive and responsive) (Daniel, 1996; Phillips, 1995). Mothers, too, consider child care quality important, but their ideas about quality are sometimes different from those of the "experts" (e.g., Kontos et al., 1995).

Recent attempts have been made to learn how mothers' ideas about quality relate to their choice of care (e.g., Eggers-Pierola, Holloway, Fuller, & Rambaud, 1995; Holloway, Rambaud, Fuller, & Eggers-Pierola, 1995; Kontos et al., 1995). These efforts are timely as the private and public sectors in the United States and elsewhere are gearing up to meet the anticipated rise in the demand for child care. Some of the increase in demand, as noted above, is linked to women's growing participation in the labor force. In 1950, 14% of U.S. women with children under the age of 6 were in the labor force; this figure rose to 58% in 1990 (Kisker, Hofferth, Phillips, & Farquhar, 1991). Today, the number of U.S. women with young children working is likely to be even higher, in part because of welfare reform. In Australia, women made up 33% of the labor force in 1970, and 45% in 1995 (VandenHeuvel, 1996). And, in Kenya, Botswana, Ghana, Sierra Leone, and Lesotho, over 40% of rural households are headed by women. This is an indication of African women entering the formal labor market if you consider head of household a proxy for women in the labor force (Youssef & Hamman, 1985, as cited in Myers, 1992). However, the demand for child care is not limited to women who work. U.S. mothers were as likely to use center care for their 3- to 5-year-olds whether or not they were working, and whether or not they were working full time (West, Hausken, & Collins, 1993).

Mothers may not always get what they want when selecting nonmaternal care for their children. Child care selections are influenced by a number of factors like cost of care, mother's employment status, job characteristics, educational level, household composition, and income level (e.g., Becerra & Chi, 1992; Fuller et al., 1996; Hofferth & Wissoker, 1992). The availability of care also may be a deciding factor. Fuller and Liang (1996) suggested that there is an uneven distribution of preschools across regions in the United States and across local communities within regions. Preschools, in their analysis of 100 counties, were more heavily concentrated in counties marked by higher median income levels and higher parental educational levels. While differences in demand for preschools among communities may help to explain this finding, other factors appear to play a role. For example, the inequities in the availability of preschools were less evident in Massachusetts, a state known for its support of preschool facilities in low-income neighborhoods. Even in this state, however, preschools were less available in working-class and middle-income communities, and communities with a higher concentration of single-parent families.

☐ The Nonmaternal Care Arrangements Mothers Make for Their Children

In this section, we look at some of the nonmaternal care arrangements available to mothers in many communities around the world. Care by relatives and friends is typically a part of the informal market care system because payment often is not monetary, although this is not always the case. Formal market care, by comparison, is paid for.

Care By Relatives and Friends

Care by relatives and friends for regular or extended periods of time is an arrangement that many women prefer, especially for infants and young children (Anderson, 1988, as cited in Myers, 1992; Meyers & van Leuwen, 1992; Sonenstein & Wolf, 1991). However, kith and kin may not always be available, as is often the case when women move away from home to seek, for example, job or educational opportunities (Becerra & Chi, 1992; Weisner, 1979). In these instances, women rely on care that is less preferred, or they resort to caring for their children themselves, which often means leaving their jobs or training programs.

A number of surveys and studies conducted in the United States over the years consistently have shown that poor families ask relatives and friends to help them care for their children more so than nonpoor families. For example, a 1994 report from the General Accounting Office indicated that 55% of poor families using nonmaternal care relied on relatives and friends, compared to 21% of families who were not poor (U.S. General Accounting Office, 1994). These figures are comparable to findings reported in the 1993 SIPP and the 1990 National Child Care Survey (NCCS) (e.g., Casper, 1996; Phillips, 1995).

While the findings suggested that poor mothers rely more than nonpoor mothers on relatives and friends to help with their children's care, mothers' ethnic membership also seemed to matter. For example, in a study on low income women in California, Mexican American mothers were reported to ask relatives to care for their infants and toddlers (65%) more often than White (37%) or Chinese American mothers (43%) (Becerra & Chi, 1992). When these women were asked to select their ideal child care arrangements, most Mexican American mothers indicated that relative care was their ideal form of care; many Chinese American and non-Hispanic White mothers, on the other hand, selected center care.

The decision of Mexican American mothers to use relative care rather than center care may reflect a trend among Latino families in the United States. For example, national figures have indicated that only 39% of Latino families using nonparental forms of care select center care (Fuller et al., 1996). It is reasonable to assume that many of these families rely on relatives to care for their children, based on what we know about Latino families' discomfort with the values promoted in preschools (Fuller et al., 1996).

The relation between poverty and preference for relative care, however, does not seem to hold up in other places around the world. For example, over half of employed Australian women participating in a survey on working arrangements relied on friends and relatives to care for their young children. This percentage dropped to around 45% when mothers of 6- to 11-year-olds were queried (VandenHeuvel, 1996).

Formal Market Child Care

With increased labor force participation and decreasing availability of extended family and friends to help with child care, more women are using organized forms of care. However, mothers also select this type of care for other reasons.

One option available to mothers is family care, an arrangement where providers care for children in their homes. According to the NCCS, about 19% of preschool-age children whose mothers were employed attended family care arrangements (Hofferth & Kisker, 1992). However, many family care providers may not meet state regulation or licensing standards, which is a concern because licensing appears related to the quality of care (Frankel, 1994; Hofferth & Kisker, 1992; Howes, Smith, & Galinsky, 1995). Concerns about family care quality also are shared by policymakers and early child care specialists in European countries, even though mothers typically rely on this type of care (Cochran, 1995). For example, Cochran (1995) reported that, in the early 1990s, 70% of French children age 2 or younger, 44% of Finnish children, and about 30% of Swedish children were cared for in homes.

A second option available to mothers is center care which differs from family care in terms of size, personnel, atmosphere, and curriculum (Frankel, 1994). Approximately 27% of preschool-age children with mothers who work were in center programs (Hofferth & Kisker, 1992).

Whether a mother chooses family or center care seems to depend on the age of her child. Mothers of infants, young children (i.e., 1- and 2-year-olds), and school-age children tend to use family care; whereas mothers of 3- to 5-year-olds tend not to (Hofferth & Kisker, 1992; Hofferth & Phillips, 1987; Klysz & Flannery, 1995). For example, mothers living in three U.S. cities who were receiving federal assistance were more likely to select center care for their 4- and 5-year-olds than they were for children younger than age 2 (25% compared to 10%) (Sonenstein & Wolf, 1991). Child's age also seemed to matter when selecting family or center care for a significant proportion of parents participating in a multicountry study (Cochran, 1995).

There also is some indication that ethnic membership and employment status relates to the type of market care used. African American mothers of preschool-age children living in Detroit were more likely to select center care than family care whether or not they were employed (66% of employed mothers, 100% of nonemployed mothers). Employed non-African American mothers, however, were equally likely to use family and center care, while nonemployed non-African American mothers used center care (about 81%) (Kuhlthau & Oppenheim Mason, 1996).

This brief look at the decisions that mothers make regarding the nonmaternal care of their children illustrates trends noted in the United States and elsewhere, and demonstrates that the factors involved in decision making are quite complex (Fuller et al., 1996). For example, though African American mothers use center care more often than family care, analyses by Fuller and his colleagues (Fuller et al., 1996) suggested that access to subsidies plays a role. As families become ineligible to receive subsidies, their ability to use center care declines.

☐ Qualities, but for What Purpose?

In this section, we look at the qualities mothers value in the nonmaternal care they select for their children. We limit our discussion to qualities that are clearly associated with children's needs, although we recognize that mothers' and children's needs are related in intricate ways. We learn that, even though mothers may value the same things in their children's care, they sometimes select different types of care arrangements for them. This is not surprising, given the many factors mothers must consider when deciding on their children's care as well as the differences among mothers in the emphasis they place on the importance of each of these different factors.

The qualities of care we consider were selected because they appear over and over again in the literature as valued by mothers. They include the safety of the care environment; personal attributes of the care provider; ethnic, child rearing, and linguistic considerations; and school readiness and social opportunities for children. Yet, even though mothers' views about quality care may be similar, what they mean by quality may differ. Mothers, for example, may agree that caregiver sensitivity, warmth, and responsiveness is important, but disagree on what constitutes sensitivity, warmth, and responsiveness.

Custodial Aspect of Care

Mothers want their children to be healthy and safe in their nonmaternal care settings. For example, working Nigerian mothers (98% were employed full or part time) living in Osun State were asked to rate the function and role of their children's care centers (Ogbimi, 1992). Features of children's care such as health were rated the highest, and most mothers (90% of them) chose care settings based on them. Similarly, in the United States, children's safety was ranked as the most important feature of child care quality by White, African American, and Latino[2] mothers (Kontos et al., 1995). These mothers used family and relative care as their primary nonmaternal arrangement. Likewise, mothers living in squatter settlements in Lima, Peru, wanted providers who would feed their children, and who maintained clean and well-equipped facilities (Anderson, 1988, as cited in Myers, 1992).

Personal Qualities of the Care Provider

Mothers want providers they can trust; it is as simple as that. Indeed, this attribute probably would be agreed on as essential by mothers everywhere. Who is trustworthy, however, is a matter of opinion. For example, women interviewed in a six-country study of children's care and women's work believed that only family members and friends were motivated and able to provide the type of quality care they wanted for their children (Overseas Education Fund, 1979). This view is shared by many poor families in the United States (Phillips, 1995). About a third of low-income families surveyed in the NCCS chose relatives as an important feature of care, while middle-income (37%) and high-income families (45%) chose "quality." However, relatives and "quality" seemed to mean the same thing to these families—a provider who was reliable, warm, and loving. The difference among families was that low-income families equated these attributes with relative care whereas middle- and high-income families did not (Phillips, 1995). Perhaps middle- and high-income families, who more often choose family or center care arrangements, consider these attributes as something that providers learn about as part of the training they receive. Indeed, there has been evidence suggesting that regulation status (and, therefore, provider training) is related to attributes similar to provider warmth (e.g., Howes et al., 1995; Kontos et al., 1995).

Kontos et al. (1995) also reported that provider warmth and attentiveness were qualities many mothers looked for when selecting nonmaternal care. Though these qualities were valued in a similar way (i.e., they were ranked among the top 5 of 19 aspects of child care) by White, African American, and Latino mothers, mothers differed in their choice of care arrangements. African American and Latino mothers were more likely to choose relative care (42% and 44%), and relied on it more often than did White mothers

(17%). White mothers, by comparison, were more likely to choose regulated care (53%), and relied on it more often than did African American and Latino mothers (35% and 13%). Perhaps mothers using nonrelative care were able to form an opinion ahead of time about provider warmth and sensitivity because more than half of them had a previous relationship with the provider or had selected the provider based on advice from friends or relatives. (Nigerian mothers studied by Ogbimi, 1992, were also likely to choose centers based on the recommendations of kith and kin.)

Ethnic, Childrearing, and Linguistic Considerations

There is less agreement among studies conducted in the United States on whether mothers favor providers who share their ethnic, linguistic, or religious background. Agreement between providers and mothers on issues related to child rearing philosophies was noted in a study conducted on mostly White, middle-class mothers living in two suburban areas in a mid-Atlantic state (Britner & Phillips, 1995). In addition, Kontos et al. (1995) found that 87% of African American mothers selected African American providers, 86% of White mothers selected White providers, and 83% of Latino mothers selected Latino providers. However, only Latino mothers noted that they highly valued providers who were able to teach their children cultural and religious values. This might be one reason why Latino mothers, and other mothers who valued these features, were more likely to rely on relatives to care for their young children.

Fuller et al. (1996) also showed that Latino mothers seek child care providers based on their views about how children should behave (e.g., showing respect for adult authority, contributing to the welfare of others). These mothers believe that the characteristics they value in their children tend to conflict with the characteristics fostered by the child-centered curriculum found in many center care arrangements. Because of this, many mothers prefer to care for their children themselves, or to ask friends and relatives to help with child care (Fuller et al., 1996; Holloway et al., 1995).

Other studies show, however, that ethnic considerations may not always play a role in mothers' choice of providers. U.S. mothers living in the Midwest did not choose their provider based on the provider's ethnicity, values, or beliefs (Kontos, 1994). However, Kontos (1994) believed that the homogeneity of the community may explain why mothers did not mention this as an important reason in selecting a child care provider. This interpretation may require more thought since the majority of low-income mothers (mostly Hispanic and African American) living in an ethnically diverse East Coast urban center did not express a preference for providers who were ethnically similar to themselves (Herscovitch, 1996).

School Readiness Opportunities

Mothers in many communities around the world also value nonmaternal care arrangements that help children prepare for learning in schools (although the age of the child seems to matter) (Cochran, 1995; Sonenstein & Wolf, 1991). Nigerian mothers rated school preparation third in their list of the function and role of child care centers (Ogbimi, 1992). (This was rated higher than providing children with the opportunity to be with other children.) And, a majority of U.S. mothers taking part in the Profile of Child Care Settings (73%) expressed the same opinion (Willer et al., 1991), as did mothers participating in other studies on child care arrangements in the United States (e.g., Fuller et al., 1996; Kontos et al., 1995) and elsewhere (Carlson & Stenmalm, 1989).

However, mothers sometimes differ in their views on what activities prepare children for school, and the differences among mothers—at least in the United States—appear related to factors like ethnic membership and income level. For example, less-educated mothers and mothers from ethnic minorities are more likely to support a didactic approach to teaching children than are White, middle-class mothers (Rosier & Corsaro, 1993; Stipek, Milburn, Clements, & Daniels, 1992). Didactic approaches often include early introduction of formal, teacher directed instruction in which the products of learning are valued. This style is contrasted with a more child-centered approach favored by many early childhood specialists that includes child-initiated, exploratory activities. Child-centered approaches often emphasize the process (not products) of learning (Stipek et al., 1992).

Yet, while poor and ethnic minority mothers in the United States seem to favor didactic teaching styles, there is some indication that they appreciate a range of experiences for their children that include the type of hands-on experiences typically associated with child-centered approaches. Many of the low-income mothers interviewed by Holloway et al. (1995) seemed pleased that their children were going on field trips, participating in cooking and art projects, and learning songs. And, while they failed to see the value of play as an educational activity, they realized that children played in centers for other reasons.

Philosophical differences in preferred teaching styles are not limited to the United States. Many Israeli mothers believe that direct instruction by an adult best promotes children's development (Rosenthal, 1994). And, some European countries like France are moving toward a preschool curriculum that promotes school success, while others like Poland are moving toward a preschool curriculum that promotes personal development (Cochran, 1995).

Even though mothers might favor a more eclectic approach to educational styles, there appears to be a fair amount of agreement between mothers' preferred teaching style and the arrangements they select for their children. Stipek et al. (1992) found that U.S. parents of 4- to 5-year-olds who valued independence and initiative typically chose child-centered programs, while parents who valued basic skill training typically chose didactic programs. In a like manner, low-income U.S. mothers expressed dissatisfaction with their child's care arrangement if there was not enough of an emphasis on learning, indicated by reliance on didactic approaches (Holloway et al., 1995).

Social Opportunities

Children's social experiences in their care arrangements appear to be important to many U.S. mothers. For example, when mothers in Kontos et al.'s (1995) study were asked what they thought were important learning experiences for their children, more than half of them indicated social experiences. In fact, social experiences were more important than academic experiences for many of these mothers. However, the extent to which mothers valued this quality of care seemed to vary by ethnic membership. White mothers were more likely to endorse this set of experiences (62%) than were African American or Latino mothers (52% and 48%).

Social experiences seem less important for some mothers as a criteria to evaluate children's care arrangements. Nigerian mothers ranked this feature fourth in their list of the function of child care (Ogbimi, 1992). It may be that, when children have a lot of opportunity to be with one another, as often is the case in many African communities (e.g., Weisner & Gallimore, 1977), mothers do not look for this feature in their children's care arrangements.

☐ Mothers' Ideas about Motherhood

In this section, we continue our discussion of the role that culture plays in the decisions mothers make by looking at how dominant cultural ideology regarding notions of motherhood relates to who else besides mothers cares for and raises children. The value a community places on mothers raising their children with little if any regular help from others affects the child care options available to women, and the role that providers are expected to play in the lives of children (Myers, 1992). For example, Uttal (1996) found that employed women from different ethnic and economic groups living in a U.S. West Coast community distinguished between two types of care: child care and child rearing. This distinction was related both to women's views of motherhood and to the way they organized the nonmaternal care of their children. Some mothers saw themselves as primarily responsible for the socialization of their children, even though their children spent long hours in nonmaternal care. These mothers did not consider it important to select providers who shared their caregiving styles or values. Care for them was perceived as custodial in nature, providing for their children's health and safety, but not much more. Other mothers, however, saw themselves as entering into a partnership with providers, sharing with them the responsibility for raising their children. These mothers looked for providers who shared their values and practices regarding children, and who taught children what they wanted them to learn.

The view that the care of infants and young children ought to be the primary responsibility of mothers is not held by all communities in the United States. Collins (1994) described the value placed on the sharing of child care in many African American communities, which leads to a more "collective" form of care. This system of care also is seen in Stack's (1974) portrayal of life in a midwestern U.S. African American community. In this community, women share many things including the care of each other's children, which may last weeks, months, or years. This practice is seen as one way that women and children are able to survive economic uncertainty.

Child rearing as a social responsibility is also described for communities outside the United States where it is common for children and adults to participate in the care of young children (Weisner & Gallimore, 1977). An example of shared care is seen among the Efe, a group of hunters and gatherers living in the Ituri rain forest of the Democratic Republic of Congo (formerly Zaire). The Efe are one of several groups of foragers and farmers inhabiting the Ituri, and they make a living by hunting and gathering, but also by exchanging field labor for agricultural goods and services. The Efe reside in camps that consist mostly of brothers and their families. Most of their day-to-day activities occur in this setting, with their leaf huts used primarily as a place to sleep and store valued items, and to protect people from the rain. This living arrangement means that the Efe spend most of their time in public situations, making it easy for people to help each other out.

One of the more noteworthy features of Efe child care is that the Efe appear to engage in the most extensive form of multiple caregiving described so far. We have found that, starting at birth, children are cared for extensively by individuals other than their mothers. Three-week-old Efe infants spend about 40% of their awake time in physical contact with people besides their mothers. By 18 weeks of age, this figure rises to about 60%, with the number of different people caring for Efe infants averaging about 14. An important aspect of care includes being nursed by caregivers, whether or not they are lactating.

Children's experiences with many caregivers seems to continue throughout early childhood. One-year-old Efe infants spend only about half of their day in social contact with their mothers. The rest of their day is spent with fathers, other men, women, and children, with few if any differences noted in the amount of time they spend with each of these different caregivers. By 3 years of age, children spend only about 20% of their day involved with their mothers (Morelli & Tronick, 1991, 1992; Tronick & Morelli, 1992).

Efe children learn about the role community members play in their lives through their involvement with them as caregivers, but also by the language they use to address certain people. For example, the word *ema* is used by children to address their biological mother, but also their mother's sisters and other female relatives; the word *afa* is used to address their father, but also their father's brothers and other male relatives.

Caregiving as a social responsibility is part of Efe life, and Efe women's notion of motherhood allows for others to fully participate in the care of children. This view of motherhood is shared by many communities in Africa and elsewhere, including the Nso of northwestern Cameroon.

☐ The Nso of Cameroon

The Nso hold a view of motherhood that regards the sharing of child care by friends and relatives as normal. It is well accepted in this community for children to spend a portion of their childhood being reared by individuals other than their birth parents (Nsamenang, 1992a). However, the decision of who cares for children is based on the qualities of care valued by parents as well as the experiences parents want their children to have.

This section reports on Nso perceptions of child care quality and how they play out in individual child care decisions. Parents and caregivers were asked to talk about how children came to stay with caregivers for an extended period of time, and what they believed this meant for those involved. The findings of this work help to extend our knowledge of the cultural similarities and differences in mothers' ideas about child care quality and the nonmaternal care arrangements they make for their children.

Holding a Child

When children are sent to stay with kith and kin for an extended period of time, North Americans and Europeans often call this "foster care" and assume that this arrangement is a result of some dramatic negative event in the life of a child. Yet, many communities, like those of the Nso in Cameroon, hold a broader view of this practice. The movement of children between relatives and friends, often referred to as *holding* a child, is usually seen in the context of raising a child within the extended family. Choosing who in one's wider circle of family and friends should help care for a child is one of the most common child care decisions a parent can make, and around a quarter of children in northwestern Cameroon spend months or years under the care of someone other than a biological parent (Page, 1989). In these cases, biological parents generally maintain regular contact with their children, visiting them and their caregivers whenever their schedules and finances permit.

In this case study, we adopt this broader view of child care, attempting to understand from the community's perspective how mothers and others go about choosing who should be put in charge of a child—who should hold a child. Like mothers in many communities, Nso mothers also consider custodial aspects of care, personal qualities of the care provider, child rearing philosophies, school preparation and support, and social opportunities when they make child care decisions. Yet, how they think about these issues and how they choose who will help them raise their children reflect the complexities of balancing such issues as where one lives and works, traditional child rearing values, and one's relative closeness to particular friends and family members.

☐ The Study

Study Site

The largest urban center in the Northwest Province (and the sixth largest city in Cameroon), Bamenda, is home to the Nkwen, Mankon, and Mendomkwe peoples as well as numerous migrants from other areas in Cameroon (e.g., Nso, Bafut, Kom) and from Nigeria (mostly, Ibo traders and Hausa herders). Most people in Bamenda speak Pidgin, the lingua franca throughout the Northwest and Southwest Provinces, as well as English, the official language taught in schools. In addition, people speak their local dialect, although it is becoming increasingly common for children to learn only Pidgin and English, especially in cases where children spend most of their time with neighborhood children and family members do not consider it a priority to talk to them in their local dialect.

Virtually all households, although urban, supplement their income by raising small livestock (e.g., pigs, goats, ducks, chickens) and by growing at least some portion of their own food. In most cases, their small gardens (e.g., maize, plantains, cassava, groundnuts, and vegetables) are located either within or adjacent to their compounds or are scattered throughout Bamenda (e.g., on the hillsides, in vacant lots, in old tires, on the outskirts of town). Women are the primary workers in gardens (hoe agriculture), but children from around 5 years of age begin helping them with farmwork.

The Nso of Bamenda

Many Nso families have lived in town for generations, but Nso from traditional rural areas (about 65 miles west) are still migrating into the city in large numbers. Most Nso households in Bamenda are extended, and family members from elsewhere often arrive at frequent intervals to stay for short or more extended periods (Nsamenang, 1992a). Social networks between kin in urban and rural Nso communities are important and grandparents, uncles, aunts, and cousins frequently exchange food and money, in addition to playing major roles in making important decisions affecting children (Nsamenang, 1992c).

The majority of Nso women in Bamenda work outside the household, engaging in farming and trading in the informal economy.[3] More often than not, they combine multiple responsibilities (teaching, nursing, small-scale trading, child care, farmwork, preparation for family functions, cooking), although they usually are helped with at least some of these tasks by others (e.g., children, relatives, friends, neighbors). Nso men are also engaged in wage employment outside the home (e.g., large-scale trading, teaching, military). However, it is not uncommon to see them passing the afternoons and evenings in off-licenses and drinking spots (local bars)—talking; drinking palm wine, corn beer, and beer; and sharing kola nuts.

Nso Children. Like many children in sub-Saharan Africa, Nso children in Bamenda spend much of their time in groups made up of siblings and peers (Nsamenang & Lamb, 1993), either wandering freely about the neighborhood or within the family compound. Older children are put "in charge" of younger children whom they have the authority to reprimand, correct, and assign tasks (Nsamenang, 1992b). In small and large groups, children are seen throughout the streets of Bamenda participating in activities such as selling puffpuffs (fried dough) and roasted groundnuts (peanuts), "driving" and building motos (toy cars fabricated out of sticks, old flip-flops, bottle caps, and so forth), and harvesting guavas and mangos from local trees.

Children's help with household chores is highly valued in Nso communities (both rural and urban) (Nsamenang, 1992c), and parents consider it a child's social responsibility to contribute to the welfare of the family. From an early age (around age 4), children begin to help their family by "fetching" items within the household compound and, by age 5, they often are sent on small errands such as buying sugar or bread from a local store or delivering messages to neighbors. In addition, many children also participate in family businesses by carrying food from the market, assisting in food and drink preparation, guarding stores, or selling food or other small items.

The Nso are known throughout the Northwest Province and even throughout Cameroon as a relatively well-educated community. The majority of Nso parents have received at least some education with many having completed primary school, some progressing to secondary school, and a select few, to university. Presently, almost all Nso children in Bamenda are sent to primary school (usually Catholic mission schools as the majority of Nso families are Catholic[4]), and many go on to secondary school. Wealthier families are able to send their children to university for further education in Cameroon, Nigeria, and, if the means are available, abroad to the United States, Germany, and the United Kingdom.

Families Participating in the Study

Fifteen families in Bamenda were recruited through social visits to neighbors and referrals from participants. Each was caring for an Nso child of a relative or friend between the age of 5 and 8 when the study began. After these caregivers were interviewed, the birth parents of these children were contacted and asked to participate in an interview.

All participants worked outside the home, either formally as nurses, teachers, and seamstresses, or informally as traders and farmers. Most of them had at least a primary school education, and a few had received some university training. Three of the 15 birth mothers and 10 of the 15 caregivers were married.

The aim of the interviews with caregivers and birth parents was to elicit community-based understandings of a variety of different child care arrangements, and to focus on ideas around children's transitions between households. All interviews were semistructured so as to allow participants to highlight the child care issues which were particularly salient to them. Interviews were tape-recorded or handwritten depending on the participant's preference and conducted in her preferred language. After each interview, notes were subsequently expanded and tapes transcribed with the assistance of a native Lamnso speaker when needed.

Child Care among the Nso

In the Nso community, parents often are not the only ones who participate in decisions around who will care for a child. Parents, siblings, aunts and uncles, grandparents, and even great grandparents are often involved in choosing who a child will live with and in highlighting important qualities of care that should be considered. Extended family members, friends, and, as will be seen below, the children themselves co-construct views of what is and should be desired in an extended child care arrangement.

Custodial Aspect of Child Care.   As in Nigeria and elsewhere, children's safety and health are of prime importance in the Nso community. Mothers and others talk about transferring their children between homes for a variety of safety and health reasons, often after reflecting on or having their attention drawn to a certain aspect of the environment in which the child was living. For example, Patience, a single mother and seamstress, had not thought about changing her 8 year-old daughter's living arrangement until her brother alerted her to the dangers of the busy thoroughfare she lived on.

> I know it's crowded and noisy here and that there's lots of traffic, but I'm always with Victorine. So, I didn't really think about it until my brother offered to take her. And I thought, yeah, I guess it is pretty dangerous. I guess there really is nowhere for her to move around here. And Karine [her brother's daughter] is there for her to play with.

Geraldine, a married seamstress, had a similar view of what spurred her and her husband to send their son to her husband's uncle in another part of town:

> Our main reason for giving Elvis to my husband's uncle was that our environment is not so healthy. We are close to a main road. Accidents, being robbed. Bad things like that happen. And he can get mixed-up with the wrong kind of people here. But, where he lives now, they can lock their gate. So he has the space to play and, for hours, they [he and his cousin] will play inside the compound. So, it's a good place for him.

That their son was in a place away from a main road and protected by a fenced-in compound was a salient issue for the couple. They were aware that they wanted to find a place for their son where, as much as was possible, he could live a protected, sheltered life.

Other parents focused more directly on health, highlighting such issues as their children's rashes, respiratory problems, weight, or jiggers (sand fleas) as motives behind their children's transition between households. Maxeline, a single mother, was posted in a teaching position in a rural village. She brought along her son, but he never quite adjusted to his environment.

> I sent Ema back to my mother in Bamenda. He just did not respond well to his new environment. Jiggers, he had jiggers everywhere on him. And then there was the time my neighbor found him stuck in a stream. I don't know what he was thinking. If she hadn't walked by and seen him, he would have drowned. He just couldn't get used to village life and I was afraid what he would do next.

Maxeline believed that if Ema went back to a familiar environment, he would be healthier and safer than he was with her. Moreover, to her, safety and health were related to lack of supervision. Maxeline was concerned about the potential trouble he could get into while unsupervised in the village:

> Mom really assists me. Most of the time when he [Ema] was with me, I would be very busy teaching. So, it would be difficult for me to bathe him and wash his clothes. Things like that. I had a hard time keeping an eye on him and making sure he didn't hurt himself. Mom is better at that.

Mothers and others in this community often equate safety with an environment where their children feel comfortable and free to move around without risk, whether it be in urban or rural environments.

Personal Qualities of the Care Provider.   Nso parents, like many other parents around the world, generally believe that relatives, especially close ones (often sisters and mothers), are less likely to maltreat a child under their care and, therefore, make better caregivers than strangers, friends, or distant relatives. But, more importantly, parents feel that it is essential for them to have a close personal relationship with the caregiver, one based on mutual trust and cooperation. Pascaline, a married teacher, sent all three of her children to her husband's parents so they could attend better schools. She mused, "If I didn't get along with and trust my husband's parents, I can tell you that the children wouldn't be staying there. But, lucky for me and lucky for them, we get along so well. I just consider them like my own parents."

Yet, not only do parents want caregivers with whom they have a personal relationship, they also want someone who connects with—who loves—their child; someone who welcomes him or her into the household. In fact, many of the mothers defined a "good caregiver" as someone who does not differentiate between her own children and other children under her care, someone who does not treat her own children preferentially. Clementine, a widow with four children, talked about her daughter's difficulty fitting into her new house and compared it to her son's situation:

> My daughter, when she went to stay with my brother, they did not hold her well. It wasn't that they punished her too much or didn't feed her well. But, if you are holding a child, you need to train her right. And they were training her in a way, a way that she knew that their house was not her own house. They treated her in a way that their children knew she was not their sister. She did not feel free or comfortable in the house. She did feel like she belonged. But, with Bless [her son], when I go to Bamenda, I see how he feels free to open cupboards, sit in chairs, climb on chairs, whatever. That house is his house.

Mothers want caregivers to treat children as their own. They want someone who not only has the skill to hold their child, but also someone who cares for and loves the child the way they do. As Clementine put it:

> I gave Bless to my sister to hold, and for the first 5 months, I was worried about him. But, then I thought about it. What am I worrying about? I know my sister well. She used to love me and hold me well when I was a child. So, why would she not do the same for my child?

For Nso mothers, at least two relationships—that between oneself and the caregiver and that between one's child and the caregiver—must be considered when decisions are made about where to place one's child.

Ethnic, Child Rearing, and Linguistic Considerations.   Although almost all parents sought child care within the Nso community, none specifically mentioned that they wanted their child to be cared for in an Nso household. It seems as if it were generally taken for granted that another Nso household was the best option for the child. Claudine, the grandmother of Loretta, put it this way:

> Yes, I married outside of Nso. But, I guess I would really think twice about giving any of my children or Loretta to my husband's family. I don't know if I could really trust them. I don't know how they would hold her because they have different ways of raising children there.

Linguistic considerations also were rarely addressed in the interviews, although one mother mentioned that she wanted her child to be in a household where English was spoken. Pascaline, a teacher, pointed out the importance of her children speaking English in their household: "I didn't want my children to be confused. I wanted them only to speak English in their home. I think this is the only way they will really learn it."

Yet, ethnic and linguistic considerations are minor in this community, in comparison with issues related to child rearing philosophies. Parents express their desire for structure, discipline, and routine for their children. They are afraid that they themselves will spoil their child too much and ruin his or her chances of becoming a respected part of the Nso community. Rose, a single mother and hotel receptionist, talked of the structure her daughter receives by staying with her parents, "I think Julette staying with them, she is more controlled and more disciplined than if she were living with me. My parents are real consistent and stable with her. I don't know if I would be able to give that to her." Her parents added to this, pointing out, "Rose spoils her and gives her sweets. And when she returned from staying with her [Rose] over the holidays, she would not follow directions. What would become of her if she remained like that?"

Mothers want their children to learn from caregivers that they are part of extended families and that this membership translates into responsibility and obligations toward helping others. They do not want a caregiver who allows the child to run wild—"only to sit and eat"—but one who has expectations for the child including chores and homework.[5] Anastasia, a housewife and farmer, talked about why Elvis' parents allowed her to care for him for the past year:

> He didn't get the discipline, the structure [with his parents]. But, for me, I feel that he's gaining so many things by staying here. There is always work for him. So, when he gets up in the morning, he washes the floor. Our house has a schedule. He knows, "If I get up in the morning, I must do this before I go to school." And when he comes home from school, he washes dishes. Over there, he was not doing that. The mother was always doing everything for him. And then, in the evening too, we always help him, we make sure he reads and does his homework. And if he doesn't, we punish him. He knows there are expectations and consequences. So, because of that, he always makes sure he does his schoolwork and housework. Over there, they were petting [spoiling] him so much that he wasn't learning anything. There he would say, "I don't want to read today." And they would say, "Okay, just leave it." Or, "I don't want to go to school." And they would say, "Okay, stay home." Here, he's learning how to be responsible. And he's studying.

Parents believe that this kind of responsibility training, this kind of help from the caregiver, will guide the child toward understanding the value of contributing to family welfare. By learning the value of work and studies in conjunction with that of reciprocity between family members, children will be prepared to give back, especially by educating and raising younger relatives.

School Readiness Opportunities.   Formal schooling is highly valued in the Nso community and mothers often move their children into extended care with kith and kin in areas with good schools. They look for caregivers who can support their children's school experience by making sure the children attend school, helping them with their homework, paying school fees, and hiring tutors. In many ways, this relates to the structure and discipline a caregiver provides for a child. Grace talked about how village life was not conducive to her son's school performance, "In our compound in the village, he had too much freedom. He played a lot and didn't have any time to do his schoolwork. And since we are busy with farmwork, I really had no time to discipline him, to sit down and make him read."

Parents want caregivers who will, through actions as well as words, stress the value of education to their children. Clementine, a widow, was happy with her extended child care arrangement with her sister. She was impressed with her sister's active involvement in her son's schooling.

The thing was, Bless was very stubborn. He didn't like to stay at school. He was always leaving school to come home and eat—sometimes several times a day. I didn't have the heart to discipline him. But, with my sister, I see a difference. Now, he does well in school. But, when he was here with me, he repeated Class 1 twice. With my sister, he passes his exams and passes them well. Good numbers. The main reason I sent him there [Bamenda] was that I knew my sister would care how he did in school. That she would want him to be well-educated.

Although most parents focus on the caregiver's responsibility for financially or personally supporting the child's school performance, a few also raised the role of other children in this process. One mother, Mirabelle, said she wanted her daughter to be familiar with numbers and letters before she entered school, and was pleased that other children around her could teach her these things:

I thought it was good that her cousins are older than her. And she likes them so much. She follows them everywhere and imitates what they do. So I thought, I mean here she is the only child. But, there, they are always playing school, teaching her numbers and letters and songs and things.

Mirabelle saw the caregivers' children as important supporters of her daughter's academic performance.

Social Opportunities. Although Nso mothers seldom raised the issue of children's social experiences, when it was raised, it often was in the context of helping the child adjust to a new care arrangement. Judith talked about how her sister's transition to her new child care arrangement was facilitated by Christabelle, the caregiver's daughter:

I think with her [my sister], it was really Christabelle who made things easier for her. She [Christabelle] was the youngest in the family and all her brothers and sisters were away at school. So, really, she needed Claire as much as Claire needed her. If you saw them, they were always together. Always doing the same thing. Claire's fine.

Parents wanted their children in a household where the children already present would welcome the child into the home. They tried to avoid arrangements where the child would feel left out and, instead, sought ones where children in the household actively facilitated the child's integration into the family. Mirabelle drew attention to the role of her sister's children in Nadine's transition to her new household:

When she went there, my sister's children really welcomed her as one of their gang. I don't think she even missed me. They played with her. They sang songs. And she eats better there. You know lots of children grow pale [they don't eat well] when they first go to a new home. But, Nadine, she eats better there. And it's not that she doesn't have plenty of food when she's with me. It's just that she enjoys eating with other children. She never liked eating alone.

Mirabelle believed that this arrangement was a good one for her daughter because of the consequences of social experiences available to her child there. Quality child care for her was a place where the child received lots of attention from other children—attention that translated into better health and school performance.

Letting Children Have a Voice in Child Care Decisions

Like mothers all over the world, Nso mothers are trying to find the best quality arrangements for their child. Yet, in this community, it seems as if this cannot be accomplished without the child's seal of approval. People in Nso generally believe that you cannot force a child to do something that he or she does not want to. You can persuade. You can coax. But, if a child refuses, that is it; he or she refuses. For instance, Geraldine, whose son was living with her husband's uncle in a more residential part of town, talked about her daughter's response to going to live in what they perceived to be a safer place for both of their children:

But, for Eunice, Eunice is a person born with her own character. When I say, Eunice, go and stay there for a day, Eunice will not feel fine. No matter what. They [the uncle and his wife] can cook meat for her, bring her small things to play with, or give her roasted peanuts; she will not change. She wants to be with us, and no matter what, no one can force her to go there.

In the same light, children who decide that they want to go and stay with their favorite relative are difficult to dissuade. Parents talked in terms of their children arranging their own child care. Nadine, the only child of a single mother and farmer in a rural village, let her mother know in no uncertain terms that she was going to go and stay with her aunts and cousins in Bamenda. The mother recounted:

Nadine is staying there because she likes her cousins a lot. Whenever my sister would come here for a visit, she [Nadine] would be crying behind her that she wanted to go and see Yolan and Gotran [her cousins]. She was always talking about her auntie in Bamenda, her brothers and sister in Bamenda. So, when my sister arrived here one time, Nadine had already packed her bags. She was ready to go back to Bamenda. So, I told Nadine that the next time she [my sister] came to the village to visit us, she could go back with her. But, Nadine said, "No, I'm going this time." She just cried and cried. So, I said "okay."

In other cases, children are not as outspoken about their desires, but parents or siblings might solicit the child's opinion, often visiting the child in the relative's care and making sure that he or she is happy with the arrangement. They ask the child such questions as "Do you want to come back home?" "Do you feel fine here?" albeit indirectly or out of earshot so as not to offend the caregiver. In this way, Nso children are consulted in an effort to ensure their satisfaction and to avoid major conflicts over child care. For instance, Comfort and Judith went to visit their younger sister who was being cared for by a family friend:

When we went there, we saw that she feels at home. She doesn't worry. When she saw us, yes, she was very happy. But, when we were coming home, she just, well, you know, with some other children they are crying to go with you. But, for her, there is no problem. I even asked her, when we were returning, whether she would like to come with us. She said "no." She only wanted to come for a visit. But, not to stay. She really feels at home there.

In the Nso community, those directly impacted by child care decisions, the children themselves, also are given a voice in expressing what they feel is most important in an extended child care arrangement.

Without the Family

This extended form of child care that is seen in the Nso community highlights the importance of the extended family in raising children. The mothers whom we interviewed strongly believed that a good child care arrangement familiarizes their children with important members of their extended family and teaches them, at the same time, about their obligations as family members. Just as children are helped by their caregivers, they will be expected to help others. As one of the mothers highlighted for us, "What is the use of sending her there if all she does is take the opportunities they provide her and only help herself. Without her family, she has no future."

☐ Experts Ideas about Qualities of Nonmaternal Care

More and more, families in the United States and elsewhere are sharing the task of raising children with experts and paid professionals who design, oversee, and provide child care services (Edwards, Gandini, & Giovaninni, 1996). We need to ask whether the standards of care established by experts are congruent with those valued by the families they serve. Discontinuity between families and professionals in perceptions of child care standards may lead some families to rely less on market care that conforms closely to professional standards but does not meet family needs. For example, the rift between qualities of care valued by care professionals and families may be one of the reasons why recent immigrants in European countries are underrepresented in their use of preschools. Countries like France and Norway are responding to the problem by putting in place policies that support the development of care facilities sensitive to the diverse cultural needs of families and children (Cochran, 1995). In this section, we explore the views of professionals regarding qualities of care, and compare their views with mothers' views.

There appears to be a growing consensus among professionals in the international community about the course of children's development. Edwards et al. (1996) found that cultural background strongly predicted parents' expectations regarding their children's developmental trajectories in Pistoia, Italy, and in Amherst, Massachusetts. However, few differences were noted between the professionals from these two communities. Edwards et al. (1996) suggested that the similarity among professionals in their ideas about children's development may be due to the sharing of educational and scientific resources.

Professionals also agree on what constitutes quality care. Features typically used to indicate program quality include staff qualification and training; staff to child ratios; low staff turnover; child development curriculum; group size; provisions for health, safety, and nutrition; appropriate evaluation practices; and parental involvement (Daniel, 1996; Smith et al., 1997). Provider sensitivity, warmth, and responsiveness also are considered important to promoting children's development, and these qualities are more likely to occur when structural features of the care setting like group size is small, the staff to child ratio is high, and when providers are trained.

These features of quality are reflected in the child care policies of third world countries. For instance, the National Policy for School Education in Nigeria lists as examples of their preprimary education objectives preparing children for primary education and promoting inquisitiveness and creativity through exploratory and play activities (Ogbimi, 1992). Staff training, staff to child ratios, and child-centered curriculum were also identified by the National Policy for Pre-Primary Education as elements of care related to quality.

There are some qualities of child care that both mothers and experts agree are important. These include child health and safety, and personal characteristics of the care provider such as attentiveness, warmth, and sensitivity. Yet, there are other qualities that they are less likely to agree on. Many U.S. mothers do not consider the education or training of the provider or the regulatory status of the arrangement as important indicators of quality, even though both of these elements are related to quality care as defined by the experts (Philips, 1995).

Yet, even when mothers do value provider training, they tend to represent it in different ways. Training to handle special problems was mentioned most often by White mothers; training in child development was mentioned most often by African American mothers. Some mothers, however, did not think that training was important because they felt that common sense and patience, or experience was enough (Kontos et al., 1995).

There is some disagreement as to whether parents know enough about the characteristics of quality care to make informed decisions when selecting care arrangements. For example, Kontos et al. (1995) are of the opinion that mothers are knowledgeable in the regulatory aspects of care such as the licensing status of the provider, the number of children in each age group, and the ratio of children to adults. Yet, even though mothers were able to recognize many of the features of quality care as articulated by experts, they did not select care based on them.

☐ Whose Views of Quality?

The factors involved in decisions about children's nonmaternal care are many, and the ideas mothers have about care are one of them. These ideas are not the same for mothers everywhere, although there is some agreement among them on what constitutes quality care. Yet, even though mothers may agree on features of quality, the types of care that they opt for may vary. Similarly, what mothers and experts look for in children's care arrangements is not always the same. This raises the question, Is it reasonable or appropriate to use the standards of quality developed by professionals as the only metric to develop and evaluate child care programs? While it is fitting to ask this question of formal market care, it is especially appropriate to ask it of relative care. For example, many mothers believe that relatives are the only ones they can trust to provide children with care that meets their concern for a safe and healthy environment, and that satisfies their desire for promoting culturally appropriate behaviors in their children. Can our current way of conceptualizing quality that relies solely on expert opinion capture those features of care that clearly are important to mothers?

The disparity between parental and expert opinions on what constitutes quality child care means that traditional ways of conceptualizing and measuring quality may need to be revised (e.g., Kontos et al., 1995; National Center for Children in Poverty, 1996). If mothers are disinclined to make use of available child care facilities because they do not meet their standards of quality, then child care programs have failed in their mission. This suggests that child care programs must advocate for the establishment of an array of child care facilities that offer a range of approaches to child care, so that mothers can place their children in care that best approximates their definition of quality.

However, developing and supporting facilities that take into account mothers' and children's needs will be challenging. Clearly, arrangements must promote children's health and safety, and they must promote children's development. But, what features of development should be emphasized? This brings us back to the question—whose views of quality should be given priority?

Addressing this question requires knowledge about the mothers who use non-maternal child care arrangements, including an understanding of what qualities they look for in their children's care and what they mean by quality. It also requires asking the right questions—questions that make sense to mothers.

Now, more than ever, women need child care if they are to participate effectively in today's market economy. Options should be available that support women in their work, and children in their development, in ways that are responsive to what mothers and children need from their child care arrangements in the contexts in which they live. Child care experts and policymakers in countries like the United States must recognize the special role they play not only in guiding their own child care policies, but also those of others. We must be proactive about advocating and supporting a diversity of nonmaternal child care arrangements so that women, wherever they live, can make decisions that best meet their goals.

☐ Notes

1. We recognize the role that others play in the lives of children. However, much of the research in this area focuses on mothers since child care typically is considered a part of women's reproductive roles. As a result, we often use the term *mothers* or *women* when talking about children's care, although we know that child care is sometimes a shared activity.

2. Twenty-nine mothers who participated in this study were Asian or Native American. Their data were grouped with data on Latino mothers.

3. In many cases, this involvement in the informal economy means that the mother spends a portion of time in the home preparing foodstuffs (e.g., frying *akra* [donuts], roasting peanuts) or drinks (e.g., cooking corn beer),and a portion of time outside the home selling them (if she does not send her children out selling).

4. The remaining minority of urban Nso households are Muslim, Baptist, and Presbyterian.

5. This does not necessarily mean that parents want the same thing for toddlers and infants.

☐ References

Becerra, R. M., & Chi, I. (1992). Child care preferences among low-income minority families. *International Social Work, 35*, 35–47.

Britner, P. A., & Phillips, D. A. (1995). Predictors of parent and provider satisfaction with child day care dimensions: A comparison of center-based and family child day care. *Child Welfare, 74*, 1135–1168.

Carlson, H. L., & Stenmalm, L. (1989). Professional and parent views of early childhood programs: A cross cultural study. *Early Child Development and Care, 50*, 51–64.

Casper, L. M. (1996). *"Who's minding our preschoolers?"* (No. P70-53). Washington, DC: Bureau of the Census, U.S. Department of Commerce.

Casper, L. M., Hawkins, M., & O'Connell, M. (1994). *"Who's minding the kids?"* (No. P70-53). Washington, DC: Bureau of Census, U.S. Department of Commerce.

Cochran, M. (1995). European child care in global perspective. *European Early Childhood Education Research Journal, 3*, 61–71.

Collins, P. H. (1994). The meaning of motherhood in Black culture. In R. Staples (Ed.), *The Black family*. Belmont, CA: Wadsworth.

Corsaro, W. A., & Rizzo, T. A. (1988). *Discussione* and friendship: Socialization processes in the peer culture of Italian nursery school children. *American Sociological Review, 53*, 879–894.

Daniel, J. (1996). The complexities of child care. In E. J. Erwin (Ed.), *Putting children first* (pp. 173–195). Baltimore: Brookes.

Edwards, C. P., Gandini, L., & Giovaninni, D. (1996). The contrasting developmental timetables of parents and preschool teachers in two cultural communities. In S. Harkness & C. M. Super (Eds.), *Parents' cultural belief systems* (pp. 270–288). New York: Guilford Press.

Eggers-Pierola, C., Holloway, S. D., Fuller, B., & Rambaud, M. F. (1995, May). *Raising them right: Individualism and collectivism in low-income and immigrant mothers' socialization goals.* Paper presented at the annual meeting of the American Educational Research Association, San Francisco, CA.

Frankel, A. J. (1994). Family day care in the United States. *Families in Society: The Journal of Contemporary Human Services,* 550–560.

Fuller, B., Holloway, S. D., & Liang, X. (1996). Family selection of child-care centers: The influence of household support, ethnicity, and parental practices. *Child Development, 67*(6), 3320–3337.

Fuller, B., & Liang, X. (1996). Market failure? Estimating inequality in preschool availability. *Educational Evaluation and Policy Analysis, 18*(1), 31–49.

Goodnow, J. J. (1988). Parents' ideas, actions, and feelings: Models and methods from developmental and social psychology. *Child Development, 59*, 286–320.

Harkness, S., & Super, C. M. (1995). Culture and parenting. In M. Bornstein (Ed.), *Handbook of parenting: Vol. 2. Biology and ecology of parenting* (pp. 211–234). Newark, NJ: Erlbaum.

Harkness, S., & Super, C. M. (1996). *Parents' cultural belief systems*. New York: Guilford Press.

Herscovitch, L. B. (1996). Child care choices: Low income mothers in Bridgeport, Connecticut. *Child and Youth Care Forum, 25*(3), 139–153.

Hofferth, S. L., & Kisker, E. E. (1992). The changing demographics of family day care in the United States. In D. L. Peters & A. R. Pence (Eds.), *Family day care* (pp. 28–57). New York: Teachers College Press.

Hofferth, S. L., & Phillips, D. A. (1987). Child care in the United States, 1970 to 1985. *Journal of Marriage and the Family, 49*, 559–571.

Hofferth, S. L., & Wissoker, D. A. (1992). Price, quality, and income in child care choice. *The Journal of Human Resources, 27*, 70–111.

Holloway, S. D., Rambaud, M. F., Fuller, B., & Eggers-Pierola, C. (1995). What is "appropriate practice" at home and in child care?: Low-income mothers' views on preparing their children for school. *Early Childhood Research Quarterly, 10*, 451–473.

Howes, C., Smith, E., & Galinsky, E. (1995). *The Florida Child Care Quality Improvement Study*. New York: Families and Work Institute.

Kisker, E. E., Hofferth, S. L., Phillips, D. A., & Farquhar, E. (1991). *A profile of child care settings: Early education and care in 1990*. Washington, DC: U.S. Department of Education.

Klysz, M. A., & Flannery, B. A. (1995). Family characteristics and child care arrangements. *Child and Youth Care Forum, 24*(3), 175–194.

Kontos, S. (1994). The ecology of family day care. *Early Childhood Research Quarterly, 9*, 87–110.

Kontos, S., Howes, C., Shinn, M., & Galinsky, E. (1995). *Quality in family child care and relative care*. New York: Teachers College Press.

Kuhlthau, K., & Oppenheim Mason, K. (1996). Market child care versus care by relatives: Choices made by employed and non-employed mothers. *Journal of Family Issues, 17*, 561–578.

McGillicuddy-De Lisi, A. V., & Subramanian, S. (1996). How do children develop knowledge? Beliefs of Tanzanian and American mothers. In S. Harkness & C. M. Super (Eds.), *Parents' cultural belief systems* (pp. 143–168). New York: Guilford Press.

Meyers, M. K., Gilbert, N., & Duerr-Berrick, J. (1992). *Gain family life and child care study*. Berkeley, CA: Family Welfare Research Group.

Meyers, M. K., & van Leuwen, K. (1992). Child care preferences and choices: Are AFDC recipients unique? *Social Work Research and Abstracts, 28*, 28–35.

Morelli, G. A., Rogoff, B., Oppenheim, D., & Goldsmith, D. (1992). Cultural variation in infants' sleeping arrangements: Questions of independence. *Developmental Psychology, 28*, 604–613.

Morelli, G. A., & Tronick, E. (1991). Parenting and child development in the Efe foragers and Lese farmers of northeastern Zaire. In M. Bornstein (Ed.), *Cultural approaches to parenting* (pp. 91–113). Hillsdale, NJ: Erlbaum.

Morelli, G. A., & Tronick, E. (1992). Efe fathers: One among many? A comparison of forager children's involvement with fathers and other males. *Social Development, 1*, 36–54.

Myers, R. (1992). *The twelve who survive*. New York: Routledge.

National Center for Children in Poverty. (1996). *Child care provided by kith and kin: Thinking "out of the box."* New York: Columbia School of Public Health.

Nsamenang, A. B. (1992a). Early childhood care and education in Cameroon. In M. E. Lamb, K. Sternberg, C. Hwang, & A. Broberg (Eds.), *Child care in context: Cross-cultural perspectives* (pp. 419–439). Hillsdale, NJ: Erlbaum.

Nsamenang, A. B. (1992b). *Human development in cultural context: A third world perspective*. Beverly Hills, CA: Sage.

Nsamenang, A. B. (1992c). Perceptions of parenting among the Nso of Cameroon. In B. Hewlett (Ed.), *Father-child relations: Cultural and biosocial contexts* (pp. 321–343). New York: Aldine de Gruyter.

Nsamenang, A. B., & Lamb, M. E. (1993). Socialization of Nso children in the Bamenda grassfields of northwest Cameroon. *International Journal of Behavioral Development, 16*, 429–441.

Ogbimi, G. E. (1992). The impact of mothers' perceptions of child care services and utilization. *Early Child Development and Care, 80*, 53–61.

Oregon Child Care Research Partnership (1997). *Patterns of work, family, and caregiver flexibility* [On-line]. Available Internet: http://www.teleport.com/ ~emlenart/open_res/flex.html

Overseas Education Fund. (1979). *Child care needs of low income mothers in less developed countries*. Washington, DC: Author.

Page, H. J. (1989). Childrearing versus childbearing: Coresidence of mother and child in sub-Saharan Africa. In R. Lesthaeghe (Ed.), *Reproduction and social organization in sub-Saharan Africa* (pp. 410–441). Berkeley: University of California Press.

Phillips, D.A. (1995). *Child care for low-income families: Summary of two workshops*. Washington, DC: National Academy Press.

Presser, H. B., & Cox, A. G. (1997). The work schedule of low-educated American women and welfare reform. *Monthly Labor Review, 120*(4), 25–34.

Rosenthal, M. K. (1994). *An ecological approach to the study of child care: Family day care in Israel*. Hillsdale, NJ: Erlbaum.

Rosier, K. B., & Corsaro, W. A. (1993). Competent parents, complex lives. *Journal of Contemporary Ethnography, 22*, 171–204.

Smith, S. L., Fairchild, M., & Groginsky, S. (1997). *Early childhood care and education*. Denver, CO: National Conference of State Legislatures.

Sonenstein, F. L., & Wolf, D. A. (1991). Satisfaction with child care: Perspectives of welfare mothers. *Journal of Social Issues, 47*(2), 15–31.

Stack, C. (1974). *All our kin*. New York: Basic Books.

Stipek, D., Milburn, S., Clements, D., & Daniels, D. H. (1992). Parents' beliefs about appropriate education for young children. *Developmental Psychology, 13*, 293–310.

Tronick, E., & Morelli, G. A. (1992). The Efe forager infant and toddler's pattern of social relationships: Multiple and simultaneous. *Developmental Psychology, 28*, 568–577.

U.S. General Accounting Office. (1994). *Child care: Child care subsidies increase likelihood that low-income women will work* (No. HEHS95-20). Washington, DC: Author.

Uttal, L. (1996). Custodial care, surrogate care, and coordinated care: Employed mothers and the meaning of child care. *Gender and Society, 10*(3), 291–311.

Valsiner, J. (1988). Epilogue: Ontogeny of co-construction of culture within socially organized environmental settings. In J. Valsiner (Ed.), *Child development within culturally constructed environments: Vol. 2. Social co-construction and environmental guidance in development* (pp. 283–297). Norwood, NJ: Ablex.

Valsiner, J., & Litvinovic, G. (1996). Processes of generalization in parental reasoning. In S. Harkness & C. M. Super (Eds.), *Parents' cultural belief systems* (pp. 56–83). New York: Guilford.

VandenHeuvel, A. (1996). The relationship between women's working arrangements and their child care arrangements. *Australian Bulletin of Labour, 22*(4), 288–305.

Weisner, T. S. (1979). Urban-rural differences in sociable and disruptive behavior of Kenya children. *Ethnology, 18*(2), 153–172.

Weisner, T. S., & Gallimore, R. (1977). My brother's keeper: Child and sibling caretaking. *Current Anthropology, 18*, 169–190.

West, J., Hausken, E. G., & Collins, M. (1993). *Readiness for kindergarten: Parent and teacher beliefs* (pp. 93–257). Washington, DC: National Center for Education Statistics.

Willer, B., Hofferth, S. L., Kisker, E. E., Divine-Hawkins, P., Farquhar, E., & Glantz, F. B. (1991). *The demand and supply of child care in 1990: Joint findings from the National Child Care Survey 1990 and a profile of child care settings*. Washington, DC: NAEYC.

Youssef, N., & Hamman, N. (1985). *Continuity in women's productive and reproductive roles: Implications for food aid and children's well being*. New York: UNICEF.

CHAPTER

Stephen J. Suomi

Behavioral Inhibition and Impulsive Aggressiveness: Insights from Studies with Rhesus Monkeys

☐ Introduction

It can be persuasively argued that, throughout the past century, the study of developmental phenomena has been dominated by three basic issues. These issues, which have profoundly influenced developmental theory and research alike, have traditionally been presented as dichotomies, although it is clear that such "either or" characterizations are overly simplistic. The first issue "nature vs. nurture," addresses fundamental causes of developmental phenomena. The second issue, "continuity versus change," involves basic descriptions of developmental processes and outcomes. The third issue, "stability versus instability of individual differences," encompasses questions of prediction, prevention, and intervention. Together, these issues transcend different developmental disciplines, research topic areas, levels of analysis, developmental periods across the life span, and species under investigation. Each has fostered seemingly endless theoretical discussions and generated countless empirical efforts over the years.

Studies of infant temperament and social-emotional development provide prime examples of the ubiquity and pervasiveness of these three issues. Temperament has classically been conceptualized as reflecting characteristics that are "inborn" or "constitutional" in nature, the implication being that they are most likely of genetic origin. In contrast, most (but not all) theories of social-emotional or personality development have emphasized experiential factors in accounting both for normative developmental change and the emergence of individual differences. The data, of course, are not so clear cut in either direction, reflecting the now widely accepted view that virtually all developmental phenomena, including temperament and social-emotional development, are the product of both nature and nurture rather than one or the other, and that the more relevant task lies in characterizing and understanding their inevitable interactions and transactions (e.g., Gottlieb, 1996).

The issue of developmental continuity versus change also is widely represented in the temperament and social-emotional development literature. Some theorists have argued that primary emotions are present at, or shortly after birth, and retain their basic defining characteristics throughout development, whereas others have argued that fear in a newborn is fundamentally different from fear in an adult—or even in a 5-year-old. Reality most likely lies somewhere between the extremes of unaltered continuity and total change, and the challenge for theorists and researchers alike has been to discover and characterize some more appropriate "middle ground."

Finally, the issue of relative stability of individual differences also is central to considerations of temperament and social-emotional development. Most definitions of temperament presume some degree of stability across situations and over time, and many empirical studies have tried to document long-term

510

stabilities across different temperamental dimensions throughout infancy, into childhood, and beyond. On the other hand, many preventive and therapeutic interventions targeted for "at-risk" individuals or populations have been based on the assumption that extreme cases can somehow be moved into the mainstream and that such movement is desirable.

Over the past 15 years, extensive research efforts have been focused on two aspects of temperament and social-emotional development: behavioral inhibition and impulsively aggressive behavioral tendencies. Seminal research carried out by Kagan and his colleagues demonstrated that children selected at 2 years of age for extreme behavioral inhibition (fearful, shy, and wary behavior in novel settings and with strange peers) tend to retain such tendencies throughout the childhood years, albeit with some exceptions (Kagan, Reznick, Clarke, Snidman, & Garcia-Coll, 1984). These children also typically exhibit characteristic patterns of physiological response to novel or challenging stimuli and circumstances—high and stable heart rate, a heightened adrenocortical response, and other indicators of autonomic arousal—that also tend to be preserved throughout childhood (Kagan, Reznick, & Snidman, 1988). More recent work in this area has (a) broadened the range of documented situations in which extremely inhibited individuals differ behaviorally from other children (Kagan & Snidman, 1991a); (b) expanded the list of physiological and physical measures that reliably differentiate inhibited children from their peers (Davidson, 1991; Davidson & Fox, 1989; Fox, 1991; Kagan, Snidman, Arcus, & Resnick, 1994); (c) identified specific patterns of behavioral and physiological reactivity exhibited during infancy that are highly predictive of subsequent behavioral inhibition (Calkins, Fox, & Marshall, 1996; Kagan & Snidman, 1991b); (d) accumulated evidence suggesting that, at least some, correlates of behavioral inhibition are heritable (e.g., Rosenberg & Kagan, 1987); (e) demonstrated that the behavioral tendencies of some inhibited children can be modified following certain types of experiences (Arcus, 1991; Putallaz, 1987); and (f) suggested that inhibited children may be at increased risk for a variety of child and adolescent behavioral problems, most notably certain anxiety and affective disorders (Biederman et al., 1990).

The three basic developmental issues described at the outset loom large in discussions concerning behavioral inhibition. With respect to nature-nurture issues, it is clear that, despite accumulating evidence regarding the heritability of certain features common to most behaviorally inhibited children, substantial modification of behavioral (and, possibly, physiological) patterns can occur (e.g., Arcus, 1991). Indeed, the question of precisely what is inherited and what can be modified (and to what degree and at what times during development) is of major interest in current behavioral inhibition research. Moreover, there also has been considerable argument as to whether behavioral inhibition is better characterized as basically categorical or basically dimensional in nature (i.e., whether behaviorally inhibited individuals represent a distinctive temperamental "type" or are merely exhibiting extreme scores on essentially continuous temperamental dimensions).

Similarly, the basic issues of developmental continuity versus change and of relative stability of individual differences over time have been at the heart of most longitudinal studies of behavioral inhibition. Just as the overall behavioral repertoires of individuals undergo dramatic change from infancy through childhood and into adolescence, so too do the specific behavioral patterns that optimally define "inhibition." Indeed, a major challenge for these studies has been to demonstrate some sort of linkage between different patterns of behavior thought to reflect inhibition at different ages. Physiological measures have posed similar problems of interpretation, although most of the developmental changes documented to date have tended to be more quantitative than qualitative in nature, with some marked exceptions. Finally, a major goal of most longitudinal studies of behavioral inhibition has been to demonstrate long-term stability of the phenomenon, typically by showing strong positive correlations for behavioral and physiological measures (or composite scores incorporating these measures) across different ages. Yet, these correlations have never been found to be perfect and often have accounted for only trivial proportions of total variance over time. Precise characterization of what is stable and what is not, over what time periods, and under what conditions, currently is far from complete.

Nature-nurture, continuity-discontinuity, and individual difference stability issues also have been central to recent studies of impulsive aggression in childhood, adolescence, and adulthood. An increasing body of prospective evidence has suggested that children (especially boys) who display high levels of such aggression on entry into the school system are likely to continue to be highly aggressive throughout adolescence and even into adulthood (e.g., Olweus, 1979). In addition, both prospective and retrospective studies have shown that such individuals are at greatly increased risk for developing a wide range of behavioral problems or more serious psychopathologies, including attentional difficulties and externalizing behavioral disorders in childhood and delinquency, substance abuse, violent criminality, and suicide in adolescence and adulthood (e.g., Tremblay, 1992).

Research in this topic area increasingly has been focused on the apparent relationship between extreme behavioral tendencies of this nature and abnormal serotonergic functioning. For example, unusually low concentrations of the primary central serotonin metabolite 5-hydroxyindoleacetic acid (5-HIAA) in cerebrospinal fluid (CSF) have been found in children who are unusually aggressive toward peers and hostile toward mothers (Kruesi et al., 1990); children who torture animals (Kruesi, 1989); children and adolescents with disruptive behavior disorders (Kruesi et al., 1990); offenders convicted of violent aggressive acts, property destruction or both (Linnoila et al., 1983); men with personality disorders having extreme scores for aggression, irritability, hostility, and psychopathic deviance on standardized tests (Brown, Linnoila, & Goodwin, 1990; Linnoila, 1988); men expelled from the marines for excessive violence and psychopathic deviance (Brown, Goodwin, Ballenger, Croyer, & Major, 1979); suicide victims (e.g., Mann, Arango, & Underwood, 1990); and sons of men arrested for violence and arson (Linnoila, DeJong, & Virkkunen, 1989). The precise nature of this linkage (i.e., what causes what) and basic developmental questions concerning its initial appearance, developmental continuity, and long-term stability all are of obvious theoretical, clinical, and even societal interest; yet, to date, definitive answers to such questions have remained largely elusive.

☐ Primate Analogs of Inhibition and Impulsive Aggressiveness

Developmental studies of humans, whether focusing on behavioral inhibition, impulsive violence, and aggression, or other phenomena, are inevitably constrained in efforts to address nature-nurture, continuity-discontinuity, and stability issues by very real ethical and practical matters. Nature-nurture questions are most clearly resolved when a range of specific genotypes can be studied across systematically varied environmental settings; yet, that is never ethically proper and seldom practically feasible with human subjects. Questions regarding issues of developmental continuity and stability are best studied via prospective longitudinal experiments, but such studies tend to be expensive, are often subject to nonrandom sample attrition, and usually take a long time to complete because humans take a long time to grow up. Many of these problems and constraints can be reduced substantially (if not eliminated) in studies with animals. Of course, the degree to which animal research can answer questions or address issues concerning human developmental phenomena is largely dependent on the degree to which the phenomena of interest generalize from the human case to the animal under study (cf., Harlow et al., 1972). In the cases of both behavioral inhibition (and its physiological concomitants) and impulsive aggression (and its apparent link with 5-HIAA deficits), a growing body of evidence has suggested considerable cross-species generality between humans and advanced nonhuman primates.

Numerous studies conducted over the past 15 years have reported highly consistent differences, both between and within different primate species, in prototypical patterns of behavioral and physiological response to environmental novelty or challenge (e.g., Capitanio, Rasmussen, Snyder, Laudenslager, & Reite, 1986; Clarke, Mason, & Moberg, 1988; Mendoza & Mason, 1986; Suomi, 1981). Much of this research has been carried out with rhesus monkeys (*Macaca mulatta*), representatives of a highly successsful Old World monkey species indigenous to the Indian subcontinent, who share approximately 94% of their genes with *Homo sapiens* (Lovejoy, 1981; Sibley, Comstock, & Alquist, 1990).

By way of background, in their natural habitats, rhesus monkeys typically reside in large social groups (termed "troops"), each containing several multigenerational female lineages (matrilines) plus numerous immigrant adult males. This form of social organization derives from the fact that rhesus monkey females spend their entire life in the troop in which they were born, whereas virtually all males emigrate from their natal troop around the time of puberty, when they are 3 to 5 years old, eventually joining other nearby troops. Rhesus monkey infants spend virtually all of their initial days and weeks of life in physical contact or within arm's reach of their biological mother, during which time they form a strong, specific attachment bond with her. In their second month of life, rhesus monkey infants begin to explore their immediate physical and social environment, typically using their mother as a "secure base" to support such exploration (cf., Suomi, 1995). Over the next few months, these infants spend increasing amounts of time engaging in extensive social interactions with other group members, especially peers. Weaning to solid food typically begins during the fourth month and is usually completed by 6 months of age. Shortly thereafter, play with peers becomes the predominant social activity and remains so throughout rhesus monkey "childhood" (i.e., the rest of the first year, all of the second, and most if not all of the third year of life). During this time, play interactions become increasingly complex, involving patterns of behavior that appear to simulate virtually all adult social activities, including courtship and reproductive behaviors and dominance-aggressive interactions.

The onset of puberty is associated with major life transitions for both genders. Although rhesus monkey females remain in their natal troop throughout adolescence and thereafter, their interactions with peers decline dramatically as they redirect much of their social activities toward matrilineal kin, including the infants they subsequently bear and rear. Adolescent males, by contrast, leave their natal troop permanently and typically join all-male "gangs" for varying periods before they attempt to enter a different troop. This period of transition for adolescent and young adult males represents a time of major stress, with a mortality rate that approaches 50% in some rhesus monkey populations. Some surviving males stay in their new troop for the rest of their lives, whereas other males may transfer from one troop to another several times during their adult years. This overall pattern of social group organization and general sequence of behavioral development is relatively common among Old World monkey species, especially within the genus *Macaca* (Lindburg, 1991).

Approximately 15% to 20% of rhesus monkeys studied in both field and captive environments consistently respond to novel or mildly challenging situations with dramatic behavioral disruption and pronounced physiological arousal. Whereas most other monkeys typically find novel stimuli interesting and will readily explore them, usually with minimal physiological arousal, these "high-reactive" individuals instead tend to avoid such stimuli and, if that is not possible, they generally display obvious physiognomic expressions of fear and anxious-like behavior (Suomi, Kraemer, Baysinger, & Delizio, 1981). In addition, high-reactive rhesus monkeys exhibit many of the same physiological patterns in response to environmental challenges as have been reported for behaviorally inhibited human infants and children. They tend to react with higher and more stable heart rates, higher levels of cortisol (both in plasma and saliva), and greater noradrenergic turnover, than do their same-age cohorts whose behavioral responses to the same circumstances are mild at best. However, just as with behaviorally inhibited young humans, high-reactive young rhesus monkeys are usually indistinguishable from the rest of their age cohort when they are in familiar and benign settings. In the absence of obvious stress, they look perfectly normal, both behaviorally and physiologically.

With respect to possible primate analogs to human impulsive aggressiveness, investigators from several laboratories working with different primate species have reported dramatic individual differences in levels and types of aggression displayed (e.g., Bernstein, Williams, & Ramsay, 1983; Steklis, Brammen, Raleigh, & McGuire, 1985). Some of these investigators also have documented, in vervet monkeys (*Cercopithecus aethiops*), strong links between high rates of unprovoked aggression (and generally incompetent social interaction patterns) and low levels of CSF 5-HIAA (e.g., Raleigh, McGuire, & Brammer, 1989; Raleigh et al., 1986). Research with rhesus monkeys also has consistently found negative correlations between levels of impulsive-like aggression and CSF 5-HIAA concentrations in comparisons involving captive subjects of different ages, sex, rearing backgrounds, and even different individuals within the same-age–same-sex rearing class (Higley, Suomi, & Linnoila, 1990). Furthermore, the finding of an inverse relationship between expressions of impulsive aggression and CSF 5-HIAA concentrations has been replicated in populations of rhesus monkeys living in naturalistic habitats (e.g., Higley et al., 1992).

Thus, there appear to be at least some features common to behavioral inhibition, as seen in human infants and children, and high reactivity, as seen in almost a fifth of rhesus monkey populations. Both involve physiognomic and behavioral expressions associated with fear and anxiety that are consistently displayed in the face of environmental novelty or challenge, but not noticeably so in familiar, stable settings, and both are also marked by similar physiological response patterns that tend to accompany these behavioral reactions (e.g., high and stable heart rates, increased adrenocortical activity, and greater autonomic arousal). Similarly, there clearly are some features common to the expressions of impulsive aggression shown by some humans and by some rhesus monkeys, most notably the inverse relationship between these behavioral patterns and CSF concentrations of the primary central metabolite of serotonin. What do we know about the developmental continuity and relative stability of individual differences in the expression of these two distinctive response patterns shown by some rhesus monkeys? What do we know about nature-nurture issues regarding these phenomena? And, in what ways might such information inform and advance our understanding of behavioral inhibition and impulsive aggression in humans? Each of these questions will be addressed in the sections that follow.

☐ Developmental Continuity and Interindividual Stability in the Expression of High Reactivity and Impulsive Aggressiveness

High Reactivity

Over the past decade, numerous studies investigating developmental aspects of high reactivity have been carried out with rhesus monkeys growing up in captive settings at the National Institutes of Health Animal Center in rural Maryland as well as at two field sites on Cayo Santiago, a small island off the east coast of Puerto Rico, and on Morgan Island, a sea island on the South Carolina Atlantic coast, respectively. As a result, there now exists a substantial database regarding its behavioral and physiological expression in rhesus monkeys of differing age and gender. Individuals who seem prone to exhibit exaggerated responses to mildly challenging situations can be readily identified in their first few months of life. Most begin leaving their mothers later chronologically and explore their immediate physical and social environment less than other infants in their birth cohort. High-reactive youngsters also tend to be shy and withdrawn in their initial encounters with peers. Laboratory studies have shown that, at 4 months of age, they exhibit significantly higher and more stable heart rates and greater cortisol secretion in such interactions than do their more outgoing age-mates (Suomi, 1991). However, when these individuals are in familiar and stable settings they are virtually indistinguishable, both behaviorally and physiologically, from others in their peer group.

On the other hand, behavioral and physiological differences between high-reactive and other infants and juveniles tend to be exacerbated when environmental perturbations are extreme, prolonged, or both. For example, in their natural habitat, rhesus monkey infants and juveniles typically experience numerous functional separations from their mother during the 2- to 3-month-long annual breeding season, when she repeatedly leaves her resident social group for brief periods to consort and mate with selected males. The departure of its mother clearly represents a major social stressor for any young rhesus monkey, and virtually all youngsters initially react to loss of physical access to her with short-term behavioral agitation and acute physiological arousal, consistent with Bowlby's descriptions of the immediate consequences of involuntary maternal separation in human infants and young children (Bowlby, 1960, 1973). However, whereas most young monkeys soon begin to adapt to the separations and readily seek out the company of others in their social group (Berman, Rasmussen, & Suomi, 1994), high-reactive individuals may lapse into a behavioral depression characterized by increasing lethargy, lack of apparent interest in social stimulation, eating and sleeping difficulties, altered immune response, and a characteristic hunched over, fetal-like posture (Suomi, 1995).

Over the past 30 years, numerous studies of maternal and other types of social separation in captive settings have both replicated and extended these findings from the field. In these studies, carried out at the University of Wisconsin Harlow Primate Laboratory, the National Institutes of Health Animal Center, and several other primate facilities, subjects typically have been removed from their familiar physical and social settings and housed individually for periods ranging from several hours to several days before being returned to their home environment, permitting the repeated collection of a variety of behavioral and physiological data under standardized conditions prior to, during, and following each separation (cf., Mineka & Suomi, 1978). High-reactive infant and juvenile rhesus monkeys consistently react to such separations with more extreme and prolonged behavioral and physiological response patterns than do others in their social group. As infants, they are more likely to exhibit depressive-like huddling and social withdrawal following separation; as juveniles and adolescents, they are more likely to engage in agitated stereotypic movements when separated. At every age, they are likely to show significantly greater and more prolonged adrenocortical elevation, more rapid central noradrenergic turnover, and altered immune responses (Suomi, 1991). Thus, despite developmental changes in the form of their behavioral response to separation, high reactive monkeys consistently respond to such separations with the most extreme behavioral responses among their age cohort throughout development. Furthermore, despite significant developmental changes in the magnitude of separation response for some physiological measures (e.g., the size and duration of plasma cortisol elevations following separation tend to decrease dramatically from year 1 to year 2 and gradually thereafter until puberty), high-reactive individuals tend to have extreme values for each physiological measure at every age tested (Suomi, 1991).

Current information regarding high reactivity during adolescence and adulthood also points to considerable continuity throughout the latter part of the life span. Cross-sectional studies of natural groups of wild rhesus monkeys have found that the relative incidence of high physiological reactivity, operationally defined in terms of specific heart rate patterns and adrenocortical responses following short-term capture and confinement, approximates that observed in laboratory colonies (i.e., about 20%) from adolescence to adulthood (e.g., Rasmussen & Suomi, 1989; Suomi et al., 1989). Recent field studies of free-ranging rhesus monkeys on Cayo Santiago have demonstrated that high-reactive adolescent males tend to delay permanent emigration from their natal social group; follow-up studies have suggested that high-reactive males also tend to follow relatively conservative strategies in their subsequent efforts to join other established monkey groups (Suomi, Rasmussen, & Higley, 1992). Field studies of adult female maternal behavioral "styles" have reported that physiologically high-reactive multiparous females tend to have higher rates of infant rejection and punishment, and take a less active role in initiating and maintaining physical contact and proximity with their infant than do multiparous females with lower and more variable heart rates and levels of plasma cortisol (Rasmussen, Timme, & Suomi, 1997). Laboratory studies of primiparous females have shown that high-reactive new mothers are at greater risk to neglect and even abuse their infant when isolated from group members than are other primiparous females of comparable age and housing backround (Suomi & Ripp, 1983). Long-term longitudinal investigation of group-living rhesus monkeys throughout adulthood has shown that behavioral tendencies expressed during early adulthood can be remarkably persistent even into old age (Suomi, Novak, & Well, 1997).

In sum, a substantial body of developmental data has suggested that high reactivity in rhesus monkeys is characterized by considerable behavioral and physiological continuity throughout the life span. The most obvious behavioral feature common to high-reactive monkeys of all ages is their tendency to show more extreme behavioral responses of a generally fearful nature for longer periods when faced with new and challenging situations than their cohorts. What does change during development is the specific behavioral patterns that become extreme, notably in the same general manner as "normative" expressions of fear change developmentally among their less reactive peers (cf., Suomi & Harlow, 1976). Moreover, there is substantial developmental continuity in the nature, if not the degree, of physiological reaction to the same challenging situations: high-reactive monkeys of all ages tend to show exaggerated adrenocortical, monoamine, psychophysiological, and immunological responses relative to those of their peers. On the other hand, such conspicuous biobehavioral response patterns essentially are nonexistent in the absence of obvious stress at any age. Thus, the apparent developmental continuity of the characteristic biobehavioral response patterns shown by high-reactive monkeys also remains situationally dependent across the life span.

Some of the longitudinal data sets contributing to current knowledge about the developmental continuity of biobehavioral expressions of high reactivity in monkeys also have been used to determine the relative stability of individual differences in measures of reactivity throughout development. These findings regarding interindividual stability have been quite consistent from study to study, from laboratory to field settings, and across different periods of development. In general (and, especially, in the absence of major environmental change), individuals who exhibit high-reactive responses to challenge as infants are prone to do so as juveniles, adolescents, and even adults, whereas those individuals who show no evidence of high reactivity early in life seem unlikely to develop its characteristic response patterns during their later years.

For example, laboratory studies of rhesus monkey infants have found significant stability of individual differences in vocal and locomotor behaviors and in levels of plasma and salivary cortisol following brief social separations at 3, 4, and 5 months of age. Those individual differences, in turn, were predictive of behavioral, adrenocortical, and even noradrenergic and immunological responses to longer separations at 6 months of age, and then again when the monkeys were 18 months old. Field studies of mother-infant separations associated with the breeding season found that the best predictor of a 2-year-old juvenile's behavioral response to its mother's consort activity was its reaction to similar separations during the previous year's breeding season: Monkeys who exhibited the most extreme behavioral reactions during their first separation experiences tended to exhibit the most extreme reactions to separation a year later, even though those latter reactions were much milder than the reactions they had shown in their first year (Rasmussen et al., 1997). Another field study examining the relationship between psychophysiological reactivity and natal group emigration by pubertal males reported remarkable concordance between individual differences in heart rate and heart rate variability sampled in the year prior to emigration and those sampled during the year following emigration, despite developmental decreases in absolute heart rate levels and enormous social changes for the males during the course of that year (Rasmussen & Suomi, 1989). Finally, the long-term longitudinal study of behavioral continuity and change throughout adulthood cited above also reported significant stability of individual differences for some (but not all) categories of specific behaviors, and remarkable interindividual stability of overall behavioral profiles, from early adulthood to old age (Suomi et al., 1997).

Two qualifications with regard to the findings of strong stability of individual differences in biobehavioral measures of reactivity throughout development are in order. First, although the short-term stability for individual categories of behavior has been impressive in many studies, it generally has been much less so over longer periods of development (e.g., individual differences in activity levels during separations are very stable from 3 to 6 months of age, but those levels are not predictive of activity levels during separations at 2 or 3 years of age, or during adulthood). Second, as was the case for issues regarding developmental continuity, the findings of strong interindividual stability of response patterns largely have been limited to conditions involving significant environmental challenge. Behavioral and physiological measures collected in benign settings have not proven to be particularly useful for predicting individual differences in either stressful or nonstressful settings later in life. The one obvious exception to both these qualifications involves a specific behavioral pattern that perhaps is best described as "vigilance": active visual monitoring of one's environment while remaining passive in other respects. Individual differences in passive visual monitoring during the first year of life are surprisingly predictive of differences in visual monitoring expressed in old age. In general, however, the impressive developmental continuities and stability of individual differences found for rhesus monkey biobehavioral reactivity largely have been limited to situations that involved some degree of environmental stress.

Impulsive Agressiveness

In many respects, the findings regarding developmental continuity and stability of individual differences in impulsive aggressiveness among rhesus monkeys parallel those for high reactivity. Impulsively aggressive rhesus monkeys can be identified on the basis of both behavioral and physiological measures relatively early in life, and these biobehavioral features show substantial developmental continuity and interindividual stability from late infancy to early adulthood, if not beyond. The parallels are not perfect, however. Impulsive aggressiveness seems less widespread (rarely involving more than 5% to 10% of any social group) than high reactivity; it first becomes behaviorally obvious somewhat later developmentally (in late rather than early infancy); and some of its physiological features, especially the unusually low concentrations of CSF 5-HIAA, appear to be less situationally dependent than most aspects of high reactivity.

Monkeys who can be characterized as impulsively agressive, especially males, typically begin to distinguish themselves from same-sex peers in their early play interactions. They seem to lack the ability to moderate their behavioral responses to playful invitations from peers and, by late childhood, their rough-and-tumble play interactions often escalate into tissue-damaging aggressive exchanges, disproportionately at their own expense. Not surprisingly, most of these individuals come to be avoided by peers, and they become increasingly isolated socially. In the wild, impulsively aggressive young males also display a propensity for making dangerous leaps from treetop to treetop, occasionally with painful outcomes. CSF samples obtained from free-ranging groups have shown that monkeys who make the greatest number of such impulsive leaps also have the lowest CSF 5-HIAA concentrations within their birth cohort (Mehlman et al., 1994).

Recent field studies carried out on the Morgan Island rhesus monkey population also have found that most impulsive young males are permanently expelled from their natal group prior to puberty, long before the rest of their male cohort begins the normal emigration process (Mehlman et al., 1995). These males tend to be grossly incompetent socially and, lacking the requisite social skills necessary for entry into another social group, most become solitary and typically perish within a year (Higley, Mehlman, et al., 1996b). Juvenile females who exhibit excessive impulsively aggressive behavior also characteristically have chronically low CSF concentrations of 5-HIAA, and they retain these distinguishing features throughout childhood and into puberty. In contrast to impulsive males, these females are unlikely to be expelled from their natal troop at any time thereafter, although laboratory studies have indicated that they typically remain at the bottom of their social hierarchy (Higley, King, et al., 1996a) and often are relatively incompetent , if not neglectful, mothers. Thus, the behavioral features of impulsive agressiveness show substantial developmental continuity and striking interindividual stability throughout much of behavioral ontogeny. Rhesus monkeys who exhibit excessive impulsive and aggressive behavior early in life tend to follow developmental trajectories that often result in premature death among males and chronically low social status and poor parenting among females.

The developmental continuity and relative stability of CSF 5-HIAA concentrations have been found to be at least as strong as any behavioral indexes of impulsivity, aggressiveness, or both. Both laboratory and field studies of rhesus monkeys across a wide age range have documented major developmental changes in CSF 5-HIAA concentrations, with levels dropping sharply during the first year and more slowly thereafter until puberty, only to typically rise slightly during the adult years. Despite these developmental changes, interindividual differences remain strikingly stable, both in the short term (Higley et al., 1992; Higley, Mehlman, et al., 1996b; Mehlman et al., 1995) and over the 5-year period from late infancy to early adulthood (Higley et al., 1997). Indeed, the developmental continuity and interindividual stability data for 5-HIAA are every bit as impressive as for any behavioral or physiological measure of high reactivity cited above. Furthermore, the 5-HIAA data differ from virtually all measures of rhesus monkey biobehavioral reactivity in one fundamental respect: Whereas the reactivity measures appear to be highly situationally dependent, CSF 5-HIAA concentrations, by comparison, show relatively little change from situation to situation, even ones involving forcible social separations or intense aggression (e.g., Higley et al., 1992; Mehlman et al., 1994). These findings therefore suggest that CSF concentrations of 5-HIAA may serve as a robust marker of an individual's propensity to engage in impulsively aggressive actions, even when assessed in relatively benign environmental settings.

☐ Nature-Nurture Issues Regarding High Reactivity and Impulsive Aggressiveness in Rhesus Monkeys

The research reviewed in the previous section identified certain behavioral and physiological features of high reactivity and impulsive aggressiveness, respectively, that show considerable continuity and interindividual stability throughout much, if not all, of the rhesus monkey life span. What factors underlie these developmental phenomena—which features might be heritable or subject to various environmental influences or, more likely, be the product of both nature and nurture?

Several studies of rhesus monkeys raised in both laboratory and field environments have examined the relative heritability of many of the behavioral and physiological characteristics of high reactivity and impulsive aggressiveness, respectively. Laboratory studies utilizing half sibling comparisons and cross-fostering rearing procedures have demonstrated significant heritability for the primary central metabolites of norepinepherine, dopamine, and serotonin, as well as for plasma cortisol output during separations, although the specific pattern of heritability appears to be different for each physiological measure (Higley et al., 1993). Other laboratory studies comparing half siblings or members of different genetic "strains" reared in identical nursery environments have reported suggestive evidence of heritability for a variety of infant state and temperament measures (Champoux, Higley, & Suomi, 1997; Champoux, Suomi, & Schnieder, 1994; Scanlan, 1988), heart rate response patterns (Suomi, 1981), plasma corticotrophin and cortisol concentrations (Scanlan, 1988; Suomi, 1984), and behavioral reactions to separation (Suomi, 1983, 1991). Field studies have found significant concordance of heart rate and adrenocortical response patterns between mothers and their adolescent sons, (Rasmussen & Suomi, 1991) and significant differences in both heart rate patterns and characteristic maternal "styles" between adult females from different matrilineal families (Rasmussen et al., 1997). Thus, there is substantial evidence that at least some of the developmentally stable interindividual variability seen in both behavioral and physiological indexes of stress reactivity and impulsivity can be attributed to heritable factors.

On the other hand, the fact that individual differences in various features of stress reactivity and impulsivity tend to be quite stable in rhesus monkeys from infancy to adulthood and, at least in part, are heritable does not mean that these biobehavioral features necessarily are fixed at birth or are immune to subsequent environmental influence. To the contrary, an increasing body of evidence from laboratory studies has clearly demonstrated that prototypical patterns of biobehavioral response to environmental novelty and stress, on the one hand, and propensity to develop patterns of impulsive aggressiveness, on the other, can be modified substantially by certain early experiences, particularly, those involving early social attachment relationships.

Peer Rearing Studies

A common practice in many primate facilities over the years has been to rear monkey infants with peers instead of with their biological mother (e.g., Chamove et al., 1973; Novak & Sackett, 1997). In one form of this general rearing paradigm, infants are permanently separated from their mothers at birth, hand reared in a neonatal nursery for their first month of life, housed with same-age, like-reared peers for the rest of their first 6 months, and then moved into larger social groups containing both peer-reared and mother-reared age-mates (e.g., Scanlan, 1988). During their initial months, these infants readily develop strong social attachment bonds to each other, much as mother-reared infants develop attachment relationships with their own mothers. However, because peers are not nearly as effective as a normal monkey mother in reducing fear in the face of stress or in providing a "secure base" for exploration, the attachment relationships that these peer-reared infants develop almost always are "anxious" or "insecure" in nature (Suomi, 1995). As a consequence, whereas peer-reared monkeys show completely normal physical and motor development, their early exploratory behavior is somewhat limited. They seem reluctant to approach novel objects, and they tend to be shy in their initial encounters with unfamiliar peers. Moreover, even when they interact with their same-age cagemates in familiar settings, their emerging social play repertoires usually are retarded in both frequency and complexity. For example, peer-reared monkeys are more likely to play with only one partner at a time rather than with multiple partners simultaneously, as mother-reared youngsters quickly come to prefer, and their play bouts usually are limited to relatively brief exchanges rather than the extended interactions that may go on for several minutes at a time among mother-reared peers. One explanation for their relatively poor play performance is that their cagemates must serve both as attachment objects and as playmates, a dual role that neither mothers nor mother-reared peers have to fulfill. It also is difficult for peer-reared youngsters to develop sophisticated play repertoires with basically incompetent play partners. Perhaps as a result, they typically drop to the bottom of their respective dominance hierarchies when they are grouped with mother-reared monkeys of their own age (cf., Higley, Suomi, & Linnoila, 1996).

In addition, peer-reared monkeys consistently exhibit more extreme behavioral, adrenocortical, and noradrenergic reactions to social separations than do their mother-reared cohorts, even after they have been living with them in the same social groups for extended periods. Such differences in prototypical biobehavioral reactions to separation persist from infancy to adolescence, if not beyond. Interestingly, the general nature of the separation reactions of peer-reared monkeys seems to mirror that of "naturally occuring" high-reactive mother-reared subjects. In this sense, early peer rearing appears to have the effect of making rhesus monkey infants generally more high reactive than they might have been if reared by their biological mother (Suomi, 1995).

Early peer-rearing has another long-term developmental consequence for rhesus monkeys: It tends to make them more impulsive, especially if they are males. Like the previously described impulsive monkeys growing up in the wild, peer-reared males initially exhibit aggressive tendencies in the context of juvenile play and, as they approach puberty, the frequency and severity of their aggressive episodes usually exceeds that of mother-reared group members of similar age. Peer-reared females tend to groom (and be groomed by) others in their social group less frequently and for shorter durations than their mother-reared counterparts and, as before, they usually stay at the bottom of their respective dominance heirarchies. These differences between peer-reared and mother-reared age-mates in aggression, grooming, and dominance remain relatively robust when the monkeys subsequently are moved into new social groups, and they generally are quite stable throughout the juvenile and adolescent years. Peer-reared monkeys also consistently show lower CSF concentrations of 5-HIAA than their mother-reared counterparts. These differences in 5-HIAA concentrations appear well before 6 months of age, they persist during the transition to mixed group housing, and they remain stable at least throughout adolescence and into early adulthood. Thus, peer-reared monkeys as a group resemble the impulsive subgroup of wild-living (and mother-reared) monkeys not only behaviorally but also in terms of decreased serotonergic functioning (Suomi, 1997). An additional risk that peer-reared females carry into adulthood concerns their maternal behavior. Peer-reared mothers are significantly more likely to exhibit neglectful or abusive treatment of their first-born offspring than are their mother-reared counterparts, although their care of subsequent offspring tends to improve dramatically (Ruppenthal, Arling, Harlow, Sakett, & Suomi, 1976).

In summary, early peer rearing seems to make rhesus monkeys both more highly reactive *and* more impulsive, and their resulting developmental trajectories not only resemble those of naturally occurring subgroups of rhesus monkeys growing up in the wild, but also persist in that vein long after their period of exclusive exposure to peers has been completed and they have been living in more species-typical social groups. Indeed, some effects of these inadequate early attachment realtionships may well be passed on to the next generation via aberrant patterns of maternal care, as appears to be the case for both high-reactive and impulsive mothers rearing infants in their natural habitat (Suomi & Levine, 1998). Interestingly, Bowlby (1988) and other attachment researchers have argued persuasively that the effects of inadequate early social attachments also may be both lifelong and cross-generational in nature for humans as well.

Cross-Fostering Studies

What about the opposite situation: Are there any consequences, either short or long terrm, of enhanced early social attachment relationships for rhesus monkeys? To address this question, rhesus monkey neonates selectively bred for differences in temperamental reactivity were raised by foster mothers who differed in their characteristic maternal "style," as determined by their patterns of care of previous offspring. In this work, specific members of a captive breeding colony were selectively bred to produce offspring who, on the basis of their genetic pedigree, were either unusually high reactive or within the normal range of reactivity. Within hours of birth these selectively bred infants were switched from their biological mothers to unrelated multiparous females preselected to be either unusually "nurturant" or within the normal range of maternal care. The "nurturant" foster mothers had been selected on the basis of their care of previous offspring, especially their consistency in providing a "secure base" and their relatively high rates of grooming and low rates of rejecting and punishing those previous offspring. The selectively bred infants were then reared by their respective foster mothers for their first 6 months of life, after which they were moved to larger social groups containing both other cross-fostered age-mates and those reared by their biological mother (Suomi, 1987).

During the period of cross-fostering, control infants (i.e., those whose pedigree suggested normative patterns of reactivity) exhibited essentially normal patterns of biobehavioral development, independent of the relative nurturance of their foster mother. In contrast, dramatic differences emerged among genetically high-reactive infants as a function of their foster mother's style. Whereas high-reactive infants foster reared by control females exhibited expected deficits in early exploration and exaggerated responses to minor environmental perturbations, high-reactive infants cross-fostered to nurturant females actually appeared to be behaviorally precocious. They left their mothers earlier, explored their environment more, and displayed less behavioral disturbance during weaning than not only the high-reactive infants cross-fostered to control mothers but even control infants reared by either type of foster mother (Suomi, 1987).

When these monkeys were separated from their foster mothers and moved into larger social groups at 6 months of age, additional temperament-rearing interaction effects appeared, marked by optimal outcomes for those high-reactive youngsters who had been reared by nurturant foster mothers. These individuals became especially adept at recruiting and retaining other group members as allies during agonistic encounters and, perhaps as a consequence, most rose to and maintained top positions in their group's dominance hierarchy. In contrast, high-reactive youngsters who had been foster reared by control females tended to drop to and remain at the bottom of the same hierarchies (Suomi, 1991).

Finally, some of the cross-fostered females from this study have since become mothers themselves, and their maternal behavior toward their firstborn offspring has been assessed. It appears that these young mothers have adapted the same general maternal style as that shown by their foster mother, independent of both their own original reactivity profile and the type of maternal style shown by their own biological mother (Suomi, 1995). Thus, the apparent benefits accrued by high-reactive females raised by nurturant foster mothers seemingly can be transmitted to the next generation of offspring, even though the mode of transmission clearly is nongenetic in nature (cf., Suomi & Levine, 1998). Clearly, high reactivity need not always be associated with adverse outcomes. Instead, following certain early experiences high-reactive infants appear to have relatively normal, if not actually optimal, long-term developmental trajectories which, in turn, can be amenable to cross-generational transmission. Whether the same possibilities exist for genetically impulsive rhesus monkey infants currently is the focus of extensive ongoing research.

These and other findings from studies with monkeys have demonstrated that differential early social experiences can have major long-term influences on an individual's behavioral and physiological propensities over and above any heritable predispositions (Suomi, 1997). The nature of early attachment experiences appears to be especially relevant. Whereas insecure early attachments tend to make monkeys more reactive and impulsive, unusually secure early attachments seem to have the opposite effect, at least for some individuals. In either case, how a rhesus monkey mother rears her infant can markedly affect its biobehavioral developmental trajectory, even long after its interactions with her have ceased.

☐ Conclusions and Implications for Understanding Behavioral Inhibition and Impulsive Aggressiveness in Humans

At the beginning of this chapter, it was argued that many of the obstacles to rigorous developmental study of nature-nurture, continuity-discontinuity, and stability of individual differences issues in humans could be overcome or even avoided by investigating parallel phenomena in animals. To what extent have studies of reactivity and impulsive aggressiveness in rhesus monkeys been informative with respect to each of those basic developmental issues?

First, the results of these studies have clearly demonstrated that both nature and nurture are at play in the development of most, if not all, biobehavioral aspects of rhesus monkey reactivity and impulsive aggressiveness. On the one hand, evidence of significant heritability has been found for certain neonatal reflex and activity patterns, measures of psychophysiological reactivity, CSF monoamine metabolite concentrations, and behavioral and adrenocortical responsiveness to separation and other environmental challenges. Notably, however, there appears to be considerable variation in the precise nature and magnitude of the heritability across these different behavioral and physiological systems, suggesting, at the very least, that multiple genes operating at multiple loci must be involved in the expression of high-reactive or impulsive biobehavioral response patterns.

On the other hand, the results of prospective longitudinal studies with rhesus monkeys also have demonstrated significant effects of differential early rearing experiences on the developmental trajectories of virtually all of these very same behavioral and physiological systems, their specific heritabilities notwithstanding. Thus, how a rhesus monkey is reared can markedly affect its pattern of neonatal reflex development; its daily distribution of activity states; its behavioral, adrenocortical, and noradrenergic responses to separation; its liklihood of escalating play bouts into aggressive episodes; and its chronic CSF concentrations of 5-HIAA, respectively, no matter how many genes might be involved in each instance. Clearly, both nature and nurture can contribute to the expression of high reactivity and impulsive aggressiveness by individual rhesus monkeys.

Perhaps, the more interesting issue concerns the manner and degree to which heritable factors interact with environmental influences to shape individual developmental trajectories regarding reactivity and impulsive aggressiveness. That such interactions can occur is clearly indicated by the results of the cross-fostering study reported above, in which infants selectively bred for high reactivity clearly benefited from being reared by a highly nurturant, as opposed to a "control," foster mother, whereas "control" infants accrued no apparent benefits from highly nurturant foster mothers. Whether comparable instances of gene-environment interactions can be demonstrated for other characteristics (e.g., impulsivity), other biological systems (e.g., immunological), other developmental periods (e.g., prenatal, adolescence, and old age), and other forms of environmental influences (e.g., dietary, pharmacologic, and social) currently are the topics of rigorous ongoing research. Nevertheless, even highly definitive findings from such studies of gene-environment interactions could scarcely begin to address issues regarding the identity of the actual genes involved; their biochemical expression; the extent and manner in which their expression was enhanced, blocked, or otherwise modified by specific environmental factors; and the pathways and mechanisms through which such expression was translated into specific physiological and behavioral activities exhibited by individual monkeys. While nature and nurture can obviously interact, exactly how, when, and why has yet to be fully determined. Yet, all of these issues can be translated into empirical questions that could readily be asked in rhesus monkeys and other organisms, and indeed many of those empirical questions are already in the process of being formulated, if not actually tested.

Questions regarding issues of developmental continuity-discontinuity in the expression of high reactivity and impulsive aggressiveness have been thoroughly addressed in several prospective longitudinal studies with rhesus monkeys living in both laboratory and field settings. These studies have revealed significant developmental changes in the behavioral expression of high reactivity from infancy to adolescence and young adulthood and, to a lesser extent, from young adulthood to senescence. Nevertheless, there clearly are common behavioral features in the expression of high reactivity at any age. Moreover, some patterns of physiological activity that consistently accompany these behavioral expressions seem quite similar in nature, if not degree, at all ages (e.g., high and stable heart rates and exaggerated adrenocortical responses). The more obvious discontinuity with respect to rhesus monkey reactivity appears to be more situational than developmental in nature: Biobehavioral expressions of high reactivity are largely limited to circumstances in which some degree of environmental novelty or challenge is present. High-reactive monkeys of any age do not typically appear to be high reactive, behaviorally or physiologically, when they are in familiar, stable, and benign settings; indeed, under these circumstances, they usually are indistinguishable from others in their age-sex cohort.

The data regarding developmental continuity-discontinuity in the biobehavioral expression of impulsive aggressiveness by rhesus monkeys are not as extensive and encompass less of the life span than for high reactivity but, in some ways, they may be more definitive. Obvious behavioral expressions of impulsive agressiveness are not readily apparent during infancy (although, there may be some powerful predictors in certain neonatal reflex and activity state patterns, e.g., Champoux et al., 1997), and no study to date has looked for possible expressions of impulsive aggressiveness in older monkeys. Moreover, while other "impulsive-like" behaviors (e.g., dangerous leaps) covary with the expression of unprovoked, escalating aggressive bouts, little presently is known about other potentially impulsive "tendencies" (e.g., poor or nonexistent delay of gratification capacities) that might be shown by impulsively aggressive individuals. On the other hand, each of these patterns of behavioral expression are associated with low CSF 5-HIAA concentrations at all ages tested. Although CSF 5-HIAA concentrations change dramatically in absolute terms throughout development, at every age, the lowest concentrations always are associated with the greatest prevalence of impulsive-like behavior. Furthermore, those associations with CSF 5-HIAA concentrations remain relatively unchanged regardless of the situations in which the CSF samples are obtained. Thus, CSF 5-HIAA concentrations appear to show the strongest developmental continuities, across both stressful and nonstressful situations, of any behavioral or physiological measure of reactivity or impulsiveness, with the possible exception of one measure of visual vigilance.

In somewhat parallel fashion, prospective longitudinal studies of rhesus monkeys also have demonstrated remarkable stability of individual differences in the expression of specific behavioral and physiological aspects of both high reactivity and impulsive aggressiveness across major portions of the life span. The more extensive data are for high reactivity: In general, monkeys who, as infants, display extreme behavioral and physiological reactions to minor stressors tend to display the same or similar reactions as juveniles, adolescents, and even adults, whereas those individuals who fail to exhibit extreme reactions as infants also tend not to do so later in life. While there are substantial differences in the relative strength of these patterns of interindividual stability as a function both of the specific measures being examined and the particular developmental period under scrutiny, the overall picture is quite impressive. However, as mentioned earlier, such stabilities tend to be highly situationally specific. For example, individual differences in heart rate patterns recorded during periods of brief separation are highly predictive of heart rate patterns recorded under comparable circumstances 1 year later, but they are not at all predictive of heart rate patterns recorded an hour before or a day after the original separation. In contrast, the evidence regarding stability of individual differences in biobehavioral measures and correlates of impulsive aggressiveness is not as extensive and encompasses less of the life span than is the case for high reactivity, but what evidence that does exist is every bit as solid statistically and (at least for CSF 5-HIAA) much less situationally dependent.

It should be pointed out that many of the studies which have identified strong developmental continuities and the impressive stabilities of individual differences for both reactive and impulsive tendencies were carried out in settings that remained relatively stable throughout most, if not all, of each study. Indeed, in the various rearing studies described above the differential rearing conditions were maintained for only the first 6 months of life; thereafter, all monkeys grew up in the same or comparable physical and social environments, during which time most measures showed predictable developmental continuity and interindividual stability. It remains a relatively open question to what extent such developmental trajectories would remain "predictable" in the face of massive environmental change or experimental intervention at later points in or periods of the life span. Indeed, it could be argued that many of these issues could be resolved, in part, by many of the same types of studies designed to investigate various aspects of the nature-nurture question, as outlined above.

What might the relevance of past, present, and proposed studies of high reactivity and impulsive aggressiveness in rhesus monkeys and other nonprimates be for advancing our understanding of phenomena associated with behavioral inhibition and impulsive aggressiveness in humans? To be sure, rhesus monkeys clearly are not furry little humans with tails, and many important aspects of human behavioral inhibition and impulsive aggressiveness indeed may be uniquely human (e.g., verbal expressions of future fears or written confessions of impulsive activities). Moreover, one always should be cautious in making direct comparisons between humans and other animals, even our closest phylogenetic relatives; the tendency to anthromorphize, particularly in the face of compelling behavioral and physiological parallels, can lead to unsubstantiated assumptions of total homologies when only partial analogies or similarities actually exist. Nevertheless, the same compelling behavioral and physiological parallels between high reactivity and impulsive aggressiveness in rhesus monkeys and behavioral inhibition and impulsive aggresiveness in humans does argue strongly for at least parallel principles regarding the basic issues of nature-nurture, continuity-discontinuity, and interindividual stability throughout development. The research to date with rhesus monkeys has strongly indicated that each of these issues is neither simple nor likely to be resolved by either-or answers. It is hard to imagine that the human phenomena would be any less complex.

☐ References

Arcus, D. M. (1991). *The experimental modification of temperamental bias in inhibited and uninhibited children.* Unpublished doctoral dissertation, Harvard University, Cambridge, MA.

Berman, C. M., Rasmussen, K. L. R., & Suomi, S. J. (1994). Responses of free-ranging rhesus monkeys to a natural form of social separation: I. Parallels with mother-infant separation in captivity. *Child Development, 65,* 1028–1041.

Bernstein, I. S., Williams, L., & Ramsay, M. (1983). The expression of aggression in Old World monkeys. *International Journal of Primatology, 4,* 113–125.

Biederman, J., Rosenbaum, J. F., Hirshfield, D. R., Faraone, S. V., Bolduc, E. A., Gersten, M., Meminger, S. R., Kagan, J., Snidman, N., & Reznick, S. J. (1990). Psychiatric correlates of behavioral inhibition in young children of parents with and without psychiatric disorders. *Archives of General Psychiatry, 47,* 21–26.

Bowlby, J. (1960). Grief and mourning in infancy and early childhood. *Psychoanalytic Study of the Child, 15,* 9–52.

Bowlby, J. (1973). *Separation: Anger and anxiety.* New York: Basic Books.

Bowlby, J. (1988). *A secure base.* New York: Basic Books.

Brown, G. L., Goodwin F. K., Ballenger, J. C., Goyer, P. F., & Major, L. F. (1979). Aggression in humans correlates with cerebrospinal fluid amine metabolites. *Psychiatry Research, 1,* 131–139.

Brown, G. L., Linnoila, M., & Goodwin, F. K. (1990). Clinical assessment of human aggression and impulsivity in relation to biochemical measures. In H. M. Van Praag, R. Plutchik, & A. Apter (Eds.), *Violence and suicidality: Perspectives in clinical and psychobiological research* (pp. 184–217). New York: Bruner/Mazel.

Calkins, S. D., Fox, N. A., & Marshall, T. R. (1996). Behavioral and physiological antecedents of inhibited and uninhibited behavior. *Child Development, 67,* 523–540.

Capitanio, J. P., Rasmussen, K. L. R., Snyder, D. S., Laudenslager, M. L., & Reite, M. (1986). Long-term follow-up of previously separated pigtail macaques: Group and individual differences in response to novel situations. *Journal of Child Psychology and Psychiatry, 27,* 531–537.

Chamove, A. S, Rosenblum, L. A., & Harlow, H. F. (1973). Monkeys (*Macaca mulatta*) raised only with peers: A pilot study. *Animal Behavior, 21,* 316–325.

Champoux, M., Higley, J. D., & Suomi, S. J. (1997). Behavioral and physiological characteristics of Indian and Chinese-Indian hybrid rhesus macaque infants. *Developmental Psychobiology, 31,* 49–63.

Champoux, M., Suomi, S. J., & Schneider, M. L. (1994). Temperamental differences between captive Indian and Chinese-Indian hybrid rhesus macaque infants. *Laboratory Animal Science, 44,* 351–357.

Clarke, A. S., Mason, W. A., & Moberg, G. P. (1988). Differential behavioral and adrenocortical responses to stress among three macaque species. *American Journal of Primatology, 14*, 37–52.

Davidson, R. J. (1991). Emotional and affective style: Hemispheric substrates. *Psychological Science, 1*, 39–43.

Davidson, R. J., & Fox, N. A. (1989). The relation between tonic EEG asymmetry and ten month old infant emotional response to separation. *Journal of Abnormal Psychology, 98*, 127–131.

Fox, N. A. (1991). If it's not left, it's right. *American Psychologist, 46*, 863–872.

Gottlieb, G. (1996). Epigenetic models of development. In R. B. Cairns, G. H. Elder, & E. J. Costello (Eds.), *Developmental Science* (pp. 51–74). Cambridge, England: Cambridge University Press.

Harlow, H. F., Suomi, S. J. & Gluck, J. P. (1972). Generalization of behavioral data between nonhuman and human primates. *American Psychologist, 27*, 709–716.

Higley, J. D., King, S. T., Hasert, M. F., Champoux, M., Suomi, S. J., & Linnoila, M. (1996a). Stability of interindividual differences in serotonin function and its relationship to severe aggression and competent social behavior in rhesus macaque females. *Neuropsychopharmacology, 14*, 67–76.

Higley, J. D., Mehlman, P. T., Taub, D. M., Higley, S., Fernald, B., Vickers, J. H., Suomi, S. J., & Linnoila, M. (1996b). Excessive mortality in young free-ranging male nonhuman primates with low CSF 5-HIAA concentrations. *Archives of General Psychiatry, 53*, 537–543.

Higley, J. D., Mehlman, P. T., Taub, D. M., Higley, S. B., Vickers, J. H., Suomi, S. J., & Linnoila, M. (1992). Cerebrospinal fluid moneamine and adrenal correlates of aggression in free-ranging rhesus monkeys. *Archives of General Psychiatry, 49*, 436–441.

Higley, J. D., Suomi, S. J., & Linnoila, M. (1990). Parallels in aggression and serotonin: Consideration of development, rearing history, and sex differences. In H. L. Van Praag, R. Plutchik, & A. Apter (Eds.), *Violence and suicidality: Perspectives in clinical and psychobiological research* (pp. 245–256). New York: Bruner/Mazel.

Higley, J. D., Suomi, S. J., & Linnoila, M. (1996). A nonhuman primate model of Type II alcoholism? (II.): Diminished social competence and excessive aggression correlates with low CSF 5-HIAA concentrations. *Alcoholism: Clinical and Experimental Research, 20*, 643–650.

Higley, J. D., Suomi, S. J., & Linnoila, M. (1997). Progress in the development of a nonhuman primate model of alcohol abuse. *Journal of the Alcoholic Beverage Foundation, 7*, 67–78.

Higley, J. D., Thompson, W. T., Champoux, M., Goldman, D., Hasert, M. F., Kraemer, G. W., Scanlan, J. M., Suomi, S. J., & Linnoila, M. (1993). Paternal and maternal genetic and environmental contributions to CSF monoamine metabolites in rhesus monkeys (*Macaca mulatta*). *Archives of General Psychiatry, 50*, 615–623.

Kagan, J., Reznick, J. S., Clarke, S., Snidman, N., & Garcia-Coll, C. (1984). Behavioral inhibition to the unfamiliar. *Child Development, 55*, 2212–2225.

Kagan, J., Reznick, J. S., & Snidman, N. (1988). Biological basis of childhood shyness. *Science, 240*, 167–171.

Kagan, J., & Snidman, N. (1991a). Temperamental factors in human development. *American Psychologist, 46*, 856–862.

Kagan, J., & Snidman, N. (1991b). Infant predictors of inhibited and uninhibited profiles. *Psychological Science, 2*, 40–44.

Kagan, J., Snidman, N., Arcus, D. M., & Reznick, S. J. (1994). *Galen's prophecy: Temperament in human nature.* New York: Basic Books.

Kruesi, M. J. (1989). Cruelty to animals and CSF 5-HIAA. *Psychiatry Research, 28*, 115–116.

Kruesi, M. J., Rapoport, J. L., Hamburder, S., Hibbs, E., Potter, W. Z., Lenane, M., & Brown, G. L. (1990). Cerebrospinal fluid monoamine metabolites, aggression, and impulsivity in disruptive behavior disorders of children and adolescents. *Archives of General Psychiatry, 47*, 419–426.

Lindburg, D. G. (1991). Ecological requirements of macaques. *Laboratory Animal Science, 41*, 315–322.

Linnoila, M. (1988). Monoamines and impulse control. In J. A. Swinkels & W. Blijeven (Eds.), *Depression, anxiety, and aggression* (pp. 167–172). Houten, The Netherlands: Medidact.

Linnoila, M., DeJong, J., & Virkkunen, M. (1989). Monoamines, glucose metabolism, and impulse control. *Psychopharmacy Bulletin, 25*, 404–406.

Linnoila, M., Virkkunen, M., Scheinin, M., Nuutila, A., Rimon, R., & Goodwin, F. K. (1983). Low cerebrospinal fluid 5-hydroxyindoleacetic acid concentration differentiates impulsive from nonimpulsive violent behavior. *Life Sciences, 33*, 2609–2614.

Lovejoy, C. O. (1981). The origins of man. *Science, 211*, 341–350.

Mann, J. J., Arango, V., & Underwood, M. E. (1990). Serotonin and suicidal behavior. *Annals of the New York Academy of Science, 600*, 476–485.

Mehlman, P. T., Higley, J. D., Faucher, I., Lilly, A. A., Taub, D. M., Vickers, J. H., Suomi, S. J., & Linnoila, M. (1994). Low cerebrospinal fluid 5-hydroxyindoleacetic acid concentrations are correlated with severe aggression and reduced impulse control in free-ranging primates. *American Journal of Psychiatry, 151*, 1485–1491.

Mehlman, P. T., Higley, J. D., Faucher, I., Lilly, A. A., Taub, D. M., Vickers, J. H., Suomi, S. J., & Linnoila, M. (1995). CSF 5-HIAA concentrations are correlated with sociality and the timing of emigration in free-ranging primates. *American Journal of Psychiatry, 152*, 901–913.

Mendoza, S. P., & Mason, W. A. (1986). Contrasting responses to intruders and to involuntary separations by monogamous and polygymous New World monkeys. *Physiology and Behavior, 38*, 795–801.

Mineka, S., & Suomi, S. J. (1978). Social separation in monkeys. *Psychological Bulletin, 85,* 1376–1400.

Novak, F. S. X., & Sackett, G. P. (1997). Pair-rearing infant monkeys (*Macaca nemestrina*) using a "rotating peer" strategy. *American Journal of Primatology, 41,* 141–149.

Olweus, D. (1979). Stability of aggressive reaction patterns in males: A review. *Psychological Bulletin, 86,* 852–875.

Putallaz, M. (1987). Maternal behavior and children's socioeconomic status. *Child Development, 58,* 324–340.

Raleigh, M. J., Branner, G. L., Rivto, E. R., Geller, E., McGuire, M. T., & Yulviler, A. (1986). Effects of chronic fenfluramine on blood serotonin, cerebrospinal fluid metabolites, and behavior in monkeys. *Psychopharmacology, 90,* 503–508.

Raleigh, M. J., McGuire, M. T., & Brammer, G. L. (1989). Subjective assessment of behavioral style: Links to overt behavior and physiology in vervet monkeys. *American Journal of Primatology, 18,* 161–162.

Rasmussen, K. L. R., & Suomi, S. J. (1989). Heart rate and endocrine responses to stress in adolescent male monkeys on Cayo Santiago. *Puerto Rico Health Science Journal, 8,* 65–71.

Rasmussen, K. L. R., & Suomi, S. J. (1991). Mothers and sons: Somatic and physiological characteristics of adult females rhesus and their adolescent male offspring. *American Journal of Primatology, 24,* 129–131.

Rasmussen, K. L R., Timme, A., & Suomi, S. J. (1997). Comparison of physiological measures of Cayo Santiago rhesus monkey females within and between social groups. *Primate Reports, 47,* 49–55.

Rosenberg, A., & Kagan, J. (1987). Iris pigmentation and behavioral inhibition. *Developmental Psychobiology, 20,* 377–392.

Ruppenthal, G. C., Arling, G. L., Harlow, H. F., Sackett, G. P., & Suomi, S. J. (1976). A 10-year perspective of motherless mother monkey maternal behavior. *Journal of Abnormal Behavior, 85,* 341–349.

Scanlan, J. M. (1988). *Continuity of stress responsivity in infant rhesus monkeys* (Macaca mulatta): *State, hormonal, dominance, and genetic influences.* Unpublished doctoral dissertation, University of Wisconsin-Madison.

Sibley, C. O., Comstock, J. A., & Alquist, J. E. (1990). DNA hybridization evidence of hominid phylogeny: A reanalysis of the data. *Journal of Molecular Evolution, 30,* 202–236.

Steklis, H. D., Brammen, G. L., Raleigh, M. J., & McGuire, M. T. (1985). Serum testosterone, male dominance, and aggression in captive groups of vervet monkeys (*Cercopithecus aethiops sabacus*). *Hormones and Behavior, 19,* 156–165.

Suomi, S. J. (1981). Genetic, maternal, and environmental influences on social development in rhesus monkeys. In A. B. Chiarelli & R. S. Corruccini (Eds.), *Primate behavior and sociobiology* (pp. 81–87). Heidelburg: Springer Verlag.

Suomi, S. J. (1983). Social development in rhesus monkeys: Consideration of individual differences. In A. Oliverio & M. Zapella (Eds.), *The behavior of human infants* (pp. 71–92). New York: Plenum Press.

Suomi, S. J. (1984). Individual differences in separation anxiety and depression in rhesus monkeys: Biological correlates. *Clinical Neuropharmocology, 7,* 454–455.

Suomi, S. J. (1987). Genetic and maternal contributions to individual differences in rhesus monkey biobehavioral development. In N. Krasnagor, E. Blass, M. Hofer, & W. Smotherman (Eds.), *Perinatal development: A psychobiological perspective* (pp. 397–420). New York: Academic Press.

Suomi, S. J. (1991). Uptight and laid-back monkeys: Individual differences in response to social challenges. In S. Brauth, W. Hall, & R. Dooling (Eds.), *Plasticity of development* (pp. 17–56). Cambridge, MA: MIT Press.

Suomi, S. J. (1995). Influence of Bowlby's attachment theory on research on nonhuman primate biobehavioral development. In S. Goldberg, R. Muir, & J. Kerr (Eds.), *Attachment theory: Social, developmental, and clinical perspectives* (pp.185–301). Hillsdale, NJ: Analytic Press.

Suomi, S. J. (1997). Early determinants of behaviour: Evidence from primate studies. *British Medical Bulletin, 53,* 170–184.

Suomi, S. J., & Harlow, H. F. (1976). The facts and functions of fear. In M. Zuckerman & C. D. Spielberger (Eds.), *Emotions and anxiety: New concepts, methods, and applications* (pp. 3–34). Hillsdale, NJ: Erlbaum.

Suomi, S. J., Kraemer, G. W., Baysinger, C. M., & Delizio, R. D. (1981). Inherited and experiential factors associated with individual differences in anxious behavior displayed by rhesus monkeys. In D. G. Klein & J. Rabkin (Eds.), *Anxiety: New reseach and changing concepts* (pp. 179–200). New York: Raven Press.

Suomi, S. J. , & Levine, S. (1998). Psychobiology of intergenerational effects of trauma: Evidence from animal studies. In Y. Daniele (Ed.), *International handbook of multigenerational legacies of trauma* (pp. 623–627). New York: Plenum Press.

Suomi, S. J., Novak, M. A., & Well, A. (1997). Aging in rhesus monkeys: Different windows on behavioral continuity and change. *Developmental Psychology, 32,* 1116–1128.

Suomi, S. J., Rasmussen, K. L. R., & Higley, J. D. (1992). Primate models of behavioral and physiological change in adolescence. In E. R. McAnarney, R. E. Kriepe, D. P. Ore, & G. D. Comerci (Eds.), *Textbook of Adolescent Medicine* (pp. 135–139). Philadelphia: Saunders.

Suomi, S. J., & Ripp, C. (1983). A history of motherless mother monkey mothering at the University of Wisconsin Primate Laboratory. In M. Reite & N. Caine (Ed.), *Child abuse: The nonhuman primate data* (pp. 49–77). New York: Alan R. Liss.

Suomi, S. J., Scanlan, J. M., Rasmussen, K. L. R., Davidson, M., Boinski, S., Higley, J. D., & Marriott, B. (1989). Pituitary-adrenal response to capture in Cayo-derived M-troop rhesus monkeys. *Puerto Rico Health Sciences Journal, 8,* 171–176.

Tremblay, R. E. (1992). The prediction of delinquent behavior from childhood behavior: Personality theory revisited. In J. McCord (Ed.), *Facts, frameworks, and forecasts: Advances in criminological theory* (Vol. 3., pp. 192–230). New Brunswick, NJ: Transactions.

INDEX

Goodwyn, Susan W., 118, 122
Gopnik, A., 127–128, 264, 460, 462
Gormican, S., 96
Gottfried, A. E., 344, 345
Gottfried, A. W., 344, 345
Gottman, J. M., 237–238, 249
Graf, P., 264, 460, 462
Grandparents, role of, 354, 401
Gratification delay, 6
Gray, C., 346
Gray, J. T., 450
Greco, C., 196
Green, F., 263
Greenspan, S. I., 12
Gringlas, M., 435
Grolnick, Wendy S., 10
Grossman, D., 417
"Gun culture," 414
Gunnar, M. R., 12, 15, 36

H
Habituation:
   infant memory, 448
   in infant visual processing, xiii, 65, 66, 67, 68,
      72–73, 74, 76, 77, 78, 79
Haden, C. A., 231, 451
Hagen, J., 267
Halverson, C. F., 364
Halverson, D., 23
Hamond, N. R., 195, 450
Han, J. J., 451, 452
Hankins, E. M., 94
Harlow Primate Laboratory, 514
Harold, R., 310
Harris, Paul L., 161, 172, 178, 202, 250
Harter, S., 314
Hartup, W. W., 239
Haskins, R., 396
Hay, D., 145
Hayne, H., 196
Head Start, 394
Health insurance subsides, xv, 405
Hedelin, L., 303
Herman, Judith, 419
Herz, E. J., 351
Hess, D. L., 241, 250
Hetherington, E. M., 438
Heyman, G. D., 291, 292
Hiebert, J., 187
High-elaborative mothers, childhood memory,
   451
High-risk infants, discriminant validity, 66–67
Highly inhibited, emotion-relevant regulation type,
   323
Hill, K. T., 306
Hinde, R., 59, 149
Hirsh-Pasek, K., 128
Hite, T., 368
Hoeksma, J., 35
Hofer, B., 277
Hoffman, M. L., 320

Hokoda, A., 307
Holding a child, Nso conception, 499
"Holding environment," 12
Hollingshead Four Factor Index of Social Status,
   219
Holloway, S. D., 497–498
Home environment;
   concept of, 341–342
   poverty mediation, 400
   protective factors, 341
HOME inventory, xv, 339, 342–347, 350–353, 351t,
   355
   poverty mediation, 399
   versions of, 342
Hort, B. E., 369
Howard, C., 474, 475,476, 477, 478
Howe, M. L., 195, 196, 200
Howes, Carollee, 143, 145, 147–150, 151, 154
Hrncir, E., 343
Hubbard, J. A., 240, 242, 253
Hudson, Judith A., 195
Huesmann, L. R., 389
Hughes, M., 187, 474
Hui, C. H., 352
Human development research, impact of poverty, 393,
   394
Humans, categorical representations of, 103f,
   103–104
Hume, David, 171
Hunt, E., 72
Hurley, Jennifer C., 248
Huston, Aletha, 365, 366, 368
Huttenlocher, J., 174
Hybrid traits, temperament, 26f, 26–27
Hymel, S., 251

I
Implicit memory, 448, 450
Impulsive aggression:
   developmental debate, 511–512, 521
   in rhesus monkeys, 513, 516–519
Income Maintenance Experiment, 396, 397f, 398
Independent-interdependent style, childhood
   recollections, xvi, 452–453
Index of Productive Syntax (IPSyn), 219–220, 228t,
   232
Individual variation
   attachment relationship, xii–xii, 45
   in child development, xi, xii
   in emotional regulation, xiv
   gender development, 370
   in infant visual processing, xiii
   intrinsic motivation, 303–304
   middle school development, 293–296
   peer groups, 143, 147–149
Infant-father attachment, 45, 48, 54–55, 55f, 56
Infant Health and Development Program
   (IHDP)Study, 351, 395
Infant information processing, 64
Infant-mother, attachment theory, 48, 49–50, 54–55,
   59

Leinbach, M. D., 369
Lesbian households, xvi, 429, 435–441
Leslie, A., 263
Letters, dual representation hypothesis, 187–189
Levy, A., 57
Levy, G. D., 370
Lewis, M., 33, 77, 253, 347
"Lexical" words, 118
Liang, X., 494
Liben, L. S., 364
"Linguistic signs," 119
"Locutionary phase,"118
Loehlin, J., 346
Loftus, E. F., 459
Lomonaco, S., 78
Long term memory:
    childhood amnesia, xvi, 447, 448
    in infants/toddlers, 194, 196, 199, 199f, 203t, 205, 208, 211, 447
Longitudinal studies, temperament-contextual linkage, 31
Look duration, infant visual processing, 67
Lord, S. E., 310
Lounsbury, M., 35
Low-elaborative mothers, childhood memory, 451

M
Mac Iver, D. J., 301
MacArthur Communicative Development Inventory (CDI), 125, 134, 219–220, 220t, 228t
MacArthur Foundation's Research Network on Mid-life Development (MIDMAC), 479, 480, 481t, 482–485, 485f, 486f
MacArthur Network on Successful Pathways Through Middle Childhood, 405
Maccoby, E., 37
MacPhee, D., 32
Magnet, human representations, 104, 105, 111
Mammals, object formation, 101–102
Mandler, J. M., 194, 449
Mangelsdorf, S. C., 10, 11, 15
Manipulatives, 186–187, 189, 190
Manpower Demonstration Research Corporation (MDRC), 405
Map learning, 107, 110
Marital quality, attachment relationship, xii–xii, 45
Marital relationship, temperament domain, 23
Markman, E., 268, 278
Markus, H. R., 452
Marsh, H. W., 291
Marshall, S., 473, 474, 476, 479
Marshall, T. R., 12
Martin, C. L., 364
Martin, E., 107
Martin, R., 23
Martinez, P., 413
Marzolf, D., 10
Masking, emotional expression, 242, 244
Mass media, poverty mediation, xv, 404–405
Mastery motivation, 78

Maternal age, HOME inventory, 350
Maternal behavior, in rhesus monkeys, 515, 517, 519–520
Maternal sensitivity:
    attachment security, 47, 49, 50, 58, 59
    infant visual processing, 75–76
Maternal separation, in rhesus monkeys, 514–515
Materpasqua, F., 443
Mathematical manipulatives, 186–187, 189
Mathematical symbols, dual representation hypothesis, 185–187, 188f
Matheny, A., 32, 36
Maudry, M., 144
Maximization, emotional expression, 242
McAdoo, H. P., 474–475
McCabe, A., 219, 231
McCall, R. B., 65, 67, 72
McClintic, S. M., 292
McClure, J., 73
McDevitt, S., 23
McDonough, L., 194, 449
McGrath, M., 35
Means-end belief, control theories, 298
Mediation model, poverty, 398–399, 399f
Meltzoff, A. N., 127–128, 194, 203, 205, 449
Memory:
    category information storage, 98–99, 104
    cues, xiv, 193
    in infants, 71, 136
    restatement, in toddlers, xiv, 193–212
    storage/retrieval, in toddlers, 193
Mental health, academic self-perception, 309–310
Mermelstein, R., 366
Mervis, C. B., 128
Metacognition, 259–261, 262t
    abilities, in childhood, xiv
    competence, in childhood, xiv, 260, 272–273, 278–279
    environment, 281
Meta-knowing:
    attainment of, 279–281
    in childhood, xiv, 261, 262t, 263–272, 270t
    concept, 260, 272–276, 274t, 278–279
    epistemological basis of, 276–278
    origin of, 261, 263
Meta-memory literature, limitations of, 267–268
Metastrategic competence, in childhood, xiv, 268, 275–276, 279
Metastrategic knowing, in childhood, xiv, 261, 262t, 266–272, 270t, 272–276, 274t
Mettetal, G., 237–238, 249
Michaelson, L., 253
Michel, M. K., 19
Michigan Study in Adolescent Life Transitions (MSALT), 292
Microgenetic method, cognition, 269
Middle childhood, gender development, 366–368
Middle Childhood HOME inventory, 342, 344, 345, 346, 355
Miller, K. F., 185